TALES·FROM
THE·ARABIAN·NIGHTS

SELECTED·FROM
THE·BOOK·OF·THE·THOUSAND
NIGHTS·AND·A·NIGHT

TRANSLATED · AND · ANNOTATED · BY

RICHARD·F·BURTON

EDITED·BY·DAVID·SHUMAKER
FROM·THE·EDITION
PRIVATELY·PRINTED
BY·THE·BURTON·CLUB

AVENEL · BOOKS · NEW · YORK

The illustrations in this volume
have been selected from the 1859
three-volume edited edition of the
E. W. Lane translation.

This edition is published by Avenel Books, distributed by
Crown Publishers, Inc.
a b c d e f g h
Printed in the United States of America.

Library of Congress Cataloging in Publication Data
Arabian nights.
Tales from the Arabian nights.
I. Burton, Richard Francis, Sir, 1821–1890.
II. Shumaker, David. III. Title.
PN7716.A1B8 1978 398.2 78-17311
ISBN 0-517-265753
ISBN 0-517-261847 lib. bdg.

EDITOR'S FOREWORD.

❖

IT is little more than 250 years since *The Book of the Thousand Nights and a Night* made its first appearance in Europe. The man who let the Jinni out of the bottle was a French scholar, Antoine Galland, whose translation from the Arabic into French (1704-17) brought this imaginative collection of tales before the Western world. Galland intended his version of the *Arabian Nights Entertainments* to be popular and this he achieved by emphasizing the strange and miraculous, and ignoring much that was characteristic of the original: the very frank treatment of sex and its perversions, the more savage stories of brutality and corruption, the historical and semihistorical anecdotes.

The first attempt to render a complete and faithful translation of the *Nights* was made by Henry Torrens (1838), but he died prematurely and only one out of his projected nine or ten volumes was completed. The principal value of E. W. Lane's translation (1839-41) lies in the notes, for his knowledge of Cairo society was encyclopedic; the work was intended for "the drawing-room table" and is a mere castrated selection of the original. The first complete translation was made by John Payne (1882-84) and published by the Villon Society in a limited edition of 500 copies. To these three translations Sir Richard Burton frankly admitted his indebtedness when he published openly, but privately, an unexpurgated sixteen-volume edition (1885-88). Burton's translation is acknowledged as the definitive rendering of the *Nights* into English for its exceptional accuracy, masculine vitality, and literary discernment, and still brooks no competition.

Burton's qualifications as a translator of the *Nights* were formidable, not only because of his extensive knowledge of Arabic (he was also fluent in Persian and Hindustani, not to mention several lesser Eastern languages and dialects) but because of his extraordinary personality. In 1853 he successfully made a pilgrimage disguised as an Afghanistan Muslim to Cairo, Suez, and Medina, then on to the sacred city of Mecca, where he measured and sketched the mosque and holy Muslim shrine, the Ka'bah. His account of the journey is not only a classic of English travel literature but also a brilliant commentary of Muslim life and manners. No enterprise could have borne more powerful testimony to his knowledge of Eastern customs and beliefs than the expedition he later made to the forbidden East African city of Harer (1854-55) as he became the first European to enter this Muslim citadel without being executed. Burton is in the first rank of English explorers and is credited with the discovery of Lake Tanganyika.

The structure of the *Arabian Nights* consists of the following whimsical plot arrangement: Shahyrár, King of India, is inflamed with jealousy by his wife's wanton ways, and after executing her, he resolves to take his revenge on all womankind. Night after night he marries some beautiful girl, only to order her beheaded the next morning. But at last he meets Shahrázád (Scheherazade), the beautiful and clever daughter of his vizier. Knowing that Shahyrár loves a good story, she begins on the night of their wedding to spin a bewildering number of yarns which she suspends just as the climax is being reached. Devoured by curiosity to know the end of each story, Shahryár stays the hand of the executioner and after a thousand and one nights is cured of his mania.

The story of Shahrázád's ingenuity is of Persian origin. Mas'udi speaks of it in 944, and it is also referred to in the *Fihrist* (987) as appearing in the *Hezar Afsane (Thousand Tales)* which was attributed to the Princess Homai, daughter of Artaxerxes I. However, the tales are more Arabian than Persian in flavor. It is possible that they were collected in Cairo by a professional storyteller around the fifteenth century. The involuted form of the *Arabian Nights Entertainments* has been a source of admiration as a miracle of narrative architecture. Boccaccio's *Decameron*, Chaucer's *Canterbury Tales*, and the *Fables of Bidpai* are all similar in construction, but the Arabian work is infinitely more complicated.

Over fifty of the choicest tales told by Shahrázád are presented in this volume. To preserve the integrity of the original Burton editions, the chronology of the nights has been maintained for the tales included in Part I from the ten-volume *Book of the Thousand Nights and a Night* and in Part II which contains selections from the six-volume *Supplemental Nights* including "Alaeddin; or, the Wonderful Lamp" and "Ali Baba and the Forty Thieves," which have become common heritage. All the text in this volume has been faithfully reproduced from the privately printed Burton Club edition. The illustrations have been selected from the 1859 edited edition of the E. W. Lane translation.

DAVID SHUMAKER
NEW YORK, APRIL, 1978

لا لابرار كل شى ثر

"TO THE PURE ALL THINGS ARE PURE"
(Puris omnia pura)
— *Arab Proverb.*

"Niuna corrotta mente intese mai sanamente parole."
— *"Decameron"* — *conclusion.*

"Erubuit, posuitque meum Lucretia librum
Sed coram Bruto. Brute! recede, leget."
— MARTIAL.

"Miculx est de ris que de larmes escripre,
Pour ce que rire est le propre des hommes."
— RABELAIS.

"The pleasure we derive from perusing the Thousand-
and-One Stories makes us regret that we possess only
a comparatively small part of these truly enchanting
fictions."
— CRICHTON's *"History of Arabia."*

CONTENTS

PART I

PART II

PART
ONE

J. JACKSON

THE BOOK OF THE
THOUSAND NIGHTS AND A NIGHT

(*ALF LAYLAH WA LAYLAH.*)

In the Name of Allah,
the Compassionating, the Compassionate!

PRAISE BE TO ALLAH * THE BENEFICENT KING * THE CREATOR OF THE UNIVERSE * LORD OF THE THREE WORLDS * WHO SET UP THE FIRMAMENT WITHOUT PILLARS IN ITS STEAD * AND WHO STRETCHED OUT THE EARTH EVEN AS A BED * AND GRACE, AND PRAYER-BLESSING BE UPON OUR LORD MOHAMMED * LORD OF APOSTOLIC MEN * AND UPON HIS FAMILY AND COMPANION-TRAIN * PRAYER AND BLESSINGS ENDURING AND GRACE WHICH UNTO THE DAY OF DOOM SHALL REMAIN * AMEN! * O THOU OF THE THREE WORLDS SOVEREIGN!

AND AFTERWARDS. Verily the works and words of those gone before us have become instances and examples to men of our modern day, that folk may view what admonishing chances befel other folk and may therefrom take warning; and that they may peruse the annals of antique peoples and all that hath betided them, and be thereby ruled and restrained:—Praise, therefore, be to Him who hath made the histories of the Past an admonition unto the Present! Now of such instances are the tales called "A Thousand Nights and a Night," together with their far-famed legends and wonders. Therein it is related (but Allah is All-knowing of His hidden things and All-ruling and All-honoured and All-giving and All-gracious and All-merciful![1]) that, in tide of yore and in time long gone before, there was a King of the Kings of the Banu Sásán in the Islands of India and China, a Lord of armies and guards and servants and dependents.[2] He left only two sons, one in the prime of manhood and the other yet a youth, while both were Knights and Braves, albeit the elder was a doughtier horseman than the younger. So he succeeded to the empire; when he ruled the land and lorded it over his lieges with justice so exemplary that he was beloved by all the peoples of his capital and of his kingdom. His name was King Shahryár[3], and he made his younger brother, Shah Zamán hight, King of Samarcand in Barbarian-land. These two ceased not to abide in their several realms and the law was ever carried out in their dominions; and each ruled his own kingdom, with equity and fair-dealing to his subjects, in extreme solace and enjoyment; and this condition continually endured for a score of years. But at the end of the twentieth twelvemonth the elder King yearned for a sight of his younger brother and felt that he must look upon him once more. So he took counsel with his Wazír[4] about visiting him, but the Minister, finding the project unadvisable, recommended that a letter be written and a present be sent under his charge to the younger brother with an invita-

---

[1] Allaho A'alam, a deprecatory formula, used because the writer is going to indulge in a series of what may possibly be untruths.

[2] The "Sons of Sásán" are the famous Sassanides whose dynasty ended with the Arabian Conquest (A.D.641). "Island" (Jazírah) in Arabic also means "Peninsula," and causes much confusion in geographical matters.

[3] Shahryár not Shahriyar (Persian) = "City-friend." The Bulak edition corrupts it to Shahrbáz (City-hawk), and the Breslau to Shahrbán or "Defender of the City," like Marz-ban = Warden of the Marshes. Shah Zamán (Persian) = "King of the Age:" Galland prefers Shah Zenan, or "King of women," and the Bul. edit. changes it to Shah Rummán, "Pomegranate King." Al-Ajam denotes all regions not Arab (Gentiles opposed to Jews, Mlechchhas to Hindus, Tajiks to Turks, etc., etc.), and especially Persia; Ajami (a man of Ajam) being an equivalent of the Gr. Βάρβαρος. See Vol. ii., p. 1.

[4] Galland writes "Vizier," a wretched frenchification of a mincing Turkish mispronunciation; Torrens, "Wuzeer" (Anglo-Indian and Gilchristian); Lane, "Wezeer"; (Egyptian or rather Cairene); Payne, "Vizier," according to his system; Burckhardt (Proverbs), "Vizír;" and Mr. Keith-Falconer, "Vizir." The root is popularly supposed to be "wizr" (burden) and the meaning "Minister;" Wazir al-Wuzará being "Premier." In the Koran (chapt. xx., 30) Moses says, "Give me a Wazir of my family, Harun (Aaron) my brother." Sale, followed by the excellent version of the Rev. J. M. Rodwell, translates a "Counsellor," and explains by "One who has the chief administration of affairs under a prince." But both learned Koranists learnt their Orientalism in London, and, like such students generally, fail only upon the easiest points, familiar to all old dwellers in the East.

tion to visit the elder. Having accepted this advice the King
forthwith bade prepare handsome gifts, such as horses with saddles of gem-encrusted gold; Mamelukes, or white slaves; beautiful handmaids, high-breasted virgins, and splendid stuffs and
costly. He then wrote a letter to Shah Zaman expressing his
warm love and great wish to see him, ending with these words,
"We therefore hope of the favour and affection of the beloved
brother that he will condescend to bestir himself and turn his
face us-wards. Furthermore we have sent our Wazir to make
all ordinance for the march, and our one and only desire is to
see thee ere we die; but if thou delay or disappoint us we shall
not survive the blow. Wherewith peace be upon thee!" Then
King Shahryar, having sealed the missive and given it to the
Wazir with the offerings aforementioned, commanded him to
shorten his skirts and strain his strength and make all expedition
in going and returning. "Harkening and obedience!" quoth the
Minister, who fell to making ready without stay and packed
up his loads and prepared all his requisites without delay. This
occupied him three days, and on the dawn of the fourth he took
leave of his King and marched right away, over desert and hill-
way, stony waste and pleasant lea without halting by night or
by day. But whenever he entered a realm whose ruler was subject to his Suzerain, where he was greeted with magnificent gifts
of gold and silver and all manner of presents fair and rare, he
would tarry there three days,[1] the term of the guest-rite; and,
when he left on the fourth, he would be honourably escorted for
a whole day's march. As soon as the Wazir drew near Shah
Zaman's court in Samarcand he despatched to report his arrival
one of his high officials, who presented himself before the King;
and, kissing ground between his hands, delivered his message.
Hereupon the King commanded sundry of his Grandees and
Lords of his realm to fare forth and meet his brother's Wazir at
the distance of a full day's journey; which they did, greeting him
respectfully and wishing him all prosperity and forming an escort
and a procession. When he entered the city he proceeded
straightway to the palace, where he presented himself in the
royal presence; and, after kissing ground and praying for the
King's health and happiness and for victory over all his enemies,

---

[1] This three-days term (rest-day, drest-day and departure day) seems to be an instinct-
made rule in hospitality. Among Moslems it is a Sunnat or practice of the Prophet.

he informed him that his brother was yearning to see him, and prayed for the pleasure of a visit. He then delivered the letter which Shah Zaman took from his hand and read: it contained sundry hints and allusions which required thought; but, when the King had fully comprehended its import, he said, "I hear and I obey the commands of the beloved brother!" adding to the Wazir, "But we will not march till after the third day's hospitality." He appointed for the Minister fitting quarters of the palace; and, pitching tents for the troops, rationed them with whatever they might require of meat and drink and other necessaries. On the fourth day he made ready for wayfare and got together sumptuous presents befitting his elder brother's majesty, and stablished his chief Wazir viceroy of the land during his absence. Then he caused his tents and camels and mules to be brought forth and encamped, with their bales and loads, attendants and guards, within sight of the city, in readiness to set out next morning for his brother's capital. But when the night was half spent he bethought him that he had forgotten in his palace somewhat which he should have brought with him, so he returned privily and entered his apartments, where he found the Queen, his wife, asleep on his own carpet-bed, embracing with both arms a black cook of loathsome aspect and foul with kitchen grease and grime. When he saw this the world waxed black before his sight and he said, "If such case happen while I am yet within sight of the city what will be the doings of this damned whore during my long absence at my brother's court?" So he drew his scymitar and, cutting the two in four pieces with a single blow, left them on the carpet and returned presently to his camp without letting anyone know of what had happened. Then he gave orders for immediate departure and set out at once and began his travel; but he could not help thinking over his wife's treason and he kept ever saying to himself, "How could she do this deed by me? How could she work her own death?," till excessive grief seized him, his colour changed to yellow, his body waxed weak and he was threatened with a dangerous malady, such an one as bringeth men to die. So the Wazir shortened his stages and tarried long at the watering-stations and did his best to solace the King. Now when Shah Zaman drew near the capital of his brother he despatched vaunt-couriers and messengers of glad tidings to announce his arrival, and Shahryar came forth to meet him with his Wazirs and Emirs and Lords and

Grandees of his realm; and saluted him and joyed with exceeding joy and caused the city to be decorated in his honour. When, however, the brothers met, the elder could not but see the change of complexion in the younger and questioned him of his case whereto he replied, "'Tis caused by the travails of wayfare and my case needs care, for I have suffered from the change of water and air! but Allah be praised for reuniting me with a brother so dear and so rare!" On this wise he dissembled and kept his secret, adding, "O King of the time and Caliph of the tide, only toil and moil have tinged my face yellow with bile and hath made my eyes sink deep in my head." Then the two entered the capital in all honour; and the elder brother lodged the younger in a palace overhanging the pleasure garden; and, after a time, seeing his condition still unchanged, he attributed it to his separation from his country and kingdom. So he let him wend his own ways and asked no questions of him till one day when he again said, "O my brother, I see thou art grown weaker of body and yellower of colour." "O my brother," replied Shah Zaman "I have an internal wound:"[1] still he would not tell him what he had witnessed in his wife. Thereupon Shahryar summoned doctors and surgeons and bade them treat his brother according to the rules of art, which they did for a whole month; but their sherbets and potions naught availed, for he would dwell upon the deed of his wife, and despondency, instead of diminishing, prevailed, and leach-craft treatment utterly failed. One day his elder brother said to him, "I am going forth to hunt and course and to take my pleasure and pastime; maybe this would lighten thy heart." Shah Zaman, however, refused, saying, "O my brother, my soul yearneth for naught of this sort and I entreat thy favour to suffer me tarry quietly in this place, being wholly taken up with my malady." So King Shah Zaman passed his night in the palace and, next morning, when his brother had fared forth, he removed from his room and sat him down at one of the lattice-windows overlooking the pleasure-grounds; and there he abode thinking with saddest thought over his wife's betrayal and burning sighs issued from his tortured breast. And as he continued in this case lo! a postern of the palace, which was carefully kept private, swung open and out of it

---

[1] *i.e.*, I am sick at heart.

came twenty slave girls surrounding his brother's wife who was wondrous fair, a model of beauty and comeliness and symmetry and perfect loveliness and who paced with the grace of a gazelle which panteth for the cooling stream. Thereupon Shah Zaman drew back from the window, but he kept the bevy in sight espying them from a place whence he could not be espied. They walked under the very lattice and advanced a little way into the garden till they came to a jetting fountain amiddlemost a great basin of water; then they stripped off their clothes and behold, ten of them were women, concubines of the King, and the other ten were white slaves. Then they all paired off, each with each: but the Queen, who was left alone, presently cried out in a loud voice, "Here to me, O my lord Saeed!" and then sprang with a drop-leap from one of the trees a big slobbering blackamoor with rolling eyes which showed the whites, a truly hideous sight.[1] He walked boldly up to her and threw his arms round her neck while she embraced him as warmly; then he bussed her and winding his legs round hers, as a button-loop clasps a button, he threw her and enjoyed her. On like wise did the other slaves with the girls till all had satisfied their passions, and they ceased not from kissing and clipping, coupling and carousing till day began to wane; when the Mamelukes rose from the damsels' bosoms and the blackamoor slave dismounted from the Queen's breast; the men resumed their disguises and all, except the negro who swarmed up the tree, entered the palace and closed the postern-door as before. Now, when Shah Zaman saw this conduct of his sister-in-law he said in himself, "By Allah, my calamity is lighter than this! My brother is a greater King among the kings than I am, yet this infamy goeth on in his very palace, and his wife is in love with that filthiest of filthy slaves. But this only

---

[1] Debauched women prefer negroes on account of the size of their parts. I measured one man in Somali-land who, when quiescent, numbered nearly six inches. This is a characteristic of the negro race and of African animals; *e.g.* the horse; whereas the pure Arab, man and beast, is below the average of Europe; one of the best proofs by the by, that the Egyptian is not an Asiatic, but a negro partially white-washed. Moreover, these imposing parts do not increase proportionally during erection; consequently, the "deed of kind" takes a much longer time and adds greatly to the woman's enjoyment. In my time no honest Hindi Moslem would take his women-folk to Zanzibar on account of the huge attractions and enormous temptations there and thereby offered to them. Upon the subject of Imsák = retention of semen and "prolongation of pleasure," I shall find it necessary to say more.

showeth that they all do it[1] and that there is no woman but who cuckoldeth her husband, then the curse of Allah upon one and all and upon the fools who lean against them for support or who place the reins of conduct in their hands." So he put away his melancholy and despondency, regret and repine, and allayed his sorrow by constantly repeating those words, adding, " 'Tis my conviction that no man in this world is safe from their malice!" When supper-time came they brought him the trays and he ate with voracious appetite, for he had long refrained from meat, feeling unable to touch any dish however dainty. Then he returned grateful thanks to Almighty Allah, praising Him and blessing Him, and he spent a most restful night, it having been long since he had savoured the sweet food of sleep. Next day he broke his fast heartily and began to recover health and strength, and presently regained excellent condition. His brother came back from the chase ten days after, when he rode out to meet him and they saluted each other; and when King Shahryar looked at King Shah Zaman he saw how the hue of health had returned to him, how his face had waxed ruddy and how he ate with an appetite after his late scanty diet. He wondered much and said, "O my brother, I was so anxious that thou wouldst join me in hunting and chasing, and wouldst take thy pleasure and pastime in my dominion!" He thanked him and excused himself; then the two took horse and rode into the city and, when they were seated at their ease in the palace, the food-trays were set before them and they ate their sufficiency. After the meats were removed and they had washed their hands, King Shahryar turned to his brother and said, "My mind is overcome with wonderment at thy condition. I was desirous to carry thee with me to the chase but I saw thee changed in hue, pale and wan to view, and in sore trouble of mind too. But now Alhamdolillah—glory be to God!—I see thy natural colour hath returned to thy face and that thou art again in the best of case. It was my belief that thy sickness came of severance from thy family and friends, and absence from capital and country, so I refrained from troubling thee with further questions. But now I beseech thee to expound to me the cause of thy complaint and thy change of colour, and to explain the reason of thy recovery

---

1 The very same words were lately spoken in England proving the eternal truth of The Nights which the ignorant call "downright lies."

and the return to the ruddy hue of health which I am wont to view. So speak out and hide naught!" When Shah Zaman heard this he bowed groundwards awhile his head, then raised it and said, "I will tell thee what caused my complaint and my loss of colour; but excuse my acquainting thee with the cause of its return to me and the reason of my complete recovery: indeed I pray thee not to press me for a reply." Said Shahryar, who was much surprised by these words, "Let me hear first what produced thy pallor and thy poor condition." "Know, then, O my brother," rejoined Shah Zaman, "that when thou sentest thy Wazir with the invitation to place myself between thy hands, I made ready and marched out of my city; but presently I minded me having left behind me in the palace a string of jewels intended as a gift to thee. I returned for it alone and found my wife on my carpet-bed and in the arms of a hideous black cook. So I slew the twain and came to thee, yet my thoughts brooded over this business and I lost my bloom and became weak. But excuse me if I still refuse to tell thee what was the reason of my complexion returning." Shahryar shook his head, marvelling with extreme marvel, and with the fire of wrath flaming up from his heart, he cried, "Indeed, the malice of woman is mighty!" Then he took refuge from them with Allah and said, "In very sooth, O my brother, thou hast escaped many an evil by putting thy wife to death,[1] and right excusable were thy wrath and grief for such mishap which never yet befel crowned King like thee. By Allah, had the case been mine, I would not have been satisfied without slaying a thousand women and that way madness lies! But now praise be to Allah who hath tempered to thee thy tribulation, and needs must thou acquaint me with that which so suddenly restored to thee complexion and health, and explain to me what causeth this concealment." "O King of the Age, again I pray thee excuse my so doing!" "Nay, but thou must." "I fear, O my brother, lest the recital cause thee more anger and sorrow than afflicted me." "That were but a better reason," quoth Shahryar, "for telling me the whole history, and I conjure thee by Allah not to keep back aught from me." Thereupon Shah Zaman told him all he had seen, from commencement to conclusion, ending with these words, "When I beheld thy calamity and the treason of thy wife, O my brother, and I reflected that

---

[1] The Arab's *Tue la!*

thou art in years my senior and in sovereignty my superior, mine
own sorrow was belittled by the comparison, and my mind
recovered tone and temper: so throwing off melancholy and
despondency, I was able to eat and drink and sleep, and thus
I speedily regained health and strength. Such is the truth and
the whole truth." When King Shahryar heard this he waxed
wroth with exceeding wrath, and rage was like to strangle him;
but presently he recovered himself and said, "O my brother, I
would not give thee the lie in this matter, but I cannot credit it
till I see it with mine own eyes." "An thou wouldst look upon
thy calamity," quoth Shah Zaman, "rise at once and make ready
again for hunting and coursing,[1] and then hide thyself with me, so
shalt thou witness it and thine eyes shall verify it." "True,"
quoth the King; whereupon he let make proclamation of his intent to travel, and the troops and tents fared forth without the
city, camping within sight, and Shahryar sallied out with them
and took seat amidmost his host, bidding the slaves admit no man
to him. When night came on he summoned his Wazir and said
to him, "Sit thou in my stead and let none wot of my absence till
the term of three days." Then the brothers disguised themselves
and returned by night with all secrecy to the palace, where they
passed the dark hours: and at dawn they seated themselves at the
lattice overlooking the pleasure grounds, when presently the
Queen and her handmaids came out as before, and passing under
the windows made for the fountain. Here they stripped, ten
of them being men to ten women, and the King's wife cried out,
"Where art thou, O Saeed?" The hideous blackamoor dropped
from the tree straightway; and, rushing into her arms without
stay or delay, cried out, "I am Sa'ad al-Din Saood!"[2] The lady
laughed heartily, and all fell to satisfying their lusts, and remained so occupied for a couple of hours, when the white slaves
rose up from the handmaidens' breasts and the blackamoor dismounted from the Queen's bosom: then they went into the basin
and, after performing the Ghusl, or complete ablution, donned
their dresses and retired as they had done before. When King

---

[1] Arab. "Sayd wa kanas": the former usually applied to fishing; hence Sayda (Sidon)
= fish-town. But noble Arabs (except the Caliph Al-Amin) do not fish; so here it means
simply "sport," chasing, coursing, birding (oiseler), and so forth.

[2] In the Mac. Edit. the negro is called "Mas'úd"; here he utters a kind of war-cry and
plays upon the name, "Sa'ád, Sa'íd, Sa'úd," and "Mas'ud", all being derived from one
root, "Sa'ad" = auspiciousness, prosperity.

Shahryar saw this infamy of his wife and concubines he became as one distraught and he cried out, "Only in utter solitude can man be safe from the doings of this vile world! By Allah, life is naught but one great wrong." Presently he added, "Do not thwart me, O my brother, in what I propose;" and the other answered, "I will not." So he said, "Let us up as we are and depart forthright hence, for we have no concern with Kingship, and let us overwander Allah's earth, worshipping the Almighty till we find some one to whom the like calamity hath happened; and if we find none then will death be more welcome to us than life." So the two brothers issued from a second private postern of the palace; and they never stinted wayfaring by day and by night, until they reached a tree a-middle of a meadow hard by a spring of sweet water on the shore of the salt sea. Both drank of it and sat down to take their rest; and when an hour of the day had gone by, lo! they heard a mighty roar and uproar in the middle of the main as though the heavens were falling upon the earth; and the sea brake with waves before them, and from it towered a black pillar, which grew and grew till it rose skywards and began making for that meadow. Seeing it, they waxed fearful exceedingly and climbed to the top of the tree, which was a lofty; whence they gazed to see what might be the matter. And behold, it was a Jinni,[1] huge of height and burly of breast and bulk, broad of brow and black of blee, bearing on his head a coffer of crystal. He strode to land, wading through the deep, and coming to the tree whereupon were the two Kings, seated himself beneath it. He then set down the coffer on its bottom and out it drew a casket, with seven padlocks of steel, which he

---

[1] The Arab. singular (whence the French "génie"); fem. Jinniyah; the Div and Rakshah of old Guebre-land and the "Rakshasa," or "Yaksha," of Hinduism. It would be interesting to trace the evident connection, by no means "accidental," of "Jinn" with the "Genius" who came to the Romans through the Asiatic Etruscans, and whose name I cannot derive from "gignomai" or "genitus." He was unknown to the Greeks, who had the Daimon (δαίμων), a family which separated, like the Jinn and the Genius, into two categories, the good (Agatho-dæmons) and the bad (Kako-dæmons). We know nothing concerning the status of the Jinn amongst the pre-Moslemitic or pagan Arabs: the Moslems made him a supernatural anthropoid being, created of subtile fire (Koran, chapts. xv. 27; lv. 14), not of earth like man, propagating his kind, ruled by mighty kings, the last being Ján bin Ján, missionarised by Prophets and subject to death and Judgment. From the same root are "Junún" = madness (*i.e.*, possession or obsession by the Jinn) and "Majnún" = a madman. According to R. Jeremiah bin Eliazar in Psalm xli. 5, Adam was excommunicated for one hundred and thirty years, during which he begat children in his own image (Gen. v. 3) and these were Mazikeen or Shedeem— Jinns. Further details anent the Jinn will presently occur.

unlocked with seven keys of steel he took from beside his thigh, and out of it a young lady to come was seen, white-skinned and of winsomest mien, of stature fine and thin, and bright as though a moon of the fourteenth night she had been, or the sun raining lively sheen. Even so the poet Utayyah hath excellently said:—

She rose like the morn as she shone through the night * And she gilded the
  grove with her gracious sight:
From her radiance the sun taketh increase when * She unveileth and shameth
  the moonshine bright.
Bow down all beings between her hands * As she showeth charms with her
  veil undight.
And she floodeth cities[1] with torrent tears * When she flasheth her look of
  leven-light.

The Jinni seated her under the tree by his side and looking at her said, "O choicest love of this heart of mine! O dame of noblest line, whom I snatched away on thy bride-night that none might prevent me taking thy maidenhead or tumble thee before I did, and whom none save myself hath loved or hath enjoyed: O my sweetheart! I would lief sleep a little while." He then laid his head upon the lady's thighs; and, stretching out his legs which extended down to the sea, slept and snored and snarked like the roll of thunder. Presently she raised her head towards the tree-top and saw the two Kings perched near the summit; then she softly lifted off her lap the Jinni's pate which she was tired of supporting and placed it upon the ground; then standing upright under the tree signed to the Kings, "Come ye down, ye two, and fear naught from this Ifrít."[2] They were in a terrible fright when they found that she had seen them and answered her in the same manner, "Allah upon thee[3] and by thy modesty, O lady, excuse us from coming down!" But she rejoined by saying, "Allah upon you both, that ye come down forthright, and if ye come not, I will rouse upon you my husband, this Ifrit, and he shall do you to die by the illest of deaths;" and she continued making signals to

---

[1] Arab. "Amsár" (cities): in Bul. Edit. "Amtár" (rains), as in Mac. Edit. So Mr. Payne (I., 5) translates:—
    And when she flashes forth the lightning of her glance, She maketh eyes
       to rain, like showers, with many a tear.
I would render it, "She makes whole cities shed tears;" and prefer it for a reason which will generally influence me—its superior exaggeration and impossibility.
[2] Not "A-frit," pronounced Aye-frit, as our poets have it. This variety of the Jinn, who, as will be shown, are divided into two races like mankind, is generally, but not always, a malignant being, hostile and injurious to mankind (Koran xxvii. 39).
[3] i.e., "I conjure thee by Allah;" the formula is technically called "Inshád."

them. So, being afraid, they came down to her and she rose before them and said, "Stroke me a strong stroke, without stay or
delay, otherwise will I arouse and set upon you this Ifrit who
shall slay you straightway." They said to her, "O our lady, we
conjure thee by Allah, let us off this work, for we are fugitives
from such and in extreme dread and terror of this thy husband.
How then can we do it in such a way as thou desirest?" "Leave
this talk: it needs must be so;" quoth she, and she swore them by
Him[1] who raised the skies on high, without prop or pillar, that,
if they worked not her will, she would cause them to be slain
and cast into the sea. Whereupon out of fear King Shahryar said
to King Shah Zaman, "O my brother, do thou what she biddeth
thee do;" but he replied, "I will not do it till thou do it before I
do." And they began disputing about futtering her. Then quoth
she to the twain, "How is it I see you disputing and demurring;
if ye do not come forward like men and do the deed of kind ye
two, I will arouse upon you the Ifrit." At this, by reason of their
sore dread of the Jinni, both did by her what she bade them do;
and, when they had dismounted from her, she said, "Well
done!" She then took from her pocket a purse and drew out a
knotted string, whereon were strung five hundred and seventy[2]
seal rings, and asked, "Know ye what be these?" They answered her saying, "We know not!" Then quoth she; "These be
the signets of five hundred and seventy men who have all
futtered me upon the horns of this foul, this foolish, this filthy
Ifrit; so give me also your two seal rings, ye pair of brothers."
When they had drawn their two rings from their hands and given
them to her, she said to them, "Of a truth this Ifrit bore me off on
my bride-night, and put me into a casket and set the casket in a
coffer and to the coffer he affixed seven strong padlocks of steel
and deposited me on the deep bottom of the sea that raves, dashing and clashing with waves; and guarded me so that I might re-

---

[1] This introducing the name of Allah into an indecent tale is essentially Egyptian and
Cairene. But see Boccaccio ii. 6; and vii. 9.

[2] So in the Mac. Edit.; in others "ninety." I prefer the greater number as exaggeration is a part of the humour. In the Hindu "Kathá Sárit Ságara" (Sea of the Streams of
Story), the rings are one hundred and the catastrophe is more moral; the good youth
Yashodhara rejects the wicked one's advances; she awakes the water-sprite, who is about
to slay him, but the rings are brought as testimony and the improper young person's nose
is duly cut off. (Chap. lxiii.; p. 80, of the excellent translation by Prof. C. H. Tawney:
for the Bibliotheca Indica: Calcutta, 1881.) The Kathá, etc., by Somadeva (century xi),
is a poetical version of the prose compendium, the "Vrihat Kathá" (Great Story) by
Gunadhya (cent. vi).

main chaste and honest, quotha! that none save himself might have connexion with me. But I have lain under as many of my kind as I please, and this wretched Jinni wotteth not that Destiny may not be averted nor hindered by aught, and that whatso woman willeth the same she fulfilleth however man nilleth. Even so saith one of them:—

Rely not on women;	* Trust not to their hearts,
Whose joys and whose sorrows	* Are hung to their parts!
Lying love they will swear thee	* Whence guile ne'er departs:
Take Yusuf[1] for sample	* 'Ware sleights and 'ware smarts!
Iblis[2] ousted Adam	* (See ye not?) thro' their arts.

And another saith:—

Stint thy blame, man! 'Twill drive to a passion without bound; * My fault is not so heavy as fault in it hast found.
If true lover I become, then to me there cometh not * Save what happened unto many in the by-gone stound.
For wonderful is he and right worthy of our praise * Who from wiles of female wits kept him safe and kept him sound."

Hearing these words they marvelled with exceeding marvel, and she went from them to the Ifrit and, taking up his head on her thigh as before, said to them softly, "Now wend your ways and bear yourselves beyond the bounds of his malice." So they fared forth saying either to other, "Allah! Allah!" and, "There be no Majesty and there be no Might save in Allah, the Glorious, the Great; and with Him we seek refuge from women's malice and sleight, for of a truth it hath no mate in might. Consider, O my brother, the ways of this marvellous lady with an Ifrit who is so much more powerful than we are. Now since there hath happened to him a greater mishap than that which befel us and which should bear us abundant consolation, so return we to our countries and capitals, and let us decide never to intermarry with

---

1 The Joseph of the Koran, very different from him of Genesis. We shall meet him often enough in The Nights.

2 "Iblis," vulgarly written "Eblis," from a root meaning The Despairer, with a suspicious likeness to Diabolos; possibly from "Balas," a profligate. Some translate it The Calumniator, as Satan is the Hater. Iblis (who appears in the Arab. version of the N. Testament) succeeded another revolting angel Al-Haris; and his story of pride, refusing to worship Adam, is told four times in the Koran from the Talmud (Sanhedrim 29). He caused Adam and Eve to lose Paradise (ii. 34); he still betrays mankind (xxv. 31), and at the end of time he, with the other devils, will be "gathered together on their knees round Hell" (xix. 69). He has evidently had the worst of the game, and we wonder, with Origen, Tillotson, Burns and many others, that he does not throw up the cards.

womankind and presently we will show them what will be our action." Thereupon they rode back to the tents of King Shahryar, which they reached on the morning of the third day; and, having mustered the Wazirs and Emirs, the Chamberlains and high officials, he gave a robe of honour to his Viceroy and issued orders for an immediate return to the city. There he sat him upon his throne and sending for the Chief Minister, the father of the two damsels who (Inshallah!) will presently be mentioned, he said, "I command thee to take my wife and smite her to death; for she hath broken her plight and her faith." So he carried her to the place of execution and did her die. Then King Shahryar took brand in hand and repairing to the Serraglio slew all the concubines and their Mamelukes.[1] He also sware himself by a binding oath that whatever wife he married he would abate her maidenhead at night and slay her next morning to make sure of his honour; "For," said he, "there never was nor is there one chaste woman upon face of earth." Then Shah Zaman prayed for permission to fare homewards; and he went forth equipped and escorted and travelled till he reached his own country. Meanwhile Shahryar commanded his Wazir to bring him the bride of the night that he might go in to her; so he produced a most beautiful girl, the daughter of one of the Emirs and the King went in unto her at eventide and when morning dawned he bade his Minister strike off her head; and the Wazir did accordingly for fear of the Sultan. On this wise he continued for the space of three years; marrying a maiden every night and killing her the next morning, till folk raised an outcry against him and cursed him, praying Allah utterly to destroy him and his rule; and women made an uproar and mothers wept and parents fled with their daughters till there remained not in the city a young person fit for carnal copulation. Presently the King ordered his Chief Wazir, the same who was charged with the executions, to bring him a virgin as was his wont; and the Minister went forth and searched and found none; so he returned home in sorrow and anxiety fearing for his life from the King. Now he had two daughters, Shahrázád and Dunyázád hight,[2] of whom the

---

[1] A similiar tale is still told at Akká (St. John d'Acre) concerning the terrible "butcher"—Jazzár (Djezzar) Pasha. One can hardly pity women who are fools enough to run such risks. According to Frizzi, Niccolò, Marquis of Este, after beheading Parisina, ordered all the faithless wives of Ferrara to be treated in like manner.

[2] "Shahrázád" (Persian) = City-freer; in the older version Scheherazade (probably both from Shirzád = lion-born). "Dunyázád" = World-freer. The Bres. Edit. corrupts the

elder had perused the books, annals and legends of preceding
Kings, and the stories, examples and instances of by-gone men
and things; indeed it was said that she had collected a thousand
books of histories relating to antique races and departed rulers.
She had perused the works of the poets and knew them by heart;
she had studied philosophy and the sciences, arts and accomplishments; and she was pleasant and polite, wise and witty, well read
and well bred. Now on that day she said to her father, "Why
do I see thee thus changed and laden with cark and care? Concerning this matter quoth one of the poets:—

> Tell whoso hath sorrow　　* Grief never shall last:
> E'en as joy hath no morrow　* So woe shall go past."

When the Wazir heard from his daughter these words he related
to her, from first to last, all that had happened between him and
the King. Thereupon said she, "By Allah, O my father, how
long shall this slaughter of women endure? Shall I tell thee what
is in my mind in order to save both sides from destruction?"
"Say on, O my daughter," quoth he, and quoth she, "I wish thou
wouldst give me in marriage to this King Shahryar; either I shall
live or I shall be a ransom for the virgin daughters of Moslems and
the cause of their deliverance from his hands and thine."[1] "Allah
upon thee!" cried he in wrath exceeding that lacked no feeding,
"O scanty of wit, expose not thy life to such peril! How durst
thou address me in words so wide from wisdom and un-far from
foolishness? Know that one who lacketh experience in worldly
matters readily falleth into misfortune; and whoso considereth
not the end keepeth not the world to friend, and the vulgar
say:—I was lying at mine ease: nought but my officiousness
brought me unease." "Needs must thou," she broke in, "make
me a doer of this good deed, and let him kill me an he will: I shall
only die a ransom for others." "O my daughter," asked he, "and
how shall that profit thee when thou shalt have thrown away
thy life?" and she answered, "O my father it must be, come of it
what will!" The Wazir was again moved to fury and blamed and

---

former to Sháhrzád or Sháhrazád; and the Mac. and Calc. to Shahrzád or Shehrzád. I
have ventured to restore the name as it should be. Galland for the second prefers
Dinarzade (?) and Richardson Dinazade (Dinázád = Religion-freer): here I have followed
Lane and Payne; though in "First Footsteps" I was misled by Galland. See Vol. ii. p. 1.

[1] Probably she proposed to "Judith" the King. These learned and clever young
ladies are very dangerous in the East.

reproached her, ending with, "In very deed I fear lest the same befal thee which befel the Bull and the Ass with the Husband-man." "And what," asked she, "befel them, O my father?" Whereupon the Wazir began the

Tale of the Bull[1] and the Ass.

KNOW, O my daughter, that there was once a merchant who owned much money and many men, and who was rich in cattle and camels; he had also a wife and family and he dwelt in the country, being experienced in husbandry and devoted to agricul-ture. Now Allah Most High had endowed him with under-standing the tongues of beasts and birds of every kind, but under pain of death if he divulged the gift to any. So he kept it secret for very fear. He had in his cow-house a Bull and an Ass each tethered in his own stall one hard by the other. As the merchant was sitting near hand one day with his servants and his children were playing about him, he heard the Bull say to the Ass, "Hail and health to thee O Father of Waking![2] for that thou enjoyest rest and good ministering; all under thee is clean-swept and fresh-sprinkled; men wait upon thee and feed thee, and thy provaunt is sifted barley and thy drink pure spring-water, while I (unhappy creature!) am led forth in the middle of the night, when they set on my neck the plough and a something called Yoke; and I tire at cleaving the earth from dawn of day till set of sun. I am forced to do more than I can and to bear all manner of ill-treatment from night to night; after which they take me back with my sides torn, my neck flayed, my legs aching and mine eyelids sored with tears. Then they shut me up in the byre and throw me beans and crushed-straw,[3] mixed with dirt and chaff; and I lie in dung and filth and foul stinks through the livelong night. But thou art ever in a place swept and sprinkled and cleansed, and thou art always

---

[1] In Egypt, etc., the bull takes the place of the Western ox. The Arab. word is "Taur" (Thaur, Saur); in old Persian "Tora" and Lat. "Taurus," a venerable remnant of the days before the "Semitic" and "Aryan" families of speech had split into two distinct growths. "Taur" ends in the Saxon "Steor" and the English "Steer."

[2] Arab. "Abú Yakzán" = the Wakener, because the ass brays at dawn.

[3] Arab. "Tibn"; straw crushed under the sledge: the hay of Egypt, Arabia, Syria, etc. The old country custom is to pull up the corn by handfuls from the roots, leaving the land perfectly bare: hence the "plucking up" of Hebrew Holy Writ. The object is to preserve every atom of "Tibn."

lying at ease, save when it happens (and seldom enough!) that the master hath some business, when he mounts thee and rides thee to town and returns with thee forthright. So it happens that I am toiling and distrest while thou takest thine ease and thy rest; thou sleepest while I am sleepless; I hunger still while thou eatest thy fill, and I win contempt while thou winnest good will." When the Bull ceased speaking, the Ass turned towards him and said, "O Broad-o'-Brow,[1] O thou lost one! he lied not who dubbed thee Bull-head, for thou, O father of a Bull, hast neither forethought nor contrivance; thou art the simplest of simpletons,[2] and thou knowest naught of good advisers. Hast thou not heard the saying of the wise:—

For others these hardships and labours I bear * And theirs is the pleasure and mine is the care;
As the bleacher who blacketh his brow in the sun * To whiten the raiment which other men wear.[3]

But thou, O fool, art full of zeal and thou toilest and moilest before the master; and thou tearest and wearest and slayest thyself for the comfort of another. Hast thou never heard the saw that saith, None to guide and from the way go wide? Thou wendest forth at the call to dawn-prayer and thou returnest not till sundown; and through the livelong day thou endurest all manner hardships; to wit, beating and belabouring and bad language. Now hearken to me, Sir Bull! when they tie thee to thy stinking manger, thou pawest the ground with thy forehand and lashest out with thy hind hoofs and pushest with thy horns and bellowest aloud, so they deem thee contented. And when they throw thee thy fodder thou fallest on it with greed and hastenest to line thy fair fat paunch. But if thou accept my advice it will be better for thee and thou wilt lead an easier life even than mine. When thou goest a-field and they lay the thing called Yoke on thy neck, lie down and rise not again though haply they swinge thee; and, if thou rise, lie down a second time; and when they bring thee home and offer thee thy beans, fall backwards and only sniff at thy meat and withdraw thee and taste it not, and be satisfied with thy crushed straw and chaff; and on this wise feign thou

---

1 Arab. "Yá Aftah": Al-Aftah is an epithet of the bull, also of the chameleon.
2 Arab. "Balíd," a favourite Egyptianism often pleasantly confounded with "Walí" (a Santon); hence the latter comes to mean "an innocent," a "ninny."
3 From the Calc. Edit., Vol. 1., p. 29.

art sick, and cease not doing thus for a day or two days or even three days, so shalt thou have rest from toil and moil." When the Bull heard these words he knew the Ass to be his friend and thanked him, saying, "Right is thy rede;" and prayed that all blessings might requite him, and cried, "O Father Wakener![1] thou hast made up for my failings." (Now[2] the merchant, O my daughter, understood all that passed between them.) Next day the driver took the Bull, and settling the plough on his neck,[3] made him work as wont; but the Bull began to shirk his plough-ing, according to the advice of the Ass, and the ploughman drubbed him till he broke the yoke and made off; but the man caught him up and leathered him till he despaired of his life. Not the less, however, would he do nothing but stand still and drop down till the evening. Then the herd led him home and stabled him in his stall: but he drew back from his manger and neither stamped nor ramped nor butted nor bellowed as he was wont to do; whereat the man wondered. He brought him the beans and husks, but he sniffed at them and left them and lay down as far from them as he could and passed the whole night fasting. The peasant came next morning; and, seeing the manger full of beans, the crushed-straw untasted and the ox lying on his back in sor-riest plight, with legs outstretched and swollen belly, he was concerned for him, and said to himself, "By Allah, he hath assuredly sickened and this is the cause why he would not plough yesterday." Then he went to the merchant and reported, "O my master, the Bull is ailing; he refused his fodder last night; nay more, he hath not tasted a scrap of it this morning." Now the merchant-farmer understood what all this meant, because he had overheard the talk between the Bull and the Ass, so quoth he, "Take that rascal donkey, and set the yoke on his neck, and bind him to the plough and make him do Bull's work." Thereupon the ploughman took the Ass, and worked him through the live-long day at the Bull's task; and, when he failed for weakness, he made him eat stick till his ribs were sore and his sides were sunken and his neck was flayed by the yoke; and when he came home in the evening he could hardly drag his limbs along, either fore-hand or hind-legs. But as for the Bull, he had passed the day lying at full length and had eaten his fodder with an excellent

---

[1] Arab. "Abu Yakzán" is hardly equivalent with "Père l'Eveillé."

[2] In Arab. the wa (‏و‎) is the sign of parenthesis.

[3] In the nearer East the light little plough is carried afield by the bull or ass.

appetite, and he ceased not calling down blessings on the Ass for his good advice, unknowing what had come to him on his account. So when night set in and the Ass returned to the byre the Bull rose up before him in honour, and said, "May good tidings gladden thy heart, O Father Wakener! through thee I have rested all this day and I have eaten my meat in peace and quiet." But the Ass returned no reply, for wrath and heart-burning and fatigue and the beating he had gotten; and he repented with the most grievous of repentance; and quoth he to himself: "This cometh of my folly in giving good counsel; as the saw saith, I was in joy and gladness, nought save my officiousness brought me this sadness. But I will bear in mind my innate worth and the nobility of my nature; for what saith the poet?

Shall the beautiful hue of the Basil[1] fail * Tho' the beetle's foot o'er the Basil crawl?
And though spider and fly be its denizens * Shall disgrace attach to the royal hall?
The cowrie,[2] I ken, shall have currency * But the pearl's clear drop, shall its value fall?

And now I must take thought and put a trick upon him and return him to his place, else I die." Then he went aweary to his manger, while the Bull thanked him and blessed him. And even so, O my daughter, said the Wazir, thou wilt die for lack of wits; therefore sit thee still and say naught and expose not thy life to such stress; for, by Allah, I offer thee the best advice, which cometh of my affection and kindly solicitude for thee." "O my father," she answered, "needs must I go up to this King and be married to him." Quoth he, "Do not this deed;" and quoth she, "Of a truth I will:" whereat he rejoined, "If thou be not silent and bide still, I will do with thee even what the merchant did with his wife." "And what did he?" asked she. "Know then, answered the Wazir, that after the return of the Ass the mer-

---

[1] Ocymum basilicum, the "royal herb," so much prized all over the East, especially in India, where, under the name of "Tulsi," it is a shrub sacred to the merry god Krishna. I found the verses in a MS. copy of The Nights.

[2] Arab. "Sadaf," the Kauri, or cowrie, brought from the Maldive and Lakdive Archipelago. The Kámús describes this "Wada'" or Concha Veneris as "a white shell (whence to "shell out") which is taken out of the sea, the fissure of which is white like that of the date-stone. It is hung about the neck to avert the evil eye." The pearl in Arab. is "Murwarid," hence evidently "Margarita" and Margaris (woman's name).

chant came out on the terrace-roof with his wife and family, for it was a moonlit night and the moon at its full. Now the terrace overlooked the cowhouse and presently, as he sat there with his children playing about him, the trader heard the Ass say to the Bull, "Tell me, O Father Broad o' Brow, what thou purposest to do to-morrow?" The Bull answered, "What but continue to follow thy counsel, O Aliboron? Indeed it was as good as good could be and it hath given me rest and repose; nor will I now depart from it one tittle: so, when they bring me my meat, I will refuse it and blow out my belly and counterfeit crank." The Ass shook his head and said, "Beware of so doing, O Father of a Bull!" The Bull asked, "Why," and the Ass answered, "Know that I am about to give thee the best of counsel, for verily I heard our owner say to the herd, If the Bull rise not from his place to do his work this morning and if he retire from his fodder this day, make him over to the butcher that he may slaughter him and give his flesh to the poor, and fashion a bit of leather[1] from his hide. Now I fear for thee on account of this. So take my advice ere a calamity befal thee; and when they bring thee thy fodder eat it and rise up and bellow and paw the ground, or our master will assuredly slay thee: and peace be with thee!" Thereupon the Bull arose and lowed aloud and thanked the Ass, and said, "To-morrow I will readily go forth with them;" and he at once ate up all his meat and even licked the manger. (All this took place and the owner was listening to their talk.) Next morning the trader and his wife went to the Bull's crib and sat down, and the driver came and led forth the Bull who, seeing his owner, whisked his tail and brake wind, and frisked about so lustily that the merchant laughed a loud laugh and kept laughing till he fell on his back. His wife asked him, "Whereat laughest thou with such loud laughter as this?"; and he answered her, "I laughed at a secret something which I have heard and seen but cannot say lest I die my death." She returned, "Perforce thou must discover it to me, and disclose the cause of thy laughing even if thou come by thy death!" But he rejoined, "I cannot reveal what beasts and birds say in their lingo for fear I die." Then quoth she, "By Allah, thou liest! this is a mere pretext: thou laughest at none save me, and now thou wouldest hide

---

[1] Arab. "Kat'a" (bit of leather): some read "Nat'a;" a leather used by way of table-cloth, and forming a bag for victuals; but it is never made of bull's hide.

somewhat from me. But by the Lord of the Heavens! an thou disclose not the cause I will no longer cohabit with thee: I will leave thee at once." And she sat down and cried. Whereupon quoth the merchant, "Woe betide thee! what means thy weeping? Fear Allah and leave these words and query me no more questions." "Needs must thou tell me the cause of that laugh," said she, and he replied, "Thou wottest that when I prayed Allah to vouchsafe me understanding of the tongues of beasts and birds, I made a vow never to disclose the secret to any under pain of dying on the spot." "No matter," cried she, "tell me what secret passed between the Bull and the Ass and die this very hour an thou be so minded;" and she ceased not to importune him till he was worn out and clean distraught. So at last he said, "Summon thy father and thy mother and our kith and kin and sundry of our neighbours," which she did; and he sent for the Kazi[1] and his assessors, intending to make his will and reveal to her his secret and die the death; for he loved her with love exceeding because she was his cousin, the daughter of his father's brother, and the mother of his children, and he had lived with her a life of an hundred and twenty years. Then, having assembled all the family and the folk of his neighbourhood, he said to them, "By me there hangeth a strange story, and 'tis such that if I discover the secret to any, I am a dead man." Therefore quoth every one of those present to the woman, "Allah upon thee, leave this sinful obstinacy and recognise the right of this matter, lest haply thy husband and the father of thy children die." But she rejoined, "I will not turn from it till he tell me, even though he come by his death." So they ceased to urge her; and the trader rose from amongst them and repaired to an out-house to perform Wuzu-ablution,[2] and he purposed thereafter to return and to tell them his secret and to die. Now, daughter Shahrazad, that merchant had in his out-houses some fifty hens under one cock, and whilst making ready to farewell his folk he heard one of his many farm-dogs thus address in his own tongue the Cock, who was flapping his wings and crowing lustily and jumping from one hen's back to another and treading all in turn, saying "O Chanticleer! how mean is thy wit and how shameless is thy conduct! Be

---

[1] The older "Cadi," a judge in religious matters. The Shuhúd, or Assessors, are officers of the Mahkamah or Kazi's Court.

[2] Of which more in a future page. He thus purified himself ceremonially before death.

he disappointed who brought thee up![1]   Art thou not ashamed of thy doings on such a day as this!"   "And what," asked the Rooster, "hath occurred this day?" when the Dog answered, "Dost thou not know that our master is this day making ready for his death?   His wife is resolved that he shall disclose the secret taught to him by Allah, and the moment he so doeth he shall surely die.   We dogs are all a-mourning; but thou clappest thy wings and clarionest thy loudest and treadest hen after hen.   Is this an hour for pastime and pleasuring?   Art thou not ashamed of thyself?"[2]   "Then by Allah," quoth the Cock, "is our master a lack-wit and a man scanty of sense: if he cannot manage matters with a single wife, his life is not worth prolonging.   Now I have some fifty Dame Partlets; and I please this and provoke that and starve one and stuff another; and through my good governance they are all well under my control.   This our master pretendeth to wit and wisdom, and he hath but one wife, and yet knoweth not how to manage her."   Asked the Dog, "What then, O Cock, should the master do to win clear of his strait?" "He should arise forthright," answered the Cock, "and take some twigs from yon mulberry-tree and give her a regular back-basting and rib-roasting till she cry:—I repent, O my lord! I will never ask thee a question as long as I live!   Then let him beat her once more and soundly, and when he shall have done this he shall sleep free from care and enjoy life.   But this master of ours owns neither sense nor judgment."   "Now, daughter Shahrazad," continued the Wazir, "I will do to thee as did that husband to that wife."   Said Shahrazad, "And what did he do?" He replied, "When the merchant heard the wise words spoken by his Cock to his Dog, he arose in haste and sought his wife's chamber, after cutting for her some mulberry-twigs and hiding them there; and then he called to her, "Come into the closet that I may tell thee the secret while no one seeth me and then die." She entered with him and he locked the door and came down upon her with so sound a beating of back and shoulders, ribs, arms and legs, saying the while, "Wilt thou ever be asking questions about what concerneth thee not?" that she was well nigh senseless.   Presently she cried out, "I am of the repentant! By Allah, I will ask thee no more questions, and indeed I repent

---

[1] This is Christian rather than Moslem: a favourite Maltese curse is "Yahrak Kiddisak man rabba-k!" = burn the Saint who brought thee up!

[2] A popular Egyptian phrase: the dog and the cock speak like Fellahs.

T. WILLIAMS

sincerely and wholesomely." Then she kissed his hand and feet and he led her out of the room submissive as a wife should be. Her parents and all the company rejoiced and sadness and mourning were changed into joy and gladness. Thus the merchant learnt family discipline from his Cock and he and his wife lived together the happiest of lives until death. And thou also, O my daughter!" continued the Wazir, "Unless thou turn from this matter I will do by thee what that trader did to his wife." But she answered him with much decision, "I will never desist, O my father, nor shall this tale change my purpose. Leave such talk and tattle. I will not listen to thy words and, if thou deny me, I will marry myself to him despite the nose of thee. And first I will go up to the King myself and alone and I will say to him:—I prayed my father to wive me with thee, but he refused, being resolved to disappoint his lord, grudging the like of me to the like of thee." Her father asked, "Must this needs be?" and she answered, "Even so." Hereupon the Wazir being weary of lamenting and contending, persuading and dissuading her, all to no purpose, went up to King Shahryar and after blessing him and kissing the ground before him, told him all about his dispute with his daughter from first to last and how he designed to bring her to him that night. The King wondered with exceeding wonder; for he had made an especial exception of the Wazir's daughter, and said to him, "O most faithful of Counsellors, how is this? Thou wottest that I have sworn by the Raiser of the Heavens that after I have gone in to her this night I shall say to thee on the morrow's morning:—Take her and slay her! and, if thou slay her not, I will slay thee in her stead without fail." "Allah guide thee to glory and lengthen thy life, O King of the age," answered the Wazir, "it is she that hath so determined: all this have I told her and more; but she will not hearken to me and she persisteth in passing this coming night with the King's Majesty." So Shahryar rejoiced greatly and said, "'Tis well; go get her ready and this night bring her to me." The Wazir returned to his daughter and reported to her the command saying, "Allah make not thy father desolate by thy loss!" But Shahrazad rejoiced with exceeding joy and gat ready all she required and said to her younger sister, Dunyazad, "Note well what directions I entrust to thee! When I have gone in to the King I will send for thee and when thou comest to me and seest that he hath had his carnal will of me, do thou say to me:—O my sister,

an thou be not sleepy, relate to me some new story, delectable
and delightsome, the better to speed our waking hours;" and I
will tell thee a tale which shall be our deliverance, if so Allah
please, and which shall turn the King from his blood-thirsty
custom." Dunyazad answered "With love and gladness." So
when it was night their father the Wazir carried Shahrazad to
the King who was gladdened at the sight and asked, "Hast thou
brought me my need?" and he answered, "I have." But when the
King took her to his bed and fell to toying with her and wished
to go in to her she wept; which made him ask, "What aileth
thee?" She replied, "O King of the age, I have a younger sister
and lief would I take leave of her this night before I see the
dawn." So he sent at once for Dunyazad and she came and kissed
the ground between his hands, when he permitted her to take
her seat near the foot of the couch. Then the King arose and did
away with his bride's maidenhead and the three fell asleep. But
when it was midnight Shahrazad awoke and signalled to her
sister Dunyazad who sat up and said, "Allah upon thee, O my
sister, recite to us some new story, delightsome and delectable,
wherewith to while away the waking hours of our latter night."[1]
"With joy and goodly gree," answered Shahrazad, "if this
pious and auspicious King permit me." "Tell on," quoth the
King who chanced to be sleepless and restless and therefore was
pleased with the prospect of hearing her story. So Shahrazad
rejoiced; and thus, on the first night of the Thousand Nights and a
Night, she began with the

TALE OF THE TRADER AND THE JINNI.

IT is related, O auspicious King, that there was a merchant of
the merchants who had much wealth, and business in various
cities. Now on a day he mounted horse and went forth to recover monies in certain towns, and the heat sore oppressed him;
so he sat beneath a tree and, putting his hand into his saddle-bags,
took thence some broken bread and dry dates and began to break
his fast. When he had ended eating the dates he threw away the
stones with force and lo! an Ifrit appeared, huge of stature and
brandishing a drawn sword, wherewith he approached the merchant and said, "Stand up that I may slay thee, even as thou

---

[1] *i. e.* between the last sleep and dawn when they would rise to wash and pray.

slewest my son!" Asked the merchant, "How have I slain thy
son?" and he answered, "When thou atest dates and threwest
away the stones they struck my son full in the breast as he was
walking by, so that he died forthwith."[1] Quoth the merchant,
"Verily from Allah we proceeded and unto Allah are we returning. There is no Majesty, and there is no Might save in
Allah, the Glorious, the Great! If I slew thy son, I slew him by
chance medley. I pray thee now pardon me." Rejoined the
Jinni, "There is no help but I must slay thee." Then he
seized him and dragged him along and, casting him to the earth,
raised the sword to strike him; whereupon the merchant wept,
and said, "I commit my case to Allah," and began repeating
these couplets:—

Containeth Time a twain of days, this of blessing that of bane * And holdeth
　　Life a twain of halves, this of pleasure that of pain.
See'st not when blows the hurricane, sweeping stark and striking strong *
　　None save the forest giant feels the suffering of the strain?
How many trees earth nourisheth of the dry and of the green * Yet none but
　　those which bear the fruits for cast of stone complain.
See'st not how corpses rise and float on the surface of the tide * While pearls
　　o'price lie hidden in the deepest of the main!
In Heaven are unnumberèd the many of the stars * Yet ne'er a star but Sun
　　and Moon by eclipse is overta'en.
Well judgedst thou the days that saw thy faring sound and well*And countedst
　　not the pangs and pain whereof Fate is ever fain.
The nights have kept thee safe and the safety brought thee pride * But bliss
　　and blessings of the night are 'genderers of bane!

When the merchant ceased repeating his verses the Jinni said to
him, "Cut thy words short, by Allah! needs must I slay thee."
But the merchant spake him thus, "Know, O thou Ifrit, that I
have debts due to me and much wealth and children and a wife
and many pledges in hand; so permit me to go home and discharge to every claimant his claim; and I will come back to thee at
the head of the new year. Allah be my testimony and surety
that I will return to thee; and then thou mayest do with me as
thou wilt and Allah is witness to what I say." The Jinni took
sure promise of him and let him go; so he returned to his own city
and transacted his business and rendered to all men their dues

---

[1] Travellers tell of a peculiar knack of jerking the date-stone, which makes it strike
with great force: I never saw this "Inwá" practised, but it reminds me of the water-
splashing with one hand in the German baths.

and after informing his wife and children of what had betided him, he appointed a guardian and dwelt with them for a full year. Then he arose, and made the Wuzu-ablution to purify himself before death and took his shroud under his arm and bade farewell to his people, his neighbours and all his kith and kin, and went forth despite his own nose.[1] They then began weeping and wailing and beating their breasts over him; but he travelled until he arrived at the same garden, and the day of his arrival was the head of the New Year. As he sat weeping over what had befallen him, behold, a Shaykh,[2] a very ancient man, drew near leading a chained gazelle; and he saluted that merchant and wish-ing him long life said, "What is the cause of thy sitting in this place and thou alone and this be a resort of evil spirits?" The merchant related to him what had come to pass with the Ifrit, and the old man, the owner of the gazelle, wondered and said, "By Allah, O brother, thy faith is none other than exceeding faith and thy story right strange; were it graven with gravers on the eye-corners, it were a warner to whoso would be warned." Then seating himself near the merchant he said, "By Allah, O my brother, I will not leave thee until I see what may come to pass with thee and this Ifrit." And presently as he sat and the two were at talk the merchant began to feel fear and terror and exceeding grief and sorrow beyond relief and ever-growing care and extreme despair. And the owner of the gazelle was hard by his side; when behold, a second Shaykh approached them, and with him were two dogs both of greyhound breed and both black. The second old man after saluting them with the salam, also asked them of their tidings and said "What causeth you to sit in this place, a dwelling of the Jánn?"[3] So they told him the

---

[1] i.e., sorely against his will.

[2] Arab. "Shaykh" = an old man (primarily), an elder, a chief (of the tribe, guild, etc.); and honourably addressed to any man. Comp. among the neo-Latins "Sieur," "Signore," "Señor," "Senhor," etc. from Lat. "Senior," which gave our "Sire" and "Sir." Like many in Arabic the word has a host of different meanings and most of them will occur in the course of The Nights. Ibrahim (Abraham) was the first Shaykh or man who became grey. Seeing his hairs whiten he cried, "O Allah what is this?" and the answer came that it was a sign of dignified gravity. Hereupon he exclaimed, "O Lord increase this to me!" and so it happened till his locks waxed snowy white at the age of one hundred and fifty. He was the first who parted his hair, trimmed his mustachios, cleaned his teeth with the Miswák (tooth-stick), pared his nails, shaved his pecten, snuffed up water, used ablution after stool and wore a shirt (Tabari).

[3] The word is mostly plural = Jinnís: it is also singular = a demon; and Ján bin Ján has been noticed.

tale from beginning to end, and their stay there had not lasted long before there came up a third Shaykh, and with him a she-mule of bright bay coat; and he saluted them and asked them why they were seated in that place. So they told him the story from first to last: and of no avail, O my master, is a twice-told tale! There he sat down with them, and lo! a dust-cloud advanced and a mighty sand-devil appeared amidmost of the waste. Presently the cloud opened and behold, within it was that Jinni hending in hand a drawn sword, while his eyes were shooting fire-sparks of rage. He came up to them and, haling away the merchant from among them, cried to him, "Arise that I may slay thee, as thou slewest my son, the life-stuff of my liver."[1] The merchant wailed and wept, and the three old men began sighing and crying and weeping and wailing with their companion. Presently the first old man (the owner of the gazelle) came out from among them and kissed the hand of the Ifrit and said, "O Jinni, thou Crown of the Kings of the Jann! were I to tell thee the story of me and this gazelle and thou shouldst consider it wondrous wouldst thou give me a third part of this merchant's blood?" Then quoth the Jinni "Even so, O Shaykh! if thou tell me this tale, and I hold it a marvellous, then will I give thee a third of his blood." Thereupon the old man began to tell

The First Shaykh's Story.

KNOW O Jinni! that this gazelle is the daughter of my paternal uncle, my own flesh and blood, and I married her when she was a young maid, and I lived with her well-nigh thirty years, yet was I not blessed with issue by her. So I took me a concubine,[2] who

---

[1] With us moderns "liver" suggests nothing but malady: in Arabic and Persian as in the classic literature of Europe it is the seat of passion, the heart being that of affection. Of this more presently.

[2] Originally in Al-Islam the concubine (Surriyat, etc.) was a captive taken in war and the Koran says nothing about buying slave-girls. But if the captives were true believers the Moslem was ordered to marry not to keep them. In modern days concubinage has become an extensive subject. Practically the disadvantage is that the slave-girls, knowing themselves to be the master's property, consider him bound to sleep with them; which is by no means the mistress's view. Some wives, however, when old and childless, insist, after the fashion of Sarah, upon the husband taking a young concubine and treating her like a daughter—which is rare. The Nights abound in tales of concubines, but these are chiefly owned by the Caliphs and high officials who did much as they pleased. The only redeeming point in the system is that it obviated the necessity of prostitution which is, perhaps, the greatest evil known to modern society.

brought to me the boon of a male child fair as the full moon, with eyes of lovely shine and eyebrows which formed one line, and limbs of perfect design. Little by little he grew in stature and waxed tall; and when he was a lad fifteen years old, it became needful I should journey to certain cities and I travelled with great store of goods. But the daughter of my uncle (this gazelle) had learned gramarye and egromancy and clerkly craft[1] from her childhood; so she bewitched that son of mine to a calf, and my handmaid (his mother) to a heifer, and made them over to the herdsman's care. Now when I returned after a long time from my journey and asked for my son and his mother, she answered me, saying "Thy slave-girl is dead, and thy son hath fled and I know not whither he is sped." So I remained for a whole year with grieving heart, and streaming eyes until the time came for the Great Festival of Allah.[2] Then sent I to my herdsman bidding him choose for me a fat heifer; and he brought me one which was the damsel, my handmaid, whom this gazelle had ensorcelled. I tucked up my sleeves and skirt and, taking a knife, proceeded to cut her throat, but she lowed aloud and wept bitter tears. Thereat I marvelled and pity seized me and I held my hand, saying to the herd, "Bring me other than this." Then cried my cousin, "Slay her, for I have not a fatter nor a fairer!" Once more I went forward to sacrifice her, but she again lowed aloud upon which in ruth I refrained and commanded the herdsman to slay her and flay her. He killed her and skinned her but found in her neither fat nor flesh, only hide and bone; and I repented when penitence availed me naught. I gave her to the herdsman and said to him, "Fetch me a fat calf;" so he brought my son ensorcelled. When the calf saw me, he brake his tether and ran to me, and fawned upon me and wailed and shed tears; so that I took pity on him and said to the herdsman, "Bring me a heifer and let this calf go!" Thereupon my cousin (this gazelle) called aloud at me, saying, "Needs must thou kill this

---

[1] Arab. "Al-Kaháhah" = the craft of a "Káhin" (Heb. Cohen) a diviner, soothsayer, etc.

[2] Arab. "Id al-kabír" = The Great Festival; the Turkish Bayrám and Indian Bakar-eed (Kine-fête), the pilgrimage-time, also termed "Festival of the Kurbán" (sacrifice) because victims are slain; Al-Zuha (of Undurn or forenoon), Al-Azhá (of serene night) and Al-Nahr (of throat-cutting). For full details I must refer readers to my "Personal Narrative of a Pilgrimage to El-Medinah and Meccah" (3 vols. 8vo, London, Longmans, 1855). I shall have often to refer to it.

calf; this is a holy day and a blessed, whereon naught is slain
save what be perfect-pure; and we have not amongst our calves
any fatter or fairer than this!" Quoth I, "Look thou upon the
condition of the heifer which I slaughtered at thy bidding and
how we turn from her in disappointment and she profited us on
no wise; and I repent with an exceeding repentance of having
killed her: so this time I will not obey thy bidding for the
sacrifice of this calf." Quoth she, "By Allah the Most Great,
the Compassionating, the Compassionate! there is no help for
it; thou must kill him on this holy day, and if thou kill him not
to me thou art no man and I to thee am no wife." Now when
I heard those hard words, not knowing her object I went up to
the calf, knife in hand——And Shahrazad perceived the dawn of
day and ceased to say her permitted say.[1] Then quoth her sister
to her, "How fair is thy tale, and how grateful, and how sweet
and how tasteful!" And Shahrazad answered her, "What is
this to that I could tell thee on the coming night, were I to live
and the King would spare me?" Then said the King in himself,
"By Allah, I will not slay her, until I shall have heard the rest
of her tale." So they slept the rest of that night in mutual embrace till day fully brake. Then the King went forth to his audience-hall[2] and the Wazir went up with his daughter's shroud
under his arm. The King issued his orders, and promoted this
and deposed that, until the end of the day; and he told the Wazir
no whit of what had happened. But the Minister wondered
thereat with exceeding wonder; and when the Court broke up
King Shahryar entered his palace.

When it was the Second Night,

said Dunyazad to her sister Shahrazad, "O my sister, finish for us
that story of the Merchant and the Jinni;" and she answered
"With joy and goodly gree, if the King permit me." Then

---

[1] Arab. "Kalám al-mubáh," *i.e.*, that allowed or permitted to her by the King, her
husband.

[2] Moslem Kings are expected, like the old Guebre Monarchs, to hold "Darbar" (*i.e.*,
give public audience) at least twice a day, morning and evening. Neglect of this practice
caused the ruin of the Caliphate and of the Persian and Moghul Empires: the great
lords were left uncontrolled and the lieges revolted to obtain justice. The Guebre Kings
had two levée places, the Rozistan (day station) and the Shabistan (night-station—istán
or stán being a nominal form of istádan, to stand, as Hindo-stán). Moreover one day in
the week the sovereign acted as "Mufti" or Supreme Judge.

quoth the King, "Tell thy tale;" and Shahrazad began in these
words: It hath reached me, O auspicious King and Heaven-
directed Ruler! that when the merchant purposed the sacrifice of
the calf but saw it weeping, his heart relented and he said to the
herdsman, "Keep the calf among my cattle." All this the old
Shaykh told the Jinni who marvelled much at these strange
words. Then the owner of the gazelle continued:—O Lord of
the Kings of the Jann, this much took place and my uncle's
daughter, this gazelle, looked on and saw it, and said, "Butcher
me this calf, for surely it is a fat one;" but I bade the herdsman
take it away and he took it and turned his face homewards. On
the next day as I was sitting in my own house, lo! the herdsman
came and, standing before me said, "O my master, I will tell
thee a thing which shall gladden thy soul, and shall gain me the
gift of good tidings."[1] I answered, "Even so." Then said he,
"O merchant, I have a daughter, and she learned magic in her
childhood from an old woman who lived with us. Yesterday
when thou gavest me the calf, I went into the house to her, and
she looked upon it and veiled her face; then she wept and laughed
alternately and at last she said:—O my father, hath mine
honour become so cheap to thee that thou bringest in to me
strange men? I asked her:—Where be these strange men and
why wast thou laughing, and crying?; and she answered, Of a
truth this calf which is with thee is the son of our master, the
merchant; but he is ensorcelled by his stepdame who bewitched
both him and his mother: such is the cause of my laughing; now
the reason of his weeping is his mother, for that his father slew
her unawares. Then I marvelled at this with exceeding marvel
and hardly made sure that day had dawned before I came to tell
thee." When I heard, O Jinni, my herdsman's words, I went
out with him, and I was drunken without wine, from the excess
of joy and gladness which came upon me, until I reached his
house. There his daughter welcomed me and kissed my hand,
and forthwith the calf came and fawned upon me as before.
Quoth I to the herdsman's daughter, "Is this true that thou
sayest of this calf?" Quoth she, "Yea, O my master, he is thy
son, the very core of thy heart." I rejoiced and said to her,
"O maiden, if thou wilt release him thine shall be whatever

---

[1] Arab. "Al-Bashárah," the gift everywhere claimed in the East and in Boccaccio's
Italy by one who brings good news. Those who do the reverse expose themselves to a
sound strappado.

cattle and property of mine are under thy father's hand." She smiled and answered, "O my master, I have no greed for the goods nor will I take them save on two conditions; the first that thou marry me to thy son and the second that I may be-witch her who bewitched him and imprison her, otherwise I cannot be safe from her malice and malpractices." Now when I heard, O Jinni, these, the words of the herdsman's daughter, I replied, "Beside what thou askest all the cattle and the house-hold stuff in thy father's charge are thine and, as for the daugh-ter of my uncle, her blood is lawful to thee." When I had spoken, she took a cup and filled it with water: then she recited a spell over it and sprinkled it upon the calf, saying, "If Almighty Allah created thee a calf, remain so shaped, and change not; but if thou be enchanted, return to thy whilom form, by command of Allah Most Highest!" and lo! he trembled and became a man. Then I fell on his neck and said, "Allah upon thee, tell me all that the daughter of my uncle did by thee and by thy mother." And when he told me what had come to pass between them I said, "O my son, Allah favoured thee with one to restore thee, and thy right hath returned to thee." Then, O Jinni, I married the herdsman's daughter to him, and she transformed my wife into this gazelle, saying:—Her shape is a comely and by no means loathsome. After this she abode with us night and day, day and night, till the Almighty took her to Himself. When she deceased, my son fared forth to the cities of Hind, even to the city of this man who hath done to thee what hath been done;[1] and I also took this gazelle (my cousin) and wandered with her from town to town seeking tidings of my son, till Destiny drove me to this place where I saw the merchant sitting in tears. Such is my tale! Quoth the Jinni, "This story is indeed strange, and therefore I grant thee the third part of his blood." There-upon the second old man, who owned the two greyhounds, came up and said, "O Jinni, if I recount to thee what befel me from my brothers, these two hounds, and thou see that it is a tale even more wondrous and marvellous than what thou hast heard, wilt thou grant to me also the third of this man's blood?" Replied the Jinni, "Thou hast my word for it, if thine adven-

---

[1] A euphemistic formula, to avoid mentioning unpleasant matters. I shall note these for the benefit of students who would honestly prepare for the public service in Moslem lands.

tures be more marvellous and wondrous." Thereupon he thus began

The Second Shaykh's Story.

KNOW, O lord of the Kings of the Jann! that these two dogs are my brothers and I am the third. Now when our father died and left us a capital of three thousand gold pieces,[1] I opened a shop with my share, and bought and sold therein, and in like guise did my two brothers, each setting up a shop. But I had been in business no long while before the elder sold his stock for a thousand dinars, and after buying outfit and merchandise, went his ways to foreign parts. He was absent one whole year with the caravan; but one day as I sat in my shop, behold, a beggar stood before me asking alms, and I said to him, "Allah open thee another door!"[2] Whereupon he answered, weeping the while, "Am I so changed that thou knowest me not?" Then I looked at him narrowly, and lo! it was my brother, so I rose to him and welcomed him; then I seated him in my shop and put questions concerning his case. "Ask me not," answered he; "my wealth is awaste and my state hath waxed un-stated!" So I took him to the Hammám-bath[3] and clad him in a suit of my own and gave him lodging in my house. Moreover, after looking over the accounts of my stock-in-trade and the profits of my business, I found that industry had gained me one thousand dinars, while my principal, the head of my wealth, amounted to two thousand. So I shared the whole with him saying, "Assume that thou hast made no journey abroad but hast remained at home; and be not cast down by thine ill-luck." He took the share in great glee and opened for himself a shop; and matters

---

[1] Arab. "Dínár," from the Latin denarius (a silver coin worth ten ounces of brass) through the Greek δηνάριον: it is a Koranic word (chapt. iii.) though its Arab equivalent is "Miskál." It also occurs in the Kathá before quoted, clearly showing the derivation. In the "Book of Kalilah and Dimnah" it is represented by the Daric or Persian Dinár, δαρεικὸs, from Dárá = a King (whence Darius). The Dinar, sequin or ducat, contained at different times from 10 and 12 (Abu Hanifah's day) to 20 and even 25 dirhams or drachmas; and, as a weight, represented a drachma and a half. Its value greatly varied, but we may assume it here at nine shillings or ten francs to half a sovereign. For an elaborate article on the Dinar see Yule's "Cathay and the Way Thither" (ii., pp. 439–443).

[2] The formula used in refusing alms to an "asker" or in rejecting an insufficient offer: "Allah will open to thee!" (some door of gain—not mine)! Another favourite ejaculation is "Allah Karim" (which Turks pronounce "Kyereem") = Allah is All-beneficent! meaning Ask Him, not me.

[3] The public bath. London knows the word through "The Hummums."

went on quietly for a few nights and days. But presently my second brother (yon other dog), also setting his heart upon travel, sold off what goods and stock-in-trade he had, and albeit we tried to stay him he would not be stayed: he laid in an outfit for the journey and fared forth with certain wayfarers. After an absence of a whole year he came back to me, even as my elder brother had come back; and when I said to him, "O my brother, did I not dissuade thee from travel?" he shed tears and cried, "O my brother, this be destiny's decree: here I am a mere beggar, penniless[1] and without a shirt to my back." So I led him to the bath, O Jinni, and clothing him in new clothes of my own wear, I went with him to my shop and served him with meat and drink. Furthermore I said to him, "O my brother, I am wont to cast up my shop-accounts at the head of every year, and whatso I shall find of surplusage is between me and thee."[2] So I proceeded, O Ifrit, to strike a balance and, finding two thousand dinars of profit, I returned praises to the Creator (be He extolled and exalted!) and made over one half to my brother, keeping the other to myself. Thereupon he busied himself with opening a shop and on this wise we abode many days. After a time my brothers began pressing me to travel with them; but I refused saying, "What gained ye by travel voyage that I should gain thereby?" As I would not give ear to them we went back each to his own shop where we bought and sold as before. They kept urging me to travel for a whole twelvemonth, but I refused to do so till full six years were past and gone when I consented with these words, "O my brothers, here am I, your companion of travel: now let me see what monies you have by you." I found, however, that they had not a doit, having squandered their substance in high diet and drinking and carnal delights. Yet I spoke not a word of reproach; so far from it I looked over my shop accounts once more, and sold what goods and stock-in-trade were mine; and, finding myself the owner of six thousand ducats, I gladly proceeded to divide that sum in halves, saying to my brothers, "These three

---

[1] Arab. "Dirham" (Plur. diráhim, also used in the sense of money, "siller"), the drachuma of Plautus (Trin. 2, 4, 23). The word occurs in the Panchatantra also showing the derivation; and in the Syriac Kalilah wa Dimnah it is "Zúz." This silver piece was = 6 obols (9¾d.) and as a weight = 66½ grains. The Dirham of The Nights was worth six "Dánik," each of these being a fraction over a penny. The modern Greek Drachma is = one franc.

[2] In Arabic the speaker always puts himself first, even if he address the King, without intending incivility.

thousand gold pieces are for me and for you to trade withal," adding, "Let us bury the other moiety underground that it may be of service in case any harm befal us, in which case each shall take a thousand wherewith to open shops." Both replied, "Right is thy recking;" and I gave to each one his thousand gold pieces, keeping the same sum for myself, to wit, a thousand dinars. We then got ready suitable goods and hired a ship and, having embarked our merchandise, proceeded on our voyage, day following day, a full month, after which we arrived at a city, where we sold our venture; and for every piece of gold we gained ten. And as we turned again to our voyage we found on the shore of the sea a maiden clad in worn and ragged gear, and she kissed my hand and said, "O master, is there kindness in thee and charity? I can make thee a fitting return for them." I answered, "Even so; truly in me are benevolence and good works, even though thou render me no return." Then she said, "Take me to wife, O my master, and carry me to thy city, for I have given myself to thee; so do me a kindness and I am of those who be meet for good works and charity: I will make thee a fitting return for these and be thou not shamed by my condition." When I heard her words, my heart yearned towards her, in such sort as willed it Allah (be He extolled and exalted!); and took her and clothed her and made ready for her a fair resting-place in the vessel, and honourably entreated her. So we voyaged on, and my heart became attached to her with exceeding attachment, and I was separated from her neither night nor day, and I paid more regard to her than to my brothers. Then they were estranged from me, and waxed jealous of my wealth and the quantity of merchandise I had, and their eyes were opened covetously upon all my property. So they took counsel to murder me and seize my wealth, saying, "Let us slay our brother and all his monies will be ours;" and Satan made this deed seem fair in their sight; so when they found me in privacy (and I sleeping by my wife's side) they took us both up and cast us into the sea. My wife awoke startled from her sleep and, forthright becoming an Ifritah,[1] she bore me up and carried me to an island and disappeared for a short time; but she returned in the morning and said, "Here am I, thy faithful slave, who hath made thee due recompense; for I bore thee up in the waters and saved thee

---

[1] A she-Ifrit, not necessarily an evil spirit.

from death by command of the Almighty. Know that I am a Jinniyah, and as I saw thee my heart loved thee by will of the Lord, for I am a believer in Allah and in His Apostle (whom Heaven bless and preserve!). Thereupon I came to thee conditioned as thou sawest me and thou didst marry me, and see now I have saved thee from sinking. But I am angered against thy brothers and assuredly I must slay them." When I heard her story I was surprised and, thanking her for all she had done, I said, "But as to slaying my brothers this must not be." Then I told her the tale of what had come to pass with them from the beginning of our lives to the end, and on hearing it quoth she, "This night will I fly as a bird over them and will sink their ship and slay them." Quoth I, "Allah upon thee, do not thus, for the proverb saith, O thou who doest good to him that doth evil, leave the evil doer to his evil deeds. Moreover they are still my brothers." But she rejoined, "By Allah, there is no help for it but I slay them." I humbled myself before her for their pardon, whereupon she bore me up and flew away with me till at last she set me down on the terrace-roof of my own house. I opened the doors and took up what I had hidden in the ground; and after I had saluted the folk I opened my shop and bought me merchandise. Now when night came on I went home, and there I saw these two hounds tied up; and, when they sighted me, they arose and whined and fawned upon me; but ere I knew what happened my wife said, "These two dogs be thy brothers!" I answered, "And who hath done this thing by them?" and she rejoined, "I sent a message to my sister and she entreated them on this wise, nor shall these two be released from their present shape till ten years shall have passed." And now I have arrived at this place on my way to my wife's sister that she may deliver them from this condition, after their having endured it for half a score of years. As I was wending onwards I saw this young man, who acquainted me with what had befallen him, and I determined not to fare hence until I should see what might occur between thee and him. Such is my tale! Then said the Jinni, "Surely this is a strange story and therefor I give thee the third portion of his blood and his crime." Thereupon quoth the third Shaykh, the master of the mare-mule, to the Jinni, "I can tell thee a tale more wondrous than these two, so thou grant me the remainder of his blood and of his offence," and the Jinni answered, "So be it!" Then the old man began

The Third Shaykh's Story.

KNOW, O Sultan and head of the Jann, that this mule was my wife. Now it so happened that I went forth and was absent one whole year; and when I returned from my journey I came to her by night, and saw a black slave lying with her on the carpet-bed and they were talking, and dallying, and laughing, and kissing and playing the close-buttock game. When she saw me, she rose and came hurriedly at me with a gugglet[1] of water; and, muttering spells over it, she besprinkled me and said, "Come forth from this thy shape into the shape of a dog;" and I became on the instant a dog. She drove me out of the house, and I ran through the doorway nor ceased running until I came to a butcher's stall, where I stopped and began to eat what bones were there. When the stall-owner saw me, he took me and led me into his house, but as soon as his daughter had sight of me she veiled her face from me, crying out, "Dost thou bring men to me and dost thou come in with them to me?" Her father asked, "Where is the man?"; and she answered, "This dog is a man whom his wife hath ensorcelled and I am able to release him." When her father heard her words, he said, "Allah upon thee, O my daughter, release him." So she took a gugglet of water and, after uttering words over it, sprinkled upon me a few drops, saying, "Come forth from that form into thy former form." And I returned to my natural shape. Then I kissed her hand and said, "I wish thou wouldest transform my wife even as she transformed me." Thereupon she gave me some water, saying, "As soon as thou see her asleep, sprinkle this liquid upon her and speak what words thou heardest me utter, so shall she become whatsoever thou desirest." I went to my wife and found her fast asleep; and, while sprinkling the water upon her, I said, "Come forth from that form into the form of a mare-mule." So she became on the instant a she-mule, and she it is whom thou

---

1 Arab. "Kullah" (in Egypt pron. "gulleh"), the wide-mouth j jug, called in the Hijaz "baradiyah;" "daurak" being the narrow. They are used eithe for water or sherbet and, being made of porous clay, "sweat," and keep the contents cool; hence all old Anglo-Egyptians drink from them, not from bottles. Sometimes they are perfumed with smoke of incense, mastich or Kafal (Amyris Kafal). For their graceful shapes see Lane's "Account of the Manners and Customs of the Modern Egyptians" (chapt. v) I quote, here and elsewhere, from the fifth edition, London, Murray, 1860.

seest with thine eyes, O Sultan and head of the Kings of the
Jann! Then the Jinni turned towards her and said, "Is this
sooth?" And she nodded her head and replied by signs, "Indeed, 'tis the truth: for such is my tale and this is what hath befallen me." Now when the old man had ceased speaking the
Jinni shook with pleasure and gave him the third of the merchant's blood.——And Shahrazad perceived the dawn of day
and ceased saying her permitted say. Then quoth Dunyazad,
"O, my sister, how pleasant is thy tale, and how tasteful; how
sweet and how grateful!" She replied, "And what is this compared with that I could tell thee, the night to come, if I live and
the King spare me?"[1] Then thought the King, "By Allah, I will
not slay her until I hear the rest of her tale, for truly it is wondrous." So they rested that night in mutual embrace until the
dawn. After this the King went forth to his Hall of Estate, and the
Wazir and the troops came in and the court was crowded, and
the King gave orders and judged and appointed and deposed,
bidding and forbidding during the rest of the day. Then the
Divan broke up, and King Shahryar entered his palace.

When it was the Third Night,

And the King had had his will of the Wazir's daughter, Dunyazad, her sister, said to her, "Finish for us that tale of thine;"
and she replied, "With joy and goodly gree! It hath reached me,
O auspicious King, that when the third old man told a tale to the
Jinni more wondrous than the two preceding, the Jinni marvelled with exceeding marvel; and, shaking with delight, cried,
"Lo! I have given thee the remainder of the merchant's punishment and for thy sake have I released him." Thereupon
the merchant embraced the old men and thanked them, and these
Shaykhs wished him joy on being saved and fared forth each one
for his own city. Yet this tale is not more wondrous than the
fisherman's story." Asked the King, "What is the fisherman's
story?" And she answered by relating the tale of

---

1 "And what is?" etc. A popular way of expressing great difference. So in India:—
"Where is Rajah Bhoj (the great King) and where is Gangá the oilman?"

THE FISHERMAN AND THE JINNI.

It hath reached me, O auspicious King, that there was a Fisherman well stricken in years who had a wife and three children, and
withal was of poor condition. Now it was his custom to cast
his net every day four times, and no more. On a day he went
forth about noontide to the sea shore, where he laid down his
basket; and, tucking up his shirt and plunging into the water,
made a cast with his net and waited till it settled to the bottom.
Then he gathered the cords together and haled away at it, but
found it weighty; and however much he drew it landwards, he
could not pull it up; so he carried the ends ashore and drove a
stake into the ground and made the net fast to it. Then he stripped
and dived into the water all about the net, and left not off
working hard until he had brought it up. He rejoiced thereat
and, donning his clothes, went to the net, when he found in it a
dead jackass which had torn the meshes. Now when he saw it,
he exclaimed in his grief, "There is no Majesty, and there is
no Might save in Allah the Glorious, the Great!" Then quoth
he, "This is a strange manner of daily bread;" and he began reciting in extempore verse:—

O toiler through the glooms of night in peril and in pain * Thy toiling stint for
    daily bread comes not by might and main!
Seest thou not the fisher seek afloat upon the sea * His bread, while glimmer
    stars of night as set in tangled skein.
Anon he plungeth in despite the buffet of the waves * The while to sight the
    bellying net his eager glances strain;
Till joying at the night's success, a fish he bringeth home * Whose gullet by the
    hook of Fate was caught and cut in twain.
When buys that fish of him a man who spent the hours of night * Reckless
    of cold and wet and gloom in ease and comfort fain,
Laud to the Lord who gives to this, to that denies his wishes * And dooms one
    toil and catch the prey and other eat the fishes.[1]

Then quoth he, "Up and to it; I am sure of His beneficence,
Inshallah!" So he continued:—

When thou art seized of Evil Fate, assume * The noble soul's long-suffering:
    'tis thy best:
Complain not to the creature; this be 'plaint * From one most Ruthful to the
    ruthlessest.

---

[1] Here, as in other places, I have not preserved the monorhyme, but have ended like the
English sonnet with a couplet; as a rule the last two lines contain a "Husn makta'" or
climax.

The Fisherman, when he had looked at the dead ass, got it free of the toils and wrung out and spread his net; then he plunged into the sea, saying, "In Allah's name!" and made a cast and pulled at it, but it grew heavy and settled down more firmly than the first time. Now he thought that there were fish in it, and he made it fast, and doffing his clothes went into the water, and dived and haled until he drew it up upon dry land. Then found he in it a large earthen pitcher which was full of sand and mud; and seeing this he was greatly troubled and began repeating these verses[1]:—

Forbear, O troubles of the world, * And pardon an ye nill forbear:
I went to seek my daily bread * I find that breadless I must fare:
For neither handcraft brings me aught * Nor Fate allots to me a share:
How many fools the Pleiads reach * While darkness whelms the wise and ware.

So he prayed pardon of Allah and, throwing away the jar, wrung his net and cleansed it and returned to the sea the third time to cast his net and waited till it had sunk. Then he pulled at it and found therein potsherds and broken glass; whereupon he began to speak these verses:—

He is to thee that daily bread thou canst nor loose nor bind * Nor pen nor
    writ avail thee aught thy daily bread to find:
For joy and daily bread are what Fate deigneth to allow; * This soil is sad and
    sterile ground, while that makes glad the hind.
The shafts of Time and Life bear down full many a man of worth * While
    bearing up to high degree wights of ignoble mind.
So come thou, Death! for verily life is not worth a straw * When low the
    falcon falls withal the mallard wings the wind:
No wonder 'tis thou seest how the great of soul and mind * Are poor, and
    many a losel carle to height of luck designed.
This bird shall overfly the world from east to furthest west * And that shall
    win her every wish though ne'er she leave the nest.

Then raising his eyes heavenwards he said, "O my God![2] verily

---

[1] Lit. "he began to say (or speak) poetry," such improvising being still common amongst the Badawin as I shall afterwards note. And although Mohammed severely censured profane poets, who "rove as bereft of their senses through every valley" and were directly inspired by devils (Koran xxvi.), it is not a little curious to note that he himself spoke in "Rajaz" (which see) and that the four first Caliphs all "spoke poetry." In early ages the verse would not be written, if written at all, till after the maker's death. I translate "inshád" by "versifying" or "repeating" or "reciting," leaving it doubtful if the composition be or be not original. In places, however, it is clearly improvised and then as a rule it is model doggrel.

[2] Arab. "Allahumma" = Yá Allah (O Allah) but with emphasis; the Fath being a substitute for the voc. part. Some connect it with the Heb. "Alihím," but that fancy

Thou wottest that I cast not my net each day save four times;[1] the third is done and as yet Thou hast vouchsafed me nothing. So this time, O my God, deign give me my daily bread." Then, having called on Allah's name,[2] he again threw his net and waited its sinking and settling; whereupon he haled at it but could not draw it in for that it was entangled at the bottom. He cried out in his vexation "There is no Majesty and there is no Might save in Allah!" and he began reciting:—

Fie on this wretched world, an so it be * I must be whelmed by grief and misery:
Tho' gladsome be man's lot when dawns the morn * He drains the cup of woe ere eve he see:
Yet was I one of whom the world when asked * "Whose lot is happiest?" oft would say "'Tis he!"

Thereupon he stripped and, diving down to the net, busied himself with it till it came to land. Then he opened the meshes and found therein a cucumber-shaped jar of yellow copper,[3] evidently full of something, whose mouth was made fast with a leaden cap, stamped with the seal-ring of our Lord Sulayman son of David (Allah accept the twain!). Seeing this the Fisherman rejoiced and said, "If I sell it in the brass-bazar 'tis worth ten golden dinars." He shook it and finding it heavy continued, "Would to Heaven I knew what is herein. But I must and will open it and look to its contents and store it in my bag and sell it in the brass-market." And taking out a knife he worked at the lead till he had loosened it from the jar; then he laid the cup on the ground and shook the vase to pour out whatever might be inside. He found nothing in it; whereat he marvelled with an exceeding marvel. But presently there came forth from the jar a smoke which spired heavenwards into æther (whereat he again marvelled with mighty marvel), and which trailed along earth's surface till presently, having reached its full height, the thick vapour condensed, and became an Ifrit, huge of bulk, whose crest touched

---

is not Arab. In Al-Hariri and the rhetoricians it sometimes means to be sure; of course; unless indeed; unless possibly.

[1] Probably in consequence of a vow. These superstitious practices, which have many a parallel amongst ourselves, are not confined to the lower orders in the East.

[2] *i.e.*, saying "Bismillah!" the pious ejaculation which should precede every act. In Boccaccio (viii., 9) it is "remembering Iddio e' Santi."

[3] Arab. Nahás asfar = brass, opposed to "Nahás" and "Nahás ahmar," = copper.

the clouds while his feet were on the ground. His head was as a dome, his hands like pitchforks, his legs long as masts and his mouth big as a cave; his teeth were like large stones, his nostrils ewers, his eyes two lamps and his look was fierce and lowering. Now when the Fisherman saw the Ifrit his side muscles quivered, his teeth chattered, his spittle dried up and he became blind about what to do. Upon this the Ifrit looked at him and cried, "There is no god but *the* God, and Sulayman is the prophet of God;" presently adding, "O Apostle of Allah, slay me not; never again will I gainsay thee in word nor sin against thee in deed."[1] Quoth the Fisherman, "O Márid,[2] diddest thou say, Sulayman the Apostle of Allah; and Sulayman is dead some thousand and eight hundred years ago,[3] and we are now in the last days of the world! What is thy story, and what is thy account of thyself, and what is the cause of thy entering into this cucurbit?" Now when the Evil Spirit heard the words of the Fisherman, quoth he; "There is no god but *the* God: be of good cheer, O Fisherman!" Quoth the Fisherman, "Why biddest thou me to be of good cheer?" and he replied, "Because of thy having to die an ill death in this very hour." Said the Fisherman, "Thou deservest for thy good tidings the withdrawal of Heaven's protection, O thou distant one![4] Wherefore shouldest thou kill me and what thing have I done to deserve death, I who freed thee from the jar, and saved thee from the depths of the sea, and brought thee up on the dry land?" Replied the Ifrit, "Ask of me only what mode of death thou wilt die, and by what manner of slaughter shall I slay thee." Rejoined the Fisherman, "What is my crime and wherefore such retribution?" Quoth the Ifrit,

---

1 This alludes to the legend of Sakhr al-Jinni, a famous fiend cast by Solomon Davidson into Lake Tiberias whose storms make it a suitable place. Hence the "Bottle imp," a world-wide fiction of folk-lore: we shall find it in the "Book of Sindibad," and I need hardly remind the reader of Le Sage's "Diable Boiteux," borrowed from "El Diablo Cojuelo," the Spanish novel by Luiz Velez de Guevara.

2 Márid (lit. "contumacious" from the Heb. root Marad to rebel, whence "Nimrod" in late Semitic) is one of the tribes of the Jinn, generally but not always hostile to man. His female is "Máridah."

3 As Solomon began to reign (according to vulgar chronometry) in B.C. 1015, the text would place the tale circ. A.D. 785, = A.H. 169. But we can lay no stress on this date which may be merely fanciful. Professor Tawney very justly compares this Moslem Solomon with the Hindu King, Vikramáditya, who ruled over the seven divisions of the world and who had as many devils to serve him as he wanted.

4 Arab. "Yá Ba'íd;" a euphemism here adopted to prevent using grossly abusive language. Others will occur in the course of these pages.

"Hear my story, O Fisherman!" and he answered, "Say on, and be brief in thy saying, for of very sooth my life-breath is in my nostrils."[1] Thereupon quoth the Jinni, "Know, that I am one among the heretical Jann and I sinned against Sulayman, David-son (on the twain be peace!) I together with the famous Sakhr al Jinni;"[2] whereupon the Prophet sent his minister, Asaf son of Barkhiyá, to seize me; and this Wazir brought me against my will and led me in bonds to him (I being downcast despite my nose) and he placed me standing before him like a suppliant. When Sulayman saw me, he took refuge with Allah and bade me embrace the True Faith and obey his behests; but I refused, so sending for this cucurbit[3] he shut me up therein, and stopped it over with lead whereon he impressed the Most High Name, and gave his orders to the Jann who carried me off, and cast me into the midmost of the ocean. There I abode an hundred years, during which I said in my heart, "Whoso shall release me, him will I enrich for ever and ever." But the full century went by and, when no one set me free, I entered upon the second five score saying, "Whoso shall release me, for him I will open the hoards of the earth." Still no one set me free and thus four hundred years passed away. Then quoth I, "Whoso shall release me, for him will I fulfil three wishes." Yet no one set me free. Thereupon I waxed wroth with exceeding wrath and said to myself, "Whoso shall release me from this time forth, him will I slay and I will give him choice of what death he will die; and now, as thou hast released me, I give thee full choice of deaths." The Fisherman, hearing the words of the Ifrit, said, "O Allah! the wonder of it that I have not come to free thee save in these

---

[1] *i. e.* about to fly out; "My heart is in my mouth." The Fisherman speaks with the dry humour of a Fellah.

[2] "Sulayman," when going out to ease himself, entrusted his seal-ring upon which his kingdom depended to a concubine "Amínah" (the "Faithful"), when Sakhr, transformed to the King's likeness, came in and took it. The prophet was reduced to beggary, but after forty days the demon fled throwing into the sea the ring which was swallowed by a fish and eventually returned to Sulayman. This Talmudic fable is hinted at in the Koran (chapt. xxxviii.), and commentators have extensively embroidered it. Asaf, son of Barkhiya, was Wazir to Sulayman and is supposed to be the "one with whom was the knowledge of the Scriptures" (Koran, chapt. xxxvii.), *i.e.* who knew the Ineffable Name of Allah. See the manifest descendant of the Talmudic-Koranic fiction in the "Tale of the Emperor Jovinian" (No. lix.) of the Gesta Romanorum, the most popular book of mediæval Europe composed in England (or Germany) about the end of the thirteenth century.

[3] Arab. "Kumkum," a gourd-shaped bottle of metal, china or glass, still used for sprinkling scents. Lane gives an illustration (chapt. viii., Mod. Egypt.).

days!" adding, "Spare my life, so Allah spare thine; and slay me not, lest Allah set one to slay thee." Replied the Contumacious One, "There is no help for it; die thou must; so ask me by way of boon what manner of death thou wilt die." Albeit thus certified the Fisherman again addressed the Ifrit saying, "Forgive me this my death as a generous reward for having freed thee;" and the Ifrit, "Surely I would not slay thee save on account of that same release." "O Chief of the Ifrits," said the Fisherman, "I do thee good and thou requitest me with evil! in very sooth the old saw lieth not when it saith:—

We wrought them weal, they met our weal with ill; * Such, by my life! is every
    bad man's labour:
To him who benefits unworthy wights * Shall hap what hapt to Ummi-Amir's
    neighbour.[1]"

Now when the Ifrit heard these words he answered, "No more of this talk, needs must I kill thee." Upon this the Fisherman said to himself, "This is a Jinni; and I am a man to whom Allah hath given a passably cunning wit, so I will now cast about to compass his destruction by my contrivance and by mine intelligence; even as he took counsel only of his malice and his frowardness."[2] He began by asking the Ifrit, "Hast thou indeed resolved to kill me?" and, receiving for all answer, "Even so," he cried, "Now in the Most Great Name, graven on the seal-ring of Sulayman the Son of David (peace be with the holy twain!), an I question thee on a certain matter wilt thou give me a true answer?" The Ifrit replied "Yea;" but, hearing mention of the Most Great Name, his wits were troubled and he said with trembling, "Ask and be brief." Quoth the Fisherman, "How didst thou fit into this bottle which would not hold thy hand; no, nor even thy foot, and how came it to be large enough to contain the whole of thee?" Replied the Ifrit, "What! dost not believe that I was all there?" and the Fisherman rejoined, "Nay! I will never believe it until I see thee inside with my own eyes."——And Shahrazad perceived the dawn of day and ceased to say her permitted say.

---

[1] Arab. meaning "the Mother of Amir," a nickname for the hyena, which bites the hand that feeds it.

[2] The intellect of man is stronger than that of the Jinni; the Ifrit, however, enters the jar because he has been adjured by the Most Great Name and not from mere stupidity. The seal-ring of Solomon according to the Rabbis contained a chased stone which told him everything he wanted to know.

When it was the Fourth Night,

Her sister said to her, "Please finish us this tale, an thou be not sleepy!" so she resumed:—It hath reached me, O auspicious King, that when the Fisherman said to the Ifrit, "I will never and nowise believe thee until I see thee inside it with mine own eyes;" the Evil Spirit on the instant shook[1] and became a vapour, which condensed, and entered the jar little and little, till all was well inside when lo! the Fisherman in hot haste took the leaden cap with the seal and stoppered therewith the mouth of the jar and called out to the Ifrit, saying, "Ask me by way of boon what death thou wilt die! By Allah, I will throw thee into the sea[2] before us and here will I build me a lodge; and whoso cometh hither I will warn him against fishing and will say:—In these waters abideth an Ifrit who giveth as a last favour a choice of deaths and fashion of slaughter to the man who saveth him!" Now when the Ifrit heard this from the Fisherman and saw himself in limbo, he was minded to escape, but this was prevented by Solomon's seal; so he knew that the Fisherman had cozened and outwitted him, and he waxed lowly and submissive and began humbly to say, "I did but jest with thee." But the other answered, "Thou liest, O vilest of the Ifrits, and meanest and filthiest!" and he set off with the bottle for the sea side; the Ifrit calling out "Nay! Nay!" and he calling out "Aye! Aye!" Thereupon the Evil Spirit softened his voice and smoothed his speech and abased himself, saying, "What wouldest thou do with me, O Fisherman?" "I will throw thee back into the sea," he answered; "where thou hast been housed and homed for a thousand and eight hundred years; and now I will leave thee therein till Judgment-day: did I not say to thee:—Spare me and Allah shall spare thee; and slay me not lest Allah slay thee? yet thou spurnedst my supplication and hadst no intention save to deal ungraciously by me, and Allah hath now thrown thee into my hands and I am cunninger than thou." Quoth the Ifrit, "Open for me and I may bring thee weal." Quoth the Fisherman, "Thou liest, thou accursed! my case with thee is that of the

---

[1] The Mesmerist will notice this shudder which is familiar to him as preceding the "magnetic" trance.

[2] Arab. "Bahr" which means a sea, a large river, a sheet of water, etc., lit. water cut or trenched in the earth. Bahri in Egypt means Northern; so Yamm (Sea, Mediterranean) in Hebrew is West.

Wazir of King Yúnán with the sage Dúbán."[1] "And who was the Wazir of King Yunan and who was the sage Duban; and what was the story about them?" quoth the Ifrit, whereupon the Fisherman began to tell

The Tale of the Wazir and the Sage Duban.

KNOW, O thou Ifrit, that in days of yore and in ages long gone before, a King called Yunan reigned over the city of Fars of the land of the Roum.[2] He was a powerful ruler and a wealthy, who had armies and guards and allies of all nations of men; but his body was afflicted with a leprosy which leaches and men of science failed to heal. He drank potions and he swallowed powders and he used unguents, but naught did him good and none among the host of physicians availed to procure him a cure. At last there came to his city a mighty healer of men and one well stricken in years, the sage Duban hight. This man was a reader of books, Greek, Persian, Roman, Arabian, and Syrian; and he was skilled in astronomy and in leechcraft, the theorick as well as the practick; he was experienced in all that healeth and that hurteth the body; conversant with the virtues of every plant, grass and herb, and their benefit and bane; and he understood philosophy and had compassed the whole range of medical science and other branches of the knowledge tree. Now this physician passed but few days in the city, ere he heard of the King's malady and all his bodily sufferings through the leprosy with which Allah had smitten him; and how all the doctors and wise men had failed to heal him. Upon this he sat up through the night in deep thought and, when broke the dawn and appeared the morn and light was again born, and the Sun greeted the Good whose beauties the world adorn,[3] he donned his handsomest dress and going in to King Yunan, he kissed the ground before him: then he prayed for the endurance of his honour and prosperity in fairest language

---

[1] In the Bul. Edit. "Ruyán," evidently a clerical error. The name is fanciful not significant.

[2] The geography is ultra-Shakespearean. "Fárs" (whence "Persia") is the central Province of the grand old Empire now a mere wreck; "Rúm" (which I write Roum, in order to avoid Jamaica) is the neo-Roman or Byzantine Empire; while "Yunan" is the classical Arab term for Greece (Ionia) which unlearned Moslems believe to be now under water.

[3] The Sun greets Mohammed every morning even as it dances on Easter-Day for Christendom. Risum teneatis?

and made himself known saying, "O King, tidings have reached me of what befel thee through that which is in thy person; and how the host of physicians have proved themselves unavailing to abate it; and lo! I can cure thee, O King; and yet will I not make thee drink of draught or anoint thee with ointment." Now when King Yunan heard his words he said in huge surprise, "How wilt thou do this? By Allah, if thou make me whole I will enrich thee even to thy son's son and I will give thee sump-tuous gifts; and whatso thou wishest shall be thine and thou shalt be to me a cup-companion[1] and a friend." The King then robed him with a dress of honour and entreated him graciously and asked him, "Canst thou indeed cure me of this complaint without drug and unguent?" and he answered, "Yes! I will heal thee without the pains and penalties of medicine." The King marvelled with exceeding marvel and said, "O physician, when shall be this whereof thou speakest, and in how many days shall it take place? Haste thee, O my son!" He replied, "I hear and I obey; the cure shall begin to-morrow." So saying he went forth from the presence, and hired himself a house in the city for the better storage of his books and scrolls, his medicines and his aromatic roots. Then he set to work at choosing the fittest drugs and simples and he fashioned a bat hollow within, and furnished with a handle without, for which he made a ball; the two being prepared with consummate art. On the next day when both were ready for use and wanted nothing more, he went up to the King; and, kissing the ground between his hands bade him ride forth on the parade ground[2] there to play at pall and mall. He was accompanied by his suite, Emirs and Chamberlains, Wazirs and Lords of the realm and, ere he was seated, the sage Duban came up to him, and handing him the bat said, "Take this mall

---

[1] Arab. "Nadím," a term often occurring. It denotes one who was intimate enough to drink with the Caliph, a very high honour and a dangerous. The last who sat with "Nudamá" was Al-Razi bi'llah A.H. 329 = 940. See Al-Siyuti's famous "History of the Caliphs" translated and admirably annotated by Major H. S. Jarrett, for the Bibliotheca Indica, Calcutta, 1880.

[2] Arab. Maydán (from Persian); Lane generally translates it "horse-course," and Payne "tilting-yard." It is both and something more; an open space, in or near the city, used for reviewing troops, races, playing the Jeríd (cane-spear) and other sports and exercises: thus Al-Maydan = Gr. hippodrome. The game here alluded to is our "polo," or hockey on horseback, a favourite with the Persian Kings, as all old illustrations of the Shahnamah show. Maydan is also a natural plain for which copious Arabic has many terms; Fayhah or Sath (a plain generally), Khabt (a low-lying plain), Bat'há (a low sandy flat), Mahattah (a plain fit for halting) and so forth. (Pilgrimage iii., 11.)

and grip it as I do; so! and now push for the plain and leaning well over thy horse drive the ball with all thy might until thy palm be moist and thy body perspire: then the medicine will penetrate through thy palm and will permeate thy person. When thou hast done with playing and thou feelest the effects of the medicine, return to thy palace, and make the Ghusl-ablution[1] in the Hammam-bath, and lay thee down to sleep; so shalt thou become whole; and now peace be with thee!" Thereupon King Yunan took the bat from the Sage and grasped it firmly; then, mounting steed, he drove the ball before him and gallopped after it till he reached it, when he struck it with all his might, his palm gripping the bat handle the while; and he ceased not malling the ball till his hand waxed moist and his skin, perspiring, imbibed the medicine from the wood. Then the sage Duban knew that the drugs had penetrated his person and bade him return to the palace and enter the Hammam without stay or delay; so King Yunan forthright returned and ordered them to clear for him the bath. They did so, the carpet spreaders making all haste, and the slaves all hurry and got ready a change of raiment for the King. He entered the bath and made the total ablution long and thoroughly; then donned his clothes within the Hammam and rode therefrom to his palace where he lay him down and slept. Such was the case with King Yunan, but as regards the sage Duban, he returned home and slept as usual and when morning dawned he repaired to the palace and craved audience. The King ordered him to be admitted; then, having kissed the ground between his hands, in allusion to the King he recited these couplets with solemn intonation:—

Happy is Eloquence when thou art named her sire * But mourns she whenas other man the title claimed.
O Lord of fairest presence, whose illuming rays * Clear off the fogs of doubt aye veiling deeds high famed,
Ne'er cease thy face to shine like Dawn and rise of Morn * And never show Time's face with heat of ire inflamed!
Thy grace hath favoured us with gifts that worked such wise * As rain-clouds raining on the hills by wolds enframed:
Freely thou lavishedst thy wealth to rise on high * Till won from Time the heights whereat thy grandeur aimed.

Now when the Sage ceased reciting, the King rose quickly to his

---

[1] For details concerning the "Ghusl" see Night xliv.

feet and fell on his neck; then, seating him by his side he bade
dress him in a sumptuous dress; for it had so happened that
when the King left the Hammam he looked on his body and saw
no trace of leprosy: the skin was all clean as virgin silver. He
joyed thereat with exceeding joy, his breast broadened[1] with
delight and he felt thoroughly happy. Presently, when it was
full day he entered his audience-hall and sat upon the throne
of his kingship whereupon his Chamberlains and Grandees
flocked to the presence and with them the Sage Duban. Seeing
the leach the King rose to him in honour and seated him by his
side; then the food trays furnished with the daintiest viands
were brought and the physician ate with the King, nor did he
cease companying him all that day. Moreover, at nightfall he
gave the physician Duban two thousand gold pieces, besides the
usual dress of honour and other gifts galore, and sent him home
on his own steed. After the Sage had fared forth King Yunan
again expressed his amazement at the leach's art, saying, "This
man medicined my body from without nor anointed me with
aught of ointments: by Allah, surely this is none other than
consummate skill! I am bound to honour such a man with re-
wards and distinction, and take him to my companion and my
friend during the remainder of my days." So King Yunan
passed the night in joy and gladness for that his body had been
made whole and had thrown off so pernicious a malady. On the
morrow the King went forth from his Serraglio and sat upon his
throne, and the Lords of Estate stood about him, and the Emirs
and Wazirs sat as was their wont on his right hand and on his
left. Then he asked for the Sage Duban, who came in and kissed
the ground before him, when the King rose to greet him and,
seating him by his side, ate with him and wished him long life.
Moreover he robed him and gave him gifts, and ceased not conversing with him until night approached. Then the King ordered him, by way of salary, five dresses of honour and a thousand
dinars.[2] The physician returned to his own house full of gratitude to the King. Now when next morning dawned the King
repaired to his audience-hall, and his Lords and Nobles surrounded

---

[1] A popular idiom and highly expressive, contrasting the upright bearing of the self-
satisfied man with the slouch of the miserable and the skirt-trailing of the woman in grief.
I do not see the necessity of such Latinisms as "dilated" or "expanded."

[2] All these highest signs of favour foreshow, in Eastern tales and in Eastern life, an
approaching downfall of the heaviest; they are so great that they arouse general jealousy.
Many of us have seen this at native courts.

him and his Chamberlains and his Ministers, as the white en-
closeth the black of the eye.[1] Now the King had a Wazir among
his Wazirs, unsightly to look upon, an ill-omened spectacle; sor-
did, ungenerous, full of envy and evil will. When this Minister
saw the King place the physician near him and give him all these
gifts, he jaloused him and planned to do him a harm, as in the
saying on such subject, "Envy lurks in every body;" and the saying, "Oppression hideth in every heart: power revealeth it and
weakness concealeth it." Then the Minister came before the
King and, kissing the ground between his hands, said, "O King
of the age and of all time, thou in whose benefits I have grown
to manhood, I have weighty advice to offer thee, and if I withhold
it I were a son of adultery and no true-born man; wherefore an
thou order me to disclose it I will so do forthwith." Quoth the
King (and he was troubled at the words of the Minister), "And
what is this counsel of thine?" Quoth he, "O glorious monarch,
the wise of old have said:—Whoso regardeth not the end, hath
not Fortune to friend; and indeed I have lately seen the King on
far other than the right way; for he lavisheth largesse on his
enemy, on one whose object is the decline and fall of his kingship: to this man he hath shown favour, honouring him with
over honour and making of him an intimate. Wherefore I fear for
the King's life." The King, who was much troubled and
changed colour, asked, "Whom dost thou suspect and anent
whom doest thou hint?" and the Minister answered, "O King,
an thou be asleep, wake up! I point to the physician Duban."
Rejoined the King, "Fie upon thee! This is a true friend who is
favoured by me above all men, because he cured me with something which I held in my hand, and he healed my leprosy which
had baffled all physicians; indeed he is one whose like may not be
found in these days—no, not in the whole world from furthest
east to utmost west! And it is of such a man thou sayest such
hard sayings. Now from this day forward I allot him a settled
solde and allowances, every month a thousand gold pieces; and,
were I to share with him my realm 'twere but a little matter.
Perforce I must suspect that thou speakest on this wise from
mere envy and jealousy as they relate of the King Sindibád."——
And Shahrazad perceived the dawn of day, and ceased saying her

---

[1] This phrase is contained in the word "ihdák" = encompassing, as the conjunctiva
does the pupil.

permitted say. Then quoth Dunyazad, "O my sister, how pleasant is thy tale, and how tasteful, how sweet, and how grateful!" She replied, "And where is this compared with what I could tell thee on the coming night if the King deign spare my life?" Then said the King in himself, "By Allah, I will not slay her until I hear the rest of her tale, for truly it is wondrous." So they rested that night in mutual embrace until the dawn. Then the King went forth to his Hall of Rule, and the Wazir and the troops came in, and the audience-chamber was thronged; and the King gave orders and judged and appointed and deposed and bade and forbade during the rest of that day till the Court broke up, and King Shahryar returned to his palace.

When it was the Fifth Night,

Her sister said, "Do you finish for us thy story if thou be not sleepy," and she resumed:—It hath reached me, O auspicious King and mighty Monarch, that King Yunan said to his Minister, "O Wazir, thou art one whom the evil spirit of envy hath possessed because of this physician, and thou plottest for my putting him to death, after which I should repent me full sorely, even as repented King Sindibad for killing his falcon." Quoth the Wazir, "Pardon me, O King of the age, how was that?" So the King began the story of

King Sindibad and his Falcon.

It is said (but Allah is All-knowing![1]) that there was a King of the Kings of Fars, who was fond of pleasuring and diversion, especially coursing and hunting. He had reared a falcon which he carried all night on his fist, and whenever he went a-chasing he took with him this bird; and he bade make for her a golden cuplet hung around her neck to give her drink therefrom. One day as the King was sitting quietly in his palace, behold, the high falconer of the household suddenly addressed him, "O King of the age, this is indeed a day fit for birding." The King gave orders accordingly and set out taking the hawk on fist; and they fared

---

[1] I have noted this formula, which is used even in conversation when about to relate some great unfact.

merrily forwards till they made a Wady[1] where they planted a circle of nets for the chase; when lo! a gazelle came within the toils and the King cried, "Whoso alloweth yon gazelle to spring over his head and loseth her, that man will I surely slay." They narrowed the nets about the gazelle when she drew near the King's station; and, planting herself on her hind quarter, crossed her forehand over her breast, as if about to kiss the earth before the King. He bowed his brow low in acknowledgment to the beast; when she bounded high over his head and took the way of the waste. Thereupon the King turned towards his troops and seeing them winking and pointing at him, he asked, "O Wazir, what are my men saying?" and the Minister answered, "They say thou didst proclaim that whoso alloweth the gazelle to spring over his head, that man shall be put to death." Quoth the King, "Now, by the life of my head! I will follow her up till I bring her back." So he set off galloping on the gazelle's trail and gave not over tracking till he reached the foot-hills of a mountain-chain where the quarry made for a cave. Then the King cast off at it the falcon which presently caught it up and, swooping down, drove her talons into its eyes, bewildering and blinding it;[2] and the King drew his mace and struck a blow which rolled the game over. He then dismounted; and, after cutting the antelope's throat and flaying the body, hung it to the pommel of his saddle. Now the time was that of the siesta[3] and the wold was parched and dry, nor was any water to be found anywhere; and the King thirsted and his horse also; so he went about searching till he saw a tree dropping water, as it were melted butter, from its boughs. Thereupon the King who wore gauntlets of skin to guard him against poisons took the cup from the hawk's neck, and filling it with the water set it before the bird, and lo! the falcon struck it with her pounces and upset the liquid. The King filled it a second time with the dripping drops, thinking his hawk was thirsty; but the bird again struck at the cup with her talons and overturned it. Then the

---

1 We are obliged to English the word by "valley," which is about as correct as the "brook Kedron," applied to the grisliest of ravines. The Wady (in old Coptic wah, oah, whence "Oasis") is the bed of a watercourse which flows only after rains. I have rendered it by "Fiumara" (Pilgrimage i., 5, and ii., 196, etc.), an Italian or rather a Sicilian word which exactly describes the "wady."

2 I have described this scene which Mr. T. Wolf illustrated by an excellent lithograph in "Falconry, etc." (London, Van Voorst, MDCCCLII.)

3 Arab. "Kaylúlah," mid-day sleep; called siesta from the sixth canonical hour.

King waxed wroth with the hawk and filling the cup a third time offered it to his horse: but the hawk upset it with a flirt of wings. Quoth the King, "Allah confound thee, thou unluckiest of flying things! thou keepest me from drinking, and thou deprivest thyself also, and the horse." So he struck the falcon with his sword and cut off her wing; but the bird raised her head and said by signs, "Look at that which hangeth on the tree!" The King lifted up his eyes accordingly and caught sight of a brood of vipers, whose poison-drops he mistook for water; thereupon he repented him of having struck off his falcon's wing, and mounting horse, fared on with the dead gazelle, till he arrived at the camp, his starting place. He threw the quarry to the cook saying, "Take and broil it," and sat down on his chair, the falcon being still on his fist when suddenly the bird gasped and died; whereupon the King cried out in sorrow and remorse for having slain that falcon which had saved his life. Now this is what occurred in the case of King Sindibad; and I am assured that were I to do as thou desirest I should repent even as the man who killed his parrot." Quoth the Wazir, "And how was that?" And the King began to tell

The Tale of the Husband and the Parrot.[1]

A CERTAIN man and a merchant to boot had married a fair wife, a woman of perfect beauty and grace, symmetry and loveliness, of whom he was mad-jealous, and who contrived successfully to keep him from travel. At last an occasion compelling him to leave her, he went to the bird-market and bought him for one hundred gold pieces a she-parrot which he set in his house to act as duenna, expecting her to acquaint him on his return with what had passed during the whole time of his absence; for the bird was kenning and cunning and never forgot what she had seen and heard. Now his fair wife had fallen in love with a young

---

[1] This parrot-story is world-wide in folk-lore and the belief in metempsychosis, which prevails more or less over all the East, there lends it probability. The "Book of Sindibad" (see Night dlxxix. and "The Academy," Sept. 20, 1884, No. 646) converts it into the "Story of the Confectioner, his Wife and the Parrot;" and it is the base of the Hindostani text-book, "Tota-Kaháni" (Parrot-chat), an abridgement of the Tutinámah (Parrot-book) of Nakhshabi (circ. A.D. 1300), a congener of the Sanskrit "Suka Saptati," or Seventy Parrot-stories. The tale is not in the Bul. or Mac. Edits. but occurs in the Bresl. (i., pp. 90, 91) much mutilated; and better in the Calc. Edit. I cannot here refrain from noticing how vilely the twelve vols. of the Breslau Edit. have been edited; even a table of contents being absent from the first four volumes.

Turk,[1] who used to visit her, and she feasted him by day and lay with him by night. When the man had made his journey and won his wish he came home; and, at once causing the Parrot be brought to him, questioned her concerning the conduct of his consort whilst he was in foreign parts. Quoth she, "Thy wife hath a man-friend who passed every night with her during thine absence." Thereupon the husband went to his wife in a violent rage and bashed her with a bashing severe enough to satisfy any body. The woman, suspecting that one of the slave-girls had been tattling to the master, called them together and questioned them upon their oaths, when all swore that they had kept the secret, but that the Parrot had not, adding, "And we heard her with our own ears." Upon this the woman bade one of the girls to set a hand-mill under the cage and grind therewith and a second to sprinkle water through the cage-roof and a third to run about, right and left, flashing a mirror of bright steel through the livelong night. Next morning when the husband returned home after being entertained by one of his friends, he bade bring the Parrot before him and asked what had taken place whilst he was away. "Pardon me, O my master," quoth the bird, "I could neither hear nor see aught by reason of the exceeding murk and the thunder and lightning which lasted throughout the night." As it happened to be the summer-tide the master was astounded and cried, "But we are now in mid Tammúz,[2] and this is not the time for rains and storms." "Ay, by Allah," rejoined the bird, "I saw with these eyes what my tongue hath told thee." Upon this the man, not knowing the case nor smoking the plot, waxed exceeding wroth; and, holding that his wife had been wrongously accused, put forth his hand and pulling the Parrot from her cage dashed her upon the ground with such force that he killed her on the spot. Some days afterwards one of his slave-girls confessed to him the whole truth,[3]

---

[1] The young "Turk" is probably a late addition, as it does not appear in many of the MSS., e. g. the Bresl. Edit. The wife usually spreads a cloth over the cage; this in the Turkish translation becomes a piece of leather.

[2] The Hebrew-Syrian month July used to express the height of summer. As Herodotus tells us (ii. 4) the Egyptians claimed to be the discoverers of the solar year and the portioners of its course into twelve parts.

[3] This proceeding is thoroughly characteristic of the servile class; they conscientiously conceal everything from the master till he finds a clew; after which they tell him everything and something more.

yet would he not believe it till he saw the young Turk, his wife's lover, coming out of her chamber, when he bared his blade[1] and slew him by a blow on the back of the neck; and he did the same by the adulteress; and thus the twain, laden with mortal sin, went straightways to Eternal Fire. Then the merchant knew that the Parrot had told him the truth anent all she had seen and he mourned grievously for her loss, when mourning availed him not. The Minister, hearing the words of King Yunan, rejoined, "O Monarch, high in dignity, and what harm have I done him, or what evil have I seen from him that I should compass his death? I would not do this thing, save to serve thee, and soon shalt thou sight that it is right; and if thou accept my advice thou shalt be saved, otherwise thou shalt be destroyed even as a certain Wazir who acted treacherously by the young Prince." Asked the King, "How was that?" and the Minister thus began

The Tale of the Prince and the Ogress.

A certain King, who had a son over much given to hunting and coursing, ordered one of his Wazirs to be in attendance upon him whithersoever he might wend. One day the youth set out for the chase accompanied by his father's Minister; and, as they jogged on together, a big wild beast came in sight. Cried the Wazir to the King's son, "Up and at yon noble quarry!" So the Prince followed it until he was lost to every eye and the chase got away from him in the waste; whereby he was confused and he knew not which way to turn, when lo! a damsel appeared ahead and she was in tears. The King's son asked, "Who art thou?" and she answered, "I am daughter to a King among the Kings of Hind, and I was travelling with a caravan in the desert when drowsiness overcame me, and I fell from my beast unwittingly; whereby I am cut off from my people and sore bewildered." The Prince, hearing these words, pitied her case and, mounting her on his horse's crupper, travelled until he passed by an old ruin,[2] when the damsel said to him, "O my master, I wish to obey a call of nature": he therefore set her down at the ruin where she delayed so long that the King's son thought that she

---

[1] Until late years, merchants and shopkeepers in the nearer East all carried swords, and held it a disgrace to leave the house unarmed.

[2] The Bresl. Edit. absurdly has Jazírah (an island).

was only wasting time; so he followed her without her knowledge and behold, she was a Ghúlah,[1] a wicked Ogress, who was
saying to her brood, "O my children, this day I bring you a fine
fat youth[2] for dinner;" whereto they answered, "Bring him
quick to us, O our mother, that we may browse upon him our
bellies full." The Prince hearing their talk, made sure of death
and his side-muscles quivered in fear for his life, so he turned
away and was about to fly. The Ghulah came out and seeing
him in sore affright (for he was trembling in every limb) cried,
"Wherefore art thou afraid?" and he replied, "I have hit upon
an enemy whom I greatly fear." Asked the Ghulah, "Diddest
thou not say:—I am a King's son?" and he answered, "Even so."
Then quoth she, "Why dost not give thine enemy something of
money and so satisfy him?" Quoth he, "He will not be satisfied with my purse but only with my life, and I mortally fear
him and am a man under oppression." She replied, "If thou be
so distressed, as thou deemest, ask aid against him from Allah,
who will surely protect thee from his ill-doing and from the evil
whereof thou art afraid." Then the Prince raised his eyes
heavenwards and cried, "O Thou who answerest the neces-
sitous when he calleth upon Thee and dispellest his distress;
O my God! grant me victory over my foe and turn him from me,
for Thou over all things art Almighty." The Ghulah, hearing
his prayer, turned away from him, and the Prince returned to
his father, and told him the tale of the Wazir; whereupon the
King summoned the Minister to his presence and then and
there slew him. Thou likewise, O King, if thou continue to
trust this leach, shalt be made to die the worst of deaths. He
verily thou madest much of and whom thou entreatedest as an
intimate, will work thy destruction. Seest thou not how he
healed the disease from outside thy body by something grasped
in thy hand? Be not assured that he will not destroy thee by
something held in like manner! Replied King Yunan, "Thou

---

[1] The Ghúlah (fem. of Ghúl) is the Heb. Lilith or Lilis; the classical Lamia; the
Hindu Yogini and Dakini; the Chaldean Utug and Gigim (desert-demons) as opposed
to the Mas (hill-demon) and Telal (who steal into towns); the Ogress of our tales and
the Bala yaga (Granny-witch) of Russian folk-lore. Etymologically "Ghul" is a calamity,
a panic fear; and the monster is evidently the embodied horror of the grave and the
graveyard.
[2] Arab. "Shább" (Lat. juvenis) between puberty and forty or according to some fifty;
when the patient becomes a "Rajul ikhtiyár" (man of free will) politely termed, and then
a Shaykh or Shaybah (grey-beard, oldster).

hast spoken sooth, O Wazir, it may well be as thou hintest O my well-advising Minister; and belike this Sage hath come as a spy searching to put me to death; for assuredly if he cured me by a something held in my hand, he can kill me by a something given me to smell." Then asked King Yunan, "O Minister, what must be done with him?" and the Wazir answered, "Send after him this very instant and summon him to thy presence; and when he shall come strike him across the neck; and thus shalt thou rid thyself of him and his wickedness, and deceive him ere he can deceive thee." "Thou hast again spoken sooth, O Wazir," said the King and sent one to call the Sage who came in joyful mood for he knew not what had appointed for him the Compassionate; as a certain poet saith by way of illustration:—

O Thou who fearest Fate, confiding fare * Trust all to Him who built the world and wait:
What Fate saith "Be" perforce must be, my lord! * And safe art thou from th' undecreed of Fate.

As Duban the physician entered he addressed the King in these lines:—

An fail I of my thanks to thee nor thank thee day by day * For whom composed I prose and verse, for whom my say and lay?
Thou lavishedst thy generous gifts ere they were craved by me * Thou lavishedst thy boons unsought sans pretext or delay:
How shall I stint my praise of thee, how shall I cease to laud * The grace of thee in secresy and patentest display?
Nay; I will thank thy benefits, for aye thy favours lie * Light on my thought and tongue, though heavy on my back they weigh.

And he said further on the same theme:—

Turn thee from grief nor care a jot! * Commit thy needs to Fate and Lot!
Enjoy the Present passing well * And let the Past be clean forgot;
For whatso haply seemeth worse * Shall work thy weal as Allah wot:
Allah shall do whate'er He wills * And in His will oppose Him not.

And further still:—

To th' All-wise Subtle One trust worldly things * Rest thee from all whereto the worldling clings:
Learn wisely well naught cometh by thy will * But e'en as willeth Allah, King of Kings.

And lastly:—

Gladsome and gay forget thine every grief * Full often grief the wisest hearts
     outwore:
Thought is but folly in the feeble slave * Shun it and so be savèd evermore.

Said the King for sole return, "Knowest thou why I have summoned thee?" and the Sage replied, "Allah Most Highest alone
kenneth hidden things!" But the King rejoined, "I summoned
thee only to take thy life and utterly to destroy thee." Duban the
Wise wondered at this strange address with exceeding wonder
and asked, "O King, and wherefore wouldest thou slay me, and
what ill have I done thee?" and the King answered, "Men tell me
thou art a spy sent hither with intent to slay me; and lo! I will
kill thee ere I be killed by thee;" then he called to his Sworder,
and said, "Strike me off the head of this traitor and deliver us
from his evil practices." Quoth the Sage, "Spare me and Allah will
spare thee; slay me not or Allah shall slay thee." And he repeated to him these very words, even as I to thee, O Ifrit, and
yet thou wouldst not let me go, being bent upon my death.
King Yunan only rejoined, "I shall not be safe without slaying
thee; for, as thou healedst me by something held in hand, so am I
not secure against thy killing me by something given me to smell
or otherwise." Said the physician, "This then, O King, is thy
requital and reward; thou returnest only evil for good." The
King replied, "There is no help for it; die thou must and without
delay." Now when the physician was certified that the King
would slay him without waiting, he wept and regretted the
good he had done to other than the good. As one hath said on
this subject:—

Of wit and wisdom is Maymúnah[1] bare * Whose sire in wisdom all the wits
     outstrippeth:
Man may not tread on mud or dust or clay * Save by good sense, else trippeth
     he and slippeth.

Hereupon the Sworder stepped forward and bound the Sage
Duban's eyes and bared his blade, saying to the King, "By thy
leave;" while the physician wept and cried, "Spare me and Allah

---

[1] Some proverbial name now forgotten. Torrens (p. 48) translates it "the giglot"
(Fortune?) but "cannot discover the drift."

will spare thee, and slay me not or Allah shall slay thee," and began repeating:—

I was kind and 'scapèd not, they were cruel and escaped;'* And my kindness
    only led me to Ruination Hall;
If I live I'll ne'er be kind; if I die, then all be damned * Who follow me, and
    curses their kindliness befal.

"Is this," continued Duban, "the return I meet from thee? Thou givest me, meseems, but crocodile-boon." Quoth the King,"What is the tale of the crocodile?", and quoth the physician, "Impossible for me to tell it in this my state; Allah upon thee, spare me, as thou hopest Allah shall spare thee." And he wept with exceeding weeping. Then one of the King's favourites stood up and said, "O King! grant me the blood of this physician; we have never seen him sin against thee, or doing aught save healing thee from a disease which baffled every leach and man of science." Said the King, "Ye wot not the cause of my putting to death this physician, and this it is. If I spare him, I doom myself to certain death; for one who healed me of such a malady by something held in my hand, surely can slay me by something held to my nose; and I fear lest he kill me for a price, since haply he is some spy whose sole purpose in coming hither was to compass my destruction. So there is no help for it; die he must, and then only shall I be sure of my own life." Again cried Duban, "Spare me and Allah shall spare thee; and slay me not or Allah shall slay thee." But it was in vain. Now when the physician, O Ifrit, knew for certain that the King would kill him, he said, "O King, if there be no help but I must die, grant me some little delay that I may go down to my house and release myself from mine obligations and direct my folk and my neighbours where to bury me and distribute my books of medicine. Amongst these I have one, the rarest of rarities, which I would present to thee as an offering: keep it as a treasure in thy treasury." "And what is in the book?" asked the King and the Sage answered, "Things beyond compt; and the least of secrets is that if, directly after thou hast cut off my head, thou open three leaves and read three lines of the page to thy left hand, my head shall speak and answer every question thou deignest ask of it." The King wondered with exceeding wonder and shaking[1] with delight at the novelty, said, "O

---

[1] Arab. "Ihtizáz," that natural and instinctive movement caused by good news suddenly given, etc.

physician, dost thou really tell me that when I cut off thy head
it will speak to me?" He replied, "Yes, O King!" Quoth the
King, "This is indeed a strange matter!" and forthwith sent him
closely guarded to his house, and Duban then and there settled
all his obligations. Next day he went up to the King's audience
hall, where Emirs and Wazirs, Chamberlains and Nabobs,
Grandees and Lords of Estate were gathered together, making
the presence-chamber gay as a garden of flower-beds. And lo!
the physician came up and stood before the King, bearing a
worn old volume and a little étui of metal full of powder, like
that used for the eyes.[1] Then he sat down and said, "Give me a
tray." So they brought him one and he poured the powder
upon it and levelled it and lastly spake as follows: "O King,
take this book but do not open it till my head falls; then set it
upon this tray, and bid press it down upon the powder, when
forthright the blood will cease flowing. That is the time to open
the book." The King thereupon took the book and made a sign
to the Sworder, who arose and struck off the physician's head,
and placing it on the middle of the tray, pressed it down upon
the powder. The blood stopped flowing, and the Sage Duban
unclosed his eyes and said, "Now open the book, O King!" The
King opened the book, and found the leaves stuck together; so he
put his finger to his mouth and, by moistening it, he easily
turned over the first leaf, and in like way the second, and the
third, each leaf opening with much trouble; and when he had un-
stuck six leaves he looked over them and, finding nothing written
thereon, said, "O physician, there is no writing here!" Duban replied, "Turn over yet more;" and he turned over three others in

---

[1] Arab. "Kohl," in India, Surmah, not a "collyrium," but powdered antimony for
the eyelids. That sold in the bazars is not the real grey ore of antimony but a galena
or sulphuret of lead. Its use arose as follows. When Allah showed Himself to Moses on
Sinai through an opening the size of a needle, the Prophet fainted and the Mount took
fire: thereupon Allah said, "Henceforth shalt thou and thy seed grind the earth of this
mountain and apply it to your eyes!" The powder is kept in an étui called Makhalah
and applied with a thick blunt needle to the inside of the eyelid, drawing it along the rim;
hence etui and probe denote the sexual *rem in re* and in cases of adultery the question
will be asked, "Didst thou see the needle in the Kohl-pot?" Women mostly use a
preparation of soot or lamp-black (Hind. Kajala, Kajjal) whose colour is easily distinguished from that of Kohl. The latter word, with the article (Al-Kohl) is the origin
of our "alcohol;" though even M. Littré fails to show how "fine powder" became "spirits
of wine." I found this powder (wherewith Jezebel "painted" her eyes) a great preservative
from ophthalmia in desert-travelling: the use in India was universal, but now European
example is gradually abolishing it.

the same way. Now the book was poisoned; and before long the venom penetrated his system, and he fell into strong convulsions and he cried out, "The poison hath done its work!" Whereupon the Sage Duban's head began to improvise:—

There be rulers who have ruled with a foul tyrannic sway * But they soon became as though they had never, never been:
Just, they had won justice: they oppressed and were opprest * By Fortune, who requited them with ban and bane and teen:
So they faded like the morn, and the tongue of things repeats * "Take this for that, nor vent upon Fortune's ways thy spleen."

No sooner had the head ceased speaking than the King rolled over dead. Now I would have thee know, O Ifrit, that if King Yunan had spared the Sage Duban, Allah would have spared him; but he refused so to do and decreed to do him dead, wherefore Allah slew him; and thou too, O Ifrit, if thou hadst spared me, Allah would have spared thee.——And Shahrazad perceived the dawn of day and ceased saying her permitted say: then quoth Dunyazad, "O my sister, how pleasant is thy tale, and how tasteful; how sweet, and how grateful!" She replied, "And where is this compared with what I could tell thee this coming night, if I live and the King spare me?" Said the King in himself, "By Allah, I will not slay her until I hear the rest of her story, for truly it is wondrous." They rested that night in mutual embrace until dawn: then the King went forth to his Darbar; the Wazirs and troops came in and the audience-hall was crowded; so the King gave orders and judged and appointed and deposed and bade and forbade the rest of that day, when the court broke up, and King Shahryar entered his palace.

When it was the Sixth Night,

Her sister, Dunyazad, said to her, "Pray finish for us thy story;" and she answered, "I will if the King give me leave." "Say on," quoth the King. And she continued:—It hath reached me, O auspicious King, that when the Fisherman said to the Ifrit, "If thou hadst spared me I would have spared thee, but nothing would satisfy thee save my death; so now I will do thee die by jailing thee in this jar and I will hurl thee into this sea." Then the Marid roared aloud and cried, "Allah upon thee, O Fisherman, don't! Spare me, and pardon my past doings; and, as I have

been tyrannous, so be thou generous, for it is said among sayings
that go current:—O thou who doest good to him who hath done
thee evil, suffice for the ill-doer his ill-deeds, and do not deal with
me as did Umamah to 'Atikah."[1]   Asked the Fisherman, "And
what was their case?" and the Ifrit answered, "This is not the
time for story-telling and I in this prison; but set me free and I
will tell thee the tale." Quoth the Fisherman, "Leave this language: there is no help but that thou be thrown back into the sea
nor is there any way for thy getting out of it for ever and ever.
Vainly I placed myself under thy protection,[2] and I humbled myself to thee with weeping, while thou soughtest only to slay me,
who had done thee no injury deserving this at thy hands; nay,
so far from injuring thee by any evil act, I worked thee nought
but weal in releasing thee from that jail of thine.   Now I knew
thee to be an evil-doer when thou diddest to me what thou
didst, and know, that when I have cast thee back into the sea,
I will warn whomsoever may fish thee up of what hath befallen
me with thee, and I will advise him to toss thee back again; so
shalt thou abide here under these waters till the End of Time
shall make an end of thee."   But the Ifrit cried aloud, "Set me
free; this is a noble occasion for generosity and I make covenant
with thee and vow never to do thee hurt and harm; nay, I will
help thee to what shall put thee out of want."   The Fisherman
accepted his promises on both conditions, not to trouble him as
before, but on the contrary to do him service; and, after making
firm the plight and swearing him a solemn oath by Allah Most
Highest he opened the cucurbit.   Thereupon the pillar of smoke
rose up till all of it was fully out; then it thickened and once
more became an Ifrit of hideous presence, who forthright administered a kick to the bottle and sent it flying into the sea.
The Fisherman, seeing how the cucurbit was treated and making
sure of his own death, piddled in his clothes and said to himself,
"This promiseth badly;" but he fortified his heart, and cried,
"O Ifrit, Allah hath said[3]:—Perform your covenant; for the
performance of your covenant shall be inquired into hereafter.

---

[1] The tale of these two women is now forgotten.

[2] Arab. "Atadakhkhal." When danger threatens it is customary to seize a man's
skirt and cry "Dakhíl-ak!" (= under thy protection).   Among noble tribes the Badawi
thus invoked will defend the stranger with his life.   Foreigners have brought themselves
into contempt by thus applying to women or to mere youths.

[3] The formula of quoting from the Koran.

Thou hast made a vow to me and hast sworn an oath not to play me false lest Allah play thee false, for verily he is a jealous God who respiteth the sinner, but letteth him not escape. I say to thee as said the Sage Duban to King Yunan, "Spare me so Allah may spare thee!" The Ifrit burst into laughter and stalked away, saying to the Fisherman, "Follow me;" and the man paced after him at a safe distance (for he was not assured of escape) till they had passed round the suburbs of the city. Thence they struck into the uncultivated grounds, and crossing them descended into a broad wilderness, and lo! in the midst of it stood a mountain-tarn. The Ifrit waded in to the middle and again cried, "Follow me;" and when this was done he took his stand in the centre and bade the man cast his net and catch his fish. The Fisherman looked into the water and was much astonished to see therein vari-coloured fishes, white and red, blue and yellow; however he cast his net and, hauling it in, saw that he had netted four fishes, one of each colour. Thereat he rejoiced greatly and more when the Ifrit said to him, "Carry these to the Sultan and set them in his presence; then he will give thee what shall make thee a wealthy man; and now accept my excuse, for by Allah at this time I wot none other way of benefiting thee, inasmuch I have lain in this sea eighteen hundred years and have not seen the face of the world save within this hour. But I would not have thee fish here save once a day." The Ifrit then gave him God-speed, saying, "Allah grant we meet again;"[1] and struck the earth with one foot, whereupon the ground clove asunder and swallowed him up. The Fisherman, much marvelling at what had happened to him with the Ifrit, took the fish and made for the city; and as soon as he reached home he filled an earthen bowl with water and therein threw the fish which began to struggle and wriggle about. Then he bore off the bowl upon his head and, repairing to the King's palace (even as the Ifrit had bidden him) laid the fish before the presence; and the King wondered with exceeding wonder at the sight, for never in his lifetime had he seen fishes like these in quality or in conformation. So he said, "Give those fish to the stranger slave-girl who now cooketh for us," meaning the bond-maiden whom the King of Roum had sent to him only three days before, so that he had not yet made trial of her talents in the dressing of meat. Thereupon the Wazir carried the fish to the cook and bade her fry them[1] saying, "O damsel, the King sendeth this say to thee:—I have not treasured thee, O tear o' me! save for stress-time of me; approve, then, to us this day thy delicate handiwork and thy savoury cooking; for this dish of fish is a present sent to the Sultan and evidently a rarity." The Wazir, after he had carefully charged her, returned to the King, who commanded him to give the Fisherman four hundred dinars: he gave them accordingly, and the man took them to his bosom and ran off home stumbling and falling and rising again and deeming the whole thing to be a dream. However, he bought for his family all they wanted and lastly he went to his wife in huge joy and gladness. So far concerning him; but as regards the cookmaid, she took the fish and cleansed them and set them in the frying pan, basting them with oil till one side was dressed. Then she turned them over and, behold, the kitchen wall clave asunder, and therefrom came a young lady, fair of form, oval of face, perfect in grace, with eyelids which Kohl-lines enchase.[2] Her dress was a silken head-kerchief fringed and tasseled with blue: a large ring hung from either ear; a pair of bracelets adorned her wrists; rings with bezels of priceless gems were on her fingers; and she hent in hand a long rod of rattan-cane which she thrust into the frying-pan, saying, "O fish! O fish! be ye constant to your covenant?" When the cookmaiden saw this apparition she swooned away. The young lady repeated her words a second time and a third time, and at last the fishes raised their heads from the pan, and saying in articulate speech "Yes! Yes!" began with one voice to recite:—

Come back and so will I! Keep faith and so will I! * And if ye fain forsake,
   I'll requite till quits we cry!

---

[1] Charming simplicity of manners when the Prime Minister carries the fish (shade of Vattel!) to the cookmaid. The "Gesta Romanorum" is nowhere more naïve.

[2] Arab. "Kahílat al-taraf" = lit. eyelids lined with Kohl; and figuratively "with black lashes and languorous look." This is a phrase which frequently occurs in The Nights and which, as will appear, applies to the "lower animals" as well as to men. Moslems in Central Africa apply Kohl not to the thickness of the eyelid but upon both outer lids, fixing it with some greasy substance. The peculiar Egyptian (and Syrian) eye with its thick fringes of jet-black lashes, looking like lines of black drawn with soot, easily suggests the simile. In England I have seen the same appearance amongst miners fresh from the colliery.

After this the young lady upset the frying-pan and went forth by the way she came in and the kitchen wall closed upon her. When the cook-maiden recovered from her fainting-fit, she saw the four fishes charred black as charcoal, and crying out, "His staff brake in his first bout,"[1] she again fell swooning to the ground. Whilst she was in this case the Wazir came for the fish and looking upon her as insensible she lay, not knowing Sunday from Thursday, shoved her with his foot and said, "Bring the fish for the Sultan!" Thereupon recovering from her fainting-fit she wept and informed him of her case and all that had befallen her. The Wazir marvelled greatly and exclaiming, "This is none other than a right strange matter!", he sent after the Fisherman and said to him, "Thou, O Fisherman, must needs fetch us four fishes like those thou broughtest before." Thereupon the man repaired to the tarn and cast his net; and when he landed it, lo! four fishes were therein exactly like the first. These he at once carried to the Wazir, who went in with them to the cook-maiden and said, "Up with thee and fry these in my presence, that I may see this business." The damsel arose and cleansed the fish, and set them in the frying-pan over the fire; however they remained there but a little while ere the wall clave asunder and the young lady appeared, clad as before and holding in hand the wand which she again thrust into the frying-pan, saying, "O fish! O fish! be ye constant to your olden covenant?" And behold, the fish lifted their heads, and repeated "Yes! Yes!" and recited this couplet:

Come back and so will I! Keep faith and so will I! *But if ye fain forsake,
　　I'll requite till quits we cry!

And Shahrazad perceived the dawn of day and ceased saying her permitted say.

When it was the Seventh Night,

She continued, It hath reached me, O auspicious King, that when the fishes spoke, and the young lady upset the frying-pan with her rod, and went forth by the way she came and the wall closed up, the Wazir cried out, "This is a thing not to be hidden from the King." So he went and told him what had happened, whereupon quoth the King, "There is no help for it but that I see this

---

[1] Of course applying to her own case.

with mine own eyes." Then he sent for the Fisherman and commanded him to bring four other fish like the first and to take with
him three men as witnesses. The Fisherman at once brought the
fish: and the King, after ordering them to give him four hundred
gold pieces, turned to the Wazir and said, "Up and fry me the
fishes here before me!" The Minister, replying "To hear is to
obey," bade bring the frying-pan, threw therein the cleansed fish
and set it over the fire; when lo! the wall clave asunder, and out
burst a black slave like a huge rock or a remnant of the tribe Ad[1]
bearing in hand a branch of a green tree; and he cried in loud
and terrible tones, "O fish! O fish! be ye all constant to your
antique covenant?" whereupon the fishes lifted their heads from
the frying-pan and said, "Yes! Yes! we be true to our vow;" and
they again recited the couplet:

Come back and so will I! Keep faith and so will I! *But if ye fain forsake,
    I'll requite till quits we cry!

Then the huge blackamoor approached the frying-pan and upset
it with the branch and went forth by the way he came in. When
he vanished from their sight the King inspected the fish; and
finding them all charred black as charcoal, was utterly bewildered
and said to the Wazir, "Verily this is a matter whereanent silence
cannot be kept, and as for the fishes, assuredly some marvellous
adventure connects with them." So he bade bring the Fisherman
and asked him, saying "Fie on thee, fellow! whence came these
fishes?" and he answered, "From a tarn between four heights
lying behind this mountain which is in sight of thy city." Quoth
the King, "How many days' march?" Quoth he, "O our lord the
Sultan, a walk of half hour." The King wondered and, straightway ordering his men to march and horsemen to mount, led off the
Fisherman who went before as guide, privily damning the Ifrit.
They fared on till they had climbed the mountain and descended
unto a great desert which they had never seen during all their
lives; and the Sultan and his merry men marvelled much at the
wold set in the midst of four mountains, and the tarn and its
fishes of four colours, red and white, yellow and blue. The King
stood fixed to the spot in wonderment and asked his troops and
all present, "Hath any one among you ever seen this piece of

---

[1] Prehistoric Arabs who measured from 60 to 100 cubits high: Koran, chapt. xxvi.,
etc. They will often be mentioned in The Nights.

water before now?" and all made answer, "O King of the age, never did we set eyes upon it during all our days." They also questioned the oldest inhabitants they met, men well stricken in years, but they replied, each and every, "A lakelet like this we never saw in this place." Thereupon quoth the King, "By Allah I will neither return to my capital nor sit upon the throne of my forbears till I learn the truth about this tarn and the fish therein." He then ordered his men to dismount and bivouac all around the mountain; which they did; and summoning his Wazir, a Minister of much experience, sagacious, of penetrating wit and well versed in affairs, said to him, "'Tis in my mind to do a certain thing, whereof I will inform thee; my heart telleth me to fare forth alone this night and root out the mystery of this tarn and its fishes. Do thou take thy seat at my tent-door, and say to the Emirs and Wazirs, the Nabobs and the Chamberlains, in fine to all who ask thee:—The Sultan is ill at ease, and he hath ordered me to refuse all admittance;[1] and be careful thou let none know my design." And the Wazir could not oppose him. Then the King changed his dress and ornaments and, slinging his sword over his shoulder, took a path which led up one of the mountains and marched for the rest of the night till morning dawned; nor did he cease wayfaring till the heat was too much for him. After his long walk he rested for a while, and then resumed his march and fared on through the second night till dawn, when suddenly there appeared a black point in the far distance. Hereat he rejoiced and said to himself, "Haply some one here shall acquaint me with the mystery of the tarn and its fishes." Presently drawing near the dark object he found it a palace built of swart stone plated with iron; and, while one leaf of the gate stood wide open, the other was shut. The King's spirits rose high as he stood

---

[1] Arab. "Dastúr" (from Persian) = leave, permission. The word has two meanings (see Burckhardt, Arab. Prov. No. 609) and is much used, *e.g.* before walking up stairs or entering a room where strange women might be met. So "Tarík" = Clear the way (Pilgrimage, iii., 319). The old Persian occupation of Egypt, not to speak of the Persian-speaking Circassians and other rulers has left many such traces in popular language. One of them is that horror of travellers—"Bakhshísh" pron. bakh-sheesh and shortened to shísh from the Pers. "bakhshish." Our "Christmas *box*" has been most unnecessarily derived from the same, despite our reading:—

Gladly the boy, with Christmas box in hand.

And, as will be seen, Persians have bequeathed to the outer world worse things than bad language, *e.g.* heresy and sodomy.

before the gate and rapped a light rap; but hearing no answer he knocked a second knock and a third; yet there came no sign. Then he knocked his loudest but still no answer, so he said, "Doubtless 'tis empty." Thereupon he mustered up resolution and boldly walked through the main gate into the great hall and there cried out aloud, "Holla, ye people of the palace! I am a stranger and a wayfarer; have you aught here of victual?" He repeated his cry a second time and a third but still there came no reply; so strengthening his heart and making up his mind he stalked through the vestibule into the very middle of the palace and found no man in it. Yet it was furnished with silken stuffs gold-starred; and the hangings were let down over the door-ways. In the midst was a spacious court off which set four open saloons each with its raised daïs, saloon facing saloon; a canopy shaded the court and in the centre was a jetting fount with four figures of lions made of red gold, spouting from their mouths water clear as pearls and diaphanous gems. Round about the palace birds were let loose and over it stretched a net of golden wire, hindering them from flying off; in brief there was everything but human beings. The King marvelled mightily thereat, yet felt he sad at heart for that he saw no one to give him account of the waste and its tarn, the fishes, the mountains and the palace itself. Presently as he sat between the doors in deep thought behold, there came a voice of lament, as from a heart grief-spent and he heard the voice chanting these verses:—

I hid what I endured of him[1] and yet it came to light, * And nightly sleep mine eyelids fled and changed to sleepless night:
Oh world! Oh Fate! withhold thy hand and cease thy hurt and harm * Look and behold my hapless sprite in dolour and affright:
Wilt ne'er show ruth to highborn youth who lost him on the way * Of Love, and fell from wealth and fame to lowest basest wight.
Jealous of Zephyr's breath was I as on your form he breathed * But whenas Destiny descends she blindeth human sight,[2]
What shall the hapless archer do who when he fronts his foe * And bends his bow to shoot the shaft shall find his string undight?
When cark and care so heavy bear on youth[3] of generous soul * How shall he 'scape his lot and where from Fate his place of flight?

---

[1] He speaks of his wife, but euphemistically in the masculine.
[2] A popular saying throughout Al-Islam.
[3] Arab. "Fata": lit. = a youth; a generous man, one of noble mind (as youth-tide should be). It corresponds with the Lat. "vir," and has much the meaning of the Ital. "Giovane," the Germ. "Junker" and our "gentleman."

Now when the Sultan heard the mournful voice he sprang to his feet; and, following the sound, found a curtain let down over a chamber-door. He raised it and saw behind it a young man sitting upon a couch about a cubit above the ground; and he fair to the sight, a well shaped wight, with eloquence dight; his forehead was flower-white, his cheek rosy bright, and a mole on his cheek-breadth like an ambergris-mite; even as the poet doth indite:—

A youth slim-waisted from whose locks and brow * The world in blackness and
  in light is set.
Throughout Creation's round no fairer show * No rarer sight thine eye hath
  ever met:
A nut-brown mole sits throned upon a cheek * Of rosiest red beneath an eye
  of jet.[1]

The King rejoiced and saluted him, but he remained sitting in his caftan of silken stuff purfled with Egyptian gold and his crown studded with gems of sorts; but his face was sad with the traces of sorrow. He returned the royal salute in most courteous wise adding, "O my lord, thy dignity demandeth my rising to thee; and my sole excuse is to crave thy pardon."[2] Quoth the King, "Thou art excused, O youth; so look upon me as thy guest come hither on an especial object. I would thou acquaint me with the secrets of this tarn and its fishes and of this palace and thy loneliness therein and the cause of thy groaning and wailing." When the young man heard these words he wept with sore weeping;[3] till his bosom was drenched with tears and began reciting:—

Say him who careless sleeps what while the shaft of Fortune flies * How many
  doth this shifting world lay low and raise to rise?
Although thine eye be sealed in sleep, sleep not th' Almighty's eyes * And who
  hath found Time ever fair, or Fate in constant guise?

Then he sighed a long-fetched sigh and recited:—

Confide thy case to Him, the Lord who made mankind; * Quit cark and care
  and cultivate content of mind;
Ask not the Past or how or why it came to pass: * All human things by Fate
  and Destiny were designed!

---

[1] From the Bul. Edit.

[2] The vagueness of his statement is euphemistic.

[3] This readiness of shedding tears contrasts strongly with the external stoicism of modern civilization; but it is true to Arab character; and Easterns, like the heroes of Homer and Italians of Boccaccio, are not ashamed of what we look upon as the result of feminine hysteria—"a good cry."

The King marvelled and asked him, "What maketh thee weep, O young man?" and he answered, "How should I not weep, when this is my case!" Thereupon he put out his hand and raised the skirt of his garment, when lo! the lower half of him appeared stone down to his feet while from his navel to the hair of his head he was man. The King, seeing this his plight, grieved with sore grief and of his compassion cried, "Alack and well-away! in very sooth, O youth, thou heapest sorrow upon my sorrow. I was minded to ask thee the mystery of the fishes only: whereas now I am concerned to learn thy story as well as theirs. But there is no Majesty and there is no Might save in Allah, the Glorious, the Great![1] Lose no time, O youth, but tell me forthright thy whole tale." Quoth he, "Lend me thine ears, thy sight and thine insight;" and quoth the King, "All are at thy service!" Thereupon the youth began, "Right wondrous and marvellous is my case and that of these fishes; and were it graven with gravers upon the eye-corners it were a warner to whoso would be warned." "How is that?" asked the King, and the young man began to tell

The Tale of the Ensorcelled Prince.

Know then, O my lord, that whilome my sire was King of this city, and his name was Mahmúd, entitled Lord of the Black Islands, and owner of what are now these four mountains. He ruled three score and ten years, after which he went to the mercy of the Lord and I reigned as Sultan in his stead. I took to wife my cousin, the daughter of my paternal uncle,[2] and she loved me with such abounding love that whenever I was absent she ate not

---

[1] The formula (constantly used by Moslems) here denotes displeasure, doubt how to act and so forth. Pronounce, "Lá haula wa lá kuwwata illá bi 'lláhi 'l-Aliyyi 'l-Azim." As a rule mistakes are marvellous: Mandeville (chapt. xii.) for "Lá iláha illa 'lláhu wa Muhammadun Rasúlu 'llah" writes "La ellec sila, Machomete rores alla." The former (lá haula, etc.), on account of the four peculiar Arabic letters, is everywhere pronounced differently; and the exclamation is called "Haulak" or "Haukal."

[2] An Arab holds that he has a right to marry his first cousin, the daughter of his father's brother, and if any win her from him a death and a blood-feud may result. It was the same in a modified form amongst the Jews and in both races the consanguineous marriage was not attended by the evil results (idiotcy, congenital deafness, etc.) observed in mixed races like the English and the Anglo-American. When a Badawi speaks of "the daughter of my uncle" he means wife; and the former is the dearer title, as a wife can be divorced, but blood is thicker than water.

and she drank not until she saw me again. She cohabited with me for five years till a certain day when she went forth to the Hammam bath; and I bade the cook hasten to get ready all requisites for our supper. And I entered this palace and lay down on the bed where I was wont to sleep and bade two damsels to fan my face, one sitting by my head and the other at my feet. But I was troubled and made restless by my wife's absence and could not sleep; for although my eyes were closed my mind and thoughts were wide awake. Presently I heard the slave-girl at my head say to her at my feet, "O Mas'údah, how miserable is our master and how wasted in his youth and oh! the pity of his being so betrayed by our mistress, the accursed whore!"[1] The other replied, "Yes indeed: Allah curse all faithless women and adulterous; but the like of our master, with his fair gifts, deserveth something better than this harlot who lieth abroad every night." Then quoth she who sat by my head, "Is our lord dumb or fit only for bubbling that he questioneth her not!" and quoth the other, "Fie on thee! doth our lord know her ways or doth she allow him his choice? Nay, more, doth she not drug every night the cup she giveth him to drink before sleep-time, and put Bhang[2] into it? So he sleepeth and wotteth not whither she goeth,

---

[1] Arab. "Kahbah;" the coarsest possible term. Hence the unhappy "Cava" of Don Roderick the Goth, which simply means The Whore.

[2] The Arab "Banj" and Hindú "Bhang" (which I use as most familiar) both derive from the old Coptic "Nibanj" meaning a preparation of hemp (*Cannabis sativa* seu *Indica*); and here it is easy to recognise the Homeric "Nepenthe." Al-Kazwini explains the term by "garden hemp (Kinnab bostáni or Sháhdánaj). On the other hand not a few apply the word to the henbane (*hyoscyamus niger*) so much used in mediæval Europe. The Kámús evidently means henbane distinguishing it from Hashish al haráfísh" = rascals' grass, *i.e.* the herb Pantagruelion. The "Alfáz Adwiya" (French translation) explains "Tabannuj" by "Endormir quelqu'un en lui faisant avaler de la jusquiame." In modern parlance Tabannuj is = our anæsthetic administered before an operation, a deadener of pain like myrrh and a number of other drugs. For this purpose hemp is always used (at least I never heard of henbane); and various preparations of the drug are sold at an especial bazar in Cairo. See the "powder of marvellous virtue" in Boccaccio, iii., 8; and iv., 10. Of these intoxicants, properly so termed, I shall have something to say in a future page.

The use of Bhang doubtless dates from the dawn of civilisation, whose earliest social pleasures would be inebriants. Herodotus (iv. c. 75) shows the Scythians burning the seeds (leaves and capsules) in worship and becoming drunken with the fumes, as do the S. African Bushmen of the present day. This would be the earliest form of smoking: it is still doubtful whether the pipe was used or not. Galen also mentions intoxication by hemp. Amongst Moslems, the Persians adopted the drink as an ecstatic, and about our thirteenth century Egypt, which began the practice, introduced a number of preparations to be noticed in the course of The Nights.

nor what she doeth; but we know that after giving him
the drugged wine, she donneth her richest raiment and per-
fumeth herself and then she fareth out from him to be away
till break of day; then she cometh to him, and burneth a
pastile under his nose and he awaketh from his deathlike
sleep." When I heard the slave-girl's words, the light became
black before my sight and I thought night would never fall.
Presently the daughter of my uncle came from the baths; and they
set the table for us and we ate and sat together a fair half-hour
quaffing our wine as was ever our wont. Then she called for the
particular wine I used to drink before sleeping and reached me
the cup; but, seeming to drink it according to my wont, I poured
the contents into my bosom; and, lying down, let her hear that I
was asleep. Then, behold, she cried, "Sleep out the night, and
never wake again: by Allah, I loathe thee and I loathe thy whole
body, and my soul turneth in disgust from cohabiting with thee;
and I see not the moment when Allah shall snatch away thy
life!" Then she rose and donned her fairest dress and perfumed
her person and slung my sword over her shoulder; and, opening
the gates of the palace, went her ill way. I rose and followed her
as she left the palace and she threaded the streets until she came
to the city gate, where she spoke words I understood not, and
the padlocks dropped of themselves as if broken and the gate-
leaves opened. She went forth (and I after her without her
noticing aught) till she came at last to the outlying mounds[1]
and a reed fence built about a round-roofed hut of mud-bricks.
As she entered the door, I climbed upon the roof which commanded a view of the interior, and lo! my fair cousin had gone in to a
hideous negro slave with his upper lip like the cover of a pot,
and his lower like an open pot; lips which might sweep up sand
from the gravel-floor of the cot. He was to boot a leper and a
paralytic, lying upon a strew of sugar-cane trash and wrapped in
an old blanket and the foulest rags and tatters. She kissed the
earth before him, and he raised his head so as to see her and said,
"Woe to thee! what call hadst thou to stay away all this time?
Here have been with me sundry of the black brethren, who
drank their wine and each had his young lady, and I was not
content to drink because of thine absence." Then she, "O my

---

[1] The rubbish heaps which outlie Eastern cities, some (near Cairo) are over a hundred feet high.

lord, my heart's love and coolth of my eyes,[1] knowest thou not
that I am married to my cousin whose very look I loathe, and
hate myself when in his company? And did not I fear for thy
sake, I would not let a single sun arise before making his city a
ruined heap wherein raven should croak and howlet hoot, and
jackal and wolf harbour and loot; nay I had removed its very
stones to the back side of Mount Káf."[2] Rejoined the slave,
"Thou liest, damn thee! Now I swear an oath by the valour and
honour of blackamoor men (and deem not our manliness to be
the poor manliness of white men), from today forth if thou stay
away till this hour, I will not keep company with thee nor will
I glue my body with thy body and strum and belly-bump.
Dost play fast and loose with us, thou cracked pot, that we may
satisfy thy dirty lusts? stinkard! bitch! vilest of the vile whites!"
When I heard his words, and saw with my own eyes what
passed between these two wretches, the world waxed dark before my face and my soul knew not in what place it was. But
my wife humbly stood up weeping before and wheedling the
slave, and saying, "O my beloved, and very fruit of my heart,
there is none left to cheer me but thy dear self; and, if thou cast
me off who shall take me in, O my beloved, O light of my eyes?"
And she ceased not weeping and abasing herself to him until he
deigned be reconciled with her. Then was she right glad and
stood up and doffed her clothes, even to her petticoat-trousers,
and said, "O my master what hast thou here for thy handmaiden
to eat?" "Uncover the basin," he grumbled, "and thou shalt find
at the bottom the broiled bones of some rats we dined on; pick
at them, and then go to that slop-pot where thou shalt find some
leavings of beer[3] which thou mayest drink." So she ate and drank

---

[1] Arab. "Kurrat al-ayn;" coolness of eyes as opposed to a hot eye ("sakhin") *i.e.*
one red with tears. The term is true and picturesque so I translate it literally. All
coolness is pleasant to dwellers in burning lands: thus in Al-Hariri Abu Zayd says of
Bassorah, "I found there whatever could fill the eye with coolness." And a "cool booty"
(or prize) is one which has been secured without plunging into the flames of war, or
simply a pleasant prize.

[2] Popularly rendered Caucasus (see Night cdxcvi): it corresponds so far with the
Hindu "Udaya" that the sun rises behind it; and the "false dawn" is caused by a hole
or gap. It is also the Persian Alborz, the Indian Meru (Sumeru), the Greek Olympus,
and the Rhiphæan Range (Veliki Camenypoys) or great starry girdle of the world, etc.

[3] Arab. "Mizr" or "Mizar;" vulg. Búzah; hence the medical Lat. Buza, the Russian
Buza (millet beer), our "booze," the O. Dutch "buyzen" and the German "busen."
This is the old ποτὸς θεῖος of negro and negroid Africa; the beer of Osiris, of which
dried remains have been found in jars amongst Egyptian tombs. In Equatorial Africa it
is known as "Pombe;" on the Upper Nile "Merissa" or "Mirisi" and amongst the

and washed her hands, and went and lay down by the side of the
slave, upon the cane-trash and, stripping herself stark naked, she
crept in with him under his foul coverlet and his rags and tatters.
When I saw my wife, my cousin, the daughter of my uncle, do
this deed[1] I clean lost my wits, and climbing down from the roof, I
entered and took the sword which she had with her and drew it,
determined to cut down the twain. I first struck at the slave's
neck and thought that the death decree had fallen on him:"——
And Shahrazad perceived the dawn of day and ceased to say her
permitted say.

When it was the Eighth Night,

She continued, It hath reached me, O auspicious King, that the
young ensorcelled Prince said to the King, "When I smote the
slave with intent to strike off his head, I thought that I had slain
him; for he groaned a loud hissing groan, but I had cut only the
skin and flesh of the gullet and the two arteries! It awoke the
daughter of my uncle, so I sheathed the sword and fared forth for
the city; and, entering the palace, lay upon my bed and slept till

Kafirs (Caffers) "Tshuala," "Oala" or "Boyala:" I have also heard of "Buswa" in
Central Africa which may be the origin of "Buzah." In the West it became ζῦθος, (Romaic
πίρρα), Xythum and cerevisia or cervisia, the humor ex hordeo, long before the days
of King Gambrinus. Central Africans drink it in immense quantities: in Unyamwezi the
standing bedsteads, covered with bark-slabs, are all made sloping so as to drain off the
liquor. A chief lives wholly on beef and Pombe which is thick as gruel below. Hops
are unknown: the grain, mostly Holcus, is made to germinate, then pounded, boiled and
left to ferment. In Egypt the drink is affected chiefly by Berbers, Nubians and slaves
from the Upper Nile; but it is a superior article and more like that of Europe than the
"Pombe." I have given an account of the manufacture in The Lake Regions of Central
Africa, vol. ii., p. 286. There are other preparations, Umm-bulbul (mother nightingale), Dinzáyah and Súbiyah, for which I must refer to the Shaykh El-Tounsy.

1 There is a terrible truth in this satire, which reminds us of the noble dame who preferred to her handsome husband the palefrenier laid, ord et infâme of Queen Margaret
of Navarre (Heptameron No. xx.). We have all known women who sacrificed everything despite themselves, as it were, for the most worthless of men. The world stares
and scoffs and blames and understands nothing. There is for every woman one man and
one only in whose slavery she is "ready to sweep the floor." Fate is mostly opposed to
her meeting him but, when she does, adieu husband and children, honour and religion,
life and "soul." Moreover Nature (human) commands the union of contrasts, such as
fair and foul, dark and light, tall and short; otherwise mankind would be like the
canines, a race of extremes, dwarf as toy-terriers, giants like mastiffs, bald as Chinese
"remedy dogs," or hairy as Newfoundlands. The famous Wilkes said only a half-truth
when he backed himself, with an hour's start, against the handsomest man in England;
his uncommon and remarkable ugliness (he was, as the Italians say, un bel brutto) was the
highest recommendation in the eyes of very beautiful women.

morning when my wife aroused me and I saw that she had cut off her hair and had donned mourning garments. Quoth she:—O son of my uncle, blame me not for what I do; it hath just reached me that my mother is dead, and my father hath been killed in holy war, and of my brothers one hath lost his life by a snake-sting and the other by falling down some precipice; and I can and should do naught save weep and lament. When I heard her words I refrained from all reproach and said only:—Do as thou list; I certainly will not thwart thee. She continued sorrowing, weeping and wailing one whole year from the beginning of its circle to the end, and when it was finished she said to me:— I wish to build me in thy palace a tomb with a cupola, which I will set apart for my mourning and will name the House of Lamentations.[1] Quoth I again:—Do as thou list! Then she builded for herself a cenotaph wherein to mourn, and set on its centre a dome under which showed a tomb like a Santon's sepulchre. Thither she carried the slave and lodged him; but he was exceeding weak by reason of his wound, and unable to do her love-service; he could only drink wine and from the day of his hurt he spake not a word, yet he lived on because his appointed hour[2] was not come. Every day, morning and evening, my wife went to him and wept and wailed over him and gave him wine and strong soups, and left not off doing after this manner a second year; and I bore with her patiently and paid no heed to her. One day, however, I went in to her unawares; and I found her weeping and beating her face and crying:—Why art thou absent from my sight, O my heart's delight? Speak to me, O my life; talk with me, O my love? Then she recited these verses:—

For your love my patience fails and albeit you forget * I may not; nor to
    other love my heart can make reply:

---

[1] Every Moslem burial-ground has a place of the kind where honourable women may sit and weep unseen by the multitude. These visits are enjoined by the Apostle:— Frequent the cemetery, 'twill make you think of futurity! Also:—Whoever visiteth the graves of his parents (or one of them) every Friday, he shall be written a pious son, even though he might have been in the world, before that, a disobedient. (Pilgrimage, ii., 71.) The buildings resemble our European "mortuary chapels." Said, Pasha of Egypt, was kind enough to erect one on the island off Suez, for the "use of English ladies who would like shelter whilst weeping and wailing for their dead." But I never heard that any of the ladies went there.

[2] Arab. "Ajal" = the period of life, the appointed time of death: the word is of constant recurrence and is also applied to sudden death. See Lane's Dictionary, s.v.

Bear my body, bear my soul wheresoever you may fare * And where you pitch
   the camp let my body buried lie:
Cry my name above my grave, and an answer shall return * The moaning of
   my bones responsive to your cry.[1]

Then she recited, weeping bitterly the while:—

The day of my delight is the day when draw you near * And the day of mine
   affright is the day you turn away:
Though I tremble through the night in my bitter dread of death * When I hold
   you in my arms I am free from all affray.

Once more she began reciting:—

Though a-morn I may awake with all happiness in hand * Though the world
   all be mine and like Kisra-kings[2] I reign;
To me they had the worth of the winglet of the gnat * When I fail to see thy
   form, when I look for thee in vain.

When she had ended for a time her words and her weeping I said
to her:—O my cousin, let this thy mourning suffice, for in pouring forth tears there is little profit! Thwart me not, answered
she, in aught I do, or I will lay violent hands on myself! So I held
my peace and left her to go her own way; and she ceased not to

---

   [1] "The dying Badawi to his tribe" (and lover) appears to me highly pathetic. The
wild people love to be buried upon hill-slopes whence they can look down upon the camp;
and they still call out the names of kinsmen and friends as they pass by the grave yards.
A similar piece occurs in Wetzstein (p. 27, "Reisebericht ueber Hauran," etc.):—

O bear with you my bones where the camel bears his load * And bury me before you, if
   buried I must be;
And let me not be buried 'neath the burden of the vine * But high upon the hill whence
   your sight I ever see!
As you pass along my grave cry aloud and name your names * The crying of your names
   shall revive the bones of me:
I have fasted through my life with my friends, and in my death, * I will feast when we
   meet, on that day of joy and glee.

   [2] The Akásirah (plur. of Kasrá=Chosroës) is here a title of the four great dynasties of
Persian Kings. 1. The Peshdadian or Assyrian race, proto-historics for whom dates
fail; 2. The Káyánián (Medes and Persians) who ended with the Alexandrian invasion
in B. C. 331; 3. The Ashkánián (Parthenians or Arsacides) who ruled till A. D. 202;
and 4. The Sassanides which have already been mentioned.   But strictly speaking
" Kisri" and "Kasra" are titles applied only to the latter dynasty and especially to the
great King Anushirwan. They must not be confounded with "Khusrau" (P. N. Cyrus,
Ahasuerus? Chosroës?); and yet the three seem to have combined in "Cæsar," Kaysar
and Czar. For details especially connected with Zoroaster see vol. I, p. 380 of the Dabistan or School of Manners, translated by David Shea and Anthony Troyer, Paris, 1843.
The book is most valuable, but the proper names are so carelessly and incorrectly printed
that the student is led into perpetual error.

cry and keen and indulge her affliction for yet another year. At the end of the third year I waxed aweary of this longsome mourning, and one day I happened to enter the cenotaph when vexed and angry with some matter which had thwarted me, and suddenly I heard her say:—O my lord, I never hear thee vouch-safe a single word to me! Why dost thou not answer me, O my master? and she began reciting:—

O thou tomb! O thou tomb! be his beauty set in shade? * Hast thou darkened
    that countenance all-sheeny as the noon?
O thou tomb! neither earth nor yet heaven art to me * Then how cometh it in
    thee are conjoined my sun and moon?

When I heard such verses as these rage was heaped upon my rage; I cried out:—Well-away! how long is this sorrow to last? and I began repeating:—

O thou tomb! O thou tomb! be his horrors set in blight? * Hast thou dark-
    enèd his countenance that sickeneth the soul?
O thou tomb! neither cess-pool nor pipkin art to me * Then how cometh it
    in thee are conjoinèd soil and coal?

When she heard my words she sprang to her feet crying:—Fie upon thee, thou cur! all this is of thy doings; thou hast wounded my heart's darling and thereby worked me sore woe and thou hast wasted his youth so that these three years he hath lain abed more dead than alive! In my wrath I cried:—O thou foulest of harlots and filthiest of whores ever futtered by negro slaves who are hired to have at thee![1] Yes indeed it was I who did this good deed; and snatching up my sword I drew it and made at her to cut her down. But she laughed my words and mine intent to scorn crying: To heel, hound that thou art! Alas[2] for the past which shall no more come to pass nor shall any one avail the dead to raise. Allah hath indeed now given into my hand him who did to me this thing, a deed that hath burned my heart with a fire which died not and a flame which might not be quenched! Then she stood up; and, pronouncing some words to me unintelligible, she said:—By virtue of my egromancy become thou half stone and half man; whereupon I became what thou seest, unable to

---

[1] The words are the very lowest and coarsest; but the scene is true to Arab life.
[2] Arab. "Hayhát:" the word, written in a variety of ways is onomatopoetic, like our "heigh-ho!" it sometimes means "far from me (or you) be it!" but in popular usage it is simply "Alas."

rise or to sit, and neither dead nor alive. Moreover she ensorcelled the city with all its streets and garths, and she turned
by her gramarye the four islands into four mountains around the
tarn whereof thou questionest me; and the citizens, who were
of four different faiths, Moslem, Nazarene, Jew and Magian,
she transformed by her enchantments into fishes; the Moslems
are the white, the Magians red, the Christians blue and the Jews
yellow.[1] And every day she tortureth me and scourgeth me
with an hundred stripes, each of which draweth floods of blood
and cutteth the skin of my shoulders to strips; and lastly she
clotheth my upper half with a hair-cloth and then throweth
over them these robes." Hereupon the young man again shed
tears and began reciting:—

In patience, O my God, I endure my lot and fate; * I will bear at will of Thee
    whatsoever be my state:
They oppress me; they torture me; they make my life a woe * Yet haply
    Heaven's happiness shall compensate my strait:
Yea, straitened is my life by the bane and hate o' foes * But Mustafá and
    Murtazá[2] shall ope me Heaven's gate.

After this the Sultan turned towards the young Prince and said,
"O youth, thou hast removed one grief only to add another grief;
but now, O my friend, where is she; and where is the mausoleum
wherein lieth the wounded slave?" "The slave lieth under yon
dome," quoth the young man, "and she sitteth in the chamber
fronting yonder door. And every day at sunrise she cometh
forth, and first strippeth me, and whippeth me with an hundred
strokes of the leathern scourge, and I weep and shriek; but there
is no power of motion in my lower limbs to keep her off me. After

---

[1] Lane (i., 134) finds a date for the book in ·this passage. The Soldan of Egypt, Mohammed ibn Kala'ún, in the early eighth century (Hijrah = our fourteenth), issued a sump-
tuary law compelling Christians and Jews to wear indigo-blue and saffron-yellow turbans,
the white being reserved for Moslems. But the custom was much older and Mandeville
(chapt. ix.) describes it in A. D. 1322 when it had become the rule. And it still endures;
although abolished in the cities it is the rule for Christians, at least in the country parts of
Egypt and Syria. I may here remark that such detached passages as these are absolutely
useless for chronology: they may be simply the additions of editors or mere copyists.

[2] The ancient "Mustapha" = the Chosen (prophet, i. e. Mohammed), also titled Al-
Mujtabá, the Accepted (Pilgrimage, ii., 309). "Murtazá"=the Elect, i. e. the Caliph
Ali is the older "Mortada" or "Mortadi" of Ockley and his day, meaning "one pleasing to
(or acceptable to) Allah." Still older writers corrupted it to "Mortis Ali" and readers
supposed this to be the Caliph's name.

ending her tormenting me she visiteth the slave, bringing him wine and boiled meats. And to-morrow at an early hour she will be here." Quoth the King, "By Allah, O youth, I will assuredly do thee a good deed which the world shall not willingly let die, and an act of derring-do which shall be chronicled long after I am dead and gone by." Then the King sat him by the side of the young Prince and talked till nightfall, when he lay down and slept; but, as soon as the false dawn[1] showed, he arose and doffing his outer garments[2] bared his blade and hastened to the place wherein lay the slave. Then was he ware of lighted candles and lamps, and the perfume of incenses and unguents; and, directed by these, he made for the slave and struck him one stroke killing him on the spot: after which he lifted him on his back and threw him into a well that was in the palace. Presently he returned and, donning the slave's gear, lay down at length within the mausoleum with the drawn sword laid close to and along his side. After an hour or so the accursed witch came; and, first going to her husband, she stripped off his clothes and, taking a whip, flogged him cruelly while he cried out, "Ah! enough for me the case I am in! take pity on me, O my cousin!" But she replied, "Didst thou take pity on me and spare the life of my true love on whom I doated?" Then she drew the cilice over his raw and bleeding skin and threw the robe upon all and went down to the slave with a goblet of wine and a bowl of meat-broth in her hands. She entered under the dome weeping and wailing, "Well-away!" and crying, "O my lord! speak a word to me! O my master! talk awhile with me!" and began to recite these couplets:—

How long this harshness, this unlove, shall bide? * Suffice thee not tear-floods
    thou hast espied?
Thou dost prolong our parting purposely * And if wouldst please my foe,
    thou'rt satisfied!

Then she wept again and said, "O my lord! speak to me, talk with me!" The King lowered his voice and, twisting his tongue, spoke

---

[1] The gleam (zodiacal light) preceding the true dawn; the Persians call the former Subh-i-kázib (false or lying dawn) opposed to Subh-i-sádik (true dawn) and suppose that it is caused by the sun shining through a hole in the world-encircling Mount Kaf.

[2] So the Heb. "Arún" = naked, means wearing the lower robe only; = our "in his shirt."

after the fashion of the blackamoors and said " 'lack! 'lack! there be no Ma'esty and there be no Might save in Allauh, the Gloriose, the Greät!" Now when she heard these words she shouted for joy, and fell to the ground fainting; and when her senses returned she asked, "O my lord, can it be true that thou hast power of speech?" and the King making his voice small and faint answered, "O my cuss! dost thou deserve that I talk to thee and speak with thee?" "Why and wherefore?" rejoined she; and he replied "The why is that all the livelong day thou tormentest thy hubby; and he keeps calling on 'eaven for aid until sleep is strange to me even from evenin' till mawnin', and he prays and damns, cussing us two, me and thee, causing me disquiet and much bother: were this not so, I should long ago have got my health; and it is this which prevents my answering thee." Quoth she, "With thy leave I will release him from what spell is on him;" and quoth the King, "Release him and let's have some rest!" She cried, "To hear is to obey;" and, going from the cenotaph to the palace, she took a metal bowl and filled it with water and spake over it certain words which made the contents bubble and boil as a cauldron seetheth over the fire. With this she sprinkled her husband saying, "By virtue of the dread words I have spoken, if thou becamest thus by my spells, come forth out of that form into thine own former form." And lo and behold! the young man shook and trembled; then he rose to his feet and, rejoicing at his deliverance, cried aloud, "I testify that there is no god but *the* God, and in very truth Mohammed is His Apostle, whom Allah bless and keep!" Then she said to him, "Go forth and return not hither, for if thou do I will surely slay thee;" screaming these words in his face. So he went from between her hands; and she returned to the dome and, going down to the sepulchre, she said, "O my lord, come forth to me that I may look upon thee and thy goodliness!" The King replied in faint low words, "What[1] thing hast thou done? Thou hast rid me of the branch but not of the root." She asked, "O my darling! O my negro-ling! what is the root?" And he answered, "Fie on thee, O my cuss! The people of this city and of the four islands every night when it's half passed lift their heads from the tank in which thou hast turned them to fishes and cry to Heaven and

---

[1] Here we have the vulgar Egyptian colloquialism "Aysh" (=Ayyu shayyin) for the classical "Má" = what.

call down its anger on me and thee; and this is the reason why
my body's baulked from health. Go at once and set them free;
then come to me and take my hand, and raise me up, for a little
strength is already back in me." When she heard the King's
words (and she still supposed him to be the slave) she cried joyously, "O my master, on my head and on my eyes be thy command, Bismillah[1]!" So she sprang to her feet and, full of joy
and gladness, ran down to the tarn and took a little of its water
in the palm of her hand——And Shahrazad perceived the dawn
of day and ceased to say her permitted say.

When it was the Ninth Night,

She said, It hath reached me, O auspicious King, that when the
young woman, the sorceress, took in hand some of the tarn-water
and spake over it words not to be understood, the fishes lifted
their heads and stood up on the instant like men, the spell on the
people of the city having been removed. What was the lake
again became a crowded capital; the bazars were thronged with
folk who bought and sold; each citizen was occupied with his
own calling and the four hills became islands as they were
whilome. Then the young woman, that wicked sorceress, returned to the King and (still thinking he was the negro) said to
him, "O my love! stretch forth thy honoured hand that I may
assist thee to rise." "Nearer to me," quoth the King in a faint
and feigned tone. She came close as to embrace him when he
took up the sword lying hid by his side and smote her across the
breast, so that the point showed gleaming behind her back.
Then he smote her a second time and cut her in twain and cast
her to the ground in two halves. After which he fared forth
and found the young man, now freed from the spell, awaiting
him and gave him joy of his happy release while the Prince
kissed his hand with abundant thanks. Quoth the King, "Wilt
thou abide in this city or go with me to my capital?" Quoth the
youth, "O King of the age, wottest thou not what journey is
between thee and thy city?" "Two days and a half," answered
he; whereupon said the other, "An thou be sleeping, O King,
awake! Between thee and thy city is a year's march for a well-
girt walker, and thou haddest not come hither in two days and
a half save that the city was under enchantment. And I, O

---

[1] "In the name of Allah!" here said before taking action.

King, will never part from thee; no, not even for the twinkling
of an eye." The King rejoiced at his words and said, "Thanks
be to Allah who hath bestowed thee upon me! From this hour
thou art my son and my only son, for that in all my life I have
never been blessed with issue." Thereupon they embraced and
joyed with exceeding great joy; and, reaching the palace, the
Prince who had been spell-bound informed his lords and his
grandees that he was about to visit the Holy Places as a pilgrim,
and bade them get ready all things necessary for the occasion.
The preparations lasted ten days, after which he set out with
the Sultan, whose heart burned in yearning for his city whence
he had been absent a whole twelvemonth. They journeyed with
an escort of Mamelukes[1] carrying all manners of precious gifts
and rarities, nor stinted they wayfaring day and night for a full
year until they approached the Sultan's capital, and sent on
messengers to announce their coming. Then the Wazir and the
whole army came out to meet him in joy and gladness, for they
had given up all hope of ever seeing their King; and the troops
kissed the ground before him and wished him joy of his safety.
He entered and took seat upon his throne and the Minister
came before him and, when acquainted with all that had befallen the young Prince, he congratulated him on his narrow
escape. When order was restored throughout the land the King
gave largesse to many of his people, and said to the Wazir,
"Hither the Fisherman who brought us the fishes!" So he sent
for the man who had been the first cause of the city and the
citizens being delivered from enchantment and, when he came into the presence, the Sultan bestowed upon him a dress of honour,
and questioned him of his condition and whether he had children.
The Fisherman gave him to know that he had two daughters and
a son, so the King sent for them and, taking one daughter to wife,
gave the other to the young Prince and made the son his head
treasurer. Furthermore he invested his Wazir with the Sultanate

---

[1] Arab. "Mamlúk" (plur. Mamálik) lit. a chattel; and in The Nights a white slave
trained to arms. The "Mameluke Beys" of Egypt were locally called the "Ghuzz," I use
the convenient word in its old popular sense;

> 'Tis sung, there's a valiant Mameluke
> In foreign lands ycleped (*Sir Luke*)—
> HUDIBRAS.

And hence, probably, Molière's "Mamamouchi"; and the modern French use "Mama-
luc." See Savary's Letters, No. xl.

of the City in the Black Islands whilome belonging to the young Prince, and dispatched with him the escort of fifty armed slaves together with dresses of honour for all the Emirs and Grandees. The Wazir kissed hands and fared forth on his way; while the Sultan and the Prince abode at home in all the solace and the de-light of life; and the Fisherman became the richest man of his age, and his daughters wived with the Kings, until death came to them. And yet, O King! this is not more wondrous than the story of

THE PORTER AND THE THREE LADIES OF BAGHDAD.

ONCE upon a time there was a Porter in Baghdad, who was a bachelor and who would remain unmarried. It came to pass on a certain day, as he stood about the street leaning idly upon his crate, behold, there stood before him an honourable woman in a mantilla of Mosul[1] silk, broidered with gold and bordered with brocade; her walking-shoes were also purfled with gold and her hair floated in long plaits. She raised her face-veil[2] and, showing two black eyes fringed with jetty lashes, whose glances were soft and languishing and whose perfect beauty was ever blandishing, she accosted the Porter and said in the suavest tones and choicest language, "Take up thy crate and follow me." The Porter was so dazzled he could hardly believe that he heard her aright, but he shouldered his basket in hot haste saying in himself, "O day of good luck! O day of Allah's grace!" and walked after her till she stopped at the door of a house. There she rapped, and presently came out to her an old man, a Nazarene, to whom she gave a gold piece, receiving from him in return what she required of strained wine clear as olive oil; and she set it safely in the hamper, saying "Lift and follow." Quoth the Porter, "This, by Allah, is indeed an auspicious day, a day propitious for the granting of all a man wisheth." He again hoisted up the crate and followed her; till she

---

[1] The name of this celebrated successor of Nineveh, where some suppose The Nights were written, is orig. Μεσοπύλαι (middle-gates) because it stood on the way where four great highways meet. The Arab. form "Mausil" (the vulgar "Mosul") is also signifi-cant, alluding to the "junction" of Assyria and Babylonia. Hence our "muslin."

[2] This is Mr. Thackeray's "nose-bag." I translate by "walking-shoes" the Arab "Khuff" which are a manner of loose boot covering the ankle; they are not usually em-broidered, the ornament being reserved for the inner shoe.

stopped at a fruiterer's shop and bought from him Shámi[1] apples and Osmáni quinces and Ománi[2] peaches, and cucumbers of Nile growth, and Egyptian limes and Sultáni oranges and citrons; besides Aleppine jasmine, scented myrtle berries, Damascene nenuphars, flower of privet[3] and camomile, blood-red anemones, violets, and pomegranate-bloom, eglantine and narcissus, and set the whole in the Porter's crate, saying, "Up with it." So he lifted and followed her till she stopped at a butcher's booth and said, "Cut me off ten pounds of mutton." She paid him his price and he wrapped it in a banana-leaf, whereupon she laid it in the crate and said "Hoist, O Porter." He hoisted accordingly, and followed her as she walked on till she stopped at a grocer's, where she bought dry fruits and pistachio-kernels, Tihámah raisins, shelled almonds and all wanted for dessert, and said to the Porter, "Lift and follow me." So he up with his hamper and after her till she stayed at the confectioner's, and she bought an earthen platter, and piled it with all kinds of sweetmeats in his shop, open-worked tarts and fritters scented with musk and "soap-cakes," and lemon-loaves and melon-preserves,[4] and "Zay-nab's combs," and "ladies' fingers," and "Kazi's tit-bits" and goodies of every description; and placed the platter in the Porter's

---

[1] *i. e.* Syria (says Abulfeda) the "land on the left" (of one facing the east) as opposed to Al-Yaman the "land on the right." Osmani would mean Turkish, Ottoman. When Bernard the Wise (Bohn, p. 24) speaks of "Bagada and Axiam" (Mabillon's text) or "Axinarri" (still worse), he means Baghdad and Ash-Shám (Syria, Damascus), the latter word puzzling his Editor. Richardson (Dissert. lxxii.) seems to support a hideous attempt to derive Shám from Shámat, a mole or wart, because the country is studded with hillocks! Al-Shám is often applied to Damascus-city whose proper name Dimishk belongs to books: this term is generally derived from Dimáshik b. Káli b. Málik b. Sham (Shem). Lee (Ibn Batútah, 29) denies that ha-Dimishki means "Eliezer of Damascus."

[2] From Oman = Eastern Arabia.

[3] Arab. "Tamar Hanná" lit. date of Henna, but applied to the flower of the eastern privet (*Lawsonia inermis*) which has the sweet scent of freshly mown hay. The use of Henna as a dye is known even in England. The "myrtle" alluded to may either have been for a perfume (as it is held an anti-intoxicant) or for eating, the bitter aromatic berries of the "Ás" being supposed to flavour wine and especially Raki (raw brandy).

[4] Lane. (i. 211) pleasantly remarks, "A list of these sweets is given in my original, but I have thought it better to omit the names" (!) Dozy does not shirk his duty, but he is not much more satisfactory in explaining words interesting to students because they are unfound in dictionaries and forgotten by the people. "Akrás (cakes) Laymuniyah (of limes) wa Maymuniyah" appears in the Bresl. Edit. as "Ma'amuniyah" which may mean "Ma'amun's cakes" or "delectable cakes." "Amshát"=(combs) perhaps refers to a fine kind of Kunáfah (vermicelli) known in Egypt and Syria as "Ghazl al-banát" =girl's spinning.

crate. Thereupon quoth he (being a merry man), "Thou shouldest have told me, and I would have brought with me a pony or a she-camel to carry all this market-stuff." She smiled and gave him a little cuff on the nape saying, "Step out and exceed not in words for (Allah willing!) thy wage will not be wanting." Then she stopped at a perfumer's and took from him ten sorts of waters, rose scented with musk, orange-flower, water-lily, willow-flower, violet and five others; and she also bought two loaves of sugar, a bottle for perfume-spraying, a lump of male incense, aloe-wood, ambergris and musk, with candles of Alexandria wax; and she put the whole into the basket, saying, "Up with thy crate and after me." He did so and followed until she stood before the greengrocer's, of whom she bought pickled safflower and olives, in brine and in oil; with tarragon and cream-cheese and hard Syrian cheese; and she stowed them away in the crate saying to the Porter, "Take up thy basket and follow me." He did so and went after her till she came to a fair mansion fronted by a spacious court, a tall, fine place to which columns gave strength and grace: and the gate thereof had two leaves of ebony inlaid with plates of red gold. The lady stopped at the door and, turning her face-veil sideways, knocked softly with her knuckles whilst the Porter stood behind her, thinking of naught save her beauty and loveliness. Presently the door swung back and both leaves were opened, whereupon he looked to see who had opened it; and behold, it was a lady of tall figure, some five feet high; a model of beauty and loveliness, brilliance and symmetry and perfect grace. Her forehead was flower-white; her cheeks like the anemone ruddy bright; her eyes were those of the wild heifer or the gazelle, with eyebrows like the crescent-moon which ends Sha'abán and begins Ramazán;[1] her mouth was the ring of Sulayman,[2] her lips coral-red, and her teeth like a line of strung pearls or of camomile petals. Her throat recalled the antelope's, and her breasts, like two pomegranates of even size, stood at bay as it were,[3] her body rose and fell in waves below her dress like the rolls of a piece of brocade, and her navel[4]

---

[1] The new moon carefully looked for by all Moslems because it begins the Ramazán-fast.

[2] Solomon's signet ring has before been noticed.

[3] The "high-bosomed" damsel, with breasts firm as a cube, is a favourite with Arab tale-tellers. *Fanno baruffa* is the Italian term for hard breasts pointing outwards.

[4] A large hollow navel is looked upon not only as a beauty, but in children it is held a promise of good growth.

would hold an ounce of benzoin ointment.   In fine she was like
her of whom the poet said:—

On Sun and Moon of palace cast thy sight * Enjoy her flower-like face, her
    fragrant light:
Thine eyes shall never see in hair so black * Beauty encase a brow so purely
    white:
The ruddy rosy cheek proclaims her claim * Though fail her name whose
    beauties we indite:
As sways her gait I smile at hips so big * And weep to see the waist they bear
    so slight.

When the Porter looked upon her his wits were waylaid, and his
senses were stormed so that his crate went nigh to fall from his
head, and he said to himself, "Never have I in my life seen a day
more blessed than this day!" Then quoth the lady-portress to the
lady-cateress, "Come in from the gate and relieve this poor man of
his load." So the provisioner went in followed by the portress
and the Porter and went on till they reached a spacious ground-
floor hall,[1] built with admirable skill and beautified with all manner colours and carvings; with upper balconies and groined
arches and galleries and cupboards and recesses whose curtains
hung before them. In the midst stood a great basin full of water
surrounding a fine fountain, and at the upper end on the raised
daïs was a couch of juniper-wood set with gems and pearls, with a
canopy like mosquito-curtains of red satin-silk looped up with
pearls as big as filberts and bigger. Thereupon sat a lady bright of
blee, with brow beaming brilliancy, the dream of philosophy,
whose eyes were fraught with Babel's gramarye[2] and her eyebrows were arched as for archery; her breath breathed ambergris
and perfumery and her lips were sugar to taste and carnelian to
see. Her stature was straight as the letter I[3] and her face
shamed the noon-sun's radiancy; and she was even as a galaxy, or

---

1 Arab. "Ka'ah," a high hall opening upon the central court: we shall find the word
used for a mansion, barrack, men's quarters, etc.

2 Babel═Gate of God (El), or Gate of Ilu (P. N. of God), which the Jews ironically
interpreted "Confusion." The tradition of Babylonia being the very centre of witchcraft and enchantment by means of its Seven Deadly Spirits, has survived in Al-Islam;
the two fallen angels(whose names will occur) being confined in a well; Nimrod attempting
to reach Heaven from the Tower in a magical car drawn by monstrous birds and so forth.
See p. 114, Francois Lenormant's "Chaldean Magic," London, Bagsters.

3 Arab. "Kámat Alfíyyah" ═ like the letter Alif, a straight perpendicular stroke.
In the Egyptian hieroglyphs, the origin of every alphabet (not syllabarium) known to
man, one form was a flag or leaf of water-plant standing upright. Hence probably the
Arabic Alif-shape; while other nations preferred other modifications of the letter (ox's
head, etc.), which in Egyptian number some thirty-six varieties, simple and compound.

a dome with golden marquetry or a bride displayed in choicest finery or a noble maid of Áraby.[1] Right well of her sang the bard when he said:—

Her smiles twin rows of pearls display * Chamomile-buds or rimey spray
Her tresses stray as night let down * And shames her light the dawn o' day.

[2]The third lady rising from the couch stepped forward with graceful swaying gait till she reached the middle of the saloon, when she said to her sisters, "Why stand ye here? take it down from this poor man's head!" Then the cateress went and stood before him, and the portress behind him while the third helped them, and they lifted the load from the Porter's head; and, emptying it of all that was therein, set everything in its place. Lastly they gave him two gold pieces, saying, "Wend thy ways, O Porter." But he went not, for he stood looking at the ladies and admiring what uncommon beauty was theirs, and their pleasant manners and kindly dispositions (never had he seen goodlier); and he gazed wistfully at that good store of wines and sweet-scented flowers and fruits and other matters. Also he marvelled with exceeding marvel, especially to see no man in the place and delayed his going; whereupon quoth the eldest lady, "What aileth thee that goest not; haply thy wage be too little?" And, turning to her sister the cateress, she said, "Give him another dinar!" But the Porter answered, "By Allah, my lady, it is not for the wage; my hire is never more than two dirhams; but in very sooth my heart and my soul are taken up with you and your condition. I wonder to see you single with ne'er a man about you and not a soul to bear you company; and well you wot that the minaret toppleth o'er unless it stand upon four, and you want this same fourth; and women's pleasure without man is short of measure, even as the poet said:—

Seest not we want for joy four things all told * The harp and lute, the flute and
    flageolet;
And be they companied with scents four-fold * Rose, myrtle, anemone and
    violet;
Nor please all eight an four thou wouldst withold * Good wine and youth and
    gold and pretty pet.

---

1 I have not attempted to order this marvellous confusion of metaphors so characteristic of The Nights and the exigencies of Al-Saj'a=rhymed prose.

2 Here and elsewhere I omit the "kála (dice Turpino)" of the original: Torrens preserves "Thus goes the tale" (which it only interrupts). This is simply letter-wise and sense-foolish.

You be there and want a fourth who shall be a person of good sense and prudence; smart witted, and one apt to keep careful counsel." His words pleased and amused them much; and they laughed at him and said, "And who is to assure us of that? We are maidens and we fear to entrust our secret where it may not be kept, for we have read in a certain chronicle the lines of one Ibn al-Sumam:—

Hold fast thy secret and to none unfold * Lost is a secret when that secret's told:
An fail thy breast thy secret to conceal * How canst thou hope another's breast shall hold?

And Abu Nowás[1] said well on the same subject:—

Who trusteth secret to another's hand * Upon his brow deserveth burn of brand!"

When the Porter heard their words he rejoined, "By your lives! I am a man of sense and a discreet, who hath read books and perused chronicles; I reveal the fair and conceal the foul and I act as the poet adviseth:—

None but the good a secret keep   * And good men keep it unrevealed:
It is to me a well-shut house   * With keyless locks and door ensealed"[2]

When the maidens heard his verse and its poetical application addressed to them they said, "Thou knowest that we have laid out all our monies on this place. Now say, hast thou aught to offer us in return for entertainment? For surely we will not suffer thee to sit in our company and be our cup-companion, and gaze upon our faces so fair and so rare without paying a round sum.[3] Wottest thou not the saying:—

Sans hope of gain
Love's not worth a grain?"

Whereto the lady-portress added, "If thou bring anything thou art a something; if no thing, be off with thee, thou art a nothing;" but the procuratrix interposed, saying, "Nay, O my sisters, leave

---

1 Of this worthy more at a future time.
2 i. e., sealed with the Kazi or legal authority's seal of office.
3 "Nothing for nothing" is a fixed idea with the Eastern woman: not so much for greed as for a sexual *point d'honneur* when dealing with the adversary—man.

teasing him for by Allah he hath not failed us this day, and had he been other he never had kept patience with me, so whatever be his shot and scot I will take it upon myself." The Porter, over-joyed, kissed the ground before her and thanked her saying, "By Allah, these monies are the first fruits this day hath given me." Hearing this they said, "Sit thee down and welcome to thee," and the eldest lady added, "By Allah, we may not suffer thee to join us save on one condition, and this it is, that no questions be asked as to what concerneth thee not, and frowardness shall be soundly flogged." Answered the Porter, "I agree to this, O my lady, on my head and my eyes be it! Lookye, I am dumb, I have no tongue." Then arose the provisioneress and tightening her girdle set the table by the fountain and put the flowers and sweet herbs in their jars, and strained the wine and ranged the flasks in row and made ready every requisite. Then sat she down, she and her sisters, placing amidst them the Porter who kept deeming himself in a dream; and she took up the wine flagon, and poured out the first cup and drank it off, and likewise a second and a third.[1] After this she filled a fourth cup which she handed to one of her sisters; and, lastly, she crowned a goblet and passed it to the Porter, saying:—

"Drink the dear draught, drink free and fain * What healeth every grief and pain."

He took the cup in his hand and, louting low, returned his best thanks and improvised:—

"Drain not the bowl save with a trusty friend * A man of worth whose good old blood all know:
For wine, like wind, sucks sweetness from the sweet * And stinks when over stench it haply blow:"

Adding:—

"Drain not the bowl, save from dear hand like thine * The cup recalls thy gifts; thou, gifts of wine."

---

1 She drinks first, the custom of the universal East, to show that the wine she had bought was unpoisoned. Easterns, who utterly ignore the "social glass" of Western civilisation, drink honestly to get drunk; and, when far gone are addicted to horse-play (in Pers. "Badmasti"=*le vin mauvais*) which leads to quarrels and bloodshed. Hence it is held highly irreverent to assert of patriarchs, prophets and saints that they "drank wine;" and Moslems agree with our "Teatotallers" in denying that, except in the case of Noah, inebriatives are anywhere mentioned in Holy Writ.

After repeating this couplet he kissed their hands and drank and was drunk and sat swaying from side to side and pursued:—

"All drinks wherein is blood the Law unclean * Doth hold save one, the bloodshed of the vine:
Fill! fill! take all my wealth bequeathed or won * Thou fawn! a willing ransom for those eyne."

Then the cateress crowned a cup and gave it to the portress, who took it from her hand and thanked her and drank. Thereupon she poured again and passed to the eldest lady who sat on the couch, and filled yet another and handed it to the Porter. He kissed the ground before them; and, after drinking and thanking them, he again began to recite:—

"Here! Here! by Allah, here! * Cups of the sweet, the dear!
Fill me a brimming bowl   * The Fount o' Life I speer"

Then the Porter stood up before the mistress of the house and said, "O lady, I am thy slave, thy Mameluke, thy white thrall, thy very bondsman;" and he began reciting:—

"A slave of slaves there standeth at thy door * Lauding thy generous boons and
   gifts galore:
Beauty! may he come in awhile to 'joy * Thy charms? for Love and I part
   nevermore!"

She said to him, "Drink; and health and happiness attend thy drink." So he took the cup and kissed her hand and recited these lines in sing-song:—

"I gave her brave old wine that like her cheeks * Blushed red or flame from
   furnace flaring up:
She bussed the brim and said with many a smile * How durst thou deal folk's
   cheek for folk to sup?
"Drink!" (said I) "these are tears of mine whose tinct * Is heart-blood sighs
   have boilèd in the cup."

She answered him in the following couplet:—

"An tears of blood for me, friend, thou hast shed * Suffer me sup them, by thy
   head and eyes!"

Then the lady took the cup, and drank it off to her sisters' health, and they ceased not drinking (the Porter being in the midst of them), and dancing and laughing and reciting verses and singing ballads and ritornellos. All this time the Porter was carrying on with them, kissing, toying, biting, handling, groping, fingering; whilst one thrust a dainty morsel in his mouth, and another slapped him; and this cuffed his cheeks, and that threw sweet flowers at him; and he was in the very paradise of pleasure, as though he were sitting in the seventh sphere among the Houris[1] of Heaven. They ceased not doing after this fashion until the wine played tricks in their heads and worsted their wits; and, when the drink got the better of them, the portress stood up and doffed her clothes till she was mother-naked. However, she let down her hair about her body by way of shift, and throwing herself into the basin disported herself and dived like a duck and swam up and down, and took water in her mouth, and spurted it all over the Porter, and washed her limbs, and between her breasts, and inside her thighs and all around her navel. Then she came up out of the cistern and throwing herself on the Porter's lap said, "O my lord, O my love, what callest thou this article?" pointing to her slit, her solution of continuity. "I call that thy cleft," quoth the Porter, and she rejoined, "Wah! wah, art thou not ashamed to use such a word?" and she caught him by the collar and soundly cuffed him. Said he again, "Thy womb, thy vulva;" and she struck him a second slap crying, "O fie, O fie, this is another ugly word; is there no shame in thee?" Quoth he, "Thy coynte;" and she cried, "O thou! art wholly destitute of modesty?" and thumped him and bashed him. Then cried the Porter, "Thy clitoris,"[2] whereat the eldest lady came down upon him with a yet sorer beating, and said, "No;" and he said, " 'Tis so," and the Porter went on calling the same commodity by sundry other names, but whatever he said they beat him more and more till his neck ached and swelled with the blows he had gotten; and on this wise they made him a butt and a laughing-stock. At last he turned upon them asking, "And what do you women call this article?" Whereto

---

[1] Arab. "Húr al-Ayn," lit. (maids) with eyes of lively white and black, applied to the virgins of Paradise who will wive with the happy Faithful. I retain our vulgar "Houri," warning the reader that it is a masc. for a fem. ("Huríyah") in Arab, although accepted in Persian, a genderless speech.

[2] Arab. "Zambúr," whose head is amputated in female circumcision. See Night ccclxxiv.

the damsel made answer, "The basil of the bridges."[1] Cried the
Porter, "Thank Allah for my safety: aid me and be thou propitious, O basil of the bridges!" They passed round the cup and
tossed off the bowl again, when the second lady stood up; and,
stripping off all her clothes, cast herself into the cistern and did as
the first had done; then she came out of the water and throwing
her naked form on the Porter's lap pointed to her machine and
said, "O light of mine eyes, do tell me what is the name of this
concern?" He replied as before, "Thy slit;" and she rejoined,
"Hath such term no shame for thee?" and cuffed him and
buffeted him till the saloon rang with the blows. Then quoth she,
"O fie! O fie! how canst thou say this without blushing?" He
suggested, "The basil of the bridges;" but she would not have it
and she said, "No! no!" and struck him and slapped him on the
back of the neck. Then he began calling out all the names he
knew, "Thy slit, thy womb, thy coynte, thy clitoris;" and the
girls kept on saying, "No! no!" So he said, "I stick to the
basil of the bridges;" and all the three laughed till they fell on
their backs and laid slaps on his neck and said, "No! no! that's
not its proper name." Thereupon he cried, "O my sisters, what *is*
its name?" and they replied, "What sayest thou to the husked
sesame-seed?" Then the cateress donned her clothes and they fell
again to carousing, but the Porter kept moaning, "Oh! and Oh!"
for his neck and shoulders, and the cup passed merrily round and
round again for a full hour. After that time the eldest and handsomest lady stood up and stripped off her garments, whereupon
the Porter took his neck in hand, and rubbed and shampoo'd
it, saying, "My neck and shoulders are on the way of Allah!"[2]
Then she threw herself into the basin, and swam and dived,
sported and washed; and the Porter looked at her naked figure
as though she had been a slice of the moon[3] and at her face with
the sheen of Luna when at full, or like the dawn when it bright-
eneth, and he noted her noble stature and shape, and those

---

1 Ocymum basilicum noticed in Introduction; the bassilico of Boccaccio iv. 5. The
Book of Kalilah and Dimnah represents it as "sprouting with something also whose
smell is foul and disgusting and the sower at once sets to gather it and burn it with fire."
(The Fables of Bidpai translated from the later Syriac version by I. G. N. Keith-Falconer,
etc., etc., etc., Cambridge University Press, 1885). Here, however, Habk is a pennyroyal
(*mentha puligium*), and probably alludes to the pecten.

2 *i. e.* common property for all to beat.

3 "A digit of the moon" is the Hindú equivalent.

glorious forms that quivered as she went; for she was naked as the Lord made her. Then he cried "Alack! Alack!" and began to address her, versifying in these couplets:—

"If I liken thy shape to the bough when green * My likeness errs and I sore mistake it;
For the bough is fairest when clad the most * And thou art fairest when mother-naked."

When the lady heard his verses she came up out of the basin and, seating herself upon his lap and knees, pointed to her genitory and said, "O my lordling, what be the name of this?" Quoth he, "The basil of the bridges;" but she said, "Bah, bah!" Quoth he, "The husked sesame;" quoth she, "Pooh, pooh!" Then said he, "Thy womb;" and she cried, "Fie, Fie! art thou not ashamed of thyself?" and cuffed him on the nape of the neck. And whatever name he gave declaring " 'Tis so," she beat him and cried "No! no!" till at last he said, "O my sisters, and what *is* its name?" She replied, "It is entitled the Khan[1] of Abu Mansur;" whereupon the Porter replied, "Ha! ha! O Allah be praised for safe deliverance! O Khan of Abu Mansur!" Then she came forth and dressed and the cup went round a full hour. At last the Porter rose up, and stripping off all his clothes, jumped into the tank and swam about and washed under his bearded chin and armpits, even as they had done. Then he came out and threw himself into the first lady's lap and rested his arms upon the lap of the portress, and reposed his legs in the lap of the cateress and pointed to his prickle[2] and said, "O my mistresses, what is the name of this article?" All laughed at his words till they fell on their backs, and one said, "Thy pintle!" But he replied, "No!" and gave each one of them a bite by way of forfeit. Then said they, "Thy pizzle!" but he cried "No," and gave each of them a hug;——And Shahrazad perceived the dawn of day and ceased saying her permitted say.

---

[1] Better known to us as Caravanserai, the "Travellers' Bungalow" of India: in the Khan, however, shelter is to be had, but neither bed nor board.

[2] Arab. "Zubb." I would again note that this and its synonyms are the equivalents of the Arabic, which is of the lowest. The tale-teller's evident object is to accentuate the contrast with the tragical stories to follow.

When it was the Tenth Night,

Quoth her sister Dunyazad, "Finish for us thy story;" and she answered, "With joy and goodly gree." It hath reached me, O auspicious King, that the damsels stinted not saying to the Porter "Thy prickle, thy pintle, thy pizzle,"and he ceased not kissing and biting and hugging until his heart was satisfied, and they laughed on till they could no more. At last one said, "O our brother, what, then, is it called?" Quoth he, "Know ye not?" Quoth they, "No!" "Its veritable name," said he, "is mule Burst-all, which browseth on the basil of the bridges, and muncheth the husked sesame, and nighteth in the Khan of Abu Mansur." Then laughed they till they fell on their backs, and returned to their carousal, and ceased not to be after this fashion till night began to fall. Thereupon said they to the Porter, "Bismillah,[1] O our master, up and on with those sorry old shoes of thine and turn thy face and show us the breadth of thy shoulders!" Said he, "By Allah, to part with my soul would be easier for me than departing from you: come let us join night to day, and to-morrow morning we will each wend our own way." "My life on you," said the procuratrix, "suffer him to tarry with us, that we may laugh at him: we may live out our lives and never meet with his like, for surely he is a right merry rogue and a witty."[2] So they said, "Thou must not remain with us this night save on condition that thou submit to our commands, and that whatso thou seest, thou ask no questions thereanent, nor enquire of its cause." "All right," rejoined he, and they said, "Go read the writing over the door." So he rose and went to the entrance and there found written in letters of gold wash; WHOSO SPEAKETH OF WHAT CONCERNETH HIM NOT, SHALL HEAR WHAT PLEASETH HIM NOT!"[3] The Porter said, "Be ye wit-

---

1 "In the name of Allah," is here a civil form of dismissal.

2 Lane (i. 124) is scandalised and naturally enough by this scene, which is the only blot in an admirable tale admirably told. Yet even here the grossness is but little more pronounced than what we find in our old drama (e. g., Shakespeare's King Henry V.) written for the stage, whereas tales like The Nights are not read or recited before both sexes. Lastly "nothing follows all this palming work:" in Europe the orgie would end very differently. These "nuns of Theleme" are physically pure: their debauchery is of the mind, not the body. Galland makes them five, including the two doggesses.

3 So Sir Francis Walsingham's "They which do that they should not, should hear that they would not."

nesses against me that I will not speak on whatso concerneth me not." Then the cateress arose, and set food before them and they ate; after which they changed their drinking-place for another, and she lighted the lamps and candles and burned ambergris and aloes-wood, and set on fresh fruit and the wine service, when they fell to carousing and talking of their lovers. And they ceased not to eat and drink and chat, nibbling dry fruits and laughing and playing tricks for the space of a full hour when lo! a knock was heard at the gate. The knocking in no wise disturbed the seance, but one of them rose and went to see what it was and presently returned, saying, "Truly our pleasure for this night is to be perfect." "How is that?" asked they; and she answered, "At the gate be three Persian Kalandars[1] with their beards and heads and eyebrows shaven; and all three blind of the left eye—which is surely a strange chance. They are foreigners from Roum-land with the mark of travel plain upon them; they have just entered Baghdad, this being their first visit to our city; and the cause of their knocking at our door is simply because they cannot find a lodging. Indeed one of them said to me:—Haply the owner of this mansion will let us have the key of his stable or some old out-house wherein we may pass this night; for evening had surprised them and, being strangers in the land, they knew none who would give them shelter. And, O my sisters, each of them is a figure o' fun after his own fashion; and if we let them in we shall have matter to make sport of." She gave not over persuading them till they said to her, "Let them in, and make thou the usual condition with them that they speak not of what concerneth them not, lest they hear what pleaseth them not." So she rejoiced and going to the door presently returned with the three monoculars whose beards and mustachios were clean

---

[1] The old "Calendar," pleasantly associated with that form of almanac. The Mac. Edit. has "Karandaliyah," a vile corruption, like Ibn Batutah's "Karandar" and Torrens' "Kurundul:" so in English we have the accepted vulgarism of "Kernel" for Colonel. The Bul. Edit. uses for synonym "Su'ulúk"=an asker, a beggar. Of these mendicant monks, for such they are, much like the Sarabaites of mediæval Europe, I have treated, and of their institutions and its founder, Shaykh Sharif Bu Ali Kalandar (ob. A. H. 724 =1323–24), at some length in my "History of Sindh," chapt. viii. See also the Dabistan (i. 136) where the good Kalandar exclaims:—

> If the thorn break in my body, how trifling the pain!
> But how sorely I feel for the poor broken thorn!

D'Herbelot is right when he says that the Kalandar is not generally approved by Moslems: he labours to win free from every form and observance and he approaches the Malámati who conceals all his good deeds and boasts of his evil doings—our "Devil's hypocrite."

shaven.[1] They salam'd and stood afar off by way of respect;
but the three ladies rose up to them and welcomed them and
wished them joy of their safe arrival and made them sit down.
The Kalandars looked at the room and saw that it was a pleasant
place, clean swept and garnished with flowers; and the lamps
were burning and the smoke of perfumes was spireing in air; and
beside the dessert and fruits and wine, there were three fair girls
who might be maidens; so they exclaimed with one voice, "By
Allah, 'tis good!" Then they turned to the Porter and saw that
he was a merry-faced wight, albeit he was by no means sober and
was sore after his slappings. So they thought that he was one of
themselves and said, "A mendicant like us! whether Arab or
foreigner."[2] But when the Porter heard these words, he rose up,
and fixing his eyes fiercely upon them, said, "Sit ye here without
exceeding in talk! Have you not read what is writ over the door?
surely it befitteth not fellows who come to us like paupers to wag
your tongues at us." "We crave thy pardon, O Fakír,"[3] rejoined
they, "and our heads are between thy hands." The ladies laughed
consumedly at the squabble; and, making peace between the
Kalandars and the Porter, seated the new guests before meat and
they ate. Then they sat together, and the portress served them
with drink; and, as the cup went round merrily, quoth the Porter
to the askers, "And you, O brothers mine, have ye no story or
rare adventure to amuse us withal?" Now the warmth of wine
having mounted to their heads they called for musical instruments; and the portress brought them a tambourine of Mosul,
and a lute of Irák, and a Persian harp; and each mendicant
took one and tuned it; this the tambourine and those the lute
and the harp, and struck up a merry tune while the ladies sang
so lustily that there was a great noise.[4]   And whilst they were
carrying on, behold, some one knocked at the gate, and the
portress went to see what was the matter there. Now the cause
of that knocking, O King (quoth Shahrazad) was this, the Caliph,
Hárún al-Rashíd, had gone forth from the palace, as was his wont

---

1 The "Kalandar" disfigures himself in this manner to show "mortification."
2 Arab. "Gharíb:" the porter is offended because the word implies "poor devil;" esp.
one out of his own country.
3 A religious mendicant generally.
4 Very scandalous to Moslem "respectability": Mohammed said the house was accursed when the voices of women could be heard out of doors. Moreover the neighbours have a right to interfere and abate the scandal.

now and then, to solace himself in the city that night, and to see and hear what new thing was stirring; he was in merchant's gear, and he was attended by Ja'afar, his Wazir, and by Masrúr his Sworder of Vengeance.[1] As they walked about the city, their way led them towards the house of the three ladies; where they heard the loud noise of musical instruments and singing and merriment; so quoth the Caliph to Ja'afar, "I long to enter this house and hear those songs and see who sing them." Quoth Ja'afar, "O Prince of the Faithful; these folk are surely drunken with wine, and I fear some mischief betide us if we get amongst them." "There is no help but that I go in there," replied the Caliph, "and I desire thee to contrive some pretext for our appearing among them." Ja'afar replied, "I hear and I obey;"[2] and knocked at the door, whereupon the portress came out and opened. Then Ja'afar came forward and kissing the ground before her said, "O my lady, we be merchants from Tiberias-town: we arrived at Baghdad ten days ago; and, alighting at the merchants' caravanserai, we sold all our merchandise. Now a certain trader invited us to an entertainment this night; so we went to his house and he set food before us and we ate: then we sat at wine and wassail with him for an hour or so when he gave us leave to depart; and we went out from him in the shadow of the night and, being strangers, we could not find our way back to our Khan. So haply of your kindness and courtesy you will suffer us to tarry with you this night, and Heaven will reward you!"[3] The portress looked upon them and seeing them dressed like merchants and men of grave looks and solid, she returned to her sisters and repeated to them Ja'afar's story; and they took compassion upon the strangers and said to her, "Let them enter." She opened the door to them, when said they to her, "Have we thy leave to come in?" "Come in," quoth she; and the Caliph entered followed by Ja'afar and Masrur; and when the girls saw them they stood up to them in respect and made them sit down and looked to their wants, saying, "Welcome, and well come and

---

1 I need hardly say that these are both historical personages; they will often be mentioned, and Ja'afar will be noticed in the Terminal Essay.

2 Arab. "Sama 'an wa tá'atan"; a popular phrase of assent generally translated "to hear is to obey;" but this formula may be and must be greatly varied. In places it means "Hearing (the word of Allah) and obeying" (His prophet, viceregent, etc.)

3 Arab. "Sawáb"=reward in Heaven. This word for which we have no equivalent has been naturalised in all tongues (e. g. Hindostani) spoken by Moslems.

good cheer to the guests, but with one condition!" "What is that?" asked they, and one of the ladies answered, "Speak not of what concerneth you not, lest ye hear what pleaseth you not." "Even so," said they; and sat down to their wine and drank deep. Presently the Caliph looked on the three Kalandars and, seeing them each and every blind of the left eye, wondered at the sight; then he gazed upon the girls and he was startled and he marvelled with exceeding marvel at their beauty and loveliness. They continued to carouse and to converse and said to the Caliph, "Drink!" but he replied, "I am vowed to Pilgrimage;"[1] and drew back from the wine. Thereupon the portress rose and spreading before him a table-cloth worked with gold, set thereon a porcelain bowl into which she poured willow-flower water with a lump of snow and a spoonful of sugar-candy. The Caliph thanked her and said in himself, "By Allah, I will recompense her to-morrow for the kind deed she hath done." The others again addressed themselves to conversing and carousing; and, when the wine gat the better of them, the eldest lady who ruled the house rose and making obeisance to them took the cateress by the hand, and said, "Rise, O my sister and let us do what is our devoir." Both answered "Even so!" Then the portress stood up and proceeded to remove the table-service and the remnants of the banquet; and renewed the pastiles and cleared the middle of the saloon. Then she made the Kalandars sit upon a sofa at the side of the estrade, and seated the Caliph and Ja'afar and Masrur on the other side of the saloon; after which she called the Porter, and said, "How scanty is thy courtesy! now thou art no stranger; nay, thou art one of the household." So he stood up and, tightening his waist-cloth, asked, "What would ye I do?" and she answered, "Stand in thy place." Then the procuratrix rose and set in the midst of the saloon a low chair and, opening a closet, cried to the Porter, "Come help me." So he went to help her and saw two black bitches with chains round their necks; and she said to him, "Take hold of them;" and he took them and led them into the middle of the saloon. Then the lady of the house arose and tucked up her sleeves above her wrists and, seizing a scourge, said to the Porter, "Bring forward one of the bitches." He

---

1 Wine-drinking, at all times forbidden to Moslems, vitiates the Pilgrimage-rite: the Pilgrim is vowed to a strict observance of the ceremonial law and many men date their "reformation" from the "Hajj." Pilgrimage, iii., 126.

brought her forward, dragging her by the chain, while the bitch wept, and shook her head at the lady who, however, came down upon her with blows on the sconce; and the bitch howled and the lady ceased not beating her till her forearm failed her. Then, casting the scourge from her hand, she pressed the bitch to her bosom and, wiping away her tears with her hands, kissed her head. Then she said to the Porter, "Take her away and bring the second;" and, when he brought her, she did with her as she had done with the first. Now the heart of the Caliph was touched at these cruel doings; his chest straitened and he lost all patience in his desire to know why the two bitches were so beaten. He threw a wink at Ja'afar wishing him to ask, but the Minister turning towards him said by signs, "Be silent!" Then quoth the portress to the mistress of the house, "O my lady, arise and go to thy place that I in turn may do my devoir."[1] She answered, "Even so"; and, taking her seat upon the couch of juniper-wood, pargetted with gold and silver, said to the portress and cateress, "Now do ye what ye have to do." Thereupon the portress sat upon a low seat by the couch side; but the procuratrix, entering a closet, brought out of it a bag of satin with green fringes and two tassels of gold. She stood up before the lady of the house and shaking the bag drew out from it a lute which she tuned by tightening its pegs; and when it was in perfect order, she began to sing these quatrains:—

"Ye are the wish, the aim of me *And when, O Love, thy sight I see[2]
The heavenly mansion openeth; [3]* But Hell I see when lost thy sight.
From thee comes madness; nor the less * Comes highest joy, comes ecstasy:
Nor in my love for thee I fear * Or shame and blame, or hate and spite.
When Love was throned within my heart * I rent the veil of modesty;
And stints not Love to rend that veil * Garring disgrace on grace to alight;
The robe of sickness then I donned * But rent to rags was secrecy:
Wherefore my love and longing heart * Proclaim your high supremest might;
The tear-drop railing adown my cheek * Telleth my tale of ignomy:
And all the hid was seen by all * And all my riddle ree'd aright.

---

[1] Here some change has been necessary; as the original text confuses the three "ladies."
[2] In Arab. the plural masc. is used by way of modesty when a girl addresses her lover; and for the same reason she speaks of herself as a man.
[3] Arab. "Al-Na'ím"; in ful "Jannat-al-Na'ím" = the Garden of Delights, *i.e.* the fifth Heaven made of white silver. The generic name of Heaven (the place of reward) is "Jannat," lit. a garden; "Firdaus" being evidently derived from the Persian through the Greek παράδεισος, and meaning a chase, a hunting park. Writers on this subject should bear in mind Mandeville's modesty, "Of Paradise I cannot speak properly, for I was not there."

Heal then my malady, for thou   * Art malady and remedy!
But she whose cure is in thy hand   * Shall ne'er be free of bane and blight;
Burn me those eyne that radiance rain * Slay me the swords of phantasy;
How many hath the sword of Love   * Laid low, their high degree despite?
Yet will I never cease to pine   * Nor to oblivion will I flee.
Love is my health, my faith, my joy   * Public and private, wrong or right.
O happy eyes that sight thy charms   * That gaze upon thee at their gree!
Yea, of my purest wish and will   * The slave of Love I'll aye be hight."

When the damsel heard this elegy in quatrains she cried out "Alas! Alas!" and rent her raiment, and fell to the ground fainting; and the Caliph saw scars of the palm-rod[1] on her back and welts of the whip; and marvelled with exceeding wonder. Then the portress arose and sprinkled water on her and brought her a fresh and very fine dress and put it on her. But when the company beheld these doings their minds were troubled, for they had no inkling of the case nor knew the story thereof; so the Caliph said to Ja'afar, "Didst thou not see the scars upon the damsel's body? I cannot keep silence or be at rest till I learn the truth of her condition and the story of this other maiden and the secret of the two black bitches." But Ja'afar answered, "O our lord, they made it a condition with us that we speak not of what concerneth us not, lest we come to hear what pleaseth us not." Then said the portress, "By Allah, O my sister, come to me and complete this service for me." Replied the procuratrix, "With joy and goodly gree;" so she took the lute; and leaned it against her breasts and swept the strings with her finger-tips, and began singing:—

"Give back mine eyes their sleep long ravishèd * And say me whither be my
    reason fled:
I learnt that lending to thy love a place * Sleep to mine eyelids mortal foe
    was made.
They said, "We held thee righteous, who waylaid * Thy soul?" "Go ask his
    glorious eyes," I said.
I pardon all my blood he pleased to spill * Owning his troubles drove him
    blood to shed.
On my mind's mirror sun-like sheen he cast * Whose keen reflection fire in
    vitals bred
Waters of Life let Allah waste at will * Suffice my wage those lips of dewy red:

---

[1] Arab. "Mikra'ah," the dried mid-rib of a date-frond used for many purposes, especially the bastinado.

An thou address my love thou'lt find a cause * For plaint and tears or ruth or
    lustihed.
In water pure his form shall greet your eyne * When fails the bowl nor need
    ye drink of wine.[1]"

Then she quoted from the same ode:—

"I drank, but the draught of his glance, not wine; * And his swaying gait
    swayed to sleep these eyne:
'Twas not grape-juice gript me but grasp of Past * 'Twas not bowl o'erbowled
    me but gifts divine:
His coiling curl-lets my soul ennetted   * And his cruel will all my wits
    outwitted.[2]"

After a pause she resumed:—

"If we 'plain of absence what shall we say? * Or if pain afflict us where wend
    our way?
An I hire a truchman[3] to tell my tale * The lover's plaint is not told for pay:
If I put on patience, a lover's life * After loss of love will not last a day:
Naught is left me now but regret, repine * And tears flooding cheeks for ever
    and aye:
O thou who the babes of these eyes[4] hast fled * Thou art homed in heart
    that shall never stray;
Would heaven I wot hast thou kept our pact * Long as stream shall flow, to
    have firmest fay?
Or hast forgotten the weeping slave * Whom groans afflict and whom griefs
    waylay?
Ah, when severance ends and we side by side * Couch, I'll blame thy rigours
    and chide thy pride!"

Now when the portress heard her second ode she shrieked aloud
and said, "By Allah! 'tis right good!"; and laying hands on her
garments tore them, as she did the first time, and fell to the
ground fainting. Thereupon the procuratrix rose and brought her
a second change of clothes after she had sprinkled water on her.
She recovered and sat upright and said to her sister the cateress,

---

[1] According to Lane (i., 229) these and the immediately following verses are from an
ode by Ibn Sahl al-Ishbili. They are in the Bul. Edit. not the Mac. Edit.

[2] The original is full of conceits and plays on words which are not easily rendered in
English.

[3] Arab. "Tarjumán," same root as Chald. Targum (= a translation), the old "Truchman," and through the Ital. "tergomano" our "Dragoman;" here a messenger.

[4] Lit. the "person of the eyes," our "babe of the eyes," a favourite poetical conceit
in all tongues; much used by the Elizabethans, but now neglected as a silly kind of conceit. See Night ccix.

"Onwards, and help me in my duty, for there remains but this one song." So the provisioneress again brought out the lute and began to sing these verses:—

"How long shall last, how long this rigour rife of woe * May not suffice thee all these tears thou seest flow?
Our parting thus with purpose fell thou dost prolong * Is't not enough to glad the heart of envious foe?
Were but this lying world once true to lover-heart * He had not watched the weary night in tears of woe:
Oh pity me whom overwhelmed thy cruel will * My lord, my king, 'tis time some ruth to me thou show:
To whom reveal my wrongs, O thou who murdered me? * Sad, who of broken troth the pangs must undergo!
Increase wild love for thee and phrenzy hour by hour * And days of exile minute by so long, so slow;
O Moslems, claim *vendetta*[1] for this slave of Love * Whose sleep Love ever wastes, whose patience Love lays low:
Doth law of Love allow thee, O my wish! to lie * Lapt in another's arms and unto me cry "Go!"?
Yet in thy presence, say, what joys shall I enjoy * When he I love but works my love to overthrow?"

When the portress heard the third song she cried aloud; and, laying hands on her garments, rent them down to the very skirt and fell to the ground fainting a third time, again showing the scars of the scourge. Then said the three Kalandars, "Would Heaven we had never entered this house, but had rather nighted on the mounds and heaps outside the city! for verily our visit hath been troubled by sights which cut to the heart." The Caliph turned to them and asked, "Why so?" and they made answer, "Our minds are sore troubled by this matter." Quoth the Caliph, "Are ye not of the household?" and quoth they, "No; nor indeed did we ever set eyes on the place till within this hour." Hereat the Caliph marvelled and rejoined, "This man who sitteth by you, would he not know the secret of the matter?" and so saying he winked and made signs at the Porter. So they questioned the man but he replied, "By the All-might of Allah, in love all are alike!"[2] I am the growth of Baghdad, yet never in my born days did I darken these doors till to-day and my com-

---

[1] Arab. "Sár" (Thár) the revenge-right recognised by law and custom (Pilgrimage, iii., 69).
[2] That is "We all swim in the same boat."

panying with them was a curious matter." "By Allah," they rejoined, "we took thee for one of them and now we see thou art
one like ourselves." Then said the Caliph, "We be seven men,
and they only three women without even a fourth to help them;
so let us question them of their case; and, if they answer us not,
fain we will be answered by force." All of them agreed to this
except Ja'afar who said,[1] "This is not my recking; let them be;
for we are their guests and, as ye know, they made a compact
and condition with us which we accepted and promised to
keep: wherefore it is better that we be silent concerning this
matter; and, as but little of the night remaineth, let each and
every of us gang his own gait." Then he winked at the Caliph
and whispered to him, "There is but one hour of darkness left
and I can bring them before thee to-morrow, when thou canst
freely question them all concerning their story." But the
Caliph raised his head haughtily and cried out at him in wrath,
saying, "I have no patience left for my longing to hear of them:
let the Kalandars question them forthright." Quoth Ja'afar,
"This is not my rede." Then words ran high and talk answered
talk, and they disputed as to who should first put the question,
but at last all fixed upon the Porter. And as the jingle increased
the house-mistress could not but notice it and asked them, "O ye
folk! on what matter are ye talking so loudly?" Then the Porter
stood up respectfully before her and said, "O my lady, this
company earnestly desire that thou acquaint them with the
story of the two bitches and what maketh thee punish them so
cruelly; and then thou fallest to weeping over them and kissing
them; and lastly they want to hear the tale of thy sister and why
she hath been bastinado'd with palm-sticks like a man. These
are the questions they charge me to put, and peace be with
thee."[2] Thereupon quoth she who was the lady of the house to
the guests, "Is this true that he saith on your part?" and all
replied, "Yes!" save Ja'afar who kept silence. When she heard
these words she cried, "By Allah, ye have wronged us, O
our guests, with grievous wronging; for when you came before us

---

[1] Ja'afar ever acts, on such occasions, the part of a wise and sensible man compelled
to join in a foolish frolic. He contrasts strongly with the Caliph, a headstrong despot
who will not be gainsaid, whatever be the whim of the moment. But Easterns would
look upon this as a proof of his "kingliness."

[2] Arab. "Wa'l-Salám" (pronounced Was-Salám); meaning "and here ends the matter."
In our slang we say, "All right, and the child's name is Antony."

we made compact and condition with you, that whoso should speak of what concerneth him not should hear what pleaseth him not. Sufficeth ye not that we took you into our house and fed you with our best food? But the fault is not so much yours as hers who let you in." Then she tucked up her sleeves from her wrists and struck the floor thrice with her hand crying, "Come ye quickly;" and lo! a closet door opened and out of it came seven negro slaves with drawn swords in hand to whom she said, "Pinion me those praters' elbows and bind them each to each." They did her bidding and asked her, "O veiled and virtuous! is it thy high command that we strike off their heads?"; but she answered, "Leave them awhile that I question them of their condition, before their necks feel the sword." "By Allah, O my lady!" cried the Porter, "slay me not for other's sin; all these men offended and deserve the penalty of crime save myself. Now by Allah, our night had been charming had we escaped the mortification of those monocular Kalandars whose entrance into a populous city would convert it into a howling wilderness." Then he repeated these verses:—

"How fair is ruth the strong man deigns not smother! * And fairest fair when
    shown to weakest brother:
By Love's own holy tie between us twain, * Let one not suffer for the sin of
    other."

When the Porter ended his verse the lady laughed——And Shahrazad perceived the dawn of day and ceased to say her permitted say.

𝔚𝔥𝔢𝔫 𝔦𝔱 𝔴𝔞𝔰 𝔱𝔥𝔢 𝔈𝔩𝔢𝔳𝔢𝔫𝔱𝔥 𝔑𝔦𝔤𝔥𝔱,

She said, It hath reached me, O auspicious King, that the lady, after laughing at the Porter despite her wrath, came up to the party and spake thus, "Tell me who ye be, for ye have but an hour of life; and were ye not men of rank and, perhaps, notables of your tribes, you had not been so froward and I had hastened your doom." Then said the Caliph, "Woe to thee, O Ja'afar, tell her who we are lest we be slain by mistake; and speak her fair before some horror befal us." "'Tis part of thy deserts," replied he; whereupon the Caliph cried out at him saying, "There is a time for witty words and there is a time for serious work." Then the lady accosted the three Kalandars and asked them, "Are ye brothers?"; when they answered, "No, by Allah, we be naught but Fakirs and foreigners." Then quoth she to one among them, "Wast thou born blind of one eye?"; and quoth he, "No, by Allah, 'twas a marvellous matter and a wondrous mischance which caused my eye to be torn out, and mine is a tale which, if it were written upon the eye-corners with needle-gravers, were a warner to whoso would be warned." [1] She questioned the second and third Kalandar; but all replied like the first, "By Allah, O our mistress, each one of us cometh from a different country, and we are all three the sons of Kings, sovereign Princes ruling over suzerains and capital cities." Thereupon she turned towards them and said, "Let each and every of you tell me his tale in due order and explain the cause of his coming to our place; and if his story please us let him stroke his head[2] and wend his way." The first to come forward was the Hammál, the Porter, who said, "O my lady, I am a man and a porter. This dame, the cateress, hired me to carry a load and took me first to the shop of a vintner, then to the booth of a butcher; thence to the stall of a fruiterer; thence to a grocer who also sold dry fruits; thence to a confectioner and a perfumer-cum-druggist and from him to this place where there happened to me with you what happened. Such is my story and peace be on us all!" At this the lady laughed and said, "Rub thy head and wend thy ways!"; but he cried, "By Allah, I will not stump it till I hear the stories of my companions." Then came forward one of the Monoculars and began to tell her

The First Kalandar's Tale.

KNOW, O my lady, that the cause of my beard being shorn and my eye being out-torn was as follows. My father was a King and he had a brother who was a King over another city; and it came to pass that I and my cousin, the son of my paternal uncle, were

---

[1] This is a favourite jingle; the play being upon "ibrat" (a needle-graver) and " 'ibrat" (an example, a warning).

[2] That is "make his bow;" as the English peasant pulls his forelock. Lane (i., 249) suggests, as an afterthought, that it means:—"Recover thy senses; in allusion to a person's drawing his hand over his head after sleep or a fit." But it occurs elsewhere in the sense of "cut thy stick."

both born on one and the same day. And years and days rolled
on; and, as we grew up, I used to visit my uncle every now and
then and to spend a certain number of months with him. Now
my cousin and I were sworn friends; for he ever entreated me
with exceeding kindness; he killed for me the fattest sheep and
strained the best of his wines, and we enjoyed long conversing
and carousing. One day when the wine had gotten the better of
us, the son of my uncle said to me, "O my cousin, I have a great
service to ask of thee; and I desire that thou stay me not in whatso
I desire to do!" And I replied, "With joy and goodly will."
Then he made me swear the most binding oaths and left me;
but after a little while he returned leading a lady veiled and
richly apparelled with ornaments worth a large sum of money.
Presently he turned to me (the woman being still behind him)
and said, "Take this lady with thee and go before me to such a
burial ground" (describing it, so that I knew the place), "and
enter with her into such a sepulchre[1] and there await my coming."
The oaths I swore to him made me keep silence and suffered me
not to oppose him; so I led the woman to the cemetery and both I
and she took our seats in the sepulchre; and hardly had we sat
down when in came my uncle's son, with a bowl of water, a
bag of mortar and an adze somewhat like a hoe. He went straight
to the tomb in the midst of the sepulchre and, breaking it open
with the adze set the stones on one side; then he fell to digging
into the earth of the tomb till he came upon a large iron plate,
the size of a wicket door; and on raising it there appeared below
it a staircase vaulted and winding. Then he turned to the lady
and said to her, "Come now and take thy final choice!" She at
once went down by the staircase and disappeared; then quoth
he to me, "O son of my uncle, by way of completing thy kindness, when I shall have descended into this place, restore the
trap-door to where it was, and heap back the earth upon it as it
lay before; and then of thy goodness mix this unslaked lime
which is in the bag with this water which is in the bowl and,
after building up the stones, plaster the outside so that none
looking upon it shall say:—This is a new opening in an old

---

[1] This would be a separate building like our family tomb and probably domed, resembling that mentioned in "The King of the Black Islands." Europeans usually call
it "a little Wali;" or, as they write it, "Wely;" the contained for the container; the "Santon" for the "Santon's tomb." I have noticed this curious confusion (which begins with
Robinson, i. 322) in "Unexplored Syria," i. 161.

tomb. For a whole year have I worked at this place whereof none knoweth but Allah, and this is the need I have of thee;" presently adding, "May Allah never bereave thy friends of thee nor make them desolate by thine absence, O son of my uncle, O my dear cousin!" And he went down the stairs and disappeared for ever. When he was lost to sight I replaced the iron plate and did all his bidding till the tomb became as it was before; and I worked almost unconsciously for my head was heated with wine. Returning to the palace of my uncle, I was told that he had goneforth a-sporting and hunting; so I slept that night without seeing him; and, when the morning dawned, I remembered the scenes of the past evening and what happened between me and my cousin; I repented of having obeyed him when penitence was of no avail, I still thought, however, that it was a dream. So I fell to asking for the son of my uncle; but there was none to answer me concerning him; and I went out to the grave-yard and the sepulchres, and sought for the tomb under which he was, but could not find it; and I ceased not wandering about from sepulchre to sepulchre, and tomb to tomb, all without success, till night set in. So I returned to the city, yet I could neither eat nor drink; my thoughts being engrossed with my cousin, for that I knew not what was become of him; and I grieved with exceeding grief and passed another sorrowful night, watching until the morning. Then went I a second time to the cemetery, pondering over what the son of mine uncle had done; and, sorely repenting my hearkening to him, went round among all the tombs, but could not find the tomb I sought. I mourned over the past, and remained in my mourning seven days, seeking the place and ever missing the path. Then my torture of scruples[1] grew upon me till I well nigh went mad, and I found no way to dispel my grief save travel and return to my father. So I set out and journeyed homeward; but as I was entering my father's capital a crowd of rioters sprang upon me and pinioned me.[2] I wondered thereat with all wonderment, seeing that I was the son of the Sultan, and these men were my father's subjects and amongst them were some of my own slaves. A great fear fell

---

[1] Arab. "Wiswás;" = diabolical temptation or suggestion. The "Wiswásí" is a man with scruples (scrupulus, a pebble in the shoe), *e.g.* one who fears that his ablutions were deficient, etc.

[2] Arab. "Katf" = pinioning by tying the arms behind the back and shoulders (Kitf), a dire disgrace to free-born men.

upon me, and I said to my soul,[1] "Would heaven I knew what
hath happened to my father!" I questioned those that bound me
of the cause of their doing, but they returned me no answer.
However, after a while one of them said to me (and he had been
a hired servant of our house), "Fortune hath been false to thy
father; his troops betrayed him and the Wazir who slew him now
reigneth in his stead and we lay in wait to seize thee by the
bidding of him." I was well-nigh distraught and felt ready to
faint on hearing of my father's death; when they carried me off
and placed me in presence of the usurper. Now between me
and him there was an olden grudge, the cause of which was this.
I was fond of shooting with the stone-bow,[2] and it befel one day
as I was standing on the terrace-roof of the palace, that a bird
lighted on the top of the Wazir's house when he happened to
be there. I shot at the bird and missed the mark; but I hit the
Wazir's eye and knocked it out as fate and fortune decreed.
Even so saith the poet:—

We tread the path where Fate hath led * The path Fate writ we fain must
    tread:
And man in one land doomed to die   * Death no where else shall do him
    dead.

And on like wise saith another:—

Let Fortune have her wanton way * Take heart and all her words obey:
Nor joy nor mourn at anything   * For all things pass and no things stay.

Now when I knocked out the Wazir's eye he could not say a
single word, for that my father was King of the city; but he hated
me everafter and dire was the grudge thus caused between us
twain. So when I was set before him hand-bound and pinioned,
he straightway gave orders for me to be beheaded. I asked,
"For what crime wilt thou put me to death?"; whereupon he
answered, "What crime is greater than this?" pointing the while

---

[1] Arab. "Nafs." = Hebr. Nephesh (Nafash) = soul, life, as opposed to "Ruach" =
spirit and breath. In these places it is equivalent to "I said to myself." Another form
of the root is "Nafas," breath, with an idea of inspiration: so "Sáhib Nafas" (= master
of breath) is a minor saint who heals by expiration, a matter familiar to mesmerists
(Pilgrimage, i., 86).

[2] Arab. "Kaus al-Banduk;" the "pellet-bow" of modern India; with two strings
joined by a bit of cloth which supports a ball of dry clay or stone. It is chiefly used for
birding.

to the place where his eye had been Quoth I, "This I did by accident not of malice prepense;" and quoth he, "If thou didst it by accident, I will do the like by thee with intention."[1] Then cried he, "Bring him forward," and they brought me up to him, when he thrust his finger into my left eye and gouged it out; whereupon I became one-eyed as ye see me. Then he bade bind me hand and foot, and put me into a chest and said to the sworder, "Take charge of this fellow, and go off with him to the waste lands about the city; then draw thy scymitar and slay him, and leave him to feed the beasts and birds." So the headsman fared forth with me and when he was in the midst of the desert, he took me out of the chest (and I with both hands pinioned and both feet fettered) and was about to bandage my eyes before striking off my head. But I wept with exceeding weeping until I made him weep with me and, looking at him I began to recite these couplets:—

"I deemed you coat-o'-mail that should withstand * The foeman's shafts; and you proved foeman's brand;
I hoped your aidance in mine every chance * Though fail my left to aid my dexter hand:
Aloof you stand and hear the railer's gibe * While rain their shafts on me the giber-band:
But an ye will not guard me from my foes * Stand clear, and succour neither these nor those!"

And I also quoted:—

"I deemed my brethren mail of strongest steel * And so they were—from foes to fend my dart!
I deemed their arrows surest of their aim; * And so they were—when aiming at my heart!"

When the headsman heard my lines (he had been sworder to my sire and he owed me a debt of gratitude) he cried, "O my lord, what can I do, being but a slave under orders?" presently adding,

---

[1] In the East blinding was a common practice, especially in the case of junior princes not required as heirs. A deep perpendicular incision was made down each corner of the eyes; the lids were lifted and the balls removed by cutting the optic nerve and the muscles. The later Caliphs blinded their victims by passing a red-hot sword blade close to the orbit or a needle over the eye-ball. About the same time in Europe the operation was performed with a heated metal basin—the well-known *bacinare* (used by Ariosto), as happened to Pier delle Vigne (Petrus de Vineâ), the "godfather of modern Italian."

"Fly for thy life and nevermore return to this land, or they will slay thee and slay me with thee, even as the poet said:—

Take thy life and fly whenas evils threat; * Let the ruined house tell its
owner's fate:
New land for the old thou shalt seek and find * But to find new life thou must
not await.
Strange that men should sit in the stead of shame, * When Allah's world is so
wide and great!
And trust not other, in matters grave * Life itself must act for a life beset:
Ne'er would prowl the lion with maned neck, * Did he reckon on aid or of
others reck."

Hardly believing in my escape, I kissed his hand and thought the loss of my eye a light matter in consideration of my escaping from being slain. I arrived at my uncle's capital; and, going in to him, told him of what had befallen my father and myself; whereat he wept with sore weeping and said, "Verily thou addest grief to my grief, and woe to my woe; for thy cousin hath been missing these many days; I wot not what hath happened to him, and none can give me news of him." And he wept till he fainted. I sorrowed and condoled with him; and he would have applied certain medicaments to my eye, but he saw that it was become as a walnut with the shell empty. Then said he, "O my son, better to lose eye and keep life!" After that I could no longer remain silent about my cousin, who was his only son and one dearly loved, so I told him all that had happened. He rejoiced with extreme joyance to hear news of his son and said, "Come now and show me the tomb;" but I replied, "By Allah, O my uncle, I know not its place, though I sought it carefully full many times, yet could not find the site." However, I and my uncle went to the grave-yard and looked right and left, till at last I recognised the tomb and we both rejoiced with exceeding joy. We entered the sepulchre and loosened the earth about the grave; then, up-raising the trap-door, descended some fifty steps till we came to the foot of the staircase when lo! we were stopped by a blinding smoke. Thereupon said my uncle that saying whose sayer shall never come to shame, "There is no Majesty and there is no Might, save in Allah, the Glorious, the Great!" and we advanced till we suddenly came upon a saloon, whose floor was strewed with flour and grain and provisions and all manner neces-saries; and in the midst of it stood a canopy sheltering a couch. Thereupon my uncle went up to the couch and inspecting it found his son and the lady who had gone down with him into the tomb, lying in each other's embrace; but the twain had become black as charred wood; it was as if they had been cast into a pit of fire. When my uncle saw this spectacle, he spat in his son's face and said, "Thou hast thy deserts, O thou hog![1] this is thy judgment in the transitory world, and yet remaineth the judgment in the world to come, a durer and a more enduring."—— And Shahrazad perceived the dawn of day and ceased saying her permitted say.

Mhen it was the Twelfth Right,

She continued, It hath reached me, O auspicious King, that the Kalandar thus went on with his story before the lady and the Caliph and Ja'afar:—My uncle struck his son with his slipper[2] as he lay there a black heap of coal. I marvelled at his hardness of heart, and grieving for my cousin and the lady, said, "By Allah, O my uncle, calm thy wrath: dost thou not see that all my thoughts are occupied with this misfortune, and how sorrowful I am for what hath befallen thy son, and how horrible it is that naught of him remaineth but a black heap of charcoal? And is not that enough, but thou must smite him with thy slipper?" Answered he, "O son of my brother, this youth from his boyhood was madly in love with his own sister;[3] and often and often I forbade

---

[1] Arab. "Khinzír" (by Europeans pronounced "Hanzír"), prop. a wild-boar; but popularly used like our "you pig!"

[2] Striking with the shoe, the pipe-stick and similar articles is highly insulting, because they are not made, like whips and scourges, for such purpose. Here the East and the West differ diametrically. "Wounds which are given by instruments which are in one's hands by chance do not disgrace a man," says Cervantes (D. Q. i., chapt. 15), and goes on to prove that if a Zapatero (cobbler) cudgel another with his form or last, the latter must not consider himself cudgelled. The reverse in the East where a blow of a pipe-stick cost Mahommed Ali Pasha's son his life: Ishmail Pasha was burned to death by Malik Nimr, chief of Shendy (Pilgrimage, i., 203). Moreover, the actual wound is less considered in Moslem law than the instrument which caused it: so sticks and stones are venial weapons, whilst sword and dagger, gun and pistol are felonious. See *ibid.* (i., 336) for a note upon the weapons with which nations are policed.

[3] Incest is now abominable everywhere except amongst the overcrowded poor of great and civilised cities. Yet such unions were common and lawful amongst ancient and highly cultivated peoples, as the Egyptians (Isis and Osiris), Assyrians and ancient Persians. Physiologically they are injurious only when the parents have constitutional defects: if both are sound, the issue, as amongst the so-called "lower animals," is viable and healthy.

himfromher,sayingtomyself:—Theyarebutlittleones.However,
when they grew up sin befel between them; and, although I
could hardly believe it, I confined him and chided him and
threatened him with the severest threats; and the eunuchs and
servants said to him:—Beware of so foul a thing which none before thee ever did, and which none after thee will ever do; and
have a care lest thou be dishonoured and disgraced among the
Kings of the day, even to the end of time.   And I added:—Such
a report as this will be spread abroad by caravans, and take heed
not to give them cause to talk or I will assuredly curse thee and do
thee to death. After that I lodged them apart and shut her up; but
the accursed girl loved him with passionate love, for Satan had got
the mastery of her as well as of him and made their foul sin seem
fair in their sight.   Now when my son saw that I separated them,
he secretly built this souterrain and furnished it and transported
to it victuals, even as thou seest; and, when I had gone out a-
sporting, came here with his sister and hid from me.   Then His
righteous judgment fell upon the twain and consumed them
with fire from Heaven; and verily the last judgment will deal
them durer pains and more enduring!" Then he wept and I wept
with him; and he looked at me and said, "Thou art my son in his
stead." And I bethought me awhile of the world and of its
chances, how the Wazir had slain my father and had taken his
place and had put out my eye; and how my cousin had come to
his death by the strangest chance: and I wept again and my uncle
wept with me.   Then we mounted the steps and let down the
iron plate and heaped up the earth over it; and, after restoring
the tomb to its former condition, we returned to the palace.
But hardly had we sat down ere we heard the tomtoming of the
kettle-drum and tantara of trumpets and clash of cymbals;
and the rattling of war-men's lances; and the clamours of as-
sailants and the clanking of bits and the neighing of steeds;
while the world was canopied with dense dust and sand-clouds
raised by the horses' hoofs.[1] We were amazed at sight and
sound, knowing not what could be the matter; so we asked and
were told us that the Wazir who usurped my father's kingdom
had marched his men; and that after levying his soldiery and

---

[1] Dwellers in the Northern Temperates can hardly imagine what a dust-storm is in
sun-parched tropical lands. In Sind we were often obliged to use candles at mid-day,
while above the dust was a sun that would roast an egg.

taking a host of wild Arabs[1] into service, he had come down upon
us with armies like the sands of the sea; their number none could
tell and against them none could prevail. They attacked the city
unawares; and the citizens, being powerless to oppose them, sur-
rendered the place: my uncle was slain and I made for the suburbs
saying to myself, "If thou fall into this villain's hands he will
assuredly kill thee." On this wise all my troubles were renewed;
and I pondered all that had betided my father and my uncle and
I knew not what to do; for if the city people or my father's troops
had recognised me they would have done their best to win favour
by destroying me; and I could think of no way to escape save by
shaving off my beard and my eyebrows. So I shore them off and,
changing my fine clothes for a Kalandar's rags, I fared forth from
my uncle's capital and made for this city; hoping that peradventure some one would assist me to the presence of the Prince of
the Faithful,[2] and the Caliph who is the Viceregent of Allah upon

---

[1] Arab. " 'Urban," now always used of the wild people, whom the French have
taught us to call *les Bedouins*; "Badw" being a waste or desert; and Badawi (fem.
Badawíyah, plur. Badáwi and Bidwán), a man of the waste. Europeans have also
learnt to miscall the Egyptians "Arabs": the difference is as great as between an
Englishman and a Spaniard. Arabs proper divide their race into sundry successive
families. "The Arab al-Arabá" (or al-Aribah, or al-Urubíyat) are the autochthones, prehistoric, proto-historic and extinct tribes; for instance, a few of the Adites who being at
Meccah escaped the destruction of their wicked nation, but mingled with other classes.
The "Arab al-Muta'arribah," (Arabised Arabs) are the first advenæ represented by
such noble strains as the Koraysh (Koreish), some still surviving. The "Arab al-
Musta'aribah" (insititious, naturalised or instituted Arabs, men who claim to be Arabs)
are Arabs like the Sinaites, the Egyptians and the Maroccans descended by inter-
marriage with other races. Hence our "Mosarabians" and the "Marrabais" of Rabelais
(not, "a word compounded of Maurus and Arabs"). Some genealogists, however, make
the Muta'arribah descendants of Kahtan (possibly the Joktan of Genesis x., a comparatively modern document, B.C. 700?); and the Musta'aribah those descended from
Adnán the origin of Arab genealogy. And, lastly, are the "Arab al-Musta'ajimah,"
barbarised Arabs, like the present population of Meccah and Al-Medinah. Besides
these there are other tribes whose origin is still unknown; such as the Mahrah tribes
of Hazramaut, the "Akhdám" (= serviles) of Oman (Maskat); and the "Ebná" of
Al-Yaman: Ibn Ishak supposes the latter to be descended from the Persian soldiers
of Anushirwan who expelled the Abyssinian invader from Southern Arabia. (Pilgrimage,
iii., 31, etc.)

[2] Arab. "Amír al-Muuminín." The title was assumed by the Caliph Omar to obviate
the inconvenience of calling himself "Khalífah" (successor) of the Khalífah of the
Apostle of Allah (*i.e.* Abu Bakr); which after a few generations would become impossible. It means "Emir (chief or prince) of the Muumins;" men who hold to the (true
Moslem) Faith, the "Imán" (theory, fundamental articles) as opposed to the "Dín,"
ordinance or practice of the religion. It once became a Wazirial time conferred by Sultan
Malikshah (King King-king) on his Nizám al-Mulk. (Richardson's Dissert. lviii.)

earth. Thus have I come hither that I might tell him my tale and lay my case before him. I arrived here this very night, and was standing in doubt whither I should go, when suddenly I saw this second Kalandar; so I salam'd to him saying:—"I am a stranger!" and he answered:—"I too am a stranger!" And as we were conversing behold, up came our companion, this third Kalandar, and saluted us saying:—"I am a stranger!" And we answered:—"We too be strangers!" Then we three walked on and together till darkness overtook us and Destiny drave us to your house. Such, then, is the cause of the shaving of my beard and mustachios and eyebrows; and the manner of my losing my right eye. They marvelled much at this tale and the Caliph said to Ja'afar, "By Allah, I have not seen nor have I heard the like of what hath happened to this Kalandar!" Quoth the lady of the house, "Rub thy head and wend thy ways;" but he replied, "I will not go, till I hear the history of the two others." Thereupon the second Kalandar came forward; and, kissing the ground, began to tell

The Second Kalandar's Tale.

KNOW, O my lady, that I was not born one-eyed and mine is a strange story; an it were graven with needle-graver on the eye-corners, it were a warner to whoso would be warned. I am a King, son of a King, and was brought up like a Prince. I learned intoning the Koran according the seven schools;[1] and I read all manner books, and held disputations on their contents with the doctors and men of science; moreover I studied star-lore and the fair sayings of poets and I exercised myself in all branches of learning until I surpassed the people of my time; my skill in calligraphy exceeded that of all the scribes; and my fame was bruited abroad over all climes and cities, and all the kings learned to know my name. Amongst others the King of Hind heard of me and sent to my father to invite me to his court, with offerings and presents and rarities such as befit royalties. So my father fitted out six ships for me and my people; and we put to sea and sailed

---

[1] This may also mean "according to the seven editions of the Koran," the old revisions and so forth (Sale, Sect. iii. and D'Herbelot "Alcoran.") The schools of the "Mukri," who teach the right pronunciation wherein a mistake might be sinful, are seven, Hamzah, Ibn Katír, Ya'akúb, Ibn Amir, Kisái, Asim and Hafs, the latter being the favourite with the Hanafis and the only one now generally known in Al-Islam.

for the space of a full month till we made the land. Then we brought out the horses that were with us in the ships; and, after loading the camels with our presents for the Prince, we set forth inland. But we had marched only a little way, when behold, a dust-cloud up-flew, and grew until it walled[1] the horizon from view. After an hour or so the veil lifted and discovered beneath it fifty horsemen, ravening lions to the sight, in steel armour dight. We observed them straightly and lo! they were cutters-off of the highway, wild as wild Arabs. When they saw that we were only four and had with us but the ten camels carrying the presents, they dashed down upon us with lances at rest. We signed to them, with our fingers, as it were saying, "We be messengers of the great King of Hind, so harm us not!" but they answered on like wise, "We are not in his dominions to obey nor are we subject to his sway." Then they set upon us and slew some of my slaves and put the lave to flight; and I also fled after I had gotten a wound, a grievous hurt, whilst the Arabs were taken up with the money and the presents which were with us. I went forth unknowing whither I went, having become mean as I was mighty; and I fared on until I came to the crest of a mountain where I took shelter for the night in a cave. When day arose I set out again, nor ceased after this fashion till I arrived at a fair city and a well-filled. Now it was the season when Winter was turning away with his rime and to greet the world with his flowers came Prime, and the young blooms were springing and the streams flowed ringing, and the birds were sweetly singing, as saith the poet concerning a certain city when describing it:—

A place secure from every thought of fear * Safety and peace for ever lord it here:
Its beauties seem to beautify its sons * And as in Heaven its happy folk appear.

---

[1] Arab. "Sadd" = wall, dyke, etc. the "bund" or "band" of Anglo-India. Hence the "Sadd" on the Nile, the banks of grass and floating islands which "wall" the stream. There are few sights more appalling than a sandstorm in the desert, the "Zauba'ah" as the Arabs call it. Devils, or pillars of sand, vertical and inclined, measuring a thousand feet high, rush over the plain lashing the sand at their base like a sea surging under a furious whirlwind; shearing the grass clean away from the roots, tearing up trees, which are whirled like leaves and sticks in air and sweeping away tents and houses as if they were bits of paper. At last the columns join at the top and form, perhaps three thousand feet above the earth, a gigantic cloud of yellow sand which obliterates not only the horizon but even the mid-day sun. These sand-spouts are the terror of travellers. In Sind and the Punjab we have the dust-storm which for darkness, I have said, beats the blackest London fog.

I was glad of my arrival for I was wearied with the way, and
yellow of face for weakness and want; but my plight was pitiable
and I knew not whither to betake me. So I accosted a Tailor
sitting in his little shop and saluted him; he returned my salam,
and bade me kindly welcome and wished me well and entreated
me gently and asked me of the cause of my strangerhood. I told
him all my past from first to last; and he was concerned on my
account and said, "O youth, disclose not thy secret to any: the
King of this city is the greatest enemy thy father hath, and there
is blood-wit[1] between them and thou hast cause to fear for thy
life." Then he set meat and drink before me; and I ate and drank
and he with me; and we conversed freely till night-fall, when
he cleared me a place in a corner of his shop and brought me a carpet and a coverlet. I tarried with him three days; at the end
of which time he said to me, "Knowest thou no calling whereby
to win thy living, O my son?" "I am learned in the law," I
replied, "and a doctor of doctrine; an adept in art and science,
a mathematician and a notable penman." He rejoined, "Thy
calling is of no account in our city, where not a soul under-
standeth science or even writing or aught save money-making."
Then said I, "By Allah, I know nothing but what I have mentioned;" and he answered, "Gird thy middle and take thee a
hatchet and a cord, and go and hew wood in the wold for thy
daily bread, till Allah send thee relief; and tell none who thou
art lest they slay thee." Then he bought me an axe and a rope
and gave me in charge to certain wood-cutters; and with these
guardians I went forth into the forest, where I cut fuel-wood
the whole of my day and came back in the evening bearing my
bundle on my head. I sold it for half a dinar, with part of which
I bought provision and laid by the rest. In such work I spent a
whole year and when this was ended I went out one day, as was
my wont, into the wilderness; and, wandering away from my
companions, I chanced on a thickly grown lowland[2] in which

---

[1] Arab. Sár = the vendetta, before mentioned, as dreaded in Arabia as in Corsica.

[2] Arab. "Ghútah," usually a place where irrigation is abundant. It especially applies
(in books) to the Damascus-plain because "it abounds with water and fruit trees." The
Ghutah is one of the four earthly paradises, the others being Basrah (Bassorah), Shiraz
and Samarcand. Its peculiarity is the likeness to a seaport; the Desert which rolls up
almost to its doors being the sea and its ships being the camels. The first Arab to whom
we owe this admirable term for the "Companion of Job" is "Tarafah" one of the poets
of the Suspended Poems: he likens (v. v. 3, 4) the camels which bore away his beloved
to ships sailing from Aduli. But "ships of the desert" is doubtless a term of the highest
antiquity.

there was an abundance of wood. So I entered and I found the
gnarled stump of a great tree and loosened the ground about it
and shovelled away the earth.. Presently my hatchet rang
upon a copper ring; so I cleared away the soil and behold, the
ring was attached to a wooden trap-door. This I raised and there
appeared beneath it a staircase. I descended the steps to the
bottom and came to a door, which I opened and found myself in a
noble hall strong of structure and beautifully built, where was a
damsel like a pearl of great price, whose favour banished from my
heart all grief and cark and care; and whose soft speech healed
the soul in despair and captivated the wise and ware. Her figure
measured five feet in height; her breasts were firm and upright;
her cheek a very garden of delight; her colour lively bright; her
face gleamed like dawn through curly tresses which gloomed like
night, and above the snows of her bosom glittered teeth of a
pearly white.[1] As the poet said of one like her:—

Slim-waisted loveling, jetty hair-encrowned * A wand of willow on a sandy
    mound:

And as saith another:—

Four things that meet not, save they here unite * To shed my heart-blood and
    to rape my sprite:
Brilliantest forehead; tresses jetty bright; * Cheeks rosy red and stature
    beauty-dight.

When I looked upon her I prostrated myself before Him who had
created her, for the beauty and loveliness He had shaped in her,
and she looked at me and said, "Art thou man or Jinni?" "I am
a man," answered I, and she, "Now who brought thee to this
place where I have abided five-and-twenty years without even
yet seeing man in it?" Quoth I (and indeed I found her words
wonder-sweet, and my heart was melted to the core by them),
"O my lady, my good fortune led me hither for the dispelling of
my cark and care." Then I related to her all my mishap from first
to last, and my case appeared to her exceeding grievous; so she
wept and said, "I will tell thee my story in my turn. I am the
daughter of the King Ifitamus, lord of the Islands of Abnùs,[2]
who married me to my cousin, the son of my paternal uncle;

---

[1] The exigencies of the "Saj'a," or rhymed prose, disjoint this and many similar passages.
[2] The "Ebony" Islands; Scott's "Isle of Ebene," i., 217.

but on my wedding night an Ifrit named Jirjís[1] bin Rajmús,
first cousin that is, mother's sister's son, of Iblís, the Foul
Fiend, snatched me up and, flying away with me like a bird, set
me down in this place, whither he conveyed all I needed of
fine stuffs, raiment and jewels and furniture, and meat and drink
and other else. Once in every ten days he comes here and lies
a single night with me, and then wends his way, for he took me
without the consent of his family; and he hath agreed with me
that if ever I need him by night or by day, I have only to pass
my hand over yonder two lines engraved upon the alcove, and
he will appear to me before my fingers cease touching. Four
days have now passed since he was here; and, as there remain
six days before he come again, say me, wilt thou abide with me
five days, and go hence the day before his coming?" I replied
"Yes, and yes again! O rare, if all this be not a dream!" Hereat
she was glad and, springing to her feet, seized my hand and
carried me through an arched doorway to a Hammam-bath, a
fair hall and richly decorate. I doffed my clothes, and she
doffed hers; then we bathed and she washed me; and when this
was done we left the bath, and she seated me by her side upon
a high divan, and brought me sherbet scented with musk. When
we felt cool after the bath, she set food before me and we ate
and fell to talking; but presently she said to me, "Lay thee
down and take thy rest, for surely thou must be weary." So I
thanked her, my lady, and lay down and slept soundly, forgetting
all that had happened to me. When I awoke I found her rubbing
and shampooing my feet;[2] so I again thanked her and blessed her
and we sat for awhile talking. Said she, "By Allah, I was sad at
heart, for that I have dwelt alone underground for these five-and-
twenty years; and praise be to Allah, who hath sent me some one
with whom I can converse!" Then she asked, "O youth, what
sayest thou to wine?" and I answered, "Do as thou wilt." Whereupon she went to a cupboard and took out a sealed flask of right
old wine and set off the table with flowers and scented herbs
and began to sing these lines:—

"Had we known of thy coming we fain had dispread * The cores of our
    hearts or the balls of our eyes;
Our cheeks as a carpet to greet thee had thrown * And our eyelids had strown
    for thy feet to betread."

---

[1] "Jarjarís" in the Bul. Edit.

[2] Arab. "Takbís." Many Easterns can hardly sleep without this kneading of the
muscles, this "rubbing" whose hygienic properties England is now learning.

Now when she finished her verse I thanked her, for indeed love o. her had gotten hold of my heart and my grief and anguish were gone. We sat at converse and carousal till nightfall, and with her I spent the night—such night never spent I in all my life! On the morrow delight followed delight till midday, by which time I had drunken wine so freely that I had lost my wits, and stood up, staggering to the right and to the left, and said "Come, O my charmer, and I will carry thee up from this underground vault and deliver thee from the spell of thy Jinni." She laughed and replied "Content thee and hold thy peace: of every ten days one is for the Ifrit and the other nine are thine." Quoth I (and in good sooth drink had got the better of me), "This very instant will I break down the alcove whereon is graven the talisman and summon the Ifrit that I may slay him, for it is a practise of mine to slay Ifrits!" When she heard my words her colour waxed wan and she said, "By Allah, do not!" and she began repeating:—

"This is a thing wherein destruction lies * I rede thee shun it an thy wits be wise."

And these also:—

"O thou who seekest severance, draw the rein * Of thy swift steed nor seek o'ermuch t' advance;
Ah stay! for treachery is the rule of life, * And sweets of meeting end in severance."

I heard her verse but paid no heed to her words, nay, I raised my foot and administered to the alcove a mighty kick——And Shahrazad perceived the dawn of day and ceased to say her permitted say.

Wh̄en it was the Thirteenth Night,

She said, It hath reached me, O auspicious King, that the second Kalandar thus continued his tale to the lady:—But when, O my mistress, I kicked that alcove with a mighty kick, behold, the air starkened and darkened and thundered and lightened; the earth trembled and quaked and the world became invisible. At once the fumes of wine left my head: I cried to her, "What is the matter?" and she replied, "The Ifrit is upon us! did I not warn thee of this? By Allah, thou hast brought ruin upon me; but fly for thy life and go up by the way thou camest down!" So I fled up the staircase; but, in the excess of my fear, I forgot sandals and hatchet. And when I had mounted two steps I turned to look for them, and lo! I saw the earth cleave asunder, and there arose from it an Ifrit, a monster of hideousness, who said to the damsel "What trouble and pother be this wherewith thou disturbest me? What mishap hath betided thee?" "No mishap hath befallen me" she answered, "save that my breast was straitened[1] and my heart heavy with sadness! so I drank a little wine to broaden it and to hearten myself; then I rose to obey a call of Nature, but the wine had gotten into my head and I fell against the alcove." "Thou liest, like the whore thou art!" shrieked the Ifrit; and he looked around the hall right and left till he caught sight of my axe and sandals and said to her, "What be these but the belongings of some mortal who hath been in thy society?" She answered, "I never set eyes upon them till this moment: they must have been brought by thee hither cleaving to thy garments." Quoth the Ifrit, "These words are absurd; thou harlot! thou strumpet!" Then he stripped her stark naked and, stretching her upon the floor, bound her hands and feet to four stakes, like one crucified;[2] and set about torturing and trying to make her confess. I could not bear to stand listening to her cries and groans; so I climbed the stair on the quake with fear; and when I reached the top I re-placed the trap-door and covered it with earth. Then repented I of what I had done with penitence exceeding; and thought of the lady and her beauty and loveliness, and the tortures she was suffering at the hands of the accursed Ifrit, after her quiet life of five-and-twenty years; and how all that had happened to her was for the cause of me. I bethought me of my father and his kingly estate and how I had become a woodcutter; and how, after my time had been awhile serene, the world had again waxed turbid and troubled to me. So I wept bitterly and repeated this couplet:—

What time Fate's tyranny shall most oppress thee * Perpend! one day shall
    joy thee, one distress thee!

---

1 The converse of the breast being broadened, the drooping, "draggle-tail" gait com-pared with the head held high and the chest inflated.

2 This penalty is mentioned in the Koran (chapt. v.) as fit for those who fight against Allah and his Apostle; but commentators are not agreed if the sinners are first to be put to death or to hang on the cross till they die. Pharaoh (chapt. xx.) threatens to crucify his magicians on palm-trees, and is held to be the first crucifier.

Then I walked till I reached the home of my friend, the Tailor, whom I found most anxiously expecting me; indeed he was, as the saying goes, on coals of fire for my account. And when he saw me he said, "All night long my heart hath been heavy, fearing for thee from wild beasts or other mischances. Now praise be to Allah for thy safety!" I thanked him for his friendly solicitude and, retiring to my corner, sat pondering and musing on what had befallen me; and I blamed and chided myself for my meddlesome folly and my frowardness in kicking the alcove. I was calling myself to account when behold, my friend, the Tailor, came to me and said, "O youth, in the shop there is an old man, a Persian,[1] who seeketh thee: he hath thy hatchet and thy sandals which he had taken to the woodcutters,[2] saying, "I was going out at what time the Mu'azzin began the call to dawn-prayer, when I chanced upon these things and know not whose they are; so direct me to their owner." The woodcutters rec-ognised thy hatchet and directed him to thee: he is sitting in my shop, so fare forth to him and thank him and take thine axe and sandals." When I heard these words I turned yellow with fear and felt stunned as by a blow; and, before I could recover myself, lo! the floor of my private room clove asunder, and out of it rose the Persian who was the Ifrit. He had tortured the lady with exceeding tortures, natheless she would not confess to him aught; so he took the hatchet and sandals and said to her, "As surely as I am Jirjis of the seed of Iblis, I will bring thee back the owner of this and these!"[3] Then he went to the woodcutters with the pretence aforesaid and, being directed to me, after waiting a while in the shop till the fact was confirmed, he sud-denly snatched me up as a hawk snatcheth a mouse and flew high in air; but presently descended and plunged with me under the earth (I being aswoon the while), and lastly set me down in the subterranean palace wherein I had passed that blissful night. And there I saw the lady stripped to the skin, her limbs bound to four stakes and blood welling from her sides. At the sight my eyes ran over with tears; but the Ifrit covered her person and

---

[1] Arab. "'Ajami"=foreigner, esp. a Persian: the latter in The Nights is mostly a villain. I must here remark that the contemptible condition of Persians in Al-Hijáz (which I noted in 1852, Pilgrimage, i., 327) has completely changed. They are no longer, "The slippers of Ali and hounds of Omar:" they have learned the force of union and now, instead of being bullied, they bully.

[2] The Calc. Edit. turns into Tailors (Khayyátín) and Torrens does not see the misprint.

[3] i. e. Axe and sandals.

said, "O wanton, is not this man thy lover?" She looked upon me and replied, "I wot him not nor have I ever seen him before this hour!" Quoth the Ifrit, "What! this torture and yet no confessing;" and quoth she, "I never saw this man in my born days, and it is not lawful in Allah's sight to tell lies on him." "If thou know him not," said the Ifrit to her, "take this sword and strike off his head."[1] She hent the sword in hand and came close up to me; and I signalled to her with my eyebrows, my tears the while flowing adown my cheeks. She understood me and made answer, also by signs, "How couldest thou bring all this evil upon me?" and I rejoined after the same fashion, "This is the time for mercy and forgiveness." And the mute tongue of my case[2] spake aloud saying:—

Mine eyes were dragomans for my tongue betied * And told full clear the love
    I fain would hide:
When last we met and tears in torrents railed * For tongue struck dumb my
    glances testified:
She signed with eye-glance while her lips were mute * I signed with fingers
    and she kenned th' implied:
Our eyebrows did all duty 'twixt us twain; * And we being speechless Love
    spake loud and plain.

Then, O my mistress, the lady threw away the sword and said, "How shall I strike the neck of one I wot not, and who hath done me no evil? Such deed were not lawful in my law!" and she held her hand. Said the Ifrit, "'Tis grievous to thee to slay thy lover; and, because he hath lain with thee, thou endurest these torments and obstinately refusest to confess. After this it is clear to me that only like loveth and pitieth like." Then he turned to me and asked me, "O man, haply thou also dost not know this woman;" whereto I answered, "And pray who may she be? assuredly I never saw her till this instant." "Then take the sword," said he "and strike off her head and I will believe that thou wottest her not and will leave thee free to go, and will not deal hardly with thee." I replied, "That will I do;" and, taking the sword went forward sharply and raised my hand to smite. But she signed to me with her eyebrows, "Have I failed thee in aught of love; and is it thus that thou requitest me?" I understood what her looks implied and answered her with an eye-

---

[1] Lit. "Strike his neck."
[2] A phrase which will frequently recur; meaning the situation suggested such words as these.

glance, "I will sacrifice my soul for thee." And the tongue of the case wrote in our hearts these lines:—

How many a lover with his eyebrows speaketh * To his beloved, as his passion pleadeth:
With flashing eyne his passion he inspireth * And well she seeth what his pleading needeth.
How sweet the look when each on other gazeth; * And with what swiftness and how sure it speedeth:
And this with eyebrows all his passion writeth; * And that with eyeballs all his passion readeth.

Then my eyes filled with tears to overflowing and I cast the sword from my hand saying, "O mighty Ifrit and hero, if a woman lacking wits and faith deem it unlawful to strike off my head, how can it be lawful for me, a man, to smite her neck whom I never saw in my whole life. I cannot do such misdeed though thou cause me drink the cup of death and perdition." Then said the Ifrit, "Ye twain show the good understanding between you; but I will let you see how such doings end." He took the sword, and struck off the lady's hands first, with four strokes, and then her feet; whilst I looked on and made sure of death and she farewelled me with her dying eyes. So the Ifrit cried at her, "Thou whorest and makest me a wittol with thine eyes;" and struck her so that her head went flying. Then he turned to me and said, "O mortal, we have it in our law that, when the wife committeth advowtry it is lawful for us to slay her. As for this damsel I snatched her away on her bride-night when she was a girl of twelve and she knew no one but myself. I used to come to her once every ten days and lie with her the night, under the semblance of a man, a Persian; and when I was well assured that she had cuckolded me, I slew her. But as for thee I am not well satisfied that thou hast wronged me in her; nevertheless I must not let thee go unharmed; so ask a boon of me and I will grant it." Then I rejoiced, O my lady, with exceeding joy and said, "What boon shall I crave of thee?" He replied, "Ask me this boon; into what shape I shall bewitch thee; wilt thou be a dog, or an ass or an ape?" I rejoined (and indeed I had hoped that mercy might be shown me), "By Allah, spare me, that Allah spare thee for sparing a Moslem and a man who never wronged thee." And I humbled myself before him with exceeding humility, and remained standing in his presence, saying, "I am sore oppressed by circumstance." He replied "Talk me no long talk, it is in my power to slay thee; but I give thee instead thy choice." Quoth I, "O thou Ifrit, it would besit thee to pardon me even as the Envied pardoned the Envier." Quoth he, "And how was that?" and I began to tell him

The Tale of the Envier and the Envied.

THEY relate, O Ifrit, that in a certain city were two men who dwelt in adjoining houses, having a common party-wall; and one of them envied the other and looked on him with an evil eye,[1] and did his utmost endeavour to injure him; and, albeit at all times he was jealous of his neighbour, his malice at last grew on him till he could hardly eat or enjoy the sweet pleasures of sleep. But the Envied did nothing save prosper; and the more the other strove to injure him, the more he got and gained and throve. At last the malice of his neighbour and the man's constant endeavour to work him a harm came to his knowledge; so he said, "By Allah! God's earth is wide enough for its people;" and, leaving the neighbourhood, he repaired to another city where he bought himself a piece of land in which was a dried up draw-well,[2] old and in ruinous condition. Here he built him an oratory and, furnishing it with a few necessaries, took up his abode therein, and devoted himself to prayer and worshipping Allah Almighty; and Fakirs and holy mendicants flocked to him from all quarters; and his fame went abroad through the city and that country side. Presently the news reached his envious neighbour, of what good fortune had befallen him and how the city notables had become his disciples; so he travelled to the place and presented himself at the holy man's hermitage, and was met by the Envied with welcome and greeting and all honour. Then quoth the Envier, "I have a word to say to thee; and this is the cause of my faring hither, and I wish to give thee a piece of good news; so come with me to thy

---

[1] The smiter with the evil eye is called "A'in" and the person smitten "Ma'ín" or "Ma'ún."

[2] Arab. "Sákiyah," the well-known Persian wheel with pots and buckets attached to the tire. It is of many kinds, the boxed, etc., etc.; and it is possibly alluded to in the "pitcher broken at the fountain" (Ecclesiastes xii. 6) an accident often occurring to the modern "Noria." Travellers mostly abuse its "dismal creaking" and "mournful monotony": I have defended the music of the water-wheel in Pilgrimage ii. 198.

cell." Thereupon the Envied arose and took the Envier by the hand, and they went in to the inmost part of the hermitage; but the Envier said, "Bid thy Fakirs retire to their cells, for I will not tell thee what I have to say, save in secret where none may hear us." Accordingly the Envied said to his Fakirs, "Retire to your private cells;" and, when all had done as he bade them, he set out with his visitor and walked a little way until the twain reached the ruinous old well. And as they stood upon the brink the Envier gave the Envied a push which tumbled him headlong into it, unseen of any; whereupon he fared forth, and went his ways, thinking to have had slain him. Now this well happened to be haunted by the Jann who, seeing the case, bore him up and let him down little by little, till he reached the bottom, when they seated him upon a large stone. Then one of them asked his fellows, "Wot ye who be this man?" and they answered, "Nay." "This man," continued the speaker, "is the Envied hight who, flying from the Envier, came to dwell in our city, and here founded this holy house, and he hath edified us by his litanies[1] and his lections of the Koran; but the Envier set out and journeyed till he rejoined him, and cunningly contrived to deceive him and cast him into the well where we now are. But the fame of this good man hath this very night come to the Sultan of our city who designeth to visit him on the morrow on account of his daughter." "What aileth his daughter?" asked one, and another answered "She is possessed of a spirit; for Maymun, son of Damdam, is madly in love with her; but, if this pious man knew the remedy, her cure would be as easy as could be." Hereupon one of them inquired, "And what is the medicine?" and he replied, "The black tom-cat which is with him in the oratory hath, on the end of his tail, a white spot, the size of a dirham; let him pluck seven white hairs from the spot, then let him fumigate her therewith and the Marid will flee from her and not return; so she shall be sane for the rest of her life." All this took place, O Ifrit, within earshot of the

---

[1] Arab. "Zikr" lit. remembering, mentioning (*i. e.* the names of Allah), here refers to the meetings of religious for devotional exercises; the "Zikkirs," as they are called, mostly standing or sitting in a circle while they ejaculate the Holy Name. These "rogations" are much affected by Darwayshes, or begging friars, whom Europe politely divides into "dancing" and "howling"; and, on one occasion, greatly to the scandal of certain Engländerinns to whom I was showing the Ezbekiyah I joined the ring of "howlers." Lane (Mod. Egypt, see index) is profuse upon the subject of "Zikrs" and Zikkíts. It must not be supposed that they are uneducated men: the better class, however, prefers more privacy.

Envied who listened readily.   When dawn broke and morn arose
in sheen and shone, the Fakirs went to seek the Shaykh and found
him climbing up the wall of the well; whereby he was magnified
in their eyes.[1]   Then, knowing that naught save the black tom-
cat could supply him with the remedy required, he plucked the
seven tail-hairs from the white spot and laid them by him; and
hardly had the sun risen ere the Sultan entered the hermitage,
with the great lords of his estate, bidding the rest of his retinue
to remain standing outside.   The Envied gave him a hearty welcome, and seating him by his side asked him, "Shall I tell thee the
cause of thy coming?"   The King answered, "Yes."   He continued, "Thou hast come upon pretext of a visitation;[2] but it is
in thy heart to question me of thy daughter."   Replied the King,
" 'Tis even so, O thou holy Shaykh;" and the Envied continued,
"Send and fetch her, and I trust to heal her forthright (an such
it be the will of Allah!)"   The King in great joy sent for his
daughter, and they brought her pinioned and fettered.   The
Envied made her sit down behind a curtain and taking out the
hairs fumigated her therewith; whereupon that which was in her
head cried out and departed from her.   The girl was at once
restored to her right mind and veiling her face, said, "What
hath happened and who brought me hither?"   The Sultan rejoiced with a joy that nothing could exceed, and kissed his
daughter's eyes,[3] and the holy man's hand; then, turning to his
great lords, he asked, "How say ye! What fee deserveth he who
hath made my daughter whole?" and all answered, "He deserveth
her to wife;" and the King said, "Ye speak sooth!"   So he
married him to her and the Envied thus became son-in-law to the
King.   And after a little the Wazir died and the King said,
"Whom can I make Minister in his stead?" "Thy son-in-law,"
replied the courtiers.   So the Envied became a Wazir; and after a
while the Sultan also died and the lieges said, "Whom shall we
make King?" and all cried, "The Wazir."   So the Wazir was
forthright made Sultan, and he became King regnant, a true ruler
of men.   One day as he had mounted his horse; and, in the emi-

---

1 As they thought he had been there for prayer or penance.
2 Arab. "Ziyárat," a visit to a pious person or place.
3 This is a paternal salute in the East where they are particular about the part kissed.
A witty and not unusually gross Persian book, called the "Al-Námah" because all questions
begin with "Al" (the Arab article) contains one "Al-Wajib al-busidan?" (what best de-
serves bussing?) and the answer is "Kus-i-nau-pashm," (a bobadilla with a young bush).

nence of his kinglihood, was riding amidst his Emirs and Wazirs and the Grandees of his realm his eye fell upon his old neighbour, the Envier, who stood afoot on his path; so he turned to one of his Ministers, and said, "Bring hither that man and cause him no affright." The Wazir brought him and the King said, "Give him a thousand miskáls[1] of gold from the treasury, and load him ten camels with goods for trade, and send him under escort to his own town." Then he bade his enemy farewell and sent him away and forbore to punish him for the many and great evils he had done. See, O Ifrit, the mercy of the Envied to the Envier, who had hated him from the beginning and had borne him such bitter malice and never met him without causing him trouble; and had driven him from house and home, and then had journeyed for the sole purpose of taking his life by throwing him into the well. Yet he did not requite his injurious dealing, but forgave him and was bountiful to him.[2] Then I wept before him, O my lady, with sore weeping, never was there sorer, and I recited:—

"Pardon my fault, for 'tis the wise man's wont * All faults to pardon and revenge forgo:
In sooth all manner faults in me contain * Then deign of goodness mercy-grace to show:
Whoso imploreth pardon from on High * Should hold his hand from sinners here below."

Said the Ifrit, "Lengthen not thy words! As to my slaying thee fear it not, and as to my pardoning thee hope it not; but from my bewitching thee there is no escape." Then he tore me from the ground which closed under my feet and flew with me into the firmament till I saw the earth as a large white cloud or a saucer[3] in the midst of the waters. Presently he set me down on a mountain, and taking a little dust, over which he muttered some magical words, sprinkled me therewith, saying, "Quit that shape and take thou the shape of an ape!" And on the instant I became an ape, a tail-less baboon, the son of a century[4]. Now when he had left me and I saw myself in this ugly and hateful shape, I wept for myself, but resigned my soul to the tyranny of Time and Circumstance, well weeting that Fortune is fair and constant to no man.

---

[1] A weight of 71–72 English grains in gold; here equivalent to the dinar.
[2] Compare the tale of The Three Crows in Gammer Grethel, Evening ix.
[3] The comparison is peculiarly apposite; the earth seen from above appears hollow with a raised rim.
[4] A hundred years old.

I descended the mountain and found at the foot a desert plain, long and broad, over which I travelled for the space of a month till my course brought me to the brink of the briny sea.[1] After standing there awhile, I was ware of a ship in the offing which ran before a fair wind making for the shore. I hid myself behind a rock on the beach and waited till the ship drew near, when I leaped on board. I found her full of merchants and passengers and one of them cried, "O Captain, this ill-omened brute will bring us ill-luck!" and another said, "Turn this ill-omened beast out from among us;" the Captain said, "Let us kill it!" another said, "Slay it with the sword;" a third, "Drown it;" and a fourth, "Shoot it with an arrow." But I sprang up and laid hold of the Rais's[2] skirt, and shed tears which poured down my chops. The Captain took pity on me, and said, "O merchants! this ape hath appealed to me for protection and I will protect him; henceforth he is under my charge: so let none do him aught hurt or harm, otherwise there will be bad blood between us." Then he en-treated me kindly and whatsoever he said I understood and ministered to his every want and served him as a servant, albeit my tongue would not obey my wishes; so that he came to love me. The vessel sailed on, the wind being fair, for the space of fifty days; at the end of which we cast anchor under the walls of a great city wherein was a world of people, especially learned men, none could tell their number save Allah. No sooner had we arrived than we were visited by certain Mameluke-officials from the King of that city; who, after boarding us, greeted the merchants and giving them joy of safe arrival said, "Our King welcometh you, and sendeth you this roll of paper, whereupon each and every of you must write a line. For ye shall know that the King's Minister, a calligrapher of renown, is dead, and the King hath sworn a solemn oath that he will make none Wazir in his stead who cannot write as well as he could." He then gave us the scroll which measured ten cubits long by a breadth of one, and each of the merchants who knew how to write wrote a line thereon, even to the last of them; after which I stood up (still in the shape of an ape) and snatched the roll out of their hands. They feared lest I should tear it or throw it overboard;

---

[1] "Bahr" in Arab. means sea, river, piece of water; hence the adjective is needed.

[2] The Captain or Master of the ship (not the owner). In Al-Yaman the word also means a "barber," in virtue of the root, Rass, a head.

so they tried to stay me and scare me, but I signed to them that I could write, whereat all marvelled, saying, "We never yet saw an ape write." And the Captain cried, "Let him write; and if he scribble and scrabble we will kick him out and kill him; but if he write fair and scholarly I will adopt him as my son; for surely I never yet saw a more intelligent and well-mannered monkey than he. Would Heaven my real son were his match in morals and manners." I took the reed, and stretching out my paw, dipped it in ink and wrote, in the hand used for letters,[1] these two couplets:—

Time hath recorded gifts she gave the great; * But none recorded thine which be far higher;
Allah ne'er orphan men by loss of thee * Who be of Goodness mother, Bounty's sire.

And I wrote in Rayháni or larger letters elegantly curved[2]:—

Thou hast a reed[3] of rede to every land, * Whose driving causeth all the world to thrive;
Nil is the Nile of Misraim by thy boons * Who makest misery smile with fingers five.

Then I wrote in the Suls[4] character:—

There be no writer who from Death shall fleet, * But what his hand hath writ men shall repeat:
Write, therefore, naught save what shall serve thee when * Thou see't on Judgment-Day an so thou see't!

Then I wrote in the character Naskh[5]:—

---

[1] The text has "in the character Ruká'í," or Riká'í, the correspondence-hand.

[2] A curved character supposed to be like the basil-leaf (rayhán). Richardson calls it "Rohani."

[3] I need hardly say that Easterns use a reed, a Calamus (Kalam applied only to the cut reed) for our quills and steel pens.

[4] Famous for being inscribed on the Kiswah (cover) of Mohammed's tomb; a large and more formal hand still used for engrossing and for mural inscriptions. Only seventy-two varieties of it are known (Pilgrimage, ii., 82).

[5] The copying and transcribing hand which is either Arabi or Ajami. A great discovery has been lately made which upsets all our old ideas of Cufic, etc. Mr. Löytved of Bayrut has found, amongst the Hauranic inscriptions, one in pure Naskhi, dating A. D. 568, or fifty years before the Hijrah; and it is accepted as authentic by my learned friend M. Ch. Clermont-Ganneau (p. 193, Pal. Explor. Fund; July 1884). In D'Herbelot and Sale's day the Koran was supposed to have been written in rude characters, like those subsequently called "Cufic," invented shortly before Mohammed's birth by Murámir ibn Murrah of Anbar in Irák, introduced into Meccah by Bashar the Kindian, and perfected by Ibn Muklah (Al-Wazir, ob. A. H. 328=940). We must now change all that. See Catalogue of Oriental Caligraphs, etc., by G. P. Badger, London, Whiteley, 1885.

When to sore parting Fate our love shall doom, * To distant life by Destiny
    decreed,
We cause the inkhorn's lips to 'plain our pains, * And tongue our utterance
    with the talking reed.

And I wrote in the Túmár character[1]:—

Kingdom with none endures; if thou deny * This truth, where be the Kings
    of earlier earth?
Set trees of goodliness while rule endures, * And when thou art fallen they
    shall tell thy worth.

And I wrote in the character Muhakkak[2]:—

When oped the inkhorn of thy wealth and fame * Take ink of generous heart
    and gracious hand;
Write brave and noble deeds while write thou can * And win thee praise from
    point of pen and brand.

Then I gave the scroll to the officials and, after we all had written
our line, they carried it before the King. When he saw the paper
no writing pleased him save my writing; and he said to the
assembled courtiers, "Go seek the writer of these lines and dress
him in a splendid robe of honour; then mount him on a she-mule,[3]

---

1 Capital and uncial letters; the hand in which the Ka'abah veil is inscribed (Pilgrimage iii. 299, 300).

2 A "Court hand" says Mr. Payne (i. 112); I know nothing of it. Other hands are:
the Ta'alík; hanging or oblique, used for finer MSS. and having, according to Richardson, "the same analogy to the Naskhi as our Italic has to the Roman." The Nasta'
lík (not Naskh-Ta'alik) much used in India, is, as the name suggests, a mixture of the
Naskhi (writing of transactions) and the Ta'alik. The Shikastah (broken hand) everywhere represents our running hand and becomes a hard task to the reader. The Kirmá
is another cursive character, mostly confined to the receipts and disbursements of the
Turkish treasury. The Diváni, or Court (of Justice) is the official hand, bold and round,
a business character, the lines often rising with a sweep or curve towards the (left) end.
The Jáli or polished has a variety, the Jali-Ta'alik: the Sulsi (known in many books)
is adopted for titles of volumes, royal edicts, diplomas and so forth; "answering much
the same purpose as capitals with us, or the flourished letters in illuminated manuscripts"
(Richardson). The Tughrái is that of the Tughrá, the Prince's cypher or flourishing
signature in ceremonial writings, and containing some such sentence as: Let this be executed. There are others e. g. Yákuti and Sirenkil known only by name. Finally the
Maghribi (Moorish) hand differs in form and diacritical points from the characters used
further east almost as much as German running hand does from English. It is curious
that Richardson omits the Jali (intricate and convoluted) and the divisions of the Sulusí,
Sulsi or Sulus (Thuluth) character, the Sulus al-Khafíf, etc.

3 Arab. "Baghlah"; the male (Baghl) is used only for loads. This is everywhere the
rule: nothing is more unmanageable than a restive "Macho"; and he knows that he
can always get you off his back when so minded. From "Baghlah" is derived the name of
the native craft Anglo-Indicè a "Buggalow."

let a band of music precede him and bring him to the presence." At these words they smiled and the King was wroth with them and cried, "O accursed! I give you an order and you laugh at me?" "O King," replied they, "if we laugh 'tis not at thee and not without a cause." "And what is it?" asked he; and they answered, "O King, thou orderest us to bring to thy presence the man who wrote these lines; now the truth is that he who wrote them is not of the sons of Adam,[1] but an ape, a tailless baboon, belonging to the ship-captain." Quoth he, "Is this true that you say?" Quoth they, "Yea! by the rights of thy munificence!" The King marvelled at their words and shook with mirth and said, "I am minded to buy this ape of the Captain." Then he sent messengers to the ship with the mule, the dress, the guard and the state-drums, saying, "Not the less do you clothe him in the robe of honour and mount him on the mule and let him be surrounded by the guards and preceded by the band of music." They came to the ship and took me from the Captain and robed me in the robe of honour and, mounting me on the she-mule, carried me in state-procession through the streets; whilst the people were amazed and amused. And folk said to one another, "Halloo! is our Sultan about to make an ape his Minister?"; and came all agog crowding to gaze at me, and the town was astir and turned topsy-turvy on my account. When they brought me up to the King and set me in his presence, I kissed the ground before him three times, and once before the High Chamberlain and great officers, and he bade me be seated, and I sat respectfully on shins and knees,[2] and all who were present marvelled at my fine manners, and the King most of all. Thereupon he ordered the lieges to retire; and, when none remained save the King's majesty, the Eunuch on duty and a little white slave, he bade them set before me the table of food, containing all manner of birds, whatever hoppeth and flieth and treadeth in nest, such as quail and sand-grouse. Then he signed me to eat with him; so I rose and kissed ground before him, then sat me down and ate with him. And when the table was re-

---

[1] In Heb. "Ben-Adam" is any man opp. to "Beni ish" (Psalm iv. 3) = *filii viri*, not *homines*.

[2] This posture is terribly trying to European legs; and few white men (unless brought up to it) can squat for any time on their heels. The "tailor-fashion," with crossed legs, is held to be free and easy.

moved I washed my hands in seven waters and took the reed case and reed; and wrote instead of speaking these couplets:—

Wail for the little partridges on porringer and plate; * Cry for the ruin of the fries and stews well marinate:
Keen as I keen for loved, lost daughters of the Katá-grouse,[1] * And omelette round the fair enbrownèd fowls agglomerate:
O fire in heart of me for fish, those *deux poissons* I saw, * Bedded on new made scones[2] and cakes in piles to laniate.
For thee, O vermicelli! aches my very maw! I hold * Without thee every taste and joy are clean annihilate.
Those eggs have rolled their yellow eyes in torturing pains of fire * Ere served with hash and fritters hot, that delicatest cate.
Praisèd be Allah for His baked and roast and ah! how good * This pulse, these pot-herbs steeped in oil with eysill combinate!
When hunger sated was, I elbow-propt fell back upon * Meat-pudding[3] wherein gleamed the bangles that my wits amate.
Then woke I sleeping appetite to eat as though in sport * Sweets from bro-caded trays and kickshaws most elaborate.
Be patient, soul of me! Time is a haughty, jealous wight; * To-day he seems dark-lowering and to-morrow fair to sight.[4]

Then I rose and seated myself at a respectful distance while the King read what I had written, and marvelled, exclaiming, "O the miracle, that an ape should be gifted with this graceful style and this power of penmanship! By Allah, 'tis a wonder of wonders!"

---

[1] Arab. "Katá" = Pterocles Alchata, the well-known sand-grouse of the desert. It is very poor white flesh.

[2] Arab. "Khubz" which I do not translate "cake" or "bread," as that would suggest the idea of our loaf. The staff of life in the East is a thin flat circle of dough baked in the oven or on the griddle, and corresponding with the Scotch "scone," the Spanish "tortilla" and the Australian "flap-jack."

[3] Arab. "Harísah," a favourite dish of wheat (or rice) boiled and reduced to a paste with shredded meat, spices and condiments. The "bangles" is a pretty girl eating with him.

[4] These lines are repeated with a difference in Night cccxxx. They affect *Rims cars*, out of the way, heavy rhymes: e. g. here Sakáríj (plur. of Sakrúj, platters, porringers); Tayáhíj (plur. of Tayhúj, the smaller caccabis-partridge); Tabáhíj (Persian Tabahjah, an omelet or a stew of meat, onions, eggs, etc.) Ma'áríj ("in stepped piles" like the pyramids; which Lane ii. 495, renders "on the stairs"); Makáríj (plur. of Makraj, a small pot); Damálíj (plur. of dumlúj, a bracelet, a bangle); Dayábíj (brocades) and Tafáríj (openings, enjoyments). In Night cccxxx. we find also Sikábíj (plur. of Sikbáj, marinated meat else-where explained); Faráríj (plur. of farrúj, a chicken, vulg. farkh) and Dakákíj (plur. of dakújah, a small jar). In the first line we have also (though not a rhyme) Gharánik Gr. Τεραυòς, a crane, preserved in Romaic. The weeping and wailing are caused by the remembrance that all these delicacies have been demolished like a Badawi camp.

Presently they set before the King choice wines in flagons of glass and he drank: then he passed on the cup to me; and I kissed the ground and drank and wrote on it:—

With fire they boilèd me to loose my tongue,[1] * And pain and patience gave
    for fellowship:
Hence comes it hands of men upbear me high * And honey-dew from lips of
    maid I sip!

And these also:—

Morn saith to Night, "withdraw and let me shine;" * So drain we draughts
    that dull all pain and pine:[2]
I doubt, so fine the glass, the wine so clear, * If 'tis the wine in glass or glass
    in wine.

The King read my verse and said with a sigh, "Were these gifts[3] in a man, he would excel all the folk of his time and age!" Then he called for the chess-board, and said, "Say, wilt thou play with me?"; and I signed with my head, "Yes." Then I came forward and ordered the pieces and played with him two games, both of which I won. He was speechless with surprise; so I took the pen-case and, drawing forth a reed, wrote on the board these two couplets:—

Two hosts fare fighting thro' the livelong day * Nor is their battling ever
    finishèd,
Until, when darkness girdeth them about, * The twain go sleeping in a
    single bed.[4]

The King read these lines with wonder and delight and said to his Eunuch,[5] "O Mukbil, go to thy mistress, Sitt al-Husn,[6] and say her, 'Come, speak the King who biddeth thee hither to take

---

[1] This is the *vinum coctum*, the boiled wine, still a favourite in Southern Italy and Greece.

[2] Eastern topers delight in drinking at dawn: upon this subject I shall have more to say in other Nights.

[3] Arab. "Adab," a *crux* to translators, meaning anything between good education and good manners. In mod. Turk. "Edibiyyet" (Adabiyat) = belles lettres and "Edebi" or "Edíb" = a littérateur.

[4] The Caliph Al-Maamún, who was a bad player, used to say, "I have the administration of the world and am equal to it, whereas I am straitened in the ordering of a space of two spans by two spans." The "board" was then "a square field of well-dressed leather."

[5] The Rabbis (after Matth. xix. 12) count three kinds of Eunuchs; (1) Seris chammah = of the sun, *i.e.* natural; (2) Seris Adam = manufactured *per homines*; and (3) Seris Chammayim = of God (*i.e.* religious abstainer). Seris (castrated) or Abd (slave) is the general Hebrew name.

[6] The "Lady of Beauty."

thy solace in seeing this right wondrous ape!'" So the Eunuch went out and presently returned with the lady who, when she saw me veiled her face and said, "O my father! hast thou lost all sense of honour? How cometh it thou art pleased to send for me and show me to strange men?" "O Sitt al-Husn," said he, "no man is here save this little foot-page and the Eunuch who reared thee and I, thy father. From whom, then, dost thou veil thy face?" She answered, "This whom thou deemest an ape is a young man, a clever and polite, a wise and learned and the son of a King; but he is ensorcelled and the Ifrit Jirjaris, who is of the seed of Iblis, cast a spell upon him, after putting to death his own wife the daughter of King Ifitamus lord of the Islands of Abnus." The King marvelled at his daughter's words and, turning to me, said, "Is this true that she saith of thee?"; and I signed by a nod of my head the answer, "Yea, verily;" and wept sore. Then he asked his daughter, "Whence knewest thou that he is ensorcelled?"; and she answered, "O my dear papa, there was with me in my childhood an old woman, a wily one and a wise and a witch to boot, and she taught me the theory of magic and its practice; and I took notes in writing and therein waxed perfect, and have committed to memory an hundred and seventy chapters of egromantic formulas, by the least of which I could transport the stones of thy city behind the Mountain Kaf and the Circumambient Main,[1] or make its site an abyss of the sea and its people fishes swimming in the midst of it." "O my daughter," said her father, "I conjure thee, by my life, disenchant this young man, that I may make him my Wazir and marry thee to him, for indeed he is an ingenious youth and a deeply learned." "With joy and goodly gree," she replied and, hending in hand an iron knife whereon was inscribed the name of Allah in Hebrew characters, she described a wide circle——And Shahrazad perceived the dawn of day and ceased saying her permitted say.

𝔚hen it was the 𝔉ourteenth 𝔑ight,

She said, It hath reached me, O auspicious King, that the Kalandar continued his tale thus:—O my lady, the King's daughter hent in

---

1 "Káf" has been noticed as the mountain which surrounds earth as a ring does the finger: it is popularly used like our Alp and Alpine. The "circumambient Ocean" (Bahr al-muhit) is the Homeric Ocean-stream.

hand a knife whereon were inscribed Hebrew characters and described a wide circle in the midst of the palace-hall, and therein wrote in Cufic letters mysterious names and talismans; and she uttered words and muttered charms, some of which we understood and others we understood not. Presently the world waxed dark before our sight till we thought that the sky was falling upon our heads, and lo! the Ifrit presented himself in his own shape and aspect. His hands were like many-pronged pitch-forks, his legs like the masts of great ships, and his eyes like cressets of gleaming fire. We were in terrible fear of him but the King's daughter cried at him, "No welcome to thee and no greeting, O dog!" whereupon he changed to the form of a lion and said, "O traitress, how is it thou hast broken the oath we sware that neither should contraire other!" "O accursed one," answered she, "how could there be a compact between me and the like of thee?" Then said he, "Take what thou has brought on thyself;" and the lion opened his jaws and rushed upon her; but she was too quick for him; and, plucking a hair from her head, waved it in the air muttering over it the while; and the hair straightway became a trenchant sword-blade, wherewith she smote the lion and cut him in twain. Then the two halves flew away in air and the head changed to a scorpion and the Princess became a huge serpent and set upon the accursed scorpion, and the two fought, coiling and uncoiling, a stiff fight for an hour at least. Then the scorpion changed to a vulture and the serpent became an eagle which set upon the vulture, and hunted him for an hour's time, till he became a black tom-cat, which miauled and grinned and spat. Thereupon the eagle changed into a piebald wolf and these two battled in the palace for a long time, when the cat, seeing himself overcome, changed into a worm and crept into a huge red pomegranate,[1] which lay beside the jetting fountain in the midst of the palace hall. Whereupon the pomegranate swelled to the size of a water-melon in air; and, falling upon the marble pavement of the palace, broke to pieces, and all the grains fell out and were scattered about till they covered the whole floor. Then the wolf shook himself and became a snow-white cock, which fell to picking up

---

[1] The pomegranate is probably chosen here because each fruit is supposed to contain one seed from Eden-garden. Hence a host of superstitions (Pilgrimage iii., 104) possibly connected with the Chaldaic-Babylonian god Rimmon or Ramanu. Hence Persephone or Ishtar tasted the "rich pomegranate's seed." Lenormant, loc. cit. pp. 166, 182.

the grains purposing not to leave one; but by doom of destiny one seed rolled to the fountain-edge and there lay hid. The cock fell to crowing and clapping his wings and signing to us with his beak as if to ask, "Are any grains left?" But we understood not what he meant, and he cried to us with so loud a cry that we thought the palace would fall upon us. Then he ran over all the floor till he saw the grain which had rolled to the fountain edge, and rushed eagerly to pick it up when behold, it sprang into the midst of the water and became a fish and dived to the bottom of the basin. Thereupon the cock changed to a big fish, and plunged in after the other, and the two disappeared for a while and lo! we heard loud shrieks and cries of pain which made us tremble. After this the Ifrit rose out of the water, and he was as a burning flame; casting fire and smoke from his mouth and eyes and nostrils. And immediately the Princess likewise came forth from the basin and she was one live coal of flaming lowe; and these two, she and he, battled for the space of an hour, until their fires entirely compassed them about and their thick smoke filled the palace. As for us we panted for breath, being well-nigh suffocated, and we longed to plunge into the water fearing lest we be burnt up and utterly destroyed; and the King said, "There is no Majesty and there is no Might save in Allah the Glorious, the Great! Verily we are Allah's and unto Him are we returning! Would Heaven I had not urged my daughter to attempt the disenchantment of this ape-fellow, whereby I have imposed upon her the terrible task of fighting yon accursed Ifrit against whom all the Ifrits in the world could not prevail. And would Heaven we had never seen this ape, Allah never assain nor bless the day of his coming! We thought to do a good deed by him before the face of Allah,[1] and to release him from enchantment, and now we have brought this trouble and travail upon our heart." But I, O my lady, was tongue-tied and powerless to say a word to him. Suddenly, ere we were ware of aught, the Ifrit yelled out from under the flames and, coming up to us as we stood on the estrade, blew fire in our faces. The damsel overtook him and breathed blasts of fire at his face and the sparks from her and from him rained down upon us, and her sparks did us no harm, but one of his sparks alighted upon my eye and destroyed it making me a monocular ape; and another fell on the King's face

---

[1] i.e. for the love of God—a favourite Moslem phrase.

scorching the lower half, burning off his beard and mustachios and causing his under teeth to fall out; while a third alighted on the Castrato's breast, killing him on the spot. So we despaired of life and made sure of death when lo! a voice repeated the say-ing, "Allah is most Highest! Allah is most Highest! Aidance and victory to all who the Truth believe; and disappointment and disgrace to all who the religion of Mohammed, the Moon of Faith, unbelieve." The speaker was the Princess who had burnt the Ifrit, and he was become a heap of ashes. Then she came up to us and said, "Reach me a cup of water." They brought it to her and she spoke over it words we understood not, and sprinkling me with it cried, "By virtue of the Truth, and by the Most Great name of Allah, I charge thee return to thy former shape." And behold, I shook, and became a man as before, save that I had utterly lost an eye. Then she cried out, "The fire! The fire! O my dear papa an arrow from the accursed hath wounded me to the death, for I am not used to fight with the Jann; had he been a man I had slain him in the beginning. I had no trouble till the time when the pomegranate burst and the grains scattered, but I overlooked the seed wherein was the very life of the Jinni. Had I picked it up he had died on the spot, but as Fate and Fortune decreed, I saw it not; so he came upon me all unawares and there befel between him and me a sore struggle under the earth and high in air and in the water; and, as often as I opened on him a gate,[1] he opened on me another gate and a stronger, till at last he opened on me the gate of fire, and few are saved upon whom the door of fire openeth. But Destiny willed that my cunning prevail over his cunning; and I burned him to death after I vainly exhorted him to embrace the religion of Al-Islam. As for me I am a dead woman; Allah supply my place to you!" Then she called upon Heaven for help and ceased not to implore relief from the fire; when lo! a black spark shot up from her robed feet to her thighs; then it flew to her bosom and thence to her face. When it reached her face she wept and said, "I testify that there is no god but *the* God and that Mahommed is the Apostle of God!" And we looked at her and saw naught but a heap of ashes by the side of the heap

---

[1] Arab. "Báb," also meaning a chapter (of magic, of war, etc.), corresponding with the Persian "Dar" as in Sad-dar, the Hundred Doors. Here, however, it is figurative "I tried a new mode." This scene is in the Mabinogion.

that had been the Ifrit. We mourned for her and I wished I had
been in her place, so had I not seen her lovely face who had
worked me such weal become ashes; but there is no gainsaying
the will of Allah. When the King saw his daughter's terrible
death, he plucked out what was left of his beard and beat his face
and rent his raiment; and I did as he did and we both wept over
her. Then came in the Chamberlains and Grandees and were
amazed to find two heaps of ashes and the Sultan in a fainting
fit; so they stood round him till he revived and told them what
had befallen his daughter from the Ifrit; whereat their grief was
right grievous and the women and the slave-girls shrieked and
keened,[1] and they continued their lamentations for the space of
seven days. Moreover the King bade build over his daughter's
ashes a vast vaulted tomb, and burn therein wax tapers and
sepulchral lamps: but as for the Ifrit's ashes they scattered them
on the winds, speeding them to the curse of Allah. Then the
Sultan fell sick of a sickness that well nigh brought him to his
death for a month's space; and, when health returned to him and
his beard grew again and he had been converted by the mercy of
Allah to Al-Islam, he sent for me and said, "O youth, Fate had
decreed for us the happiest of lives, safe from all the chances and
changes of Time, till thou camest to us, when troubles fell upon
us. Would to Heaven we had never seen thee and the foul face
of thee! For we took pity on thee and thereby we have lost our
all. I have on thy account first lost my daughter who to me was
well worth an hundred men, secondly I have suffered that which
befel me by reason of the fire and the loss of my teeth, and my
Eunuch also was slain. I blame thee not, for it was out of thy
power to prevent this: the doom of Allah was on thee as well as
on us and thanks be to the Almighty for that my daughter delivered thee, albeit thereby she lost her own life! Go forth now,
O my son, from this my city, and suffice thee what hath befallen
us through thee, even although 'twas decreed for us. Go forth
in peace; and if I ever see thee again I will surely slay thee."

---

[1] I use this Irish term = crying for the dead; as English wants the word for the præfica
or myrialogist. The practice is not encouraged in Al-Islam; and Caliph Abu Bakr said,
"Verily a corpse is sprinkled with boiling water by reason of the lamentations of the living," i. e. punished for not having taken measures to prevent their profitless lamentations.
But the practice is from Negroland whence it reached Egypt; and the people have there
developed a curious system in the "weeping-song": I have noted this in "The Lake-
Regions of Central Africa." In Zoroastrianism (Dabistan, chapt. xcvii.) tears shed for
the dead form a river in hell, black and frigid.

And he cried out at me. So I went forth from his presence, O
my lady, weeping bitterly and hardly believing in my escape
and knowing not whither I should wend. And I recalled all
that had befallen me, my meeting the tailor, my love for the
damsel in the palace beneath the earth, and my narrow escape
from the Ifrit, even after he had determined to do me die; and
how I had entered the city as an ape and was now leaving it a
man once more. Then I gave thanks to Allah and said, "My
eye and not my life!" and before leaving the place I entered the
bath and shaved my poll and beard and mustachios and eyebrows; and cast ashes on my head and donned the coarse black
woollen robe of a Kalandar. Then I fared forth, O my lady,
and every day I pondered all the calamities which had betided me,
and I wept and repeated these couplets:—

"I am distraught, yet verily His ruth abides with me, * Tho' round me
    gather hosts of ills, whence come I cannot see:
Patient I'll be till Patience self with me impatient wax; * Patient for ever till
    the Lord fulfil my destiny:
Patient I'll bide without complaint, a wronged and vanquisht man; * Patient
    as sunparcht wight that spans the desert's sandy sea:
Patient I'll be till Aloe's¹ self unwittingly allow * I'm patient under bitterer
    things than bitterest aloë:
No bitterer things than aloes or than patience for mankind; * Yet bitterer
    than the twain to me were Patience' treachery:
My sere and seamed and seared brow would dragoman my sore * If soul could
    search my sprite and there unsecret secrecy:
Were hills to bear the load I bear they'd crumble 'neath the weight; * 'Twould
    still the roaring wind, 'twould quench the flame-tongue's flagrancy,
And whoso saith the world is sweet certès a day he'll see * With more than
    aloes' bitterness and aloes' pungency."

Then I journeyed through many regions and saw many a city
intending for Baghdad, that I might seek audience, in the House

---

¹ These lines are hardly translatable. Arab. "Sabr" means "patience" as well as
"aloes," hereby lending itself to a host of puns and double entendres more or less vile.
The aloe, according to Burckhardt, is planted in graveyards as a lesson of patience: it
is also slung, like the dried crocodile, over house-doors to prevent evil spirits entering:
"thus hung without earth and water," says Lane (M. E., chapt. xi.), "it will live for
several years and even blossom. Hence (?) it is called *Sabr*, which signifies patience."
But Sibr as well as Sabr (a root) means "long-sufferance." I hold the practise to be
one of the many Inner African superstitions. The wild Gallas to the present day plant
aloes on graves, and suppose that when the plant sprouts the deceased has been admitted
to the gardens of Wák, the Creator. (Pilgrimage iii. 350.)

of Peace,[1] with the Commander of the Faithful and tell him all
that had befallen me. I arrived here this very night and found
my brother in Allah, this first Kalandar, standing about as one
perplexed; so I saluted him with "Peace be upon thee," and entered into discourse with him. Presently up came our brother,
this third Kalandar, and said to us, "Peace be with you! I am a
stranger;" whereto we replied, "And we too be strangers, who
have come hither this blessed night." So we all three walked on
together, none of us knowing the other's history, till Destiny
drave us to this door and we came in to you. Such then is my
story and my reason for shaving my beard and mustachios, and
this is what caused the loss of my eye. Said the house-mistress,
"Thy tale is indeed a rare; so rub thy head and wend thy ways;"
but he replied, "I will not budge till I hear my companions'
stories." Then came forward the third Kalandar, and said, "O
illustrious lady! my history is not like that of these my comrades,
but more wondrous and far more marvellous. In their case Fate
and Fortune came down on them unawares; but I drew down
destiny upon my own head and brought sorrow on mine own
soul, and shaved my own beard and lost my own eye. Hear then

The Third Kalandar's Tale.

KNOW, O my lady, that I also am a King and the son of a King
and my name is Ajíb son of Khazíb. When my father died I
succeeded him; and I ruled and did justice and dealt fairly by all
my lieges. I delighted in sea trips, for my capital stood on the
shore, before which the ocean stretched far and wide; and nearhand were many great islands with sconces and garrisons in the
midst of the main. My fleet numbered fifty merchantmen, and as
many yachts for pleasance, and an hundred and fifty sail ready
fitted for holy war with the Unbelievers. It fortuned that I had
a mind to enjoy myself on the islands aforesaid, so I took ship with
my people in ten keel; and, carrying with me a month's victual,
I set out on a twenty days' voyage. But one night a head wind
struck us, and the sea rose against us with huge waves; the
billows sorely buffeted us and a dense darkness settled round us.
We gave ourselves up for lost and I said, "Whoso endangereth his

---

[1] Every city in the East has its specific title: this was given to Baghdad either on account of its superior police or simply because it was the Capital of the Caliphate. The
Tigris was also called the "River of Peace (or Security)."

days, e'en an he 'scape deserveth no praise." Then we prayed
to Allah and besought Him; but the storm-blasts ceased not to
blow against us nor the surges to strike us till morning broke,
when the gale fell, the seas sank to mirrory stillness and the sun
shone upon us kindly clear. Presently we made an island where
we landed and cooked somewhat of food, and ate heartily and
took our rest for a couple of days. Then we set out again
and sailed other twenty days, the seas broadening and the land
shrinking. Presently the current ran counter to us, and we
found ourselves in strange waters, where the Captain had lost
his reckoning, and was wholly bewildered in this sea; so said we
to the look-out man,[1] "Get thee to the mast-head and keep thine
eyes open." He swarmed up the mast and looked out and cried
aloud, "O Rais, I espy to starboard something dark, very like a
fish floating on the face of the sea, and to larboard there is a
loom in the midst of the main, now black and now bright." When
the Captain heard the look-out's words he dashed his turband on
the deck and plucked out his beard and beat his face saying,
"Good news indeed! we be all dead men; not one of us can be
saved." And he fell to weeping and all of us wept for his weeping and also for our lives; and I said, "O Captain, tell us what it is
the look-out saw." "O my Prince," answered he, "know that
we lost our course on the night of the storm, which was followed
on the morrow by a two-days' calm during which we made no
way; and we have gone astray eleven days reckoning from that
night, with ne'er a wind to bring us back to our true course.
To-morrow by the end of the day we shall come to a mountain of
black stone, hight the Magnet Mountain;[2] for thither the currents carry us willy-nilly. As soon as we are under its lea, the

---

[1] This is very characteristic: the passengers finding themselves in difficulties at once
take command. See in my Pilgrimage (I. chapt. xi.) how we beat and otherwise mal-
treated the Captain of the "Golden Wire."

[2] The fable is probably based on the currents which, as in Eastern Africa, will carry a
ship fifty miles a day out of her course. We first find it in Ptolemy (vii. 2) whose Man-
iólai Islands, of India extra Gangem, cause iron nails to fly out of ships, the effect of
the Lapis Herculeus (Loadstone). Rabelais (v. c. 37) alludes to it and to the vulgar idea
of magnetism being counteracted by Skordon (*Scordon* or garlic). Hence too the Adamant
(Loadstone) Mountains of Mandeville (chapt. xxvii.) and the "Magnetic Rock" in Mr.
Puttock's clever "Peter Wilkins." I presume that the myth also arose from seeing craft
built, as on the East African Coast, without iron nails. We shall meet with the legend
again. The word Jabal ("Jebel" in Egypt) often occurs in these pages. The Arabs
apply it to any rising ground or heap of rocks; so it is not always = our mountain. It
has found its way to Europe *e. g.* Gibraltar and Monte Gibello (or Mongibel in poetry) =
"Mt. Ethne that men clepen Mounte Gybelle." Other special senses of Jabal will occur.

ship's sides will open and every nail in plank will fly out and cleave fast to the mountain; for that Almighty Allah hath gifted the loadstone with a mysterious virtue and a love for iron, by reason whereof all which is iron travelleth towards it; and on this mountain is much iron, how much none knoweth save the Most High, from the many vessels which have been lost there since the days of yore. The bright spot upon its summit is a dome of yellow laton from Andalusia, vaulted upon ten columns; and on its crown is a horseman who rideth a horse of brass and holdeth in hand a lance of laton; and there hangeth on his bosom a tablet of lead graven with names and talismans." And he presently added, "And, O King, none destroyeth folk save the rider on that steed, nor will the egromancy be dispelled till he fall from his horse."[1] Then, O my lady, the Captain wept with exceeding weeping and we all made sure of death-doom and each and every one of us farewelled his friend and charged him with his last will and testament in case he might be saved. We slept not that night and in the morning we found ourselves much nearer the Loadstone Mountain, whither the waters drave us with a violent send. When the ships were close under its lea they opened and the nails flew out and all the iron in them sought the Magnet Mountain and clove to it like a network; so that by the end of the day we were all struggling in the waves round about the mountain. Some of us were saved, but more were drowned and even those who had escaped knew not one another, so stupefied were they by the beating of the billows and the raving of the winds. As for me, O my lady, Allah (be His name exalted!) preserved my life that I might suffer whatso He willed to me of hardship, misfortune and calamity; for I scrambled upon a plank from one of the ships, and the wind and waters

---

1 As we learn from the Nubian Geographer the Arabs in early ages explored the Fortunate Islands (Jazírát al-Khálidát = Eternal Isles), or Canaries, on one of which were reported a horse and horseman in bronze with his spear pointing west. Ibn al-Wardi notes "two images of hard stone, each an hundred cubits high, and upon the top of each a figure of copper pointing with its hand backwards, as though it would say:—Return for there is nothing behind me!" But this legend attaches to older doings. The 23rd Tobba (who succeeded Bilkis), Malik bin Sharhabíl, (or Sharabíl or Sharahíl) surnamed Náshir al-Ni'ám = scatterer of blessings, lost an army in attempting the Western sands and set up a statue of copper upon whose breast was inscribed in antique characters:—

There is no access behind me,
Nothing beyond,
(Saith) The Son of Sharabíl.

threw it at the feet of the Mountain. There I found a practicable path leading by steps carven out of the rock to the summit, and I called on the name of Allah Almighty"[1]——And Shahrazad perceived the dawn of day and ceased to say her permitted say.

When it was the Fifteenth Night,

She continued, It hath reached me, O auspicious King, that the third Kalandar said to the lady (the rest of the party sitting fast bound and the slaves standing with swords drawn over their heads):—And after calling on the name of Almighty Allah and passionately beseeching Him, I breasted the ascent, clinging to the steps and notches hewn in the stone, and mounted little by little. And the Lord stilled the wind and aided me in the ascent, so that I succeeded in reaching the summit. There I found no resting-place save the dome, which I entered, joying with exceeding joy at my escape; and made the Wuzu-ablution[2] and prayed a two-bow prayer,[3] a thanksgiving to God for my preservation. Then I fell asleep under the dome, and heard in my dream a mysterious Voice[4] saying, "O son of Khazib! when thou wakest from thy sleep dig under thy feet and thou shalt find a bow of brass and three leaden arrows, inscribed with talismans and characts. Take the bow and shoot the arrows at the horseman on the dome-top and free mankind from this sore calamity. When thou hast shot him he shall fall into the sea, and the horse will also drop at thy feet: then bury it in the place of the bow. This done, the main will swell and rise till it is level with the mountain-head, and there will appear on it a skiff carrying a man of laton (other than he thou shalt have shot) holding in his hand a pair of paddles. He will come to thee and do thou embark with him but beware of saying Bismillah or of otherwise naming Allah Almighty. He will row thee for a space of ten days, till he bring thee to certain Islands called the Islands of Safety, and thence thou shalt easily reach a port and find those who will convey thee

---

[1] *i. e.* I exclaimed "Bismillah!"

[2] The lesser ablution of hands, face and feet; a kind of "washing the points." More in Night ccccxl.

[3] Arab. "Ruka'tayn"; the number of these bows which are followed by the prostrations distinguishes the five daily prayers.

[4] The "Beth Kol" of the Hebrews; also called by the Moslems "Hátif"; for which ask the Spiritualists. It is the Hindu "voice divine" or "voice from heaven."

to thy native land; and all this shall be fulfilled to thee so thou call not on the name of Allah." Then I started up from my sleep in joy and gladness and, hastening to do the bidding of the mysterious Voice, found the bow and arrows and shot at the horseman and tumbled him into the main, whilst the horse dropped at my feet; so I took it and buried it. Presently the sea surged up and rose till it reached the top of the mountain; nor had I long to wait ere I saw a skiff in the offing coming towards me. I gave thanks to Allah; and, when the skiff came up to me, I saw therein a man of brass with a tablet of lead on his breast inscribed with talismans and characts; and I embarked without uttering a word. The boatman rowed on with me through the first day and the second and the third, in all ten whole days, till I caught sight of the Islands of Safety; whereat I joyed with exceeding joy and for stress of gladness exclaimed, "Allah! Allah! In the name of Allah! There is no god but *the* God and Allah is Almighty."[1] Thereupon the skiff forthwith upset and cast me upon the sea; then it righted and sank deep into the depths. Now I am a fair swimmer, so I swam the whole day till nightfall, when my forearms and shoulders were numbed with fatigue and I felt like to die; so I testified to my faith, expecting naught but death. The sea was still surging under the violence of the winds, and presently there came a billow like a hillock; and, bearing me up high in air, threw me with a long cast on dry land, that His will might be fulfilled. I crawled up the beach and doffing my raiment wrung it out to dry and spread it in the sunshine: then I lay me down and slept the whole night. As soon as it was day, I donned my clothes and rose to look whither I should walk. Presently I came to a thicket of low trees; and, making a cast round it, found that the spot whereon I stood was an islet, a mere holm, girt on all sides by the ocean; whereupon I said to myself, "Whatso freeth me from one great calamity casteth me into a greater!" But while I was pondering my case and longing for death behold, I saw afar off a ship making for the island; so I clomb a tree and hid myself among the branches. Presently the ship anchored and landed ten slaves, blackamoors, bearing iron hoes and baskets, who walked on till they reached the middle of the island. Here they dug deep into the ground, until they uncovered a plate of metal

---

[1] These formulæ are technically called Tasmiyah, Tahlíl (before noted) and Takbír: the "testifying" is Tashhíd.

which they lifted, thereby opening a trap-door. After this they returned to the ship and thence brought bread and flour, honey and fruits, clarified butter,[1] leather bottles containing liquors and many household stuffs; also furniture, table-service and mirrors; rugs, carpets and in fact all needed to furnish a dwelling; and they kept going to and fro, and descending by the trap-door, till they had transported into the dwelling all that was in the ship. After this the slaves again went on board and brought back with them garments as rich as may be, and in the midst of them came an old, old man, of whom very little was left, for Time had dealt hardly and harshly with him, and all that remained of him was a bone wrapped in a rag of blue stuff through which the winds whistled west and east. As saith the poet of him:—

Time gars me tremble Ah, how sore the baulk! * While Time in pride of
    strength doth ever stalk:
Time was I walked nor ever felt I tired, * Now am I tired albe I never
    walk!

And the Shaykh held by the hand a youth cast in beauty's mould, all elegance and perfect grace; so fair that his comeliness deserved to be proverbial; for he was as a green bough or the tender young of the roe, ravishing every heart with his loveliness and subduing every soul with his coquetry and amorous ways.[2] It was of him the poet spake when he said:—

Beauty they brought with him to make compare; * But Beauty hung her head
    in shame and care:
Quoth they, "O Beauty, hast thou seen his like?" * And Beauty cried, "His
    like? not anywhere!"

They stinted not their going, O my lady, till all went down by the trap-door and did not reappear for an hour, or rather more; at the end of which time the slaves and the old man came up without

---

[1] Arab. "Samn," (Pers. "Raughan" Hind. "Ghi") the "single sauce" of the East; fresh butter set upon the fire, skimmed and kept (for a century if required) in leather bottles and demijohns. Then it becomes a hard black mass, considered a panacea for wounds and diseases. It is very "filling": you say jocosely to an Eastern threatened with a sudden inroad of guests, "Go, swamp thy rice with Raughan." I once tried training, like a Hindu Pahlawan or athlete, on Gur (raw sugar), milk and Ghi; and the result was being blinded by bile before the week ended.

[2] These handsome youths are always described in the terms we should apply to women.

the youth and, replacing the iron plate and carefully closing the door-slab as it was before, they returned to the ship and made sail and were lost to my sight. When they turned away to depart, I came down from the tree and, going to the place I had seen them fill up, scraped off and removed the earth; and in patience possessed my soul till I had cleared the whole of it away. Then appeared the trap-door which was of wood, in shape and size like a millstone; and when I lifted it up it disclosed a winding stair-case of stone. At this I marvelled and, descending the steps till I reached the last, found a fair hall, spread with various kinds of carpets and silk stuffs, wherein was a youth sitting upon a raised couch and leaning back on a round cushion with a fan in his hand and nosegays and posies of sweet scented herbs and flowers before him;[1] but he was alone and not a soul near him in the great vault. When he saw me he turned pale; but I saluted him cour-teously and said, "Set thy mind at ease and calm thy fears; no harm shall come near thee; I am a man like thyself and the son of a King to boot; whom the decrees of Destiny have sent to bear thee company and cheer thee in thy loneliness. But now tell me, what is thy story and what causeth thee to dwell thus in solitude under the ground?" When he was assured that I was of his kind and no Jinni, he rejoiced and his fine colour returned; and, making me draw near to him he said, "O my brother, my story is a strange story and 'tis this. My father is a merchant-jeweller possessed of great wealth, who hath white and black slaves travelling and trading on his account in ships and on camels, and trafficking with the most distant cities; but he was not blessed with a child, not even one. Now on a certain night he dreamed a dream that he should be favoured with a son, who would be short lived; so

---

1 The Bul. Edit. (i. 43) reads otherwise:—I found a garden and a second and a third and so on till they numbered thirty and nine; and, in each garden, I saw what praise will not express, of trees and rills and fruits and treasures. At the end of the last I sighted a door and said to myself, "What may be in this place?; needs must I open it and look in!" I did so accordingly and saw a courser ready saddled and bridled and picketed; so I loosed and mounted him; and he flew with me like a bird till he set me down on a terrace-roof; and, having landed me, he struck me a whisk with his tail and put out mine eye and fled from me. Thereupon I descended from the roof and found ten youths all blind of one eye who, when they saw me exclaimed, "No welcome to thee, and no good cheer!" I asked them, "Do ye admit me to your home and society?" and they answered, "No, by Allah, thou shalt not live amongst us." So I went forth with weeping eyes and grieving heart, but Allah had written my safety on the Guarded Tablet so I reached Baghdad in safety, etc. This is a fair specimen of how the work has been curtailed in that issue.

the morning dawned on my father bringing him woe and weeping. On the following night my mother conceived and my father
noted down the date of her becoming pregnant.[1] Her time being
fulfilled she bare me; whereat my father rejoiced and made banquets and called together the neighbors and fed the Fakirs and
the poor, for that he had been blessed with issue near the end of
his days. Then he assembled the astrologers and astronomers
who knew the places of the planets, and the wizards and wise
ones of the time, and men learned in horoscopes and nativities;[2]
and they drew out my birth scheme and said to my father, "Thy
son shall live to fifteen years, but in his fifteenth there is a sinister
aspect; an he safely tide it over he shall attain a great age. And
the cause that threateneth him with death is this. In the Sea of
Peril standeth the Mountain Magnet hight; on whose summit is a
horseman of yellow laton seated on a horse also of brass and
bearing on his breast a tablet of lead. Fifty days after this rider
shall fall from his steed thy son will die and his slayer will be he
who shoots down the horseman, a Prince named Ajib son of King
Khazib." My father grieved with exceeding grief to hear these
words; but reared me in tenderest fashion and educated me excellently well until my fifteenth year was told. Ten days ago news
came to him that the horseman had fallen into the sea and he who
shot him down was named Ajib son of King Khazib. My father
thereupon wept bitter tears at the need of parting with me and
became like one possessed of a Jinni. However, being in mortal
fear for me, he built me this place under the earth; and, stocking it
with all required for the few days still remaining, he brought me
hither in a ship and left me here. Ten are already past and, when
the forty shall have gone by without danger to me, he will come
and take me away; for he hath done all this only in fear of Prince
Ajib. Such, then, is my story and the cause of my loneliness."

---

[1] Arabs date pregnancy from the stopping of the menses, upon which the fœtus is
supposed to feed. Kalilah wa Dimnah says, "The child's navel adheres to that of his
mother and thereby he sucks" (i. 263).

[2] This is contrary to the commands of Al-Islam; Mohammed expressly said "The
Astrologers are liars, by the Lord of the Ka'abah!"; and his saying is known to almost
all Moslems, lettered or unlettered. Yet, the further we go East (Indiawards) the more
we find these practises held in honour. Turning westwards we have:

Iuridicis, Erebo, Fisco, fas vivere rapto:
Militibus, Medicis, Tortori occidere ludo est;
Mentiri Astronomis, Pictoribus atque Poetis.

When I heard his history I marvelled and said in my mind, "I am the Prince Ajib who hath done all this; but as Allah is with me I will surely not slay him!" So said I to him, "O my lord, far from thee be this hurt and harm and then, please Allah, thou shalt not suffer cark nor care nor aught disquietude, for I will tarry with thee and serve thee as a servant, and then wend my ways; and after having borne thee company during the forty days, I will go with thee to thy home where thou shalt give me an escort of some of thy Mamelukes with whom I may journey back to my own city; and the Almighty shall requite thee for me." He was glad to hear these words, when I rose and lighted a large wax-candle and trimmed the lamps and the three lanterns; and I set on meat and drink and sweetmeats. We ate and drank and sat talking over various matters till the greater part of the night was gone; when he lay down to rest and I covered him up and went to sleep myself. Next morning I arose and warmed a little water, then lifted him gently so as to awake him and brought him the warm water wherewith he washed his face[1] and said to me, "Heaven requite thee for me with every blessing, O youth! By Allah, if I get quit of this danger and am saved from him whose name is Ajib bin Khazib, I will make my father reward thee and send thee home healthy and wealthy; and, if I die, then my blessing be upon thee." I answered, "May the day never dawn on which evil shall betide thee; and may Allah make my last day before thy last day!" Then I set before him somewhat of food and we ate; and I got ready perfumes for fumigating the hall, wherewith he was pleased. Moreover I made him a Mankalah-cloth;[2] and we played and ate sweetmeats and we played again and took our pleasure till nightfall, when I rose and lighted the lamps, and set before him somewhat to eat, and sat telling him stories till the hours of darkness were far spent. Then he lay down to rest and I covered him up and rested also. And thus I continued to do, O my lady, for days and nights and affection for him took root in my heart and my sorrow was eased, and I said to myself, "The

---

1 He does not perform the Wuzu or lesser ablution because he neglects his dawn prayers.
2 For this game see Lane (M. E. Chapt. xvii.) It is usually played on a checked cloth not on a board like our draughts; and Easterns are fond of eating, drinking and smoking between and even during the games. Torrens (p. 142) translates "I made up some dessert," confounding "Mankalah" with "Nukl" (dried fruit, quatre-mendiants).

astrologers lied[1] when they predicted that he should be slain by
Ajib bin Khazib: by Allah, I will not slay him." I ceased not
ministering to him and conversing and carousing with him and
telling him all manner tales for thirty-nine days. On the fortieth
night[2] the youth rejoiced and said, "O my brother, Alhamdolillah!—praise be to Allah—who hath preserved me from death
and this is by thy blessing and the blessing of thy coming to me;
and I pray God that He restore thee to thy native land. But
now, O my brother, I would thou warm me some water for the
Ghusl-ablution and do thou kindly bathe me and change my
clothes." I replied, "With love and gladness;" and I heated
water in plenty and carrying it in to him washed his body all over,
the washing of health,[3] with meal of lupins[4] and rubbed him well
and changed his clothes and spread him a high bed whereon he
lay down to rest, being drowsy after bathing. Then said he, "O
my brother, cut me up a water-melon, and sweeten it with a little
sugar-candy."[5] So I went to the store-room and bringing out a
fine water-melon I found there, set it on a platter and laid it before
him saying, "O my master hast thou not a knife?" "Here it
is," answered he, "over my head upon the high shelf." So I got
up in haste and taking the knife drew it from its sheath; but my
foot slipped in stepping down and I fell heavily upon the youth
holding in my hand the knife which hastened to fulfil what had
been written on the Day that decided the destinies of man, and
buried itself, as if planted, in the youth's heart. He died on the
instant. When I saw that he was slain and knew that I had slain
him, maugre myself, I cried out with an exceeding loud and
bitter cry and beat my face and rent my raiment and said, "Verily
we be Allah's and unto Him we be returning, O Moslems! O folk
fain of Allah! there remained for this youth but one day of the
forty dangerous days which the astrologers and the learned had
foretold for him; and the predestined death of this beautiful one
was to be at my hand. Would Heaven I had not tried to cut the
water-melon. What dire misfortune is this I must bear lief or

---

[1] Quoted from Mohammed whose saying has been given.

[2] We should say "the night of the thirty-ninth."

[3] The bath first taken after sickness.

[4] Arab. "Dikák" used by way of soap or rather to soften the skin: the meal is usually
of lupins, "Adas"="*Revalenta Arabica*," which costs a penny in Egypt and half-a-crown
in England.

[5] Arab. "Sukkar-nabát." During my day (1842-49) we had no other sugar in the
Bombay Presidency.

loath? What a disaster! What an affliction! O Allah mine, I implore thy pardon and declare to Thee my innocence of his death. But what God willeth let that come to pass."[1]——And Shahrazad perceived the dawn of day and ceased to say her permitted say.

When it was the Sixteenth Night,

She said, It hath reached me, O auspicious King, that Ajib thus continued his tale to the lady:—When I was certified that I had slain him, I arose and ascending the stairs replaced the trap-door and covered it with earth as before. Then I looked out seawards and saw the ship cleaving the waters and making for the island, wherefore I was afeard and said, "The moment they come and see the youth done to death, they will know 'twas I who slew him and will slay me without respite." So I climbed up into a high tree and concealed myself among its leaves; and hardly had I done so when the ship anchored and the slaves landed with the ancient man, the youth's father, and made direct for the place and when they removed the earth they were surprised to see it soft.[2] Then they raised the trap-door and went down and found the youth lying at full length, clothed in fair new garments, with a face beaming after the bath, and the knife deep in his heart. At the sight they shrieked and wept and beat their faces, loudly cursing the murderer; whilst a swoon came over the Shaykh so that the slaves deemed him dead, unable to survive his son. At last they wrapped the slain youth in his clothes and carried him up and laid him on the ground covering him with a shroud of silk. Whilst they were making for the ship the old man revived; and, gazing on his son who was stretched out, fell on the ground and strewed dust over his head and smote his face and plucked out his beard; and his weeping redoubled as he thought of his murdered son and he swooned away once more. After awhile a slave went and fetched a strip of silk whereupon they lay the old man and sat down at his head. All this took place and I was on the tree above them watching everything that came to pass; and my heart

---

1 This is one of the myriad Arab instances that the decrees of "Anagké," Fate, Destiny, Weird, are inevitable. The situation is highly dramatic; and indeed The Nights, as will appear in the Terminal Essay, have already suggested a national drama.
2 Having lately been moved by Ajib.

became hoary before my head waxed grey, for the hard lot which was mine, and for the distress and anguish I had undergone, and I fell to reciting:—

"How many a joy by Allah's will hath fled * With flight escaping sight of
     wisest head!
How many a sadness shall begin the day, * Yet grow right gladsome ere the
     day is sped!
How many a weal trips on the heels of ill, * Causing the mourner's heart
     with joy to thrill!"[1]

But the old man, O my lady, ceased not from his swoon till near sunset, when he came to himself and, looking upon his dead son, he recalled what had happened, and how what he had dreaded had come to pass; and he beat his face and head and recited these couplets:—

"Racked is my heart by parting fro' my friends * And two rills ever fro' my
     eyelids flow:
With them[2] went forth my hopes, Ah, well-away! * What shift remaineth me
     to say or do?
Would I had never looked upon their sight, * What shift, fair sirs, when paths
     e'er straiter grow?
What charm shall calm my pangs when this wise burn * Longings of love
     which in my vitals glow?
Would I had trod with them the road of Death! * Ne'er had befel us twain
     this parting-blow:
Allah: I pray the Ruthful show me ruth * And mix our lives nor part them
     evermo'e!
How blest were we as 'neath one roof we dwelt * Conjoined in joys nor
     recking aught of woe;
Till Fortune shot us with the severance shaft; * Ah who shall patient bear
     such parting throe?
And dart of Death struck down amid the tribe * The age's pearl that Morn
     saw brightest show:
I cried the while his case took speech and said:— * Would Heaven, my son,
     Death mote his doom foreslow!
Which be the readiest road wi' thee to meet * My Son! for whom I would my
     soul bestow?
If sun I call him no! the sun doth set; * If moon I call him, wane the moons;
     Ah no!

---

[1] Mr. Payne (i. 131) omits these lines which appear out of place; but this mode of inappropriate quotation is a characteristic of Eastern tales.
[2] Anglicè "him."

O sad mischance o' thee, O doom of days, * Thy place none other love shall
    ever know:
Thy sire distracted sees thee, but despairs * By wit or wisdom Fate to over-
    throw:
Some evil eye this day hath cast its spell * And foul befal him as it foul
    befel!"

Then he sobbed a single sob and his soul fled his flesh. The
slaves shrieked aloud, "Alas, our lord!" and showered dust on
their heads and redoubled their weeping and wailing. Presently
they carried their dead master to the ship side by side with his
dead son and, having transported all the stuff from the dwelling
to the vessel, set sail and disappeared from mine eyes. I descended from the tree and, raising the trap-door, went down into
the underground dwelling where everything reminded me of the
youth; and I looked upon the poor remains of him and began
repeating these verses:—

"Their tracks I see, and pine with pain and pang * And on deserted hearths
    I weep and yearn:
And Him I pray who doomèd them depart * Some day vouchsafe the boon of
    safe return."[1]

Then, O my lady, I went up again by the trap-door, and every day
I used to wander round about the island and every night I returned to the underground hall. Thus I lived for a month, till at
last, looking at the western side of the island, I observed that
every day the tibe ebbed, leaving shallow water for which the
flow did not compensate; and by the end of the month the sea
showed dry land in that direction. At this I rejoiced making
certain of my safety; so I arose and fording what little was left
of the water got me to the main land, where I fell in with great
heaps of loose sand in which even a camel's hoof would sink up
to the knee.[2] However I emboldened my soul and wading
through the sand behold, a fire shone from afar burning with a
blazing light.[3] So I made for it hoping haply to find succour, and
broke out into these verses:—

---

[1] This march of the tribe is a *lieu commun* of Arab verse *e. g.* the poet Labid's noble
elegy on the "Deserted Camp." We shall find scores of instances in The Nights.

[2] I have heard of such sands in the Desert east of Damascus which can be crossed only
on boards or camel furniture; and the same is reported of the infamous Region "Al-
Ahkláf" ("Unexplored Syria").

[3] Hence the Arab. saying "The bark of a dog and not the gleam of a fire;" the tired
traveller knows from the former that the camp is near, whereas the latter shows from
great distances.

"Belike my Fortune may her bridle turn * And Time bring weal although he's
    jealous hight;
Forward my hopes, and further all my needs, * And passèd ills with present
    weals requite."

And when I drew near the fire aforesaid lo! it was a palace with
gates of copper burnished red which, when the rising sun shone
thereon, gleamed and glistened from afar showing what had
seemed to me a fire. I rejoiced in the sight, and sat down over
against the gate, but I was hardly settled in my seat before there
met me ten young men clothed in sumptuous gear and all were
blind of the left eye which appeared as plucked out. They were
accompanied by a Shaykh, an old, old man, and much I marvelled
at their appearance, and their all being blind of the same eye.
When they saw me, they saluted me with the Salam and asked
me of my case and my history; whereupon I related to them all
what had befallen me, and what full measure of misfortune was
mine. Marvelling at my tale they took me to the mansion, where
I saw ranged round the hall ten couches each with its blue
bedding and coverlet of blue stuff[1] and amiddlemost stood a
smaller couch furnished like them with blue and nothing else. As
we entered each of the youths took his seat on his own couch and
the old man seated himself upon the smaller one in the middle
saying to me, "O youth, sit thee down on the floor and ask not of
our case nor of the loss of our eyes." Presently he rose up and set
before each young man some meat in a charger and drink in a
large mazer, treating me in like manner; and after that they sat
questioning me concerning my adventures and what had betided
me: and I kept telling them my tale till the night was far spent.
Then said the young men, "O our Shaykh, wilt not thou set before us our ordinary? The time is come." He replied, "With love
and gladness," and rose and entering a closet disappeared, but
presently returned bearing on his head ten trays each covered
with a strip of blue stuff. He set a tray before each youth and,

---

[1] Dark blue is the colour of mourning in Egypt as it was of the Roman Republic. The
Persians hold that this tint was introduced by Kay Kawús (B. C. 600) when mourning
for his son Siyáwush. It was continued till the death of Husayn on the 10th of Mu-
harram (the first month, then representing the vernal equinox) when it was changed
for black. As a rule Moslems do not adopt this symbol of sorrow (called "Hidád"),
looking upon the practice as somewhat idolatrous and foreign to Arab manners. In
Egypt and especially on the Upper Nile women dye their hands with indigo and stain
their faces black or blacker.

lighting ten wax candles, he stuck one upon each tray, and drew off the covers and lo! under them was naught but ashes and pow-dered charcoal and kettle soot. Then all the young men tucked up their sleeves to the elbows and fell a-weeping and wailing and they blackened their faces and smeared their clothes and buffetted their brows and beat their breasts, continually ex-claiming, "We were sitting at our ease but our frowardness brought us unease!" They ceased not to do this till dawn drew nigh, when the old man rose and heated water for them; and they washed their faces, and donned other and clean clothes. Now when I saw this, O my lady, for very wonderment my senses left me and my wits went wild and heart and head were full of thought, till I forgot what had betided me and I could not keep silence feeling I fain must speak out and question them of these strangenesses; so I said to them, "How come ye to do this after we have been so open-hearted and frolicksome? Thanks be to Allah ye be all sound and sane, yet actions such as these befit none but mad men or those possessed of an evil spirit. I conjure you by all that is dearest to you, why stint ye to tell me your history, and the cause of your losing your eyes and your blackening your faces with ashes and soot?" Hereupon they turned to me and said, "O young man, hearken not to thy youthtide's suggestions and question us no questions." Then they slept and I with them and when they awoke the old man brought us somewhat of food; and, after we had eaten and the plates and goblets had been re-moved, they sat conversing till night-fall when the old man rose and lit the wax candles and lamps and set meat and drink before us. After we had eaten and drunken we sat conversing and carousing in companionage till the noon of night, when they said to the old man, "Bring us our ordinary, for the hour of sleep is at hand!" So he rose and brought them the trays of soot and ashes; and they did as they had done on the preceding night, nor more, nor less. I abode with them after this fashion for the space of a month during which time they used to blacken their faces with ashes every night, and to wash and change their raiment when the morn was young; and I but marvelled the more and my scruples and curiosity increased to such a point that I had to forego even food and drink. At last, I lost command of myself, for my heart was aflame with fire unquenchable and lowe unconcealable and I said, "O young men, will ye not relieve my trouble and acquaint me with the reason of thus blackening your faces and the meaning of your words:—We were sitting at our ease but our frowardness brought us unease?" Quoth they " 'Twere better to keep these things secret." Still I was bewildered by their doings to the point of abstaining from eating and drinking and, at last wholly losing patience, quoth I to them, "There is no help for it: ye must acquaint me with what is the reason of these doings." They replied, "We kept our secret only for thy good: to gratify thee will bring down evil upon thee and thou wilt become a monocular even as we are." I repeated, "There is no help for it and, if ye will not, let me leave you and return to mine own people and be at rest from seeing these things, for the proverb saith:—

Better ye 'bide and I take my leave: * For what eye sees not heart shall never grieve."

Thereupon they said to me, "Remember, O youth, that should ill befal thee we will not again harbour thee nor suffer thee to abide amongst us;" and bringing a ram they slaughtered it and skinned it. Lastly they gave me a knife saying, "Take this skin and stretch thyself upon it and we will sew it around thee; presently there shall come to thee a certain bird, hight Rukh,[1] that will catch thee up in his pounces and tower high in air and then set thee down on a mountain. When thou feelest he is no longer flying, rip open the pelt with this blade and come out of it; the bird will be scared and will fly away and leave thee free. After this fare for half a day, and the march will place thee at a palace wondrous fair to behold, towering high in air and builded of Khalanj,[2] lign-aloes and sandal-wood, plated with red gold, and studded with all manner emeralds and costly gems fit for seal-rings. Enter it and thou shalt win to thy wish for we have all entered that palace; and such is the cause of our losing our eyes and of our blackening our faces. Were we now to tell thee our stories it would take too long a time; for each and every of us lost his left eye by an adventure of his own." I rejoiced at their words and they did with me as they said; and the bird Rukh bore

---

[1] The older Roc, of which more in the Tale of Sindbad. Meanwhile the reader curious about the Persian Símurgh (thirty bird) will consult the Dabistan, i., 55, 191 and iii., 237, and Richardson's Diss. p. xlviii. For the Anka (Enka or Unka = long-necked bird) see Dab. iii., 249 and for the Humá (bird of Paradise) Richardson lxix. We still lack details concerning the Ben or Bennu (nycticorax) of Egypt which with the Article pi gave rise to the Greek "phœnix."

[2] Probably the *Haledj* of Forskal (p. xcvi. Flor. Ægypt. Arab.), "lignum tenax, durum, obscuri generis." The Bres. Edit. has "ákúl" = teak wood, vulg. "Sáj."

me off and set me down on the mountain. Then I came out of the skin and walked on till I reached the palace. The door stood open as I entered and found myself in a spacious and goodly hall, wide exceedingly, even as a horse-course; and around it were an hundred chambers with doors of sandal and aloes woods plated with red gold and furnished with silver rings by way of knockers.[1] At the head or upper end[2] of the hall I saw forty damsels, sumptuously dressed and ornamented and one and all bright as moons; none could ever tire of gazing upon them and all so lovely that the most ascetic devotee on seeing them would become their slave and obey their will. When they saw me the whole bevy came up to me and said "Welcome and well come and good cheer[3] to thee, O our lord! This whole month have we been expecting thee. Praised be Allah who hath sent us one who is worthy of us, even as we are worthy of him!" Then they made me sit down upon a high divan and said to me, "This day thou art our lord and master, and we are thy servants and thy handmaids, so order us as thou wilt." And I marvelled at their case. Presently one of them arose and set meat before me and I ate and they ate with me; whilst others warmed water and washed my hands and feet and changed my clothes and others made ready sherbets and gave us to drink; and all gathered around me being full of joy and gladness at my coming. Then they sat down and conversed with me till nightfall, when five of them arose and laid the trays and spread them with flowers and fragrant herbs and fruits, fresh and dried, and confections in profusion. At last they brought out a fine wine-service with rich old wine; and we sat down to drink and some sang songs and others played the lute and psaltery and recorders and other instruments, and the bowl went merrily round. Hereupon such gladness possessed me that I forgot the sorrows of the world one and all and said, "This is indeed life; O sad that 'tis fleeting!" I enjoyed their company till the time came for rest; and our heads were all warm with wine, when they said, "O our lord, choose from amongst us her who shall be thy bed-fellow this night and not lie with thee again till forty days be past." So I chose a girl fair of face and

---

[1] The knocker ring is an invention well known to the Romans.
[2] Arab. "Sadr"; the place of honour; hence the "Sudder Adawlut" (Supreme Court) in the Anglo-Indian jargon.
[3] Arab. "Ahlan wa sahlan wa marhabá," the words still popularly addressed to a guest.

perfect in shape, with eyes Kohl-edged by nature's hand;[1] hair long and jet black with slightly parted teeth[2] and joining brows: 'twas as if she were some limber graceful branchlet or the slender stalk of sweet basil to amaze and to bewilder man's fancy; even as the poet said of such an one:—

To even her with greeny bough were vain * Fool he who finds her beauties in
  the roe:
When hath the roe those lively lovely limbs * Or honey dews those lips alone
  bestow?
Those eyne, soul-piercing eyne, which slay with love, * Which bind the victim by their shafts laid low?
My heart to second childhood they beguiled * No wonder: love-sick man
  again is child!

And I repeated to her the maker's words who said:—

"None other charms but thine shall greet mine eyes, * Nor other image can
  my heart surprize:
Thy love, my lady, captives all my thoughts * And on that love I'll die and
  I'll arise."

So I lay with her that night; none fairer I ever knew; and, when it was morning, the damsels carried me to the Hammam-bath and bathed me and robed me in fairest apparel. Then they served up food, and we ate and drank and the cup went round till nightfall when I chose from among them one fair of form and face, soft-sided and a model of grace, such an one as the poet described when he said:—

On her fair bosom caskets twain I scanned, * Sealed fast with musk-seals
  lovers to withstand;
With arrowy glances stand on guard her eyes, * Whose shafts would shoot
  who dares put forth a hand.

With her I spent a most goodly night; and, to be brief, O my mistress, I remained with them in all solace and delight of life, eating and drinking, conversing and carousing and every night

---

[1] This may mean "liquid black eyes"; but also, as I have noticed, that the lashes were long and thick enough to make the eyelids appear as if Kohl-powder had been applied to the inner rims.

[2] A slight parting between the two front incisors, the upper only, is considered a beauty by Arabs; why it is hard to say except for the racial love of variety. "Sughr" (Thugr) in the text means, primarily, the opening of the mouth, the gape: hence the front teeth.

lying with one or other of them. But at the head of the new year they came to me in tears and bade me farewell, weeping and crying out and clinging about me; whereat I wondered and said, "What may be the matter? verily you break my heart!" They exclaimed, "Would Heaven we had never known thee; for, though we have companied with many, yet never saw we a pleasanter than thou or a more courteous." And they wept again. "But tell me more clearly," asked I, "what causeth this weeping which maketh my gall-bladder[1] like to burst;" and they answered, "O our lord and master, it is severance which maketh us weep; and thou, and thou only, art the cause of our tears. If thou hearken to us we need never be parted and if thou hearken not we part for ever; but our hearts tell us that thou wilt not listen to our words and this is the cause of our tears and cries." "Tell me how the case standeth?" "Know, O our lord, that we are the daughters of Kings who have met here and have lived together for years; and once in every year we are perforce absent for forty days; and afterwards we return and abide here for the rest of the twelve-month eating and drinking and taking our pleasure and enjoying delights: we are about to depart according to our custom; and we fear lest after we be gone thou contraire our charge and disobey our injunctions. Here now we commit to thee the keys of the palace which containeth forty chambers and thou mayest open of these thirty and nine, but beware (and we conjure thee by Allah and by the lives of us!) lest thou open the fortieth door, for therein is that which shall separate us for ever."[2] Quoth I, "Assuredly I will not open it, if it contain the cause of severance from you." Then one among them came up to me and falling on my neck wept and recited these verses:—

"If Time unite us after absent-while, * The world harsh frowning on our lot
    shall smile;
And if thy semblance deign adorn mine eyes,[3] * I'll pardon Time past wrongs
    and by-gone guile."

---

[1] *i. e.* makes me taste the bitterness of death, "bursting the gall-bladder" (Marárah) being our "breaking the heart."

[2] Almost needless to say that forbidden doors and rooms form a *lieu-commun* in Fairie: they are found in the Hindu Katha Sarit Sagara and became familiar to our childhood by "Bluebeard."

[3] Lit. "apply Kohl to my eyes," even as Jezebel "painted her face," in Heb. put her eyes in painting (2 Kings ix. 30).

And I recited the following:—

"When drew she near to bid adieu with heart unstrung, * While care and
    longing on that day her bosom wrung;
Wet pearls she wept and mine like red carnelians rolled * And, joined in sad
    rivière, around her neck they hung."

When I saw her weeping I said, "By Allah I will never open that
fortieth door, never and no wise!" and I bade her farewell.
Thereupon all departed flying away like birds; signalling with
their hands farewells as they went and leaving me alone in the
palace. When evening drew near I opened the door of the first
chamber and entering it found myself in a place like one of the
pleasaunces of Paradise. It was a garden with trees of freshest
green and ripe fruits of yellow sheen; and its birds were singing
clear and keen and rills ran wimpling through the fair terrene.
The sight and sounds brought solace to my sprite; and I walked
among the trees, and I smelt the breath of the flowers on the
breeze; and heard the birdies sing their melodies hymning
the One, the Almighty in sweetest litanies; and I looked upon
the apple whose hue is parcel red and parcel yellow; as said the
poet:—

Apple whose hue combines in union mellow * My fair's red cheek, her hapless
    lover's yellow.

Then I looked upon the quince, and inhaled its fragrance which
putteth to shame musk and ambergris, even as the poet hath
said:—

Quince every taste conjoins; in her are found * Gifts which for queen of
    fruits the Quince have crowned;
Her taste is wine, her scent the waft of musk; * Pure gold her hue, her shape
    the Moon's fair round.

Then I looked upon the pear whose taste surpasseth sherbet and
sugar; and the apricot[1] whose beauty striketh the eye with admiration, as if she were a polished ruby. Then I went out of the place
and locked the door as it was before. When it was the morrow I
opened the second door; and entering found myself in a spacious

---

[1] Arab. "Al-Barkúk," whence our older "Apricock." Classically it is "Burkúk" and
Pers. for Arab. "Mishmish," and it also denotes a small plum or damson. In Syria the
"side next the sun" shows a glowing red flush.

plain set with tall date-palms and watered by a running stream
whose banks were shrubbed with bushes of rose and jasmine,
while privet and eglantine, oxe-eye, violet and lily, narcissus,
origane and the winter gilliflower carpeted the borders; and the
breath of the breeze swept over these sweet-smelling growths
diffusing their delicious odours right and left, perfuming the
world and filling my soul with delight. After taking my pleasure
there awhile I went from it and, having closed the door as it was
before, opened the third door wherein I saw a high open hall
pargetted with parti-coloured marbles and *pietra dura* of price
and other precious stones, and hung with cages of sandal-wood
and eagle-wood; full of birds which made sweet music, such as
the Thousand-voiced,[1] and the cushat, the merle, the turtle-
dove and the Nubian ring-dove. My heart was filled with pleasure thereby; my grief was dispelled and I slept in that aviary till
dawn. Then I unlocked the door of the fourth chamber and therein
found a grand saloon with forty smaller chambers giving upon it.
All their doors stood open: so I entered and found them full of
pearls and jacinths and beryls and emeralds and corals and car-
buncles, and all manner precious gems and jewels, such as tongue
of man may not describe. My thought was stunned at the
sight and I said to myself, "These be things methinks united
which could not be found save in the treasuries of a King of
Kings, nor could the monarchs of the world have collected the
like of these!" And my heart dilated and my sorrows ceased,
"For," quoth I, "now verily am I the monarch of the age, since
by Allah's grace this enormous wealth is mine; and I have forty
damsels under my hand nor is there any to claim them save
myself." Then I gave not over opening place after place until
nine and thirty days were passed and in that time I had entered
every chamber except that one whose door the Princesses had
charged me not to open. But my thoughts, O my mistress, ever
ran on that forbidden fortieth[2] and Satan urged me to open it for
my own undoing; nor had I patience to forbear, albeit there
wanted of the trysting time but a single day. So I stood before
the chamber aforesaid and, after a moment's hesitation, opened
the door which was plated with red gold, and entered. I was

---

[1] Arab. "Hazár" (in Persian, a thousand) = a kind of mocking bird.
[2] Some Edits. make the doors number a hundred, but the Princesses were forty and
these coincidences, which seem to have significance and have none save for Arab sym-
metromania, are common in Arab stories.

met by a perfume whose like I had never before smelt; and so sharp and subtle was the odour that it made my senses drunken as with strong wine, and I fell to the ground in a fainting fit which lasted a full hour. When I came to myself I strengthened my heart and, entering, found myself in a chamber whose floor was bespread with saffron and blazing with light from branched candelabra of gold and lamps fed with costly oils, which diffused the scent of musk and ambergris. I saw there also two great censers each big as a mazer-bowl,[1] flaming with lign-aloes, nadd-perfume,[2] ambergris and honied scents; and the place was full of their fragrance. Presently, O my lady, I espied a noble steed, black as the murks of night when murkiest, standing, ready saddled and bridled (and his saddle was of red gold) before two mangers, one of clear crystal wherein was husked sesame, and the other also of crystal containing water of the rose scented with musk. When I saw this I marvelled and said to myself, "Doubt-less in this animal must be some wondrous mystery;" and Satan cozened me, so I led him without the palace and mounted him, but he would not stir from his place. So I hammered his sides with my heels, but he moved not, and then I took the rein-whip,[3] and struck him withal. When he felt the blow, he neighed a neigh with a sound like deafening thunder and, opening a pair of wings[4] flew up with me in the firmament of heaven far beyond the eyesight of man. After a full hour of flight he descended and alighted on a terrace roof and shaking me off his back lashed me on the face with his tail and gouged out my left eye causing it roll along my cheek. Then he flew away. I went down from the terrace and found myself again amongst the ten one-eyed youths sitting upon their ten couches with blue covers; and they cried out when they saw me, "No welcome to thee, nor aught of good cheer! We all lived of lives the happiest and we ate and drank of the best; upon brocades and cloths of gold we took rest and we slept with our heads on beauty's breast, but we could not await one day to gain the delights of a year!" Quoth I, "Behold I have become one like unto you and now I would have you bring me a tray full of blackness, wherewith to blacken my

---

[1] Arab. "Májúr": hence possibly our "mazer," which is popularly derived from Masarn, a maple.

[2] A compound scent of ambergris, musk and aloes.

[3] The ends of the bridle-reins forming the whip.

[4] The flying horse is Pegasus which is a Greek travesty of an Egyptian myth developed in India.

face, and receive me into your society." "No, by Allah," quoth
they, "thou shalt not sojourn with us and now get thee hence!"
So they drove me away. Finding them reject me thus I foresaw
that matters would go hard with me, and I remembered the many
miseries which Destiny had written upon my forehead; and I
fared forth from among them heavy-hearted and tearful-eyed,
repeating to myself these words, "I was sitting at mine ease but
my frowardness brought me to unease." Then I shaved beard
and mustachios and eye-brows, renouncing the world, and wandered in Kalandar-garb about Allah's earth; and the Almighty
decreed safety for me till I arrived at Baghdad, which was on
the evening of this very night. Here I met these two other Kalandars standing bewildered; so I saluted them saying, "I am a
stranger!" and they answered, "And we likewise be strangers!"
By the freak of Fortune we were like to like, three Kalandars and
three monoculars all blind of the left eye. Such, O my lady, is the
cause of the shearing of my beard and the manner of my losing an
eye. Said the lady to him, "Rub thy head and wend thy ways;"
but he answered, "By Allah, I will not go until I hear the stories
of these others." Then the lady, turning towards the Caliph
and Ja'afar and Masrur, said to them, "Do ye also give an account of yourselves, you men!" Whereupon Ja'afar stood forth
and told her what he had told the portress as they were entering
the house; and when she heard his story of their being merchants
and Mosul-men who had outrun the watch, she said, "I grant
you your lives each for each sake, and now away with you all."
So they all went out and when they were in the street, quoth
the Caliph to the Kalandars, "O company, whither go ye now,
seeing that the morning hath not yet dawned?" Quoth they,
"By Allah, O our lord, we know not where to go." "Come and
pass the rest of the night with us," said the Caliph and, turning
to Ja'afar, "Take them home with thee and to-morrow bring
them to my presence that we may chronicle their adventures."
Ja'afar did as the Caliph bade him and the Commander of the
Faithful returned to his palace; but sleep gave no sign of visiting
him that night and he lay awake pondering the mishaps of the
three Kalandar-princes and impatient to know the history of the
ladies and the two black bitches. No sooner had morning
dawned than he went forth and sat upon the throne of his
sovereignty; and, turning to Ja'afar, after all his Grandees and
Officers of state were gathered together, he said, "Bring me the

three ladies and the two bitches and the three Kalandars." So Ja'afar fared forth and brought them all before him (and the ladies were veiled); then the Minister turned to them and said in the Caliph's name, "We pardon you your maltreatment of us and your want of courtesy, in consideration of the kindness which forewent it, and for that ye knew us not: now however I would have you to know that ye stand in presence of the fifth[1] of the sons of Abbas, Harun al-Rashid, brother of Caliph Músá al-Hádi, son of Al-Mansúr; son of Mohammed the brother of Al-Saffáh bin Mohammed who was first of the royal house. Speak ye therefore before him the truth and the whole truth!" When the ladies heard Ja'afar's words touching the Commander of the Faithful, the eldest came forward and said, "O Prince of True Believers, my story is one which, were it graven with needle-gravers upon the eye-corners were a warner for whoso would be warned and an example for whoso can take profit from example." ——And Shahrazad perceived the dawn of day and ceased to say her permitted say.

When it was the Seventeenth Night,

She said, It hath reached me, O auspicious King, that she stood forth before the Commander of the Faithful and began to tell

The Eldest Lady's Tale.

VERILY a strange tale is mine and 'tis this:—Yon two black bitches are my eldest sisters by one mother and father; and these two others, she who beareth upon her the signs of stripes and the third our procuratrix are my sisters by another mother. When my father died, each took her share of the heritage and, after a while my mother also deceased, leaving me and my sisters-german three thousand dinars; so each daughter received her portion of a thousand dinars and I the same, albe the youngest. In due course of time my sisters married with the usual festivities and lived with their husbands, who bought merchandise with their wives' monies and set out on their travels together. Thus they threw me off. My brothers-in-law were absent with their wives five years, during which period they spent all the money they had and, becoming bankrupt, deserted my sisters in foreign parts amid stranger folk. After five years my eldest sister returned to

---

[1] The Bres. Edit. wrongly says "the seventh."

me in beggar's gear with her clothes in rags and tatters[1] and a dirty old mantilla;[2] and truly she was in the foulest and sorriest plight. At first sight I did not know my own sister; but presently I recognised her and said "What state is this?" "O our sister," she replied, "Words cannot undo the done; and the reed of Destiny hath run through what Allah decreed." Then I sent her to the bath and dressed her in a suit of mine own, and boiled for her a bouillon and brought her some good wine and said to her, "O my sister, thou art the eldest, who still standest to us in the stead of father and mother; and, as for the inheritance which came to me as to you twain, Allah hath blessed it and prospered it to me with increase; and my circumstances are easy, for I have made much money by spinning and cleaning silk; and I and you will share my wealth alike." I entreated her with all kindliness and she abode with me a whole year, during which our thoughts and fancies were always full of our other sister. Shortly after she too came home in yet fouler and sorrier plight than that of my eldest sister; and I dealt by her still more honorably than I had done by the first, and each of them had a share of my substance. After a time they said to me, "O our sister, we desire to marry again, for indeed we have not patience to drag on our days without husbands and to lead the lives of widows bewitched;" and I replied, "O eyes of me![3] ye have hitherto seen scanty weal in wedlock, for now-a-days good men and true are become rarities and curiosities; nor do I deem your projects advisable, as ye have already made trial of matrimony and have failed." But they would not accept my advice and married without my consent: nevertheless I gave them outfit and dowries out of my money; and they fared forth with their mates. In a mighty little time their husbands played them false and, taking whatever they could lay hands upon, levanted and left them in the lurch. Thereupon they came to me ashamed and in abject case and made their excuses to me, saying, "Pardon our fault and

---

1 Arab. "Sharmutah" (plur. Sharámít) from the root Sharmat, to shred, a favourite Egyptian word also applied in vulgar speech to a strumpet, a punk, a piece. It is also the popular term for strips of jerked or boucaned meat hung up in the sun to dry, and classically called "Kadíd."

2 Arab. "Izár," the man's waistcloth opposed to the Ridá or shoulder-cloth, is also the sheet of white calico worn by the poorer Egyptian women out of doors and covering head and hands. See Lane (M. E., chapt. i.). The rich prefer a "Habárah" of black silk, and the poor, when they have nothing else, use a bed-sheet.

3 i. e. "My dears."

be not wroth with us;[1] for although thou art younger in years yet
art thou older in wit; henceforth we will never make mention of
marriage; so take us back as thy hand-maidens that we may eat
our mouthful." Quoth I, "Welcome to you, O my sisters, there
is naught dearer to me than you." And I took them in and redoubled my kindness to them. We ceased not to live after this
loving fashion for a full year, when I resolved to sell my wares
abroad and first to fit me a conveyance for Bassorah; so I equipped
a large ship, and loaded her with merchandise and valuable goods
for traffic, and with provaunt and all needful for a voyage, and
said to my sisters, "Will ye abide at home whilst I travel, or
would ye prefer to accompany me on the voyage?" "We will
travel with thee," answered they, "for we cannot bear to be
parted from thee." So I divided my monies into two parts, one to
accompany me and the other to be left in charge of a trusty person, for, as I said to myself, "Haply some accident may happen
to the ship and yet we remain alive; in which case we shall
find on our return what may stand us in good stead." I took my
two sisters and we went a-voyaging some days and nights; but
the master was careless enough to miss his course, and the ship
went astray with us and entered a sea other than the sea we
sought. For a time we knew naught of this; and the wind blew
fair for us ten days, after which the look-out man went aloft to
see about him and cried, "Good news!" Then he came down rejoicing and said, "I have seen what seemeth to be a city as 'twere
a pigeon." Hereat we rejoiced and, ere an hour of the day had
passed, the buildings showed plain in the offing and we asked
the Captain, "What is the name of yonder city?" and he answered
"By Allah I wot not, for I never saw it before and never sailed
these seas in my life: but, since our troubles have ended in safety,
remains for you only to land there with your merchandise and, if
you find selling profitable, sell and make your market of what is
there; and if not, we will rest here two days and provision ourselves and fare away." So we entered the port and the Captain
went up town and was absent awhile, after which he returned to
us and said, "Arise; go up into the city and marvel at the works
of Allah with His creatures and pray to be preserved from His
righteous wrath!" So we landed and going up into the city, saw
at the gate men hending staves in hand; but when we drew near

---

[1] Arab. "Lá tawákhizná:" lit. "do not chastise (or blame) us;" the pop. expression
for, "excuse (or pardon) us."

them, behold, they had been translated[1] by the anger of Allah
and had become stones. Then we entered the city and found all
who therein woned into black stones enstoned: not an inhabited
house appeared to the espier, nor was there a blower of fire.[2] We
were awe struck at the sight and threaded the market streets
where we found the goods and gold and silver left lying in their
places; and we were glad and said, "Doubtless there is some
mystery in all this." Then we dispersed about the thorough-
fares and each busied himself with collecting the wealth and
money and rich stuffs, taking scanty heed of friend or comrade.
As for myself I went up to the castle which was strongly fortified; and, entering the King's palace by its gate of red gold,
found all the vaiselle of gold and silver, and the King himself
seated in the midst of his Chamberlains and Nabobs and Emirs
and Wazirs; all clad in raiment which confounded man's art. I
drew nearer and saw him sitting on a throne incrusted and inlaid with pearls and gems; and his robes were of gold-cloth
adorned with jewels of every kind, each one flashing like a star.
Around him stood fifty Mamelukes, white slaves, clothed in
silks of divers sorts holding their drawn swords in their hands;
but when I drew near to them lo! all were black stones. My
understanding was confounded at the sight, but I walked on and
entered the great hall of the Harím,[3] whose walls I found hung
with tapestries of gold-striped silk and spread with silken carpets
embroidered with golden flowers. Here I saw the Queen lying
at full length arrayed in robes purfled with fresh young[4] pearls;
on her head was a diadem set with many sorts of gems each fit
for a ring[5] and around her neck hung collars and necklaces. All
her raiment and her ornaments were in natural state but she had
been turned into a black stone by Allah's wrath. Presently I

---

[1] Arab. "Maskhút," mostly applied to change of shape as man enchanted to monkey,
and in vulgar parlance applied to a statue (of stone, etc.). The list of metamorphoses
in Al-Islam is longer than that known to Ovid. Those who have seen Petra, the Greek
town of the Haurán and the Roman ruins in Northern Africa will readily detect the basis
upon which these stories are built. I shall return to this subject in The City of Iram
(Night cclxxvi.) and The City of Brass (dlxvii.).

[2] A picturesque phrase enough to express a deserted site, a spectacle familiar to the
Nomades and always abounding in pathos to the citizens.

[3] The olden "Harem" (or gynæceum, Pers. Zenanah, Serraglio): Harím is also used
by synecdoche for the inmates; especially the wife.

[4] The pearl is supposed in the East to lose 1% per ann. of its splendour and value.

[5] Arab. "Fass," properly the bezel of a ring; also a gem cut en cabochon and generally
the contenant for the contenu.

espied an open door for which I made straight and found leading
to it a flight of seven steps. So I walked up and came upon a
place pargetted with marble and spread and hung with gold-
worked carpets and tapestry, amiddlemost of which stood a
throne of juniper-wood inlaid with pearls and precious stones
and set with bosses of emeralds. In the further wall was an
alcove whose curtains, bestrung with pearls, were let down
and I saw a light issuing therefrom; so I drew near and perceived that the light came from a precious stone as big as an
ostrich-egg, set at the upper end of the alcove upon a little
chryselephantine couch of ivory and gold; and this jewel,
blazing like the sun, cast its rays wide and side. The couch
also was spread with all manner of silken stuffs amazing the
gazer with their richness and beauty. I marvelled much at all
this, especially when seeing in that place candles ready lighted;
and I said in my mind, "Needs must some one have lighted these
candles." Then I went forth and came to the kitchen and thence
to the buttery and the King's treasure-chambers; and continued
to explore the palace and to pace from place to place; I forgot myself in my awe and marvel at these matters and I was drowned in
thought till the night came on. Then I would have gone forth,
but knowing not the gate I lost my way, so I returned to the
alcove whither the lighted candles directed me and sat down
upon the couch; and wrapping myself in a coverlet, after I had
repeated somewhat from the Koran, I would have slept but
could not, for restlessness possessed me. When night was at its
noon I heard a voice chanting the Koran in sweetest accents;
but the tone thereof was weak; so I rose, glad to hear the silence
broken, and followed the sound until I reached a closet whose
door stood ajar. Then peeping through a chink I considered
the place and lo! it was an oratory wherein was a prayer-niche[1]
with two wax candles burning and lamps hanging from the

---

[1] Arab. "Mihráb" = the arch-headed niche in the Mosque-wall facing Meccah-wards.
Here, with his back to the people and fronting the Ka'abah or Square House of Meccah
(hence called the "Kiblah" = direction of prayer), stations himself the Imám, antistes
or fugleman, lit. "one who stands *before* others;" and his bows and prostrations give the
time to the congregation. I have derived the Mihrab from the niche in which the
Egyptian God was shrined: the Jews ignored it, but the Christians preserved it for their
statues and altars. Maundrell suggests that the empty niche denotes an invisible God.
As the niche (symbol of Venus) and the minaret (symbol of Priapus) date only from the
days of the tenth Caliph, Al-Walid (A.H. 86–96 = 105–115), the Hindus charge the
Moslems with having borrowed the two from their favourite idols—The Linga-Yoni or
Cunnus-phallus (Pilgrimage ii. 140), and plainly call the Mihrab a Bhaga = Cunnus

ceiling. In it too was spread a prayer-carpet whereupon sat a
youth fair to see; and before him on its stand[1] was a copy of the
Koran, from which he was reading. I marvelled to see him alone
alive amongst the people of the city and entering saluted him;
whereupon he raised his eyes and returned my salam. Quoth I,
"Now by the Truth of what thou readest in Allah's Holy Book,
I conjure thee to answer my question." He looked upon me
with a smile and said, "O handmaid of Allah, first tell me the
cause of thy coming hither, and I in turn will tell what hath
befallen both me and the people of this city, and what was the
reason of my escaping their doom." So I told him my story
whereat he wondered; and I questioned him of the people of the
city, when he replied, "Have patience with me for a while, O
my sister!" and, reverently closing the Holy Book, he laid it up
in a satin bag. Then he seated me by his side; and I looked at him
and behold, he was as the moon at its full, fair of face and rare
of form, soft-sided and slight, of well-proportioned height, and
cheek smoothly bright and diffusing light; in brief a sweet, a
sugar-stick,[2] even as saith the poet of the like of him in these
couplets:—

That night th' astrologer a scheme of planets drew, * And lo! a graceful shape
  of youth appeared in view:
Saturn had stained his locks with Saturninest jet, * And spots of nut-brown
  musk on rosy side-face blew:[3]
Mars tinctured either cheek with tinct of martial red; * Sagittal shots from
  eyelids Sagittarius threw:
Dowered him Mercury with bright mercurial wit; * Bore off the Bear[4] what all
  man's evil glances grew:
Amazed stood Astrophil to sight the marvel-birth * When louted low the
  Moon at full to buss the Earth.

And of a truth Allah the Most High had robed him in the raiment

---

(Dabistan ii. 152). The Guebres further term Meccah "Mah-gah," locus Lunæ, and Al-
Medinah, "Mahdinah," = Moon of religion. See Dabistan i., 49, etc.

[1] Arab. "Kursi," a stool of palm-fronds, etc., X-shaped (see Lane's illustration,
Nights i., 197), before which the reader sits. Good Moslems will not hold the Holy
Volume below the waist nor open it except when ceremonially pure. Englishmen in the
East should remember this, for to neglect the "Adab al-Kúran" (respect due to Holy
Writ) gives great scandal.

[2] Mr. Payne (i. 148) quotes the German Zuckerpüppchen.

[3] The Persian poets have a thousand conceits in praise of the "mole," (Khál or
Shámah) for which Hafiz offered "Samarkand and Bokhara" (they not being his, as his
friends remarked). Another "topic" is the flight of arrows shot by eyelashes.

[4] Arab. "Suhá" a star in the Great Bear introduced only to balance "wushát" = spies,
enviers, enemies, whose "evil eye" it will ward off.

of perfect grace and had purfled and fringed it with a cheek all beauty and loveliness, even as the poet saith of such an one:—

By his eyelids shedding perfume and his fine slim waist I swear, * By the
    shooting of his shafts barbed with sorcery passing rare;
By the softness of his sides,[1] and glances' lingering light; * And brow of
    dazzling day-tide ray and night within his hair;
By his eyebrows which deny to who look upon them rest, * Now bidding now
    forbidding, ever dealing joy and care;
By the rose that decks his cheek, and the myrtle of its moss;[2] * By jacinths
    bedded in his lips and pearl his smile lays bare;
By his graceful bending neck and the curving of his breast; * Whose polished
    surface beareth those granados, lovely pair;
By his heavy hips that quiver as he passeth in his pride; * Or he resteth with
    that waist which is slim beyond compare;
By the satin of his skin, by that fine unsullied sprite; * By the beauty that con-
    taineth all things bright and debonnair;
By that ever-open hand; by the candour of his tongue; * By noble blood and
    high degree whereof he's hope and heir;
Musk from him borrows muskiness she loveth to exhale * And all the airs of
    ambergris through him perfume the air;
The sun, methinks, the broad bright sun, before my love would pale * And sans
    his splendour would appear a paring of his nail.[3]

I glanced at him with one glance of eyes which caused me a thousand sighs; and my heart was at once taken captive-wise; so I asked him, "O my lord and my love, tell me that whereof I questioned thee;" and he answered, "Hearing is obeying! Know, O handmaid of Allah, that this city was the capital of my father who is the King thou sawest on the throne transfigured by Allah's wrath to a black stone, and the Queen thou foundest in the alcove is my mother. They and all the people of the city were Magians who fire adored in lieu of the Omnipotent Lord[4] and were wont to swear by lowe and heat and shade and light, and the spheres revolving day and night. My father had ne'er a son till he was blest with me near the last of his days; and he reared me till I grew up and prosperity anticipated me in all

---

[1] In Arab tales beauty is always "soft-sided," and a smooth skin is valued in proportion to its rarity.
[2] The myrtle is the young hair upon the side-face.
[3] In other copies of these verses the fourth couplet swears "by the scorpions of his
brow" i.e. the accroche-cœurs, the beau-catchers, bell-ropes or "aggravators," as the
B.P. calls them. In couplet eight the poet alludes to his love's "Unsur," or element,
his nature made up of the four classicals, and in the last couplet he makes the nail paring
refer to the moon not the sun.
[4] This is regular formula when speaking of Guebres.

things. Now it so fortuned that there was with us an old woman well stricken in years, a Moslemah who, inwardly believing in Allah and His Apostle, conformed outwardly with the religion of my people; and my father placed thorough confidence in her for that he knew her to be trustworthy and virtuous; and he treated her with ever-increasing kindness believing her to be of his own belief. So when I was well-nigh grown up my father committed me to her charge saying:—Take him and educate him and teach him the rules of our faith; let him have the best instructions and cease not thy fostering care of him. So she took me and taught me the tenets of Al-Islam with the divine ordinances[1] of the Wuzu-ablution and the five daily prayers and she made me learn the Koran by rote, often repeating:—Serve none save Allah Almighty! When I had mastered this much of knowledge she said to me:—O my son, keep this matter concealed from thy sire and reveal naught to him lest he slay thee. So I hid it from him and I abode on this wise for a term of days when the old woman died, and the people of the city redoubled in their impiety[2] and arrogance and the error of their ways. One day, while they were as wont, behold, they heard a loud and terrible sound and a crier crying out with a voice like roaring thunder so every ear could hear, far and near, "O folk of this city, leave ye your fire-worshipping and adore Allah the All-compassionate King!" At this, fear and terror fell upon the citizens and they crowded to my father (he being King of the city) and asked him, "What is this awesome voice we have heard, for it hath confounded us with the excess of its terror?" and he answered, "Let not a voice fright you nor shake your steadfast sprite nor turn you back from the faith which is right." Their hearts inclined to his words and they ceased not to worship the fire and they persisted in rebellion for a full year from the time

---

[1] Arab. "Faráiz"; the orders expressly given in the Koran which the reader will remember, is Uncreate and Eternal. In India "Farz" is applied to injunctions thrice repeated; and "Wájib" to those given twice over. Elsewhere scanty difference is made between them.

[2] Arab. "Kufr" = rejecting the True Religion, *i.e.* Al-Islam, such rejection being "Tughyán" or rebellion against the Lord. The "terrible sound" is taken from the legend of the prophet Sálih and the proto-historic tribe of Thámúd which for its impiety was struck dead by an earthquake and a noise from heaven. The latter, according to some commentators, was the voice of the Archangel Gabriel crying "Die all of you" (Koran, chapts. vii., xviii., etc.). We shall hear more of it in the "City of many-columned Iram." According to some, Salih, a mysterious Badawi prophet, is buried in the Wady al-Shaykh of the so-called Sinaitic Peninsula.

they heard the first voice; and on the anniversary came a second cry, and a third at the head of the third year, each year once. Still they persisted in their malpractises till one day at break of dawn, judgment and the wrath of Heaven descended upon them with all suddenness, and by the visitation of Allah all were metamorphosed into black stones,[1] they and their beasts and their cattle; and none was saved save myself who at the time was engaged in my devotions. From that day to this I am in the case thou seest, constant in prayer and fasting and reading and reciting the Koran; but I am indeed grown weary by reason of my loneliness, having none to bear me company." Then said I to him (for in very sooth he had won my heart and was the lord of my life and soul), "O youth, wilt thou fare with me to Baghdad city and visit the Olema and men learned in the law and doctors of divinity and get thee increase of wisdom and understanding and theology? And know that she who standeth in thy presence will be thy handmaid, albeit she be head of her family and mistress over men and eunuchs and servants and slaves. Indeed my life was no life before it fell in with thy youth. I have here a ship laden with merchandise; and in very truth Destiny drove me to this city that I might come to the knowledge of these matters, for it was fated that we should meet." And I ceased not to persuade him and speak him fair and use every art till he consented.——And Shahrazad perceived the dawn of day and ceased to say her permitted say.

𝔚𝔥𝔢𝔫 𝔦𝔱 𝔴𝔞𝔰 𝔱𝔥𝔢 𝔈𝔦𝔤𝔥𝔱𝔢𝔢𝔫𝔱𝔥 𝔑𝔦𝔤𝔥𝔱,

She continued, It hath reached me, O auspicious King, that the lady ceased not persuading with soft speech the youth to depart with her till he consented and said "Yes." She slept that night lying at his feet and hardly knowing where she was for excess of joy. As soon as the next morning dawned (she pursued, addressing the Caliph), I arose and we entered the treasuries and took thence whatever was light in weight and great in worth; then we went down side by side from the castle to the city, where we were met by the Captain and my sisters and slaves who had been

---

[1] Yet they kept the semblance of man, showing that the idea arose from the basaltic statues found in Hauranic ruins. Mohammed in his various marches to Syria must have seen remnants of Greek and Roman settlements; and as has been noticed "Sesostris" left his mark near Meccah. (Pilgrimage iii. 137.)

seeking for me. When they saw me they rejoiced and asked what had stayed me, and I told them all I had seen and related to them the story of the young Prince and the transformation wherewith the citizens had been justly visited. Hereat all marvelled, but when my two sisters (these two bitches, O Commander of the Faith-ful!) saw me by the side of my young lover they jaloused me on his account and were wroth and plotted mischief against me. We awaited a fair wind and went on board rejoicing and ready to fly for joy by reason of the goods we had gotten, but my own greatest joyance was in the youth; and we waited awhile till the wind blew fair for us and then we set sail and fared forth. Now as we sat talking, my sisters asked me, "And what wilt thou do with this handsome young man?"; and I answered, "I purpose to make him my husband!" Then I turned to him and said, "O my lord, I have that to propose to thee wherein thou must not cross me; and this it is that, when we reach Baghdad, my native city, I offer thee my life as thy handmaiden in holy matrimony, and thou shalt be to me baron and I will be femme to thee." He answered, "I hear and I obey!; thou art my lady and my mistress and whatso thou doest I will not gainsay." Then I turned to my sisters and said, "This is my gain; I content me with this youth and those who have gotten aught of my property let them keep it as their gain with my good will." "Thou sayest and doest well," answered the twain, but they imagined mischief against me. We ceased not spooning before a fair wind till we had exchanged the sea of peril for the seas of safety and, in a few days, we made Bassorah-city, whose buildings loomed clear before us as evening fell. But after we had retired to rest and were sound alseep, my two sisters arose and took me up, bed and all, and threw me into the sea: they did the same with the young Prince who, as he could not swim, sank and was drowned and Allah enrolled him in the noble army of Martyrs.[1] As for me would Heaven I had been drowned with him, but Allah deemed that I should be

---

[1] Arab. "Shuhadá"; highly respected by Moslems as by other religionists; although their principal if not only merit seems as a rule to have been intense obstinacy and devo-tion to one idea for which they were ready to sacrifice even life. The Martyrs-category is extensive including those killed by falling walls; victims to the plague, pleurisy and pregnancy; travellers drowned or otherwise lost when journeying honestly, and chaste lovers who die of "broken hearts" *i.e.* impaired digestion. Their souls are at once stowed away in the crops of green birds where they remain till Resurrection Day, "eating of the fruits and drinking of the streams of Paradise," a place however, whose topography is wholly uncertain. Thus the young Prince was rewarded with a manner of anti-Purga-tory, a preparatory heaven.

of the saved; so when I awoke and found myself in the sea and saw the ship making off like a flash of lightning, He threw in my way a piece of timber which I bestrided, and the waves tossed me to and fro till they cast me upon an island coast, a high land and an uninhabited. I landed and walked about the island the rest of the night and, when morning dawned, I saw a rough track barely fit for child of Adam to tread, leading to what proved a shallow ford connecting island and mainland. As soon as the sun had risen I spread my garments to dry in its rays; and ate of the fruits of the island and drank of its waters; then I set out along the foot-track and ceased not walking till I reached the mainland. Now when there remained between me and the city but a two hours' journey behold, a great serpent, the bigness of a date-palm, came fleeing towards me in all haste, gliding along now to the right then to the left till she was close upon me, whilst her tongue lolled ground-wards a span long and swept the dust as she went. She was pursued by a Dragon[1] who was not longer than two lances, and of slender build about the bulk of a spear and, although her terror lent her speed, and she kept wriggling from side to side, he overtook her and seized her by the tail, whereat her tears streamed down and her tongue was thrust out in her agony. I took pity on her and, picking up a stone and calling upon Allah for aid, threw it at the Dragon's head with such force that he died then and there; and the serpent opening a pair of wings flew into the lift and disappeared from before my eyes. I sat down marvelling over that adventure, but I was weary and, drowsiness overcoming me, I slept where I was for a while. When I awoke I found a jet-black damsel sitting at my feet shampooing them; and by her side stood two black bitches (my sisters, O Commander of the Faithful!). I was ashamed before her[2] and, sitting up, asked her, "O my sister, who and what art thou?"; and she answered, "How soon hast thou forgotten me! I am she for whom thou wroughtest a good deed and sowedest the seed of gratitude and slewest her foe; for I am the serpent whom by Allah's aidance thou didst

---

[1] Arab. "Su'ubán:" the Badawin give the name to a variety of serpents all held to be venomous; but in tales the word, like "Tannín," expresses our "dragon" or "cockatrice."

[2] She was ashamed to see the lady doing servile duty by rubbing her feet. This massage, which B. de la Brocquière describes in 1452 as "kneading and pinching," has already been noticed. The French term is apparently derived from the Arab. "Mas-h."

just now deliver from the Dragon. I am a Jinniyah and he was a Jinn who hated me, and none saved my life from him save thou. As soon as thou freedest me from him I flew on the wind to the ship whence thy sisters threw thee, and removed all that was therein to thy house. Then I ordered my attendant Marids to sink the ship and I transformed thy two sisters into these black bitches; for I know all that hath passed between them and thee; but as for the youth, of a truth he is drowned." So saying, she flew up with me and the bitches, and presently set us down on the terrace-roof of my house, wherein I found ready stored the whole of what property was in my ship, nor was aught of it missing. "Now (continued the serpent that was), I swear by all engraven on the seal-ring of Solomon[1] (with whom be peace!) unless thou deal to each of these bitches three hundred stripes every day I will come and imprison thee forever under the earth." I answered, "Hearkening and obedience!"; and away she flew. But before going she again charged me saying, "I again swear by Him who made the two seas flow[2] (and this be my second oath) if thou gainsay me I will come and transform thee like thy sisters." Since then I have never failed, O Commander of the Faithful, to beat them with that number of blows till their blood flows with my tears, I pitying them the while, and well they wot that their being scourged is no fault of mine and they accept my excuses. And this is my tale and my history! The Caliph marvelled at her adventures and then signed to Ja'afar who said to the second lady, the Portress, "And thou, how camest thou by the welts and wheals upon thy body?" So she began the

Tale of the Portress.

KNOW, O Commander of the Faithful, that I had a father who, after fulfilling his time, deceased and left me great store of wealth. I remained single for a short time and presently married one of the richest of his day. I abode with him a year when he also died, and my share of his property amounted to eighty thousand dinars

---

1 Alluding to the Most High Name, the hundredth name of God, the Heb. Shem hamphorash, unknown save to a favoured few who by using it perform all manner of miracles.
2 *i. e.* the Mediterranean and the Indian Ocean.

in gold according to the holy law of inheritance.[1] Thus I became passing rich and my reputation spread far and wide, for I had made me ten changes of raiment, each worth a thousand dinars. One day as I was sitting at home, behold, there came in to me an old woman[2] with lantern jaws and cheeks sucked in, and eyes rucked up, and eyebrows scant and scald, and head bare and bald; and teeth broken by time and mauled, and back bending and neck-nape nodding, and face blotched, and rheum running, and hair like a snake black-and-white-speckled, in complexion a very fright, even as saith the poet of the like of her:—

Ill-omened hag! unshriven be her sins * Nor mercy visit her on dying bed:
Thousand head-strongest he-mules would her guiles, * Despite their bolting,
    lead with spider thread.

And as saith another:—

A hag to whom th' unlawful lawfullest * And witchcraft wisdom in her
    sight are grown:
A mischief-making brat, a demon-maid, * A whorish woman and a pimping
    crone.[3]

When the old woman entered she salamed to me and kissing the ground before me, said, "I have at home an orphan daughter and this night are her wedding and her displaying.[4] We be poor folks and strangers in this city knowing none inhabitant and we are broken-hearted. So do thou earn for thyself a recompense and a reward in Heaven by being present at her displaying and, when the ladies of this city shall hear that thou art to make act of presence, they also will present themselves; so shalt thou comfort her affliction, for she is sore bruised in spirit and she hath none to

---

[1] i. e. Settled by the Koran.

[2] The uglier the old woman the better procuress she is supposed to make. See the Santa Verdiana in Boccaccio v., 10. In Arab. "Ajuz" (old woman) is highly insulting and if addressed to an Egyptian, whatever be her age she will turn fiercely and resent it. The polite term is Shaybah (Pilgrimage iii., 200).

[3] The four ages of woman, considered after Demosthenes in her three-fold character, prostitute for pleasure, concubine for service and wife for breeding.

[4] Arab. "Jilá" (the Hindostani Julwa) = the displaying of the bride before the bride-groom for the first time, in different dresses, to the number of seven which are often borrowed for the occasion. The happy man must pay a fee called "the tax of face-unveiling" before he can see her features. Amongst Syrian Christians he sometimes tries to lift the veil by a sharp movement of the sword which is parried by the women present, and the blade remains entangled in the cloth. At last he succeeds, the bride sinks to the ground covering her face with her hands and the robes of her friends: presently she is raised up, her veil is readjusted and her face is left bare.

look to save Allah the Most High." Then she wept and kissed my feet reciting these couplets:—

"Thy presence bringeth us a grace * We own before thy winsome face:
And wert thou absent ne'er an one * Could stand in stead or take thy place."

So pity gat hold on me and compassion and I said, "Hearing is consenting and, please Allah, I will do somewhat more for her; nor shall she be shown to her bridegroom save in my raiment and ornaments and jewelry." At this the old woman rejoiced and bowed her head to my feet and kissed them, saying, "Allah requite thee weal, and comfort thy heart even as thou hast comforted mine! But, O my lady, do not trouble thyself to do me this service at this hour; be thou ready by supper-time,[1] when I will come and fetch thee." So saying she kissed my hand and went her ways. I set about stringing my pearls and donning my brocades and making my toilette, little recking what Fortune had in womb for me, when suddenly the old woman stood before me, simpering and smiling till she showed every tooth stump, and quoth she, "O my mistress, the city madams have arrived and when I apprized them that thou promisedst to be present, they were glad and they are now awaiting thee and looking eagerly for thy coming and for the honour of meeting thee." So I threw on my mantilla and, making the old crone walk before me and my handmaidens behind me, I fared till we came to a street well watered and swept neat, where the winnowing breeze blew cool and sweet. Here we were stopped by a gate arched over with a dome of marble stone firmly seated on solidest foundation, and leading to a Palace whose walls from earth rose tall and proud, and whose pinnacle was crowned by the clouds,[2] and over the doorway were writ these couplets:—

I am the wone where Mirth shall ever smile; * The home of Joyance through
    my lasting while:
And 'mid my court a fountain jets and flows, * Nor tears nor troubles shall
    that fount defile:
The marge with royal Nu'uman's[3] bloom is dight, * Myrtle, Narcissus-
    flower and Chamomile.

---

[1] Arab. "Ishá"= the first watch of the night, twilight, supper-time, supper. Moslems have borrowed the four watches of the Romans from 6 (a.m. or p.m.) to 6; and ignore the three original watches of the Jews, even, midnight and cockcrow (Sam. ii. 19, Judges vii. 19, and Exodus xiv. 24).

[2] A popular Arab hyperbole.

[3] Arab. "Shakáik al-Nu'umán," lit. the fissures of Nu'uman, the beautiful anemone, which a tyrannical King of Hirah, Nu'uman Al-Munzir, a contemporary of Mohammed, attempted to monopolize.

Arrived at the gate, before which hung a black curtain, the old woman knocked and it was opened to us; when we entered and found a vestibule spread with carpets and hung around with lamps all alight and wax candles in candelabra adorned with pendants of precious gems and noble ores. We passed on through this passage till we entered a saloon, whose like for grandeur and beauty is not to be found in this world. It was hung and carpeted with silken stuffs, and was illuminated with branches, sconces and tapers ranged in double row, an avenue abutting on the upper or noble end of the saloon, where stood a couch of juniper-wood encrusted with pearls and gems and surmounted by a baldaquin with mosquito-curtains of satin looped up with margarites. And hardly had we taken note of this when there came forth from the baldaquin a young lady and I looked, O Commander of the Faithful, upon a face and form more perfect than the moon when fullest, with a favour brighter than the dawn gleaming with saffron-hued light, even as the poet sang when he said:—

Thou pacest the palace a marvel-sight, * A bride for a Kisrá's or Kaisar's night!
Wantons the rose on thy roseate cheek, * O cheek as the blood of the dragon[1] bright!
Slim-waisted, languorous, sleepy-eyed, * With charms which promise all love-delight:
And the tire which attires thy tiara'd brow * Is a night of woe on a morn's glad light.

The fair young girl came down from the estrade and said to me, "Welcome and well come and good cheer to my sister, the dearly-beloved, the illustrious, and a thousand greetings!" Then she recited these couplets:—

"An but the house could know who cometh 'twould rejoice, * And kiss the very dust whereon thy foot was placed;
And with the tongue of circumstance the walls would say, * "Welcome and hail to one with generous gifts engraced!"

Then sat she down and said to me, "O my sister, I have a brother who hath had sight of thee at sundry wedding-feasts and festive seasons: he is a youth handsomer than I, and he hath fallen

---

[1] Arab. "Andam" = here the gum called dragon's blood; in other places the dye-wood known as brazil.

desperately in love with thee, for that bounteous Destiny hath garnered in thee all beauty and perfection; and he hath given silver to this old woman that she might visit thee; and she hath contrived on this wise to foregather us twain. He hath heard that thou art one of the nobles of thy tribe nor is he aught less in his; and, being desirous to ally his lot with thy lot, he hath practised this device to bring me in company with thee; for he is fain to marry thee after the ordinance of Allah and his Apostle; and in what is lawful and right there is no shame." When I heard these words and saw myself fairly entrapped in the house, I said, "Hearing is consenting." She was delighted at this and clapped her hands;[1] whereupon a door opened and out of it came a young man blooming in the prime of life, exquisitely dressed, a model of beauty and loveliness and symmetry and perfect grace, with gentle winning manners and eyebrows like a bended bow and shaft on cord, and eyes which bewitched all hearts with sorcery lawful in the sight of the Lord; even as saith some rhymer describing the like of him:—

His face as the face of the young moon shines * And Fortune stamps him with
    pearls for signs.[2]

And Allah favour him who said:—

Blest be his beauty; blest the Lord's decree * Who cast and shaped a thing so
    bright of blee:
All gifts of beauty he conjoins in one; * Lost in his love is all humanity;
For Beauty's self inscribed on his brow * "I testify there be no Good but he!"[3]

When I looked at him my heart inclined to him and I loved him; and he sat by my side and talked with me a while, when the young lady again clapped her hands and behold, a side-door opened and out of it came the Kazi with his four assessors as witnesses; and they saluted us and, sitting down, drew up and wrote out the marriage-contract between me and the youth and retired. Then he turned to me and said, "Be our night blessed," presently adding, "O my lady, I have a condition to lay on thee."

---

1 I need hardly say that in the East, where bells are unused, clapping the hands summons the servants. In India men cry "Quy hye" (Koi hái?) and in Brazil whistle "Pst!" after the fashion of Spain and Portugal.

2 The moles are here compared with pearls; a simile by no means common or appropriate.

3 A parody on the testification of Allah's Unity.

Quoth I, "O my lord, what is that?" Whereupon he arose and fetching a copy of the Holy Book presented it to me saying, "Swear hereon thou wilt never look at any other than myself nor incline thy body or thy heart to him." I swore readily enough to this and he joyed with exceeding joy and embraced me round the neck while love for him possessed my whole heart. Then they set the table[1] before us and we ate and drank till we were satisfied; but I was dying for the coming of the night. And when night did come he led me to the bride-chamber and slept with me on the bed and continued to kiss and embrace me till the morning—such a night I had never seen in my dreams. I lived with him a life of happiness and delight for a full month, at the end of which I asked his leave[2] to go on foot to the bazar and buy me certain especial stuffs and he gave me permission. So I donned my mantilla and, taking with me the old woman and a slave-girl,[3] I went to the khan of the silk-mercers, where I seated myself in the shop-front of a young merchant whom the old woman recommended, saying to me, "This youth's father died when he was a boy and left him great store of wealth: he hath by him a mighty fine[4] stock of goods and thou wilt find what thou seekest with him, for none in the bazar hath better stuffs than he." Then she said to him, "Show this lady the most costly stuffs thou hast by thee;" and he replied, "Hearkening and obedience!" Then she whispered me, "Say a civil word to him!"; but I replied, "I am pledged to address no man save my lord." And as she began to sound his praise I said sharply to her, "We want nought of thy sweet speeches; our wish is to buy of him whatsoever we need, and return home." So he

---

[1] Arab. "Simát" (prop. "Sumát"); the "dinner-table," composed of a round wooden stool supporting a large metal tray, the two being called "Sufrah" (or "Simat"): thus "Sufrah házirah!" means dinner is on the table. After the meal they are at once removed.

[2] In the text "Dastúr," the Persian word before noticed; "Izn" would be the proper Arabic equivalent.

[3] In the Moslem East a young woman, single or married, is not allowed to appear alone in the streets; and the police have a right to arrest delinquents. As a preventive of intrigues the precaution is excellent. During the Crimean war hundreds of officers, English, French and Italian, became familiar with Constantinople; and not a few flattered themselves on their success with Turkish women. I do not believe that a single *bona fide* case occurred: the "conquests" were all Greeks, Wallachians, Armenians or Jewesses.

[4] Arab. "Azím": translators do not seem to know that this word in The Nights often bears its Egyptian and slang sense, somewhat equivalent to our "deuced" or "mighty" or "awfully fine."

brought me all I sought and I offered him his money, but he
refused to take it saying, "Let it be a gift offered to my guest this
day!"   Then quoth I to the old woman, "If he will not take the
money, give him back his stuff."   "By Allah," cried he, "not a
thing will I take from thee: I sell it not for gold or for silver,
but I give it all as a gift for a single kiss; a kiss more precious to
me than everything the shop containeth."   Asked the old woman,
"What will the kiss profit thee?"; and, turning to me, whispered,
"O my daughter, thou hearest what this young fellow saith?
What harm will it do thee if he get a kiss from thee and thou
gettest what thou seekest at that price?"   Replied I, "I take refuge with Allah from such action!   Knowest thou not that I am
bound by an oath?"[1]   But she answered, "Now whist! just let
him kiss thee and neither speak to him nor lean over him, so shalt
thou keep thine oath and thy silver, and no harm whatever shall
befal thee."   And she ceased not to persuade me and importune
me and make light of the matter till evil entered into my mind and
I put my head in the poke[2] and, declaring I would ne'er consent,
consented.   So I veiled my eyes and held up the edge of my
mantilla between me and the people passing and he put his
mouth to my cheek under the veil.   But while kissing me he bit
me so hard a bite that it tore the flesh from my cheek,[3] and blood
flowed fast and faintness came over me.   The old woman caught
me in her arms and, when I came to myself, I found the shop shut
up and her sorrowing over me and saying, "Thank Allah for
averting what might have been worse!"   Then she said to me,
"Come, take heart and let us go home before the matter become
public and thou be dishonoured.   And when thou art safe inside
the house feign sickness and lie down and cover thyself up; and
I will bring thee powders and plasters to cure this bite withal,
and thy wound will be healed at the latest in three days."   So
after a while I arose and I was in extreme distress and terror came
full upon me; but I went on little by little till I reached the house
when I pleaded illness and lay me down.   When it was night my
husband came in to me and said, "What hath befallen thee, O my

---

[1] This is a very serious thing amongst Moslems and scrupulous men often make great
sacrifices to avoid taking an oath.

[2] We should say "into the noose."

[3] The man had fallen in love with her and determined to mark her so that she might
be his.

darling, in this excursion of thine?"; and I replied, "I am not
well: my head acheth badly." Then he lighted a candle and
drew near me and looked hard at me and asked, "What is that
wound I see on thy cheek and in the tenderest part too?" And I
answered, "When I went out to-day with thy leave to buy stuffs,
a camel laden with firewood jostled me and one of the pieces tore
my veil and wounded my cheek as thou seest; for indeed the ways
of this city are strait." "To-morrow," cried he, "I will go complain to the Governor, so shall he gibbet every fuel-seller in
Baghdad." "Allah upon thee," said I, "burden not thy soul with
such sin against any man. The fact is I was riding on an ass and
it stumbled, throwing me to the ground; and my cheek lighted
upon a stick or a bit of glass and got this wound." "Then," said
he, "to-morrow I will go up to Ja'afar the Barmaki and tell
him the story, so shall he kill every donkey-boy in Baghdad."
"Wouldst thou destroy all these men because of my wound,"
said I, "when this which befel me was by decree of Allah and
His destiny?" But he answered, "There is no help for it;" and,
springing to his feet, plied me with words and pressed me till I
was perplexed and frightened; and I stuttered and stammered
and my speech waxed thick and I said, "This is a mere accident
by decree of Allah." Then, O Commander of the Faithful, he
guessed my case and said, "Thou hast been false to thine oath."
He at once cried out with a loud cry, whereupon a door opened
and in came seven black slaves whom he commanded to drag me
from my bed and throw me down in the middle of the room.
Furthermore, he ordered one of them to pinion my elbows and
squat upon my head; and a second to sit upon my knees and
secure my feet; and drawing his sword he gave it to a third and
said, "Strike her, O Sa'ad, and cut her in twain and let each one
take half and cast it into the Tigris[1] that the fish may eat her;
for such is the retribution due to those who violate their vows
and are unfaithful to their love." And he redoubled in wrath
and recited these couplets:—

"An there be one who shares with me her love, * I'd strangle Love tho' life
    by Love were slain;
Saying, O Soul, Death were the nobler choice, * For ill is Love when shared
    'twixt partners twain."

Then he repeated to the slave, "Smite her, O Sa'ad!" And when

---

[1] Arab. "Dajlah," in which we find the Heb. Hid-dekel.

the slave who was sitting upon me made sure of the command he bent down to me and said, "O my mistress, repeat the profession of Faith and bethink thee if there be any thing thou wouldst have done; for verily this is the last hour of thy life." "O good slave," said I, "wait but a little while and get off my head that I may charge thee with my last injunctions." Then I raised my head and saw the state I was in, how I had fallen from high degree into lowest disgrace; and into death after life (and such life!) and how I had brought my punishment on myself by my own sin; whereupon the tears streamed from mine eyes and I wept with exceeding weeping. But he looked on me with eyes of wrath, and began repeating:—

"Tell her who turneth from our love to work it injury sore, * And taketh her
    a fine new love the old love tossing o'er:
We cry enough o' thee ere thou enough of us shalt cry! * What past between
    us doth suffice and haply something more."[1]

When I heard this, O Commander of the Faithful, I wept and looked at him and began repeating these couplets:—

"To severance you doom my love and all unmoved remain; * My tear-sore
    lids you sleepless make and sleep while I complain:
You make firm friendship reign between mine eyes and insomny; * Yet can my
    heart forget you not, nor tears can I restrain:
You made me swear with many an oath my troth to hold for aye; * But when
    you reigned my bosom's lord you wrought me traitor-bane:
I loved you like a silly child who wots not what is Love; * Then spare the
    learner, let her not be by the master slain!
By Allah's name I pray you write, when I am dead and gone, * Upon my
    tomb, This died of Love whose senses Love had ta'en:
Then haply one shall pass that way who fire of Love hath felt, * And tread-
    ing on a lover's heart with ruth and woe shall melt."

When I ended my verses tears came again; but the poetry and the weeping only added fury to his fury, and he recited:—

" 'Twas not satiety bade me leave the dearling of my soul, * But that she
    sinned a mortal sin which clipt me in its clip:
She sought to let another share the love between us twain, * But my True
    Faith of Unity refuseth partnership."[2]

---

[1] Such an execution would be contrary to Moslem law: but people would look leniently upon the peccadillo of beheading or sacking a faithless wife. Moreover the youth was of the blood royal and *A quoi bon être prince?* as was said by a boy of viceroyal family in Egypt to his tutor who reproached him for unnecessarily shooting down a poor old man.

[2] Arab. "Shirk," partnership, evening or associating gods with God; polytheism: especially levelled at the Hindu triadism, Guebre dualism and Christian Trinitarianism.

When he ceased reciting I wept again and prayed his pardon and humbled myself before him and spoke him softly, saying to my-self, "I will work on him with words; so haply he will refrain from slaying me, even though he take all I have." So I com-plained of my sufferings and began to repeat these couplets:—

"Now, by thy life and wert thou just my life thou hadst not ta'en, * But who
    can break the severance-law which parteth lovers twain!
Thou loadest me with heavy weight of longing love, when I * Can hardly
    bear my chemisette for weakness and for pain:
I marvel not to see my life and soul in ruin lain: * I marvel much to see my
    frame such severance-pangs sustain."

When I ended my verse I wept again; and he looked at me and reviled me in abusive language,[1] repeating these couplets:—

"Thou wast all taken up with love of other man, not me; * 'Twas thine to
    show me severance-face, 'twas only mine to see:
I'll leave thee for that first thou wast of me to take thy leave * And patient
    bear that parting blow thou borest so patiently:
E'en as thou soughtest other love, so other love I'll seek, * And make the
    crime of murdering love thine own atrocity."

When he had ended his verses he again cried out to the slave, "Cut her in half and free us from her, for we have no profit of her." So the slave drew near me, O Commander of the Faithful, and I ceased bandying verses and made sure of death and, despair-ing of life, committed my affairs to Almighty Allah, when behold, the old woman rushed in and threw herself at my husband's feet and kissed them and wept and said, "O my son, by the rights of my fosterage and by my long service to thee, I conjure thee pardon this young lady, for indeed she hath done nothing deserv-ing such doom. Thou art a very young man and I fear lest her death be laid at thy door; for it is said:—Whoso slayeth shall be slain. As for this wanton (since thou deemest her such) drive her out from thy doors, from thy love and from thy heart." And she ceased not to weep and importune him till he relented and said, "I pardon her, but needs must I set on her my mark which shall show upon her all my life." Then he bade the slaves drag me along the ground and lay me out at full length, after stripping

---

[1] Arab. "Shatm" = abuse, generally couched in foulest language with especial reference to the privy parts of female relatives.

me of all my clothes;[1] and when the slaves had so sat upon me that I could not move, he fetched in a rod of quince-tree and came down with it upon my body, and continued beating me on the back and sides till I lost consciousness from excess of pain, and I despaired of life.   Then he commanded the slaves to take me away as soon as it was dark, together with the old woman to show them the way and throw me upon the floor of the house wherein I dwelt before my marriage.   They did their lord's bidding and cast me down in my old home and went their ways. I did not revive from my swoon till dawn appeared, when I applied myself to the dressing of my wounds with ointments and other medicaments; and I medicined myself, but my sides and ribs still showed signs of the rod as thou hast seen.   I lay in weakly case and confined to my bed for four months before I was able to rise and health returned to me.   At the end of that time I went to the house where all this had happened and found it a ruin; the street had been pulled down endlong and rubbish-heaps rose where the building erst was; nor could I learn how this had come about.   Then I betook myself to this my sister on my father's side and found her with these two black bitches.   I saluted her and told her what had betided me and the whole of my story and she said, "O my sister, who is safe from the despite of Time and secure?   Thanks be to Allah who has brought thee off safely;" and she began to say:—

"Such is the World, so bear a patient heart * When riches leave thee and
    when friends depart!"

Then she told me her own story, and what had happened to her with her two sisters and how matters had ended; so we abode together and the subject of marriage was never on our tongues for all these years.   After a while we were joined by our other sister, the procuratrix, who goeth out every morning and buyeth all we require for the day and night; and we continued in such condition till this last night.   In the morning our sister went out, as usual, to make her market and then befel us what befel from bringing the Porter into the house and admitting these three Kalandar-men.   We entreated them kindly and honourably and

---

[1] When a woman is bastinadoed in the East they leave her some portion of dress and pour over her sundry buckets of water for a delicate consideration.   When the hands are beaten they are passed through holes in the curtain separating the sufferer from mankind, and made fast to a "falakah" or pole.

a quarter of the night had not passed ere three grave and respectable merchants from Mosul joined us and told us their
adventures. We sat talking with them but on one condition
which they violated, whereupon we treated them as sorted with
their breach of promise, and made them repeat the account they
had given of themselves. They did our bidding and we forgave
their offence; so they departed from us and this morning we
were unexpectedly summoned to thy presence. And such is
our story! The Caliph wondered at her words and bade the
tale be recorded and chronicled and laid up in his muniment-
chambers.——And Shahrazad perceived the dawn of day and
ceased saying her permitted say.

When it was the Nineteenth Night,

She continued, It hath reached me, O auspicious King, that the
Caliph commanded this story and those of the sister and the
Kalandars to be recorded in the archives and be set in the royal
muniment-chambers. Then he asked the eldest lady, the mistress of the house, "Knowest thou the whereabouts of the Ifritah
who spelled thy sisters?"; and she answered, "O Commander of
the Faithful, she gave me a ringlet of her hair saying:—Whenas
thou wouldest see me, burn a couple of these hairs and I will be
with thee forthright, even though I were beyond Caucasus-
mountain." Quoth the Caliph, "Bring me hither the hair." So
she brought it and he threw the whole lock upon the fire. As
soon as the odour of the burning hair dispread itself, the palace
shook and trembled, and all present heard a rumbling and rolling
of thunder and a noise as of wings and lo! the Jinniyah who had
been a serpent stood in the Caliph's presence. Now she was a
Moslemah, so she saluted him and said, "Peace be with thee O
Vicar[1] of Allah;" whereto he replied, "And with thee also be
peace and the mercy of Allah and His blessing." Then she continued, "Know that this damsel sowed for me the seed of kindness, wherefor I cannot enough requite her, in that she delivered
me from death and destroyed mine enemy. Now I had seen how
her sisters dealt with her and felt myself bound to avenge her

---

[1] Arab. "Khalifah," Caliph. The word is also used for the successor of a Santon or
holy man.

on them. At first I was minded to slay them, but I feared it
would be grievous to her, so I transformed them to bitches;
but if thou desire their release, O Commander of the Faithful, I
will release them to pleasure thee and her for I am of the Moslems." Quoth the Caliph, "Release them and after we will look
into the affair of the beaten lady and consider her case carefully;
and if the truth of her story be evidenced I will exact retaliation[1]
from him who wronged her." Said the Ifritah, "O Commander
of the Faithful, I will forthwith release them and will discover
to thee the man who did that deed by this lady and wronged her
and took her property, and he is the nearest of all men to thee!"
So saying she took a cup of water and muttered a spell over it
and uttered words there was no understanding; then she
sprinkled some of the water over the faces of the two bitches,
saying, "Return to your former human shape!" whereupon they
were restored to their natural forms and fell to praising their
Creator. Then said the Ifritah, "O Commander of the Faithful,
of a truth he who scourged this lady with rods is thy son Al-Amin
brother of Al-Maamun;[2] for he had heard of her beauty and loveliness and he played a lover's stratagem with her and married her
according to the law and committed the crime (such as it is) of
scourging her. Yet indeed he is not to be blamed for beating her,
for he laid a condition on her and swore her by a solemn oath not
to do a certain thing; however, she was false to her vow and he
was minded to put her to death, but he feared Almighty Allah
and contented himself with scourging her, as thou hast seen, and
with sending her back to her own place. Such is the story of the
second lady and the Lord knoweth all." When the Caliph heard
these words of the Ifritah, and knew who had beaten the damsel,
he marvelled with mighty marvel and said, "Praise be to Allah,
the Most High, the Almighty, who hath shown his exceeding
mercy towards me, enabling me to deliver these two damsels
from sorcery and torture, and vouchsafing to let me know the
secret of this lady's history! And now by Allah, we will do a
deed which shall be recorded of us after we are no more." Then
he summoned his son Al-Amin and questioned him of the story
of the second lady, the portress; and he told it in the face of truth;

---

[1] Arab. "Sár;" here the Koranic word for carrying out the venerable and undying
lex talionis the original basis of all criminal jurisprudence. Its main fault is that justice
repeats the offence.
[2] Both these sons of Harun became Caliphs, as we shall see in The Nights.

whereupon the Caliph bade call into presence the Kazis and their witnesses and the three Kalandars and the first lady with her sisters-german who had been ensorcelled; and he married the three to the three Kalandars whom he knew to be princes and sons of Kings and he appointed them chamberlains about his person, assigning to them stipends and allowances and all that they required, and lodging them in his palace at Baghdad. He returned the beaten lady to his son, Al-Amin, renewing the marriage-contract between them and gave her great wealth and bade rebuild the house fairer than it was before. As for himself he took to wife the procuratrix and lay with her that night: and next day he set apart for her an apartment in his Serraglio, with handmaidens for her service and a fixed daily allowance. And the people marvelled at their Caliph's generosity and natural beneficence and princely widsom; nor did he forget to send all these histories to be recorded in his annals. When Shahrazad ceased speaking Dunyazad exclaimed, "O my own sister, by Allah in very sooth this is a right pleasant tale and a delectable; never was heard the like of it, but prithee tell me now another story to while away what yet remaineth of the waking hours of this our night." She replied, "With love and gladness if the King give me leave;" and he said, "Tell thy tale and tell it quickly." So she began, in these words,

THE TALE OF THE THREE APPLES.

THEY relate, O King of the age and lord of the time and of these days, that the Caliph Harun al-Rashid summoned his Wazir Ja'afar one night and said to him, "I desire to go down into the city and question the common folk concerning the conduct of those charged with its governance; and those of whom they complain we will depose from office and those whom they commend we will promote." Quoth Ja'afar, "Hearkening and obedience!" So the Caliph went down with Ja'afar and Eunuch Masrur to the town and walked about the streets and markets and, as they were threading a narrow alley, they came upon a very old man with a fishing-net and crate to carry small fish on his head, and in his hand a staff; and, as he walked at a leisurely pace, he repeated these lines:—

"They say me:—Thou shinest a light to mankind * With thy lore as the night
    which the Moon doth uplight!
I answer, "A truce to your jests and your gibes; * Without luck what is learn-
    ing?—a poor-devil wight!
If they take me to pawn with my lore in my pouch, * With my volumes to read
    and my ink-case to write,
For one day's provision they never could pledge me; * As likely on Doomsday
    to draw bill at sight:"
How poorly, indeed, doth it fare wi' the poor, * With his pauper existence and
    beggarly plight:
In summer he faileth provision to find; * In winter the fire-pot's his only
    delight:
The street-dogs with bite and with bark to him rise, * And each losel receives
    him with bark and with bite:
If he lift up his voice and complain of his wrong, * None pities or heeds him,
    however he's right;
And when sorrows and evils like these he must brave * His happiest home-
    stead were down in the grave."

When the Caliph heard his verses he said to Ja'afar, "See this
poor man and note his verses, for surely they point to his neces-
sities." Then he accosted him and asked, "O Shaykh, what be
thine occupation?" and the poor man answered, "O my lord, I
am a fisherman with a family to keep and I have been out between
mid-day and this time; and not a thing hath Allah made my portion
wherewithal to feed my family. I cannot even pawn myself to
buy them a supper and I hate and disgust my life and I hanker
after death." Quoth the Caliph, "Say me, wilt thou return with
us to Tigris' bank and cast thy net on my luck, and whatsoever
turneth up I will buy of thee for an hundred gold pieces?" The
man rejoiced when he heard these words and said, "On my head
be it! I will go back with you;" and, returning with them riverwards, made a cast and waited a while; then he hauled in the rope
and dragged the net ashore and there appeared in it a chest padlocked and heavy. The Caliph examined it and lifted it finding it
weighty; so he gave the fisherman two hundred dinars and sent
him about his business; whilst Masrur, aided by the Caliph,
carried the chest to the palace and set it down and lighted the
candles. Ja'afar and Masrur then broke it open and found therein
a basket of palm-leaves corded with red worsted. This they cut
open and saw within it a piece of carpet which they lifted out,
and under it was a woman's mantilla folded in four, which they
pulled out; and at the bottom of the chest they came upon a
young lady, fair as a silver ingot, slain and cut into nineteen

pieces. When the Caliph looked upon her he cried, "Alas!" and tears ran down his cheeks and turning to Ja'afar he said, "O dog of Wazirs,[1] shall folk be murdered in our reign and be cast into the river to be a burden and a responsibility for us on the Day of Doom? By Allah, we must avenge this woman on her murderer and he shall be made die the worst of deaths!" And presently he added, "Now, as surely as we are descended from the Sons of Abbas,[2] if thou bring us not him who slew her, that we do her justice on him, I will hang thee at the gate of my palace, thee and forty of thy kith and kin by thy side." And the Caliph was wroth with exceeding rage. Quoth Ja'afar, "Grant me three days' delay;" and quoth the Caliph, "We grant thee this." So Ja'afar went out from before him and returned to his own house, full of sorrow and saying to himself, "How shall I find him who murdered this damsel, that I may bring him before the Caliph? If I bring other than the murderer, it will be laid to my charge by the Lord: in very sooth I wot not what to do." He kept his house three days and on the fourth day the Caliph sent one of the Chamberlains for him and, as he came into the presence, asked him, "Where is the murderer of the damsel?" to which answered Ja'afar, "O Commander of the Faithful, am I inspector of murdered folk that I should ken who killed her?" The Caliph was furious at his answer and bade hang him before the palace-gate and commanded that a crier cry through the streets of Baghdad, "Whoso would see the hanging of Ja'afar, the Barmaki, Wazir of the Caliph, with forty of the Barmecides,[3] his cousins and kinsmen, before the palace-gate, let him come and let him look!" The people flocked out from all the quarters of the city to witness the execution of Ja'afar and his kinsmen, not knowing the cause. Then they set up the gallows and made Ja'afar and the others stand underneath in readiness for execu-

---

[1] "Dog" and "hog" are still highly popular terms of abuse. The Rabbis will not defile their lips with "pig;" but say "Dabhar akhir"="another thing."

[2] The "hero eponymus" of the Abbaside dynasty, Abbas having been the brother of Abdullah, the father of Mohammed. He is a famous personage in Al-Islam (D'Herbelot).

[3] Europe translates the word "Barmecides." It is Persian from bar (up) and makidan (to suck). The vulgar legend is that Ja'afar, the first of the name, appeared before the Caliph Abd al-Malik with a ring poisoned for his own need; and that the Caliph, warned of it by the clapping of two stones which he wore ad hoc, charged the visitor with intention to murder him. He excused himself and in his speech occurred the Persian word "Barmakam," which may mean "I shall sup it up," or "I am a Barmak," that is, a high priest among the Guebres. See D'Herbelot s.v.

tion, but whilst every eye was looking for the Caliph's signal, and the crowd wept for Ja'afar and his cousins of the Barmecides, lo and behold! a young man fair of face and neat of dress and of favour like the moon raining light, with eyes black and bright, and brow flower-white, and cheeks red as rose and young down where the beard grows, and a mole like a grain of ambergris, pushed his way through the people till he stood immediately before the Wazir and said to him, "Safety to thee from this strait, O Prince of the Emirs and Asylum of the poor! I am the man who slew the woman ye found in the chest, so hang me for her and do her justice on me!" When Ja'afar heard the youth's confession he rejoiced at his own deliverance, but grieved and sorrowed for the fair youth; and whilst they were yet talking behold, another man well stricken in years pressed forwards through the people and thrust his way amid the populace till he came to Ja'afar and the youth, whom he saluted saying, "Ho thou the Wazir and Prince sans-peer! believe not the words of this youth. Of a surety none murdered the damsel but I; take her wreak on me this moment; for, an thou do not thus, I will require it of thee before Almighty Allah." Then quoth the young man, "O Wazir, this is an old man in his dotage who wotteth not whatso he saith ever, and I am he who murdered her, so do thou avenge her on me!" Quoth the old man, "O my son, thou art young and desirest the joys of the world and I am old and weary and surfeited with the world: I will offer my life as a ransom for thee and for the Wazir and his cousins. No one murdered the damsel but I, so Allah upon thee, make haste to hang me, for no life is left in me now that hers is gone." The Wazir marvelled much at all this strangeness and, taking the young man and the old man, carried them before the Caliph, where, after kissing the ground seven times between his hands, he said, "O Commander of the Faithful, I bring thee the murderer of the damsel!" "Where is he?", asked the Caliph and Ja'afar answered, "This young man saith, I am the murderer, and this old man giving him the lie saith, I am the murderer, and behold, here are the twain standing before thee." The Caliph looked at the old man and the young man and asked, "Which of you killed the girl?" The young man replied, "No one slew her save I;" and the old man answered, "Indeed none killed her but myself." Then said the Caliph to Ja'afar, "Take the twain and hang them both;" but Ja'afar rejoined, "Since one of them was the murderer, to hang the other were mere injustice."[1] "By Him who raised the firmament and dispread the earth like a carpet," cried the youth, "I am he who slew the damsel;" and he went on to describe the manner of her murder and the basket, the mantilla and the bit of carpet, in fact all that the Caliph had found upon her. So the Caliph was certified that the young man was the murderer; whereat he wondered and asked him, "What was the cause of thy wrongfully doing this damsel to die and what made thee confess the murder without the bastinado, and what brought thee here to yield up thy life, and what made thee say Do her wreak upon me?" The youth answered, "Know, O Commander of the Faithful, that this woman was my wife and the mother of my children; also my first cousin and the daughter of my paternal uncle, this old man who is my father's own brother. When I married her she was a maid[2] and Allah blessed me with three male children by her; she loved me and served me and I saw no evil in her, for I also loved her with fondest love. Now on the first day of this month she fell ill with grievous sickness and I fetched in physicians to her; but recovery came to her little by little and, when I wished her to go to the Hammam-bath, she said, "There is a something I long for before I go to the bath and I long for it with an exceeding longing." "To hear is to comply," said I, "And what is it?" Quoth she, "I have a queasy craving for an apple, to smell it and bite a bit of it." I replied, "Hadst thou a thousand longings I would try to satisfy them!" So I went on the instant into the city and sought for apples but could find none; yet, had they cost a gold piece each, would I have bought them. I was vexed at this and went home and said, "O daughter of my uncle, by Allah I can find none!" She was distressed, being yet very weakly, and her weakness increased greatly on her that night and I felt anxious and alarmed on her account. As soon as morning dawned I went out again and made the round of the gardens, one by one, but found no apples anywhere. At last there met me an old gardener, of whom I asked about them and he answered, "O my son, this fruit is a

---

[1] Arab. "Zulm," the deadliest of monarch's sins. One of the sayings of Mohammed, popularly quoted, is, "Kingdom endureth with Kufr or infidelity (*i. e.* without accepting Al-Islam) but endureth not with Zulm or injustice." Hence the good Moslem will not complain of the rule of Kafirs or Unbelievers, like the English, so long as they rule him righteously and according to his own law.

[2] All this aggravates his crime: had she been a widow she would not have had upon him "the claims of maidenhead," the premio della verginita of Boccaccio, x. 10.

rarity with us and is not now to be found save in the garden of
the Commander of the Faithful at Bassorah, where the gardener
keepeth it for the Caliph's eating." I returned to my house
troubled by my ill-success; and my love for my wife and my
affection moved me to undertake the journey. So I gat me ready
and set out and travelled fifteen days and nights, going and
coming, and brought her three apples which I bought from the
gardener for three dinars. But when I went in to my wife and
set them before her, she took no pleasure in them and let them
lie by her side; for her weakness and fever had increased on her
and her malady lasted without abating ten days, after which
time she began to recover health. So I left my house and betaking me to my shop sat there buying and selling; and about
midday behold, a great ugly black slave, long as a lance and
broad as a bench, passed by my shop holding in hand one of the
three apples wherewith he was playing. Quoth I, "O my good
slave, tell me whence thou tookest that apple, that I may get the
like of it?" He laughed and answered, "I got it from my mistress, for I had been absent and on my return I found her lying ill
with three apples by her side, and she said to me, 'My horned
wittol of a husband made a journey for them to Bassorah and
bought them for three dinars.' So I ate and drank with her and
took this one from her."[1] When I heard such words from the
slave, O Commander of the Faithful, the world grew black before
my face, and I arose and locked up my shop and went home
beside myself for excess of rage. I looked for the apples and
finding only two of the three asked my wife, "O my cousin,
where is the third apple?"; and raising her head languidly she
answered, "I wot not, O son of my uncle, where 'tis gone!"
This convinced me that the slave had spoken the truth, so I took
a knife and coming behind her got upon her breast without a
word said and cut her throat. Then I hewed off her head and
her limbs in pieces and, wrapping her in her mantilla and a rag of
carpet, hurriedly sewed up the whole which I set in a chest and,

---

[1] It is supposed that slaves cannot help telling these fatal lies. Arab story-books are
full of ancient and modern instances and some have become "Joe Millers." Moreover
it is held unworthy of a free-born man to take over-notice of these servile villanies; hence
the scoundrel in the story escapes unpunished. I have already noticed the predilection
of debauched women for these "skunks of the human race;" and the young man in the
text evidently suspected that his wife had passed herself this "little caprice." The excuse
which the Caliph would find for him is the *pundonor* shown in killing one he loved so fondly.

locking it tight, loaded it on my he-mule and threw it into the Tigris with my own hands. So Allah upon thee, O Commander of the Faithful, make haste to hang me, as I fear lest she appeal for vengeance on Resurrection Day. For, when I had thrown her into the river and none knew aught of it, as I went back home I found my eldest son crying and yet he knew naught of what I had done with his mother. I asked him, "What hath made thee weep, my boy?" and he answered, "I took one of the three apples which were by my mammy and went down into the lane to play with my brethren when behold, a big long black slave snatched it from my hand and said, 'Whence hadst thou this?' Quoth I, 'My father travelled far for it, and brought it from Bassorah for my mother who was ill and two other apples for which he paid three ducats.' He took no heed of my words and I asked for the apple a second and a third time, but he cuffed me and kicked me and went off with it. I was afraid lest my mother should swinge me on account of the apple, so for fear of her I went with my brother outside the city and stayed there till evening closed in upon us; and indeed I am in fear of her; and now by Allah, O my father, say nothing to her of this or it may add to her ailment!" When I heard what my child said I knew that the slave was he who had foully slandered my wife, the daughter of my uncle, and was certified that I had slain her wrongfully. So I wept with exceeding weeping and presently this old man, my paternal uncle and her father, came in; and I told him what had happened and he sat down by my side and wept and we ceased not weeping till midnight. We have kept up mourning for her these last five days and we lamented her in the deepest sorrow for that she was unjustly done to die. This came from the gratuitous lying of the slave, the blackamoor, and this was the manner of my killing her; so I conjure thee, by the honour of thine ancestors, make haste to kill me and do her justice upon me, as there is no living for me after her!" The Caliph marvelled at his words and said, "By Allah, the young man is excusable: I will hang none but the accursed slave and I will do a deed which shall comfort the ill-at-ease and suffering, and which shall please the All-glorious King."——And Shahrazad perceived the dawn of day and ceased saying her permitted say.

When it was the Twentieth Night,

She said, It hath reached me, O auspicious King, that the Caliph swore he would hang none but the slave, for the youth was excusable. Then he turned to Ja'afar and said to him, "Bring before me this accursed slave who was the sole cause of this calamity; and, if thou bring him not before me within three days, thou shalt be slain in his stead." So Ja'afar fared forth weeping and saying, "Two deaths have already beset me, nor shall the crock come off safe from every shock.[1] In this matter craft and cunning are of no avail; but He who preserved my life the first time can preserve it a second time. By Allah, I will not leave my house during the three days of life which remain to me and let the Truth (whose perfection be praised!) do e'en as He will." So he kept his house three days, and on the fourth day he summoned the Kazis and legal witnesses and made his last will and testament, and took leave of his children weeping. Presently in came a messenger from the Caliph and said to him, "The Commander of the Faithful is in the most violent rage that can be, and he sendeth to seek thee and he sweareth that the day shall certainly not pass without thy being hanged unless the slave be forthcoming." When Ja'afar heard this he wept, and his children and slaves and all who were in the house wept with him. After he had bidden adieu to everybody except his youngest daughter, he proceeded to farewell her; for he loved this wee one, who was a beautiful child, more than all his other children; and he pressed her to his breast and kissed her and wept bitterly at parting from her; when he felt something round inside the bosom of her dress and asked her, "O my little maid, what is in thy bosom pocket?"; "O my father," she replied, "it is an apple with the name of our Lord the Caliph written upon it. Rayhán our slave brought it to me four days ago and would not let me have it till I gave him two dinars for it." When Ja'afar heard speak of the slave and the apple, he was glad and put his hand into his child's pocket[2] and drew out the apple and knew it and rejoiced saying, "O ready Dispeller of trouble!"[3] Then he bade them bring the

---

[1] The Arab equivalent of our pitcher and well.
[2] *i.e.* Where the dress sits loosely about the bust.
[3] He had trusted in Allah and his trust was justified.

slave and said to him, "Fie upon thee, Rayhan! whence haddest thou this apple?" "By Allah, O my master," he replied, "though a lie may get a man once off, yet may truth get him off, and well off, again and again. I did not steal this apple from thy palace nor from the gardens of the Commander of the Faithful. The fact is that five days ago, as I was walking along one of the alleys of this city, I saw some little ones at play and this apple in hand of one of them. So I snatched it from him and beat him and he cried and said, 'O youth this apple is my mother's and she is ill. She told my father how she longed for an apple, so he travelled to Bassorah and bought her three apples for three gold pieces, and I took one of them to play withal.' He wept again, but I paid no heed to what he said and carried it off and brought it here, and my little lady bought it of me for two dinars of gold. And this is the whole story." When Ja'afar heard his words he marvelled that the murder of the damsel and all this misery should have been caused by his slave; he grieved for the relation of the slave to himself, while rejoicing over his own deliverance, and he repeated these lines:—

"If ill betide thee through thy slave, * Make him forthright thy sacrifice:
A many serviles thou shalt find, * But life comes once and never twice."

Then he took the slave's hand and, leading him to the Caliph, related the story from first to last and the Caliph marvelled with extreme astonishment, and laughed till he fell on his back and ordered that the story be recorded and be made public amongst the people. But Ja'afar said, "Marvel not, O Commander of the Faithful, at this adventure, for it is not more wondrous than the History of the Wazir Núr al-Dín Ali of Egypt and his brother Shams al-Dín Mohammed." Quoth the Caliph, "Out with it; but what can be stranger than this story?" And Ja'afar answered, "O Commander of the Faithful, I will not tell it thee, save on condition that thou pardon my slave;" and the Caliph rejoined, "If it be indeed more wondrous than that of the three apples, I grant thee his blood, and if not I will surely slay thy slave." So Ja'afar began in these words the

TALE OF NUR AL-DIN ALI AND HIS SON.

KNOW, O Commander of the Faithful, that in times of yore the land of Egypt was ruled by a Sultan endowed with justice and generosity, one who loved the pious poor and companied with the Olema and learned men; and he had a Wazir, a wise and an experienced, well versed in affairs and in the art of government. This Minister, who was a very old man, had two sons, as they were two moons; never man saw the like of them for beauty and grace, the elder called Shams al-Din Mohammed and the younger Nur al-Din Ali; but the younger excelled the elder in seemliness and pleasing semblance, so that folk heard his fame in far countries and men flocked to Egypt for the purpose of seeing him. In course of time their father, the Wazir, died and was deeply regretted and mourned by the Sultan, who sent for his two sons and, investing them with dresses of honour,[1] said to them, "Let not your hearts be troubled, for ye shall stand in your father's stead and be joint Ministers of Egypt." At this they rejoiced and kissed the ground before him and performed the ceremonial mourning[2] for their father during a full month; after which time they entered upon the Wazirate, and the power passed into their hands as it had been in the hands of their father, each doing duty for a week at a time. They lived under the same roof and their word was one; and whenever the Sultan desired to travel they took it by turns to be in attendance on him. It fortuned one night that the Sultan purposed setting out on a journey next morning, and the elder, whose turn it was to accompany him, was sitting conversing with his brother and said to him, "O my brother, it is my wish that we both marry, I and thou, two sisters; and go in to our wives on one and the same night." "Do, O my brother, as thou desirest," the younger replied, "for right is thy recking and surely I will comply with thee in whatso thou sayest." So they agreed upon this and quoth Shams al-

---

[1] Arab. "Khila'ah" prop. what a man strips from his person: gen. an honorary gift. It is something more than the "robe of honour" of our chivalrous romances, as it includes a horse, a sword (often gold-hilted), a black turban (amongst the Abbasides) embroidered with gold, a violet-coloured mantle, a waist-shawl and a gold neck-chain and shoe-buckles.

[2] Arab. "Izá," *i.e.* the visits of condolence and so forth which are long and terribly wearisome in the Moslem East.

Din, "If Allah decree that we marry two damsels and go in to them on the same night, and they shall conceive on their bride-nights and bear children to us on the same day, and by Allah's will thy wife bear thee a son and my wife bear me a daughter, let us wed them either to other, for they will be cousins." Quoth Nur al-Din, "O my brother, Shams al-Din, what dower[1] wilt thou require from my son for thy daughter?" Quoth Shams al-Din, "I will take three thousand dinars and three pleasure gardens and three farms; and it would not be seemly that the youth make contract for less than this." When Nur al-Din heard such demand he said, "What manner of dower is this thou wouldest impose upon my son? Wottest thou not that we are brothers and both by Allah's grace Wazirs and equal in office? It behoveth thee to offer thy daughter to my son without marriage settlement; or, if one need be, it should represent a mere nominal value by way of show to the world: for thou knowest that the masculine is worthier than the feminine, and my son is a male and our memory will be preserved by him, not by thy daughter." "But what," said Shams al-Din, "is she to have?"; and Nur al-Din continued, "Through her we shall not be remembered among the Emirs of the earth; but I see thou wouldest do with me according to the saying:—An thou wouldst bluff off a buyer, ask him high price and higher; or as did a man who, they say, went to a friend and asked something of him being in necessity and was answered, 'Bismillah,[2] in the name of Allah, I will do all what thou requirest but come to-morrow!' Whereupon the other replied in this verse:—

'When he who is asked a favour saith "To-morrow," * The wise man wots 'tis vain to beg or borrow.'"

Quoth Shams al-Din, "Basta![3] I see thee fail in respect to me by making thy son of more account than my daughter; and 'tis plain

---

[1] Arab. "Mahr," the money settled by the man before marriage on the woman and without which the contract is not valid. Usually half of it is paid down on the marriage-day and the other half when the husband dies or divorces his wife. But if she take a divorce she forfeits her right to it, and obscene fellows, especially Persians, often compel her to demand divorce by unnatural and preposterous use of her person.

[2] Bismillah here means "Thou art welcome to it."

[3] Arab. "Bassak," half Pers. (bas = enough) and -ak = thou; for thee. "Bas" sounds like our "buss" (to kiss) and there are sundry good old Anglo-Indian jokes of feminine mistakes on the subject.

T.WILLIAMS.SC.

that thine understanding is of the meanest and that thou lackest manners.   Thou remindest me of thy partnership in the Wazirate, when I admitted thee to share with me only in pity for thee, and not wishing to mortify thee; and that thou mightest help me as a manner of assistant.   But since thou talkest on this wise, by Allah, I will never marry my daughter to thy son; no, not for her weight in gold!"   When Nur al-Din heard his brother's words he waxed wroth and said, "And I too, I will never, never marry my son to thy daughter; no, not to keep from my lips the cup of death."   Shams al-Din replied, "I would not accept him as a husband for her, and he is not worth a paring of her nail.   Were I not about to travel I would make an example of thee; however when I return thou shalt see, and I will show thee, how I can assert my dignity and vindicate my honour.   But Allah doeth whatso He willeth."[1]   When Nur al-Din heard this speech from his brother, he was filled with fury and lost his wits for rage; but he hid what he felt and held his peace; and each of the brothers passed the night in a place far apart, wild with wrath against the other.   As soon as morning dawned the Sultan fared forth in state and crossed over from Cairo[2] to Jízah[3] and made for the Pyramids, accompanied by the Wazir Shams al-Din, whose turn of duty it was, whilst his brother Nur al-Din, who passed the night in sore rage, rose with the light and prayed the dawn-prayer.   Then he betook himself to his treasury and, taking a small pair of saddle-bags, filled them with gold; and he called to mind his brother's threats and the contempt wherewith he had treated him, and he repeated these couplets:—

"Travel! and thou shalt find new friends for old ones left behind; * Toil! for
     the sweets of human life by toil and moil are found:
The stay-at-home no honour wins nor aught attains but want; * So leave
     thy place of birth[4] and wander all the world around!

---

[1] This saving clause makes the threat worse.   The scene between the two brothers is written with characteristic Arab humour; and it is true to nature.   In England we have heard of a man who separated from his wife because he wished to dine at six and she preferred half-past six.

[2] Arab. "Misr." (vulg. Masr).   The word, which comes of a very ancient house, was applied to the present Capital about the time of its conquest by the Osmanli Turks A.H. 923 = 1517.

[3] The Arab. "Jízah," = skirt, edge; the modern village is the site of an ancient Egyptian city, as the "Ghizah inscription" proves (Brugsch, History of Egypt, ii. 415).

[4] Arab. "Watan" literally meaning "birth-place" but also used for "patria, native country"; thus "Hubb al-Watan" = patriotism.   The Turks pronounce it "Vatan," which the French have turned into Va-t'en!

I've seen, and very oft I've seen, how standing water stinks, * And only flowing
  sweetens it and trotting makes it sound:
And were the moon for ever full and ne'er to wax or wane, * Man would not
  strain his watchful eyes to see its gladsome round:
Except the lion leave his lair he ne'er would fell his game; * Except the arrow
  leave the bow ne'er had it reached its bound:
Gold-dust is dust the while it lies untravelled in the mine, * And aloes-wood
  mere fuel is upon its native ground:
And gold shall win his highest worth when from his goal ungoal'd; * And aloes
  sent to foreign parts grows costlier than gold."

When he ended his verse he bade one of his pages saddle him his
Nubian mare-mule with her padded selle. Now she was a dapple-
grey,[1] with ears like reed-pens and legs like columns and a back
high and strong as a dome builded on pillars; her saddle was of
gold-cloth and her stirrups of Indian steel, and her housing of
Ispahan velvet; she had trappings which would serve the Chosroës, and she was like a bride adorned for her wedding night.
Moreover he bade lay on her back a piece of silk for a seat, and a
prayer-carpet under which were his saddle-bags. When this was
done he said to his pages and slaves, "I purpose going forth
a-pleasuring outside the city on the road to Kalyúb-town,[2] and I
shall lie three nights abroad; so let none of you follow me, for
there is something straiteneth my breast." Then he mounted
the mule in haste; and, taking with him some provaunt for the
way, set out from Cairo and faced the open and uncultivated
country lying around it.[3] About noontide he entered Bilbays-
city,[4] where he dismounted and stayed awhile to rest himself
and his mule and ate some of his victual. He bought at Bilbays
all he wanted for himself and forage for his mule and then fared
on the way of the waste. Towards night-fall he entered a town
called Sa'adiyah[5] where he alighted and took out somewhat of
his viaticum and ate; then he spread his strip of silk on the sand
and set the saddle-bags under his head and slept in the open air;

---

[1] Arab. "Zarzariyah" = the colour of a stare or starling (Zurzúr).

[2] Now a Railway Station on the Alexandria-Cairo line.

[3] Even as late as 1852, when I first saw Cairo, the city was girt by waste lands and the
climate was excellent. Now cultivation comes up to the house walls; while the Mah-
mudiyah Canal, the planting the streets with avenues and over-watering have seriously
injured it; those who want the air of former Cairo must go to Thebes. Gout, rheumatism
and hydrophobia (before unknown) have become common of late years.

[4] This is the popular pronunciation: Yákút calls it "Bilbís."

[5] An outlying village on the "Long Desert," between Cairo and Palestine.

for he was still overcome with anger. When morning dawned he mounted and rode onward till he reached the Holy City,[1] Jerusalem, and thence he made Aleppo, where he dismounted at one of the caravanserais and abode three days to rest himself and the mule and to smell the air.[2] Then, being determined to travel afar and Allah having written safety in his fate, he set out again, wending without wotting whither he was going; and, having fallen in with certain couriers, he stinted not travelling till he had reached Bassorah-city albeit he knew not what the place was. It was dark night when he alighted at the Khan, so he spread out his prayer-carpet and took down the saddle-bags from the back of the mule and gave her with her furniture in charge of the door-keeper that he might walk her about. The man took her and did as he was bid. Now it so happened that the Wazir of Bassorah, a man shot in years, was sitting at the lattice-window of his palace opposite the Khan and he saw the porter walking the mule up and down. He was struck by her trappings of price and thought her a nice beast fit for the riding of Wazirs or even of royalties; and the more he looked the more was he perplexed till at last he said to one of his pages, "Bring hither yon door-keeper." The page went and returned to the Wazir with the porter who kissed the ground between his hands, and the Minister asked him, "Who is the owner of yonder mule and what manner of man is he?"; and he answered, "O my lord, the owner of this mule is a comely young man of pleasant manners, withal grave and dignified, and doubtless one of the sons of the merchants." When the Wazir heard the door-keeper's words

---

[1] Arab. "Al-Kuds" = holiness. There are few cities which in our day have less claim to this title than Jerusalem; and, curious to say, the "Holy Land" shows Jews, Christians and Moslems all in their worst form. The only religion (if it can be called one) which produces men in Syria is the Druse. "Heiligen-landes Jüden" are proverbial and nothing can be meaner than the Christians while the Moslems are famed for treachery.

[2] Arab. "Shamm al-hawá." In vulgar parlance to "smell the air" is to take a walk, especially out of town. There is a peculiar Egyptian festival called "Shamm al-Nasím" (smelling the Zephyr) which begins on Easter-Monday (O.S.), thus corresponding with the Persian Nau-roz, vernal equinox and introducing the fifty days of "Khammasín" or "Mirísi" (hot desert winds). On awakening, the people smell and bathe their temples with vinegar in which an onion has been soaked and break their fast with a "fisikh" or dried "búri" = mullet from Lake Menzalah: the late Hekekiyan Bey had the fish-heads counted in one public garden and found 70,000. The rest of the day is spent out of doors "Gypsying," and families greatly enjoy themselves on these occasions. For a longer description see a paper by my excellent friend Yacoub Artin Pasha, in the Bulletin de l'Institut Égyptien, 2nd series, No. 4, Cairo, 1884. I have noticed the Mirísi (south-wester) and other winds in the Land of Midian, i., 23.

he arose forthright; and, mounting his horse, rode to the Khan[1] and went in to Nur al-Din who, seeing the Minister making towards him, rose to his feet and advanced to meet him and saluted him. The Wazir welcomed him to Bassorah and dismounting, embraced him and made him sit down by his side and said, "O my son, whence comest thou and what dost thou seek?" "O my lord," Nur al-Din replied, "I have come from Cairo-city of which my father was whilome Wazir; but he hath been removed to the grace of Allah;" and he informed him of all that had befallen him from beginning to end, adding, "I am resolved never to return home before I have seen all the cities and countries of the world." When the Wazir heard this, he said to him, "O my son, hearken not to the voice of passion lest it cast thee into the pit; for indeed many regions be waste places and I fear for thee the turns of Time." Then he let load the saddle-bags and the silk and prayer-carpets on the mule and carried Nur al-Din to his own house, where he lodged him in a pleasant place and entreated him honourably and made much of him, for he inclined to love him with exceeding love. After a while he said to him, "O my son, here am I left a man in years and have no male children, but Allah hath blessed me with a daughter who eveneth thee in beauty; and I have rejected all her many suitors, men of rank and substance. But affection for thee hath entered into my heart; say me, then, wilt thou be to her a husband? If thou accept this, I will go up with thee to the Sultan of Bassorah[2] and will tell him that thou art my nephew, the son of my brother, and bring thee to be appointed Wazir in my place that I may keep the house for, by Allah, O my son, I am

---

[1] So in the days of the "Mameluke Beys" in Egypt a man of rank would not cross the street on foot.

[2] Arab. Basrah. The city now in decay and not to flourish again till the advent of the Euphrates Valley R.R., is a modern place, founded in A.H. 15, by the Caliph Omar upon the Aylah, a feeder of the Tigris. Here, according to Al-Hariri, the "whales and the lizards meet;" and, as the tide affects the river,

Its stream shows prodigy, ebbing and flowing.

In its far-famed market-place, Al-Marbad, poems used to be recited; and the city was famous for its mosques and Saint-shrines, fair women and school of Grammar which rivalled that of Kúfah. But already in Al-Hariri's day (nat. A.H. 446 = A.D. 1030) Baghdad had drawn off much of its population.

stricken in years and aweary." When Nur al-Din heard the
Wazir's words, he bowed his head in modesty and said, "To hear
is to obey!" At this the Wazir rejoiced and bade his servants
prepare a feast and decorate the great assembly-hall, wherein they
were wont to celebrate the marriages of Emirs and Grandees.
Then he assembled his friends and the notables of the reign and
the merchants of Bassorah and when all stood before him he said
to them, "I had a brother who was Wazir in the land of Egypt,
and Allah Almighty blessed him with two sons, whilst to me, as
well ye wot, He hath given a daughter. My brother charged me
to marry my daughter to one of his sons, whereto I assented; and,
when my daughter was of age to marry, he sent me one of his
sons, the young man now present, to whom I purpose marrying
her, drawing up the contract and celebrating the night of unveil-
ing with due ceremony: for he is nearer and dearer to me than a
stranger and, after the wedding, if he please he shall abide with
me, or if he desire to travel I will forward him and his wife to
his father's home." Hereat one and all replied, "Right is thy
recking;" and they looked at the bridegroom and were pleased
with him. So the Wazir sent for the Kazi and legal witnesses and
they wrote out the marriage-contract, after which the slaves perfumed the guests with incense,[1] and served them with sherbet of
sugar and sprinkled rose-water on them and all went their ways.
Then the Wazir bade his servants take Nur al-Din to the Ham-
mam-baths and sent him a suit of the best of his own especial
raiment, and napkins and towelry and bowls and perfume-burners
and all else that was required. After the bath, when he came
out and donned the dress, he was even as the full moon on the
fourteenth night; and he mounted his mule and stayed not till
he reached the Wazir's palace. There he dismounted and went in
to the Minister and kissed his hands, and the Wazir bade him
welcome.——And Shahrazad perceived the dawn of day and
ceased to say her permitted say.

---

[1] This fumigation (Bukhúr) is still used. A little incense or perfumed wood is burnt
upon an open censer (Mibkharah) of earthenware or metal, and passed round, each guest
holding it for a few moments under his beard. In the Somali Country, the very home
of incense, both sexes fumigate the whole person after carnal intercourse. Lane (Mod.
Egypt, chapt. viii) gives an illustration of the Mibkharah.

When it was the Twenty-first Night,

She said, It hath reached me, O auspicious King, that the Wazir stood up to him and welcoming him said, "Arise and go in to thy wife this night, and on the morrow I will carry thee to the Sultan, and pray Allah bless thee with all manner of weal." So Nur al-Din left him and went in to his wife the Wazir's daughter. Thus far concerning him, but as regards his elder brother, Shams al-Din, he was absent with the Sultan a long time and when he returned from his journey he found not his brother; and he asked of his servants and slaves who answered, "On the day of thy departure with the Sultan, thy brother mounted his mule fully caparisoned as for state procession saying, 'I am going towards Kalyub-town and I shall be absent one day or at most two days; for my breast is straitened, and let none of you follow me.' Then he fared forth and from that time to this we have heard no tidings of him." Shams al-Din was greatly troubled at the sudden disappearance of his brother and grieved with exceeding grief at the loss and said to himself, "This is only because I chided and upbraided him the night before my departure with the Sultan; haply his feelings were hurt and he fared forth a-travelling; but I must send after him." Then he went in to the Sultan and acquainted him with what had happened and wrote letters and dispatches, which he sent by running footmen to his deputies in every province. But during the twenty days of his brother's absence Nur al-Din had travelled far and had reached Bassorah; so after diligent search the messengers failed to come at any news of him and returned. Thereupon Shams al-Din despaired of finding his brother and said, "Indeed I went beyond all bounds in what I said to him with reference to the marriage of our children. Would that I had not done so! This all cometh of my lack of wit and want of caution." Soon after this he sought in marriage the daughter of a Cairene merchant,[1] and drew up the marriage contract and went in to her. And it so chanced that, on the very

---

[1] The reader of The Nights will remark that the merchant is often a merchant-prince, consorting and mating with the highest dignitaries. Even amongst the Romans, a race of soldiers, statesmen and lawyers, "mercatura" on a large scale was "not to be vituperated." In Boccaccio (x. 19) they are netti e delicati uomini. England is perhaps the only country which has made her fortune by trade, and much of it illicit trade, like that in slaves which built Liverpool and Bristol, and which yet disdains or affects to disdain the trader. But the unworthy prejudice is disappearing with the last generation, and men who formerly would have half starved as curates and ensigns, barristers and *carabins* are now only too glad to become merchants.

same night when Shams al-Din went in to his wife, Nur al-Din also went in to his wife the daughter of the Wazir of Bassorah; this being in accordance with the will of Almighty Allah, that He might deal the decrees of Destiny to His creatures. Furthermore, it was as the two brothers had said; for their two wives became pregnant by them on the same night and both were brought to bed on the same day; the wife of Shams al-Din, Wazir of Egypt, of a daughter, never in Cairo was seen a fairer; and the wife of Nur al-Din of a son, none more beautiful was ever seen in his time, as one of the poets said concerning the like of him:—

> That jetty hair, that glossy brow,
> My slender-waisted youth, of thine,
> Can darkness round creation throw,
> Or make it brightly shine.
> The dusky mole that faintly shows
> Upon his cheek, ah! blame it not:
> The tulip-flower never blows
> Undarkened by its spot.[1]

And as another also said:—

His scent was musk and his cheek was rose; * His teeth are pearls and his lips drop wine;
His form is a brand and his hips a hill; * His hair is night and his face moonshine.

They named the boy Badr al-Din Hasan and his grandfather, the Wazir of Bassorah, rejoiced in him and, on the seventh day after his birth, made entertainments and spread banquets which would befit the birth of Kings' sons and heirs. Then he took Nur al-Din and went up with him to the Sultan, and his son-in-law, when he came before the presence of the King, kissed the ground between his hands and repeated these verses, for he was ready of speech, firm of sprite and good in heart as he was goodly in form:—

"The world's best joys long be thy lot, my lord! * And last while darkness and the dawn o'erlap:
O thou who makest, when we greet thy gifts, * The world to dance and Time his palms to clap."[2]

---

1 These lines in the Calc. and Bul. Edits. have already occurred (Night vii.) but such carelessness is characteristic despite the proverb, "In repetition is no fruition." I quote Torrens (p. 60) by way of variety. As regards the anemone (here called a tulip) being named "Shakík" = fissure, I would conjecture that it derives from the flower often forming long lines of red like stripes of blood in the landscape. Travellers in Syria always observe this.

2 Such an address to a royalty (Eastern) even in the present day, would be a passport to future favours.

Then the Sultan rose up to honour them and, thanking Nur al-Din for his fine compliment, asked the Wazir, "Who may be this young man?"; and the Minister answered, "This is my brother's son," and related his tale from first to last. Quoth the Sultan, "And how comes he to be thy nephew and we have never heard speak of him?" Quoth the Minister, "O our lord the Sultan, I had a brother who was Wazir in the land of Egypt and he died, leaving two sons, whereof the elder hath taken his father's place and the younger, whom thou seest, came to me. I had sworn I would not marry my daughter to any but to him; so when he came I married him to her.[1] Now he is young and I am old; my hearing is dulled and my judgment is easily fooled; wherefore I would solicit our lord the Sultan[2] to set him in my stead, for he is my brother's son and my daughter's husband; and he is fit for the Wazirate, being a man of good counsel and ready contrivance." The Sultan looked at Nur al-Din and liked him, so he stablished him in office as the Wazir had requested and formally appointed him, presenting him with a splendid dress of honour and a she-mule from his private stud; and assigning to him solde, stipends and supplies. Nur al-Din kissed the Sultan's hand and went home, he and his father-in-law, joying with exceeding joy and saying, "All this followeth on the heels of the boy Hasan's birth!" Next day he presented himself before the King and, kissing the ground, began repeating:—

"Grow thy weal and thy welfare day by day: * And thy luck prevail o'er the envier's spite;
And ne'er cease thy days to be white as day, * And thy foeman's day to be black as night!"

The Sultan bade him be seated on the Wazir's seat, so he sat down and applied himself to the business of his office and went

---

[1] In England the man marries and the woman is married: there is no such distinction in Arabia.

[2] "Sultan" (and its corruption "Soldan") etymologically means lord, victorious, ruler, ruling over. In Arabia it is a not uncommon proper name; and as a title it is taken by a host of petty kinglets. The Abbaside Caliphs (as Al-Wásik who has been noticed) formally created these Sultans as their regents. Al-Tá'i bi'llah (regn. A. H. 363 = 974), invested the famous Sabuktagin with the office; and, as Alexander-Sikandar was wont to do,fashioned for him two flags, one of silver, after the fashion of nobles, and the other of gold, as Viceroy-designate. Sabuktagin's son, the famous Mahmúd of the Ghaznavite dynasty in A. H. 393 = 1002, was the first to adopt "Sultan" as an independent title some two hundred years after the death of Harun al-Rashid. In old writers we have the Soldan of Egypt, the Soudan of Persia, and the Sowdan of Babylon; three modifications of one word.

into the cases of the lieges and their suits, as is the wont of Ministers; while the Sultan watched him and wondered at his wit and good sense, judgment and insight. Wherefor he loved him and took him into intimacy. When the Divan was dismissed Nur al-Din returned to his house and related what had passed to his father-in-law who rejoiced. And thenceforward Nur al-Din ceased not so to administer the Wazirate that the Sultan would not be parted from him night or day; and increased his stipends and supplies till his means were ample and he became the owner of ships that made trading voyages at his command, as well as of Mamelukes and blackamoor slaves; and he laid out many estates and set up Persian wheels and planted gardens. When his son Hasan was four years of age, the old Wazir deceased, and he made for his father-in-law a sumptuous funeral ceremony ere he was laid in the dust. Then he occupied himself with the education of this son and, when the boy waxed strong and came to the age of seven, he brought him a Fakih, a doctor of law and religion, to teach him in his own house and charged him to give him a good education and instruct him in politeness and good manners. So the tutor made the boy read and retain all varieties of useful knowledge, after he had spent some years in learning the Koran by heart;[1] and he ceased not to grow in beauty and stature and symmetry, even as saith the poet:—

In his face-sky shines the fullest moon; * In his cheeks' anemone glows the sun:
He so conquered Beauty that he hath won * All charms of humanity one by one.

The professor brought him up in his father's palace teaching him reading, writing and cyphering, theology and belles lettres. His grandfather the old Wazir had bequeathed to him the whole of his property when he was but four years of age. Now during all the time of his earliest youth he had never left the house, till on a certain day his father, the Wazir Nur al-Din, clad him in his best clothes and, mounting him on a she-mule of the finest, went up

---

1 i. e. he was a "Háfiz," one who commits to memory the whole of the Koran. It is a serious task and must be begun early. I learnt by rote the last "Juzw" (or thirtieth part) and found that quite enough. This is the vulgar use of "Hafiz": technically and theologically it means the third order of Traditionists (the total being five) who know by heart 300,000 traditions of the Prophet with their ascriptions. A curious "spiritualist" book calls itself "Hafed, Prince of Persia," proving by the very title that the Spirits are equally ignorant of Arabic and Persian.

with him to the Sultan. The King gazed at Badr al-Din Hasan and marvelled at his comeliness and loved him. As for the city-folk, when he first passed before them with his father, they marvelled at his exceeding beauty and sat down on the road expecting his return, that they might look their fill on his beauty and loveliness and symmetry and perfect grace; even as the poet said in these verses:—

> As the sage watched the stars, the semblance clear
> Of a fair youth on 's scroll he saw appear.
> Those jetty locks Canopus o'er him threw,
> And tinged his temple curls a musky hue;
> Mars dyed his ruddy cheek; and from his eyes
> The Archer-star his glittering arrow flies;
> His wit from Hermes came; and Soha's care,
> (The half-seen star that dimly haunts the Bear)
> Kept off all evil eyes that threaten and ensnare,
> The sage stood mazed to see such fortunes meet,
> And Luna kissed the earth beneath his feet.[1]

And they blessed him aloud as he passed and called upon Almighty Allah to bless him.[2] The Sultan entreated the lad with especial favour and said to his father, "O Wazir, thou must needs bring him daily to my presence;" whereupon he replied, "I hear and I obey." Then the Wazir returned home with his son and ceased not to carry him to court till he reached the age of twenty. At that time the Minister sickened and, sending for Badr al-Din Hasan, said to him, "Know, O my son, that the world of the Present is but a house of mortality, while that of the Future is a house of eternity. I wish, before I die, to bequeath thee certain charges and do thou take heed of what I say and incline thy heart to my words." Then he gave him last instructions as to the properest way of dealing with his neighbours and the due management of his affairs; after which he called to mind his brother and his home and his native land and wept over his separation from those he had first loved. Then he wiped away his tears and, turning to his son, said to him, "Before I proceed, O my son, to my last charges and injunctions, know that I have a brother, and thou hast an uncle, Shams

---

[1] Here again the Cairo Edit. repeats the six couplets already given in Night xvii. I take them from Torrens (p. 163).

[2] This naïve admiration of beauty in either sex characterised our chivalrous times. Now it is mostly confined to "professional beauties" or what is conventionally called the "fair sex"; as if there could be any comparison between the beauty of man and the beauty of woman, the Apollo Belvidere with the Venus de Medici.

al-Din hight, the Wazir of Cairo, with whom I parted, leaving him against his will. Now take thee a sheet of paper and write upon it whatso I say to thee." Badr al-Din took a fair leaf and set about doing his father's bidding and he wrote thereon a full account of what had happened to his sire first and last; the dates of his arrival at Bassorah and of his foregathering with the Wazir; of his marriage, of his going in to the Minister's daughter and of the birth of his son; brief, his life of forty years from the day of his dispute with his brother, adding the words, "And this is written at my dictation and may Almighty Allah be with him when I am gone!" Then he folded the paper and sealed it and said, "O Hasan, O my son, keep this paper with all care; for it will enable thee to stablish thine origin and rank and lineage and, if anything contrary befal thee, set out for Cairo and ask for thine uncle and show him this paper and say to him that I died a stranger far from mine own people and full of yearning to see him and them." So Badr al-Din Hasan took the document and folded it; and, wrapping it up in a piece of waxed cloth, sewed it like a talisman between the inner and outer cloth of his skull-cap and wound his light turband[1] round it. And he fell to weeping over his father and at parting with him, and he but a boy. Then Nur al-Din lapsed into a swoon, the forerunner of death; but presently recovering himself he said, "O Hasan, O my son, I will now bequeath to thee five last behests. The FIRST BEHEST is, Be over-intimate with none, nor frequent any, nor be familiar with any; so shalt thou be safe from his mischief;[2] for security lieth in seclusion of thought and a certain retirement from the society of thy fellows; and I have heard it said by a poet:—

In this world there is none thou mayst count upon * To befriend thy case in
    the nick of need:
So live for thyself nursing hope of none * Such counsel I give thee: enow, take
    heed!

The SECOND BEHEST is, O my son: Deal harshly with none lest fortune with thee deal hardly; for the fortune of this world is one day with thee and another day against thee and all worldly goods are but a loan to be repaid. And I have heard a poet say:—

Take thought nor haste to win the thing thou wilt; * Have ruth on man for
    ruth thou may'st require:
No hand is there but Allah's hand is higher; * No tyrant but shall rue worse
    tyrant's ire!

---

[1] Arab. "Shásh" (in Pers. urine), a light turband generally of muslin.
[2] This is a *lieu commun* of Eastern worldly wisdom. Quite true! Very unadvisable to

The THIRD BEHEST is, Learn to be silent in society and let thine own faults distract thine attention from the faults of other men: for it is said:—In silence dwelleth safety, and thereon I have heard the lines that tell us:—

Reserve's a jewel, Silence safety is; * Whenas thou speakest many a word withhold:
For an of Silence thou repent thee once, * Of speech thou shalt repent times manifold.

The FOURTH BEHEST, O my son, is Beware of wine-bibbing, for wine is the head of all frowardness and a fine solvent of human wits. So shun, and again I say, shun mixing strong liquor; for I have heard a poet say[1]:—

From wine[2] I turn and whoso wine-cups swill; * Becoming one of those who deem it ill:
Wine driveth man to miss salvation-way,[3] * And opes the gateway wide to sins that kill.

The FIFTH BEHEST, O my son, is Keep thy wealth and it will keep thee; guard thy money and it will guard thee; and waste not thy substance lest haply thou come to want and must fare a-begging from the meanest of mankind. Save thy dirhams and deem them the sovereignest salve for the wounds of the world. And here again I have heard that one of the poets said:—

When fails my wealth no friend will deign befriend: * When wealth abounds all friends their friendship tender:
How many friends lent aid my wealth to spend; * But friends to lack of wealth no friendship render."

---

dive below the surface of one's acquaintances, but such intimacy is like marriage of which Johnson said, "Without it there is no pleasure in life."

[1] The lines are attributed to the famous Al-Mutanabbi = the claimant to "Prophecy," of whom I have given a few details in my Pilgrimage iii. 60, 62. He led the life of a true poet, somewhat Chauvinistic withal; and, rather than run away, was killed in A.H. 354 = 965.

[2] Arab. "Nabíz" = wine of raisins or dates; any fermented liquor; from a root to "press out" in Syriac, like the word "Talmiz" (or Tilmiz, says the Kashf al-Ghurrah) a pupil, student. Date-wine (fermented from the fruit, not the Tádi, or juice of the stem, our "toddy") is called Fazikh. Hence the Masjid al-Fazikh at Al-Medinah where the Ansar or Auxiliaries of that city were sitting cup in hand when they heard of the revelation forbidding inebriants and poured the liquor upon the ground (Pilgrimage ii. 322).

[3] Arab. "Huda" = direction (to the right way), salvation, a word occurring in the Opening Chapter of the Koran. Hence to a Kafir who offers the Salam-salutation many Moslems reply "Allah-yahdík" = Allah direct thee! (i.e. make thee a Moslem), instead of Allah yusallimak = Allah lead thee to salvation. It is the root word of the Mahdi and Mohdi.

On this wise Nur al-Din ceased not to counsel his son Badr al-Din Hasan till his hour came and, sighing one sobbing sigh, his life went forth. Then the voice of mourning and keening rose high in his house and the Sultan and all the grandees grieved for him and buried him; but his son ceased not lamenting his loss for two months, during which he never mounted horse, nor attended the Divan nor presented himself before the Sultan. At last the King, being wroth with him, stablished in his stead one of his Chamberlains and made him Wazir, giving orders to seize and set seals on all Nur al-Din's houses and goods and domains. So the new Wazir went forth with a mighty posse of Chamberlains and people of the Divan, and watchmen and a host of idlers to do this and to seize Badr al-Din Hasan and carry him before the King, who would deal with him as he deemed fit. Now there was among the crowd of followers a Mameluke of the deceased Wazir who, when he heard this order, urged his horse and rode at full speed to the house of Badr al-Din Hasan; for he could not endure to see the ruin of his old master's son. He found him sitting at the gate with head hung down and sorrowing, as was his wont, for the loss of his father; so he dismounted and kissing his hand said to him, "O my lord and son of my lord, haste ere ruin come and lay waste!" When Hasan heard this he trembled and asked, "What may be the matter?"; and the man answered, "The Sultan is angered with thee and hath issued a warrant against thee, and evil cometh hard upon my track; so flee with thy life!" At these words Hasan's heart flamed with the fire of bale, and his rose-red cheek turned pale, and he said to the Mameluke, "O my brother, is there time for me to go in and get me some worldly gear which may stand me in stead during my strangerhood?" But the slave replied, "O my lord, up at once and save thyself and leave this house, while it is yet time." And he quoted these lines:—

"Escape with thy life, if oppression betide thee, * And let the house tell of its builder's fate!
Country for country thou'lt find, if thou seek it; * Life for life never, early or late.
It is strange men should dwell in the house of abjection, * When the plain of God's earth is so wide and so great!"[1]

At these words of the Mameluke, Badr al-Din covered his head

---

[1] These lines have already occurred in The First Kalandar's Story (Night xi). I quote by way of change and with permission Mr. Payne's version (i. 93).

with the skirt of his garment and went forth on foot till he stood
outside of the city, where he heard folk saying, "The Sultan hath
sent his new Wazir to the house of the old Wazir, now no more, to
seal his property and seize his son Badr al-Din Hasan and take
him before the presence, that he may put him to death;" and all
cried, "Alas for his beauty and his loveliness!" When he heard
this he fled forth at hazard, knowing not whither he was going,
and gave not over hurrying onwards till Destiny drove him to his
father's tomb. So he entered the cemetery and, threading his way
through the graves, at last he reached the sepulchre where he sat
down and let fall from his head the skirt of his long robe[1] which
was made of brocade with a gold-embroidered hem whereon were
worked these couplets:—

O thou whose forehead, like the radiant East, * Tells of the stars of Heaven
    and bounteous dews:
Endure thine honour to the latest day,   * And Time thy growth of glory
    ne'er refuse!

While he was sitting by his father's tomb behold, there came to
him a Jew as he were a Shroff,[2] a money-changer, with a pair of
saddle-bags containing much gold, who accosted him and kissed
his hand, saying, "Whither bound, O my lord: 'tis late in the day
and thou art clad but lightly and I read signs of trouble in thy
face?" "I was sleeping within this very hour," answered Hasan,
"when my father appeared to me and chid me for not having
visited his tomb; so I awoke trembling and came hither forthright
lest the day should go by without my visiting him, which would
have been grievous to me." "O my lord," rejoined the Jew,[3] "thy
father had many merchantmen at sea and, as some of them are
now due, it is my wish to buy of thee the cargo of the first ship
that cometh into port with this thousand dinars of gold." "I
consent," quoth Hasan, whereupon the Jew took out a bag full
of gold and counted out a thousand sequins which he gave to

---

[1] Arab. "Farajíyah," a long-sleeved robe worn by the learned (Lane, M. E., chapt. i.).
[2] Arab. "Sarráf" (vulg. Sayrafi), whence the Anglo-Indian "Shroff," a familiar corruption.
[3] Arab. "Yahúdi" which is less polite than "Banú Isráíl" = Children of Israel. So in
Christendom "Israelite" when in favour and "Jew" (with an adjective or a participle)
when nothing is wanted of him.

Hasan, the son of the Wazir, saying, "Write me a letter of sale and seal it." So Hasan took a pen and paper and wrote these words in duplicate, "The writer, Hasan Badr al-Din, son of Wazir Nur al-Din, hath sold to Isaac the Jew all the cargo of the first of his father's ships which cometh into port, for a thousand dinars, and he hath received the price in advance." And after he had taken one copy the Jew put it into his pouch and went away; but Hasan fell a-weeping as he thought of the dignity and prosperity which had erst been his and he began reciting:—

"This house, my lady, since you left is now a home no more * For me, nor
    neighbours, since you left, prove kind and neighbourly:
The friend, whilere I took to heart, alas! no more to me * Is friend; and even
    Luna's self displayeth lunacy:
You left and by your going left the world a waste, a wold, * And lies a gloomy
    murk upon the face of hill and lea:
O may the raven-bird whose cry our hapless parting croaked * Find ne'er a
    nesty home and eke shed all his plumery!
At length my patience fails me; and this absence wastes my flesh; * How many
    a veil by severance rent our eyes are doomèd see:
Ah! shall I ever sight again our fair past nights of yore; * And shall a single
    house become a home for me once more?"

Then he wept with exceeding weeping and night came upon him; so he leant his head against his father's grave and sleep overcame him: Glory to Him who sleepeth not! He ceased not slumbering till the moon rose, when his head slipped from off the tomb and he lay on his back, with limbs outstretched, his face shining bright in the moonlight. Now the cemetery was haunted day and night by Jinns who were of the True Believers, and presently came out a Jinniyah who, seeing Hasan asleep, marvelled at his beauty and loveliness and cried, "Glory to God! this youth can be none other than one of the Wuldán of Paradise."[1] Then she flew firmament-wards to circle it, as was her custom, and met an Ifrit on the wing

---

[1] Also called "Ghilmán"= the beautiful youths appointed to serve the True Believers in Paradise. The Koran says (chapt. lvi. 9 etc.) "Youths, which shall continue in their bloom for ever,shall go round about to attend them, with goblets, and beakers, and a cup of flowing wine," etc. Mohammed was an Arab (not a Persian, a born pederast) and he was too fond of women to be charged with love of boys: even Tristram Shandy (vol. vii. chapt. 7; "No, quoth a third; the gentleman has been committing——") knew that the two tastes are incompatibles. But this and other passages in the Koran have given the Chevaliers de la Pallie a hint that the use of boys, like that of wine, here forbidden, will be permitted in Paradise.

who saluted her and she said to him, "Whence comest thou?" "From Cairo," he replied. "Wilt thou come with me and look upon the beauty of a youth who sleepeth in yonder burial place?" she asked, and he answered, "I will." So they flew till they lighted at the tomb and she showed him the youth and said, "Now diddest thou ever in thy born days see aught like this?" The Ifrit looked upon him and exclaimed, "Praise be to Him that hath no equal! But, O my sister, shall I tell thee what I have seen this day?" Asked she, "What is that?" and he answered, "I have seen the counterpart of this youth in the land of Egypt. She is the daughter of the Wazir Shams al-Din and she is a model of beauty and loveliness, of fairest favour and formous form, and dight with symmetry and perfect grace. When she had reached the age of nineteen,[1] the Sultan of Egypt heard of her and, sending for the Wazir her father, said to him, 'Hear me, O Wazir: it hath reached mine ear that thou hast a daughter and I wish to demand her of thee in marriage.' The Wazir replied, 'O our lord the Sultan, deign accept my excuses and take compassion on my sorrows, for thou knowest that my brother, who was partner with me in the Wazirate, disappeared from amongst us many years ago and we wot not where he is. Now the cause of his departure was that one night, as we were sitting together and talking of wives and children to come, we had words on the matter and he went off in high dudgeon. But I swore that I would marry my daughter to none save to the son of my brother on the day her mother gave her birth, which was nigh upon nineteen years ago. I have lately heard that my brother died at Bassorah, where he had married the daughter of the Wazir and that she bare him a son; and I will not marry my daughter but to him in honour of my brother's memory. I recorded the date of my marriage and the conception of my wife and the birth of my daughter; and from her horoscope I find that her name is conjoined

---

[1] Which, by the by, is the age of an oldish old maid in Egypt. I much doubt puberty being there earlier than in England where our grandmothers married at fourteen. But Orientals are aware that the period of especial feminine devilry is between the first menstruation and twenty when, according to some, every girl is a "possible murderess." So they wisely marry her and get rid of what is called the "lump of grief," the "domestic calamity"—a daughter. Amongst them we never hear of the abominable egotism and cruelty of the English mother, who disappoints her daughter's womanly cravings in order to keep her at home for her own comfort; and an "old maid" in the house, especially a stout, plump old maid, is considered not "respectable." The ancient virgin is known by being lean and scraggy; and perhaps this diagnosis is correct.

with that of her cousin;[1] and there are damsels in foison for our
lord the Sultan.' The King, hearing his Minister's answer and
refusal, waxed wroth with exceeding wrath and cried, 'When
the like of me asketh a girl in marriage of the like of thee, he
conferreth an honour, and thou rejectest me and puttest me off
with cold[2] excuses! Now, by the life of my head I will marry her
to the meanest of my men in spite of the nose of thee!'[3] There
was in the palace a horse-groom which was a Gobbo with a
bunch to his breast and a hunch to his back; and the Sultan sent
for him and married him to the daughter of the Wazir, lief or
loath, and hath ordered a pompous marriage procession for him
and that he go in to his bride this very night. I have now just
flown hither from Cairo, where I left the Hunchback at the door
of the Hammam-bath amidst the Sultan's white slaves who were
waving lighted flambeaux about him. As for the Minister's
daughter she sitteth among her nurses and tirewomen, weeping
and wailing; for they have forbidden her father to come near her.
Never have I seen, O my sister, more hideous being than this
Hunchback[4] whilst the young lady is the likest of all folk to this
young man, albeit even fairer than he."——And Shahrazad perceived the dawn of day and ceased saying her permitted say.

When it was the Twenty-second Night,

She said, It hath reached me, O auspicious King, that when the
Jinni narrated to the Jinniyah how the King had caused the
wedding contract to be drawn up between the hunchbacked
groom and the lovely young lady who was heart-broken for
sorrow; and how she was the fairest of created things and even
more beautiful than this youth, the Jinniyah cried at him
"Thou liest! this youth is handsomer than any one of his day."

---

1 This prognostication of destiny by the stars and a host of follies that end in -mancy is
an intricate and extensive subject. Those who would study it are referred to chapt. xiv.
of the "Qanoon-e-Islam, or the Customs of the Mussulmans of India; etc., etc., by Jaffur
Shurreeff and translated by G. A. Herklots, M. D. of Madras." This excellent work first
appeared in 1832 (Allen and Co., London) and thus it showed the way to Lane's "Modern
Egyptians" (1833–35). The name was unfortunate as "Kuzzilbash" (which rhymed to
guzzle and hash), and kept the book back till a second edition appeared in 1863 (Madras:
J. Higginbotham).

2 Arab. "Bárid," lit. cold: metaph. vain, foolish, insipid.

3 Not to "spite thee" but "in spite of thee." The phrase is still used by high and low.

4 Arab. "Ahdab," the common hunchback: in classical language the Gobbo in the
text would be termed "Ak'as" from "Ka'as," one with protruding back and breast; sometimes used for hollow back and protruding breast.

The Ifrit gave her the lie again, adding, "By Allah, O my sister, the damsel I speak of is fairer than this; yet none but he deserveth her, for they resemble each other like brother and sister or at least cousins. And, well-away! how she is wasted upon that Hunchback!" Then said she, "O my brother, let us get under him and lift him up and carry him to Cairo, that we may compare him with the damsel of whom thou speakest and so determine whether of the twain is the fairer." "To hear is to obey!" replied he, "thou speakest to the point; nor is there a righter recking than this of thine, and I myself will carry him." So he raised him from the ground and flew with him like a bird soaring in upper air, the Ifritah keeping close by his side at equal speed, till he alighted with him in the city of Cairo and set him down on a stone bench and woke him up. He roused himself and finding that he was no longer at his father's tomb in Bassorah-city he looked right and left and saw that he was in a strange place; and he would have cried out; but the Ifrit gave him a cuff which persuaded him to keep silence. Then he brought him rich raiment and clothed him therein and, giving him a lighted flambeau, said, "Know that I have brought thee hither, meaning to do thee a good turn for the love of Allah: so take this torch and mingle with the people at the Hammam-door and walk on with them without stopping till thou reach the house of the wedding-festival; then go boldly forward and enter the great saloon; and fear none, but take thy stand at the right hand of the Hunchback bridegroom; and, as often as any of the nurses and tirewomen and singing-girls come up to thee,[1] put thy hand into thy pocket which thou wilt find filled with gold. Take it out and throw to them and spare not; for as often as thou thrustest fingers in pouch thou shalt find it full of coin.

[1] This is the custom with such gentry, who, when they see a likely man sitting, are allowed by custom to ride astraddle upon his knees with most suggestive movements, till he buys them off. These Ghawází are mostly Gypsies who pretend to be Moslems; and they have been confused with the Almahs or Moslem dancing-girls proper (Awálim, plur. of Alimah, a learned feminine) by a host of travellers. They call themselves Barámikah or Barmecides only to affect Persian origin. Under native rule they were perpetually being banished from and returning to Cairo (Pilgrimage i., 202). Lane (M. E., chapts. xviii. and xix.) discusses the subject, and would derive Al'mah, often so pronounced, from Heb. Almah, girl, virgin, singing-girl, hence he would translate Al-Alamoth shir (Psalm xlvi.) and Nebalim al-alamoth (1. Chron., xv. 20) by a "song for singing-girls" and "harps for singing-girls." He quotes also St. Jerome as authority that Alma in Punic (Phœnician) signified a virgin, not a common article, I may observe, amongst singing-girls. I shall notice in a future page Burckhardt's description of the Ghawazi, p. 173, "Arabic Proverbs;" etc., etc. Second Edition. London: Quaritch, 1875.

Give largesse by handsful and fear nothing, but set thy trust upon Him who created thee, for this is not by thine own strength but by that of Allah Almighty, that His decrees may take effect upon his creatures." When Badr al-Din Hasan heard these words from the Ifrit he said to himself, "Would Heaven I knew what all this means and what is the cause of such kindness!" However, he mingled with the people and, lighting his flambeau, moved on with the bridal procession till he came to the bath where he found the Hunchback already on horseback. Then he pushed his way in among the crowd, a veritable beauty of a man in the finest apparel, wearing tarbush[1] and turband and a long-sleeved robe purfled with gold; and, as often as the singing-women stopped for the people to give them largesse, he thrust his hand into his pocket and, finding it full of gold, took out a handful and threw it on the tambourine[2] till he had filled it with gold pieces for the music-girls and the tirewomen. The singers were amazed by his bounty and the people marvelled at his beauty and loveliness and the splendour of his dress. He ceased not to do thus till he reached the mansion of the Wazir (who was his uncle), where the Chamberlains drove back the people and forbade them to go forward; but the singing-girls and the tirewomen said, "By Allah we will not enter unless this young man enter with us, for he hath given us length o' life with his largesse and we will not display the bride unless he be present." Therewith they carried him into the bridal hall and made him sit down defying the evil glances of the hunchbacked bridegroom. The wives of the Emirs and Wazirs and Chamberlains and Courtiers all stood in double line, each holding a massy cierge ready lighted; all wore thin face-veils and the two rows right and left extended from the bride's throne[3] to the head of the hall adjoining the chamber whence she was to come forth. When the ladies saw Badr al-Din Hasan and noted his beauty and loveliness and his face that shone like the

---

[1] I need hardly describe the Tarbúsh, a corruption of the Pers. "Sar-púsh" (head-cover) also called "Fez," from its old home; and "Tarbrush" by the travelling Briton. In old days it was a calotte worn under the turban; and it was protected from scalp-perspiration by an "Arakiyah" (Pers. Arak-chin), a white skull-cap. Now it is worn without either and as a head-dress nothing can be worse (Pilgrimage ii. 275).

[2] Arab. "Tár.": the custom still prevails. Lane (M. E., chapt. xviii.) describes and figures this hoop-drum.

[3] The couch on which she sits while being displayed. It is her throne, for she is the Queen of the occasion, with all the Majesty of Virginity.

new moon, their hearts inclined to him and the singing-girls said
to all that were present, "Know that this beauty crossed our
hands with naught but red gold; so be not chary to do him
womanly service and comply with all he says, no matter what he
ask."[1]   So all the women crowded round Hasan with their
torches and gazed on his loveliness and envied him his beauty;
and one and all would gladly have lain on his bosom an hour or
rather a year.   Their hearts were so troubled that they let fall
their veils from before their faces and said, "Happy she who
belongeth to this youth or to whom he belongeth!"; and they
called down curses on the crooked groom and on him who
was the cause of his marriage to the girl-beauty; and as often
as they blessed Badr al-Din Hasan they damned the Hunchback, saying, "Verily this youth and none else deserveth our
Bride: ah, well-away for such a lovely one with this hideous
Quasimodo; Allah's curse light on his head and on the Sultan
who commanded the marriage!"   Then the singing-girls beat
their tabrets and lulliloo'd with joy, announcing the appearing
of the bride; and the Wazir's daughter came in surrounded by
her tirewomen who had made her goodly to look upon; for they
had perfumed her and incensed her and adorned her hair;
and they had robed her in raiment and ornaments befitting
the mighty Chosroës Kings.   The most notable part of her
dress was a loose robe worn over her other garments: it was
diapered in red gold with figures of wild beasts, and birds
whose eyes and beaks were of gems, and claws of red rubies
and green beryl; and her neck was graced with a necklace of
Yamani work, worth thousands of gold pieces, whose bezels
were great round jewels of sorts, the like of which was never
owned by Kaysar or by Tobba King.[2] And the bride was as the
full moon when at fullest on fourteenth night; and as she paced

---

[1] This is a solemn "chaff;" such liberties being permitted at weddings and festive
occasions.

[2] The pre-Islamític dynasty of Al-Yaman in Arabia Felix, a region formerly famed for
wealth and luxury. Hence the mention of Yamani work. The caravans from Sana'á,
the capital, used to carry patterns of vases to be made in China and bring back the porce-
lains at the end of the third year: these are the Arabic inscriptions which have puzzled so
many collectors. The Tobba, or Successors, were the old Himyarite Kings, a dynastic
name like Pharaoh, Kisra (Persia), Negush (Abyssinia), Khakan or Khan (Tartary), etc.,
who claimed to have extended their conquests to Samarcand and made war on China.
Any history of Arabia (as Crichton I., chapt iv.) may be consulted for their names and
annals. I have been told by Arabs that "Tobba" (or Tubba) is still used in the old Himyar-
land = the Great or the Chief.

into the hall she was like one of the Houris of Heaven—praise
be to Him who created her in such splendour of beauty! The
ladies encompassed her as the white contains the black of the
eye, they clustering like stars whilst she shone amongst them
like the moon when it eats up the clouds. Now Badr al-Din
Hasan of Bassorah was sitting in full gaze of the folk, when the
bride came forward with her graceful swaying and swimming
gait, and her hunchbacked bridegroom stood up to meet[1] and
receive her: she, however, turned away from the wight and
walked forward till she stood before her cousin Hasan, the son
of her uncle. Whereat the people laughed. But when the
wedding-guests saw her thus attracted towards Badr al-Din
they made a mighty clamour and the singing-women shouted
their loudest; whereupon he put his hand into his pocket and,
pulling out a handful of gold, cast it into their tambourines and
the girls rejoiced and said, "Could we win our wish this bride
were thine!" At this he smiled and the folk came round him,
flambeaux in hand like the eyeball round the pupil, while the
Gobbo bridegroom was left sitting alone much like a tail-less
baboon; for every time they lighted a candle for him it went out
willy-nilly, so he was left in darkness and silence and looking at
naught but himself.[2] When Badr al-Din Hasan saw the bridegroom sitting lonesome in the dark, and all the wedding-guests
with their flambeaux and wax candles crowding about himself,
he was bewildered and marvelled much; but when he looked at
his cousin, the daughter of his uncle, he rejoiced and felt an
inward delight: he longed to greet her and gazed intently on
her face which was radiant with light and brilliancy. Then the
tirewomen took off her veil and displayed her in the first bridal
dress which was of scarlet satin; and Hasan had a view of her
which dazzled his sight and dazed his wits, as she moved to and
fro, swaying with graceful gait;[3] and she turned the heads of all
the guests, women as well as men, for she was even as saith the
surpassing poet:—

A sun on wand in knoll of sand she showed, * Clad in her cramoisy-hued
    chemisette:
Of her lips honey-dew she gave me drink, * And with her rosy cheeks
    quencht fire she set.

---

[1] Lane and Payne (as well as the Bres. Edit.) both render the word "to kiss her," but
this would be clean contrary to Moslem usage.
[2] i. e. he was full of rage which he concealed.
[3] The Hindus (as the Katha shows) compare this swimming gait with an elephant's roll.

Then they changed that dress and displayed her in a robe of azure; and she reappeared like the full moon when it riseth over the horizon, with her coal-black hair and cheeks delicately fair; and teeth shown in sweet smiling and breasts firm rising and crowning sides of the softest and waist of the roundest. And in this second suit she was as a certain master of high conceits saith of the like of her:—

She came apparelled in an azure vest, * Ultramarine, as skies are deckt and dight:
I view'd th' unparallel'd sight, which show'd my eyes * A moon of Summer on a Winter-night.

Then they changed that suit for another and, veiling her face in the luxuriance of her hair, loosed her lovelocks, so dark, so long that their darkness and length outvied the darkest nights, and she shot through all hearts with the magical shaft of her eye-babes. They displayed her in the third dress and she was as said of her the sayer:—

Veiling her cheeks with hair a-morn she comes, * And I her mischiefs with the cloud compare:
Saying, "Thou veilest morn with night!" "Ah no!" * Quoth she, "I shroud full moon with darkling air!"

Then they displayed her in the fourth bridal dress and she came forward shining like the rising sun and swaying to and fro with lovesome grace and supple ease like a gazelle-fawn. And she clave all hearts with the arrows of her eyelashes, even as saith one who described a charmer like her:—

The sun of beauty she to sight appears * And, lovely-coy, she mocks all loveliness;
And when he fronts her favour and her smile * A-morn, the Sun of day in clouds must dress.

Then she came forth in the fifth dress, a very light of loveliness like a wand of waving willow or a gazelle of the thirsty wold. Those locks which stung like scorpions along her cheeks were bent, and her neck was bowed in blandishment, and her hips quivered as she went. As saith one of the poets describing her in verse:—

She comes like fullest moon on happy night; * Taper of waist, with shape of magic might:
She hath an eye whose glances quell mankind, * And Ruby on her cheeks reflects his light:

Enveils her hips the blackness of her hair; * Beware of curls that bite with
    viper-bite!
Her sides are silken-soft, the while the heart * Mere rock behind that surface
    lurks from sight:
From the fringed curtains of her eyne she shoots * Shafts which at farthest
    range on mark alight:
When round her neck or waist I throw my arms * Her breasts repel me with
    their hardened height.
Ah, how her beauty all excels! ah how * That shape transcends the graceful
    waving bough!

Then they adorned her with the sixth toilette, a dress which was
green. And now she shamed in her slender straightness the nut-
brown spear; her radiant face dimmed the brightest beams of full
moon and she outdid the bending branches in gentle movement
and flexile grace. Her loveliness exalted the beauties of earth's
four quarters and she broke men's hearts by the significance of her
semblance; for she was even as saith one of the poets in these
lines:—

A damsel 'twas the tirer's art had decked with snares and sleight:[1] * And robed
    in rays as though the sun from her had borrowed light:
She came before us wondrous clad in chemisette of green, * As veilèd by its
    leafy screen pomegranate hides from sight:
And when he said "How callest thou the manner of thy dress?" * She answered
    us in pleasant way with double meaning dight;
"We call this garment crève-cœur; and rightly is it hight, * For many a heart
    wi' this we broke[2] and conquered many a sprite!"

Then they displayed her in the seventh dress, coloured between
safflower[3] and saffron, even as one of the poets saith:—

In vest of saffron pale and safflower red * Musk'd, sandal'd, ambergris'd, she
    came to front:
"Rise!" cried her youth, "go forth and show thyself!" * "Sit!" said her hips,
    "we cannot bear the brunt!"
And when I craved a bout, her Beauty said * "Do, do!" and said her pretty
    shame, "Don't, don't!"

---

[1] Arab. "Fitnah," a word almost as troublesome as "Adab." Primarily, revolt, seduction,
mischief: then a beautiful girl (or boy), and lastly a certain aphrodisiac perfume extracted
from mimosa-flowers (Pilgrimage i., 118).

[2] Lit. bu.. the "gall-bladder:" In this and in the "liver" allusions I dare not be baldly
literal.

[3] Arab. "Usfur" the seeds of Carthamus tinctorius = Safflower (Forskal, Flora, etc. lv.).
The seeds are crushed for oil and the flowers, which must be gathered by virgins or the
colour will fail, are extensively used for dyeing in Southern Arabia and Eastern Africa.

Thus they displayed the bride in all her seven toilettes before Hasan al-Basri, wholly neglecting the Gobbo who sat moping alone; and, when she opened her eyes[1] she said, "O Allah make this man my goodman and deliver me from the evil of this hunch-backed groom." As soon as they had made an end of this part of the ceremony they dismissed the wedding guests who went forth, women, children and all, and none remained save Hasan and the Hunchback, whilst the tirewomen led the bride into an inner room to change her garb and gear and get her ready for the bride-groom. Thereupon Quasimodo came up to Badr al-Din Hasan and said, "O my lord, thou hast cheered us this night with thy good company and overwhelmed us with thy kindness and courtesy; but now why not get thee up and go?" "Bismillah;" he answered, "In Allah's name so be it!"; and rising, he went forth by the door, where the Ifrit met him and said, "Stay in thy stead, O Badr al-Din, and when the Hunchback goes out to the closet of ease go in without losing time and seat thyself in the alcove; and when the bride comes say to her, ' 'Tis I am thy hus-band, for the King devised this trick only fearing for thee the evil eye, and he whom thou sawest is but a Syce, a groom, one of our stablemen.' Then walk boldly up to her and unveil her face; for jealousy hath taken us of this matter." While Hasan was still talking with the Ifrit behold, the groom fared forth from the hall and entering the closet of ease sat down on the stool. Hardly had he done this when the Ifrit came out of the tank,[2] wherein the water was, in semblance of a mouse and squeaked out "Zeek!" Quoth the Hunchback, "What ails thee?"; and the mouse grew and grew till it became a coal-black cat and caterwauled "Meeao! Meeao!"[3] Then it grew still more and more till it became a dog and barked out "Owh! Owh!" When the bridegroom saw this he was frightened and exclaimed "Out with thee, O unlucky

---

[1] On such occasions Miss Modesty shuts her eyes and looks as if about to faint.

[2] After either evacuation the Moslem is bound to wash or sand the part; first however he should apply three pebbles, or potsherds or clods of earth. Hence the allusion in the Koran (chapt. ix.), "men who love to be purified." When the Prophet was ques-tioning the men of Kuba, where he founded a mosque (Pilgrimage ii., 215), he asked them about their legal ablutions, especially after evacuation; and they told him that they used three stones before washing. Moslems and Hindus (who prefer water mixed with earth) abhor the unclean and unhealthy use of paper without ablution; and the people of India call European draught-houses, by way of opprobrium, "Kághaz-khánah"= paper closets. Most old Anglo-Indians, however, learn to use water.

[3] "Miao" or "Mau" is the generic name of the cat in the Egyptian of the hieroglyphs.

one!"[1] But the dog grew and swelled till it became an ass-colt
that brayed and snorted in his face "Hauk! Hauk!"[2] Whereupon
the Hunchback quaked and cried, "Come to my aid, O people of
the house!" But behold, the ass-colt grew and became big as a
buffalo and walled the way before him and spake with the voice
of the sons of Adam, saying, "Woe to thee, O thou Bunch-back,
thou stinkard, O thou filthiest of grooms!" Hearing this the
groom was seized with a colic and he sat down on the jakes in
his clothes with teeth chattering and knocking together. Quoth
the Ifrit, "Is the world so strait to thee thou findest none to
marry save my lady-love?" But as he was silent the Ifrit continued, "Answer me or I will do thee dwell in the dust!" "By
Allah," replied the Gobbo, "O King of the Buffaloes, this is no
fault of mine, for they forced me to wed her; and verily I wot not
that she had a lover amongst the buffaloes; but now I repent, first
before Allah and then before thee." Said the Ifrit to him, "I
swear to thee that if thou fare forth from this place, or thou
utter a word before sunrise, I assuredly will wring thy neck.
When the sun rises wend thy went and never more return to
this house." So saying, the Ifrit took up the Gobbo bridegroom
and set him head downwards and feet upwards in the slit of the
privy,[3] and said to him, "I will leave thee here but I shall be on
the look-out for thee till sunrise; and, if thou stir before then, I
will seize thee by the feet and dash out thy brains against the
wall: so look out for thy life!" Thus far concerning the Hunchback, but as regards Badr al-Din Hasan of Bassorah he left the
Gobbo and the Ifrit jangling and wrangling and, going into the
house, sat him down in the very middle of the alcove; and behold,
in came the bride attended by an old woman who stood at the
door and said, "O Father of Uprightness,[4] arise and take what

---

[1] Arab. "Ya Mash'úm" addressed to an evil spirit.

[2] "Heehaw!" as we should say. The Bresl. Edit. makes the cat cry "Nauh! Nauh!"
and the ass-colt "Manu! Manu!" I leave these onomatopœics as they are in Arabic;
they are curious, showing the unity in variety of hearing inarticulate sounds. The bird
which is called "Whip poor Will" in the U. S. is known to the Brazilians as "Joam corta
páo" (John cut wood); so differently do they hear the same notes.

[3] It is usually a slab of marble with a long slit in front and a round hole behind. The
text speaks of a Kursi (=stool); but this is now unknown to native houses which have not
adopted European fashions.

[4] This again is chaff as she addresses the Hunchback. The Bul. Edit. has "O Abu
Shiháb" (Father of the shooting-star = evil spirit); the Bresl. Edit. "O son of a heap!
O son of a Something!" (al-Afsh, a vulgarism).

God giveth thee." Then the old woman went away and the
bride, Sitt al-Husn or the Lady of Beauty hight, entered the inner
part of the alcove broken-hearted and saying in herself, "By
Allah I will never yield my person to him; no, not even were
he to take my life!" But as she came to the further end she saw
Badr al-Din Hasan and she said, "Dearling! art thou still sitting
here? By Allah I was wishing that thou wert my bridegroom
or, at least, that thou and the hunchbacked horse-groom were
partners in me." He replied, "O beautiful lady, how should the
Syce have access to thee, and how should he share in thee with
me?" "Then," quoth she, "who is my husband, thou or he?" "Sitt
al-Husn," rejoined Hasan, "we have not done this for mere fun,[1]
but only as a device to ward off the evil eye from thee; for when
the tirewomen and singers and wedding guests saw thy beauty
being displayed to me, they feared fascination and thy father
hired the horse-groom for ten dinars and a porringer of meat to
take the evil eye off us; and now he hath received his hire and
gone his gait." When the Lady of Beauty heard these words
she smiled and rejoiced and laughed a pleasant laugh. Then she
whispered him, "By the Lord thou hast quenched a fire which
tortured me and now, by Allah, O my little dark-haired darling,
take me to thee and press me to thy bosom!" Then she began
singing:—

"By Allah, set thy foot upon my soul; * Since long, long years for this alone
        I long:
And whisper tale of love in ear of me; * To me 'tis sweeter than the sweetest
        song!
No other youth upon my heart shall lie; * So do it often, dear, and do it long."

Then she stripped off her outer gear and she threw open her chemise
from the neck downwards and showed her parts genital and all
the rondure of her hips. When Badr al-Din saw the glorious
sight his desires were roused, and he arose and doffed his clothes,
and wrapping up in his bag-trousers[2] the purse of gold which

---

[1] As the reader will see, Arab ideas of "fun" and practical jokes are of the largest,
putting the Hibernian to utter rout, and comparing favourably with those recorded in
Don Quixote.

[2] Arab. "Saráwil" a corruption of the Pers. "Sharwál"; popularly called "libás" which,
however, may also mean clothing in general and especially outer-clothing. I translate
"bag-trousers" and "petticoat-trousers," the latter being the divided skirt of our future.
In the East, where Common Sense, not Fashion, rules dress, men, who have a protuberance
to be concealed, wear petticoats and women wear trousers. The feminine article is mostly

he had taken from the Jew and which contained the thousand
dinars, he laid it under the edge of the bedding.   Then he took
off his turband and set it upon the settle[1] atop of his other clothes,
remaining in his skull-cap and fine shirt of blue silk laced with
gold.   Whereupon the Lady of Beauty drew him to her and
he did likewise.   Then he took her to his embrace and set her
legs round his waist and point-blanked that cannon[2] placed where
it battereth down the bulwark of maidenhead and layeth it waste.
And he found her a pearl unpierced and unthridden and a filly
by all men save himself unridden; and he abated her virginity and
had joyance of her youth in his virility and presently he withdrew sword from sheath; and then returned to the fray right
eath; and when the battle and the siege had finished, some fifteen
assaults he had furnished and she conceived by him that very
night.   Then he laid his hand under her head and she did the
same and they embraced and fell asleep in each other's arms, as a
certain poet said of such lovers in these couplets:—

Visit thy lover, spurn what envy told; * No envious churl shall smile on love
    ensoul'd.
Merciful Allah made no fairer sight * Than coupled lovers single couch doth
    hold;
Breast pressing breast and robed in joys their own, * With pillowed forearms
    cast in finest mould:
And when heart speaks to heart with tongue of love, * Folk who would part
    them hammer steel ice-cold:
If a fair friend[3] thou find who cleaves to thee, * Live for that friend, that
    friend in heart enfold.
O ye who blame for love us lover kind * Say, can ye minister to diseasèd
    mind?

This much concerning Badr al-Din Hasan and Sitt al-Husn his

---

baggy but sometimes, as in India, *collant*-tight.   A quasi-sacred part of it is the inkle,
tape or string, often a most magnificent affair, with tassels of pearl and precious stones;
and "laxity in the trouser-string" is equivalent to the loosest conduct.   Upon the subject
of "libás," "sarwál" and its variants the curious reader will consult Dr. Dozy's "Dictionnaire Détaillé des Noms des Vêtements chez les Arabes," a most valuable work.

[1] The turban out of respect is not put upon the ground (Lane, M. E., chapt. i.).

[2] Arab. "Madfa" showing the modern date or the modernization of the tale.   In Lebid
"Madáfi" (plur. of Madfa') means water-courses or leats.

[3] In Arab. the "he" is a "she;" and Habíb ("friend") is the Attic φίλος, a euphemism
for lover.   This will occur throughout The Nights.   So the Arabs use a phrase corresponding
with the Stoic φιλεῖ, i. e. is wont, is fain.

cousin; but as regards the Ifrit, as soon as he saw the twain asleep, he said to the Ifritah, "Arise; slip thee under the youth and let us carry him back to his place ere dawn overtake us; for the day is nearhand." Thereupon she came forward and, getting under him as he lay asleep, took him up clad only in his fine blue shirt, leaving the rest of his garments; and ceased not flying (and the Ifrit vying with her in flight) till the dawn advised them that it had come upon them mid-way, and the Muezzin began his call from the Minaret, "Haste ye to salvation! Haste ye to salvation!"[1] Then Allah suffered his angelic host to shoot down the Ifrit with a shooting star,[2] so he was consumed, but the Ifritah escaped and she descended with Badr al-Din at the place where the Ifrit was burnt, and did not carry him back to Bassorah, fearing lest he come to harm. Now by the order of Him who predestineth all things, they alighted at Damascus of Syria, and the Ifritah set down her burden at one of the city-gates and flew away. When day arose and the doors were opened, the folk who came forth saw a handsome youth, with no other raiment but his blue shirt of gold-embroidered silk and skull-cap,[3] lying upon the ground drowned in sleep after the hard labour of the night which had not suffered him to take his rest. So the folk looking at him said, "O her luck with whom this one spent the night! but would he had waited to don his garments." Quoth another, "A sorry lot are the sons of great families! Haply he but now came forth of the tavern on some occasion of his own and his wine flew to his head,[4] whereby he hath missed the place he was making for and strayed till he came to the gate of the city; and finding it shut lay him down and went to by-by!" As the people were bandying guesses about him suddenly the morning breeze blew upon Badr al-Din and raising his shirt to his middle showed a stomach and navel with something below it,[5] and legs and thighs clear as crystal

---

[1] Part of the Azán, or call to prayer.

[2] Arab. "Shiháb," these meteors being the flying shafts shot at evil spirits who approach too near heaven. The idea doubtless arose from the showers of August and November meteors (The Perseides and Taurides) which suggest a battle raging in upper air. Christendom also has its superstition concerning them and called those of August the "fiery tears of Saint Lawrence," whose festival was on August 10.

[3] Arab. "Tákiyah"= Pers. Arak-chin; the calotte worn under the Fez. It is, I have said, now obsolete and the red woollen cap (mostly made in Europe) is worn over the hair; an unclean practice.

[4] Often the effect of cold air after a heated room.

[5] i. e. He was not a Eunuch, as the people guessed.

and smooth as cream. Cried the people, "By Allah he is a pretty
fellow!"; and at the cry Badr al-Din awoke and found himself
lying at a city-gate with a crowd gathered around him. At this
he greatly marvelled and asked, "Where am I, O good folk; and
what causeth you thus to gather round me, and what have I had
to do with you?"; and they answered, "We found thee lying
here asleep during the call to dawn-prayer and this is all we
know of the matter, but where diddest thou lie last night?"[1]
"By Allah, O good people," replied he, "I lay last night in
Cairo." Said somebody, "Thou hast surely been eating Hashish;"[2] and another, "He is a fool;" and a third, "He is a citrou-
ille;" and a fourth asked him, "Art thou out of thy mind? thou
sleepest in Cairo and thou wakest in the morning at the gate of
Damascus-city!"[3] Cried he, "By Allah, my good people, one
and all, I lie not to you: indeed I lay yesternight in the land of
Egypt and yesternoon I was at Bassorah." Quoth one, "Well!
well!"; and quoth another, "Ho! ho!"; and a third, "So! so!";
and a fourth cried, "This youth is mad, is possessed of the Jinni!"
So they clapped hands at him and said to one another, "Alas,
the pity of it for his youth: by Allah a madman! and madness is
no respecter of persons." Then said they to him, "Collect thy
wits and return to thy reason! How couldest thou be in Bassorah
yesterday and in Cairo yesternight and withal awake in Damascus
this morning?" But he persisted, "Indeed I was a bridegroom in
Cairo last night." "Belike thou hast been dreaming," rejoined
they, "and sawest all this in thy sleep." So Hasan took thought
for a while and said to them, "By Allah, this is no dream; nor
vision-like doth it seem! I certainly was in Cairo where they
displayed the bride before me, in presence of a third person, the
Hunchback groom who was sitting hard by. By Allah, O my
brother, this be no dream, and if it were a dream, where is the
bag of gold I bore with me and where are my turband and my
robe, and my trousers?" Then he rose and entered the city,
threading its highways and by-ways and bazar-streets; and the
people pressed upon him and jeered at him, crying out "Madman! madman!" till he, beside himself with rage, took refuge in

---

[1] In Arab. "this night" for the reason before given.

[2] Meaning especially the drink prepared of the young leaves and florets of Cannabis
Sativa. The word literally means "day grass" or "herbage." This intoxicant was much
used by magicians to produce ecstasy and thus to "deify themselves and receive the homage
of the genii and spirts of nature."

[3] Torrens, being an Irishman, translates "and woke in the morning sleeping at Damascus."

a cook's shop.   Now that Cook had been a trifle too clever, that
is, a rogue and thief; but Allah had made him repent and turn
from his evil ways and open a cook-shop; and all the people of
Damascus stood in fear of his boldness and his mischief.   So when
the crowd saw the youth enter his shop, they dispersed being
afraid of him, and went their ways.   The Cook looked at Badr
al-Din and, noting his beauty and loveliness, fell in love with him
forthright and said, "Whence comest thou, O youth?   Tell me at
once thy tale, for thou art become dearer to me than my soul."
So Hasan recounted to him all that had befallen him from
beginning to end (but in repetition there is no fruition) and the
Cook said, "O my lord Badr al-Din, doubtless thou knowest that
this case is wondrous and this story marvellous; therefore, O my
son, hide what hath betided thee, till Allah dispel what ills be
thine; and tarry with me here the meanwhile, for I have no child
and I will adopt thee."   Badr al-Din replied, "Be it as thou wilt,
O my uncle!"   Whereupon the Cook went to the bazar and
bought him a fine suit of clothes and made him don it; then fared
with him to the Kazi, and formally declared that he was his son.
So Badr al-Din Hasan became known in Damascus-city as the
Cook's son and he sat with him in the shop to take the silver,
and on this wise he sojourned there for a time.   Thus far concerning him; but as regards his cousin, the Lady of Beauty, when
morning dawned she awoke and missed Badr al-Din Hasan from
her side; but she thought that he had gone to the privy and she
sat expecting him for an hour or so; when behold, entered her
father Shams al-Din Mohammed, Wazir of Egypt.   Now he was
disconsolate by reason of what had befallen him through the
Sultan, who had entreated him harshly and had married his
daughter by force to the lowest of his menials and he too a lump
of a groom bunch-backed withal, and he said to himself, "I will
slay this daughter of mine if of her own free will she have yielded
her person to this accursed carle."   So he came to the door of the
bride's private chamber and said, "Ho!   Sitt al-Husn."   She
answered him, "Here am I! here am I![1] O my lord," and came

---

[1] Arab. "Labbayka," the cry technically called "Talbiyah" and used by those entering
Meccah (Pilgrimage iii. 125–232).   I shall also translate it by "Adsum."   The full cry is:—
Here am I, O Allah, here am I!
No partner hast Thou, here am I:
Verily the praise and the grace and the kingdom are thine:
No partner hast Thou: here am I!

out unsteady of gait after the pains and pleasures of the night; and she kissed his hand, her face showing redoubled brightness and beauty for having lain in the arms of that gazelle, her cousin. When her father, the Wazir, saw her in such case, he asked her, "O thou accursed, art thou rejoicing because of this horse-groom?", and Sitt al-Husn smiled sweetly and answered, "By Allah, don't ridicule me: enough of what passed yesterday when folk laughed at me, and evened me with that groom-fellow who is not worthy to bring my husband's shoes or slippers; nay who is not worth the paring of my husband's nails! By the Lord, never in my life have I nighted a night so sweet as yesternight!, so don't mock by reminding me of the Gobbo." When her parent heard her words he was filled with fury, and his eyes glared and stared, so that little of them showed save the whites and he cried, "Fie upon thee! What words are these? 'Twas the hunchbacked horse-groom who passed the night with thee!" "Allah upon thee," replied the Lady of Beauty, "do not worry me about the Gobbo, Allah damn his father;[1] and leave jesting with me; for this groom was only hired for ten dinars and a porringer of meat and he took his wage and went his way. As for me I entered the bridal-chamber, where I found my true bridegroom sitting, after the singer-women had displayed me to him; the same who had crossed their hands with red gold, till every pauper that was present waxed wealthy; and I passed the night on the breast of my bonny man, a most lively darling, with his black eyes and joined eyebrows."[2] When her parent heard these words the light before his face became night, and he cried out at her saying, "O thou whore! What is this thou tellest me? Where be thy wits?" "O my father," she rejoined, "thou breakest my heart; enough for thee that thou hast been so hard upon me! Indeed my husband who took my virginity is but just now gone to the draught-house and I feel that I have conceived by him."[3] The

---

A single Talbiyah is a "Shart" or positive condition: and its repetitiun is a Sunnat or Custom of the Prophet. See Night xci.

[1] The staple abuse of the vulgar is cursing parents and relatives, especially feminine, with specific allusions to their "shame." And when dames of high degree are angry, Nature, in the East as in the West, sometimes speaks out clearly enough, despite Mistress Chapone and all artificial restrictions.

[2] A great beauty in Arabia and the reverse in Denmark, Germany and Slav-land, where it is a sign of being a were-wolf or a vampire. In Greece also it denotes a "Brukolak" or vampire.

[3] This is not physiologically true: a bride rarely conceives the first night, and certainly would not know that she had conceived. Moreover the number of courses furnished by

Wazir rose in much marvel and entered the privy where he found the hunchbacked horse-groom with his head in the hole and his heels in the air. At this sight he was confounded and said, "This is none other than he, the rascal Hunchback!" So he called to him, "Ho, Hunchback!" The Gobbo grunted out, "*Taghúm! Taghúm!*" thinking it was the Ifrit spoke to him; so the Wazir shouted at him and said, "Speak out, or I'll strike off thy pate with this sword." Then quoth the Hunchback, "By Allah, O Shaykh of the Ifrits, ever since thou settest me in this place, I have not lifted my head; so Allah upon thee, take pity and entreat me kindly!" When the Wazir heard this he asked, "What is this thou sayest? I'm the bride's father and no Ifrit." "Enough for thee that thou hast well nigh done me die," answered Quasimodo; "now go thy ways before he come upon thee who hath served me thus. Could ye not marry me to any save the lady-love of buffaloes and the beloved of Ifrits? Allah curse her and curse him who married me to her and was the cause of this my case."——And Shahrazad perceived the dawn of day, and ceased to say her permitted say.

When it was the Twenty-third Night,

She said, It hath reached me, O auspicious King, that the hunchbacked groom spake to the bride's father saying, "Allah curse him who was the cause of this my case!" Then said the Wazir to him, "Up and out of this place!" "Am I mad," cried the groom, "that I should go with thee without leave of the Ifrit whose last words to me were:—"When the sun rises, arise and go thy gait." So hath the sun risen or no?; for I dare not budge from this place till then." Asked the Wazir, "Who brought thee hither?"; and he answered "I came here yesternight for a call of nature and to

---

the bridegroom would be against conception. It is popularly said that a young couple often undoes in the morning what it has done during the night.

[1] Torrens (Notes, xxiv.) quotes "Fleisher" upon the word "Ghamghama" (Diss. Crit. de Glossis Habichtionis), which he compares with "Dumduma" and "Humbuma," determining them to be onomatopœics, "an incomplete and an obscure murmur of a sentence as it were lingering between the teeth and lips and therefore difficult to be understood." Of this family is "Taghúm"; not used in modern days. In my Pilgrimage (i. 313) I have noticed another, "Khyas', Khyas'!" occurring in a Hizb al-Bahr (Spell of the Sea). Herklots gives a host of them; and their sole characteristics are harshness and strangeness of sound, uniting consonants which are not joined in Arabic. The old Egyptians and Chaldeans had many such words composed at will for theurgic operations.

do what none can do for me, when lo! a mouse came out of the
water, and squeaked at me and swelled and waxed gross till it was
big as a buffalo, and spoke to me words that entered my ears.
Then he left me here and went away, Allah curse the bride and
him who married me to her!" The Wazir walked up to him and
lifted his head out of the cesspool hole; and he fared forth running for dear life and hardly crediting that the sun had risen; and
repaired to the Sultan to whom he told all that had befallen him
with the Ifrit. But the Wazir returned to the bride's private
chamber, sore troubled in spirit about her, and said to her, "O my
daughter, explain this strange matter to me!" Quoth she, "'Tis
simply this. The bridegroom to whom they displayed me yester-
eve lay with me all night, and took my virginity and I am with
child by him. He is my husband and if thou believe me not, there
are his turband, twisted as it was, lying on the settle and his
dagger and his trousers beneath the bed with a something, I wot
not what, wrapped up in them." When her father heard this he
entered the private chamber and found the turband which had
been left there by Badr al-Din Hasan, his brother's son, and he
took it in hand and turned it over, saying, "This is the turband
worn by Wazirs, save that it is of Mosul stuff."[1] So he opened it
and, finding what seemed to be an amulet sewn up in the Fez, he
unsewed the lining and took it out; then he lifted up the trousers
wherein was the purse of the thousand gold pieces and, opening
that also, found in it a written paper. This he read and it was
the sale-receipt of the Jew in the name of Badr al-Din Hasan, son
of Nur al-Din Ali, the Egyptian; and the thousand dinars were
also there. No sooner had Shams al-Din read this than he cried out
with a loud cry and fell to the ground fainting; and as soon as he
revived and understood the gist of the matter he marvelled and
said, "There is no god, but *the* God, whose All-might is over all
things! Knowest thou, O my daughter, who it was that became
the husband of thy virginity?" "No," answered she, and he said
"Verily he is the son of my brother, thy cousin, and this thousand
dinars is thy dowry. Praise be to Allah! and would I wot how
this matter came about!" Then opened he the amulet which was
sewn up and found therein a paper in the handwriting of his
deceased brother, Nur al-Din the Egyptian, father of Badr al-Din

---

[1] This may mean either "it is of Mosul fashion" or, it is of muslin.

Hasan; and, when he saw the hand-writing, he kissed it again and again; and he wept and wailed over his dead brother and improvised these lines:—

"I see their traces and with pain I melt, * And on their whilome homes I
     weep and yearn:
And Him I pray who dealt this parting-blow * Some day he deign vouchsafe a
     safe return."[1]

When he ceased versifying, he read the scroll and found in it recorded the dates of his brother's marriage with the daughter of the Wazir of Bassorah, and of his going in to her, and her conception, and the birth of Badr al-Din Hasan and all his brother's history and doings up to his dying day. So he marvelled much and shook with joy and, comparing the dates with his own marriage and going in unto his wife and the birth of his daughter, Sitt al-Husn, he found that they perfectly agreed. So he took the document and, repairing with it to the Sultan, acquainted him with what had passed, from first to last; whereat the King marvelled and commanded the case to be at once recorded.[2] The Wazir abode that day expecting to see his brother's son but he came not; and he waited a second day, a third day and so on to the seventh day, without any tidings of him. So he said, "By Allah, I will do a deed such as none hath ever done before me!"; and he took reed-pen and ink and drew upon a sheet of paper the plan of the whole house, showing whereabouts was the private chamber with the curtain in such a place and the furniture in such another and so on with all that was in the room. Then he folded up the sketch and, causing all the furniture to be collected, he took Badr al-Din's garments and the turband and Fez and robe and purse, and carried the whole to his house and locked them up, against the coming of his nephew, Badr al-Din Hasan, the son of his lost brother, with an iron padlock on which he set his seal. As for the Wazir's daughter, when her tale of months was fulfilled, she bare a son like the full moon, the image of his father in beauty and

---

[1] To the English reader these lines would appear the reverse of apposite; but Orientals have their own ways of application, and all allusions to Badawi partings are effective and affecting. The civilised poets of Arab cities throw the charm of the Desert over their verse by images borrowed from its scenery, the dromedary, the mirage and the well as naturally as certain of our bards who hated the country, babbled of purling rills, etc. Thoroughly to feel Arabic poetry one must know the Desert (Pilgrimage iii., 63).

[2] In those days the Arabs and the Portuguese recorded everything which struck them, as the Chinese and Japanese do in our times. And yet we complain of the amount of our modern writing!

loveliness and fair proportions and perfect grace. They cut his navel-string[1] and Kohl'd his eyelids to strengthen his eyes, and gave him over to the nurses and nursery governesses,[2] naming him Ajíb, the Wonderful. His day was as a month and his month was as a year;[3] and, when seven years had passed over him, his grandfather sent him to school, enjoining the master to teach him Koran-reading, and to educate him well. He remained at the school four years, till he began to bully his schoolfellows and abuse them and bash them and thrash them and say, "Who among you is like me? I am the son of the Wazir of Egypt!" At last the boys came in a body to complain to the Monitor[4] of what hard usage they were wont to have from Ajib, and he said to them, "I will tell you somewhat you may do to him so that he shall leave off coming to the school, and it is this. When he enters to-morrow, sit ye down about him and say some one of you to some other, 'By Allah none shall play with us at this game except he tell us the names of his mamma and his papa; for he who knows not the names of his mother and his father is a bastard, a son of adultery,[5] and he shall not play with us.' " When morning dawned the boys came to school, Ajib being one of them, and all flocked round him saying, "We will play a game wherein none shall join save he can tell the name of his mamma and his papa." And they all cried, "By Allah, good!" Then quoth one of them, "My name is Májid and my mammy's name is Alawiyah and my daddy's Izz al-Din." Another spoke in like guise and yet a third, till Ajib's turn came, and he said, "My name is Ajib, and my mother's is Sitt al-Husn, and my father's Shams al-Din, the Wazir of Cairo." "By Allah," cried they, "the Wazir is not thy true father." Ajib answered, "The Wazir is my father in very deed." Then the boys all laughed and clapped their hands at him, saying "He does not know who is his papa: get out from among us, for none shall play with us except he know his father's name." Thereupon they dispersed from around him and laughed him to

---

1 This is mentioned because it is the act preliminary to naming the babe.

2 Arab. "Kahramánát" from Kahramán, an old Persian hero who conversed with the Simurgh-Griffon. Usually the word is applied to women-at-arms who defend the Harem, like the Urdu-begani of India, whose services were lately offered to England (1885), or the "Amazons" of Dahome.

3 Meaning he grew as fast in one day as other children in a month.

4 Arab. Al-Aríf; the tutor, the assistant-master.

5 Arab. "Ibn harám," a common term of abuse; and not a factual reflection on the parent. I have heard a mother apply the term to her own son.

scorn; so his breast was straitened and he well nigh choked with tears and hurt feelings. Then said the Monitor to him, "We know that the Wazir is thy grandfather, the father of thy mother, Sitt al-Husn, and not thy father. As for thy father, neither dost thou know him nor yet do we; for the Sultan married thy mother to the hunchbacked horse-groom; but the Jinni came and slept with her and thou hast no known father. Leave, then, comparing thyself too advantageously with the little ones of the school, till thou know that thou hast a lawful father; for until then thou wilt pass for a child of adultery amongst them. Seest thou not that even a huckster's son knoweth his own sire? Thy grandfather is the Wazir of Egypt; but as for thy father we wot him not and we say indeed that thou hast none. So return to thy sound senses!" When Ajib heard these insulting words from the Monitor and the school boys and understood the reproach they put upon him, he went out at once and ran to his mother, Sitt al-Husn, to complain; but he was crying so bitterly that his tears prevented his speech for a while. When she heard his sobs and saw his tears her heart burned as though with fire for him, and she said, "O my son, why dost thou weep? Allah keep the tears from thine eyes! Tell me what hath betided thee?" So he told her all that he heard from the boys and from the Monitor and ended with asking, "And who, O my mother, is my father?" She answered, "Thy father is the Wazir of Egypt;" but he said, "Do not lie to me. The Wazir is thy father, not mine! who then is my father? Except thou tell me the very truth I will kill myself with this hanger."[1] When his mother heard him speak of his father she wept, remembering her cousin and her bridal night with him and all that occurred there and then, and she repeated these couplets:—

"Love in my heart they lit and went their ways, * And all I love to furthest
    lands withdrew;
And when they left me sufferance also left, * And when we parted Patience
    bade adieu:
They fled and flying with my joys they fled, * In very constancy my spirit flew:
They made my eyelids flow with severance tears * And to the parting-pang
    these drops are due:

---

[1] Arab. "Khanjar" from the Persian, a syn. with the Arab. "Jambiyah." It is noticed in my Pilgrimage iii., pp. 72, 75. To "silver the dagger," means to become a rich man. From "Khanjar," not from its fringed loop or strap, I derive our silly word "hanger." Dr. Steingass would connect it with Germ. Fänger, *e. g.*, Hirschfänger.

And when I long to see reunion-day, * My groans prolonging sore for ruth
    I sue:
Then in my heart of hearts their shapes I trace, * And love and longing care
    and cark renew:
O ye, whose names cling round me like a cloak, * Whose love yet closer than a
    shirt I drew,
Belovèd ones! how long this hard despite? * How long this severance and
    this coy shy flight?"

Then she wailed and shrieked aloud and her son did the like; and
behold, in came the Wazir whose heart burnt within him at the
sight of their lamentations, and he said, "What makes you weep?"
So the Lady of Beauty acquainted him with what had happened
between her son and the school boys; and he also wept, calling
to mind his brother and what had past between them and what
had betided his daughter and how he had failed to find out what
mystery there was in the matter. Then he rose at once and,
repairing to the audience-hall, went straight to the King and told
his tale and craved his permission[1] to travel eastward to the city
of Bassorah and ask after his brother's son. Furthermore he besought the Sultan to write for him letters patent, authorising him
to seize upon Badr al-Din, his nephew and son-in-law, wheresoever
he might find him. And he wept before the King, who had pity on
him and wrote royal autographs to his deputies in all climes[2] and
countries and cities; whereat the Wazir rejoiced and prayed for
blessings on him. Then, taking leave of his Sovereign, he returned
to his house, where he equipped himself and his daughter and his
adopted child Ajib, with all things meet for a long march; and set
out and travelled the first day and the second and the third and so
forth till he arrived at Damascus-city. He found it a fair place
abounding in trees and streams, even as the poet said of it:—

When I nighted and dayed in Damascus town, * Time sware such another
    he ne'er should view:
And careless we slept under wing of night, * Till dappled Morn 'gan her
    smiles renew:
And dew-drops on branch in their beauty hung, * Like pearls to be dropt
    when the Zephyr blew:
And the Lake[3] was the page where birds read and note, * And the clouds set
    points to what breezes wrote.

---

1 Again we have "Dastur" for "Izn."
2 Arab. "Iklím"; the seven climates of Ptolemy.
3 Arab. "Al-Ghadir," lit. a place where water sinks, a lowland: here the drainage-
lakes east of Damascus into which the Baradah (Abana?) discharges. The higher eastern
plain is "Al-Ghutah" before noticed.

The Wazir encamped on the open space called Al-Hasá;[1] and, after pitching tents, said to his servants, "A halt here for two days!" So they went into the city upon their several occasions, this to sell and that to buy; this to go to the Hammam and that to visit the Cathedral-mosque of the Banu Umayyah, the Ommiades, whose like is not in this world.[2] Ajib also went, with his attendant eunuch, for solace and diversion to the city and the servant followed with a quarter-staff[3] of almond-wood so heavy that if he struck a camel therewith the beast would never rise again.[4] When the people of Damascus saw Ajib's beauty and brilliancy and perfect grace and symmetry (for he was a marvel of comeliness and winning loveliness, softer than the cool breeze of the North, sweeter than limpid waters to man in drowth, and pleasanter than the health for which sick man sueth), a mighty many followed him, whilst others ran on before, and sat down on the road until he should come up, that they might gaze on him, till, as Destiny had decreed, the Eunuch stopped opposite the shop of Ajib's father, Badr al-Din Hasan. Now his beard had grown long and thick and his wits had ripened during the twelve years which had passed over him, and the Cook and ex-rogue having died, the so-called Hasan of Bassorah had succeeded to his goods and shop, for that he had been formally adopted before the Kazi and witnesses. When his son and the Eunuch stepped before him he gazed on Ajib and, seeing how very beautiful he was, his heart fluttered and throbbed, and blood drew to blood and natural affection spake out and his bowels yearned over him. He had just dressed a conserve of pomegranate-grains with sugar, and Heaven-implanted love wrought within him; so he called to his son Ajib and said, "O my lord, O thou who hast gotten the mastery of my heart and my very vitals and to whom my bowels yearn; say me, wilt thou enter my house and solace my soul by eating of my meat?" Then his eyes streamed with tears which he could not stay, for he bethought him of what he had been and what he had become. When Ajib heard his father's words his

---

[1] The "Plain of Pebbles" still so termed at Damascus; an open space west of the city.
[2] Every Guide-book, even the Reverend Porter's "Murray," gives a long account of this Christian Church 'verted to a Mosque.
[3] Arab. "Nabút"; Pilgrimage i. 336.
[4] The Bres. Edit. says, "would have knocked him into Al-Yaman" (Southern Arabia), something like our slang phrase "into the middle of next week."

heart also yearned himwards and he looked at the Eunuch and said to him, "Of a truth, O my good guard, my heart yearns to this cook; he is as one that hath a son far away from him: so let us enter and gladden his heart by tasting of his hospitality. Per-chance for our so doing Allah may reunite me with my father." When the Eunuch heard these words he cried, "A fine thing this, by Allah! Shall the sons of Wazirs be seen eating in a common cook-shop? Indeed I keep off the folk from thee with this quarter-staff lest they even look upon thee; and I dare not suffer thee to enter this shop at all." When Hasan of Bassorah heard his speech he marvelled and turned to the Eunuch with the tears pouring down his cheeks; and Ajib said, "Verily my heart loves him!" But he answered, "Leave this talk, thou shalt not go in." There-upon the father turned to the Eunuch and said, "O worthy sir, why wilt thou not gladden my soul by entering my shop? O thou who art like a chestnut, dark without but white of heart within! O thou of the like of whom a certain poet said * * * " The Eunuch burst out a-laughing and asked—"Said what? Speak out by Allah and be quick about it." So Hasan the Bassorite began reciting these couplets:—

"If not master of manners or aught but discreet * In the household of Kings
  no trust could he take:
And then for the Harem! What Eunuch¹ is he * Whom angels would serve
  for his service sake."

The Eunuch marvelled and was pleased at these words, so he took Ajib by the hand and went into the cook's shop: whereupon Hasan the Bassorite ladled into a saucer some conserve of pomegranate-grains wonderfully good, dressed with almonds and sugar, saying, "You have honoured me with your company: eat then and health and happiness to you!" Thereupon Ajib said to his father, "Sit thee down and eat with us; so perchance Allah may unite us with him we long for." Quoth Hasan, "O my son, hast thou then been afflicted in thy tender years with parting from those thou lovest?" Quoth Ajib, "Even so, O nuncle mine; my heart burns for the loss of a beloved one who is none other than

---

¹ Arab. "Khádim": lit. a servant, politely applied (like Aghá = master) to a castrato. These gentry wax furious if baldly called "Tawáshi"=Eunuch. A mauvais plaisant in Egypt used to call me The Agha because a friend had placed his wife under my charge.

my father; and indeed I come forth, I and my grandfather,[1] to circle and search the world for him. Oh, the pity of it, and how I long to meet him!" Then he wept with exceeding weeping, and his father also wept seeing him weep and for his own bereave-ment, which recalled to him his long separation from dear friends and from his mother; and the Eunuch was moved to pity for him. Then they ate together till they were satisfied; and Ajib and the slave rose and left the shop. Hereat Hasan the Bassorite felt as though his soul had departed his body and had gone with them; for he could not lose sight of the boy during the twinkling of an eye, albeit he knew not that Ajib was his son. So he locked up his shop and hastened after them; and he walked so fast that he came up with them before they had gone out of the western gate. The Eunuch turned and asked him, "What ails thee?"; and Badr al-Din answered, "When ye went from me, meseemed my soul had gone with you; and, as I had business without the city-gate, I purposed to bear you company till my matter was ordered and so return." The Eunuch was angered and said to Ajib, "This is just what I feared! we ate that unlucky mouthful (which we are bound to respect), and here is the fellow following us from place to place; for the vulgar are ever the vulgar." Ajib, turning and seeing the Cook just behind him, was wroth and his face reddened with rage and he said to the servant, "Let him walk the highway of the Moslems; but, when we turn off it to our tents, and find that he still follows us, we will send him about his business with a flea in his ear." Then he bowed his head and walked on, the Eunuch walking behind him. But Hasan of Bas-sorah followed them to the plain Al-Hasa; and, as they drew near to the tents, they turned round and saw him close on their heels; so Ajib was very angry, fearing that the Eunuch might tell his grandfather what had happened. His indignation was the hotter for apprehension lest any say that after he had entered a cook-shop the cook had followed him. So he turned and looked at Hasan of Bassorah and found his eyes fixed on his own, for the father had become a body without a soul; and it seemed to Ajib that his eye was a treacherous eye or that he was some lewd fellow. So his rage redoubled and, stooping down, he took up a stone weighing half a pound and threw it at his father. It struck him

---

[1] This sounds absurd enough in English, but Easterns always put themselves first for respect.

on the forehead, cutting it open from eye-brow to eye-brow and causing the blood to stream down: and Hasan fell to the ground in a swoon whilst Ajib and the Eunuch made for the tents. When the father came to himself he wiped away the blood and tore off a strip from his turband and bound up his head, blaming himself the while, and saying, "I wronged the lad by shutting up my shop and following, so that he thought I was some evil-minded fellow." Then he returned to his place where he busied himself with the sale of his sweetmeats; and he yearned after his mother at Bassorah, and wept over her and broke out repeating:—

"Unjust it were to bid the World[1] be just * And blame her not: She ne'er
        was made for justice:
Take what she gives thee, leave all grief aside, * For now to fair and then to foul
        her lust is."

So Hasan of Bassorah set himself steadily to sell his sweetmeats; but the Wazir, his uncle, halted in Damascus three days and then marched upon Emesa, and passing through that town he made enquiry there and at every place where he rested. Thence he fared on by way of Hamah and Aleppo and thence through Diyár Bakr and Máridin and Mosul, still enquiring, till he arrived at Bassorah-city. Here, as soon as he had secured a lodging, he presented himself before the Sultan, who entreated him with high honour and the respect due to his rank, and asked the cause of his coming. The Wazir acquainted him with his history and told him that the Minister Nur al-Din was his brother; whereupon the Sultan exclaimed, "Allah have mercy upon him!" and added, "My good Sahib![2]; he was my Wazir for fifteen years and I loved him exceedingly. Then he died leaving a son who abode only a single month after his father's death; since which time he has disappeared and we could gain no tidings of him. But his mother, who is the daughter of my former Minister, is still among us." When the Wazir Shams al-Din heard that his nephew's mother was alive and well, he rejoiced and said, "O King I much desire to meet her." The King on the instant gave him

---

[1] In Arabic the World is feminine.
[2] Arab. "Sáhib"= lit. a companion; also a friend and especially applied to the Companions of Mohammed. Hence the Sunnis claim for them the honour of "friendship" with the Apostle; but the Shia'hs reply that the Arab says "Sahaba-hu'l-himár" (the Ass was his Sahib or companion). In the text it is a Wazirial title, in modern India it is = gentleman, e. g. "Sahib log" (the Sahib people) means their white conquerors, who, by the by, mostly mispronounce the word "Sáb."

leave to visit her; so he betook himself to the mansion of his brother, Nur al-Din, and cast sorrowful glances on all things in and around it and kissed the threshold. Then he bethought him of his brother, Nur al-Din Ali, and how he had died in a strange land far from kith and kin and friends; and he wept and repeated these lines:—

"I wander 'mid these walls, my Layla's walls, * And kissing this and other wall
    I roam:
'Tis not the walls or roof my heart so loves, * But those who in this house had
    made their home."

Then he passed through the gate into a courtyard and found a vaulted doorway builded of hardest syenite[1] inlaid with sundry kinds of multi-coloured marble. Into this he walked and wandered about the house and, throwing many a glance around, saw the name of his brother, Nur al-Din, written in gold wash upon the walls. So he went up to the inscription and kissed it and wept and thought of how he had been separated from his brother and had now lost him for ever, and he recited these couplets:—

"I ask of you from every rising sun, * And eke I ask when flasheth leven-
    light:
Restless I pass my nights in passion-pain, * Yet ne'er I 'plain me of my pain-
    ful plight:
My love! if longer last this parting throe * Little by little shall it waste my
    sprite.
An thou wouldst bless these eyne with sight of thee * One day on earth, I
    crave none other sight:
Think not another could possess my mind * Nor length nor breadth for other
    love I find."

Then he walked on till he came to the apartment of his brother's widow, the mother of Badr al-Din Hasan, the Egyptian. Now from the time of her son's disappearance she had never ceased weeping and wailing through the light hours and the dark; and, when the years grew longsome with her, she built for him a tomb of marble in the midst of the saloon and there used to weep for him day and night, never sleeping save thereby. When the Wazir drew near her apartment, he heard her voice and stood behind the door while she addressed the sepulchre in verse and said:—

---

[1] Arab. "Suwán," prop. Syenite, from Syene (Al-Suwan) but applied to flint and any hard stone.

"Answer, by Allah! Sepulchre, are all his beauties gone? * Hath change the
  power to blight his charms, that Beauty's paragon?
Thou art not earth, O Sepulchre! nor art thou sky to me; * How comes it,
  then, in thee I see conjoint the branch and moon?"

While she was bemoaning herself after this fashion, behold, the
Wazir went in to her and saluted her and informed her that he was
her husband's brother; and, telling her all that had passed between them, laid open before her the whole story, how her son
Badr al-Din Hasan had spent a whole night with his daughter full
ten years ago but had disappeared in the morning. And he ended
with saying, "My daughter conceived by thy son and bare a
male child who is now with me, and he is thy son and thy son's
son by my daughter." When she heard the tidings that her boy,
Badr al-Din, was still alive and saw her brother-in-law, she rose
up to him and threw herself at his feet and kissed them, reciting
these lines:—

"Allah be good to him that gives glad tidings of thy steps; * In very sooth for
  better news mine ears would never sue:
Were he content with worn-out robe, upon his back I'd throw * A heart to
  pieces rent and torn when heard the word Adieu."

Then the Wazir sent for Ajib and his grandmother stood up and
fell on his neck and wept; but Shams al-Din said to her, "This is
no time for weeping; this is the time to get thee ready for travelling with us to the land of Egypt; haply Allah will reunite me and
thee with thy son and my nephew." Replied she, "Hearkening
and obedience;" and, rising at once, collected her baggage and
treasures and her jewels, and equipped herself and her slave-girls
for the march, whilst the Wazir went to take his leave of the
Sultan of Bassorah, who sent by him presents and rarities for the
Soldan of Egypt. Then he set out at once upon his homeward
march and journeyed till he came to Damascus-city where he
alighted in the usual place and pitched tents, and said to
his suite, "We will halt a se'nnight here to buy presents and
rare things for the Soldan." Now Ajib bethought him of
the past so he said to the Eunuch, "O Láik, I want a little
diversion; come, let us go down to the great bazar of Damascus,[1] and see what hath become of the cook whose sweetmeats we ate and whose head we broke, for indeed he was

---

1 It was famous in the middle ages, and even now it is, perhaps, the most interesting
to travellers after that "Sentina Gentium," the "Bhendi Bazar" of unromantic Bombay.

kind to us and we entreated him scurvily." The Eunuch answered, "Hearing is obeying!" So they went forth from the tents; and the tie of blood drew Ajib towards his father, and forthwith they passed through the gateway, Báb al-Farádís[1] hight, and entered the city and ceased not walking through the streets till they reached the cookshop, where they found Hasan of Bassorah standing at the door. It was near the time of mid-afternoon prayer[2] and it so fortuned that he had just dressed a confection of pomegranate-grains. When the twain drew near to him and Ajib saw him, his heart yearned towards him, and noticing the scar of the blow, which time had darkened on his brow, he said to him, "Peace be on thee, O man!;[3] know that my heart is with thee." But when Badr al-Din looked upon his son his vitals yearned and his heart fluttered, and he hung his head earthwards and sought to make his tongue give utterance to his words, but he could not. Then he raised his head humbly and suppliant-wise towards his boy and repeated these couplets:—

"I longed for my beloved but when I saw his face, * Abashed I held my tongue
    and stood with downcast eye;
And hung my head in dread and would have hid my love, * But do whatso I
    would hidden it would not lie:
Volumes of plaints I had prepared, reproach and blame, * But when we met,
    no single word remembered I."

And then said he to them, "Heal my broken heart and eat of my sweetmeats; for, by Allah, I cannot look at thee but my heart flutters. Indeed I should not have followed thee the other day, but that I was beside myself." "By Allah," answered Ajib, "thou dost indeed love us! We ate in thy house a mouthful when we were here before and thou madest us repent of it, for that thou followedst us and wouldst have disgraced us; so now we will not eat aught with thee save on condition that thou make oath not to go out after us nor dog us. Otherwise we will not visit thee again during our present stay; for we shall halt a week here, whilst my

---

[1] "The Gate of the Gardens," in the northern wall, a Roman archway of the usual solid construction shaming not only our modern shams, but our finest masonry.

[2] Arab. "Al-Asr," which may mean either the hour or the prayer. It is also the moment at which the Guardian Angels relieve each other (Sale's Koran, chapt. v.).

[3] Arab. "Ya házá"= O this (one)! a somewhat slighting address equivalent to "Heus tu! O thou, whoever thou art." Another form is "Yá hú"= O he! Can this have originated Swift's "Yahoo"?

grandfather buys certain presents for the King." Quoth Hasan of Bassorah, "I promise you this." So Ajib and the Eunuch entered the shop, and his father set before them a saucer-full of conserve of pomegranate-grains. Said Ajib, "Sit thee down and eat with us, so haply shall Allah dispel our sorrows." Hasan the Bassorite was joyful and sat down and ate with them; but his eyes kept gazing fixedly on Ajib's face, for his very heart and vitals clove to him; and at last the boy said to him, "Did I not tell thee thou art a most noyous dotard?; so do stint thy staring in my face!" But when Hasan of Bassorah heard his son's words he repeated these lines:—

"Thou hast some art the hearts of men to clip;* Close-veiled, far-hidden
    mystery dark and deep:
O thou whose beauties shame the lustrous moon, * Wherewith the saffron
    Morn fears rivalship!
Thy beauty is a shrine shall ne'er decay; * Whose signs shall grow until they
    all outstrip;[1]
Must I be thirst-burnt by that Eden-brow * And die of pine to taste that
    Kausar[2]-lip?"

Hasan kept putting morsels into Ajib's mouth at one time and at another time did the same by the Eunuch and they ate till they were satisfied and could no more. Then all rose up and the cook poured water on their hands;[3] and, loosing a silken waist-shawl, dried them and sprinkled them with rose-water from a casting-bottle he had by him. Then he went out and presently returned with a gugglet of sherbet flavoured with rose-water, scented with musk and cooled with snow; and he set this before them saying,

---

[1] Alluding to the τήρατα ("minor miracles which cause surprise") performed by Saints' tombs, the mildest form of thaumaturgy. One of them gravely recorded in the Dabistan (ii. 226) is that of the holy Jamen, who opened the Sámran or bead-bracelet from the arm of the beautiful Chistápá with member erect, "thus evincing his manly strength and his command over himself"(!)

[2] The River of Paradise, a *lieu commun* of poets (Koran, chapt. cviii.): the water is whiter than milk or silver, sweeter than honey, smoother than cream, more odorous than musk; its banks are of chrysolite and it is drunk out of silver cups set around it thick as stars. Two pipes conduct it to the Prophet's Pond which is an exact square, one month's journey in compass. Kausar is spirituous like wine; Salsabil sweet like clarified honey; the Fount of Mildness is like milk and the Fount of Mercy like liquid crystal.

[3] The Moslem does not use the European basin because water which has touched an impure skin becomes impure. Hence it is poured out from a ewer ("ibrík" Pers. Ab-ríz) upon the hands and falls into a basin ("tisht") with an open-worked cover.

"Complete your kindness to me!" So Ajib took the gugglet and drank and passed it to the Eunuch; and it went round till their stomachs were full and they were surfeited with a meal larger than their wont. Then they went away and made haste in walk-ing till they reached the tents, and Ajib went in to his grand-mother, who kissed him and, thinking of her son, Badr al-Din Hasan, groaned aloud and wept and recited these lines:—

"I still had hoped to see thee and enjoy thy sight, * For in thine absence life had lost its kindly light:
I swear my vitals wot none other love but thine * By Allah, who can read the secrets of the sprite!"

Then she asked Ajib, "O my son! where hast thou been?"; and he answered, "In Damascus-city;" Whereupon she rose and set before him a bit of scone and a saucer of conserve of pomegranate-grains (which was too little sweetened), and she said to the Eunuch, "Sit down with thy master!" Said the servant to him-self, "By Allah, we have no mind to eat: I cannot bear the smell of bread;" but he sat down and so did Ajib, though his stomach was full of what he had eaten already and drunken. Nevertheless he took a bit of the bread and dipped it in the pomegranate-con-serve and made shift to eat it, but he found it too little sweetened, for he was cloyed and surfeited, so he said, "Faugh; what be this wild-beast¹ stuff?" "O my son," cried his grandmother, "dost thou find fault with my cookery? I cooked this myself and none can cook it as nicely as I can save thy father, Badr al-Din Hasan." "By Allah, O my lady," Ajib answered, "this dish is nasty stuff; for we saw but now in the city of Bassorah a cook who so dresseth pomegranate-grains that the very smell openeth a way to the heart and the taste would make a full man long to eat; and, as for this mess compared with his, 'tis not worth either much or little." When his grandmother heard his words she waxed wroth with exceeding wrath and looked at the servant——And Shahrazad perceived the dawn of day and ceased to say her permitted say.

---

¹ Arab. "Wahsh," a word of many meanings; nasty, insipid, savage, etc. The off-side of a horse is called Wahshi opposed to Insi, the near side. The Amir Taymur ("Lord Iron") whom Europeans unwittingly call after his Persian enemies' nickname, "Tamerlane," i. e. Taymur-i-lang, or limping Taymur, is still known as "Al-Wahsh" (the wild beast) at Damascus, where his Tartars used to bury men up to their necks and play at bowls with their heads for ninepins.

When it was the Twenty-fourth Night,

She said, It hath reached me, O auspicious King, that when Ajib's grandmother heard his words, she waxed wroth and looked at the servant and said, "Woe to thee! dost thou spoil my son,[1] and dost take him into common cookshops?" The Eunuch was frightened and denied, saying, "We did not go into the shop; we only passed by it." "By Allah," cried Ajib, "but we *did* go in and we ate till it came out of our nostrils, and the dish was better than thy dish!" Then his grandmother rose and went and told her brother-in-law, who was incensed against the Eunuch, and sending for him asked him, "Why didst thou take my son into a cookshop?"; and the Eunuch being frightened answered, "We did not go in." But Ajib said, "We *did* go inside and ate conserve of pomegranate-grains till we were full; and the cook gave us to drink of iced and sugared sherbet." At this the Wazir's indignation redoubled and he questioned the Castrato but, as he still denied, the Wazir said to him, "If thou speak sooth, sit down and eat before us." So he came forward and tried to eat, but could not and threw away the mouthful crying "O my lord! I am surfeited since yesterday." By this the Wazir was certified that he had eaten at the cook's and bade the slaves throw him[2] which they did. Then they came down on him with a rib basting which burned him till he cried for mercy and help from Allah, saying, "O my master, beat me no more and I will tell thee the truth;" whereupon the Wazir stopped the bastinado and said, "Now speak thou sooth." Quoth the Eunuch, "Know then that we did enter the shop of a cook while he was dressing conserve of pomegranate-grains and he set some of it before us: by Allah! I never ate in my life its like, nor tasted aught nastier than this stuff which is now before us."[3] Badr al-Din Hasan's mother was angry at this and said, "Needs must thou go back to the cook and bring me a saucer of conserved pomegranate-grains from that which is in his shop and show it to thy master, that he may say

---

1 For "grandson" as being more affectionate. Easterns have not yet learned that clever Western saying:—The enemies of our enemies are our friends.

2 This was a simple bastinado on the back, not the more ceremonious affair of beating the feet-soles. But it is surprising what the Egyptians can bear; some of the rods used in the time of the Mameluke Beys are nearly as thick as a man's wrist.

3 The woman-like spite of the eunuch intended to hurt the grandmother's feelings.

which be the better and the nicer, mine or his." Said the un-
sexed "I will." So on the instant she gave him a saucer and a
half dinar and he returned to the shop and said to the cook, "O
Shaykh of all Cooks,[1] we have laid a wager concerning thy
cookery in my lord's house, for they have conserve of pomegranate-grains there also; so give me this half-dinar's worth and
look to it; for I have eaten a full meal of stick on account of thy
cookery, and so do not let me eat aught more thereof." Hasan of
Bassorah laughed and answered, "By Allah, none can dress this
dish as it should be dressed save myself and my mother, and she
at this time is in a far country." Then he ladled out a saucer-full;
and, finishing it off with musk and rose-water, put it in a cloth
which he sealed[2] and gave it to the Eunuch, who hastened back
with it. No sooner had Badr al-Din Hasan's mother tasted it
and perceived its fine flavour and the excellence of the cookery,
than she knew who had dressed it, and she screamed and fell
down fainting. The Wazir, sorely startled, sprinkled rose-water
upon her and after a time she recovered and said, "If my son
be yet of this world, none dressed this conserve of pomegranate-
grains but he; and this Cook is my very son Badr al-Din Hasan;
there is no doubt of it nor can there be any mistake, for only I and
he knew how to prepare it and I taught him." When the Wazir
heard her words he joyed with exceeding joy and said, "Oh the
longing of me for a sight of my brother's son! I wonder if the
days will ever unite us with him! Yet it is to Almighty Allah
alone that we look for bringing about this meeting." Then he
rose without stay or delay and, going to his suite said to them,
"Be off, some fifty of you with sticks and staves to the Cook's shop
and demolish it; then pinion his arms behind him with his own
turband, saying, 'It was thou madest that foul mess of pomegranate-grains!' and drag him here perforce but without doing him
a harm." And they replied, "It is well." Then the Wazir rode
off without losing an instant to the Palace and, foregathering with
the Viceroy of Damascus, showed him the Sultan's orders. After
careful perusal he kissed the letter, and placing it upon his head
said to his visitor, "Who is this offender of thine?" Quoth the
Wazir, "A man which is a cook." So the Viceroy at once sent
his apparitors to the shop; which they found demolished and

---

[1] The usual Cairene "chaff."
[2] A necessary precaution against poison (Pilgrimage i. 84, and iii. 43).

everything in it broken to pieces; for whilst the Wazir was riding to the palace his men had done his bidding. Then they awaited his return from the audience, and Hasan of Bassorah who was their prisoner kept saying, "I wonder what they have found in the conserve of pomegranate-grains to bring things to this pass!"[1] When the Wazir returned to them, after his visit to the Viceroy who had given him formal permission to take up his debtor and depart with him, on entering the tents he called for the Cook. They brought him forward pinioned with his turband; and, when Badr al-Din Hasan saw his uncle, he wept with exceeding weeping and said, "O my lord, what is my offence against thee?"   "Art thou the man who dressed that conserve of pomegranate-grains?"; asked the Wazir, and he answered "Yes! didst thou find in it aught to call for the cutting off of my head?"   Quoth the Wazir, "That were the least of thy deserts!"   Quoth the cook, "O my lord, wilt thou not tell me my crime and what aileth the conserve of pomegranate-grains?"   "Presently," replied the Wazir and called aloud to his men, saying "Bring hither the camels."   So they struck the tents and by the Wazir's orders the servants took Badr al-Din Hasan, and set him in a chest which they padlocked and put on a camel. Then they departed and stinted not journeying till nightfall, when they halted and ate some victual, and took Badr al-Din Hasan out of his chest and gave him a meal and locked him up again. They set out once more and travelled till they reached Kimrah, where they took him out of the box and brought him before the Wazir who asked him, "Art thou he who dressed that conserve of pomegranate-grains?"   He answered "Yes, O my lord!"; and the Wazir said "Fetter him!"   So they fettered him and returned him to the chest and fared on again till they reached Cairo and lighted at the quarter called Al-Raydaniyah.[2]   Then the Wazir gave order to take Badr al-Din Hasan out of the chest and sent for a carpenter and said to him, "Make me a cross of wood[3] for this fellow!"   Cried Badr al-

---

[1] The Bresl. Edit. (ii. 108) describes the scene at greater length.

[2] The Bul. Edit. gives by mistake of diacritical points, "Zabdaniyah:" Raydaniyah is or rather was a camping ground to the North of Cairo.

[3] Arab. "La'abat"= a plaything, a puppet, a lay figure. Lane (i. 326) conjectures that the cross is so called because it resembles a man with arms extended. But Moslems never heard of the fanciful ideas of mediæval Christian divines who saw the cross everywhere and in everything. The former hold that Pharaoh invented the painful and ignominious punishment. (Koran, chapt. vii.)

Din Hasan "And what wilt thou do with it?"; and the Wazir replied, "I mean to crucify thee thereon, and nail thee thereto and parade thee all about the city." "And why wilt thou use me after this fashion?" "Because of thy villanous cookery of con-served pomegranate-grains; how durst thou dress it and sell it lacking pepper?" "And for that it lacked pepper wilt thou do all this to me? Is it not enough that thou hast broken my shop and smashed my gear and boxed me up in a chest and fed me only once a day?" "Too little pepper! too little pepper! this is a crime which can be expiated only upon the cross!" Then Badr al-Din Hasan marvelled and fell a-mourning for his life; whereupon the Wazir asked him, "Of what thinkest thou?"; and he answered him, "Of maggoty heads like thine;[1] for an thou had one ounce of sense thou hadst not treated me thus." Quoth the Wazir, "It is our duty to punish thee lest thou do the like again." Quoth Badr al-Din Hasan, "Of a truth my offence were over-punished by the least of what thou hast already done to me; and Allah damn all conserve of pomegranate-grains and curse the hour when I cooked it and would I had died ere this!" But the Wazir rejoined, "There is no help for it: I must crucify a man who sells conserve of pomegranate-grains lacking pepper." All this time the carpenter was shaping the wood and Badr al-Din looked on; and thus they did till night, when his uncle took him and clapped him into the chest, saying, "The thing shall be done to-morrow!" Then he waited till he knew Badr al-Din Hasan to be asleep, when he mounted; and, taking the chest up before him, entered the city and rode on to his own house, where he alighted and said to his daughter, Sitt al-Husn, "Praised be Allah who hath reunited thee with thy husband, the son of thine uncle! Up now, and order the house as it was on thy bridal night." So the servants arose and lit the candles; and the Wazir took out his plan of the nuptial chamber, and directed them what to do till they had set everything in its stead, so that whoever saw it would have no doubt but it was the very night of the mar-riage. Then he bade them put down Badr al-Din Hasan's tur-band on the settle, as he had deposited it with his own hand, and

---

[1] Here good blood, driven to bay, speaks out boldly. But, as a rule, the humblest and mildest Eastern when in despair turns round upon his oppressors like a wild cat. Some of the criminals whom Fath Ali Shah of Persia put to death by chopping down the fork, begin-ning at the scrotum, abused his mother till the knife reached their vitals and they could no longer speak.

in like manner his bag-trousers and the purse which were under
the mattress: and told his daughter to undress herself and go to
bed in the private chamber as on her wedding-night, adding,
"When the son of thine uncle comes in to thee, say to him:—
Thou hast loitered while going to the privy; and call him to lie
by thy side and keep him in converse till daybreak, when we will
explain the whole matter to him." Then he bade take Badr al-
Din Hasan out of the chest, after loosing the fetters from his feet
and stripping off all that was on him save the fine shirt of blue
silk in which he had slept on his wedding-night; so that he was
well-nigh naked and trouserless. All this was done whilst he
was sleeping on utterly unconscious. Then, by doom of Destiny,
Badr al-Din Hasan turned over and awoke; and, finding himself
in a lighted vestibule, said to himself, "Surely I am in the mazes
of some dream." So he rose and went on a little to an inner door
and looked in and lo! he was in the very chamber wherein the
bride had been displayed to him; and there he saw the bridal
alcove and the settle and his turband and all his clothes. When
he saw this he was confounded and kept advancing with one
foot, and retiring with the other, saying, "Am I sleeping or
waking?" And he began rubbing his forehead and saying (for
indeed he was thoroughly astounded), "By Allah, verily this is the
chamber of the bride who was displayed before me! Where
am I then? I was surely but now in a box!" Whilst he was
talking with himself, Sitt al-Husn suddenly lifted the corner of
the chamber-curtain and said, "O my lord, wilt thou not come
in? Indeed thou hast loitered long in the water-closet." When
he heard her words and saw her face he burst out laughing and
said, "Of a truth this is a very nightmare among dreams!" Then
he went in sighing, and pondered what had come to pass with
him and was perplexed about his case, and his affair became yet
more obscure to him when he saw his turband and bag-trousers
and when, feeling the pocket, he found the purse containing the
thousand gold pieces. So he stood still and muttered, "Allah is
all knowing! Assuredly I am dreaming a wild waking dream!"
Then said the Lady of Beauty to him, "What ails thee to look
puzzled and perplexed?"; adding, "Thou wast a very different
man during the first of the night!" He laughed and asked her,
"How long have I been away from thee?"; and she answered him,
"Allah preserve thee and His Holy Name be about thee! Thou
didst but go out an hour ago for an occasion and return. Are thy

wits clean gone?" When Badr al-Din Hasan heard this, he laughed,[1] and said, "Thou hast spoken truth; but, when I went out from thee, I forgot myself awhile in the draught-house and dreamed that I was a cook at Damascus and abode there ten years; and there came to me a boy who was of the sons of the great, and with him an Eunuch." Here he passed his hand over his forehead and, feeling the scar, cried, "By Allah, O my lady, it must have been true, for he struck my forehead with a stone and cut it open from eye-brow to eye-brow; and here is the mark: so it must have been on wake." Then he added, "But perhaps I dreamt it when we fell asleep, I and thou, in each other's arms, for meseems it was as though I travelled to Damascus without tarbush and trousers and set up as a cook there." Then he was perplexed and considered for awhile, and said, "By Allah, I also fancied that I dressed a conserve of pomegranate-grains and put too little pepper in it. By Allah, I must have slept in the numero-cent and have seen the whole of this in a dream; but how long was that dream!" "Allah upon thee," said Sitt al-Husn, "and what more sawest thou?" So he related all to her; and presently said, "By Allah had I not woke up they would have nailed me to a cross of wood!" "Wherefore?" asked she; and he answered, "For putting too little pepper in the conserve of pomegranate-grains, and meseemed they demolished my shop and dashed to pieces my pots and pans, destroyed all my stuff and put me in a box; they then sent for the carpenter to fashion a cross for me and would have crucified me thereon. Now Alhamdolillah! thanks be to Allah, for that all this happened to me in sleep, and not on wake." Sitt al-Husn laughed and clasped him to her bosom and he her to his: then he thought again and said, "By Allah, it could not be save while I was awake: truly I know not what to think of it." Then he lay him down and all the night he was bewildered about his case, now saying, "I was dreaming!" and then saying, "I was awake!", till morning, when his uncle Shams al-Din, the Wazir, came to him and saluted him. When Badr al-Din Hasan saw him he said, "By Allah, art thou not he who bade bind my hands behind me and smash my shop and nail me to a cross on a matter of conserved pomegranate-grains be-cause the dish lacked a sufficiency of pepper?" Whereupon the

---

[1] These repeated "laughs" prove the trouble of his spirit. Noble Arabs "show their back-teeth" so rarely that their laughter is held worthy of being recorded by their bi-ographers.

Wazir said to him, "Know, O my son, that truth hath shown it soothfast and the concealed hath been revealed![1] Thou art the son of my brother, and I did all this with thee to certify myself that thou wast indeed he who went in unto my daughter that night. I could not be sure of this, till I saw that thou knewest the chamber and thy turband and thy trousers and thy gold and the papers in thy writing and in that of thy father, my brother; for I had never seen thee afore that and knew thee not; and as to thy mother I have prevailed upon her to come with me from Bassorah." So saying, he threw himself on his nephew's breast and wept for joy; and Badr al-Din Hasan, hearing these words from his uncle, marvelled with exceeding marvel and fell on his neck and also shed tears for excess of delight. Then said the Wazir to him, "O my son, the sole cause of all this is what passed between me and thy sire;" and he told him the manner of his father wayfaring to Bassorah and all that had occurred to part them. Lastly the Wazir sent for Ajib; and when his father saw him he cried, "And this is he who struck me with the stone!" Quoth the Wazir "This is thy son!" And Badr al-Din Hasan threw himself upon his boy and began repeating:—

"Long have I wept o'er severance' ban and bane, * Long from mine eyelids
    tear-rills rail and rain:
And vowèd I if Time reunion bring * My tongue from name of "Severance"
    I'll restrain:
Joy hath o'ercome me to this stress that I * From joy's revulsion to shed tears
    am fain:
Ye are so trained to tears, O eyne of me! * You weep with pleasure as you
    weep with pain."[2]

When he had ended his verse his mother came in and threw herself upon him and began reciting:—

"When we met we complained, * Our hearts were sore wrung:
But plaint is not pleasant * Fro' messenger's tongue."

Then she wept and related to him what had befallen her since his departure, and he told her what he had suffered, and they thanked

---

[1] A popular phrase, derived from the Koranic "Truth is come, and falsehood is vanished: for falsehood is of short continuance" (chapt. xvii.). It is an equivalent of our adaptation from 1 Esdras iv. 41, "Magna est veritas et prævalebit." But the great question still remains, What is Truth?

[2] In Night lxxv. these lines will occur with variants.

Allah Almighty for their reunion. Two days after his arrival the Wazir Shams al-Din went in to the Sultan and, kissing the ground between his hands, greeted him with the greeting due to Kings. The Sultan rejoiced at his return and his face brightened and, placing him hard by his side,[1] asked him to relate all he had seen in his wayfaring and whatso had betided him in his going and coming. So the Wazir told him all that had passed from first to last and the Sultan said, "Thanks be to Allah for thy victory[2] and the winning of thy wish and thy safe return to thy children and thy people! And now I needs must see the son of thy brother, Hasan of Bassorah, so bring him to the audience-hall to-morrow." Shams al-Din replied, "Thy slave shall stand in thy presence to-morrow, Inshallah, if it be God's will." Then he saluted him and, returning to his own house, informed his nephew of the Sultan's desire to see him, whereto replied Hasan, whilome the Bassorite, "The slave is obedient to the orders of his lord." And the result was that next day he accompanied his uncle, Shams al-Din, to the Divan; and, after saluting the Sultan and doing him reverence in most ceremonious obeisance and with most courtly obsequious-ness, he began improvising these verses:—

"The first in rank to kiss the ground shall deign * Before you, and all ends
  and aims attain:
You are Honour's fount; and all that hope of you, * Shall gain more honour
  than Hope hoped to gain."

The Sultan smiled and signed to him to sit down. So he took a seat close to his uncle, Shams al-Din, and the King asked him his name. Quoth Badr al-Din Hasan, "The meanest of thy slaves is known as Hasan the Bassorite, who is instant in prayer for thee day and night." The Sultan was pleased at his words and, being minded to test his learning and prove his good breeding, asked him, "Dost thou remember any verses in praise of the mole on the cheek?" He answered, "I do," and began reciting:—

"When I think of my love and our parting-smart, * My groans go forth and
  my tears upstart:
He's a mole that reminds me in colour and charms * O' the black o' the eye
  and the grain[3] of the heart."

---

[1] This is always mentioned: the nearer the seat the higher the honour.
[2] Alluding to the phrase "Al-safar zafar"= voyaging is victory (Pilgrimage i., 127).
[3] Arab. "Habb;" alluding to the black drop in the human heart which the Archangel Gabriel removed from Mohammed by opening his breast.

The King admired and praised the two couplets and said to him, "Quote something else; Allah bless thy sire and may thy tongue never tire!" So he began:—

"That cheek-mole's spot they evened with a grain * Of musk, nor did they here the simile strain:
Nay, marvel at the face comprising all * Beauty, nor falling short by single grain."

The King shook with pleasure[1] and said to him, "Say more: Allah bless thy days!" So he began:—

"O you whose mole on cheek enthroned recalls * A dot of musk upon a stone of ruby,
Grant me your favours! Be not stone at heart! * Core of my heart whose only sustenance *you* be!"

Quoth the King, "Fair comparison, O Hasan![2] thou hast spoken excellently well and hast proved thyself accomplished in every accomplishment! Now explain to me how many meanings be there in the Arabic language[3] for the word *Khál* or *mole*." He replied, "Allah keep the King! Seven and fifty and some by tradition say fifty." Said the Sultan, "Thou sayest sooth," presently adding, "Hast thou knowledge as to the points of excellence in beauty?" "Yes," answered Badr al-Din Hasan, "Beauty consisteth in brightness of face, clearness of complexion, shapeliness of nose, gentleness of eyes, sweetness of mouth, cleverness of speech, slenderness of shape and seemliness of all attributes. But the acme of beauty is in the hair and, indeed, al-Shiháb the Hijazi hath brought together all these items in his doggrel verse of the metre Rajaz[4] and it is this:

---

1 This phrase, I have said, often occurs: it alludes to the horripilation (Arab. Kush'-arírah), horror or gooseflesh which, in Arab as in Hindu fables, is a symptom of great joy. So Boccaccio's "pelo arriciato" v., 8: Germ. Gänsehaut.

2 Arab. "Hasanta ya Hasan"= Bene detto, Benedetto! the usual word-play vulgarly called "pun": Hasan (not Hassan, as we *will* write it) meaning "beautiful."

3 Arab. "Loghah" also = a vocabulary, a dictionary; the Arabs had them by camelloads.

4 The seventh of the sixteen "Bahr" (metres) in Arabic prosody; the easiest because allowing the most licence and, consequently, a favourite for didactic, homiletic and gnomic themes. It means literally "agitated" and was originally applied to the rude song of the Cameleer. De Sacy calls this doggrel "the poet's ass" (Torrens, Notes xxvi.). It was the only metre in which Mohammed the Apostle ever spoke: he was no poet (Koran xxxvi., 69) but he occasionally recited a verse and recited it wrongly (Dabistan iii., 212). In Persian prosody Rajaz is the seventh of nineteen and has six distinct varieties (pp. 79–81, "Gladwin's Dissertations on Rhetoric," etc. Calcutta, 1801). I shall have more to say about it in the Terminal Essay.

Say thou to skin "Be soft," to face "Be fair," * And gaze, nor shall they blame
    howso thou stare:
Fine nose in Beauty's list is high esteemed; * Nor less an eye full, bright and
    debonnair:
Eke did they well to laud the lovely lips   * (Which e'en the sleep of me
    will never spare);
A winning tongue, a stature tall and straight;[1] * A seemly union of gifts rarest
    rare:
But Beauty's acme in the hair one views it; * So hear my strain and with
    some few excuse it!"

The Sultan was captivated by his converse and, regarding him as
a friend, asked, "What meaning is there in the saw 'Shurayh is
foxier than the fox'?" And he answered, "Know, O King (whom
Almighty Allah keep!) that the legist Shurayh[2] was wont, during
the days of the plague, to make a visitation to Al-Najaf; and,
whenever he stood up to pray, there came a fox which would
plant himself facing him and which, by mimicking his movements,
distracted him from his devotions. Now when this became longsome to him, one day he doffed his shirt and set it upon a cane
and shook out the sleeves; then placing his turband on the top
and girding its middle with a shawl, he stuck it up in the place
where he used to pray. Presently up trotted the fox according
to his custom and stood over against the figure, whereupon
Shurayh came behind him, and took him. Hence the sayer saith,
'Shurayh foxier than the fox.'" When the Sultan heard Badr al-
Din Hasan's explanation he said to his uncle, Shams al-Din,
"Truly this the son of thy brother is perfect in courtly breeding
and I do not think that his like can be found in Cairo." At this
Hasan arose and kissed the ground before him and sat down again
as a Mameluke should sit before his master. When the Sultan had
thus assured himself of his courtly breeding and bearing and his
knowledge of the liberal arts and belles-lettres, he joyed with
exceeding joy and invested him with a splendid robe of honour
and promoted him to an office whereby he might better his

---

    [1] "Her stature tall—I hate a dumpy woman" (Don Juan).
    [2] A worthy who was Kazi of Kufah (Cufa) in the seventh century. Al-Najaf, gene-
rally entitled "Najaf al-Ashraf" (the Venerand) is the place where Ali, the son-in-law
of Mohammed, lies or is supposed to lie buried, and has ever been a holy place to the
Shi'ahs. I am not certain whether to translate "Sa'alab" by fox or jackal; the Arabs
make scant distinction between them. "Abu Hosayn" (Father of the Fortlet) is certainly the fox, and as certainly "Sha'arhar" is the jackal from the Pehlevi Shagál or
Shaghál.

condition.[1] Then Badr al-Din Hasan arose and, kissing the ground
before the King, wished him continuance of glory and asked
leave to retire with his uncle, the Wazir Shams al-Din. The Sultan gave him leave and he issued forth and the two returned
home, where food was set before them and they ate what Allah
had given them. After finishing his meal Hasan repaired to the
sitting-chamber of his wife, the Lady of Beauty, and told her
what had past between him and the Sultan; whereupon quoth
she, "He cannot fail to make thee a cup-companion and give
thee largesse in excess and load thee with favours and bounties;
so shalt thou, by Allah's blessing, dispread, like the greater
light, the rays of thy perfection wherever thou be, on shore or
on sea." Said he to her, "I purpose to recite a Kasídah, an ode,
in his praise, that he may redouble in affection for me." "Thou
art right in thine intent," she answered, "so gather thy wits together and weigh thy words, and I shall surely see my husband
favoured with his highest favour." Thereupon Hasan shut himself up and composed these couplets on a solid base and abounding in inner grace and copied them out in a hand-writing of the
nicest taste. They are as follows:—

Mine is a Chief who reached most haught estate, * Treading the pathways of
 the good and great:
His justice makes all regions safe and sure, * And against froward foes bars
 every gate:
Bold lion, hero, saint, e'en if you call * Seraph or Sovran[2] he with all may
 rate!
The poorest suppliant rich from him returns, * All words to praise him were
 inadequate.

---

1 Usually by all manner of extortions and robbery, corruption and bribery, the ruler's
motto being
                    Fiat *in*justitia ruat Coelum.
                                                   •
There is no more honest man than the Turkish peasant or the private soldier; but the
process of deterioration begins when he is made a corporal and culminates in the
Pasha. Moreover official dishonesty is permitted by public opinion, because it belongs
to the condition of society. A man buys a place (as in England two centuries ago)
and retains it by presents to the heads of offices. Consequently he must recoup himself
in some way, and he mostly does so by grinding the faces of the poor and by spoiling
the widow and the orphan. The radical cure is high pay; but that phase of society refuses
to afford it.
 2 Arab. "Malik" (King) and "Malak" (angel) the words being written the same when
lacking vowels and justifying the jingle.

He to the day of peace is saffron Morn, * And murky Night in furious warfare's
   bate.
Bow 'neath his gifts our necks, and by his deeds * As King of freeborn[1] souls
   he 'joys his state:
Allah increase for us his term of years, * And from his lot avert all risks and
   fears!

When he had finished transcribing the lines, he despatched them,
in charge of one of his uncle's slaves, to the Sultan, who perused
them and his fancy was pleased; so he read them to those present
and all praised them with the highest praise. Thereupon he sent
for the writer to his sitting-chamber and said to him, "Thou art
from this day forth my boon-companion and I appoint to thee a
monthly solde of a thousand dirhams, over and above that I
bestowed on thee aforetime." So Hasan rose and, kissing the
ground before the King several times, prayed for the continuance
of his greatness and glory and length of life and strength. Thus
Badr al-Din Hasan the Bassorite waxed high in honour and his
fame flew forth to many regions and he abode in all comfort and
solace and delight of life with his uncle and his own folk till Death
overtook him. When the Caliph Harun al-Rashid heard this
story from the mouth of his Wazir, Ja'afar the Barmecide, he
marvelled much and said, "It behoves that these stories be written
in letters of liquid gold." Then he set the slave at liberty and
assigned to the youth who had slain his wife such a monthly
stipend as sufficed to make his life easy; he also gave him a concubine from amongst his own slave-girls and the young man became one of his cup-companions. "Yet this story" (continued
Shahrazad) "is in no wise stranger than the tale of the Tailor and
the Hunchback and the Jew and the Reeve and the Nazarene,
and what betided them." Quoth the King, "And what may
that be?" So Shahrazad began, in these words,[2]

---

[1] Arab. "Hurr"; the Latin "ingenuus," lit. freeborn; metaph. noble as opp. to
a slave who is not expected to do great or good deeds. In pop. use it corresponds, like
"Fatá," with our "gentleman."

[2] This is one of the best tales for humour and movement, and Douce and Madden
show what a rich crop of fabliaux, whose leading incident was the disposal of a dead body,
it produced.

THE HUNCHBACK'S TALE.

IT hath reached me, O auspicious King, that there dwelt during times of yore, and years and ages long gone before, in a certain city of China,[1] a Tailor who was an open-handed man that loved pleasuring and merry-making; and who was wont, he and his wife, to solace themselves from time to time with public diversions and amusements. One day they went out with the first of the light and were returning in the evening when they fell in with a Hunchback, whose semblance would draw a laugh from care and dispel the horrors of despair. So they went up to enjoy looking at him and invited him to go home with them and converse and carouse with them that night. He consented and accompanied them afoot to their home; whereupon the Tailor fared forth to the bazar (night having just set in) and bought a fried fish and bread and lemons and dry sweetmeats for dessert; and set the victuals before the Hunchback and they ate. Presently the Tailor's wife took a great fid of fish and gave it in a gobbet to the Gobbo, stopping his mouth with her hand and saying, "By Allah, thou must down with it at a single gulp; and I will not give thee time to chew it." So he bolted it; but therein was a stiff bone which stuck in his gullet and, his hour being come, he died.——And Shahrazad perceived the dawn of day and ceased saying her permitted say.

𝔚𝔥𝔢𝔫 𝔦𝔱 𝔴𝔞𝔰 𝔱𝔥𝔢 𝔗𝔴𝔢𝔫𝔱𝔶=𝔣𝔦𝔣𝔱𝔥 𝔑𝔦𝔤𝔥𝔱,

She said, It hath reached me, O auspicious King, that when the Tailor's wife gave the Hunchback that mouthful of fish which ended his term of days he died on the instant. Seeing this the Tailor cried aloud, "There is no Majesty and there is no Might save in Allah! Alas, that this poor wretch should have died in so foolish fashion at our hands!" and the woman rejoined, "Why this idle talk? Hast thou not heard his saying who said:—

---

[1] Other editions read, "at Bassorah" and the Bresl. (ii. 123) "at Bassorah and Kájkár" (Káshghár): somewhat like in Dover and Sebastopol. I prefer China because further off and making the improbabilities more notable.

Why then waste I my time in grief, until * I find no friend to bear my weight
　　of woe?
How sleep upon a fire that flames unquenched? * Upon the flames to rest were
　　hard enow!"

Asked her husband, "And what shall I do with him?"; and she
answered, "Rise and take him in thine arms and spread a silken
kerchief over him; then I will fare forth, with thee following me,
this very night and if thou meet any one say, 'This is my son,
and his mother and I are carrying him to the doctor that he may
look at him.' " So he rose and taking the Hunchback in his arms
bore him along the streets, preceded by his wife who kept crying,
"O my son, Allah keep thee! what part paineth thee and where
hath this small-pox¹ attacked thee?" So all who saw them said
" 'Tis a child sick of small-pox."² They went along asking for
the physician's house till folk directed them to that of a leach
which was a Jew. They knocked at the door, and there came
down to them a black slave-girl who opened and, seeing a man
bearing a babe, and a woman with him, said to them, "What is
the matter?" "We have a little one with us," answered the
Tailor's wife, "and we wish to show him to the physician: so take
this quarter-dinar and give it to thy master and let him come
down and see my son who is sore sick." The girl went up to tell
her master, whereupon the Tailor's wife walked into the vestibule and said to her husband, "Leave the Hunchback here and let
us fly for our lives." So the Tailor carried the dead man to the top
of the stairs and propped him upright against the wall and ran
away, he and his wife. Meanwhile the girl went in to the Jew

---

¹ Arab. "Judri," lit. "small stones" from the hard gravelly feeling of the pustules
(Rodwell, p. 20). The disease is generally supposed to be the growth of Central Africa
where it is still a plague and passed over to Arabia about the birth-time of Mohammed.
Thus is usually explained the "war of the elephant" (Koran, chapt. cv.) when the
Abyssinian army of Abrahah, the Christian, was destroyed by swallows (Ababíl which
Major Price makes the plural of Abilah = a vesicle) which dropped upon them "stones
of baked clay," like vetches (Pilgrimage ii. 175). See for details Sale (*in loco*) who seems
to accept the miraculous defence of the Ka'abah. For the horrors of small-pox in
Central Intertropical Africa the inoculation, known also to the Badawin of Al-Hijáz and
other details, readers will consult "The Lake Regions of Central Africa" (ii. 318). The
Hindus "take the bull by the horns" and boldly make "Sítlá" (small-pox) a goddess,
an incarnation of Bhawáni, deëss of destruction-reproduction. In China small-pox is
believed to date from B.C. 1200; but the chronology of the Middle Kingdom still awaits
the sceptic.
² In Europe we should add "and all fled, especially the women." But the fatalism
inherent in the Eastern mind makes the great difference.

and said to him, "At the door are a man and a woman with a sick child and they have given me a quarter-dinar for thee, that thou mayest go down and look at the little one and prescribe for it." As soon as the Jew saw the quarter-dinar he rejoiced and rose quickly in his greed of gain and went forth hurriedly in the dark; but hardly had he made a step when he stumbled on the corpse and threw it over, when it rolled to the bottom of the staircase. So he cried out to the girl to hurry up with the light, and she brought it, whereupon he went down and examining the Hunch-back found that he was stone dead. So he cried out, "O for Esdras![1] O for Moses! O for Aaron! O for Joshua, son of Nun! O the Ten Commandments! I have stumbled against the sick one and he hath fallen downstairs and he is dead! How shall I get this man I have killed out of my house? O by the hoofs of the ass of Esdras!" Then he took up the body and, carrying it into the house, told his wife what had happened and she said to him, "Why dost thou sit still? If thou keep him here till day-break we shall both lose our lives. Let us two carry him to the terrace-roof and throw him over into the house of our neighbour, the Moslem, for if he abide there a night the dogs will come down on him from the adjoining terraces and eat him up." Now his neighbour was a Reeve, the controller of the Sultan's kitchen, and was wont to bring back great store of oil and fat and broken meats; but the cats and rats used to eat it, or, if the dogs scented a fat sheep's tail they would come down from the nearest roofs and tear at it; and on this wise the beasts had already damaged much of what he brought home. So the Jew and his wife carried the Hunchback up to the roof; and, letting him down by his hands and feet through the wind-shaft[2] into the Reeve's house,

---

[1] Arab. "Uzayr." Esdras was a manner of Ripp van Winkle. He was riding over the ruins of Jerusalem when it had been destroyed by the Chaldeans and he doubted by what means Allah would restore it; whereupon he died and at the end of a hundred years he revived. He found his basket of figs and cruse of wine as they were; but of his ass only the bones remained. These were raised to life as Ezra looked on and the ass began at once to bray. Which was a lesson to Esdras. (Koran, chapt. ii.) The oath by the ass's hoofs is to ridicule the Jew. Mohammed seems to have had an *idée fixe* that "the Jews say, Ezra is the son of God" (Koran ix.); it may have arisen from the heterodox Jewish belief that Ezra, when the Law was utterly lost, dictated the whole anew to the scribes of his own memory. His tomb with the huge green dome is still visited by the Jews of Baghdad.

[2] Arab. "Bádhanj," the Pers. Bád. (wind) -gír (catcher): a wooden pent-house on the terrace-roof universal in the nearer East.

propped him up against the wall and went their ways. Hardly had they done this when the Reeve, who had been passing an evening with his friends hearing a recitation of the Koran, came home and opened the door and, going up with a lighted candle, found a son of Adam standing in the corner under the ventilator. When he saw this, he said, "Wah! by Allah, very good forsooth! He who robbeth my stuff is none other than a man." Then he turned to the Hunchback and said, "So 'tis thou that stealest the meat and the fat! I thought it was the cats and dogs, and I kill the dogs and cats of the quarter and sin against them by killing them. And all the while 'tis thou comest down from the house terrace through the wind-shaft. But I will avenge myself upon thee with my own hand!" So he snatched up a heavy hammer and set upon him and smote him full on the breast and he fell down. Then he examined him and, finding that he was dead, cried out in horror, thinking that he had killed him, and said, "There is no Majesty and there is no Might save in Allah, the Glorious, the Great!" And he feared for his life, and added, "Allah curse the oil and the meat and the grease and the sheep's tails to boot! How hath fate given this man his quietus at my hand!" Then he looked at the body and seeing it was that of a Gobbo, said, "Was it not enough for thee to be a hunchback,[1] but thou must likewise be a thief and prig flesh and fat! O thou Veiler,[2] deign to veil me with Thy curtain of concealment!" So he took him up on his shoulders and, going forth with him from his house about the latter end of the night, carried him to the nearest end of the bazar, where he set him up on his feet against the wall of a shop at the head of a dark lane, and left him and went away. After a while up came a Nazarene,[3] the Sultan's broker who, much bemused with liquor, was purposing for the Hammam-bath as his drunkenness whispered in his ear, "Verily the call to matins[4] is nigh." He came plodding along and staggering about till he drew near the Hunchback and squatted down to make

---

[1] The hunchback, in Arabia as in Southern Europe, is looked upon by the vulgar with fear and aversion. The reason is that he is usually sharper-witted than his neighbours.

[2] Arab. "Yá Sattár" = Thou who veilest the discreditable secrets of Thy creatures.

[3] Arab. "Nasráni," a follower of Him of Nazareth and an older name than "Christian" which (Acts xi., 26) was first given at Antioch about A.D. 43. The cry in Alexandria used to be "Ya Nasráni, Kalb awáni!" = O Nazarene! O dog obscene! (Pilgrimage, i., 160). "Christian" in Arabic can be expressed only by "Masíhi" = follower of the Messiah.

[4] Arab. "Tasbíh," = Saluting in the Subh (morning).

water[1] over against him; when he happened to glance around and saw a man standing against the wall. Now some person had snatched off the Christian's turband[2] in the first of the night; so when he saw the Hunchback hard by he fancied that he also meant to steal his head-dress. Thereupon he clenched his fist and struck him on the neck, felling him to the ground, and called aloud to the watchman of the bazar, and came down on the body in his drunken fury and kept on belabouring and throttling the corpse. Presently the Charley came up and, finding a Nazarene kneeling on a Moslem and frapping him, asked, "What harm hath this one done?"; and the Broker answered, "The fellow meant to snatch off my turband." "Get up from him," quoth the watch-man. So he arose and the Charley went up to the Hunchback and finding him dead, exclaimed, "By Allah, good indeed! A Chris-tian killing a Mahometan!" Then he seized the Broker and, tying his hands behind his back, carried him to the Governor's house,[3] and all the while the Nazarene kept saying to himself, "O Mes-siah! O Virgin! how came I to kill this fellow? And in what a hurry he must have been to depart this life when he died of a single blow!" Presently, as his drunkenness fled, came dolour in its stead. So the Broker and the body were kept in the Governor's place till morning morrowed, when the Wali came out and gave order to hang the supposed murderer and commanded the executioner[4] make proclamation of the sentence. Forthwith they

---

[1] In the East women stand on minor occasions while men squat on their hunkers in a way hardly possible to an untrained European. The custom is old. Herodotus (ii., 35) says, "The women stand up when they make water, but the men sit down." Will it be believed that Canon Rawlinson was too modest to leave this passage in his translation? The custom was perpetuated by Al-Islam because the position prevents the ejection touching the clothes and making them ceremonially impure; possibly they borrowed it from the Guebres. Dabistan, Gate xvi. says, "It is improper, whilst in an erect posture, to make water; it is therefore necessary to sit at squat and force it to some distance, repeating the Avesta mentally."

[2] This is still a popular form of the "Kinchin lay," and as the turbands are often of fine stuff, the *petite industrie* pays well.

[3] Arab. "Wali" = Governor; the term still in use for the Governor-General of a Province as opposed to the "Muháfiz," or district-governor. In Eastern Arabia the Wali is the Civil Governor opposed to the Amir or Military Commandant. Under the Caliphate the Wali acted also as Prefect of Police (the Indian Faujdár), who is now called "Zábit." The older name for the latter was "Sáhib al-Shartah" (= chief of the watch) or "Mutawalli"; and it was his duty to go the rounds in person. The old "Charley," with his lantern and cudgel, still guards the bazars in Damascus.

[4] Arab. "Al-Mashá ilí" = the bearer of a cresset (Mash'al) who was also Jack Ketch. In Anglo-India the name is given to a lower body-servant. The "Mash'al" which Lane (M. E., chapt. vi.) calls "Mesh'al" and illustrates, must not be confounded with its congener the "Sha'ílah" or link (also lamp, wick, etc.).

set up a gallows under which they made the Nazarene stand and the torch-bearer, who was hangman, threw the rope round his neck and passed one end through the pulley, and was about to hoist him up[1] when lo! the Reeve, who was passing by, saw the Broker about to be hanged; and, making his way through the people, cried out to the executioner, "Hold! Hold! I am he who killed the Hunchback!" Asked the Governor, "What made thee kill him?"; and he answered, "I went home last night and there found this man who had come down the ventilator to steal my property; so I smote him with a hammer on the breast and he died forthright. Then I took him up and carried him to the bazar and set him up against the wall in such a place near such a lane;" adding, "Is it not enough for me to have killed a Moslem without also killing a Christian? So hang none other but me." When the Governor heard these words he released the Broker and said to the torch-bearer, "Hang up this man on his own confession." So he loosed the cord from the Nazarene's neck and threw it round that of the Reeve and, making him stand under the gallows-tree, was about to string him up when behold, the Jewish physician pushed through the people and shouted to the executioner, "Hold! Hold! It was I and none else killed the Hunchback! Last night I was sitting at home when a man and a woman knocked at the door carrying this Gobbo who was sick, and gave my handmaid a quarter-dinar, bidding her hand me the fee and tell me to come down and see him. Whilst she was gone the man and the woman brought him into the house and, setting him on the stairs, went away; and presently I came down and not seeing him, for I was in the dark, stumbled over him and he fell to the foot of the staircase and died on the moment. Then we took him up, I and my wife, and carried him on to the top terrace; and, the house of this Reeve being next door to mine, we let the body down through the ventilator. When he came home and found the Hunchback in his house, he fancied he was a thief and struck him with a hammer, so that he fell to the ground, and our neighbour made certain that he had slain him. Now is it not enough for me to have killed one Moslem unwittingly, without burdening myself with taking the life of another Moslem wittingly?" When the Governor heard this he said to the hangman, "Set free the Reeve and hang the Jew." Thereupon the torch-bearer took him

---

[1] I need hardly say that the civilised "drop" is unknown to the East where men are strung up as to a yardarm. This greatly prolongs the suffering.

and slung the cord round his neck when behold, the Tailor pushed through the people, and shouted to the executioner, "Hold! Hold! It was I and none else killed the Hunchback; and this was the fashion thereof. I had been out a-pleasuring yesterday and, coming back to supper, fell in with this Gobbo, who was drunk and drumming away and singing lustily to his tambourine. So I accosted him and carried him to my house and bought a fish, and we sat down to eat. Presently my wife took a fid of fish and, making a gobbet of it,[1] crammed it into his mouth; but some of it went down the wrong way or stuck in his gullet and he died on the instant. So we lifted him up, I and my wife, and carried him to the Jew's house where the slave-girl came down and opened the door to us and I said to her, 'Tell thy master that there are a man and a woman and a sick person for thee to see!' I gave her a quarter-dinar and she went up to tell her master; and, whilst she was gone, I carried the Hunchback to the head of the staircase and propped him up against the wall, and went off with my wife. When the Jew came down he stumbled over him and thought that he had killed him." Then he asked the Jew, "Is this the truth?"; and the Jew answered, "Yes." Thereupon the Tailor turned to the Governor, and said, "Leave go the Jew and hang me." When the Governor heard the Tailor's tale he marvelled at the matter of this Hunchback and exclaimed. "Verily this is an adventure which should be recorded in books!" Then he said to the hangman, "Let the Jew go and hang the Tailor on his own confession." The executioner took the Tailor and put the rope around his neck and said, "I am tired of such slow work: we bring out this one and change him for that other, and no one is hanged after all!" Now the Hunchback in question was, they relate, jester to the Sultan of China who could not bear him out of his sight; so when the fellow got drunk and did not make his appearance that night or the next day till noon, the Sultan asked some of his courtiers about him and they answered, "O our lord, the Governor hath come upon him dead and hath ordered his murderer to be hanged; but, as the hangman was about to hoist him up there came a second and a third and a fourth and each one said, 'It is I, and none else killed the Hunchback!' and each gave a full

---

[1] Arab. "Lukmah"; = a mouthful. It is still the fashion amongst Easterns of primitive manners to take up a handful of rice, etc., ball it and put it into a friend's mouth *honoris causâ*. When the friend is a European the expression of his face is generally a study.

and circumstantial account of the manner of the jester being killed." When the King heard this he cried aloud to the Chamberlain-in-waiting, "Go down to the Governor and bring me all four of them." So the Chamberlain went down at once to the place of execution, where he found the torch-bearer on the point of hanging the Tailor and shouted to him, "Hold! Hold!" Then he gave the King's command to the Governor who took the Tailor, the Jew, the Nazarene and the Reeve (the Hunchback's body being borne on men's shoulders) and went up with one and all of them to the King. When he came into the presence, he kissed the ground and acquainted the ruler with the whole story which it is needless to relate for, as they say, There is no avail in a thrice-told tale. The Sultan hearing it marvelled and was moved to mirth and commanded the story to be written in letters of liquid gold, saying to those present, "Did ye ever hear a more wondrous tale than that of my Hunchback?" Thereupon the Nazarene broker came forward and said, "O King of the age, with thy leave I will tell thee a thing which happened to myself and which is still more wondrous and marvellous and pleasurable and delectable than the tale of the Hunchback." Quoth the King, "Tell us what thou hast to say!" So he began in these words

The Nazarene Broker's Story.

O KING of the age, I came to this thy country with merchandise and Destiny stayed me here with you: but my place of birth was Cairo, in Egypt, where I also was brought up, for I am one of the Copts and my father was a broker before me. When I came to man's estate he departed this life and I succeeded to his business. One day, as I was sitting in my shop, behold, there came up to me a youth as handsome as could be, wearing sumptuous raiment and riding a fine ass.[1] When he saw me he saluted me, and I stood up

---

[1] I need hardly note that this is an old Biblical practice. The ass is used for city-work as the horse for fighting and travelling, the mule for burdens and the dromedary for the desert. But the Badawi, like the Indian, despises the monture and sings:—

The back of the steed is a noble place;
But the mule's dishonour, the ass disgrace!

The fine white asses, often thirteen hands high, sold by the Banu Salíb and other Badawi tribes, will fetch £100, and more. I rode a little brute from Meccah to Jedda (42 miles) in one night and it came in with me cantering.

to do him honour: then he took out a kerchief containing a sample
of sesame and asked, "How much is this worth per Ardabb?";[1]
whereto I answered, "An hundred dirhams." Quoth he, "Take
porters and gaugers and metesmen and come to-morrow to the
Khan al-Jawáli,[2] by the Gate of Victory quarter where thou wilt
find me." Then he fared forth leaving with me the sample of
sesame in his kerchief; and I went the round of my customers and
ascertained that every Ardabb would fetch an hundred and
twenty dirhams. Next day I took four metesmen and walked
with them to the Khan, where I found him awaiting me. As soon
as he saw me he rose and opened his magazine, when we measured
the grain till the store was empty; and we found the contents fifty
Ardabbs, making five thousand pieces of silver. Then said he,
"Let ten dirhams on every Ardabb be thy brokerage; so take the
price and keep in deposit four thousand and five hundred dirhams
for me; and, when I have made an end of selling the other wares
in my warehouses, I will come to thee and receive the amount."
"I will well," replied I and kissing his hand went away, having
made that day a profit of a thousand dirhams. He was absent a
month, at the end of which he came to me and asked, "Where be
the dirhams?" I rose and saluted him and answered to him,
"Wilt thou not eat somewhat in my house?" But he refused with
the remark, "Get the monies ready and I will presently return and
take them." Then he rode away. So I brought out the dirhams
and sat down to await him, but he stayed away for another
month, when he came back and said to me, "Where be the dirhams?" I rose and saluting him asked, "Wilt thou not eat something in my house?" But he again refused adding, "Get me the
monies ready and I will presently return and take them." Then
he rode off. So I brought out the dirhams and sat down to await
his return; but he stayed away from me a third month, and I
said, "Verily this young man is liberality in incarnate form." At
the end of the month he came up, riding a mare-mule and wearing
a suit of sumptuous raiment; he was as the moon on the night of
fullness, and he seemed as if fresh from the baths, with his cheeks
rosy bright, and his brow flower-white, and a mole-spot like a

---

[1] A dry measure of about five bushels (Cairo). The classical pronunciation is Irdabb
and it measured 24 sa'a (gallons) each filling four outstretched hands.

[2] "Al-Jawáli" should be Al-Jáwali (Al-Makrizi) and the Bab al-Nasr (Gate of Victory)
is that leading to Suez. I lived in that quarter as shown by my Pilgrimage (i. 62).

grain of ambergris delighting the sight; even as was said of such an one by the poet:—

Full moon with sun in single mansion * In brightest sheen and fortune rose and shone,
With happy splendour changing every sprite: * Hail to what guerdons prayer with blissfull boon!
Their charms and grace have gained perfection's height, * All hearts have conquered and all wits have won.
Laud to the Lord for works so wonder-strange, * And what th' Almighty wills His hand hath done!

When I saw him I rose to him and invoking blessings on him asked, "O my lord, wilt thou not take thy monies?" "Whence the hurry?"[1] quoth he, "Wait till I have made an end of my business and then I will come and take them." Again he rode away and I said to myself, "By Allah, when he comes next time needs must I make him my guest; for I have traded with his dirhams and have gotten large gains thereby." At the end of the year he came again, habited in a suit of clothes more sumptuous than the former; and, when I conjured him by the Evangel to alight at my house and eat of my guest-food, he said, "I consent, on condition that what thou expendest on me shall be of my monies still in thy hands." I answered, "So be it," and made him sit down whilst I got ready what was needful of meat and drink and else besides; and set the tray before him, with the invitation "Bismillah"![2] Then he drew near the tray and put out his left hand[3] and ate with me; and I marvelled at his not using the right hand. When we had done eating, I poured water on his hand and gave him wherewith to wipe it. Upon this we sat down to converse after I had set before him some sweetmeats; and I said to him, "O my master, prithee relieve me by telling me why thou eatest with thy

---

[1] Arab. "Al-'ajalah," referring to a saying in every Moslem mouth, "Patience is from the Protector (Allah): Hurry is from Hell." That and "Inshallah bukra!" (Please God to-morrow!) are the traveller's *bêtes noires.*

[2] Here it is a polite equivalent for "fall to!"

[3] The left hand is used throughout the East for purposes of ablution and is considered unclean. To offer the left hand would be most insulting and no man ever strokes his beard with it or eats with it: hence, probably, one never sees a left-handed man throughout the Moslem east. In the Brazil for the same reason old-fashioned people will not take snuff with the right hand. And it is related of the Khataians that they prefer the left hand, "Because the heart, which is the Sultan of the city of the Body, hath his mansion on that side" (Rauzat al-Safá).

left hand? Perchance something aileth thy other hand?" When he heard my words, he repeated these verses:—

"Dear friend, ask not what burneth in my breast, * Lest thou see fiery pangs
    eye never saw:
Wills not my heart to harbour Salmá in stead * Of Laylá's[1] love, but need
    hath ne'er a law!"

And he put out his right arm from his sleeve and behold, the hand was cut off, a wrist without a fist. I was astounded at this but he said, "Marvel not, and think not that I ate with my left hand for conceit and insolence, but from necessity; and the cutting off my right hand was caused by an adventure of the strangest." Asked I, "And what caused it?"; and he answered:—Know that I am of the sons of Baghdad and my father was of notables of that city. When I came to man's estate I heard the pilgrims and wayfarers, travellers and merchants talk of the land of Egypt and their words sank deep into my mind till my parent died, when I took a large sum of money and furnished myself for trade with stuffs of Baghdad and Mosul and, packing them up in bales, set out on my wanderings; and Allah decreed me safety till I entered this your city. Then he wept and began repeating:—

The blear-eyed scapes the pits * Wherein the lynx-eyed fall:
A word the wise man slays * And saves the natural:
The Moslem fails of food * The Káfir feasts in hall:
What art or act is man's? * God's will obligeth all!

Now when he had ended his verse he said, So I entered Cairo and took off my loads and stored my stuffs in the Khan "Al-Masrúr."[2] Then I gave the servant a few silvers wherewith to buy me some food and lay down to sleep awhile. When I awoke I went to the street called "Bayn al-Kasrayn"—Between the two Palaces—and presently returned and rested my night in the Khan. When it was morning I opened a bale and took out some stuff saying to myself, "I will be off and go through some of the bazars and see the state of the market." So I loaded the stuff on some of my slaves and fared forth till I reached the Kaysariyah or Exchange

---

[1] Two feminine names; as we might say Mary and Martha.
[2] It was near the Caliph's two Palaces (Al-Kasrayn); and was famous in the 15th century A. D. The Kazi's Mahkamah (Court-house) now occupies the place of the Two Palaces.

of Jahárkas;[1] where the brokers who knew of my coming came to meet me. They took the stuffs and cried them for sale, but could not get the prime cost of them. I was vexed at this, however the Shaykh of the brokers said to me, "O my lord, I will tell thee how thou mayest make a profit of thy goods. Thou shouldest do as the merchants do and sell thy merchandise at credit for a fixed period, on a contract drawn up by a notary and duly witnessed; and employ a Shroff to take thy dues every Monday and Thursday. So shalt thou gain two dirhams and more, for every one; and thou shalt solace and divert thyself by seeing Cairo and the Nile." Quoth I, "This is sound advice," and carried the brokers to the Khan. They took my stuffs and went with them on 'Change where I sold them well taking bonds for the value. These bonds I deposited with a Shroff, a banker, who gave me a receipt with which I returned to the Khan. Here I stayed a whole month, every morning breaking my fast with a cup of wine and making my meals on pigeon's meat, mutton and sweetmeats, till the time came when my receipts began to fall due. So, every Monday and Thursday I used to go on 'Change and sit in the shop of one or other of the merchants, whilst the notary and money-changer went round to recover the monies from the traders, till after the time of mid-afternoon prayer, when they brought me the amount, and I counted it and, sealing the bags, returned with them to the Khan. On a certain day which happened to be a Monday,[2] I went to the Hammam and thence back to my Khan, and sitting in my own room[3] broke my fast with a cup of wine, after which I slept a little. When I awoke I ate a chicken and, perfuming my person, repaired to the shop of a merchant hight Badr al-Din al-Bostáni, or the Gardener,[4] who welcomed me; and we sat talking awhile till the bazar should open. Presently, behold, up came a lady of stately figure wearing

---

[1] A Kaysariah is a superior kind of bazar, a "bezestein." That in the text stood to the east of the principal street in Cairo and was built in A. H. 502 (=1108–9) by a Circassian Emir, known as Fakhr al-Din Jahárkas, a corruption of the Persian "Chehárkas" = four persons (Lane, i. 422, from Al-Makrizi and Ibn Khallikan). For Jahárkas the Mac. Edit. has Jirjís (George) a common Christian name. I once lodged in a "Wakálah (the modern Khan) Jirjis." Pilgrimage, i. 255.

[2] Arab. "Second Day," i.e. after Saturday, the true Sabbath, so marvellously ignored by Christendom.

[3] Readers who wish to know how a traveller is lodged in a Wakálah, Khan, or Caravanserai, will consult my Pilgrimage, i. 60.

[4] The original occupation of the family had given it a name, as amongst us.

a headdress of the most magnificent, perfumed with the sweetest of scents and walking with graceful swaying gait; and seeing me she raised her mantilla allowing me a glimpse of her beautiful black eyes. She saluted Badr al-Din who returned her salutation and stood up, and talked with her; and the moment I heard her speak, the love of her gat hold of my heart. Presently she said to Badr al-Din, "Hast thou by thee a cut piece of stuff woven with thread of pure gold?" So he brought out to her a piece from those he had bought of me and sold it to her for one thousand two hundred dirhams; when she said, "I will take the piece home with me and send thee its price." "That is impossible, O my lady," the merchant replied, "for here is the owner of the stuff and I owe him a share of profit." "Fie upon thee!" she cried, "Do I not use to take from thee entire rolls of costly stuff, and give thee a greater profit than thou expectest, and send thee the money?" "Yes," rejoined he; "but I stand in pressing need of the price this very day." Hereupon she took up the piece and threw it back upon his lap, saying "Out on thee! Allah confound the tribe of you which estimates none at the right value;" and she turned to go. I felt my very soul going with her; so I stood up and stayed her, saying, "I conjure thee by the Lord, O my lady, favour me by retracing thy gracious steps." She turned back with a smile and said, "For thy sake I return," and took a seat opposite me in the shop. Then quoth I to Badr al-Din, "What is the price they asked thee for this piece?"; and quoth he, "Eleven hundred dirhams." I rejoined, "The odd hundred shall be thy profit: bring me a sheet of paper and I will write thee a discharge for it." Then I wrote him a receipt in my own handwriting and gave the piece to the lady, saying, "Take it away with thee and, if thou wilt, bring me its price next bazar-day; or better still, accept it as my guest-gift to thee." "Allah requite thee with good," answered she, "and make thee my husband and lord and master of all I have!"[1] And Allah favoured her prayer. I saw the Gates of Paradise swing open before me and said, "O my lady, let this piece of stuff be now thine and another like it is ready for thee; only let me have one look at thy face." So she raised her veil and I saw a face the sight of which bequeathed to me a thousand sighs, and my heart was so captivated by her love that I was

---

[1] The usual "chaff" or banter allowed even to modest women when shopping, and— many a true word is spoken in jest.

no longer ruler of my reason. Then she let fall her face-veil and taking up the piece of stuff said, "O my lord make me not desolate by thine absence!" and turned away and disappeared from my sight. I remained sitting on 'Change till past the hour of after-noon prayer, lost to the world by the love which had mastered me; and the violence of my passion compelled me to make en-quiries concerning her of the merchant, who answered me, "This is a lady and a rich: she is the daughter of a certain Emir who lately died and left her a large fortune." Then I took leave of him and returned home to the Khan where they set supper before me; but I could not eat for thinking of her and when I lay down to sleep, sleep came not near me. So I watched till morning, when I arose and donned a change of raiment and drank a cup of wine; and, after breaking my fast on some slight matter, I went to the merchant's shop where I saluted him and sat down by him. Pres-ently up came the lady as usual, followed by a slave-girl and wear-ing a dress more sumptuous than before; and she saluted me with-out noticing Badr al-Din and said in fluent graceful speech (never heard I voice softer or sweeter), "Send one with me to take the thousand and two hundred dirhams, the price of the piece." "Why this hurry?" asked I and she answered, "May we never lose thee!"[1] and handed me the money. Then I sat talking with her and presently I signed to her in dumb show, whereby she un-derstood that I longed to enjoy her person,[2] and she rose up in haste with a show of displeasure. My heart clung to her and I went forth from the bazar and followed on her track. As I was walking suddenly a black slave-girl stopped me and said, "O my master, come speak with my mistress."[3] At this I was surprised and replied, "There is none who knows me here;" but she re-joined, "O my lord, how soon hast thou forgotten her! My lady is the same who was this day at the shop of such a merchant." Then I went with her to the Shroff's, where I found the lady who drew me to her side and said, "O my beloved, thine image is firmly stamped upon my fancy, and love of thee hath gotten hold of my heart: from the hour I first saw thee nor sleep nor food nor drink hath given me aught of pleasure." I replied, "The double

---

[1] "La adamnák" = Heaven deprive us not of thee, *i.e.* grant I see thee often!

[2] This is a somewhat cavalier style of advance; but Easterns under such circumstances go straight to the point, hating to filer the parfait amour.

[3] The peremptory formula of a slave delivering such a message.

of that suffering is mine and my state dispenseth me from complaint." Then said she, "O my beloved, at thy house, or at mine?"
"I am a stranger here and have no place of reception save the
Khan, so by thy favour it shall be at thy house." "So be it; but
this is Friday[1] night and nothing can be done till to-morrow after
public prayers; go to the Mosque and pray; then mount thine ass,
and ask for the Habbániyah[2] quarter; and, when there, look out
for the mansion of Al-Nakib[3] Barakát, popularly known as Abu
Shámah the Syndic; for I live there: so do not delay as I shall
be expecting thee." I rejoiced with still greater joy at this; and
took leave of her and returned to my Khan, where I passed a
sleepless night. Hardly was I assured that morning had dawned
when I rose, changed my dress, perfumed myself with essences
and sweet scents and, taking fifty dinars in a kerchief, went from
the Khan Masrúr to the Zuwaylah[4] gate, where I mounted an ass
and said to its owner, "Take me to the Habbaniyah." So he set
off with me and brought up in the twinkling of an eye at a street
known as Darb al-Munkari, where I said to him, "Go in and ask
for the Syndic's mansion." He was absent a while and then
returned and said, "Alight." "Go thou before me to the house,"
quoth I, adding, "Come back with the earliest light and bring me
home;" and he answered, "In Allah's name;" whereupon I gave
him a quarter-dinar of gold, and he took it and went his ways.
Then I knocked at the door and out came two white slave-girls,
both young; high-bosomed virgins, as they were moons, and said
to me, "Enter, for our mistress is expecting thee and she hath not

---

[1] This would be our Thursday night, preceding the day of public prayers which can
be performed only when in a state of ceremonial purity. Hence many Moslems go to
the Hammam on Thursday and have no connection with their wives till Friday night.

[2] Lane (i. 423) gives ample details concerning the Habbániyah, or grain-sellers' quarter
in the southern part of Cairo; and shows that when this tale was written (or transcribed?)
the city was almost as extensive as it is now.

[3] Nakíb is a caravan-leader, a chief, a syndic; and "Abú Shámah" = Father of a
cheek mole, while "Abú Shámmah" = Father of a smeller, a nose, a snout. The
"Kuniyah," bye-name, patronymic or matronymic, is necessary amongst Moslems whose
list of names, all connected more or less with religion, is so scanty. Hence Buckingham
the traveller was known as Abu Kidr, the Father of a Cooking-pot and Hajj Abdullah
as Abu Shawárib, Father of Mustachios (Pilgrimage, iii., 263).

[4] More correctly Bab Zawilah from the name of a tribe in Northern Africa. This
gate dates from the same age as the Eastern or Desert gate, Bab al-Nasr (A.D. 1087)
and is still much admired. M. Jomard describes it (Description, etc., ii. 670) and lately
my good friend Yacoub Artin Pasha has drawn attention to it in the Bulletin de l'Inst.
Egypt., Deuxième Série, No. 4, 1883.

slept the night long for her delight in thee." I passed through the vestibule into a saloon with seven doors, floored with parti-coloured marbles and furnished with curtains and hangings of coloured silks: the ceiling was *cloisonné* with gold and corniced with inscriptions[1] emblazoned in lapis lazuli; and the walls were stuccoed with Sultání gypsum[2] which mirrored the beholder's face. Around the saloon were latticed windows overlooking a garden full of all manner of fruits; whose streams were railing and rilling and whose birds were trilling and shrilling; and in the heart of the hall was a jetting fountain at whose corners stood birds fashioned in red gold crusted with pearls and gems and spouting water crystal-clear. When I entered and took a seat, ——And Shahrazad perceived the dawn of day and ceased saying her permitted say.

When it was the Twenty-sixth Night,

She said, It hath reached me, O auspicious King, that the young merchant continued, When I entered and took a seat, the lady at once came in crowned with a diadem[3] of pearls and jewels; her face dotted with artificial moles in indigo,[4] her eyebrows pencilled with Kohl and her hands and feet reddened with Henna. When she saw me she smiled in my face and took me to her embrace and clasped me to her breast; then she put her mouth to my mouth and sucked my tongue[5] (and I did likewise) and said,

---

[1] This ornament is still seen in the older saloons of Damascus: the inscriptions are usually religious sentences, extracts from the Koran, etc., in uncial characters. They take the place of our frescos; and, as a work of art, are generally far superior.

[2] Arab. "Bayáz al-Sultání," the best kind of gypsum which shines like polished marble. The stucco on the walls of Alexandria, built by Alexander of the two Horns, was so exquisitely tempered and beautifully polished that men had to wear masks for fear of blindness.

[3] This Iklíl, a complicated affair, is now obsolete, its place having been taken by the "Kurs," a gold plate, some five inches in diameter, set with jewels, etc. Lane (M. E. Appendix A) figures it.

[4] The woman-artist who applies the dye is called "Munakkishah."

[5] "Kissing with th' inner lip," as Shakespeare calls it; the French *langue fourrée:* and Sanskrit "Samputa." The subject of kissing is extensive in the East. Ten different varieties are duly enumerated in the "Ananga-Ranga;" or, The Hindu Art of Love (Ars Amoris Indica) translated from the Sanskrit, and annotated by A. F. F. and B. F. R. It is also connected with unguiculation, or impressing the nails, of which there are seven kinds; morsication (seven kinds); handling the hair and tappings or pattings with the fingers and palm (eight kinds).

"Can it be true, O my little darkling, thou art come to me?"
adding, "Welcome and good cheer to thee! By Allah, from the
day I saw thee sleep hath not been sweet to me nor hath food
been pleasant." Quoth I, "Such hath also been my case: and I
am thy slave, thy negro slave." Then we sat down to converse
and I hung my head earthwards in bashfulness, but she delayed
not long ere she set before me a tray of the most exquisite viands,
marinated meats, fritters soaked in bee's honey[1] and chickens
stuffed with sugar and pistachio-nuts, whereof we ate till we were
satisfied. Then they brought basin and ewer and I washed my
hands and we scented ourselves with rose-water musk'd and
sat down again to converse. So she began repeating these
couplets[2]:—

> "Had we wist of thy coming, thy way had been strown
>   With the blood of our heart and the balls of our sight:
> Our cheek as a foot-cloth to greet thee been thrown,
>   That thy step on our eyelids should softly alight."

And she kept plaining of what had befallen her and I of what
had betided me; and love of her gat so firm hold of my heart
that all my wealth seemed a thing of naught in comparison with
her. Then we fell to toying and groping and kissing till nightfall, when the handmaidens set before us meats and a complete
wine service, and we sat carousing till the noon of night, when
we lay down and I lay with her; never in my life saw I a night
like that night. When morning morrowed I arose and took leave
of her, throwing under the carpet-bed the kerchief wherein were
the dinars[3] and as I went out she wept and said, "O my lord,
when shall I look upon that lovely face again?" "I will be with
thee at sunset," answered I, and going out found the donkey-boy,
who had brought me the day before, awaiting at the door. So I
mounted ass and rode to the Khan of Masrur where I alighted
and gave the man a half-dinar, saying, "Return at sunset;" and
he said "I will." Then I breakfasted and went out to seek the
price of my stuffs; after which I returned, and taking a roast lamb
and some sweetmeats, called a porter and put the provision in his

---

[1] Arab. "asal-nahl," to distinguish it from "honey" *i.e.* syrup of sugar-cane and
fruits.
[2] The lines have occurred in Night xii. By way of variety I give Torrens' version
p. 273.
[3] The way of carrying money in the corner of a pocket-handkerchief is still common.

crate, and sent it to the lady paying the man his hire.[1] I went back to my business till sunset, when the ass-driver came to me; and I took fifty dinars in a kerchief and rode to her house where I found the marble floor swept, the brasses burnisht, the branch-lights burning, the wax-candles ready lighted, the meat served up and the wine strained.[2] When my lady saw me she threw her arms about my neck, and cried, "Thou hast desolated me by thine absence." Then she set the tables before me and we ate till we were satisfied, when the slave-girls carried off the trays and served up wine. We gave not over drinking till half the night was past; and, being well warmed with drink, we went to the sleeping-chamber and lay there till morning. I then arose and fared forth from her leaving the fifty dinars with her as before; and, finding the donkey-boy at the door, rode to the Khan and slept awhile. After that I went out to make ready the evening meal and took a brace of geese with gravy on two platters of dressed and peppered rice, and got ready colocasia[3]-roots fried and soaked in honey, and wax-candles and fruits and conserves and nuts and almonds and sweet-scented flowers; and I sent them all to her. As soon as it was night I again tied up fifty dinars in a kerchief and, mounting the ass as usual, rode to the mansion where we ate and drank and lay together till morning when I threw the kerchief and dinars to her[4] and rode back to the Khan. I ceased not doing after that fashion till, after a sweet night, I woke one fine morning and found myself beggared, dinar-less and dirham-less. So said I to myself "All this be Satan's work;" and began to recite these couplets:—

"Poverty dims the sheen of man whate'er his wealth has been, * E'en as the
    sun about to set shines with a yellowing light:
Absent he falls from memory, forgotten by his friends; * Present he shareth
    not their joys for none in him delight:
He walks the market shunned of all, too glad to hide his head; * In desert
    places tears he sheds and moans his bitter plight:
By Allah, 'mid his kith and kin a man, however good, * Waylaid by want and
    penury is but a stranger-wight!"

---

[1] He sent the provisions not to be under an obligation to her in this matter. And she received them to judge thereby of his liberality.

[2] Those who have seen the process of wine-making in the Libanus will readily understand why it is always strained.

[3] Arab. "Kulkasá," a kind of arum or yam, eaten boiled like our potatoes.

[4] At first he slipped the money into the bed-clothes: now he gives it openly and she accepts it for a reason.

I fared forth from the Khan and walked down "Between the
Palaces" street till I came to the Zuwaylah Porte, where I found
the people crowding and the gateway blocked for the much folk.
And by the decree of Destiny I saw there a trooper against whom
I pressed unintentionally, so that my hand came upon his bosom-
pocket and I felt a purse inside it. I looked and seeing a string
of green silk hanging from the pocket knew it for a purse; and
the crush grew greater every minute and just then, a camel laden
with a load of fuel happened to jostle the trooper on the opposite
side, and he turned round to fend it off from him, lest it tear his
clothes; and Satan tempted me, so I pulled the string and drew
out a little bag of blue silk, containing something which chinked
like coin. But the soldier, feeling his pocket suddenly lightened,
put his hand to it and found it empty; whereupon he turned to
me and, snatching up his mace from his saddle-bow, struck me
with it on the head. I fell to the ground, whilst the people came
round us and seizing the trooper's mare by the bridle said to him,
"Strikest thou this youth such a blow as this for a mere push!"
But the trooper cried out at them, "This fellow is an accursed
thief!" Whereupon I came to myself and stood up, and the
people looked at me and said, "Nay, he is a comely youth: he
would not steal anything;" and some of them took my part and
others were against me and question and answer waxed loud and
warm. The people pulled at me and would have rescued me
from his clutches; but as fate decreed behold, the Governor, the
Chief of Police, and the watch[1] entered the Zuwaylah Gate at this
moment and, seeing the people gathered together around me and
the soldier, the Governor asked, "What is the matter?" "By
Allah! O Emir," answered the trooper, "this is a thief! I had
in my pocket a purse of blue silk lined with twenty good gold
pieces and he took it, whilst I was in the crush." Quoth the
Governor, "Was any one by thee at the time?"; and quoth the
soldier, "No." Thereupon the Governor cried out to the Chief of
Police who seized me, and on this wise the curtain of the Lord's
protection was withdrawn from me. Then he said "Strip him;"
and, when they stripped me, they found the purse in my clothes.
The Wali took it, opened it and counted it; and, finding in it
twenty dinars as the soldier had said, waxed exceeding wroth and

---

[1] Arab. Al-Zalamah: lit. = tyrants, oppressors, applied to the police and generally to
the employés of Government. It is a word which tells a history.

bade his guard bring me before him. Then said he to me, "Now, O youth, speak truly: didst thou steal this purse?"[1] At this I hung my head to the ground and said to myself, "If I deny having stolen it, I shall get myself into terrible trouble." So I raised my head and said, "Yes, I took it." When the Governor heard these words he wondered and summoned witnesses who came forward and attested my confession. All this happened at the Zuwaylah Gate. Then the Governor ordered the link-bearer to cut off my right hand, and he did so; after which he would have struck off my left foot also; but the heart of the soldier softened and he took pity on me and interceded for me with the Governor that I should not be slain.[2] Thereupon the Wali left me, and went away and the folk remained round me and gave me a cup of wine to drink. As for the trooper he pressed the purse upon me, and said, "Thou art a comely youth and it befitteth not thou be a thief." So I repeated these verses:—

"I swear by Allah's name, fair sir! no thief was I, * Nor, O thou best of men! was I a bandit bred:
But Fortune's change and chance o'erthrew me suddenly, * And cark and care and penury my course misled:
I shot it not, indeed, 'twas Allah shot the shaft   * That rolled in dust the Kingly diadem from my head."[3]

The soldier turned away after giving me the purse; and I also went my ways having wrapped my hand in a piece of rag and thrust it into my bosom. My whole semblance had changed, and my colour had waxed yellow from the shame and pain which had befallen me. Yet I went on to my mistress's house where, in extreme perturbation of spirit I threw myself down on the carpet-

---

[1] Moslem law is never completely satisfied till the criminal confess. It also utterly ignores circumstantial evidence and for the best of reasons: amongst so sharp-witted a people the admission would lead to endless abuses. I greatly surprised a certain Governor-General of India by giving him this simple information.

[2] Cutting off the right hand is the Koranic punishment (chapt. v.) for one who robs an article worth four dinars, about forty francs to shillings. The left foot is to be cut off at the ankle for a second offence and so on; but death is reserved for a hardened criminal. The practice is now obsolete and theft is punished by the bastinado, fine or imprisonment. The old Guebres were as severe. For stealing one dirham's worth they took a fine of two, cut off the ear-lobes, gave ten stick-blows and dismissed the criminal who had been subjected to an hour's imprisonment. A second theft caused the penalties to be doubled; and after that the right hand was cut off or death was inflicted according to the proportion stolen.

[3] Koran viii. 17.

bed. She saw me in this state and asked me, "What aileth thee and why do I see thee so changed in looks?"; and I answered, "My head paineth me and I am far from well." Whereupon she was vexed and was concerned on my account and said, "Burn not my heart, O my lord, but sit up and raise thy head and recount to me what hath happened to thee to-day, for thy face tells me a tale." "Leave this talk," replied I. But she wept and said, "Me-seems thou art tired of me, for I see thee contrary to thy wont." But I was silent; and she kept on talking to me albeit I gave her no answer, till night came on. Then she set food before me, but I refused it fearing lest she see me eating with my left hand and said to her, "I have no stomach to eat at present." Quoth she, "Tell me what hath befallen thee to-day, and why art thou so sorrowful and broken in spirit and heart?" Quoth I, "Wait awhile; I will tell thee all at my leisure." Then she brought me wine, saying, "Down with it, this will dispel thy grief: thou must indeed drink and tell me of thy tidings." I asked her, "Perforce must I tell thee?"; and she answered, "Yes." Then said I, "If it needs must be so, then give me to drink with thine own hand." She filled and drank,[1] and filled again and gave me the cup which I took from her with my left hand and wiped the tears from my eyelids and began repeating:—

"When Allah willeth aught befal a man * Who hath of ears and eyes and wits full share;
His ears He deafens and his eyes He blinds * And draws his wits e'en as we draw a hair[2]
Till, having wrought His purpose, He restores * Man's wits, that warned more circumspect he fare."

When I ended my verses I wept, and she cried out with an ex-ceeding loud cry, "What is the cause of thy tears? Thou burnest my heart! What makes thee take the cup with thy left hand?" Quoth I, "Truly I have on my right hand a boil;" and quoth she, "Put it out and I will open it for thee."[3] "It is not yet time to open it," I replied, "so worry me not with thy words, for I will not take it out of the bandage at this hour." Then I drank off

---

[1] A universal custom in the East, the object being originally to show that the draught was not poisoned.

[2] Out of paste or pudding.

[3] Boils and pimples are supposed to be caused by broken hair-roots and in Hindostani are called Bál-tor.

the cup, and she gave not over plying me with drink until drunkenness overcame me and I fell asleep in the place where I was sitting; whereupon she looked at my right hand and saw a wrist without a fist. So she searched me closely and found with me the purse of gold and my severed hand wrapped up in the bit of rag.[1] With this such sorrow came upon her as never overcame any and she ceased not lamenting on my account till the morning. When I awoke I found that she had dressed me a dish of broth of four boiled chickens, which she brought to me together with a cup of wine. I ate and drank and laying down the purse, would have gone out; but she said to me, "Whither away?"; and I answered, "Where my business calleth me;" and said she, "Thou shalt not go: sit thee down." So I sat down and she resumed, "Hath thy love for me so overpowered thee that thou hast wasted all thy wealth and hast lost thine hand on my account? I take thee to witness against me and also Allah be my witness that I will never part with thee, but will die under thy feet; and soon thou shalt see that my words are true." Then she sent for the Kazi and witnesses and said to them, "Write my contract of marriage with this young man, and bear ye witness that I have received the marriage-settlement."[2] When they had drawn up the document she said, "Be witness that all my monies which are in this chest and all I have in slaves and handmaidens and other property is given in free gift to this young man." So they took act of this statement enabling me to assume possession in right of marriage; and then withdrew, after receiving their fees. Thereupon she took me by the hand and, leading me to a closet, opened a large chest and said to me, "See what is herein;" and I looked and behold, it was full of kerchiefs. Quoth she, "This is the money I had from thee and every kerchief thou gavest me, containing fifty dinars, I wrapped up and cast into this chest; so now take thine own, for it returns to thee, and this day thou art become of high estate. Fortune and Fate afflicted thee so that thou didst lose thy right hand for my sake; and I can never requite thee; nay, although I gave my life 't were but little and I should still

---

[1] He intended to bury it decently, a respect which Moslems always show even to the exuviæ of the body, as hair and nail parings. Amongst Guebres the latter were collected and carried to some mountain. The practice was intensified by fear of demons or wizards getting possession of the spoils.

[2] Without which the marriage was not valid. The minimum is ten dirhams (drachmas) now valued at about five francs to shillings; and if a man marry without naming the sum, the woman, after consummation, can compel him to pay this minimum.

remain thy debtor." Then she added, "Take charge of thy property;" so I transferred the contents of her chest to my chest,
and added my wealth to her wealth which I had given her, and
my heart was eased and my sorrow ceased. I stood up and kissed
her and thanked her; and she said, "Thou hast given thy hand
for love of me and how am I able to give thee an equivalent?
By Allah, if I offered my life for thy love, it were indeed but little
and would not do justice to thy claim upon me." Then she made
over to me by deed all that she possessed in clothes and ornaments
of gold and pearls, and goods and farms and chattels, and lay not
down to sleep that night, being sorely grieved for my grief, till
I told her the whole of what had befallen me. I passed the night
with her. But before we had lived together a month's time she
fell sorely sick and illness increased upon her, by reason of her
grief for the loss of my hand, and she endured but fifty days
before she was numbered among the folk of futurity and heirs of
immortality. So I laid her out and buried her body in mother
earth and let make a pious perlection of the Koran[1] for the
health of her soul, and gave much money in alms for her; after
which I turned me from the grave and returned to the house.
There I found that she had left much substance in ready money
and slaves, mansions, lands and domains, and among her storehouses was a granary of sesame-seed, whereof I sold part to thee;
and I had neither time nor inclination to take count with thee till
I had sold the rest of the stock in store; nor, indeed, even now
have I made an end of receiving the price. So I desire thou baulk
me not in what I am about to say to thee: twice have I eaten of
thy food and I wish to give thee as a present the monies for the
sesame which are by thee. Such is the cause of the cutting off
my right hand and my eating with my left. "Indeed," said I,
"thou hast shown me the utmost kindness and liberality." Then
he asked me, "Why shouldst thou not travel with me to my
native country whither I am about to return with Cairene and
Alexandrian stuffs? Say me, wilt thou accompany me?"; and I
answered "I will." So I agreed to go with him at the head of
the month, and I sold all I had and bought other merchandise;
then we set out and travelled, I and the young man, to this
country of yours, where he sold his venture and bought other

---

[1] Arab. "Khatmah" = reading or reciting the whole Koran, by one or more persons,
usually in the house, not over the tomb. Like the "Zikr," Litany or Rogation, it is a
pious act confined to certain occasions.

investment of country stuffs and continued his journey to Egypt. But it was my lot to abide here, so that these things befel me in my strangerhood which befel last night, and is not this tale, O King of the age, more wondrous and marvellous than the story of the Hunchback? "Not so," quoth the King, "I cannot accept it: there is no help for it but that you be hanged, every one of you."——And Shahrazad perceived the dawn of day, and ceased saying her permitted say.

When it was the Twenty-seventh Night,

She said, It hath reached me, O auspicious King, that when the King of China declared "There is no help for it but that you be hanged," the Reeve of the Sultan's Kitchen came forward and said, "If thou permit me I will tell thee a tale of what befel me just before I found this Gobbo; and, if it be more wondrous than his story, do thou grant us our lives." And when the King answered "Yes" he began to recount

The Reeve's Tale.

KNOW, O King, that last night I was at a party where they made a perlection of the Koran and got together doctors of law and religion skilled in recitation and intoning; and, when the readers ended, the table was spread and amongst other things they set before us was a marinated ragout[1] flavoured with cumin-seed. So we sat down, but one of our number held back and refused to touch it. We conjured him to eat of it but he swore he would not; and, when we again pressed him, he said, "Be not instant with me; sufficeth me that which hath already befallen me through eating it"; and he began reciting:—

"Shoulder thy tray and go straight to thy goal; * And, if suit thee this Kohl,
       why,—use this Kohl!"[2]

When he ended his verse we said to him, "Allah upon thee, tell us thy reason for refusing to eat of the cumin-ragout?" "If so it be," he replied, "and needs must I eat of it, I will not do so except I wash my hand forty times with soap, forty times with potash

---

[1] Arab. "Zirbájah" = meat dressed with vinegar, cumin-seed (Pers. Zír) and hot spices. More of it in the sequel of the tale.

[2] A saying not uncommon meaning, let each man do as he seems fit; also = "age quod agis": and at times corresponding with our saw about the cap fitting.

and forty times with galangale,[1] the total being one hundred and twenty washings." Thereupon the hospitable host bade his slaves bring water and whatso he required; and the young man washed his hand as afore mentioned. Then he sat down, as if disgusted and frightened withal, and dipping his hand in the ragout, began eating and at the same time showing signs of anger. And we wondered at him with extreme wonderment, for his hand trembled and the morsel in it shook and we saw that his thumb had been cut off and he ate with his four fingers only. So we said to him, "Allah upon thee, what happened to thy thumb? Is thy hand thus by the creation of God or hath some accident befallen it?" "O my brothers," he answered, "it is not only thus with this thumb, but also with my other thumb and with both my great toes, as you shall see." So saying he uncovered his left hand and his feet, and we saw that the left hand was even as the right and in like manner that each of his feet lacked its great toe. When we saw him after this fashion, our amazement waxed still greater and we said to him, "We have hardly patience enough to await thy history and to hear the manner of the cutting off of thy thumbs, and the reason of thy washing both hands one hundred and twenty times." Know then, said he, that my father was chief of the merchants and the wealthiest of them all in Baghdad-city during the reign of the Caliph Harun al-Rashid; and he was much given to wine-drinking and listening to the lute and the other instruments of pleasaunce; so that when he died he left nothing. I buried him and had perlections of the Koran made for him, and mourned for him days and nights: then I opened his shop and found that he had left in it few goods, while his debts were many. However I compounded with his creditors for time to settle their demands and betook myself to buying and selling, paying them something from week to week on account; and I gave not over doing this till I had cleared off his obligations in full and began adding to my principal. One day, as I sat in my shop, suddenly and unexpectedly there appeared before me a young lady, than whom I never saw a fairer, wearing the richest raiment and ornaments and riding a she-mule, with one negro-slave walking before her and another behind her. She drew rein at the head of the exchange-bazar and entered followed by an eunuch who said to

---

[1] Arab. "Su'úd," an Alpinia with pungent rhizome like ginger; here used as a counter-odour.

her, "O my lady come out and away without telling any one, lest thou light a fire which will burn us all up." Moreover he stood before her guarding her from view whilst she looked at the merchants' shops. She found none open but mine; so she came up with the eunuch behind her and sitting down in my shop saluted me; never heard I aught fairer than her speech or sweeter than her voice. Then she unveiled her face, and I saw that she was like the moon and I stole a glance at her whose sight caused me a thousand sighs, and my heart was captivated with love of her, and I kept looking again and again upon her face repeating these verses:—

"Say to the charmer in the dove-hued veil, * Death would be welcome to abate
    thy bale!
Favour me with thy favours that I live: * See, I stretch forth my palm to
    take thy vail!"

When she heard my verse she answered me saying:—

"I've lost all patience by despite of you; * My heart knows nothing save love-
    plight to you!
If aught I sight save charms so bright of you; * My parting end not in the
    sight of you!
I swear I'll ne'er forget the right of you; * And fain this breast would soar to
    height of you:
You made me drain the love-cup, and I lief * A love-cup tender for delight of
    you:
Take this my form where'er you go, and when * You die, entomb me in the
    site of you:
Call on me in my grave, and hear my bones * Sigh their responses to the
    shright of you:
And were I asked 'Of God what wouldst thou see?' * I answer, 'first His will
    then Thy decree!' "

When she ended her verse she asked me, "O youth, hast thou any fair stuffs by thee?"; and I answered, "O my lady, thy slave is poor; but have patience till the merchants open their shops, and I will suit thee with what thou wilt." Then we sat talking, I and she (and I was drowned in the sea of her love, dazed in the desert[1] of my passion for her), till the merchants opened their shops; when I rose and fetched her all she sought to the tune of five thousand dirhams. She gave the stuff to the eunuch and, going forth by the door of the Exchange, she mounted mule and went

---

[1] Arab. "Tá'ih" = lost in the "Tíh," a desert wherein man *may* lose himself, translated in our maps "The Desert of the Wanderings," scil. of the children of Israel. "Credat Judæus."

away, without telling me whence she came, and I was ashamed to speak of such trifle. When the merchants dunned me for the price, I made myself answerable for five thousand dirhams and went home, drunken with the love of her. They set supper before me and I ate a mouthful, thinking only of her beauty and loveliness, and sought to sleep, but sleep came not to me. And such was my condition for a whole week, when the merchants required their monies of me, but I persuaded them to have patience for another week, at the end of which time she again appeared mounted on a she-mule and attended by her eunuch and two slaves. She saluted me and said, "O my master, we have been long in bringing thee the price of the stuffs; but now fetch the Shroff and take thy monies." So I sent for the money-changer and the eunuch counted out the coin before him and made it over to me. Then we sat talking, I and she, till the market opened, when she said to me, "Get me this and that." So I got her from the merchants whatso she wanted, and she took it and went away without saying a word to me about the price. As soon as she was out of sight, I repented me of what I had done; for the worth of the stuffs bought for her amounted to a thousand dinars, and I said in my soul, "What manner of love is this? She hath brought me five thousand dirhams, and hath taken goods for a thousand dinars."[1] I feared lest I should be beggared through having to pay the merchants their money, and I said, "They know none other but me; this lovely lady is naught but a cheat and a swindler, who hath diddled me with her beauty and grace; for she saw that I was a mere youth and laughed at me for not asking her address." I ceased not to be troubled by these doubts and fears, as she was absent more than a month, till the merchants pestered me for their money and were so hard upon me that I put up my property for sale and stood on the very brink of ruin. However, as I was sitting in my shop one day, drowned in melancholy musings, she suddenly rode up and, dismounting at the bazar-gate, came straight towards me. When I saw her all my cares fell from me and I forgot every trouble. She came close up to me and greeted me with her sweet voice and pleasant speech and presently said, "Fetch me the Shroff and weigh thy money."[2] So she gave me the price of what goods I had gotten for her and more, and fell to

---

[1] *i.e.*, £125 and £500.
[2] A large sum was weighed by a professional instead of being counted, the reason

talking freely with me, till I was like to die of joy and delight. Presently she asked me, "Hast thou a wife?"; and I answered "No, indeed: I have never known woman"; and began to shed tears. Quoth she "Why weepest thou?" Quoth I "It is nothing!" Then giving the eunuch some of the gold pieces, I begged him to be go-between[1] in the matter; but he laughed and said, "She is more in love with thee than thou with her: she hath no occasion for the stuffs she hath bought of thee and did all this only for the love of thee; so ask of her what thou wilt and she will deny thee nothing." When she saw me giving the dinars to the eunuch, she returned and sat down again; and I said to her, "Be charitable to thy slave and pardon him what he is about to say." Then I told her what was in my mind and she assented and said to the eunuch, "Thou shalt carry my message to him," adding to me, "And do thou whatso the eunuch biddeth thee." Then she got up and went away, and I paid the merchants their monies and they all profited; but as for me, regret at the breaking off of our inter-course was all my gain; and I slept not the whole of that night. However, before many days passed her eunuch came to me, and I entreated him honourably and asked him after his mistress. "Truly she is sick with love of thee," he replied and I rejoined, "Tell me who and what she is." Quoth he, "The Lady Zubay-dah, queen-consort of Harun al-Rashid, brought her up as a rear-ling[2] and hath advanced her to be stewardess of the Harim, and gave her the right of going in and out of her own sweet will. She spoke to her lady of thee and begged her to marry her to thee; but she said, 'I will not do this, till I see the young man; and, if he be worthy of thee, I will marry thee to him.' So now we look for the moment to smuggle thee into the Palace and if thou suc-ceed in entering privily thou wilt win thy wish to wed her; but if the affair get wind, the Lady Zubaydah will strike off thy head.[3]

---

being that the coin is mostly old and worn: hence our words "pound" and "pension" (or what is weighed out).

[1] The eunuch is the best possible go-between on account of his almost unlimited power over the Harem.

[2] i.e., a slave-girl brought up in the house and never sold except for some especial reason, as habitual drunkenness, etc.

[3] Smuggling men into the Harem is a stock "topic" of eastern tales. "By means of their female attendants, the ladies of the royal harem generally get men into their apart-ments in the disguise of women," says Vatsyayana in The Kama Sutra, Part V., London: Printed for the Hindoo Kamashastra Society, 1883. For private circulation only.

What sayest thou to this?" I answered, "I will go with thee and abide the risk whereof thou speakest." Then said he, "As soon as it is night, go to the Mosque built by the Lady Zubaydah on the Tigris and pray the night-prayers and sleep there." "With love and gladness," cried I. So at nightfall I repaired to the Mosque, where I prayed and passed the night. With earliest dawn, behold, came sundry eunuchs in a skiff with a number of empty chests which they deposited in the Mosque; then all of them went their ways but one, and looking curiously at him, I saw he was our go-between. Presently in came the handmaiden, my mistress, walking straight up to us; and I rose to her and embraced her while she kissed me and shed tears.[1] We talked awhile; after which she made me get into one of the chests which she locked upon me. Presently the other eunuchs came back with a quantity of packages and she fell to stowing them in the chests, which she locked down, one by one, till all were shut. When all was done the eunuchs embarked the chests in the boat and made for the Lady Zubaydah's palace. With this, thought began to beset me and I said to myself, "Verily thy lust and wantonness will be the death of thee; and the question is after all shalt thou win to thy wish or not?" And I began to weep, boxed up as I was in the box and suffering from cramp; and I prayed Allah that He deliver me from the dangerous strait I was in, whilst the boat gave not over going on till it reached the Palace-gate where they lifted out the chests and amongst them that in which I was. Then they carried them in, passing through a troop of eunuchs, guardians of the Harim and of the ladies behind the curtain, till they came to the post of the Eunuch-in-Chief[2] who started up from his slumbers and shouted to the damsel "What is in those chests?" "They are full of wares for the Lady Zubaydah!" "Open them,

---

[1] These tears are shed over past separation. So the "Indians" of the New World never meet after long parting without beweeping mutual friends they have lost.

[2] A most important Jack in office whom one can see with his smooth chin and blubber lips, starting up from his lazy snooze in the shade and delivering his orders more peremptorily than any Dogberry. These epicenes are as curious and exceptional in character as in external conformation. Disconnected, after a fashion, with humanity, they are brave, fierce and capable of any villany or barbarity (as Agha Mohammed Khan in Persia 1795-98). The frame is unnaturally long and lean, especially the arms and legs; with high, flat, thin shoulders; big protruding joints and a face by contrast extraordinarily large, a veritable mask; the Castrato is expert in the use of weapons and sits his horse admirably, riding well "home" in the saddle for the best of reasons; and his hoarse thick voice, which apparently does not break, as in the European "Cáppone," invests him with all the circumstance of command.

one by one, that I may see what is in them." "And wherefore
wouldst thou open them?" "Give me no words and exceed not
in talk! these chests must and shall be opened." So saying, he
sprang to his feet, and the first which they brought to him to open
was that wherein I was; and, when I felt his hands upon it, my
senses failed me and I bepissed myself in my funk, the water running out of the box. Then said she to the Eunuch-in-Chief, "O
steward! thou wilt cause me to be killed and thyself too, for thou
hast damaged goods worth ten thousand dinars. This chest contains coloured dresses, and four gallon flasks of Zemzem water;[1]
and now one of them hath got unstoppered and the water is running out over the clothes and it will spoil their colours." The
eunuch answered, "Take up thy boxes and get thee gone to the
curse of God!" So the slaves carried off all the chests, including
mine; and hastened on with them till suddenly I heard the voice
of one saying, "Alack, and alack! the Caliph! the Caliph!" When
that cry struck mine ears I died in my skin and said a saying which
never yet shamed the sayer, "There is no Majesty and there is no
Might save in Allah, the Glorious, the Great! I and only I have
brought this calamity upon myself." Presently I heard the
Caliph say to my mistress, "A plague on thee, what is in those
boxes?"; and she answered, "Dresses for the Lady Zubaydah";[2]
whereupon he, "Open them before me!" When I heard this I
died my death outright and said to myself, "By Allah, to-day is
the very last of my days in this world: if I come safe out of this I
am to marry her and no more words, but detection stares me in
the face and my head is as good as stricken off." Then I repeated
the profession of Faith, saying, "There is no god but *the* God,
and Mohammed is the Apostle of God!"——And Shahrazad
perceived the dawn of day and ceased to say her permitted say.

When it was the Twenty-eighth Night,

She said, It hath reached me, O auspicious King, that the young
merchant continued as follows: Now when I testified, "I bear witness that there is no god save *the* God," I heard my mistress the

---

[1] From the Meccan well used by Moslems much like Eau de Lourdes by Christians:
the water is saltish, hence the touch of Arab humour (Pilgrimage iii., 201-202).

[2] Such articles would be sacred from Moslem eyes.

handmaid declare to the Caliph, "These chests, O Commander of
the Faithful, have been committed to my charge by the Lady
Zubaydah, and she doth not wish their contents to be seen by
any one." "No matter!" quoth the Caliph, "needs must they be
opened, I *will* see what is in them"; and he cried aloud to the
eunuchs, "Bring the chests here before me." At this I made sure
of death (without benefit of a doubt) and swooned away. Then
the eunuchs brought the chests up to him one after another and
he fell to inspecting the contents, but he saw in them only ottars
and stuffs and fine dresses; and they ceased not opening the
chests and he ceased not looking to see what was in them, finding
only clothes and such matters, till none remained unopened but
the box in which I was boxed. They put forth their hands to
open it, but my mistress the handmaid made haste and said to the
Caliph, "This one thou shalt see only in the presence of the Lady
Zubaydah, for that which is in it is her secret." When he heard
this he gave orders to carry in the chests; so they took up that
wherein I was and bore it with the rest into the Harim and set it
down in the midst of the saloon; and indeed my spittle was dried
up for very fear.[1] Then my mistress opened the box and took me
out, saying, "Fear not: no harm shall betide thee now nor dread;
but broaden thy breast and strengthen thy heart and sit thee
down till the Lady Zubaydah come, and surely thou shalt win thy
wish of me." So I sat down and, after a while, in came ten handmaidens, virgins like moons, and ranged themselves in two rows,
five facing five; and after them twenty other damsels, high-
bosomed virginity, surrounding the Lady Zubaydah who could
hardly walk for the weight of her raiment and ornaments. As
she drew near, the slave-girls dispersed from around her, and I
advanced and kissed the ground between her hands. She signed
to me to sit and, when I sat down before her chair, she began questioning me of my forbears and family and condition, to which I
made such answers that pleased her, and she said to my mistress,
"Our nurturing of thee, O damsel, hath not disappointed us."
Then she said to me, "Know that this handmaiden is to us even
as our own child and she is a trust committed to thee by Allah."
I again kissed the ground before her, well pleased that I should
marry my mistress, and she bade me abide ten days in the palace.
So I abode there ten days, during which time I saw not my mis-

---

[1] Physiologically true, but not generally mentioned in describing the emotions.

tress nor any body save one of the concubines, who brought me the morning and evening meals. After this the Lady Zubaydah took counsel with the Caliph on the marriage of her favourite handmaid, and he gave leave and assigned to her a wedding portion of ten thousand gold pieces. So the Lady Zubaydah sent for the Kazi and witnesses who wrote our marriage-contract, after which the women made ready sweetmeats and rich viands and distributed them among all the Odahs[1] of the Harim. Thus they did other ten days, at the end of which time my mistress went to the baths.[2] Meanwhile, they set before me a tray of food whereon were various meats and among those dishes, which were enough to daze the wits, was a bowl of cumin-ragout containing chickens' breasts, fricandoed[3] and flavoured with sugar, pistachios, musk and rose-water. Then, by Allah, fair sirs, I did not long hesitate; but took my seat before the ragout and fell to and ate of it till I could no more. After this I wiped my hands, but forgot to wash them; and sat till it grew dark, when the wax-candles were lighted and the singing-women came in with their tambourines and proceeded to display the bride in various dresses and to carry her in procession from room to room all round the palace, getting their palms crossed with gold. Then they brought her to me and disrobed her. When I found myself alone with her on the bed I embraced her, hardly believing in our union; but she smelt the strong odours of the ragout upon my hands and forthwith cried out with an exceeding loud cry, at which the slave-girls came running to her from all sides. I trembled with alarm, unknowing what was the matter, and the girls asked her, "What aileth thee, O our sister?" She answered them, "Take this madman away from me: I had thought he was a man of sense!" Quoth I to her, "What makes thee think me mad?" Quoth she, "Thou madman! what made thee eat of cumin-ragout and forget to wash thy hand? By Allah, I will requite thee for thy misconduct. Shall the like of thee come to bed with the like of me with unclean hands?"[4] Then she took from her side a plaited scourge and came down with it on my back and the place where I sit till her forearms were benumbed and I fainted away from the

---

[1] Properly "Uta," the different rooms, each "Odalisque," or concubine, having her own.

[2] Showing that her monthly ailment was over.

[3] Arab. "Muhammarah" = either browned before the fire or artificially reddened.

[4] The insolence and licence of these palace-girls was (and is) unlimited; especially when, as in the present case, they have to deal with a "softy." On this subject numberless stories are current throughout the East.

mucn beating; when she said to the handmaids, "Take him and carry him to the Chief of Police, that he may strike off the hand wherewith he ate of the cumin-ragout, and which he did not wash." When I heard this I said, "There is no Majesty and there is no Might save in Allah! Wilt thou cut off my hand, because I ate of a cumin-ragout and did not wash?" The handmaidens also interceded with her and kissed her hand saying, "O our sister, this man is a simpleton, punish him not for what he hath done this nonce;" but she answered, "By Allah, there is no help but that I dock him of somewhat, especially the offending member." Then she went away and I saw no more of her for ten days, during which time she sent me meat and drink by a slave-girl who told me that she had fallen sick from the smell of the cumin-ragout. After that time she came to me and said, "O black of face![1] I will teach thee how to eat cumin-ragout without washing thy hands!" Then she cried out to the handmaids, who pinioned me; and she took a sharp razor and cut off my thumbs and great toes; even as you see, O fair assembly! Thereupon I swooned away, and she sprinkled some powder of healing herbs upon the stumps and when the blood was staunched, I said, "Never again will I eat of cumin-ragout without washing my hands forty times with potash and forty times with galangale and forty times with soap!" And she took of me an oath and bound me by a covenant to that effect. When, therefore, you brought me the cumin-ragout my colour changed and I said to myself, "It was this very dish that caused the cutting off of my thumbs and great toes;" and, when you forced me, I said, "Needs must I fulfil the oath I have sworn." "And what befel thee after this?" asked those present; and he answered, "When I swore to her, her anger was appeased and I slept with her that night. We abode thus awhile till she said to me one day, 'Verily the Palace of the Caliph is not a pleasant place for us to live in, and none ever entered it save thyself; and thou only by grace of the Lady Zubaydah. Now she hath given me fifty thousand dinars,' adding, 'Take this money and go out and buy us a fair dwelling-house.' So I fared forth and bought a fine and spacious mansion, whither she removed all the wealth she owned and what riches I had gained in stuffs and costly rarities. Such is the cause of the cutting off of my thumbs and great toes." We ate (continued the Reeve), and were returning to our homes

---

[1] *i.e.*, blackened by the fires of Jehannam.

when there befel me with the Hunchback that thou wottest of.
This then is my story, and peace be with thee! Quoth the King,
"This story is on no wise more delectable than the story of the
Hunchback; nay, it is even less so, and there is no help for the
hanging of the whole of you." Then came forward the Jewish
physician and kissing the ground said, "O King of the age, I will
tell thee an history more wonderful than that of the Hunchback."
"Tell on," said the King of China; so he began the

Tale of the Jewish Doctor.

RIGHT marvellous was a matter which came to pass to me in my
youth. I lived in Damascus of Syria studying my art and, one
day, as I was sitting at home behold, there came to me a Mameluke from the household of the Sáhib and said to me, "Speak with
my lord!" So I followed him to the Viceroy's house and, entering
the great hall, saw at its head a couch of cedar plated with gold
whereon lay a sickly youth beautiful withal; fairer than he one
could not see. I sat down by his head and prayed to Heaven for
a cure; and he made me a sign with his eyes, so I said to him,
"O my lord! favour me with thy hand, and safety be with thee!"[1]
Then he put forth his left hand and I marvelled thereat and said,
"By Allah, strange that this handsome youth, the son of a great
house, should so lack good manners. This can be nothing but
pride and conceit!" However I felt his pulse and wrote him a pre-
scription and continued to visit him for ten days, at the end of
which time he recovered and went to the Hammam,[2] whereupon
the Viceroy gave me a handsome dress of honour and appointed
me superintendent of the hospital which is in Damascus.[3] I ac-

---

[1] Arab. "Bi'l-Salámah" = in safety (to avert the evil eye). When visiting the sick
it is usual to say something civil; "The Lord heal thee! No evil befal thee!" etc.

[2] Washing during sickness is held dangerous by Arabs; and "going to the Hammam"
is, I have said, equivalent to convalescence.

[3] Arab. "Máristán" (pronounced Múristan) a corruption of the Pers. "Bímá-
ristán" = place of sickness, a hospital much affected by the old Guebres (Dabistan,
i., 165, 166). That of Damascus was the first Moslem hospital, founded by Al-Walid
Son of Abd al-Malik the Ommiade in A. H. 88 = 706-7. Benjamin of Tudela (A. D.
1164) calls it "Dar-al-Maraphtan" which his latest Editor explains by "Dar-al-Mora-
bittan" (abode of those who require being chained). Al-Makrizi (Khitat) ascribes
the invention of "Spitals" to Hippocrates; another historian to an early Pharaoh
"Manákiyush;" thus ignoring the Persian Kings, Saint Ephrem (or Ephraim), Syru,
etc. In modern parlance "Maristan" is a madhouse where the maniacs are treated

companied him to the baths, the whole of which they had kept private for his accommodation; and the servants came in with him and took off his clothes within the bath, and when he was stripped I saw that his right hand had been newly cut off, and this was the cause of his weakliness. At this I was amazed and grieved for him: then, looking at his body, I saw on it the scars of scourge-stripes whereto he had applied unguents. I was troubled at the sight and my concern appeared in my face. The young man looked at me and, comprehending the matter, said, "O Physician of the age, marvel not at my case; I will tell thee my story as soon as we quit the baths." Then we washed and, returning to his house, ate somewhat of food and took rest awhile; after which he asked me, "What sayest thou to solacing thee by inspecting the supper-hall?"; and I answered "So let it be." Thereupon he ordered the slaves to carry out the carpets and cushions required and roast a lamb and bring us some fruit. They did his bidding and we ate together, he using the left hand for the purpose. After a while I said to him, "Now tell me thy tale." "O Physician of the age," replied he, "hear what befel me. Know that I am of the sons of Mosul, where my grandfather died leaving nine children of whom my father was the eldest. All grew up and took to them wives, but none of them was blessed with offspring except my father, to whom Providence vouchsafed me. So I grew up amongst my uncles who rejoiced in me with exceeding joy, till I came to man's estate. One day which happened to be a Friday, I went to the Cathedral-mosque of Mosul with my father and my uncles, and we prayed the congregational prayers, after which the folk went forth, except my father and uncles, who sat talking of wondrous things in foreign parts and the marvellous sights of strange cities. At last they mentioned Egypt, and one of my uncles said, "Travellers tell us that there is not on earth's face aught fairer than Cairo and her Nile;" and these words made me

---

with all the horrors which were universal in Europe till within a few years and of which occasional traces occur to this day. In A. D. 1399 Katherine de la Court held a "hospital in the Court called Robert de Paris;" but the first madhouse in Christendom was built by the legate Ortiz in Toledo A. D. 1483, and was therefore called Casa del Nuncio. The Damascus "Maristan" was described by every traveller of the last century: and it showed a curious contrast between the treatment of the maniac and the idiot or omadhaun, who is humanely allowed to wander about unharmed, if not held a Saint. When I saw it last (1870) it was all but empty and mostly in ruins. As far as my experience goes, the United States is the only country where the insane are rationally treated by the sane.

long to see Cairo. Quoth my father, "Whoso hath not seen Cairo hath not seen the world. Her dust is golden and her Nile a miracle holden; and her women are as Houris fair; puppets, beautiful pictures; her houses are palaces rare; her water is sweet and light[1] and her mud a commodity and a medicine beyond compare, even as said the poet in this his poetry:—

The Nile[2]-flood this day is the gain you own; * You alone in such gain and
    bounties wone:
The Nile is my tear-flood of severance, * And here none is forlorn
    but I alone.

Moreover temperate is her air, and with fragrance blent, which surpasseth aloes-wood in scent; and how should it be otherwise, she being the Mother of the World? And Allah favour him who wrote these lines:—

An I quit Cairo and her pleasaunces, * Where can I wend to find so glad-
    some ways?
Shall I desert that site, whose grateful scents * Joy every soul and call for
    loudest praise?
Where every palace, as another Eden, * Carpets and cushions richly wrought
    displays;
A city wooing sight and sprite to glee, * Where Saint meets Sinner and
    each 'joys his craze;
Where friend meets friend, by Providence united * In greeny garden and
    in palmy maze:
People of Cairo, an by Allah's doom * I fare, with you in thoughts I wone
    always!
Whisper not Cairo in the ear of Zephyr, * Lest for her like of garden scents
    he reave her.[3]

And if your eyes saw her earth, and the adornment thereof with bloom, and the purfling of it with all manner blossoms, and the islands of the Nile and how much is therein of wide-spread and

---

[1] Hence the trite saying "Whoso drinks the water of the Nile will ever long to drink it again." "Light" means easily digested water; and the great test is being able to drink it at night between the sleeps, without indigestion.

[2] "Níl" in popular parlance is the Nile in flood, although also used for the River as a proper name. Egyptians (modern as well as ancient) have three seasons, Al-Shitá (winter), Al-Sayf (summer) and Al-Níl (the Nile i.e. flood season, our mid-summer); corresponding with the Growth-months; Housing (or granary)-months and Flood-months of the older race.

[3] These lines are in the Mac. Edit.

goodly prospect, and if you bent your sight upon the Abyssinian Pond,[1] your glance would not revert from the scene quit of wonder; for nowhere would you behold the fellow of that lovely view; and, indeed, the two arms of the Nile embrace most luxuriant verdure,[2] as the white of the eye encompasseth its black or like filagree'd silver surrounding chrysolites. And divinely gifted was the poet who thereanent said these couplets:—

By th' Abyssinian Pond, O day divine! sunny shine: * In morning twilight and in

The water prisoned in its verdurous walls, shrinking eyne: * Like sabre flashes before

And in The Garden sat we while it drains sides dyed finest fine: * Slow draught, with purfled

The stream is rippled by the hands of clouds; * We too, a-rippling, on our rugs recline,

Passing pure wine, and whoso leaves us there woes design: * Shall ne'er arise from fall his

Draining long draughts from large and brimming bowls, * Administ'ring thirst's only medicine—wine.

And what is there to compare with the Rasad, the Observatory, and its charms whereof every viewer as he approacheth saith, 'Verily this spot is specialised with all manner of excellence!' And if thou speak of the Night of Nile-full,[3] give the rainbow and distribute it![4] And if thou behold The Garden at eventide, with the cool shades sloping far and wide, a marvel thou wouldst see and wouldst incline to Egypt in ecstasy. And wert thou by Cairo's river-side,[5] when the sun is sinking and the stream dons mail-coat and habergeon[6] over its other vestments, thou wouldst be quickened to new life by its gentle zephyrs and by its all-sufficient

---

[1] Arab. "Birkat al-Habash," a tank formerly existing in Southern Cairo: Galland (Night 128) says "en remontant vers l'Éthiopie."

[2] The Bres. Edit. (ii., 190), from which I borrow this description, here alludes to the well-known Island, Al-Rauzah (Rodah) = The Garden.

[3] Arab. "Laylat al-Wafá," the night of the completion or abundance of the Nile (-flood), usually between August 6th and 16th, when the government proclaims that the Nilometer shows a rise of 16 cubits. Of course it is a great festival and a high ceremony, for Egypt is still the gift of the Nile (Lane M. E. chapt. xxvi—a work which would be much improved by a better index).

[4] i.e., admiration will be complete.

[5] Arab. "Sáhil Masr" (Misr): hence I suppose Galland's villes maritimes.

[6] A favourite simile, suggested by the broken glitter and shimmer of the stream under the level rays and the breeze of eventide.

shade." So spake he and the rest fell to describing Egypt and her Nile. As I heard their accounts, my thoughts dwelt upon the subject and when, after talking their fill, all arose and went their ways, I lay down to sleep that night, but sleep came not because of my violent longing for Egypt; and neither meat pleased me nor drink. After a few days my uncles equipped themselves for a trade-journey to Egypt; and I wept before my father till he made ready for me fitting merchandise, and he consented to my going with them, saying however, "Let him not enter Cairo, but leave him to sell his wares at Damascus." So I took leave of my father and we fared forth from Mosul and gave not over travelling till we reached Aleppo[1] where we halted certain days. Then we marched onwards till we made Damascus and we found her a city as though she were a Paradise, abounding in trees and streams and birds and fruits of all kinds. We alighted at one of the Khans, where my uncles tarried awhile selling and buying; and they bought and sold also on my account, each dirham turning a profit of five on prime cost, which pleased me mightily. After this they left me alone and set their faces Egyptwards; whilst I abode at Damascus, where I had hired from a jeweller, for two dinars a month, a mansion[2] whose beauties would beggar the tongue. Here I remained, eating and drinking and spending what monies I had in hand till, one day, as I was sitting at the door of my house behold, there came up a young lady clad in costliest raiment—never saw my eyes richer. I winked[3] at her and she stepped inside without hesitation and stood within. I entered with her and shut the door upon myself and her; whereupon she raised her face-veil and threw off her mantilla, when I found her like a pictured moon of rare and marvellous loveliness; and love of her gat hold of my heart. So I rose and brought a tray of the most delicate eatables and fruits and whatso befitted the occasion, and we ate and played and after that we drank till the wine turned our heads. Then I lay with her the sweetest of nights and in the morning I offered her ten gold pieces; when her face lowered and her eye-

---

[1] Arab. "Halab," derived by Moslems from "He (Abraham) milked (*halaba*) the white and dun cow." But the name of the city occurs in the Cuneiforms as Halbun or Khalbun, and the classics knew it as Βέροια, Beroea, written with variants.

[2] Arab. "Ká'ah," usually a saloon; but also applied to a fine house here and elsewhere in The Nights.

[3] Arab. "Ghamz" = winking, signing with the eye which, amongst Moslems, is not held "vulgar."

brows wrinkled and shaking with wrath she cried, "Fie upon thee, O my sweet companion! dost thou deem that I covet thy money?" Then she took out from the bosom of her shift[1] fifteen dinars and, laying them before me, said, "By Allah! unless thou take them I will never come back to thee." So I accepted them and she said to me, "O my beloved! expect me again in three days' time, when I will be with thee between sunset and supper-tide; and do thou prepare for us with these dinars the same entertainment as yesternight." So saying, she took leave of me and went away and all my senses went with her. On the third day she came again, clad in stuff weft with gold wire, and wearing raiment and ornaments finer than before. I had prepared the place for her ere she arrived and the repast was ready; so we ate and drank and lay together, as we had done, till the morning, when she gave me other fifteen gold pieces and promised to come again after three days. Accordingly, I made ready for her and, at the appointed time, she presented herself more richly dressed than on the first and second occasions, and said to me, "O my lord, am I not beautiful?" "Yea, by Allah thou art!" answered I, and she went on, "Wilt thou allow me to bring with me a young lady fairer than I, and younger in years, that she may play with us and thou and she may laugh and make merry and rejoice her heart, for she hath been very sad this long time past, and hath asked me to take her out and let her spend the night abroad with me?" "Yea, by Allah!" I replied; and we drank till the wine turned our heads and slept till the morning, when she gave me other fifteen dinars, saying, "Add something to thy usual provision on account of the young lady who will come with me." Then she went away, and on the fourth day I made ready the house as usual, and soon after sunset behold, she came, accompanied by another damsel carefully wrapped in her mantilla. They entered and sat down; and when I saw them I repeated these verses:—

"How dear is our day and how lucky our lot,   * When the cynic's away
     with his tongue malign!
When love and delight and the swimming of head * send cleverness trotting,—
     the best boon of wine.

---

[1] Arab. "Kamís" from low Lat. "Camicia," first found in St. Jerome:—"Solent militantes habere lineas, quas Camicias vocant." Our shirt, chemise, chemisette, etc., was unknown to the Ancients of Europe.

When the full moon shines from the cloudy veil, * And the branchlet sways in
　　her greens that shine:
When the red rose mantles in freshest cheek, 　 * And Narcissus[1] opeth his
　　love-sick eyne:
When pleasure with those I love is so sweet, 　 * When friendship with those
　　I love is complete!"

I rejoiced to see them, and lighted the candles after receiving them
with gladness and delight. They doffed their heavy outer dresses
and the new damsel uncovered her face when I saw that she was
like the moon at its full—never beheld I aught more beautiful.
Then I rose and set meat and drink before them, and we ate and
drank; and I kept giving mouthfuls to the new comer, crowning
her cup and drinking with her till the first damsel, waxing inwardly jealous, asked me, "By Allah, is she not more delicious
than I?"; whereto I answered, "Ay, by the Lord!" "It is my
wish that thou lie with her this night; for I am thy mistress but
she is our visitor." "Upon my head be it, and my eyes." Then
she rose and spread the carpets for our bed[2] and I took the young
lady and lay with her that night till morning, when I awoke and
found myself wet, as I thought, with sweat. I sat up and tried to
arouse the damsel; but when I shook her by the shoulders my
hand became crimson with blood and her head rolled off the pillow. Thereupon my senses fled and I cried aloud, saying, "O
All-powerful Protector, grant me Thy protection!" Then finding her neck had been severed, I sprung up and the world waxed
black before my eyes, and I looked for the lady, my former love,
but could not find her. So I knew that it was she who had mur-

---

[1] Arab. "Narjís." The Arabs borrowed nothing, but the Persians much, from Greek
Mythology. Hence the eye of Narcissus, an idea hardly suggested by the look of the
daffodil (or asphodel) -flower, is at times the glance of a spy and at times the die-away look
of a mistress. Some scholars explain it by the form of the flower, the internal calyx resembling the iris, and the stalk being bent just below the petals suggesting drooping
eyelids and languid eyes. Hence a poet addresses the Narcissus:—

O Narjis, look away! Before those eyes 　　 * I may not kiss her as a-breast she lies.
What! Shall the lover close his eyes in sleep 　 * While thine watch all things between
　　earth and skies?

The fashionable lover in the East must affect a frantic jealousy if he does not feel it.

[2] In Egypt there are neither bedsteads nor bedrooms: the carpets and mattresses,
pillows and cushions (sheets being unknown), are spread out when wanted, and during
the day are put into chests or cupboards, or only rolled up in a corner of the room
(Pilgrimage i., 53).

dered the damsel in her jealousy,[1] and said, "There is no Majesty and there is no Might save in Allah, the Glorious, the Great! What is to be done now?" I considered awhile then, doffing my clothes, dug a hole in the middle of the court-yard, wherein I laid the murdered girl with her jewellery and golden ornaments; and, throwing back the earth on her, replaced the slabs of the marble[2] pavement. After this I made the Ghusl or total ablution,[3] and put on pure clothes; then, taking what money I had left, locked up the house and summoned courage and went to its owner to whom I paid a year's rent, saying, "I am about to join my uncles in Cairo." Presently I set out and, journeying to Egypt, foregathered with my uncles who rejoiced in me, and I found that they had made an end of selling their merchandise. They asked me, "What is the cause of thy coming?"; and I answered "I longed for a sight of you;" but did not let them know that I had any money with me. I abode with them a year, enjoying the pleasures of Cairo and her Nile,[4] and squandering the rest of my money in feasting and carousing till the time drew near for the departure of my uncles, when I fled from them and hid myself. They made enquiries and sought for me, but hearing no tidings they said, "He will have gone back to Damascus." When they departed I came forth from my hiding-place and abode in Cairo three years, until naught remained of my money. Now every year I used to send the rent of the Damascus house to its owner, until at last I had nothing left but enough to pay him for one year's rent and my breast was straitened. So I travelled to Damascus and alighted at the house whose owner, the jeweller, was glad to see me and I found everything locked up as I had left it. I opened the closets and took out my clothes and necessaries and came upon, beneath the carpet-bed whereon I had lain that night with the girl who had been beheaded, a golden necklace set

---

[1] The women of Damascus have always been famed for the sanguinary jealousy with which European story-books and novels credit the "Spanish lady." The men were as celebrated for intolerance and fanaticism, which we first read of in the days of Bertrandon de la Brocquière and which culminated in the massacre of 1860. Yet they are a notoriously timid race and make, physically and morally, the worst of soldiers: we proved that under my late friend Fred. Walpole in the Bashi-Buzuks during the old Crimean war. The men looked very fine fellows and after a month in camp fell off to the condition of old women.

[2] Arab. "Rukhám," properly = alabaster and "Marmar" = marble; but the two are often confounded.

[3] He was ceremonially impure after touching a corpse.

[4] The phrase is perfectly appropriate: Cairo without "her Nile" would be nothing.

with ten gems of passing beauty. I took it up and, cleansing it of the blood, sat gazing upon it and wept awhile. Then I abode in the house two days and on the third I entered the Hammam and changed my clothes. I had no money by me now; so Satan whispered temptation to me that the Decree of Destiny be carried out. Next day I took the jewelled necklace to the bazar and handed it to a broker who made me sit down in the shop of the jeweller, my landlord, and bade me have patience till the market was full,[1] when he carried off the ornament and proclaimed it for sale, privily and without my knowledge. The necklet was priced as worth two thousand dinars, but the broker returned to me and said, "This collar is of copper, a mere counterfeit after the fashion of the Franks[2] and a thousand dirhams have been bidden for it." "Yes," I answered, "I knew it to be copper, as we had it made for a certain person that we might mock her: now my wife hath inherited it and we wish to sell it; so go and take over the thousand dirhams."——And Shahrazad perceived the dawn of day and ceased to say her permitted say.

When it was the Twenty-ninth Night,

She said, It hath reached me, O auspicious King, that the beautiful youth said to the broker, "Take over the thousand dirhams;" and when the broker heard this, he knew that the case was suspicious. So he carried the collar to the Syndic of the bazar, and the Syndic took it to the Governor who was also prefect of police, and said to him falsely enough, "This necklet was stolen from my house, and we have found the thief in traders' dress." So before I was aware of it the watch got round me and, making me their prisoner, carried me before the Governor who questioned me of the collar. I told him the tale I had told to the broker; but he laughed and said, "These words are not true." Then, before I knew what was doing, the guard stripped off my clothes and came down with palm-rods upon my ribs, till for the smart of the stick I confessed, "It was I who stole it;" saying to myself, " 'Tis

---

[1] "The market was hot" say the Hindustanis. This would begin between 7 and 8 a.m.
[2] Arab. Al-Faranj, Europeans generally. It is derived from "Gens Francorum," and dates from Crusading days when the French played the leading part. Hence the Lingua Franca, the Levantine jargon, of which Molière has left such a witty specimen.

better for thee to say, I stole it, than to let them know that its owner was murdered in thy house, for then would they slay thee to avenge her." So they wrote down that I had stolen it and they cut off my hand and scalded the stump in oil,[1] when I swooned away for pain; but they gave me wine to drink and I recovered and, taking up my hand, was going to my fine house, when my landlord said to me, "Inasmuch, O my son, as this hath befallen thee, thou must leave my house and look out for another lodging for thee, since thou art convicted of theft. Thou art a handsome youth, but who will pity thee after this?" "O my master" said I, "bear with me but two days or three, till I find me another place." He answered, "So be it," and went away and left me. I returned to the house where I sat weeping and saying, "How shall I go back to my own people with my hand lopped off and they know not that I am innocent? Perchance even after this Allah may order some matter for me." And I wept with exceeding weeping; grief beset me and I remained in sore trouble for two days; but on the third day my landlord came suddenly in to me, and with him some of the guard and the Syndic of the bazar, who had falsely charged me with stealing the necklet. I went up to them and asked, "What is the matter?" however, they pinioned me without further parley and threw a chain about my neck, saying, "The necklet which was with thee hath proved to be the property of the Wazir of Damascus who is also her Viceroy;" and they added, "It was missing from his house three years ago at the same time as his younger daughter." When I heard these words, my heart sank within me and I said to myself, "Thy life is gone beyond a doubt! By Allah, needs must I tell the Chief my story; and, if he will, let him kill me, and if he please, let him pardon me." So they carried me to the Wazir's house and made me stand between his hands. When he saw me, he glanced at me out of the corner of his eye and said to those present, "Why did ye lop off his hand? This man is unfortunate, and there is no fault in him; indeed ye have wronged him in cutting off his hand." When I heard this, I took heart and, my soul presaging good, I said to him, "By Allah, O my lord, I am no thief; but they calumniated me with a vile calumny, and they scourged me midmost the market, bidding me confess till, for the pain of the rods, I lied against myself and confessed the theft, albeit I am altogether

---

[1] A process familiar to European surgery of the same date.

innocent of it." "Fear not," quoth the Viceroy, "no harm shall come to thee." Then he ordered the Syndic of the bazar to be imprisoned and said to him, "Give this man the blood-money for his hand; and, if thou delay I will hang thee and seize all thy property." Moreover he called to his guards who took him and dragged him away, leaving me with the Chief. Then they loosed by his command the chain from my neck and unbound my arms; and he looked at me, and said, "O my son, be true with me, and tell me how this necklace came to thee." And he repeated these verses:—

"Truth best befits thee, albeit truth * Shall bring thee to burn on the threatened fire."

"By Allah, O my lord," answered I, "I will tell thee nothing but the truth." Then I related to him all that had passed between me and the first lady, and how she had brought me the second and had slain her out of jealousy, and I detailed for him the tale to its full. When he heard my story, he shook his head and struck his right hand upon the left,[1] and putting his kerchief over his face wept awhile and then repeated:—

"I see the woes of the world abound, * And worldings sick with spleen and teen;
There's One who the meeting of two shall part, * And who part not are few and far between!"

Then he turned to me and said, "Know, O my son, that the elder damsel who first came to thee was my daughter whom I used to keep closely guarded. When she grew up, I sent her to Cairo and married her to her cousin, my brother's son. After a while he died and she came back: but she had learnt wantonness and ungraciousness from the people of Cairo;[2] so she visited thee four

---

[1] In sign of disappointment, regret, vexation; a gesture still common amongst Moslems and corresponding in significance to a certain extent with our stamping, wringing the hands and so forth. It is not mentioned in the Koran where, however, we find "biting fingers' ends out of wrath" against a man (chapt. iii.).

[2] This is no unmerited scandal. The Cairenes, especially the feminine half (for reasons elsewhere given), have always been held exceedingly debauched. Even the modest Lane gives a "shocking" story of a woman enjoying her lover under the nose of her husband and confining the latter in a madhouse (chapt. xiii.). With civilisation, which objects to the good old remedy, the sword, they become worse: and the Kazi's court is crowded with would-be divorcees. Under English rule the evil has reached its

times and at last brought her younger sister. Now they were
sisters-german and much attached to each other; and, when that
adventure happened to the elder, she disclosed her secret to her
sister who desired to go out with her. So she asked thy leave and
carried her to thee; after which she returned alone and, finding
her weeping, I questioned her of her sister, but she said, 'I know
nothing of her.' However, she presently told her mother privily
of what had happened and how she had cut off her sister's head
and her mother told me. Then she ceased not to weep and say,
'By Allah! I shall cry for her till I die.' Nor did she give over
mourning till her heart broke and she died; and things fell out
after that fashion. See then, O my son, what hath come to pass;
and now I desire thee not to thwart me in what I am about to
offer thee, and it is that I purpose to marry thee to my youngest
daughter; for she is a virgin and born of another mother;[1] and I
will take no dower of thee but, on the contrary, will appoint thee
an allowance, and thou shalt abide with me in my house in the
stead of my son." "So be it," I answered, "and how could I
hope for such good fortune?" Then he sent at once for the Kazi
and witnesses, and let write my marriage-contract with his
daughter and I went in to her. Moreover, he got me from the
Syndic of the bazar a large sum of money and I became in high
favour with him. During this year news came to me that my
father was dead and the Wazir despatched a courier, with letters
bearing the royal sign-manual, to fetch me the money which my
father had left behind him, and now I am living in all the solace

---

acme because it goes unpunished: in the avenues of the new Isma'iliyah Quarter,
inhabited by Europeans, women, even young women, will threaten to expose their persons unless they receive "bakhshísh." It was the same in Sind when husbands were
assured that they would be hanged for cutting down adulterous wives: at once after its
conquest the women broke loose; and in 1843–50, if a young officer sent to the bazar
for a girl, half-a-dozen would troop to his quarters. Indeed more than once the professional prostitutes threatened to memorialise Sir Charles Napier because the "modest
women," the "ladies" were taking the bread out of their mouths. The same was the
case at Kabul (Caboul) of Afghanistan in the old war of 1840; and here the women had
more excuse, the husbands being notable sodomites as the song has it:—

> The worth of slit the Afghan knows;
> The worth of hole the Kábul-man.

[1] So that he might not have to do with three sisters-german. Moreover amongst
Moslems a girl's conduct is presaged by that of her mother; and if one sister go wrong,
the other is expected to follow suit. Practically the rule applies everywhere, "like mother
like daughter."

of life. Such was the manner of the cutting off my right hand."
I marvelled at his story (continued the Jew), and I abode with
him three days after which he gave me much wealth, and I set out
and travelled Eastward till I reached this your city and the
sojourn suited me right well; so I took up my abode here and
there befel me what thou knowest with the Hunchback. Thereupon the King of China shook his head[1] and said, "This story of
thine is not stranger and more wondrous and marvellous and
delectable than the tale of the Hunchback; and so needs must I
hang the whole number of you. However there yet remains the
Tailor who is the head of all the offence;" and he added, "O
Tailor, if thou canst tell me any thing more wonderful than the
story of the Hunchback, I will pardon you all your offences."
Thereupon the man came forward and began to tell the

Tale of the Tailor.

KNOW, O King of the age, that most marvellous was that which
befel me but yesterday, before I foregathered with the Hunchback. It so chanced that in the early day I was at the marriage-
feast of one of my companions, who had gotten together in his
house some twenty of the handicraftsmen of this city, amongst
them tailors and silk-spinners and carpenters and others of the
same kidney. As soon as the sun had risen, they set food[2] before
us that we might eat when behold, the master of the house entered, and with him a foreign youth and a well-favoured of the
people of Baghdad, wearing clothes as handsome as handsome
could be; and he was of right comely presence save that he was
lame of one leg. He came and saluted us and we stood up to receive him; but when he was about to sit down he espied amongst
us a certain man which was a Barber; whereupon he refused to be
seated and would have gone away. But we stopped him and our

---

[1] In sign of dissent; as opposed to nodding the head which signifies assent. These
are two items, apparently instinctive and universal, of man's gesture-language which has
been so highly cultivated by sundry North American tribes and by the surdo-mute estab-
lishments of Europe.

[2] This "Futur" is the real "breakfast" of the East, the "Chhoti házri" (petit
déjeûner) of India, a bit of bread, a cup of coffee or tea and a pipe on rising. In the
text, however, it is a ceremonious affair.

host also stayed him, making oath that he should not leave us and asked him, "What is the reason of thy coming in and going out again at once?"; whereto he answered, "By Allah, O my lord, do not hinder me; for the cause of my turning back is yon Barber of bad omen,[1] yon black o' face, yon ne'er-do-well!" When the house-master heard these words he marvelled with extreme marvel and said, "How cometh this young man, who haileth from Baghdad, to be so troubled and perplexed about this Barber?" Then we looked at the stranger and said, "Explain the cause of thine anger against the Barber." "O fair company," quoth the youth, "there befel me a strange adventure with this Barber in Baghdad (which is my native city); he was the cause of the breaking of my leg and of my lameness, and I have sworn never to sit in the same place with him, nor even tarry in any town where he happens to abide; and I have bidden adieu to Baghdad and travelled far from it and came to stay in this your city; yet I have hardly passed one night before I meet him again. But not another day shall go by ere I fare forth from here." Said we to him, "Allah upon thee, tell us the tale;" and the youth replied (the Barber changing colour from brown to yellow as he spoke): —Know, O fair company, that my father was one of the chief merchants of Baghdad, and Almighty Allah had blessed him with no son but myself. When I grew up and reached man's estate, my father was received into the mercy of Allah (whose Name be exalted!) and left me money and eunuchs, servants and slaves; and I used to dress well and diet well. Now Allah had made me a hater of women-kind and one day, as I was walking along a street in Baghdad, a party of females met me face to face in the footway; so I fled from them and, entering an alley which was no thoroughfare, sat down upon a stone-bench at its other end. I had not sat there long before the latticed window of one of the houses opposite was thrown open, and there appeared at it a young lady, as she were the full moon at its fullest; never in my life saw I her like; and she began to water some flowers on the window-sill.[2] She turned right and left and, seeing me watching her, shut the window and went away. Thereupon fire was sud-

---

[1] Arab. "Nahs," a word of many meanings; a sinister aspect of the stars (as in Hebr. and Aram.) or, adjectively, sinister, of ill-omen. Vulgarly it is used as the reverse of nice and corresponds, after a fashion, with our "nasty."

[2] "Window-gardening," new in England, is an old practice in the East.

denly enkindled in my heart; my mind was possessed with her
and my woman-hate turned to woman-love. I continued sitting
there, lost to the world, till sunset when lo! the Kazi of the city
came riding by with his slaves before him and his eunuchs behind
him, and dismounting entered the house in which the damsel had
appeared. By this I knew that he was her father; so I went home
sorrowful and cast myself upon my carpet-bed in grief. Then
my handmaids flocked in and sat about me, unknowing what
ailed me; but I addressed no speech to them, and they wept and
wailed over me. Presently in came an old woman who looked at
me and saw with a glance what was the matter with me: so she
sat down by my head and spoke me fair, saying, "O my son, tell
me all about it and I will be the means of thy union with her."[1]
So I related to her what had happened and she answered, "O my
son, this one is the daughter of the Kazi of Baghdad who keepeth
her in the closest seclusion; and the window where thou sawest
her is her floor, whilst her father occupies the large saloon in the
lower story. She is often there alone and I am wont to visit at the
house; so thou shalt not win to her save through me. Now set
thy wits to work and be of good cheer." With these words she
went away and I took heart at what she said and my people rejoiced that day, seeing me rise in the morning safe and sound. By
and by the old woman returned looking chopfallen,[2] and said, "O
my son, do not ask me how I fared with her! When I told her
that, she cried at me, 'If thou hold not thy peace, O hag of ill-
omen, and leave not such talk, I will entreat thee as thou deservest and do thee die by the foulest of deaths.' But needs must I
have at her a second time."[3] When I heard this it added ailment
to my ailment and the neighbours visited me and judged that I
was not long for this world; but after some days, the old woman
came to me and, putting her mouth close to my ear, whispered,
"O my son; I claim from thee the gift of good news." With this
my soul returned to me and I said, "Whatever thou wilt shall be
thine." Thereupon she began, "Yesterday I went to the young
lady who, seeing me broken in spirit and shedding tears from

---

[1] Her pimping instinct at once revealed the case to her.
[2] The usual "pander-dodge" to get more money.
[3] The writer means that the old woman's account was all false, to increase apparent
difficulties and *pour se faire valoir*.

reddened eyes, asked me, 'O naunty[1] mine, what ails thee, that
I see thy breast so straitened?'; and I answered her, weeping bitterly, 'O my lady, I am just come from the house of a youth who
loves thee and who is about to die for sake of thee!' Quoth she
(and her heart was softened), 'And who is this youth of whom
thou speakest?'; and quoth I, 'He is to me as a son and the fruit
of my vitals. He saw thee, some days ago, at the window water-
ing thy flowers and espying thy face and wrists he fell in love at
first sight. I let him know what happened to me the last time I
was with thee, whereupon his ailment increased, he took to the
pillow and he is naught now but a dead man, and no doubt whatever of it.' At this she turned pale and asked, 'All this for my
sake?'; and I answered, 'Ay, by Allah![2] what wouldst thou have
me do?' Said she, 'Go back to him and greet him for me and tell
him that I am twice more heartsick than he is. And on Friday,
before the hour of public prayer, bid him here to the house, and I
will come down and open the door for him. Then I will carry
him up to my chamber and foregather with him for a while, and
let him depart before my father return from the Mosque.' "
When I heard the old woman's words, all my sickness suddenly
fell from me, my anguish ceased and my heart was comforted; I
took off what clothes were on me and gave them to her and, as
she turned to go, she said, "Keep a good heart!" "I have not a jot
of sorrow left," I replied. My household and intimates rejoiced
in my recovery and I abode thus till Friday, when behold, the
old woman came in and asked me how I did, to which I answered
that I was well and in good case. Then I donned my clothes and
perfumed myself and sat down to await the congregation going
in to prayers, that I might betake myself to her. But the old
woman said to me, "Thou hast time and to spare: so thou wouldst
do well to go to the Hammam and have thy hair shaven off (especially after thy ailment), so as not to show traces of sickness."

---

[1] Arab. "Yá Khálati" = mother's sister; a familiar address to the old, as uncle or
nuncle (father's brother) to a man. The Arabs also hold that as a girl resembles her
mother so a boy follows his uncle (mother's brother): hence the address "Ya tayyib
al-Khál!" = O thou nephew of a good uncle. I have noted that physically this is often
fact.

[2] "Ay w' Alláhi," contracted popularly to Aywa, a word in every Moslem mouth and
shunned by Christians because against orders Hebrew and Christian. The better educated
Turks now eschew that eternal reference to Allah which appears in The Nights and
which is still the custom of the vulgar throughout the world of Al-Islam.

"This were the best way," answered I, "I have just now bathed in hot water, but I will have my head shaved." Then I said to my page, "Go to the bazar and bring me a barber, a discreet fellow and one not inclined to meddling or impertinent curiosity or likely to split my head with his excessive talk."[1] The boy went out at once and brought back with him this wretched old man, this Shaykh of ill-omen. When he came in he saluted me and I returned his salutation; then quoth he, "Of a truth I see thee thin of body;" and quoth I, "I have been ailing." He continued, "Allah drive far away from thee thy woe and thy sorrow and thy trouble and thy distress." "Allah grant thy prayer!" said I. He pursued, "All gladness to thee, O my master, for indeed recovery is come to thee. Dost thou wish to be polled or to be blooded? Indeed it was a tradition of Ibn Abbas[2] (Allah accept of him!) that the Apostle said, 'Whoso cutteth his hair on a Friday, the Lord shall avert from him threescore and ten calamities;' and again is related of him also that he said, 'Cupping on a Friday keepeth from loss of sight and a host of diseases.'" "Leave this talk," I cried; "come, shave me my head at once for I can't stand it." So he rose and put forth his hand in most leisurely way and took out a kerchief and unfolded it, and lo! it contained an astrolabe[3] with seven parallel plates mounted in silver. Then he went to the middle of the court and raised head and instrument towards the sun's rays and looked for a long while. When this was over, he came back and said to me, "Know that there have elapsed of this our day, which be Friday, and this Friday be the tenth of the month Safar in the six hundred and fifty-third year since the Hegira or Flight of the Apostle (on whom be the bestest of blessings and peace!) and the seven thousand three hundred and twentieth year of the era of Alexander, eight degrees and six minutes. Furthermore the ascendant of this our day is, according

---

[1] The "Muzayyin" or barber in the East brings his basin and budget under his arm: he is not content only to shave, he must scrape the forehead, trim the eyebrows, pass the blade lightly over the nose and correct the upper and lower lines of the mustachios, opening the central parting and so forth. He is not a whit less a tattler and a scandalmonger than the old Roman tonsor or Figaro his *confrère* in Southern Europe. The whole scene of the Barber is admirable, an excellent specimen of Arab humour and not over-caricatured. We all have met him.

[2] Abdullah ibn Abbas was a cousin and a companion of the Apostle; also a well-known Commentator on the Koran and conserver of the traditions of Mohammed.

[3] I have noticed the antiquity of this father of our sextant, a fragment of which was found in the Palace of Sennacherib. More concerning the "Arstable" (as Chaucer calls it) is given in my "Camoens: his Life and his Lusiads," p. 381.

to the exactest science of computation, the planet Mars; and it so happeneth that Mercury is in conjunction with him, denoting an auspicious moment for hair-cutting; and this also maketh manifest to me that thou desirest union with a certain person and that your intercourse will not be propitious. But after this there occurreth a sign respecting a matter which will befal thee and whereof I will not speak." "O thou," cried I, "by Allah, thou weariest me and scatterest my wits and thy forecast is other than good; I sent for thee to poll my head and naught else: so up and shave me and prolong not thy speech." "By Allah," replied he, "if thou but knew what is about to befal thee, thou wouldst do nothing this day, and I counsel thee to act as I tell thee by computation of the constellations." "By Allah," said I, "never did I see a barber who excelled in judicial astrology save thyself: but I think and I know that thou art most prodigal of frivolous talk. I sent for thee only to shave my head, but thou comest and pesterest me with this sorry prattle." "What more wouldst thou have?" replied he. "Allah hath bounteously bestowed on thee a Barber who is an astrologer, one learned in alchemy and white magic;[1] syntax, grammar, and lexicology; the arts of logic, rhetoric and elocution; mathematics, arithmetic and algebra; astronomy, astromancy and geometry; theology, the Traditions of the Apostle and the Commentaries on the Koran. Furthermore, I have read books galore and digested them and have had experience of affairs and comprehended them. In short I have learned the theorick and the practick of all the arts and sciences; I know everything of them by rote and I am a past master *in totâ re scibili.* Thy father loved me for my lack of officiousness, argal, to serve thee is a religious duty incumbent on me. I am no busy-body as thou seemest to suppose, and on this account I am known as The Silent Man, also, The Modest Man. Wherefore it behoveth thee to render thanks to Allah Almighty and not cross me, for I am a true counsellor to thee and benevolently minded towards thee. Would that I were in thy service a whole year that thou mightest

---

[1] Arab. "Simiyá" to rhyme with Kímiyá (alchemy proper). It is a subordinate branch of the Ilm al-Ruháni which I would translate "Spiritualism," and which is divided into two great branches, "Ilwí or Rahmáni" (the high or related to the Deity) and Siflí or Shaytáni (low, Satanic). To the latter belongs Al-Sahr, magic or the black art proper, gramarye, egromancy, while Al-Simiyá is white magic, electro-biology, a kind of natural and deceptive magic, in which drugs and perfumes exercise an important action. One of its principal branches is the Darb al-Mandal or magic mirror, of which more in a future page. See Boccaccio's Day x. Novel 5.

do me justice; and I would ask thee no wage for all this." When I heard his flow of words, I said to him, "Doubtless thou wilt be my death this day!"——And Shahrazad perceived the dawn of day and ceased saying her permitted say.

When it was the Thirtieth Night,

She said, It hath reached me, O auspicious King, that the young man said to the Barber, "Thou certainly will be the death of me this very day!" "O master mine," replied he, "I am he, The Silent Man hight, by reason of the fewness of my words, to distinguish me from my six brothers. For the eldest is called Al-Bakbúk, the prattler; the second Al-Haddár, the babbler; the third Al-Fakík, the gabbler; the fourth, his name is Al-Kuz al-aswáni, the long-necked Gugglet, from his eternal chattering; the fifth is Al-Nashshár, the tattler and tale-teller; the sixth Shakáshik, or many-clamours; and the seventh is famous as Al-Sámit, The Silent Man, and this is my noble self!" Whilst he redoubled his talk, I thought my gall-bladder would have burst; so I said to the servant, "Give him a quarter-dinar and dismiss him and let him go from me in the name of God who made him. I won't have my head shaved to-day." "What words be these, O my lord?" cried he. "By Allah! I will accept no hire of thee till I have served thee and have ministered to thy wants; and I care not if I never take money of thee. If thou know not my quality, I know thine; and I owe thy father, honest man, on whom Allah Almighty have mercy! many a kindness, for he was a liberal soul and a generous. By Allah, he sent for me one day, as it were this blessed day, and I went in to him and found a party of his intimates about him. Quoth he to me, 'Let me blood;' so I pulled out my astrolabe and, taking the sun's altitude for him, I ascertained that the ascendant was inauspicious and the hour unfavourable for blooding. I told him of this, and he did according to my bidding and awaited a better opportunity. So I made these lines in honour of him:—

I went to my patron some blood to let him, * But found that the moment was
    far from good:
So I sat and I talked of all strangenesses, * And with jests and jokes his good
    will I wooed:
They pleased him and cried he, 'O man of wit, * Thou hast proved thee per-
    fect in merry mood!'

Quoth I, 'O thou Lord of men, save thou * Lend me art and wisdom I'm fou
  and wood:
In thee gather grace, boon, bounty, suavity; * And I guerdon the world with
  lore, science and gravity.'

Thy father was delighted and cried out to the servant, 'Give him
an hundred and three gold pieces with a robe of honour!' The
man obeyed his orders, and I awaited an auspicious moment,
when I blooded him; and he did not baulk me; nay he thanked me
and I was also thanked and praised by all present. When the
blood-letting was over I had no power to keep silence and asked
him, 'By Allah, O my lord, what made thee say to the servant,
Give him an hundred and *three* dinars?'; and he answered, 'One
dinar was for the astrological observation, another for thy pleasant conversation, the third for the phlebotomisation, and the remaining hundred and the dress were for thy verses in my com-
mendation.' " "May Allah show small mercy to my father,"
exclaimed I, "for knowing the like of thee." He laughed and
ejaculated, "There is no god but *the* God and Mohammed is the
Apostle of God! Glory to Him that changeth and is changed not!
I took thee for a man of sense, but I see thou babblest and dotest
for illness. Allah hath said in the Blessed Book,[1] 'Paradise is prepared for the goodly who bridle their anger and forgive men,' and
so forth; and in any case thou art excused. Yet I cannot conceive
the cause of thy hurry and flurry; and thou must know that thy
father and thy grandfather did nothing without consulting me,
and indeed it hath been said truly enough, 'Let the adviser be
prized'; and, 'There is no vice in advice'; and it is also said in
certain saws, 'Whoso hath no counsellor elder than he, will never
himself an elder be';[2] and the poet says:—

Whatever needful thing thou undertake, * Consult th' experienced and contraire him not!

And indeed thou shalt never find a man better versed in affairs
than I, and I am here standing on my feet to serve thee. I am
not vexed with thee: why shouldest thou be vexed with me? But
whatever happen I will bear patiently with thee in memory of the
much kindness thy father shewed me." "By Allah," cried I, "O

---

[1] Chap. iii., 128. See Sale (in loco) for the noble application of this text by the Imam
Hasan, son of the Caliph Ali.

[2] These proverbs at once remind us of our old friend Sancho Panza and are equally
true to nature in the mouth of the Arab and of the Spaniard.

thou with tongue long as the tail of a jackass, thou persistest in pestering me with thy prate and thou becomest more longsome in thy long speeches, when all I want of thee is to shave my head and wend thy way!" Then he lathered my head saying, "I per-ceive thou art vexed with me, but I will not take it ill of thee, for thy wit is weak and thou art but a laddy: it was only yesterday I used to take thee on my shoulder[1] and carry thee to school." "O my brother," said I, "for Allah's sake do what I want and go thy gait!" And I rent my garments.[2] When he saw me do this he took the razor and fell to sharpening it and gave not over strop-ping it until my senses were well-nigh leaving me. Then he came up to me and shaved part of my head; then he held his hand and then he said, "O my lord, haste is Satan's gait whilst patience is of Allah the Compassionate. But thou, O my master, I ken thou knowest not my rank; for verily this hand alighteth upon the heads of Kings and Emirs and Wazirs, and sages and doctors learned in the law, and the poet said of one like me:—

All crafts are like necklaces strung on a string, * But this Barber's the union
     pearl of the band:
High over all craftsmen he ranketh, and why? * The heads of the Kings are
     under his hand!"[3]

---

[1] Our nurses always carry in the arms: Arabs place the children astraddle upon the hip and when older on the shoulder.

[2] Eastern clothes allow this biblical display of sorrow and vexation, which with our European garb would look absurd: we must satisfy ourselves with maltreating our hats.

[3] Koran xlviii., 8. It may be observed that according to the Ahádis (sayings of the Prophet) and the Sunnat (sayings and doings of Mahommed), all the hair should be allowed to grow or the whole head be clean shaven. Hence the "Shúshah," or topknot, supposed to be left as a handle for drawing the wearer into Paradise, and the Zulf, or side-locks, somewhat like the ringlets of the Polish Jews, are both vain "Bida'at," or innovations, and therefore technically termed "Makrúh," a practice not laudable, neither "Halál" (perfectly lawful) nor "Harám" (forbidden by the law). When boys are first shaved, generally in the second or third year, a tuft is left on the crown and another over the forehead; but this is not the fashion amongst adults. Abu Hanifah, if I am rightly informed, wrote a treatise on the Shushah or long lock growing from the Násiyah (head-poll) which is also a precaution lest the decapitated Moslem's mouth be defiled by an impure hand; and thus it would resemble the chivalry-lock by which the Redskin brave (and even the "cowboy" of better times) facilitated the removal of his own scalp. Possibly the Turks had learned the practice from the Chinese and intro-duced it into Baghdad (Pilgrimage i., 240). The Badawi plait their locks in Kurún (horns) or Jadáil (ringlets) which are undone only to be washed with the water of the she-camel. The wild Sherifs wear Haffah, long elf-locks hanging down both sides of the throat, and shaved away about a finger's breadth round the forehead and behind the neck (Pilgrimage iii., 35-36). I have elsewhere noted the accroche-cœurs, the "idiot-fringe," etc.

Then said I, "Do leave off talking about what concerneth thee
not: indeed thou hast straitened my breast and distracted my
mind." Quoth he, "Meseems thou art a hasty man;" and quoth
I, "Yes! yes! yes!" and he, "I rede thee practise restraint of self,
for haste is Satan's pelf which bequeatheth only repentance and
ban and bane, and He (upon whom be blessings and peace!) hath
said, 'The best of works is that wherein deliberation lurks;' but I,
by Allah! have some doubt about thine affair; and so I should
like thee to let me know what it is thou art in such haste to do;
for I fear me it is other than good." Then he continued, "It wanteth three hours yet to prayer-time; but I do not wish to be in
doubt upon this matter; nay, I must know the moment exactly,
for truly, 'A guess shot in times of doubt, oft brings harm about;'
especially in the like of me, a superior person whose merits are
famous amongst mankind at large; and it doth not befit me to
talk at random, as do the common sort of astrologers." So saying,
he threw down the razor and taking up the astrolabe, went forth
under the sun and stood there a long time; after which he returned and counting on his fingers said to me, "There remain still
to prayer-time three full hours and complete, neither more nor
yet less, according to the most learned astronomicals and the
wisest makers of almanacks." "Allah upon thee," cried I, "hold
thy tongue with me, for thou breakest my liver in pieces." So he
took the razor and, after sharpening it as before and shaving other
two hairs of my head, he again held his hand and said, "I am concerned about thy hastiness and indeed thou wouldst do well to
let me into the cause of it; 't were the better for thee, as thou
knowest that neither thy father nor thy grandfather ever did a
single thing save by my advice." When I saw that there was no
escape from him I said to myself, "The time for prayer draws
near and I wish to go to her before the folk come out of the
mosque. If I am delayed much longer, I know not how to come
at her." Then said I aloud, "Be quick and stint this talk and im-
pertinence, for I have to go to a party at the house of some of my
intimates." When he heard me speak of the party, he said, "This
thy day is a blessed day for me! In very sooth it was but yesterday I invited a company of my friends and I have forgotten to
provide anything for them to eat. This very moment I was
thinking of it: Alas, how I shall be disgraced in their eyes!" "Be
not distressed about this matter," answered I; "have I not told
thee that I am bidden to an entertainment this day? So every-

thing in my house, eatable and drinkable, shall be thine, if thou wilt only get through thy work and make haste to shave my head." He replied, "Allah requite thee with good! Specify to me what is in thy house for my guests that I may be ware of it." Quoth I, "Five dishes of meat and ten chickens with reddened breasts[1] and a roasted lamb." "Set them before me," quoth he, "that I may see them." So I told my people to buy, borrow or steal them and bring them in anywise, and had all this set before him. When he saw it he cried, "The wine is wanting," and I replied, "I have a flagon or two of good old grape-juice in the house," and he said, "Have it brought out!" So I sent for it and he exclaimed, "Allah bless thee for a generous disposition! But there are still the essences and perfumes." So I bade them set before him a box containing Nadd,[2] the best of compound perfumes, together with fine lign-aloes, ambergris and musk unmixed, the whole worth fifty dinars. Now the time waxed strait and my heart straitened with it; so I said to him, "Take it all and finish shaving my head by the life of Mohammed (whom Allah bless and keep!)." "By Allah," said he, "I will not take it till I see all that is in it." So I bade the page open the box and the Barber laid down the astrolabe, leaving the greater part of my head unpolled; and, sitting on the ground, turned over the scents and incense and aloes-wood and essences till I was well-nigh distraught. Then he took the razor and coming up to me shaved off some few hairs and repeated these lines:—

"The boy like his father shall surely show, * As the tree from its parent root
    shall grow."[3]

Then said he, "By Allah, O my son, I know not whether to thank thee or thy father; for my entertainment this day is all due to thy bounty and beneficence; and, although none of my company be worthy of it, yet I have a set of honourable men, to wit Zantút the bath-keeper and Salí'a the corn-chandler; and Sílat the bean-

---

[1] Meats are rarely coloured in modern days; but Persian cooks are great adepts in staining rice for the "Puláo" (which we call after its Turkish corruption "pilaff"): it sometimes appears in rainbow-colours, red, yellow and blue; and in India is covered with gold and silver leaf. Europe retains the practice in tinting Pasch (Easter) eggs, the survival of the mundane ovum which was hatched at Easter-tide; and they are dyed red in allusion to the Blood of Redemption.

[2] As I have noticed, this is a mixture.

[3] We say:—'Tis rare the father in the son we see:
    He sometimes rises in the third degree.

seller; and Akrashah the greengrocer; and Humayd the scavenger; and Sa'íd the camel-man; and Suwayd the porter; and Abu Makárish the bathman;[1] and Kasím the watchman; and Karím the groom. There is not among the whole of them a bore or a bully in his cups; nor a meddler nor a miser of his money, and each and every hath some dance which he danceth and some of his own couplets which he caroleth; and the best of them is that, like thy servant, thy slave here, they know not what much talking is nor what forwardness means. The bath-keeper sings to the tom-tom[2] a song which enchants; and he stands up and dances and chants,

> 'I am going, O mammy, to fill up my pot.'

As for the corn-chandler he brings more skill to it than any; he dances and sings,

> 'O Keener,[3] O sweetheart, thou fallest not short'

and he leaves no one's vitals sound for laughing at him. But the scavenger sings so that the birds stop to listen to him and dances and sings,

> 'News my wife wots is not locked in a box!'[4]

And he hath privilege, for 'tis a shrewd rogue and a witty;[5] and speaking of his excellence I am wont to say,

---

1 Arab. "Ballán" *i.e.* the body-servant: "Ballánah" is a tire-woman.

2 Arab. "Darabukkah" a drum made of wood or earthen-ware (Lane, M. E., xviii.), and used by all in Egypt.

3 Arab. "Naihah" more generally "Naddábah" Lat. præfica or carina, a hired mourner, the Irish "Keener" at the conclamatio or coronach, where the Hullabaloo, Hulululu or Ululoo showed the survivors' sorrow.

4 These doggrels, which are like our street melodies, are now forgotten and others have taken their place. A few years ago one often heard, "Dus ya lallí" (Tread, O my joy) and "Názil il'al-Ganínah" (Down into the garden) and these in due turn became obsolete. Lane (M. E. chapt. xviii.) gives the former *e.g.*

> Tread, O my joy! Tread, O my joy!
> Love of my love brings sore annoy,

A chorus to such stanzas as:—

> Alexandrian damsels rare!   * Daintily o'er the floor ye fare:
> Your lips are sweet, are sugar-sweet, * And purfled Cashmere shawls ye wear!

It may be noted that "humming" is not a favourite practice with Moslems; if one of the company begin, another will say, "Go to the Kahwah" (the coffee-house, the proper music-hall) "and sing there!" I have elsewhere observed their dislike to Al-sifr or whistling.

5 Arab. Khalí'a = worn out, crafty, an outlaw; used like Span. "Perdido."

My life for the scavenger! right well I love him, * Like a waving bough he is
　　sweet to my sight:
Fate joined us one night, when to him quoth I * (The while I grew weak and
　　love gained more might)
'Thy love burns my heart!' 'And no wonder,' quoth he * 'When the drawer
　　of dung turns a stoker wight.'[1]

And indeed each is perfect in whatso can charm the wit with joy
and jollity;" adding presently, "But hearing is not seeing; and
indeed if thou make up thy mind to join us and put off going to
thy friends, 'twill be better for us and for thee. The traces of illness are yet upon thee and haply thou art going among folk who
be mighty talkers, men who commune together of what concerneth them not; or there may be amongst them some forward fellow
who will split thy head, and thou half thy size from sickness."
"This shall be for some other day," answered I, and laughed with
heart angered: "finish thy work and go, in Allah Almighty's
guard, to thy friends, for they will be expecting thy coming."
"O my lord," replied he, "I seek only to introduce thee to these
fellows of infinite mirth, the sons of men of worth, amongst whom
there is neither procacity nor dicacity nor loquacity; for never,
since I grew to years of discretion, could I endure to consort with
one who asketh questions concerning what concerneth him not,
nor have I ever frequented any save those who are, like myself,
men of few words. In sooth if thou were to company with them
or even to see them once, thou wouldst forsake all thy intimates."
"Allah fulfil thy joyance with them," said I, "needs must I come
amongst them some day or other." But he said, "Would it were
this very day, for I had set my heart upon thy making one of us;
yet if thou must go to thy friends to-day, I will take these good
things, wherewith thou hast honoured and favoured me, to my
guests and leave them to eat and drink and not wait for me;
whilst I will return to thee in haste and accompany thee to thy
little party; for there is no ceremony between me and my intimates to prevent my leaving them. Fear not, I will soon be back
with thee and wend with thee whithersoever thou wendest.
There is no Majesty and there is no Might save in Allah, the
Glorious, the Great!" I shouted, "Go thou to thy friends and
make merry with them; and *do* let me go to mine and be with

---

[1] "Zabbál" is the scavenger, lit. a dung-drawer, especially for the use of the Hammam
which is heated with the droppings of animals. "Wakkád" (stoker) is the servant who
turns the fire. The verses are mere nonsense to suit the Barber's humour.

them this day, for they expect me." But the Barber cried, "I will not let thee go alone;" and I replied, "The truth is none can enter where I am going save myself." He rejoined, "I suspect that to-day thou art for an assignation with some woman, else thou hadst taken me with thee; yet am I the right man to take, one who could aid thee to the end thou wishest. But I fear me thou art running after strange women and thou wilt lose thy life; for in this our city of Baghdad one cannot do any thing in this line, especially on a day like Friday: our Governor is an angry man and a mighty sharp blade." "Shame on thee, thou wicked, bad, old man!" cried I, "Be off! what words are these thou givest me?" "O cold of wit,"[1] cried he, "thou sayest to me what is not true and thou hidest thy mind from me, but I know the whole busi-ness for certain and I seek only to help thee this day with my best endeavour." I was fearful lest my people or my neighbours should hear the Barber's talk, so I kept silence for a long time whilst he finished shaving my head; by which time the hour of prayer was come and the Khutbah, or sermon, was about to follow. When he had done, I said to him, "Go to thy friends with their meat and drink, and I will await thy return. Then we will fare together." In this way I hoped to pour oil on troubled waters and to trick the accursed loon, so haply I might get quit of him; but he said, "Thou art cozening me and thou wouldst go alone to thy appointment and cast thyself into jeopardy, whence there will be no escape for thee. Now by Allah! and again by Allah! do not go till I return, that I may accompany thee and watch the issue of thine affair." "So be it," I replied, "do not be long absent." Then he took all the meat and drink I had given him and the rest of it and went out of my house; but the accursed carle gave it in charge of a porter to carry to his home but hid himself in one of the alleys. As for me I rose on the instant, for the Muezzins had already called the Salám of Friday, the saluta-tion to the Apostle;[2] and I dressed in haste and went out alone

---

[1] Arab. "Yá bárid" = O fool.

[2] This form of blessing is chanted from the Minaret about half-an-hour before midday, when the worshippers take their places in the mosque. At noon there is the usual Azán or prayer-call, and each man performs a two-bow, in honour of the mosque and its gathering, as it were. The Prophet is then blessed and a second Salám is called from the raised ambo or platform ("dikkah") by the divines who repeat the midday-call. Then an Imam recites the first Khutbah, or sermon "of praise"; and the congregation worships in silence. This is followed by the second exhortation "of Wa'az," dispensing

and, hurrying to the street, took my stand by the house wherein I had seen the young lady. I found the old woman on guard at the door awaiting me, and went up with her to the upper story, the damsel's apartment. Hardly had I reached it when behold, the master of the house returned from prayers and entering the great saloon, closed the door. I looked down from the window and saw this Barber (Allah's curse upon him!) sitting over against the door and said, "How did this devil find me out?" At this very moment, as Allah had decreed it for rending my veil of secrecy, it so happened that a handmaid of the house-master committed some offence for which he beat her. She shrieked out and his slave ran in to intercede for her, whereupon the Kazi beat him to boot, and he also roared out. The damned Barber fancied that it was I who was being beaten; so he also fell to shouting and tore his garments and scattered dust on his head and kept on shrieking and crying "Help! Help!" So the people came round about him and he went on yelling, "My master is being murdered in the Kazi's house!" Then he ran clamouring to my place with the folk after him, and told my people and servants and slaves; and, before I knew what was doing, up they came tearing their clothes and letting loose their hair[1] and shouting, "Alas, our master!"; and this Barber leading the rout with his clothes rent and in sorriest plight; and he also shouting like a madman and saying, "Alas for our murdered master!" And they all made an assault upon the house in which I was. The Kazi, hearing the yells and the uproar at his door, said to one of his servants, "See what is the matter"; and the man went forth and returned and said, "O my master, at the gate there are more than ten thousand souls what with men and women, and all crying out, 'Alas for our murdered master!'; and they keep pointing to our house." When the Kazi heard this, the matter seemed serious and he waxed wroth; so he rose and opening the door saw a great crowd of people; whereat he was astounded and said, "O folk! what is

---

the words of wisdom. The Imam now stands up before the Mihráb (prayer niche) and recites the Ikámah which is the common Azan with one only difference: after "Hie ye to salvation" it adds "Come is the time of supplication"; whence the name, "causing" (prayer) "to stand" (i.e., to begin). Hereupon the worshippers recite the Farz or Koran-commanded noon-prayer of Friday; and the unco' guid add a host of superogatories. Those who would study the subject may consult Lane (M. E. chapt. iii. and its abstract in his "Arabian Nights," I, p. 430, or note 69 to chapt. v.).

[1] i.e., the women loosed their hair; an immodesty sanctioned only by a great calamity.

there to do?" "O accursed! O dog! O hog!" my servants replied; "'Tis thou who hast killed our master!" Quoth he, "O good
folk, and what hath your master done to me that I should kill
him?"——And Shahrazad perceived the dawn of day and ceased
saying her permitted say.

When it was the Thirty-first Night,

She said, It hath reached me, O auspicious King, that the Kazi
said to the servants, "What hath your master done to me that I
should kill him? This is my house and it is open to you all."
Then quoth the Barber, "Thou didst beat him and I heard him
cry out;" and quoth the Kazi, "But what was he doing that I
should beat him, and what brought him in to my house; and
whence came he and whither went he?" "Be not a wicked, perverse old man!" cried the Barber, "for I know the whole story;
and the long and short of it is that thy daughter is in love with
him and he loves her; and when thou knewest that he had entered
the house, thou badest thy servants beat him and they did so: by
Allah, none shall judge between us and thee but the Caliph; or
else do thou bring out our master that his folk may take him,
before they go in and save him perforce from thy house, and thou
be put to shame." Then said the Kazi (and his tongue was bridled
and his mouth was stopped by confusion before the people), "An
thou say sooth, do thou come in and fetch him out." Whereupon
the Barber pushed forward and entered the house. When I saw
this I looked about for a means of escape and flight, but saw no
hiding-place except a great chest in the upper chamber where I
was. So I got into it and pulled the lid down upon myself and
held my breath. The Barber was hardly in the room before he
began to look about for me, then turned him right and left and
came straight to the place where I was, and stepped up to the
chest and, lifting it on his head, made off as fast as he could. At
this, my reason forsook me, for I knew that he would not let me
be; so I took courage and opening the chest threw myself to the
ground. My leg was broken in the fall, and the door being open
I saw a great concourse of people looking in. Now I carried in
my sleeve much gold and some silver, which I had provided for
an ill day like this and the like of such occasion; so I kept scattering it amongst the folk to divert their attention from me and,

whilst they were busy scrambling for it, I set off, hopping as fast as I could, through the by-streets of Baghdad, shifting and turning right and left. But whithersoever I went this damned Barber would go in after me, crying aloud, "They would have bereft me of my maa-a-ster! They would have slain him who was a benefactor to me and my family and my friends! Praised be Allah who made me prevail against them and delivered my lord from their hands!" Then to me, "Where wilt thou go now? Thou wouldst persist in following thine own evil devices, till thou broughtest thyself to this ill pass; and, had not Allah vouchsafed me to thee, ne'er hadst thou escaped this strait into which thou hast fallen, for they would have cast thee into a calamity whence thou never couldest have won free. But I will not call thee to account for thine ignorance, as thou art so little of wit and inconsequential and addicted to hastiness!" Said I to him, "Doth not what thou hast brought upon me suffice thee, but thou must run after me and talk me such talk in the bazar-streets?" And I well-nigh gave up the ghost for excess of rage against him. Then I took refuge in the shop of a weaver amiddlemost of the market and sought protection of the owner who drove the Barber away; and, sitting in the back-room,[1] I said to myself, "If I return home I shall never be able to get rid of this curse of a Barber, who will be with me night and day; and I cannot endure the sight of him even for a breathing-space." So I sent out at once for witnesses and made a will, dividing the greater part of my property among my people, and appointed a guardian over them, to whom I committed the charge of great and small, directing him to sell my houses and domains. Then I set out on my travels that I might be free of this pimp;[2] and I came to settle in your town where I have lived some time. When you invited me and I came hither, the first thing I saw was this accursed pander seated in the place of honour. How then can my heart be glad and my stay be pleasant in company with this fellow who brought all this upon me, and who was the cause of the breaking of my leg and of my exile from home and native land? And the youth refused to sit down and went away. When we heard his story (continued the Tailor) we were amazed beyond measure and amused and said to the Barber, "By Allah,

---

[1] These small shops are composed of a "but" and a "ben." (Pilgrimage i., 99.)

[2] Arab. "Kawwád," a popular term of abuse; hence the Span. and Port. "Alco-viteiro." The Italian "Galeotto" is from Galahalt, not Galahad.

is it true what this young man saith of thee?" "By Allah," replied he, "I dealt thus by him of my courtesy and sound sense and generosity. Had it not been for me he had perished and none but I was the cause of his escape. Well it was for him that he suffered in his leg and not in his life! Had I been a man of many words, a meddler, a busy-body, I had not acted thus kindly by him; but now I will tell you a tale which befel me, that you may be well assured I am a man sparing of speech in whom is no forwardness and a very different person from those six Brothers of mine; and this it is."

The Barber's Tale of Himself.

I was living in Baghdad during the times of Al-Mustansir bi'llah,[1] son of Al-Mustazi bi'llah the then Caliph, a prince who loved the poor and needy and companied with the learned and pious. One day it happened to him that he was wroth with ten persons, high-waymen who robbed on the Caliph's highway, and he ordered the Prefect of Baghdad to bring them into the presence on the anni-versary of the Great Festival.[2] So the Prefect sallied out and, making them his prisoners, embarked with them in a boat. I caught sight of them as they were embarking and said to myself, "These are surely assembled for a marriage-feast; methinks they are spending their day in that boat eating and drinking, and none shall be companion of their cups but I myself." So I rose, O fair assembly; and, of the excess of my courtesy and the gravity of my understanding, I embarked with them and entered into conver-sation with them. They rowed across to the opposite bank, where they landed and there came up the watch and guardians of the peace with chains, which they put round the robbers' necks. They chained me among the rest of them; and, O people, is it not

---

[1] i.e., "one seeking assistance in Allah." He was the son of Al-Záhir bi'lláh (one pre-eminent by the decree of Allah). Lane says (i. 430), "great-grandson of Harun al-Rashid," alluding to the first Mustansir son of Al-Mutawakkil (regn. A. H. 247-248 = 861-862). But this is the 56th Abbaside and regn. A. H. 623-640 (= 1226-1242).

[2] Arab. "Yaum al-Id," the Kurban Bairam of the Turks, the Pilgrimage festival. The story is historical. In the "Akd," a miscellany compiled by Ibn Abd Rabbuh (vulg. Rabbi-hi) of Cordova, who ob. A. H. 328 = 940 we read:—A sponger found ten criminals and followed them, imagining they were going to a feast; but lo, they were going to their deaths! And when they were slain and he remained, he was brought before the Khalifah (Al-Maamun) and Ibrahim son of Al-Mahdi related a tale to procure pardon for the man, whereupon the Khalifah pardoned him. (Lane ii., 506.)

a proof of my courtesy and spareness of speech, that I held my peace and did not please to speak? Then they took us away in bilbos and next morning carried us all before Al-Mustansir bi'llah, Commander of the Faithful, who bade smite the necks of the ten robbers. So the Sworder came forward after they were seated on the leather of blood;[1] then drawing his blade, struck off one head after another until he had smitten the neck of the tenth; and I alone remained. The Caliph looked at me and asked the Heads-man, saying, "What ails thee that thou hast struck off only nine heads?"; and he answered, "Allah forbid that I should behead only nine, when thou biddest me behead ten!" Quoth the Caliph, "Meseems thou hast smitten the necks of only nine, and this man before thee is the tenth." "By thy beneficence!" replied the Headsman, "I have beheaded ten." "Count them!" cried the Caliph and whenas they counted heads, lo! there were ten. The Caliph looked at me and said, "What made thee keep silence at a time like this and how camest thou to company with these men of blood? Tell me the cause of all this, for albeit thou art a very old man, assuredly thy wits are weak." Now when I heard these words from the Caliph I sprang to my feet and replied, "Know, O Prince of the Faithful, that I am the Silent Shaykh and am thus called to distinguish me from my six brothers. I am a man of im-mense learning whilst, as for the gravity of my understanding, the wiliness of my wits and the spareness of my speech, there is no end of them; and my calling is that of a barber. I went out early on yesterday morning and saw these men making for a skiff; and, fancying they were bound for a marriage-feast, I joined them and mixed with them. After a while up came the watch and guardians of the peace, who put chains round their necks and round mine with the rest; but, in the excess of my courtesy, I held my peace and spake not a word; nor was this other but generosity on my part. They brought us into thy presence, and thou gavest an order to smite the necks of the ten; yet did I not make myself known to thee and remained silent before the Sworder, purely of my great generosity and courtesy which led

---

[1] Arab. "Nata' al-Dam"; the former word was noticed in the Tale of the Bull and the Ass. The leather of blood was not unlike the Sufrah and could be folded into a bag by a string running through rings round the edges. Moslem executioners were very expert and seldom failed to strike off the head with a single blow of the thin narrow blade with razor-edge, hard as diamond withal, which contrasted so strongly with the great coarse chopper of the European headsman.

me to share with them in their death. But all my life long have I
dealt thus nobly with mankind, and they requite me the foulest
and evillest requital!" When the Caliph heard my words and
knew that I was a man of exceeding generosity and of very few
words, one in whom is no forwardness (as this youth would have
it whom I rescued from mortal risk and who hath so scurvily
repaid me), he laughed with excessive laughter till he fell upon
his back. Then said he to me, "O Silent Man, do thy six brothers
favour thee in wisdom and knowledge and spareness of speech?"
I replied, "Never were they like me! Thou puttest reproach upon
me, O Commander of the Faithful, and it becomes thee not to
even my brothers with me; for, of the abundance of their speech
and their deficiency of courtesy and gravity, each one of them
hath gotten some maim or other. One is a monocular, another
palsied, a third stone-blind, a fourth cropped of ears and nose and
a fifth shorn of both lips, while the sixth is a hunchback and a
cripple. And conceive not, O Commander of the Faithful, that I
am prodigal of speech; but I must perforce explain to thee that I
am a man of greater worth and fewer words than any of them.
From each one of my brothers hangs a tale of how he came by
his bodily defect and these I will relate to thee." So the Caliph
gave ear to

The Barber's Tale of his First Brother.

KNOW then, O Commander of the Faithful, that my first brother,
Al-Bakbuk, the Prattler, is a Hunchback who took to tailoring in
Baghdad, and he used to sew in a shop hired from a man of much
wealth, who dwelt over the shop,[1] and there was also a flour-mill
in the basement. One day as my brother, the Hunchback, was
sitting in his shop a-tailoring, he chanced to raise his head and
saw a lady like the rising full moon at a balconied window of his
landlord's house, engaged in looking out at the passers-by.[2] When
my brother beheld her, his heart was taken with love of her and
he passed his whole day gazing at her and neglected his tailoring

---

[1] The ground floor, which in all hot countries is held, and rightly so, unwholesome
during sleep, is usually let for shops. This is also the case throughout Southern Europe,
and extends to the Canary Islands and the Brazil.
[2] This serious contemplation of street-scenery is one of the pleasures of the Harems.

till eventide. Next morning he opened his shop and sat him down to sew; but, as often as he stitched a stitch, he looked to the window and saw her as before; and his passion and infatuation for her increased. On the third day as he was sitting in his usual place, gazing on her, she caught sight of him and, perceiving that he had been captivated with love of her, laughed in his face,[1] and he smiled back at her. Then she disappeared and presently sent her slave-girl to him with a bundle containing a piece of red flowered silk. The handmaid accosted him and said, "My lady salameth to thee and desireth thee, of thy skill and good will, to fashion for her a shift of this piece and to sew it handsomely with thy best sewing." He replied, "Hearkening and obedience"; and shaped for her a chemise and finished sewing it the same day. When the morning morrowed the girl came back and said to him, "My lady salameth to thee and asks how thou hast passed yesternight; for she hath not tasted sleep by reason of her heart being taken up with thee." Then she laid before him a piece of yellow satin and said, "My lady biddeth thee cut her two pair of petticoat-trousers out of this piece and sew them this very day." "Hearkening and obedience!" replied he, "greet her for me with many greetings and say to her, Thy slave is obedient to thine order; so command him as thou wilt." Then he applied himself to cutting out and worked hard at sewing the trousers; and after an hour the lady appeared at the lattice and saluted him by signs, now casting down her eyes, then smiling in his face, and he began to assure himself that he would soon make a conquest. She did not let him stir till he had finished the two pair of trousers, when she withdrew and sent the handmaid to whom he delivered them; and she took them and went her ways. When it was night, he threw himself on his carpet-bed, and lay tossing about from side to side till morning, when he rose and sat down in his place. Presently the damsel came to him and said, "My master calleth for thee." Hearing these words he feared with exceeding fear; but the slave-girl, seeing his affright, said to him, "No evil is meant to thee: naught but good awaiteth thee. My lady would have thee make acquaintance with my lord." So my brother the tailor, rejoicing with great joy, went with her; and when he came into the presence of his landlord, the lady's husband, he kissed the ground before him, and the master of the house returned his greeting and

---

[1] We should say "smiled at him": the laugh was not intended as an affront.

gave him a great piece of linen saying, "Shape me shirts out of this
stuff and sew them well;" and my brother answered, "To hear is
to obey." Thereupon he fell to work at once, snipping, shaping
and sewing till he had finished twenty shirts by supper time,
without stopping to taste food. The house-master asked him,
"How much the wage for this?"; and he answered, "Twenty
dirhams." So the gentleman cried out to the slave-girl, "Bring
me twenty dirhams," and my brother spake not a word; but the
lady signed, "Take nothing from him;" whereupon my brother
said, "By Allah I will take naught from thy hand." And he
carried off his tailor's gear and returned to his shop, although he
was destitute even to a red cent.[1] Then he applied himself to do
their work; eating, in his zeal and diligence, but a bit of bread
and drinking only a little water for three days. At the end of this
time came the handmaid and said to him, "What hast thou
done?" Quoth he, "They are finished," and carried the shirts to
the lady's husband, who would have paid him his hire: but he
said, "I will take nothing," for fear of her and, returning to his
shop, passed the night without sleep because of his hunger. Now
the dame had informed her husband how the case stood (my
brother knowing naught of this); and the two had agreed to make
him tailor for nothing, the better to mock and laugh at him. Next
morning he went to his shop, and, as he sat there, the handmaid
came to him and said, "Speak with my master." So he accompanied her to the husband who said to him, "I wish thee to cut
out for me five long-sleeved robes."[2] So he cut them out[3] and
took the stuff and went away. Then he sewed them and carried
them to the gentleman, who praised his sewing and offered him a
purse of silver. He put out his hand to take it, but the lady
signed to him from behind her husband not to do so, and he
replied, "O my lord, there is no hurry, we have time enough for
this." Then he went forth from the house meaner and meeker

---

[1] Arab. "Fals ahmar." Fals is a fish-scale, also the smaller coin and the plural
"Fulús" is the vulgar term for money (= Ital. *quattrini*) without specifying the coin.
It must not be confounded with the "Fazzah," alias "Nuss," alias "Páráh" (Turk.);
the latter being made, not of "red copper" but of a vile alloy containing, like the Greek
"Asper," some silver; and representing, when at par, the fortieth of a piastre, the latter
being = 2d. ⅗ths.

[2] Arab. "Farajiyah," a long-sleeved robe; Lane's "Farageeyeh," (M. E., chapt. i.)

[3] The tailor in the East, as in Southern Europe, is made to cut out the cloth in presence
of its owner, to prevent "cabbaging."

than a donkey, for verily five things were gathered together in him viz.:—love, beggary, hunger, nakedness and hard labour. Nevertheless he heartened himself with the hope of gaining the lady's favours. When he had made an end of all their jobs, they played him another trick and married him to their slave-girl; but, on the night when he thought to go in to her, they said to him, "Lie this night in the mill; and to-morrow all will go well." My brother concluded that there was some good cause for this and nighted alone in the mill. Now the husband had set on the miller to make the tailor turn the mill: so when night was half spent the man came in to him and began to say, "This bull of ours hath become useless and standeth still instead of going round: he will not turn the mill this night, and yet we have great store of corn to be ground. However, I'll yoke him perforce and make him finish grinding it before morning, as the folk are impatient for their flour." So he filled the hoppers with grain and, going up to my brother with a rope in his hand, tied it round his neck and said to him, "Gee up! Round with the mill! thou, O bull, wouldst do nothing but grub and stale and dung!" Then he took a whip and laid it on the shoulders and calves of my brother, who began to howl and bellow; but none came to help him; and he was forced to grind the wheat till hard upon dawn, when the house-master came in and, seeing my brother still tethered to the yoke and the man flogging him, went away. At day-break the miller returned home and left him still yoked and half dead; and soon after in came the slave-girl who unbound him, and said to him, "I and my lady are right sorry for what hath happened and we have borne thy grief with thee." But he had no tongue wherewith to answer her from excess of beating and mill-turning. Then he retired to his lodging and behold, the clerk who had drawn up the marriage-deed came to him[1] and saluted him, saying, "Allah give thee long life! May thy espousal be blessed! This face telleth of pleasant doings and dalliance and kissing and clipping from dusk to dawn." "Allah grant the liar no peace, O thou thousandfold cuckold!", my brother replied, "by Allah, I did nothing but turn the mill in the place of the bull all night till morning!" "Tell me thy tale," quoth he; and my brother recounted what had befallen him and he said, "Thy star agrees not with her star; but an thou wilt I can alter the contract for thee," adding, " 'Ware lest another

---

1.Expecting a present.

cheat be not in store for thee." And my brother answered him, "See if thou have not another contrivance." Then the clerk left him and he sat in his shop, looking for some one to bring him a job whereby he might earn his day's bread. Presently the handmaid came to him and said, "Speak with my lady." "Begone, O my good girl," replied he, "there shall be no more dealings between me and thy lady." The handmaid returned to her mistress and told her what my brother had said and presently she put her head out of the window, weeping and saying, "Why, O my beloved, are there to be no more dealings 'twixt me and thee?" But he made her no answer. Then she wept and conjured him, swearing that all which had befallen him in the mill was not sanctioned by her and that she was innocent of the whole matter. When he looked upon her beauty and loveliness and heard the sweetness of her speech, the sorrow which had possessed him passed from his heart; he accepted her excuse and he rejoiced in her sight. So he saluted her and talked with her and sat tailoring awhile, after which the handmaid came to him and said, "My mistress greeteth thee and informeth thee that her husband purposeth to lie abroad this night in the house of some intimate friends of his; so, when he is gone, do thou come to us and spend the night with my lady in de-lightsomest joyance till the morning." Now her husband had asked her, "How shall we manage to turn him away from thee?"; and she answered, "Leave me to play him another trick and make him a laughing-stock for all the town." But my brother knew naught of the malice of women. As soon as it was dusk, the slave-girl came to him and carried him to the house, and when the lady saw him she said to him, "By Allah, O my lord, I have been long-ing exceedingly for thee." "By Allah," cried he, "kiss me quick before thou give me aught else."[1] Hardly had he spoken, when the lady's husband came in from the next room[2] and seized him, saying, "By Allah, I will not let thee go, till I deliver thee to the chief of the town watch." My brother humbled himself to him; but he would not listen to him and carried him before the Prefect who gave him an hundred lashes with a whip and, mounting him on a camel, promenaded him round about the city, whilst the guards proclaimed aloud, "This is his reward who violateth the

---

[1] Alluding to the saying, "Kiss is the key to Kitty."
[2] The "panel-dodge" is fatally common throughout the East, where a man found in the house of another is helpless.

Harims of honourable men!" Moreover, he fell off the camel and broke his leg and so became lame. Then the Prefect banished him from the city; and he went forth unknowing whither he should wend; but I heard of him and fearing for him went out after him, and brought him back secretly to the city and restored him to health and took him into my house where he still liveth. The Caliph laughed at my story and said, "Thou hast done well, O Samit, O Silent Man, O spare of speech!"; and he bade me take a present and go away. But I said, "I will accept naught of thee except I tell thee what befel all my other brothers; and do not think me a man of many words." So the Caliph gave ear to

The Barber's Tale of his Second Brother.

KNOW, O Commander of the Faithful, that my second brother's name was Al-Haddár, that is the Babbler, and he was the para-lytic. Now it happened to him one day, as he was going about his business, that an old woman accosted him and said, "Stop a little, my good man, that I may tell thee of somewhat which, if it be to thy liking, thou shalt do for me and I will pray Allah to give thee good of it!" My brother stopped and she went on, "I will put thee in the way of a certain thing, so thou not be prodigal of speech." "On with thy talk," quoth he; and she, "What sayest thou to handsome quarters and a fair garden with flowing waters, flowers blooming, and fruit growing, and old wine going and a pretty young face whose owner thou mayest embrace from dark till dawn? If thou do whatso I bid thee thou shalt see something greatly to thy advantage." "And is all this in the world?" asked my brother; and she answered, "Yes, and it shall be thine, so thou be reasonable and leave idle curiosity and many words, and do my bidding." "I will indeed, O my lady," said he, "how is it thou hast preferred me in this matter before all men and what is it that so much pleaseth thee in me?" Quoth she, "Did I not bid thee be spare of speech? Hold thy peace and follow me. Know, that the young lady, to whom I shall carry thee, loveth to have her own way and hateth being thwarted and all who gainsay; so, if thou humour her, thou shalt come to thy desire of her." And my brother said, "I will not cross her in anything." Then she went on and my brother followed her, an-hungering after what she de-

scribed to him till they entered a fine large house, handsome and
choicely furnished, full of eunuchs and servants and showing
signs of prosperity from top to bottom. And she was carrying
him to the upper story when the people of the house said to him,
"What dost thou here?" But the old woman answered them,
"Hold your peace and trouble him not: he is a workman and we
have occasion for him." Then she brought him into a fine great
pavilion, with a garden in its midst, never eyes saw a fairer; and
made him sit upon a handsome couch. He had not sat long, before he heard a loud noise and in came a troop of slave-girls surrounding a lady like the moon on the night of its fullest. When
he saw her, he rose up and made an obeisance to her, whereupon
she welcomed him and bade him be seated. So he sat down and
she said to him, "Allah advance thee to honour! Is all well with
thee?" "O my lady," he answered, "all with me is right well."
Then she bade bring in food, and they set before her delicate
viands; so she sat down to eat, making a show of affection to my
brother and jesting with him, though all the while she could not
refrain from laughing; but as often as he looked at her, she signed
towards her handmaidens as though she were laughing at them.
My brother (the ass!) understood nothing; but, in the excess of
his ridiculous passion, he fancied that the lady was in love with
him and that she would soon grant him his desire. When they
had done eating, they set on the wine and there came in ten
maidens like moons, with lutes ready strung in their hands, and
fell to singing with full voices, sweet and sad, whereupon delight
gat hold upon him and he took the cup from the lady's hands and
drank it standing. Then she drank a cup of wine and my brother
(still standing) said to her "Health," and bowed to her. She
handed him another cup and he drank it off, when she slapped
him hard on the nape of his neck.[1] Upon this my brother would
have gone out of the house in anger; but the old woman followed
him and winked to him to return. So he came back and the lady
bade him sit and he sat down without a word. Then she again
slapped him on the nape of his neck; and the second slapping did
not suffice her, she must needs make all her handmaidens also slap
and cuff him, while he kept saying to the old woman, "I never
saw aught nicer than this." She on her side ceased not exclaiming, "Enough, enough, I conjure thee, O my mistress!"; but the

---

[1] This was the beginning of horseplay which often ends in a bastinado.

women slapped him till he well-nigh swooned away. Presently my brother rose and went out to obey a call of nature, but the old woman overtook him, and said, "Be patient a little and thou shalt win to thy wish." "How much longer have I to wait," my brother replied, "this slapping hath made me feel faint." "As soon as she is warm with wine," answered she, "thou shalt have thy desire." So he returned to his place and sat down, where-upon all the handmaidens stood up and the lady bade them per-fume him with pastiles and besprinkle his face with rose-water. Then said she to him, "Allah advance thee to honour! Thou hast entered my house and hast borne with my conditions, for whoso thwarteth me I turn him away, and whoso is patient hath his desire." "O mistress mine," said he, "I am thy slave and in the hollow of thine hand!" "Know, then," continued she, "that Allah hath made me passionately fond of frolic; and whoso falleth in with my humour cometh by whatso he wisheth." Then she ordered her maidens to sing with loud voices till the whole com-pany was delighted; after which she said to one of them, "Take thy lord, and do what is needful for him and bring him back to me forthright." So the damsel took my brother (and he not knowing what she would do with him); but the old woman over-took him and said, "Be patient; there remaineth but little to do." At this his face brightened and he stood up before the lady while the old woman kept saying, "Be patient; thou wilt now at once win to thy wish!"; till he said, "Tell me what she would have the maiden do with me?" "Nothing but good," replied she, "as I am thy sacrifice! She wisheth only to dye thy eyebrows and pluck out thy mustachios." Quoth he, "As for the dyeing of my eye-brows, that will come off with washing,[1] but for the plucking out of my mustachios, that indeed is a somewhat painful process." "Be cautious how thou cross her," cried the old woman; "for she hath set her heart on thee." So my brother patiently suffered her to dye his eyebrows and pluck out his mustachios; after which the maiden returned to her mistress and told her. Quoth she, "Remaineth now only one other thing to be done; thou must

---

[1] Hair-dyes, in the East, are all of vegetable matter, henna, indigo-leaves, galls, etc.: our mineral dyes are, happily for them, unknown. Herklots will supply a host of recipes. The Egyptian mixture which I quoted in Pilgrimage (ii., 274) is sulphate of iron and ammoniure of iron one part and gall nuts two parts, infused in eight parts of distilled water. It is innocuous but very poor as a dye.

shave his beard and make him a smooth o' face."[1] So the maiden
went back and told him what her mistress had bidden her do; and
my brother (the blockhead!) said to her, "How shall I do what
will disgrace me before the folk?" But the old woman said, "She
would do on this wise only that thou mayst be as a beardless
youth and that no hair be left on thy face to scratch and prick her
delicate cheeks; for indeed she is passionately in love with thee.
So be patient and thou shalt attain thine object." My brother
was patient and did her bidding and let shave off his beard and,
when he was brought back to the lady, lo! he appeared dyed red
as to his eyebrows, plucked of both mustachios, shorn of his
beard, rouged on both cheeks. At first she was affrighted at him;
then she made mockery of him and, laughing till she fell upon her
back, said, "O my lord, thou hast indeed won my heart by thy
good nature!" Then she conjured him, by her life, to stand up
and dance, and he arose, and capered about, and there was not a
cushion in the house but she threw it at his head, and in like
manner did all her women who also kept pelting him with oranges
and lemons and citrons till he fell down senseless from the cuffing
on the nape of the neck, the pillowing and the fruit-pelting.
"Now thou hast attained thy wish," said the old woman when
he came round; "there are no more blows in store for thee and
there remaineth but one little thing to do. It is her wont, when
she is in her cups, to let no one have her until she put off her dress
and trousers and remain stark naked.[2] Then she will bid thee
doff thy clothes and run; and she will run before thee as if she
were flying from thee; and do thou follow her from place to place
till thy prickle stands at fullest point, when she will yield to
thee;"[3] adding, "Strip off thy clothes at once." So he rose, well-
nigh lost in ecstasy and, doffing his raiment, showed himself
mother-naked.——And Shahrazad perceived the dawn of day
and ceased to say her permitted say.

---

[1] Arab. Amrad, etymologically "beardless and handsome," but often used in a bad
sense, to denote an effeminate, a catamite.

[2] The Hindus prefer "having the cardinal points as her sole garment." "Vêtu de climat,"
says Madame de Stael. In Paris nude statues are "draped in cerulean blue." Rabelais
(iv., 29) robes King Shrovetide in grey and gold of a comical cut, nothing before, nothing
behind, with sleeves of the same.

[3] This scene used to be enacted a few years ago in Paris for the benefit of concealed
spectators, a young American being the victim. It was put down when one of the lookers-
on lost his eye by a pen-knife thrust into the "crevice."

When it was the Thirty-second Night,

She said, It hath reached me, O auspicious King, that when the
old woman said to the Barber's second brother, "Doff thy
clothes," he rose, well-nigh lost in ecstasy; and, stripping off his
raiment, showed himself mother-naked. Whereupon the lady
stripped also and said to my brother, "If thou want anything run
after me till thou catch me." Then she set out at a run and he ran
after her while she rushed into room after room and rushed out
of room after room, my brother scampering after her in a rage of
desire like a veritable madman, with yard standing terribly tall.
After much of this kind she dashed into a darkened place, and he
dashed after her; but suddenly he trod upon a yielding spot,
which gave way under his weight; and, before he was aware
where he was, he found himself in the midst of a crowded market,
part of the bazar of the leather-sellers who were crying the prices
of skins and hides and buying and selling. When they saw him
in his plight, naked, with standing yard, shorn of beard and
mustachios, with eyebrows dyed red, and cheeks ruddied with
rouge, they shouted and clapped their hands at him, and set to
flogging him with skins upon his bare body till a swoon came over
him. Then they threw him on the back of an ass and carried him
to the Chief of Police. Quoth the Chief, "What is this?" Quoth
they, "This fellow fell suddenly upon us out of the Wazir's
house[1] in this state." So the Prefect gave him an hundred lashes
and then banished him from Baghdad. However I went out after
him and brought him back secretly into the city and made him a
daily allowance for his living: although, were it not for my
generous humour, I could not have put up with the like of him.
Then the Caliph gave ear to

The Barber's Tale of his Third Brother.

My third brother's name was Al-Fakík, the Gabbler, who was
blind. One day Fate and Fortune drove him to a fine large house,
and he knocked at the door, desiring speech of its owner that he

---

[1] Meaning that the trick had been played by the Wazir's wife or daughter. I could
mention sundry names at Cairo whose charming owners have done worse things than
this unseemly frolic.

might beg somewhat of him. Quoth the master of the house, "Who is at the door?" But my brother spake not a word and presently he heard him repeat with a loud voice, "Who is this?" Still he made no answer and immediately heard the master walk to the door and open it and say, "What dost thou want?" My brother answered "Something for Allah Almighty's sake."[1] "Art thou blind?" asked the man, and my brother answered "Yes." Quoth the other, "Stretch me out thy hand." So my brother put out his hand thinking that he would give him something; but he took it and, drawing him into the house, carried him up from stair to stair till they reached the terrace on the house-top, my brother thinking the while that he would surely give him something of food or money. Then he asked my brother, "What dost thou want, O blind man?" and he answered, "Something for the Almighty's sake." "Allah open for thee some other door!" "O thou! why not say so when I was below stairs?" "O cadger, why not answer me when I first called to thee?" "And what meanest thou to do for me now?" "There is nothing in the house to give thee." "Then take me down the stair." "The path is before thee." So my brother rose and made his way downstairs, till he came within twenty steps of the door, when his foot slipped and he rolled to the bottom and broke his head. Then he went out, unknowing whither to turn, and presently fell in with two other blind men, companions of his, who said to him, "What didst thou gain to-day?" He told them what had befallen him and added, "O my brothers, I wish to take some of the money in my hands and provide myself with it." Now the master of the house had followed him and was listening to what they said; but neither my brother nor his comrades knew of this. So my brother went to his lodging and sat down to await his companions, and the house-owner entered after him without being perceived. When the other blind men arrived, my brother said to them, "Bolt the door and search the house lest any stranger have followed us." The man, hearing this, caught hold of a cord that hung from the ceiling and clung to it, whilst they went round about the house and searched but found no one. So they came back, and, sitting beside my brother, brought out their money which they counted and lo! it was twelve thousand dirhams. Each took what he

---

[1] Arab. "Shayyun li'lláhi," a beggar's formula = per amor di Dio.

wanted and they buried the rest in a corner of the room. Then they set on food and sat down, to eat. Presently my brother, hearing a strange pair of jaws munching by his side,[1] said to his friends, "There is a stranger amongst us;" and, putting forth his hand, caught hold of that of the house-master. Thereupon all fell on him and beat him;[2] and when tired of belabouring him they shouted, "O ye Moslems! a thief is come in to us, seeking to take our money!" A crowd gathered around them, whereupon the intruder hung on to them; and complained with them as they complained; and, shutting his eyes like them, so that none might doubt his blindness, cried out, "O Moslems, I take refuge with Allah and the Governor, for I have a matter to make known to him!" Suddenly up came the watch and, laying hands on the whole lot (my brother being amongst them), drove them[3] to the Governor's who set them before him and asked, "What news with you?" Quoth the intruder, "Look and find out for thyself, not a word shall be wrung from us save by torture, so begin by beating me and after me beat this man our leader."[4] And he pointed to my brother. So they threw the man at full length and gave him four hundred sticks on his backside. The beating pained him, whereupon he opened one eye and, as they redoubled their blows, he opened the other eye. When the Governor saw this he said to him, "What have we here, O accursed?"; whereto he replied, "Give me the seal-ring of pardon! We four have shammed blind, and we impose upon people that we may enter houses and look upon the unveiled faces of the women and contrive for their corruption. In this way we have gotten great gain

---

[1] Noting how sharp-eared the blind become.

[2] The blind in Egypt are notorious for insolence and violence, fanaticism and rapacity. Not a few foreigners have suffered from them (Pilgrimage i., 148). In former times many were blinded in infancy by their mothers, and others blinded themselves to escape conscription or honest hard work. They could always obtain food, especially as Mu'ezzins; and were preferred because they could not take advantage of the minaret by spying into their neighbours' households. The Egyptian race is chronically weak-eyed, the effect of the damp hot climate of the valley, where ophthalmia prevailed even during the pre-Pharaohnic days. The great Sesostris died stone-blind and his successor lost his sight for ten years (Pilgrimage ii., 176). That the Fellahs are now congenitally weak-eyed, may be seen by comparing them with negroes imported from Central Africa. Ophthalmia rages, especially during the damp season, in the lower Nile-valley; and the best cure for it is a fortnight's trip to the Desert where, despite glare, sand and wind, the eye readily recovers tone.

[3] *i.e.*, with kicks and cuffs and blows, as is the custom. (Pilgrimage i., 174.)

[4] Arab. Káid (whence "Alcayde") a word still much used in North Western Africa.

and our store amounts to twelve thousand dirhams. Said I to my
company, 'Give me my share, three thousand;' but they rose and
beat me and took away my money, and I seek refuge with Allah
and with thee; better thou have my share than they. So, if thou
wouldst know the truth of my words, beat one and every of the
others more than thou hast beaten me, and he will surely open his
eyes." The Governor gave orders for the question to begin with
my brother, and they bound him to the whipping-post,[1] and the
Governor said, "O scum of the earth, do ye abuse the gracious
gifts of Allah and make as if ye were blind!" "Allah! Allah!"
cried my brother, "by Allah, there is none among us who can
see." Then they beat him till he swooned away and the Governor cried, "Leave him till he come to and then beat him again."
After this he caused each of the companions to receive more than
three hundred sticks, whilst the sham-abraham kept saying to
them "Open your eyes or you will be beaten afresh." At last the
man said to the Governor, "Dispatch some one with me to bring
thee the money; for these fellows will not open their eyes, lest
they incur disgrace before the folk." So the Governor sent to
fetch the money and gave the man his pretended share, three
thousand dirhams; and, keeping the rest for himself, banished the
three blind men from the city. But I, O Commander of the Faithful, went out and overtaking my brother questioned him of his
case; whereupon he told me of what I have told thee, so I brought
him secretly into the city, and appointed him (in the strictest
privacy) an allowance for meat and drink! The Caliph laughed at
my story and said, "Give him a gift and let him go;" but I said,
"By Allah! I will take naught till I have made known to the Commander of the Faithful what came to pass with the rest of my
brothers; for truly I am a man of few words and spare of speech."
Then the Caliph gave ear to

The Barber's Tale of his Fourth Brother.

Now as for my fourth brother, O Commander of the Faithful,
Al-Kuz al-aswáni, or the long-necked Gugglet hight, from his
brimming over with words, the same who was blind of one eye, he

---

1 Arab. "Sullam" = lit. a ladder; a frame-work of sticks, used by way of our triangles
or whipping-posts.

became a butcher in Baghdad and he sold flesh and fattened rams; and great men and rich bought their meat of him, so that he amassed much wealth and got him cattle and houses. He fared thus a long while, till one day, as he was sitting in his shop, there came up an old man and long o' the beard, who laid down some silver and said, "Give me meat for this." He gave him his money's worth of flesh and the oldster went his ways. My brother examined the Shaykh's silver, and, seeing that the dirhams were white and bright, he set them in a place apart. The greybeard continued to return to the shop regularly for five months, and my brother ceased not to lay up all the coin he received from him in its own box. At last he thought to take out the money to buy sheep; so he opened the box and found in it nothing, save bits of white paper cut round to look like coin;[1] so he buffeted his face and cried aloud till the folk gathered about him, whereupon he told them his tale which made them marvel exceedingly. Then he rose as was his wont, and slaughtering a ram hung it up inside his shop; after which he cut off some of the flesh, and hanging it outside kept saying to himself, "O Allah, would the ill-omened old fellow but come!" And an hour had not passed before the Shaykh came with his silver in hand; whereupon my brother rose and caught hold of him calling out, "Come aid me, O Moslems, and learn my story with this villain!" When the old man heard this, he quietly said to him, "Which will be the better for thee, to let go of me or to be disgraced by me amidst the folk?" "In what wilt thou disgrace me?" "In that thou sellest man's flesh for mutton!" "Thou liest, thou accursed!" "Nay, he is the accursed who hath a man hanging up by way of meat in his shop." "If the matter be as thou sayest, I give thee lawful leave to take my money and my life." Then the old man cried out aloud, "Ho, ye people! if you would prove the truth of my words, enter this man's shop." The folk rushed in and found that the ram was become a dead man[2] hung up for sale. So they set upon my brother crying out, "O Infidel! O villain!"; and his best friends fell to cuffing and kicking him and kept saying, "Dost thou make us eat flesh of the sons of Adam?" Furthermore, the old

---

[1] This is one of the feats of Al-Símiyá = white magic; fascinating the eyes. In Europe it has lately taken the name of "Electro-biology."

[2] Again by means of the "Símiyá" or power of fascination possessed by the old scoundrel.

man struck him on the eye and put it out. Then they carried the carcass, with the throat cut, before the Chief of the city-watch, to whom the old man said, "O Emir, this fellow butchers men and sells their flesh for mutton and we have brought him to thee; so arise and execute the judgments of Allah (to whom be honour and glory!)." My brother would have defended himself, but the Chief refused to hear him and sentenced him to receive five hundred sticks and to forfeit the whole of his property. And, indeed, had it not been for that same property which he expended in bribes, they would have surely slain him. Then the Chief banished him from Baghdad; and my brother fared forth at a venture, till he came to a great town, where he thought it best to set up as a cobbler; so he opened a shop and sat there doing what he could for his livelihood. One day, as he went forth on his business, he heard the distant tramp of horses and, asking the cause, was told that the King was going out to hunt and course; so my brother stopped to look at the fine suite. It so fortuned that the King's eye met my brother's; whereupon the King hung down his head and said, "I seek refuge with Allah from the evil of this day!";[1] and turned the reins of his steed and returned home with all his retinue. Then he gave orders to his guards, who seized my brother and beat him with a beating so painful that he was well-nigh dead; and my brother knew not what could be the cause of his maltreatment, after which he returned to his place in sorriest plight. Soon afterwards he went to one of the King's household and related what had happened to him; and the man laughed till he fell upon his back and cried, "O brother mine, know that the King cannot bear to look at a monocular, especially if he be blind of the right eye, in which case he doth not let him go without killing him." When my brother heard this, he resolved to fly from that city; so he went forth from it to another wherein none knew him and there he abode a long while. One day, being full of sorrowful thought for what had befallen him, he sallied out to solace himself; and, as he was walking along, he heard the distant tramp of horses behind him and said, "The judgment of Allah is upon me!" and looked about for a hiding-

---

[1] A formula for averting "Al-Ayn," the evil eye. It is always unlucky to meet a one-eyed man, especially the first thing in the morning and when setting out on any errand. The idea is that the fascinated one will suffer from some action of the physical eye. Monoculars also are held to be rogues: so the Sanskrit saying "Few one-eyed men be honest men."

place but found none. At last he saw a closed door which he pushed hard: it yielded and he entered a long gallery in which he took refuge, but hardly had he done so, when two men set upon him crying out, "Allah be thanked for having delivered thee into our hands, O enemy of God! These three nights thou hast robbed us of our rest and sleep, and verily thou hast made us taste of the death-cup." My brother asked, "O folk, what ails you?"; and they answered, "Thou givest us the change and goest about to disgrace us and plannest some plot to cut the throat of the house-master! Is it not enough that thou hast brought him to beggary, thou and thy fellows? But now give us up the knife wherewith thou threatenest us every night." Then they searched him and found in his waist-belt the knife used for his shoe-leather; and he said, "O people, have the fear of Allah before your eyes and mal-treat me not, for know that my story is a right strange!" "And what is thy story?" said they: so he told them what had befallen him, hoping they would let him go; however they paid no heed to what he said and, instead of showing some regard, beat him grievously and tore off his clothes: then, finding on his sides the scars of beating with rods, they said, "O accursed! these marks are the manifest signs of thy guilt!" They carried him before the Governor, whilst he said to himself, "I am now punished for my sins and none can deliver me save Allah Almighty!" The Gov-ernor addressing my brother asked him, "O villain, what led thee to enter their house with intention to murther?"; and my brother answered, "I conjure thee by Allah, O Emir, hear my words and be not hasty in condemning me!" But the Governor cried, "Shall we listen to the words of a robber who hath beggared these people, and who beareth on his back the scar of his stripes?" add-ing, "They surely had not done this to thee, save for some great crime." So he sentenced him to receive an hundred cuts with the scourge, after which they set him on a camel and paraded him about the city, proclaiming, "This is the requital and only too little to requite him who breaketh into people's houses." Then they thrust him out of the city, and my brother wandered at random, till I heard what had befallen him; and, going in search of him, questioned him of his case; so he acquainted me with his story and all his mischances, and I carried him secretly to the city where I made him an allowance for his meat and drink. Then the Caliph gave ear to

The Barber's Tale of his Fifth Brother.

My fifth brother, Al-Nashshár,[1] the Babbler, the same who was cropped of both ears, O Commander of the Faithful, was an asker wont to beg of folk by night and live on their alms by day. Now when our father, who was an old man well stricken in years, sickened and died, he left us seven hundred dirhams whereof each son took his hundred; but, as my fifth brother received his portion, he was perplexed and knew not what to do with it. While in this uncertainty he bethought him to lay it out on glassware of all sorts and turn an honest penny on its price. So he bought an hundred dirhams worth of verroterie and, putting it into a big tray, sat down to sell it on a bench at the foot of a wall against which he leant back. As he sat with the tray before him he fell to musing and said to himself, "Know, O my good Self, that the head of my wealth, my principal invested in this glassware, is an hundred dirhams. I will assuredly sell it for two hundred, with which I will forthright buy other glass and make by it four hundred; nor will I cease to sell and buy on this wise, till I have gotten four thousand and soon find myself the master of much money. With these coins I will buy merchandise and jewels and ottars[2] and gain great profit on them; till, Allah willing, I will make my capital an hundred thousand dirhams. Then I will purchase a fine house with white slaves and eunuchs and horses; and I will eat and drink and disport myself; nor will I leave a singing man or a singing woman in the city, but I will summon them to my palace and make them perform before me."

---

[1] Al-Nashshár from Nashr = sawing: so the fiddler in Italian is called the "village-saw" (*Sega del villaggio*). He is the Alnaschar of the Englished Galland and Richardson. The tale is very old. It appears as the Brahman and the Pot of Rice in the Panchatantra; and Professor Benfey believes (as usual with him) that this, with many others, derives from a Buddhist source. But I would distinctly derive it from Æsop's market-woman who kicked over her eggs; whence the Lat. prov. Ante victoriam canere triumphum = to sell the skin before you have caught the bear. In the "Kalilah and Dimnah" and its numerous offspring it is the "Ascetic with his Jar of oil and honey;" in Rabelais (i., 33) Echephron's shoemaker spills his milk, and so La Perette in La Fontaine. See M. Max Muller's "Chips," (vol. iii., appendix). The curious reader will compare my version with that which appears at the end of Richardson's Arabic Grammar (Edit. of 1811): he had a better, or rather a fuller MS. (p. 199) than any yet printed.

[2] Arab. "Atr" = any perfume, especially oil of roses; whence our word "Ottar," through the Turkish corruption.

All this he counted over in his mind, while the tray of glass-ware, worth an hundred dirhams, stood on the bench before him, and, after looking at it, he continued, "And when, Inshallah! my capital shall have become one hundred thousand[1] dinars, I will send out marriage-brokeresses to require for me in wedlock the daughters of Kings and Wazirs; and I will demand to wife the eldest daughter of the Prime Minister; for it hath reached me that she is perfect in beauty and prime in loveliness and rare in accomplishments. I will give a marriage-settlement of one thousand dinars; and, if her father consent, well: but if not I will take her by force from under his very nose. When she is safely homed in my house, I will buy ten little eunuchs[2] and for myself a robe of the robes of Kings and Sultans; and get me a saddle of gold and a bridle set thick with gems of price. Then I will mount with the Mamelukes preceding me and surrounding me, and I will make the round of the city whilst the folk salute me and bless me; after which I will repair to the Wazir (he that is father of the girl), with armed white slaves before and behind me and on my right and on my left. When he sees me, the Wazir stands up, and seating me in his own place sits down much below me; for that I am to be his son-in-law. Now I have with me two eunuchs carrying purses, each containing a thousand dinars; and of these I deliver to him the thousand, his daughter's marriage-settlement, and make him a free gift of the other thousand, that he may have reason to know my generosity and liberality and my greatness of spirit and the littleness of the world in my eyes. And for ten words he addresses to me I answer him two. Then back I go to my house, and if one come to me on the bride's part, I make him a present of money and throw on him a dress of honour; but if he bring me a gift, I give it back to him and refuse to accept it,[3] that they may learn what a proud spirit is mine which never condescends to derogate. Thus I establish my rank and status. When this is done I appoint her wedding night and adorn my house showily! gloriously! And as the time for parading the

---

[1] The texts give "dirhams" (100,000 = 5,000 dinars) for "dinars," a clerical error as the sequel shows.

[2] "Young slaves," says Richardson, losing "colour."

[3] Nothing more calculated to give affront than such a refusal. Richardson (p. 204), who, however, doubts his own version (p. 208), here translates, "and I will not give liberty to my soul (spouse) but in her apartments." The Arabic, or rather Cairene, is, "wa lá akhalli rúhi" = I will not let myself go, i.e., be my everyday self, etc.

bride is come, I don my finest attire and sit down on a mattress of gold brocade, propping up my elbow with a pillow, and turning neither to the right nor to the left; but looking only straight in front for the haughtiness of my mind and the gravity of my understanding. And there before me stands my wife in her raiment and ornaments, lovely as the full moon; and I, in my loftiness and dread lordliness,[1] will not glance at her till those present say to me, 'O our lord and our master, thy wife, thy handmaid, standeth before thee; vouchsafe her one look, for standing wearieth her.' Then they kiss the ground before me many times; whereupon I raise my eyes and cast at her one single glance and turn my face earthwards again. Then they bear her off to the bride-chamber,[2] and I arise and change my clothes for a far finer suit; and, when they bring in the bride a second time, I deign not to throw her a look till they have begged me many times; after which I glance at her out of the corner of one eye, and then bend down my head. I continue acting after this fashion till the parading and displaying are completed[3]"——And Shahrazad perceived the dawn of day and ceased saying her permitted say.

When it was the Thirty-third Night,

She said, It hath reached me, O auspicious King, that the Barber's fifth brother proceeded:—"Then I bend down my head and continue acting after this fashion till her parading and displaying are completed. Thereupon I order one of my eunuchs to bring me a bag of five hundred dinars which I give as largesse to the tire-women present and bid them one and all lead me to the bride-chamber. When they leave me alone with her I neither look at her nor speak to her, but lie[4] by her side with my face to the wall showing my contempt, that each and every may again remark how high and haughty I am. Presently her mother comes in to me; and kissing[5] my head and hand, says to me, 'O my lord, look upon thine handmaid who longs for thy favour; so heal her broken spirit!' I give her no answer; and when she sees this she

---

1 "Whilst she is in astonishment and terror." (Richardson.)
2 "Chamber of robes," Richardson, whose text has "Nám" for "Manám."
3 "Till I compleat her distress," Richardson, whose text is corrupt.
4 "Sleep by her side," R. the word "Náma" bearing both senses.
5 "Will take my hand," R. "takabbal" being also ambiguous.

rises and busses my feet many times and says, 'O my lord, in very sooth my daughter is a beautiful maid, who hath never known man; and if thou show her this backwardness and aversion, her heart will break; so do thou incline to her and speak to her and soothe her mind and spirit.' Then she rises and fetches a cup of wine; and says to her daughter, 'Take it and hand it to thy lord.' But as she approaches me I leave her standing between my hands and sit, propping my elbow on a round cushion purfled with gold thread, leaning lazily back, and without looking at her in the majesty of my spirit, so that she may deem me indeed a Sultan and a mighty man. Then she says to me, 'O my lord, Allah upon thee, do not refuse to take the cup from the hand of thine hand-maid, for verily I am thy bondswoman.' But I do not speak to her and she presses me, saying, 'There is no help but that thou drink it;' and she puts it to my lips. Then I shake my fist in her face and kick her with my foot thus." So he let out with his toe and knocked over the tray of glass-ware which fell to the ground and, falling from the bench, all that was on it was broken to bits. "O foulest of pimps,[1] this comes from the pride of my spirit!" cried my brother; and then, O Commander of the Faithful, he buffeted his face and rent his garments, and kept on weeping and beating himself. The folk who were flocking to their Friday prayers saw him; and some of them looked at him and pitied him, whilst others paid no heed to him, and in this way my brother lost both capital and profit. He remained weeping a long while, and at last up came a beautiful lady, the scent of musk ex-haling from her, who was going to Friday prayers riding a mule with a gold saddle and followed by several eunuchs. When she saw the broken glass and my brother weeping, her kind heart was moved to pity for him, and she asked what ailed him and was told that he had a tray full of glass-ware by the sale of which he hoped to gain his living, but it was broken, and (said they), "there befel him what thou seest." Thereupon she called up one of her eunuchs and said to him, "Give what thou hast with thee to this poor fellow!" And he gave my brother a purse in which he found five hundred dinars; and when it touched his hand he was well-

---

[1] Arab. "Mu'arras" one who brings about " 'Ars," marriages, etc. So the Germ. "Kupplerinn," a Coupleress. It is one of the many synonyms for a pimp, and a word in general use (Pilgrimage i., 276). The most insulting term, like Dayyús, insinuates that the man panders for his own wife.

nigh dying for excess of joy and he offered up blessings for her. Then he returned to his abode a substantial man; and, as he sat considering, some one rapped at the door. So he rose and opened and saw an old woman whom he had never seen. "O my son," said she, "know that prayertide is near and I have not yet made my Wuzu-ablution;[1] so kindly allow me the use of thy lodging for the purpose." My brother answered, "To hear is to comply;" and going in bade her follow him. So she entered and he brought her an ewer wherewith to wash, and sat down like to fly with joy because of the dinars which he had tied up in his belt for a purse. When the old woman had made an end of her ablution, she came up to where he sat, and prayed a two-bow prayer; after which she blessed my brother with a godly benediction, and he while thanking her put his hand to the dinars and gave her two, saying to himself "These are my voluntaries."[2] When she saw the gold she cried, "Praise be to Allah! why dost thou look on one who loveth thee as if she were a beggar? Take back thy money: I have no need of it; or, if thou want it not, return it to her who gave it thee when thy glass-ware was broken. Moreover, if thou wish to be united with her, I can manage the matter, for she is my mistress." "O my mother," asked my brother, "by what manner of means can I get at her?"; and she answered, "O my son! she hath an inclination for thee, but she is the wife of a wealthy man; so take the whole of thy money with thee and follow me, that I may guide thee to thy desire: and when thou art in her company spare neither persuasion nor fair words, but bring them all to bear upon her; so shalt thou enjoy her beauty and wealth to thy heart's content." My brother took all his gold and rose and followed the old woman, hardly believing in his luck. She ceased not faring on, and my brother following her, till they came to a tall gate at which she knocked and a Roumi slave-girl[3] came out and opened to them. Then the old woman led my brother into a great sitting-room spread with wondrous fine carpets and hung

---

1 Of hands and face, etc. See Night cccclxiv.

2 Arab. "Sadakah" (sincerity), voluntary or superogatory alms, opposed to "Zakát" (purification), legal alms which are indispensable. "Prayer carries us half way to Allah; fasting brings us to the door of His palace and alms-deeds (Sadakah) cause us to enter." For "Zakát" no especial rate is fixed, but it should not be less than one-fortieth of property or two and a half per cent. Thus Al-Islam is, as far as I know, the only faith which makes a poor-rate (Zakát) obligatory and which has invented a property-tax, as opposed to the unjust and unfair income-tax upon which England prides herself.

3 A Greek girl.

with curtains, where he sat down with his gold before him, and his turband on his knee.[1] He had scarcely taken seat before there came to him a young lady (never eye saw fairer) clad in garments of the most sumptuous; whereupon my brother rose to his feet, and she smiled in his face and welcomed him, signing to him to be seated. Then she bade shut the door and, when it was shut, she turned to my brother, and taking his hand conducted him to a private chamber furnished with various kinds of brocades and gold-cloths. Here he sat down and she sat by his side and toyed with him awhile; after which she rose and saying, "Stir not from thy seat till I come back to thee;" disappeared. Meanwhile as he was on this wise, lo! there came in to him a black slave big of body and bulk and holding a drawn sword in hand, who said to him, "Woe to thee! Who brought thee hither and what dost thou want here?" My brother could not return him a reply, being tongue-tied for terror; so the blackamoor seized him and stripped him of his clothes and bashed him with the flat of his sword-blade till he fell to the ground, swooning from excess of belabouring. The ill-omened nigger fancied that there was an end of him and my brother heard him cry, "Where is the salt-wench?"[2] Where-upon in came a handmaid holding in hand a large tray of salt, and the slave kept rubbing it into my brother's wounds;[3] but he did not stir fearing lest the slave might find out that he was not dead and kill him outright. Then the salt-girl went away, and the slave cried "Where is the souterrain[4]-guardianess?" Hereupon in came the old woman and dragged my brother by his feet to a souterrain and threw him down upon a heap of dead bodies. In this place he lay two full days, but Allah made the salt the means of preserving his life by staunching the blood and staying its flow. Presently, feeling himself able to move, Al-Nashshar rose and

---

[1] This was making himself very easy; and the idea is that the gold in pouch caused him to be so bold. Lane's explanation (in loco) is all wrong. The pride engendered by sudden possession of money is a *lieu commun* amongst Eastern story-tellers; even in the beast-fables the mouse which has stolen a few gold pieces becomes confident and stout-hearted.

[2] Arab. "Al-Málihah" also means the beautiful (fem.), from "Milh" = salt, splendour, etc., the Mac. Edit. has "Mumallihah" = a salt-vessel.

[3] *i.e.*, to see if he felt the smart.

[4] Arab. "Sardábeh" (Persian) = an underground room used for coolness in the hot season. It is unknown in Cairo, but every house in Baghdad, in fact throughout the Mesopotamian cities, has one. It is on the principle of the underground cellar without which wine will not keep: Lane (i., 406) calls it a "vault."

opened the trap-door in fear and trembling and crept out into the open; and Allah protected him, so that he went on in the darkness and hid himself in the vestibule till dawn, when he saw the accursed beldam sally forth in quest of other quarry. He followed in her wake without her knowing it, and made for his own lodging where he dressed his wounds and medicined himself till he was whole. Meanwhile he used to watch the old woman, tracking her at all times and seasons, and saw her accost one man after another and carry them to the house. However he uttered not a word; but, as soon as he waxed hale and hearty, he took a piece of stuff and made it into a bag which he filled with broken glass and bound about his middle. He also disguised himself as a Persian that none might know him, and hid a sword under his clothes of foreign cut. Then he went out and presently, falling in with the old woman, said to her, speaking Arabic with a Persian accent, "Venerable lady,[1] I am a stranger arrived but this day here where I know no one. Hast thou a pair of scales wherein I may weigh eleven hundred dinars? I will give thee somewhat of them for thy pains." "I have a son, a money-changer, who keepeth all kinds of scales," she answered, "so come with me to him before he goeth out and he will weigh thy gold." My brother answered "Lead the way!" She led him to the house and the young lady herself came out and opened it, whereupon the old woman smiled in her face and said, "I bring thee fat meat to-day."[2] Then the damsel took my brother by the hand, and led him to the same chamber as before; where she sat with him awhile then rose and went forth saying, "Stir not from thy seat till I come back to thee." Presently in came the accursed slave with the drawn sword and cried to my brother, "Up and be damned to thee!" So he rose, and as the slave walked on before him he drew the sword from under his clothes and smote him with it, making head fly from body. Then he dragged the corpse by the feet to the souterrain and called out, "Where is the salt-wench?" Up came the girl carrying the tray of salt and, seeing my brother sword in hand, turned to fly; but he followed her and struck off her head. Then he called out, "Where is the souterrain-guardianess?"; and in came the old woman to whom he said, "Dost know me again, O ill-omened hag?" "No my lord," she replied, and he said, "I am

---

[1] In the orig. "O old woman!" which is insulting.
[2] So the Italians say "a quail to skin."

the owner of the five hundred gold pieces, whose house thou
enteredst to make the ablution and to pray, and whom thou didst
snare hither and betray." "Fear Allah and spare me," cried she;
but he regarded her not and struck her with the sword till he had
cut her in four. Then he went to look for the young lady; and
when she saw him her reason fled and she cried out piteously
"Amán![1] Mercy!" So he spared her and asked, "What made thee
consort with this blackamoor?"; and she answered, "I was slave
to a certain merchant, and the old woman used to visit me till I
took a liking to her. One day she said to me, 'We have a marriage
festival at our house the like of which was never seen and I wish
thee to enjoy the sight.' 'To hear is to obey,' answered I, and
rising arrayed myself in my finest raiment and ornaments, and
took with me a purse containing an hundred gold pieces. Then
she brought me hither and hardly had I entered the house when
the black seized on me, and I have remained in this case three
whole years through the perfidy of the accursed beldam." Then
my brother asked her, "Is there anything of his in the house?";
whereto she answered, "Great store of wealth, and if thou art
able to carry it away, do so and Allah give thee good of it!" My
brother went with her and she opened to him sundry chests
wherein were money bags, at which he was astounded; then she
said to him, "Go now and leave me here, and fetch men to remove
the money." He went out and hired ten men, but when he returned he found the door wide open, the damsel gone and nothing left but some small matter of coin and the household stuffs.[2]
By this he knew that the girl had overreached him; so he opened
the store rooms and seized what was in them, together with the
rest of the money, leaving nothing in the house. He passed the
night rejoicing, but when morning dawned he found at the door
some twenty troopers who laid hands on him saying, "The
Governor wants thee!" My brother implored them hard to let
him return to his house; and even offered them a large sum of
money; but they refused and, binding him fast with cords, carried
him off. On the way they met a friend of my brother who clung
to his skirt and implored his protection, begging him to stand by
him and help to deliver him out of their hands. The man stopped,

---

[1] "Amán" is the word used for quarter on the battle-field; and there are Joe Millers
about our soldiers in India mistaking it for "a man" or (*Scotticè*) "a mon."
[2] Illustrating the Persian saying "Allah himself cannot help a fool."

and asked them what was the matter, and they answered, "The Governor hath ordered us to bring this fellow before him and, look ye, we are doing so." My brother's friend urged them to release him, and offered them five hundred dinars to let him go, saying, "When ye return to the Governor tell him that you were unable to find him." But they would not listen to his words and took my brother, dragging him along on his face, and set him before the Governor who asked him, "Whence gottest thou these stuffs and monies?"; and he answered, "I pray for mercy!" So the Governor gave him the kerchief of mercy;[1] and he told him all that had befallen him from first to last with the old woman and the flight of the damsel; ending with, "Whatso I have taken, take of it what thou wilt, so thou leave me sufficient to support life."[2] But the Governor took the whole of the stuffs and all the money for himself; and, fearing lest the affair come to the Sultan's ears, he summoned my brother and said, "Depart from this city, else I will hang thee." "Hearing and obedience" quoth my brother and set out for another town. On the way thieves fell foul of him and stripped and beat him and docked his ears; but I heard tidings of his misfortunes and went out after him taking him clothes; and brought him secretly into the city where I assigned to him an allowance for meat and drink. And presently the Caliph gave ear to

The Barber's Tale of his Sixth Brother.

My sixth brother, O Commander of the Faithful, Shakashik,[3] or Many-clamours, the shorn of both lips, was once rich and became poor; so one day he went out to beg somewhat to keep life in him. As he was on the road he suddenly caught sight of a large and handsome mansion, with a detached building wide and lofty at the entrance, where sat sundry eunuchs bidding and forbidding.[4]

---

1 Any article taken from the person and given to a criminal is a promise of pardon, of course on the implied condition of plenary confession and of becoming "King's evidence."

2 A naïve proposal to share the plunder.

3 In popular literature "Schacabac." And from this tale comes our saying "A Barmecide's Feast," *i.e.*, an illusion.

4 The Castrato at the door is still (I have said) the fashion of Cairo and he acts "Suisse" with a witness.

My brother enquired of one of those idling there and he replied, "The palace belongs to a scion of the Barmaki house;" so he stepped up to the door-keepers and asked an alms of them. "Enter," said they, "by the great gate and thou shalt get what thou seekest from the Wazir our master." Accordingly he went in and, passing through the outer entrance, walked on a while and presently came to a mansion of the utmost beauty and elegance, paved with marble, hung with curtains and having in the midst of it a flower garden whose like he had never seen.[1] My brother stood awhile as one bewildered not knowing whither to turn his steps; then, seeing the farther end of the sitting-chamber tenanted, he walked up to it and there found a man of handsome presence and comely beard. When this personage saw my brother he stood up to him and welcomed him and asked him of his case; whereto he replied that he was in want and needed charity. Hearing these words the grandee showed great concern and, putting his hand to his fine robe, rent it exclaiming, "What! am I in a city, and thou here an-hungered? I have not patience to bear such disgrace!" Then he promised him all manner of good cheer and said, "There is no help but that thou stay with me and eat of my salt."[2] "O my lord," answered my brother, "I can wait no longer; for I am indeed dying of hunger." So he cried, "Ho boy! bring basin and ewer;" and, turning to my brother, said, "O my guest come forward and wash thy hands." My brother rose to do so but he saw neither ewer nor basin; yet his host kept washing his hands with invisible soap in imperceptible water and cried, "Bring the table!" But my brother again saw nothing. Then said the host, "Honour me by eating of this meat and be not ashamed." And he kept moving his hand to and fro as if he ate and saying to my brother, "I wonder to see thee eating thus sparely: do not stint thyself for I am sure thou art famished." So my brother began to make as though he were eating whilst

---

[1] As usual in the East, the mansion was a hollow square surrounding what in Spain is called *Patio:* the outer entrance was far from the inner, showing the extent of the grounds.

[2] "Nahnu málihín" = we are on terms of salt, said and say the Arabs. But the traveller must not trust in these days to the once sacred tie; there are tribes which will give bread with one hand and stab with the other. The Eastern use of salt is a curious contrast with that of Westerns, who made it an invidious and inhospitable distinction, *e.g.*, to sit above the salt-cellar and below the salt. Amongst the ancients, however, "he took bread and salt" means he swore, the food being eaten when an oath was taken. Hence the "Bride cake" of salt, water and flour.

his host kept saying to him, "Fall to, and note especially the ex-cellence of this bread and its whiteness!" But still my brother saw nothing. Then said he to himself, ";This man is fond of pok-ing fun at people;" and replied, "O my lord, in all my days I never knew aught more winsome than its whiteness or sweeter than its savour." The Barmecide said, "This bread was baked by a hand-maid of mine whom I bought for five hundred dinars." Then he called out, "Ho boy, bring in the meat pudding[1] for our first dish, and let there be plenty of fat in it;" and, turning to my brother said, "O my guest, Allah upon thee, hast ever seen anything better than this meat-pudding? Now by my life, eat and be not abashed." Presently he cried out again, "Ho boy, serve up the marinated stew[2] with the fatted sand-grouse in it;" and he said to my brother, "Up and eat, O my guest, for truly thou art hungry and needest food." So my brother began wagging his jaws and made as if champing and chewing,[3] whilst the host con-tinued calling for one dish after another and yet produced noth-ing save orders to eat. Presently he cried out, "Ho boy, bring us the chickens stuffed with pistachio nuts;" and said to my brother, "By thy life, O my guest, I have fattened these chickens upon pistachios; eat, for thou hast never eaten their like." "O my lord," replied my brother, "they are indeed first-rate." Then the host began motioning with his hand as though he were giving my brother a mouthful; and ceased not to enumerate and expatiate upon the various dishes to the hungry man whose hunger waxt still more violent, so that his soul lusted after a bit of bread, even a barley-scone.[4] Quoth the Barmecide, "Didst thou ever taste anything more delicious than the seasoning of these dishes?"; and quoth my brother, "Never, O my lord!" "Eat heartily and be not ashamed," said the host, and the guest, "I have eaten my fill

---

1 Arab. "Harísah," the meat-pudding before explained.
2 Arab. "Sikbáj," before explained; it is held to be a lordly dish, invented by Khusraw Parwiz. "Fatted duck" says the Bresl. Edit. ii., 308, with more reason.
3 I was reproved in Southern Abyssinia for eating without this champing, "Thou feedest like a beggar who muncheth silently in his corner;" and presently found that it was a sign of good breeding to eat as noisily as possible.
4 Barley in Arabia is, like our oats, food for horses: it fattens at the same time that it cools them. Had this been known to our cavalry when we first occupied Egypt in 1883-4 our losses in horse-flesh would have been far less; but official ignorance persisted in feeding the cattle upon heating oats and the riders upon beef, which is indigestible, instead of mutton, which is wholesome.

of meat." So the entertainer cried, "Take away and bring in the sweets;" and turning to my brother said, "Eat of this almond conserve for it is prime and of these honey-fritters; take this one, by my life, the syrup runs out of it." "May I never be bereaved of thee, O my lord," replied the hungry one and began to ask him about the abundance of musk in the fritters. "Such is my custom," he answered: "they put me a dinar-weight of musk in every honey-fritter and half that quantity of ambergris." All this time my brother kept wagging head and jaws till the master cried, "Enough of this. Bring us the dessert!" Then said he to him, "Eat of these almonds and walnuts and raisins; and of this and that (naming divers kinds of dried fruits), and be not abashed." But my brother replied, "O my lord, indeed I am full: I can eat no more." "O my guest," repeated the host, "if thou have a mind to these good things eat: Allah! Allah![1] do not remain hungry;" but my brother rejoined, "O my lord, he who hath eaten of all these dishes how can he be hungry?" Then he considered and said to himself, "I will do that shall make him repent of these pranks." Presently the entertainer called out "Bring me the wine;" and, moving his hands in the air, as though they had set it before them, he gave my brother a cup and said, "Take this cup and, if it please thee, let me know." "O my lord," he replied, "it is notable good as to nose but I am wont to drink wine some twenty years old." "Knock then at this door,"[2] quoth the host, "for thou canst not drink of aught better." "By thy kindness," said my brother, motioning with his hand as though he were drinking. "Health and joy to thee," exclaimed the house-master, and feigned to fill a cup and drink it off; then he handed another to my brother who quaffed it and made as if he were drunken. Presently he took the host unawares; and, raising his arm till the white of his armpit appeared, dealt him such a cuff on the nape of his neck that the palace echoed to it. Then he came down upon him with a second cuff and the entertainer cried aloud, "What is this, O thou scum of the earth?" "O my lord," replied my brother, "thou hast shown much kindness to thy slave, and admitted him into thine abode and given him to eat of thy victual; then thou madest him drink of thine old wine till he

---

[1] i.e. "I conjure thee by God."
[2] i.e. "This is the very thing for thee."

became drunken and boisterous; but thou art too noble not to bear with his ignorance and pardon his offence." When the Barmaki heard my brother's words he laughed his loudest and said, "Long have I been wont to make mock of men and play the madcap among my intimates, but never yet have I come across a single one who had the patience and the wit to enter into all my humours save thyself: so I forgive thee, and thou shalt be my boon-companion in very sooth and never leave me." Then he ordered the servants to lay the table in earnest and they set on all the dishes of which he had spoken in sport; and he and my brother ate till they were satisfied; after which they removed to the drinking-chamber, where they found damsels like moons who sang all manner songs and played on all manner instruments. There they remained drinking till their wine got the better of them and the host treated my brother like a familiar friend, so that he became as it were his brother, and bestowed on him a robe of honour and loved him with exceeding love. Next morning the two fell again to feasting and carousing, and ceased not to lead this life for a term of twenty years; at the end of which the Barmecide died and the Sultan took possession of all his wealth and squeezed my brother of his savings, till he was left a pauper without a penny to handle. So he quitted the city and fled forth following his face;[1] but, when he was half way between two towns, the wild Arabs fell on him and bound him and carried him to their camp, where his captor proceeded to torture him, saying, "Buy thy life of me with thy money, else I will slay thee!" My brother began to weep and replied, "By Allah, I have nothing, neither gold nor silver; but I am thy prisoner; so do with me what thou wilt." Then the Badawi drew a knife, broad-bladed and so sharp-grided that if plunged into a camel's throat[2] it would sever it clean across from one jugular to the other, and cut off my brother's lips and waxed more instant in requiring money. Now this Badawi had a fair wife who in her husband's absence used to make advances to my brother and offer him her favours, but he held off from her. One day she began to tempt him as usual and

---

[1] *i.e.*, at random.
[2] This is the way of slaughtering the camel, whose throat is never cut on account of the thickness of the muscles. "Égorger un chameau" is a mistake often made in French books.

he played with her and made her sit on his lap, when behold, in
came the Badawi who, seeing this, cried out, "Woe to thee, O
accursed villain, wouldest thou debauch my wife for me?" Then
he took out a knife and cut off my brother's yard, after which he
bound him on the back of a camel and, carrying him to a mountain, left him there. He was at last found by some who recognised him and gave him meat and drink and acquainted me with
his condition; whereupon I went forth to him and brought him
back to Baghdad where I made him an allowance sufficient to live
on. This, then, O Commander of the Faithful, is the history of
my six brothers, and I feared to go away without relating it all to
thee and leave thee in the error of judging me to be like them.
And now thou knowest that I have six brothers upon my hands
and, being more upright than they, I support the whole family.
When the Caliph heard my story and all I told him concerning
my brothers, he laughed and said, "Thou sayest sooth, O Silent
Man! thou art indeed spare of speech nor is there aught of forwardness in thee; but now go forth out of this city and settle in
some other." And he banished me under edict. I left Baghdad
and travelled in foreign parts till I heard of his death and the
accession of another to the Caliphate. Then I returned to Baghdad where I found all my brothers dead and chanced upon this
young man, to whom I rendered the kindliest service, for without
me he had surely been killed. Indeed he slanders me and accuses
me of a fault which is not in my nature; and what he reports concerning impudence and meddling and forwardness is idle and
false; for verily on his account I left Baghdad and travelled about
full many a country till I came to this city and met him here in
your company. And was not this, O worthy assemblage, of the
generosity of my nature?

The End of the Tailor's Tale.

THEN quoth the Tailor to the King of China:—When we heard
the Barber's tale and saw the excess of his loquacity and the way
in which he had wronged this young man, we laid hands on him
and shut him up, after which we sat down in peace, and ate and
drank and enjoyed the good things of the marriage-feast till the

time of the call to mid-afternoon prayer, when I left the party and returned home. My wife received me with sour looks and said, "Thou goest a-pleasuring among thy friends and thou leavest me to sit sorrowing here alone. So now, unless thou take me abroad and let me have some amusement for the rest of the day, I will cut the rope[1] and it will be the cause of my separation from thee." So I took her out and we amused ourselves till supper time, when we returned home and fell in with this Hunchback who was brimful of drink and trolling out these rhymes:—

"Clear's the wine, the cup's fine; * Like to like they combine:
It is wine and not cup!   * 'Tis a cup and not wine!"

So I invited him to sup with us and went out to buy fried fish; after which we sat down to eat; and presently my wife took a piece of bread and a fid of fish and stuffed them into his mouth and he choked; and, though I slapped him long and hard between the shoulders, he died. Then I carried him off and contrived to throw him into the house of this leach, the Jew; and the leach contrived to throw him into the house of the Reeve; and the Reeve contrived to throw him on the way of the Nazarene broker. This, then, is my adventure which befel me but yesterday. Is not it more wondrous than the story of the Hunchback? When the King of China heard the Tailor's tale he shook his head for pleasure; and, showing great surprise, said, "This that passed between the young man and the busy-body of a Barber is indeed more pleasant and wonderful than the story of my lying knave of a Hunchback." Then he bade one of his Chamberlains go with the Tailor and bring the Barber out of jail, saying, "I wish to hear the talk of this Silent Man and it shall be the cause of your deliverance one and all: then we will bury the Hunchback, for that he is dead since yesterday, and set up a tomb over him."——And Shahrazad perceived the dawn of day and ceased to say her permitted say.

𝔚𝔥𝔢𝔫 𝔦𝔱 𝔴𝔞𝔰 𝔱𝔥𝔢 𝔗𝔥𝔦𝔯𝔱𝔶-𝔣𝔬𝔲𝔯𝔱𝔥 𝔑𝔦𝔤𝔥𝔱,

She said, It hath reached me, O auspicious King, that the King of China bade, "Bring me the Barber who shall be the cause of your

---

[1] i.e. I will break bounds.

deliverance; then we will bury this Hunchback, for that he is dead since yesterday and set up a tomb over him." So the Chamberlain and the Tailor went to the jail and, releasing the Barber, presently returned with him to the King. The Sultan of China looked at him and considered him carefully and lo and behold! he was an ancient man, past his ninetieth year; swart of face, white of beard, and hoar of eyebrows; lop-eared and proboscis-nosed,[1] with a vacant, silly and conceited expression of countenance. The King laughed at this figure o' fun and said to him, "O Silent Man, I desire thee to tell me somewhat of thy history." Quoth the Barber, "O King of the age, allow me first to ask thee what is the tale of this Nazarene and this Jew and this Moslem and this Hunchback (the corpse) I see among you? And prithee what may be the object of this assemblage?" Quoth the King of China, "And why dost thou ask?" "I ask," he replied, "in order that the King's majesty may know that I am no forward fellow or busy-body or impertinent meddler; and that I am innocent of their calumnious charges of overmuch talk; for I am he whose name is the Silent Man, and indeed peculiarly happy is my sobriquet, as saith the poet:—

When a nickname or little name men design, * Know that nature with name shall full oft combine."

Then said the King, "Explain to the Barber the case of this Hunchback and what befel him at supper-time; also repeat to him the stories told by the Nazarene, the Jew, the Reeve, and the Tailor; and of no avail to me is a twice-told tale." They did his bidding, and the Barber shook his head and said, "By Allah, this is a marvel of marvels! Now uncover me the corpse of yonder Hunchback." They undid the winding-sheet and he sat down and, taking the Hunchback's head in his lap, looked at his face, and laughed and guffaw'd[2] till he fell upon his back and said,

---

[1] The Arabs have a saying corresponding with the dictum of the Salernitan school:—
   Noscitur a labiis quantum sit virginis antrum:
   Noscitur a naso quanta sit hasta viro;
   (A maiden's mouth shows what's the make of her *chose;*
   And man's mentule one knows by the length of his nose.)
Whereto I would add:—
   And the eyebrows disclose how the lower wig grows.
The observations are purely empirical but, as far as my experience extends, correct.
   [2] Arab. "Kahkahah," a very low proceeding.

"There is wonder in every death,[1] but the death of this Hunchback is worthy to be written and recorded in letters of liquid
gold!" The bystanders were astounded at his words and the
King marvelled and said to him, "What ails thee, O Silent Man?
Explain to us thy words!" "O King of the age," said the Barber,
"I swear by thy beneficence that there is still life in this Gobbo
Golightly!" Thereupon he pulled out of his waist-belt a
barber's budget, whence he took a pot of ointment and anointed
therewith the neck of the Hunchback and its arteries. Then he
took a pair of iron tweezers and, inserting them into the Hunchback's throat, drew out the fid of fish with its bone; and, when
it came to sight, behold, it was soaked in blood. Thereupon the
Hunchback sneezed a hearty sneeze and jumped up as if nothing
had happened and passing his hand over his face said, "I testify
that there is no god, but the God, and I testify that Mohammed
is the Apostle of God." At this sight all present wondered; the
King of China laughed till he fainted and in like manner did the
others. Then said the Sultan, "By Allah, of a truth this is the
most marvellous thing I ever saw! O Moslems, O soldiers all,
did you ever in the lives of you see a man die and be quickened
again? Verily had not Allah vouchsafed to him this Barber, he
had been a dead man!" Quoth they, "By Allah, 'tis a marvel of
marvels." Then the King of China bade record this tale, so they
recorded it and placed it in the royal muniment-rooms; after
which he bestowed costly robes of honour upon the Jew, the
Nazarene and the Reeve, and bade them depart in all esteem.
Then he gave the Tailor a sumptuous dress and appointed him
his own tailor, with suitable pay and allowances; and made peace
between him and the Hunchback, to whom also he presented a
splendid and expensive suit with a suitable stipend. He did as
generously with the Barber, giving him a gift and a dress of
honour; moreover he settled on him a handsome solde and
created him Barber-surgeon[2] of state and made him one of his cup-
companions. So they ceased not to live the most pleasurable life
and the most delectable, till there came to them the Destroyer of

---

[1] Or "for every death there is a cause;" but the older Arabs had a saying corresponding with "Deus non fecit mortem."
[2] The King's barber is usually a man of rank for the best of reasons, that he holds his
Sovereign's life between his fingers. One of these noble Figaros in India married an
English lady who was, they say, unpleasantly surprised to find out what were her husband's official duties.

all delights and the Sunderer of all societies, the Depopulator of palaces and the Garnerer for graves. Yet, O most auspicious King! (continued Shahrazad) this tale is by no means more wonderful than that of the two Wazirs and Anís al-Jalís. Quoth her sister Dunyazad, "And what may that be?"; whereupon she began to relate the following tale of

THE EBONY HORSE.[1]

THERE was once in times of yore and ages long gone before, a great and puissant King, of the Kings of the Persians, Sábúr by name, who was the richest of all the Kings in store of wealth and dominion and surpassed each and every in wit and wisdom. He was generous, open handed and beneficent, and he gave to those who sought him and repelled not those who resorted to him; and he comforted the broken-hearted and honourably entreated those who fled to him for refuge. Moreover, he loved the poor and was hospitable to strangers and did the oppressed justice upon the oppressor. He had three daughters, like full moons of shining light or flower-gardens blooming bright; and a son as he were the moon; and it was his wont to keep two festivals in the twelve-month, those of the Nau-Roz, or New Year, and Mihrgán the Autumnal Equinox,[2] on which occasions he threw open his palaces and gave largesse and made proclamation of safety and security and promoted his chamberlains and viceroys; and the people of his realm came in to him and saluted him and gave him joy of the holy day, bringing him gifts and servants and eunuchs. Now he loved

---

[1] This tale (one of those translated by Galland) is best and fullest in the Bresl. Edit. iii. 329.

[2] Europe has degraded this autumnal festival, the Sun-fête Mihrgán (which balanced the vernal Nau-roz) into Michaelmas and its goose-massacre. It was so called because it began on the 16th of Mihr, the seventh month; and lasted six days, with feasts, festivities and great rejoicings in honour of the Sun, who now begins his southing-course to gladden the other half of the world.

science and geometry, and one festival-day as he sat on his kingly throne there came in to him three wise men, cunning artificers and past masters in all manner of craft and inventions, skilled in making things curious and rare, such as confound the wit; and versed in the knowledge of occult truths and perfect in mysteries and subtleties. And they were of three different tongues and countries, the first a Hindi or Indian,[1] the second a Roumi or Greek and the third a Farsi or Persian. The Indian came forwards and, prostrating himself before the King, wished him joy of the festival and laid before him a present befitting his dignity; that is to say, a man of gold, set with precious gems and jewels of price and hending in hand a golden trumpet. When Sabur[2] saw this, he asked, "O sage, what is the virtue of this figure?"; and the Indian answered, "O my lord, if this figure be set at the gate of thy city, it will be a guardian over it; for, if an enemy enter the place, it will blow this clarion against him and he will be seized with a palsy and drop down dead." Much the King marvelled at this and cried, "By Allah, O sage, an this thy word be true, I will grant thee thy wish and thy desire." Then came forward the Greek and, prostrating himself before the King, presented him with a basin of silver, in whose midst was a peacock of gold, surrounded by four-and-twenty chicks of the same metal. Sabur looked at them and turning to the Greek, said to him, "O sage, what is the virtue of this peacock?" "O my lord," answered he, "as often as an hour of the day or night passeth, it pecketh one of its young and crieth out and flappeth its wings, till the four-and-twenty hours are accomplished; and when the month cometh to an end, it will open its mouth and thou shalt see the crescent therein." And the King said, "An thou speak sooth, I will bring thee to thy wish and thy desire." Then came forward the Persian sage and, prostrating himself before the King, presented him with a horse[3] of the

---

[1] "Hindí" is an Indian Moslem as opposed to "Hindú," a pagan, or Gentoo.

[2] The orig. Persian word is "Sháh-púr"=King's son: the Greeks (who had no *sh*) (preferred Σαбώρ); the Romans turned it into Sapor and the Arabs (who lack the *p*) into Sábúr. See p. x. Hamzæ ıspahanensis Annalium Libri x.: Gottwaldt, Lipsiæ mdcccxlviii.

[3] The magic horse may have originated with the Hindu tale of a wooden Garuda (the bird of Vishnu) built by a youth for the purpose of a vehicle. It came with the "Moors" to Spain and appears in "Le Cheval de Fust," a French poem of the thirteenth Century. Thence it passed over to England as shown by Chaucer's "Half-told tale of Cambuscan (Janghíz Khan?) bold," as

"The wondrous steed of brass
On which the Tartar King did ride;"

blackest ebony-wood inlaid with gold and jewels, and ready
harnessed with saddle, bridle and stirrups such as befit Kings;
which when Sabur saw, he marvelled with exceeding marvel and
was confounded at the beauty of its form and the ingenuity of its
fashion. So he asked, "What is the use of this horse of wood, and
what is its virtue and what the secret of its movement?"; and the
Persian answered, "O my lord, the virtue of this horse is that, if
one mount him, it will carry him whither he will and fare with its
rider through the air and cover the space of a year in a single
day." The King marvelled and was amazed at these three
wonders, following thus hard upon one another on the same day,
and turning to the sage, said to him, "By Allah the Omnipotent,
and our Lord the Beneficent, who created all creatures and feedeth
them with meat and drink, an thy speech be veritable and the
virtue of thy contrivance appear, I will assuredly give thee whatsoever thou lustest for and will bring thee to thy desire and thy
wish!"[1] Then he entertained the sages three days, that he might
make trial of their gifts; after which they brought the figures
before him and each took the creature he had wroughten and
showed him the mystery of its movement. The trumpeter blew the
trump; the peacock pecked its chicks and the Persian sage mounted
the ebony horse, whereupon it soared with him high in air and
descended again. When King Sabur saw all this, he was amazed
and perplexed and felt like to fly for joy and said to the three
sages, "Now I am certified of the truth of your words and it
behoveth me to quit me of my promise. Ask ye, therefore, what
ye will, and I will give you that same." Now the report of the
King's daughters had reached the sages, so they answered, "If the
King be content with us and accept of our gifts and allow us to
prefer a request to him, we crave of him that he give us his three
daughters in marriage, that we may be his sons-in-law; for that the
stability of Kings may not be gainsaid." Quoth the King, "I grant

And Leland (Itinerary) derives "Rutlandshire" from "a man named Rutter who rode
round it on a wooden horse constructed by art magic." Lane (ii. 548) quotes the parallel
story of Cleomades and Claremond which Mr. Keightley (Tales and Popular Fictions,
chapt. ii) dates from our thirteenth century. See Vol. i., p. 160.

[1] All Moslems, except those of the Máliki school, hold that the maker of an image representing anything of life will be commanded on the Judgment Day to animate it, and failing
will be duly sent to the Fire. This severity arose apparently from the necessity of putting
down idol-worship and, perhaps, for the same reason the Greek Church admits pictures
but not statues. Of course the command has been honoured with extensive breaching:
for instance all the Sultans of Stambul have had their portraits drawn and painted.

you that which you wish and you desire," and bade summon the
Kazi forthright, that he might marry each of the sages to one of
his daughters. Now it fortuned that the Princesses were behind
a curtain, looking on; and when they heard this, the youngest
considered her husband to be and behold, he was an old man,[1] an
hundred years of age, with hair frosted, forehead drooping, eyebrows mangy, ears slitten, beard and mustachios stained and
dyed; eyes red and goggle; cheeks bleached and hollow; flabby
nose like a brinjall, or egg-plant[2]; face like a cobbler's apron, teeth
overlapping and lips like camel's kidneys, loose and pendulous; in
brief a terror, a horror, a monster, for he was of the folk of his time
the unsightliest and of his age the frightfullest; sundry of his
grinders had been knocked out and his eye-teeth were like the
tusks of the Jinni who frighteneth poultry in hen-houses. Now
the girl was the fairest and most graceful of her time, more elegant
than the gazelle however tender, than the gentlest zephyr blander
and brighter than the moon at her full; for amorous fray right
suitable; confounding in graceful sway the waving bough and
outdoing in swimming gait the pacing roe; in fine she was fairer
and sweeter by far than all her sisters. So, when she saw her
suitor, she went to her chamber and strewed dust on her head and
tore her clothes and fell to buffeting her face and weeping and
wailing. Now the Prince, her brother, Kamar al-Akmár, or the
Moon of Moons hight, was then newly returned from a journey
and, hearing her weeping and crying came in to her (for he loved
her with fond affection, more than his other sisters) and asked her,
"What aileth thee? What hath befallen thee? Tell me and
conceal naught from me." So she smote her breast and answered,
"O my brother and my dear one, I have nothing to hide. If the
palace be straitened upon thy father, I will go out; and if he be
resolved upon a foul thing, I will separate myself from him, though
he consent not to make provision for me; and my Lord will
provide." Quoth he, "Tell me what meaneth this talk and what
hath straitened thy breast and troubled thy temper." "O my

---

[1] This description of ugly old age is written with true Arab *verve*.

[2] Arab. "Badinján": Hind. Bengan: Pers. Bádingán or Badilján; the Mala insana (*Sol-anum pomiferum* or *S. Melongena*) of the Romans, well known in Southern Europe. It is of two kinds, the red (*Solanum lycopersicum*) and the black (*S. Melongena*). The Spaniards know it as "berengeria" and when Sancho Panza (Part ii. chapt. 2) says, "The Moors are fond of egg-plants" he means more than appears. The vegetable is held to be exceedingly heating and thereby to breed melancholia and madness; hence one says to a man that has done something eccentric, "Thou hast been eating brinjalls."

brother and my dear one," answered the Princess, "Know that my father hath promised me in marriage to a wicked magician who brought him, as a gift, a horse of black wood, and hath bewitched him with his craft and his egromancy; but, as for me, I will none of him, and would, because of him, I had never come into this world!" Her brother soothed her and solaced her, then fared to his sire and said, "What be this wizard to whom thou hast given my youngest sister in marriage, and what is this present which he hath brought thee, so that thou hast killed[1] my sister with chagrin? It is not right that this should be." Now the Persian was standing by and, when he heard the Prince's words, he was mortified and filled with fury and the King said, "O my son, an thou sawest this horse, thy wit would be confounded and thou wouldst be amated with amazement." Then he bade the slaves bring the horse before him and they did so; and, when the Prince saw it, it pleased him. So (being an accomplished cavalier) he mounted it forthright and struck its sides with the shovel-shaped stirrup-irons; but it stirred not and the King said to the Sage, "Go show him its movement, that he also may help thee to win thy wish." Now the Persian bore the Prince a grudge because he willed not he should have his sister; so he showed him the pin of ascent on the right side of the horse and saying to him, "Trill this," left him. Thereupon the Prince trilled the pin and lo! the horse forthwith soared with him high in ether, as it were a bird, and gave not overflying till it disappeared from men's espying, whereat the King was troubled and perplexed about his case and said to the Persian, "O sage, look how thou mayst make him descend." But he replied, "O my lord, I can do nothing, and thou wilt never see him again till Resurrection-day, for he, of his ignorance and pride, asked me not of the pin of descent and I forgot to acquaint him therewith." When the King heard this, he was enraged with sore rage; and bade bastinado the sorcerer and clap him in jail, whilst he himself cast the crown from his head and beat his face and smote his breast. Moreover, he shut the doors of his palaces and gave himself up to weeping and keening, he and his wife and daughters and all the folk of the city; and thus their joy was turned to annoy and their gladness changed into sore affliction and sadness. Thus far concerning them; but as regards the Prince, the horse gave not over soaring with him till he drew

---

[1] Again to be understood *Hibernice* "kilt."

near the sun, whereat he gave himself up for lost and saw death in the skies, and was confounded at his case, repenting him of having mounted the horse and saying to himself, "Verily, this was a device of the Sage to destroy me on account of my youngest sister; but there is no Majesty and there is no Might save in Allah, the Glorious, the Great! I am lost without recourse; but I wonder, did not he who made the ascent-pin make also a descent-pin?" Now he was a man of wit and knowledge and intelligence; so he fell to feeling all the parts of the horse, but saw nothing save a screw, like a cock's head, on its right shoulder and the like on the left, when quoth he to himself, "I see no sign save these things like buttons." Presently he turned the right-hand pin, whereupon the horse flew heavenwards with increased speed. So he left it and looking at the sinister shoulder and finding another pin, he wound it up and immediately the steed's upwards motion slowed and ceased and it began to descend, little by little, towards the face of the earth, while the rider became yet more cautious and careful of his life.——And Shahrazad perceived the dawn of day and ceased to say her permitted say.

When it was the Three Hundred and Fifty-eighth Night,

She said, It hath reached me, O auspicious King, that when the Prince wound up the sinister screw, the steed's upward motion slowed and ceased, and it began to descend, little by little, towards the earth while the rider became yet more cautious and careful of his life. And when he saw this and knew the uses of the horse, his heart was filled with joy and gladness and he thanked Almighty Allah for that He had deigned deliver him from destruction. Then he began to turn the horse's head whithersoever he would, making it rise and fall at pleasure, till he had gotten complete mastery over its every movement. He ceased not to descend the whole of that day, for that the steed's ascending flight had borne him afar from the earth; and, as he descended, he diverted himself with viewing the various cities and countries over which he passed and which he knew not, never having seen them in his life. Amongst the rest, he descried a city ordered after the fairest fashion in the midst of a verdant and riant land, rich in trees and streams, with gazelles pacing daintily over the plains; whereat he fell a-musing and said to himself, "Would I knew the name of yon town and in what land it is!" And he took to circling about it and observing it right and left. By this time, the day began to decline and the sun drew near to its downing; and he said in his mind, "Verily I find no goodlier place to night in than this city; so I will lodge here and early on the morrow I will return to my kith and kin and my kingdom; and tell my father and family what hath passed and acquaint him with what mine eyes have seen." Then he addressed himself to seeking a place wherein he might safely bestow himself and his horse and where none should descry him, and presently behold, he espied a-middle-most of the city a palace rising high in upper air surrounded by a great wall with lofty crenelles and battlements, guarded by forty black slaves, clad in complete mail and armed with spears and swords, bows and arrows. Quoth he, "This is a goodly place," and turned the descent-pin, whereupon the horse sank down with him like a weary bird, and alighted gently on the terrace-roof of the palace. So the Prince dismounted and ejaculating "Alhamdolillah"—praise be to Allah[1]—he began to go round about the horse and examine it, saying, "By Allah, he who fashioned thee with these perfections was a cunning craftsman, and if the Almighty extend the term of my life and restore me to my country and kinsfolk in safety and reunite me with my father, I will assuredly bestow upon him all manner bounties and benefit him with the utmost beneficence." By this time night had overtaken him and he sat on the roof till he was assured that all in the palace slept; and indeed hunger and thirst were sore upon him, for that he had not tasted food nor drunk water since he parted from his sire. So he said within himself, "Surely the like of this palace will not lack of victual;" and, leaving the horse above, went down in search of somewhat to eat. Presently, he came to a staircase and descending it to the bottom, found himself in a court paved with white marble and alabaster, which shone in the light of the moon. He marvelled at the place and the goodliness of its fashion, but sensed no sound of speaker and saw no living soul and stood in perplexed surprise, looking right and left and knowing not whither he should wend. Then said he to himself, "I may not do better than return to where I left my horse and pass the night by it; and as soon as day shall dawn I will mount and ride away."——And Shahrazad perceived the dawn of day and ceased saying her permitted say.

---

[1] *i.e.* for fear of the evil eye injuring the palace and, haply, himself.

When it was the Three Hundred and Fifty-ninth Night,

She said, It hath reached me, O auspicious King, that quoth the
king's son to himself, "I may not do better than pass the night
by my horse; and as soon as day shall dawn I will mount and
ride away." However, as he tarried talking to himself, he espied
a light within the palace, and making towards it, found that it
came from a candle that stood before a door of the Harim, at the
head of a sleeping eunuch, as he were one of the Ifrits of Solomon
or a tribesman of the Jinn, longer than lumber and broader than
a bench. He lay before the door, with the pommel of his sword
gleaming in the flame of the candle, and at his head was a bag
of leather[1] hanging from a column of granite. When the Prince
saw this, he was affrighted and said, "I crave help from Allah the
Supreme! O mine Holy One, even as Thou hast already delivered me from destruction, so vouchsafe me strength to quit
myself of the adventure of this palace!" So saying, he put out
his hand to the budget and taking it, carried it aside and opened
it and found in it food of the best. He ate his fill and refreshed
himself and drank water, after which he hung up the provision-
bag in its place and drawing the eunuch's sword from its sheath,
took it, whilst the slave slept on, knowing not whence destiny
should come to him. Then the Prince fared forwards into the
palace and ceased not till he came to a second door, with a curtain
drawn before it; so he raised the curtain and behold, on entering
he saw a couch of the whitest ivory, inlaid with pearls and jacinths
and jewels, and four slave-girls sleeping about it. He went up to
the couch, to see what was thereon, and found a young lady lying
asleep, chemised with her hair[2] as she were the full moon rising[3]
over the Eastern horizon, with flower-white brow and shining hair-
parting and cheeks like blood-red anemones and dainty moles
thereon. He was amazed at her as she lay in her beauty and
loveliness, her symmetry and grace, and he recked no more
of death. So he went up to her, trembling in every nerve and,

---

[1] The "Sufrah" before explained as acting provision-bag and table-cloth.

[2] Eastern women in hot weather, lie mother-nude under a sheet here represented by the
hair. The Greeks and Romans also slept stripped and in mediæval England the most
modest women saw nothing indelicate in sleeping naked by their naked husbands. The
"night-cap" and the "night-gown" are comparatively modern inventions.

[3] Hindu fable turns this simile into better poetry, "She was like a second and a more
wondrous moon made by the Creator."

shuddering with pleasure, kissed her on the right cheek; whereupon she awoke forthright and opened her eyes, and seeing the
Prince standing at her head, said to him, "Who art thou and
whence comest thou?" Quoth he, "I am thy slave and thy
lover." Asked she, "And who brought thee hither?" and he
answered, "My Lord and my fortune." Then said Shams
al-Nahár[1] (for such was her name), "Haply thou art he who
demanded me yesterday of my father in marriage and he rejected
thee, pretending that thou wast foul of favour. By Allah, my sire
lied in his throat when he spoke this thing, for thou art not other
than beautiful." Now the son of the King of Hind had sought
her in marriage, but her father had rejected him, for that he was
ugly and uncouth, and she thought the Prince was he. So, when
she saw his beauty and grace (for indeed he was like the radiant
moon) the syntheism[2] of love gat hold of her heart as it were a
flaming fire, and they fell to talk and converse. Suddenly, her
waiting-women awoke and, seeing the Prince with their mistress,
said to her, "Oh my lady, who is this with thee?" Quoth she,
"I know not; I found him sitting by me, when I woke up: haply
'tis he who seeketh me in marriage of my sire." Quoth they,
"O my lady, by Allah the All-Father, this is not he who seeketh
thee in marriage, for he is hideous and this man is handsome
and of high degree. Indeed, the other is not fit to be his servant."[3]
Then the handmaidens went out to the eunuch, and finding him
slumbering awoke him, and he started up in alarm. Said they,
"How happeth it that thou art on guard at the palace and yet men
come in to us, whilst we are asleep?" When the black heard this,
he sprang in haste to his sword, but found it not; and fear took him

---

[1] "Sun of the Day."

[2] Arab. "Shirk"=worshipping more than one God. A theological term here most ap-
propriately used.

[3] The Bul. Edit. as usual abridges (vol. i. 534). The Prince lands on the palace-roof
where he leaves his horse, and finding no one in the building goes back to the terrace.
Suddenly he sees a beautiful girl approaching him with a party of her women, suggesting
to him these couplets,

"She came without tryst in the darkest hour, * Like full moon lighting horizon's night:
Slim-formed, there is not in the world her like * For grace of form or for gifts of sprite:
'Praise him who made her from semen-drop,' * I cried, when her beauty first struck
    my sight:
I guard her from eyes, seeking refuge with * The Lord of mankind and of morning-
    light."

The two then made acquaintance and "follows what follows."

and trembling. Then he went in, confounded, to his mistress and seeing the Prince sitting at talk with her, said to him, "O my lord, art thou man or Jinni?" Replied the Prince, "Woe to thee, O unluckiest of slaves: how darest thou even the sons of the royal Chosroes[1] with one of the unbelieving Satans?" And he was as a raging lion. Then he took the sword in his hand and said to the slave, "I am the King's son-in-law, and he hath married me to his daughter and bidden me go in to her." And when the eunuch heard these words he replied, "O my lord, if thou be indeed of kind a man as thou avouchest, she is fit for none but for thee, and thou art worthier of her than any other." Thereupon the eunuch ran to the King, shrieking loud and rending his raiment and heaving dust upon his head; and when the King heard his outcry, he said to him, "What hath befallen thee?: speak quickly and be brief; for thou hast fluttered my heart." Answered the eunuch, "O King, come to thy daughter's succour; for a devil of the Jinn, in the likeness of a King's son, hath got possession of her; so up and at him!" When the King heard this, he thought to kill him and said, "How camest thou to be careless of my daughter and let this demon come at her?" Then he betook himself to the Princess's palace, where he found her slave-women standing to await him and asked them, "What is come to my daughter?" "O King," answered they, "slumber overcame us and, when we awoke, we found a young man sitting upon her couch in talk with her, as he were the full moon; never saw we aught fairer of favour than he. So we questioned him of his case and he declared that thou hadst given him thy daughter in marriage. More than this we know not, nor do we know if he be a man or a Jinni; but he is modest and well bred, and doth nothing unseemly or which leadeth to disgrace." Now when the King heard these words, his wrath cooled and he raised the curtain little by little and looking in, saw sitting at talk with his daughter a Prince of the goodliest with a face like the full moon for sheen. At this sight he could not contain himself, of his jealousy for his daughter's honour; and, putting aside the curtain, rushed in upon them drawn sword in hand like a furious Ghul. Now when the Prince saw him he asked the Princess, "Is this thy sire?"; and she answered, "Yes."——And Shahrazad perceived the dawn of day and ceased to say her permitted say.

---

[1] Arab. "Akásirah," explained (vol. i., 75) as the plur. of Kisrá.

She said, It hath reached me, O auspicious King, that when the
Prince saw the King rushing in upon them, drawn sword in hand,
like a furious Ghul he asked the Princess, "Is this thy sire?";
and she answered, "Yes." Whereupon he sprang to his feet and,
seizing his sword, cried out at the King with so terrible a cry that
he was confounded. Then the youth would have fallen on him
with the sword; but the King seeing that the Prince was doughtier
than he, sheathed his scymitar and stood till the young man came
up to him, when he accosted him courteously and said to him, "O
youth, art thou a man or a Jinni?" Quoth the Prince, "Did I not
respect thy right as mine host and thy daughter's honour, I would
spill thy blood! How darest thou fellow me with devils, me that
am a Prince of the sons of the royal Chosroes who, had they
wished to take thy kingdom, could shake thee like an earthquake
from thy glory and thy dominions and spoil thee of all thy possessions?" Now when the King heard his words, he was confounded
with awe and bodily fear of him and rejoined, "If thou indeed be
of the sons of the Kings, as thou pretendest, how cometh it that
thou enterest my palace without my permission, and smirchest
mine honour, making thy way to my daughter and feigning that
thou art her husband and claiming that I have given her to thee
to wife, I that have slain Kings and Kings' sons, who sought her
of me in marriage? And now who shall save thee from my might
and majesty when, if I cried out to my slaves and servants and
bade them put thee to the vilest of deaths they would slay thee
forthright? Who shall deliver thee out of my hand?" When
the Prince heard this speech of the King he answered, "Verily, I
wonder at thee and at the shortness and denseness of thy wit!
Say me, canst covet for thy daughter a mate comelier than myself,
and hast ever seen a stouter hearted man or one better fitted for
a Sultan or a more glorious in rank and dominion than I?"
Rejoined the King, "Nay, by Allah! but I would have had thee,
O youth, act after the custom of Kings and demand her from me
to wife before witnesses, that I might have married her to thee
publicly; and now, even were I to marry her to thee privily, yet
hast thou dishonoured me in her person." Rejoined the Prince,
"Thou sayest sooth, O King, but if thou summon thy slaves and
thy soldiers and they fall upon me and slay me, as thou pretendest,

thou wouldst but publish thine own disgrace, and the folk would
be divided between belief in thee and disbelief in thee. Wherefore,
O King, thou wilt do well, meseemeth, to turn from this thought
to that which I shall counsel thee." Quoth the King, "Let me
hear what thou hast to advise;" and quoth the Prince, "What I
have to propose to thee is this: either do thou meet me in combat
singular, I and thou; and he who slayeth his adversary shall be
held the worthier and having a better title to the kingdom; or
else, let me be this night and, whenas dawns the morn, draw out
against me thy horsemen and footmen and servants; but first tell
me their number." Said the King, "They are forty thousand
horse, besides my own slaves and their followers,[1] who are the like
of them in number." Thereupon said the Prince, "When the day
shall break, do thou array them against me and say to them"——
And Shahrazad perceived the dawn of day and ceased saying her
permitted say.

When it was the Three Hundred and Sixty-first Night,

She continued, It hath reached me, O auspicious King, that quoth
the Prince, "When day shall break, do thou array them against me
and say to them: 'This man is a suitor to me for my daughter's
hand, on condition that he shall do battle single-handed against
you all; for he pretendeth that he will overcome you and put you
to the rout, and indeed that ye cannot prevail against him.' After
which, leave me to do battle with them: if they slay me, then is thy
secret surer guarded and thine honour the better warded; and
if I overcome them and see their backs, then is it the like of me a
King should covet to his son-in-law." So the King approved of
his opinion and accepted his proposition, despite his awe at the
boldness of his speech and amaze at the pretensions of the Prince
to meet in fight his whole host, such as he had described it to him,
being at heart assured that he would perish in the fray and so he
should be quit of him and freed from the fear of dishonour. Thereupon he called the eunuch and bade him go to his Wazir without
stay and delay and command him to assemble the whole of the

---

[1] The dearest ambition of a slave is not liberty but to have a slave of his own. This was
systematised by the servile rulers known in history as the Mameluke Beys and to the
Egyptians as the Ghuzz. Each had his household of servile pages and squires, who looked
forward to filling the master's place as knight or baron.

army and cause them don their arms and armour and mount their
steeds. So the eunuch carried the King's order to the Minister,
who straightway summoned the Captains of the host and the
Lords of the realm and bade them don their harness of derring-do
and mount horse and sally forth in battle array. Such was their
case; but as regards the King, he sat a long while conversing with
the young Prince, being pleased with his wise speech and good
sense and fine breeding. And when it was day-break he returned
to his palace and, seating himself on his throne, commanded his
merry men to mount and bade them saddle one of the best of the
royal steeds with handsome selle and housings and trappings and
bring it to the Prince. But the youth said, "O King, I will not
mount horse, till I come in view of the troops and review them."
"Be it as thou wilt," replied the King. Then the two repaired to
the parade-ground, where the troops were drawn up, and the
young Prince looked upon them and noted their great number;
after which the King cried out to them, saying, "Ho, all ye men,
there is come to me a youth who seeketh my daughter in marriage;
and in very sooth never have I seen a goodlier than he; no, nor a
stouter of heart nor a doughtier of arm, for he pretendeth that he
can overcome you, single-handed, and force you to flight and that,
were ye an hundred thousand in number, yet for him would ye be
but few. Now when he chargeth down on you, do ye receive him
upon point of pike and sharp of sabre; for, indeed, he hath undertaken a mighty matter." Then quoth the King to the Prince,
"Up, O my son, and do thy devoir on them." Answered he, "O
King, thou dealest not justly and fairly by me: how shall I go
forth against them, seeing that I am afoot and the men be
mounted?" The King retorted, "I bade thee mount, and thou
refusedst; but choose thou which of my horses thou wilt." Then
he said, "Not one of thy horses pleaseth me, and I will ride none
but that on which I came." Asked the King, "And where is thy
horse?" "Atop of thy palace." "In what part of my palace?"
"On the roof." Now when the King heard these words, he cried,
"Out on thee! this is the first sign thou hast given of madness.
How can the horse be on the roof? But we shall at once see if
thou speak the truth or lies." Then he turned to one of his chief
officers and said to him, "Go to my palace and bring me what
thou findest on the roof." So all the people marvelled at the
young Prince's words, saying one to other, "How can a horse
come down the steps from the roof? Verily this is a thing whose

like we never heard." In the meantime the King's messenger repaired to the palace and mounting to the roof, found the horse standing there and never had he looked on a handsomer; but when he drew near and examined it, he saw that it was made of ebony and ivory. Now the officer was accompanied by other high officers, who also looked on and they laughed to one another, saying, "Was it of the like of this horse that the youth spake? We cannot deem him other than mad; however, we shall soon see the truth of his case."——And Shahrazad perceived the dawn of day and ceased to say her permitted say.

When it was the Three Hundred and Sixty-second Night,

She said, It hath reached me, O auspicious King, that when the high officials looked upon the horse, they laughed one to other and said, "Was it of the like of this horse that the youth spake? We cannot deem him other than mad; however, we shall soon see the truth of his case. Peradventure herein is some mighty matter, and he is a man of high degree." Then they lifted up the horse bodily and, carrying it to the King, set it down before him, and all the lieges flocked round to look at it, marvelling at the beauty of its proportions and the richness of its saddle and bridle. The King also admired it and wondered at it with extreme wonder; and he asked the Prince, "O youth, is this thy horse?" He answered, "Yes, O King, this is my horse, and thou shalt soon see the marvel it showeth." Rejoined the King, "Then take and mount it," and the Prince retorted, "I will not mount till the troops withdraw afar from it." So the King bade them retire a bowshot from the horse; whereupon quoth its owner, "O King, see thou; I am about to mount my horse and charge upon thy host and scatter them right and left and split their hearts asunder." Said the King, "Do as thou wilt; and spare not their lives, for they will not spare thine." Then the Prince mounted, whilst the troops ranged themselves in ranks before him, and one said to another, "When the youth cometh between the ranks, we will take him on the points of our pikes and the sharps of our sabres." Quoth another, "By Allah, this a mere misfortune: how shall we slay a youth so comely of face and shapely of form?" And a third continued, "Ye will have hard work to get the better of him; for the youth had not done this, but for what he knew of his own prowess and pre-eminence of valour." Meanwhile, having settled himself in his saddle, the Prince turned the pin of ascent; whilst all eyes were strained to see what he would do, whereupon the horse began to heave and rock and sway to and fro and make the strangest of movements steed ever made, till its belly was filled with air and it took flight with its rider and soared high into the sky. When the King saw this, he cried out to his men, saying, "Woe to you! catch him, catch him, ere he 'scape you!" But his Wazirs and Viceroys said to him, "O King, can a man overtake the flying bird? This is surely none but some mighty magician or Marid of the Jinn or devil, and Allah save thee from him. So praise thou the Almighty for deliverance of thee and of all thy host from his hand." Then the King returned to his palace after seeing the feat of the Prince and, going in to his daughter, acquainted her with what had befallen them both on the parade-ground. He found her grievously afflicted for the Prince and bewailing her separation from him; wherefore she fell sick with violent sickness and took to her pillow. Now when her father saw her on this wise, he pressed her to his breast and kissing her between the eyes, said to her, "O my daughter, praise Allah Almighty and thank Him for that He hath delivered us from this crafty enchanter, this villain, this low fellow, this thief who thought only of seducing thee!" And he repeated to her the story of the Prince and how he had disappeared in the firmament; and he abused him and cursed him knowing not how dearly his daughter loved him. But she paid no heed to his words and did but re-double in her tears and wails, saying to herself, "By Allah, I will neither eat meat nor drain drink, till Allah reunite me with him!" Her father was greatly concerned for her case and mourned much over her plight; but, for all he could do to soothe her, love-longing only increased on her.——And Shahrazad perceived the dawn of day and ceased saying her permitted say.

When it was the Three Hundred and Sixty-third Night,

She said, It hath reached me, O auspicious King, that the King mourned much over his daughter's plight but, for all he could do to soothe her, love-longing only increased on her. Thus far concerning the King and Princess Shams al-Nahár; but as regards Prince Kamar al-Akmar, when he had risen high in air, he turned his horse's head towards his native land, and being alone mused upon the beauty of the Princess and her loveliness. Now he had enquired of the King's people the name of the city and of its King and his daughter; and men had told him that it was the city of Sana'á.[1] So he journeyed with all speed, till he drew near his father's capital and, making an airy circuit about the city, alighted on the roof of the King's palace, where he left his horse, whilst he descended into the palace and seeing its threshold strewn with ashes, thought that one of his family was dead. Then he entered, as of wont, and found his father and mother and sisters clad in mourning raiment of black, all pale of faces and lean of frames. When his sire descried him and was assured that it was indeed his son, he cried out with a great cry and fell down in a fit, but after a time coming to himself, threw himself upon him and embraced him, clipping him to his bosom and rejoicing in him with exceeding joy and extreme gladness. His mother and sisters heard this; so they came in and seeing the Prince, fell upon him, kissing him and weeping, and joying with exceeding joyance. Then they questioned him of his case; so he told them all that had passed from first to last, and his father said to him, "Praised be Allah for thy safety, O coolth of my eyes and core of my heart!" Then the King bade hold high festival, and the glad tidings flew through the city. So

---

[1] The well-known capital of Al-Yaman, a true Arabia Felix, a Paradise inhabited by demons in the shape of Turkish soldiery and Arab caterans. According to Moslem writers Sana'a was founded by Shem son of Noah who, wandering southward with his posterity after his father's death, and finding the site delightful, dug a well and founded the citadel, Ghamdán, which afterwards contained a *Maison Carrée* rivalling (or attempting to rival) the Meccan Ka'abah. The builder was Surahbíl who, says M. C. de Perceval coloured its four faces red, white, golden and green; the central quadrangle had seven stories (the planets) each forty cubits high, and the lowest was a marble hall ceiling'd with a single slab. At the four corners stood hollow lions through whose mouths the winds roared. This palatial citadel-temple was destroyed by order of Caliph Omar. The city's ancient name was Azal or Uzal whom some identify with one of the thirteen sons of Joktan (Genesis xi. 27): it took its present name from the Ethiopian conquerors (they say) who, seeing it for the first time, cried "Hazá Sana'ah!" meaning in their tongue, this is commodious, etc. I may note that the word is Kisawahili (Zanzibarian) *e.g.* "Yámbo *sáná*—is the state *good?*" Sana'a was the capital of the Tabábi'ah or Tobba Kings who judaized; and the Abyssinians with their Negush made it Christian while the Persians under Anushirwán converted it to Guebrism. It is now easily visited but to little purpose; excursions in the neighbourhood being deadly dangerous. Moreover the Turkish garrison would probably murder a stranger who sympathised with the Arabs, and the Arabs kill one who took part with their hated and hateful conquerors. The late Mr. Shapira of Jerusalem declared that he had visited it and Jews have great advantages in such travel. But his friends doubted him.

they beat drums and cymbals and, doffing the weed of mourning, they donned the gay garb of gladness and decorated the streets and markets; whilst the folk vied with one another who should be the first to give the King joy, and the King proclaimed a general pardon and opening the prisons, released those who were therein prisoned. Moreover, he made banquets for the people, with great abundance of eating and drinking, for seven days and nights and all creatures were gladsomest; and he took horse with his son and rode out with him, that the folk might see him and rejoice. After awhile the Prince asked about the maker of the horse, saying, "O my father, what hath fortune done with him?"; and the King answered, "Allah never bless him nor the hour wherein I set eyes on him! For he was the cause of thy separation from us, O my son, and he hath lain in gaol since the day of thy disappearance." Then the King bade release him from prison and, sending for him, invested him in a dress of satisfaction and entreated him with the utmost favour and munificence, save that he would not give him his daughter to wife; whereat the Sage raged with sore rage and repented of that which he had done, knowing that the Prince had secured the secret of the steed and the manner of its motion. Moreover, the King said to his son, "I reck thou wilt do well not to go near the horse henceforth and more especially not to mount it after this day; for thou knowest not its properties, and belike thou art in error about it." Now the Prince had told his father of his adventure with the King of Sana'a and his daughter and he said, "Had the King intended to kill thee, he had done so; but thine hour was not yet come." When the rejoicings were at an end, the people returned to their places and the King and his son to the palace, where they sat down and fell to eating and drinking and making merry. Now the King had a handsome handmaiden who was skilled in playing the lute; so she took it and began to sweep the strings and sing thereto before the King and his son of separation of lovers, and she chanted the following verses:—

"Deem not that absence breeds in me aught of forgetfulness; * What should
    remember I did you fro' my remembrance wane?
Time dies but never dies the fondest love for you we bear; * And in your
    love I'll die and in your love I'll arise again."[1]

---

[1] The Bresl. Edit. (iii. 347) prints three vile errors in four lines.

When the Prince heard these verses, the fires of longing flamed up in his heart and pine and passion redoubled upon him. Grief and regret were sore upon him and his bowels yearned in him for love of the King's daughter of Sana'a; so he rose forthright and, escaping his father's notice, went forth the palace to the horse and mounting it, turned the pin of ascent, whereupon bird-like it flew with him high in air and soared towards the upper regions of the sky. In early morning his father missed him and, going up to the pinnacle of the palace, in great concern, saw his son rising into the firmament; whereat he was sore afflicted and repented in all penitence that he had not taken the horse and hidden it; and he said to himself, "By Allah, if but my son return to me, I will destroy the horse, that my heart may be at rest concerning my son." And he fell again to weeping and bewailing himself.——And Shahrazad perceived the dawn of day and ceased to say her permitted say.

When it was the Three Hundred and Sixty-fourth Night,

She said, It hath reached me, O auspicious King, that the King again fell to weeping and bewailing himself for his son. Such was his case; but as regards the Prince, he ceased not flying on through air till he came to the city of Sana'a and alighted on the roof as before. Then he crept down stealthily and, finding the eunuch asleep, as of wont, raised the curtain and went on little by little, till he came to the door of the Princess's alcove[1]-chamber and stopped to listen; when lo! he heard her shedding plenteous tears and reciting verses, whilst her women slept round her. Presently, overhearing her weeping and wailing quoth they, "O our mistress, why wilt thou mourn for one who mourneth not for thee?" Quoth she, "O ye little of wit, is he for whom I mourn of those who forget or who are forgotten?" And she fell again to wailing and weeping, till sleep overcame her. Hereat the Prince's heart melted for her and his gall-bladder was like to burst, so he entered and, seeing her lying asleep without covering,[2] touched her with his hand;

---

[1] Alcove is a corruption of the Arab. Al-Kubbah (the dome) through Span. and Port.

[2] Easterns as a rule sleep with head and body covered by a sheet or in cold weather a blanket. The practice is doubtless hygienic, defending the body from draughts when the

whereupon she opened her eyes and espied him standing by her. Said he, "Why all this crying and mourning?" And when she knew him, she threw herself upon him, and took him around the neck and kissed him and answered, "For thy sake and because of my separation from thee." Said he, "O my lady, I have been made desolate by thee all this long time!" But she replied, " 'Tis thou who hast desolated *me;* and hadst thou tarried longer, I had surely died!" Rejoined he, "O my lady, what thinkest thou of my case with thy father and how he dealt with me? Were it not for my love of thee, O temptation and seduction of the Three Worlds, I had certainly slain him and made him a warning to all beholders; but, even as I love thee, so I love him for thy sake." Quoth she, "How couldst thou leave me: can my life be sweet to me after thee?" Quoth he, "Let what hath happened suffice: I am now hungry, and thirsty." So she bade her maidens make ready meat and drink, and they sat eating and drinking and conversing till night was well nigh ended; and when day broke he rose to take leave of her and depart, ere the eunuch should awake. Shams al-Nahar asked him, "Whither goest thou?"; and he answered, "To my father's house, and I plight thee my troth that I will come to thee once in every week." But she wept and said, "I conjure thee, by Allah the Almighty, take me with thee whereso thou wendest and make me not taste anew the bitter-gourd[1] of separation from thee." Quoth he, "Wilt thou indeed go with me?" and quoth she, "Yes." "Then," said he, "arise that we depart." So she rose forthright and going to a chest, arrayed herself in what was richest and dearest to her of her trinkets of gold and jewels of price, and she fared forth, her handmaids recking naught. So he carried her up to the roof of the palace and, mounting the ebony horse, took her up behind him and made her fast to himself, binding her with strong bonds; after which he

---

pores are open; but Europeans find it hard to adopt; it seems to stop their breathing. Another excellent practice in the East and, indeed amongst barbarians and savages generally, is training children to sleep with mouths shut: in after life they never snore and in malarious lands they do not require Outram's "fever-guard," a swathe of muslin over the mouth. Mr. Catlin thought so highly of the "shut mouth" that he made it the subject of a book.

[1] Arab. "Hanzal" = coloquintida, an article often mentioned by Arabs in verse and prose; the bright coloured little gourd attracts every eye by its golden glance when travelling through the brown-yellow waste of sand and clay. A favourite purgative (enough for a horse) is made by filling the inside with sour milk which is drunk after a night's soaking: it is as active as the croton-nut of the Gold Coast.

turned the shoulder-pin of ascent, and the horse rose with him
high in air. When her slave-women saw this, they shrieked aloud
and told her father and mother, who in hot haste ran to the palace-
roof and looking up, saw the magical horse flying away with the
Prince and Princess. At this the King was troubled with ever-
increasing trouble and cried out, saying, "O King's son, I conjure
thee, by Allah, have ruth on me and my wife and bereave us not
of our daughter!" The Prince made him no reply; but, thinking
in himself that the maiden repented of leaving father and mother,
asked her, "O ravishment of the age, say me, wilt thou that I
restore thee to thy mother and father?": whereupon she answered,
"By Allah, O my lord, that is not my desire: my only wish is to
be with thee, wherever thou art; for I am distracted by the love
of thee from all else, even from my father and mother." Hearing
these words the Prince joyed with great joy, and made the horse
fly and fare softly with them, so as not to disquiet her; nor did
they stay their flight till they came in sight of a green meadow,
wherein was a spring of running water. Here they alighted and
ate and drank; after which the Prince took horse again and set her
behind him, binding her in his fear for her safety; after which they
fared on till they came in sight of his father's capital. At this,
the Prince was filled with joy and bethought himself to show his
beloved the seat of his dominion and his father's power and dignity
and give her to know that it was greater than that of her sire.
So he set her down in one of his father's gardens without the city
where his parent was wont to take his pleasure; and, carrying her
into a domed summer-house prepared there for the King, left the
ebony horse at the door and charged the damsel keep watch over
it, saying, "Sit here, till my messenger come to thee; for I go
now to my father, to make ready a palace for thee and show thee
my royal estate." She was delighted when she heard these words
and said to him, "Do as thou wilt;"——And Shahrazad perceived
the dawn of day and ceased saying her permitted say.

When it was the Three Hundred and Sixty-fifth Night,

She said, It hath reached me, O auspicious King, that the maiden
was delighted when she heard these words and said to him, "Do as
thou wilt;" for she thereby understood that she should not enter
the city but with due honour and worship, as became her rank.

Then the Prince left her and betook himself to the palace of the King his father, who rejoiced in his return and met him and welcomed him; and the Prince said to him, "Know that I have brought with me the King's daughter of whom I told thee; and have left her without the city in such a garden and come to tell thee, that thou mayst make ready the procession of estate and go forth to meet her and show her thy royal dignity and troops and guards." Answered the King, "With joy and gladness"; and straightway bade decorate the town with the goodliest adornment. Then he took horse and rode out in all magnificence and majesty, he and his host, high officers and household, with drums and kettle-drums, fifes and clarions and all manner instruments; whilst the Prince drew forth of his treasuries jewellery and apparel and what else of the things which Kings hoard and made a rare display of wealth and splendour: moreover he got ready for the Princess a canopied litter of brocades, green, red and yellow, wherein he set Indian and Greek and Abyssinian slave-girls. Then he left the litter and those who were therein and preceded them to the pavilion where he had set her down; and searched but found naught, neither Princess nor horse. When he saw this, he beat his face and rent his raiment and began to wander round about the garden, as he had lost his wits; after which he came to his senses and said to himself, "How could she have come at the secret of this horse, seeing I told her nothing of it? Maybe the Persian sage who made the horse hath chanced upon her and stolen her away, in revenge for my father's treatment of him." Then he sought the guardians of the garden and asked them if they had seen any pass the precincts; and said, "Hath any one come in here? Tell me the truth and the whole truth or I will at once strike off your heads." They were terrified by his threats; but they answered with one voice, "We have seen no man enter save the Persian sage, who came to gather healing herbs." So the Prince was certified that it was indeed he that had taken away the maiden,——And Shahrazad perceived the dawn of day and ceased to say her permitted say.

When it was the Three Hundred and Sixty-sixth Night,

She said, It hath reached me, O auspicious King, that when the Prince heard their answer, he was certified that the Sage had taken away the maiden and abode confounded and perplexed concerning his case. And he was abashed before the folk and, turning to his sire, told him what had happened and said to him, "Take the troops and march them back to the city. As for me, I will never return till I have cleared up this affair." When the King heard this, he wept and beat his breast and said to him, "O my son, calm thy choler and master thy chagrin and come home with us and look what King's daughter thou wouldst fain have, that I may marry thee to her." But the Prince paid no heed to his words and farewelling him departed, whilst the King returned to the city and their joy was changed into sore annoy. Now, as Destiny issued her decree, when the Prince left the Princess in the garden-house and betook himself to his father's palace, for the ordering of his affair, the Persian entered the garden to pluck certain simples and, scenting the sweet savour of musk and perfumes that exhaled from the Princess and impregnated the whole place, followed it till he came to the pavilion and saw standing at the door the horse which he had made with his own hands. His heart was filled with joy and gladness, for he had bemourned its loss much since it had gone out of his hand: so he went up to it and, examining its every part, found it whole and sound; whereupon he was about to mount and ride away, when he bethought himself and said, "Needs must I first look what the Prince hath brought and left here with the horse." So he entered the pavilion and, seeing the Princess sitting there, as she were the sun shining sheen in the sky serene, knew her at the first glance to be some high-born lady and doubted not but the Prince had brought her thither on the horse and left her in the pavilion, whilst he went to the city, to make ready for her entry in state procession with all splendour. Then he went up to her and kissed the earth between her hands, whereupon she raised her eyes to him and, finding him exceedingly foul of face and favour, asked, "Who art thou?"; and he answered, "O my lady, I am a messenger sent by the Prince who hath bidden me bring thee to another pleasance nearer the city; for that my lady the Queen cannot walk so far and is unwilling, of her joy in thee, that another should forestall her with thee." Quoth she, "Where is the Prince?"; and quoth the Persian, "He is in the city, with his sire and forthwith he shall come for thee in great state." Said she, "O thou! say me, could he find none handsomer to send to me?"; whereat loud laughed the Sage and said, "Yea verily, he hath not a Mameluke as ugly as I am; but, O my lady, let not the ill-

favour of my face and the foulness of my form deceive thee.
Hadst thou profited of me as hath the Prince, verily thou wouldst
praise my affair. Indeed, he chose me as his messenger to thee,
because of my uncomeliness and loathsomeness in his jealous
love of thee: else hath he Mamelukes and negro slaves, pages,
eunuchs and attendants out of number, each goodlier than
other." Whenas she heard this, it commended itself to her
reason and she believed him; so she rose forthright;——And
Shahrazad perceived the dawn of day and ceased saying her
permitted say.

When it was the Three Hundred and Sixty-seventh Night,

She said, It hath reached me, O auspicious King, that when the
Persian sage acquainted the Princess with the case of the King's
son, she believed him; so she rose forthright; and, putting her
hand in his, said, "O my father, what hast thou brought me to
ride?" He replied, "O my lady, thou shalt ride the horse thou
camest on;" and she, "I cannot ride it by myself." Whereupon
he smiled and knew that he was her master and said, "I will ride
with thee myself." So he mounted and, taking her up behind him
bound her to himself with firm bonds, while she knew not what he
would with her. Then he turned the ascent-pin, whereupon the
belly of the horse became full of wind and it swayed to and fro like
a wave of the sea, and rose with them high in air nor slackened
in its flight, till it was out of sight of the city. Now when Shams
al-Nahar saw this, she asked him, "Ho thou! what is become of
that thou toldest me of my Prince, making me believe that he
sent thee to me?" Answered the Persian, "Allah damn the Prince!
he is a mean and skin-flint knave." She cried, "Woe to thee!
How darest thou disobey thy lord's commandment?" Whereto the
Persian replied, "He is no lord of mine: knowest thou who I
am?" Rejoined the Princess, "I know nothing of thee save what
thou toldest me;" and retorted he, "What I told thee was a trick
of mine against thee and the King's son: I have long lamented
the loss of this horse which is under us; for I constructed it and
made myself master of it. But now I have gotten firm hold of it and
of thee too, and I will burn his heart even as he hath burnt mine;
nor shall he ever have the horse again; no, never! So be of good
cheer and keep thine eyes cool and clear; for I can be of more

use to thee than he; and I am generous as I am wealthy; my servants and slaves shall obey thee as their mistress; I will robe thee in finest raiment and thine every wish shall be at thy will." When she heard this, she buffeted her face and cried out, saying, "Ah, well-away! I have not won my beloved and I have lost my father and mother!" And she wept bitter tears over what had befallen her, whilst the Sage fared on with her, without ceasing, till he came to the land of the Greeks[1] and alighted in a verdant mead, abounding in streams and trees. Now this meadow lay near a city wherein was a King of high puissance, and it chanced that he went forth that day to hunt and divert himself. As he passed by the meadow, he saw the Persian standing there, with the damsel and the horse by his side; and, before the Sage was ware, the King's slaves fell upon him and carried him and the lady and the horse to their master who, noting the foulness of the man's favour and his loathsomeness and the beauty of the girl and her loveliness, said, "O my lady, what kin is this oldster to thee?" The Persian made haste to reply, saying, "She is my wife and the daughter of my father's brother." But the lady at once gave him the lie and said, "O King, by Allah, I know him not, nor is he my husband; nay, he is a wicked magician who hath stolen me away by force and fraud." Thereupon the King bade bastinado the Persian and they beat him till he was well-nigh dead; after which the King commanded to carry him to the city and cast him into jail; and, taking from him the damsel and the ebony horse (though he knew not its properties nor the secret of its motion), set the girl in his serraglio and the horse amongst his hoards. Such was the case with the Sage and the lady; but as regards Prince Kamar al-Akmar, he garbed himself in travelling gear and taking what he needed of money, set out tracking their trail in very sorry plight; and journeyed from country to country and city to city seeking the Princess and enquiring after the ebony horse, whilst all who heard him marvelled at him and deemed his talk extravagant. Thus he continued doing a long while; but, for all his enquiry and quest, he could hit on no news of her. At last he came to her father's city of Sana'a and there asked for her, but could get no tidings of her and found her father mourning her loss. So he turned back and made for the land of the Greeks, continuing to

---

[1] The Bresl. Edit. iii. 354 sends him to the "land of Sín" (China).

enquire concerning the twain as he went,——And Shahrazad perceived the dawn of day and ceased to say her permitted say.

When it was the Three Hundred and Sixty-eighth Night,

She said, It hath reached me, O auspicious King, that the King's
son made for the land of the Greeks, continuing to enquire concerning the two as he went along, till, as chance would have it, he
alighted at a certain Khan and saw a company of merchants
sitting at talk. So he sat down near them and heard one say, "O
my friends, I lately witnessed a wonder of wonders." They asked,
"What was that?" and he answered, "I was visiting such a district in such a city (naming the city wherein was the Princess),
and I heard its people chatting of a strange thing which had
lately befallen. It was that their King went out one day hunting
and coursing with a company of his courtiers and the lords of his
realm; and, issuing from the city, they came to a green meadow
where they espied an old man standing, with a woman sitting hard
by a horse of ebony. The man was foulest-foul of face and loathly
of form, but the woman was a marvel of beauty and loveliness and
elegance and perfect grace; and as for the wooden horse, it was a
miracle, never saw eyes aught goodlier than it nor more gracious
than its make." Asked the others, "And what did the King
with them?"; and the merchant answered, "As for the man the
King seized him and questioned him of the damsel and he pretended that she was his wife and the daughter of his paternal
uncle; but she gave him the lie forthright and declared that he
was a sorcerer and a villain. So the King took her from the old
man and bade beat him and cast him into the trunk-house. As
for the ebony horse, I know not what became of it." When the
Prince heard these words, he drew near to the merchant and began
questioning him discreetly and courteously touching the name of
the city and of its King; which when he knew, he passed the
night full of joy. And as soon as dawned the day he set out and
travelled sans surcease till he reached that city; but, when he
would have entered, the gate-keepers laid hands on him, that they
might bring him before the King to question him of his condition
and the craft in which he was skilled and the cause of his coming
thither—such being the usage and custom of their ruler. Now
it was supper-time when he entered the city, and it was then

impossible to go in to the King or take counsel with him respecting the stranger. So the guards carried him to the jail, thinking
to lay him by the heels there for the night; but, when the warders
saw his beauty and loveliness, they could not find it in their hearts
to imprison him: they made him sit with them without the walls;
and, when food came to them, he ate with them what sufficed him.
As soon as they had made an end of eating, they turned to the
Prince and said, "What countryman art thou?" "I come from
Fars," answered he, "the land of the Chosroës." When they
heard this they laughed and one of them said, "O Chosroan,[1] I
have heard the talk of men and their histories and I have looked
into their conditions; but never saw I or heard I a bigger liar
than the Chosroan which is with us in the jail." Quoth another,
"And never did I see aught fouler than his favour or more hideous
than his visnomy." Asked the Prince, "What have ye seen of his
lying?"; and they answered, "He pretendeth that he is one of the
wise! Now the King came upon him, as he went a-hunting, and
found with him a most beautiful woman and a horse of the
blackest ebony, never saw I a handsomer. As for the damsel, she
is with the King, who is enamoured of her and would fain marry
her; but she is mad, and were this man a leach as he claimeth to
be, he would have healed her, for the King doth his utmost to
discover a cure for her case and a remedy for her disease, and this
whole year past hath he spent treasures upon physicians and
astrologers, on her account; but none can avail to cure her. As
for the horse, it is in the royal hoard-house, and the ugly man
is here with us in prison; and as soon as night falleth, he weepeth
and bemoaneth himself and will not let us sleep."——And
Shahrazad perceived the dawn of day and ceased to say her
permitted say.

When it was the Three Hundred and Sixty-ninth Night,

She said, It hath reached me, O auspicious King, that when the
warders had recounted the case of the Persian egromancer they

---

[1] Arab. "Yá Kisrawi!"=O subject of the Kisrá or Chosroë; the latter explained in
vol. i., 75. "Fars" is the origin of "Persia"; and there is a hit at the prodigious lying of the
modern race, whose forefathers were so famous as truth-tellers. "I am a Persian, but I am
not lying now," is a phrase familiar to every traveller.

held in prison and his weeping and wailing, the Prince at once devised a device whereby he might compass his desire; and presently the guards of the gate, being minded to sleep, led him into the jail and locked the door. So he overheard the Persian weeping and bemoaning himself, in his own tongue, and saying, "Alack, and alas for my sin, that I sinned against myself and against the King's son, in that which I did with the damsel; for I neither left her nor won my will of her! All this cometh of my lack of sense, in that I sought for myself that which I deserved not and which befitted not the like of me; for whoso seeketh what suiteth him not at all, falleth with the like of my fall." Now when the King's son heard this, he accosted him in Persian, saying, "How long will this weeping and wailing last? Say me, thinkest thou that hath befallen thee that which never befel other than thou?" Now when the Persian heard this, he made friends with him and began to complain to him of his case and misfortunes. And as soon as the morning morrowed, the warders took the Prince and carried him before their King, informing him that he had entered the city on the previous night, at a time when audience was impossible. Quoth the King to the Prince, "Whence comest thou and what is thy name and trade and why hast thou travelled hither?" He replied, "As to my name I am called in Persian Harjah;[1] as to my country I come from the land of Fars; and I am of the men of art and especially of the art of medicine and healing the sick and those whom the Jinns drive mad. For this I go round about all countries and cities, to profit by adding knowledge to my knowledge, and whenever I see a patient I heal him and this is my craft."[2] Now when the King heard this, he rejoiced with exceeding joy and said, "O excellent Sage, thou hast indeed come to us at a time when we need thee." Then he acquainted him with the case of the Princess, adding, "If thou cure her and recover her from her madness, thou shalt have of me everything thou seekest." Replied the Prince,

---

[1] There is no such name: perhaps it is a clerical error for "Har jáh" = (a man of) any place. I know an Englishman who in Persian called himself "Mirza Abdullah-i-Hích-makáni" = Master Abdullah of Nowhere.

[2] The Bresl. Edit. (loc. cit.) gives a comical description of the Prince assuming the dress of an astrologer-doctor, clapping an old book under his arm, fumbling a rosary of beads, enlarging his turband, lengthening his sleeves and blackening his eyelids with antimony. Here, however, it would be out of place. Very comical also is the way in which he pretends to cure the maniac by "muttering unknown words, blowing in her face, biting her ear," etc.

"Allah save and favour the King: describe to me all thou hast seen of her insanity and tell me how long it is since the access attacked her; also how thou camest by her and the horse and the Sage." So the King told him the whole story, from first to last, adding, "The Sage is in goal." Quoth the Prince, "O auspicious King, and what hast thou done with the horse?" Quoth the King, "O youth, it is with me yet, laid up in one of my treasure-chambers," whereupon said the Prince within himself, "The best thing I can do is first to see the horse and assure myself of its condition. If it be whole and sound, all will be well and end well; but, if its motor-works be destroyed, I must find some other way of delivering my beloved." Thereupon he turned to the King and said to him, "O King, I must see the horse in question: haply I may find in it somewhat that will serve me for the recovery of the damsel." "With all my heart," replied the King, and taking him by the hand, showed him into the place where the horse was. The Prince went round about it, examining its condition, and found it whole and sound, whereat he rejoiced greatly and said to the King, "Allah save and exalt the King! I would fain go in to the damsel, that I may see how it is with her; for I hope in Allah to heal her by my healing hand through means of the horse." Then he bade them take care of the horse and the King carried him to the Princess's apartment, where her lover found her wringing her hands and writhing and beating herself against the ground, and tearing her garments to tatters as was her wont; but there was no madness of Jinn in her, and she did this but that none might approach her. When the Prince saw her thus, he said to her, "No harm shall betide thee, O ravishment of the three worlds;" and went on to soothe her and speak her fair, till he managed to whisper, "I am Kamar al-Akmar;" whereupon she cried out with a loud cry and fell down fainting for excess of joy; but the King thought this was epilepsy[1] brought on by her fear of him, and by her suddenly being startled. Then the Prince put his mouth to her ear and said to her, "O Shams al-Nahar, O seduction of the universe, have a care for thy life and mine and be patient and constant; for this our position needeth sufferance and skilful contrivance to make shift for our delivery from this tyrannical King. My first move will be now to go out to him and tell him that thou

---

[1] Arab. "Sar'a" = falling sickness. Here again we have in all its simplicity the old nursery idea of "possession" by evil spirits.

art possessed of a Jinn and hence thy madness; but that I will engage to heal thee and drive away the evil spirit, if he will at once unbind thy bonds. So when he cometh in to thee, do thou speak him smooth words, that he may think I have cured thee, and all will be done for us as we desire." Quoth she, "Hearkening and obedience;" and he went out to the King in joy and gladness, and said to him, "O august King, I have, by thy good fortune, discovered her disease and its remedy, and have cured her for thee. So now do thou go in to her and speak her softly and treat her kindly, and promise her what may please her; so shall all thou desirest of her be accomplished to thee."——And Shahrazad per-ceived the dawn of day and ceased to say her permitted say.

𝔚𝔥𝔢𝔫 𝔦𝔱 𝔴𝔞𝔰 𝔱𝔥𝔢 𝔗𝔥𝔯𝔢𝔢 𝔥𝔲𝔫𝔡𝔯𝔢𝔡 𝔞𝔫𝔡 𝔖𝔢𝔳𝔢𝔫𝔱𝔦𝔢𝔱𝔥 𝔑𝔦𝔤𝔥𝔱.

She said, It hath reached me, O auspicious King, that when the Prince feigned himself a leach and went in to the damsel and made himself known to her and told her how he purposed to deliver her, she cried "Hearkening and obedience!" He then fared forth from her and sought the King and said, "Go thou in to her and speak her softly and promise her what may please her; so shall all thou desirest of her be accomplished to thee." Thereupon the King went in to her and when she saw him, she rose and kissing the ground before him, bade him welcome and said, "I admire how thou hast come to visit thy handmaid this day;" whereat he was ready to fly for joy and bade the waiting-women and the eunuchs attend her and carry her to the Hammam and make ready for her dresses and adornment. So they went in to her and saluted her, and she returned their salams with the goodliest language and after the pleasantest fashion; whereupon they clad her in royal apparel and, clasping a collar of jewels about her neck, carried her to the bath and served her there. Then they brought her forth, as she were the full moon; and, when she came into the King's presence, she saluted him and kissed ground before him; whereupon he joyed in her with joy exceeding and said to the Prince, "O Sage, O philosopher, all this is of thy blessing. Allah increase to us the benefit of thy healing breath!"[1] The Prince

---

[1] Arab. "Nafahát" = breathings, benefits, the Heb. Neshamah opp. to Nephesh (soul) and Ruach (spirit). Healing by the breath is a popular idea throughout the East and not unknown to Western Magnetists and Mesmerists. The miraculous cures of the Messiah

replied, "O King, for the completion of her cure it behoveth that thou go forth, thou and all thy troops and guards, to the place where thou foundest her, not forgetting the beast of black wood which was with her; for therein is a devil; and, unless I exorcise him, he will return to her and afflict her at the head of every month." "With love and gladness," cried the King, "O thou Prince of all philosophers and most learned of all who see the light of day." Then he brought out the ebony horse to the meadow in question and rode thither with all his troops and the Princess, little weeting the purpose of the Prince. Now when they came to the appointed place, the Prince, still habited as a leach, bade them set the Princess and the steed as far as eye could reach from the King and his troops, and said to him, "With thy leave, and at thy word, I will now proceed to the fumigations and conjurations, and here imprison the adversary of mankind, that he may never more return to her. After this, I shall mount this wooden horse which seemeth to be made of ebony, and take the damsel up behind me; where-upon it will shake and sway to and fro and fare forwards, till it come to thee, when the affair will be at an end; and after this thou mayst do with her as thou wilt." When the King heard his words, he rejoiced with extreme joy; so the Prince mounted the horse, and, taking the damsel up behind him, whilst the King and his troops watched him, bound her fast to him. Then he turned the ascending-pin and the horse took flight and soared with them high in air, till they disappeared from every eye. After this the King abode half the day, expecting their return; but they returned not. So when he despaired of them, repenting him greatly of that which he had done and grieving sore for the loss of the damsel, he went back to the city with his troops. He then sent for the Persian who was in prison and said to him, "O thou traitor, O thou villain, why didst thou hide from me the mystery of the ebony horse? And now a sharper hath come to me and hath carried it off, together with a slave-girl whose ornaments are worth a mint of money, and I shall never see anyone or anything of them again!" So the Persian related to him all his past, first and last, and the

---

were, according to Moslems, mostly performed by aspiration. They hold that in the days of Isa, physic had reached its highest development, and thus his miracles were mostly miracles of medicine; whereas, in Mohammed's time, eloquence had attained its climax and accordingly his miracles were those of eloquence, as shown in the Koran and Ahádís.

King was seized with a fit of fury which well-nigh ended his life. He shut himself up in his palace for a while, mourning and afflicted; but at last his Wazirs came in to him and applied themselves to comfort him, saying, "Verily, he who took the damsel is an enchanter, and praised be Allah who hath delivered thee from his craft and sorcery!" And they ceased not from him, till he was comforted for her loss. Thus far concerning the King; but as for the Prince, he continued his career towards his father's capital in joy and cheer, and stayed not till he alighted on his own palace, where he set the lady in safety; after which he went in to his father and mother and saluted them and acquainted them with her coming, whereat they were filled with solace and gladness. Then he spread great banquets for the towns-folk,——And Shahrazad perceived the dawn of day and ceased saying her permitted say.

When it was the Three Hundred and Seventy-first Night,

She said, It hath reached me, O auspicious King, that the King's son spread great banquets for the towns-folk and they held high festival a whole month, at the end of which time he went in to the Princess and they took their joy of each other with exceeding joy. But his father brake the ebony horse in pieces and destroyed its mechanism for flight; moreover the Prince wrote a letter to the Princess's father, advising him of all that had befallen her and informing him how she was now married to him and in all health and happiness, and sent it by a messenger, together with costly presents and curious rarities. And when the messenger arrived at the city which was Sana'a and delivered the letter and the presents to the King, he read the missive and rejoiced greatly thereat and accepted the presents, honouring and rewarding the bearer handsomely. Moreover, he forwarded rich gifts to his son-in-law by the same messenger, who returned to his master and acquainted him with what had passed; whereat he was much cheered. And after this the Prince wrote a letter every year to his father-in-law and sent him presents till, in course of time, his sire King Sabur deceased and he reigned in his stead, ruling justly over his lieges and conducting himself well and righteously towards them, so that the land submitted to him and his subjects did him loyal service; and Kamar al-Akmar and his wife Shams al-Nahar abode in the enjoyment of all satisfaction and solace of life, till there came to them the Destroyer of delights and Sunderer of societies; the Plunderer of palaces, the Caterer for cemeteries and the Garnerer of graves. And now glory be to the Living One who dieth not and in whose hand is the dominion of the worlds visible and invisible!

SINDBAD THE SEAMAN[1] AND SINDBAD THE LANDSMAN.

THERE lived in the city of Baghdad, during the reign of the Commander of the Faithful, Harun al-Rashid, a man named Sindbád the Hammál,[2] one in poor case who bore burdens on his head for hire. It happened to him one day of great heat that whilst he was carrying a heavy load, he became exceeding weary and sweated profusely, the heat and the weight alike oppressing him. Presently, as he was passing the gate of a merchant's house, before which the ground was swept and watered, and there the air was temperate, he sighted a broad bench beside the door; so he set his load thereon, to take rest and smell the air,——And Shahrazad perceived the dawn of day and ceased saying her permitted say.

---

[1] Lane (vol. iii. 1) calls our old friend "Es-Sindibád of the Sea," and Benfey derives the name from the Sanskrit "Siddhapati"=lord of sages. The etymology (in Heb. Sandabar and in Greek Syntipas) is still uncertain, although the term often occurs in Arab stories; and some look upon it as a mere corruption of "Bidpai" (Bidyápati). The derivation offered by Hole (Remarks on the Arabian Nights' Entertainments, by Richard Hole, LL.D. London, Cadell, 1797) from the Persian ábád (a region) is impossible. It is, however, not a little curious that this purely Persian word (=a "habitation") should be found in Indian names as early as Alexander's day, e.g. the "Dachina bades" of the Periplus is "Dakhshin-ábád," the Sanskr. being "Dakshinapatha."

[2] A porter like the famous Armenians of Constantinople. Some edits. call him "Al-Hindibád."

When it was the Five Hundred and Thirty-seventh Night,

She said, It hath reached me, O auspicious King, that when the Hammal set his load upon the bench to take rest and smell the air, there came out upon him from the court-door a pleasant breeze and a delicious fragrance. He sat down on the edge of the bench, and at once heard from within the melodious sound of lutes and other stringed instruments, and mirth-exciting voices singing and reciting, together with the song of birds warbling and glorifying Almighty Allah in various tunes and tongues; turtles, mocking-birds, merles, nightingales, cushats and stone-curlews,[1] whereat he marvelled in himself and was moved to mighty joy and solace. Then he went up to the gate and saw within a great flower-garden wherein were pages and black slaves and such a train of servants and attendants and so forth as is found only with Kings and Sultans; and his nostrils were greeted with the savoury odours of all manner meats rich and delicate, and delicious and generous wines. So he raised his eyes heavenwards and said, "Glory to Thee, O Lord, O Creator and Provider, who providest whomso Thou wilt without count or stint! O mine Holy One, I cry Thee pardon for all sins and turn to Thee repenting of all offences! O Lord, there is no gainsaying Thee in Thine ordinance and Thy dominion, neither wilt Thou be questioned of that Thou dost, for Thou indeed over all things art Almighty! Extolled be Thy perfection: whom Thou wilt Thou makest poor and whom Thou wilt Thou makest rich! Whom Thou wilt Thou exaltest and whom Thou wilt Thou abasest and there is no god but Thou! How mighty is Thy majesty and how enduring Thy dominion and how excellent Thy government! Verily, Thou favourest whom Thou wilt of Thy servants, whereby the owner of this place abideth in all joyance of life and delighteth himself with pleasant scents and delicious meats and exquisite wines of all kinds. For indeed Thou appointest unto Thy creatures that which Thou wilt and that which Thou hast foreordained unto them; wherefore are some weary and others are at rest and some enjoy fair fortune and affluence, whilst others suffer the extreme of travail and misery, even as I do." And he fell to reciting,

---

[1] Arab. "Karawán" (Charadrius œdicnemus, Linn.) : its shrill note is admired by Egyptians and hated by sportsmen.

"How many by my labours, that evermore endure, * All goods of life enjoy
 and in cooly shade recline?
Each morn that dawns I wake in travail and in woe, * And strange is my
 condition and my burden gars me pine:
Many others are in luck and from miseries are free, * And Fortune never
 loads them with loads the like o' mine:
They live their happy days in all solace and delight; * Eat, drink and dwell
 in honour 'mid the noble and the digne:
All living things were made of a little drop of sperm, * Thine origin is mine
 and my provenance is thine;
Yet the difference and distance 'twixt the twain of us are far * As the
 difference of savour 'twixt vinegar and wine:
But at Thee, O God All-wise! I venture not to rail * Whose ordinance is
 just and whose justice cannot fail."

When Sindbad the Porter had made an end of reciting his verses,
he bore up his burden and was about to fare on, when there came
forth to him from the gate a little foot-page, fair of face and
shapely of shape and dainty of dress who caught him by the hand
saying, "Come in and speak with my lord, for he calleth for thee."
The Porter would have excused himself to the page but the lad
would take no refusal; so he left his load with the doorkeeper in
the vestibule and followed the boy into the house, which he found
to be a goodly mansion, radiant and full of majesty, till he brought
him to a grand sitting-room wherein he saw a company of nobles
and great lords, seated at tables garnished with all manner of
flowers and sweet-scented herbs, besides great plenty of dainty
viands and fruits dried and fresh and confections and wines of the
choicest vintages. There also were instruments of music and
mirth and lovely slave-girls playing and singing. All the company
was ranged according to rank; and in the highest place sat a man
of worshipful and noble aspect whose beard-sides hoariness had
stricken; and he was stately of stature and fair of favour, agreeable
of aspect and full of gravity and dignity and majesty. So Sindbad
the Porter was confounded at that which he beheld and said in
himself, "By Allah, this must be either a piece of Paradise or
some King's palace!" Then he saluted the company with much
respect praying for their prosperity, and kissing the ground before
them, stood with his head bowed down in humble attitude.———
And Shahrazad perceived the dawn of day and ceased to say
her permitted say.

When it was the Five Hundred and Thirty-eighth Night,

She said, It hath reached me, O auspicious King, that Sindbad the Porter, after kissing ground between their hands stood with his head bowed down in humble attitude. The master of the house bade him draw near and be seated and bespoke him kindly, bidding him welcome. Then he set before him various kinds of viands, rich and delicate and delicious, and the Porter, after saying his Bismillah, fell to and ate his fill, after which he exclaimed, "Praised be Allah whatso be our case![1]" and, washing his hands, returned thanks to the company for his entertainment. Quoth the host, "Thou art welcome and thy day is a blessed. But what is thy name and calling?" Quoth the other, "O my lord, my name is Sindbad the Hammal, and I carry folk's goods on my head for hire." The house-master smiled and rejoined, "Know, O Porter that thy name is even as mine, for I am Sindbad the Seaman; and now, O Porter, I would have thee let me hear the couplets thou recitedst at the gate anon." The Porter was abashed and replied, "Allah upon thee! Excuse me, for toil and travail and lack of luck when the hand is empty, teach a man ill manners and boorish ways." Said the host, "Be not ashamed; thou art become my brother; but repeat to me the verses, for they pleased me whenas I heard thee recite them at the gate. Hereupon the Porter repeated the couplets and they delighted the merchant, who said to him, "Know, O Hammal, that my story is a wonderful one, and thou shalt hear all that befel me and all I underwent ere I rose to this state of prosperity and became the lord of this place wherein thou seest me; for I came not to this high estate save after travail sore and perils galore, and how much toil and trouble have I not suffered in days of yore! I have made seven voyages, by each of which hangeth a marvellous tale, such as confoundeth the reason, and all this came to pass by doom of fortune and fate; for from what destiny doth write there is neither refuge nor flight. Know, then, good my lords (continued he) that I am about to relate the

First Voyage of Sindbad the Seaman."[2]

My father was a merchant, one of the notables of my native place, a monied man and ample of means, who died whilst I was yet a

---

[1] This ejaculation, still popular, averts the evil eye. In describing Sindbad the Seaman the Arab writer seems to repeat what one reads of Marco Polo returned to Venice.

[2] Our old friend must not be confounded with the eponym of the "Sindibád-námah;" the Persian book of Sindbad the Sage. See Night dlxxviii.

child, leaving me much wealth in money and lands and farm-houses. When I grew up, I laid hands on the whole and ate of the best and drank freely and wore rich clothes and lived lavishly, companioning and consorting with youths of my own age, and considering that this course of life would continue for ever and ken no change. Thus did I for a long time, but at last I awoke from my heedlessness and, returning to my senses, I found my wealth had become unwealth and my condition ill-conditioned and all I once hent had left my hand. And recovering my reason I was stricken with dismay and confusion and bethought me of a saying of our lord Solomon, son of David (on whom be peace!), which I had heard aforetime from my father, "Three things are better than other three; the day of death is better than the day of birth, a live dog is better than a dead lion and the grave is better than want."[1] Then I got together my remains of estates and property and sold all, even my clothes, for three thousand dirhams, with which I resolved to travel to foreign parts, remembering the saying of the poet,

"By means of toil man shall scale the height; * Who to fame aspires mustn't sleep o' night:
Who seeketh pearl in the deep must dive, * Winning weal and wealth by his main and might:
And who seeketh Fame without toil and strife * Th' impossible seeketh and wasteth life."

So taking heart I bought me goods, merchandise and all needed for a voyage and, impatient to be at sea, I embarked, with a com-pany of merchants, on board a ship bound for Bassorah. There we again embarked and sailed many days and nights, and we passed from isle to isle and sea to sea and shore to shore, buying and selling and bartering everywhere the ship touched, and con-tinued our course till we came to an island as it were a garth of the gardens of Paradise. Here the captain cast anchor and making fast to the shore, put out the landing planks. So all on board landed and made furnaces[2] and lighting fires therein, busied themselves in various ways, some cooking and some

---

[1] The first and second are from Eccles. chapts. vii. 1, and ix. 4. The Bul. Edit. reads for the third, "The grave is better than the palace." None are from Solomon, but Easterns do not "verify quotations."

[2] Arab. "Kánún"; a furnace, a brasier before noticed (vol. v., p. 272); here a pot full of charcoal sunk in the ground, or a little hearth of clay shaped like a horseshoe and opening down wind.

washing, whilst other some walked about the island for solace,
and the crew fell to eating and drinking and playing and sporting.
I was one of the walkers but, as we were thus engaged, behold the
master who was standing on the gunwale cried out to us at the
top of his voice, saying, "Ho there! passengers, run for your lives
and hasten back to the ship and leave your gear and save yourselves from destruction, Allah preserve you!   For this island
whereon ye stand is no true island, but a great fish stationary
a-middlemost of the sea, whereon the sand hath settled and trees
have sprung up of old time, so that it is become like unto an
island;[1] but, when ye lighted fires on it, it felt the heat and
moved; and in a moment it will sink with you into the sea and ye
will all be drowned.   So leave your gear and seek your safety
ere ye die!"———And Shahrazad perceived the dawn of day and
ceased saying her permitted say.

When it was the Five Hundred and Thirty-ninth Night,

She said, It hath reached me, O auspicious King, that when the
ship-master cried to the passengers, "Leave your gear and seek
safety, ere ye die;" all who heard him left gear and goods, clothes
washed and unwashed, fire pots and brass cooking-pots, and fled
back to the ship for their lives, and some reached it while others
(amongst whom was I) did not, for suddenly the island shook and
sank into the abysses of the deep, with all that were thereon, and
the dashing sea surged over it with clashing waves.   I sank with
the others down, down into the deep, but Almighty Allah preserved me from drowning and threw in my way a great wooden
tub of those that had served the ship's company for tubbing.   I
gripped it for the sweetness of life and, bestriding it like one
riding, paddled with my feet like oars, whilst the waves tossed me
as in sport right and left.   Meanwhile the captain made sail and

---

[1] These fish-islands are common in the Classics, *e.g.* the Pristis of Pliny (xvii. 4), which
Olaus Magnus transfers to the Baltic (xxi. 6) and makes timid as the whales of Nearchus.
C. J. Solinus (*Plinii Simia*) says, "Indica maria balænas habent ultra spatia quatuor
jugerum." See also Bochart's Hierozoicon (i. 50) for Job's Leviathan (xli. 16–17). Hence
Boiardo (Orl. Innam, lib. iv.) borrowed his magical whale and Milton (P.L. i.) his Leviathan
deemed an island. A basking whale would readily suggest the Kraken and Cetus of Olaus
Magnus (xxi. 25). Al-Kazwíni's famous treatise on the "Wonders of the World" (Ajáib
al-Makhlúkát) tells the same tale of the "Sulahfah" tortoise, the colossochelys, for which
see Night dl.

departed with those who had reached the ship, regardless of the
drowning and the drowned; and I ceased not following the vessel
with my eyes, till she was hid from sight and I made sure of death.
Darkness closed in upon me while in this plight and the winds and
waves bore me on all that night and the next day, till the tub
brought to with me under the lee of a lofty island, with trees overhanging the tide.   I caught hold of a branch and by its aid
clambered up on to the land, after coming nigh upon death; but
when I reached the shore, I found my legs cramped and numbed
and my feet bore traces of the nibbling of fish upon their soles;
withal I had felt nothing for excess of anguish and fatigue.   I
threw myself down on the island ground, like a dead man, and
drowned in desolation swooned away, nor did I return to my
senses till next morning, when the sun rose and revived me.   But I
found my feet swollen, so made shift to move by shuffling on my
breech and crawling on my knees, for in that island were found
store of fruits and springs of sweet water. I ate of the fruits which
strengthened me; and thus I abode days and nights, till my life
seemed to return and my spirits began to revive and I was better
able to move about.   So, after due consideration, I fell to exploring
the island and diverting myself with gazing upon all things that
Allah Almighty had created there; and rested under the trees
from one of which I cut me a staff to lean upon.   One day as I
walked along the marge, I caught sight of some object in the distance and thought it a wild beast or one of the monster-creatures
of the sea; but, as I drew near it, looking hard the while, I saw
that it was a noble mare, tethered on the beach.   Presently I went
up to her, but she cried out against me with a great cry, so that
I trembled for fear and turned to go away, when there came forth
a man from under the earth and followed me, crying out and
saying, "Who and whence art thou, and what caused thee to
come hither?"   "O my lord," answered I, "I am in very sooth,
a waif, a stranger, and was left to drown with sundry others by
the ship we voyaged in;[1] but Allah graciously sent me a wooden
tub; so I saved myself thereon and it floated with me, till the
waves cast me up on this island."   When he heard this, he took
my hand and saying, "Come with me," carried me into a great
Sardáb, or underground chamber, which was spacious as a saloon.

---

[1] Sindbad does not say that he was a shipwrecked man, being a model in the matter
of "travellers' tales," *i.e.* he always tells the truth when an untruth would not serve him.

He made me sit down at its upper end; then he brought me somewhat of food and, being anhungered, I ate till I was satisfied and
refreshed; and when he had put me at mine ease he questioned
me of myself, and I told him all that had befallen me from first
to last; and, as he wondered at my adventure, I said, "By Allah,
O my lord, excuse me; I have told thee the truth of my case and
the accident which betided me; and now I desire that thou tell
me who thou art and why thou abidest here under the earth and
why thou hast tethered yonder mare on the brink of the sea."
Answered he, "Know, that I am one of the several who are
stationed in different parts of this island, and we are of the grooms
of King Mihrján[1] and under our hand are all his horses. Every
month, about new-moon tide we bring hither our best mares which
have never been covered, and picket them on the sea-shore and
hide ourselves in this place under the ground, so that none may
espy us. Presently, the stallions of the sea scent the mares and
come up out of the water and seeing no one, leap the mares and
do their will of them. When they have covered them, they try to
drag them away with them, but cannot, by reason of the leg-ropes;
so they cry out at them and butt at them and kick them, which
we hearing, know that the stallions have dismounted; so we run
out and shout at them, whereupon they are startled and return in
fear to the sea. Then the mares conceive by them and bear colts
and fillies worth a mint of money, nor is their like to be found on
earth's face. This is the time of the coming forth of the sea-
stallions; and Inshallah! I will bear thee to King Mihrjan"——
And Shahrazad perceived the dawn of day and ceased to say her
permitted say.

---

[1] Lane (iii. 83) would make this a corruption of the Hindu "Maharáj"=great Rajah:
but it is the name of the great autumnal fête of the Guebres; a term composed of two good
old Persian words "Mihr" (the sun, whence "Mithras") and "ján"=life. As will presently
appear, in the days of the Just King Anushirwán, the Persians possessed Southern Arabia
and East Africa south of Cape Guardafui (Jird Háfún). On the other hand, supposing
the word to be a corruption of Maharaj, Sindbad may allude to the famous Narsinga
kingdom in Mid-south India whose capital was Vijaya-nagar; or to any great Indian
Rajah even he of Kachch (Cutch), famous in Moslem story as the Balhará (Ballaba Rais,
who founded the Ballabhi era; or the Zamorin of Camoens, the Samdry Rajah of Malabar).
For Mahrage, or Mihrage, see Renaudot's "Two Mohammedan Travellers of the Ninth
Century." In the account of Ceylon by Wolf (English Transl. p. 168) it adjoins the "Ilhas
de Cavalos" (of wild horses) to which the Dutch merchants sent their brood-mares. Sir
W. Jones (Description of Asia, chapt. ii.) makes the Arabian island Soborma or Mahráj=
Borneo.

When it was the Five Hundred and Fortieth Night,

She continued, It hath reached me, O auspicious King, that the Syce[1] said to Sindbad the Seaman, "I will bear thee to King Mihrjan and show thee our country. And know that hadst thou not happened on us thou hadst perished miserably and none had known of thee: but I will be the means of the saving of thy life and of thy return to thine own land." I called down blessings on him and thanked him for his kindness and courtesy; and, while we were yet talking, behold, the stallion came up out of the sea; and, giving a great cry, sprang upon the mare and covered her. When he had done his will of her, he dismounted and would have carried her away with him, but could not by reason of the tether. She kicked and cried out at him, whereupon the groom took a sword and target[2] and ran out of the underground saloon, smiting the buckler with the blade and calling to his company, who came up shouting and brandishing spears; and the stallion took fright at them and plunging into the sea, like a buffalo, disappeared under the waves.[3] After this we sat awhile, till the rest of the grooms came up, each leading a mare, and seeing me with their fellow-Syce, questioned me of my case and I repeated my story to them. Thereupon they drew near me and spreading the table, ate and invited me to eat; so I ate with them, after which they took horse and mounting me on one of the mares, set out with me and fared on without ceasing, till we came to the capital city of King Mihr-jan, and going in to him acquainted him with my story. Then he sent for me, and when they set me before him and salams had been exchanged, he gave me a cordial welcome and wishing me long life bade me tell him my tale. So I related to him all that

---

[1] Arab. "Sáis"; the well-known Anglo-Indian word for a groom or rather a "horse-keeper."

[2] Arab. "Darakah"; whence our word.

[3] The myth of mares being impregnated by the wind was known to the Classics of Europe; and the "sea-stallion" may have arisen from the Arab practice of picketing mare asses to be covered by the wild ass. Colonel J. D. Watson of the Bombay Army suggests to me that Sindbad was wrecked at the mouth of the Ran of Kachch (Cutch) and was carried in a boat to one of the Islands there formed during the rains and where the wild ass (*Equus Onager*, Khar-gadh, in Pers. Gor-khar) still breeds. This would explain the "stallions of the sea" and we find traces of the ass blood in the true Kathiawár horse, with his dun colour, barred legs and dorsal stripe.

I had seen and all that had befallen me from first to last, whereat he marvelled and said to me, "By Allah, O my son, thou hast indeed been miraculously preserved! Were not the term of thy life a long one, thou hadst not escaped from these straits; but praised be Allah for safety!" Then he spoke cheerily to me and entreated me with kindness and consideration: moreover, he made me his agent for the port and registrar of all ships that entered the harbour. I attended him regularly, to receive his command-ments, and he favoured me and did me all manner of kindness and invested me with costly and splendid robes. Indeed, I was high in credit with him, as an intercessor for the folk and an intermediary between them and him, when they wanted aught of him. I abode thus a great while and, as often as I passed through the city to the port, I questioned the merchants and travellers and sailors of the city of Baghdad; so haply I might hear of an occasion to return to my native land, but could find none who knew it or knew any who resorted thither. At this I was chagrined, for I was weary of long strangerhood; and my disappointment endured for a time till one day, going in to King Mihrjan, I found with him a company of Indians. I saluted them and they returned my salam; and politely welcomed me and asked me of my country. ——And Shahrazad perceived the dawn of day and ceased saying her permitted say.

When it was the Five Hundred and Forty-first Night,

She continued, It hath reached me, O auspicious King, that Sindbad the Seaman said:—When they asked me of my country I questioned them of theirs and they told me that they were of various castes, some being called Shakiriyah[1] who are the noblest of their castes and neither oppress nor offer violence to any, and others Brahmans, a folk who abstain from wine, but live in delight and solace and merriment and own camels and horses and cattle. Moreover, they told me that the people of India are divided into two-and-seventy castes, and I marvelled at this with exceeding

---

[1] The second or warrior caste (Kshatriya), popularly supposed to have been annihilated by Battle-axe Ráma (Parashu Ráma); but several tribes of Rajputs and other races claim the honourable genealogy. Colonel Watson would explain the word by "Shakháyát" or noble Káthis (Kathiawar-men), or by "Shikári," the professional hunter here acting as stable-groom.

marvel. Amongst other things that I saw in King Mihrjan's dominions was an island called Kásil,[1] wherein all night is heard the beating of drums and tabrets; but we were told by the neighbouring islanders and by travellers that the inhabitants are people of diligence and judgment.[2] In this sea I saw also a fish two hundred cubits long and the fishermen fear it; so they strike together pieces of wood and put it to flight.[3] I also saw another fish, with a head like that of an owl, besides many other wonders and rarities, which it would be tedious to recount. I occupied myself thus in visiting the islands till, one day, as I stood in the port, with a staff in my hand, according to my custom, behold, a great ship, wherein were many merchants, came sailing for the harbour. When it reached the small inner port where ships anchor under the city, the master furled his sails and making fast to the shore, put out the landing-planks, whereupon the crew fell to breaking bulk and landing cargo whilst I stood by, taking written note of them. They were long in bringing the goods ashore so I asked the master, "Is there aught left in thy ship?"; and he answered, "O my lord, there are divers bales of merchandise in the hold, whose owner was drowned from amongst us at one of the islands on our course; so his goods remained in our charge by way of trust and we purpose to sell them and note their price, that we may convey it to his people in the city of Baghdad, the Home of Peace." "What was the merchant's name?" quoth I, and quoth he, "Sindbad the Seaman;" whereupon I straitly considered him and knowing him, cried out to him with a great cry, saying, "O captain, I am that Sindbad the Seaman who travelled with other merchants; and when the fish heaved and thou calledst to us

---

[1] In Bul. Edit. "Kábil." Lane (iii. 88) supposes it to be the "Bartail" of Al-Kazwini near Borneo and quotes the Spaniard B. L. de Argensola (History of the Moluccas), who places near Banda a desert island, Poelsatton, infamous for cries, whistlings, roarings and dreadful apparitions, suggesting that it was peopled by devils (Stevens, vol. i., p. 168).

[2] Some texts substitute for this last phrase, "And the sailors say that Al-Dajjál is there." He is a manner of Moslem Antichrist, the Man of Sin per excellentiam, who will come in the latter days and lay waste the earth, leading 70,000 Jews, till encountered and slain by Jesus at the gate of Lud. (Sale's Essay, sect. 4.)

[3] Also from Al-Kazwini: it is an exaggerated description of the whale still common off the East African Coast. My crew was dreadfully frightened by one between Berberah and Aden. Nearchus scared away the whales in the Persian Gulf by trumpets (Strabo, lib. xv.). The owl-faced fish is unknown to me: it may perhaps be a seal or a manatee. Hole says that Father Martini, the Jesuit (seventeenth century), placed in the Canton Seas, an "animal with the head of a bird and the tail of a fish,"—a parrot-beak?

some saved themselves and others sank, I being one of them. But Allah Almighty threw in my way a great tub of wood, of those the crew had used to wash withal, and the winds and waves carried me to this island, where by Allah's grace, I fell in with King Mihrjan's grooms and they brought me hither to the King their master. When I told him my story, he entreated me with favour and made me his harbour-master, and I have prospered in his service and found acceptance with him. These bales, therefore are mine, the goods whch God hath given me."——And Shahrazad perceived the dawn of day and ceased to say her permitted say.

When it was the Five Hundred and Forty-second Night,

She continued, It hath reached me, O auspicious King, that when Sindbad the Seaman said to the captain, "These bales are mine, the goods which Allah hath given me," the other exclaimed, "There is no Majesty and there is no Might save in Allah, the Glorious, the Great! Verily, there is neither conscience nor good faith left among men!" said I, "O Rais,[1] what mean these words, seeing that I have told thee my case?" And he answered, "Because thou heardest me say that I had with me goods whose owner was drowned, thou thinkest to take them without right; but this is forbidden by law to thee, for we saw him drown before our eyes, together with many other passengers, nor was one of them saved. So how canst thou pretend that thou art the owner of the goods?" "O captain," said I, "listen to my story and give heed to my words, and my truth will be manifest to thee; for lying and leasing are the letter-marks of the hypocrites." Then I recounted to him all that had befallen me since I sailed from Baghdad with him to the time when we came to the fish-island where we were nearly drowned; and I reminded him of certain matters which had passed between us; whereupon both he and the merchants were certified at the truth of my story and recognized me and gave me joy of my deliverance, saying, "By Allah, we thought not that thou hadst escaped drowning! But the Lord hath granted thee new life." Then they delivered my bales to me, and I found my name written thereon, nor was aught thereof lacking. So I opened them and making up a present for King

---

[1] The captain or master (not owner) of a ship.

Mihrjan of the finest and costliest of the contents, caused the sailors carry it up to the palace, where I went in to the King and laid my present at his feet, acquainting him with what had happened, especially concerning the ship and my goods; whereat he wondered with exceeding wonder and the truth of all that I had told him was made manifest to him. His affection for me redoubled after that and he showed me exceeding honour and bestowed on me a great present in return for mine. Then I sold my bales and what other matters I owned making a great profit on them, and bought me other goods and gear of the growth and fashion of the island-city. When the merchants were about to start on their homeward voyage, I embarked on board the ship all that I possessed, and going in to the King, thanked him for all his favours and friendship and craved his leave to return to my own land and friends. He farewelled me and bestowed on me great store of the country-stuffs and produce; and I took leave of him and embarked. Then we set sail and fared on nights and days, by the permission of Allah Almighty; and Fortune served us and Fate favoured us, so that we arrived in safety at Bassorah-city where I landed rejoiced at my safe return to my natal soil. After a short stay, I set out for Baghdad, the House of Peace, with store of goods and commodities of great price. Reaching the city in due time, I went straight to my own quarter and entered my house where all my friends and kinsfolk came to greet me. Then I bought me eunuchs and concubines, servants and negro slaves till I had a large establishment, and I bought me houses, and lands and gardens, till I was richer and in better case than before, and returned to enjoy the society of my friends and familiars more assiduously than ever, forgetting all I had suffered of fatigue and hardship and strangerhood and every peril of travel; and I applied myself to all manner joys and solaces and delights, eating the daintiest viands and drinking the deliciousest wines; and my wealth allowed this state of things to endure. "This, then, is the story of my first voyage, and to-morrow, Inshallah! I will tell you the tale of the second of my seven voyages." (Saith he who telleth the tale), Then Sindbad the Seaman made Sindbad the Landsman sup with him and bade give him an hundred gold pieces, saying, "Thou hast cheered us with thy company this day."[1] The

---

[1] The kindly Moslem feeling, shown to a namesake, however humble.

Porter thanked him and, taking the gift, went his way, pondering that which he had heard and marvelling mightily at what things betide mankind. He passed the night in his own place and with early morning repaired to the abode of Sindbad the Seaman, who received him with honour and seated him by his side. As soon as the rest of the company was assembled, he set meat and drink before them and, when they had well eaten and drunken and were merry and in cheerful case, he took up his discourse and recounted to them in these words the narrative of

The Second Voyage of Sindbad the Seaman.

KNOW, O my brother, that I was living a most comfortable and enjoyable life, in all solace and delight, as I told you yesterday, ——And Shahrazad perceived the dawn of day and ceased saying her permitted say.

When it was the Five Hundred and Forty-third Night,

She continued, It hath reached me, O auspicious King, that when Sindbad the Seaman's guests were all gathered together he thus bespake them:—I was living a most enjoyable life until one day my mind became possessed with the thought of travelling about the world of men and seeing their cities and islands; and a longing seized me to traffic and to make money by trade. Upon this resolve I took a great store of cash and, buying goods and gear fit for travel, bound them up in bales. Then I went down to the river-bank, where I found a noble ship and brand-new about to sail, equipped with sails of fine cloth and well manned and provided; so I took passage in her, with a number of other merchants, and after embarking our goods we weighed anchor the same day. Right fair was our voyage and we sailed from place to place and from isle to isle; and whenever we anchored we met a crowd of merchants and notables and customers, and we took to buying and selling and bartering. At last Destiny brought us to an island, fair and verdant, in trees abundant, with yellow-ripe fruits luxuriant, and flowers fragrant and birds warbling soft descant; and streams crystalline and radiant; but no sign of man showed to the descrier, no, not a blower of the fire.[1] The captain made fast with us to this island, and the merchants and sailors landed and walked about, enjoying the shade of the trees and the song of the birds, that chanted the praises of the One, the Victorious, and marvelling at the works of the Omnipotent King.[2] I landed with the rest; and, sitting down by a spring of sweet water that welled up among the trees, took out some vivers I had with me and ate of that which Allah Almighty had allotted unto me. And so sweet was the zephyr and so fragrant were the flowers, that presently I waxed drowsy and, lying down in that place, was soon drowned in sleep. When I awoke, I found myself alone, for the ship had sailed and left me behind, nor had one of the merchants or sailors bethought himself of me. I searched the island right and left, but found neither man nor Jinn, whereat I was beyond measure troubled and my gall was like to burst for stress of chagrin and anguish and concern, because I was left quite alone, without aught of wordly gear or meat or drink, weary and heart-broken. So I gave myself up for lost and said, "Not always doth the crock escape the shock. I was saved the first time by finding one who brought me from the desert island to an inhabited place, but now there is no hope for me." Then I fell to weeping and wailing and gave myself up to an access of rage, blaming myself for having again ventured upon the perils and hardships of voyage, whenas I was at my ease in mine own house in mine own land, taking my pleasure with good meat and good drink and good clothes and lacking nothing, neither money nor goods. And I repented me of having left Baghdad, and this the more after all the travails and dangers I had undergone in my first voyage, wherein I had so narrowly escaped destruction, and exclaimed "Verily we are Allah's and unto Him we are returning!" I was indeed even as one mad and Jinn-struck and presently I rose and walked about the island, right and left and every whither, unable for trouble to sit or tarry in any one place. Then I climbed a tall tree and looked in all directions, but saw nothing save sky and sea and trees and birds and isles and sands. However, after a while my eager glances fell upon some great white thing, afar off in the

---

[1] A popular phrase to express utter desolation.

[2] The literature of all peoples contains this physiological perversion. Birds do not sing hymns; the song of the male is simply to call the female and when the pairing-season ends all are dumb.

interior of the island; so I came down from the tree and made for that which I had seen; and behold, it was a huge white dome rising high in air and of vast compass. I walked all around it, but found no door thereto, nor could I muster strength or nimbleness by reason of its exceeding smoothness and slipperiness. So I marked the spot where I stood and went round about the dome to measure its circumference which I found fifty good paces. And as I stood, casting about how to gain an entrance the day being near its fall and the sun being near the horizon, behold, the sun was suddenly hidden from me and the air became dull and dark. Methought a cloud had come over the sun, but it was the season of summer; so I marvelled at this and lifting my head looked steadfastly at the sky, when I saw that the cloud was none other than an enormous bird, of gigantic girth and inordinately wide of wing which, as it flew through the air, veiled the sun and hid it from the island. At this sight my wonder redoubled and I remembered a story,——And Shahrazad perceived the dawn of day and ceased to say her permitted say.

When it was the Five Hundred and Forty-fourth Night,

She said, It hath reached me, O auspicious King, that Sindbad the Seaman continued in these words:—My wonder redoubled and I remembered a story I had heard aforetime of pilgrims and travellers, how in a certain island dwelleth a huge bird, called the "Rukh"[1] which feedeth its young on elephants; and I was certi-

---

[1] The older "roc." The word is Persian, with many meanings, *e.g.* a cheek (Lalla "Rookh"); a "rook" (hero) at chess; a rhinoceros, etc. The fable world-wide of the *wundervogel* is, as usual, founded upon fact: man remembers and combines but does not create. The Egyptian Bennu (Ti-bennu = phœnix) may have been a reminiscence of gigantic pterodactyls and other winged monsters. From the Nile the legend fabled by these Oriental "putters out or five for one" overspread the world and gave birth to the Eorosh of the Zend, whence the Pers. "Símurgh" (= the "thirty-fowl-like"), the "Bar Yuchre" of the Rabbis, the "Garuda" of the Hindus; the "Anká" ("long-neck") of the Arabs; the "Hathilinga bird," of Buddhagosha's Parables, which had the strength of five elephants; the "Kerkes" of the Turks; the "Gryps" of the Greeks; the Russian "Norka"; the sacred dragon of the Chinese; the Japanese "Pheng" and "Kirni"; the "wise and ancient Bird" which sits upon the ash-tree yggdrasil, and the dragons, griffins, basilisks, etc. of the Middle Ages. A second basis wanting only a superstructure of exaggeration (M. Polo's Ruch had wing-feathers twelve paces long) would be the huge birds but lately

fied that the dome which caught my sight was none other than a Rukh's egg. As I looked and wondered at the marvellous works of the Almighty, the bird alighted on the dome and brooded over it with its wings covering it and its legs stretched out behind it on the ground, and in this posture it fell asleep, glory be to Him who sleepeth not! When I saw this, I arose and, unwinding my turband from my head, doubled it and twisted it into a rope, with which I girt my middle and bound my waist fast to the legs of the Rukh, saying in myself, "Peradventure, this bird may carry me to a land of cities and inhabitants, and that will be better than abiding in this desert island." I passed the night watching and fearing to sleep, lest the bird should fly away with me unawares; and, as soon as the dawn broke and morn shone, the Rukh rose off its egg and spreading its wings with a great cry flew up into the air dragging me with it; nor ceased it to soar and to tower till I thought it had reached the limit of the firmament; after which it descended, earthwards, little by little, till it lighted on the top of a high hill. As soon as I found myself on the hard ground, I made haste to unbind myself, quaking for fear of the bird, though it took no heed of me nor even felt me; and, loosing my turband from its feet, I made off with my best speed. Presently, I saw it catch up in its huge claws something from the earth and rise with it high in air, and observing it narrowly I saw it to be a serpent big of bulk and gigantic of girth, wherewith it flew away clean out of sight. I marvelled at this and faring forwards found myself on a peak overlooking a valley, exceeding great and wide and deep, and bounded by vast mountains that spired high in air: none could descry their summits, for the excess of their height, nor was any able to climb up thereto. When I saw this, I blamed myself for that which I had done and said, "Would Heaven I had tarried in the island!

---

killed out. Sindbad may allude to the Æpyornus of Madagascar, a gigantic ostrich whose egg contains 2.35 gallons. The late Herr Hildebrand discovered on the African coast, facing Madagascar, traces of another huge bird. Bochart (Hierozoicon ii. 854) notices the Avium Avis Ruch and taking the *pulli* was followed by lapidation on the part of the parent bird. A Persian illustration in Lane (iii. 90) shows the Rukh carrying off three elephants in beak and pounces with the proportions of a hawk and field mice: and the Rukh hawking at an elephant is a favourite Persian subject. It is possible that the "Twelve Knights of the Round Table" were the twelve Rukhs of Persian story. We need not go, with Faber, to the Cherubim which guarded the Paradise-gate. The curious reader will consult Dr. H. H. Wilson's Essays, edited by my learned correspondent, Dr. Rost, Librarian of the India House (vol. i. pp. 192–3).

It was better than this wild desert; for there I had at least fruits to eat and water to drink, and here are neither trees nor fruits nor streams. But there is no Majesty and there is no Might save in Allah, the Glorious, the Great! Verily, as often as I am quit of one peril, I fall into a worse danger and a more grievous." However, I took courage and walking along the Wady found that its soil was of diamond, the stone wherewith they pierce minerals and precious stones and porcelain and the onyx, for that it is a dense stone and a dure, whereon neither iron nor hardhead hath effect, neither can we cut off aught therefrom nor break it, save by means of leadstone.[1] Moreover, the valley swarmed with snakes and vipers, each big as a palm tree, that would have made but one gulp of an elephant; and they came out by night, hiding during the day, lest the Rukhs and eagles pounce on them and tear them to pieces, as was their wont, why I wot not. And I repented of what I had done and said, "By Allah, I have made haste to bring destruction upon myself!" The day began to wane as I went along and I looked about for a place where I might pass the night, being in fear of the serpents; and I took no thought of meat and drink in my concern for my life. Presently, I caught sight of a cave nearhand, with a narrow doorway; so I entered and seeing a great stone close to the mouth, I rolled it up and stopped the entrance, saying to myself, "I am safe here for the night; and as soon as it is day, I will go forth and see what destiny will do." Then I looked within the cave and saw at the upper end a great serpent brooding on her eggs, at which my flesh quaked and my hair stood on end; but I raised my eyes to Heaven and, committing my case to fate and lot, abode all that night without sleep

---

[1] It is not easy to explain this passage unless it be a garbled allusion to the steel-plate of the diamond-cutter. Nor can we account for the wide diffusion of this tale of perils unless to enhance the value of the gem. Diamonds occur in alluvial lands mostly open and comparatively level, as in India, the Brazil and the Cape. Archbishop Epiphanius of Salamis (ob. A.D. 403) tells this story about the jacinth or ruby (Epiphanii Opera, a Petaio, Coloniæ 1682); and it was transferred to the diamond by Marco Polo (iii. 29, "of Eagles bring up diamonds") and Nicolò de Conti, whose "mountain Albenigaras" must be Vijayanagar in the kingdom of Golconda. Major Rennel places the famous mines of Pauna or Purna in a mountain-tract of more than 200 miles square to the south-west of the Jumna. Al-Kazwini locates the "Chaos" in the "Valley of the Moon amongst the mountains of Serendib" (Ceylon); the Chinese tell the same tale in the campaigns of Hulaku; and it is known in Armenia. Col. Yule (M. P. ii. 349) suggests that all these are ramifications of the legend told by Herodotus concerning the Arabs and their cinnamon (iii. 3). But whence did Herodotus borrow the tale?

till daybreak, when I rolled back the stone from the mouth of the cave and went forth, staggering like a drunken man and giddy with watching and fear and hunger. As in this sore case I walked along the valley, behold, there fell down before me a slaughtered beast; but I saw no one, whereat I marvelled with great marvel and presently remembered a story I had heard aforetime of traders and pilgrims and travellers; how the mountains where are the diamonds are full of perils and terrors, nor can any fare through them; but the merchants who traffic in diamonds have a device by which they obtain them, that is to say, they take a sheep and slaughter and skin it and cut it in pieces and cast them down from the mountain-tops into the valley-sole, where the meat being fresh and sticky with blood, some of the gems cleave to it. There they leave it till mid-day, when the eagles and vultures swoop down upon it and carry it in their claws to the mountain-summits, whereupon the merchants come and shout at them and scare them away from the meat. Then they come and, taking the diamonds which they find sticking to it, go their ways with them and leave the meat to the birds and beasts; nor can any come at the diamonds but by this device,——And Shahrazad perceived the dawn of day and ceased saying her permitted say.

When it was the Five Hundred and Forty-tifth Night,

She said, it hath reached me, O auspicious King, that Sind-bad the Seaman continued his relation of what befel him in the Mountain of Diamonds, and informed them that the merchants cannot come at the diamonds save by the device aforesaid. So, when I saw the slaughtered beast fall (he pursued) and bethought me of the story, I went up to it and filled my pockets and shawl-girdle and turband and the folds of my clothes with the choicest diamonds; and, as I was thus engaged, down fell before me another great piece of meat. Then with my unrolled turband and lying on my back, I set the bit on my breast so that I was hidden by the meat, which was thus raised above the ground. Hardly had I gripped it, when an eagle swooped down upon the flesh and, seizing it with his talons, flew up with it high in air and me cling-ing thereto, and ceased not its flight till it alighted on the head of one of the mountains where, dropping the carcass he fell to rend-

ing it; but, behold, there arose behind him a great noise of shouting and clattering of wood, whereat the bird took fright and flew
away. Then I loosed off myself the meat, with clothes daubed with
blood therefrom, and stood up by its side; whereupon up came
the merchant, who had cried out at the eagle, and seeing me standing there, bespoke me not, but was affrighted at me and shook
with fear. However, he went up to the carcass and turning it
over, found no diamonds sticking to it, whereat he gave a great
cry and exclaimed, "Harrow, my disappointment! There is no Majesty and there is no Might save in Allah with whom we seek refuge from Satan the stoned!" And he bemoaned himself and beat
hand upon hand, saying, "Alas, the pity of it! How cometh
this?" Then I went up to him and he said to me, "Who art
thou and what causeth thee to come hither?" And I, "Fear not,
I am a man and a good man and a merchant. My story is a
wondrous and my adventures marvellous and the manner of my
coming hither is prodigious. So be of good cheer, thou shalt
receive of me what shall rejoice thee, for I have with me great
plenty of diamonds and I will give thee thereof what shall suffice
thee; for each is better than aught thou couldst get otherwise. So
fear nothing." The man rejoiced thereat and thanked and blessed
me; then we talked together till the other merchants, hearing me
in discourse with their fellow, came up and saluted me; for each
of them had thrown down his piece of meat. And as I went off
with them I told them my whole story, how I had suffered hardships at sea and the fashion of my reaching the valley. But I
gave the owner of the meat a number of the stones I had by me,
so they all wished me joy of my escape, saying, "By Allah a new
life hath been decreed to thee, for none ever reached yonder
valley and came off thence alive before thee; but praised be Allah
for thy safety!" We passed the night together in a safe and
pleasant place, beyond measure rejoiced at my deliverance from
the Valley of Serpents and my arrival in an inhabited land; and
on the morrow we set out and journeyed over the mighty range
of mountains, seeing many serpents in the valley, till we came to
a fair great island, wherein was a garden of huge camphor trees
under each of which an hundred men might take shelter. When
the folk have a mind to get camphor, they bore into the upper
part of the bole with a long iron; whereupon the liquid camphor,
which is the sap of the tree, floweth out and they catch it in
vessels, where it concreteth like gum; but, after this, the tree

dieth and becometh firewood.[1] Moreover, there is in this island a kind of wild beast, called "Rhinoceros,"[2] that pastureth as do steers and buffalos with us; but it is a huge brute, bigger of body than the camel and like it feedeth upon the leaves and twigs of trees. It is a remarkable animal with a great and thick horn, ten cubits long, amiddleward its head; wherein, when cleft in twain, is the likeness of a man. Voyagers and pilgrims and travellers declare that this beast called "Karkadan" will carry off a great elephant on its horn and graze about the island and the sea-coast therewith and take no heed of it, till the elephant dieth and its fat, melting in the sun, runneth down into the rhinoceros's eyes and blindeth him, so that he lieth down on the shore. Then comes the bird Rukh and carrieth off both the rhinoceros and that which is on its horn to feed its young withal. Moreover, I saw in this island many kinds of oxen and buffalos, whose like are not found in our country. Here I sold some of the diamonds which I had by me for gold dinars and silver dirhams and bartered others for the produce of the country; and, loading them upon beasts of burden, fared on with the merchants from valley to valley and town to town, buying and selling and viewing foreign countries and the works and creatures of Allah, till we came to Bassorah-city, where we abode a few days, after which I continued my journey to Baghdad.——And Shahrazad perceived the dawn of day and ceased to say her permitted say.

---

[1] Sindbad correctly describes the primitive way of extracting camphor, a drug unknown to the Greeks and Romans, introduced by the Arabs and ruined in reputation by M. Raspail. The best Laurus Camphora grows in the Malay Peninsula, Sumatra and Borneo: although Marsden (Marco Polo) declares that the tree is not found South of the Equator. In the Calc. Edit. of two hundred Nights the camphor-island (or peninsula) is called "Al-Ríhah" which is the Arab name for Jericho-town.

[2] In Bul. Edit. Kazkazan: Calc. Karkaddan and others Karkand and Karkadan; the word being Persian, Karg or Kargadan; the καρτάζυνον of Ælian (Hist. Anim. xvi. 21). The length of the horn (greatly exaggerated) shows that the white species is meant; and it supplies only walking-sticks. Cups are made of the black horn (a bundle of fibres) which, like Venetian glass, sweat at the touch of poison. A section of the horn is supposed to show white lines in the figure of a man, and sundry likenesses of birds; but these I never saw. The rhinoceros gives splendid sport and the African is perhaps the most dangerous of noble game. It has served to explain away and abolish the unicorn among the Scientists of Europe. But Central Africa with one voice assures us that a horse-like animal with a single erectile horn on the forehead exists. The late Dr. Baikie, of Niger fame, thoroughly believed in it and those curious on the subject will read about Abu Karn (Father of a Horn) in Preface (pp. xvi.–xviii.) of the Voyage au Darfour, by Mohammed ibn Omar al-Tounsy (Al-Tunisi), Paris, Duprat, 1845.

When it was the Five Hundred and Forty-sixth Night,

She said, It hath reached me, O auspicious King, that when Sindbad the Seaman returned from his travel to Baghdad, the House of Peace, he arrived at home with great store of diamonds and money and goods. (Continued he) I foregathered with my friends and relations and gave alms and largesse and bestowed curious gifts and made presents to all my friends and companions. Then I betook myself to eating well and drinking well and wearing fine clothes and making merry with my fellows, and forgot all my sufferings in the pleasures of return to the solace and delight of life, with light heart and broadened breast. And every one who heard of my return came and questioned me of my adventures and of foreign countries, and I related to them all that had befallen me, and the much I had suffered, whereat they wondered and gave me joy of my safe return. "This, then, is the end of the story of my second voyage; and to-morrow, Inshallah! I will tell you what befel me in my third voyage." The company marvelled at his story and supped with him; after which he ordered an hundred dinars of gold to be given to the Porter, who took the sum with many thanks and blessings (which he stinted not even when he reached home) and went his way, wondering at what he had heard. Next morning as soon as day came in its sheen and shone, he rose and praying the dawn-prayer, repaired to the house of Sindbad the Seaman, even as he had bidden him, and went in and gave him good-morrow. The merchant welcomed him and made him sit with him, till the rest of the company arrived; and when they had well eaten and drunken and were merry with joy and jollity, their host began by saying, "Hearken, O my brothers, to what I am about to tell you; for it is even more wondrous than what you have already heard; but Allah alone kenneth what things His Omniscience concealed from man! And listen to

The Third Voyage of Sindbad the Seaman."

As I told you yesterday, I returned from my second voyage over-joyed at my safety and with great increase of wealth, Allah having requited me all that I had wasted and lost, and I abode awhile in Baghdad-city savouring the utmost ease and prosperity and comfort and happiness, till the carnal man was once more seized with longing for travel and diversion and adventure, and yearned after traffic and lucre and emolument, for that the human heart is naturally prone to evil. So making up my mind I laid in great plenty of goods suitable for a sea-voyage and repairing to Bassorah, went down to the shore and found there a fine ship ready to sail, with a full crew and a numerous company of merchants, men of worth and substance; faith, piety and consideration. I embarked with them and we set sail on the blessing of Allah Almighty and on His aidance and His favour to bring our voyage to a safe and prosperous issue and already we congratulated one another on our good fortune and boon voyage. We fared on from sea to sea and from island to island and city to city, in all delight and contentment, buying and selling wherever we touched, and taking our solace and our pleasure, till one day when, as we sailed athwart the dashing sea, swollen with clashing billows, behold, the master (who stood on the gunwale examining the ocean in all directions) cried out with a great cry, and buffeted his face and pluckt out his beard and rent his raiment, and bade furl the sail and cast the anchors. So we said to him, "O Rais, what is the matter?" "Know, O my brethren (Allah preserve you!), that the wind hath gotten the better of us and hath driven us out of our course into mid-ocean, and destiny, for our ill luck, hath brought us to the Mountain of the Zughb, a hairy folk like apes,[1] among whom no man ever fell and came forth alive; and my heart presageth that we all be dead men." Hardly had the master made an end of his speech when the apes were upon us. They surrounded the ship on all sides swarming like locusts and crowding the shore. They were the most frightful of wild creatures, covered with black hair like felt, foul of favour and small of stature, being but four spans high, yellow-eyed and black-faced; none knoweth their language

---

[1] Ibn al-Wardi mentions an "Isle of Apes" in the Sea of China and Al-Idrísi places it two days' sail from Sukutra (Dwipa Sukhatra, Socotra). It is a popular error to explain the Homeric and Herodotean legend of the Pygmies by anthropoid apes. The Pygmy fable (Pygmæi Spithamai = 1 cubit = 3 spans) was, as usual, based upon fact, as the explorations of late years have proved: the dwarfs are homunculi of various tribes, the Akka, Doko, Tiki-Tiki, Wambilikimo ("two-cubit men"), the stunted race that share the central regions of Intertropical Africa with the abnormally tall peoples who speak dialects of the Great South African tongue, miscalled the "Bantu." Hole makes the Pygmies "monkeys," a word we have borrowed from the Italians (monichio à mono = ape) and quotes Ptolemy, Νῆσοι τῶν Σατυρῶν (Ape-islands) East of Sunda.

nor what they are, and they shun the company of men. We feared to slay them or strike them or drive them away, because of their inconceivable multitude; lest, if we hurt one, the rest fall on us and slay us, for numbers prevail over courage; so we let them do their will, albeit we feared they would plunder our goods and gear. They swarmed up the cables and gnawed them asunder, and on like wise they did with all the ropes of the ship, so that it fell off from the wind and stranded upon their mountainous coast. Then they laid hands on all the merchants and crew, and landing us on the island, made off with the ship and its cargo and went their ways, we wot not whither. We were thus left on the island, eating of its fruits and pot-herbs and drinking of its streams till, one day, we espied in its midst what seemed an inhabited house. So we made for it as fast as our feet could carry us and behold, it was a castle strong and tall, compassed about with a lofty wall, and having a two-leaved gate of ebony-wood both of which leaves open stood. We entered and found within a space wide and bare like a great square, round which stood many high doors open thrown, and at the farther end a long bench of stone and brasiers, with cooking gear hanging thereon and about it great plenty of bones; but we saw no one and marvelled thereat with exceeding wonder. Then we sat down in the courtyard a little while and presently falling asleep, slept from the forenoon till sundown, when lo! the earth trembled under our feet and the air rumbled with a terrible tone. Then there came down upon us, from the top of the castle, a huge creature in the likeness of a man, black of colour, tall and big of bulk, as he were a great date-tree, with eyes like coals of fire and eye-teeth like boar's tusks and a vast big gape like the mouth of a well. Moreover, he had long loose lips like camel's, hanging down upon his breast, and ears like two Jarms[1] falling over his shoulder-blades and the nails of his hands were like the claws of a lion.[2] When we saw this frightful giant, we were like to faint and every moment increased our fear and terror; and we became as dead

---

[1] A kind of barge (Arab. Bárijah, plur. Bawárij) used on the Nile of sub-pyriform shape when seen in bird's eye. Lane translates "ears like two mortars" from the Calc. Edit.

[2] This giant is distinctly Polyphemus; but the East had giants and cyclopes of her own (Hierozoicon ii. 845). The Ajáib al-Hind (chapt. cxxii.) makes Polyphemus copulate with the sheep. Sir John Mandeville (if such person ever existed) mentions men fifty feet high in the Indian Islands; and Al-Kazwini and Al-Idrisi transfer them to the Sea of China, a Botany Bay for monsters in general.

men for excess of horror and affright.——And Shahrazad perceived the dawn of day and ceased saying her permitted say.

When it was the Five Hundred and Forty-seventh Night,

She said, It hath reached me, O auspicious King, that Sindbad the
Seaman continued:—When we saw this frightful giant we were
struck with exceeding terror and horror. And after trampling
upon the earth, he sat awhile on the bench; then he arose and
coming to us seized me by the arm choosing me out from among
my comrades the merchants. He took me up in his hand and
turning me over felt me, as a butcher feeleth a sheep he is about to
slaughter, and I but a little mouthful in his hands; but finding me
lean and fleshless for stress of toil and trouble and weariness, let
me go and took up another, whom in like manner he turned over
and felt and let go; nor did he cease to feel and turn over the rest
of us, one after another, till he came to the master of the ship.
Now he was a sturdy, stout, broad-shouldered wight, fat and in
full vigour; so he pleased the giant, who seized him, as a butcher
seizeth a beast, and throwing him down, set his foot on his neck
and brake it; after which he fetched a long spit and thrusting it
up his backside, brought it forth of the crown of his head. Then,
lighting a fierce fire, he set over it the spit with the Rais thereon,
and turned it over the coals, till the flesh was roasted, when he
took the spit off the fire and set it like a Kabáb-stick before him.
Then he tare the body, limb from limb, as one jointeth a chicken
and, rending the flesh with his nails, fell to eating of it and gnaw-
ing the bones, till there was nothing left but some of these, which
he threw on one side of the wall. This done, he sat for a while;
then he lay down on the stone-bench and fell asleep, snarking and
snoring like the gurgling of a lamb or a cow with its throat cut;
nor did he awake till morning, when he rose and fared forth and
went his ways. As soon as we were certified that he was gone,
we began to talk with one another, weeping and bemoaning ourselves for the risk we ran, and saying, "Would Heaven we had
been drowned in the sea or that the apes had eaten us! That
were better than to be roasted over the coals; by Allah, this is a
vile, foul death! But whatso the Lord willeth must come to pass
and there is no Majesty and there is no Might, save in Him, the
Glorious, the Great! We shall assuredly perish miserably and

none will know of us; as there is no escape for us from this place."
Then we arose and roamed about the island, hoping that haply we
might find a place to hide us in or a means of flight, for indeed
death was a light matter to us, provided we were not roasted over
the fire[1] and eaten. However, we could find no hiding-place and
the evening overtook us; so, of the excess of our terror, we returned to the castle and sat down awhile. Presently, the earth
trembled under our feet and the black ogre came up to us and
turning us over, felt one after other, till he found a man to his
liking, whom he took and served as he had done the captain,
killing and roasting and eating him: after which he lay down on
the bench[2] and slept all night, snarking and snoring like a beast
with its throat cut, till daybreak, when he arose and went out as
before. Then we drew together and conversed and said one to
other, "By Allah, we had better throw ourselves into the sea and
be drowned than die roasted; for this is an abominable death!"
Quoth one of us, "Hear ye my words! let us cast about to kill
him, and be at peace from the grief of him and rid the Moslems of
his barbarity and tyranny." Then said I, "Hear me, O my brothers; if there is nothing for it but to slay him, let us carry some of
this firewood and planks down to the sea-shore and make us a boat
wherein, if we succeed in slaughtering him, we may either embark
and let the waters carry us whither Allah willeth, or else abide
here till some ship pass, when we will take passage in it. If we fail
to kill him, we will embark in the boat and put out to sea; and if
we be drowned, we shall at least escape being roasted over a kitch-
en fire with sliced weasands; whilst, if we escape, we escape, and if
we be drowned, we die martyrs." "By Allah," said they all, "this
rede is a right;" and we agreed upon this, and set about carrying
it out. So we haled down to the beach the pieces of wood which
lay about the bench; and, making a boat, moored it to the strand,
after which we stowed therein somewhat of victual and returned to

---

[1] Fire is forbidden as a punishment amongst Moslems, the idea being that it should
be reserved for the next world. Hence the sailors fear the roasting more than the eating:
with ours it would probably be the reverse. The Persian insult "Pidar-sokhtah" = (son
of a) burnt father, is well known. I have noted the advisability of burning the Moslem's
corpse under certain circumstances: otherwise the murderer may come to be canonised.

[2] Arab. "Mastabah" = the bench or form of masonry before noticed. In olden Europe
benches were much more used than chairs, these being articles of luxury. So King Horne
"sett him abenche;" and hence our "King's Bench" (Court).

the castle. As soon as evening fell the earth trembled under our feet and in came the blackamoor upon us, snarling like a dog about to bite. He came up to us and feeling us and turning us over one by one, took one of us and did with him as he had done before and ate him, after which he lay down on the bench and snored and snorted like thunder. As soon as we were assured that he slept, we arose and taking two iron spits of those standing there, heated them in the fiercest of the fire, till they were red-hot, like burning coals, when we gripped fast hold of them and going up to the giant, as he lay snoring on the bench, thrust them into his eyes and pressed upon them, all of us, with our united might, so that his eyeballs burst and he became stone blind. Thereupon he cried with a great cry, whereat our hearts trembled, and springing up from the bench, he fell a-groping after us, blind-fold. We fled from him right and left and he saw us not, for his sight was altogether blent; but we were in terrible fear of him and made sure we were dead men despairing of escape. Then he found the door, feeling for it with his hands and went out roaring aloud; and behold, the earth shook under us, for the noise of his roaring, and we quaked for fear. As he quitted the castle we followed him and betook ourselves to the place where we had moored our boat, saying to one another, "If this accursed abide absent till the going down of the sun and come not to the castle, we shall know that he is dead; and if he come back, we will embark in the boat and paddle till we escape, committing our affair to Allah." But, as we spoke, behold, up came the blackamoor with other two as they were Ghuls, fouler and more frightful than he, with eyes like red-hot coals; which when we saw, we hurried into the boat and casting off the moorings paddled away and pushed out to sea.[1] As soon as the ogres caught sight of us, they cried out at us and running down to the sea-shore, fell a-pelting us with rocks, whereof some fell amongst us and others fell into the sea. We paddled with all our might till we were beyond their reach, but the most part of us were slain by the rock-throwing, and the winds and waves sported with us and carried us into the midst of the dashing sea, swollen with billows clashing. We knew not whither we went and my fellows died one after another, till there remained but three,

---

[1] This is from the Bresl. Edit. vol. iv. 32: the Calc. Edit. gives only an abstract and in the Bul. Edit. the Ogre returned "accompanied by a female, greater than he and more hideous." We cannot accept Mistress Polyphemus.

myself and two others;——And Shahrazad perceived the dawn of day and ceased to say her permitted say.

When it was the Five Hundred and Forty-eighth Night,

She said, It hath reached me, O auspicious King, that Sindbad the Seaman thus continued:——Most part of us were slain by the rock-throwing and only three of us remained on board the boat for, as often as one died, we threw him into the sea. We were sore exhausted for stress of hunger, but we took courage and heartened one another and worked for dear life and paddled with main and might, till the winds cast us upon an island, as we were dead men for fatigue and fear and famine. We landed on the island and walked about it for a while, finding that it abounded in trees and streams and birds; and we ate of the fruits and rejoiced in our escape from the black and our deliverance from the perils of the sea; and thus we did till nightfall, when we lay down and fell asleep for excess of fatigue. But we had hardly closed our eyes before we were aroused by a hissing sound, like the sough of wind, and awaking, saw a serpent like a dragon, a seld-seen sight, of monstrous make and belly of enormous bulk which lay in a circle around us. Presently it reared its head and, seizing one of my companions, swallowed him up to his shoulders; then it gulped down the rest of him, and we heard his ribs crack in its belly. Presently it went its way, and we abode in sore amazement and grief for our comrade and mortal fear for ourselves, saying, "By Allah, this is a marvellous thing! Each kind of death that threatened us is more terrible than the last. We were rejoicing in our escape from the black ogre and our deliverance from the perils of the sea; but now we have fallen into that which is worse. There is no Majesty and there is no Might save in Allah! By the Almighty, we have escaped from the blackamoor and from drowning: but how shall we escape from this abominable and viperish monster?" Then we walked about the island, eating of its fruits and drinking of its streams till dusk, when we climbed up into a high tree and went to sleep there, I being on the topmost bough. As soon as it was dark night, up came the serpent, looking right and left; and, making for the tree whereon we were, climbed up to my comrade and swallowed him down to his shoulders.

Then it coiled about the bole[1] with him, whilst I, who could not take my eyes off the sight, heard his bones crack in its belly, and it swallowed him whole, after which it slid down from the tree. When the day broke and the light showed me that the serpent was gone, I came down, as I were a dead man for stress of fear and anguish, and thought to cast myself into the sea and be at rest from the woes of the world; but could not bring myself to this, for verily life is dear. So I took five pieces of wood, broad and long, and bound one crosswise to the soles of my feet and others in like fashion on my right and left sides and over my breast; and the broadest and largest I bound across my head and made them fast with ropes. Then I lay down on the ground on my back, so that I was completely fenced in by the pieces of wood, which enclosed me like a bier.[2] So as soon as it was dark, up came the serpent, as usual, and made towards me, but could not get at me to swallow me for the wood that fenced me in. So it wriggled round me on every side, whilst I looked on, like one dead by reason of my terror; and every now and then it would glide away and come back; but as often as it tried to come at me, it was hindered by the pieces of wood wherewith I had bound myself on every side. It ceased not to beset me thus from sundown till dawn, but when the light of day shone upon the beast it made off, in the utmost fury and extreme disappointment. Then I put out my hand and unbound myself, well-nigh down among the dead men for fear and suffering; and went down to the island-shore, whence a ship afar off in the midst of the waves suddenly struck my sight. So I tore off a great branch of a tree and made signs with it to the crew, shouting out the while; which when the ship's company saw they said to one another, "We must stand in and see what this

---

[1] This is from Al-Kazwini, who makes the serpent "wind itself round a tree or a rock, and thus break to pieces the bones of the breast in its belly."

[2] "Like a closet," in the Calc. Edit. The serpent is an exaggeration of the python which grows to an enormous size. Monstrous Ophidia are mentioned in sober history, *e.g.* that which delayed the army of Regulus. Dr. de Lacerda, a sober and sensible Brazilian traveller, mentions his servants sitting down upon a tree-trunk in the Captaincy of San Paulo (Brasil), which began to move and proved to be a huge snake. F. M. Pinto (the Sindbad of Portugal though not so respectable) when in Sumatra takes refuge in a tree from "tigers, crocodiles, copped adders and serpents which slay men with their breath." Father Lobo in Tigre (chapt. x.) was nearly killed by the poison-breath of a huge snake, and healed himself with a bezoar carried *ad hoc*. Maffæus makes the breath of crocodiles suavissimus, but that of the Malabar serpents and vipers "adeo teter ac noxius ut afflatu ipso necare perhibeantur."

is; peradventure 'tis a man." So they made for the island and
presently heard my cries, whereupon they took me on board and
questioned me of my case. I told them all my adventures from
first to last, whereat they marvelled mightily and covered my
shame[1] with some of their clothes. Moreover, they set before me
somewhat of food and I ate my fill and I drank cold sweet water
and was mightily refreshed; and Allah Almighty quickened me
after I was virtually dead. So I praised the Most Highest and
thanked Him for His favours and exceeding mercies, and my heart
revived in me after utter despair, till meseemed as if all I had
suffered were but a dream I had dreamed. We sailed on with a
fair wind the Almighty sent us till we came to an island, called
Al-Saláhitah,[2] which aboundeth in sandal-wood when the captain
cast anchor,——And Shahrazad perceived the dawn of day and
ceased saying her permitted say.

When it was the Five Hundred and Forty-ninth Night,

She said, It hath reached me, O auspicious King, that Sindbad
the Seaman continued:—And when we had cast anchor, the
merchants and the sailors landed with their goods to sell and to
buy. Then the captain turned to me and said, "Hark'ee, thou art
a stranger and a pauper and tellest us that thou hast undergone
frightful hardship; wherefore I have a mind to benefit thee with
somewhat that may further thee to thy native land, so thou wilt
ever bless me and pray for me." "So be it," answered I; "thou
shalt have my prayers." Quoth he, "Know then that there was
with us a man, a traveller, whom we lost, and we know not if he
be alive or dead, for we had no news of him; so I purpose to
commit his bales of goods to thy charge, that thou mayst sell them
in this island. A part of the proceeds we will give thee as an
equivalent for thy pains and service, and the rest we will keep till
we return to Baghdad, where we will enquire for his family and

---

[1] Arab. "Aurat": the word has been borrowed by the Hindostani jargon, and means
a woman, a wife.

[2] So in Al-Idrísi and Langlès: the Bres. Edit. has "Al-Kalásitah"; and Al-Kazwini
"Al-Salámit." The latter notes in it a petrifying spring which Camoens (The Lus. x. 104),
places in Sunda, *i.e.* Java-Minor of M. Polo. Some read Salabat-Timor, one of the Moluccas famed for sanders, cloves, cinnamon, etc. (Purchas ii. 1784.)

deliver it to them, together with the unsold goods. Say me then, wilt thou undertake the charge and land and sell them as other merchants do?" I replied "Hearkening and obedience to thee, O my lord; and great is thy kindness to me," and thanked him; whereupon he bade the sailors and porters bear the bales in question ashore and commit them to my charge. The ship's scribe asked him, "O master, what bales are these and what merchant's name shall I write upon them?"; and he answered, "Write on them the name of Sindbad the Seaman, him who was with us in the ship and whom we lost at the Rukh's island, and of whom we have no tidings; for we mean this stranger to sell them; and we will give him a part of the price for his pains and keep the rest till we return to Baghdad where, if we find the owner we will make it over to him, and if not, to his family." And the clerk said, "Thy words are apposite and thy rede is right." Now when I heard the captain give orders for the bales to be inscribed with my name, I said to myself, "By Allah, I am Sindbad the Seaman!" So I armed myself with courage and patience and waited till all the merchants had landed and were gathered together, talking and chaffering about buying and selling; then I went up to the captain and asked him, "O my lord, knowest thou what manner of man was this Sindbad, whose goods thou hast committed to me for sale?"; and he answered, "I know of him naught save that he was a man from Baghdad-city, Sindbad hight the Seaman, who was drowned with many others when we lay anchored at such an island and I have heard nothing of him since then." At this I cried out with a great cry and said, "O captain, whom Allah keep! know that I am that Sindbad the Seaman and that I was not drowned, but when thou castest anchor at the island, I landed with the rest of the merchants and crew; and I sat down in a pleasant place by myself and ate somewhat of food I had with me and enjoyed myself till I became drowsy and was drowned in sleep; and when I awoke, I found no ship and none near me. These goods are my goods and these bales are my bales; and all the merchants who fetch jewels from the Valley of Diamonds saw me there and will bear me witness that I am the very Sindbad the Seaman; for I related to them everything that had befallen me and told them how you forgot me and left me sleeping on the island, and that betided me which betided me." When the passengers and crew heard my words, they gathered about me and some of them believed me and others disbelieved; but presently, behold, one of the merchants, hearing me mention the Valley of Diamonds, came up to me and said to them, "Hear what I say, good people! When I related to you the most wonderful thing in my travels, and I told you that, at the time we cast down our slaughtered animals into the Valley of Serpents (I casting with the rest as was my wont), there came up a man hanging to mine, ye believed me not and gave me the lie." "Yes," quoth they, "thou didst tell us some such tale, but we had no call to credit thee." He resumed, "Now this is the very man, by token that he gave me diamonds of great value, and high price whose like are not to be found, requiting me more than would have come up sticking to my quarter of meat; and I companied with him to Bassorah-city, where he took leave of us and went on to his native stead, whilst we returned to our own land. This is he; and he told us his name, Sindbad the Seaman, and how the ship left him on the desert island. And know ye that Allah hath sent him hither, so might the truth of my story be made manifest to you. More-over, these are his goods for, when he first foregathered with us, he told us of them; and the truth of his words is patent." Hearing the merchant's speech the captain came up to me and considered me straitly awhile, after which he said, "What was the mark on thy bales?" "Thus and thus," answered I, and reminded him of somewhat that had passed between him and me, when I shipped with him from Bassorah. Thereupon he was convinced that I was indeed Sindbad the Seaman and took me round the neck and gave me joy of my safety, saying, "By Allah, O my lord, thy case is indeed wondrous and thy tale marvellous; but lauded be Allah who hath brought thee and me together again, and who hath restored to thee thy goods and gear!"——And Shahrazad per-ceived the dawn of day and ceased to say her permitted say.

𝔚𝔥𝔢𝔫 𝔦𝔱 𝔴𝔞𝔰 𝔱𝔥𝔢 𝔉𝔦𝔳𝔢 𝔥𝔲𝔫𝔡𝔯𝔢𝔡 𝔞𝔫𝔡 𝔉𝔦𝔣𝔱𝔦𝔢𝔱𝔥 𝔑𝔦𝔤𝔥𝔱,

She said, It hath reached me, O auspicious King, that Sindbad the Seaman thus continued:—"Alhamdolillah!" quoth the cap-tain, "lauded be Allah who hath restored unto thee thy goods and gear." Then I disposed of my merchandise to the best of my skill, and profited largely on them whereat I rejoiced with exceed-ing joy and congratulated myself on my safety and the recovery of my goods. We ceased not to buy and sell at the several islands till we came to the land of Hind, where we bought cloves and ginger and all manner spices; and thence we fared on to the land of Sind, where also we bought and sold. In these Indian seas, I saw wonders without number or count, amongst others a fish like a cow which bringeth forth its young and suckleth them like human beings; and of its skin bucklers are made.[1]   There were eke fishes like asses and camels[2] and tortoises twenty cubits wide.[3] And I saw also a bird that cometh out of a sea-shell and layeth eggs and hatcheth her chicks on the surface of the water, never coming up from the sea to the land.[4]   Then we set sail again with a fair wind and the blessing of Almighty Allah; and, after a prosperous voyage, arrived safe and sound at Bassorah. Here I abode a few days and presently returned to Baghdad where I went at once to my quarter and my house and saluted my family and familiars and friends.   I had gained on this voyage what was beyond count and reckoning, so I gave alms and largesse and clad the widow and the orphan, by way of thanksgiving for my happy return, and fell to feasting and making merry with my companions

---

[1] Evidently the hippopotamus (Pliny, viii. 25; ix. 3 and xxiii. 11). It can hardly be the Mulaccan Tapir, as shields are not made of the hide. Hole suggests the buffalo which found its way to Egypt from India *viâ* Persia; but this would not be a speciosum miraculum.

[2] The ass-headed fish is from Pliny (ix. cap. 3); all those tales are founded upon the manatee (whose dorsal protuberance may have suggested the camel), the seal and the dugong or sea-calf. I have noticed (Zanzibar i. 205) legends of ichthyological marvels current on the East African seaboard; and even the monsters of the Scottish waters are not all known: witness the mysterious "brigdie." See Bochart De Cetis i. 7; and Purchas iii. 930.

[3] The colossal tortoise is noticed by Ælian (De Nat. Animal. xvi. 17), by Strabo (Lib. xv.), by Pliny (ix. 10) and Diodorus Siculus (iv. 1) who had heard of a tribe of Chelonophagi. Ælian makes them 16 cubits long near Taprobane and serving as house-roofs; and others turn the shell into boats and coracles. A colossochelys was first found on the Scwalik Hills by Dr. Falconer and Major (afterwards Sir Proby) Cantley. In 1867 M. Emile Blanchard exhibited to the Académie des Sciences a monster crab from Japan 1.20 metres long (or 2.50 including legs); and other travellers have reported 4 metres. These crustaceæ seem never to cease growing and attain great dimensions under favourable circumstances, *i.e.* when not troubled by man.

[4] Lane suggests (iii. 97), and with some probability, that the "bird" was a nautilus; but the wild traditions concerning the barnacle-goose may perhaps have been the base of the fable. The albatross also was long supposed never to touch land. Possibly the barnacle, like the barometz or Tartarean lamb, may be a survivor of the day when the animal and vegetable kingdoms had not yet branched off into different directions.

and intimates and forgot, while eating well and drinking well and dressing well, everything that had befallen me and all the perils and hardships I had suffered. "These, then, are the most admirable things I sighted on my third voyage, and to-morrow, an it be the will of Allah, you shall come to me and I will relate the adventures of my fourth voyage, which is still more wonderful than those you have already heard." (Saith he who telleth the tale), Then Sindbad the Seaman bade give Sindbad the Landsman an hundred golden dinars as of wont and called for food. So they spread the tables and the company ate the night-meal and went their ways, mar-velling at the tale they had heard. The Porter after taking his gold passed the night in his own house, also wondering at what his namesake the Seaman had told him, and as soon as day broke and the morning showed with its sheen and shone, he rose and praying the dawn-prayer betook himself to Sindbad the Seaman, who returned his salute and received him with an open breast and cheerful favour and made him sit with him till the rest of the company arrived, when he caused set on food and they ate and drank and made merry. Then Sindbad the Seaman bespake them and related to them the narrative of

The Fourth Voyage of Sindbad the Seaman.

KNOW, O my brethren that after my return from my third voyage and foregathering with my friends, and forgetting all my perils and hardships in the enjoyment of ease and comfort and repose, I was visited one day by a company of merchants who sat down with me and talked of foreign travel and traffic, till the old bad man within me yearned to go with them and enjoy the sight of strange countries, and I longed for the society of the various races of mankind and for traffic and profit. So I resolved to travel with them and buying the necessaries for a long voyage, and great store of costly goods, more than ever before, transported them from Baghdad to Bassorah where I took ship with the merchants in question, who were of the chief of the town. We set out, trusting in the blessing of Almighty Allah; and with a favouring breeze and the best conditions we sailed from island to island and sea to

sea, till, one day, there arose against us a contrary wind and the
captain cast out his anchors and brought the ship to a standstill,
fearing lest she should founder in mid-ocean. Then we all fell to
prayer and humbling ourselves before the Most High; but, as we
were thus engaged there smote us a furious squall which tore the
sails to rags and tatters: the anchor-cable parted and, the ship
foundering, we were cast into the sea, goods and all. I kept myself afloat by swimming half the day, till, when I had given myself
up for lost, the Almighty threw in my way one of the planks of
the ship, whereon I and some others of the merchants scrambled.
——And Shahrazad perceived the dawn of day and ceased saying
her permitted say.

When it was the Five Hundred and Fifty-first Night,

She said, It hath reached me, O auspicious King, that Sindbad
the Seaman continued as follows:—And when the ship foundered
I scrambled on to a plank with some others of the merchants and,
mounting it as we would a horse, paddled with our feet in the sea.
We abode thus a day and a night, the wind and waves helping us
on, and on the second day shortly before the mid-time between
sunrise and noon[1] the breeze freshened and the sea wrought and
the rising waves cast us upon an island, well-nigh dead bodies for
weariness and want of sleep, cold and hunger and fear and thirst.
We walked about the shore and found abundance of herbs, whereof we ate enough to keep breath in body and to stay our failing
spirits, then lay down and slept till morning hard by the sea.
And when morning came with its sheen and shone, we arose and
walked about the island to the right and left, till we came in sight
of an inhabited house afar off. So we made towards it, and ceased
not walking till we reached the door thereof when lo! a number
of naked men issued from it and without saluting us or a word
said, laid hold of us masterfully and carried us to their king, who
signed us to sit. So we sat down and they set food before us such

---

[1] Arab. "Zahwah," also meaning a luncheon. The five daily prayers made all
Moslems take strict account of time, and their nomenclature of its division is extensive.

as we knew not[1] and whose like we had never seen in all our lives. My companions ate of it, for stress of hunger, but my stomach revolted from it and I would not eat; and my refraining from it was, by Allah's favour, the cause of my being alive till now: for no sooner had my comrades tasted of it than their reason fled and their condition changed and they began to devour it like madmen possessed of an evil spirit. Then the savages gave them to drink of cocoa-nut oil and anointed them therewith; and straightway after drinking thereof, their eyes turned into their heads and they fell to eating greedily, against their wont. When I saw this, I was confounded and concerned for them, nor was I less anxious about myself, for fear of the naked folk. So I watched them narrowly, and it was not long before I discovered them to be a tribe of Magian cannibals whose King was a Ghul.[2] All who came to their country or whoso they caught in their valleys or on their roads they brought to this King and fed them upon that food and anointed them with that oil, whereupon their stomachs dilated that they might eat largely, whilst their reason fled and they lost the power of thought and became idiots. Then they stuffed them with cocoa-nut oil and the aforesaid food, till they became fat and gross, when they slaughtered them by cutting their throats and roasted them for the King's eating; but, as for the savages themselves, they ate human flesh raw.[3] When I saw this, I was sore dismayed

---

[1] This is the "insane herb." Davis, who visited Sumatra in 1599 (Purchas i. 120) speaks "of a kind of seed, whereof a little being eaten, maketh a man to turn foole, all things seeming to him to be metamorphosed." Linschoten's "Dutroa" was a poppy-like bud containing small kernels like melons which stamped and administered as a drink make a man "as if he were foolish, or out of his wits." This is Father Lobo's "Vanguini" of the Cafres, called by the Portuguese *dutro* (*Datura Stramonium*) still used by dishonest confectioners. It may be Dampier's Ganga (Ganjah) or Bang (Bhang) which he justly describes as acting differently "according to different constitutions; for some it stupefies, others it makes sleepy, others merry and some quite mad." (Harris, Collect. ii. 900.) Dr. Fryer also mentions Duty, Bung and Post, the Poust of Bernier, an infusion of poppy-seed.

[2] Arab. "Ghul," here an ogre, a cannibal. I cannot but regard the "Ghul of the waste" as an embodiment of the natural fear and horror which a man feels when he faces a really dangerous desert. As regards cannibalism, Al-Islam's religion of common sense freely allows it when necessary to save life, and unlike our mawkish modern sensibility, never blames those who

> Alimentis talibus usi
> Produxere animos.

[3] For Cannibals, see the Massagetæ of Herod (i.), the Padæi of India (iii.), and the Essedones near Mæotis (iv.); Strabo (lib. iv.) of the Luci; Pomponius Mela (iii. 7) and

for myself and my comrades, who were now become so stupefied that they knew not what was done with them and the naked folk committed them to one who used every day to lead them out and pasture them on the island like cattle.   And they wandered amongst the trees and rested at will, thus waxing very fat. As for me, I wasted away and became sickly for fear and hunger and my flesh shrivelled on my bones; which when the savages saw, they left me alone and took no thought of me and so far forgot me that one day I gave them the slip and walking out of their place made for the beach which was distant and there espied a very old man seated on a high place, girt by the waters. I looked at him and knew him for the herdsman, who had charge of pasturing my fellows, and with him were many others in like case. As soon as he saw me, he knew me to be in possession of my reason and not afflicted like the rest whom he was pasturing; so signed to me from afar, as who should say, "Turn back and take the right-hand road, for that will lead thee into the King's highway." So I turned back, as he bade me, and followed the right-hand road, now running for fear and then walking leisurely to rest me, till I was out of the old man's sight. By this time, the sun had gone down and the darkness set in; so I sat down to rest and would have slept, but sleep came not to me that night, for stress of fear and famine and fatigue. When the night was half spent, I rose and walked on, till the day broke in all its beauty and the sun rose over the heads of the lofty hills and athwart the low gravelly plains. Now I was weary and hungry and thirsty; so I ate my fill of herbs and grasses that grew in the island and kept life in body and stayed my stomach, after which I set out again and fared on all that day and the next night, staying my greed with roots and herbs; nor

---

St. Jerome (ad Jovinum) of Scoti. M. Polo locates them in Dragvia, a kingdom of Sumatra (iii. 17), and in Angaman (the Andamanian Isles?), possibly the ten Maniolai which Ptolemy (vii.), confusing with the Nicobars, places on the Eastern side of the Bay of Bengal; and thence derives the Heraklian stone (magnet) which attracts the iron of ships (See Serapion, De Magnete, fol. 6, Edit. of 1479, and Brown's Vulgar Errors, p. 74, 6th Edit.).   Mandeville finds his cannibals in Lamaray (Sumatra) and Barthema in the "Isle of Gyava" (Java).   Ibn Al-Wardi and Al-Kazwini notice them in the Isle Saksar, in the Sea of the Zanj (Zanzibar): the name is corrupted Persian "Sag-Sar" (Dogs'-heads) hence the dog-descended race of Camoens in Pegu (The Lus. x. 122). The Bresl. Edit. (iv. 52) calls them "Khawárij" = certain sectarians in Eastern Arabia. Needless to say that cocoa-nut oil would have no stupefying effect unless mixed with opium or datura, hemp or henbane.

did I cease walking for seven days and their nights, till the morn of the eighth day, when I caught sight of a faint object in the distance. So I made towards it, though my heart quaked for all I had suffered first and last, and behold it was a company of men gathering pepper-grains.[1] As soon as they saw me, they hastened up to me and surrounding me on all sides, said to me, "Who art thou and whence come?" I replied, "Know, O folk, that I am a poor stranger," and acquainted them with my case and all the hardships and perils I had suffered,——And Shahrazad perceived the dawn of day and ceased to say her permitted say.

When it was the Five Hundred and Fifty-second Night,

She said, It hath reached me, O auspicious King, that Sindbad the Seaman continued:——And the men gathering pepper in the island questioned me of my case, when I acquainted them with all the hardships and perils I had suffered and how I had fled from the savages; whereat they marvelled and gave me joy of my safety, saying, "By Allah, this is wonderful! But how didst thou escape from these blacks who swarm in the island and devour all who fall in with them; nor is any safe from them, nor can any get out of their clutches?" And after I had told them the fate of my companions, they made me sit by them, till they got quit of their work; and fetched me somewhat of good food, which I ate, for I was hungry, and rested awhile, after which they took ship with me and carrying me to their island-home brought me before their King, who returned my salute and received me honourably and questioned me of my case. I told him all that had befallen me, from the day of my leaving Baghdad-city, whereupon he wondered with great wonder at my adventures, he and his courtiers, and bade me sit by him; then he called for food and I ate with him what sufficed me and washed my hands and returned thanks to Almighty Allah for all His favours praising Him and glorifying Him. Then I left the King and walked for solace about the city,

---

[1] Black pepper is produced in the Goanese but we must go south to find the "Bilád al-Filfíl" (home of pepper) *i.e.* Malabar. The exorbitant prices demanded by Venice for this spice led directly to the discovery of The Cape route by the Portuguese; as the "Grains of Paradise" (Amomum Granum Paradisi) induced the English to explore the West African Coast.

which I found wealthy and populous, abounding in market-streets well stocked with food and merchandise and full of buyers and sellers. So I rejoiced at having reached so pleasant a place and took my ease there after my fatigues; and I made friends with the townsfolk, nor was it long before I became more in honour and favour with them and their King than any of the chief men of the realm. Now I saw that all the citizens, great and small, rode fine horses, high-priced and thorough-bred, without saddles or housings, whereat I wondered and said to the King, "Wherefore, O my lord, dost thou not ride with a saddle? Therein is ease for the rider and increase of power." "What is a saddle?" asked he: "I never saw nor used such a thing in all my life;" and I answered, "With thy permission I will make thee a saddle, that thou mayest ride on it and see the comfort thereof." And quoth he, "Do so." So quoth I to him, "Furnish me with some wood," which being brought, I sought me a clever carpenter and sitting by him showed him how to make the saddle-tree, portraying for him the fashion thereof in ink on the wood. Then I took wool and teased it and made felt of it, and, covering the saddle-tree with leather, stuffed it and polished it and attached the girth and stirrup leathers; after which I fetched a blacksmith and described to him the fashion of the stirrups and bridle-bit. So he forged a fine pair of stirrups and a bit, and filed them smooth and tinned[1] them. Moreover, I made fast to them fringes of silk and fitted bridle-leathers to the bit. Then I fetched one of the best of the royal horses and saddling and bridling him, hung the stirrups to the saddle and led him to the King. The thing took his fancy and he thanked me; then he mounted and rejoiced greatly in the saddle and rewarded me handsomely for my work. When the King's Wazir saw the saddle, he asked of me one like it and I made it for him. Furthermore, all the grandees and officers of state came for saddles to me; so I fell to making saddles (having taught the craft to the carpenter and blacksmith), and selling them to all who sought, till I amassed great wealth and became in high honour and great favour with the King and his household and grandees. I abode thus till, one day, as I was sitting with the King in all respect and contentment, he

---

[1] Arab. "Kazdír." Sansk. "Kastír." Gr. "Kassiteron." Lat. "Cassiteros," evidently derived from one root. The Heb. is "Badih," a substitute, an alloy. "Tanakah" is the vulg. Arab. word, a congener of the Assyrian "Anaku," and "Kala-i" is the corrupt Arab. term used in India.

said to me, "Know thou, O such an one, thou art become one of us, dear as a brother, and we hold thee in such regard and affection that we cannot part with thee nor suffer thee to leave our city; wherefore I desire of thee obedience in a certain matter, and I will not have thee gainsay me." Answered I, "O King, what is it thou desirest of me? Far be it from me to gainsay thee in aught, for I am indebted to thee for many favours and bounties and much kindness, and (praised be Allah!) I am become one of thy servants." Quoth he, "I have a mind to marry thee to a fair, clever and agreeable wife who is wealthy as she is beautiful; so thou mayst be naturalised and domiciled with us: I will lodge thee with me in my palace; wherefore oppose me not neither cross me in this." When I heard these words I was ashamed and held my peace nor could make him any answer,[1] by reason of my much bashfulness before him. Asked he, "Why dost thou not reply to me, O my son?"; and I answered, saying, "O my master, it is thine to command, O King of the age!" So he summoned the Kazi and the witnesses and married me straightway to a lady of a noble tree and high pedigree; wealthy in moneys and means; the flower of an ancient race; of surpassing beauty and grace, and the owner of farms and estates and many a dwelling-place.——And Shahrazad perceived the dawn of day and ceased saying her permitted say.

When it was the Five Hundred and Fifty-third Night,

She said, It hath reached me, O auspicious King, that Sindbad the Seaman continued in these words:—Now after the King my master had married me to this choice wife, he also gave me a great and goodly house standing alone, together with slaves and officers, and assigned me pay and allowances. So I became in all ease and contentment and delight and forgot everything which had befallen me of weariness and trouble and hardship; for I loved my wife with fondest love and she loved me no less, and we were as one and abode in the utmost comfort of life and in its happiness. And I said in myself, "When I return to my native land, I will carry her with me." But whatso is predestined to a man, that needs must be, and none knoweth what shall befal him. We lived thus a

---

[1] Our Arabian Ulysses had probably left a Penelope or two at home and finds a Calypso in this Ogygia. His modesty at the mention of womankind is notable.

great while, till Almighty Allah bereft one of my neighbours of his wife. Now he was a gossip of mine; so hearing the cry of the keeners I went in to condole with him on his loss and found him in very ill plight, full of trouble and weary of soul and mind. I condoled with him and comforted him, saying, "Mourn not for thy wife who hath now found the mercy of Allah; the Lord will surely give thee a better in her stead and thy name shall be great and thy life shall be long in the land, Inshallah!"[1] But he wept bitter tears and replied, "O my friend, how can I marry another wife and how shall Allah replace her to me with a better than she, whenas I have but one day left to live?" "O my brother," said I, "return to thy senses and announce not the glad tidings of thine own death, for thou art well, sound and in good case." "By thy life, O my friend," rejoined he, "to-morrow thou wilt lose me and wilt never see me again till the Day of Resurrection." I asked, "How so?" and he answered, "This very day they bury my wife, and they bury me with her in one tomb; for it is the custom with us, if the wife die first, to bury the husband alive with her and in like manner the wife, if the husband die first; so that neither may enjoy life after losing his or her mate." "By Allah," cried I, "this is a most vile, lewd custom and not to be endured of any!" Meanwhile, behold, the most part of the townsfolk came in and fell to condoling with my gossip for his wife and for himself. Presently they laid the dead woman out, as was their wont; and, setting her on a bier, carried her and her husband without the city, till they came to a place in the side of a mountain at the end of the island by the sea; and here they raised a great rock and discovered the mouth of a stone-rivetted pit or well,[2] leading down into a vast underground cavern that ran beneath the mountain. Into this pit they threw the corpse, then tying a rope of palm-fibres under the husband's armpits, they let him down into the cavern, and with him a great pitcher of fresh water and seven scones by way of viaticum.[3] When he came to the bottom, he loosed himself from the rope and they drew it up; and, stopping the mouth of the pit with the great stone, they returned to the

---

[1] These are the commonplaces of Moslem consolation on such occasions: the artistic part is their contrast with the unfortunate widower's prospect.

[2] Lit. "a margin of stone, like the curb-stone of a well."

[3] I am not aware that this vivisepulture of the widower is the custom of any race, but the fable would be readily suggested by the Sati (Suttee)-rite of the Hindus. Simple vivisepulture was and is practised by many people.

city, leaving my friend in the cavern with his dead wife. When I saw this, I said to myself, "By Allah, this fashion of death is more grievous than the first!" And I went in to the King and said to him, "O my lord, why do ye bury the quick with the dead?" Quoth he, "It hath been the custom, thou must know, of our forbears and our olden Kings from time immemorial, if the husband die first, to bury his wife with him, and the like with the wife, so we may not sever them, alive or dead." I asked, "O King of the age, if the wife of a foreigner like myself die among you, deal ye with him as with yonder man?"; and he answered, "Assuredly, we do with him even as thou hast seen." When I heard this, my gall-bladder was like to burst, for the violence of my dismay and concern for myself: my wit became dazed; I felt as if in a vile dungeon; and hated their society; for I went about in fear lest my wife should die before me and they bury me alive with her. However, after a while, I comforted myself, saying, "Haply I shall predecease her, or shall have returned to my own land before she die, for none knoweth which shall go first and which shall go last." Then I applied myself to diverting my mind from this thought with various occupations; but it was not long before my wife sickened and complained and took to her pillow and fared after a few days to the mercy of Allah; and the King and the rest of the folk came, as was their wont, to condole with me and her family and to console us for her loss and not less to condole with me for myself. Then the women washed her and arraying her in her richest raiment and golden ornaments, necklaces and jewellery, laid her on the bier and bore her to the mountain aforesaid, where they lifted the cover of the pit and cast her in; after which all my intimates and ac-quaintances and my wife's kith and kin came round me, to farewell me in my lifetime and console me for my own death, whilst I cried out among them, saying, "Almighty Allah never made it lawful to bury the quick with the dead! I am a stranger, not one of your kind; and I cannot abear your custom, and had I known it I never would have wedded among you!" They heard me not and paid no heed to my words, but laying hold of me, bound me by force and let me down into the cavern, with a large gugglet of sweet water and seven cakes of bread, according to their custom. When I came to the bottom, they called out to me to cast myself loose from the cords, but I refused to do so; so they threw them down on me and, closing the mouth of the pit with the stones

aforesaid, went their ways,——And Shahrazad perceived the
dawn of day and ceased to say her permitted say.

When it was the Five Hundred and Fifty-fourth Night,

She said, It hath reached me, O auspicious King, that Sindbad
the Seaman continued:—When they left me in the cavern with
my dead wife and, closing the mouth of the pit, went their ways,
I looked about me and found myself in a vast cave full of dead
bodies, that exhaled a fulsome and loathsome smell and the air
was heavy with the groans of the dying. Thereupon I fell to
blaming myself for what I had done, saying, "By Allah, I deserve
all that hath befallen me and all that shall befal me! What curse
was upon me to take a wife in this city? There is no Majesty and
there is no Might save in Allah, the Glorious, the Great! As often
as I say, I have escaped from one calamity, I fall into a worse.
By Allah, this is an abominable death to die! Would Heaven
I had died a decent death and been washed and shrouded like
a man and a Moslem. Would I had been drowned at sea
or perished in the mountains! It were better than·to die this
miserable death!" And on such wise I kept blaming my own
folly and greed of gain in that black hole, knowing not night from
day; and I ceased not to ban the Foul Fiend and to bless the
Almighty Friend. Then I threw myself down on the bones of the
dead and lay there, imploring Allah's help and in the violence of
my despair, invoking death which came not to me, till the fire
of hunger burned my stomach and thirst set my throat aflame
when I sat up and feeling for the bread, ate a morsel and
upon it swallowed a mouthful of water. After this, the worst
night I ever knew, I arose, and exploring the cavern, found that
it extended a long way with hollows in its sides; and its floor
was strewn with dead bodies and rotten bones, that had lain there
from olden time. So I made myself a place in a cavity of the
cavern, afar from the corpses lately thrown down and there slept.
I abode thus a long while, till my provision was like to give
out; and yet I ate not save once every day or second day;
nor did I drink more than an occasional draught, for fear my
victual should fail me before my death; and I said to myself,
"Eat little and drink little; belike the Lord shall vouchsafe
deliverance to thee!" One day, as I sat thus, pondering my case

and bethinking me how I should do, when my bread and water should be exhausted, behold, the stone that covered the opening was suddenly rolled away and the light streamed down upon me. Quoth I, "I wonder what is the matter: haply they have brought another corpse." Then I espied folk standing about the mouth of the pit, who presently let down a dead man and a live woman, weeping and bemoaning herself, and with her an ampler supply of bread and water than usual.[1] I saw her and she was a beautiful woman; but she saw me not; and they closed up the opening and went away. Then I took the leg-bone of a dead man and, going up to the woman, smote her on the crown of the head; and she cried one cry and fell down in a swoon. I smote her a second and a third time, till she was dead, when I laid hands on her bread and water and found on her great plenty of ornaments and rich apparel, necklaces, jewels and gold trinkets;[2] for it was their custom to bury women in all their finery. I carried the vivers to my sleeping place in the cavern-side and ate and drank of them sparingly, no more than sufficed to keep the life in me, lest the provaunt come speedily to an end and I perish of hunger and thirst. Yet did I never wholly lose hope in Almighty Allah. I abode thus a great while, killing all the live folk they let down into the cavern and taking their provisions of meat and drink; till one day, as I slept, I was awakened by something scratching and burrowing among the bodies in a corner of the cave and said, "What can this be?" fearing wolves or hyænas. So I sprang up and seizing the leg-bone aforesaid, made for the noise. As soon as the thing was ware of me, it fled from me into the inward of the cavern, and lo! it was a wild beast. However, I followed it to the further end, till I saw afar off a point of light not bigger than a star, now appearing and then disappearing. So I made for it, and as I drew near, it grew larger and brighter, till I was certified that it was a crevice in the rock, leading to the open country; and I said to myself, "There must be some reason for this opening: either it is the mouth of a second pit, such as that by which they let me down, or else it is a natural fissure in the stonery." So I bethought me awhile and nearing the light, found that it came

---

[1] Because she was weaker than a man. The Bresl. Edit. however, has "a gugglet of water and five scones."

[2] The confession is made with true Eastern sang-froid and probably none of the hearers "disapproved" of the murders which saved the speaker's life.

from a breach in the back side of the mountain, which the wild beasts had enlarged by burrowing, that they might enter and devour the dead and freely go to and fro. When I saw this, my spirits revived and hope came back to me and I made sure of life, after having died a death. So I went on, as in a dream, and making shift to scramble through the breach found myself on the slope of a high mountain, overlooking the salt sea and cutting off all access thereto from the island, so that none could come at that part of the beach from the city.[1] I praised my Lord and thanked Him, rejoicing greatly and heartening myself with the prospect of deliverance; then I returned through the crack to the cavern and brought out all the food and water I had saved up and donned some of the dead folk's clothes over my own; after which I gath-ered together all the collars and necklaces of pearls and jewels and trinkets of gold and silver set with precious stones and other ornaments and valuables I could find upon the corpses; and, making them into bundles with the grave clothes and raiment of the dead, carried them out to the back of the mountain facing the sea-shore, where I established myself, purposing to wait there till it should please Almighty Allah to send me relief by means of some passing ship. I visited the cavern daily and as often as I found folk buried alive there, I killed them all indifferently, men and women, and took their victual and valuables and trans-ported them to my seat on the sea-shore. Thus I abode a long while,——And Shahrazad perceived the dawn of day and ceased saying her permitted say.

When it was the Five Hundred and Fifty-fifth Night,

She said, It hath reached me, O auspicious King, that Sindbad the Seaman continued:—And after carrying all my victuals and valu-ables from the cavern to the coast I abode a long while by the sea, pondering my case, till one day I caught sight of a ship passing in the midst of the clashing sea, swollen with dashing billows. So I took a piece of a white shroud I had with me and, tying it to a

---

[1] This tale is evidently taken from the escape of Aristomenes the Messenian from the pit into which he had been thrown, a fox being his guide. The Arabs in an early day were eager students of Greek literature. Hole (p. 140) noted the coincidence.

staff, ran along the sea-shore, making signals therewith and calling to the people in the ship, till they espied me and hearing my shouts, sent a boat to fetch me off. When it drew near, the crew called out to me, saying, "Who art thou and how camest thou to be on this mountain, whereon never saw we any in our born days?" I answered, "I am a gentleman[1] and a merchant, who hath been wrecked and saved myself on one of the planks of the ship, with some of my goods; and by the blessing of the Almighty and the decrees of Destiny and my own strength and skill, after much toil and moil I have landed with my gear in this place where I awaited some passing ship to take me off." So they took me in their boat together with the bundles I had made of the jewels and valu-ables from the cavern, tied up in clothes and shrouds, and rowed back with me to the ship, where the captain said to me, "How camest thou, O man, to yonder place on yonder mountain behind which lieth a great city? All my life I have sailed these seas and passed to and fro hard by these heights; yet never saw I here any living thing save wild beasts and birds." I repeated to him the story I had told the sailors,[2] but acquainted him with nothing of that which had befallen me in the city and the cavern, lest there should be any of the islandry in the ship. Then I took out some of the best pearls I had with me and offered them to the captain, saying, "O my lord, thou hast been the means of saving me off this mountain. I have no ready money; but take this from me in requital of thy kindness and good offices." But he refused to accept it of me, saying, "When we find a shipwrecked man on the sea-shore or on an island, we take him up and give him meat and drink, and if he be naked we clothe him; nor take we aught from him; nay, when we reach a port of safety, we set him ashore with a present of our own money and entreat him kindly and charita-bly, for the love of Allah the Most High." So I prayed that his life be long in the land and rejoiced in my escape, trusting to be de-livered from my stress and to forget my past mishaps; for every time I remembered being let down into the cave with my dead wife I shuddered in horror. Then we pursued our voyage and sailed from island to island and sea to sea, till we arrived at the Island of

---

[1] Bresl. Edit. "Khwájah," our "Howajee," meaning a schoolmaster, a man of letters, a gentleman.

[2] And he does repeat at full length what the hearers must have known right well. I abridge.

the Bell, which containeth a city two days' journey in extent, whence after a six days' run we reached the Island Kala, hard by the land of Hind.[1]   This place is governed by a potent and puissant King and it produceth excellent camphor and an abun-dance of the Indian rattan: here also is a lead mine.   At last by the decree of Allah, we arrived in safety at Bassorah-town where I tarried a few days, then went on to Baghdad-city, and, finding my quarter, entered my house with lively pleasure.   There I fore-gathered with my family and friends, who rejoiced in my happy return and gave me joy of my safety.   I laid up in my storehouses all the goods I had brought with me, and gave alms and largesse to Fakirs and beggars and clothed the widow and the orphan.   Then I gave myself up to pleasure and enjoyment, returning to my old merry mode of life. "Such, then, be the most marvellous adven-tures of my fourth voyage, but to-morrow if you will kindly come to me, I will tell you that which befel me in my fifth voyage, which was yet rarer and more marvellous than those which forewent it. And thou, O my brother Sindbad the Landsman, shalt sup with me as thou art wont." (Saith he who telleth the tale), When Sindbad the Seaman had made an end of his story, he called for supper; so they spread the table and the guests ate the evening meal; after which he gave the Porter an hundred dinars as usual, and he and the rest of the company went their ways, glad at heart and marvelling at the tales they had heard, for that each story was more extraordinary than that which forewent it.   The porter Sind-bad passed the night in his own house, in all joy and cheer and wonderment; and, as soon as morning came with its sheen and shone, he prayed the dawn-prayer and repaired to the house of Sindbad the Seaman, who welcomed him and bade him sit with him till the rest of the company arrived, when they ate and drank and made merry and the talk went round amongst them. Presently, their host began the narrative of the fifth voyage,——And Shahra-zad perceived the dawn of day and ceased to say her permitted say.

---

[1] Island of the Bell (Arab. "Nákús" = a wooden gong used by Christians but forbidden to Moslems).   "Kala" is written "Kela," "Kullah" and a variety of ways.   Baron Walck-enaer places it at Keydah in the Malay peninsula opposite Sumatra.   Renaudot identifies it with Calabar, "somewhere about the point of Malabar."

She said, It hath reached me, O auspicious King, that the host
began in these words the narrative of

The Fifth Voyage of Sindbad the Seaman.

KNOW, O my brothers, that when I had been awhile on shore after
my fourth voyage; and when, in my comfort and pleasures and
merry-makings and in my rejoicing over my large gains and profits,
I had forgotten all I had endured of perils and sufferings, the
carnal man was again seized with the longing to travel and to
see foreign countries and islands.[1]   Accordingly I bought costly
merchandise suited to my purpose and, making it up into bales,
repaired to Bassorah, where I walked about the river-quay till I
found a fine tall ship, newly builded with gear unused and fitted
ready for sea.   She pleased me; so I bought her and, embarking
my goods in her, hired a master and crew, over whom I set certain
of my slaves and servants as inspectors.   A number of merchants
also brought their outfits and paid me freight and passage-money;
then, after reciting the Fatihah we set sail over Allah's pool in all
joy and cheer, promising ourselves a prosperous voyage and much
profit.   We sailed from city to city and from island to island and
from sea to sea viewing the cities and countries by which we
passed, and selling and buying in not a few till one day we came to
a great uninhabited island, deserted and desolate, whereon was a
white dome of biggest bulk half buried in the sands.   The merchants landed to examine this dome, leaving me in the ship; and
when they drew near, behold, it was a huge Rukh's egg.   They
fell a-beating it with stones, knowing not what it was, and presently broke it open, whereupon much water ran out of it and the
young Rukh appeared within.   So they pulled it forth of the shell
and cut its throat and took of it great store of meat. Now I was in
the ship and knew not what they did; but presently one of the

---

[1] Islands, because Arab cosmographers love to place their *speciosa miracula* in such
places.

passengers came up to me and said, "O my lord, come and look at the egg that we thought to be a dome." So I looked and seeing the merchants beating it with stones, called out to them, "Stop, stop! do not meddle with that egg, or the bird Rukh will come out and break our ship and destroy us."[1] But they paid no heed to me and gave not over smiting upon the egg, when behold, the day grew dark and dun and the sun was hidden from us, as if some great cloud had passed over the firmament.[2] So we raised our eyes and saw that what we took for a cloud was the Rukh poised between us and the sun, and it was his wings that darkened the day. When he came and saw his egg broken, he cried a loud cry, whereupon his mate came flying up and they both began circling about the ship, crying out at us with voices louder than thunder. I called to the Rais and crew, "Put out to sea and seek safety in flight, before we be all destroyed." So the merchants came on board and we cast off and made haste from the island to gain the open sea. When the Rukhs saw this, they flew off and we crowded all sail on the ship, thinking to get out of their country; but presently the two re-appeared and flew after us and stood over us, each carrying in its claws a huge boulder which it had brought from the mountains. As soon as the he-Rukh came up with us, he let fall upon us the rock he held in his pounces; but the master put about ship, so that the rock missed her by some small matter and plunged into the waves with such violence, that the ship pitched high and then sank into the trough of the sea and the bottom of the ocean appeared to us. Then the she-Rukh let fall her rock, which was bigger than that of her mate, and as Destiny had decreed, it fell on the poop of the ship and crushed it, the rudder flying into twenty pieces; whereupon the vessel foundered and all and everything on board were cast into the main.[3] As for me I struggled for sweet life, till Almighty Allah threw in my way one

---

[1] Like the companions of Ulysses who ate the sacred oxen (Od. xii.).

[2] So the enormous kingfisher of Lucian's True History (lib. ii.).

[3] This tale is borrowed from Ibn Al-Wardi, who adds that the greybeards awoke in the morning after eating the young Rukh with black hair which never turned white. The same legend is recounted by Al-Dimiri (ob. A.H. 808 = 1405–6) who was translated into Latin by Bochart (Hierozoicon ii. p. 854) and quoted by Hole and Lane (iii. 103). An excellent study of Marco Polo's Rukh was made by my learned friend the late Prof. G. G. Bianconi of Bologna, "Dell'Uccello Ruc," Bologna, Gamberini, 1868. Prof. Bianconi predicted that other giant birds would be found in Madagascar on the East African Coast opposite; but he died before hearing of Hildebrand's discovery.

of the planks of the ship, to which I clung and bestriding it, fell a-paddling with my feet. Now the ship had gone down hard by an island in the midst of the main and the winds and waves bore me on till, by permission of the Most High, they cast me up on the shore of the island, at the last gasp for toil and distress and half dead with hunger and thirst. So I landed more like a corpse than a live man and throwing myself down on the beach, lay there awhile, till I began to revive and recover spirits, when I walked about the island and found it as it were one of the garths and gardens of Paradise. Its trees, in abundance dight, bore ripe-yellow fruit for freight; its streams ran clear and bright; its flowers were fair to scent and to sight and its birds warbled with delight the praises of Him to whom belong permanence and all-might. So I ate my fill of the fruits and slaked my thirst with the water of the streams till I could no more and I returned thanks to the Most High and glorified Him;——And Shahrazad perceived the dawn of day and ceased saying her permitted say.

When it was the Five Hundred and Fifty-seventh Night,

She said, It hath reached me, O auspicious King, that Sindbad the Seaman continued:—So when I escaped drowning and reached the island which afforded me fruit to eat and water to drink, I returned thanks to the Most High and glorified Him; after which I sat till nightfall, hearing no voice and seeing none inhabitant. Then I lay down, well-nigh dead for travail and trouble and terror, and slept without surcease till morning, when I arose and walked about under the trees, till I came to the channel of a draw-well fed by a spring of running water, by which well sat an old man of venerable aspect, girt about with a waist-cloth[1] made of the fibre of palm-fronds.[2] Quoth I to myself, "Haply this Shaykh is of those who were wrecked in the ship and hath made his way to this island." So I drew near to him and saluted him, and he returned my salam by signs, but spoke not; and I said to him, "O nuncle

---

[1] Arab. "Izár," the earliest garb of Eastern man; and, as such preserved in the Meccan pilgrimage. The "waist-cloth" is either tucked in or kept in place by a girdle.
[2] Arab. "Líf," a succedaneum for the unclean sponge, not unknown in the "Turkish Baths" of London.

mine, what causeth thee to sit here?" He shook his head and moaned and signed to me with his hand as who should say, "Take me on thy shoulders and carry me to the other side of the well-channel." And quoth I in my mind, "I will deal kindly with him and do what he desireth; it may be I shall win me a reward in Heaven for he may be a paralytic." So I took him on my back and carrying him to the place whereat he pointed, said to him, "Dismount at thy leisure." But he would not get off my back and wound his legs about my neck. I looked at them and seeing that they were like a buffalo's hide for blackness and roughness,[1] was affrighted and would have cast him off; but he clung to me and gripped my neck with his legs, till I was well-nigh choked, the world grew black in my sight and I fell senseless to the ground like one dead. But he still kept his seat and raising his legs drummed with his heels and beat harder than palm-rods my back and shoulders, till he forced me to rise for excess of pain. Then he signed to me with his hand to carry him hither and thither among the trees which bore the best fruits; and if ever I refused to do his bidding or loitered or took my leisure he beat me with his feet more grievously than if I had been beaten with whips. He ceased not to signal with his hand wherever he was minded to go; so I carried him about the island, like a captive slave, and he bepissed and conskited my shoulders and back, dismounting not night nor day, and whenas he wished to sleep he wound his legs about my neck and leaned back and slept awhile, then arose and beat me; whereupon I sprang up in haste, unable to gainsay him because of the pain he inflicted on me. And indeed I blamed myself and sore repented me of having taken compassion on him

---

[1] The Persians have a Plinian monster called "Tasmeh-pá" = Strap-legs without bones. The "Old Man" is not an ourang-outang nor an Ifrít as in Sayf al-Mulúk, Night dcclxxi., but a jocose exaggeration of a custom prevailing in parts of Asia and especially in the African interior where the Tsetse-fly prevents the breeding of burden-beasts. Ibn Batútah tells us that in Malabar everything was borne upon men's backs. In Central Africa the kinglet rides a slave, and on ceremonious occasions mounts his Prime Minister. I have often been reduced to this style of conveyance and found man the worst imaginable riding: there is no hold and the sharpness of the shoulder-ridge soon makes the legs ache intolerably. The classicists of course find the Shaykh of the Sea in the Tritons and Nereus, and Bochart (Hiero. ii. 858, 880) notices the homo aquaticus, Senex Judæus and Senex Marinus. Hole (p. 151) suggests the inevitable ouran-outan (man o' wood), one of "our humiliating copyists," and quotes "Destiny" in Scarron's comical romance (Part ii. chapt. i) and "Jealousy" enfolding Rinaldo. (O.F. lib. 42.)

and continued in this condition, suffering fatigue not to be de- scribed, till I said to myself, "I wrought him a weal and he requited me with my ill; by Allah, never more will I do any man a service so long as I live!" And again and again I besought the Most High that I might die, for stress of weariness and misery; and thus I abode a long while till, one day, I came with him to a place wherein was abundance of gourds, many of them dry. So I took a great dry gourd and, cutting open the head, scooped out the inside and cleaned it; after which I gathered grapes from a vine which grew hard by and squeezed them into the gourd, till it was full of the juice. Then I stopped up the mouth and set it in the sun, where I left it for some days, until it became strong wine; and every day I used to drink of it, to comfort and sustain me under my fatigues with that froward and obstinate fiend; and as often as I drank myself drunk, I forgot my troubles and took new heart. One day he saw me drinking and signed to me with his hand, as who should say, "What is that?" Quoth I, "It is an excel- lent cordial, which cheereth the heart and reviveth the spirits." Then, being heated with wine, I ran and danced with him among the trees, clapping my hands and singing and making merry; and I staggered under him by design. When he saw this, he signed to me to give him the gourd that he might drink, and I feared him and gave it him. So he took it and, draining it to the dregs, cast it on the ground, whereupon he grew frolicsome and began to clap hands and jig to and fro on my shoulders and he made water upon me so copiously that all my dress was drenched. But pre- sently the fumes of the wine rising to his head, he became help- lessly drunk and his side-muscles and limbs relaxed and he swayed to and fro on my back. When I saw that he had lost his senses for drunkenness, I put my hand to his legs and, loosing them from my neck, stooped down well-nigh to the ground and threw him at full length,——And Shahrazad perceived the dawn of day and ceased to say her permitted say.

When it was the Five Hundred and Fifty-eighth Night,

She said, It hath reached me, O auspicious King, that Sindbad the Seaman continued:—So I threw the devil off my shoulders, hardly crediting my deliverance from him and fearing lest he should shake off his drunkenness and do me a mischief. Then I took up a great stone from among the trees and coming up to him smote him therewith on the head with all my might and crushed in his skull as he lay dead drunk. Thereupon his flesh and fat and blood being in a pulp, he died and went to his deserts, The Fire, no mercy of Allah be upon him! I then returned, with a heart at ease, to my former station on the sea-shore and abode in that island many days, eating of its fruits and drinking of its waters and keeping a look-out for passing ships; till one day, as I sat on the beach, recalling all that had befallen me and saying, "I wonder if Allah will save me alive and restore me to my home and family and friends!" behold, a ship was making for the island through the dashing sea and clashing waves. Presently, it cast anchor and the passengers landed; so I made for them, and when they saw me all hastened up to me and gathering round me questioned me of my case and how I came thither. I told them all that had betided me, whereat they marvelled with exceeding marvel and said, "He who rode on thy shoulder is called the 'Shaykh al-Bahr' or Old Man of the Sea,[1] and none ever felt his legs on neck and came off alive but thou; and those who die under him he eateth: so praised be Allah for thy safety!" Then they set somewhat of food before me, whereof I ate my fill, and gave me somewhat of clothes wherewith I clad myself anew and covered my nakedness; after which they took me up into the ship, and we sailed days and nights, till fate brought us to a place called the City of Apes, builded with lofty houses, all of which gave upon the sea and it had a single gate studded and strengthened with iron nails. Now every night, as soon as it is dusk the dwellers in this city use to come forth of the gates and, putting out to sea in boats and ships, pass the night upon the waters in their fear lest the apes should come down on them from the mountains. Hearing this I was sore troubled remembering what I had before suffered from the ape-kind. Presently I landed to solace myself in the city, but meanwhile the ship set sail without me and I repented of having

---

[1] More literally "The Chief of the Sea (-Coast)," Shaykh being here a chief rather than an elder (eoldermann, alderman). So the "Old Man of the Mountain," famous in crusading days, was the Chief who lived on the Nusayriyah or Ansári range, a northern prolongation of the Libanus. Our "old man" of the text may have been suggested by the Koranic commentators on chapt. vi. When an Infidel rises from the grave, a hideous figure meets him and says, "Why wonderest thou at my loathsomeness? I am thine Evil Deeds: thou didst ride upon me in the world and now I will ride upon thee." (Suiting the action to the words.)

gone ashore, and calling to mind my companions and what had befallen me with the apes, first and after, sat down and fell a-weeping and lamenting. Presently one of the townsfolk accosted me and said to me, "O my lord, meseemeth thou art a stranger to these parts?" "Yes," answered I, "I am indeed a stranger and a poor one, who came hither in a ship which cast anchor here, and I landed to visit the town; but when I would have gone on board again, I found they had sailed without me." Quoth he, "Come and embark with us, for if thou lie the night in the city, the apes will destroy thee." "Hearkening and obedience," replied I, and rising, straightway embarked with him in one of the boats, where-upon they pushed off from shore and anchoring a mile or so from the land, there passed the night. At daybreak, they rowed back to the city and landing, went each about his business. Thus they did every night, for if any tarried in the town by night the apes came down on him and slew him. As soon as it was day, the apes left the place and ate of the fruits of the gardens, then went back to the mountains and slept there till nightfall, when they again came down upon the city.[1] Now this place was in the farthest part of the country of the blacks, and one of the strangest things that befel me during my sojourn in the city was on this wise. One of the company with whom I passed the night in the boat, asked me, "O my lord, thou art apparently a stranger in these parts; hast thou any craft whereat thou canst work?"; and I answered, "By Allah, O my brother, I have no trade nor know I any handicraft, for I was a merchant and a man of money and substance and had a ship of my own, laden with great store of

---

[1] In parts of West Africa and especially in Gorilla-land there are many stories of women and children being carried off by apes, and all believe that the former bear issue to them. It is certain that the anthropoid ape is lustfully excited by the presence of women and I have related how at Cairo (1856) a huge cynocephalus would have raped a girl had it not been bayonetted. Young ladies who visited the Demidoff Gardens and menagerie at Florence were often scandalised by the vicious exposure of the baboons' parti-coloured persons. The female monkey equally solicits the attentions of man and I heard in India from my late friend, Mirza Ali Akbar of Bombay, that to his knowledge connection had taken place. Whether there would be issue and whether such issue would be viable are still disputed points: the produce would add another difficulty to the pseudo-science called psychology, as such mule would have only half a soul and issue by a congener would have a quarter-soul. A traveller well known to me once proposed to breed pithecoid men who might be useful as hewers of wood and drawers of water: his idea was to put the highest races of apes to the lowest of humanity. I never heard what became of his "breed-ing stables."

goods and merchandise; but it foundered at sea and all were drowned excepting me who saved myself on a piece of plank which Allah vouchsafed to me of His favour." Upon this he brought me a cotton bag and giving it to me, said, "Take this bag and fill it with pebbles from the beach and go forth with a company of the townsfolk to whom I will give a charge respecting thee. Do as they do and belike thou shalt gain what may further thy return voyage to thy native land." Then he carried me to the beach, where I filled my bag with pebbles large and small, and presently we saw a company of folk issue from the town, each bearing a bag like mine, filled with pebbles. To these he committed me, commending me to their care, and saying, "This man is a stranger, so take him with you and teach him how to gather, that he may get his daily bread, and you will earn your reward and recompense in Heaven." "On our head and eyes be it!" answered they and bidding me welcome, fared on with me till we came to a spacious Wady, full of lofty trees with trunks so smooth that none might climb them. Now sleeping under these trees were many apes, which when they saw us rose and fled from us and swarmed up among the branches; whereupon my companions began to pelt them with what they had in their bags, and the apes fell to plucking of the fruit of the trees and casting them at the folk. I looked at the fruits they cast at us and found them to be Indian[1] or cocoa-nuts; so I chose out a great tree, full of apes, and going up to it, began to pelt them with stones, and they in return pelted me with nuts, which I collected, as did the rest; so that even before I had made an end of my bagful of pebbles, I had gotten great plenty of nuts; and as soon as my companions had in like manner gotten as many nuts as they could carry, we returned to the city, where we arrived at the fag-end of day. Then I went in to the kindly man who had brought me in company with the nut-gatherers and gave him all I had gotten, thanking him for his kindness; but he would not accept them, saying, "Sell them and make profit by the price; and presently he added (giving me the key of a closet in his house) "Store thy nuts in this safe place and go thou forth every morning and gather them as thou

---

[1] Arab. "Jauz al-Hindi": our word cocoa is from the Port. "Coco," meaning a "bug" (bugbear) in allusion to its caricature of the human face, hair, eyes and mouth. I may here note that a cocoa-tree is easily climbed with a bit of rope or a handkerchief.

hast done to-day, and choose out the worst for sale and supplying thyself; but lay up the rest here, so haply thou mayst collect enough to serve thee for thy return home." Allah requite thee!" answered I and did as he advised me, going out daily with the cocoa-nut gatherers, who commended me to one another and showed me the best-stocked trees.[1] Thus did I for some time, till I had laid up great store of excellent nuts, besides a large sum of money, the price of those I had sold. I became thus at my ease and bought all I saw and had a mind to, and passed my time pleasantly greatly enjoying my stay in the city, till, as I stood on the beach, one day, a great ship steering through the heart of the sea presently cast anchor by the shore and landed a company of merchants, who proceeded to sell and buy and barter their goods for cocoa-nuts and other commodities. Then I went to my friend and told him of the coming of the ship and how I had a mind to return to my own country; and he said, " 'Tis for thee to decide." So I thanked him for his bounties and took leave of him; then, going to the captain of the ship, I agreed with him for my passage and embarked my cocoa-nuts and what else I pos-sessed. We weighed anchor,——And Shahrazad perceived the dawn of day and ceased saying her permitted say.

When it was the Five Hundred and Fifty-ninth Night,

She said, It hath reached me, O auspicious King, that Sindbad the Seaman continued:—So I left the City of the Apes and em-barked my cocoa-nuts and what else I possessed. We weighed anchor the same day and sailed from island to island and sea to sea; and whenever we stopped, I sold and traded with my cocoa-nuts, and the Lord requited me more than I erst had and lost. Amongst other places, we came to an island abounding in cloves[2] and cinna-mon and pepper; and the country people told me that by the side of each pepper-bunch groweth a great leaf which shadeth it from the sun and casteth the water off it in the wet season; but, when the rain ceaseth the leaf turneth over and droopeth down by the

---

[1] Tomb-pictures in Egypt show tame monkeys gathering fruits and Grossier (Descrip-tion of China, quoted by Hole and Lane) mentions a similar mode of harvesting tea by irritating the monkeys of the Middle Kingdom.

[2] Bresl. Edit. Cloves and cinnamon in those days grew in widely distant places.

side of the bunch.[1] Here I took in great store of pepper and
cloves and cinnamon, in exchange for cocoa-nuts, and we passed
thence to the Island of Al-Usirát,[2] whence cometh the Comorin
aloes-wood and thence to another island, five days' journey in
length, where grows the Chinese lign-aloes, which is better than
the Comorin; but the people of this island[3] are fouler of condition
and religion than those of the other, for that they love fornication
and wine-bibbing, and know not prayer nor call to prayer. Thence
we came to the pearl-fisheries, and I gave the divers some of my
cocoa-nuts and said to them, "Dive for my luck and lot!" They
did so and brought up from the deep bight[4] great store of large
and priceless pearls; and they said to me, "By Allah, O my master,
thy luck is a lucky!" Then we sailed on, with the blessing of
Allah (whose name be exalted!); and ceased not sailing till we
arrived safely at Bassorah. There I abode a little and then went on
to Baghdad, where I entered my quarter and found my house and
foregathered with my family and saluted my friends who gave me
joy of my safe return, and I laid up all my goods and valuables
in my storehouses.   Then I distributed alms and largesse and
clothed the widow and the orphan and made presents to my
relations and comrades; for the Lord had requited me fourfold
that I had lost. After which I returned to my old merry way of
life and forgot all I had suffered in the great profit and gain I had
made.   "Such, then, is the history of my fifth voyage and its
wonderments, and now to supper; and to-morrow, come again and
I will tell you what befel me in my sixth voyage; for it was still
more wonderful than this." (Saith he who telleth the tale), Then
he called for food; and the servants spread the table, and
when they had eaten the evening-meal, he bade give Sindbad the

---

[1] In pepper-plantations it is usual to set bananas (*Musa Paradisiaca*) for shading the
young shrubs which bear bunches like ivy-fruit, not pods.

[2] The Bresl. Edit. has "Al-Ma'arat."   Langlès calls it the Island of Al-Kamárí.   See
Lane, iii. 86.

[3] Insula, pro. peninsula.   "Comorin" is a corrupt. of "Kanyá" (=Virgo, the goddess
Durgá) and "Kumári" (a maid, a princess); from a temple of Shiva's wife: hence Ptolemy's
Κῶϱυ ἄϰϱον and near it to the N. East Κομαϱία ἄϰϱον καὶ πόλις, "Promontorium
Cori quod Comorini caput insulæ vocant," says Maffæus (Hist. Indic. i. p. 16).   In the
text "Al 'úd" refers to the eagle-wood (Aloekylon Agallochum) so called because spotted
like the bird's plume.   That of Champa (Cochin-China, mentioned by Camoens, The Lus.
x. 129) is still famous.

[4] Arab. "Birkat"=tank, pool, reach, bight.   Hence Birkat Far'aun in the Suez Gulf.
(Pilgrimage i. 297.)

porter an hundred golden dinars and the Landsman returned home and lay him down to sleep, much marvelling at all he had heard. Next morning, as soon as it was light, he prayed the dawn-prayer; and, after blessing Mohammed the Cream of all creatures, betook himself to the house of Sindbad the Seaman and wished him a good day. The merchant bade him sit and talked with him, till the rest of the company arrived. Then the servants spread the table and when they had well eaten and drunken and were mirth-ful and merry, Sindbad the Seaman began in these words the narrative of

The Sixth Voyage of Sindbad the Seaman.

KNOW, O my brothers and friends and companions all, that I abode some time, after my return from my fifth voyage, in great solace and satisfaction and mirth and merriment, joyance and enjoyment; and I forgot what I had suffered, seeing the great gain and profit I had made till, one day, as I sat making merry and enjoying myself with my friends, there came in to me a com-pany of merchants whose case told tales of travel, and talked with me of voyage and adventure and greatness of pelf and lucre. Hereupon I remembered the days of my return from abroad, and my joy at once more seeing my native land and foregathering with my family and friends; and my soul yearned for travel and traffic. So compelled by Fate and Fortune I resolved to undertake another voyage; and, buying me fine and costly merchandise meet for foreign trade, made it up into bales, with which I journeyed from Baghdad to Bassorah. Here I found a great ship ready for sea and full of merchants and notables, who had with them goods of price; so I embarked my bales therein. And we left Bassorah in safety and good spirits under the safeguard of the King, the Preserver.——And Shahrazad perceived the dawn of day and ceased to say her permitted say.

When it was the Five Hundred and Sixtieth Night,

She said, It hath reached me, O auspicious King, that Sindbad the Seaman continued:—And after embarking my bales and leaving Bassorah in safety and good spirits, we continued our voyage from place to place and from city to city, buying and selling and profiting and diverting ourselves with the sight of countries where strange folk dwell. And Fortune and the voyage smiled upon us, till one day, as we went along, behold, the captain suddenly cried with a great cry and cast his turband on the deck. Then he buffeted his face like a woman and plucked out his beard and fell down in the waist of the ship well nigh fainting for stress of grief and rage, and crying, "Oh and alas for the ruin of my house and the orphanship of my poor children!" So all the merchants and sailors came round about him and asked him, "O master, what is the matter?"; for the light had become night before their sight. And he answered, saying, "Know, O folk, that we have wandered from our course and left the sea whose ways we wot, and come into a sea whose ways I know not; and unless Allah vouchsafe us a means of escape, we are all dead men; wherefore pray ye to the Most High, that He deliver us from this strait. Haply amongst you is one righteous whose prayers the Lord will accept." Then he arose and clomb the mast to see an there were any escape from that strait; and he would have loosed the sails; but the wind redoubled upon the ship and whirled her round thrice and drave her backwards; whereupon her rudder brake and she fell off towards a high mountain. With this the captain came down from the mast, saying, "There is no Majesty and there is no Might save in Allah, the Glorious, the Great; nor can man prevent that which is fore-ordained of fate! By Allah, we are fallen on a place of sure destruction, and there is no way of escape for us, nor can any of us be saved!" Then we all fell a-weeping over ourselves and bidding one another farewell for that our days were come to an end, and we had lost all hopes of life. Presently the ship struck the mountain and broke up, and all and everything on board of her were plunged into the sea. Some of the merchants were drowned and others made shift to reach the shore and save themselves upon the mountain; I amongst the number, and when we got ashore, we found a great island, or rather peninsula[1] whose base was strewn with wreckage of crafts and goods and gear cast up by the sea from broken ships whose passengers had been drowned; and the quantity confounded compt and calculation.

---

[1] Probably Cape Comorin; to judge from the river, but the text names Sarandib (Ceylon Island) famous for gems. This was noticed by Marco Polo, iii. cap. 19; and ancient authors relate the same of "Taprobane."

So I climbed the cliffs into the inward of the isle and walked on inland, till I came to a stream of sweet water, that welled up at the nearest foot of the mountains and disappeared in the earth under the range of hills on the opposite side. But all the other passengers went over the mountains to the inner tracts; and, dispersing hither and thither, were confounded at what they saw and became like madmen at the sight of the wealth and treasures wherewith the shores were strewn. As for me I looked into the bed of the stream aforesaid and saw therein great plenty of rubies, and great royal pearls[1] and all kinds of jewels and precious stones which were as gravel in the bed of the rivulets that ran through the fields, and the sands sparkled and glittered with gems and precious ores. Moreover we found in the island abundance of the finest lign-aloes, both Chinese and Comorin; and there also is a spring of crude ambergris[2] which floweth like wax or gum over the stream-banks, for the great heat of the sun, and runneth down to the sea-shore, where the monsters of the deep come up and swallowing it, return into the sea. But it burneth in their bellies; so they cast it up again and it congealeth on the surface of the water, whereby its colour and quantities are changed; and at last, the waves cast it ashore, and the travellers and merchants who know it, collect it and sell it. But as to the raw ambergris which is not swallowed, it floweth over the channel and congealeth on the banks and when the sun shineth on it, it melteth and scenteth the whole valley with a musk-like fragrance: then, when the sun ceaseth from it, it congealeth again. But none can get to this place where is the crude ambergris, because of the mountains

---

[1] I need hardly trouble the reader with a note on pearl-fisheries: the descriptions of travellers are continuous from the days of Pliny (ix. 35), Solinus (cap. 56) and Marco Polo (iii. 23). Maximilian of Transylvania, in his narrative of Magellan's voyage (Novus Orbis, p. 532) says that the Celebes produce pearls big as turtle-doves' eggs; and the King of Porne (Borneo) had two unions as great as goose's eggs. Pigafetta (in Purchas) reduces this to hen's eggs and Sir Thomas Herbert to dove's eggs.

[2] Arab. "Anbar" pronounced "Ambar;" wherein I would derive "Ambrosia." Ambergris was long supposed to be a fossil, a vegetable which grew upon the sea-bottom or rose in springs; or a "substance produced in the water like naphtha or bitumen" (!): now it is known to be the egesta of a whale. It is found in lumps weighing several pounds upon the Zanzibar Coast and is sold at a high price, being held a potent aphrodisiac. A small hollow is drilled in the bottom of the cup and the coffee is poured upon the bit of ambergris it contains; when the oleaginous matter shows in dots amidst the "Kaymagh" (coffee-cream), the bubbly froth which floats upon the surface and which an expert "coffee servant" distributes equally among the guests. Argensola mentions in Ceylon, "springs of liquid bitumen thicker than our oil and some of pure balsam."

which enclose the island on all sides and which foot of man cannot ascend.[1] We continued thus to explore the island, marvelling at the wonderful works of Allah and the riches we found there, but sore troubled for our own case, and dismayed at our prospects. Now we had picked up on the beach some small matter of victual from the wreck and husbanded it carefully, eating but once every day or two, in our fear lest it should fail us and we die miserably of famine and affright. Moreover, we were weak for colic brought on by sea-sickness and low diet, and my companions deceased, one after other, till there was but a small company of us left. Each that died we washed and shrouded in some of the clothes and linen cast ashore by the tides; and after a little, the rest of my fellows perished, one by one, till I had buried the last of the party and abode alone on the island, with but a little provision left, I who was wont to have so much. And I wept over myself, saying, "Would Heaven I had died before my companions and they had washed me and buried me! It had been better than I should perish and none wash me and shroud me and bury me. But there is no Majesty and there is no Might save in Allah, the Glorious, the Great!"——And Shahrazad perceived the dawn of day and ceased saying her permitted say.

When it was the Five Hundred and Sixty-first Night,

She said, It hath reached me, O auspicious King, that Sind-bad the Seaman continued in these words:—Now after I had buried the last of my party and abode alone on the island, I arose and dug me a deep grave on the sea-shore, saying to myself, "Whenas I grow weak and know that death cometh to me, I will cast myself into the grave and die there, so the wind may drift the sand over me and cover me and I be buried therein."[2] Then I fell to reproaching myself for my little wit in leaving my native land and betaking me again to

---

[1] The tale-teller forgets that Sindbad and his companions have just ascended it; but this *inconséquence* is a characteristic of the Eastern Saga. I may note that the description of ambergris in the text tells us admirably well what it is not.

[2] This custom is alluded to by Lane (Mod. Egypt, ch. xv.) : it is the rule of pilgrims to Meccah when too ill to walk or ride (Pilgrimage i. 180). Hence all men carry their shrouds : mine, after being dipped in the Holy Water of Zemzem, was stolen from me by the rascally Somal of Berberah.

travel, after all I had suffered during my first five voyages, and
when I had not made a single one without suffering more horrible
perils and more terrible hardships than in its forerunner and
having no hope of escape from my present stress; and I repented
me of my folly and bemoaned myself, especially as I had no need
of money, seeing that I had enough and more than enough and
could not spend what I had, no, nor a half of it in all my life.
However, after a while Allah sent me a thought and I said to
myself, "By God, needs must this stream have an end as well as
a beginning; ergo an issue somewhere, and belike its course may
lead to some inhabited place; so my best plan is to make me a
little boat[1] big enough to sit in, and carry it and launching it on
the river, embark therein and drop down the stream. If I escape,
I escape, by God's leave; and if I perish, better die in the river
than here." Then, sighing for myself, I set to work collecting
a number of pieces of Chinese and Comorin aloes-wood and
I bound them together with ropes from the wreckage; then I
chose out from the broken-up ships straight planks of even size
and fixed them firmly upon the aloes-wood, making me a boat-
raft a little narrower than the channel of the stream; and I tied
it tightly and firmly as though it were nailed. Then I loaded it
with the goods, precious ores and jewels: and the union pearls
which were like gravel and the best of the ambergris crude and
pure, together with what I had collected on the island and what
was left me of victual and wild herbs. Lastly I lashed a piece
of wood on either side, to serve me as oars; and launched it, and
embarking, did according to the saying of the poet,

"Fly, fly with life whenas evils threat; * Leave the house to tell of its
builder's fate!
Land after land shalt thou seek and find * But no other life on thy wish shall
wait:
Fret not thy soul in thy thoughts o' night; * All woes shall end or sooner or
late.
Whoso is born in one land to die, * There and only there shall gang his
gait:
Nor trust great things to another wight, * Soul hath only soul for confederate."[2]

My boat-raft drifted with the stream, I pondering the issue of my
affair; and the drifting ceased not till I came to the place where

---

[1] Arab. "Fulk;" some Edits. read "Kalak" and "Ramaz" (= a raft).
[2] These lines occur in modified form in Night xi.

it disappeared beneath the mountain. I rowed my conveyance into the place which was intensely dark; and the current carried the raft with it down the underground channel.[1] The thin stream bore me on through a narrow tunnel where the raft touched either side and my head rubbed against the roof, return therefrom being impossible. Then I blamed myself for having thus risked my life, and said, "If this passage grow any straiter, the raft will hardly pass, and I cannot turn back; so I shall inevitably perish miserably in this place." And I threw myself down upon my face on the raft, by reason of the narrowness of the channel, whilst the stream ceased not to carry me along, knowing not night from day, for the excess of the gloom which encompassed me about and my terror and concern for myself lest I should perish. And in such condi-tion my course continued down the channel which now grew wider and then straiter till, sore aweary by reason of the darkness which could be felt, I fell asleep, as I lay prone on the raft, and I slept knowing not an the time were long or short. When I awoke at last, I found myself in the light of Heaven and opening my eyes I saw myself in a broad of the stream and the raft moored to an is-land in the midst of a number of Indians and Abyssinians. As soon as these blackamoors[2] saw that I was awake, they came up to me and bespoke me in their speech; but I understood not what they said and thought that this was a dream and a vision which had be-tided me for stress of concern and chagrin. But I was delighted at my escape from the river. When they saw I understood them not and made them no answer, one of them came forward and said to me in Arabic, "Peace be with thee, O my brother! Who art thou and whence faredst thou thither? How camest thou into this river and what manner of land lies behind yonder mountains, for never knew we any one make his way thence to us?" Quoth I, "And

---

[1] These underground rivers (which Dr. Livingstone derided) are familar to every geographer from Spenser's "Mole" to the Poika of Adelberg and the Timavo near Trieste. Hence "Peter Wilkins" borrowed his cavern which led him to Grandevolet. I have some experience of Sindbad's sorrows, having once attempted to descend the Poika on foot. The Classics had the Alpheus (Pliny v. 31; and Seneca, Nat. Quæ. vi.), and the Tigris-Euphrates supposed to flow underground: and the Mediævals knew the Abana of Damascus and the Zenderúd of Isfahan.

[2] Abyssinians can hardly be called "blackamoors," but the arrogance of the white skin shows itself in Easterns (e.g. Turks and Brahmans) as much as, if not more than, amongst Europeans. Southern India at the time it was explored by Vasco da Gama was crowded with Abyssinian slaves imported by the Arabs.

upon thee be peace and the ruth of Allah and his blessing! Who
are ye and what country is this?" "O my brother," answered he,
"we are husbandmen and tillers of the soil, who came out to
water our fields and plantations; and, finding thee asleep on this
raft, laid hold of it and made it fast by us, against thou shouldst
awake at thy leisure. So tell us how thou camest hither?" I
answered, "For Allah's sake, O my lord, ere I speak give me somewhat to eat, for I am starving, and after ask me what thou
wilt." So he hastened to fetch me food and I ate my fill, till
I was refreshed and my fear was calmed by a good belly-full
and my life returned to me. Then I rendered thanks to the
Most High for mercies great and small, glad to be out of the
river and rejoicing to be amongst them, and I told them all my
adventures from first to last, especially my troubles in the narrow
channel.——And Shahrazad perceived the dawn of day and
ceased to say her permitted say.

When it was the Five Hundred and Sixty-second Night,

She said, It hath reached me, O auspicious King, that Sindbad the
Seaman continued:—When I landed and found myself amongst
the Indians and Abyssinians and had taken some rest, they consulted among themselves and said to one another, "There is
no help for it but we carry him with us and present him to our
King, that he may acquaint him with his adventures." So they
took me, together with the raft-boat and its lading of monies and
merchandise; jewels, minerals and golden gear, and brought me
to their King, who was King of Sarandib,[1] telling him what had
happened; whereupon he saluted me and bade me welcome.
Then he questioned me of my condition and adventures through
the man who had spoken Arabic and I repeated to him my story
from beginning to end, whereat he marvelled exceedingly and gave
me joy of my deliverance; after which I arose and fetched from

---

[1] "Sarandib" and "Ceylon" (the Taprobane of Ptolemy and Diodorus Siculus) derive
from the Pali "Sihalam" (not the Sansk. "Sinhala") shortened to Silam and Ilam in old
Tamul. Van der Tunk would find it in the Malay "Pulo Selam"=Isle of Gems (the
Ratna-dwípa or Jewel Isle of the Hindus and the Jazirat al-Yakút or Ruby-Island of the
Arabs); and the learned Colonel Yule (Marco Polo ii. 296) remarks that we have adopted
many Malayan names, *e.g.* Pegu, China and Japan. Sarandib is clearly "Selan-dwípa,"
which Mandeville reduced to "Silha."

the raft great store of precious ores and jewels and ambergris and lign-aloes and presented them to the King, who accepted them and entreated me with the utmost honour, appointing me a lodging in his own palace. So I consorted with the chief of the islanders, and they paid me the utmost respect. And I quitted not the royal palace. Now the Island Sarandib lieth under the equinoctial line, its night and day both numbering twelve hours. It measureth eighty leagues long by a breadth of thirty and its width is bounded by a lofty mountain[1] and a deep valley. The mountain is conspicuous from a distance of three days and it containeth many kinds of rubies and other minerals, and spice-trees of all sorts. The surface is covered with emery wherewith gems are cut and fashioned; diamonds are in its rivers and pearls are in its valleys. I ascended that mountain and solaced myself with a view of its marvels which are indescribable and afterwards I returned to the King.[2] Thereupon, all the travellers and merchants who came to the place questioned me of the affairs of my native land and of the Caliph Harun al-Rashid and his rule and I told them of him and of that wherefor he was renowned, and they praised him because of this; whilst I in turn questioned them of the manners and customs of their own countries and got the knowledge I desired. One day, the King himself asked me of the fashions and form of government of my country, and I acquainted him with the circumstance of the Caliph's sway in the city of Baghdad and the justice of his rule. The King marvelled at my account of his appointments and said, "By Allah, the Caliph's ordinances are indeed wise and his fashions of praiseworthy guise and thou hast made me love him by what thou tellest me; wherefore I have a mind to make him a present and send it by thee." Quoth I, "Hearkening and obedience, O my lord; I will bear thy gift to him and inform him that thou art his sincere lover and true friend." Then I abode with the King in great honour and regard and consideration for a long while till, one day, as I sat in his palace, I heard news of a company of merchants, that were fitting out a ship for Bassorah, and said to myself, "I cannot do better

---

[1] This is the well-known Adam's Peak, the Jabal al-Ramun of the Arabs where Adam fell when cast out of Eden in the lowest or lunar sphere. Eve fell at Jeddah (a modern myth) and the unhappy pair met at Mount Arafat (*i.e.* recognition) near Meccah. Thus their fall was a fall indeed. (Pilgrimage iii. 259.)

[2] He is the Alcinous of our Arabian Odyssey.

than voyage with these men." So I rose without stay or delay and kissed the King's hand and acquainted him with my longing to set out with the merchants, for that I pined after my people and mine own land. Quoth he, "Thou art thine own master; yet, if it be thy will to abide with us, on our head and eyes be it, for thou gladdenest us with thy company." "By Allah, O my lord," answered I, "thou hast indeed overwhelmed me with thy favours and well-doings; but I weary for a sight of my friends and family and native country." When he heard this, he summoned the merchants in question and commended me to their care, paying my freight and passage-money. Then he bestowed on me great riches from his treasuries and charged me with a magnificent present for the Caliph Harun al-Rashid. Moreover he gave me a sealed letter, saying, "Carry this with thine own hand to the Commander of the Faithful and give him many salutations from us!" "Hearing and obedience," I replied. The missive was written on the skin of the Kháwi[1] (which is finer than lamb-parchment and of yellow colour), with ink of ultramarine and the contents were as follows. "Peace be with thee from the King of Al-Hind, before whom are a thousand elephants and upon whose palace-crenelles are a thousand jewels. But after (laud to the Lord and praises to His Prophet!): we send thee a trifling gift which be thou pleased to accept. Thou art to us a brother and a sincere friend; and great is the love we bear for thee in heart; favour us therefore with a reply. The gift besitteth not thy dignity: but we beg of thee, O our brother, graciously to accept it and peace be with thee." And the present was a cup of ruby a span high[2] the inside of which was adorned with precious pearls; and a bed covered with the skin of the serpent which swalloweth the elephant, which skin hath spots each like a dinar and whoso sitteth upon it never sickeneth;[3] and an hundred thousand miskals of Indian

---

[1] This word is not in the dictionaries; Hole (p. 192) and Lane understand it to mean the hog-deer; but why, one cannot imagine. The animal is neither "beautiful" nor "uncommon" and most men of my day have shot dozens in the Sind-Shikárgáhs.

[2] M. Polo speaks of a ruby in Seilan (Ceylon) a palm long and three fingers thick: William of Tyre mentions a ruby weighing twelve Egyptian drams (Gibbon ii. 123), and Mandeville makes the King of Mammera wear about his neck a "rubye orient" one foot long by five fingers large.

[3] The fable is from Al-Kazwini and Ibn Al-Wardi who place the serpent (an animal sacred to Æsculapius, Pliny, xxix. 4) "in the sea of Zanj" (*i.e.* Zanzibar). In the "garrow hills" of N. Eastern Bengal the skin of the snake Burrawar (?) is held to cure pain. (Asiat. Res. vol. iii.)

lign-aloes and a slave-girl like a shining moon.   Then I took leave
of him and of all my intimates and acquaintances in the island and
embarked with the merchants aforesaid.   We sailed with a fair
wind, committing ourselves to the care of Allah (be He extolled
and exalted!) and by His permission arrived at Bassorah, where
I passed a few days and nights equipping myself and packing up
my bales.   Then I went on to Baghdad-city, the House of Peace,
where I sought an audience of the Caliph and laid the King's
presents before him.   He asked me whence they came and I said
to him, "By Allah, O Commander of the Faithful, I know not the
name of the city nor the way thither!"   He then asked me, "O
Sindbad, is this true which the King writeth?"; and I answered,
after kissing the ground, "O my lord, I saw in his kingdom much
more than he hath written in his letter.   For state processions a
throne is set for him upon a huge elephant, eleven cubits high:
and upon this he sitteth having his great lords and officers and
guests standing in two ranks, on his right hand and on his left.
At his head is a man hending in hand a golden javelin and behind
him another with a great mace of gold whose head is an emerald[1]
a span long and as thick as a man's thumb.   And when he
mounteth horse there mount with him a thousand horsemen clad
in gold brocade and silk; and as the King proceedeth a man
precedeth him, crying, 'This is the King of great dignity, of high
authority!'   And he continueth to repeat his praises in words I
remember not, saying at the end of his panegyric, 'This is the
King owning the crown whose like nor Solomon nor the Mihraj[2]
ever possessed.'   Then he is silent and one behind him proclaimeth,
saying, 'He will die!   Again I say he will die!;' and the other
addeth, 'Extolled be the perfection of the Living who dieth not!'[3]
Moreover by reason of his justice and ordinance and intelligence,
there is no Kazi in his city, and all his lieges distinguish between
Truth and Falsehood."   Quoth the Caliph, "How great is this

---

[1] For "Emerald," Hole (p. 177) would read emery or adamantine spar.

[2] Evidently Maháráj=Great Rajah, Rajah in Chief, an Hindu title common to the
three potentates before alluded to, the Narsinga, Balhara or Samiry.

[3] This is probably classical.   So the page said to Philip of Macedon every morning,
"Remember, Philip, thou art mortal"; also the slave in the Roman Triumph,

"Respice poste te: hominem te esse memento!"

And the dying Severus, "Urnlet, soon shalt thou enclose what hardly a whole world
could contain."   But the custom may also have been Indian: the contrast of external
pomp with the real vanity of human life suggests itself to all.

King! His letter hath shown me this; and as for the mightiness
of his dominion thou hast told us what thou hast eye-witnessed.
By Allah, he hath been endowed with wisdom as with wide rule."
Then I related to the Commander of the Faithful all that had
befallen me in my last voyage; at which he wondered exceedingly
and bade his historians record my story and store it up in his
treasuries, for the edification of all who might see it. Then he
conferred on me exceeding great favours, and I repaired to my
quarter and entered my home, where I warehoused all my goods
and possessions. Presently, my friends came to me and I distributed presents among my family and gave alms and largesse;
after which I yielded myself to joyance and enjoyment, mirth
and merry-making, and forgot all that I had suffered. "Such, then,
O my brothers, is the history of what befel me in my sixth voyage,
and to-morrow, Inshallah! I will tell you the story of my seventh
and last voyage, which is still more wondrous and marvellous than
that of the first six." (Saith he who telleth the tale), Then he bade
lay the table, and the company supped with him; after which he
gave the Porter an hundred dinars, as of wont, and they all went
their ways, marvelling beyond measure at that which they had
heard.——And Shahrazad perceived the dawn of day and ceased
saying her permitted say.

𝔚𝔥𝔢𝔫 𝔦𝔱 𝔴𝔞𝔰 𝔱𝔥𝔢 𝔉𝔦𝔳𝔢 ℌ𝔲𝔫𝔡𝔯𝔢𝔡 𝔞𝔫𝔡 𝔖𝔦𝔵𝔱𝔶-𝔱𝔥𝔦𝔯𝔡 𝔑𝔦𝔤𝔥𝔱,

She said, It hath reached me, O auspicious King, that when
Sindbad the Seaman had related the history of what befel
him in his sixth voyage, and all the company had dispersed,
Sindbad the Landsman went home and slept as of wont. Next
day he rose and prayed the dawn-prayer and repaired to his
namesake's house where, after the company was all assembled,
the host began to relate

The Seventh Voyage of Sindbad the Seaman.

KNOW, O company, that after my return from my sixth voyage,
which brought me abundant profit, I resumed my former life in
all possible joyance and enjoyment and mirth and making merry
day and night; and I tarried some time in this solace and satis-

faction till my soul began once more to long to sail the seas and
see foreign countries and company with merchants and hear new
things.   So having made up my mind, I packed up in bales a
quantity of precious stuffs suited for sea-trade and repaired with
them from Baghdad-city to Bassorah-town, where I found a ship
ready for sea, and in her a company of considerable merchants.   I
shipped with them and becoming friends, we set forth on our venture, in health and safety; and sailed with a fair wind, till we came
to a city called Madínat-al-Sín; but after we had left it, as we fared
on in all cheer and confidence, devising of traffic and travel, behold,
there sprang up a violent head-wind and a tempest of rain fell on
us and drenched us and our goods.   So we covered the bales with
our cloaks and garments and drugget and canvas, lest they be
spoiled by the rain, and betook ourselves to prayer and supplication to Almighty Allah and humbled ourselves before Him for
deliverance from the peril that was upon us.   But the captain
arose and tightening his girdle tucked up his skirts and, after
taking refuge with Allah from Satan the Stoned, clomb to the
mast-head, whence he looked out right and left and gazing at the
passengers and crew fell to buffeting his face and plucking out his
beard.   So we cried to him, "O Rais, what is the matter?"; and
he replied saying, "Seek ye deliverance of the Most High from
the strait into which we have fallen and bemoan yourselves and
take leave of one another; for know that the wind hath gotten the
mastery of us and hath driven us into the uttermost of the seas of
the world." Then he came down from the mast-head and opening
his sea-chest, pulled out a bag of blue cotton, from which he took
a powder like ashes.   This he set in a saucer wetted with a little
water and, after waiting a short time, smelt and tasted it; and then
he took out of the chest a booklet, wherein he read awhile and said
weeping, "Know, O ye passengers, that in this book is a marvellous matter, denoting that whoso cometh hither shall surely die,
without hope of escape; for that this ocean is called the Sea of the
Clime of the King, wherein is the sepulchre of our lord Solomon,
son of David (on both be peace!) and therein are serpents of vast
bulk and fearsome aspect: and what ship soever cometh to these
climes there riseth to her a great fish[1] out of the sea and swalloweth her up with all and everything on board her." Hearing these

---

[1] Arab. "Hút"; a term applied to Jonah's whale and to monsters of the deep, "Samak"
being the common fishes.

words from the captain great was our wonder, but hardly had he
made an end of speaking, when the ship was lifted out of the water
and let fall again and we applied to praying the death-prayer[1] and
committing our souls to Allah. Presently we heard a terrible great
cry like the loud-pealing thunder, whereat we were terror-struck
and became as dead men, giving ourselves up for lost. Then behold,
there came up to us a huge fish, as big as a tall mountain, at whose
sight we became wild for affright and, weeping sore, made ready
for death, marvelling at its vast size and gruesome semblance;
when lo! a second fish made its appearance than which we had
seen naught more monstrous. So we bemoaned ourselves of our
lives and farewelled one another; but suddenly up came a third
fish bigger than the two first; whereupon we lost the power of
thought and reason and were stupefied for the excess of our fear
and horror. Then the three fish began circling round about the
ship and the third and biggest opened his mouth to swallow it,
and we looked into its mouth and behold, it was wider than the
gate of a city and its throat was like a long valley. So we besought
the Almighty and called for succour upon His Apostle (on whom
be blessing and peace!), when suddenly a violent squall of wind
arose and smote the ship, which rose out of the water and settled
upon a great reef, the haunt of sea-monsters, where it broke up
and fell asunder into planks and all and everything on board were
plunged into the sea. As for me, I tore off all my clothes but my
gown and swam a little way, till I happened upon one of the ship's
planks whereto I clung and bestrode it like a horse, whilst the
winds and the waters sported with me and the waves carried me
up and cast me down; and I was in most piteous plight for fear
and distress and hunger and thirst. Then I reproached myself
for what I had done and my soul was weary after a life of ease
and comfort; and I said to myself, "O Sindbad, O Seaman, thou
repentest not and yet thou art ever suffering hardships and travails; yet wilt thou not renounce sea-travel; or, an thou say, 'I renounce,' thou liest in thy renouncement. Endure then with patience that which thou sufferest, for verily thou deservest all that
betideth thee!"——And Shahrazad perceived the dawn of day
and ceased to say her permitted say.

---

[1] Usually a two-bow prayer.

When it was the Five Hundred and Sixty-fourth Night,

She said, It hath reached me, O auspicious King, that Sindbad the Seaman continued:—But when I had bestridden the plank, quoth I to myself, "Thou deservest all that betideth thee. All this is decreed to me of Allah (whose name be exalted!), to turn me from my greed of gain, whence ariseth all that I endure, for I have wealth galore." Then I returned to my senses and said, "In very sooth, this time I repent to the Most High, with a sincere repentance, of my lust for gain and venture; and never will I again name travel with tongue nor in thought." And I ceased not to humble myself before Almighty Allah and weep and bewail myself, recalling my former estate of solace and satisfaction and mirth and merriment and joyance; and thus I abode two days, at the end of which time I came to a great island abounding in trees and streams. There I landed and ate of the fruits of the island and drank of its waters, till I was refreshed and my life returned to me and my strength and spirits were restored and I recited,

"Oft when thy case shows knotty and tangled skein, * Fate downs from
    Heaven and straightens every ply:
In patience keep thy soul till clear thy lot * For He who ties the knot can
    eke untie."

Then I walked about, till I found on the further side, a great river of sweet water, running with a strong current; whereupon I called to mind the boat-raft I had made aforetime and said to myself, "Needs must I make another; haply I may free me from this strait. If I escape, I have my desire and I vow to Allah Almighty to foreswear travel; and if I perish I shall be at peace and shall rest from toil and moil." So I rose up and gathered together great store of pieces of wood from the trees (which were all of the finest sanders-wood, whose like is not albe I knew it not), and made shift to twist creepers and tree-twigs into a kind of rope, with which I bound the billets together and so contrived a raft. Then saying, "An I be saved, 'tis of God's grace," I embarked thereon and committed myself to the current, and it bore me on for the first day and the second and the third after leaving the island; whilst I lay in the raft, eating not and drinking, when I was athirst, of the water of the river, till I was weak and giddy as a chicken, for

stress of fatigue and famine and fear. At the end of this time
I came to a high mountain, whereunder ran the river; which when
I saw, I feared for my life by reason of the straitness I had suffered
in my former journey, and I would fain have stayed the raft and
landed on the mountain-side; but the current overpowered me and
drew it into the subterranean passage like an archway; whereupon
I gave myself up for lost and said, "There is no Majesty and there
is no Might save in Allah, the Glorious, the Great!" However,
after a little, the raft glided into open air and I saw before me a
wide valley, whereinto the river fell with a noise like the rolling
of thunder and a swiftness as the rushing of the wind. I held on to
the raft, for fear of falling off it, whilst the waves tossed me right
and left; and the craft continued to descend with the current nor
could I avail to stop it nor turn it shorewards, till it stopped with
me at a great and goodly city, grandly edified and containing much
people. And when the townsfolk saw me on the raft, dropping
down with the current, they threw me out ropes which I had not
strength enough to hold; then they tossed a net over the craft and
drew it ashore with me, whereupon I fell to the ground amidst
them, as I were a dead man, for stress of fear and hunger and lack
of sleep. After a while, there came up to me out of the crowd an
old man of reverend aspect, well stricken in years, who welcomed
me and threw over me abundance of handsome clothes, wherewith
I covered my nakedness. Then he carried me to the Hammam-
bath and brought me cordial sherbets and delicious perfumes;
moreover, when I came out, he bore me to his house, where his
people made much of me and, seating me in a pleasant place, set
rich food before me, whereof I ate my fill and returned thanks to
God the Most High for my deliverance. Thereupon his pages
fetched me hot water, and I washed my hands, and his handmaids
brought me silken napkins, with which I dried them and wiped
my mouth. Also the Shaykh set apart for me an apartment in a
part of his house and charged his pages and slave-girls to wait
upon me and do my will and supply my wants. They were
assiduous in my service, and I abode with him in the guest-
chamber three days, taking my ease of good eating and good
drinking and good scents till life returned to me and my terrors
subsided and my heart was calmed and my mind was eased. On
the fourth day the Shaykh, my host, came in to me and said,
"Thou cheerest us with thy company, O my son, and praised be
Allah for thy safety! Say: wilt thou now come down with me to

the beach and the bazar and sell thy goods and take their price?
Belike thou mayst buy thee wherewithal to traffic. I have ordered
my servants to remove thy stock-in-trade from the sea and they
have piled it on the shore." I was silent awhile and said to myself, "What mean these words and what goods have I?" Then
said he, "O my son, be not troubled nor careful, but come with
me to the market and if any offer for thy goods what price con-
tenteth thee, take it; but, an thou be not satisfied, I will lay them
up for thee in my warehouse, against a fitting occasion for sale."
So I bethought me of my case and said to myself, "Do his bidding
and see what are these goods!"; and I said to him, "O my nuncle
the Shaykh, I hear and I obey; I may not gainsay thee in aught
for Allah's blessing is on all thou dost." Accordingly he guided
me to the market-street, where I found that he had taken in pieces
the raft which carried me and which was of sandal-wood and I
heard the broker crying it for sale.——And Shahrazad perceived
the dawn of day and ceased saying her permitted say.

𝔚𝔥𝔢𝔫 𝔦𝔱 𝔴𝔞𝔰 𝔱𝔥𝔢 𝔉𝔦𝔳𝔢 𝔥𝔲𝔫𝔡𝔯𝔢𝔡 𝔞𝔫𝔡 𝔖𝔦𝔵𝔱𝔶-𝔣𝔦𝔣𝔱𝔥 𝔑𝔦𝔤𝔥𝔱,

She said, It hath reached me, O auspicious King, that Sindbad
the Seaman thus resumed his tale:—I found that the Shaykh had
taken to pieces my raft which lay on the beach and the broker was
crying the sandal-wood for sale. Then the merchants came and
opened the gate of bidding for the wood and bid against one
another till its price reached a thousand dinars, when they left
bidding and my host said to me, "Hear, O my son, this is the current price of thy goods in hard times like these: wilt thou sell
them for this or shall I lay them up for thee in my storehouses, till
such time as prices rise?" "O my lord," answered I, "the business is in thy hands: do as thou wilt." Then asked he, "Wilt
thou sell the wood to me, O my son, for an hundred gold pieces
over and above what the merchants have bidden for it?" and I
answered, "Yes, I have sold it to thee for monies received."[1] So
he bade his servants transport the wood to his storehouses and,
carrying me back to his house, seated me and counted out to me
the purchase money; after which he laid it in bags and setting

---

[1] This is the recognised formula of Moslem sales.

them in a privy place, locked them up with an iron padlock and
gave me its key. Some days after this, the Shaykh said to me,
"O my son, I have somewhat to propose to thee, wherein I trust
thou wilt do my bidding." Quoth I, "What is it?" Quoth he,
"I am a very old man and have no son; but I have a daughter
who is young in years and fair of favour and endowed with
abounding wealth and beauty. Now I have a mind to marry her
to thee, that thou mayst abide with her in this our country, and I
will make thee master of all I have in hand for I am an old man
and thou shalt stand in my stead." I was silent for shame and
made him no answer, whereupon he continued, "Do my desire in
this, O my son, for I wish but thy weal; and if thou wilt but do
as I say, thou shalt have her at once and be as my son; and all
that is under my hand or that cometh to me shall be thine. If
thou have a mind to traffic and travel to thy native land, none
shall hinder thee, and thy property will be at thy sole disposal; so
do as thou wilt." "By Allah, O my uncle," replied I, "thou art
become to me even as my father, and I am a stranger and have
undergone many hardships: while for stress of that which I have
suffered naught of judgment or knowledge is left to me. It is for
thee, therefore, to decide what I shall do." Hereupon he sent his
servants for the Kazi and the witnesses and married me to his
daughter making for us a noble marriage-feast[1] and high festival.
When I went in to her, I found her perfect in beauty and loveliness and symmetry and grace, clad in rich raiment and covered
with a profusion of ornaments and necklaces and other trinkets of
gold and silver and precious stones, worth a mint of money, a price
none could pay. She pleased me and we loved each other; and I
abode with her in all solace and delight of life, till her father was
taken to the mercy of Allah Almighty. So we shrouded him and
buried him, and I laid hands on the whole of his property and all
his servants and slaves became mine. Moreover, the merchants
installed me in his office, for he was their Shaykh and their Chief;
and none of them purchased aught but with his knowledge and by
his leave. And now his rank passed on to me. When I became acquainted with the townsfolk, I found that at the beginning of each
month they were transformed, in that their faces changed and they
became like unto birds and they put forth wings wherewith they

---

[1] Arab. "Walímah"; like our wedding-breakfast but a much more ceremonious and
important affair.

flew unto the upper regions of the firmament and none remained in the city save the women and children; and I said in my mind, "When the first of the month cometh, I will ask one of them to carry me with them, whither they go." So when the time came and their complexion changed and their forms altered, I went in to one of the townsfolk and said to him, "Allah upon thee! carry me with thee, that I might divert myself with the rest and return with you." "This may not be," answered he; but I ceased not to solicit him and I importuned him till he consented. Then I went out in his company, without telling any of my family[1] or servants or friends, and he took me on his back and flew up with me so high in air, that I heard the angels glorifying God in the heavenly dome, whereat I wondered and exclaimed, "Praised be Allah! Extolled be the perfection of Allah!" Hardly had I made an end of pronouncing the Tasbíh—praised be Allah!—when there came out a fire from heaven and all but consumed the company; whereupon they fled from it and descended with curses upon me and, casting me down on a high mountain, went away, exceeding wroth with me, and left me there alone. As I found myself in this plight, I repented of what I had done and reproached myself for having undertaken that for which I was unable, saying, "There is no Majesty and there is no Might, save in Allah, the Glorious, the Great! No sooner am I delivered from one affliction than I fall into a worse." And I continued in this case knowing not whither I should go, when lo! there came up two young men, as they were moons, each using as a staff a rod of red gold. So I approached them and saluted them; and when they returned my salam, I said to them, "Allah upon you twain; who are ye and what are ye?" Quoth they, "We are of the servants of the Most High Allah, abiding in this mountain;" and, giving me a rod of red gold they had with them, went their ways and left me. I walked on along the mountain-ridge staying my steps with the staff and pondering the case of the two youths, when behold, a serpent came forth from under the mountain, with a man in her[2] jaws, whom she had swallowed even to below his navel, and he was crying out and saying, "Whoso delivereth me, Allah will

---

[1] *i.e.* his wife (euphemistically). I remember an Italian lady being much hurt when a Maltese said to her "Mia moglie—con rispetto parlando" (my wife, saving your presence). "What," she cried, "he speaks of his wife as he would of the sweepings!"

[2] The serpent in Arabic is mostly feminine.

deliver him from all adversity!" So I went up to the serpent and smote her on the head with the golden staff, whereupon she cast the man forth of her mouth.——And Shahrazad perceived the dawn of day and ceased to say her permitted say.

When it was the Five Hundred and Sixty-sixth Night,

She said, It hath reached me, O auspicious King, that Sindbad the Seaman thus continued:—When I smote the serpent on the head with my golden staff she cast the man forth of her mouth. Then I smote her a second time, and she turned and fled; where-upon he came up to me and said, "Since my deliverance from yonder serpent hath been at thy hands I will never leave thee, and thou shalt be my comrade on this mountain." "And welcome," answered I; so we fared on along the mountain, till we fell in with a company of folk, and I looked and saw amongst them the very man who had carried me and cast me down there. I went up to him and spake him fair, excusing myself to him and saying, "O my comrade, it is not thus that friend should deal with friend." Quoth he, "It was thou who well-nigh destroyed us by thy Tasbih and thy glorifying God on my back." Quoth I, "Pardon me, for I had no knowledge of this matter; but, if thou wilt take me with thee, I swear not to say a word." So he relented and consented to carry me with him, but he made an express condition that, so long as I abode on his back, I should abstain from pro-nouncing the Tasbih or otherwise glorifying God. Then I gave the wand of gold to him whom I had delivered from the serpent and bade him farewell, and my friend took me on his back and flew with me as before, till he brought me to the city and set me down in my own house. My wife came to meet me and saluting me gave me joy of my safety and then said, "Beware of going forth hereafter with yonder folk, neither consort with them, for they are brethren of the devils, and know not how to mention the name of Allah Almighty; neither worship they Him." "And how did thy father with them?" asked I; and she answered, "My father was not of them, neither did he as they; and as now he is dead methinks thou hadst better sell all we have and with the price buy merchandise and journey to thine own country and people, and I with thee; for I care not to tarry in this city, my father and my mother being dead." So I sold all the Shaykh's property piecemeal, and looked for one who should be journeying thence to Bassorah that I might join myself to him. And while thus doing I heard of a company of townsfolk who had a mind to make the voyage, but could not find them a ship; so they bought wood and built them a great ship wherein I took passage with them, and paid them all the hire. Then we embarked, I and my wife, with all our moveables, leaving our houses and domains and so forth, and set sail, and ceased not sailing from island to island and from sea to sea, with a fair wind and a favouring, till we arrived at Bassorah safe and sound. I made no stay there, but freighted another vessel and, transferring my goods to her, set out forthright for Baghdad-city, where I arrived in safety, and entering my quarter and repairing to my house, foregathered with my family and friends and familiars and laid up my goods in my warehouses. When my people who, reckoning the period of my absence on this my seventh voyage, had found it to be seven and twenty years, and had given up all hope of me, heard of my return, they came to welcome me and to give me joy of my safety; and I related to them all that had befallen me; whereat they mar-velled with exceeding marvel. Then I forswore travel and vowed to Allah the Most High I would venture no more by land or sea, for that this seventh and last voyage had surfeited me of travel and adventure; and I thanked the Lord (be He praised and glorified!), and blessed Him for having restored me to my kith and kin and country and home. "Consider, therefore, O Sindbad, O Landsman," continued Sindbad the Seaman, "what sufferings I have undergone and what perils and hardships I have endured before coming to my present state." "Allah upon thee, O my Lord!" answered Sindbad the Landsman, "pardon me the wrong I did thee."[1] And they ceased not from friendship and fellowship, abiding in all cheer and pleasures and solace of life, till there came to them the Destroyer of delights and the Sunderer of Societies, and the Shatterer of palaces and the Caterer for Ceme-teries to wit, the Cup of Death, and glory be to the Living One who dieth not!"[2]

---

[1] *i.e.* in envying his wealth, with the risk of the evil eye.

[2] I subjoin a translation of the Seventh Voyage from the Calc. Edit. of the two hundred Nights which differs in essential points from the above. All respecting Sindbad the Sea-man has an especial interest. In one point this world-famous tale is badly ordered. The most exciting adventures are the earliest and the falling off of the interest has a somewhat depressing effect. The Rukh, the Ogre and the Old Man o' the Sea should come last.

JULNAR THE SEA-BORN AND HER SON KING BADR BASIM OF PERSIA.

THERE was once in days of yore and in ages and times long gone before, in Ajam-land, a King Shahrimán[1] hight, whose abiding-place was Khorásán. He owned an hundred concubines, but by

---

none of them had he been blessed with boon of child, male or female, all the days of his life. One day, among the days, he bethought him of this and fell lamenting for that the most part of his existence was past and he had not been vouchsafed a son, to inherit the kingdom after him, even as he had inherited it from his fathers and forebears; by reason whereof there betided him sore cark and care and chagrin exceeding. As he sat thus one of his Mamelukes came in to him and said, "O my lord, at the door is a slave-girl with her merchant, and fairer than she eye hath never seen." Quoth the King, "Hither to me with merchant and maid!"; and both came in to him. Now when Shahriman beheld the girl, he saw that she was like a Rudaynian lance,[1] and she was wrapped in a veil of gold-purfled silk. The merchant uncovered her face, whereupon the place was illumined by her beauty and her seven tresses hung down to her anklets like horses' tails. She had Nature-kohl'd eyes, heavy hips and thighs and waist of slenderest guise; her sight healed all maladies and quenched the fire of sighs, for she was even as the poet cries,

"I love her madly for she is perfect fair, * Complete in gravity and gracious
    way;
Nor overtall nor overshort, the while * Too full for trousers are those hips
    that sway:
Her shape is midmost 'twixt o'er small and tall, * Nor long to blame nor
    little to gainsay:
O'erfall her anklets tresses black as night * Yet in her face resplends eternal
    day."

The King seeing her marvelled at her beauty and loveliness, her symmetry and perfect grace and said to the merchant, "O Shaykh, how much for this maiden?" Replied the merchant, "O my lord, I bought her for two thousand dinars of the merchant who owned her before myself, since when I have travelled with her three years and she hath cost me, up to the time of my coming hither, other three thousand gold pieces; but she is a gift from me to thee." The King robed him with a splendid robe of honour and ordered him ten thousand ducats, whereupon he kissed his hands, thanking him for his bounty and beneficence, and went his ways. Then the King committed the damsel to the tire-women,

---

[1] For a note on this subject see vol. ii. 2.

saying, "Amend ye the case of this maiden[1] and adorn her and furnish her a bower and set her therein." And he bade his chamberlains carry her everything she needed and shut all the doors upon her. Now his capital wherein he dwelt, was called the White City and was seated on the sea-shore; so they lodged her in a chamber, whose latticed casements overlooked the main.——— And Shahrazad perceived the dawn of day and ceased saying her permitted say.

When it was the Seven Hundred and Thirty-ninth Night,

She said, It hath reached me, O auspicious King, that the King after taking the maiden, committed her to the tire-women bidding them amend her case and set her in a bower, and ordered his chamberlains to shut all the doors upon her when they had lodged her in a chamber whose latticed casements overlooked the main. Then Shahriman went in to her; but she spake not to him neither took any note of him.[2] Quoth he, " 'Twould seem she hath been with folk who have not taught her manners." Then he looked at the damsel and saw her surpassing beauty and loveliness and symmetry and perfect grace, with a face like the rondure of the moon at its full or the sun shining in the sheeny sky. So he marvelled at her charms of favour and figure and he praised Allah the Creator (magnified be His might!), after which he walked up to her and sat him down by her side; then he pressed her to his bosom and seating her on his thighs, sucked the dew of her lips, which he found sweeter than honey. Presently he called for trays spread with richest viands of all kinds and ate and fed her by mouthfuls, till she had enough; yet she spoke not one word. The King began to talk to her and asked her of her name; but she abode still silent and uttered not a syllable nor made him any answer, neither ceased to hang down her head groundwards; and it was but the excess of her beauty and loveliness and the amorous

---

[1] *i.e.* bathe her and apply cosmetics to remove all traces of travel.

[2] These pretentious and curious displays of coquetry are not uncommon in handsome slave-girls when newly bought; and it is a kind of pundonor to humour them. They may also refuse their favours and a master who took possession of their persons by brute force would be blamed by his friends, men and women. Even the most despotic of despots, Fath Ali Shah of Persia, put up with refusals from his slave-girls and did not, as would the mean-minded, marry them to the grooms or cooks of the palace.

grace that saved her from the royal wrath. Quoth he to himself, "Glory be to God, the Creator of this girl! How charming she is, save that she speaketh not! But perfection belongeth only to Allah the Most High." And he asked the slave-girls whether she had spoken, and they said, "From the time of her coming until now she hath not uttered a word nor have we heard her address us." Then he summoned some of his women and concubines and bade them sing to her and make merry with her, so haply she might speak. Accordingly they played before her all manner instruments of music and sports and what not and sang, till the whole company was moved to mirth, except the damsel, who looked at them in silence, but neither laughed nor spoke. The King's breast was straitened; thereupon he dismissed the women and abode alone with that damsel: after which he doffed his clothes and disrobing her with his own hand, looked upon her body and saw it as it were a silvern ingot. So he loved her with exceeding love and falling upon her, took her maidenhead and found her a pure virgin; whereat he rejoiced with excessive joy and said in himself, "By Allah, 'tis a wonder that a girl so fair of form and face should have been left by the merchants a clean maid as she is!"[1] Then he devoted himself altogether to her, heeding none other and forsaking all his concubines and favourites, and tarried with her a whole year as it were a single day. Still she spoke not till, one morning he said to her (and indeed the love of her and longing waxed upon him), "O desire of souls, verily passion for thee is great with me, and I have forsaken for thy sake all my slave-girls and concubines and women and favourites and I have made thee my portion of the world and had patience with thee a whole year; and now I beseech Almighty Allah, of His favour, to soften thy heart to me, so thou mayst speak to me. Or, an thou be dumb, tell me by a sign, that I may give up hope of thy speech. I pray the Lord (extolled be He!) to vouchsafe me by thee a son child, who shall inherit the kingdom after me; for I am old and lone and have none to be my heir. Wherefore, Allah upon thee, an thou love me, return me a reply." The damsel bowed her head awhile in thought, and presently raising it, smiled in his face; whereat it seemed to him as if lightning filled the chamber. Then she said, "O magnanimous liege lord, and

---

[1] Such continence is rarely shown by the young Jallabs or slave-traders; when older they learn how much money is lost with the chattel's virginity.

valorous lion, Allah hath answered thy prayer, for I am with
child by thee and the time of my delivery is near at hand, though
I know not if the unborn babe be male or female.[1] But, had I not
conceived by thee, I had not spoken to thee one word." When
the King heard her speech, his face shone with joy and gladness
and he kissed her head and hands for excess of delight, saying,
"Alhamdolillah—laud to Lord—who hath vouchsafed me the
things I desired!; first, thy speech, and secondly, thy tidings that
thou art with child by me." Then he rose up and went forth from
her and, seating himself on the throne of his kingship, in an
ecstasy of happiness, bade his Wazir distribute to the poor and
needy and widows and others an hundred thousand dinars, by way
of thank-offering to Allah Most High and alms on his own
account. The Minister did as bidden by the King who, returning
to the damsel, sat with her and embraced and pressed her to his
breast, saying, "O my lady, my queen, whose slave I am, prithee
what was the cause of this thy silence? Thou hast been with me
a whole year, night and day, waking and sleeping, yet hast not
spoken to me till this day." She replied, "Hearken, O King of
the Age, and know that I am a wretched exile, broken-hearted and
far-parted from my mother and my family and my brother." When
the King heard her words, he knew her desire and said, "As for
thy saying that thou art wretched, there is for such speech no
ground, inasmuch as my kingdom and good and all I possess are
at thy service and I also am become thy bondman; but, as for thy
saying, 'I am parted from my mother and brother and family', tell
me where they are and I will send and fetch them to thee." Thereupon she answered, "Know, then, O auspicious King, that I am called
Julnár[2] the Sea-born and that my father was of the Kings of the

---

[1] Midwives in the East, as in the less civilised parts of the West, have many nostrums
for divining the sex of the unborn child.

[2] Arabic (which has no written "g") from Pers. Gulnár (Gul-i-anár) pomegranate-flower,
the "Gulnare" of Byron who learnt his Orientalism at the Mekhitarist (Armenian) Convent, Venice. I regret to see the little honour now paid to the gallant poet in the land
where he should be honoured the most. The systematic depreciation was begun by the
late Mr. Thackeray, perhaps the last man to value the noble independence of Byron's
spirit; and it has been perpetuated, I regret to see, by better judges. These critics seem
wholly to ignore the fact that Byron founded a school which covered Europe from Russia
to Spain, from Norway to Sicily, and which from England passed over to the two Americas.
This exceptional success, which has not yet fallen even to Shakespeare's lot, was due to
genius only, for the poet almost ignored study and poetic art. His great misfortune was
being born in England under the Georgium Sidus. Any Continental people would have
regarded him as one of the prime glories of his race.

Main.   He died and left us his reign, but while we were yet
unsettled, behold, one of the other Kings arose against us and took
the realm from our hands.   I have a brother called Sálih, and my
mother also is a woman of the sea; but I fell out with my brother
'The Pious' and swore that I would throw myself into the hands
of a man of the folk of the land.   So I came forth of the sea and
sat down on the edge of an island in the moonshine,[1] where a
passer-by found me and, carrying me to his house, besought me of
love-liesse; but I smote him on the head, so that he all but died;
whereupon he carried me forth and sold me to the merchant from
whom thou hadst me, and this was a good man and a virtuous;
pious, loyal and generous.   Were it not that thy heart loved me
and that thou promotedest me over all thy concubines, I had not
remained with thee a single hour, but had cast myself from this
window into the sea and gone to my mother and family; but I was
ashamed to fare themwards, being with child by thee; for they
would have deemed evilly of me and would not have credited me,
even although I swore to them, an I told them that a King had
bought me with his gold and made me his portion of the world
and preferred me over all his wives and every thing that his right
hand possessed.   This then is my story and—the Peace!"——And
Shahrazad perceived the dawn of day and ceased to say her
permitted say.

When it was the Seben Hundred and Fortieth Night,

She resumed, It hath reached me, O auspicious King, that when
Julnar[2] the Sea-born, answering the question of King Shahriman,
told him her past from first to last, the King thanked her and
kissed her between the eyes, saying, "By Allah, O my lady and
light of mine eyes, I cannot bear to be parted from thee one hour;
and given thou leave me, I shall die forthright.   What then is to
be done?"   Replied she, "O my lord, the time of my delivery

---

[1] Arab. "Fí al-Kamar," which Lane renders "in the moonlight." It seems to me that
the allusion is to the Comorin Islands; but the sequel speaks simply of an island.

[2] The Mac. Edit. misprints Julnár as Julnáz (so the Bul. Edit. ii. 233), and Lane's
Jullanár is an Egyptian vulgarism.   He is right in suspecting the "White City" to be
imaginary; but its sea has no apparent connection with the Caspian.   The mermen and
mermaids appear to him to be of an inferior order of the Jinn, termed Al-Ghawwásah, the
Divers, who fly through air and are made of fire which at times issues from their mouths.

is at hand and my family needs must be present, that they may tend me; for the women of the land know not the manner of child-bearing of the women of the sea, nor do the daughters of the ocean know the manner of the daughters of the earth; and when my people come, I shall be reconciled to them and they will be reconciled to me." Quoth the King, "How do the people of the sea walk therein, without being wetted?"; and quoth she, "O King of the Age, we walk in the waters with our eyes open, as do ye on the ground, by the blessing of the names graven upon the seal-ring of Solomon David-son (on whom be peace!). But, O King, when my kith and kin come, I will tell them how thou boughtest me with thy gold, and hast entreated me with kindness and benevolence. It behoveth that thou confirm my words to them and that they witness thine estate with their own eyes and they learn that thou art a King, son of a King." He rejoined, "O my lady, do what seemeth good to thee and what pleaseth thee; and I will consent to thee in all thou wouldst do." The damsel continued, "Yes, we walk in the sea and see what is therein and behold the sun, moon, stars and sky, as it were on the surface of earth; and this irketh us naught. Know also that there be many peoples in the main and various forms and creatures of all kinds that are on the land, and that all that is on the land compared with that which is in the main is but a very small matter." And the King marvelled at her words. Then she pulled out from her bosom two bits of Comorin lign-aloes and, kindling fire in a chafing-dish, chose somewhat of them and threw it in, then she whistled a loud whistle and spake words none understood. Thereupon arose a great smoke and she said to the King, who was looking on, "O my lord, arise and hide thyself in a closet, that I may show thee my brother and mother and family, whilst they see thee not; for I design to bring them hither, and thou shalt presently espy a wondrous thing and shalt marvel at the several creatures and strange shapes which Almighty Allah hath created." So he arose without stay or delay and entering a closet, fell a-watching what she should do. She continued her fumigations and conjurations till the sea foamed and frothed turbid and there rose from it a handsome young man of a bright favour, as he were the moon at its full, with brow flower-white, cheeks of ruddy light and teeth like the marguerite. He was the likest of all creatures to his sister and the tongue of the case spoke in his praise these two couplets,

"The full moon groweth perfect once a month　* But thy face each day we
　　see perfectèd.
And the full moon dwelleth in single sign,　　* But to thee all hearts be a
　　dwelling stead."

After him there came forth of the sea an ancient dame with hair
speckled gray and five maidens, as they were moons, bearing a
likeness to the damsel hight Julnar. The King looked upon them
as they all walked upon the face of the water, till they drew near the
window and saw Julnar, whereupon they knew her and went in to
her. She rose to them and met them with joy and gladness, and
they embraced her and wept with sore weeping. Then said they
to her, "O Julnar, how couldst thou leave us four years, and we
unknowing of thine abiding place? By Allah the world hath
been straitened upon us for stress of severance from thee, and we
have had no delight of food or drink; no, not for one day, but
have wept with sore weeping night and day for the excess of our
longing after thee!" Then she fell to kissing the hands of the
youth her brother and her mother and cousins, and they sat with
her awhile, questioning her of her case and of what had betided
her, as well as of her present estate. "Know," replied she, "that,
when I left you, I issued from the sea and sat down on the shore
of an island, where a man found me and sold me to a merchant,
who brought me to this city and sold me for ten thousand dinars
to the King of the country, who entreated me with honour and
forsook all his concubines and women and favourites for my sake
and was distracted by me from all he had and all that was in his
city." Quoth her brother, "Praised be Allah, who hath reunited us
with thee! But now, O my sister, 'tis my purpose that thou arise
and go with us to our country and people." When the King
heard these words, his wits fled him for fear lest the damsel accept
her brother's words and he himself avail not to stay her, albeit he
loved her passionately, and he became distracted with fear of
losing her. But Julnar answered, "By Allah, O my brother, the
mortal who bought me is lord of this city and he is a mighty King
and a wise man, good and generous with extreme generosity.
Moreover, he is a personage of great worth and wealth and hath
neither son nor daughter. He hath entreated me with honour and
done me all manner of favour and kindness; nor, from the day of
his buying me to this time have I heard from him an ill word to
hurt my heart; but he hath never ceased to use me courteously;
doing nothing save with my counsel, and I am in the best of case

with him and in the perfection of fair fortune. Furthermore, were
I to leave him, he would perish; for he cannot endure to be parted
from me an hour; and if I left him, I also should die, for the
excess of the love I bear him, by reason of his great goodness to
me during the time of my sojourn with him; for, were my father
alive, my estate with him would not be like my estate with this
great and glorious and puissant potentate. And verily, ye see
me with child by him and praise be to Allah, who hath made me
a daughter of the Kings of the sea, and my husband the mightiest
of the Kings of the land, and Allah, in very sooth, he hath compensated me for whatso I lost."——And Shahrazad perceived the
dawn of day and ceased saying her permitted say.

When it was the Seven Hundred and Forty-first Night,

She said, It hath reached me, O auspicious King, that Julnar the
Sea-born told her brother all her tale, adding "Allah hath not cut
me off, but hath compensated me for whatso I lost. Now this
King hath no issue, male or female, so I pray the Almighty to
vouchsafe me a son who shall inherit of this mighty sovran that
which the Lord hath bestowed upon him of lands and palaces and
possessions." Now when her brother and the daughters of her
uncle heard this her speech, their eyes were cooled thereby and
they said, "O Julnar, thou knowest thy value with us and thou
wottest the affection we bear thee and thou art certified that thou
art to us the dearest of all creatures and thou art assured that we
seek but ease for thee, without travail or trouble. Wherefore, an
thou be in unease, arise and go with us to our land and our folk;
but, an thou be at thine ease here, in honour and happiness, this
is our wish and our will; for we desire naught save thy welfare in
any case."[1] Quoth she, "By Allah, I am here in the utmost ease
and solace and honour and grace!" When the King heard what
she said, he joyed with a heart set at rest and thanked her silently
for this; the love of her redoubled on him and entered his heart-
core and he knew that she loved him as he loved her and that she
desired to abide with him, that she might see his child by her.
Then Julnar bade her women lay the tables and set on all sorts
of viands, which had been cooked in kitchen under her own eyes,

---

[1] Arab. "'Alà Kulli hál," a popular phrase, like the Anglo-American "anyhow."

and fruits and sweetmeats, whereof she ate, she and her kinsfolk. But, presently, they said to her, "O Julnar, thy lord is a stranger to us, and we have entered his house, without his leave or weeting. Thou hast extolled to us his excellence and eke thou hast set before us of his victual whereof we have eaten; yet have we not companied with him nor seen him, neither hath he seen us nor come to our presence and eaten with us, so there might be between us bread and salt."   And they all left eating and were wroth with her, and fire issued from their mouths, as from cressets; which when the King saw, his wits fled for excess of fear of them.   But Julnar arose and soothed them and going to the closet where was the King her lord, said to him, "O my lord, hast thou seen and heard how I praised thee and extolled thee to my people and hast thou noted what they said to me of their desire to carry me away with them?"   Quoth he, "I both heard and saw: May the Almighty abundantly requite thee for me! By Allah, I knew not the full measure of thy fondness until this blessed hour, and now I doubt not of thy love to me!"   Quoth she, "O my lord, is the reward of kindness aught but kindness? Verily, thou hast dealt generously with me and hast entreated me with worship and I have seen that thou lovest me with the utmost love, and thou hast done me all manner of honour and kindness and preferred me above all thou lovest and desirest. So how should my heart be content to leave thee and depart from thee, and how should I do thus after all thy goodness to me? But now I desire of thy courtesy that thou come and salute my family, so thou mayst see them and they thee and pure love and friendship may be between you; for know, O King of the Age, that my brother and mother and cousins love thee with exceeding love, by reason of my praises of thee to them, and they say, 'We will not depart from thee nor go to our homes till we have foregathered with the King and saluted him.' For indeed they desire to see thee and make acquaintance with thee."   The King replied, "To hear is to obey, for this is my very own wish."   So saying, he rose and went in to them and saluted them with the goodliest salutation; and they sprang up to him and received him with the utmost worship, after which he sat down in the palace and ate with them; and he entertained them thus for the space of thirty days. Then, being desirous of returning home, they took leave of the King and Queen and departed with due permission to their own land, after he had done them all possible honour. Awhile after this, Julnar completed the days of her pregnancy and the time of her delivery being come, she bore a boy, as he were the moon at its full; whereat the utmost joy betided the King, for that he had never in his life been vouchsafed son or daughter. So they held high festival and decorated the city seven days, in the extreme of joy and jollity: and on the seventh day came Queen Julnar's mother, Faráshah hight,[1] and brother and cousins, whenas they knew of her delivery.———And Shahrazad perceived the light of day and ceased to say her permitted say.

When it was the Seben Hundred and Forty=second Night,

She said, It hath reached me, O auspicious King, that when Julnar was brought to bed and was visited by her people, the King received them with joy at their coming and said to them, "I said that I would not give my son a name till you should come and name him of your knowledge." So they named him Badr Básim,[2] and all agreed upon this name. Then they showed the child to his uncle Salih, who took him in his arms and arising began to walk about the chamber with him in all directions right and left. Presently he carried him forth of the palace and going down to the salt sea, fared on with him, till he was hidden from the King's sight. Now when Shahriman saw him take his son and disappear with him in the depth of the sea, he gave the child up for lost and fell to weeping and wailing; but Julnar said to him, "O King of the Age, fear not, neither grieve for thy son, for I love my child more than thou and he is with my brother; so reck thou not of the sea neither fear for him drowning. Had my brother known that aught of harm would betide the little one, he had not done this deed; and he will presently bring thee thy son safe, Inshallah —an it please the Almighty." Nor was an hour past before the sea became turbid and troubled and King Salih came forth and flew from the sea till he came up to them with the child lying quiet and showing a face like the moon on the night of fulness. Then, looking at the King he said, "Haply thou fearedst harm for thy son, whenas I plunged into the sea with him?" Replied the father, "Yes, O my lord, I did indeed fear for him and thought he

---

[1] In the text the name does not appear till near the end of the tale.
[2] *i.e.* Full moon smiling.

would never be saved therefrom." Rejoined Salih, "O King of
the land, we pencilled his eyes with an eye-powder we know of
and recited over him the names graven upon the seal-ring of
Solomon David-son (on whom be the Peace!), for this is what we
use to do with children newly born among us; and now thou
needst not fear for him drowning or suffocation in all the oceans
of the world, if he should go down into them; for, even as ye walk
on the land, so walk we in the sea." Then he pulled out of his
pocket a casket, graven and sealed and, breaking open the seals,
emptied it; whereupon there fell from it strings of all manner
jacinths and other jewels, besides three hundred bugles of emerald
and other three hundred hollow gems, as big as ostrich eggs,
whose light dimmed that of sun and moon. Quoth Salih, "O
King of the Age, these jewels and jacinths are a present from me
to thee. We never yet brought thee a gift, for that we knew not
Julnar's abiding-place neither had we of her any tidings or trace;
but now that we see thee to be united with her and we are all
become one thing, we have brought thee this present; and every
little while we will bring thee the like thereof, Inshallah! for that
these jewels and jacinths are more plentiful with us than pebbles
on the beach and we know the good and the bad of them and their
whereabouts and the way to them, and they are easy to us."
When the King saw the jewels, his wits were bewildered and his
sense was astounded and he said, "By Allah, one single gem of
these jewels is worth my realm!" Then he thanked for his bounty
Salih the Sea-born and, looking towards Queen Julnar, said, "I
am abashed before thy brother, for that he hath dealt munificently
by me and bestowed on me this splendid gift, which the folk of
the land were unable to present." So she thanked her brother
for his deed and he said, "O King of the Age, thou hast the prior
claim on us and it behoves us to thank thee, for thou hast entreated
our sister with kindness and we have entered thy dwelling and
eaten of thy victual; and the poet saith[1],

'Had I wept before she did in my passion for Saada, * I had healed my soul
    before repentance came.
But she wept before I did: her tears drew mine; and I said, * The merit
    belongs to the precedent.' "

"And" (resumed Salih the Pious) "if we stood on our faces in thy

---

[1] These lines have occurred in vol. iii. 264. so I quote Lane ii. 499.

service, O King of the Age, a thousand years, yet had we not the might to requite thee, and this were but a scantling of thy due." The King thanked him with heartiest thanks and the Merman and Merwomen abode with him forty days' space, at the end of which Salih arose and kissed the ground before his brother-in-law, who asked "What wantest thou, O Salih?" He answered, "O King of the Age, indeed thou hast done us overabundant favours, and we crave of thy bounties that thou deal charitably with us and grant us permission to depart; for we yearn after our people and country and kinsfolk and our homes; so will we never forsake thy service nor that of my sister and my nephew; and by Allah, O King of the Age, 'tis not pleasant to my heart to part from thee; but how shall we do, seeing that we have been reared in the sea and that the sojourn of the shore liketh us not?" When the King heard these words he rose to his feet and farewelled Salih the Sea-born and his mother and his cousins, and all wept together, because of parting and presently they said to him, "Anon we will be with thee again, nor will we forsake thee, but will visit thee every few days." Then they flew off and descending into the sea, disappeared from sight.——And Shahrazad perceived the dawn of day and ceased saying her permitted say.

When it was the Seven Hundred and Forty-third Night,

She continued, It hath reached me, O auspicious King, that the relations of Julnar the Sea-born farewelled the King and her, weeping together because of parting; then they flew off and descending into the depths disappeared from sight. After this King Shahriman showed the more kindness to Julnar and honoured her with increase of honour; and the little one grew up and flourished, whilst his maternal uncle and grandam and cousins visited the King every few days and abode with him a month or two months at a time. The boy ceased not to increase in beauty and loveliness with increase of years, till he attained the age of fifteen and was unique in his perfection and symmetry. He learnt writing and Koran-reading; history, syntax and lexicography; archery, spearplay and horsemanship and what not else behoveth the sons of Kings; nor was there one of the children of the folk of the city, men or women, but would talk of the youth's charms, for he was of surpassing beauty and perfection, even such an one as is praised in the saying of the poet,[1]

"The whiskers write upon his cheek, with ambergris on pearl, * Two lines, as
    'twere with jet upon an apple, line for line.
Death harbours in his languid eye and slays with every glance, * And in his
    cheek is drunkenness, and not in any wine."

And in that of another,

"Upsprings from table of his lovely cheek[2] * A growth like broidery my
    wonder is:
As 'twere a lamp that burns through night hung up * Beneath the gloom[3]
    in chains of ambergris."

And indeed the King loved him with exceeding love, and summoning his Wazir and Emirs and the Chief Officers of state and Grandees of his realm, required of them a binding oath that they would make Badr Basim King over them after his sire; and they sware the oath gladly, for the sovran was liberal to the lieges, pleasant in parley and a very compend of goodness, saying naught but that wherein was advantage for the people. On the morrow Shahriman mounted, with all his troops and Emirs and Lords, and went forth into the city and returned. When they drew near the palace, the King dismounted, to wait upon his son who abode on horseback, and he and all the Emirs and Grandees bore the saddle-cloth of honour before him, each and every of them bearing it in his turn, till they came to the vestibule of the palace, where the Prince alighted and his father and the Emirs embraced him and seated him on the throne of Kingship, whilst they (including his sire) stood before him. Then Badr Basim judged the people, deposing the unjust and promoting the just and continued so doing till near upon noon, when he descended from the throne and went in to his mother, Julnar the Sea-born, with the crown upon his head, as he were the moon. When she saw him, with the King standing before him, she rose and kissing him, gave him joy of the Sultanate and wished him and his sire length of life and victory over their foes. He sat with her and rested till the hour of mid-afternoon prayer, when he took horse and repaired,

---

[1] These lines occurred in vol. ii. 301. I quote Mr. Payne.

[2] Arab. "Khadd"=cheek from the eye-orbit to the place where the beard grows; also applied to the side of a rough highland, the side-planks of a litter, etc. etc.

[3] The black hair of youth.

with the Emirs before him, to the Maydán-plain, where he played at
arms with his father and his lords, till night-fall, when he returned
to the palace, preceded by all the folk. He rode forth thus every
day to the tilting-ground, returning to sit and judge the people
and do justice between carl and churl; and thus he continued
doing a whole year, at the end of which he began to ride out
a-hunting and a-chasing and to go round about in the cities and
countries under his rule, proclaiming security and satisfaction and
doing after the fashion of Kings; and he was unique among the
people of his day for glory and valour and just dealing among the
subjects. And it chanced that one day the old King fell sick
and his fluttering heart forebode him of translation to the Mansion
of Eternity. His sickness grew upon him till he was nigh upon
death, when he called his son and commended his mother and
subjects to his care and caused all the Emirs and Grandees
once more swear allegiance to the Prince and assured himself of
them by strongest oaths; after which he lingered a few days and
departed to the mercy of Almighty Allah. His son and widow
and all the Emirs and Wazirs and Lords mourned over him, and
they built him a tomb and buried him therein. They ceased not
ceremonially to mourn for him a whole month, till Salih and his
mother and cousins arrived and condoled with their grieving for
the King and said, "O Julnar, though the King be dead, yet hath
he left this noble and peerless youth, and not dead is whoso
leaveth the like of him, the rending lion and the shining moon."
——And Shahrazad perceived the dawn of day and ceased to say
her permitted say.

When it was the Seven Hundred and Forty-fourth Night,

She pursued, It hath reached me, O auspicious King, that Salih
brother of Julnar and her mother and cousins said to her, "Albeit
the King be dead, yet hath he left behind him as successor this
noble and peerless youth, the rending lion and the shining moon."
Thereupon the Grandees and notables of the Empire went in to
King Badr Basim and said to him, "O King, there is no harm in
mourning for the late sovran: but over-mourning beseemeth none
save women; wherefore occupy thou not thy heart and our hearts
with mourning for thy sire; inasmuch as he hath left thee behind
him, and whoso leaveth the like of thee is not dead." Then they
comforted him and diverted him and lastly carried him to the bath.

When he came out of the Hammam, he donned a rich robe, purfled with gold and embroidered with jewels and jacinths; and,
setting the royal crown on his head, sat down on his throne of
kingship and ordered the affairs of the folk, doing equal justice
between strong and weak, and exacting from the prince the dues
of the pauper; wherefore the people loved him with exceeding
love. Thus he continued doing for a full year, whilst, every now
and then, his kinsfolk of the sea visited him, and his life was
pleasant and his eye was cooled. Now it came to pass that his
uncle Salih went in one night of the nights to Julnar and saluted
her; whereupon she rose and embracing him seated him by her
side and asked him, "O my brother, how art thou and my mother
and my cousins?" He answered, "O my sister, they are well and
glad and in good case, lacking naught save a sight of thy face."
Then she set somewhat of food before him and he ate, after which
talk ensued between the twain and they spake of King Badr Basim
and his beauty and loveliness, his symmetry and skill in cavalarice
and cleverness and good breeding. Now Badr was propped upon
his elbow hard by them; and, hearing his mother and uncle
speak of him, he feigned sleep and listened to their talk.[1]
Presently Salih said to his sister, "Thy son is now seventeen years
old and is unmarried, and I fear lest mishap befal him and he
have no son; wherefore it is my desire to marry him to a Princess
of the princesses of the sea, who shall be a match for him in beauty
and loveliness." Quoth Julnar, "Name them to me for I know
them all." So Salih proceeded to enumerate them to her, one by
one, but to each she said, "I like not this one for my son; I will
not marry him but to one who is his equal in beauty and loveliness
and wit and piety and good breeding and magnanimity and
dominion and rank and lineage."[2] Quoth Salih, "I know none
other of the daughters of the Kings of the sea, for I have
numbered to thee more than an hundred girls and not one of
them pleaseth thee: but see, O my sister, whether thy son be
asleep or no." So she felt Badr and finding on him the signs of
slumber said to Salih, "He is asleep; what hast thou to say and

---

[1] This manner of listening is not held dishonourable amongst Arabs or Easterns generally;
who, however, hear as little good of themselves as Westerns declare in proverb.

[2] Arab. "Hasab wa nasab," before explained as inherited degree and acquired dignity.
See vol. iv. 171.

what is thine object in making sure his sleeping?"   Replied he,
"O my sister, know that I have bethought me of a Mermaid of
the mermaids who befitteth thy son; but I fear to name her, lest
he be awake and his heart be taken with her love and maybe we
shall be unable to win to her; so should he and we and the
Grandees of the realm be wearied in vain and trouble betide us
through this; for, as saith the poet,

'Love, at first sight, is a spurt of spray;[1]   * But a spreading sea when it
      gaineth sway.' "

When she heard these words, she cried, "Tell me the condition of
this girl, and her name for I know all the damsels of the sea,
Kings' daughters and others; and, if I judge her worthy of him, I
will demand her in marriage for him of her father, though I spend
on her whatso my hand possesseth.   So recount to me all anent
her and fear naught, for my son sleepeth."   Quoth Salih, "I fear
lest he be awake; and the poet saith,

'I loved him, soon as his praise I heard; * For ear oft loveth ere eye survey.' "

But Julnar said, "Speak out and be brief and fear not, O my
brother."   So he said, "By Allah, O my sister, none is worthy of
thy son save the Princess Jauharah, daughter of King Al-Samandal,[2] for that she is like unto him in beauty and loveliness and brilliancy and perfection; nor is there found, in sea or on land, a
sweeter or pleasanter of gifts than she; for she is prime in comeliness and seemlihead of face and symmetrical shape of perfect
grace; her cheek is ruddy dight, her brow flower white, her teeth
gem-bright, her eyes blackest black and whitest white, her hips of
heavy weight, her waist slight and her favour exquisite.   When
she turneth she shameth the wild cattle[3] and the gazelles and when
she walketh, she breedeth envy in the willow branch: when she
unveileth her face outshineth sun and moon and all who look upon
her she enslaveth soon: sweet-lipped and soft-sided indeed is she."

---

[1] Arab. "Mujájat"=spittle running from the mouth: hence Lane, "is like running
saliva," which, in poetry is not pretty.

[2] Arab. and Heb. "Salmandra" from Pers. Samandal (—dar—duk—dun, etc.), a Sala-
mander, a mouse which lives in fire, some say a bird in India and China and others confuse
with the chameleon (Bochart Hiero. Part ii. chapt. vi).

[3] Arab. "Mahá" one of the four kinds of wild cows or bovine antelopes, bubalus, Antelope defassa, A. leucoryx, etc.

Now when Julnar heard what Salih said, she replied, "Thou sayest sooth, O my brother! By Allah, I have seen her many and many a time and she was my companion, when we were little ones; but now we have no knowledge of each other, for constraint of distance; nor have I set eyes on her for eighteen years. By Allah, none is worthy of my son but she!" Now Badr heard all they said and mastered what had passed, first and last, of these praises bestowed on Jauharah daughter of King Al-Samandal; so he fell in love with her on hearsay, pretending sleep the while, wherefore fire was kindled in his heart on her account full sore and he was drowned in a sea without bottom or shore.——And Shahrazad perceived the dawn of day and ceased saying her permitted say.

𝔚𝔥𝔢𝔫 𝔦𝔱 𝔴𝔞𝔰 𝔱𝔥𝔢 𝔖𝔢𝔳𝔢𝔫 𝔥𝔲𝔫𝔡𝔯𝔢𝔡 𝔞𝔫𝔡 𝔉𝔬𝔯𝔱𝔶-𝔣𝔦𝔣𝔱𝔥 𝔑𝔦𝔤𝔥𝔱,

She resumed, It hath reached me, O auspicious King, that when King Badr Basim heard the words of his uncle Salih and his mother Julnar, praising the daughter of King Al-Samandal, a flame of fire burnt in his heart full sore and he was drowned in a sea which hath nor bottom nor shore. Then Salih, looking at his sister, exclaimed, "By Allah, O my sister, there is no greater fool among the Kings of the sea than her father nor one more violent of temper than he! So name thou not the girl to thy son, till we demand her in marriage of her father. If he favour us with his assent, we will praise Allah Almighty; and if he refuse us and will not give her to thy son to wife, we will say no more about it and seek another match." Answered Julnar, "Right is thy rede;" and they parleyed no more: but Badr passed the night with a heart on fire with passion for Princess Jauharah. However he concealed his case and spake not of her to his mother or his uncle, albeit he was on coals of fire for love of her. Now when it was morning, the King and his uncle went to the Hammam-bath and washed, after which they came forth and drank wine and the servants set food before them, whereof they and Julnar ate their sufficiency, and washed their hands. Then Salih rose and said to his nephew and sister, "With your leave, I would fain go to my mother and my folk for I have been with you some days and their hearts are troubled with awaiting me." But Badr Basim said to him, "Tarry with us this day;" and he consented. Then quoth the King, "Come, O my uncle, let us go forth to the garden." So they sallied forth and promenaded about the pastures and took their solace awhile, after which King Badr lay down under a shady tree, thinking to rest and sleep; but he remembered his uncle's description of the maiden and her beauty and loveliness and shed railing tears, reciting these two couplets[1],

"Were it said to me while the flame is burning within me, * And the fire blazing in my heart and bowels,
'Wouldst thou rather that thou shouldest behold them * Or a draught of pure water?'—I would answer, 'Them.' "

Then he sighed and wept and lamented, reciting these verses also,

"Who shall save me from love of a lovely gazelle, * Brighter browed than the sunshine, my bonnibel!
My heart, erst free from her love, now burns * With fire for the maid of Al-Samandal."

When Salih heard what his nephew said, he smote hand upon hand and said, "There is no god but *the* God! Mohammed is the Apostle of God and there is no Majesty and there is no Might save in Allah, the Glorious, the Great!" adding, "O my son, heardest thou what passed between me and thy mother respecting Princess Jauharah?" Replied Badr Basim, "Yes, O my uncle, and I fell in love with her by hearsay through what I heard you say. Indeed, my heart cleaveth to her and I cannot live without her." Rejoined his uncle, "O King, let us return to thy mother and tell her how the case standeth and crave her leave that I may take thee with me and seek the Princess in marriage of her sire; after which we will farewell her and I and thou will return. Indeed, I fear to take thee and go without her leave, lest she be wroth with me; and verily the right would be on her side, for I should be the cause of her separation from us. Moreover, the city would be left without king and there would be none to govern the citizens and look to their affairs; so should the realm be disordered against thee and the kingship depart from thy hands." But Badr Basim, hearing these words, cried, "O my uncle, if I return to my mother and consult her on such matter, she will not suffer me to do this; wherefore I will not return to

---

[1] These lines have occurred in vol. iii. 279; so I quote Lane (iii. 274) by way of variety; although I do not like his "bowels."

my mother nor consult her." And he wept before him and presently added, "I will go with thee and tell her not and after will return." When Salih heard what his nephew said, he was confused anent his case and said, "I crave help of the Almighty in any event." Then, seeing that Badr Basim was resolved to go with him, whether his mother would let him or no, he drew from his finger a seal-ring, whereon were graven certain of the names of Allah the Most High, and gave it to him, saying, "Put this on thy finger, and thou shalt be safe from drowning and other perils and from the mischief of sea-beasts and great fishes." So King Badr Basim took the ring and set it on his finger. Then they dove into the deep——And Shahrazad perceived the dawn of day and ceased to say her permitted say.

𝕴𝖍𝖊𝖓 𝖎𝖙 𝖜𝖆𝖘 𝖙𝖍𝖊 𝕾𝖊𝖛𝖊𝖓 𝕳𝖚𝖓𝖉𝖗𝖊𝖉 𝖆𝖓𝖉 𝕱𝖔𝖗𝖙𝖞-𝖘𝖎𝖝𝖙𝖍 𝕹𝖎𝖌𝖍𝖙,

She said, It hath reached me, O auspicious King, that Badr Basim and his uncle, after diving into the deep, fared on till they came to Salih's palace, where they found Badr Basim's grandmother, the mother of his mother, seated with her kinsfolk; and, going in to them, kissed their hands. When the old Queen saw Badr, she rose to him and embracing him, kissed him between the eyes and said to him, "A blessed coming, O my son! How didst thou leave thy mother Julnar?" He replied, "She is well in health and fortune, and saluteth thee and her uncle's daughters." Then Salih related to his mother what had occurred between him and his sister and how King Badr Basim had fallen in love with the Princess Jauharah daughter of Al-Samandal by report and told her the whole tale from beginning to end adding, "He hath not come save to demand her in wedlock of her sire;" which when the old Queen heard, she was wroth against her son with exceeding wrath and sore troubled and concerned and said, "O Salih, O my son, in very sooth thou diddest wrong to name the Princess before thy nephew, knowing, as thou dost, that her father is stupid and violent, little of wit and tyrannical of temper, grudging his daughter to every suitor; for all the Monarchs of the Main have sought her hand, but he rejected them all; nay, he would none of them, saying, 'Ye are no match for her in beauty or in loveliness or in aught else.' Wherefore we fear to demand her in wedlock of him, lest he reject us, even as he hath rejected

others; and we are a folk of high spirit and should return broken-
hearted." Hearing these words Salih answered, "O my mother,
what is to do? For King Badr Basim saith, 'There is no help
but that I seek her in marriage of her sire, though I expend my
whole kingdom'; and he avoucheth that, an he take her not to
wife, he will die of love for her and longing." And Salih continued, "He is handsomer and goodlier than she; his father was
King of all the Persians, whose King he now is, and none is worthy
of Jauharah save Badr Basim. Wherefore I purpose to carry her
father a gift of jacinths and jewels befitting his dignity, and
demand her of him in marriage. An he object to us that he is a
King, behold, our man also is a King and the son of a King; or, if
he object to us her beauty, behold our man is more beautiful
than she; or, again, if he object to us the vastness of his dominion,
behold our man's dominion is vaster than hers and her father's
and numbereth more troops and guards, for that his kingdom is
greater than that of Al-Samandal. Needs must I do my endeavour
to further the desire of my sister's son, though it relieve me of my
life; because I was the cause of whatso hath betided; and, even
as I plunged him into the ocean of her love, so will I go about
to marry him to her, and may Almighty Allah help me thereto!"
Rejoined his mother, "Do as thou wilt, but beware of giving
her father rough words, whenas thou speakest with him; for thou
knowest his stupidity and violence and I fear lest he do thee a
mischief, for he knoweth not respect for any." And Salih
answered, "Hearkening and obedience." Then he sprang up
and taking two bags full of gems such as rubies and bugles of
emerald, noble ores and all manner jewels gave them to his
servants to carry and set out with his nephew for the palace of
Al-Samandal. When they came thither, he sought audience of
the King and being admitted to his presence, kissed ground
before him and saluted him with the goodliest Salam. The
King rose to him and honouring him with the utmost honour,
bade him be seated. So he sat down and presently the King
said to him, "A blessed coming: indeed thou hast desolated us, O
Salih! But what bringeth thee to us? Tell me thine errand
that we may fulfil it to thee." Whereupon Salih arose and,
kissing the ground a second time, said, "O King of the Age, my
errand is to Allah and the magnanimous liege lord and the valiant
lion, the report of whose good qualities the caravans far and near
have dispread and whose renown for benefits and beneficence and

clemency and graciousness and liberality to all climes and countries hath sped." Thereupon he opened the two bags and, displaying their contents before Al-Samandal, said to him, "O King of the Age, haply wilt thou accept my gift and by showing favour to me heal my heart."——And Shahrazad perceived the dawn of day and ceased saying her permitted say.

When it was the Seven Hundred and Forty-seventh Night,

She continued, It hath reached me, O auspicious King, that when Salih offered his gift to the King, saying, "My aim and end is that the Sovran show favour to me and heal my heart by accepting my present," King Al-Samandal asked, "With what object dost thou gift me with this gift? Tell me thy tale and acquaint me with thy requirement. An its accomplishment be in my power I will straightway accomplish it to thee and spare thee toil and trouble; and if I be unable thereunto, Allah compelleth not any soul aught beyond its power."[1] So Salih rose and kissing ground three times, said, "O King of the Age, that which I desire thou art indeed able to do; it is in thy power and thou art master thereof; and I impose not on the King a difficulty, nor am I Jinn-demented, that I should crave of the King a thing whereto he availeth not; for one of the sages saith, 'An thou wouldst be complied with ask that which can be readily supplied'. Wherefore, that of which I am come in quest, the King (whom Allah preserve!) is able to grant." The King replied, "Ask what thou wouldst have, and state thy case and seek thy need." Then said Salih,[2] "O King of the Age, know that I come as a suitor, seeking the unique pearl and the hoarded jewel, the Princess Jauharah, daughter of our lord the King; wherefore, O King disappoint thou not thy suitor." Now when the King heard this, he laughed till he fell backwards, in mockery of him and said, "O Salih, I had thought thee a man of worth and a youth of sense, seeking naught save what was reasonable and speaking not save advisedly. What then hath befallen thy reason and urged thee to this monstrous matter and mighty hazard,

---

[1] The last verse (286) of chapt. ii. The Cow: "compelleth" in the sense of "burdeneth."
[2] Salih's speeches are euphuistic.

that thou seekest in marriage daughters of Kings, lords of cities and climates? Say me, art thou of a rank to aspire to this great eminence and hath thy wit failed thee to this extreme pass that thou affrontest me with this demand?" Replied Salih, "Allah amend the King! I seek her not for myself (albeit, an I did, I am her match and more than her match, for thou knowest that my father was King of the Kings of the sea, for all thou art this day our King), but I seek her for King Badr Basim, lord of the lands of the Persians and son of King Shahriman, whose puissance thou knowest. An thou object that thou art a mighty great King, King Badr is a greater; and if thou object thy daughter's beauty, King Badr is more beautiful than she and fairer of form and more excellent of rank and lineage; and he is the champion of the people of his day. Wherefore, if thou grant my request, O King of the Age thou wilt have set the thing in its stead; but, if thou deal arrogantly with us, thou wilt not use us justly nor travel with us the 'road which is straght'.[1] Moreover, O King, thou knowest that the Princess Jauharah, the daughter of our lord the King, must needs be wedded and bedded, for the sage saith, a girl's lot is either grace of marriage or the grave.[2] Wherefore, an thou mean to marry her, my sister's son is worthier of her than any other man." Now when King Al-Samandal heard Salih's words, he was wroth with exceeding wrath; his reason well nigh fled and his soul was like to depart his body for rage, and he cried, "O dog, shall the like of thee dare to bespeak me thus and name my daughter in the assemblies,[3] saying that the son of thy sister Julnar is a match for her? Who art thou and who is this sister of thine and who is her son and who was his father,[4] that thou durst say to me such say and address me with such address? What are ye all, in comparison with my daughter, but dogs?" And he cried out to his pages, saying, "Take yonder gallows-bird's head!" So they drew their swords and made for Salih, but he fled and for the palace-gate sped; and reaching the entrance, he found of his cousins and kinsfolk and servants, more than a thousand horse armed cap-à-pie in iron and close knitted

---

[1] From the Fátihah.

[2] A truly Eastern saying, which ignores the "old maids" of the West.

[3] *i.e.* naming her before the lieges as if the speaker were her and his superior. It would have been more polite not to have gone beyond "the unique pearl and the hoarded jewel:" the offensive part of the speech was using the girl's name.

[4] Meaning emphatically that one and all were nobodies.

mail-coats, hending in hand spears and naked swords glittering white. And these when they saw Salih come running out of the palace (they having been sent by his mother to his succour), questioned him and he told them what was to do; whereupon they knew that the King was a fool and violent-tempered to boot. So they dismounted and baring their blades, went in to the King Al-Samandal, whom they found seated upon the throne of his Kingship, unaware of their coming and enraged against Salih with furious rage; and they beheld his eunuchs and pages and officers unprepared. When the King saw them enter, drawn brand in hand, he cried out to his people, saying "Woe to you! Take me the heads of these hounds!" But ere an hour had sped Al-Samandal's party were put to the route and relied upon flight, and Salih and his kinsfolk seized upon the King and pinioned him.——And Shahrazad perceived the dawn of day and ceased to say her permitted say.

When it was the Seven Hundred and Forty-eighth Night,

She pursued, It hath reached me, O auspicious King, that when Salih and his kinsfolk pinioned the King, Princess Jauharah awoke and knew that her father was a captive and his guards slain. So she fled forth the palace to a certain island, and climbing up into a high tree, hid herself in its summit. Now when the two parties came to blows, some of King Al-Samandal's pages fled and Badr Basim meeting them, questioned them of their case and they told him what had happened. But when he heard that the King was a prisoner, Badr feared for himself and fled, saying in his heart, "Verily, all this turmoil is on my account and none is wanted but I." So he sought safety in flight, security to sight, knowing not whither he went; but destiny from Eternity fore-ordained drave him to the very island where the Princess had taken refuge, and he came to the very tree whereon she sat and threw himself down, like a dead man, thinking to lie and repose himself and knowing not there is no rest for the pursued, for none knoweth what Fate hideth for him in the future. As he lay down, he raised his eyes to the tree and they met the eyes of the Princess. So he looked at her and seeing her to be like the moon rising in the East, cried, "Glory to Him who fashioned yonder perfect form, Him who is the Creator of all

things and who over all things is Almighty! Glory to the Great
God, the Maker, the Shaper and Fashioner! By Allah, if
my presentiments be true, this is Jauharah, daughter of King
Al-Samandal! Methinks that, when she heard of our coming to
blows with her father, she fled to this island and, happening upon
this tree, hid herself on its head; but, if this be not the Princess
herself, 'tis one yet goodlier than she." Then he bethought himself of her case and said in himself, "I will arise and lay hands
on her and question her of her condition; and, if she be indeed
the she, I will demand her in wedlock of herself and so win my
wish." So he stood up and said to her, "O end of all desire, who
art thou and who brought thee hither?" She looked at Badr
Basim and seeing him to be as the full moon,[1] when it shineth from
under the black cloud, slender of shape and sweet of smile,
answered, "O fair of fashion, I am Princess Jauharah, daughter
of King Al-Samandal, and I took refuge in this place, because
Salih and his host came to blows with my sire and slew his
troops and took him prisoner, with some of his men; wherefore I fled, fearing for my very life," presently adding, "And I
weet not what fortune hath done with my father." When King
Badr Basim heard these words he marvelled with exceeding
marvel at this strange chance, and thought: "Doubtless I have
won my wish by the capture of her sire." Then he looked at
Jauharah and said to her, "Come down, O my lady; for I am
slain for love of thee and thine eyes have captivated me. On
my account and thine are all these broils and battles; for thou
must know that I am King Badr Basim, Lord of the Persians
and Salih is my mother's brother and he it is who came to thy
sire to demand thee of him in marriage. As for me, I have
quitted my kingdom for thy sake, and our meeting here is the
rarest coincidence. So come down to me and let us twain fare
for thy father's palace, that I may beseech uncle Salih to release
him and I may make thee my lawful wife." When Jauharah heard
his words, she said in herself, " 'Twas on this miserable gallows
bird's account, then, that all this hath befallen and that my father
hath fallen prisoner and his chamberlains and suite have been
slain and I have been departed from my palace, a miserable exile
and have fled for refuge to this island. But, an I devise not
against him some device to defend myself from him, he will

---

[1] Arab. Badr, the usual pun.

possess himself of me and take his will of me; for he is in
love and for aught that he doeth a lover is not blamed." Then
she beguiled him with winning words and soft speeches, whilst
he knew not the perfidy against him she purposed, and asked
him, "O my lord and light of my eyes, say me, art thou indeed
King Badr Basim, son of Queen Julnar?" And he answered,
"Yes, O my lady."——And Shahrazad perceived the dawn of day
and ceased saying her permitted say.

When it was the Seben Hundred and Forty-ninth Night,

She resumed, It hath reached me, O auspicious King, that Jauharah,
daughter of King Al-Samandal, asked the youth, "Art thou in
very sooth King Badr Basim, son of Queen Julnar?" And he
answered, "Yes, O my lady!" Then she, "May Allah cut off my
father and gar his kingdom cease from him and heal not his heart
neither avert from him strangerhood, if he could desire a comelier
than thou or aught goodlier than these fair qualities of thine! By
Allah, he is of little wit and judgment!" presently adding, "But,
O King of the Age, punish him not for that he hath done; more
by token that an thou love me a span, verily I love thee a cubit.
Indeed, I have fallen into the net of thy love and am become of
the number of thy slain. The love that was with thee hath transferred itself to me and there is left thereof with thee but a tithe of
that which is with me." So saying, she came down from the tree
and drawing near him strained him to her bosom and fell to kissing
him; whereat passion and desire for her redoubled on him and
doubting not but she loved him, he trusted in her, and returned
her kisses and caresses. Presently he said to her, "By Allah, O
Princess, my uncle Salih set forth to me not a fortieth part of thy
charms; no, nor a quarter-carat[1] of the four-and-twenty." Then
Jauharah pressed him to her bosom and pronounced some unintelligible words; then spat on his face, saying, "Quit this form of
man and take shape of bird, the handsomest of birds, white of
robe, with red bill and legs." Hardly had she spoken, when

---

[1] Arab. "Kirát" (κεράτιον) the bean of the *Abrus precatorius*, used as a weight in Arabia
and India and as a bead for decoration in Africa. It is equal to four Kamhahs or wheat-
grains and about 3 grs. avoir.; and being the twenty-fourth of a miskal, it is applied to that
proportion of everything. Thus the Arabs say of a perfect man, "He is of four-and-twenty
Kirát" *i.e.* pure gold. See vol. iii. 239.

King Badr Basim found himself transformed into a bird, the hand-somest of birds, who shook himself and stood looking at her. Now Jauharah had with her one of her slave-girls, by name Mar-sínah;[1] so she called her and said to her, "By Allah, but that I fear for the life of my father, who is his uncle's prisoner, I would kill him! Allah never requite him with good! How unlucky was his coming to us; for all this trouble is due to his hard-headed-ness! But do thou, O slave-girl, bear him to the Thirsty Island and leave him there to die of thirst." So Marsinah carried him to the island in question and would have returned and left him there; but she said in herself, "By Allah, the lord of such beauty and loveliness deserveth not to die of thirst!" So she went forth from that island and brought him to another abounding in trees and fruits and rills and, setting him down there, returned to her mistress and told her, "I have left him on the Thirsty Island." Such was the case with Badr Basim; but as regards King Salih, he sought for Jauharah after capturing the King and killing his folk; but, finding her not, returned to his palace and said to his mother, "Where is my sister's son, King Badr Basim?" "By Allah, O my son," replied she, "I know nothing of him! For when it reached him that you and King Al-Samandal had come to blows and that strife and slaughter had betided between you, he was affrighted and fled." When Salih heard this, he grieved for his nephew and said, "O my mother, by Allah, we have dealt negli-gently by King Badr and I fear lest he perish or lest one of King Al-Samandal's soldiers or his daughter Jauharah fall in with him. So should we come to shame with his mother and no good betide us from her, for that I took him without her leave." Then he despatched guards and scouts throughout the sea and elsewhere to seek for Badr; but they could learn no tidings of him; so they returned and told King Salih, wherefore cark and care redoubled on him and his breast was straitened for King Badr Basim. So far concerning nephew and uncle, but as for Julnar the Sea-born, after their departure she abode in expectation of them, but her son returned not and she heard no report of him. So when many days of fruitless waiting had gone by, she arose and going down into the sea, repaired to her mother, who sighting her rose to her and kissed her and embraced her, as did the Mermaids her cousins.

---

[1] The (she) myrtle: Kazimirski (A. de Biberstein) Dictionnaire Arabe-Francais (Paris Maisonneuve 1867) gives Marsín = Rose de Jericho: myrte.

Then she questioned her mother of King Badr Basim, and she answered, saying, "O my daughter, of a truth he came hither with his uncle, who took jacinths and jewels and carrying them to King Al-Samandal, demanded his daughter in marriage for thy son; but he consented not and was violent against thy brother in words. Now I had sent Salih nigh upon a thousand horse and a battle befel between him and King Al-Samandal; but Allah aided thy brother against him, and he slew his guards and troops and took himself prisoner. Meanwhile, tidings of this reached thy son, and it would seem as if he feared for himself; wherefore he fled forth from us, without our will, and returned not to us, nor have we heard any news of him." Then Julnar enquired for King Salih, and his mother said, "He is seated on the throne of his kingship, in the stead of King Al-Samandal, and hath sent in all directions to seek thy son and Princess Jauharah." When Julnar heard the maternal words, she mourned for her son with sad mourning and was highly incensed against her brother Salih for that he had taken him and gone down with him into the sea without her leave; and she said, "O my mother, I fear for our realm; as I came to thee without letting any know; and I dread tarrying with thee, lest the state fall into disorder and the kingdom pass from our hands. Wherefore I deem best to return and govern the reign till it please Allah to order our son's affair for us. But look ye forget him not neither neglect his case; for should he come to any harm, it would infallibly kill me, since I see not the world save in him and delight but in his life." She replied, "With love and gladness, O my daughter. Ask not what we suffer by reason of his loss and absence." Then she sent to seek for her grandson, whilst Julnar returned to her kingdom, weeping-eyed and heavy-hearted, and indeed the gladness of the world was straitened upon her.——And Shahrazad perceived the dawn of day and ceased to say her permitted say.

When it was the Seven Hundred and Fiftieth Night,

She said, It hath reached me, O auspicious King, that when Queen Julnar returned from her mother to her own realm, her breast was straitened and she was in ill-case. So fared it with her; but as regards King Badr Basim, after Princess Jauharah had ensorcelled him and had sent him with her handmaid to the Thirsty Island, saying, "Leave him there to die of thirst," and Marsinah had set him down in a green islet, he abode days and nights in the semblance of a bird eating of its fruits and drinking of its waters and knowing not whither to go nor how to fly; till, one day, there came a certain fowler to the island to catch somewhat wherewithal to get his living. He espied King Badr Basim in his form of a white-robed bird, with red bill and legs, captivating the sight and bewildering the thought; and, looking thereat, said in himself, "Verily, yonder is a beautiful bird: never saw I its like in fairness or form." So he cast his net over Badr and taking him, carried him to the town, mentally resolved to sell him for a high price. On his way one of the townsfolk accosted him and said, "For how much this fowl, O fowler?" Quoth the fowler, "What wilt thou do with him an thou buy him?" Answered the other, "I will cut his throat and eat him;" whereupon said the birder, "Who could have the heart to kill this bird and eat him? Verily, I mean to present him to our King, who will give me more than thou wouldest give me and will not kill him, but will divert himself by gazing upon his beauty and grace, for in all my life, since I have been a fowler, I never saw his like among land game or water fowl. The utmost thou wouldst give me for him, however much thou covet him, would be a dirham, and, by Allah Almighty, I will not sell him!" Then he carried the bird up to the King's palace and when the King saw it, its beauty and grace pleased him and the red colour of its beak and legs. So he sent an eunuch to buy it, who accosted the fowler and said to him, "Wilt thou sell this bird?" Answered he, "Nay, 'tis a gift from me to the King."[1] So the eunuch carried the bird to the King and told him what the man had said; and he took it and gave the fowler ten dinars, whereupon he kissed ground and fared forth. Then the eunuch carried the bird to the palace and placing him in a fine cage, hung him up after setting meat and drink by him. When the King came down from the Divan, he said to the eunuch, "Where is the bird? Bring it to me, that I may look upon it; for, by Allah, 'tis beautiful!" So the eunuch brought the cage and set it between the hands of the King, who looked and seeing the food untouched, said, "By Allah, I wis not what it will eat, that I may nourish it!"

---

[1] Needless to note that the fowler had a right to expect a return present worth double or treble the price of his gift. Such is the universal practice of the East: in the West the extortioner says, "I leave it to you, sir!"

Then he called for food and they laid the tables and the King ate. Now when the bird saw the flesh and meats and fruits and sweet-meats, he ate of all that was upon the trays before the King, whereat the Sovran and all the bystanders marvelled and the King said to his attendants, eunuchs and Mamelukes, "In all my life I never saw a bird eat as doth this bird!"   Then he sent an eunuch to fetch his wife that she might enjoy looking upon the bird, and he went in to summon her and said, "O my lady, the King desireth thy presence, that thou mayst divert thyself with the sight of a bird he hath bought.   When we set on the food, it flew down from its cage and perching on the table, ate of all that was thereon.   So arise, O my lady, and solace thee with the sight for it is goodly of aspect and is a wonder of the wonders of the age."   Hearing these words she came in haste; but, when she noted the bird, she veiled her face and turned to fare away.   The King rose up and looking at her, asked, "Why dost thou veil thy face when there is none in presence save the women and eunuchs who wait on thee and thy husband?"   Answered she, "O King, this bird is no bird, but a man like thyself."   He rejoined, "Thou liest, this is too much of a jest.   How should he be other than a bird?"; and she "O King, by Allah, I do not jest with thee nor do I tell thee aught but the truth; for verily this bird is King Badr Basim, son of King Shahriman, Lord of the land of the Persians, and his mother is Julnar the Sea-born."———And Shahrazad perceived the dawn of day and ceased saying her permitted say.

When it was the Seven Hundred and Fifty-first Night,

She continued, It hath reached me, O auspicious King, that when the King's wife said to the King, "Verily, this is no bird but a man like thyself: he is King Badr Basim son of King Shariman and his mother is Julnar the Sea-born," quoth the King, "And how came he in this shape?"; and quoth she, "Princess Jauharah, daughter of King Al-Samandal, hath enchanted him:" and told him all that had passed with King Badr Basim from first to last.[1] The King marvelled exceedingly at his wife's words and conjured her, on his life, to free Badr from his enchantment (for she was the notablest enchantress of her age), and not leave him in torment,

---

[1] And she does tell him all that the reader well knows.

saying, "May Almighty Allah cut off Jauharah's hand, for a foul witch as she is! How little is her faith and how great her craft and perfidy!" Said the Queen, "Do thou say to him, 'O Badr Basim, enter yonder closet!' " So the King bade him enter the closet and he went in obediently. Then the Queen veiled her face and taking in her hand a cup of water,[1] entered the closet where she pronounced over the water certain incomprehensible words ending with, "By the virtue of these mighty names and holy verses and by the majesty of Allah Almighty, Creator of heaven and earth, the Quickener of the dead and Appointer of the means of daily bread and the terms determined, quit this thy form wherein thou art and return to the shape in which the Lord created thee!" Hardly had she made an end of her words, when the bird trembled once and became a man; and the King saw before him a handsome youth, than whom on earth's face was none goodlier. But when King Badr Basim found himself thus restored to his own form he cried, "There is no god but *the* God and Mohammed is the Apostle of God! Glory be to the Creator of all creatures and Provider of their provision, and Ordainer of their life-terms preordained!" Then he kissed the King's hand and wished him long life, and the King kissed his head and said to him, "O Badr Basim, tell me thy history from commencement to conclusion." So he told him his whole tale, concealing naught; and the King marvelled thereat and said to him, "O Badr Basim, Allah hath saved thee from the spell: but what hath thy judgment decided and what thinkest thou to do?" Replied he, "O King of the Age, I desire thy bounty that thou equip me a ship with a company of thy servants and all that is needful; for 'tis long since I have been absent and I dread lest the kingdom depart from me. And I misdoubt me my mother is dead of grief for my loss; and this doubt is the stronger for that she knoweth not what is come of me nor whether I am alive or dead. Wherefore, I beseech thee, O King, to crown thy favours to me by granting me what I seek." The King, after beholding the beauty and grace of Badr Basim and listening to his sweet speech, said, "I hear and obey." So he fitted him out a ship, to which he transported all that was needful

---

[1] This was for sprinkling him, but the texts omit that operation. Arabic has distinct terms for various forms of metamorphosis. "Naskh" is change from a lower to a higher, as beast to man; "Maskh" (the common expression) is the reverse; "Raskh" is from animate to inanimate (man to stone) and "Faskh" is absolute wasting away to corruption.

and which he manned with a company of his servants; and Badr Basim set sail in it, after having taken leave of the King. They sailed over the sea ten successive days with a favouring wind; but, on the eleventh day, the ocean became troubled with exceeding trouble, the ship rose and fell and the sailors were powerless to govern her. So they drifted at the mercy of the waves, till the craft neared a rock in mid-sea which fell upon her[1] and broke her up and all on board were drowned, save King Badr Basim who got astride one of the planks of the vessel, after having been nigh upon destruction. The plank ceased not to be borne by the set of the sea, whilst he knew not whither he went and had no means of directing its motion, as the wind and waves wrought for three whole days. But on the fourth the plank grounded with him on the sea-shore where he sighted a white city, as it were a dove passing white, builded upon a tongue of land that jutted out into the deep and it was goodly of ordinance, with high towers and lofty walls against which the waves beat. When Badr Basim saw this, he rejoiced with exceeding joy, for he was well-nigh dead of hunger and thirst, and dismounting from the plank, would have gone up the beach to the city; but there came down to him mules and asses and horses, in number as the sea-sands and fell to striking at him and staying him from landing. So he swam round to the back of the city, where he waded to shore and entering the place, found none therein and marvelled at this, saying, "Would I knew to whom doth this city belong, wherein is no lord nor any liege, and whence came these mules and asses and horses that hindered me from landing." And he mused over his case. Then he walked on at hazard till he espied an old man, a grocer.[2] So he saluted him and the other returned his salam and seeing him to be a handsome young man, said to him, "O youth, whence comest thou and what brought thee to this city?" Badr told him his story; at which the old man marvelled and said, "O my son, didst thou see any on thy way?" He replied, "Indeed, O my father, I wondered in good sooth to sight a city void of folk." Quoth the

---

[1] I render this improbable detail literally: it can only mean that the ship was dashed against a rock.

[2] Who was probably squatting on his shop-counter. The "Bakkál" (who must not be confounded with the *épicier*), lit. "vender of herbs" = greengrocer, and according to Richardson used incorrectly for Baddál (?) vendor of provisions. Popularly it is applied to a seller of oil, honey, butter and fruit, like the Ital. "Pizzicagnolo" = Salsamentarius, and in North-West Africa to an inn-keeper.

Shaykh, "O my son, come up into the shop, lest thou perish." So
Badr Basim went up into the shop and sat down; whereupon the
old man set before him somewhat of food, saying, "O my son,
enter the inner shop; glory be to Him who hath preserved thee
from yonder she-Sathanas!" King Badr Basim was sore affrighted
at the grocer's words; but he ate his fill and washed his hands;
then glanced at his host and said to him, "O my lord, what is the
meaning of these words? Verily thou hast made me fearful of
this city and its folk." Replied the old man, "Know, O my son,
that this is the City of the Magicians and its Queen is as she were
a she-Satan, a sorceress and a mighty enchantress, passing crafty
and perfidious exceedingly. All thou sawest of horses and mules
and asses were once sons of Adam like thee and me; they were
also strangers, for whoever entereth this city, being a young man
like thyself, this miscreant witch taketh him and hometh him for
forty days, after which she enchanteth him, and he becometh a
mule or a horse or an ass, of those animals thou sawest on the
sea-shore."——And Shahrazad perceived the dawn of day and
ceased to say her permitted say.

When it was the Seven Hundred and Fifty-second Night,

She pursued, It hath reached me, O auspicious King, that the old
grocer related to King Badr Basim the history of the enchantress
ending with, "All these people hath she spelled; and, when it was
thy intent to land they feared lest thou be transmewed like themselves; so they counselled thee by signs that said, 'Land not,' of
their solicitude for thee, fearing that haply she should do with thee
like as she had done with them. She possessed herself of this city
and seized it from its citizens by sorcery and her name is Queen
Láb, which being interpreted, meaneth in Arabic 'Almanac of the
Sun.' "[1] When Badr Basim heard what the old man said, he was
affrighted with sore affright and trembled like reed in wind saying
in himself, "Hardly do I feel me free from the affliction wherein I
was by reason of sorcery, when Destiny casteth me into yet sorrier

---

[1] Here the Shaykh is mistaken: he should have said, "The Sun in old Persian." "Almanac" simply makes nonsense of the Arabian Circe's name. In Arab. it is "Takwím,"
whence the Span. and Port. "Tacuino:" in Heb. Hakamathá-Takunah=sapientia dis-
positionis astrorum (Asiat. Research. iii. 120).

case!" And he fell a-musing over his condition and that which
had betided him. When the Shaykh looked at him and saw the
violence of his terror, he said to him, "O my son, come, sit at the
threshold of the shop and look upon yonder creatures and upon
their dress and complexion and that wherein they are by reason
of gramarye and dread not; for the Queen and all in the city love
and tender me and will not vex my heart or trouble my mind."
So King Badr Basim came out and sat at the shop-door, looking
out upon the folk; and there passed by him a world of creatures
without number. But when the people saw him, they accosted the
grocer and said to him, "O elder, is this thy captive and thy prey
gotten in these days?" The old man replied, "He is my brother's
son, I heard that his father was dead; so I sent for him and
brought him here that I might quench with him the fire of my
home-sickness." Quoth they, "Verily, he is a comely youth; but
we fear for him from Queen Lab, lest she turn on thee with
treachery and take him from thee, for she loveth handsome young
men." Quoth the Shaykh, "The Queen will not gainsay my
commandment, for she loveth and tendereth me; and when she
shall know that he is my brother's son, she will not molest him or
afflict me in him neither trouble my heart on his account." Then
King Badr Basim abode some months with the grocer, eating and
drinking, and the old man loved him with exceeding love. One
day, as he sat in the shop according to his custom, behold, there
came up a thousand eunuchs, with drawn swords and clad in
various kinds of raiment and girt with jewelled girdles: all rode
Arabian steeds and bore in baldrick Indian blades. They saluted
the grocer, as they passed his shop and were followed by a thousand damsels like moons, clad in various raiments of silks and satins
fringed with gold and embroidered with jewels of sorts, and spears
were slung to their shoulders. In their midst rode a damsel
mounted on a Rabite mare, saddled with a saddle of gold set
with various kinds of jewels and jacinths; and they reached in a
body the Shaykh's shop. The damsels saluted him and passed
on, till, lo and behold! up came Queen Lab, in great state, and
seeing King Badr Basim sitting in the shop, as he were the moon
at its full, was amazed at his beauty and loveliness and became
passionately enamoured of him, and distraught with desire of him.
So she alighted and sitting down by King Badr Basim said to the
old man, "Whence hadst thou this handsome one?"; and the
Shaykh replied, "He is my brother's son, and is lately come to

me." Quoth Lab, "Let him be with me this night, that I may
talk with him;" and quoth the old man, "Wilt thou take him
from me and not enchant him?" Said she, "Yes," and said he,
"Swear to me." So she sware to him that she would not do him
any hurt or ensorcell him, and bidding bring him a fine horse,
saddled and bridled with a golden bridle and decked with trappings
all of gold set with jewels, gave the old man a thousand dinars,
saying, "Use this."[1] Then she took Badr Basim and carried him
off, as he were the full moon on its fourteenth night, whilst all
the folk, seeing his beauty, were grieved for him and said, "By
Allah, verily, this youth deserveth not to be bewitched by yonder
sorceress, the accursed!" Now King Badr Basim heard all they
said, but was silent, committing his case to Allah Almighty, till
they came to——And Shahrazad perceived the dawn of day and
ceased saying her permitted say.

When it was the Seven Hundred and Fifty-third Night,

She resumed, It hath reached me, O auspicious King, that King
Badr Basim ceased not faring with Queen Lab and her suite till
they came to her palace-gate, where the Emirs and eunuchs and
Lords of the realm took foot and she bade the Chamberlains
dismiss her Officers and Grandees, who kissed ground and went
away, whilst she entered the palace with Badr Basim and her
eunuchs and women. Here he found a place, whose like he had
never seen at all, for it was builded of gold and in its midst was a
great basin brimfull of water midmost a vast flower-garden. He
looked at the garden and saw it abounding in birds of various
kinds and colours, warbling in all manner tongues and voices,
pleasurable and plaintive. And everywhere he beheld great state
and dominion and said, "Glory be to God, who of His bounty and
long-suffering provideth those who serve other than Himself!"
The Queen sat down at a latticed window overlooking the garden
on a couch of ivory, whereon was a high bed, and King Badr
Basim seated himself by her side. She kissed him and pressing
him to her breast, bade her women bring a tray of food. So they
brought a tray of red gold, inlaid with pearls and jewels and
spread with all manner of viands and he and she ate, till they

---

[1] *i.e.* for thy daily expenses.

were satisfied, and washed their hands; after which the waiting-
women set on flagons of gold and silver and glass, together with
all kinds of flowers and dishes of dried fruits. Then the Queen
summoned the singing-women and there came ten maidens, as
they were moons, hending all manner of musical instruments.
Queen Lab crowned a cup and drinking it off, filled another and
passed it to King Badr Basim, who took and drank; and they
ceased not to drink till they had their sufficiency. Then she bade
the damsels sing, and they sang all manner modes till it seemed
to Badr Basim as if the palace danced with him for joy. His
sense was ecstasied and his breast broadened, and he forgot his
strangerhood and said in himself, "Verily, this Queen is young
and beautiful[1] and I will never leave her; for her kingdom is
vaster than my kingdom and she is fairer than Princess Jauharah."
So he ceased not to drink with her till even-tide came, when they
lighted the lamps and waxen candles and diffused censer-
perfumes; nor did they leave drinking, till they were both
drunken, and the singing-women sang the while. Then Queen
Lab, being in liquor, rose from her seat and lay down on a bed
and dismissing her women called to Badr Basim to come and
sleep by her side. So he lay with her, in all delight of life till
the morning.——And Shahrazad perceived the dawn of day and
ceased to say her permitted say.

When it was the Seven Hundred and Fifty-fourth Night,

She said, It hath reached me, O auspicious King, that when the
Queen awoke she repaired to the Hammam-bath in the palace,
King Badr Basim being with her, and they bathed and were
purified; after which she clad him in the finest of raiment and
called for the service of wine. So the waiting women brought
the drinking-gear and they drank. Presently, the Queen arose
and taking Badr Basim by the hand, sat down with him on chairs
and bade bring food, whereof they ate, and washed their hands.
Then the damsels fetched the drinking-gear and fruits and flowers

---

[1] *Un adolescent aime toutes les femmes.* Man is by nature polygamic whereas woman as
a rule is monogamic and polyandrous only when tired of her lover. For the man, as has
been truly said, loves the woman, but the love of the woman is for the love of the man.

and confections, and they ceased not to eat and drink,[1] whilst the
singing-girls sang various airs till the evening. They gave not
over eating and drinking and merry-making for a space of forty
days, when the Queen said to him, "O Badr Basim, say me
whether is the more pleasant, this place or the shop of thine uncle
the grocer?" He replied, "By Allah, O Queen, this is the pleasanter, for my uncle is but a beggarly man, who vendeth pot-herbs."
She laughed at his words and the twain lay together in the
pleasantest of case till the morning, when King Badr Basim
awoke from sleep and found not Queen Lab by his side, so he
said, "Would Heaven I knew where can she have gone!" And
indeed he was troubled at her absence and perplexed about the
case, for she stayed away from him a great while and did not
return; so he donned his dress and went seeking her but not
finding her, and he said to himself, "Haply, she is gone to the
flower-garden." Thereupon he went out into the garden and
came to a running rill beside which he saw a white she-bird and
on the stream-bank a tree full of birds of various colours, and he
stood and watched the birds without their seeing him. And
behold, a black bird flew down upon that white she-bird and fell
to billing her pigeon-fashion, then he leapt on her and trod her
three consecutive times, after which the bird changed and became
a woman. Badr looked at her and lo! it was Queen Lab. So he
knew that the black bird was a man transmewed and that she was
enamoured of him and had transformed herself into a bird, that he
might enjoy her; wherefore jealousy got hold upon him and he
was wroth with the Queen because of the black bird. Then he
returned to his place and lay down on the carpet-bed and after an
hour or so she came back to him and fell to kissing him and
jesting with him; but being sore incensed against her he answered
her not a word. She saw what was to do with him and was
assured that he had witnessed what befel her when she was a
white bird and was trodden by the black bird; yet she discovered
naught to him but concealed what ailed her. When he had done
her need, he said to her, "O Queen, I would have thee give me
leave to go to my uncle's shop, for I long after him and have not

---

[1] I have already noted that the heroes and heroines of Eastern love-tales are always
bonnes fourchettes: they eat and drink hard enough to scandalise the sentimental amourist
of the West; but it is understood that this abundant diet is necessary to qualify them for
the Herculean labours of the love night.

seen him these forty days." She replied, "Go to him but tarry
not from me, for I cannot brook to be parted from thee, nor can I
endure without thee an hour." He said, "I hear and I obey,"
and mounting, rode to the shop of the Shaykh, the grocer, who
welcomed him and rose to him and embracing him said to him,
"How hast thou fared with yonder idolatress?" He replied, "I
was well in health and happiness till this last night," and told him
what had passed in the garden with the black bird.[1] Now when
the old man heard his words, he said, "Beware of her, for know
that the birds upon the tree were all young men and strangers,
whom she loved and enchanted and turned into birds. That
black bird thou sawest was one of her Mamelukes whom she loved
with exceeding love, till he cast his eyes upon one of her women,
wherefore she changed him into a black bird";——And Shahrazad
perceived the dawn of day and ceased saying her permitted say.

When it was the Seven Hundred and Fifty-fifth Night,

She continued, It hath reached me, O auspicious King, that when
Badr Basim acquainted the old grocer with all the doings of
Queen Lab and what he had seen of her proceedings, the Shaykh
gave him to know that all the birds upon the tree were young
men and strangers whom she had enchanted, and that the black
bird was one of her Mamelukes whom she had transmewed.
"And," continued the Shaykh, "whenas she lusteth after him she
transformeth herself into a she-bird that he may enjoy her, for she
still loveth him with passionate love. When she found that thou
knewest of her case, she plotted evil against thee, for she loveth
thee not wholly. But no harm shall betide thee from her, so long
as I protect thee; therefore fear nothing; for I am a Moslem, by
name Abdallah, and there is none in my day more magical than
I; yet do I not make use of gramarye save upon constraint.
Many a time have I put to naught the sorceries of yonder
accursed and delivered folk from her, and I care not for her,
because she can do me no hurt: nay, she feareth me with exceeding fear, as do all in the city who, like her, are magicians and
serve the fire, not the Omnipotent Sire. So to-morrow, come

---

[1] Here again a little excision is necessary; the reader already knows all about it.

thou to me and tell me what she doth with thee; for this very
night she will cast about to destroy thee, and I will tell thee how
thou shalt do with her, that thou mayst save thyself from her
malice." Then King Badr Basim farewelled the Shaykh and
returned to the Queen whom he found awaiting him. When she
saw him, she rose and seating him and welcoming him brought
him meat and drink and the two ate till they had enough and
washed their hands; after which she called for wine and they
drank till the night was well nigh half spent, when she plied him
with cup after cup till he was drunken and lost sense[1] and wit.
When she saw him thus, she said to him, "I conjure thee by
Allah and by whatso thou worshippest, if I ask thee a question
wilt thou inform me rightly and answer me truly?" And he being
drunken, answered, "Yes, O my lady." Quoth she, "O my lord
and light of mine eyes, when thou awokest last night and foundest
me not, thou soughtest me, till thou sawest me in the garden,
under the guise of a white she-bird, and also thou sawest the
black bird leap on me and tread me. Now I will tell the truth of
this matter. That black bird was one of my Mamelukes, whom I
loved with exceeding love; but one day he cast his eyes upon a
certain of my slave-girls, wherefore jealousy gat hold upon me
and I transformed him by my spells into a black bird and her I
slew. But now I cannot endure without him a single hour; so,
whenever I lust after him, I change myself into a she-bird and go
to him, that he may leap me and enjoy me, even as thou hast seen.
Art thou not therefore incensed against me, because of this, albeit,
by the virtue of Fire and Light, Shade and Heat, I love thee
more than ever and have made thee my portion of the world?"
He answered (being drunken), "Thy conjecture of the cause of
my rage is correct, and it had no reason other than this." With this
she embraced him and kissed him and made great show of love to
him; then she lay down to sleep and he by her side. Presently,
about midnight she rose from the carpet-bed and King Badr Basim
was awake; but he feigned sleep and watched stealthily to see
what she would do. She took out of a red bag a something red,
which she planted a-middlemost the chamber, and it became a
stream, running like the sea; after which she took a handful of
barley and strewing it on the ground, watered it with water from

---

[1] Arab. "Hiss," prop. speaking a perception (as of sound or motion) as opposed to
"Hadas," a surmise or opinion without proof.

the river; whereupon it became wheat in the ear, and she gathered it and ground it into flour. Then she set it aside and returning to bed, lay down by Badr Basim till morning when he arose and washed his face and asked her leave to visit the Shaykh his uncle. She gave him permission and he repaired to Abdallah and told him what had passed. The old man laughed and said, "By Allah, this miscreant witch plotteth mischief against thee; but reck thou not of her ever!" Then he gave him a pound of parched corn[1] and said to him, "Take this with thee and know that, when she seeth it, she will ask thee, 'What is this and what wilt thou do with it?' Do thou answer, 'Abundance of good things is good'; and eat of it. Then will she bring forth to thee parched grain of her own and say to thee, 'Eat of this Sawík'; and do thou feign to her that thou eatest thereof, but eat of this instead, and beware and have a care lest thou eat of hers even a grain; for, an thou eat so much as a grain thereof, her spells will have power over thee and she will enchant thee and say to thee, 'Leave this form of a man.' Whereupon thou wilt quit thine own shape for what shape she will. But, an thou eat not thereof, her enchantments will be null and void and no harm will betide thee therefrom; whereat she will be shamed with shame exceeding and say to thee, 'I did but jest with thee!' Then will she make a show of love and fondness to thee; but this will all be but hypocrisy in her and craft. And do thou also make a show of love to her and say to her, 'O my lady and light of mine eyes, eat of this parched barley and see how delicious it is.' And if she eat thereof, though it be but a grain, take water in thy hand and throw it in her face, saying, 'Quit this human form' (for what form soever thou wilt have her take). Then leave her and come to me and I will counsel thee what to do." So Badr Basim took leave of him and returning to the palace, went in to the Queen, who said to him, "Welcome and well come and good cheer to thee!" And she rose and kissed him, saying, "Thou hast tarried long from me, O my lord." He replied, "I have been with my uncle, and he gave me to eat of this Sawík." Quoth she, "We have better than that." Then she

---

[1] Arab. "Sawík," the old and modern name for native frumenty, green grain (mostly barley) toasted, pounded, mixed with dates or sugar and eaten on journeys when cooking is impracticable. M. C. de Perceval (iii. 54), gives it a different and now unknown name; and Mr. Lane also applies it to "ptisane." It named the "Day of Sawaykah" (for which see Pilgrimage ii. 19), called by our popular authors the "War of the Meal-sacks."

laid his parched Sawik in one plate and hers in another and said
to him, "Eat of this, for 'tis better than thine." So he feigned to
eat of it and when she thought he had done so, she took water in
her hand and sprinkled him therewith, saying, "Quit this form, O
thou gallows-bird, thou miserable, and take that of a mule one-
eyed and foul of favour." But he changed not; which when she
saw, she arose and went up to him and kissed him between the
eyes, saying, "O my beloved, I did but jest with thee; bear me no
malice because of this." Quoth he, "O my lady, I bear thee no
whit of malice; nay, I am assured that thou lovest me: but eat
of this my parched barley." So she ate a mouthful of Abdallah's
Sawik; but no sooner had it settled in her stomach than she was
convulsed; and King Badr Basim took water in his palm and
threw it in her face, saying, "Quit this human form and take that
of a dapple mule." No sooner had he spoken than she found
herself changed into a she-mule, whereupon the tears rolled down
her cheeks and she fell to rubbing her muzzle against his feet.
Then he would have bridled her, but she would not take the bit;
so he left her and, going to the grocer, told him what had passed.
Abdallah brought out for him a bridle and bade him rein her
forthwith. So he took it to the palace, and when she saw him,
she came up to him and he set the bit in her mouth and mounting
her, rode forth to find the Shaykh. But when the old man saw
her, he rose and said to her, "Almighty Allah confound thee, O
accursed woman!" Then quoth he to Badr, "O my son, there is
no more tarrying for thee in this city; so ride her and fare with
her whither thou wilt and beware lest thou commit the bridle[1] to
any." King Badr thanked him and farewelling him, fared on three
days, without ceasing, till he drew near another city and there
met him an old man, gray-headed and comely, who said to him,
"Whence comest thou, O my son?" Badr replied, "From the
city of this witch"; and the old man said, "Thou art my guest
to-night." He consented and went with him; but by the way
behold, they met an old woman, who wept when she saw the mule,

---

[1] Mr. Keightley (H. 122-24 Tales and Popular Fictions, a book now somewhat obsolete)
remarks, "There is nothing said about the bridle in the account of the sale (infra), but I
am sure that in the original tale, Badr's misfortunes must have been owing to his having
parted with it. In Chaucer's Squier's Tale the bridle would also appear to have been of
some importance." He quotes a story from the Notti Piacevoli of Straparola, the Milanese,
published at Venice in 1550. And there is a popular story of the kind in Germany.

and said, "There is no god but *the* God! Verily, this mule resembleth my son's she-mule, which is dead, and my heart acheth for her; so, Allah upon thee, O my lord, do thou sell her to me!" He replied, "By Allah, O my mother, I cannot sell her." But she cried, "Allah upon thee, do not refuse my request, for my son will surely be a dead man except I buy him this mule." And she importuned him, till he exclaimed, "I will not sell her save for a thousand dinars," saying in himself, "Whence should this old woman get a thousand gold pieces?" Thereupon she brought out from her girdle a purse containing a thousand ducats, which when King Badr Basim saw, he said, "O my mother, I did but jest with thee; I cannot sell her." But the old man looked at him and said, "O my son, in this city none may lie, for whoso lieth they put to death." So King Badr Basim lighted down from the mule. ——And Shahrazad perceived the dawn of day and ceased to say her permitted say.

When it was the Seven Hundred and Fifty-sixth Night,

She pursued, It hath reached me, O auspicious King, that when Badr Basim dismounted from and delivered the mule to the old woman, she drew the bit from her mouth and, taking water in her hand, sprinkled the mule therewith, saying, "O my daughter, quit this shape for that form wherein thou wast aforetime!" Upon this she was straightway restored to her original semblance and the two women embraced and kissed each other. So King Badr Basim knew that the old woman was Queen Lab's mother and that he had been tricked and would have fled; when, lo! the old woman whistled a loud whistle and her call was obeyed by an Ifrit as he were a great mountain, whereat Badr was affrighted and stood still. Then the old woman mounted on the Ifrit's back, taking her daughter behind her and King Badr Basim before her, and the Ifrit flew off with them; nor was it a full hour ere they were in the palace of Queen Lab, who sat down on the throne of kingship and said to Badr, "Gallows-bird that thou art, now am I come hither and have attained to that I desired and soon will I show thee how I will do with thee and with yonder old man the grocer! How many favours have I shown him! Yet he doth me frowardness; for thou hast not attained thine end but by means of him." Then she took water and sprinkled him therewith, saying,

"Quit the shape wherein thou art for the form of a foul-favoured fowl, the foulest of all fowls"; and she set him in a cage and cut off from him meat and drink; but one of her women seeing this cruelty, took compassion on him and gave him food and water without her knowledge. One day, the damsel took her mistress at unawares and going forth the palace, repaired to the old grocer, to whom she told the whole case, saying, "Queen Lab is minded to make an end of thy brother's son." The Shaykh thanked her and said, "There is no help but that I take the city from her and make thee Queen thereof in her stead." Then he whistled a loud whistle and there came forth to him an Ifrit with four wings, to whom he said, "Take up this damsel and carry her to the city of Julnar the Sea-born and her mother Faráshah[1] for they twain are the most powerful magicians on face of earth." And he said to the damsel, "When thou comest thither, tell them that King Badr Basim is Queen Lab's captive." Then the Ifrit took up his load and, flying off with her, in a little while set her down upon the terrace roof of Queen Julnar's palace. So she descended and going in to the Queen, kissed the earth and told her what had passed to her son, first and last, whereupon Julnar rose to her and entreated her with honour and thanked her. Then she let beat the drums in the city and acquainted her lieges and the lords of her realm with the good news that King Badr Basim was found; after which she and her mother Farashah and her brother Salih assembled all the tribes of the Jinn and the troops of the main; for the Kings of the Jinn obeyed them since the taking of King Al-Samandal. Presently they all flew up into the air and lighting down on the city of the sorceress, sacked the town and the palace and slew all the Unbelievers therein in the twinkling of an eye. Then said Julnar to the damsel, "Where is my son?" And the slave-girl brought her the cage and signing to the bird within, cried, "This is thy son." So Julnar took him forth of the cage and sprinkled him with water, saying, "Quit this shape for the form wherein thou wast aforetime;" nor had she made an end of her speech ere he shook and became a man as before: whereupon his mother, seeing him restored to human shape, embraced him and he wept with sore weeping. On like wise did his uncle Salih

---

[1] Here, for the first time we find the name of the mother who has often been mentioned in the story. Faráshah is the fem. or singular form of "Farásh," a butterfly, a moth. Lane notes that his Shaykh gives it the very unusual sense of "a locust."

and his grandmother and the daughters of his uncle and fell to
kissing his hands and feet. Then Julnar sent for Shaykh
Abdallah and thanking him for his kind dealing with her son,
married him to the damsel, whom he had despatched to her with
news of him, and made him King of the city. Moreover, she
summoned those who survived of the citizens (and they were
Moslems), and made them swear fealty to him and take the oath
of loyalty, whereto they replied, "Hearkening and obedience!"
Then she and her company farewelled him and returned to their
own capital. The townsfolk came out to meet them, with drums
beating, and decorated the place three days and held high festival,
of the greatness of their joy for the return of their King Badr
Basim. After this Badr said to his mother, "O my mother,
naught remains but that I marry and we be all united." She
replied, "Right is thy rede, O my son, but wait till we ask who
befitteth thee among the daughters of the Kings." And his grandmother Farashah, and the daughters of both his uncles said, "O
Badr Basim, we will help thee to win thy wish forthright." Then
each of them arose and fared forth questing in the lands, whilst
Julnar sent out her waiting women on the necks of Ifrits, bidding
them leave not a city nor a King's palace without noting all the
handsome girls that were therein. But, when King Badr Basim
saw the trouble they were taking in this matter, he said to Julnar,
"O my mother, leave this thing, for none will content me save
Jauharah, daughter of King Al-Samandal; for that she is indeed
a jewel,[1] according to her name." Replied Julnar, "I know that
which thou seekest;" and bade forthright bring Al-Samandal the
King. As soon as he was present, she sent for Badr Basim and
acquainted him with the King's coming, whereupon he went in to
him. Now when Al-Samandal was aware of his presence, he rose
to him and saluted him and bade him welcome; and King Badr
Basim demanded of him his daughter Jauharah in marriage.
Quoth he, "She is thine handmaid and at thy service and disposition," and despatched some of his suite bidding them seek her
abode and, after telling her that her sire was in the hands of King
Badr Basim, to bring her forthright. So they flew up into the air
and disappeared and they returned after a while, with the Princess
who, as soon as she saw her father, went up to him and threw her
arms round his neck. Then looking at her he said, "O my

---

[1] Punning upon Jauharah = "a jewel" a name which has an Hibernian smack.

daughter, know that I have given thee in wedlock to this magnanimous Sovran, and valiant lion King Badr Basim, son of Queen
Julnar the Sea-born, for that he is the goodliest of the folk of his
day and most powerful and the most exalted of them in degree
and the noblest in rank; he befitteth none but thee and thou none
but him." Answered she, "I may not gainsay thee, O my sire;
do as thou wilt, for indeed chagrin and despite are at an end, and
I am one of his handmaids." So they summoned the Kazi and
the witnesses who drew up the marriage-contract between King
Badr Basim and the Princess Jauharah, and the citizens decorated
the city and beat the drums of rejoicing, and they released all who
were in the jails, whilst the King clothed the widows and the
orphans and bestowed robes of honour upon the Lords of the
Realm and Emirs and Grandees: and they made bride-feasts and
held high festival night and morn ten days, at the end of which
time they displayed the bride, in nine different dresses, before
King Badr Basim who bestowed an honourable robe upon King
Al-Samandal and sent him back to his country and people and
kinsfolk. And they ceased not from living the most delectable of
life and the most solaceful of days, eating and drinking and
enjoying every luxury, till there came to them the Destroyer of
delights and the Sunderer of Societies; and this is the end of
their story, may Allah have mercy on them all! Moreover, O
auspicious King, a tale is also told anent

Conclusion.

Now, during this time, Shahrazad had borne the King three boy children: so, when she had made an end of the story of Ma'aruf, she rose to her feet and kissing ground before him, said, "O King of the time and unique one[1] of the age and the tide, I am thine handmaid and these thousand nights and a night have I entertained thee with stories of folk gone before and admonitory instances of the men of yore. May I then make bold to crave a boon of Thy Highness?" He replied, "Ask, O Shahrazad, and it shall be granted to thee.[2]" Whereupon she cried out to the nurses and the eunuchs, saying, "Bring me my children." So they brought them to her in haste, and they were three boy children, one walking, one crawling and one sucking. She took them and setting them before the King, again kissed the ground and said, "O King of the age, these are thy children and I crave that thou release me from the doom of death, as a dole to these infants; for, an thou kill me, they will become motherless and will find none among women to rear them as they should be reared." When the King heard this, he wept and straining the boys to his bosom, said, "By Allah, O Shahrazad, I pardoned thee before the coming of these children, for that I found thee chaste, pure, ingenuous and pious! Allah bless thee and thy father and thy mother and thy root and thy branch! I take the Almighty to witness against me that I exempt thee from aught that can harm thee." So she kissed his hands and feet and rejoiced with exceeding joy, saying, "The Lord make thy life long and increase thee in dignity and majesty[3]!"; presently adding, "Thou marvelledst at that which befel thee on the part of women; yet there betided the Kings of the Chosroës before thee greater mishaps and more grievous than that which hath befallen thee, and indeed I have set forth unto thee that which happened to Caliphs and Kings and others with their women, but the relation is longsome and hearkening groweth tedious, and in this is all-

---

[1] Arab. "Fárid" which may also mean "union-pearl."

[2] Trébutien (iii. 497) cannot deny himself the pleasure of a French touch making the King reply, "C'est assez; qu'on lui coupe la tête, car ces dernières histoires surtout m'ont causé un ennui mortel." This reading is found in some of the MSS.

[3] After this I borrow from the Bresl. Edit. inserting passages from the Mac. Edit.

sufficient warning for the man of wits and admonishment for the wise." Then she ceased to speak, and when King Shahriyar heard her speech and profited by that which she said, he summoned up his reasoning powers and cleansed his heart and caused his under· standing revert and turned to Allah Almighty and said to himself, "Since there befel the Kings of the Chosroës more than that which hath befallen me, never, whilst I live, shall I cease to blame my· self for the past. As for this Shahrazad, her like is not found in the lands; so praise be to Him who appointed her a means for delivering His creatures from oppression and slaughter!" Then he arose from his séance and kissed her head, whereat she rejoiced, she and her sister Dunyazad, with exceeding joy. When the morning morrowed, the King went forth and sitting down on the throne of the Kingship, summoned the Lords of his land; where· upon the Chamberlains and Nabobs and Captains of the host went in to him and kissed ground before him. He distinguished the Wazir, Shahrazad's sire, with special favour and bestowed on him a costly and splendid robe of honour and entreated him with the utmost kindness, and said to him, "Allah protect thee for that thou gavest me to wife thy noble daughter, who hath been the means of my repentance from slaying the daughters of folk. Indeed I have found her pure and pious, chaste and ingenuous, and Allah hath vouchsafed me by her three boy children; wherefore praised be He for his passing favour." Then he bestowed robes of honour upon his Wazirs, and Emirs and Chief Officers and he set forth to them briefly that which had betided him with Shahrazad and how he had turned from his former ways and repented him of what he had done and purposed to take the Wazir's daughter, Shahrazad, to wife and let draw up the marriage-contract with her. When those who were present heard this, they kissed the ground before him and blessed him and his betrothed[1] Shahrazad, and the Wazir thanked her. Then Shahriyar made an end of his sitting in all weal, whereupon the folk dispersed to their dwelling-places and the news was bruited abroad that the King purposed to marry the Wazir's daughter, Shahrazad. Then he proceeded to make ready the wedding gear, and presently he sent after his brother, King Shah Zaman, who came, and King Shahriyar went forth to meet him with the troops. Furthermore, they decorated the city after the goodliest fashion and diffused scents from censers and burnt

---

[1] *i.e.* whom he intended to marry with regal ceremony.

aloes-wood and other perfumes in all the markets and thorough-fares and rubbed themselves with saffron,[1] what while the drums beat and the flutes and pipes sounded and mimes and mounte-banks played and plied their arts and the King lavished on them gifts and largesse; and in very deed it was a notable day. When they came to the palace, King Shahriyar commanded to spread the tables with beasts roasted whole and sweetmeats and all manner of viands and bade the crier cry to the folk that they should come up to the Divan and eat and drink and that this should be a means of reconciliation between him and them. So, high and low, great and small came up unto him and they abode on that wise, eating and drinking, seven days with their nights. Then the King shut himself up with his brother and re-lated to him that which had betided him with the Wazir's daughter, Shahrazad, during the past three years and told him what he had heard from her of proverbs and parables, chronicles and pleasantries, quips and jests, stories and anecdotes, dialogues and histories and elegies and other verses; whereat King Shah Zaman marvelled with the uttermost marvel and said, "Fain would I take her younger sister to wife, so we may be two brothers-german to two sisters-german, and they on like wise be sisters to us; for that the calamity which befel me was the cause of our discovering that which befel thee and all this time of three years past I have taken no delight in woman, save that I lie each night with a damsel of my kingdom, and every morning I do her to death; but now I desire to marry thy wife's sister Dunyazad." When King Shahriyar heard his brother's words, he rejoiced with joy exceeding and arising forthright, went in to his wife Shahrazad and acquainted her with that which his brother purposed, namely that he sought her sister Dunyazad in wedlock; whereupon she answered, "O King of the age, we seek of him one condition, to wit, that he take up his abode with us, for that I cannot brook to be parted from my sister an hour, because we were brought up together and may not endure separation each from other.[2] If he accept this pact, she is his handmaid." King Shahriyar returned to his brother and acquainted him with that which Shahrazad had

---

[1] The use of coloured powders in sign of holiday-making is not obsolete in India. See Herklots for the use of "Huldee" (Haldí) or turmeric-powder, pp. 64-65.

[2] Many Moslem families insist upon this before giving their girls in marriage, and the practice is still popular amongst many Mediterranean peoples.

said; and he replied, "Indeed, this is what was in my mind, for that I desire nevermore to be parted from thee one hour. As for the kingdom, Allah the Most High shall send to it whomso He chooseth, for that I have no longer a desire for the kingship." When King Shahriyar heard his brother's words, he rejoiced exceedingly and said, "Verily, this is what I wished, O my brother. So Alhamdolillah—Praised be Allah—who hath brought about union between us." Then he sent after the Kazis and Olema, Captains and Notables, and they married the two brothers to the two sisters. The contracts were written out and the two Kings bestowed robes of honour of silk and satin on those who were present, whilst the city was decorated and the rejoicings were renewed. The King commanded each Emir and Wazir and Chamberlain and Nabob to decorate his palace and the folk of the city were gladdened by the presage of happiness and content-ment. King Shahriyar also bade slaughter sheep and set up kitchens and made bride-feasts and fed all comers, high and low; and he gave alms to the poor and needy and extended his bounty to great and small. Then the eunuchs went forth, that they might perfume the Hammam for the brides; so they scented it with rose-water and willow-flower-water and pods of musk and fumigated it with Kákilí[1] eagle-wood and ambergris. Then Shahrazad en-tered, she and her sister Dunyazad, and they cleansed their heads and clipped their hair. When they came forth of the Hammam-bath, they donned raiment and ornaments; such as men were wont prepare for the Kings of the Chosroës; and among Shahrazad's apparel was a dress purfled with red gold and wrought with counterfeit presentments of birds and beasts. And the two sisters encircled their necks with necklaces of jewels of price, in the like whereof Iskander[2] rejoiced not, for therein were great jewels such as amazed the wit and dazzled the eye; and the imagination was bewildered at their charms, for indeed each of them was brighter than the sun and the moon. Before them they lighted brilliant flambeaux of wax in candelabra of gold, but their faces outshone the flambeaux, for that they had eyes sharper than unsheathed swords and the lashes of their eyelids bewitched all hearts. Their cheeks were rosy red and their necks and shapes gracefully swayed and their eyes wantoned like the

---

[1] *i.e.* Sumatran.
[2] *i.e.* Alexander, according to the Arabs; see vol. v. 252.

gazelle's; and the slave-girls came to meet them with instruments of music. Then the two Kings entered the Hammam-bath, and when they came forth, they sat down on a couch set with pearls and gems, whereupon the two sisters came up to them and stood between their hands, as they were moons, bending and leaning from side to side in their beauty and loveliness. Presently they brought forward Shahrazad and displayed her, for the first dress, in a red suit; whereupon King Shahriyar rose to look upon her and the wits of all present, men and women, were bewitched for that she was even as saith of her one of her describers[1]:—

A sun on wand in knoll of sand she showed, * Clad in her cramoisy-hued
    chemisette:
Of her lips' honey-dew she gave me drink * And with her rosy cheeks quencht
    fire she set.

Then they attired Dunyazad in a dress of blue brocade and she became as she were the full moon when it shineth forth. So they displayed her in this, for the first dress, before King Shah Zaman, who rejoiced in her and well-nigh swooned away for love-longing and amorous desire; yea, he was distraught with passion for her, whenas he saw her, because she was as saith of her one of her describers in these couplets[2]:—

She comes apparelled in an azure vest * Ultramarine as skies are deckt and
    dight:
I view'd th' unparallel'd sight, which showed my eyes * A Summer-moon upon
    a Winter-night.

Then they returned to Shahrazad and displayed her in the second dress, a suit of surpassing goodliness, and veiled her face with her hair like a chin-veil.[3] Moreover, they let down her side-locks and she was even as saith of her one of her describers in these couplets:—

O hail to him whose locks his cheeks o'ershade, * Who slew my life by cruel
    hard despight:
Said I, "Hast veiled the Morn in Night?" He said, * "Nay I but veil Moon
    in hue of Night."

---

[1] These lines are in vol. i. 217.

[2] I repeat the lines from vol. i. 218.

[3] All these coquetries require as much inventiveness as a cotillon; the text alludes to fastening the bride's tresses across her mouth giving her the semblance of beard and mustachios.

Then they displayed Dunyazad in a second and a third and a fourth dress and she paced forward like the rising sun, and swayed to and fro in the insolence of beauty; and she was even as saith the poet of her in these couplets[1]:—

The sun of beauty she to all appears   * And, lovely coy she mocks all loveliness:
And when he fronts her favour and her smile * A-morn, the sun of day in clouds must dress.

Then they displayed Shahrazad in the third dress and the fourth and the fifth and she became as she were a Bán-branch snell or a thirsting gazelle, lovely of face and perfect in attributes of grace, even as saith of her one in these couplets[2]:—

She comes like fullest moon on happy night. * Taper of waist with shape of magic might:
She hath an eye whose glances quell mankind, * And ruby on her cheeks reflects his light:
Enveils her hips the blackness of her hair; * Beware of curls that bite with viper-bite!
Her sides are silken-soft, that while the heart * Mere rock behind that surface 'scapes our sight:
From the fringed curtains of her eyne she shoots * Shafts that at furthest range on mark alight.

Then they returned to Dunyazad and displayed her in the fifth dress and in the sixth, which was green, when she surpassed with her loveliness the fair of the four quarters of the world and outvied, with the brightness of her countenance, the full moon at rising tide; for she was even as saith of her the poet in these couplets[3]:—

A damsel 'twas the tirer's art had decked with snare and sleight, * And robed with rays as though the sun from her had borrowed light:
She came before us wondrous clad in chemisette of green, * As veilèd by his leafy screen Pomegranate hides from sight:
And when he said, "How callest thou the fashion of thy dress?" * She answered us in pleasant way with double meaning dight,
"We call this garment crève-cœur; and rightly is it hight, * For many a heart wi' this we brake and harried many a sprite."

---

[1] Repeated from vol. i. 218.
[2] Repeated from vol. i. 218.
[3] See vol. i. 219.

Then they displayed Shahrazad in the sixth and seventh dresses and clad her in youth's clothing, whereupon she came forward swaying from side to side and coquettishly moving and indeed she ravished wits and hearts and ensorcelled all eyes with her glances. She shook her sides and swayed her haunches, then put her hair on sword-hilt and went up to King Shahriyar, who embraced her as hospitable host embraceth guest, and threatened her in her ear with the taking of the sword;ªand she was even as saith of her the poet in these words:—

Were not the Murk[1] of gender male, * Than feminines surpassing fair,
Tirewomen they had grudged the bride, * Who made her beard and whiskers
    wear!

Thus also they did with her sister Dunyazad, and when they had made an end of the display the King bestowed robes of honour on all who were present and sent the brides to their own apartments. Then Shahrazad went in to King Shahriyar and Dunyazad to King Shah Zaman and each of them solaced himself with the company of his beloved consort and the hearts of the folk were comforted. When morning morrowed, the Wazir came in to the two Kings and kissed ground before them; wherefore they thanked him and were large of bounty to him. Presently they went forth and sat down upon couches of Kingship, whilst all the Wazirs and Emirs and Grandees and Lords of the land presented themselves and kissed ground. King Shahriyar ordered them dresses of honour and largesse and they prayed for the permanence and prosperity of the King and his brother. Then the two Sovrans appointed their sire-in-law the Wazir to be Viceroy in Samarcand and assigned him five of the Chief Emirs to accompany him, charging them attend him and do him service. The Minister kissed the ground and prayed that they might be vouchsafed length of life: then he went in to his daughters, whilst the Eunuchs and Ushers walked before him, and saluted them and farewelled them. They kissed his hands and gave him joy of the Kingship and bestowed on him immense treasures; after which he took leave of them and setting out, fared days and nights, till he came near Samarcand, where the townspeople met him at a distance of three marches and rejoiced in him with exceeding joy. So he

---

[1] Arab. Sawád = the blackness of the hair.

entered the city and they decorated the houses and it was
a notable day. He sat down on the throne of his kingship
and the Wazirs did him homage and the Grandees and Emirs
of Samarcand and all prayed that he might be vouchsafed
justice and victory and length of continuance. So he bestowed
on them robes of honour and entreated them with distinction and
they made him Sultan over them. As soon as his father-in-law
had departed for Samarcand, King Shahriyar summoned the
Grandees of his realm and made them a stupendous banquet of
all manner of delicious meats and exquisite sweetmeats. He also
bestowed on them robes of honour and guerdoned them and
divided the kingdoms between himself and his brother in their
presence, whereat the folk rejoiced. Then the two Kings abode,
each ruling a day in turn, and they were ever in harmony each
with other while on similar wise their wives continued in the love
of Allah Almighty and in thanksgiving to Him; and the peoples
and the provinces were at peace and the preachers prayed for
them from the pulpits, and their report was bruited abroad and
the travellers bore tidings of them to all lands. In due time
King Shahriyar summoned chroniclers and copyists and bade
them write all that had betided him with his wife, first and last;
so they wrote this and named it "𝕿𝖍𝖊 𝕾𝖙𝖔𝖗𝖎𝖊𝖘 𝖔𝖋 𝖙𝖍𝖊 𝕿𝖍𝖔𝖚𝖘𝖆𝖓𝖉
𝕹𝖎𝖌𝖍𝖙𝖘 𝖆𝖓𝖉 𝕬 𝕹𝖎𝖌𝖍𝖙." The book came to thirty volumes and these
the King laid up in his treasury. And the two brothers abode with
their wives in all pleasance and solace of life and its delights, for
that indeed Allah the Most High had changed their annoy into joy;
and on this wise they continued till there took them the Destroyer
of delights and the Severer of societies, the Desolator of dwelling-
places and Garnerer of grave-yards, and they were translated to
the ruth of Almighty Allah; their houses fell waste and their
palaces lay in ruins[1] and the Kings inherited their riches. Then
there reigned after them a wise ruler, who was just, keen-witted
and accomplished and loved tales and legends, especially those
which chronicle the doings of Sovrans and Sultans, and he found
in the treasury these marvellous stories and wondrous histories,
contained in the thirty volumes aforesaid. So he read in them a
first book and a second and a third and so on to the last of them,
and each book astounded and delighted him more than that which
preceded it, till he came to the end of them. Then he admired

---

[1] Because Easterns build, but never repair.

whatso he had read therein of description and discourse and rare
traits and anecdotes and moral instances and reminiscences and
bade the folk copy them and dispread them over all lands and
climes; wherefore their report was bruited abroad and the people
named them "𝕿𝖍𝖊 𝖒𝖆𝖗𝖛𝖊𝖑𝖘 𝖆𝖓𝖉 𝖜𝖔𝖓𝖉𝖊𝖗𝖘 𝖔𝖋 𝖙𝖍𝖊 𝕿𝖍𝖔𝖚𝖘𝖆𝖓𝖉 𝕹𝖎𝖌𝖍𝖙𝖘
𝖆𝖓𝖉 𝕬 𝕹𝖎𝖌𝖍𝖙."   This is all that hath come down to us of the
origin of this book, and Allah is All-knowing.[1] So Glory be to
Him whom the shifts of Time waste not away, nor doth aught
of chance or change affect His sway: whom one case diverteth not
from other case and Who is sole in the attributes of perfect grace.
And prayer and peace be upon the Lord's Pontiff and Chosen
One among His creatures, our lord MOHAMMED the Prince
of mankind through whom we supplicate Him for a goodly and
a godly

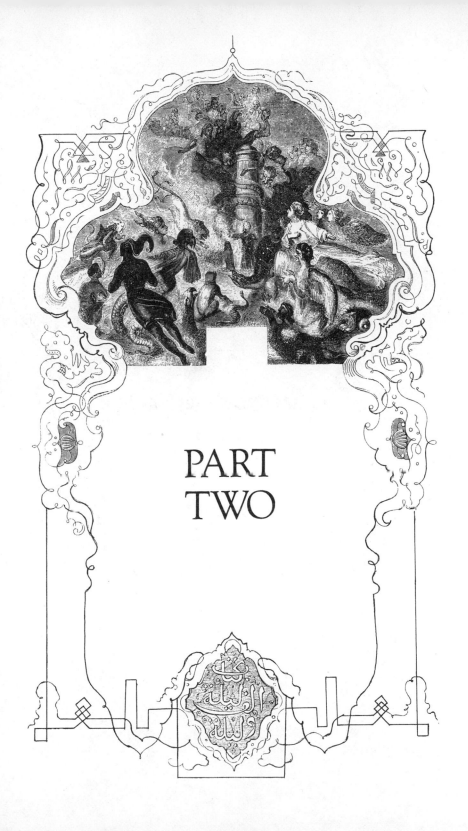

PART
TWO

J.JACKSON.Sc.

SUPPLEMENTAL NIGHTS

TO THE BOOK OF THE

THOUSAND NIGHTS AND A NIGHT

𝔚𝔥𝔢𝔫 𝔦𝔱 𝔴𝔞𝔰 𝔱𝔥𝔢 𝔉𝔬𝔲𝔯 ℌ𝔲𝔫𝔡𝔯𝔢𝔡 𝔞𝔫𝔡 𝔑𝔦𝔫𝔢𝔱𝔶=𝔰𝔢𝔳𝔢𝔫𝔱𝔥 𝔑𝔦𝔤𝔥𝔱,[1]

Quoth Dunyázád, "O sister mine, an thou be other than sleepy, tell us one of thy fair tales, so therewith we may cut short the waking hours of this our night;" and Shahrázád replied, "With love and good will! I will relate to you

THE TALE OF ZAYN AL-ASNAM.[2]

It hath reached me, O King of the Age, that in Bassorah-city[3] reigned a puissant Sultan, who was opulent exceedingly and who owned all the goods of life; but he lacked a child which might inherit his wealth and dominion. So, being sorely sorrowful on this account, he arose and fell to doing abundant alms-deeds to

---

[1] From the MS. in the Bibliothèque Nationale (Supplement Arab. No. 2523) vol. ii., p. 82, verso to p. 94, verso. The Sisters are called Dínárzád and Shahrázád, a style which I have not adopted.

[2] The old versions read "Ornament (Adornment?) of the Statues," Zierde der Pildsäulen (Weil). I hold the name to be elliptical, Zayn (al-Din = Adornment of The Faith and owner of) al-Asnám = the Images. The omission of Al-Din in proper names is very common; e.g., Fakhr (Al-Din) Al-Iftakhári (Iftikhár-al-Din) and many others given by De Sacy (Chrest. i. 30, and in the Treatise on Coffee by Abd al-Kádir). So Al-Kamál, Al-Imád, Al-Baha are = Kamal al-Dín, etc. in Ibn Khallikan, iii 493. Sanam properly = an idol is popularly applied to all artificial figures of man and beast. I may note that we must not call the hero, after Galland's fashion, unhappily adopted by Weil, *tout bonnement* "Zayn."

[3] Galland persistently writes "Balsorah," a European corruption common in his day, the childhood of Orientalism in Europe. The Hindostani versions have "Bansrá," which is worse.

Fakírs and the common poor, to the Hallows and other holy men and prayed their recourse to Allah Almighty, in order that the Lord (to whom belong Might and Majesty!) might of His grace bless him with issue. And the Compassionate accepted his prayer for his alms to the Religious and deigned grant his petition; and one night of the nights after he lay with the Queen she went away from him with child. Now as soon as the Sultan heard of the conception he rejoiced with exceeding great joyance, and when the days of delivery drew near he gathered together all the astrologers and sages who strike the sand-board,[1] and said to them, " 'Tis our desire that ye disclose and acquaint us anent the birth which is to be born during the present month whether it shall be male or female, and what shall befal it from the shifts of Time, and what shall proceed from it." Thereupon the geomantists struck their sand-boards and the astrophils ascertained their ascendants and they drew the horoscope of the babe unborn, and said to the sovran, "O King of the Age and Lord of the Time and the Tide, verily the child to which the Queen shall presently give birth will be a boy and 't will be right for thee to name him Zayn al-Asnám—Zayn of the Images." Then spake the geomantists, saying, "Know then, Ho thou the King, that this little one shall approve him when grown to man's estate valiant and intelligent; but his days shall happen upon sundry troubles and travails, and yet if he doughtily fight against all occurrence he shall become the most opulent of the Kings of the World." Exclaimed the Sultan, "An the child approve himself valorous, as ye have announced, then the toil and moil which shall be his lot may be held for naught, inasmuch as calamities but train and strengthen the sons of the Kings."[2] Shortly after this the Queen gave birth to a man-child, and Glory be to Him who fashioned the babe with such peerless beauty and loveliness! The King named his son Zayn al-Asnam, and presently he became even as the poets sang of one of his fellows in semblance,

"He showed; and they cried, 'Be Allah blest!' * And who made him and
    formed him His might attest!
This be surely the lord of all loveliness; * And all others his lieges and
    thralls be confest."

---

[1] For notes on Geomancy (Zarb Raml) see vol. iii. 269.

[2] The Hindostani Version enlarges upon this:— "Besides this, kings cannot escape perils and mishaps which serve as warnings and examples to them when dealing their decrees."

Then Zayn al-Asnam grew up and increased until his age attained its fifteenth year, when his sire the Sultan appointed for him an experienced governor, one versed in all the sciences and philosophies;[1] who fell to instructing him till such times as he waxed familiar with every branch of knowledge, and in due season he became an adult. Thereupon the Sultan bade summon his son and heir to the presence together with the Lords of his land and the Notables of his lieges and addressed him before them with excellent counsel saying, "O my son, O Zayn al-Asnam, seeing that I be shotten in years and at the present time sick of a sickness which haply shall end my days in this world and which anon shall seat thee in my stead, therefore, I bequeath unto thee the following charge. Beware, O my son, lest thou wrong any man, and incline not to cause the poor complain; but do justice to the injured after the measure of thy might. Furthermore, have a care lest thou trust to every word spoken to thee by the Great; but rather lend thou ever an ear unto the voice of the general; for that thy Grandees will betray thee as they seek only whatso suiteth them, not that which suiteth thy subjects." A few days after this time the old Sultan's distemper increased and his life-term was fulfilled and he died; whereupon his son, Zayn al-Asnam, arose and donned mourning-dress for his father during six days; and on the seventh he went forth to the Divan and took seat upon the throne of his Sultanate. He also held a levée wherein were assembled all the defenders of the realm, and the Ministers and the Lords of the land came forward and condoled with him for the loss of his parent and wished him all good fortune and gave him joy of his kingship and dominion and prayed for his endurance in honour and his permanence in prosperity. ———And Shahrazad was surprised by the dawn of day and ceased to say her permitted say.

When it was the Four Hundred and Ninety-eighth Night,

QUOTH Dunyazad, "O sister mine, an thou be other than sleepy, tell us one of thy fair tales, so therewith we may cut short the waking hours of this our night;" and quoth Shahrazad:———It hath reached me, O King of the Age, that Zayn al-Asnam seeing

---

1 In the XIXth century we should say "All the —ologies."

himself in this high honour and opulence[1] and he young in years
and void of experience, straightway inclined unto lavish expendi-
ture and commerce with the younglings, who were like him and
fell to wasting immense wealth upon his pleasures; and neglected
his government, nor paid aught of regard to his subjects.[2] Thereupon the Queen-mother began to counsel him, and forbid him
from such ill courses, advising him to abandon his perverse in-
clinations and apply his mind to rule and commandment, and to
further the policy of his kingdom, lest the lieges repudiate him
and rise up against him and depose him. But he would on no
wise hearken to a single of her words and persisted in his ignorant folly; whereat the folk murmured, inasmuch as the Lords
of the land had put forth their hands to tyranny and oppression
when they saw the King lacking in regard for his Ryots. And
presently the commons rose up against Zayn al-Asnam and would
have dealt harshly with him had not his mother been a woman of
wits and wisdom and contrivance, dearly loved of the general.
So she directed the malcontents aright and promised them every
good: then she summoned her son Zayn al-Asnam and said to
him, "Behold, O my child, that which I foretold for thee, to wit
that thou wastest thy realm and lavishest thy life to boot by
persevering in what ignorance thou art; for that thou hast placed
the governance of thy Kingdom in the hands of inexperienced
youth and hast neglected the elders and hast dissipated thy
moneys and the moneys of the monarchy, and thou hast lavished
all thy treasure upon wilfulness and carnal pleasuring." Zayn
al-Asnam, awaking from the slumber of negligence, forthright
accepted his mother's counsel and, faring forth at once to the
Díwán,[3] he entrusted the management of the monarchy to certain
old officers, men of intelligence and experience. But he acted on

---

[1] In the Hindostani Version he begins by "breaking the seal which had been set upon
the royal treasury."

[2] "Three things" (says Sa'di in the Gulistan) "lack permanency, Wealth without trading,
Learning without disputation, Government without justice." (chap. viii. max. 8). The
Bakhtiyár-námeh adds that "Government is a tree whose root is legal punishment (Siyásat);
its root-end is justice; its bough, mercy; its flower, wisdom; its leaf, liberality; and its
fruit, kindness and benevolence. The foliage of every tree whose root waxeth dry (lacketh
sap) taketh a yellow tint and beareth no fruit."

[3] For this word, see vol. ix. 108. It is the origin of the Fr. "Douane" and the Italian
"Dogana" through the Spanish Aduana (Ad-Díwán) and the Provencal "Doana." Ménage
derives it from the Gr. δοχάνη = a place where goods are received, and others from "Doge"
(Dux) for whom a tax on merchandise was levied at Venice. Littré (s. v.) will not decide,
but rightly inclines to the Oriental origin.

this wise only after Bassorah-town was ruined, inasmuch as he had not turned away from his ignorant folly before he had wasted and spoiled all the wealth of the Sultanate, and he had become utterly impoverished.   Thereupon the Prince fell to repenting and regretting that which had been done by him, until the repose of sleep was destroyed for him and he shunned meat and drink; nor did this cease until one night of the nights which had sped in such grief and thoughtfulness and vain regret until dawn drew nigh and his eyelids closed for a little while.   Then an old and venerable Shaykh appeared to him in vision[1] and said to him, "O Zayn al-Asnam, sorrow not; for after sorrow however sore cometh naught but joyance; and, would'st thou win free of this woe, up and hie thee to Egypt where thou shalt find hoards of wealth which shall replace whatso thou hast wasted and will double it more than twofold."   Now when the Prince was aroused from his sleep he recounted to his mother all he had seen in his dream; but his parent began to laugh at him, and he said to her, "Mock me not: there is no help but that I wend Egypt-wards."   Rejoined she, "O my son, believe not in swevens which be mere imbroglios of sleep and lying phantasies;" and he retorted saying, "In very sooth my vision is true and the man whom I saw therein is of the Saints of Allah and his words are veridical."   Then on a night of the nights mounting horse alone and privily, he abandoned his Kingdom and took the highway to Egypt; and he rode day and night until he reached Cairo-city.   He entered it and saw it to be a mighty fine capital; then, tethering his steed he found shelter in one of its Cathedral-mosques, and he worn out by weariness; however, when he had rested a little he fared forth and bought himself somewhat of food.   After eating, his excessive fatigue caused him fall asleep in the mosque; nor had he slept long ere the Shaykh[2] appeared to him a second time in vision and said to him, "O Zayn al-Asnam,"——And Shahrazad was surprised by the dawn of day and ceased to say her permitted say.

---

[1] A Hadís says, "The dream is the inspiration of the True Believer;" but also here, as the sequel shows, the Prince believed the Shaykh to be the Prophet, concerning whom a second Hadis declares, "Whoso seeth me in his sleep seeth me truly, for Satan may not assume my semblance."   See vol. iv. 287.   The dream as an inspiration shows early in literature, e.g.

—καὶ γάρ ὄναρ ἐκ Διός ἐστιν (Il. i. 63).

and   —Θεῖός μοι ἐνύπνιον ἦλθεν Ὄνειρος (Il. ii 55).

in which the Dream is Διὸς ἄγγελος.

[2] In the Hindostani Version he becomes a Pír = saint, spiritual guide.

When it was the Four Hundred and Ninety-ninth Night.

QUOTH Dunyazad, "O sister mine, an thou be other than sleepy, tell us one of thy fair tales, so therewith we may cut short the waking hours of this our night," and quoth Shahrazad: —— It hath reached me, O King of the Age, that the Shaykh again appeared to the Prince in a vision and said to him, "O Zayn al-Asnam, thou hast obeyed me in whatso I bade thee and I only made trial of thee to test an thou be valiant or a craven. But now I wot thy worth, inasmuch as thou hast accepted my words and thou hast acted upon my advice: so do thou return straightway to thy capital and I will make thee a wealthy ruler, such an one that neither before thee was any king like unto thee nor shall any like unto thee come after thee." Hereat Zayn al-Asnam awoke and cried "Bismillah,—in the name of Allah, the Compassion-ating, the Compassionate — what be this Shaykh who verily persecuted me until I travelled to Cairo; and I having faith in him and holding that he was either the Apostle (whom Allah save and assain!) or one of the righteous Hallows of God; and there is no Majesty and there is no Might save in Allah, the Glorious, the Great! By the Lord, but I did right well in not relating my dream to any save to my mother, and in warning none of my departure. I had full faith in this oldster; but now, me-seemeth, the man is not of those who know the Truth (be He extolled and exalted!); so by Allah I will cast off all confidence in this Shaykh and his doings." With this resolve the Prince slept that night in the Mosque and on the morrow took horse and after a few days of strenuous travel arrived at his capital Bassorah. Herein he entered by night, and forthright went in to his mother who asked him, "Say me, hast thou won aught of whatso the Shaykh promised thee?" and he answered her by acquainting her with all his adventure. Then she applied her to consoling and comforting him, saying, "Grieve not, O my son; if Almighty Allah have apportioned unto thee aught thou shalt obtain it without toil and travail.[1] But I would see thee wax sensible and

---

[1] A favourite sentiment. In Sir Charles Murray's excellent novel, "Hassan: or, the Child of the Pyramid," it takes the form, "what's past is past and what is written is written and shall come to pass."

wise, abandoning all these courses which have landed thee in poverty, O my son; and shunning songstresses and commune with the inexperienced and the society of loose livers, male and female. All such pleasures as these are for the sons of the ne'er-do-well, not for the scions of the Kings thy peers." Herewith Zayn al-Asnam sware an oath to bear in mind all she might say to him, never to gainsay her commandments, nor deviate from them a single hair's breadth; to abandon all she should forbid him, and to fix his thoughts upon rule and governance. Then he addrest himself to sleep, and as he slumbered, the Shaykh appeared to him a third time in vision, and said, "O Zayn al-Asnam, O thou valorous Prince; this very day, as soon as thou shalt have shaken off thy drowsiness, I will fulfil my covenant with thee. So take with thee a pickaxe, and hie to such a palace of thy sire, and turn up the ground, searching it well in such a place where thou wilt find that which shall enrich thee." As soon as the Prince awoke, he hastened to his mother in huge joy and told her his tale; but she fell again to laughing at him, and saying, "O my child, indeed this old man maketh mock of thee and naught else; so get thyself clear of him." But Zayn al-Asnam replied, "O mother mine, verily this Shaykh is soothfast and no liar: for the first time he but tried me and now he proposeth to perform his promise." Whereto his mother, "At all events, the work is not wearisome; so do thou whatso thou willest even as he bade thee. Make the trial and Inshallah — God willing — return to me rejoicing; yet sore I fear lest thou come back to me and say, 'Sooth thou hast spoken in thy speech, O my mother!'" However Zayn al-Asnam took up a pickaxe and, descending to that part of the palace where his sire lay entombed, began to dig and to delve; nor had he worked a long while[1] ere, lo and behold! there appeared to him a ring bedded in a marble slab. He removed the stone and saw a ladder-like flight of steps whereby he descended until he found a huge souterrain all pillar'd and propped with columns of marble and alabaster. And when he entered the inner recesses he saw within the cave-like souterrain a pavilion which bewildered his wits, and inside the same stood

---

1 In the H. V. the Prince digs a vat or cistern-shaped hole a yard deep. Under the ringed slab he also finds a door whose lock he breaks with his pickaxe and seeing a staircase of white marble lights a candle and reaches a room whose walls are of porcelain and its floor and ceiling are of crystal.

eight jars[1] of green jasper. So he said in his mind, "What may be these jars and what may be stored therein?" —— And Shahrazad was surprised by the dawn of day and ceased to say her permitted say.

When it was the full Five Hundredth Night,

Quoth Dunyazad, "O sister mine, an thou be other than sleepy, tell us one of thy fair tales, so therewith we may cut short the waking hours of this our night," and quoth Shahrazad: —— It hath reached me, O King of the Age, that when Zayn al-Asnam saw the jars, he came forwards and unlidding them found each and every full of antique[2] golden pieces; so he hent a few in hand and going to his mother gave of them to her saying, "Hast thou seen, O my mother?" She marvelled at the matter and made answer, "Beware, O my son, of wasting this wealth as thou dissipatedst other aforetime;" whereupon her son sware to her an oath saying, "Have no care, O my mother, nor be thy heart other than good before me; and I desire that thou also find satisfaction in mine actions." Presently she arose and went forth with him, and the twain descended into the cavern-like souterrain and entered the pavilion, where the Queen saw that which wildereth the wits; and she made sure with her own eyes that the jars were full of gold. But while they enjoyed the spectacle of the treasure behold, they caught sight of a smaller jar wondrously wrought in green jasper; so Zayn al-Asnam opened it and found therein a golden key; whereupon quoth the Queen-mother, "O my son, needs must this key have some door which it unlocketh." Accordingly they sought all about the souterrain and the pavilion to find if there be a door or aught like thereto, and presently, seeing a wooden lock fast barred, they knew wherefor the key was intended. Presently the Prince applied it and opened the lock, whereupon the door of a palace gave admittance, and when the twain entered they found it more spacious than the first pavilion and all illumined with a light which dazed the sight; yet not a

---

[1] Arab. Khawábi (plur. of Khábiyah) large jars usually of pottery. In the H. V. four shelves of mother o' pearl support ten jars of porphyry ranged in rows and the Prince supposes (with Galland) that the contents are good old wine.

[2] Arab. " 'Atík": the superficial similarity of the words has produced a new noun in Arabic, e.g. Abú Antíká = father of antiquities, a vendor of such articles mostly modern, "brand-new and intensely old."

wax-candle lit it up nor indeed was there a recess for lamps.
Hereat they marvelled and meditated and presently they discovered eight images[1] of precious stones, all seated upon as many
golden thrones, and each and every was cut of one solid piece;
and all the stones were pure and of the finest water and most
precious of price. Zayn al-Asnam was confounded hereat and
said to his mother, "Whence could my sire have obtained all
these rare things?" And the twain took their pleasure in gazing
at them and considering them and both wondered to see a ninth
throne unoccupied, when the Queen espied a silken hanging
whereon was inscribed, "O my son, marvel not at this mighty
wealth which I have acquired by sore stress and striving travail.
But learn also that there existeth a Ninth Statue whose value is
twenty-fold greater than these thou seest and, if thou would win
it, hie thee again to Cairo-city. There thou shalt find a whilome
slave of mine Mubárak[2] hight and he will take thee and guide
thee to the Statue; and 'twill be easy to find him on entering
Cairo: the first person thou shalt accost will point out the house
to thee, for that Mubarak is known throughout the place."
When Zayn al-Asnam had read this writ he cried, "O my mother,
'tis again my desire to wend my way Cairo-wards and seek out
this image; so do thou say how seest thou my vision, fact or
fiction, after thou assuredst me saying, 'This be an imbroglio of
sleep?' However, at all events, O my mother, now there is no
help for it but that I travel once more to Cairo." Replied she,
"O my child, seeing that thou be under the protection of the
Apostle of Allah (whom may He save and assain!) so do thou
fare in safety, while I and thy Wazir will order thy reign in thine
absence till such time as thou shalt return." Accordingly the
Prince went forth and gat him ready and rode on till he reached
Cairo where he asked for Mubarak's house. The folk answered
him saying, "O my lord, this be a man than whom none is
wealthier or greater in boon deeds and bounties, and his home is
ever open to the stranger." Then they showed him the way and
he followed it till he came to Mubarak's mansion where he

---

[1] In the text "Ashkhás" (plural of Shakhs) vulgarly used, throughout India, Persia
and other Moslem realms, in the sense of persons or individuals. For its lit. sig. see vols.
iii. 26; and viii. 159. The H. V. follows Galland in changing to pedestals the Arab. thrones,
and makes the silken hanging a "piece of white satin" which covers the unoccupied base.
[2] The blessed or well-omened: in these days it is mostly a servile name, e.g. Sidi Mubárak
Bombay. See vol. ix. 58, 330.

knocked at the door and a slave of the black slaves opened to him. —— And Shahrazad was surprised by the dawn of day and ceased to say her permitted say.

When it was the Five Hundred and First Night,

QUOTH Dunyazad, "O sister mine, an thou be other than sleepy, tell us one of thy fair tales, so therewith we may cut short the waking hours of this our night;" and quoth Shahrazad: —— It hath reached me, O King of the Age, that Zayn al-Asnam knocked at the door when a slave of Mubarak's black slaves came out to him and opening asked him, "Who[1] art thou and what is it thou wantest?" The Prince answered, "I am a foreigner from a far country, and I have heard of Mubarak thy lord that he is famed for liberality and generosity; so that I come hither purposing to become his guest." Thereupon the chattel went in to his lord and, after reporting the matter to him, came out and said to Zayn al-Asnam, "O my lord, a blessing hath descended upon us by thy footsteps. Do thou enter, for my master Mubarak awaiteth thee." Therewith the Prince passed into a court spacious exceedingly and all beautified with trees and waters, and the slave led him to the pavilion wherein Mubarak was sitting. As the guest came in the host straightway rose up and met him with cordial greeting and cried, "A benediction hath alighted upon us and this night is the most benedight of the nights by reason of thy coming to us! So who art thou, O youth, and whence is thine arrival and whither is thine intent?" He replied, "I am Zayn al-Asnam and I seek one Mubarak, a slave of the Sultan of Bassorah who deceased a year ago, and I am his son." Mubarak rejoined, "What sayest thou? Thou the son of the King of Bassorah?" and the other retorted, "Yea, verily I am his son."[2] Quoth Mubarak, "In good sooth my late lord the King of Bassorah left no son known to me! But what may be thine age, O youth?" "Twenty years or so," quoth the Prince, presently adding, "But thou, how long is it since thou leftest my sire?" "I left him eighteen years ago," said the other; "but, O my child Zayn al-Asnam, by what sign canst thou assure me of thy being

---

[1] In the text "Mín" for "Man," a Syro-Egyptian form common throughout this MS.
[2] "Ay Ni'am," an emphatic and now vulgar expression.

the son of my old master, the Sovran of Bassorah?" Said the
Prince, "Thou alone knowest that my father laid out beneath his
palace a souterrain,[1] and in this he placed forty jars of the finest
green jasper, which he filled with pieces of antique gold, also that
within a pavilion he builded a second palace and set therein eight
images of precious stones, each one of a single gem, and all seated
upon royal seats of placer-gold.[2] He also wrote upon a silken
hanging a writ which I read and which bade me repair to thee
and thou wouldst inform me concerning the Ninth Statue whereabouts it may be, assuring me that it is worth all the eight."
Now when Mubarak heard these words, he fell at the feet of
Zayn al-Asnam and kissed them exclaiming, "Pardon me, O my
lord, in very truth thou art the son of my old master;" adding,
presently, "I have spread, O my lord, a feast[3] for all the Grandees
of Cairo and I would that thy Highness honour it by thy presence." The Prince replied, "With love and the best will." Thereupon Mubarak arose and forewent Zayn al-Asnam to the saloon
which was full of the Lords of the land there gathered
together, and here he seated himself after stablishing Zayn al-
Asnam in the place of honour. Then he bade the tables be spread
and the feast be served and he waited upon the Prince with arms
crossed behind his back[4] and at times falling upon his knees. So
the Grandees of Cairo marvelled to see Mubarak, one of the
great men of the city, serving the youth and wondered with extreme wonderment, unknowing whence the stranger was. ——
And Shahrazad was surprised by the dawn of day and ceased to
say her permitted say,

When it was the Five Hundred and Second Night,

Quoth Dunyazad, "O sister mine, an thou be other than sleepy,
tell us one of thy fair tales, so therewith we may cut short the

---

[1] The MS. here has " 'Imárah" = a building, probably a clerical error for Maghárah,"
a cave, a souterrain.

[2] Arab. "Zahab-ramlí," explained in "Alaeddin." So Al-Mutanabbi sang: —

"I become not of them because homed in their ground: * Sandy earth is the gangue
wherein gold is found."

[3] Walímah prop. = a marriage-feast. For the different kinds of entertainments see vols.
vi. 74; viii. 231.

[4] Arab. Mukattaí al-Yadayn, a servile posture: see vols. iii. 218; ix. 320.

waking hours of this our night," and quoth Shahrazad: —— It
hath reached me, O King of the Age, that Mᵘbarak fell to waiting upon Zayn al-Asnam the son of his old lord, and the Grandees
of Cairo there sitting marvelled to see Mubarak, one of the great
men of the city, serving the youth and wondered with extreme
wonderment, unknowing whence the stranger was. After this
they ate and drank and supped well and were cheered till at last
Mubarak turned towards them and said, "O folk, admire not
that I wait upon this young man with all worship and honour,
for that he is the son of my old lord, the Sultan of Bassorah, who
bought me with his money and who died without manumitting
me. I am, therefore, bound to do service to his son, this my
young lord, and all that my hand possesseth of money and muni-
tion belongeth to him nor own I aught thereof at all, at all."
When the Grandees of Cairo heard these words, they stood up
before Zayn al-Asnam and salamed to him with mighty great
respect and entreated him with high regard and blessed him.
Then said the Prince, "O assembly, I am in the presence of your
worships, and be ye my witnesses. O Mubarak, thou art now
freed and all thou hast of goods, gold and gear erst belonging to us
becometh henceforth thine own and thou art endowed with them
for good each and every. Eke do thou ask whatso of importance
thou wouldst have from me, for I will on no wise let or stay thee in
thy requiring it." With this Mubarak arose and kissed the hand
of Zayn al-Asnam and thanked him for his boons, saying, "O my
lord, I wish for thee naught save thy weal, but the wealth that is
with me is altogether overmuch for my wants." Then the Prince
abode with the Freedman four days, during which all the Grandees of Cairo made act of presence day by day to offer their
salams as soon as they heard men say, "This is the master of
Mubarak and the monarch of Bassorah." And whenas the
guest had taken his rest he said to his host, "O Mubarak, my
tarrying with thee hath been long;" whereto said the other,
"Thou wottest, O my lord, that the matter whereinto thou
comest to enquire is singular-rare, but that it also involveth risk
of death, and I know not if thy valour can make the attainment
thereto possible to thee." Rejoined Zayn al-Asnam, "Know, O
Mubarak, that opulence is gained only by blood; nor cometh
aught upon mankind save by determination and predestination
of the Creator (be He glorified and magnified!); so look to thine
own stoutness of heart and take thou no thought of me." There-

upon Mubarak forthright bade his slaves get them ready for
wayfare; so they obeyed his bidding in all things and mounted
horse and travelled by light and dark over the wildest of wolds,
every day seeing matters and marvels which bewildered their
wits, sights they had never seen in all their years, until they
drew near unto a certain place. There the party dismounted
and Mubarak bade the negro slaves and eunuchs abide on the
spot saying to them, "Do ye keep watch and ward over the beasts
of burthen and the horses until what time we return to you."
After this the twain set out together afoot and quoth the Freedman to the Prince, "O my lord, here valiancy besitteth, for
that now thou art in the land of the Image¹ thou camest to seek."
And they ceased not walking till they reached a lake, a long water
and a wide, where quoth Mubarak to his companion, "Know, O
my lord, that anon will come to us a little craft bearing a banner
of azure tinct and all its planks are of chaunders and lign-aloes of
Comorin, the most precious of woods. And now I would charge
thee with a charge the which must thou most diligently observe."
Asked the other, "And what may be this charge?" Whereto
Mubarak answered, "Thou wilt see in that boat a boatman²
whose fashion is the reverse of man's; but beware, and again I
say beware, lest thou utter a word, otherwise he will at once
drown us.³ Learn also that this stead belongeth to the King of
the Jinns and that everything thou beholdest is the work of the
Jánn."——— And Shahrazad was surprised by the dawn of day
and ceased to say her permitted say.

When it was the Five Hundred and Third Night,

Quoth Dunyazad, "O sister mine, an thou be other than sleepy,
tell us one of thy fair tales, so therewith we may cut short the
waking hours of this our night," and quoth Shahrazad: ——— It
hath reached me, O King of the Age, that Mubarak and Zayn
al-Asnam came upon a lake where, behold, they found a little

---

¹ Here the Arabic has the advantage of the English; "Shakhs" meaning either a person
or an image. See supra, p. 11.

² Arab. "Kawárijí = one who uses the paddle, a paddler, a rower.

³ In the Third Kalandar's Tale (vol. i. 143) Prince 'Ajíb is forbidden to call upon the
name of Allah, under pain of upsetting the skiff paddled by the man of brass. Here the
detail is omitted.

craft whose planks were of chaunders and lign-aloes of Comorin
and therein stood a ferryman with the head of an elephant while
the rest of his body wore the semblance of a lion.[1] Presently he
approached them and winding his trunk around them[2] lifted them
both into the boat and seated them beside himself: then he fell to
paddling till he passed through the middle of the lake and he
ceased not so doing until he had landed them on the further bank.
Here the twain took ground and began to pace forwards, gazing
around them the while and regarding the trees which bore for
burthen ambergris and lign-aloes, sandal, cloves and gelsamine,[3]
all with flowers and fruits bedrest whose odours broadened the
breast and excited the sprite. There also the birds warbled, with
various voices, notes ravishing and rapturing the heart by the
melodies of their musick. So Mubarak turned to the Prince and
asked him saying, "How seest thou this place, O my lord?" and
the other answered, "I deem, O Mubarak, that in very truth this
be the Paradise promised to us by the Prophet (whom Allah save
and assain!)." Thence they fared forwards till they came upon a
mighty fine palace all builded of emeralds and rubies with gates
and doors of gold refined: it was fronted by a bridge one hundred
and fifty cubits long to a breadth of fifty, and the whole was one
rib of a fish.[4] At the further end thereof stood innumerous hosts
of the Jann, all frightful of favour and fear-inspiring of figure and
each and every hent in hand javelins of steel which flashed to the
sun like December leven. Thereat quoth the Prince to his companion, "This be a spectacle which ravisheth the wits;" and
quoth Mubarak, "It now behoveth that we abide in our places
nor advance further lest there happen to us some mishap; and
may Allah vouchsafe to us safety!" Herewith he brought forth
his pouch four strips of a yellow silken stuff and zoning himself
with one threw the other over his shoulders;[5] and he gave the

---

[1] Arab. "Wahsh," which Galland translates "Tiger," and is followed by his Hind.
translator.

[2] Arab. "Laffa 'l-isnayn bi-zulúmati-h," the latter word = Khurtúm, the trunk of an
elephant, from Zalm = the dewlap of sheep or goat.

[3] In the text "Yámin," a copyist's error, which can mean nothing else but "Yasimín."

[4] The H. V. rejects this detail for "a single piece of mother-o'-pearl twelve yards long,"
etc. Galland has *une seule écaille de poisson*. In my friend M. Zotenberg's admirable
translation of Tabari (i. 52) we read of a bridge at Baghdad made of the ribs of Og bin 'Unk
(= Og of the Neck), the fabled King of Bashan.

[5] I have noted that this is the primitive attire of Eastern man in all hot climates, and
that it still holds its ground in that grand survival of heathenry, the Meccan Pilgrimage.
In Galland the four strips are of *taffetas jaune*, the Hind. "Taftí."

two remaining pieces to the Prince that he might do with them on like wise. Next he dispread before either of them a waist shawl[1] of white sendal and then he pulled out of his poke sundry precious stones and scents and ambergris and eagle-wood;[2] and, lastly, each took his seat upon his sash, and when both were ready Mubarak repeated the following words to the Prince and taught him to pronounce them before the King of the Jann, "O my lord, Sovran of the Spirits, we stand within thy precincts and we throw ourselves on thy protection;" whereto Zayn al-Asnam added, "And I adjure him earnestly that he accept of us." But Mubarak rejoined, "O my lord, by Allah I am in sore fear. Hear me! An he determine to accept us without hurt or harm he will approach us in the semblance of a man rare of beauty and comeliness but, if not, he will assume a form frightful and terrifying. Now an thou see him in his favourable shape do thou arise forthright and salam to him and above all things beware lest thou step beyond this thy cloth." The Prince replied, "To hear is to obey," and the other continued, "And let thy salam to him be thy saying, O King of the Sprites and Sovran of the Jann and Lord of Earth, my sire, the whilome Sultan of Bassorah, whom the Angel of Death hath removed (as is not hidden from thy Highness) was ever taken under thy protection and I, like him, come to thee sueing the same safeguard." —— And Shahrazad was surprised by the dawn of day and ceased to say her permitted say.

When it was the Five Hundred and Fourth Night,

Quoth Dunyazad, "O sister mine, an thou be other than sleepy, tell us one of thy fair tales, so therewith we may cut short the waking hours of this our night," and quoth Shahrazad: —— It hath reached me, O King of the Age, that Mubarak fell to lessoning Zayn al-Asnam how he should salute the King of the Jinns, and pursued, "Likewise, O my lord, if he hail us with gladsome face of welcome he will doubtless say thee, 'Ask whatso thou wantest of me!' and the moment he giveth thee his word do thou at once prefer thy petition saying, O my lord, I require of thy

---

1 The word is Hizám = girdle, sash, waist-belt, which Galland turns into *nappes*. The object of the cloths edged with gems and gums was to form a barrier excluding hostile Jinns: the European magician usually drew a magic circle.

2 This is our corruption of the Malay Aigla = sandal wood. See vol. ix. 150.

Highness the Ninth Statue than which is naught more precious
in the world, and thou didst promise my father to vouchsafe me
that same." And after this Mubarak instructed his master how
to address the King and crave of him the boon and how to bespeak
him with pleasant speech. Then he began his conjurations and
fumigations and adjurations and recitations of words not under-
standed of any, and but little time elapsed before cold rain down
railed and lightning flashed and thunder roared and thick darkness veiled earth's face. Presently came forth a mighty rushing
wind and a voice like an earthquake, the quake of earth on Judgment Day.[1] The Prince, seeing these horrors and sighting that
which he had never before seen or heard, trembled for terror in
every limb; but Mubarak fell to laughing at him and saying,
"Fear not, O my lord: for that which thou dreadest is what we
seek, for to us it is an earnest of glad tidings and success; so be
thou satisfied and hold thyself safe."[2] After this the skies waxed
clear and serene exceedingly while perfumed winds and the
purest scents breathed upon them; nor did a long time elapse
ere the King of the Jann presented himself under the semblance of
a beautiful man who had no peer in comeliness save and excepting
Him who lacketh likeness and to Whom be honour and glory! He
gazed at Zayn al-Asnam with a gladsome aspect and a riant,
whereat the Prince arose forthright and recited the string of
benedictions taught to him by his companion and the King said to
him with a smiling favour, "O Zayn al-Asnam, verily I was wont
to love thy sire, the Sultan of Bassorah and, when he visited me
ever, I used to give him an image of those thou sawest, each cut of
a single gem; and thou also shalt presently become to me honoured
as thy father and yet more. Ere he died I charged him to write
upon the silken curtain the writ thou readest and eke I gave
promise and made covenant with him to take thee like thy parent

---

[1] Lit. = the Day of Assembly, "Yaum al-Mahshar." These lines were translated at
Cannes on Feb. 22nd, 1886, the day before the earthquake which brought desolation upon
the Riviera. It was a second curious coincidence. On Thursday, July 10th, 1863 — the
morning when the great earthquake at Accra laid in ruins the town and the stout old fort
built in the days of James II — I had been reading the Koranic chapter entitled "Earth-
quakes" (No. xcix.) to some Moslem friends who had visited my quarters. Upwards of a
decade afterwards I described the accident in "Ocean Highways" (New Series, No. II.,
Vol. I. pp. 448–461), owned by Trübner & Co., and edited by my friend Clements Mark-
ham, and I only regret that this able Magazine has been extinguished by that dullest of
Journals, "Proceedings of the R. S. S. and monthly record of Geography."

[2] Galland has *un tremblement pareil à celui qu'Israfyel* (Isráfíl) *doit causer le jour du
jugement.*

under my safeguard and to gift thee as I gifted him with an image, to wit, the ninth, which is of greater worth than all those viewed by thee. So now 'tis my desire to stand by my word and to afford thee my promised aid." —— And Shahrazad was surprised by the dawn of day and ceased to say her permitted say.

When it was the Five Hundred and Fifth Night,

QUOTH Dunyazad, "O sister mine, an thou be other than sleepy, tell us one of thy fair tales, so therewith we may cut short the waking hours of this our night," and quoth Shahrazad: —— It hath reached me, O King of the Age, that the Lord of the Jann said to the Prince, "I will take thee under my safeguard and the Shaykh thou sawest in thy swevens was myself and I also 'twas who bade thee dig under thy palace down to the souterrain wherein thou sawest the crocks of gold and the figures of fine gems. I also well know wherefore thou art come hither and I am he who caused thee to come and I will give thee what thou seekest, for all that I would not give it to thy sire. But 'tis on condition that thou return unto me bringing a damsel whose age is fifteen, a maiden without rival or likeness in loveliness; further-more she must be a pure virgin and a clean maid who hath never lusted for male nor hath ever been solicited of man;[1] and lastly, thou must keep faith with me in safeguarding the girl whenas thou returnest hither and beware lest thou play the traitor with her whilst thou bringest her to me." To this purport the Prince sware a mighty strong oath adding, "O my lord, thou hast indeed honoured me by requiring of me such service, but truly 'twill be right hard for me to find a fair one like unto this; and, grant that I find one perfectly beautiful and young in years after the requirement of thy Highness, how shall I weet if she ever longed for mating with man or that male ever lusted for her?" Replied the King, "Right thou art, O Zayn al-Asnam, and verily this be a

---

[1] The idea is Lady M. W. Montague's ("The Lady's Resolve.")

In part she is to blame that has been tried:
He comes too near that comes to be denied.

As an unknown correspondent warns me the sentiment was probably suggested by Sir Thomas Overbury ("A Wife." St. xxxvi):—

—In part to blame is she
Which hath without consent bin only tride:
He comes too near that comes to be denide.

knowledge whereunto the sons of men may on no wise attain. However, I will give thee a mirror[1] of my own whose virtue is this. When thou shalt sight a young lady whose beauty and loveliness please thee, do thou open the glass,[2] and, if thou see therein her image clear and undimmed, do thou learn forthright that she is a clean maid without aught of defect or default and endowed with every praiseworthy quality. But if, contrariwise, the figure be found darkened or clothed in uncleanness, do thou straightway know that the damsel is sullied by soil of sex. Shouldst thou find her pure and gifted with all manner good gifts, bring her to me but beware not to offend with her and do villainy, and if thou keep not faith and promise with me bear in mind that thou shalt lose thy life." Hereupon the Prince made a stable and solemn pact with the King, a covenant of the sons of the Sultans which may never be violated. —— And Shahrazad was surprised by the dawn of day and ceased to say her per-mitted say.

𝔚𝔥𝔢𝔫 𝔦𝔱 𝔴𝔞𝔰 𝔱𝔥𝔢 𝔉𝔦𝔳𝔢 𝔥𝔲𝔫𝔡𝔯𝔢𝔡 𝔞𝔫𝔡 𝔖𝔦𝔵𝔱𝔥 𝔑𝔦𝔤𝔥𝔱,

QUOTH Dunyazad, O sister mine, an thou be other than sleepy, tell us one of thy fair tales, so therewith we may cut short the

---

[1] These highly compromising magical articles are of many kinds. The ballad of The Boy and the Mantle is familiar to all, how in the case of Sir Kay's lady:—

> When she had tane the mantle
> With purpose for to wear;
> It shrunk up to her shoulder
> And left her backside bare.
>
> Percy, Vol. I., i and Book III.

Percy derives the ballad from "Le Court Mantel," an old French piece and Mr. Evans (Specimens of Welsh Poetry) from an ancient MS. of Tegan Earfron, one of Arthur's mistresses, who possessed a mantle which would not fit immodest women. See also in Spenser, Queen Florimel's Girdle (F. Q. iv. 5, 3), and the detective is a horn in the Morte d'Arthur, translated from the French, temp. Edward IV., and first printed in A. D. 1484. The Spectator (No. 579) tells us "There was a Temple upon Mount *Etna* which was guarded by dogs of so exquisite a smell, that they could discover whether the Persons who came thither were chaste or not;" and that they caused, as might be expected, immense trouble. The test-article becomes in the Tuti-námeh the Tank of Trial at Agra; also a nosegay which remains fresh or withers; in the Kathá Sarit Ságara, the red lotus of Shiva; a shirt in Story lxix. Gesta Romanorum; a cup in Ariosto; a rose-garland in "The Wright's Chaste Wife," edited by Mr. Furnival for the Early English Text Society; a magic picture in Bandello, Part I., No. 21; a ring in the Pentamerone, of Basile; and a distaff in "L'Adroite Princesse," a French imitation of the latter.

[2] Looking glasses in the East are mostly made, like our travelling mirrors, to open and shut.

waking hours of this our night," and quoth Shahrazad: —— It hath reached me, O King of the Age, that the Prince Zayn al-Asnam made a stable and trustworthy compact to keep faith with the King of the Jann and never to play traitor thereto, but to bring the maid *en tout bien et tout honneur* to that potentate who made over to him the mirror saying, "O my son, take this looking-glass whereof I bespake thee and depart straightway." Thereupon the Prince and Mubarak arose and, after blessing him, fared forth and journeyed back until they made the lakelet, where they sat but a little ere appeared the boat which had brought them bearing the Jinni with elephantine head and leonine body, and he was standing up ready for paddling.[1] The twain took passage with him (and this by command of the King of the Jann) until they reached Cairo and returned to their quarters, where they abode whilst they rested from the travails of travel. Then the Prince turned to his companion and said, "Arise with us and wend we to Baghdad-[2]city that we may look for some damsel such as the King describeth!" and Mubarak replied, "O my lord, we be in Cairo, a city of the cities, a wonder of the world, and here no doubt there is but that I shall find such a maiden, nor is there need that we fare therefor to a far country." Zayn al-Asnam rejoined, "True for thee, O Mubarak, but what be the will and the way whereby to hit upon such a girl, and who shall go about to find her for us?" Quoth the other, "Be not beaten and broken down, O my lord, by such difficulty: I have by me here an ancient dame (and cursed be the same!) who maketh marriages, and she is past mistress in wiles and guiles; nor will she be hindered by the greatest of obstacles."[3] So saying, he sent to summon the old trot, and informed her that he wanted a damsel perfect of beauty and not past her fifteenth year, whom he would

---

[1] In Eastern countries the oarsman stands to his work and lessens his labour by applying his weight which cannot be done so forcibly when sitting even upon the sliding-seat. In rowing as in swimming we have forsaken the old custom and have lost instead of gaining.

[2] I have explained this word in vol. iii. 100; viii. 51, etc., and may add the interpretation of Mr. L. C. Casartelli (p. 17) "La Philosophie Religieuse du Mazdéisme, etc., Paris Maisonneuve, 1884." "A divine name, which has succeeded little (?) is the ancient title *Bagh*, the O. P. *Baga* of the Cuneiforms (*Baga vazraka Auramazda, etc.*) and the *Bagha* of the Avesta, whose memory is preserved in Baghdad—the city created by the Gods (?). The Pahlevi books show the word in the compound *Baghôbakht*, lit.=what is granted by the Gods, popularly, Providence."

[3] The H. V. makes the old woman a "finished procuress whose skill was unrivalled in that profession."

marry to the son of his lord; and he promised her sumptuous Bakhshish and largesse if she would do her very best endeavour. Answered she, "O my lord, be at rest: I will presently contrive to satisfy thy requirement even beyond thy desire; for under my hand are damsels unsurpassable in beauty and loveliness, and all be the daughters of honourable men." But the old woman, O Lord of the Age, knew naught anent the mirror. So she went forth to wander about the city and work on her well-known ways. —— And Shahrazad was surprised by the dawn of day and ceased to say her permitted say.

𝖂𝖍𝖊𝖓 𝖎𝖙 𝖜𝖆𝖘 𝖙𝖍𝖊 𝕱𝖎𝖛𝖊 𝕳𝖚𝖓𝖉𝖗𝖊𝖉 𝖆𝖓𝖉 𝕾𝖊𝖛𝖊𝖓𝖙𝖍 𝕹𝖎𝖌𝖍𝖙,

Quoth Dunyazad, "O sister mine, an thou be other than sleepy, tell us one of thy fair tales, so therewith we may cut short the waking hours of this our night," and quoth Shahrazad: —— It hath reached me, O King of the Age, that the old woman went forth to work on her well-known ways, and she wandered about town to find a maiden for the Prince Zayn al-Asnam. Whatever notable beauty she saw she would set before Mubarak; but each semblance as it was considered in the mirror showed exceedingly dark and dull, and the inspector would dismiss the girl. This endured until the crone had brought to him all the damsels in Cairo, and not one was found whose reflection in the mirror showed clear-bright and whose honour was pure and clean, in fact such an one as described by the King of the Jann. Herewith Mubarak, seeing that he had not found one in Cairo to please him, or who proved pure and unsullied as the King of the Jann had required, determined to visit Baghdad: so they rose up and equipped them and set out and in due time they made the City of Peace where they hired them a mighty fine mansion amiddle-most the capital. Here they settled themselves in such comfort and luxury that the Lords of the land would come daily to eat at their table, even the thirsty and those who went forth betimes,[1] and what remained of the meat was distributed to the mesquin and the miserable; also every poor stranger lodging in the

---

[1] In the text "Al-Sádí w'al-Ghádí:" the latter may mean those who came for the morning meal.

Mosques would come to the house and find a meal. Therefore the bruit of them for generosity and liberality went abroad throughout the city and won for them notable name and the fairest of fame; nor did any ever speak of aught save the beneficence of Zayn al-Asnam and his generosity and his opulence. Now there chanced to be in one of the cathedral-mosques an Imám,[1] Abu Bakr hight, a ghostly man passing jealous and fulsome, who dwelt hard by the mansion wherein the Prince and Mubarak abode; and he, when he heard of their lavish gifts and alms deeds, and honourable report, smitten by envy and malice and hatred, fell to devising how he might draw them into some calamity that might despoil the goods they enjoyed and destroy their lives, for it is the wont of envy to fall not save upon the fortunate. So one day of the days, as he lingered in the Mosque after mid-afternoon prayer, he came forwards amidst the folk and cried, "O ye, my brethren of the Faith which is true and who bear testimony to the unity of the Deity, I would have you to weet that housed in this our quarter are two men which be strangers, and haply ye have heard of them how they lavish and waste immense sums of money, in fact moneys beyond measure, and for my part I cannot but suspect that they are cutpurses and brigands who commit robberies in their own country and who came hither to expend their spoils."——And Shahrazad was surprised by the dawn of day and ceased to say her permitted say.

When it was the Five Hundred and Eighth Night,

Quoth Dunyazad, "O sister mine, an thou be other than sleepy, tell us one of thy fair tales, so therewith we may cut short the waking hours of this our night," and quoth Shahrazad:——It hath reached me, O King of the Age, that the Imam in his jealousy of Zayn al-Asnam and Mubarak said to the congregation, "Verily they be brigands and cutpurses;" adding, "O believers of Mohammed, I counsel you in Allah's name that ye guard yourselves against such accurseds; for haply the Caliph shall in coming times hear of these twain and ye also shall fall with them

---

[1] An antistes, a leader in prayer (vols. ii. 203, and iv. 227); a reverend, against whom the normal skit is directed. The H. V. makes him a Muezzin, also a Mosque-man; and changes his name to Murad. Imám is a word with a host of meanings, e.g., model (and master), a Sir-Oracle, the Caliph, etc., etc.

into calamity.[1] I have hastened to caution you, and having warned you I wash my hands of your business, and after this do ye as ye judge fit." All those present replied with one voice, "Indeed we will do whatso thou wishest us to do, O Abu Bakr!" But when the Imam heard this from them he arose and, bringing forth ink-case and reed-pen and a sheet of paper, began inditing an address to the Commander of the Faithful, recounting all that was against the two strangers. However, by decree of Destiny, Mubarak chanced to be in the Mosque amongst the crowd when he heard the address of the blameworthy Imam and how he purposed applying by letter to the Caliph. So he delayed not at all but returned home forthright and, taking an hundred dinars and packing up a parcel of costly clothes, silver-wrought all, repaired in haste to the reverend's quarters and knocked at the door. The preacher came and opened to him, but sighting Mubarak he asked him in anger, " What is't thou wantest and who art thou?" Whereto the other answered, "I am Mubarak and at thy service, O my master the Imam Abu Bakr; and I come to thee from my lord the Emir Zayn al-Asnam who, hearing of and learning thy religious knowledge and right fair repute in this city, would fain make acquaintance with thy Worship and do by thee whatso behoveth him. Also he hath sent me to thee with these garments and this spending-money, hoping excuse of thee for that this be a minor matter compared with your Honour's deserts; but, Inshallah, after this he will not fail in whatever to thee is due." As soon as Abu Bakr saw the coin and gold[2] and the bundle of clothes, he answered Mubarak saying, "I crave pardon, O my lord, of thy master the Emir for that I have been ashamed of waiting upon him and repentance is right hard upon me for that I have failed to do my devoir by him; wherefore I hope that thou wilt be my deputy in imploring him to pardon my default and, the Creator willing, to-morrow I will do what is incumbent upon me and fare to offer my services and proffer the honour which beseemeth me." Rejoined Mubarak, "The end of my master's wishes is to see thy worship, O my lord Abu Bakr, and be exalted by thy presence and therethrough to win a blessing." So saying he bussed the reverend's hand and

---

[1] *i.e.* being neighbours they would become to a certain extent answerable for the crimes committed within the quarter.

[2] Arab. "Nakshat" and "Sifrat."

returned to his own place. On the next day, as Abu Bakr was leading the dawn-prayer of Friday, he took his station amongst the folk amiddlemost the Mosque and cried, "O, our brethren the Moslems great and small and folk of Mohammed one and all, know ye that envy falleth not save upon the wealthy and praiseworthy and never descendeth upon the mean and miserable. I would have you wot, as regards the two strangers whom yesterday I misspake, that one of them is an Emir high in honour and son of most reputable parents, in lieu of being (as I was informed by one of his enviers) a cutpurse and a brigand. Of this matter I have made certain that 'tis a lying report, so beware lest any of you say aught against him or speak evil in regard to the Emir even as I heard yesterday; otherwise you will cast me and cast yourselves into the sorest of calamities with the Prince of True Believers. For a man like this of exalted degree may not possibly take up his abode in our city of Baghdad unbeknown to the Caliph." —— And Shahrazad was surprised by the dawn of day and ceased to say her permitted say.

When it was the Five Hundred and Ninth Night,

QUOTH Dunyazad, "O sister mine, an thou be other than sleepy, tell us one of thy fair tales, so therewith we may cut short the waking hours of this our night," and quoth Shahrazad: —— It hath reached me, O King of the Age, that Abu Bakr the Imam uprooted on such wise from the minds of men the evil which he had implanted by his own words thrown out against the Emir Zayn al-Asnam. But when he had ended congregational prayers and returned to his home, he donned his long gaberdine[1] and made weighty his skirts and lengthened his sleeves, after which he took the road to the mansion of the Prince; and, when he went in, he stood up before the stranger and did him honour with the highmost distinction. Now Zayn al-Asnam was by nature conscientious albeit young in years; so he returned the Imam Abu Bakr's civilities with all courtesy and, seating himself beside him upon his high-raised divan, bade bring for him ambergris'd[2] coffee. Then the tables were spread for breakfast and the twain ate and

---

[1] Arab. "Farajíyah," for which see vol. i. 210, 321.
[2] For this aphrodisiac see vol. vi. 60,

drank their sufficiency, whereafter they fell to chatting like boon companions. Presently the Imam asked the Prince, saying, "O my lord Zayn al-Asnam, doth thy Highness design residing long in this our city of Baghdad?" and the other answered, "Yes indeed,[1] O our lord the Imam; 'tis my intention to tarry here for a while until such time as my requirement shall be fulfilled." The Imam enquired, "And what may be the requirement of my lord the Emir? Haply when I hear it I may devote my life thereto until I can fulfil it." Quoth the Prince, "My object is to marry a maiden who must be comely exceedingly, aged fifteen years; pure, chaste, virginal, whom man hath never soiled and who during all her days never lusted for male kind: moreover, she must be unique for beauty and loveliness." The Imam rejoined, "O my lord, this be a thing hard of finding indeed, hard exceedingly; but I know a damsel of that age who answereth to thy description. Her father, a Wazir who resigned succession and office of his own freewill, now dwelleth in his mansion jealously overwatching his daughter and her education; and I opine that this maiden will suit the fancy of thy Highness, whilst she will rejoice in an Emir such as thyself and eke her parents will be equally well pleased." The Prince replied, "Inshallah, this damsel whereof thou speakest will suit me and supply my want, and the furtherance of my desire shall be at thy hands. But, O our lord the Imam, 'tis my wish first of all things to look upon her and see if she be pure or otherwise; and, as regarding her singular comeliness, my conviction is that thy word sufficeth and thine avouchment is veridical. Of her purity, however, even thou canst not bear sure and certain testimony in respect to that condition." Asked the Imam, "How is it possible for you, O my lord the Emir, to learn from her face aught of her and her honour; also whether she be pure or not: indeed, if this be known to your Highness you must be an adept in physiognomy.[2] However, if your Highness be willing to accompany me, I will bear you to the mansion of her sire and make you acquainted with him, so shall he set her before you." —— And Shahrazad was surprised by the dawn of day and ceased to say her permitted say.

---

1 In the text "Ay ni'am," still a popular expression.
2 Arab. " 'Ilm al-Híah," gen. translated Astrology, but here meaning scientific Physiognomy. All these branches of science, including Palmistry, are nearly connected; the features and the fingers, mounts, lines, etc. being referred to the sun, moon and planets.

When it was the Five Hundred and Tenth Night,

Quoth Dunyazad, "O sister mine, an thou be other than sleepy, tell us one of thy fair tales, so therewith we may cut short the waking hours of this our night," and quoth Shahrazad: —— It hath reached me, O King of the Age, that the Imam Abu Bakr took the Prince and passed with him into the mansion of the Wazir; and, when they entered, both salam'd to the house-master and he rose and received them with greetings especially when he learned that an Emir had visited him and he understood from the Imam that Zayn al-Asnam inclined to wed his daughter. So he summoned her to his presence and she came, whereupon he bade her raise her face-veil; and, when she did his bidding, the Prince considered her and was amazed and per-plexed at her beauty and loveliness, he never having seen aught that rivalled her in brightness and brilliancy. So quoth he in his mind, "Would to Heaven I could win a damsel like this, albeit this one be to me unlawful." Thinking thus he drew forth the mirror from his pouch and considered her image carefully when, lo and behold! the crystal was bright and clean as virgin silver and when he eyed her semblance in the glass he saw it pure as a white dove's. Then sent he forthright for the Kazi and wit-nesses and they knotted the knot and wrote the writ and the bride was duly throned. Presently the Prince took the Wazir his father-in-law into his own mansion, and to the young lady he sent a present of costly jewels and it was a notable marriage-festival, none like it was ever seen; no, never. Zayn al-Asnam applied himself to inviting the folk right royally and did honour due to Abu Bakr the Imam, giving him abundant gifts, and for-warded to the bride's father offerings of notable rarities. As soon as the wedding ended, Mubarak said to the Prince, "O my lord, let us arise and wend our ways lest we lose our time in leisure, for that we sought is now found." Said the Prince, "Right thou art;" and, arising with his companion, the twain fell to equipping them for travel and gat ready for the bride a covered litter[1] to be carried by camels and they set out. Withal Mubarak well knew that the Prince was deep in love to the young lady. So he took him aside and said to him, "O my lord

---

[1] Arab. "Mihaffah bi-takhtrawán": see vols. ii. 180; v. 175.

Zayn al-Asnam, I would warn thee and enjoin thee to keep watch and ward upon thy senses and passions and to observe and preserve the pledge by thee plighted to the King of the Jann." "O Mubarak," replied the Prince, "an thou knew the love-longing and ecstasy which have befallen me of my love to this young lady, thou wouldst feel ruth for me! indeed I never think of aught else save of taking her to Bassorah and of going in unto her." Mubarak rejoined, "O my lord, keep thy faith and be not false to thy pact, lest a sore harm betide thee and the loss of thy life as well as that of the young lady.[1] Remember the oath thou swarest nor suffer lust[2] to lay thy reason low and despoil thee of all thy gains and thine honour and thy life." "Do thou, O Mubarak," retorted the Prince, "become warden over her nor allow me ever to look upon her." —— And Shahrazad was surprised by the dawn of day and ceased to say her permitted say.

Wh̕en it was the Five Hundred and Eleventh Night,

Quoth Dunyazad, "O sister mine, an thou be other than sleepy, tell us one of thy fair tales, so therewith we may cut short the waking hours of this our night," and quoth Shahrazad: —— It hath reached me, O King of the Age, that Mubarak, after warning Zayn al-Asnam to protect the virgin-bride against himself, fell also to defending her as his deputy: also he prevented the Prince from even looking upon her. They then travelled along the road unto the Island of the Jann, after[3] they had passed by the line leading unto Misr.[4] But when the bride saw that the wayfare had waxed longsome nor had beheld her bridegroom for all that time since the wedding-night, she turned to Mubarak

---

[1] The H. V. is more explicit: "do not so, or the King of the Jann will slay thee even before thou canst enjoy her and will carry her away."

[2] Arab. "Shahwah" the rawest and most direct term. The Moslem religious has no absurd shame of this natural passion. I have heard of a Persian Imam, who, suddenly excited as he was sleeping in a friend's house, awoke the master with, "Shahwah dáram"="I am lustful" and was at once gratified by a "Mut'ah," temporary and extempore marriage to one of the slave-girls. These morganatic marriages are not, I may note, allowed to the Sunnis.

[3] Arab. "Min ba'di an" for "Min ba'di má" = after that, still popular in the latter broad form.

[4] The word has been used in this tale with a threefold sense Egypt, old Cairo (Fostat) and new Cairo, in fact to the land and to its capital for the time being.

and said, "Allah upon thee; inform me, O Mubarak, by the life of thy lord the Emir, have we fared this far distance by commandment of my bridegroom Prince Zayn al-Asnam?" Said he, "Ah, O my lady, sore indeed is thy case to me, yet must I disclose to thee the secret thereof which be this. Thou imaginest that Zayn al-Asnam, the King of Bassorah, is thy bridegroom; but, alas! 'tis not so. He is no husband of thine; nay, the deed he drew up was a mere pretext in the presence of thy parents and thy people; and now thou art going as a bride to the King of the Jann who required thee of the Prince." When the young lady heard these words, she fell to shedding tears and Zayn al-Asnam wept for her, weeping bitter tears from the excess of his love and affection. Then quoth the young lady, "Ye have nor pity in you nor feeling for me; neither fear ye aught of Allah that, seeing in me a stranger maiden ye cast me into a calamity like this. What reply shall ye return to the Lord on the Day of Reckoning for such treason ye work upon me?" However her words and her weeping availed her naught, for that they stinted not wayfaring with her until they reached the King of the Jann, to whom they forthright on arrival made offer of her. When he considered the damsel she pleased him, so he turned to Zayn al-Asnam and said to him, "Verily the bride thou broughtest me is exceeding beautiful and passing of loveliness; yet lovelier and more beautiful to me appear thy true faith and the mastery of thine own passions, thy marvellous purity and valiance of heart. So hie thee to thy home and the Ninth Statue, wherefor thou askedst me, by thee shall be found beside the other images, for I will send it by one of my slaves of the Jann." Hereupon Zayn al-Asnam kissed his hand and marched back with Mubarak to Cairo, where he would not abide long with his companion, but, as soon as he was rested, of his extreme longing and anxious yearning to see the Ninth Statue, he hastened his travel homewards. Withal he ceased not to be thoughtful and sorrowful concerning his maiden-wife and on account of her beauty and loveliness, and he would fall to groaning and crying, "O for my lost joys whose cause wast thou, O singular in every charm and attraction, thou whom I bore away from thy parents and carried to the King of the Jann. Alas, and woe worth the day!" —— And Shahrazad was surprised by the dawn of day and ceased to say her permitted say.

When it was the Five Hundred and Twelfth Night,

QUOTH Dunyazad, "O sister mine, an thou be other than sleepy, tell us one of thy fair tales, so therewith we may cut short the waking hours of this our night," and quoth Shahrazad: —— It hath reached me, O King of the Age, that Zayn al-Asnam fell to chiding himself for the deceit and treason which he had practised upon the young lady's parents and for bringing and offering her to the King of the Jann. Then he set out nor ceased travelling till such time as he reached Bassorah, when he entered his palace; and, after saluting his mother, he apprised her of all things that had befallen him. She replied, "Arise, O my son, that we may look upon the Ninth Statue, for I rejoice with extreme joy at its being in our possession." So both descended into the pavilion where stood the eight images of precious gems and here they found a mighty marvel. 'Twas this. In lieu of seeing the Ninth Statue upon the golden throne, they found seated thereon the young lady whose beauty suggested the sun. Zayn al-Asnam knew her at first sight and presently she addressed him saying, "Marvel not for that here thou findest me in place of that where-for thou askedst; and I deem that thou shalt not regret nor repent when thou acceptest me instead of that thou soughtest." Said he, "No, by Allah, O life-blood of my heart, verily thou art the end of every wish of me nor would I exchange thee for all the gems of the universe. Would thou knew what was the sorrow which surcharged me on account of our separation and of my reflecting that I took thee from thy parents by fraud and I bore thee as a present to the King of the Jann. Indeed I had well nigh determined to forfeit all my profit of the Ninth Statue and to bear thee away to Bassorah as my own bride, when my comrade and councillor dissuaded me from so doing lest I bring about my death and thy death." Nor had Zayn al-Asnam ended his words ere they heard the roar of thunderings that would rend a mount and shake the earth, whereat the Queen-mother was seized with mighty fear and affright. But presently appeared the King of the Jinns who said to her, "O my lady, fear not! 'Tis I, the protector of thy son whom I fondly affect for the affection borne to me by his sire. I also am he who manifested myself to him in his sleep; and my object therein was to make trial of his valiance and to learn an he could do violence to his passions for the sake of his promise, or whether the beauty of this lady would so tempt and allure him that he could not keep his promise to me with due regard." —— And Shahrazad was surprised by the dawn of day and ceased to say her permitted say.

When it was the Five Hundred and Thirteenth Night,

QUOTH Dunyazad, "O sister mine, an thou be other than sleepy, tell us one of thy fair tales, so therewith we may cut short the waking hours of this our night," and quoth Shahrazad: —— It hath reached me, O King of the Age, that the King of the Jann said to the Queen-mother, "Indeed Zayn al-Asnam hath not kept faith and covenant with all nicety as regards the young lady, in that he longed for her to become his wife. However, I am assured that this lapse befel him from man's natural and inherent frailty albeit I repeatedly enjoined him to defend and protect her until he concealed from her his face. I now accept[1] this man's valour and bestow her upon him to wife, for she is the Ninth Statue by me promised to him and she is fairer than all these jewelled images, the like of her not being found in the whole world of men save by the rarest of chances." Then the King of the Jann turned to the Prince and said to him, "O Emir Zayn al-Asnam, this is thy bride: take her and enjoy her upon the one condition that thou love her only nor choose for thyself another one in addition to her; and I pledge myself that her faith thee-wards will be of the fairest." Hereupon the King of the Jann disappeared and the Prince, gladdened and rejoicing, went forth with the maiden and for his love and affection to her he paid to her the first ceremonious visit that same night[2] and he made bride-feasts and banquets throughout his realm and in due time he formally wedded her and went in unto her. Then he stab-lished himself upon the throne of his kingship and ruled it, bid-ding and forbidding, and his consort became Queen of Bassorah. His mother left this life a short while afterwards and they both

---

[1] Arab. "Kabbaltu" = I have accepted, i.e., I accept emphatically. Arabs use this form in sundry social transactions, such as marriages, sales, contracts, bargains and so forth, to denote that the engagement is irrevocable and that no change can be made. De Sacy neg-lected to note this in his Grammar, but explains it in his Chrestomathy (i. 44, 53), and rightly adds that the use of this energetic form peut-être serait susceptible d'applications plus étendues.

[2] La nuit de l'entrée, say the French: see Lane "Leylet ed-dukhlah" (M.E. chapt. vi.).

mourned and lamented their loss. Lastly he lived with his wife in all joyance of life till there came to them the Destroyer of delights and the Separator of societies. —— And Shahrazad ceased to say her pleasant[1] say. Quoth Dunyazad, "O sister mine, how rare is thy tale and delectable!" whereto quoth Shahrazad, "And what is this compared with that I would relate to you on the coming night concerning Alaeddin[2] and the Enchanted Lamp, an this my lord the King leave me on life?" The King said to himself, "By Allah, I will not slay her until she tell me the whole tale."

𝔚𝔥𝔢𝔫 𝔦𝔱 𝔴𝔞𝔰 𝔱𝔥𝔢 𝔉𝔦𝔳𝔢 𝔥𝔲𝔫𝔡𝔯𝔢𝔡 𝔞𝔫𝔡 𝔉𝔬𝔲𝔯𝔱𝔢𝔢𝔫𝔱𝔥 𝔑𝔦𝔤𝔥𝔱,

Quoth Dunyazad,[3] to Shahrazad, "O sister mine, an thou be other than sleepy, do tell us some of thy pleasant tales;" and Shahrazad began to relate the story of

---

[1] This MS. uses "Miláh" (pleasant) for "Mubáh" (permitted). I must remark, before parting with Zayn al-Asnam, that its object is to inculcate that the price of a good wife is "far above rubies" (Prov. xxxi. 10: see the rest of this fine chapter), a virtuous woman being "a crown to her husband" (*ibid.* xxii. 4); and "a prudent wife is from the Lord" (Prov. xix. 4). The whole tale is told with extreme delicacy and the want of roughness and energy suggests a European origin.

[2] *i.e.* the "Height or Glory ('Alá) of the Faith (al-Dín)" pron. Aláaddeen; which is fairly represented by the old form "Aladdin;" and better by De Sacy's "Ala-eddin." The name has occurred in The Nights, vol. iv. 29-33; it is a household word in England and who has not heard of Thomas Hood's "A-lad-in?" Easterns write it in five different ways and in the Paris MS. it is invariably " 'Alí al-dín," which is a palpable mistake. The others are (1) 'Alá al-Dín, (2) 'Alá yadín, (3) 'Alah Dín in the H. V. and (4) 'Aláa al-Dín (with the Hamzah), the last only being grammatical. In Galland the *Histoire de la Lampe merveilleuse* is preceded by the *Histoire du Dormeur Eveillé* which, being "The Story of Abú al-Hasan the Wag, or the Sleeper awakened," of the Bresl. Edit. (Nights cclxxi.-ccxc.), is here omitted. The Alaeddin Story exists in germ in Tale ii. of the "Dravidian Nights Entertainments," (Madana Kamara-Sankádái), by Pandit S. M. Natisa Shastri (Madras, 1868, and London, Trübner). We are told by Mr. Coote that it is well represented in Italy. The Messina version is by Pitrè, "La Lanterna Magica," also the Palermitan "Lanterne;" it is "II Matrimonio di Cajussi" of Rome (R. H. Busk's *Folk-lore*); "Il Gallo e il Mago," of Visentini's "Fiabe Mantovane," and the "Pesciolino," and "Il Contadino che aveva tre Fígli," of Imbriana. In "La Fanciulla e il Mago," of De Gubernatis ("Novelline di Sante Stefano de Calcenaja," p. 47), occurs the popular incident of the original. "The Magician was not a magician for nothing. He feigned to be a hawker and fared through the streets, crying out, 'Donne, donne, chi baratta anelli di ferro contra anelli di argento?' "

Alaeddin has ever been a favourite with the stage. Early in the present century it was introduced to the Parisian opera by M. Etienne, to the Feydeau by Théaulon's *La Clochette*: to the Gymnase by *La Petite-Lampe* of MM. Scribe and Melesville, and to the Panorama Dramatique by MM. Merle, Cartouche and Saintine (Gauttier, vii. 380).

[3] This MS. always uses Dínárzád like Galland.

ALAEDDIN; OR, THE WONDERFUL LAMP.

IT hath reached me, O King of the Age, that there dwelt in a city of the cities of China a man which was a tailor, withal a pauper, and he had one son, Alaeddin hight. Now this boy had been from his babyhood a ne'er-do-well, a scapegrace; and, when he reached his tenth year, his father inclined to teach him his own trade; and, for that he was over indigent to expend money upon his learning other work or craft or apprenticeship, he took the lad into his shop that he might be taught tailoring. But, as Alaeddin was a scapegrace and a ne'er-do-well and wont to play at all times with the gutter boys of the quarter, he would not sit in the shop for a single day; nay, he would await his father's leaving it for some purpose, such as to meet a creditor, when he would run off at once and fare forth to the gardens with the other scapegraces and low companions, his fellows. Such was his case; counsel and castigation were of no avail, nor would he obey either parent in aught or learn any trade; and presently, for his sadness and sorrowing because of his son's vicious indolence, the tailor sickened and died. Alaeddin continued in his former ill courses and, when his mother saw that her spouse had deceased, and that her son was a scapegrace and good for nothing at all[1] she sold the shop and whatso was to be found therein and fell to spinning cotton yarn. By this toilsome industry she fed herself and found food for her son Alaeddin the scapegrace who, seeing himself freed from bearing the severities of his sire, increased in idleness and low habits; nor would he ever stay at home save at meal-hours while his miserable wretched mother lived only by what her hands could spin until the youth had reached his fifteenth year. —— And Shahrazad was surprised by the dawn of day and ceased saying her permitted say.

When it was the Five Hundred and Fifteenth Night,

QUOTH Dunyazad, "O sister mine, an thou be other than sleepy, do tell us some of thy pleasant tales," whereupon Shahrazad

---

[1] Arab. " 'Abadan," a term much used in this MS. and used correctly. It refers always and only to future time, past being denoted by "Kattu" from Katta = he cut (in breadth, as opposed to Kadda = he cut lengthwise). See De Sacy, Chrestom. ii. 443.

replied, "With love and good will."——It hath reached me, O King of the Age, that when Alaeddin had come to his fifteenth year, it befel, one day of the days, that as he was sitting about the quarter at play with the vagabond boys behold, a Darwaysh from the Maghrib, the Land of the Setting Sun, came up and stood gazing for solace upon the lads and he looked hard at Alaeddin and carefully considered his semblance, scarcely no-ticing his companions the while. Now this Darwaysh was a Moorman from Inner Marocco and he was a magician who could upheap by his magic hill upon hill, and he was also an adept in astrology. So after narrowly considering Alaeddin he said in himself, "Verily, this is the lad I need and to find whom I have left my natal land." Presently he led one of the children apart and questioned him anent the scapegrace saying, "Whose[1] son is he?" And he sought all information concerning his condition and whatso related to him. After this he walked up to Alaeddin and drawing him aside asked, "O my son, haply thou art the child of Such-an-one the tailor?" and the lad answered, "Yes, O my lord, but 'tis long since he died." The Maghrabi,[2] the Magician, hearing these words threw himself upon Alaeddin and wound his arms around his neck and fell to bussing him, weeping the while with tears trickling adown his cheeks. But when the lad saw the Moorman's case he was seized with sur-prise thereat and questioned him, saying, "What causeth thee weep, O my lord: and how camest thou to know my father?" "How canst thou, O my son," replied the Moorman, in a soft voice saddened by emotion, "question me with such query after informing me that thy father and my brother is deceased; for that he was my brother-german and now I come from my adopted country and after long exile I rejoiced with exceeding joy in the hope of looking upon him once more and condoling with him

---

[1] In the text "Ibn mín," a vulgarism for "man." Galland adds that the tailor's name was Mustapha—*il y avait un tailleur nommé Mustafa.*

[2] In classical Arabic the word is "Maghribi," the local form of the root Gharaba = he went far away (the sun), set, etc., whence "Maghribi" = a dweller in the Sunset-land. The vulgar, however, prefer "Maghrab" and "Maghrabi," of which foreigners made "Mogrebin." For other information see vols. vi. 220; ix. 50. The "Moormen" are famed as magicians; so we find a Maghrabi Sahhár = wizard, who by the by takes part in a transformation scene like that of the Second Kalandar (vol. i. p. 134, The Nights), in p. 10 of Spitta Bey's "Contes Arabes Modernes," etc. I may note that "Sihr," according to Jauhari and Firozábádi = anything one can hold by a thin or subtle place, *i.e.*, easy to handle. Hence it was applied to all sciences, "Sahhár" being = to 'Alim (or sage) : and the older Arabs called poetry "Sihr al-halál"—lawful magic.

over the past; and now thou hast announced to me his demise. But blood hideth not from blood[1] and it hath revealed to me that thou art my nephew, son of my brother, and I knew thee amongst all the lads, albeit thy father, when I parted from him, was yet unmarried." —— And Shahrazad was surprised by the dawn of day and ceased to say her permitted say.

𝔚hen it was the 𝔉ive 𝔥undred and 𝔖ixteenth 𝔑ight,

Quoth Dunyazad, "O sister mine, an thou be other than sleepy, do tell us some of thy pleasant tales," whereupon Shahrazad replied, "With love and good will." —— It hath reached me, O King of the Age, that the Maghrabi, the Magician, said to the tailor's orphan, "O my son Alaeddin, and I have now failed in the mourning ceremonies and have lost the delight I expected from meeting thy father, my brother, whom after my long banishment I had hoped to see once more ere I die; but far distance wrought me this trouble nor hath the creature aught of asylum from the Creator or artifice against the commandments of Allah Almighty." Then he again clasped Alaeddin to his bosom crying, "O my son, I have none to condole with now save thyself; and thou standest in stead of thy sire, thou being his issue and representative and 'whoso leaveth issue dieth not,'[2] O my child!" So saying, the Magician put hand to purse and pulling out ten gold pieces gave them to the lad asking, "O my son, where is your house and where dwelleth she, thy mother, and my brother's widow?" Presently Alaeddin arose with him and showed him the way to their home and meanwhile quoth the Wizard, "O my son, take these moneys and give them to thy mother, greeting her from me, and let her know that thine uncle, thy father's brother, hath reappeared from his exile and that Inshallah—God willing—on the morrow I will visit her to salute her with the salam and see the house wherein my brother was homed and look upon the place where he lieth buried." Thereupon Alaeddin kissed the Maghrabi's hand, and, after running in his joy at fullest speed to his mother's dwelling, entered to her clean contrariwise to his custom, inasmuch as he never came near her save

---

[1] *i.e.* blood is thicker than water, as the Highlanders say.

[2] A popular saying amongst Moslems which has repeatedly occurred in The Nights. The son is the "lamp of a dark house." Vol. ii. 280.

at meal-times only. And when he found her, the lad exclaimed
in his delight, "O my mother, I give thee glad tidings of mine
uncle who hath returned from his exile and who now sendeth me
to salute thee." "O my son," she replied, "meseemeth thou
mockest me! Who is this uncle and how canst thou have an
uncle in the bonds of life?" He rejoined, "How sayest thou, O
my mother, that I have nor living uncles nor kinsmen, when this
man is my father's own brother? Indeed he embraced me and
bussed me, shedding tears the while, and bade me acquaint thee
herewith." She retorted, "O my son, well I wot thou haddest
an uncle, but he is now dead nor am I ware that thou hast other
eme."——And Shahrazad was surprised by the dawn of day and
ceased to say her permitted say,

When it was the Five Hundred and Seventeenth Night,

Quoth Dunyazad, "O sister mine, an thou be other than sleepy,
do tell us some of thy pleasant tales," whereupon Shahrazad replied, "With love and good will."——It hath reached me, O
King of the Age, that the Maroccan Magician fared forth next
morning and fell to finding out Alaeddin, for his heart no longer
permitted him to part from the lad; and, as he was to-ing and
fro-ing about the city-highways, he came face to face with him
disporting himself, as was his wont, amongst the vagabonds and
the scapegraces. So he drew near to him and, taking his hand,
embraced him and bussed him, then pulled out of his poke two
dinars and said, "Hie thee to thy mother and give her these couple
of ducats and tell her that thine uncle would eat the evening-
meal with you; so do thou take these two gold pieces and prepare
for us a succulent supper. But before all things show me once
more the way to your home." "On my head and mine eyes be it,
O my uncle," replied the lad and forewent him, pointing out the
street leading to the house. Then the Moorman left him and
went his ways and Alaeddin ran home and, giving the news and
the two sequins to his parent, said, "My uncle would sup with
us." So she arose straightway and going to the market-street
bought all she required; then, returning to her dwelling she borrowed from the neighbours whatever was needed of pans and
platters and so forth and when the meal was cooked and supper-
time came she said to Alaeddin, "O my child, the meat is ready

but peradventure thine uncle wotteth not the way to our dwelling; so do thou fare forth and meet him on the road." He replied, "To hear is to obey," and before the twain ended talking a knock was heard at the door. Alaeddin went out and opened when, behold, the Maghrabi, the Magician, together with an eunuch carrying the wine and the dessert-fruits; so the lad led them in and the slave went about his business. The Moorman on entering saluted his sister-in-law with the salam; then began to shed tears and to question her saying, "Where be the place whereon my brother went to sit?" She showed it to him, whereat he went up to it and prostrated himself in prayer[1] and kissed the floor crying, "Ah, how scant is my satisfaction and how luckless is my lot, for that I have lost thee, O my brother, O vein of my eye!" And after such fashion he continued weeping and wailing till he swooned away for excess of sobbing and lamentation; wherefor Alaeddin's mother was certified of his soothfastness. So coming up to him she raised him from the floor and said, "What gain is there in slaying thyself?"——And Shahrazad was surprised by the dawn of day and ceased to say her permitted say.

When it was the Five Hundred and Eighteenth Night,

QUOTH Dunyazad, "O sister mine, an thou be other than sleepy, do tell us some of thy pleasant tales," whereupon Shahrazad replied, "With love and good will."——It hath reached me, O King of the Age, that Alaeddin's mother began consoling the Maghrabi, the Magician, and placed him upon the divan; and, as soon as he was seated at his ease and before the food-trays were served up, he fell to talking with her and saying, "O wife of my brother, it must be a wonder to thee how in all thy days thou never sawest me nor learnedst thou aught of me during the life-time of my brother who hath found mercy.[2] Now the reason is that forty years ago I left this town and exiled myself from my birth-place and wandered forth over all the lands of Al-Hind and Al-Sind and entered Egypt and settled for a long time in its magnificent city,[3] which is one of the world-wonders, till at last I fared to the regions of the Setting Sun and abode for a space of

[1] Out of respect to his brother, who was probably the senior: the H. V. expressly says so.
[2] Al-Marhúm = my late brother. See vol. ii. 129, 196.
[3] This must refer to Cairo not to Al-Medinah whose title is "Al-Munawwarah" = the Illumined.

thirty years in the Maroccan interior. Now one day of the days, O wife of my brother, as I was sitting alone at home, I fell to thinking of mine own country and of my birth-place and of my brother (who hath found mercy); and my yearning to see him waxed excessive and I bewept and bewailed my strangerhood and distance from him. And at last my longings drave me homewards until I resolved upon travelling to the region which was the falling-place of my head[1] and my homestead, to the end that I might again see my brother. Then quoth I to myself, 'O man,[2] how long wilt thou wander like a wild Arab from thy place of birth and native stead? Moreover, thou hast one brother and no more; so up with thee and travel and look upon him[3] ere thou die; for who wotteth the woes of the world and the changes of the days? 'Twould be saddest regret an thou lie down to die without beholding thy brother and Allah (laud be to the Lord!) hath vouchsafed thee ample wealth; and belike he may be straitened and in poor case, when thou wilt aid thy brother as well as see him.' So I arose at once and equipped me for wayfare and recited the Fátihah; then, whenas Friday prayers ended, I mounted and travelled to this town, after suffering manifold toils and travails which I patiently endured whilst the Lord (to whom be honour and glory!) veiled me with the veil of His protection. So I entered and whilst wandering about the streets, the day before yesterday, I beheld my brother's son Alaeddin disporting himself with the boys and, by God the Great, O wife of my brother, the moment I saw him this heart of mine went forth to him (for blood yearneth unto blood!), and my soul felt and informed me that he was my very nephew. So I forgot all my travails and troubles at once on sighting him and I was like to fly for joy; but, when he told me of the dear one's departure to the ruth of Allah Almighty, I fainted for stress of distress and disappointment. Perchance, however, my nephew hath informed thee of the pains which prevailed upon me; but after a fashion I am consoled by the sight of Alaeddin, the legacy bequeathed to us by him who hath found mercy for that 'whoso leaveth issue is not wholly dead.' "[4]——And Shahrazad was surprised by the dawn of day and ceased to say her permitted say.

---

[1] A picturesque term for birth-place.
[2] In text "Yá Rájul" (for Rajul) = O man, an Egypto-Syrian form, broad as any Doric.
[3] Arab. Shúf-hu, the colloquial form of Shuf-hu.
[4] For the same sentiment see "Julnár" the "Sea-born," Nights dccxliii.-xliv.

When it was the Five Hundred and Nineteenth Night,

QUOTH Dunyazad, "O sister mine, an thou be other than sleepy, do tell us some of thy pleasant tales," whereupon Shahrazad replied, "With love and good will."——It hath reached me, O King of the Age, that the Maghrabi, the Magician, said to Alaeddin's mother, "Whoso leaveth issue is not wholly dead." And when he looked at his sister-in-law she wept at these his words; so he turned to the lad that he might cause her forget the mention of her mate, as a means of comforting her and also of completing his deceit, and asked him, saying, "O my son Alaeddin what hast thou learned in the way of work and what is thy business? Say me, hast thou mastered any craft whereby to earn a livelihood for thyself and for thy mother?" The lad was abashed and put to shame and he hung down his head and bowed his brow groundwards; but his parent spake out, "How, forsooth? By Allah, he knoweth nothing at all, a child so ungracious as this I never yet saw; no, never! All the day long he idleth away his time with the sons of the quarter, vagabonds like himself, and his father (O regret of me!) died not save of dolour for him. And I also am now in piteous plight: I spin cotton and toil at my distaff, night and day, that I may earn a couple of scones of bread which we eat together. This is his condition, O my brother-in-law; and, by the life of thee, he cometh not near me save at meal-times and none other. Indeed, I am thinking to lock the house-door nor ever open to him again but leave him to go and seek a livelihood whereby he can live, for that I am now grown a woman in years and have no longer strength to toil and go about for a maintenance after this fashion. O Allah, I am compelled to provide him with daily bread when I require to be provided!" Hereat the Moorman turned to Alaeddin and said, "Why is this, O son of my brother, thou goest about in such ungraciousness? 'Tis a disgrace to thee and unsuitable for men like thyself. Thou art a youth of sense, O my son, and the child of honest folk, so 'tis for thee a shame that thy mother, a woman in years, should struggle to support thee. And now that thou hast grown to man's estate it becometh thee to devise thee some device whereby thou canst live, O my child. Look around thee and Alhamdolillah—praise be to Allah—in this our town are many teachers of all manner of crafts and nowhere are they more numerous; so choose thee some calling which may please thee to the end that I establish thee therein; and, when thou growest up, O my son, thou shalt have some business whereby to live. Haply thy father's industry may not be to thy liking; and, if so it be, choose thee some other handicraft which suiteth thy fancy; then let me know and I will aid thee with all I can, O my son." But when the Maghrabi saw that Alaeddin kept silence and made him no reply, he knew that the lad wanted none other occupation than a scapegrace-life, so he said to him, "O son of my brother, let not my words seem hard and harsh to thee, for, if despite all I say, thou still dislike to learn a craft, I will open thee a merchant's store[1] furnished with costliest stuffs and thou shalt become famous amongst the folk and take and give and buy and sell and be well known in the city." Now when Alaeddin heard the words of his uncle the Moorman, and the design of making him a Khwájah[2]—merchant and gentleman,—he joyed exceedingly knowing that such folk dress handsomely and fare delicately. So he looked at the Maghrabi smiling and drooping his head groundwards and saying with the tongue of the case that he was content.——And Shahrazad was surprised by the dawn of day and ceased to say her permitted say.

When it was the Five Hundred and Twentieth Night,

QUOTH Dunyazad, "O sister mine, an thou be other than sleepy, do tell us some of thy pleasant tales," whereupon Shahrazad replied, "With love and good will."——It hath reached me, O King of the Age, that the Maghrabi, the Magician, looked at Alaeddin and saw him smiling, whereby he understood that the lad was satisfied to become a trader. So he said to him, "Since thou art content that I open thee a merchant's store and make thee a gentleman, do thou, O son of my brother, prove thyself a man and Inshallah—God willing—to-morrow I will take thee to

---

[1] "I will hire thee a shop in the Chauk"—Carfax or market street says the H. V.

[2] The MS. writes the word Khwájá (for Khwájah see vol. vi. 46). Here we are at once interested in the scapegrace who looked Excelsior. In fact the tale begins with a strong inducement to boyish vagabondage and scampish indolence; but the Moslem would see in it the hand of Destiny bringing good out of evil. Amongst other meanings of "Khwájah" it is a honorific title given by Khorásánis to their notables. In Arab. the similarity of the word to "Khuwáj" = hunger, has given rise to a host of conceits, more or less frigid (Ibn Khallikán, iii. 45).

the bazar in the first place and will have a fine suit of clothes cut out for thee, such gear as merchants wear; and, secondly, I will look after a store for thee and keep my word." Now Alaeddin's mother had somewhat doubted the Maroccan being her brother-in-law; but as soon as she heard his promise of opening a merchant's store for her son and setting him up with stuffs and capital and so forth, the woman decided and determined in her mind that this Maghrabi was in very sooth her husband's brother, seeing that no stranger man would do such goodly deed by her son. So she began directing the lad to the right road and teaching him to cast ignorance from out his head and to prove himself a man; moreover she bade him ever obey his excellent uncle as though he were his son and to make up for the time he had wasted in frowardness with his fellows. After this she arose and spread the table, then served up supper; so all sat down and fell to eating and drinking, while the Maghrabi conversed with Alaeddin upon matters of business and the like, rejoicing him to such degree that he enjoyed no sleep that night. But when the Moorman saw that the dark hours were passing by, and the wine was drunken, he arose and sped to his own stead; but, ere going, he agreed to return next morning and take Alaeddin and look to his suit of merchant's clothes being cut out for him. And as soon as it was dawn, behold, the Maghrabi rapped at the door which was opened by Alaeddin's mother: the Moorman, however, would not enter, but asked to take the lad with him to the market-street. Accordingly Alaeddin went forth to his uncle and, wishing him good morning, kissed his hand; and the Maroccan took him by the hand and fared with him to the Bazar. There he entered a clothier's shop containing all kinds of clothes and called for a suit of the most sumptuous; whereat the merchant brought him out his need, all wholly fashioned and ready sewn, and the Moorman said to the lad, "Choose, O my child, whatso pleaseth thee." Alaeddin rejoiced exceedingly seeing that his uncle had given him his choice, so he picked out the suit most to his own liking and the Maroccan paid to the merchant the price thereof in ready money. Presently he led the lad to the Hammám-baths where they bathed; then they came out and drank sherbets, after which Alaeddin arose and, donning his new dress in huge joy and delight, went up to his uncle and kissed his hand and thanked him for his favours. —— And Shahrazad was surprised by the dawn of day and ceased to say her permitted say.

When it was the Five Hundred and Twenty-first Night,

QUOTH Dunyazad, "O sister mine, an thou be other than sleepy, do tell us some of thy pleasant tales," whereupon Shahrazad replied, "With love and good will." —— It has reached me, O King of the Age, that the Maghrabi, the Magician, after leaving the Hammam with Alaeddin, took him and trudged with him to the Merchants' bazar; and, having diverted him by showing the market and its sellings and buyings, said to him, "O my son, it besitteth thee to become familiar with the folk, especially with the merchants, so thou mayest learn of them merchant-craft, seeing that the same hath now become thy calling." Then he led him forth and showed him the city and its cathedral-mosques together with all the pleasant sights therein; and, lastly, made him enter a cook's shop. Here dinner was served to them on platters of silver and they dined well and ate and drank their sufficiency, after which they went their ways. Presently the Moorman pointed out to Alaeddin the pleasances and noble buildings, and went in with him to the Sultan's Palace and diverted him with displaying all the apartments which were mighty fine and grand; and led him finally to the Khán of stranger merchants where he himself had his abode. Then the Maroccan invited sundry traders which were in the Caravanserai; and they came and sat down to supper, when he notified to them that the youth was his nephew, Alaeddin by name. And after they had eaten and drunken and night had fallen, he rose up and taking the lad with him led him back to his mother, who no sooner saw her boy as he were one of the merchants[1] than her wits took flight and she waxed sad for very gladness. Then she fell to thanking her false connection, the Moorman, for all his benefits and said to him, "O my brother-in-law, I can never say enough though I expressed my gratitude to thee during the rest of thy days and praised thee for the good deeds thou hast done by this my child." Thereupon quoth the Maroccan, "O wife of my brother, deem this not mere kindness of me, for that the lad is mine own son and 'tis incumbent on me to stand in the stead of my brother, his sire. So be thou fully satisfied!" And quoth she, "I pray Allah by the honour of the Hallows, the ancients and the moderns, that

---

[1] Arab. "Wáhid min al-Tujjár," the very vulgar style.

He preserve thee and cause thee to continue, O my brother-in-law, and prolong for me thy life; so shalt thou be a wing overshadowing this orphan lad; and he shall ever be obedient to thine orders nor shall he do aught save whatso thou biddest him thereunto." The Maghrabi replied, "O wife of my brother, Alaeddin is now a man of sense and the son of goodly folk, and I hope to Allah that he will follow in the footsteps of his sire and cool thine eyes. But I regret that, to-morrow being Friday, I shall not be able to open his shop, as 'tis meeting-day when all the merchants, after congregational prayer, go forth to the gardens and pleasances. On the Sabbath,[1] however, Inshallah! — an it please the Creator — we will do our business. Meanwhile to-morrow I will come to thee betimes and take Alaeddin for a pleasant stroll to the gardens and pleasances without the city which haply he may hitherto not have beheld. There also he shall see the merchants and notables who go forth to amuse themselves, so shall he become acquainted with them and they with him." —— And Shahrazad was surprised by the dawn of day and ceased to say her permitted say.

When it was the Five Hundred and Twenty-second Night,

Quoth Dunyazad, "O sister mine, an thou be other than sleepy, do tell us some of thy pleasant tales," whereupon Shahrazad replied, "With love and good will." —— It hath reached me, O King of the Age, that the Maghrabi went away and lay that night in his quarters; and early next morning he came to the tailor's house and rapped at the door. Now Alaeddin (for stress of his delight in the new dress he had donned and for the past day's enjoyment in the Hammam and in eating and drinking and

---

[1] *i.e.*, the Saturday (see vol. ii. 305) established as a God's rest by the so-called "Mosaic" commandment No. iv. How it gradually passed out of observance, after so many centuries of most stringent application, I cannot discover: certainly the text in Cor. ii. 16-17 is insufficient to abolish or supersede an order given with such singular majesty and impressiveness by God and so strictly obeyed by man. The popular idea is that the Jewish Sabbath was done away with in Christ; and that sundry of the 1604 councils, *e.g.*, Laodicea, anathematized those who kept it holy after such fashion. With the day the aim and object changed; and the early Fathers made it the "Feast of the Resurrection" which could not be kept too joyously. The "Sabbatismus" of our Sabbatarians, who return to the Israelitic practice and yet honour the wrong day, is heretical and vastly illogical; and the Sunday is better kept in France, Italy and other "Catholic" countries than in England and Scotland.

gazing at the folk; expecting furthermore his uncle to come at dawn and carry him off on pleasuring to the gardens) had not slept a wink that night, nor closed his eyelids, and would hardly believe it when day broke. But hearing the knock at the door he went out at once in hot haste, like a spark of fire, and opened and saw his uncle, the Magician, who embraced him and kissed him. Then, taking his hand, the Moorman said to him as they fared forth together, "O son of my brother, this day will I show thee a sight thou never sawest in all thy life," and he began to make the lad laugh and cheer him with pleasant talk. So doing they left the city gate, and the Maroccan took to promenading with Alaeddin amongst the gardens and to pointing out for his pleasure the mighty fine pleasances and the marvellous high-builded[1] pavilions. And whenever they stood to stare at a garth or a mansion or a palace the Maghrabi would say to his companion, "Doth this please thee, O son of my brother?" Alaeddin was nigh to fly with delight at seeing sights he had never seen in all his born days; and they ceased not[2] to stroll about and solace themselves until they waxed aweary, when they entered a mighty grand garden which was nearhand, a place that the heart delighted and the sight belighted; for that its swift-running rills flowed amidst the flowers and the waters jetted from the jaws of lions moulded in yellow brass like unto gold. So they took seat over against a lakelet and rested a little while, and Alaeddin enjoyed himself with joy exceeding and fell to jesting with his uncle and making merry with him as though the Magician were really his father's brother. Presently the Maghrabi arose and loosing his girdle drew forth from thereunder a bag full of victual, dried fruits and so forth, saying to Alaeddin, "O my nephew, haply thou art become anhungered; so come forward and eat what thou needest." Accordingly the lad fell upon the food and the Moorman ate with him and they were gladdened and cheered by rest and good cheer. Then quoth the Magician, "Arise, O son of my brother, an thou be reposed and let us stroll onwards a little and reach the end of our walk." Thereupon Alaeddin arose and the Maroccan paced with him from garden to garden until they left all behind them and reached the base of a high and naked hill;

---

[1] For "Mushayyadát" see vol. viii. 23.

[2] All these words sárú, dakhalú, jalasú, &c. are in the plur. for the dual—popular and vulgar speech. It is so throughout the MS.

when the lad who, during all his days, had never issued from the
city-gate and never in his life had walked such a walk as this,
said to the Maghrabi, "O uncle mine, whither are we wending?
We have left the gardens behind us one and all and have reached
the barren hill-country;[1] and, if the way be still long, I have no
strength left for walking: indeed I am ready to fall with fatigue.
There are no gardens before us, so let us hark back and return to
town." Said the Magician, "No, O my son; this is the right
road, nor are the gardens ended for we are going to look at one
which hath ne'er its like amongst those of the Kings and all
thou hast beheld are naught in comparison therewith. Then gird
thy courage to walk; thou art now a man, Alhamdolillah—
praise be to Allah!" Then the Maghrabi fell to soothing Alaeddin with soft words and telling him wondrous tales, lies as well
as truth, until they reached the site intended by the African
Magician who had travelled from the Sunset-land to the regions
of China for the sake thereof. And when they made the place,
the Moorman said to Alaeddin, "O son of my brother, sit thee
down and take thy rest, for this is the spot we are now seeking
and, Inshallah, soon will I divert thee by displaying marvel-
matters whose like not one in the world ever saw; nor hath any
solaced himself with gazing upon that which thou art about to
behold."——And Shahrazad was surprised by the dawn of day
and ceased to say her permitted say.

𝔚𝔥𝔢𝔫 𝔦𝔱 𝔴𝔞𝔰 𝔱𝔥𝔢 𝔉𝔦𝔳𝔢 𝔥𝔲𝔫𝔡𝔯𝔢𝔡 𝔞𝔫𝔡 𝔗𝔴𝔢𝔫𝔱𝔶=𝔱𝔥𝔦𝔯𝔡 𝔑𝔦𝔤𝔥𝔱,

QUOTH Dunyazad, "O sister mine, an thou be other than sleepy,
do tell us some of thy pleasant tales," whereupon Shahrazad
replied, "With love and good will."——It hath reached me, O
King of the Age, that the Maghrabi wizard said to Alaeddin,
"No one of created beings hath enjoyed the sights *thou* art about
to see. But when thou art rested, arise and seek some wood-
chips and fuel sticks[2] which be small and dry, wherewith we may
kindle a fire: then will I show thee, O son of my brother, matters

---

[1] The Persians apply the Arab word "Sahrá"=desert, to the waste grounds about a
town.

[2] Arab. Kashákísh from the quadril, kashkasha=he gathered fuel.

beyond the range of matter."[1] Now, when the lad heard these words, he longed to look upon what his uncle was about to do and, forgetting his fatigue, he rose forthright and fell to gathering small wood-chips and dry sticks, and continued until the Moor-man cried to him, "Enough, O son of my brother!" Presently the Magician brought out from his breast-pocket a casket which he opened, and drew from it all he needed of incense; then he fumigated and conjured and adjured, muttering words none might understand. And the ground straightway clave asunder after thick gloom and quake of earth and bellowings of thunder. Hereat Alaeddin was startled and so affrighted that he tried to fly; but, when the African Magician saw his design, he waxed wroth with exceeding wrath, for that without the lad his work would profit him naught, the hidden hoard which he sought to open being not to be opened save by means of Alaeddin. So noting this attempt to run away, the Magician arose and raising his hand smote Alaeddin on the head a buffet so sore that well nigh his back-teeth were knocked out, and he fell swooning to the ground. But after a time he revived by the magic of the Magi-cian, and cried, weeping the while, "O my uncle, what have I done that deserveth from thee such a blow as this?" Hereat the Maghrabi fell to soothing him, and said, "O my son, 'tis my intent to make thee a man; therefore, do thou not gainsay me, for that I am thine uncle and like unto thy father. Obey me, therefore, in all I bid thee, and shortly thou shalt forget all this travail and toil whenas thou shalt look upon the marvel-matters I am about to show thee." And soon after the ground had cloven asunder before the Maroccan it displayed a marble slab wherein was fixed a copper ring. The Maghrabi, striking a geomantic table[2] turned to Alaeddin, and said to him, "An thou do all I shall bid thee, indeed thou shalt become wealthier than any of the kings, and for this reason, O my son, I struck thee, because here lieth a hoard which is stored in thy name; and yet thou de-signedst to leave it and to levant. But now collect thy thoughts, and behold how I opened earth by my spells and adjurations."—— And Shahrazad was surprised by the dawn of day, and ceased to say her permitted say.

---

[1] In text "Shayy bi-lásh" which would mean lit. a thing gratis or in vain.
[2] In the text "Sabba raml" = cast in sand. It may be a clerical error for "Zaraba Raml" = he struck sand, i.e., made geomantic figures.

QUOTH Dunyazad, "O sister mine, an thou be other than sleepy, do tell us some of thy pleasant tales," whereupon Shahrazad replied, "With love and good will." —— It hath reached me, O King of the Age, that the Maghrabi, the Magician, said to Alaeddin, "O my son, now collect thy thoughts! under yon stone wherein the ring is set lieth the treasure wherewith I acquainted thee: so set thy hand upon the ring and raise the slab, for that none other amongst the folk, thyself excepted, hath power to open it, nor may any of mortal birth, save thyself, set foot within this Enchanted Treasury which hath been kept for thee. But 'tis needful that thou learn of me all wherewith I would charge thee; nor gainsay e'en a single syllable of my words. All this, O my child, is for thy good; the hoard being of immense value, whose like the kings of the world never accumulated, and do thou remember that 'tis for thee and me." So poor Alaeddin forgot his fatigue and buffet and tear-shedding, and he was dumbed and dazed at the Maghrabi's words and rejoiced that he was fated to become rich in such measure that not even the Sultans would be richer than himself. Accordingly, he cried, "O my uncle, bid me do all thou pleasest, for I will be obedient unto thy bidding." The Maghrabi replied, "O my nephew, thou art to me as my own child and even dearer, for being my brother's son and for my having none other kith and kin except thyself; and thou, O my child, art my heir and successor." So saying, he went up to Alaeddin and kissed him and said, "For whom do I intend these my labours? Indeed, each and every are for thy sake, O my son, to the end that I may leave thee a rich man and one of the very greatest. So gainsay me not in all I shall say to thee, and now go up to yonder ring and uplift it as I bade thee." Alaeddin answered, "O uncle mine, this ring is over heavy for me: I cannot raise it single-handed, so do thou also come forward and lend me strength and aidance towards uplifting it, for indeed I am young in years." The Moorman replied, "O son of my brother, we shall find it impossible to do aught if I assist thee, and all our efforts would be in vain. But do thou set thy hand upon the ring and pull it up, and thou shalt raise the slab forthright, and in very sooth I told thee that none can touch it save thyself. But whilst haling at it cease not to pronounce thy name and the names of thy father and mother, so 'twill rise at once to thee nor shalt thou feel its weight." Thereupon the lad mustered up strength and girt the loins of resolution and did as the Maroccan had bidden him, and hove up the slab with all ease when he pronounced his name and the names of his parents, even as the Magician had bidden him. And as soon as the stone was raised he threw it aside. —— And Shahrazad was surprised by the dawn of day and ceased to say her permitted say.

𝔚𝔥𝔢𝔫 𝔦𝔱 𝔴𝔞𝔰 𝔱𝔥𝔢 𝔉𝔦𝔳𝔢 𝔥𝔲𝔫𝔡𝔯𝔢𝔡 𝔞𝔫𝔡 𝔗𝔴𝔢𝔫𝔱𝔶-𝔣𝔦𝔣𝔱𝔥 𝔑𝔦𝔤𝔥𝔱,

Quoth Dunyazad, "O sister mine, an thou be other than sleepy, do tell us some of thy pleasant tales," whereupon Shahrazad replied, "With love and good will." —— It hath reached me, O King of the Age, that after Alaeddin had raised the slab from over the entrance to the Hoard there appeared before him a Sardáb, a souterrain, whereunto led a case of some twelve stairs and the Maghrabi said, "O Alaeddin, collect thy thoughts and do whatso I bid thee to the minutest detail nor fail in aught thereof. Go down with all care into yonder vault until thou reach the bottom and there shalt thou find a space divided into four halls,[1] and in each of these thou shalt see four golden jars[2] and others of virgin or and silver. Beware, however, lest thou take aught therefrom or touch them, nor allow thy gown or its skirts even to brush the jars or the walls. Leave them and fare forwards until thou reach the fourth hall without lingering for a single moment on the way; and, if thou do aught contrary thereto thou wilt be at once transformed and become a black stone. When reaching the fourth hall thou wilt find therein a door which do thou open, and pronouncing the names thou spakest over the slab, enter therethrough into a garden adorned everywhere with fruit-bearing trees. This thou must traverse by a path thou wilt see in front of thee measuring some fifty cubits long, beyond which thou wilt come upon an open saloon[3] and therein a ladder of some thirty rungs. And thou shalt also see hanging from

---

[1] Arab. Mauza' = a place, an apartment, a saloon.

[2] Galland makes each contain *quatre vases de bronze, grands comme des cuves.*

[3] The Arab. is "Líwán," for which see vols. iv. 71 and vii. 347. Galland translates it by a "terrace" and "niche."

its ceiling" —— And Shahrazad was surprised by the dawn of day and ceased to say her permitted say.

When it was the Five Hundred and Twenty-sixth Night,

QUOTH Dunyazad, "O sister mine, an thou be other than sleepy, do tell us some of thy pleasant tales," whereupon Shahrazad replied, "With love and good will." —— It hath reached me, O King of the Age, that the Maghrabi, the Magician, fell to teaching Alaeddin how he should descend into the Hoard and continued, "On reaching the saloon thou shalt there find a Lamp hanging from its ceiling; so mount the ladder and take that Lamp and place it in thy breast-pocket after pouring out its contents; nor fear evil from it for thy clothes because its contents are not common oil.[1] And on return thou art allowed to pluck from the trees whatso thou pleasest, for all is thine so long as the Lamp is in thy hand." Now when the Moorman ended his charge to Alaeddin, he drew off a seal-ring[2] and put it upon the lad's forefinger saying, "O my son, verily this signet shall free thee

---

[1] The idea is borrowed from the *lume eterno* of the Rosicrucians. It is still prevalent throughout Syria where the little sepulchral lamps buried by the Hebrews, Greeks and Romans are so called. Many tales are told of their being found burning after the lapse of centuries, but the traveller will never see the marvel.

[2] The first notice of the signet-ring and its adventures is by Herodotus in the Legend of the Samian Polycrates; and here it may be observed that the accident is probably founded on fact; every fisherman knows that fish will seize and swallow spoon-bait and other objects that glitter. The text is the Talmudic version of Solomon's seal-ring. The king of the demons, after becoming a "Bottle-imp," prayed to be set free upon condition of teaching a priceless secret, and after cajoling the Wise One flung his signet into the sea and cast the owner into a land four hundred miles distant. Here David's son begged his bread till he was made head cook to the King of Ammon at Mash Kernín. After a while, he eloped with Na'úzah, the daughter of his master, and presently when broiling a fish found therein his missing property. In the Moslem version, Solomon had taken prisoner Amínah, the daughter of a pagan prince, and had homed her in his Harem, where she taught him idolatry. One day before going to the Hammam he entrusted to her his signet-ring presented to him by the four angelic Guardians of sky, air, water and earth when the mighty Jinni Al-Sakhr (see vol. i. 41; v. 36), who was hovering about unseen, snatching away the ring, assumed the king's shape, whereby Solomon's form became so changed that his courtiers drove him from his own doors. Thereupon Al-Sakhr, taking seat upon the throne, began to work all manner of iniquity, till one of the Wazirs, suspecting the transformation, read aloud from a scroll of the law: this caused the demon to fly shrieking and to drop the signet into the sea. Presently Solomon, who had taken service with a fisherman, and received for wages two fishes a day, found his ring and made Al-Sakhr a "Bottle-imp." The legend of St. Kentigern or Mungo of Glasgow, who recovered the Queen's ring from the stomach of a salmon, is a palpable imitation of the Biblical incident which paid tribute to Cæsar.

from all hurt and fear which may threaten thee, but only on condition that thou bear in mind all I have told thee.[1] So arise straightway and go down the stairs, strengthening thy purpose and girding the loins of resolution: moreover fear not for thou art now a man and no longer a child. And in shortest time, O my son, thou shalt win thee immense riches and thou shalt become the wealthiest of the world." Accordingly, Alaeddin arose and descended into the souterrain, where he found the four halls, each containing four jars of gold and these he passed by, as the Maroccan had bidden him, with the utmost care and caution. Thence he fared into the garden and walked along its length until he entered the saloon, where he mounted the ladder and took the Lamp which he extinguished, pouring out the oil which was therein, and placed it in his breast-pocket. Presently, descending the ladder he returned to the garden where he fell to gazing at the trees whereupon sat birds glorifying with loud voices their great Creator. Now he had not observed them as he went in, but all these trees bare for fruitage costly gems; moreover each had its own kind of growth and jewels of its peculiar sort; and these were of every colour, green and white; yellow, red and other such brilliant hues and the radiance flashing from these gems paled the rays of the sun in forenoon sheen. Furthermore the size of each stone so far surpassed description that no King of the Kings of the world owned a single gem equal to the larger sort nor could boast of even one half the size of the smaller kind of them. —— And Shahrazad was surprised by the dawn of day and ceased to say her permitted say.

When it was the Five Hundred and Twenty-seventh Night,

QUOTH Dunyazad, "O sister mine, an thou be other than sleepy, do tell us some of thy pleasant tales," whereupon Shahrazad replied, "With love and good will." —— It hath reached me, O King of the Age, that Alaeddin walked amongst the trees and gazed upon them and other things which surprised the sight and bewildered the wits; and, as considered them, he saw that in lieu of common fruits the produce was of mighty fine jewels and

---

[1] The Magician evidently had mistaken the powers of the Ring. This is against all probability and possibility, but on such abnormal traits are tales and novels founded.

precious stones,[1] such as emeralds and diamonds; rubies, spinels and balasses, pearls and similar gems astounding the mental vision of man. And forasmuch as the lad had never beheld things like these during his born days nor had reached those years of discretion which would teach him the worth of such valuables (he being still but a little lad), he fancied that all these jewels were of glass or crystal. So he collected them until he had filled his breast-pockets and began to certify himself if they were or were not common fruits, such as grapes, figs and such like edibles. But seeing them of glassy substance, he, in his ignorance of precious stones and their prices, gathered into his breast-pockets every kind of growth the trees afforded; and, having failed of his purpose in finding them food, he said in his mind, "I will collect a portion of these glass fruits for playthings at home." So he fell to plucking them in quantities and cramming them in his pokes and breast-pockets till these were stuffed full; after which he picked others which he placed in his waist-shawl and then, girding himself therewith, carried off all he availed to, purposing to place them in the house by way of ornaments and, as hath been mentioned, never imagining that they were other than glass. Then he hurried his pace in fear of his uncle, the Maghrabi, until he had passed through the four halls and lastly on his return reached the souterrain where he cast not a look at the jars of gold, albeit he was able and allowed to take of the contents on his way back. But when he came to the souterrain-stairs[2] and clomb the

---

[1] These are the Gardens of the Hesperides and of King Isope (Tale of Beryn, Supplem. Canterbury Tales, Chaucer Soc. p. 84) :—

> In mydward of this gardyn stant a feirè tre
> Of alle manner levis that under sky be,
> I-forgit and i-fourmyd, eche in his degre
> Of sylver, and of golde fyne, that lusty been to see.

So in the Kathá (S. S.) there are trees with trunks of gold, branches of pearls, and buds and flowers of clear white pearls.

[2] The text causes some confusion by applying "Sullam" to staircase and ladder, hence probably the latter is not mentioned by Galland and Co., who speak only of an *escalier de cinquante marches*. "Sullam" (plur. "Salálim") in modern Egyptian is popularly used for a flight of steps: see Spitta-Bey's "Contes Arabes Modernes," p. 70. The H. V. places under the slab a hollow space measuring four paces (kadam = 2.5 feet), and at one corner a wicket with a ladder. This leads to a vault of three rooms, one with the jars of gold; the second not to be swept by the skirts, and the third opening upon the garden of gems. "There thou shalt see a path, whereby do thou fare straight forwards to a lofty palace with a flight of fifty steps leading to a flat terrace: and here shalt thou find a niche wherein a lamp burneth."

steps till naught remained but the last; and, finding this higher than all the others, he was unable alone and unassisted, burthened moreover as he was, to mount it. So he said to the Maghrabi, "O my uncle, lend me thy hand and aid me to climb;" but the Moorman answered, "O my son, give me the Lamp and lighten thy load; belike 'tis that weigheth thee down." The lad rejoined, "O my uncle, 'tis not the Lamp downweigheth me at all; but do thou lend me a hand and as soon as I reach ground I will give it to thee." Hereat the Maroccan, the Magician, whose only object was the Lamp and none other, began to insist upon Alaeddin giving it to him at once; but the lad (forasmuch as he had placed it at the bottom of his breast-pocket and his other pouches being full of gems bulged outwards)[1] could not reach it with his fingers to hand it over, so the wizard after much vain persistency in requiring what his nephew was unable to give, fell to raging with furious rage and to demanding the Lamp whilst Alaeddin could not get at it. —— And Shahrazad was surprised by the dawn of day and ceased to say her permitted say.

When it was the Five Hundred and Twenty-eighth Night,

QUOTH Dunyazad, "O sister mine, an thou be other than sleepy, do tell us some of thy pleasant tales," whereupon Shahrazad replied, "With love and good will." —— It hath reached me, O King of the Age, that Alaeddin could not get at the Lamp so as to hand it to his uncle the Maghrabi, that false felon, so the Magician waxed foolish with fury for that he could not win to his wish. Yet had the lad promised truthfully that he would give it up as soon as he might reach ground, without lying thought or ill-intent. But when the Moorman saw that he would not hand it over, he waxed wroth with wrath exceeding and cut off all his hopes of winning it; so he conjured and adjured and cast incense amiddlemost the fire, when forthright the slab made a cover of itself, and by the might of magic lidded the entrance; the earth buried the stone as it was aforetime and Alaeddin, unable to issue forth, remained underground. Now the Sorcerer was a stranger, and, as we have mentioned, no uncle of Alaeddin's,

---

[1] In the H.V. he had thrust the lamp into the bosom of his dress, which, together with his sleeves, he had filled full of fruit, and had wound his girdle tightly around him lest any fall out.

and he had misrepresented himself and preferred a lying claim,
to the end that he might obtain the Lamp by means of the lad for
whom his Hoard had been upstored. So the Accursed heaped the
earth over him and left him to die of hunger. For this Maghrabi
was an African of Afrikíyah proper, born in the Inner Sunset-
land, and from his earliest age upwards he had been addicted to
witchcraft and had studied and practised every manner of occult
science, for which unholy lore the city of Africa[1] is notorious.
And he ceased not to read and hear lectures until he had become
a past-master in all such knowledge. And of the abounding skill
in spells and conjurations which he had acquired by the perusing
and the lessoning of forty years, one day of the days he discovered by devilish inspiration that there lay in an extreme city
of the cities of China, named Al-Kal'ás,[2] an immense Hoard, the
like whereof none of the Kings in this world had ever accumulated: moreover, that the most marvellous article in this Enchanted Treasure was a wonderful Lamp which, whoso possessed,
could not possibly be surpassed by any man upon earth, either
in high degree or in wealth and opulence; nor could the mightiest
monarch of the universe attain to the all-sufficiency of this Lamp
with its might of magical means. —— And Shahrazad was surprised by the dawn of day and ceased to say her permitted say.

When it was the Five Hundred and Twenty-ninth Night,

QUOTH Dunyazad, "O sister mine, an thou be other than sleepy,
do tell us some of thy pleasant tales." whereupon Shahrazad
replied, "With love and good will." —— It hath reached me, O
King of the Age, that when the Maghrabi assured himself by his
science and saw that this Hoard could be opened only by the
presence of a lad named Alaeddin, of pauper family and abiding
in that very city, and learnt how taking it would be easy and

---

1 Africa (Arab. Afrikíyah) here is used in its old and classical sense for the limited tract
about Carthage (Tunis) *i.e.*, Africa Propria. But the scribe imagines it to be the P. N. of a
city: so in Júdar (vol. vi. 222) we find Fás and Miknás (Fez and Mequinez) converted into
one settlement. The Maghribi, Mauritanian or Maroccan is famed for sorcery throughout
the Moslem world: see vol. vi. 220. The Moslem "Kingdom of Afrikíyah" was composed
of four provinces, Tunis, Tripoli, Constantina, and Bugia: and a considerable part of it
was held by the Berber tribe of Sanhája or Sinhága, also called the Zenag, whence our modern "Senegal." Another noted tribe which held Bajaiyah (Bugia) in Afrikiyah proper was
the "Zawáwah," the European "Zouaves," (Ibn Khall. iv. 84).

2 Galland omits the name, which is outlandish enough.

without hardships, he straightway and without stay or delay equipped himself for a voyage to China (as we have already told), and he did what he did with Alaeddin fancying that he would become Lord of the Lamp. But his attempt and his hopes were baffled and his work was clean wasted; whereupon, determining to do the lad die, he heaped up the earth over him by gramarye to the end that the unfortunate might perish, reflecting that "The live man hath no murtherer."[1] Secondly, he did so with the design that, as Alaeddin could not come forth from underground, he would also be impotent to bring out the Lamp from the sou-terrain. So presently he wended his ways and retired to his own land, Africa, a sadder man and disappointed of all his expecta-tions. Such was the case with the Wizard; but as regards Alaeddin when the earth was heaped over him, he began shout-ing to the Moorman whom he believed to be his uncle, and pray-ing him to lend a hand that he might issue from the souterrain and return to earth's surface; but, however loudly he cried, none was found to reply. At that moment he comprehended the sleight which the Maroccan had played upon him, and that the man was no uncle but a liar and a wizard. Then the unhappy despaired of life, and learned to his sorrow that there was no escape for him; so he fell to beweeping with sore weeping the calamity had befallen him; and after a little while he stood up and descended the stairs to see if Allah Almighty had lightened his grief-load by leaving a door of issue. So he turned him to the right and to the left but he saw naught save darkness and four walls closed upon him, for that the Magician had by his magic locked all the doors and had shut up even the garden, where-through the lad erst had passed, lest it offer him the means of issuing out upon earth's surface, and that he might surely die. Then Alaeddin's weeping waxed sorer, and his wailing louder whenas he found all the doors fast shut, for he had thought to solace himself awhile in the garden. But when he felt that all were locked, he fell to shedding tears and lamenting like unto one who hath lost his every hope, and he returned to sit upon the stairs of the flight whereby he had entered the souterrain. ———— And Shahrazad was surprised by the dawn of day and ceased to say her permitted say.

---

[1] Meaning that he had incurred no blood-guiltiness, as he had not killed the lad and only left him to die.

When it was the Five Hundred and Thirtieth Night,

QUOTH Dunyazad, "O sister mine, an thou be other than sleepy, do tell us some of thy pleasant tales," whereupon Shahrazad replied, "With love and good will."——It hath reached me, O King of the Age, that Alaeddin sat down upon the stair of the vault weeping and wailing and wanting all hopes. But it is a light matter for Allah (be He exalted and extolled!) whenas He designeth aught to say, "Be" and it becometh; for that He createth joy in the midst of annoy; and on this wise it was with Alaeddin. Whilst the Maghrabi, the Magician, was sending him down into the souterrain he set upon his finger by way of gift, a seal-ring and said, "Verily, this signet shall save thee from every strait an thou fall into calamity and ill shifts of time; and it shall remove from thee all hurt and harm, and aid thee with a strong arm whereso thou mayest be set."[1] Now this was by destiny of God the Great, that it might be the means of Alaeddin's escape; for whilst he sat wailing and weeping over his case and cast away all hope of life, and utter misery overwhelmed him, he rubbed his hands together for excess of sorrow, as is the wont of the woeful; then, raising them in supplication to Allah, he cried, "I testify that there is no God save Thou alone, The Most Great, the Omnipotent, the All-Conquering, Quickener of the dead, Creator of man's need and Granter thereof, Resolver of his difficulties and duresse and Bringer of joy not of annoy. Thou art my sufficiency and Thou art the Truest of Trustees. And I bear witness that Mohammed is Thy servant and Thine Apostle and I supplicate Thee, O my God, by his favour with Thee to free me from this my foul plight." And whilst he implored the Lord and was chafing his hands in the soreness of his sorrow for that had befallen him of calamity, his fingers chanced to rub the Ring when, lo and behold! forthright its Familiar rose upright before him and cried, "Adsum; thy slave between thy hands is come! Ask whatso thou wantest, for that I am the thrall of him on whose hand is the Ring, the Signet of my lord and master." Hereat the lad looked at him and saw standing before him a

---

[1] The H. V. explains away the improbability of the Magician forgetting his gift. "In this sore disquietude he bethought him not of the ring which, by the decree of Allah, was the means of Alaeddin's escape; and indeed not only he but oft times those who practice the Black Art are baulked of their designs by Divine Providence."

Márid like unto an Ifrít[1] of our lord Solomon's Jinns. He trembled at the terrible sight; but, hearing the Slave of the Ring say,
"Ask whatso thou wantest, verily, I am thy thrall, seeing that
the signet of my lord be upon thy finger," he recovered his spirits
and remembered the Moorman's saying when giving him the Ring.
So he rejoiced exceedingly and became brave and cried, "Ho thou,
Slave of the Lord of the Ring, I desire thee to set me upon the
face of earth." And hardly had he spoken this speech when
suddenly the ground clave asunder and he found himself at the
door of the Hoard and outside it in full view of the world. Now
for three whole days he had been sitting in the darkness of the
Treasury underground and when the sheen of day and the shine
of sun smote his face he found himself unable to keep his eyes
open; so he began to unclose the lids a little and to close them a
little until his eyeballs regained force and got used to the light
and were purged of the noisome murk. —— And Shahrazad was
surprised by the dawn of day and ceased to say her permitted say.

When it was the Five Hundred and Thirty-first Night,

Quoth Dunyazad, "O sister mine, an thou be other than sleepy,
do tell me some of thy pleasant tales," whereupon Shahrazad
replied "With love and good will." —— It hath reached me, O
King of the Age, that Alaeddin, issuing from the Treasury,
opened his eyes after a short space of time and saw himself upon
earth's surface, the which rejoiced him exceedingly, and withal
he was astounded at finding himself without the Hoard-door
whereby he had passed in when it was opened by the Maghrabi,
the Magician; especially as the adit had been lidded and the
ground had been smoothed, showing no sign whatever of entrance. Thereat his surprise increased until he fancied himself
in another place, nor was his mind convinced that the stead was
the same until he saw the spot whereupon they had kindled the
fire of wood-chips and dried sticks, and where the African Wizard
had conjured over the incense. Then he turned him rightwards
and leftwards and sighted the gardens from afar and his eyes

---

[1] See vol. vii. 60. The word is mostly derived from " 'afar" = dust, and denotes, according to some, a man coloured like the ground or one who "dusts" all his rivals. " 'Ifr"
(fem. 'Ifrah) is a wicked and dangerous man. Al-Jannabi, I may here notice, is the chief
authority for Afrikus son of Abraha and xviiith Tobba being the eponymus of "Africa."

recognized the road whereby he had come. So he returned thanks
to Allah Almighty who had restored him to the face of earth
and had freed him from death after he had cut off all hopes of life.
Presently he arose and walked along the way to the town, which
now he well knew, until he entered the streets and passed on to
his own home. Then he went in to his mother and on seeing
her, of the overwhelming stress of joy at his escape and the
memory of past affright and the hardships he had borne and the
pangs of hunger, he fell to the ground before his parent in a
fainting-fit. Now his mother had been passing sad since the
time of his leaving her and he found her moaning and crying
about him; however on sighting him enter the house she joyed
with exceeding joy, but soon was overwhelmed with woe when
he sank upon the ground swooning before her eyes. Still,[1] she
did not neglect the matter or treat it lightly, but at once hastened
to sprinkle water upon his face and after she asked of the neighbours some scents which she made him snuff up. And when he
came round a little, he prayed her to bring him somewhat of food
saying, "O my mother 'tis now three days since I ate anything
at all." Thereupon she arose and brought him what she had by
her; then, setting it before him, said, "Come forward, O my
son; eat and be cheered[2] and, when thou shalt have rested, tell
me what hath betided and affected thee, O my child; at this
present I will not question thee for thou art aweary in very
deed."——And Shahrazad was surprised by the dawn of day
and ceased to say her permitted say.

When it was the Five Hundred and Thirty-second Night,

Quoth Dunyazad, "O sister mine, an thou be other than sleepy,
do tell me some of thy pleasant tales," whereupon Shahrazad
replied, "With love and good will." —— It hath reached me, O
King of the Age, that Alaeddin ate and drank and was cheered
and after he had rested and had recovered spirits he cried, "Ah, O
my mother, I have a sore grievance against thee for leaving me
to that accursed wight who strave to compass my destruction

---

[1] Arab. "Ghayr an" = otherwise that, except that, a favourite form in this MS. The
first word is the Syriac "Gheir" = for, a conjunction which is most unneccessarily derived
by some from the Gr. γὰϱ.

[2] Galland and the H.V. make the mother deliver a little hygienic lecture about not
feeding too fast after famine: exactly what an Eastern parent would not dream of doing.

and designed to take my life.[1] Know that I beheld Death with mine own eyes at the hand of this damned wretch, whom thou didst certify to be my uncle; and, had not Almighty Allah rescued me from him, I and thou, O my mother, had been cozened by the excess of this Accursed's promises to work my welfare, and by the great show of affection which he manifested to us. Learn, O my mother, that this fellow is a sorcerer, a Moorman, an accursed, a liar, a traitor, a hypocrite;[2] nor deem I that the devils under the earth are damnable as he. Allah abase him in his every book! Hear then, O my mother, what this abominable one did, and all I shall tell thee will be soothfast and certain. See how the damned villain brake every promise he made, certifying that he would soon work all good with me; and do thou consider the fondness which he displayed to me and the deeds which he did by me; and all this only to win his wish, for his design was to destroy me; and Alhamdolillah — laud to the Lord — for my deliverance. Listen and learn, O my mother, how this Accursed entreated me." Then Alaeddin informed his mother of all that had befallen him (weeping the while for stress of gladness); how the Maghrabi had led him to a hill wherein was hidden the Hoard and how he had conjured and fumigated, adding,[3] "After which, O my mother, mighty fear gat hold of me when the hill split and the earth gaped before me by his wizardry; and I trembled with terror at the rolling of thunder in mine ears and the murk which fell upon us when he fumigated and muttered spells. Seeing these horrors I in mine affright designed to fly; but, when he understood mine intent he reviled me and smote me a buffet so sore that it caused me to swoon. However, inasmuch as the Treasury was to be opened only by means of me, O my mother, he could not descend therein himself, it being in my name and not in his; and, for that he is an ill-omened magician, he understood that I was necessary to him and this was his need of me." —— And Shahrazad was surprised by the dawn of day and ceased to say her permitted say.

---

[1] The lad now turns the tables upon his mother and becomes her master, having "a crow to pick" with her.

[2] Arab. "Munáfik" for whose true sense, "an infidel who pretendeth to believe in Al-Islam," see vol. vi. p. 207. Here the epithet comes last being the climax of abuse, because the lowest of the seven hells (vol. viii. 111) was created for "hypocrites," i.e., those who feign to be Moslems when they are Miscreants.

[3] Here a little abbreviation has been found necessary to avoid the whole of a twice-told tale; but nothing material has been omitted.

When it was the Five Hundred and Thirty-third Night,

QUOTH Dunyazad, "O sister mine, an thou be other than sleepy, do tell me some of thy pleasant tales," whereupon Shahrazad replied, "With love and good will." —— It hath reached me, O King of the Age, that Alaeddin acquainted his mother with all that had befallen him from the Maghrabi, the Magician, and said, "After he had buffetted me, he judged it advisable to soothe me in order that he might send me down into the Enchanted Treasury; and first he drew from his finger a Ring which he placed upon mine. So I descended and found four halls all full of gold and silver which counted as naught, and the Accursed had charged me not to touch aught thereof. Then I entered a mighty fine flower-garden everywhere bedecked with tall trees whose foliage and fruitage bewildered the wits, for all, O my mother, were of vari-coloured glass, and lastly I reached the Hall wherein hung this Lamp. So I took it straightway and put it out[1] and poured forth its contents." And so saying Alaeddin drew the Lamp from his breast-pocket and showed it to his mother, together with the gems and jewels which he had brought from the garden; and there were two large bag-pockets full of precious stones, whereof not one was to be found amongst the kings of the world. But the lad knew naught anent their worth deeming them glass or crystal; and presently he resumed, "After this, O mother mine, I reached the Hoard-door carrying the Lamp and shouted to the accursed Sorcerer, which called himself my uncle, to lend me a hand and hale me up, I being unable to mount of myself the last step for the over-weight of my burthen. But he would not and said only, 'First hand me the Lamp!' As, however, I had placed it at the bottom of my breast-pocket and the other pouches bulged out beyond it, I was unable to get at it and said, 'O my uncle, I cannot reach thee the Lamp, but I will give it to thee when outside the Treasury.' His only need was the Lamp and he designed, O my mother, to snatch it from me

---

[1] Arab. "Taffaytu-hu." This is the correct term = to extinguish. They relate of the great scholar Firozábádí, author of the "Kámús" (ob. A. H. 817 = A. D. 1414), that he married a Badawi wife in order to study the purest Arabic and once when going to bed said to her, "Uktuli's-siráj," the Persian "Chirágh-rá bi-kush" = Kill the lamp. "What," she cried, "Thou an 'Álim and talk of killing the lamp instead of putting it out!"

and after that slay me, as indeed he did his best to do by heaping the earth over my head. Such then is what befel me from this foul Sorcerer." Hereupon Alaeddin fell to abusing the Magician in hot wrath and with a burning heart and crying, "Well-away! I take refuge from this damned wight, the ill-omened, the wrong-doer, the for-swearer, the lost to all humanity, the arch-traitor, the hypocrite, the annihilator of ruth and mercy."——And Shahrazad was surprised by the dawn of day and ceased to say her permitted say.

When it was the Five Hundred and Thirty-fourth Night,

QUOTH Dunyazad, "O sister mine, an thou be other than sleepy, do tell us some of thy pleasant tales," whereupon Shahrazad replied, "With love and good will."——It hath reached me, O King of the Age, that when Alaeddin's mother heard his words and what had befallen him from the Maghrabi, the Magician, she said, "Yea, verily, O my son, he is a miscreant, a hypocrite who murthereth the folk by his magic; but 'twas the grace of Allah Almighty, O my child, that saved thee from the tricks and the treachery of this accursed Sorcerer whom I deemed to be truly thine uncle."[1] Then, as the lad had not slept a wink for three days and found himself nodding, he sought his natural rest, his mother doing on like wise; nor did he awake till about noon on the second day. As soon as he shook off slumber he called for somewhat of food being sore anhungered, but said his mother, "O my son, I have no victual for thee inasmuch as yesterday thou atest all that was in the house. But wait patiently a while: I have spun a trifle of yarn which I will carry to the market-street and sell it and buy with what it may be worth some victual for thee." "O my mother," said he, "keep your yarn and sell it not; but fetch me the Lamp I brought hither that I may go vend it and with its price purchase provaunt, for that I deem 'twill bring more money than the spinnings." So Alaeddin's mother arose and fetched the Lamp for her son; but, while so doing, she saw that it was dirty exceedingly; so she said, "O my son, here is the Lamp, but 'tis very foul: after we shall have washed it and

---

[1] In the H. V. the mother takes the "fruits" and places them upon the ground; "but when darkness set in, a light shone from them like the rays of a lamp or the sheen of the sun."

polished it 'twill sell better." Then, taking a handful of sand she began to rub therewith, but she had only begun when appeared to her one of the Jánn whose favour was frightful and whose bulk was horrible big, and he was gigantic as one of the Jabá-birah.[1] And forthright he cried to her, "Say whatso thou wantest of me? Here am I, thy Slave and Slave to whoso holdeth the Lamp; and not I alone, but all the Slaves of the Wonderful Lamp which thou hendest in hand." She quaked and terror was sore upon her when she looked at that frightful form and her tongue being tied she could not return aught reply, never having been accustomed to espy similar semblances.——And Shahrazad was surprised by the dawn of day and ceased to say her permitted say.

𝔚𝔥𝔢𝔫 𝔦𝔱 𝔴𝔞𝔰 𝔱𝔥𝔢 𝔉𝔦𝔳𝔢 𝔥𝔲𝔫𝔡𝔯𝔢𝔡 𝔞𝔫𝔡 𝔗𝔥𝔦𝔯𝔱𝔶-𝔣𝔦𝔣𝔱𝔥 𝔑𝔦𝔤𝔥𝔱,

QUOTH Dunyazad, "O sister mine, an thou be other than sleepy, do tell us some of thy pleasant tales," whereupon Shahrazad replied, "With love and good will."——It hath reached me, O King of the Age, that Alaeddin's mother could not of her terror return a reply to the Márid; nay she fell to the ground oppressed by her affright.[2] Now her son was standing afar off and he had already seen the Jinní of the Ring which he had rubbed within the Treasury; so when he heard the Slave speaking to his parent, he hastened forwards and snatching the Lamp from her hand, said, "O Slave of the Lamp, I am unhungered and 'tis my desire that thou fetch me somewhat to eat and let it be something tooth-some beyond our means." The Jinni disappeared for an eye-twinkle and returned with a mighty fine tray and precious of price, for that 'twas all in virginal silver and upon it stood twelve golden platters of meats manifold and dainties delicate, with bread snowier than snow; also two silvern cups and as many black jacks[3] full of wine clear-strained and long-stored. And after

---

[1] For these fabled Giant rulers of Syria, Og King of Bashan, etc., see vols. vii. 84; ix. 109, 323. D'Herbelot (s. v. Giabbar = Giant) connects "Jabábirah" with the Heb. Ghibbor, Ghibborim and the Pers. Dív, Diván: of these were 'Ád and Shaddád, Kings of Syria: the Falastín (Philistines) 'Auj, Amálik and Banú Shayth or Seth's descendants, the sons of God (Benu-Elohim) of the Book of Genesis (vi. 2) who inhabited Mount Hermon and lived in purity and chastity.

[2] The H. V. explains that the Jinni had appeared to the mother in hideous aspect, with noise and clamour, because she had scoured the Lamp roughly; but was more gentle with Alaeddin because he had rubbed it lightly. This is from Galland.

[3] Arab. Musawwadatayn = lit. two black things, rough copies, etc.

setting all these before Alaeddin, he evanished from vision. Thereupon the lad went and sprinkled rose water upon his mother's face and caused her snuff up perfumes pure and pungent and said to her when she revived, "Rise, O mother mine, and let us eat of these meats wherewith Almighty Allah hath eased our poverty." But when she saw that mighty fine silvern tray she fell to marvelling at the matter and quoth she, "O my son, who be this generous, this beneficent one who hath abated our hunger-pains and our penury? We are indeed under obligation to him and, meseemeth, 'tis the Sultan who, hearing of our mean condition and our misery, hath sent us this food-tray." Quoth he, "O my mother, this be no time for questioning: arouse thee and let us eat for we are both a-famished." Accordingly, they sat down to the tray and fell to feeding when Alaeddin's mother tasted meats whose like in all her time she had never touched; so they devoured them with sharpened appetites and all the capacity engendered by stress of hunger; and, secondly, the food was such that marked the tables of the Kings. But neither of them knew whether the tray was or was not valuable, for never in their born days had they looked upon aught like it. As soon as they had finished the meal (withal leaving victual enough for supper and eke for the next day), they arose and washed their hands and sat at chat, when the mother turned to her son and said, "Tell me, O my child, what befel thee from the Slave, the Jinní, now that Alhamdolillah—laud to the Lord!— we have eaten our full of the good things wherewith He hath favoured us and thou hast no pretext for saying to me, 'I am anhungered.' " So Alaeddin related to her all that took place between him and the Slave what while she had sunk upon the ground aswoon for sore terror; and at this she, being seized with mighty great surprise, said, " 'Tis true; for the Jinns do present themselves before the Sons of Adam[1] but I, O my son, never saw them in all my life and meseemeth that this be the same who saved thee when thou wast within the Enchanted Hoard." "This is not he, O my mother:

---

[1] Arab. Banú Adam, as opposed to Banú Elohim (Sons of the Gods), B. al-Jánn etc. The Banú al-Asfar = sons of the yellow, are Esau's posterity in Edom, also a term applied by Arab historians to the Greeks and Romans whom Jewish fable derived from Idumæa: in my vol. ii. 220, they are the people of the yellow or tawny faces. For the legend see Ibn Khall. iii. 8, where the translator suggests that the by-name may be = the "sons of the Emperor" Flavius, confounded with "flavus," a title left by Vespasian to his successors. The Banú al-Khashkhash = sons of the (black) poppy are the Ethiopians.

this who appeared before thee is the Slave of the Lamp!" "Who may this be, O my son?" "This be a Slave of sort and shape other than he; that was the Familiar of the Ring and this his fellow thou sawest was the Slave of the Lamp thou hentest in hand."——And Shahrazad was surprised by the dawn of day and ceased to say her permitted say.

When it was the Five Hundred and Thirty-sixth Night,

QUOTH Dunyazad, "O sister mine, an thou be other than sleepy, do tell us some of thy pleasant tales," whereupon Shahrazad replied, "With love and good will."——It hath reached me, O King of the Age, that Alaeddin said, "Verily, O my mother, the Jinni who appeared to thee was the Slave of the Lamp." And when his parent heard these words she cried, "There! there![1] so this Accursed, who showed himself to me and went nigh unto killing me with affright, is attached to the Lamp." "Yes," he replied, and she rejoined, "Now I conjure thee, O my son, by the milk wherewith I suckled thee, to throw away from thee this Lamp and this Ring; because they can cause us only extreme terror and I especially can never abear a second glance at them. Moreover all intercourse with them is unlawful, for that the Prophet (whom Allah save and assain!) warned us against them with threats." He replied, "Thy commands, O my mother, be upon my head[2] and mine eyes; but, as regards this saying thou saidest, 'tis impossible that I part or with Lamp or with Ring. Thou thyself hast seen what good the Slave wrought us whenas we were famishing; and know, O my mother, that the Maghrabi, the liar, the Magician, when sending me down into the Hoard, sought nor the silver nor the gold wherewith the four halls were fulfilled, but charged me to bring him only the Lamp (naught else), because in very deed he had learned its priceless value; and, had he not been certified of it, he had never endured such toil and trouble nor had he travelled from his own land to our land in search thereof; neither had he shut me up in the Treasury when he de- spaired of the Lamp which I would not hand to him. Therefore

---

[1] Arab, Há! há! so Háka (fem. Háki) = Here for thee!
[2] So in Mediæval Europe Papal bulls and Kings' letters were placed for respect on the head. See Duffield's "Don Quixote," Part i. xxxi.

it besitteth us, O my mother, to keep this Lamp and take all care thereof nor disclose its mysteries to any; for this is now our means of livelihood and this it is shall enrich us. And likewise as regards the Ring, I will never withdraw it from my finger, inasmuch as but for this thou hadst nevermore seen me on life; nay I should have died within the Hoard underground. How then can I possibly remove it from my finger? And who wotteth that which may betide me by the lapse of Time, what trippings or calamities or injurious mishaps wherefrom this Ring may deliver me? However, for regard to thy feelings I will stow away the Lamp nor ever suffer it to be seen of thee hereafter." Now when his mother heard his words and pondered them she knew they were true and said to him, "Do, O my son, whatso thou willest; for my part I wish never to see them nor ever sight that frightful spectacle I erst saw."——And Shahrazad was surprised by the dawn of day and ceased to say her permitted say.

When it was the Five Hundred and Thirty-seventh Night,

QUOTH Dunyazad, "O sister mine, an thou be not sleepy, do tell us some of thy pleasant tales," whereupon Shahrazad replied, "With love and good will."——It hath reached me, O King of the Age, that Alaeddin and his mother continued eating of the meats brought them by the Jinni for two full told days till they were finished; but when he learned that nothing of food remained for them, he arose and took a platter of the platters which the Slave had brought upon the tray. Now they were all of the finest gold but the lad knew naught thereof; so he bore it to the Bazar and there, seeing a man which was a Jew, a viler than the Satans,[1] offered it to him for sale. When the Jew espied it he took the lad aside that none might see him, and he looked at the platter and considered it till he was certified that it was of gold refined. But he knew not whether Alaeddin was acquainted with its value or he was in such matters a raw laddie;[2] so he asked him, "For how much, O my lord, this platter?" and the other answered, "Thou wottest what be its worth." The Jew

---

[1] Galland makes the Juif only *rusé et adroit*.

[2] Arab. "Ghashím" = a "Johnny Raw" from the root "Ghashm" = iniquity: Builders apply the word to an unhewn stone; addressed to a person it is considered slighting, if not insulting. See vol. ii. 330.

debated with himself as to how much he should offer, because Alaeddin had returned him a craftsman-like reply; and he thought of the smallest valuation; at the same time he feared lest the lad, haply knowing its worth, should expect a considerable sum. So he said in his mind, "Belike the fellow is an ignoramus in such matters nor is ware of the price of the platter." Whereupon he pulled out of his pocket a dinar, and Alaeddin eyed the gold piece lying in his palm and hastily taking it went his way; whereby the Jew was certified of his customer's innocence of all such knowledge, and repented with entire repentance that he had given him a golden dinar in lieu of a copper carat,[1] a bright-polished groat. However, Alaeddin made no delay but went at once to the baker's where he bought him bread and changed the ducat; then, going to his mother, he gave her the scones and the remaining small coin and said, "O my mother, hie thee and buy thee all we require." So she arose and walked to the Bazar and laid in the necessary stock; after which they ate and were cheered. And whenever the price of the platter was expended, Alaeddin would take another and carry it to the accursed Jew who bought each and every at a pitiful price; and even this he would have minished but, seeing how he had paid a dinar for the first, he feared to offer a lesser sum, lest the lad go and sell to some rival in trade and thus lose his usurious gains. Now when all the golden platters were sold, there remained only the silver tray whereupon they stood; and, for that it was large and weighty, Alaeddin brought the Jew to his house and produced the article, when the buyer, seeing its size gave him ten dinars and these being accepted went his ways. Alaeddin and his mother lived upon the sequins until they were spent; then he brought out the Lamp and rubbed it and straightway appeared the Slave who had shown himself aforetime.——And Shahrazad was surprised by the dawn of day and ceased to say her permitted say.

𝔚hen it was the 𝔉ive 𝔥undred and 𝔗hirty-eighth 𝔑ight,

Quoth Dunyazad, "O sister mine, an thou be other than sleepy, do tell us some of thy pleasant tales," whereupon Shahrazad replied, "With love and good will."——It hath reached me, O

---

[1] The carat (Kírát) being most often, but not always, one twenty-fourth of the dinar. See vols. iii. 239; vii. 289.

King of the Age, that the Jinni, the Slave of the Lamp, on appearing to Alaeddin said, "Ask, O my lord, whatso thou wantest for
I am thy Slave and the thrall of whoso hath the Lamp;" and said
the lad, "I desire that thou bring me a tray of food like unto that
thou broughtest me erewhiles, for indeed I am famisht." Accordingly, in the glance of an eye the Slave produced a similar
tray supporting twelve platters of the most sumptuous, furnished
with requisite cates; and thereon stood clean bread and sundry
glass bottles[1] of strained wine. Now Alaeddin's mother had
gone out when she knew he was about to rub the Lamp that she
might not again look upon the Jinni; but after a while she returned and, when she sighted the tray covered with silvern[2]
platters and smelt the savour of the rich meats diffused over the
house, she marvelled and rejoiced. Thereupon quoth he, "Look,
O my mother! Thou badest me throw away the Lamp, see now
its virtues;" and quoth she, "O my son, Allah increase his[3] weal,
but I would not look upon him." Then the lad sat down with
his parent to the tray and they ate and drank until they were
satisfied; after which they removed what remained for use on the
morrow. As soon as the meats had been consumed, Alaeddin
arose and stowed away under his clothes a platter of the platters
and went forth to find the Jew, purposing to sell it to him; but
by fiat of Fate he passed by the shop of an ancient jeweller, an
honest man and a pious who feared Allah. When the Shaykh
saw the lad, he asked him saying, "O my son, what dost thou
want? for that times manifold have I seen thee passing hereby
and having dealings with a Jewish man; and I have espied thee
handing over to him sundry articles; now also I fancy thou hast
somewhat for sale and thou seekest him as a buyer thereof. But
thou wottest not, O my child, that the Jews ever hold lawful to
them the good of Moslems,[4] the Confessors of Allah Almighty's
unity, and, always defraud them; especially this accursed Jew
with whom thou hast relations and into whose hands thou hast

---

[1] Kanání, plur. of Kinnínah.

[2] Here and below silver is specified, whenas the platters in Night dxxxv. were of gold.
This is one of the many changes, contradictions and confusions which are inherent in Arab
stories. See Spitta-Bey's "Contes Arabes," Preface.

[3] i.e., the Slave of the Lamp.

[4] This may be true, but my experience has taught me to prefer dealing with a Jew than
with a Christian. The former will "jew" me perhaps, but his commercial cleverness will in-
duce him to allow me some gain in order that I may not be quite disheartened: the latter
will strip me of my skin and will grumble because he cannot gain more.

fallen. If then, O my son, thou have aught thou wouldest sell show the same to me and never fear, for I will give thee its full price by the truth of Almighty Allah." Thereupon Alaeddin brought out the platter which when the ancient goldsmith saw, he took and weighed it in his scales and asked the lad saying, "Was it the fellow of this thou soldest to the Jew?" "Yes, its fellow and its brother," he answered, and quoth the old man, "What price did he pay thee?" Quoth the lad, "One dinar." ——And Shahrazad was surprised by the dawn of day and ceased to say her permitted say.

𝔚𝔥𝔢𝔫 𝔦𝔱 𝔴𝔞𝔰 𝔱𝔥𝔢 𝔉𝔦𝔳𝔢 𝔥𝔲𝔫𝔡𝔯𝔢𝔡 𝔞𝔫𝔡 𝔗𝔥𝔦𝔯𝔱𝔶-𝔫𝔦𝔫𝔱𝔥 𝔑𝔦𝔤𝔥𝔱,

Quoth Dunyazad, "O sister mine, an thou be other than sleepy, do tell us some of thy pleasant tales," whereupon Shahrazad replied, "With love and good will."——It hath reached me, O King of the Age, that the ancient goldsmith, hearing from Alaeddin how the Jew used to give only one dinar as the price of the platter, cried, "Ah! I take refuge from this Accursed who cozeneth the servants of Allah Almighty!" Then, looking at the lad, he exclaimed, "O my son, verily yon tricksy Jew hath cheated thee and laughed at thee, this platter being pure silver and virginal. I have weighed it and found it worth seventy dinars; and, if thou please to take its value, take it." Thereupon the Shaykh counted out to him seventy gold pieces, which he accepted and presently thanked him for his kindness in exposing the Jew's rascality. And after this, whenever the price of a platter was expended, he would bring another, and on such wise he and his mother were soon in better circumstances; yet they ceased not to live after their olden fashion as middle class folk[1] without spending on diet overmuch or squandering money. But Alaeddin had now thrown off the ungraciousness of his boyhood; he shunned the society of scapegraces and he began to frequent good men and true, repairing daily to the market-street of the merchants and there companying with the great and the small of them, asking about matters of merchandise and learning the price of investments and so forth; he likewise frequented the

---

[1] Arab. "Hálah mutawassitah," a phrase which has a European touch.

Bazars of the Goldsmiths and the Jewellers[1] where he would sit and divert himself by inspecting their precious stones and by noting how jewels were sold and bought therein. Accordingly, he presently became ware that the tree-fruits, wherewith he had filled his pockets what time he entered the Enchanted Treasury, were neither glass nor crystal but gems rich and rare; and he understood that he had acquired immense wealth such as the Kings never can possess. He then considered all the precious stones which were in the Jewellers' Quarter, but found that their biggest was not worth his smallest. On this wise he ceased not every day repairing to the Bazar and making himself familiar with the folk and winning their loving will;[2] and enquiring anent selling and buying, giving and taking, the dear and the cheap, until one day of the days when, after rising at dawn and donning his dress he went forth, as was his wont, to the Jewellers' Bazar; and, as he passed along it he heard the crier crying as follows: "By command of our magnificent master, the King of the Time and the Lord of the Age and the Tide, let all the folk lock up their shops and stores and retire within their houses, for that the Lady Badr al-Budúr,[3] daughter of the Sultan, designeth to visit the Hammám; and whoso gainsayeth the order shall be punished with death-penalty and be his blood upon his own neck!" But when Alaeddin heard the proclamation, he longed to look upon the King's daughter and said in his mind, "Indeed all the lieges talk of her beauty and loveliness and the end of my desires is to see her."——And Shahrazad was surprised by the dawn of day and ceased to say her permitted say.

When it was the Five Hundred and Fortieth Night,

Quoth Dunyazad, "O sister mine an thou be other than sleepy, do tell us some of thy pleasant tales," whereupon Shahrazad replied, "With love and good will."——It hath reached me, O

---

[1] In the text "Jauharjíyyah," common enough in Egypt and Syria; an Arab. plur. of an Arabised Turkish sing.—ji for—chí = (crafts-) man.

[2] We may suppose some years may have passed in this process and that Alaeddin from a lad of fifteen had reached the age of manhood. The H. V. declares that for many a twelve-month the mother and son lived by cotton spinning and the sale of the plate.

[3] i.e. Full moon of full moons: See vol. iii. 228. It is pronounced "Badroo'l-Budoor," hence Galland's "Badr-oul-boudour."

King of the Age, that Alaeddin fell to contriving some means whereby he might look upon the Princess Badr al-Budúr and at last judged best to take his station behind the Hammam-door whence he might see her face as she entered.[1] Accordingly, without stay or delay he repaired to the Baths before she was expected and stood a-rear of the entrance, a place whereat none of the folk happened to be looking. Now when the Sultan's daughter had gone the rounds of the city and its main streets and had solaced herself by sight-seeing, she finally reached the Hammam and whilst entering she raised her veil, when her face rose before sight as it were a pearl of price or a sheeny sun, and she was as one of whom the describer sang,

"Magic Kohl enchanteth the glances so bright of her: * We pluck roses in posies
     from cheeks rosy bright of her:
   Of night's gloomiest hue is the gloom of the hair of her * And her bright brow
     uplighteth the murks of the night of her."[2]

(Quoth the reciter) when the Princess raised from her face the veil and Alaeddin saw her favour he said, "In very truth her fashion magnifieth her Almighty Fashioner and glory be to Him who created her and adorned her with this beauty and loveliness." His strength was struck down from the moment he saw her and his thoughts were distraught; his gaze was dazed, the love of her gat hold of the whole of his heart; and, when he returned home to his mother, he was as one in ecstasy. His parent addressed him, but he neither replied nor denied; and, when she set before him the morning meal he continued in like case; so quoth she, "O my son, what is't may have befallen thee? Say me, doth aught ail thee? Let me know what ill hath betided thee for, unlike thy custom, thou speakest not when I bespeak thee." Thereupon Alaeddin (who used to think that all women resembled his mother[3] and who, albeit he had heard of the charms of Badr al-Budur, daughter of the Sultan, yet knew not what "beauty"

---

[1] In the H. V. Alaeddin "bethought him of a room adjacent to the Baths where he might sit and see the Princess through the door-chinks, when she raised her veil before the hand-maids and eunuchs."

[2] This is the common conceit of the brow being white as day and the hair black as night.

[3] Such a statement may read absurdly to the West but it is true in the East. "Selim" had seen no woman's face unveiled, save that of his sable mother Rosebud in Morier's Tale of Yeldoz, the wicked woman ("The Mirza," vol. iii. 135). The H. V. adds that Alaeddin's mother was old and verily had little beauty even in her youth. So at the sight of the Princess he learnt that Allah had created women exquisite in loveliness and heart-ensnar-

and "loveliness" might signify) turned to his parent and ex-claimed, "Let me be!" However, she persisted in praying him to come forwards and eat, so he did her bidding but hardly touched food; after which he lay at full length on his bed all the night through in cogitation deep until morning morrowed. The same was his condition during the next day, when his mother was perplexed for the case of her son and unable to learn what had happened to him. So, thinking that belike he might be ailing, she drew near him and asked him saying, "O my son, an thou sense aught of pain or such like, let me know that I may fare forth and fetch thee the physician; and to-day there be in this our city a leech from the Land of the Arabs whom the Sultan hath sent to summon and the bruit abroad reporteth him to be skilful exceedingly. So, an be thou ill let me go and bring him to thee."——And Shahrazad was surprised by the dawn of day and ceased to say her permitted say.

When it was the Five Hundred and Forty-first Night,

Quoth Dunyazad, "O sister mine, an thou be other than sleepy, do tell us some of thy pleasant tales," whereupon Shahrazad replied, "With love and good will."——It hath reached me, O King of the Age, that Alaeddin, hearing his parent's offer to summon the mediciner, said, "O my mother, I am well in body and on no wise ill. But I ever thought that all women resembled thee until yesterday, when I beheld the Lady Badr al-Budur, daughter of the Sultan, as she was faring for the Baths." Then he related to her all and everything that had happened to him adding, "Haply thou also hast heard the crier a-crying, 'Let no man open shop or stand in street that the Lady Badr al-Budur may repair to the Hammam without eye seeing her.' But I have looked upon her even as she is, for she raised her veil at the door; and, when I viewed her favour and beheld that noble work of the Creator, a sore fit of ecstasy, O my mother, fell upon me for love of her and firm resolve to win her hath opened its way into every limb of me, nor is repose possible for me except I win her. Where-

---

ing; and at first glance the shaft of love pierced his heart and he fell to the ground afaint. He loved her with a thousand lives and, when his mother questioned him, "his lips formed no friendship with his speech."

for I purpose asking her to wife from the Sultan her sire in lawful
wedlock." When Alaeddin's mother heard her son's words, she
belittled his wits and cried, "O my child, the name of Allah upon
thee! meseemeth thou hast lost thy senses. But be thou rightly
guided, O my son, nor be thou as the men Jinn-maddened!" He
replied, "Nay, O mother mine, I am not out of my mind nor am
I of the maniacs; nor shall this thy saying alter one jot of what is
in my thoughts, for rest is impossible to me until I shall have won
the dearling of my heart's core, the beautiful Lady Badr al-Budur.
And now I am resolved to ask her of her sire the Sultan." She
rejoined, "O my son, by my life upon thee speak not such speech,
lest any overhear thee and say thou be insane: so cast away from
thee such nonsense! Who shall undertake a matter like this or
make such request to the King? Indeed, I know not how, supposing this thy speech to be soothfast, thou shalt manage to
crave such grace of the Sultan or through whom thou desirest to
propose it." He retorted, "Through whom shall I ask it, O my
mother, when thou art present? And who is there fonder and
more faithful to me than thyself? So my design is that thou thyself shalt proffer this my petition." Quoth she, "O my son, Allah
remove me far therefrom! What! have I lost my wits like thyself? Cast the thought away and a long way from thy heart.
Remember whose son thou art, O my child, the orphan boy of a
tailor, the poorest and meanest of the tailors toiling in this city;
and I, thy mother, am also come of pauper folk and indigent.
How then durst thou ask to wife the daughter of the Sultan,
whose sire would not deign marry her with the sons of the Kings
and the Sovrans, except they were his peers in honour and
grandeur and majesty; and, were they but one degree lower, he
would refuse his daughter to them."——And Shahrazad was
surprised by the dawn of day and ceased to say her permitted say.

𝔚𝔥𝔢𝔫 𝔦𝔱 𝔴𝔞𝔰 𝔱𝔥𝔢 𝔉𝔦𝔳𝔢 𝔥𝔲𝔫𝔡𝔯𝔢𝔡 𝔞𝔫𝔡 𝔉𝔬𝔯𝔱𝔶-𝔰𝔢𝔠𝔬𝔫𝔡 𝔑𝔦𝔤𝔥𝔱,

QUOTH Dunyazad, "O sister mine, an thou be other than sleepy,
do tell us some of thy pleasant tales," whereupon Shahrazad
replied, "With love and good will."——It hath reached me, O
King of the Age, that Alaeddin took patience until his parent
had said her say, when quoth he, "O my mother, everything
thou hast called to mind is known to me; moreover 'tis thoroughly

well known to me that I am the child of pauper parents; withal
do not these words of thee divert me from my design at all, at all.
Nor the less do I hope of thee, an I be thy son and thou truly
love me, that thou grant me this favour, otherwise thou wilt
destroy me; and present Death hovereth over my head except
I win my will of my heart's dearling; and I, O my mother, am in
every case thy child." Hearing these words, his parent wept of
her sorrow for him and said, "O my child! Yes, in very deed I
am thy mother, nor have I any son or life's blood of my liver except thyself, and the end of my wishes is to give thee a wife and
rejoice in thee. But suppose that I would seek a bride of our
likes and equals, her people will at once ask an thou have any
land or garden, merchandise or handicraft, wherewith thou canst
support her; and what is the reply I can return? Then, if I
cannot possibly answer the poor like ourselves, how shall I be
bold enough, O my son, to ask for the daughter of the Sultan of
China-land who hath no peer or behind or before him? Therefore do thou weigh this matter in thy mind. Also who shall ask
her to wife for the son of a snip? Well indeed I wot that my
saying aught of this kind will but increase our misfortunes; for
that it may be the cause of our incurring mortal danger from the
Sultan; peradventure even death for thee and me. And, as concerneth myself, how shall I venture upon such rash deed and
perilous, O my son? and in what way shall I ask the Sultan for his
daughter to be thy wife; and, indeed, how ever shall I even get
access to him? And should I succeed therein, what is to be my
answer an they ask me touching thy means? Haply the King will
hold me to be a madwoman. And, lastly, suppose that I obtain
audience of the Sultan, what offering is there I can submit to the
King's majesty?"[1] —— And Shahrazad was surprised by the
dawn of day and ceased to say her permitted say.

When it was the Five Hundred and Forty-third Night,

Quoth Dunyazad, "O sister mine, an thou be other than sleepy,
do tell us some of thy pleasant tales;" whereupon Shahrazad

---

[1] "There is not a present (Teshurah) to bring to the Man of God" (1 Sam. ix. 7), and
Menachem explains Teshurah as a gift offered with the object of being admitted to the
presence. See also the offering of oil to the King in Isaiah lvii. 9. Even in Maundriell's
Day Travels (p. 26) it was counted uncivil to visit a dignitary without an offering in hand.

replied, "With love and good will." —— It hath reached me, O
King of the Age, that Alaeddin's mother continued to her son,
" 'Tis true, O my child, that the Sultan is mild and merciful,
never rejecting any who approach him to require justice or ruth
or protection, nor any who pray him for a present; for he is liberal and lavisheth favour upon near and far. But he dealeth his
boons to those deserving them, to men who have done some
derring-do in battle under his eyes or have rendered as civilians
great service to his estate. But thou! do thou tell me what feat
thou hast performed in his presence or before the public that thou
meritest from him such grace? And, secondly, this boon thou
ambitionest is not for one of our condition, nor is it possible that
the King grant to thee the bourne of thine aspiration; for whoso
goeth to the Sultan and craveth of him a favour, him it besitteth
to take in hand somewhat that suiteth the royal majesty, as
indeed I warned thee aforetime. How, then, shalt thou risk
thyself to stand before the Sultan and ask his daughter in marriage, when thou hast with thee naught to offer him of that which
beseemeth his exalted station?" Hereto Alaeddin replied, "O
my mother, thou speakest to the point and hast reminded me
aright and 'tis meet that I revolve in mind the whole of thy re-
mindings. But, O my mother, the love of Princess Badr al-
Budur hath entered into the core of my heart; nor can I rest
without I win her. However, thou hast also recalled to me a
matter which I forgot and 'tis this emboldeneth me to ask his
daughter of the King. Albeit thou, O my mother, declarest that
I have no gift which I can submit to the Sultan, as is the wont of
the world, yet in very sooth I have an offering and a present
whose equal, O my mother, I hold none of the Kings to possess;
no, nor even aught like it." —— And Shahrazad was surprised
by the dawn of day and ceased to say her permitted say.

When it was the Five Hundred and Forty-fourth Night,

QUOTH DUNYAZAD, "O sister mine, an thou be other than sleepy,
do tell us some of thy pleasant tales," whereupon Shahrazad
replied, "With love and good will." —— It hath reached me, O
King of the Age, that Alaeddin said to his mother, "Because
verily that which I deemed glass or crystal was nothing but
precious stones and I hold that all the Kings of the World have

never possessed any thing like one of the smallest thereof. For, by frequenting the jeweller-folk, I have learned that they are the costliest gems and these are what I brought in my pockets from the Hoard, whereupon, an thou please, compose thy mind. We have in our house a bowl of China porcelain; so arise thou and fetch it, that I may fill it with these jewels, which thou shalt carry as a gift to the King, and thou shalt stand in his presence and solicit him for my requirement. I am certified that by such means the matter will become easy to thee; and, if thou be unwilling, O my mother, to strive for the winning of my wish as regards the lady Badr al-Budur, know thou that surely I shall die. Nor do thou imagine that this gift is of aught save the costliest of stones and be assured, O my mother, that in my many visits to the Jewellers' Bazar I have observed the merchants selling for sums man's judgment may not determine jewels whose beauty is not worth one quarter carat of what we possess; seeing which I was certified that ours are beyond all price. So arise, O my mother, as I bade thee and bring me the porcelain bowl afore-said, that I may arrange therein some of these gems and we will see what semblance they show." So she brought him the China bowl saying in herself, "I shall know what to do when I find out if the words of my child concerning these jewels be soothfast or not;" and she set it before her son who pulled the stones out of his pockets and disposed them in the bowl and ceased not arrang-ing therein gems of sorts till such time as he had filled it. And when it was brimful she could not fix her eyes firmly upon it; on the contrary, she winked and blinked for the dazzle of the stones and their radiance and excess of lightning-like glance; and her wits were bewildered thereat; only she was not certified of their value being really of the enormous extent she had been told. Withal she reflected that possibly her son might have spoken aright when he declared that their like was not to be found with the Kings. Then Alaeddin turned to her and said, "Thou hast seen, O my mother, that this present intended for the Sultan is magnificent, and I am certified that it will procure for thee high honour with him and that he will receive thee with all respect. And now, O my mother, thou hast no excuse; so compose thy thoughts and arise; take thou this bowl and away with it to the palace." His mother rejoined, "O my son, 'tis true that the present is high-priced exceedingly and the costliest of the costly; also that according to thy word none owneth its like. But who

would have the boldness to go and ask the Sultan for his daughter, the Lady Badr al-Badur? I indeed dare not say to him, 'I
want thy daughter!' when he shall ask me, 'What is thy want?'
for know thou, O my son, that my tongue will be tied. And,
granting that Allah assist me and I embolden myself to say to
him, 'My wish is to become a connection of thine through the
marriage of thy daughter, the Lady Badr al-Budur, to my son
Alaeddin,' they will surely decide at once that I am demented
and will thrust me forth in disgrace and despised. I will not tell
thee that I shall thereby fall into danger of death, for 'twill not
only be I but thou likewise. However, O my son, of my regard
for thine inclination, I needs must embolden myself and hie
thither; yet, O my child, if the King receive me and honour me
on account of the gift and enquire of me what thou desirest,"
—— And Shahrazad was surprised by the dawn of day and
ceased to say her permitted say.

Mhen it was the Five Hundred and Forty-fifth Night,

QUOTH Dunyazad, "O sister mine, an thou be other than sleepy,
do tell us some of thy pleasant tales," whereupon Shahrazad
replied, "With love and good will."——It hath reached me, O
King of the Age, that Alaeddin's mother said to her son, "And
in reply I ask of him that which thou desirest in the matter of thy
marriage with his daughter, how shall I answer him an he ask
me, as is man's wont, What estates hast thou, and what income?
And perchance, O my son, he will question me of this before
questioning me of thee."   Alaeddin replied, " 'Tis not possible
that the Sultan should make such demand what time he considereth the jewels and their magnificence; nor is it meet to think
of such things as these which may never occur. Now do thou
but arise and set before him this present of precious stones and
ask of him his daughter for me, and sit not yonder making much
of the difficulty in thy fancy. Ere this thou hast learned, O
mother mine, that the Lamp which we possess hath become to us
a stable income and that whatso I want of it the same is supplied
to me; and my hope is that by means thereof I shall learn how to
answer the Sultan should he ask me of that thou sayest."[1] Then

---

[1] As we shall see further on, the magical effect of the Ring and the Lamp extend far and

Alaeddin and his mother fell to talking over the subject all that
night long and when morning morrowed, the dame arose and
heartened her heart, especially as her son had expounded to her
some little of the powers of the Lamp and the virtues thereof; to
wit, that it would supply all they required of it. Alaeddin,
however, seeing his parent take courage when he explained to
her the workings of the Lamp, feared lest she might tattle to the
folk thereof;[1] so he said to her, "O my mother, beware how thou
talk to any of the properties of the Lamp and its profit, as this is
our one great good. Guard thy thoughts lest thou speak over
much concerning it before others, whoso they be; haply we
shall lose it and lose the boon fortune we possess and the benefits
we expect, for that 'tis of him."[2] His mother replied, "Fear not,
therefor, O my son," and she arose and took the bowl full of
jewels, which she wrapped up in a fine kerchief, and went forth
betimes that she might reach the Divan ere it became crowded.
When she passed into the Palace, the levée not being fully attended, she saw the Wazirs and sundry of the Lords of the land
going into the presence-room and after a short time, when the
Divan was made complete by the Ministers and high Officials
and Chieftains and Emirs and Grandees, the Sultan appeared
and the Wazirs made their obeisance and likewise did the Nobles
and the Notables. The King seated himself upon the throne of
his kingship, and all present at the levée stood before him with
crossed arms awaiting his commandment to sit; and, when they
received it, each took his place according to his degree; then the
claimants came before the Sultan who delivered sentence, after
his wonted way, until the Divan was ended, when the King
arose and withdrew into the palace[3] and the others all went
their ways. —— And Shahrazad was surprised by the dawn of
day and ceased to say her permitted say.

---

wide over the physique and morale of the owner: they turn a "raw laddie" into a finished
courtier, warrior, statesman, etc.

[1] In Eastern states the mere suspicion of having such an article would expose the suspected at least to torture. Their practical system of treating "treasure trove," as I saw
when serving with my regiment in Gujarát (Guzerat), is at once to imprison and "molest"
the finder, in order to make sure that he has not hidden any part of his find.

[2] Here the MS. text is defective, the allusion is, I suppose, to the Slave of the Lamp.

[3] In the H. V. the King retired into his private apartment; and, dismissing all save the
Grand Wazir, "took cognisance of special matters" before withdrawing to the Harem.

When it was the Five Hundred and Forty-sixth Night,

QUOTH Dunyazad, "O sister mine, an thou be other than sleepy, do tell us some of thy pleasant tales," whereupon Shahrazad replied, "With love and good will."——It hath reached me, O King of the Age, that Alaeddin's mother, having come the earliest of all, found means of entering without any addressing her or offering to lead her to the presence; and she ceased not standing there until the Divan ended, when the Sultan arose and withdrew into the palace and the others all went about their business. And when she saw the throne empty and the King passing into his Harem, she also wended her ways and returned home. But as soon as her son espied her, bowl in hand, he thought that haply something untoward had befallen her, but he would not ask of aught until such time as she had set down the bowl, when she acquainted him with that which had occurred and ended by adding, "Alhamdolillah, — laud to the Lord! — O my child, that I found courage enough and secured for myself standing-place in the levée this day; and, albe I dreaded to bespeak the King yet (Inshallah!) on the morrow I will address him. Even to-day were many who, like myself, could not get audience of the Sultan. But be of good cheer, O my son, and to-morrow needs must I bespeak him for thy sake; and what happened not may happen." When Alaeddin heard his parent's words, he joyed with excessive joy; and, although he expected the matter to be managed hour by hour, for excess of his love and longing to the Lady Badr al-Budur, yet he possessed his soul in patience. They slept well that night and betimes next morning the mother of Alaeddin arose and went with her bowl to the King's court which she found closed. So she asked the people and they told her that the Sultan did not hold a levée every day but only thrice in the se'nnight; wherefor she determined to return home; and, after this, whenever she saw the court open she would stand before the King until the reception ended and when it was shut she would go to make sure thereof; and this was the case for the whole month. The Sultan was wont to remark her presence at every levée, but, on the last day when she took her station, as was her wont, before the Council, she allowed it to close and lacked boldness to come forwards and speak even a syllable. Now as the King having risen was making for his Harem accompanied by

the Grand Wazir, he turned to him and said, "O Wazir, during
the last six or seven levée days I see yonder old woman present
herself at every reception and I also note that she always carrieth
a something under her mantilla. Say me, hast thou, O Wazir,
any knowledge of her and her intention?" "O my lord the Sultan," said the other, "verily women be weakly of wits, and haply
this goodwife cometh hither to complain before thee[1] against her
goodman or some of her people." But this reply was far from
satisfying the Sultan; nay, be bade the Wazir, in case she should
come again, set her before him; and forthright the Minister
placed hand on head and exclaimed,"To hear is to obey, O our
lord the Sultan!"——And Shahrazad was surprised by the dawn
of day and ceased to say her permitted say.

When it was the Five Hundred and Forty-seventh Night,

Quoth Dunyazad, "O sister mine, an thou be other than sleepy,
do tell us some of thy pleasant tales," whereupon Shahrazad
replied, "With love and good will." —— It hath reached me, O
King of the Age, that the mother of Alaeddin, as she made a
practice of repairing to the Divan every day and passing into
the room and standing opposite the King, albeit she was sorrowful and sore aweary, withal for her son's sake she endeavored to
make easy all her difficulties. Now one day of the days, when
she did according to her custom, the Sultan cast his eyes upon
her as she stood before him, and said to his Grand Wazir, "This
be the very woman whereof I spake to thee yesterday, so do thou
straightway bring her before me, that I may see what be her
suit and fulfil her need." Accordingly, the Minister at once
introduced her and when in the presence she saluted the King by
kissing her finger tips and raising them to her brow;[2] and, praying
for the Sultan's glory and continuance and the permanence of
his prosperity, bussed ground before him. Thereupon, quoth he,
"O woman,[3] for sundry days I have seen thee attend the levée

---

[1] The levée, Divan or Darbár being also a *lit de justice* and a Court of Cassation: See vol.
i. 29.

[2] All this is expressed by the Arabic in one word "Tamanná." Galland adds *pour mar-
quer qu'il etait prêt à la perdre s'il y manquait;* and thus he conveys a wrong idea.

[3] This would be still the popular address, nor is it considered rude or slighting. In John
(ii. 4) "Atto," the Heb. Eshah, is similarly used, not complimentarily, but in popular
speech.

sans a word said; so tell me an thou have any requirement I may grant." She kissed ground a second time and after blessing him, answered, "Yea, verily, as thy head liveth, O King of the Age, I have a want; but first of all, do thou deign grant me a promise of safety that I may prefer my suit to the ears of our lord the Sultan; for haply thy Highness[1] may find it a singular." The King, wishing to know her need, and being a man of unusual mildness and clemency, gave his word for her immunity and bade forthwith dismiss all about him, remaining without other but the Grand Wazir. Then he turned towards his suppliant and said, "Inform me of thy suit: thou hast the safeguard of Allah Almighty." "O King of the Age," replied she, "I also require of thee pardon;" and quoth he, "Allah pardon thee even as I do." Then, quoth she,"O our lord the Sultan, I have a son, Alaeddin hight; and he, one day of the days, having heard the crier commanding all men to shut shop and shun the streets, for that the Lady Badr al-Budur, daughter of the Sultan, was going to the Hammam, felt an uncontrollable longing to look upon her, and hid himself in a stead whence he could sight her right well, and that place was behind the door of the Baths. When she entered he beheld her and considered her as he wished, and but too well; for, since the time he looked upon her, O King of the Age, unto this hour, life hath not been pleasant to him. And he hath required of me that I ask her to wife for him from thy Highness, nor could I drive this fancy from his mind because love of her hath mastered his vitals and to such degree that he said to me, 'Know thou, O mother mine, that an I win not my wish surely I shall die.' Accordingly I hope that thy Highness will deign be mild and merciful and pardon this boldness on the part of me and my child and refrain to punish us therefor." When the Sultan heard her tale he regarded her with kindness and, laughing aloud, asked her, "What may be that thou carriest and what be in yonder kerchief?" And she seeing the Sultan laugh in lieu of waxing wroth at her words, forthright opened the wrapper and set before him the bowl of jewels, whereby the audience-hall was illumined as it were by lustres and candelabra;[2] and he was dazed

---

[1] This sounds ridiculous enough in English, but not in German; *e.g.* Deine Königliche Hoheit is the formula de rigueur when an Austrian officer, who always addresses brother-soldiers in the familiar second person, is speaking to a camarade who is also a royalty.

[2] "Suráyyát (lit. = the Pleiades) and "Sham'ádín" a would-be Arabic plur. of the Persian "Sham'adán"=candlestick, chandelier, for which more correctly Sham'adánát is used.

and amazed at the radiance of the rare gems, and he fell to marvelling at their size and beauty and excellence. —— And Shahrazad was surprised by the dawn of day and ceased to say her permitted say.

When it was the Five Hundred and Forty-eighth Night,'

QUOTH Dunyazad, "O sister mine, if thou be other than sleepy, do tell us some of thy pleasant tales," whereupon Shahrazad replied, "With love and good will." —— It hath reached me, O King of the Age, that when the King saw the gems he was seized by surprise and cried, "Never at all until this day saw I anything like these jewels for size and beauty and excellence: nor deem I that there be found in my treasury a single one like them." Then he turned to his Minister and asked, "What sayest thou, O Wazir? Tell me, hast thou seen in thy time such mighty fine jewels as these?" The other answered, "Never saw I such, O our lord the Sultan, nor do I think that there be in the treasures of my lord the Sultan the fellow of the least thereof." The King resumed, "Now indeed whoso hath presented to me such jewels meriteth to become bridegroom to my daughter, Badr al-Budur; because, as far as I see, none is more deserving of her than he." When the Wazir heard the Sultan's words he was tongue-tied with concern and he grieved with sore grief, for the King had promised to give the Princess in marriage to his son; so after a little while he said, "O King of the Age, thy Highness deigned promise me that the Lady Badr al-Budur should be spouse to my son; so 'tis but right that thine exalted Highness vouchsafe us a delay of three months, during which time, Inshallah! my child may obtain and present an offering yet costlier than this." Accordingly the King, albeit he knew that such a thing could not be done, or by the Wazir or by the greatest of his Grandees, yet of his grace and kindness granted him the required delay. Then he turned to the old woman, Alaeddin's mother, and said, "Go to thy son and tell him I have pledged my word that my daughter shall be in his name;[1] only 'tis needful that I make the requisite preparations of nuptial furniture for her use; and 'tis only meet that he take patience

---

[1] *i.e.*, betrothed to her—*j'agrée la proposition*, says Galland.

for the next three months." Receiving this reply, Alaeddin's
mother thanked the Sultan and blessed him; then, going forth
in hottest haste, as one flying for joy, she went home; and when
her son saw her entering with a smiling face, he was gladdened
at the sign of good news, especially because she had returned
without delay as on the past days, and had not brought back the
bowl. Presently he asked her saying, "Inshallah, thou bearest
me, O my mother, glad tidings; and peradventure the jewels
and their value have wrought their work and belike thou hast
been kindly received by the King and he hath shown thee grace
and hath given ear to thy request?" So she told him the whole
tale, how the Sultan had entreated her well and had marvelled at
the extraordinary size of the gems and their surpassing water as
did also the Wazir, adding, "And he promised that his daughter
should be thine. Only, O my child, the Wazir spake of a secret
contract made with him by the Sultan before he pledged himself
to me and, after speaking privily, the King put me off to the end
of three months: therefore I have become fearful lest the Wazir
be evilly disposed to thee and perchance he may attempt to
change the Sultan's mind." —— And Shahrazad was surprised
by the dawn of day and ceased to say her permitted say.

When it was the Five Hundred and Forty-ninth Night,

QUOTH Dunyazad, "O sister mine, an thou be other than sleepy,
do tell us some of thy pleasant tales," whereupon Shahrazad
replied, "With love and good will." —— It hath reached me, O
King of the Age, that when Alaeddin heard his mother's words
and how the Sultan had promised him his daughter, deferring,
however, the wedding until after the third month, his mind was
gladdened and he rejoiced exceedingly and said, "Inasmuch as the
King hath given his word after three months (well, it is a long
time!), at all events my gladness is mighty great." Then he
thanked his parent, showing her how her good work had exceeded her toil and travail; and said to her, "By Allah, O my
mother, hitherto I was as 'twere in my grave and therefrom thou
hast withdrawn me; and I praise Allah Almighty because I am
at this moment certified that no man in the world is happier than
I or more fortunate." Then he took patience until two of the
three months had gone by. Now one day of the days his mother

fared forth about sundown to the Bazar that she might buy somewhat of oil; and she found all the market shops fast shut and the
whole city decorated, and the folk placing waxen tapers and
flowers at their casements; and she beheld the soldiers and
household troops and Aghás[1] riding in procession and flambeaux
and lustres flaming and flaring, and she wondered at the marvellous sight and the glamour of the scene. So she went in to an
oilman's store which stood open still and bought her need of him
and said, "By thy life, O uncle, tell me what be the tidings in
town this day, that people have made all these decorations and
every house and market-street are adorned and the troops all
stand on guard?" The oilman asked her, "O woman, I suppose
thou art a stranger and not one of this city?" and she answered,
"Nay, I am thy townswoman." He rejoined, "Thou a townswoman, and yet wottest not that this very night the son of the
Grand Wazir goeth in to the Lady Badr al-Budur, daughter of the
Sultan! He is now in the Hammam and all this power of soldiery
is on guard and standing under arms to await his coming forth,
when they will bear him in bridal procession to the palace where
the Princess expecteth him." As the mother of Alaeddin heard
these words, she grieved and was distraught in thought and
perplexed how to inform her son of this sorrowful event, well
knowing that the poor youth was looking, hour by hour, to the
end of the three months. But she returned straightway home to
him and when she had entered she said, "O my son, I would give
thee certain tidings, yet hard to me will be the sorrow they shall
occasion thee." He cried, "Let me know what be thy news;"
and she replied, "Verily the Sultan hath broken his promise to
thee in the matter of the Lady Badr al-Budur, and this very night
the Grand Wazir's son goeth in to her. And for some time, O my
son, I have suspected that the Minister would change the King's
mind, even as I told thee how he had spoken privily to him before
me." Alaeddin[2] asked, "How learnedst thou that the Wazir's
son is this night to pay his first visit to the Princess?" So she
told him the whole tale, how when going to buy oil she had found
the city decorated and the eunuch-officials and Lords of the land

---

[1] Here meaning Eunuch-officers and officials. In the cdlxxvith Night of this volume the
word is incorrectly written Aghát in the singular.

[2] In the H. V. Alaeddin on hearing this became as if a thunderbolt had stricken him, and,
losing consciousness, swooned away.

with the troops under arms awaiting the bridegroom from the Baths; and that the first visit was appointed for that very night. Hearing this Alaeddin was seized with a fever of jealousy brought on by his grief: however, after a short while he remembered the Lamp and, recovering his spirits said, "By thy life, O my mother, do thou believe that the Wazir's son will not enjoy her as thou thinkest. But now leave we this discourse and arise thou and serve up supper[1] and after eating let me retire to my own chamber and all will be well and happy." —— And Shahrazad was surprised by the dawn of day and ceased to say her permitted say.

𝕸𝖍𝖊𝖓 𝖎𝖙 𝖜𝖆𝖘 𝖙𝖍𝖊 𝕱𝖎𝖛𝖊 𝕳𝖚𝖓𝖉𝖗𝖊𝖉 𝖆𝖓𝖉 𝕱𝖎𝖋𝖙𝖎𝖊𝖙𝖍 𝕹𝖎𝖌𝖍𝖙,

QUOTH Dunyazad, "O sister mine, an thou be other than sleepy, do tell us some of thy pleasant tales," whereupon Shahrazad replied, "With love and good will." —— It hath reached me, O King of the Age, that Alaeddin after he had supped retired to his chamber and, locking the door, brought out the Lamp and rubbed it, whenas forthright appeared to him its Familiar who said, "Ask whatso thou wantest, for I am thy Slave and Slave to him who holdeth the Lamp in hand; I and all the Slaves of the Lamp." He replied, "Hear me! I prayed the Sultan for his daughter to wife and he plighted her to me after three months; but he hath not kept his word; nay, he hath given her to the son of the Wazir and this very night the bridegroom will go in to her. Therefore I command thee (an thou be a trusty Servitor to the Lamp) when thou shalt see bride and bridegroom bedded together this night,[2] at once take them up and bear them hither abed; and this be what I want of thee." The Marid replied, "Hearing and obeying; and if thou have other service but this, do thou

---

[1] These calls for food at critical times, and oft-recurring allusions to eating are not yet wholly obsolete amongst the civilised of the xixth century. The ingenious M. Jules Verne often enlivens a tedious scene by *Dejeunons!* And French travellers, like English, are not unready to talk of food and drink, knowing that the subject is never displeasing to their readers.

[2] The H. V. gives a sketch of the wedding. "And when the ceremonies ended at the palace with pomp and parade and pageant, and the night was far spent, the eunuchs led the Wazir's son into the bridal chamber. He was the first to seek his couch; then the Queen, his mother-in-law, came into him leading the bride, and followed by her suite. She did with her virgin daughter as parents are wont to do, removed her wedding-raiment, and donning a night-dress, placed her in her bridegroom's arms. Then, wishing her all joy, she with her ladies went away and shut the door. At that instant came the Jinni," etc.

demand of me all thou desirest." Alaeddin rejoined, "At the
present time I require naught save that I bade thee do." Hereupon the Slave disappeared and Alaeddin returned to pass the
rest of the evening with his mother. But at the hour when he
knew that the Servitor would be coming, he arose and retired to
his chamber and after a little while, behold, the Marid came
bringing to him the newly-wedded couple upon their bridal-bed.
Alaeddin rejoiced to see them with exceeding joy; then he cried
to the Slave, "Carry yonder gallows-bird hence and lay him at
full length in the privy."[1] His bidding was done straightway;
but, before leaving him, the Slave blew upon the bridegroom a
blast so cold that it shrivelled him and the plight of the Wazir's
son became piteous. Then the Servitor returning to Alaeddin
said to him, "An thou require aught else, inform me thereof;"
and said the other, "Return a-morn that thou mayest restore
them to their stead;" whereto, "I hear and obey," quoth the
Marid and evanished. Presently Alaeddin arose, hardly believing that the affair had been such a success for him; but whenas he
looked upon the Lady Badr al-Budur lying under his own roof,
albeit he had long burned with her love yet he preserved respect
for her and said, "O Princess of fair ones, think not that I brought
thee hither to minish thy honour. Heaven forfend! Nay 'twas
only to prevent the wrong man enjoying thee, for that thy sire
the Sultan promised thee to me. So do thou rest in peace." ——
And Shahrazad was surprised by the dawn of day and ceased to
say her permitted say.

When it was the Five Hundred and Fifty-first Night,

QUOTH Dunyazad, "O sister mine, an thou be other than sleepy,
do tell us some of thy pleasant tales." whereupon Shahrazad
replied, "With love and good will." —— It hath reached me, O
King of the Age, that when the Lady Badr al-Budur, daughter of
the Sultan, saw herself in that mean and darksome lodging, and
heard Alaeddin's words, she was seized with fear and trembling
and waxed clean distraught; nor could she return aught of reply.
Presently the youth arose and stripping off his outer dress placed

---

[1] The happy idea of the wedding night in the water-closet is repeated from the tale of
Nur-al-Dín Ali Hasan (vol. i. 221), and the mishap of the Hunchback bridegroom.

a scymitar between them and lay upon the bed beside the Princess;[1] and he did no villain deed, for it sufficed him to prevent the consummation of her nuptials with the Wazir's son. On the other hand the Lady Badr al-Budur passed a night the evillest of all nights; nor in her born days had she seen a worse; and the same was the case with the Minister's son who lay in the chapel of ease and who dared not stir for the fear of the Jinni which overwhelmed him. As soon as it was morning the Slave appeared before Alaeddin, without the Lamp being rubbed, and said to him, "O my lord, an thou require aught, command me therefor, that I may do it upon my head and mine eyes." Said the other, "Go, take up and carry the bride and bridegroom to their own apartment;" so the Servitor did his bidding in an eye-glance and bore away the pair, and placed them in the palace as whilome they were and without their seeing any one; but both died of affright when they found themselves being transported from stead to stead.[2] And the Marid had barely time to set them down and wend his ways ere the Sultan came on a visit of congratulation to his daughter; and, when the Wazir's son heard the doors thrown open, he sprang straightway from his couch and donned his dress[3] for he knew that none save the King could enter at that hour. Yet it was exceedingly hard for him to leave his bed wherein he wished to warm himself a trifle after his cold night in the water-closet which he had lately left. —— And Shahrazad was surprised by the dawn of day and ceased to say her permitted say.

When it was the Five Hundred and Fifty-second Night,

Quoth Dunyazad, "O sister mine, an thou be other than sleepy, do tell us some of thy pleasant tales," whereupon Shahrazad

---

[1] For the old knightly practice of sleeping with a drawn sword separating man and maid, see vol. vii. 353 and Mr. Clouston's "Popular Tales and Fictions," vol. i. 316. In Poland the intermediary who married by procuration slept alongside the bride in all his armour. The H. V. explains, "He (Alaeddin) also lay a naked sword between him and the Princess, so she might perceive that he was ready to die by that blade should he attempt to do aught of villainy by the bride."

[2] Galland says: *Ils ne s'aperçurent que de l'ébranlement du lit et que de leur transport d'un lieu à l'autre: c'était bien assez pour leur donner une frayeur qu'il est aisé d'imaginer.*

[3] Galland very unnecessarily makes the Wazir's son pass into the wardrobe (*garderobe*) to dress himself.

replied, "With love and good will." —— It hath reached me, O
King of the Age, that the Sultan went in to his daughter Badr al-
Budur and kissing her between the eyes gave her good morning
and asked her of her bridegroom and whether she was pleased
and satisfied with him. But she returned no reply whatever and
looked at him with the eye of anger and, although he repeated his
words again and again, she held her peace nor bespake him with
a single syllable. So the King quitted her and, going to the
Queen, informed her of what had taken place between him and
his daughter; and the mother, unwilling to leave the Sultan
angered with their child, said to him, "O King of the Age, this
be the custom of most newly-married couples at least during their
first days of marriage, for that they are bashful and somewhat
coy. So deign thou excuse her and after a little while she will
again become herself and speak with the folk as before, whereas
now her shame, O King of the Age, keepeth her silent. However
'tis my wish to fare forth and see her." Thereupon the Queen
arose and donned her dress; then, going to her daughter, wished
her good morning and kissed her between the eyes. Yet would
the Princess make no answer at all, whereat quoth the Queen
to herself, "Doubtless some strange matter hath occurred to
trouble her with such trouble as this." So she asked her saying,
"O my daughter, what hath caused this thy case? Let me know
what hath betided thee that, when I come and give thee good
morning, thou hast not a word to say to me?" Thereat the Lady
Badr al-Budur raised her head and said, "Pardon me, O my
mother, 'twas my duty to meet thee with all respect and worship, seeing that thou hast honoured me by this visit. However,
I pray thee to hear the cause of this my condition and see how
the night I have just spent hath been to me the evillest of the
nights. Hardly had we lain down, O my mother, than one whose
form I wot not uplifted our bed and transported it to a darksome
place, fulsome and mean." Then the Princess related to the
Queen-mother all that had befallen her that night; how they
had taken away her bridegroom, leaving her lone and lonesome,
and how after a while came another youth who lay beside her, in
lieu of her bridegroom, after placing his scymitar between her
and himself; "and in the morning" (she continued) "he who carried
us off returned and bore us straight back to our own stead. But
at once when he arrived hither he left us and suddenly my sire

the Sultan entered at the hour and moment of our coming and I I had nor heart nor tongue to speak him withal, for the stress of the terror and trembling which came upon me. Haply such lack of duty may have proved sore to him, so I hope, O my mother, that thou wilt acquaint him with the cause of this my condition and that he will pardon me for not answering him and blame me not, but rather accept my excuses." —— And Shahrazad was surprised by the dawn of day and ceased to say her permitted say.

When it was the Five Hundred and Fifty-third Night,

Quoth Dunyazad, "O sister mine, an thou be other than sleepy, do tell us some of thy pleasant tales," whereupon Shahrazad replied, "With love and good will." —— It hath reached me, O King of the Age, that when the Queen heard these words of Princess Badr al-Budur, she said to her, "O my child, compose thy thoughts. An thou tell such tale before any, haply shall he say, 'Verily, the Sultan's daughter hath lost her wits.' And thou hast done right well in not choosing to recount thine adventure to thy father; and beware and again I say beware, O my daughter, lest thou inform him thereof." The Princess replied, "O my mother, I have spoken to thee like one sound in senses nor have I lost my wits: this be what befel me and, if thou believe it not because coming from me, ask my bridegroom." To which the Queen replied, "Rise up straightway, O my daughter, and banish from thy thoughts such fancies as these; and robe thyself and come forth to glance at the bridal feasts and festivities they are making in the city for the sake of thee and thy nuptials; and listen to the drumming and the singing and look at the decorations all intended to honour thy marriage, O my daughter." So saying, the Queen at once summoned the tirewomen who dressed and prepared the Lady Badr al-Budur; and presently she went in to the Sultan and assured him that their daughter had suffered during all her wedding-night from swevens and nightmare and said to him, "Be not severe with her for not answering thee." Then the Queen sent privily for the Wazir's son and asked of the matter, saying, "Tell me, are these words of the Lady Badr al-Budur soothfast or not?" But he, in his fear of losing his bride out of hand, answered, "O my lady, I have no knowledge of that whereof thou speakest." Accordingly the mother made sure that her daughter had seen visions and dreams. The marriage-feasts lasted throughout that day with Almahs[1] and singers and the smiting of all manner instruments of mirth and merriment, while the Queen and the Wazir and his son strave right strenuously to enhance the festivities that the Princess might enjoy herself; and that day they left nothing of what exciteth to pleasure unrepresented in her presence, to the end that she might forget what was in her thoughts and derive increase of joyance. Yet did naught of this take any effect upon her; nay, she sat in silence, sad of thought, sore perplexed at what had befallen her during the last night. It is true that the Wazir's son had suffered even more because he had passed his sleeping hours lying in the water-closet: he, however, had falsed the story and had cast out remembrance of the night; in the first place for his fear of losing his bride and with her the honour of a connection which brought him such excess of consideration and for which men envied him so much; and, secondly, on account of the wondrous loveliness of the Lady Badr al-Budur and her marvellous beauty. Alaeddin also went forth that day and looked at the merry-makings which extended throughout the city as well as the palace and he fell a-laughing, especially when he heard the folk prating of the high honour which had accrued to the son of the Wazir and the prosperity of his fortunes in having become son-in-law to the Sultan and the high consideration shown by the wedding fêtes. And he said in his mind, "Indeed ye wot not, O ye miserables, what befel him last night that ye envy him!" But after darkness fell and it was time for sleep, Alaeddin arose and, retiring to his chamber, rubbed the Lamp, whereupon the Slave incontinently appeared. —— And Shahrazad was surprised by the dawn of day and ceased to say her permitted say.

---

[1]Professional singing and dancing girls: Properly the word is the fem. of 'Álim = a learned man; but it has been anglicised by Byron's
> "The long chibouque's dissolving cloud supply,
> Where dance the Almahs to wild minstrelsy."— (The Corsair, ii. 2.)

They go about the streets with unveiled faces and are seldom admitted into respectable Harems, although on festal occasions they perform in the court or in front of the house; but even this is objected to by the Mrs. Grundy of Egypt. Lane (M.E. chap. xviii.) derives with Saint Jerome the word from the Heb. or Phœnician Almah = a virgin, a girl, a singing-girl; and thus explains "Alámoth" in Psalms xlvi. and I Chron. xv. 20. Parkhurst (s.v. 'Alamah = an undeflowered virgin) renders Job xxxix. 30, "the way of a man with a maid" (bi-álmah). The way of a man in his virgin state, shunning youthful lust and keeping himself "pure and unspotted."

When it was the Five Hundred and Fifty-fourth Night,

QUOTH Dunyazad, "O sister mine, an thou be other than sleepy, do tell us some of thy pleasant tales," whereupon Shahrazad replied, "With love and good will." —— It hath reached me, O King of the Age, that when the Slave appeared in presence of Alaeddin, he was bidden to bring him the Sultan's daughter to-gether with her bridegroom as on the past night ere the Wazir's son could abate her maidenhead. So the Marid without stay or delay evanished for a little while until the appointed time, when he returned carrying the bed whereon lay the Lady Badr al-Budur and the Wazir's son; and he did with the bridegroom as he had done before, to wit, he took him up and lay him at full length in the jakes and there left him dried up for excess of fear and trem-bling. Then Alaeddin arose, and placing the scymitar between himself and the Princess, lay down beside her; and when day broke the Slave restored the pair to their own place, leaving Alaeddin filled with delight at the state of the Minister's son. Now when the Sultan woke up amorn he resolved to visit his daughter and see if she would treat him as on the past day; so shaking off his sleep he sprang up and arrayed himself in his raiment and, going to the apartment of the Princess bade open the door. Thereat the son of the Wazir arose forthright and came down from his bed and began donning his dress whilst his ribs were wrung with cold; for when the King entered the Slave had but just brought him back. The Sultan, raising the arras,[1] drew near his daughter as she lay abed and gave her good morn-ing; then kissing her between the eyes, he asked her of her case. But he saw her looking sour and sad and she answered him not at all, only glowering at him as one in anger and her plight was pitiable. Hereat the Sultan waxed wroth with her for that she would not reply and he suspected that something evil had be-fallen her,[2] whereupon he bared his blade and cried to her, brand in hand, saying, "What be this hath betided thee? Either ac-quaint me with what happened or this very moment I will take thy life! Is such conduct the token of honour and respect I expect

---

[1] The text reads "Rafa' " (he raised) "al-Bashkhánah" which in Suppl. Nights (ii. 119) is a hanging, a curtain. Apparently it is a corruption of the Pers. "Paskhkhánah," a mos-quito-curtain.

[2] The father suspected that she had not gone to bed a clean maid.

of thee, that I address thee and thou answerest me not a word?"
When the Lady Badr al-Badur saw her sire in high dudgeon and
the naked glaive in his grip, she was freed from her fear of the
past, so she raised her head and said to him, "O my beloved
father, be not wroth with me nor be hasty in thy hot passion,
for I am excusable in what thou shalt see of my case. So do thou
lend an ear to what occurred to me and well I wot that after
hearing my account of what befel to me during these two last
nights, thou wilt pardon me and thy Highness will be softened
to pitying me even as I claim of thee affection for thy child."
Then the Princess informed her father of all that had betided her
adding, "O my sire, an thou believe me not, ask my bridegroom
and he will recount to thy Highness the whole adventure; nor
did I know either what they would do with him when they bore
him away from my side or where they would place him." ——
And Shahrazad was surprised by the dawn of day, and ceased to
say her permitted say.

When it was the Five Hundred and Fifty-fifth Night,

QUOTH Dunyazad, "O sister mine, an thou be other than sleepy,
do tell us some of thy pleasant tales," whereupon Shahrazad
replied, "With love and good will."——It hath reached me, O
King of the Age, that when the Sultan heard his daughter's
words, he was saddened and his eyes brimmed with tears; then
he sheathed his sabre and kissed her saying, "O my daughter,
wherefore[1] didst thou not tell me what happened on the past
night that I might have guarded thee from this torture and terror
which visited thee a second time? But now 'tis no matter. Rise
and cast out all such care and to-night I will set a watch to ward
thee nor shall any mishap again make thee miserable." Then
the Sultan returned to his palace and straightway bade summon
the Grand Wazir and asked him, as he stood before him in his
service, "O Wazir, how dost thou look upon this matter? Haply
thy son hath informed thee of what occurred to him and to my
daughter." The Minister replied, "O King of the Age, I have
not seen my son or yesterday or to-day." Hereat the Sultan told

---

[1] Arab. Aysh = Ayyu Shayyin and Laysh = li ayyi Shayyin. This vulgarism, or
rather popular corruption, is of olden date and was used by such a purist as Al-Mutanabbi
in such a phrase as "Aysh Khabara-k?" = how art thou? See Ibn Khallikan, iii. 79.

him all that had afflicted the Princess, adding, " 'Tis my desire
that thou at once seek tidings of thy son concerning the facts of
the case: peradventure of her fear my daughter may not be fully
aware of what really befel her; withal I hold all her words to be
truthful." So the Grand Wazir arose and, going forth, bade
summon his son and asked him anent all his lord had told him
whether it be true or untrue. The youth replied, "O my father
the Wazir, Heaven forbid that the Lady Badr al-Budur speak
falsely: indeed all she said was sooth and these two nights
proved to us the evillest of our nights instead of being nights of
pleasure and marriage-joys. But what befel me was the greater
evil because, instead of sleeping abed with my bride, I lay in the
wardrobe, a black hole, frightful, noisome of stench, truly damnable; and my ribs were bursten with cold." In fine the young
man told his father the whole tale, adding as he ended it, "O
dear father mine, I implore thee to speak with the Sultan that he
may set me free from this marriage. Yes, indeed 'tis a high
honour for me to be the Sultan's son-in-law and especially the
love of the Princess hath gotten hold of my vitals; but I have no
strength left to endure a single night like unto these two last."
And Shahrazad was surprised by the dawn of day and ceased to
say her permitted say.

When it was the Five Hundred and Fifty-sixth Night,

Quoth Dunyazad, "O sister mine, an thou be other than sleepy,
do tell us some of thy pleasant tales," whereupon Shahrazad
replied, "With love and good will." —— It hath reached me, O
King of the Age, that the Wazir, hearing the words of his son,
was saddened and sorrowful exceedingly, for it was his design to
advance and promote his child by making him son-in-law to the
Sultan. So he became thoughtful and perplexed about the affair
and the device whereby to manage it, and it was sore grievous
for him to break off the marriage, it having been a rare enjoyment
to him that he had fallen upon such high good fortune. Accordingly he said, "Take patience, O my son, until we see what may
happen this night, when we will set watchmen to ward you;
nor do thou give up the exalted distinction which hath fallen to
none save to thyself." Then the Wazir left him and, returning
to the sovran, reported that all told to him by the Lady Badr al-
Budur was a true tale; whereupon quoth the Sultan, "Since the

affair is on this wise, we require no delay," and he at once ordered all the rejoicings to cease and the marriage to be broken off. This caused the folk and the citizens to marvel at the matter, especially when they saw the Grand Wazir and his son leaving the palace in pitiable plight for grief and stress of passion; and the people fell to asking, "What hath happened and what is the cause of the wedding being made null and void?" Nor did any know aught of the truth save Alaeddin the lover who claimed the Princess's hand, and he laughed in his sleeve. But even after the marriage was dissolved, the Sultan forgot nor even recalled to mind his promise made to Alaeddin's mother; and the same was the case with the Grand Wazir, while neither had any inkling of whence befel them that which had befallen. So Alaeddin patiently awaited the lapse of the three months after which the Sultan had pledged himself to give him to wife his daughter; but, as soon as ever the term came, he sent his mother to the Sultan for the pur-pose of requiring him to keep his covenant. So she went to the palace and when the King appeared in the Divan and saw the old woman standing before him, he remembered his promise to her concerning the marriage after a term of three months, and he turned to the Minister and said "O Wazir, this be the ancient dame who presented me with the jewels and to whom we pledged our word that when the three months had elapsed we would summon her to our presence before all others." So the Minister went forth and fetched her[1] and when she went in to the Sultan's presence she saluted him and prayed for his glory and permanence of prosperity. Hereat the King asked her if she needed aught, and she answered, "O King of the Age, the three months' term thou assignedst to me is finished, and this is thy time to marry my son Alaeddin with thy daughter, the Lady Badr al-Budur." The Sultan was distraught at this demand, especially when he saw the old woman's pauper condition, one of the meanest of her kind; and yet the offering she had brought to him was of the most magnificent, far beyond his power to pay the price. Accordingly, he turned to the Grand Wazir and said, "What device is there with thee? In very sooth I did pass my word, yet meseemeth that they be pauper folk and not persons of high condition." —— And Shahrazad was surprised by the dawn of day and ceased to say her permitted say.

---

[1] In the H. V. the Minister sends the Chob-dár = rod-bearer, mace-bearer, usher, etc.

When it was the Five Hundred and Fifty-seventh Night,

QUOTH Dunyazad, "O sister mine, an thou be other than sleepy, do tell us some of thy pleasant tales," whereupon Shahrazad replied, "With love and good will." —— It hath reached me, O King of the Age, that the Grand Wazir, who was dying of envy and who was especially saddened by what had befallen his son, said to himself, "How shall one like this wed the King's daughter and my son lose this highmost honour?" Accordingly, he answered his Sovran speaking privily, "O my lord, 'tis an easy[1] matter to keep off a poor devil such as this, for he is not worthy that thy Highness give his daughter to a fellow whom none knoweth what he may be." "By what means," enquired the Sultan, "shall we put off the man when I pledged my promise; and the word of the Kings is their bond?" Replied the Wazir, "O my lord, my rede is that thou demand of him forty platters made of pure sand-gold[2] and full of gems (such as the woman brought thee aforetime), with forty white slave-girls to carry the platters and forty black eunuch-slaves." The King rejoined, "By Allah, O Wazir, thou hast spoken to the purpose, seeing that such thing is not possible and by this way we shall be freed." Then quoth he to Alaeddin's mother, "Do thou go and tell thy son that I am a man of my word even as I plighted it to him, but on condition that he have power to pay the dower of my daughter; and that which I require of him is a settlement consisting of two score platters of virgin gold, all brimming with gems the like of those thou broughtest to me, and as many white handmaids to carry them and two score black eunuch-slaves to serve and escort the bearers. An thy son avail hereto I will marry him with my daughter." Thereupon she returned home wagging her head and saying in her mind, "Whence can my poor boy procure these platters and such jewels? And granted that he return to the Enchanted Treasury and pluck them from the trees which, however, I hold impossible; yet given that he bring them

---

[1] In the text Sáhal for Sahal, again the broad "Doric" of Syria.

[2] Arab. Dahab ramli = gold dust washed out of the sand, *placer*-gold. I must excuse myself for using this Americanism, properly a diluvium or deposit of sand, and improperly (Bartlett) a find of drift gold. The word, like many mining terms in the Far West, is borrowed from the Spaniards; it is not therefore one of the many American vulgarisms which threaten hopelessly to defile the pure well of English speech.

whence shall he come by the girls and the blacks?" Nor did she leave communing with herself till she reached her home, where she found Alaeddin awaiting her, and she lost no time in saying, "O my son, did I not tell thee never to fancy that thy power would extend to the Lady Badr al-Budur, and that such a matter is not possible to folk like ourselves?" "Recount to me the news," quoth he; so quoth she, "O my child, verily the Sultan received me with all honour according to his custom and, meseemeth his intentions towards us be friendly. But thine enemy is that accursed Wazir; for, after I addressed the King in thy name as thou badest me say, 'In very sooth the promised term is past,' adding ' 'Twere well an thy Highness would deign issue commandment for the espousals of thy daughter the Lady Badr al-Budur to my son Alaeddin,' he turned to and addressed the Minister who answered privily, after which the Sultan gave me his reply." Then she enumerated the King's demands and said, "O my son, he indeed expecteth of thee an instant reply; but I fancy that we have no answer for him." —— And Shahra-zad was surprised by the dawn of day and ceased to say her permitted say.

When it was the Five Hundred and Fifty-eighth Night,

Quoth Dunyazad, "O sister mine, an thou be other than sleepy, do tell us some of thy pleasant tales," whereupon Shahrazad replied, "With love and good will." —— It hath reached me, O King of the Age, that when Alaeddin heard these words he laughed and said, "O my mother, thou affirmeth that we have no answer and thou deemest the case difficult exceedingly; but com-pose thy thoughts and arise and bring me somewhat we may eat; and, after we have dined, an the Compassionate be willing, thou shalt see my reply. Also the Sultan thinketh like thyself that he hath demanded a prodigious dower in order to divert me from his daughter, whereas the fact is that he hath required of me a matter far less than I expected. But do thou fare forth at once and purchase the provision and leave me to procure thee a reply." So she went out to fetch her needful from the Bazar and Alaeddin retired to his chamber and taking the Lamp rubbed it, when forthright appeared to him its Slave and said, "Ask, O my lord, whatso thou wantest." The other replied, "I have demanded of the Sultan his daughter to wife and he hath required of me forty bowls of purest gold each weighing ten pounds[1] and all to be filled with gems such as we find in the Gardens of the Hoard; furthermore, that they be borne on the heads of as many white handmaids, each attended by her black eunuch-slave, also forty in full rate; so I desire that thou bring all these into my presence." "Hearkening and obeying, O my lord," quoth the Slave and, disappearing for the space of an hour or so, presently returned bringing the platters and jewels, handmaids and eunuchs; then, setting them before him the Marid cried, "This be what thou demandest of me: declare now an thou want any matter or service other than this." Alaeddin rejoined, "I have need of naught else; but, an I do, I will summon thee and let thee know." The Slave now disappeared and, after a little while, Alaeddin's mother returned home and, on entering the house, saw the blacks and the handmaids.[2] Hereat she wondered and exclaimed, "All this proceedeth from the Lamp which Allah perpetuate to my son!" But ere she doffed her mantilla Alaeddin said to her, "O my mother, this be thy time before the Sultan enter his Serraglio-palace;[3] do thou carry to him what he required and wend thou with it at once, so may he know that I avail to supply all he wanteth and yet more; also that he is beguiled by his Grand Wazir and the twain imagined vainly that they would baffle me." Then he arose forthright and opened the house-door, when the handmaids and blackamoors paced forth in pairs, each girl with her eunuch beside her, until they crowded the quarter, Alaeddin's mother foregoing them. And when the folk of that ward sighted such mighty fine sight and marvellous spectacle, all stood at gaze and they considered the forms and figures of the handmaids marvelling at their beauty and loveliness, for each and every wore robes inwrought with gold and studded with jewels, no dress being worth less than a thousand dinars.[4] They stared as intently at the bowls and albeit these were

---

[1] Abra. "Ratl," by Europeans usually pronounced "Rotl" (Rotolo).

[2] In the H. V. she returns from the bazar; and, "seeing the house filled with so many persons in goodliest attire, marvelled greatly. Then setting down the meat lately bought she would have taken off her veil, but Alaeddin prevented her and said," etc.

[3] The word is popularly derived from Serai in Persian = a palace; but it comes from the Span. and Port. *Cerrar* = to shut up, and should be written with the reduplicated liquid.

[4] In the H. V. the dresses and ornaments of the slaves were priced at ten millions (Karúr = a crore) of gold coins. I have noticed that Messer Marco "Milione" did not learn his high numerals in Arabia, but that India might easily have taught them to him.

covered with pieces of brocade, also orfrayed and dubbed with precious stones, yet the sheen outshot from them dulled the shine of sun. —— And Shahrazad was surprised by the dawn of day and ceased to say her permitted say.

When it was the Five Hundred and Fifty-ninth Night,

Quoth Dunyazad, "O sister mine, an thou be other than sleepy, do tell us some of thy pleasant tales," whereupon Shahrazad replied, "With love and good will." —— It hath reached me, O King of the Age, that the folk and especially the people of the quarter stood a-marvelling at this singular scene. Then Alaeddin's mother walked forwards and all the handmaids and eunuchs paced behind her in the best of ordinance and disposition, and the citizens gathered to gaze at the beauty of the damsels, glorifying God the Most Great, until the train reached the palace and entered it accompanied by the tailor's widow. Now when the Aghas and Chamberlains and Army-officers beheld them, all were seized with surprise, notably by seeing the handmaids who each and every would ravish the reason of an anchorite. And albeit the royal Chamberlains and Officials were men of family, the sons of Grandees and Emirs, yet they could not but especially wonder at the costly dresses of the girls and the platters borne upon their heads; nor could they gaze at them open-eyed by reason of the exceeding brilliance and radiance. Then the Nabobs went in and reported to the King who forthright bade admit them to the presence-chamber, and Alaeddin's mother went in with them. When they stood before the Sultan, all saluted him with every sign of respect and worship and prayed for his glory and prosperity; then they set down from their heads the bowls at his feet and, having removed the brocade covers, rested with arms crossed behind them. The Sultan wondered with exceeding wonder and was distraught by the beauty of the handmaids and their loveliness which passed praise; and his wits were wildered when he considered the golden bowls brimful of gems which captured man's vision, and he was perplexed at the marvel until he became, like the dumb, unable to utter a syllable for the excess of his wonder. Also his sense was stupefied the more when he bethought him that within a hour or so all these treasures had been collected. Presently he com-

manded the slave-girls to enter, with what loads they bore, the
dower of the Princess; and, when they had done his bidding
Alaeddin's mother came forward and said to the Sultan, "O my
lord, this be not much wherewith to honour the Lady Badr
al-Budur, for that she meriteth these things multiplied times
manifold." Hereat the Sovran turned to the Minister and asked,
"What sayest thou, O Wazir? is not he who could produce such
wealth in a time so brief, is he not, I say, worthy to become the
Sultan's son-in-law and take the King's daughter to wife?" Then
the Minister (although he marvelled at these riches even more
than did the Sultan), whose envy was killing him and growing
greater hour by hour, seeing his liege lord satisfied with the
moneys and the dower and yet being unable to fight against fact,
made answer, " 'Tis not worthy of her." Withal he fell to
devising a device against the King that he might withhold the
Lady Badr al-Budur from Alaeddin and accordingly he continued, "O my liege, the treasures of the universe all of them are
not worth a nail-paring of thy daughter: indeed thy Highness
hath prized these things overmuch in comparison with her." ——
And Shahrazad was surprised by the dawn of day and ceased to
say her permitted say.

When it was the Five Hundred and Sixtieth Night,

Quoth Dunyazad, "O sister mine, an thou be other than sleepy,
do tell us some of thy pleasant tales," whereupon Shahrazad
replied, "With love and good will." —— It hath reached me, O
King of the Age, that when the King heard the words of his
Grand Wazir, he knew that the speech was prompted by excess
of envy; so turning to the mother of Alaeddin he said, "O
woman, go to thy son and tell him that I have accepted of him the
dower and stand to my bargain, and that my daughter be his
bride and he my son-in-law: furthermore, bid him at once make
act of presence that I may become familiar with him: he shall see
naught from me save all honour and consideration, and this night
shall be the beginning of the marriage-festivities. Only, as I said
to thee, let him come to me and tarry not." Thereupon Alaeddin's mother returned home with the speed of the stormwinds
that she might hasten her utmost to congratulate her son; and
she flew with joy at the thought that her boy was about to be-

come[1] son-in-law to the Sultan. After her departure the King dismissed the Divan and, entering the palace of the Princess, bade them bring the bowls and the handmaids before him and before her, that she also might inspect them. But when the Lady Badr al-Budur considered the jewels, she waxed distraught and cried, "Meseemeth that in the treasuries of the world there be not found one jewel rivalling these jewels." Then she looked at the handmaids and marvelled at their beauty and loveliness, and knew that all this came from her new bridegroom who had sent them in her service. So she was gladdened, albeit she had been grieved and saddened on account of her former husband, the Wazir's son, and she rejoiced with exceeding joy when she gazed upon the damsels and their charms; nor was her sire, the Sultan, less pleased and inspirited when he saw his daughter relieved of all her mourning and melancholy and his own vanished at the sight of her enjoyment. Then he asked her, "O my daughter, do these things divert thee? Indeed I deem that this suitor of thine be more suitable to thee than the son of the Wazir; and right soon (Inshallah!), O my daughter, shalt thou have fuller joy with him." Such was the case with the King; but as regards Alaeddin, as soon as he saw his mother entering the house with face laughing for stress of joy he rejoiced at the sign of glad tidings and cried, "To Allah alone be lauds! Perfected is all I desired." Rejoined his mother, "Be gladdened at my good news, O my son, and hearten thy heart and cool thine eyes for the winning of thy wish. The Sultan hath accepted thine offering, I mean the moneys and the dower of the Lady Badr al-Budur, who is now thine affianced bride; and, this very night, O my child, is your marriage and thy first visit to her; for the King, that he might assure me of his word, hath proclaimed to the world thou art his son-in-law and promised this night to be the night of going in. But he also said to me, 'Let thy son come hither forthright that I may become familiar with him and receive him with all honour and worship.' And now here am I, O my son, at the end of my labours; happen whatso may happen the rest is upon thy shoulders." Thereupon Alaeddin arose and kissed his mother's hand and thanked her, enhancing her kindly service: then he left her and entering his chamber took the Lamp and rubbed it when, lo and behold! its Slave appeared and cried, "Adsum! Ask whatso

---

[1] Arab. "Ráih yasír," peasant's language.

thou wantest." The young man replied, " 'Tis my desire that
thou take me to a Hammam whose like is not in the world; then,
fetch me a dress so costly and kingly that no royalty ever owned
its fellow." The Marid replied, "I hear and I obey," and carried
him to Baths such as were never seen by the Kings of the Chosroës, for the building was all of alabaster and carnelian and it
contained marvellous limnings which captured the sight; and the
great hall[1] was studded with precious stones. Not a soul was
therein but, when Alaeddin entered, one of the Jann in human
shape washed him and bathed[2] him to the best of his desire.——
And Shahrazad was surprised by the dawn of day and ceased to
say her permitted say.

When it was the Five Hundred and Sixty-first Night,

QUOTH Dunyazad, "O sister mine, an thou be other than sleepy,
do tell us some of thy pleasant tales," whereupon Shahrazad
replied, "With love and good will."——It hath reached me, O
King of the Age, that Alaeddin, after having been washed and
bathed, left the Baths and went into the great hall where he
found that his old dress had been removed and replaced by a
suit of the most precious and princely. Then he was served
with sherbets and ambergris'd coffee[3] and, after drinking, he
arose and a party of black slaves came forwards and clad him in
the costliest of clothing, then perfumed and fumigated him. It
is known that Alaeddin was the son of a tailor, a pauper, yet
now would none deem him to be such; nay, all would say, "This
be the greatest that is of the progeny of the Kings: praise be to

---

[1] Arab. Ká'ah, the apodyterium or undressing room upon which the vestibule of the
Hammam opens. See the plan in Lane's M. E. chapt. xvi. The Kár'ah is now usually
called "Maslakh" = stripping-room.

[2] Arab. "Hammam-hu" = went through all the operations of the Hammam, scraping,
kneading, soaping, wiping and so forth.

[3] For this aphrodisiac see vol. vi. 60. The subject of aphrodisiacs in the East would fill a
small library: almost every medical treatise ends in a long disquisition upon fortifiers,
provocatives, etc. We may briefly divide them into three great classes. The first is the
medicinal, which may be either external or internal. The second is the mechanical, such as
scarification, flagellation, and the application of insects as practised by certain savage races.
There is a venerable Joe Miller of an old Brahmin whose young wife always insisted, each
time before he possessed her, upon his being stung by a bee in certain parts. The third is
magical, superstitious and so forth.

Him who changeth and who is not changed!" Presently came the Jinni and lifting him up bore him to his home and asked, "O my lord, tell me hast thou aught of need?" He answered, "Yes, 'tis my desire that thou bring me eight and forty Mamelukes, of whom two dozen shall forego me and the rest follow me, the whole number with their war-chargers and clothing and accoutrements; and all upon them and their steeds must be of naught save of highest worth and the costliest, such as may not be found in treasuries of the Kings. Then fetch me a stallion fit for the riding of the Chosroës and let his furniture, all thereof, be of gold crusted with the finest gems:[1] fetch me also eight and forty thousand dinars that each white slave may carry a thousand gold pieces. 'Tis now my intent to fare to the Sultan, so delay thou not, for that without all these requisites whereof I bespake thee I may not visit him. Moreover set before me a dozen slave girls unique in beauty and dight with the most magnificent dresses, that they wend with my mother to the royal palace; and let every handmaid be robed in raiment that befitteth Queen's wearing." The Slave replied, "To hear is to obey;" and, disappearing for an eye-twinkling, brought all he was bidden bring and led by hand a stallion whose rival was not amongst the Arabian Arabs,[2] and its saddle cloth was of splendid brocade gold-inwrought. Thereupon, without stay or delay, Alaeddin sent for his mother and gave her the garments she should wear and committed to her charge the twelve slave-girls forming her suite to the palace. Then he sent one of the Mamelukes, whom the Jinni had brought, to see if the Sultan had left the Serraglio or not. The white slave went forth lighter than the lightning and returning in like haste, said, "O my lord, the Sultan awaiteth thee!" Hereat Alaeddin arose and took horse, his Mamelukes riding a-van and a-rear of him, and they were such that all must cry, "Laud to the Lord who created them and clothed them with such beauty and loveliness." And they scattered gold amongst the crowd in front of their master who surpassed them all in comeliness and seemlihead nor needst thou ask concerning the

---

[1] This may sound exaggerated to English ears, but a petty Indian Prince, such as the Gáikwár, or Rajah of Baroda, would be preceded in state processions by several led horses all whose housings and saddles were gold studded with diamonds. The sight made one's mouth water.

[2] *i.e.* the 'Arab al-'Arbá; for which see vols. i. 112; v. 101.

sons of the Kings,—praise be to the Bountiful, the Eternal! All this was of the virtues of the Wonderful Lamp,[1] which, whoso possessed, him it gifted with fairest favour and finest figure, with wealth and with wisdom. The folk admired Alaeddin's liberality and exceeding generosity and all were distraught seeing his charms and elegance, his gravity and his good manners, they glorified the Creator for this noble creation, they blessed him each and every and, albeit they knew him for the son of Such-an-one, the tailor, yet no man envied him; nay, all owned that he deserved his great good fortune.——And Shahrazad was surprised by the dawn of day and ceased to say her permitted say.

𝖂𝖍𝖊𝖓 𝖎𝖙 𝖜𝖆𝖘 𝖙𝖍𝖊 𝕱𝖎𝖛𝖊 𝕳𝖚𝖓𝖉𝖗𝖊𝖉 𝖆𝖓𝖉 𝕾𝖎𝖝𝖙𝖞-𝖘𝖊𝖈𝖔𝖓𝖉 𝕹𝖎𝖌𝖍𝖙,

QUOTH Dunyazad, "O sister mine, an thou be other than sleepy, do tell us some of thy pleasant tales," whereupon Shahrazad replied, "With love and good will."——It hath reached me, O King of the Age, that the people were bewildered at Alaeddin and his liberality and generosity; and all blessed and prayed for him, high and low, as he rode palace-wards with the Mamelukes before and behind him, scattering gold upon the heads of the folk. Now the Sultan had assembled the Lords of the land and, informing them of the promise he had passed to Alaeddin, touching the marriage of his daughter, had bidden them await his approach and then go forth, one and all, to meet him and greet him. Hereupon the Emirs and Wazirs, the Chamberlains, the Nabobs and the Army-officers took their stations expecting him at the palace gate. Alaeddin would fain have dismounted at the outer entrance; but one of the Nobles, whom the King had deputed for such duty, approached him and said, "O my lord, 'tis the Royal Command that thou enter riding thy steed nor dismount except at the Divan-door."[2] Then they all forewent him in a body and conducted him to the appointed place where they crowded about him, these to hold his stirrup and those supporting him on either

---

[1] Arab. "Al-Kandíl al-'ajíb:" here its magical virtues are specified and remove many apparent improbabilities from the tale.

[2] This was the highest of honours. At Abyssinian Harar even the Grandees were compelled to dismount at the door of the royal "compound." See my "First Footsteps in East Africa," p. 296.

side whilst others took him by the hands and helped him dismount; after which all the Emirs and Nobles preceded him into the Divan and led him close up to the royal throne. Thereupon the Sultan came down forthright from his seat of estate and, forbidding him to buss the carpet, embraced and kissed and seated him to the right[1] of and beside himself. Alaeddin did whatso is suitable, in the case of the Kings, of salutation and offering of blessings, and said, "O our lord the Sultan, indeed the generosity of thy Highness demanded that thou deign vouchsafe to me the hand of thy daughter, the Lady Badr al-Budur, albeit I undeserve the greatness of such gift, I being but the humblest of thy slaves. I pray Allah grant thee prosperity and perpetuance; but in very sooth, O King, my tongue is helpless to thank thee for the fullness of the favour, passing all measure, which thou hast bestowed upon me. And I hope of thy Highness that thou wilt give me a piece of ground fitted for a pavilion which shall besit thy daughter, the Lady Badr al-Budur." The Sultan was struck with admiration when he saw Alaeddin in his princely suit and looked upon him and considered his beauty and loveliness, and noted the Mamelukes standing to serve him in their comeliness and seemlihead; and still his marvel grew when the mother of Alaeddin approached him in costly raiment and sumptuous, clad as though she were a Queen, and when he gazed upon the twelve handmaids standing before her with crossed arms and with all worship and reverence doing her service. He also considered the eloquence of Alaeddin and his delicacy of speech and he was astounded thereat, he and all his who were present at the levée. Thereupon fire was kindled in the Grand Wazir's heart for envy of Alaeddin until he was like to die: and it was worse when the Sultan, after hearing the youth's succession of prayers and seeing his high dignity of demeanour, respectful withal, and his eloquence and elegance of language, clasped him to his bosom and kissed him and cried, "Alas, O my son, that I have not enjoyed thy converse before this day!"——And Shahrazad was surprised by the dawn of day and ceased to say her permitted say.

---

1 "The right hand" seems to me a European touch in Galland's translation, *leur chef mit Aladdin a sa droite.* Amongst Moslems the great man sits in the sinistral corner of the Divan as seen from the door, so the place of honour is to his left.

When it was the Five Hundred and Sixty-third Night,

QUOTH Dunyazad, "O sister mine, an thou be other than sleepy, do tell us some of thy pleasant tales," whereupon Shahrazad replied, "With love and good will."——It hath reached me, O King of the Age, that when the Sultan beheld Alaeddin after such fashion, he rejoiced in him with mighty great joy and straightway bade the music[1] and the bands strike up; then he arose and, taking the youth led him into the palace where supper had been prepared and the Eunuchs at once laid the tables. So the Sovran sat down and seated his son-in-law on his right side and the Wazirs and high officials and Lords of the land took places each according to his degree, whereupon the bands played and a mighty fine marriage-feast was dispread in the palace. The King now applied himself to making friendship with Alaeddin and conversed with the youth, who answered him with all courtesy and eloquence, as though he had been bred in the palaces of the kings or he had lived with them his daily life. And the more the talk was prolonged between them, the more did the Sultan's pleasure and delight increase, hearing his son-in-law's readiness of reply and his sweet flow of language. But after they had eaten and drunken and the trays were removed, the King bade summon the Kazis and witnesses who presently attended and knitted the knot and wrote out the contract-writ between Alaeddin and the Lady Badr al-Budur. And presently the bridegroom arose and would have fared forth, when his father-in-law withheld him and asked, "Whither away, O my child? The bride-fêtes have begun and the marriage is made and the tie is tied and the writ is written." He replied, "O my lord the King, 'tis my desire to edify, for the Lady Badr al-Budur, a pavilion befitting her station and high degree, nor can I visit her before so doing. But, Inshallah! the building shall be finished within the shortest time, by the utmost endeavor of thy slave and by the kindly regard of thy Highness; and, although I do (yes indeed!) long to enjoy the society of the Lady Badr al-Budur, yet 'tis incumbent on me first to serve her and it becometh me to set about the work forth-

---

[1] Arab. "Músiká," classically "Musikí" = Μουσική: the Pers. form is "Músikár"; and the Arab. equivalent is Al-Lahn. In the H. V. the King "made a signal and straightway drums (*dhol*) and trumpets (*trafír*) and all manner wedding instruments struck up on every side."

right." "Look around thee, O my son," replied the Sultan, "for what ground thou deemest suitable to thy design and do thou take all things into thy hands; but I deem the best for thee will be yonder broad plain facing my palace; and, if it please thee, build thy pavilion thereupon." "And this," answered Alaeddin, "is the sum of my wishes that I may be nearhand to thy Highness." So saying he farewelled the King and took horse, with his Mamelukes riding before him and behind him, and all the world blessed him and cried, "By Allah he is deserving," until such time as he reached his home. Then he alighted from his stallion and repairing to his chamber, rubbed the Lamp and behold, the Slave stood before him and said, "Ask, O my lord, whatso thou wantest;" and Alaeddin rejoined, "I require thee of a service grave and important which thou must do for me, and 'tis that thou build me with all urgency a pavilion fronting the palace of the Sultan; and it must be a marvel for it shall be provided with every requisite, such as royal furniture and so forth." The Slave replied, "To hear is to obey."——And Shahrazad was surprised by the dawn of day and ceased to say her permitted say.

When it was the Five Hundred and Sixty-fourth Night,

QUOTH Dunyazad, "O sister mine, an thou be other than sleepy, do tell us some of thy pleasant tales," whereupon Shahrazad replied, "With love and good will."——It hath reached me, O King of the Age, that the Slave evanished and, before the next dawn brake, returned to Alaeddin and said, "O my lord, the pavilion is finished to the fullest of thy fancy; and, if thou wouldst inspect it, arise forthright and fare with me." Accordingly, he rose up and the Slave carried him in the space of an eye-glance to the pavilion which, when Alaeddin looked upon it, struck him with surprise at such building, all its stones being of jasper and alabaster, Sumáki[1]-marble and mosaic-work. Then the Slave led him into the treasury which was full of all manner of gold and silver and costly gems, not to be counted or computed, priced or estimated. Thence to another place, where Alaeddin

---

[1] Arab. "Marmar Sumáki" = porphyry of which ancient Egypt supplied the finest specimens. I found a vein of it in the Anti-Libanus. Strange to say, the quarries which produced the far-famed giallo antico, verd' antico (serpentine limestone) and rosso antico (mostly a porphyry) worked by the old Nilotes, are now unknown to us.

saw all requisites for the tables, plates and dishes, spoons and
ladles, basins and covers, cups and tasses, the whole of precious
metal: thence to the kitchen, where they found the kitcheners
provided with their needs and cooking batteries, likewise golden
and silvern; thence to a warehouse piled up with chests full-
packed of royal raiment, stuffs that captured the reason, such as
gold-wrought brocades from India and China and kimcobs[1] or
orfrayed cloths; thence to many apartments replete with appointments which beggar description; thence to the stables containing
coursers whose like was not to be met with amongst the kings
of the universe; and, lastly, they went to the harness-rooms all
hung with housings, costly saddles and other furniture, everywhere studded with pearls and precious stones. And all this
was the work of one night. Alaeddin was wonder-struck and
astounded by that magnificent display of wealth which not even
the mightiest monarch on earth could produce; and more so to
see his pavilion fully provided with eunuchs and handmaids
whose beauty would seduce a saint. Yet the prime marvel of the
pavilion was an upper kiosque or belvedere of four-and-twenty
windows all made of emeralds and rubies and other gems;[2] and
one window remained unfinished at the requirement of Alaeddin
that the Sultan might prove him impotent to complete it. When
the youth had inspected the whole edifice, he was pleased and
gladdened exceedingly: then, turning to the Slave he said, "I
require of thee still one thing which is yet wanting and whereof
I had forgotten to tell thee." "Ask, O my lord, thy want,"
quoth the Servitor; and quoth the other, "demand of thee a
carpet of the primest brocade all gold-inwrought which, when
unrolled and outstretched, shall extend hence to the Sultan's
palace in order that the Lady Badr al-Budur may, when coming
hither, pace upon it[3] and not tread common earth." The Slave

---

1 i.e. velvets with gold embroidery: see vol. viii. 201.
2 The Arabic says, "There was a kiosque with four-and-twenty alcoves (Líwán, for which
see vols. iv. 71; vi. 347) all builded of emerald, etc., and one remained with the kiosque
(kushk) unfinished." I adopt Galland's reading salon à vingt-quatre croisées which are mentioned in the Arab. text towards the end of the tale, and thus avoid the confusion between kiosque and window. In the H. V. there is a domed belvedere (bárah-dari-i-gumbaz-
dár), four-sided, with six doors on each front (i. e. twenty-four), and all studded with
diamonds, etc.
3 In Persia this is called "Pá-andáz," and must be prepared for the Shah when he deigns
to visit a subject. It is always of costly stuffs, and becomes the perquisite of the royal
attendants.

departed for a short while and said on his return, "O my lord, verily that which thou demandest is here." Then he took him and showed him a carpet which wildered the wits, and it extended from palace to pavilion; and after this the Servitor bore off Alaeddin and set him down in his own home.——And Shahrazad was surprised by the dawn of day and ceased to say her permitted say.

When it was the Five Hundred and Sixty-fifth Night,

Quoth Dunyazad, "O sister mine; an thou be other than sleepy, do tell us some of thy pleasant tales," whereupon Shahrazad replied, "With love and good will."——It hath reached me, O King of the Age, that the Slave, after displaying the Carpet to Alaeddin, bore him home. Now day was brightening so the Sultan rose from his sleep and throwing open the casement looked out[1] and espied, opposite his palace, a palatial pavilion ready edified. Thereupon he fell to rubbing his eyes and opening them their widest and considering the scene, and he soon was certified that the new edifice was mighty fine and grand enough to bewilder the wits. Moreover, with amazement as great he saw the carpet dispread between palace and pavilion: like their lord also the royal door-keepers and the household, one and all, were dazed and amazed at the spectacle. Meanwhile[2] the Wazir came in and, as he entered, espied the newly-builded pavilion and the carpet, whereat he also wondered; and, when he went in to the Sultan the twain fell to talking on this marvellous matter with great surprise at a sight which distracted the gazer and attracted the heart. They said finally, "In very truth, of this pavilion we deem that none of the royalties could build its fellow;" and the King, turning to the Minister, asked him, "Hast thou seen now that Alaeddin is worthy to be the husband of the Princess my daughter? Hast thou looked upon and considered this right royal building, this magnificence of opulence, which thought of man can not contain?" But the Wazir in his envy of Alaeddin replied, "O King of the Age, indeed this foundation and this building

---

[1] Here the European hand again appears to me: the Sultan as a good Moslem should have made the Wuzú-ablution and prayed the dawn-prayers before doing anything worldly.

[2] Arab. "Fí ghuzúni zálika," a peculiar phrase; Ghazn = a crease, a wrinkle.

and this opulence may not be save by means of magic nor can any man in the world, be he the richest in good or the greatest in governance, avail to found and finish in a single night such edifice as this." The Sultan rejoined, "I am surprised to see in thee how thou dost continually harp on evil opinion of Alaeddin; but I hold that 'tis caused by thine envy and jealousy. Thou wast present when I gave him the ground at his own prayer for a place whereon he might build a pavilion wherein to lodge my daughter, and I myself favoured him with a site for the same and that too before thy very face. But however that be, shall one who could send me as dower for the Princess such store of such stones whereof the kings never obtained even a few, shall he, I say, be unable to edify an edifice like this?"———And Shahrazad was surprised by the dawn of day and ceased to say her permitted say.

When it was the Five Hundred and Sixty-sixth Night,

QUOTH Dunyazad, "O sister mine, an thou be other than sleepy, do tell us some of thy pleasant tales," whereupon Shahrazad replied, "With love and good will."———It hath reached me, O King of the Age, that when the Wazir heard the Sultan's words, he knew that his lord loved Alaeddin exceedingly; so his envy and malice increased; only, as he could do nothing against the youth, he sat silent and impotent to return a reply. But Alaeddin seeing that it was broad day, and the appointed time had come for his repairing to the palace (where his wedding was being celebrated and the Emirs and Wazirs and Grandees were gathered together about the Sultan to be present at the ceremony), arose and rubbed the Lamp, and when its Slave appeared and said, "O my lord, ask whatso thou wantest, for I stand before thee and at thy service," said he, "I mean forthright to seek the palace, this day being my wedding-festival and I want thee to supply me with ten thousand dinars." The Slave evanished for an eye-twinkling and returned bringing the moneys, when Alaeddin took horse with his Mamelukes a-van and a-rear and passed on his way, scattering as he went gold pieces upon the lieges until all were fondly affected towards him and his dignity was enhanced. But when he drew near the palace, and the Emirs and Aghas and Army-officers who were standing to await him noted his approach, they hastened straightway to the King and gave him the tidings thereof; whereupon the Sultan rose and met his son-in-law and, after embracing and kissing him, led him still holding his hand into his own apartment where he sat down and seated him by his right side. The city was all decorated and music rang through the palace and the singers sang until the King bade bring the noon-meal, when the eunuchs and Mamelukes hastened to spread the tables and trays which are such as are served to the kings. Then the Sultan and Alaeddin and the Lords of the land and the Grandees of the realm took their seats and ate and drank until they were satisfied. And it was a mighty fine wedding in city and palace and the high nobles all rejoiced therein and the commons of the kingdom were equally gladdened, while the Governors of provinces and Nabobs of districts flocked from far regions to witness Alaeddin's marriage and its processions and festivities. The Sultan also marvelled in his mind to look at Alaeddin's mother[1] and recall to mind how she was wont to visit him in pauper plight, while her son could command all this opulence and magnificence. And when the spectators, who crowded the royal palace to enjoy the wedding-feasts, looked upon Alaeddin's pavilion and the beauties of the building, they were seized with an immense surprise that so vast an edifice as this could be reared on high during a single night; and they blessed the youth and cried, "Allah gladden him! By Allah, he deserveth all this! Allah bless his days!"——And Shahrazad was surprised by the dawn of day and ceased to say her permitted say.

When it was the Five Hundred and Sixty-seventh Night,

Quoth Dunyazad, "O sister mine, an thou be other than sleepy, do tell us some of thy pleasant tales," whereupon Shahrazad replied, "With love and good will." —— It hath reached me, O King of the Age, that when dinner was done, Alaeddin rose and, farewelling the Sultan, took horse with his Mamelukes and rode to his own pavilion that he might prepare to receive therein his bride, the Lady Badr al-Budur. And as he passed, all the folk

---

[1] In the H. V. the King "marvelled to see Alaeddin's mother without her veil and magnificently adorned with costly jewels and said in his mind, 'Methought she was a grey-haired crone, but I find her still in the prime of life and comely to look upon, somewhat after the fashion of Badr al-Budúr.' " This also was one of the miracles of the Lamp.

shouted their good wishes with one voice and their words were, "Allah gladden thee! Allah increase thy glory. Allah grant thee length of life!" while immense crowds of people gathered to swell the marriage procession and they conducted him to his new home, he showering gold upon them during the whole time. When he reached his pavilion, he dismounted and walked in and sat him down on the divan, whilst his Mamelukes stood before him with arms afolded; also after a short delay they brought him sherbets and, when these were drunk, he ordered his white slaves and handmaids and eunuchs and all who were in the pavilion to make ready for meeting the Lady Badr al-Budur. Moreover, as soon as mid-afternoon came and the air had cooled and the great heat of the sun was abated, the Sultan bade his Army-officers and Emirs and Wazirs go down into the Maydán-plain[1] whither he likewise rode. And Alaeddin also took horse with his Mamelukes, he mounting a stallion whose like was not among the steeds of the Arab al-Arbá,[2] and he showed his horsemanship in the hippodrome and so played with the Jaríd[3] that none could withstand him, while his bride sat gazing upon him from the latticed balcony of her bower and, seeing in him such beauty and cavalarice, she fell headlong in love of him and was like to fly for joy. And after they had ringed their horses on the Maydan and each had displayed whatso he could of horsemanship, Alaeddin proving himself the best man of all, they rode in a body to the Sultan's palace and the youth also returned to his own pavilion. But when it was evening, the Wazirs and Nobles took the bride-groom and, falling in, escorted him to the royal Hammam (known as the Sultání), when he was bathed and perfumed. As soon as he came out he donned a dress more magnificent than the former and took horse with the Emirs and the soldier-officers riding before him and forming a grand cortège, wherein four of the Wazirs bore naked swords round about him.[4] All the citizens and the strangers and the troops marched before him in ordered throng carrying wax-candles and kettle drums and pipes and other

---

[1] For this word see vols. i. 46, vii. 326. A Joe Miller is told in Western India of an old General Officer boasting his knowledge of Hindostani. "How do you say, Tell a plain story, General?" asked one of the hearers, and the answer was, "Maydán-kí bát bolo!" = "speak a word about the plain" (or level space).

[2] The prehistoric Arabs: see supra p. 98.

[3] Popularly, Jeríd, the palm-frond used as javelin: see vol. vi. 263.

[4] In order to keep off the evil eye, one of the functions of iron and steel: see vol. ii. 316.

instruments of mirth and merriment, until they conducted him to his pavilion. Here he alighted and walking in took his seat and seated the Wazirs and Emirs who had escorted him, and the Mamelukes brought sherbets and sugared drinks, which they also passed to the people who had followed in his train. It was a world of folk whose tale might not be told; withal Alaeddin bade his Mamelukes stand without the pavilion-doors and shower gold upon the crowd. —— And Shahrazad was surprised by the dawn of day and ceased to say her permitted say.

When it was the Five Hundred and Sixty-eighth Night,

QUOTH Dunyazad, "O sister mine, an thou be other than sleepy, do tell us some of thy pleasant tales," whereupon Shahrazad replied, "With love and good will." —— It hath reached me, O King of the Age, that when the Sultan returned from the Maydan-plain to his palace he ordered the household, men as well as women, straightway to form a cavalcade for his daughter, with all ceremony, and bear her to her bridegroom's pavilion. So the nobles and soldier-officers, who had followed and escorted the bridegroom, at once mounted, and the handmaids and eunuchs went forth with wax-candles and made a mighty fine procession for the Lady Badr al-Budur and they paced on preceding her till they entered the pavilion of Alaeddin whose mother walked beside the bride. In front of the Princess also fared the wives of the Wazirs and Emirs, Grandees and Notables, and in attendance on her were the eight and forty slave-girls presented to her aforetime by her bridegroom, each hending in hand a huge cierge scented with camphor and ambergris and set in a candlestick of gem-studded gold. And reaching Alaeddin's pavilion they led her to her bower in the upper storey and changed her robes and enthroned her; then, as soon as the displaying was ended, they accompanied her to Alaeddin's apartments and presently he paid her the first visit. Now his mother was with the bride and, when the bridegroom came up and did off her veil, the ancient dame fell to considering the beauty of the Princess and her loveliness; and she looked around at the pavilion which was all litten up by gold and gems besides the manifold candelabra of precious metals encrusted with emeralds and jacinths; so she said in her mind, "Once upon a time I thought the Sultan's palace mighty fine, but this pavilion is a thing apart; nor do I deem that any of the greatest Kings of Chosroës attained in his day to aught like thereof; also am I certified that all the world could not build anything evening it." Nor less did the lady Badr al-Budur fall to gazing at the pavilion and marvelling for its magnificence. Then the tables were spread and they all ate and drank and were gladdened; after which fourscore damsels came before them each holding in hand an instrument of mirth and merriment; then they deftly moved their finger-tips and touched the strings smiting them into song, most musical, most melancholy, till they rent the hearts of the hearers. Hereat the Princess increased in marvel and quoth she to herself, "In all my life ne'er heard I songs like these,"[1] till she forsook food, the better to listen. And at last Alaeddin poured out for her wine and passed it to her with his own hand; so great joy and jubilee went round amongst them and it was a notable night, such an one as Iskander, Lord of the Two Horns,[2] had never spent in his time. When they had finished eating and drinking and the tables were removed from before them, Alaeddin arose and went in to his bride.[3] As soon as morning morrowed he left his bed and the treasurer brought him a costly suit and a mighty fine, of the most sumptuous robes worn by the kings. Then, after drinking coffee flavoured with ambergris, he ordered the horses be saddled and, mounting with his Mamelukes before and behind him, rode to the Sultan's palace and on his entering its court the eunuchs went in and reported his coming to their lord.——And Shahrazad was surprised by the dawn of day and ceased to say her permitted say.

---

[1] The H. V. adds, "Little did the Princess know that the singers were fairies whom the Slave of the Lamp had brought together."

[2] Alexander the Great: see v. 252, x. 57. The H. V. adds, "Then only one man and one woman danced together, one with other, till midnight, when Alaeddin and the Princess stood up; for it was the wont of China in those days that bride and bridegroom perform together in presence of the wedding company."

[3] The exceptional reserve of this and other descriptions makes M. H. Zotenberg suspect that the tale was written for one of the Mameluke Princesses: I own to its modesty but I doubt that such virtue would have recommended it to the dames in question. The H. V. adds a few details:—"Then, when the bride and bridegroom had glanced and gazed each at other's face, the Princess rejoiced with excessive joy to behold his comeliness, and he exclaimed, in the courtesy of his gladness, 'O happy me, whom thou deignest, O Queen of the Fair, to honour despite mine unworth, seeing that in thee all charms and graces are perfected.' "

When it was the Five Hundred and Sixty-ninth Nigh

QUOTH Dunyazad, "O sister mine, an thou be other than sleepy, do tell us some of thy pleasant tales," whereupon Shahrazad replied, "With love and good will." —— It hath reached me, O King of the Age, that when the Sultan heard of Alaeddin's approach, he rose up forthright to receive him and embraced and kissed him as though he were his own son: then, seating him on his right, he blessed and prayed for him, as did the Wazirs and Emirs, the Lords of the land and the Grandees of the realm. Presently, the King commanded bring the morning-meal which the attendants served up and all broke their fast together, and when they had eaten and drunken their sufficiency and the tables were removed by the eunuchs, Alaeddin turned to the Sultan and said, "O my lord, would thy Highness deign honour me this day at dinner, in the house of the Lady Badr al-Budur thy beloved daughter, and come accompanied by all thy Ministers and Grandees of the reign?" The King replied (and he was delighted with his son-in-law), "Thou art surpassing in liberality, O my son!" Then he gave orders to all invited and rode forth with them (Alaeddin also riding beside him) till they reached the pavilion and as he entered it and considered its construction, its architecture and its stonery, all jasper and carnelian, his sight was dazed and his wits were amazed at such grandeur and magnificence of opulence. Then turning to the Minister he thus addressed him, "What sayest thou? Tell me hast thou seen in all thy time aught like this amongst the mightiest of earth's monarchs for the abundance of gold and gems we are now beholding?" The Grand Wazir replied, "O my lord the King, this be a feat which cannot be accomplished by might of monarch amongst Adam's sons;[1] nor could the collected peoples of the universal world build a palace like unto this; nay, even builders could not be found to make aught resembling it, save (as I said to thy Highness) by force of sorcery." These words certified the King that his Minister spake not except in envy and jealousy of Alaeddin, and would stablish in the royal mind that all this splendour was

---

[1] The term has not escaped ridicule amongst Moslems. A common fellow having stood in his way the famous wit Abú al-'Ayná asked "What is that?" "A man of the Sons of Adam" was the reply. "Welcome, welcome," cried the other, "Allah grant thee length of days! I deemed that all his sons were dead." See Ibn Khallikan iii. 57.

not made of man but by means of magic and with the aid of the
Black Art. So quoth he to him, "Suffice thee so much, O Wazir:
thou hast none other word to speak and well I know what cause
urgeth thee to say this say."   Then Alaeddin preceded the
Sultan till he conducted him to the upper Kiosque where he saw
its skylights, windows and latticed casements and jalousies
wholly made of emeralds and rubies and other costly gems;
whereat his mind was perplexed and his wits were bewildered
and his thoughts were distraught. Presently he took to strolling
round the Kiosque and solacing himself with these sights which
captured the vision, till he chanced to cast a glance at the window
which Alaeddin by design had left unwrought and not finished
like the rest; and, when he noted its lack of completion, he cried,
"Woe and well-away for thee, O window, because of thine im-
perfection;"[1] and, turning to his Minister he asked, "Knowest
thou the reason of leaving incomplete this window and its frame-
work?" —— And Shahrazad was surprised by the dawn of day
and ceased to say her permitted say.

When it was the Five Hundred and Seventieth Night,

QUOTH Dunyazad, "O sister mine, an thou be other than sleepy,
do tell us some of thy pleasant tales," whereupon Shahrazad
replied, "With love and good will." —— It hath reached me, O
King of the Age, that the Wazir said to the Sultan, "O my lord, I
conceive that the want of finish in this window resulteth from
thy Highness having pushed on Alaeddin's marriage and he
lacked the leisure to complete it." Now at that time, Alaeddin
had gone in to his bride, the Lady Badr al-Budur, to inform her
of her father's presence; and, when he returned, the King asked
him, "O my son what is the reason why the window of this
Kiosque was not made perfect?" "O King of the Age, seeing the
suddenness of my wedding," answered he, "I failed to find
artists for finishing it." Quoth the Sultan, "I have a mind to
complete it myself;" and quoth Alaeddin, "Allah perpetuate

---

[1] This address to an inanimate object (here a window) is highly idiomatic and must be
cultivated by the practical Arabist. In the H. V. the unfinished part is the four-and-
twentieth door of the fictitious (ja'alí) palace.

thy glory, O thou the King; so shall thy memory endure in thy daughter's pavilion." The Sultan forthright bade summon jewellers and goldsmiths and ordered them be supplied from the treasury with all their needs of gold and gems and noble ores; and, when they were gathered together he commanded them to complete the work still wanting in the Kiosque-window. Meanwhile the Princess came forth to meet her sire the Sultan who noticed, as she drew near, her smiling face; so he embraced her and kissed her, then led her to the pavilion and all entered in a body. Now this was the time of the noon-day meal and one table had been spread for the Sovran, his daughter and his son-in-law and a second for the Wazirs, the Lords of the land, the Grandees of the realm, the Chief Officers of the host, the Chamberlains and the Nabobs. The King took seat between the Princess and her husband; and, when he put forth his hand to the food and tasted it, he was struck with surprise by the flavour of the dishes and their savoury and sumptuous cooking. Moreover, there stood before him the fourscore damsels each and every saying to the full moon, "Rise that I may seat myself in thy stead!"[1] All held instruments of mirth and merriment and they tuned the same and deftly moved their finger-tips and smote the strings into song, most musical, most melodious, which expanded the mourner's heart. Hereby the Sultan was gladdened and time was good to him and for high enjoyment he exclaimed, "In very sooth the thing is beyond the compass of King and Kaysar." Then they fell to eating and drinking; and the cup went round until they had drunken enough, when sweetmeats and fruits of sorts and other such edibles were served, the dessert being laid out in a different salon whither they removed and enjoyed of these pleasures their sufficiency. Presently the Sultan arose that he might see if the produce of his jewellers and goldsmiths favoured that of the pavilion; so he went upstairs to them and inspected their work and how they had wrought; but he noted a mighty great difference and his men were far from being able to make anything like the rest of Alaeddin's pavilion. —— And Shahrazad was surprised by the dawn of day and ceased to say her permitted say.

---

[1] This is true Orientalism, a personification or incarnation which Galland did not think proper to translate.

When it was the Five Hundred and Seventy-first Night,

QUOTH Dunyazad, "O sister mine, an thou be other than sleepy, do tell us some of thy pleasant tales," whereupon Shahrazad replied, "With love and good will." —— It hath reached me, O King of the Age, that after the King had inspected the work of his jewellers and goldsmiths, they informed him how all the gems stored in the Lesser Treasury had been brought to them and used by them but that the whole had proved insufficient; wherefor he bade open the Greater Treasury and gave the workmen all they wanted of him. Moreover he allowed them, an it sufficed not, to take the jewels wherewith Alaeddin had gifted him. They carried off the whole and pushed on their labours but they found the gems fail them, albeit had they not yet finished half the part wanting to the Kiosque-window. Herewith the King commanded them to seize all the precious stones owned by the Wazirs and Grandees of the realm; but, although they did his bidding, the supply still fell short of their requirements. Next morning Alaeddin arose to look at the jeweller's work and remarked that they had not finished a moiety of what was wanting to the Kiosque-window: so he at once ordered them to undo all they had done and restore the jewels to their owners. Accordingly, they pulled out the precious stones and sent the Sultan's to the Sultan and the Wazirs' to the Wazirs. Then the jewellers went to the King and told him of what Alaeddin had bidden; so he asked them, "What said he to you, and what was his reason and wherefore was he not content that the window be finished and why did he undo the work ye wrought?" They answered, "O our lord, we know not at all, but he bade us deface whatso we had done." Hereupon the Sultan at once called for his horse, and mounting, took the way pavilion-wards, when Alaeddin, after dismissing the goldsmiths and jewellers had retired into his closet and had rubbed the Lamp. Hereat straightway its Servitor appeared to him and said, "Ask whatso thou wantest: thy Slave is between thy hands;" and said Alaeddin, " 'Tis my desire that thou finish the window which was left unfinished." The Marid replied, "On my head be it and also upon mine eyes!" then he vanished and after a little while returned saying, "O my lord, verily that thou commandedst me do is completed." So Alaeddin went upstairs to the Kiosque and found the whole

window in wholly finished state; and, whilst he was still considering it, behold, a castrato came in to him and said, "O my
lord, the Sultan hath ridden forth to visit thee and is passing
through the pavilion-gate." So Alaeddin at once went down
and received his father-in-law. —— And Shahrazad was surprised by the dawn of day and ceased to say her permitted say.

When it was the Five Hundred and Seventy-second Night,

QUOTH Dunyazad, "O sister mine, an thou be other than sleepy,
do tell us some of thy pleasant tales," whereupon Shahrazad
replied, "With love and good will." —— It hath reached me, O
King of the Age, that the Sultan, on sighting his son-in-law, cried
to him, "Wherefore, O my child, hast thou wrought on this wise
and sufferedst not the jewellers to complete the Kiosque-window
leaving in the pavilion an unfinished place?" Alaeddin replied,
"O King of the Age, I left it not imperfect save for a design of
mine own; nor was I incapable of perfecting it nor could I purpose that thy Highness should honour me with visiting a pavilion
wherein was aught of deficiency. And, that thou mayest know
I am not unable to make it perfect, let thy Highness deign walk
upstairs with me and see if anything remain to be done therewith
or not." So the Sultan went up with him and, entering the
Kiosque, fell to looking right and left, but he saw no default at all
in any of the windows; nay, he noted that all were perfect. So
he marvelled at the sight and embraced Alaeddin and kissed him,
saying, "O my son, what be this singular feat? Thou canst
work in a single night what in months the jewellers could not do.
By Allah, I deem thou hast nor brother nor rival in this world."
Quoth Alaeddin, "Allah prolong thy life and preserve thee to
perpetuity! thy slave deserveth not this encomium;" and quoth
the King, "By Allah, O my child, thou meritest all praise for a
feat whereof all the artists of the world were incapable." Then
the Sultan came down and entered the apartments of his daughter,
the Lady Badr al-Budur, to take rest beside her, and he saw her
joyous exceedingly at the glory and grandeur wherein she was;
then, after reposing awhile he returned to his palace. Now
Alaeddin was wont every day to thread the city-streets with his
Mamelukes riding a-van and a-rear of him showering rightwards
and leftwards gold upon the folk; and all the world, stranger and

neighbour, far and near, were fulfilled of his love for the excess of his liberality and generosity. Moreover he increased the pensions of the poor Religious and the paupers and he would distribute alms to them with his own hand; by which good deed, he won high renown throughout the realm and most of the Lords of the land and Emirs would eat at his table; and men swore not at all save by his precious life. Nor did he leave faring to the chase and the Maydan-plain and the riding of horses and playing at javelin-play[1] in presence of the Sultan; and, whenever the Lady Badr al-Budur beheld him disporting himself on the backs of steeds, she loved him much the more, and thought to herself that Allah had wrought her abundant good by causing to happen whatso happened with the son of the Wazir and by preserving her virginity intact for her true bridegroom, Alaeddin. —— And Shahrazad was surprised by the dawn of day and ceased to say her permitted say.

When it was the Five Hundred and Seventy-third Night,

QUOTH Dunyazad, "O sister mine, an thou be other than sleepy, do tell us some of thy pleasant tales." whereupon Shahrazad replied, "With love and good will." —— It hath reached me, O King of the Age, that Alaeddin won for himself day by day a fairer fame and a rarer report, while affection for him increased in the hearts of all the lieges and he waxed greater in the eyes of men. Moreover it chanced that in those days certain enemies took horse and attacked the Sultan, who armed and accoutred an army to repel them and made Alaeddin commander thereof. So he marched with his men nor ceased marching until he drew near the foe whose forces were exceeding many; and, presently, when the action began he bared his brand and charged home upon the enemy. Then battle and slaughter befel and violent was the hurly-burly, but at last Alaeddin broke the hostile host and put all to flight, slaying the best part of them and pillaging their coin and cattle, property and possessions; and he despoiled them of spoils that could not be counted nor computed. Then he returned victorious after a noble victory and entered the capital

---

[1] Arab. "La'ab al-Andáb;" the latter word is from "Nadb" = brandishing or throwing the javelin.

which had decorated herself in his honour, of her delight in him; and the Sultan went forth to meet him and giving him joy embraced him and kissed him; and throughout the kingdom was held high festival with great joy and gladness. Presently, the Sovran and his son-in-law repaired to the pavilion where they were met by the Princess Badr al-Budur who rejoiced in her husband and, after kissing him between the eyes, led him to her apartments. After a time the Sultan also came and they sat down while the slave-girls brought them sherbets and confections which they ate and drank. Then the Sultan commanded that the whole kingdom be decorated for the triumph of his son-in-law and his victory over the invader; and the subjects and soldiery and all the people knew only Allah in heaven and Alaeddin on earth; for that their love, won by his liberality, was increased by his noble horsemanship and his successful battling for the country and putting to flight the foe. Such then was the high fortune of Alaeddin; but as regards the Maghrabi, the Magician, after returning to his native country, he passed all this space of time in bewailing what he had borne of toil and travail to win the Lamp and mostly that his trouble had gone vain and that the morsel when almost touching his lips had flown from his grasp. He pondered all this and mourned and reviled Alaeddin for the excess of his rage against him and at times he would exclaim, "For this bastard's death underground I am well satisfied and hope only that some time or other I may obtain the Lamp, seeing how 'tis yet safe." Now one day of the days he struck a table of sand and dotted down the figures and carefully considered their consequence; then he transferred them to paper that he might study them and make sure of Alaeddin's destruction and the safety of the Lamp preserved beneath the earth. Presently, he firmly stablished the sequence of the figures, mothers as well as daughters,[1] but still he saw not the Lamp. Thereupon rage overrode him and he made another trial to be assured of Alaeddin's death; but he saw him not in the Enchanted Treasure. Hereat his wrath still grew, and it waxed greater when he ascertained that the youth had issued from underground and was now upon earth's surface alive and alert: furthermore,

---

[1] The "mothers" are the prime figures, the daughters being the secondary. For the " 'Ilm al-Raml" = (Science of the sand) our geomancy, see vol. iii. 269, and D'Herbelot's sub. v. *Raml* or *Reml*.

that he had become owner of the Lamp, for which he had himself endured such toil and travail and troubles as man may not bear save for so great an object. Accordingly quoth he to himself, "I have suffered sore pains and penalties which none else could have endured for the Lamp's sake in order that other than I may carry it off; and this Accursed hath taken it without difficulty. And who knoweth an he wot the virtues of the Lamp, than whose owner none in the world should be wealthier?" —— And Shahrazad was surprised by the dawn of day and ceased to say her permitted say.

When it was the Five Hundred and Seventy-fourth Night,

QUOTH Dunyazad, "O sister mine, an thou be other than sleepy, do tell us some of thy pleasant tales," whereupon Shahrazad replied, "With love and good will." —— It hath reached me, O King of the Age, that the Maghrabi, the Magician, having considered and ascertained that Alaeddin had escaped from the souterrain and had gotten the boon of the Lamp, said to himself, "There is no help but that I work for his destruction." He then struck another geomantic table and examining the figures saw that the lad had won for himself unmeasurable riches and had wedded the daughter of his King; so of his envy and jealousy he was fired with the flame of wrath; and, rising without let or stay, he equipped himself and set forth for China-land, where he arrived in due season. Now when he had reached the King's capital wherein was Alaeddin, he alighted at one of the Kháns; and, when he had rested from the weariness of wayfare, he donned his dress and went down to wander about the streets, where he never passed a group without hearing them prate about the pavilion and its grandeur and vaunt the beauty of Alaeddin and his lovesomeness, his liberality and generosity, his fine manners and his good morals. Presently he entered an establishment wherein men were drinking a certain warm beverage;[1] and, going up to one of those who were loud in their lauds, he said to him, "O fair youth, who may be the man ye describe and commend?" "Apparently thou art a foreigner, O man," answered the other,

---

[1] This is from Galland, whose *certaine boisson chaude* evidently means tea. It is preserved in the H. V.

"and thou comest from a far country; but, even this granted, how happeneth it thou hast not heard of the Emir Alaeddin whose renown, I fancy, hath filled the universe and whose pavilion, known by report to far and near, is one of the Wonders of the World? How, then, never came to thine ears aught of this or the name of Alaeddin (whose glory and enjoyment our Lord increase!) and his fame?" The Moorman replied, "The sum of my wishes is to look upon this pavilion and, if thou wouldest do me a favour, prithee guide me thereunto, for I am a foreigner." The man rejoined, "To hear is to obey;" and, foregoing him, pointed out Alaeddin's pavilion, whereupon the Maroccan fell to considering it and at once understood that it was the work of the Lamp. So he cried, "Ah! Ah! needs must I dig a pit for this Accursed, this son of a snip, who could not earn for himself even an evening meal: and, if the Fates abet me, I will assuredly destroy his life and send his mother back to spinning at her wheel, e'en as she was wont erewhiles to do." So saying, he returned to his caravanserai in a sore state of grief and melancholy and regret bred by his envy and hate of Alaeddin.—— And Shahrazad was surprised by the dawn of day and ceased to say her permitted say.

𝔚𝔥𝔢𝔫 𝔦𝔱 𝔴𝔞𝔰 𝔱𝔥𝔢 𝔉𝔦𝔳𝔢 𝔥𝔲𝔫𝔡𝔯𝔢𝔡 𝔞𝔫𝔡 𝔖𝔢𝔳𝔢𝔫𝔱𝔶-𝔣𝔦𝔣𝔱𝔥 𝔑𝔦𝔤𝔥𝔱.

QUOTH Dunyazad, "O sister mine, an thou be other than sleepy, do tell us some of thy pleasant tales," whereupon Shahrazad replied, "With love and good will."—— It hath reached me, O King of the Age, that when the Maghrabi, the Magician, reached his caravanserai, he took his astrological gear[1] and geomantic table

---

1 *i.e.* his astrolabe, his "Zíj" or table of the stars, his almanack, etc. For a highly fanciful derivation of the "Arstable" see Ibn Khallikán (iii. 580). He makes it signify "balance or lines (Pers. 'Astur') of the sun," which is called "Láb" as in the case of wicked Queen Láb (The Nights, vol. vii. 296). According to him the Astrolabe was suggested to Ptolemy by an armillary sphere which had accidentally been flattened by the hoof of his beast: this is beginning late in the day, the instrument was known to the ancient Assyrians. Chardin (Voyages ii. 149) carefully describes the Persian variety of—

"The cunning man hight Sidrophil

(as Will. Lilly was called). Amongst other things he wore at his girdle an astrolabe not bigger than the hollow of a man's hand, often two to three inches in diameter and looking at a distance like a medal." These men practised both natural astrology = astronomy, as well as judicial astrology which foretells events and of which Kepler said that "she, albeit

to discover where might be the Lamp; and he found that it was in the pavilion and not upon Alaeddin's person. So he rejoiced thereat with joy exceeding and exclaimed, "Now indeed 'twill be an easy task to take the life of this Accursed and I see my way to getting the Lamp." Then he went to a coppersmith and said to him, "Do thou make me a set of lamps and take from me their full price and more; only I would have thee hasten to finish them." Replied the smith, "Hearing and obeying," and fell aworking to keep his word; and when they were ready the Moorman paid him what price he required; then taking them he carried them to the Khan and set them in a basket. Presently he began wandering about the highways and market-streets of the capital crying aloud, "Ho! who will exchange old lamps for new lamps?"[1] But when the folk heard him cry on this wise, they derided him and said, "Doubtless this man is Jinn-mad, for that he goeth about offering new for old;" and a world followed him and the children of the quarter caught him up from place to place, laughing at him the while, nor did he forbid them or care for their maltreatment. And he ceased not strolling about the streets till he came under Alaeddin's pavilion,[2] where he shouted with his loudest voice and the boys screamed at him, "A madman! A madman!" Now Destiny had decreed that the Lady Badr al-Budur be sitting in her Kiosque whence she heard one crying like a crier, and the children bawling at him; only she understood not what was going on; so she gave orders to one of her slave-girls saying,[3] "Go thou and see who 'tis that crieth and what be his cry?" The girl fared forth and looked on when she beheld a man crying, "Ho! who will exchange old lamps for new lamps?" and the little ones pursuing and laughing at him; and as loudly laughed the Princess when this strange case was told to her. Now

---

a fool, was the daughter of a wise mother, to whose support and life the silly maid was indispensable." Isidore of Seville (A. D. 600-636) was the first to distinguish between the two branches, and they flourished side by side till Newton's day. Hence the many astrological terms in our tongue, *e.g.* consider, contemplate, disaster, jovial, mercurial, saturnine, etc.

[1] In the H. V. "New brass lamps for old ones! who will exchange?" So in the story of the Fisherman's son, a Jew who had been tricked of a cock, offers to give new rings for old rings. See Jonathan Scott's excerpts from the Wortley-Montague MSS. vol. vi. pp. 210-12. This is one of the tales which I have translated for vol. iv.

[2] The H. V. adds that Alaeddin loved to ride out a-hunting and had left the city for eight days whereof three had passed by.

[3] Galland makes her say, *Hé bien, folle, veux-tu me dire pourquoi tu ris?* The H.V. renders "Cease, giddy head, why laughest thou?" and the vulgate "Well, giggler," said the Princess, etc.

Alaeddin had carelessly left the Lamp in his pavilion without hiding it and locking it up in his strong box;[1] and one of the slave-girls who had seen it said, "O my lady, I think to have noticed, in the apartment of my lord Alaeddin, an old lamp: so let us give it in change for a new lamp to this man, and see if his cry be truth or lie." —— And Shahrazad was surprised by the dawn of day and ceased to say her permitted say.

When it was the Five Hundred and Seventy-sixth Night,

QUOTH Dunyazad, "O sister mine, an thou be other than sleepy, do tell us some of thy pleasant tales," 'whereupon Shahrazad replied, "With love and good will." —— It hath reached me, O King of the Age, that hereupon the Princess said to the slave-girl, "Bring the old lamp which thou saidst to have seen in thy lord's apartment." Now the Lady Badr al-Budur knew naught of the Lamp and of the specialties thereof which had raised Alaeddin her spouse to such high degree and grandeur; and her only end and aim was to understand by experiment the mind of a man who would give in exchange the new for the old. So the handmaid fared forth and went up to Alaeddin's apartment and returned with the Lamp to her lady who, like all the others, knew nothing of the Maghrabi's cunning tricks and his crafty device. Then the Princess bade an Aghá of the eunuchry go down and barter the old Lamp for a new lamp. So he obeyed her bidding and, after taking a new lamp from the man, he returned and laid it before his lady who looking at it and seeing that it was brand-new, fell to laughing at the Moorman's wits. But the Maroccan, when he held the article in hand and recognised it for the Lamp of the Enchanted Treasury,[2] at once placed it in his breast-pocket and left all the other lamps to the folk who were bartering of him. Then he went forth running till he was clear of the city, when he

---

[1] Nothing can be more improbable than this detail, but upon such abnormal situations almost all stories, even in our most modern "Society-novels," depend and the cause is clear —without them there would be no story. And the modern will, perhaps, suggest that "the truth was withheld for a higher purpose, for the working out of certain ends." In the H. V. Alaeddin, when about to go a-hunting, always placed the Lamp high up on the cornice with all care lest any touch it.

[2] The H. V. adds, "The Magician, when he saw the Lamp, at once knew that it must be the one he sought; for he knew that all things, great and small, appertaining to the palace would be golden or silver."

walked leisurely over the level grounds and he took patience until night fell on him in desert ground where was none other but himself. There he brought out the Lamp when suddenly appeared to him the Marid who said, "Adsum! thy slave between thy hands is come: ask of me whatso thou wantest." " 'Tis my desire," the Moorman replied, "that thou upraise from its present place Alaeddin's pavilion with its inmates and all that be therein, not forgetting myself, and set it down upon my own land, Africa. Thou knowest my town and I want the building placed in the gardens hard by it." The Marid-slave replied, "Hearkening and obedience: close thine eyes and open thine eyes whenas thou shalt find thyself together with the pavilion in thine own country." This was done; and, in an eye-twinkling, the Maroccan and the pavilion with all therein were transported to the African land. Such then was the work of the Maghrabi, the Magician; but now let us return to the Sultan and his son-in-law. It was the custom of the King, because of his attachment to and his affection for his daughter, every morning when he had shaken off sleep, to open the latticed casement and look out therefrom that he might catch sight of her abode. So that day he arose and did as he was wont. —— And Shahrazad was surprised by the dawn of day and ceased to say her permitted say.

𝔚𝔥𝔢𝔫 𝔦𝔱 𝔴𝔞𝔰 𝔱𝔥𝔢 𝔉𝔦𝔳𝔢 𝔥𝔲𝔫𝔡𝔯𝔢𝔡 𝔞𝔫𝔡 𝔖𝔢𝔳𝔢𝔫𝔱𝔶-𝔰𝔢𝔳𝔢𝔫𝔱𝔥 𝔑𝔦𝔤𝔥𝔱,

QUOTH Dunyazad, "O sister mine, an thou be other than sleepy, do tell us some of thy pleasant tales," whereupon Shahrazad replied, "With love and good will." —— It hath reached me, O King of the Age, that when the Sultan drew near the latticed casement of his palace and looked out at Alaeddin's pavilion he saw naught; nay, the site was smooth as a well-trodden highway and like unto what it had been aforetime; and he could find nor edifice nor offices. So astonishment clothed him as with a garment, and his wits were wildered and he began to rub his eyes, lest they be dimmed or darkened, and to gaze intently; but at last he was certified that no trace of the pavilion remained nor sign of its being; nor wist he the why and the wherefore of its disappearance. So his surprise increased and he smote hand upon hand and the tears trickled down his cheeks over his beard, for that he knew not what had become of his daughter. Then he sent out officials forthright and summoned the Grand Wazir who at once attended; and, seeing him in this piteous plight said, "Pardon, O King of the Age, may Allah avert from thee every ill! Wherefore art thou in such sorrow?" Exclaimed the Sovran, "Methinketh thou wottest not my case?" and quoth the Minister, "On no wise. O our lord: by Allah, I know of it nothing at all." "Then," resumed the Sultan, " 'tis manifest thou hast not looked this day in the direction of Alaeddin's pavilion." "True, O my lord," quoth the Wazir, "it must still be locked and fast shut;" and quoth the King, "Forasmuch as thou hast no inkling of aught,[1] arise and look out at the window and see Alaeddin's pavilion whereof thou sayest 'tis locked and fast shut." The Minister obeyed his bidding but could not see anything, or pavilion or other place; so with mind and thoughts sore perplexed he returned to his liege lord who asked him, "Hast now learned the reason of my distress and noted yon locked-up palace and fast shut?" Answered the Wazir, "O King of the Age, erewhile I represented to thy Highness that this pavilion and these matters be all magical." Hereat the Sultan, fired with wrath, cried, "Where be Alaeddin?" and the Minister replied, "He hath gone a-hunting," when the King commanded without stay or delay sundry of his Aghas and Army-officers to go and bring to him his son-in-law chained and with pinioned elbows. So they fared forth until they found Alaeddin when they said to him, "O our lord Alaeddin, excuse us nor be thou wroth with us; for the King hath commanded that we carry thee before him pinioned and fettered, and we hope pardon from thee because we are under the royal orders which we cannot gainsay." Alaeddin, hearing these words, was seized with surprise and not knowing the reason of this remained tongue-tied for a time, after which he turned to them and asked, "O assembly, have you naught of knowledge concerning the motive of the royal mandate? Well I wot my soul to be innocent and that I never sinned against king or against kingdom." "O our lord," answered they, "we have no inkling whatever." So Alaeddin alighted from his horse and said to them, "Do ye whatso the Sultan bade you do, for that the King's command is upon the head and the eyes."[2] — And Shahrazad was surprised by the dawn of day and ceased to say her permitted say.

---

[1] In truly Oriental countries the Wazir is expected to know everything, and if he fail in this easy duty he may find himself in sore trouble.

[2] *i.e.*, must be obeyed.

When it was the Five Hundred and Seventy-eighth Night,

QUOTH Dunyazad, "O sister mine, an thou be other than sleepy, do tell us some of thy pleasant tales," whereupon Shahrazad replied, "With love and good will." —— It hath reached me, O King of the Age, that the Aghas, having bound Alaeddin in bonds and pinioned his elbows behind his back, haled him in chains and carried him into the city. But when the lieges saw him pinioned and ironed, they understood that the Sultan purposed to strike off his head; and, forasmuch as he was loved of them exceedingly, all gathered together and seized their weapons; then, swarming out of their houses, followed the soldiery to see what was to do. And when the troops arrived with Alaeddin at the palace, they went in and informed the Sultan of this, whereat he forthright commanded the Sworder to cut off the head of his son-in-law. Now as soon as the subjects were aware of this order, they barricaded the gates and closed the doors of the palace and sent a message to the King saying, "At this very moment we will level thine abode over the heads of all it containeth and over thine own,[1] if the least hurt or harm befal Alaeddin." So the Wazir went in and reported to the Sultan, "O King of the Age, thy commandment is about to seal the roll of our lives; and 'twere-more suitable that thou pardon thy son-in-law lest there chance to us a sore mischance; for that the lieges do love him far more than they love us." Now the Sworder had already dispread the carpet of blood and, having seated Alaeddin thereon, had bandaged his eyes; moreover he had walked round him several times awaiting the last orders of his lord, when the King looked out of the window and saw his subjects, who had suddenly attacked him, swarming up the walls intending to tear them down. So forthright he bade the Sworder stay his hand from Alaeddin and commanded the crier fare forth to the crowd and cry aloud that he had pardoned his son-in-law and received him back into favour. But when Alaeddin found himself free and saw the Sultan seated on his throne, he went up to him and said, "O my lord, inasmuch as thy Highness hath favoured me throughout my life, so of thy grace now deign let me

---

[1] We see that "China" was in those days the normal Oriental "despotism tempered by assassination."

know the how and the wherein I have sinned against thee?" "O
traitor," cried the King, "unto this present I knew not any sin
of thine;" then, turning to the Wazir he said, "Take him and
make him look out at the window and after let him tell us where
be his pavilion." And when the royal order was obeyed Alaeddin saw the place level as a well-trodden road, even as it had been
ere the base of the building was laid, nor was there the faintest
trace of edifice. Hereat he was astonished and perplexed knowing not what had occurred; but, when he returned to the presence, the King asked him, "What is it thou hast seen? Where is
thy pavilion and where is my daughter, the core of my heart, my
only child, than whom I have none other?" Alaeddin answered,
"O King of the Age, I wot naught thereof nor aught of what
hath befallen," and the Sultan rejoined, "Thou must know, O
Alaeddin, I have pardoned thee only that thou go forth and look
into this affair and enquire for me concerning my daughter; nor
do thou ever show thyself in my presence except she be with
thee; and, if thou bring her not, by the life of my head, I will cut
off the head of thee." The other replied, "To hear is to obey:
only vouchsafe me a delay and respite of some forty days; after
which, an I produce her not, strike off my head[1] and do with me
whatso thou wishest." —— And Shahrazad was surprised by
the dawn of day and ceased to say her permitted say.

When it was the Five Hundred and Seventy-ninth Night,

Quoth Dunyazad, "O sister mine, an thou be other than sleepy,
do tell us some of thy pleasant tales," whereupon Shahrazad
replied, "With love and good will." —— It hath reached me, O
King of the Age, that the Sultan said to Alaeddin, "Verily I have
granted thee thy request, a delay of forty days; but think not
thou canst fly from my hand, for I would bring thee back even
if thou wert above the clouds instead of being only upon earth's
surface." Replied Alaeddin, "O my lord the Sultan, as I said
to thy Highness, an I fail to bring her within the term appointed,
I will present myself for my head to be stricken off." Now when

---

1 In the H. V. Alaeddin promises, "if I fail to find and fetch the Princess, I will myself
cut off my head and cast it before the throne." Hindus are adepts in suicide and this self-
decapitation, which sounds absurd further West, is quite possible to them.

the folk and the lieges all saw Alaeddin at liberty, they rejoiced
with joy exceeding and were delighted for his release; but the
shame of his treatment and bashfulness before his friends and the
envious exultation of his foes had bowed down Alaeddin's head;
so he went forth a-wandering through the city ways and he was
perplexed concerning his case and knew not what had befallen
him. He lingered about the capital for two days, in saddest
state, wotting not what to do in order to find his wife and his
pavilion, and during this time sundry of the folk privily brought
him meat and drink. When the two days were done he left the
city to stray about the waste and open lands outlying the walls,
without a notion as to whither he should wend; and he walked
on aimlessly until the path led him beside a river where, of the
stress of sorrow that overwhelmed him, he abandoned himself
to despair and thought of casting himself into the water. Being,
however, a good Moslem who professed the unity of the God-
head, he feared Allah in his soul; and, standing upon the margin
he prepared to perform the Wuzú-ablution. But as he was baling
up the water in his right hand and rubbing his fingers,[1] it so
chanced that he also rubbed the Ring. Hereat its Marid appeared and said to him, "Adsum! thy thrall between thy hands
is come: ask of me whatso thou wantest." Seeing the Marid,
Alaeddin rejoiced with exceeding joy and cried,[2] "O Slave, I
desire of thee that thou bring before me my pavilion and therein
my wife, the Lady Badr al-Budur, together with all and everything it containeth." "O my lord," replied the Marid, " 'tis
right hard upon me that thou demandest a service whereto I may
not avail: this matter dependeth upon the Slave of the Lamp nor
dare I even attempt it." Alaeddin rejoined, "Forasmuch as the
matter is beyond thy competence, I require it not of thee, but at
least do thou take me up and set me down beside my pavilion
in what land soever that may be." The Slave exclaimed, "Hearing and obeying, O my lord;" and, uplifting him high in air, within the space of an eye-glance set him down beside his pavilion in

---

[1] In Galland Alaeddin unconsciously rubbed the ring against *un petit roc*, to which he
clung in order to prevent falling into the stream. In the H. V. "The bank was high and
difficult of descent and the youth would have rolled down headlong had he not struck upon
a rock two paces from the bottom and remained hanging over the water. This mishap was
of the happiest for during his fall he struck the stone and rubbed his ring against it," etc.
[2] In the H. V. he said, "First save me that I fall not into the stream and then tell me
where is the pavilion thou builtest for her and who hath removed it."

the land of Africa and upon a spot facing his wife's apartment. Now this was at fall of night yet one look enabled him to recognise his home; whereby his cark and care were cleared away and he recovered trust in Allah after cutting off all his hope to look upon his wife once more. Then he fell to pondering the secret and mysterious favours of the Lord (glorified be His omnipotence!); and how, after despair had mastered him, the Ring had come to gladden him and how, when all his hopes were cut off, Allah had deigned bless him with the services of its Slave. So he rejoiced and his melancholy left him; then, as he had passed four days without sleep for the excess of his cark and care and sorrow and stress of thought, he drew near his pavilion and slept under a tree hard by the building which (as we mentioned) had been set down amongst the gardens outlying the city of Africa. —— And Shahrazad was surprised by the dawn of day and ceased to say her permitted say.

𝖂𝖍𝖊𝖓 𝖎𝖙 𝖜𝖆𝖘 𝖙𝖍𝖊 𝕱𝖎𝖛𝖊 𝕳𝖚𝖓𝖉𝖗𝖊𝖉 𝖆𝖓𝖉 𝕰𝖎𝖌𝖍𝖙𝖎𝖊𝖙𝖍 𝕹𝖎𝖌𝖍𝖙.

QUOTH Dunyazad, "O sister mine, an thou be other than sleepy, do tell us some of thy pleasant tales," whereupon Shahrazad replied, "With love and good will." —— It hath reached me, O King of the Age, that Alaeddin lay that night under a tree beside his pavilion in all restfulness; but whoso weareth head hard by the headsman may not sleep o' nights save whenas slumber prevail over him. He slumbered till Morning showed her face and, when awakened by the warbling of the small birds, he arose and went down to the bank of the river which flowed thereby into the city; and here he again washed hands and face[1] and after finished his Wuzú-ablution. Then he prayed the dawn-prayer, and when he had ended his orisons he returned and sat down under the windows of the Princess's bower. Now the Lady Badr al-Budur, of her exceeding sorrow for severance from her husband and her sire the Sultan, and for the great mishap which had happened to her from the Maghrabi, the Magician, the Accursed, was wont to rise during the murk preceding dawn and to sit in tears inasmuch as she could not sleep o' nights, and had

---

[1] Alluding to the preparatory washing, a mere matter of cleanliness which precedes the formal Wuzú-ablution.

forsworn meat and drink. Her favourite slave-girl would enter her chamber at the hour of prayer-salutation in order to dress her; and this time, by decree of Destiny, when she threw open the window to let her lady comfort and console herself by looking upon the trees and rills, and she herself peered out of the lattice, she caught sight of her master sitting below, and informed the Princess of this, saying, "O my lady! O my lady! here's my lord Alaeddin seated at the foot of the wall." So her mistress arose hurriedly and gazing from the casement saw him; and her husband raising his head saw her; so she saluted him and he saluted her, both being like to fly for joy. Presently quoth she, "Up and come in to me by the private postern, for now the Accursed is not here;" and she gave orders to the slave-girl who went down and opened for him. Then Alaeddin passed through it and was met by his wife, when they embraced and exchanged kisses with all delight until they wept for overjoy. After this they sat down and Alaeddin said to her, "O my lady, before all things 'tis my desire to ask thee a question. 'Twas my wont to place an old copper lamp in such a part of my pavilion, what became of that same?" When the Princess heard these words she sighed and cried, "O my dearling, 'twas that very Lamp which garred us fall into this calamity!" Alaeddin asked her, "How befel the affair?" and she answered by recounting to him all that passed, first and last, especially how they had given in exchange an old lamp for a new lamp, adding, "And next day we hardly saw one another at dawn before we found ourselves in this land, and he who deceived us and took the lamp by way of barter informed me that he had done the deed by might of his magic and by means of the Lamp; that he is a Moorman from Africa, and that we are now in his native country."——And Shahrazad was surprised by the dawn of day and ceased to say her permitted say.

When it was the Five Hundred and Eighty-first Night,

QUOTH Dunyazad, "O sister mine, an thou be other than sleepy, do tell us some of thy pleasant tales," whereupon Shahrazad replied, "With love and good will." —— It hath reached me, O King of the Age, that when the Lady Badr al-Budur ceased speaking, Alaeddin resumed, "Tell me the intent of this Accursed in thy respect, also what he sayeth to thee and what be his will of thee?" She replied, "Every day he cometh to visit me once and no more: he would woo me to his love and he sueth that I take him to spouse in lieu of thee and that I forget thee and be con-soled for the loss of thee. And he telleth me that the Sultan my sire hath cut off my husband's head, adding that thou, the son of pauper parents, wast by him enriched. And he sootheth me with talk, but he never seeth aught from me save weeping and wailing; nor hath he heard from me one sugar-sweet word."[1] Quoth Alaeddin, "Tell me where he hath placed the Lamp an thou know anything thereof:" and quoth she, "He beareth it about on his body alway, nor is it possible that he leave it for a single hour; moreover once when he related what I have now recounted to thee, he brought it out of his breast-pocket and allowed me to look upon it." When Alaeddin heard these words, he joyed with exceeding joy and said, "O my lady, do thou lend ear to me. 'Tis my design to go from thee forthright and to return only after doffing this my dress; so wonder not when thou see me changed, but direct one of thy women to stand by the private postern alway and, whenever she espy me coming, at once to open. And now I will devise a device whereby to slay this damned loon." Herewith he arose and, issuing from the pavilion-door, walked till he met on the way a Fellah to whom he said, "O man, take my attire and give me thy garments." But the peasant refused, so Alaeddin stripped him of his dress perforce[2] and donned it, leaving to the man his own rich gear by way of gift. Then he followed the highway leading to the neigh-bouring city and entering it went to the Perfumers' Bazar where he bought of one some rarely potent Bhang, the son of a minute,[3] paying two dinars for two drachms thereof and he returned in disguise by the same road till he reached the pavilion. Here the slave-girl opened to him the private postern wherethrough he went in to the Lady Badr al-Budur. —— And Shahrazad was surprised by the dawn of day and ceased to say her permitted say.

---

[1] In the H. V. the Princess ends with, "I had made this resolve that should he approach me with the design to win his wish perforce, I would destroy my life. By day and by night I abode in fear of him; but now at the sight of thee my heart is heartened."

[2] The Fellah had a natural fear of being seen in fine gear, which all would have supposed to be stolen goods; and Alaeddin was justified in taking it perforce, because *necessitas non habet legem*. See a similar exchange of dress in Spitta-Bey's "Contes Arabes Modernes," p. 91. In Galland the peasant when pressed consents; and in the H. V. Alaeddin persuades him by a gift of money.

[3] *i.e.* which would take effect in the shortest time.

When it was the Five Hundred and Eighty-second Night,

QUOTH Dunyazad, "O sister mine, an thou be other than sleepy, do tell us some of thy pleasant tales," whereupon Shahrazad replied, "With love and good will." —— It hath reached me, O King of the Age, that when Alaeddin went in disguised to his wife he said, "Hear me! I desire of thee that thou dress and dight thyself in thy best and thou cast off all outer show and semblance of care; also when the Accursed, the Maghrabi, shall visit thee, do thou receive him with a 'Welcome and fair welcome,' and meet him with smiling face and invite him to come and sup with thee. Moreover, let him note that thou hast forgotten Alaeddin thy beloved, likewise thy father; and that thou hast learned to love him with exceeding love, displaying to him all manner joy and pleasure. Then ask him for wine which must be red and pledge him to his secret in a significant draught; and, when thou hast given him two to three cups full and hast made him wax careless, then drop these drops into his cup and fill it up with wine: no sooner shall he drink of it than he will fall upon his back senseless as one dead." Hearing these words, the Princess exclaimed," 'Tis exceedingly sore to me that I do such deed;[1] withal must I do it that we escape the defilement of this Accursed who tortured me by severance from thee and from my sire. Lawful and right therefore is the slaughter of this Accursed." Then Alaeddin ate and drank with his wife what hindered his hunger; then, rising without stay or delay, fared forth the pavilion. So the Lady Badr al-Budur summoned the tirewoman who robed and arrayed her in her finest raiment and adorned her and perfumed her; and, as she was thus, behold, the accursed Maghrabi entered. He joyed much seeing her in such case and yet more when she confronted him, contrary to her custom, with a laughing face; and his love-longing increased and his desire to have her. Then she took him and, seating him beside her, said, "O my dearling, do thou (an thou be willing) come to me this night and let us sup together. Sufficient to me hath been my sorrow for, were I to sit mourning through a thousand years or even two thousand, Alaeddin would not return to me from the tomb; and

---

[1] Her modesty was startled by the idea of sitting at meat with a strange man and allowing him to make love to her.

I depend upon thy say of yesterday, to wit, that my sire the Sultan slew him in his stress of sorrow for severance from me. Nor wonder thou an I have changed this day from what I was yester·· day; and the reason thereof is I have determined upon taking thee to friend and playfellow in lieu of and succession to Alaed- din, for that now I have none other man but thyself. So I hope for thy presence this night, that we may sup together and we may carouse and drink somewhat of wine each with other; and especially 'tis my desire that thou cause me taste the wine of thy natal soil, the African land, because belike 'tis better than aught of the wine of China we drink: I have with me some wine but 'tis the growth of my country and I vehemently wish to taste the wine produced by thine."——And Shahrazad was sur- prised by the dawn of day and ceased to say her permitted say.

When it was the Five Hundred Eighty-third Night,

QUOTH Dunyazad, "O sister mine, an thou be other than sleepy, do tell us some of thy pleasant tales," whereupon Shahrazad replied, "With love and good will."——It hath reached me, O King of the Age, that when the Maghrabi saw the love lavisht upon him by the Lady Badr al-Budur, and noted her change from the sorrowful, melancholy woman she was wont to be, he thought that she had cut off her hope of Alaeddin and he joyed exceedingly and said to her, "I hear and obey, O my lady, whatso thou wishest and all thou biddest. I have at home a jar of our country wine, which I have carefully kept and stored deep in earth for a space of eight years; and I will now fare and fill from it our need and will return to thee in all haste." But the Prin- cess, that she might wheedle him the more and yet more, replied, "O my darling, go not thou, leaving me alone, but send one of the eunuchs to fill for us thereof and do thou remain sitting beside me, that I may find in thee my consolation." He rejoined, "O my lady, none wotteth where the jar be buried save myself nor will I tarry from thee." So saying, the Moorman went out and after a short time he brought back as much wine as they wanted; whereupon quoth the Princess to him, "Thou hast been at pains and trouble to serve me and I have suffered for thy sake, O my beloved." Quoth he, "On no wise, O eyes of me; I hold myself enhonoured by thy service." Then the Lady Badr al-Budur sat with him at table, and the twain fell to eating and presently

the Princess expressed a wish to drink, when the handmaid filled
her a cup forthright and then crowned another for the Maroccan.
So she drank to his long life and his secret wishes and he also
drank to her life; then the Princess, who was unique in eloquence
and delicacy of speech, fell to making a cup-companion of him and
beguiled him by addressing him in the sweetest terms full of
hidden meaning. This was done only that he might become
more madly enamoured of her, but the Maghrabi thought that it
resulted from her true inclination for him; nor knew that it was
a snare set up to slay him. So his longing for her increased, and
he was dying of love for her when he saw her address him in such
tenderness of words and thoughts, and his head began to swim
and all the world seemed as nothing in his eyes. But when they
came to the last of the supper and the wine had mastered his
brains and the Princess saw this in him, she said, "With us there
be a custom throughout our country, but I know not an it be the
usage of yours or not." The Moorman replied, "And what may
that be?" So she said to him, "At the end of supper each lover
in turn taketh the cup of the beloved and drinketh it off;" and at
once she crowned one with wine and bade the handmaid carry
to him her cup wherein the drink was blended with the Bhang.
Now she had taught the slave-girl what to do and all the handmaids and eunuchs in the pavilion longed for the Sorcerer's
slaughter and in that matter were one with the Princess. Accordingly the damsel handed him the cup and he, when he heard
her words and saw her drinking from his cup and passing hers to
him noted all that show of love, fancied himself Iskander, Lord
of the Two Horns. Then said she to him, the while swaying
gracefully to either side and putting her hand within his hand,
"O my life, here is thy cup with me and my cup with thee, and
on this wise[1] do lovers drink from each other's cups." Then she
bussed the brim and drained it to the dregs and again she kissed
its lip and offered it to him. Thereat he flew for joy and meaning
to do the like, raised her cup to his mouth and drank off the whole
contents, without considering whether there was therein aught
harmful or not. And forthright he rolled upon his back in deathlike condition and the cup dropped from his grasp, whereupon

---

[1] In the text Kidí, pop. for Ka-zálika. In the H. V. the Magician replies to the honeyed
speech of the Princess, "O my lady, we in Africa have not so gracious customs as the men
of China. This day I have learned of thee a new courtesy which I shall ever keep in mind."

the Lady Badr al-Budur and the slave-girls ran hurriedly and opened the pavilion door to their lord Alaeddin who, disguised as a Fellah, entered therein.——And Shahrazad was surprised by the dawn of day and ceased to say her permitted say.

When it was the Five Hundred and Eighty-fourth Night,

Quoth Dunyazad, "O sister mine, an thou be other than sleepy, do tell us some of thy pleasant tales," whereupon Shahrazad replied, "With love and good will."——It hath reached me, O King of the Age, that Alaeddin entering his pavilion, went up to the apartment of his wife, whom he found still sitting at table; and facing her lay the Maghrabi as one slaughtered; so he at once drew near to her and kissed her and thanked her for this. Then rejoicing with joy exceeding he turned to her and said, "Do thou with thy handmaids betake thyself to the inner-rooms and leave me alone for the present that I may take counsel touching mine affair." The Princess hesitated not but went away at once, she and her women; then Alaeddin arose and, after locking the door upon them, walked up to the Moorman and put forth his hand to his breast-pocket and thence drew the Lamp; after which he unsheathed his sword and slew the villain.[1] Presently he rubbed the Lamp and the Marid-slave appeared and said, "Adsum, O my lord, what is it thou wantest?" "I desire of thee," said Alaeddin, "that thou take up my pavilion from this country and transport it to the land of China and there set it down upon the site where it was whilome, fronting the palace of the Sultan." The Marid replied, "Hearing and obeying, O my lord." The Alaeddin went and sat down with his wife and throwing his arms round her neck kissed her and she kissed him, and they sat in converse, what while the Jinni transported the pavilion and all therein to the place appointed. Presently Alaeddin bade the handmaids spread the table before him and he and the Lady Badr al-Budur took seat thereat and fell to eating and drinking, in all joy and gladness, till they had their sufficiency when, removing to the chamber of wine and cup-converse, they sat there and caroused in fair companionship and each kissed

---

[1] Galland makes the Princess poison the Maghrabi, which is not gallant. The H. V. follows suit and describes the powder as a mortal poison.

other with all love-liesse. The time had been long and longsome
since they enjoyed aught of pleasure; so they ceased not doing
thus until the wine-sun arose in their heads and sleep gat hold of
them, at which time they went to their bed in all ease and comfort.[1] Early on the next morning Alaeddin woke and awoke his
wife, and the slave-girls came in and donned her dress and prepared her and adorned her whilst her husband arrayed himself
in his costliest raiment and the twain were ready to fly for joy at
reunion after parting. Moreover the Princess was especially
joyous and gladsome because on that day she expected to see her
beloved father. Such was the case of Alaeddin and the Lady
Badr al-Budur; but as regards the Sultan, after he drove away
his son-in-law he never ceased to sorrow for the loss of his
daughter; and every hour of every day he would sit and weep
for her as women weep, because she was his only child and he
had none other to take to heart. And as he shook off sleep,
morning after morning, he would hasten to the window and
throw it open and peer in the direction where formerly stood
Alaeddin's pavilion and pour forth tears until his eyes were dried
up and their lids were ulcered. Now on that day he arose at dawn
and, according to his custom, looked out when, lo and behold!
he saw before him an edifice; so he rubbed his eyes and considered
it curiously when he became certified that it was the pavilion of
his son-in-law. So he called for a horse[2] without let or delay; and
as soon as his beast was saddled, he mounted and made for the
place; and Alaeddin, when he saw his father-in-law approaching,
went down and met him half way: then, taking his hand, aided
him to step upstairs to the apartment of his daughter. And the
Princess, being as earnestly desirous to see her sire, descended
and greeted him at the door of the staircase fronting the ground-
floor hall. Thereupon the King folded her in his arms and kissed
her, shedding tears of joy; and she did likewise till at last Alaeddin led them to the upper saloon where they took seats and the
Sultan fell to asking her case and what had betided her.——And
Shahrazad was surprised by the dawn of day and ceased to say
her permitted say.

---

[1] Contrast this modesty with the usual scene of reunion after severance, as in the case of
Kamar al-Zamán and immodest Queen Budúr, vol. iii. pp. 302-304.

[2] His dignity forbade him to walk even the length of a carpet: see vol. vii. for this habit
of the Mameluke Beys. When Harun al-Rashid made his famous pilgrimage afoot from

When it was the Five Hundred and Eighty-fifth Night,

QUOTH Dunyazad, "O sister mine, an thou be other than sleepy, do tell us some of thy pleasant tales," whereupon Shahrazad replied, "With love and good will."——It hath reached me, O King of the Age, that the Lady Badr al-Budur began to inform the Sultan of all which had befallen her, saying, "O my father, I recovered not life save yesterday when I saw my husband, and he it was who freed me from the thraldom of that Maghrabi, that Magician, that Accursed, than whom I believe there be none viler on the face of earth; and, but for my beloved, I had never escaped him nor hadst thou seen me during the rest of my days. But mighty sadness and sorrow gat about me, O my father, not only for losing thee but also for the loss of a husband, under whose kindness I shall be all the length of my life, seeing that he freed me from that fulsome sorcerer." Then the Princess began repeating to her sire every thing that happened to her, and relating to him how the Moorman had tricked her in the guise of a lamp-seller who offered in exchange new for old; how she had given him the Lamp whose worth she knew not, and how she had bartered it away only to laugh at the lampman's folly. "And next morning, O my father," she continued, "we found ourselves and whatso the pavilion contained in Africa-land, till such time as my husband came to us and devised a device whereby we escaped: and, had it not been for Alaeddin's hastening to our aid, the Accursed was determined to enjoy me perforce." Then she told him of the Bhang-drops administered in wine to the African and concluded, "Then my husband returned to me and how I know not, but we were shifted from Africa-land to this place." Alaeddin in his turn recounted how, finding the wizard dead drunken, he had sent away his wife and her women from the polluted place into the inner apartments; how he had taken the Lamp from the Sorcerer's breast-pocket whereto he was directed by his wife; how he had slaughtered the villain and, finally how, making use of the Lamp, he had summoned its Slave and ordered him to transport the pavilion back to its proper site, ending his tale with, "And, if thy Highness have any doubt

---

Baghdad to Meccah (and he was the last of the Caliphs who performed this rite), the whole way was spread with a "Pá-andáz" of carpets and costly cloths.

anent my words, arise with me and look upon the accursed Magician." The King did accordingly and, having considered the Moorman, bade the carcase be carried away forthright and burned and its ashes scattered in air. Then he took to embracing Alaeddin and kissing him said, "Pardon me, O my son, for that I was about to destroy thy life through the foul deeds of this damned enchanter, who cast thee into such pit of peril; and I may be excused, O my child, for what I did by thee, because I found myself forlorn of my daughter; my only one, who to me is dearer than my very kingdom. Thou knowest how the hearts of parents yearn unto their offspring, especially when like myself they have but one and none other to love." And on this wise the Sultan took to excusing himself and kissing his son-in-law. ——And Shahrazad was surprised by the dawn of day and ceased to say her permitted say.

When it was the Five Hundred and Eighty-sixth Night,

QUOTH Dunyazad, "O sister mine, an thou be other than sleepy, do tell us some of thy pleasant tales," whereupon Shahrazad replied, "With love and good will."——It hath reached me, O King of the Age, that Alaeddin said to the Sultan, "O King of the Time, thou didst naught to me contrary to Holy Law, and I also sinned not against thee; but all the trouble came from that Maghrabi, the impure, the Magician." Thereupon the Sultan bade the city be decorated and they obeyed him and held high feast and festivities. He also commanded the crier to cry about the streets saying, "This day is a mighty great fête, wherein public rejoicings must be held throughout the realm, for a full month of thirty days, in honour of the Lady Badr al-Budur and her husband Alaeddin's return to their home." On this wise befel it with Alaeddin and the Maghrabi; but withal the King's son-in-law escaped not wholly from the Accursed, albeit the body had been burnt and the ashes scattered in air. For the villain had a brother yet more villainous than himself, and a greater adept in necromancy, geomancy and astromancy; and, even as the old saw saith "A bean and 'twas split;"[1] so each one dwelt in his own quarter of the globe that he might fill it with

---

[1] The proverb suggests our "par nobile fratrum," a pair resembling each other as two halves of a split bean.

his sorcery, his fraud and his treason.[1] Now, one day of the days it fortuned that the Moorman's brother would learn how it fared with him, so he brought out his sandboard and dotted it and produced the figures which, when he had considered and carefully studied them, gave him to know that the man he sought was dead and housed in the tomb. So he grieved and was certified of his decease, but he dotted a second time seeking to learn the manner of the death and where it had taken place; so he found that the site was the China-land and that the mode was the foulest of slaughter; furthermore, that he who did him die was a young man Alaeddin hight. Seeing this he straightway arose and equipped himself for wayfare; then he set out and cut across the wilds and wolds and heights for the space of many a month until he reached China and the capital of the Sultan wherein was the slayer of his brother. He alighted at the so-called Strangers' Khan and, hiring himself a cell, took rest therein for a while; then he fared forth and wandered about the highways that he might discern some path which would aid him unto the winning of his ill-minded wish, to wit, of wreaking upon Alaeddin blood-revenge for his brother.[2] Presently he entered a coffee-house, a fine building which stood in the market-place and which collected a throng of folk to play, some at the mankalah,[3] others at the backgammon[4] and others at the chess and what not else. There he sat down and listened to those seated beside him and they chanced to be conversing about an ancient dame and a holy, by name Fátimah,[5] who dwelt alway at her devotions in a hermitage

---

[1] In the H. V. "If the elder Magician was in the East, the other was in the West; but once a year, by their skill in geomancy, they had tidings of each other."

[2] The act was religiously laudable, but to the Eastern, as to the South European mind, fair play is *not* a jewel; moreover the story-teller may insinuate that vengeance would be taken only by foul and unlawful means—the Black Art, perjury, murder and so forth.

[3] For this game, a prime favourite in Egypt, see vol. vi. 145, De Sacy (Chrestomathie i. 477) and his authorities Hyde, Syntagma Dissert. ii. 374; P. Labat, "Mémoires du Chev. d'Arvieux," iii. 321; Thevenot, "Voyage du Levant," p. 107; and Niebuhr, "Voyages," i. 139, Plate 25, fig. H.

[4] Evidently="(jeu de) dames" (supposed to have been invented in Paris during the days of the Regency: see Littré); and, although in certain Eastern places now popular, a term of European origin. It is not in Galland. According to Ibn Khallikan (iii. 69) "Nard" = tables, arose with King Ardashír son of Babuk, and was therefore called Nardashír (Nard Ardashír?). He designed it as an image of the world and its people, so the board had twelve squares to represent the months; the thirty pieces or men represented the days, and the dice were the emblems of Fate and Lot.

[5] *i.e.* a weaner, a name of good omen for a girl-child: see vol. vi. 145. The Hindi translator, Totárám Shayyán, calls her Hamídah = the Praiseworthy.

without the town, and this she never entered save only two days each month. They mentioned also that she had performed many saintly miracles[1] which, when the Maghrabi, the Necromancer, heard he said in himself, "Now have I found that which I sought: Inshallah—God willing—by means of this crone will I win to my wish."——And Shahrazad was surprised by the dawn of day and ceased to say her permitted say.

When it was the Five Hundred and Eighty-seventh Night,

QUOTH Dunyazad, "O sister mine, an thou be other than sleepy, do tell us some of thy pleasant tales," whereupon Shahrazad replied, "With love and good will."——It hath reached me, O King of the Age, that the Maghrabi, the Necromancer, went up to the folk who were talking of the miracles performed by the devout old woman and said to one of them, "O my uncle, I heard you all chatting about the prodigies of a certain saintess named Fatimah: who is she and where may be her abode?" "Marvellous!"[2] exclaimed the man: "How canst thou be in our city and yet never have heard about the miracles of the Lady Fatimah? Evidently, O thou poor fellow, thou art a foreigner, since the fastings of this devotee and her asceticism in worldly matters and the beauties of her piety never came to thine ears." The Moorman rejoined, " 'Tis true, O my lord: yes, I am a stranger and came to this your city only yesternight; and I hope thou wilt inform me concerning the saintly miracles of this virtuous woman and where may be her wone, for that I have fallen into a calamity, and 'tis my wish to visit her and crave her prayers, so haply Allah (to whom be honour and glory!) will, through her blessings, deliver me from mine evil." Hereat the man recounted to him the marvels of Fatimah the Devotee and her piety and the beauties of her worship; then, taking him by

---

[1] Arab. Kirámát: see vols. ii. 237; iv. 45. The Necromancer clearly smells a rat holding with Diderot:

> De par le Roi! Defense à Dieu
> De faire miracle en ce lieu;

and the stage properties afterwards found with the holy woman, such as the gallipot of colouring ointment, justify his suspicion.

[2] " 'Ajáib" plur. of " 'Ajíb," a common exclamation amongst the populace. It is used in Persian as well as in Arabic.

the hand went with him without the city and showed him the way to her abode, a cavern upon a hillock's head. The Necromancer acknowledged his kindness in many words and, thanking him for his good offices, returned to his cell in the caravanserai. Now by the fiat of Fate on the very next day Fatimah came down to the city, and the Maghrabi, the Necromancer, happened to leave his hostelry a-morn, when he saw the folk swarming and crowding; wherefore he went up to discover what was to do and found the Devotee standing amiddlemost the throng, and all who suffered from pain or sickness flocked to her soliciting a blessing and praying for her prayers; and each and every she touched became whole of his illness.[1] The Maroccan, the Necromancer, followed her about until she returned to her antre; then, awaiting till the evening evened, he arose and repaired to a vintner's store where he drank a cup of wine. After this he fared forth the city and finding the Devotee's cavern, entered it and saw her lying prostrate[2] with her back upon a strip of matting. So he came forward and mounted upon her belly; then he drew his dagger and shouted at her; and, when she awoke and opened her eyes, she espied a Moorish man with an unsheathed poniard sitting upon her middle as though about to kill her. She was troubled and sore terrified, but he said to her, "Hearken! an thou cry out or utter a word I will slay thee at this very moment: arise now and do all I bid thee." Then he sware to her an oath that if she obeyed his orders, whatever they might be, he would not do her die. So saying, he rose up from off her and Fatimah also arose, when he said to her, "Give me thy gear and take thou my habit;" whereupon she gave him her clothing and head-fillets, her face-kerchief and her mantilla. Then quoth he, " 'Tis also requisite that thou anoint me with somewhat shall make the colour of my face like unto thine." Accordingly she went into the inner cavern and, bringing out a gallipot of ointment, spread somewhat thereof upon her palm and with it besmeared his face until its hue

---

[1] Evidently *la force de l'imagination*, of which a curious illustration was given in Paris during the debauched days of the Second Empire. Before a highly "fashionable" assembly of men appeared a youth in fleshings who sat down upon a stool, bared his pudenda and closed his eyes when, by "force of fancy," erection and emission took place. But presently it was suspected and proved that the stool was hollow and admitted from below a hand whose titillating fingers explained the phenomenon.

[2] Moslems are curious about sleeping postures and the popular saying is:—Lying upon the right side is proper to Kings; upon the left to Sages; to sleep supine is the position of Allah's Saints and prone upon the belly is peculiar to the Devils.

favoured her own; then she gave him her staff[1] and, showing him how to walk and what to do when he entered the city, hung her rosary around his neck. Lastly she handed to him a mirror and said, "Now look! Thou differest from me in naught;" and he saw himself Fatimah's counterpart as though she had never gone or come.[2] But after obtaining his every object he falsed his oath and asked for a cord which she brought to him; then he seized her and strangled her in the cavern; and presently, when she was dead, haled the corpse outside and threw it into a pit hard by. —And Shahrazad was surprised by the dawn of day and ceased to say her permitted say.

When it was the Five Hundred and Eighty-eighth Night,

Quoth Dunyazad, "O sister mine, an thou be other than sleepy, do tell us some of thy pleasant tales," whereupon Shahrazad replied, "With love and good will."——It hath reached me, O King of the Age, that the Maghrabi, after murthering Fatimah, threw her body into a pit and went back to sleep in her cavern; and, when broke the day, he rose and repairing to the town took his stand under the walls of Alaeddin's pavilion. Hereupon flocked the folk about him, all being certified that he was Fatimah the Devotee and he fell to doing whatso she was wont to do: he laid hands on these in pain and recited for those a chapter of the Koran and made orisons for a third. Presently the thronging of the folk and the clamouring of the crowd were heard by the Lady Badr al-Budur, who said to her handmaidens, "Look what is to do and what be the cause of this turmoil!" Thereupon the Agha of the eunuchry fared forth to see what might be the matter and presently returning said, "O my lady, this clamour is caused by the Lady Fatimah, and if thou be pleased to command, I will bring her to thee; so shalt thou gain through her a blessing." The Princess answered, "Go bring her, for since many a day I am always hearing of her miracles and her virtues, and I do long to see her and get a blessing by her intervention, for the folk recount

---

[1] This " 'Asá," a staff five to six feet long, is one of the properties of Moslem Saints and reverends who, imitating that furious old Puritan, Caliph Omar, make and are allowed to make a pretty liberal distribution of its caresses.

[2] *i.e.* as she was in her own home.

her manifestations in many cases of difficulty." The Agha went
forth and brought in the Maroccan, the Necromancer, habited in
Fatimah's clothing; and, when the wizard stood before the Lady
Badr al-Budur, he began at first sight to bless her with a string of
prayers; nor did any one of those present doubt at all but that he
was the Devotee herself. The Princess arose and salam'd to him;
then seating him beside her, said, "O my Lady Fatimah, 'tis my
desire that thou abide with me alway, so might I be blessed
through thee, and also learn of thee the paths[1] of worship and
piety and follow thine example making for salvation." Now all
this was a foul deceit of the accursed African and he designed
furthermore to complete his guile, so he continued, "O my Lady,
I am a poor woman and a religious that dwelleth in the desert;
and the like of me deserveth not to abide in the palaces of the
kings." But the Princess replied, "Have no care whatever, O my
Lady Fatimah; I will set apart for thee an apartment of my pavilion, that thou mayest worship therein and none shall ever come
to trouble thee; also thou shalt avail to worship Allah in my
place better than in thy cavern." The Maroccan rejoined, "Hearkening and obedience, O my lady; I will not oppose thine order
for that the commands of the children of the kings may not be
gainsaid nor renounced. Only I hope of thee that my eating and
drinking and sitting may be within my own chamber which shall
be kept wholly private; nor do I require or desire the delicacies
of diet, but do thou favour me by sending thy handmaid every
day with a bit of bread and a sup of water;[2] and, when I feel fain
of food, let me eat by myself in my own room." Now the Accursed hereby purposed to avert the danger of haply raising his
face-kerchief at meal times, when his intent might be baffled by
his beard and mustachios discovering him to be a man. The
Princess replied, "O my Lady Fatimah, be of good heart; naught
shall happen save what thou wishest. But now arise and let me
show thee the apartment in the palace which I would prepare for
thy sojourn with us."——And Shahrazad was surprised by the
dawn of day and ceased to say her permitted say.

---

[1] Arab. "Sulúk" a Sufistical expression, the road to salvation, &c.
[2] In the H. V. her diet consisted of dry bread and fruits.

When it was the Five Hundred and Eighty-ninth Night,

QUOTH Dunyazad, "O sister mine, an thou be other than sleepy, do tell us some of thy pleasant tales," whereupon Shahrazad replied, "With love and good will."——It hath reached me, O King of the Age, that the Lady Badr al-Budur arose and taking the Necromancer who had disguised himself as the Devotee, ushered him in to the place which she had kindly promised him for a home and said, "O my Lady Fatimah, here thou shalt dwell with every comfort about thee and in all privacy and repose; and the place shall be named after thy name;" whereupon the Maghrabi acknowledged her kindness and prayed for her. Then the Princess showed him the jalousies and the jewelled Kiosque with its four and twenty windows[1] and said to him, "What thinkest thou, O my Lady Fatimah, of this marvellous pavilion?" The Moorman replied, "By Allah, O my daughter, 'tis indeed passing fine and wondrous exceedingly; nor do I deem that its fellow is to be found in the whole universe; but alas for the lack of one thing which would enhance its beauty and decoration!" The Princess asked her, "O my Lady Fatimah, what lacketh it and what be this thing would add to its adornment? Tell me thereof, inasmuch as I was wont to believe it wholly perfect." The Maroccan answered, "O my lady, all it wanteth is that there be hanging from the middle of the dome the egg of a fowl called the Rukh;[2] and, were this done, the pavilion would lack its peer all the world over." The Princess asked, "What be this bird and where can we find her egg?" and the Maroccan answered, "O my lady, the Rukh is indeed a giant fowl which carrieth off camels and elephants in her pounces and flieth away with them, such is her stature and strength; also this fowl is mostly found in Mount Káf; and the architect who built this pavilion is able to bring thee one of her eggs." They then left such talk as it was the hour for the noon-day meal and, when the handmaid had spread the table, the Lady Badr al-Budur sent down to invite the Accursed African to eat with her. But he accepted not and for a reason he

---

1 This is the first mention of the windows in the Arabic MS.
2 For this "Roc" of the older writers see vols. v. 122; vi. 16-49. I may remind the reader that the O. Egyptian "Rokh," or "Rukh," by some written "Rekhit," whose ideograph is a monstrous bird with one claw raised, also denotes pure wise Spirits, the Magi, &c. I know a man who derives from it our "rook" = beak and parson.

would on no wise consent; nay, he rose and retired to the room which the Princess had assigned to him and whither the slave-girls carried his dinner. Now when evening evened, Alaeddin returned from the chase and met his wife who salam'd to him and he clasped her to his bosom and kissed her. Presently, look-ing at her face he saw thereon a shade of sadness and he noted that contrary to her custom, she did not laugh; so he asked her, "What hath betided thee, O my dearling? tell me, hath aught happened to trouble thy thoughts?" "Nothing whatever," answered she, "but, O my beloved, I fancied that our pavilion lacked naught at all; however, O eyes of me, O Alaeddin, were the dome of the upper story hung with an egg of the fowl called Rukh, there would be naught like it in the universe." Her husband rejoined, "And for this trifle thou art saddened when 'tis the easiest of all matters to me! So cheer thyself; and, what-ever thou wantest, 'tis enough thou inform me thereof, and I will bring it from the abysses of the earth in the quickest time and at the earliest hour."——And Shahrazad was surprised by the dawn of day and ceased to say her permitted say.

When it was the Five Hundred and Ninetieth Night,

QUOTH Dunyazad, "O sister mine, an thou be other than sleepy, do tell us some of thy pleasant tales," whereupon Shahrazad re-plied, "With love and good will."——It hath reached me, O King of the Age, that Alaeddin, after refreshing the spirits of his Princess by promising her all she could desire, repaired straight-way to his chamber and taking the Lamp[1] rubbed it, when the Marid appeared without let or delay saying, "Ask whatso thou wantest." Said the other, "I desire thee to fetch me an egg of the bird Rukh and do thou hang it to the dome-crown of this my pavilion." But when the Marid heard these words, his face waxed fierce and he shouted with a mighty loud voice and a frightful, and cried, "O denier of kindly deeds, sufficeth it not for thee that I and all the Slaves of the Lamp are ever at thy service, but thou must also require me to bring thee our Liege Lady[2] for

---

[1] In the H. V. he takes the Lamp from his bosom, where he had ever kept it since his misadventure with the African Magician.

[2] Here the mythical Rukh is mixed up with the mysterious bird Símurgh, for which see vol. x. 117.

thy pleasure, and hang her up at thy pavilion-dome for the enjoyment of thee and thy wife! Now by Allah, ye deserve, thou and she, that I reduce you to ashes this very moment and scatter you upon the air; but, inasmuch as ye twain be ignorant of this matter, unknowing its inner from its outer significance, I will pardon you for indeed ye are but innocents. The offence cometh from that accursed Necromancer, brother to the Maghrabi, the Magician, who abideth here representing himself to be Fatimah, the Devotee, after assuming her dress and belongings and murthering her in the cavern: indeed he came hither seeking to slay thee by way of blood-revenge for his brother; and 'tis he who taught thy wife to require this matter of me."[1] So saying the Marid evanished. But when Alaeddin heard these words, his wits fled his head and his joints trembled at the Marid's terrible shout; but he empowered his purpose and, rising forthright, issued from his chamber and went into his wife's. There he affected an ache of head, for that he knew how famous was Fatimah for the art and mystery of healing all such pains; and, when the Lady Badr al-Budur saw him sitting hand to head and complaining of unease, she asked him the cause and he answered, "I know of none other save that my head acheth exceedingly." Hereupon she straightway bade summon Fatimah that the Devotee might impose her hand upon his head;[2] and Alaeddin asked her, "Who may this Fatimah be?" So she informed him that it was Fatimah the Devotee to whom she had given a home in the pavilion. Meanwhile the slave-girls had fared forth and summoned the Maghrabi, and when the Accursed made act of presence, Alaeddin rose up to him and, acting like one who knew naught of his purpose, salam'd to him as though he had been the real Fatimah and, kissing the hem of his sleeve, welcomed him and entreated him with honour and said, "O my Lady Fatimah, I hope thou wilt bless me with a boon, for well I wot thy practice in the healing of pains: I have gotten a mighty ache in my head." The Moorman, the Accursed, could hardly believe that he heard such words, this being all that he desired.——And Shahrazad was surprised by the dawn of day and ceased to say her permitted say.

---

[1] The H. V. adds, "hoping thereby that thou and she and all the household should fall into perdition."

[2] Rank mesmerism, which has been practised in the East from ages immemorial. In

𝔚𝔥𝔢𝔫 𝔦𝔱 𝔴𝔞𝔰 𝔱𝔥𝔢 𝔉𝔦𝔳𝔢 𝔥𝔲𝔫𝔡𝔯𝔢𝔡 𝔞𝔫𝔡 𝔑𝔦𝔫𝔢𝔱𝔶-𝔣𝔦𝔯𝔰𝔱 𝔑𝔦𝔤𝔥𝔱,

QUOTH Dunyazad, "O sister mine, an thou be other than sleepy, do tell us some of thy pleasant tales," whereupon Shahrazad replied, "With love and good will."——It hath reached me, O King of the Age, that the Maghrabi, the Necromancer, habited as Fatimah the Devotee, came up to Alaeddin that he might place hand upon his head and heal his ache; so he imposed one hand and, putting forth the other under his gown, drew a dagger wherewith to slay him. But Alaeddin watched him and, taking patience till he had wholly unsheathed the weapon, seized him with a forceful grip; and, wrenching the dagger from his grasp plunged it deep into his heart. When the Lady Badr al-Budur saw him do on this wise, she shrieked and cried out, "What hath this virtuous and holy woman done that thou hast charged thy neck with the heavy burthen of her blood shed wrongfully? Hast thou no fear of Allah that thou killest Fatimah, this saintly woman, whose miracles are far-famed?" "No," replied Alaeddin, "I have not killed Fatimah. I have slain only Fatimah's slayer, he that is the brother of the Maghrabi, the Accursed, the Magician, who carried thee off by his black art and transported my pavilion to the Africa-land; and this damnable brother of his came to our city and wrought these wiles, murthering Fatimah and assuming her habit, only that he might avenge upon me his brother's blood; and he also 'twas who taught thee to require of me a Rukh's egg, that my death might result from such require- ment. But, an thou doubt my speech, come forwards and consider the person I have slain." Thereupon Alaeddin drew aside the Moorman's face-kerchief and the Lady Badr al-Budur saw the semblance of a man with a full beard that well nigh covered his features. She at once knew the truth and said to her husband, "O my beloved, twice have I cast thee into death-risk!" but he rejoined, "No harm in that, O my lady, by the blessing of your loving eyes: I accept with all joy all things thou bringest me." The Princess, hearing these words, hastened to fold him in her arms and kissed him saying, "O my dearling, all this is for my love to thee and I knew naught thereof; but indeed I do not deem

---

Christendom Santa Guglielma worshipped at Brunate, "works many miracles, chiefly healing aches of head." In the H. V. Alaeddin feigns that he is ill and fares to the Princess with his head tied up.

lightly of thine affection." So Alaeddin kissed her and strained
her to his breast; and the love between them waxed but greater.
At that moment the Sultan appeared and they told him all that
had happened, showing him the corpse of the Maghrabi, the
Necromancer, when the King commanded the body to be burned
and the ashes scattered on air, even as had befallen the Wizard's
brother. And Alaeddin abode with his wife, the Lady Badr
al-Budur, in all pleasure and joyance of life and thenceforward
escaped every danger; and, after a while, when the Sultan deceased, his son-in-law was seated upon the throne of the Kingdom; and he commanded and dealt justice to the lieges so that
all the folk loved him, and he lived with his wife in all solace and
happiness until there came to him the Destroyer of delights and
the Severer of societies.[1] Quoth Dunyazad, "O sister mine, how
rare is thy tale and delectable!" and quoth Shahrazad, "And
what is this compared with that I could relate to you after the
coming night, an this my lord the King deign leave me on life?"
So Shahryar said to himself, "Indeed I will not slay her until she
tell me the whole tale."

𝔚𝔥𝔢𝔫 𝔦𝔱 𝔴𝔞𝔰 𝔱𝔥𝔢 𝔉𝔦𝔳𝔢 𝔥𝔲𝔫𝔡𝔯𝔢𝔡 𝔞𝔫𝔡 𝔑𝔦𝔫𝔢𝔱𝔶-𝔰𝔢𝔠𝔬𝔫𝔡 𝔑𝔦𝔤𝔥𝔱,[2]

Shahrazad began to relate the adventures of

KHUDADAD[3] AND HIS BROTHERS.

Said she, O auspicious King, this my tale relateth to the Kingdom

---

[1] Mr. Morier in "The Mirza" (vol. i. 87) says, "Had the Arabian Nights' Entertainments, with all their singular fertility of invention and never-ending variety, appeared as a
new book in the present day, translated literally and not adapted to European taste in the
manner attempted in M. Galland's translation, I doubt whether they would have been
tolerated, certainly not read with the avidity they are, even in the dress with which he has
clothed them, however imperfect that dress may be." But in Morier's day the literal
translation was so despised that an Eastern book was robbed of half its charms, both of
style and idea.

[2] In the MS. of the Bibliothèque Nationale, Supplement Arabe (No. 2523, vol. ii.
fol. 147), the story which follows "Aladdin" is that of the Ten Wazirs, for which see
Supp. Nights ii. In Galland the *Histoire de Codadad et de ses Frères* comes next to the
tale of Zayn al-Asnam: I have changed the sequence in order that the two stories directly
translated from the Arabic may be together.

[3] M. Hermann Zotenberg lately informed me that "Khudadad and his Brothers" is
to be found in a Turkish MS., "Al-Faraj ba'd al-Shiddah"—Joy after Annoy—in the
Bibliothèque Nationale of Paris. But that work is a mere derivation from the Persian
"Hazár o yek Roz," for which see my vol. x. p. 441. The name Khudadad is common to

of Diyár Bakr[1] in whose capital-city of Harrán[2] dwelt a Sultan of illustrious lineage, a protector of the people, a lover of his lieges, a friend of mankind and renowned for being gifted with every good quality. Now Allah Almighty had bestowed upon him all that his heart could desire, save boon of child, for though he had lovely wives within his Harem-door and fair concubines galore, he had been not blessed with a son; wherefor he offered up incessant worship to the Creator. One night there appeared to him in a dream a man of comely visage and holy of semblance like unto a prophet, who addressed him, saying, "O puissant King, thy vows are at length heard. Arise to-morrow at day-dawn, pray a two-bow prayer and offer up thy petitions; then haste thee to the Chief Gardener of thy palace and require of him a pomegranate whereof do thou eat as many seeds as seemeth best to thee; after which perform another two-bow prayer, and Allah will shower favours and graces upon thy head." The King, awaking at peep of day, called to mind the vision of the night, and returning thanks to the Almighty, made his orisons and kneeling invoked a benedicite. Then he rose and repaired to the garth, and receiving a pomegranate from the Head-Gardener, counted out and ate fifty grains thereof; to wit, one for each of his wives. After this he lay the night in turn with them all and by the omnipotence of the Creator all gave in due time signs of pregnancy, save one Firúzah[3] hight. So the King conceived a grudge against her, saying in his soul, "Allah holdeth this woman vile and accursed

---

most Eastern peoples, the Sansk. Devadatta, the Gr. Θεοδόσιος, Θεόδωρος, Θεοδώρητος and Dorotheus; the Lat. Deodatus, the Ital. Diodato, and Span. Diosdado, the French Dieu-donné, and the Arab.-Persic Alladád, Dívdád and Khudábaksh. Khudá is the mod. Pers. form of the old Khudái = sovereign, king, as in Máh-i-Khudái = the sovereign moon, Kám-Khudái = master of his passions, etc.

[1] Lit. Homes (or habitations) of Bakr (see vol. v. 66), by the Turks pronounced "Diyár-i-Bekír." It is the most famous of the four provinces into which Mesopotamia (Heb. Naharaym, Arab. Al-Jazírah) is divided by the Arabs; viz: Diyár Bakr (capital Amídah); Diyár Modhar (cap. Rakkah or Aracta); Diyár Rabí'ah (cap. Nisibis) and Diyár al-Jazírah or Al-Jazírah (cap. Mosul). As regards the "King of Harrán," all these ancient cities were at some time the capitals of independent chiefs who styled themselves royalties.

[2] The Heb. Charran, the Carrhæ of the classics where, according to the Moslems, Abraham was born, while the Jews and Christians make him emigrate thither from "Ur (hod. Mughayr) of the Chaldees." Hence his Arab. title "Ibrahim al-Harráni." My late friend Dr. Beke had a marvellous theory that this venerable historic Harrán was identical with a miserable village to the east of Damascus because the Fellahs call it Harrán al-'Awámíd—of the Columns—from some Græco-Roman remnants of a paltry provincial temple. See "Jacob's Flight," etc., London, Longmans, 1865.

[3] Pírozah = turquoise, is the Persian, Firúzah and Firuzakh (De Sacy, Chrest. ii. 84) the

and He willeth not that she become the mother of a Prince, and on this wise hath the curse of barrenness become her lot." He would have had her done to death but the Grand Wazir made intercession for her and suggested to the Sultan that perchance Firuzah might prove with child and withal not show outward signal thereof, as is the manner of certain women; wherefore to slay her might be to destroy a Prince with the mother. Quoth the King, "So be it! slay her not, but take heed that she abide no longer or at court or in the city, for I cannot support the sight of her." Replied the Minister, "It shall be done even as thy Highness biddeth: let her be conveyed to the care of thy brother's son, Prince Samír." The King did according to the counsel of his Wazir and despatched his loathed Queen to Samaria[1] accompanied by a writ with the following purport, to his nephew, "We forward this lady to thy care: entreat her honourably and, shouldest thou remark tokens of pregnancy in her, see that thou acquaint us therewith without stay or delay." So Firuzah journeyed to Samaria, and when her time was fulfilled she gave birth to a boy babe, and became the mother of a Prince who in favour was resplendent as the sheeny day. Hereat the lord of Samaria sent message by letter to the Sultan of Harran saying, "A Prince hath been borne by the womb of Firuzah: Allah Almighty give thee permanence of prosperity!" By these tidings the King was filled with joy; and presently he replied to his cousin, Prince Samir, "Each one of my forty-and-nine spouses hath been blessed with issue and it delighteth me beyond bounds that Firuzah hath also given me a son. Let him be named Khudadad — God's gift — do thou have due care of him and whatsoever thou mayest need for his birth-ceremonies shall be counted out to thee without regard to cost." Accordingly Prince Samir took in hand with all

---

Arab. forms. The stone is a favourite in the East where, as amongst the Russians (who affect to despise the Eastern origin of their blood to which they owe so much of its peculiar merit), it is supposed to act talisman against wounds and death in battle; and the Persians, who hold it to be a guard against the Evil Eye, are fond of inscribing "turquoise of the old rock" with one or more of the "Holy Names." Of these talismans a modern Spiritualist asks, "Are rings and charms and amulets *magnetic*, to use an analogue for what we cannot understand, and has the immemorial belief in the power of relics a natural not to say a scientific basis?"

[1] Samaria is a well-known name amongst Moslems, who call the city Shamrín and Shamrún. It was built, according to Ibn Batrik, upon Mount Samir by Amri who gave it the first name; and the Taríkh Samírí, by Abu al-Fath Abú al-Hasan, is a detailed account of its garbled annals. As Nablús (Neapolis of Herod., also called by him Sebaste) it is now familiar to the Cookite.

pleasure and delight the charge of Prince Khudadad; and, as soon as the child reached the age for receiving instruction, he caused him to be taught cavalarice and archery and all such arts and sciences which it behoveth the sons of the Kings to learn, so that he became perfect in all manner knowledge. At eighteen years of age he waxed seemly of semblance and such were his strength and valiance that none in the whole world could compare with him. Presently, feeling himself gifted with unusual vigour and virile character he addressed one day of the days Firuzah his parent, saying, "O mother mine, grant me thy leave to quit Samaria and fare in quest of fortune, especially of some battle-field where I may prove the force and prowess of me. My sire, the Sultan of Harran, hath many foes, some of whom are lusting to wage war with him; and I marvel that at such time he doth not summon me and make me his aid in this mightiest of matters. But seeing that I possess such courage and Allah-given strength it behoveth me not to remain thus idly at home. My father knoweth not of my lustihood, nor forsooth doth he think of me at all; nevertheless 'tis suitable that at such a time I present myself before him, and tender my services until my brothers be fit to fight and to front his foes." Hereto his mother made answer, "O my dear son, thine absence pleaseth me not, but in truth it becometh thee to help thy father against the enemies who are attacking him on all sides, provided that he send for thine aidance."—— And as the morn began to dawn Shahrazad held her peace till

The end of the Five Hundred and Ninety-third Night.

Then said she:—— I have heard, O auspicious King, that Khudadad replied to his mother Firuzah, "Indeed I am unable to brook delay; moreover such longing have I in heart to look upon the Sultan, my sire, that an I go not and visit him and kiss his feet I shall assuredly die. I will enter his employ as a stranger and all unknown to him, nor will I inform him that I am his son; but I shall be to him as a foreigner or as one of his hired knaves, and with such devotion will I do him suit and service that, when he learneth that I am indeed his child, he may grant me his favour and affection." Prince Samir also would not suffer him to depart and forbade him therefrom; but one day of the days the Prince suddenly set out from Samaria under pretext that he was about to hunt and chase. He mounted a milk-white steed, whose reins and stirrups were of gold and the saddle and housings were of azure satin dubbed with jewels and fringed with pendants of fresh pearls. His scymitar was hilted with a single diamond, the scabbard of chaunders-wood was crested with rubies and emeralds and it depended from a gemmed waist-belt; while his bow and richly wrought quiver hung by his side. Thus equipped and escorted by his friends and familiars he presently arrived at Harran-city after the fairest fashion; and, when occasion offered itself, he made act of presence before the King and did his obeisance at Darbár. The Sultan, remarking his beauty and comeliness, or haply by reason of an outburst of natural affection, was pleased to return his salam; and, graciously calling him to his side, asked of him his name and pedigree, whereto Khudadad answered, "O my liege, I am the son of an Emir of Cairo. A longing for travel hath made me quit my native place and wander from clime to clime till at length I have come hither; and, hearing that thou hast matters of importance in hand, I am desirous of approving to thee my valiancy." The King joyed with exceeding joy to hear this stout and doughty speech, and forthwith gave him a post of command in his army; and Khudadad by careful supervision of the troops soon won the esteem of his officers by his desire to satisfy them and the hearts of his soldiers by reason of his strength and courage, his goodly nature and his kindly disposition. He also brought the host and all its equipments and munitions of warfare into such excellent order and method that the King on inspecting them was delighted and created the stranger Chief Commandant of the forces and made him an especial favourite; while the Wazirs and Emirs, also the Nabobs and the Notables, perceiving that he was highly reputed and regarded, showed him abundant good will and affection. Presently, the other Princes, who became of no account in the eyes of the King and the lieges, waxed envious of his high degree and dignity. But Khudadad ceased not to please the Sultan his sire, at all times when they conversed together, by his prudence and discretion, his wit and wisdom, and gained his regard ever more and more; and when the invaders, who had planned a raid on the realm, heard of the discipline of the army and of Khudadad's provisions for materials of war, they abstained from all hostile intent. After a while the King committed to Khudadad the

custody and education of the forty-nine Princes, wholly relying
on his sagesse and skill; and thus, albeit Khudadad was of age
like his brothers, he became their master by reason of his sapience
and good sense. Whereupon they hated him but the more; and,
when taking counsel one day, quoth one to the other, "What be
this thing our sire hath done that he should make a stranger-
wight his cup-companion and set him to lord it over us? We can
do naught save by leave of this our governor, and our condition
is past bearing; so contrive we to rid ourselves of this foreigner
and at least render him vile and contemptible in the eyes of our
sire the Sultan." Said one, "Let us gather together and slay him
in some lonely spot;" and said another, "Not so! to kill him
would benefit us naught, for how could we keep the matter
hidden from the King? He would become our enemy and Allah
only wotteth what evil might befal us. Nay, rather let us crave
permission of him and fare a-hunting and then tarry we in some
far-off town; and after a while the King will marvel at our absence, then grief will be sore upon him and at length, waxing
displeased and suspicious, he will have this fellow expelled the
palace or haply done to death. This is the only sure and safe
way of bringing about his destruction." —— And as the morn
began to dawn Shahrazad held her peace till

The end of the Five Hundred and Ninety-fourth Night.

THEN said she: —— I have heard, O auspicious King, that the
forty-and-nine brothers agreed to hold this plan wisest and,
presently going together to Khudadad, asked leave of him to
ride about the country awhile or fare to the chase, promising they
would return by set of sun. He fell into the snare and allowed
them to go; whereupon they sallied forth a-hunting but did not
come back that day or the next. On the third morning the King
who missed them asked Khudadad wherefore it was that none of
his sons were to be seen; and he answered that three days before
they had gotten leave from him to go a-hunting and had not
returned. Hereat the father was perplexed with sore perplexity;
and, when sundry days more had passed by and still the Princes
appeared not, the old Sultan was much troubled in mind and
hardly restraining his rage summoned Khudadad and in hot wrath
exclaimed, "O thou neglectful stranger, what courage and over-
daring is this of thine that thou didst suffer my sons fare to the

chase and didst not ride with them! And now 'tis but right that
thou set out and search for them and bring them back; otherwise
thou shalt surely die." Khudadad, hearing these harsh words,
was startled and alarmed; however he got him ready and mounted
his horse forthwith and left the city in quest of the Princes his
brethren, wandering about from country to country, like unto a
herd seeking a straying flock of goats. Presently, not finding any
trace of them in homestead or on desert-ground, he became sad
and sorrowful exceedingly, saying in his soul, "O my brothers,
what hath befallen you and where can ye be dwelling? Perchance
some mighty foeman hath made you prisoners so that ye cannot
escape; and I may never return unto Harran till I find you; for
this will be a matter of bitter regret and repine to the King." So
he repented more and more having suffered them to go without
his escort and guidance. At length whilst searching for them
from plain to plain and forest to forest he chanced come upon a
large and spacious prairie in the middlemost whereof rose a castle
of black marble; so he rode on at a foot pace and when close
under the walls he espied a lady of passing beauty and loveliness
who was seated at a window in melancholy plight and with no
other ornament than her own charms. Her lovely hair hung down
in dishevelled locks; her raiment was tattered and her favour was
pale and showed sadness and sorrow. Withal she was speaking
under her breath and Khudadad, giving attentive ear, heard her
say these words, "O youth, fly this fatal site, else thou wilt fall
into the hands of the monster who dwelleth here: a man-devouring Ethiopian[1] is lord of this palace; and he seizeth all whom Fate
sendeth to this prairie and locketh them up in darksome and
narrow cells that he may preserve them for food." Khudadad
exclaimed, "O my lady, tell me I pray thee who thou art and
whereabouts was thy home;" and she answered, "I am a daughter of Cairo and of the noblest thereof. But lately, as I wended
my way to Baghdad, I alighted upon this plain and met that
Habashi, who slew all my servants and carrying me off by force
placed me in this palace. I no longer cared to live, and a thousand

---

[1] In the text Zangi-i-Adam-kh'wár afterwards called Habashi = an Abyssinian. Galland
simply says *un nègre*. In India the "Habshí" (chief) of Jinjirah (= Al-Jazirah, the Island)
was admiral of the Grand Moghul's fleets. These negroids are still dreaded by Hindús
and Hindís and, when we have another "Sepoy Mutiny," a few thousands of them bought
upon the Zanzibar coast, dressed, drilled and officered by Englishmen, will do us yeomans'
service.

times better were it for me to die; for that this Abyssinian
lusteth to enjoy me and albeit to the present time I have escaped
the caresses of the impure wretch, to-morrow an I still refuse to
gratify his desire he will surely ravish me and do me dead. So I
have given up all hope of safety; but thou, why hast thou come
hither to perish? Escape without stay or delay, for he hath gone
forth in quest of wayfarers and right soon will he return. Moreover he can see far and wide and can descry all who traverse this
wold." Now hardly had the lady spoken these words when the
Abyssinian drew in sight; and he was as a Ghúl of the Wild, big
of bulk, and fearsome of favour and figure, and he mounted a
sturdy Tartar steed, brandishing, as he rode, a weighty blade
which none save he could wield. Prince Khudadad seeing this
monstrous semblance was sore amazed and prayed Heaven that
he might be victorious over that devil: then unsheathing his
sword he stood awaiting the Abyssinian's approach with courage
and steadfastness; but the blackamoor when he drew near
deemed the Prince too slight and puny to fight and was minded
to seize him alive. Khudadad, seeing how his foe had no intent
to combat, struck him with his sword on the knee a stroke so
dour that the negro foamed with rage and yelled a yell so loud
that the whole prairie resounded with the plaint. Thereupon
the brigand, fiery with fury, rose straight in his shovel-stirrups
and struck fiercely at Khudadad with his huge sword and, but
for the Prince's cunning of fence and the cleverness of his courser,
he would have been sliced in twain like unto a cucumber. Though
the scymitar whistled through the air, the blow was harmless,
and in an eye-twinkling Khudadad dealt him a second cut and
struck off his right hand which fell to the ground with the sword
hilt it gripped, when the blackamoor losing his balance rolled
from the saddle and made earth resound with the fall. Thereupon the Prince sprang from his steed and deftly severing the
enemy's head from his body threw it aside. Now the lady had
been looking down at the lattice rigid in prayer for the gallant
youth; and, seeing the Abyssinian slain and the Prince victorious,
she was overcome with exceeding joy and cried out to her de-
liverer, "Praise be to Almighty Allah, O my lord, who by thy
hand hath defeated and destroyed this fiend. Come now to
me within the castle, whose keys are with the Abyssinian; so
take them and open the door and deliver me." Khudadad found
a large bunch of keys under the dead man's girdle wherewith he

opened the portals of the fort and entered a large saloon in which was the lady; and, no sooner did she behold him than running to meet him she was about to cast herself at his feet and kiss them when Khudadad prevented her. She praised him with highest praise and extolled him for valiancy above all the champions of the world, and he returned the salam to her who, when seen near hand seemed endued with more grace and charms than had appeared from afar. So the Prince joyed with extreme joy and the twain sat down in pleasant converse. Presently, Khudadad heard shrieks and cries and weeping and wailing with groans and moans and ever loudening lamentations; so he asked the lady, saying, "Whence are these clamours and from whom come these pitiful complaints?" And, she pointing to a wicket in a hidden corner of the court below, answered, saying, "O my lord, these sounds come therefrom. Many wretches driven by Destiny have fallen into the clutches of the Abyssinian Ghúl and are securely locked up in cells, and each day he was wont to roast and eat one of the captives." " 'Twill please me vastly," quoth Khudadad, "to be the means of their deliverance: come, O my lady, and show me where they are imprisoned." Thereupon the twain drew near to the place and the Prince forthright tried a key upon the lock of the dungeon but it did not fit; then he made essay of another wherewith they opened the wicket. As they were so doing the report of the captives' moaning and groaning increased yet more and more until Khudadad, touched and troubled at their impatience, asked the cause of it. The lady replied, "O my lord, hearing our footsteps and the rattling of the key in the lock they deem that the cannibal, according to his custom, hath come to supply them with food and to secure one of them for his evening meal. Each feareth lest his turn for roasting be come, so all are affrighted with sore affright and redouble their shouts and cries."——And as the morn began to dawn Shahrazad held her peace till

𝕿𝖍𝖊 𝖊𝖓𝖉 𝖔𝖋 𝖙𝖍𝖊 𝕱𝖎𝖛𝖊 𝕳𝖚𝖓𝖉𝖗𝖊𝖉 𝖆𝖓𝖉 𝕹𝖎𝖓𝖊𝖙𝖞-𝖋𝖎𝖋𝖙𝖍 𝕹𝖎𝖌𝖍𝖙.

THEN said she:——I have heard, O auspicious King, that the sounds from that secret place seemed to issue from under ground or from the depths of a draw-well. But when the Prince opened the dungeon door, he espied a steep staircase and descending thereby found himself in a deep pit, narrow and darksome, wherein were penned more than an hundred persons with elbows pinioned and members chained; nor saw he aught of light save through one bull's-eye. So he cried to them, "O ye unfortunates, fear ye no more! I have slain the Abyssinian; and render ye praise to Allah Almighty who hath rid you of your wrong-doer: also I come to strike off your fetters and return you to freedom." Hearing these glad tidings the prisoners were in raptures of delight and raised a general cry of joy and jubilee. Hereupon Khudadad and the lady began to loose their hands and feet; and each, as he was released from his durance, helped to unchain his fellows: brief, after a moment of time all were delivered from their bonds and bondage. Then each and every kissed Khudadad's feet and gave thanks and prayed for his welfare; and when those whilom prisoners entered the court-yard whereupon the sun was shining sheen, Khudadad recognised amongst them his brothers, in quest of whom he had so long wandered. He was amazed with exceeding amazement and exclaimed, "Laud be to the Lord, that I have found you one and all safe and sound: your father is sorely sad and sorrowful at your absence; and Heaven forfend that this devil hath devoured any from amongst you." He then counted their number, forty-and-nine, and set them apart from the rest; and all in excess of joy fell upon one another's necks and ceased not to embrace their saviour. After this the Prince spread a feast for the captives, each and every, whom he had delivered; and, when they had eaten and drunken their full, he restored to them the gold and silver, the Turkey carpets and pieces of Chinese silk and brocade and other valuables innumerable which the Abyssinian had plundered from the caravans, as also their own personal goods and chattels, directing each man to claim his own; and what remained he divided equally amongst them. "But," quoth he, "by what means can ye convey these bales to your own countries, and where can ye find beasts of burden in this wild wold?" Quoth they, "O our Lord, the Abyssinian robbed us of our camels with their loads and doubtless they are in the stables of the castle." Hereupon Khudadad fared forth with them to the stables and there found tethered and tied not only the camels but also the forty-nine horses of his brothers the princes, and accordingly he gave to each one his own animal. There were moreover in the stables hundreds of Abyssinian slave-boys who, seeing the prisoners released, were certified that their lord the cannibal was slain and fled in dismay to the forest and none thought of giving chase to them.   So the merchants loaded their merchandise upon the camels' backs and farewelling the Prince set out for their own countries.   Then quoth Khu-dadad to the lady, "O thou rare in beauty and chastity, whence camest thou when the Abyssinian seized thee and whither now wouldst thou wend?   Inform me thereof that I may restore thee to thy home;   haply these Princes, my brethren, sons of the Sultan of Harran, know thine abode;   and doubtless they will escort thee thither."   The lady turning to Khudadad presently made answer, "I live far from here and my country, the land of Egypt, is over distant for travel.   But thou, O valorous Prince, hast delivered mine honour and my life from the hands of the Abyssinian and hast shown me such favour that 'twould ill become me to conceal from thee my history.   I am the daughter of a mighty king;   reigning over the Sa'íd or upper Nile-land; and when a tyrant foeman seized him and, reaving him of life as well as of his realm, usurped his throne and seized his kingdom, I fled away to preserve my existence and mine honour."   There-upon Khudadad and his brothers prayed the lady to recount all that had befallen her and reassured her, saying, "Henceforth thou shalt live in solace and luxury: neither toil nor trouble shall betide thee."   When she saw that there was no help for her but to tell all her tale, she began in the following words to recount the

History of the Princess of Daryabar.[1]

IN an island of the islands standeth a great city called Daryábár, wherein dwelt a king of exalted degree.   But despite his virtue and his valour he was ever sad and sorrowful having naught of offspring, and he offered up without surcease prayers on that behalf.   After long years and longsome supplications a half boon was granted to him;   to wit, a daughter (myself) was born.   My father who grieved sore at first presently rejoiced with joy ex-ceeding at the unfortunate ill-fated birth of me;   and, when I

---

[1] This seems to be a fancy name for a country: the term is Persian = the Oceanland or a seaport town: from "Daryá" the sea and bár = a region, tract, as in Zanzibár = Black-land.   The learned Weil explains it (in loco) by *Gegend der Brunnen, brunnengleicher ort*, but I cannot accept Scott's note (iv. 400), "Signifying the seacoast of every country;   and hence the term is applied by Oriental geographers to the coast of Malabar."

came of age to learn, he bade me be taught to read and write; and caused me to be instructed in court-ceremonial and royal duties and the chronicles of the past, to the intent that I might succeed him as heiress to his throne and his kingship. Now it happened one day that my sire rode out a-hunting and gave chase to a wild ass[1] with such hot pursuit that he found himself at eventide separated from his suite; so, wearied with the chase, he dismounted from his steed and seating himself by the side of a forest-path, he said to himself, "The onager will doubtless seek cover in this copse." Suddenly he espied a light shining bright amidst the trees and, thinking that a hamlet might be hard by, he was minded to night there and at day-dawn to determine his further course. Hereupon he arose and walking towards the light he found that it issued from a lonely hut in the forest; then peering into the inside he espied an Abyssinian burly of bulk and in semblance like unto a Satan, seated upon a divan. Before him were ranged many capacious jars full of wine and over a fire of charcoal he was roasting a bullock whole and eating the flesh and ever and anon drinking deep draughts from one of the pitchers. Furthermore the King sighted in that hut a lady of exquisite beauty and comeliness sitting in a corner direly distressed: her hands were fast bound with cords, and at her feet a child of two or three years of age lay beweeping his mother's sorry plight.——And as the morn began to dawn Shahrazad held her peace till

The end of the Five Hundred and Ninety-sixth Night.

THEN said she:—— I have heard, O auspicious King, that seeing the doleful state of these twain, my sire was filled with ruth and longed to fall upon the ogre sword in hand; however, not being

---

[1] The onager, confounded by our older travellers with the zebra, is the Gúr-i-khár of Persia, where it is the noblest game from which kings did not disdain to take a cognomen, e.g., Bahrám-i-Gúr. It is the "wild ass" of Jeremiah (ii. 24: xiv. 6). The meat is famous in poetry for combining the flavours peculiar to all kinds of flesh (Ibn Khallikan iii. 117; iii. 239, etc.) and is noticed by Herodotus (Clio. cxxxiii.) and by Xenophon (Cyro. lib. 1) in sundry passages: the latter describes the relays of horses and hounds which were used in chasing it then as now. The traveller Olearius (A. D. 1637) found it more common than in our present day: Shah Abbas turned thirty-two wild asses into an enclosure where they were shot as an item of entertainment to the ambassadors at his court. The skin of the wild ass's back produces the famous shagreen, a word seemingly derived from the Pers.

able to cope with him he restrained his wrath and remained on stealthy watch. The giant having drained all the pitchers of wine and devoured half of the barbacued bullock presently addressed himself to the lady and said, "O loveliest of Princesses, how long wilt thou prove thee coy and keep aloof from me? Dost thou not see how desirous I am of winning thy heart and how I am dying for the love of thee? 'Tis therefore only right that thou also shouldst return my affection and know me as thine own, when I will become to thee the kindest of mankind." "O thou Ghul of the waste," cried the lady, "what be this whereof thou pratest? Never; no, never shalt thou win thy wish of me, however much thou mayest lust therefor. Torment me or, an thou wilt, destroy me downright, but for my part I will on no wise yield me to thy lusts." At these words the infuriated savage roared aloud, " 'Tis enough and more than enough: thy hate breedeth hatred in me and now I desire less to have and hold thee than to do thee die." Then he seized her with one hand, and drawing his sabre with the other, would have struck off her head from her body when my father shot at him a shaft so deftly that it pierced his heart and came out gleaming at his back and he fell to the ground and found instant admission into Jahannam. Hereupon my sire entered the hut and unbinding the lady's bonds enquired of her who she was and by what means that ogre had brought her thither. Answered she, "Not far from this site there liveth on the sea-shore a race of Saracens, like unto the demons of the desert. Sorely against my will I was wedded to their Prince and the fulsome villain thou hast now slain was one of my husband's chief officers. He fell madly in love to me and he longed with excessive longing to get me into his power and to carry me off from my home. Accordingly, one day of the days when my husband was out of the way and I was in privacy, he carried me off with this my babe from the palace to this wild wood wherein is none save He[1] and where well he wot that all search and labour would be baffled; then, hour after hour he designed guilty designs against me, but by the mercy of Almighty Allah I have ever escaped all carnal soil of that foul monster. This evening, in despair of my safety, I was reject-ing his brutal advances when he attempted to take my life and

---

"Saghrí," *e.g.* "Kyafash-i-Saghri" = slippers of shagreen, fine wear fit for a "young Duke". See in Ibn Khallikan (iv. 245) an account of a "Júr" (the Arabised "Gúr") eight hundred years old.

[1] "Dasht-i-lá-siwá-Hú" = a desert wherein is none save He (Allah), a howling wilderness.

in the attempt he was slain by thy valorous hand. This is then my story which I have told thee." My father reassured the Princess, saying, "O my lady, let thy heart be at ease; at day-break I will take thee away from this wilderness and escort thee to Daryabar, of which city I am the Sultan; and, shouldst thou become fain of that place, then dwell therein until thy husband shall come in quest of thee." Quoth the lady, "O my lord, this plan doth not displease me." So with the earliest light next morning my father took mother and child away from that forest and set forth homewards when suddenly he fell in with his Sirdars and officers who had been wandering hither and thither during the livelong night in search of him. They rejoiced with great joy on seeing the King and marvelled with exceeding marvel at the sight of a veiled one with him, admiring much that so love-some a lady should be found dwelling in a wold so wild. There-upon the King related to them the tale of the ogre and of the Princess and how he had slain the blackamoor. Presently they set forth on their homeward way; one of the Emirs seating the dame behind him on his horse's crupper while another took charge of the child. They reached the royal city, where the King ordered a large and splendid mansion to be built for his guest, the babe also received a suitable education; and thus the mother passed her days in perfect comfort and happiness. After the lapse of some months, when no tidings, however fondly expected, came of her husband, she resigned herself to marrying my father whom she had captivated by her beauty and loveliness and amorous liveliness,[1] whereupon he wedded her, and when the marriage-contract was drawn up (as was customary in those days), they sojourned together in one stead. As time went on the lad grew up to be a lusty youth of handsome mien; moreover he became perfect in courtly ceremonial and in every art and science that befit Princes. The King and all the Ministers and Emirs highly approved of him, and determined that I should be married to him, and that he should succeed the sovereign as heir to throne and kingship. The youth also was well pleased with such tokens of favour from my father, but chiefly he rejoiced with exceeding joy to hear talk of his union with his protector's only daughter. One day my sire desired to place my hand in his

---

[1] Per. "Náz o andáz" = coquetry, in a half-honest sense. The Persian "Káká Siyáh," *i.e.* "black brother" (a domestic negro) pronounces Nází-núzí.

to the intent that the marriage ceremony should at once take place, but first he would impose upon my suitor certain conditions, whereof one was that he should wed none other but his wife's daughter, that is, myself. This pledge displeased the haughty youth, who forthwith refused his consent thereto, deeming himself by the demand of such condition a despised and contemptible suitor of villain birth. —— And as the morn began to dawn Shahrazad held her peace till

The end of the Five Hundred and Ninety-seventh Night.

THEN said she: —— I have heard, O auspicious King, that, the lady continued: — On this wise the wedding was deferred, and this delay became a matter of sore displeasure to the young man, who thought in his heart that my father was his foe. Therefore he ever strove to lure him into his power till one day in a frenzy of rage he slew him and proclaimed himself King of Daryabar. Moreover the murtherer would have entered my chamber to kill me also had not the Wazir, a true and faithful servant of the crown, at the tidings of his liege lord's death speedily taken me away, and hidden me in the house of a friend where he bade me remain concealed. Two days afterwards, having fitted out a ship, he embarked me therein with a Kahramánah — an old duenna — and set sail for a country whose King was of my father's friends, to the intent that he might consign me to his charge, and obtain from him the aid of an army wherewith he might avenge himself upon the ungrateful and ungracious youth who had proved himself a traitor to the salt.[1] But a few days after our weighing anchor a furious storm began to blow making the captain and crew sore confounded and presently the waves beat upon the vessel with such exceeding violence that she brake up, and the Wazir and the duenna and all who were therein (save myself) were drowned in the billows. But I, albeit well nigh a-swoon, clung to a plank and was shortly after washed ashore by the send of the sea, for Allah of His mighty power had preserved me safe and sound from death-doom by the raging of the ocean, to the end that further troubles might befal me. When I

---

[1] In the text Nimak-harám: on this subject see vol. viii. 12.

returned to sense and consciousness, I found myself alive on the strand and offered up grateful thanks to Almighty Allah; but not seeing the Wazir or any one of the company I knew that they had perished in the waters. —— And as the morn began to dawn Shahrazad held her peace till

The end of the Five Hundred and Ninety-eighth Night.

THEN said she: —— I have heard, O auspicious King, that the Princess of Daryabar continued: — Presently, calling to remembrance the murther of my father I cried aloud with an exceeding bitter cry and was sore afraid at my lonesome plight, insomuch that I would fain have cast myself again into the sea, when suddenly the voice of man and tramp of horse-hooves fell upon my ears. Then looking about I descried a band of cavaliers in the midst of whom was a handsome prince: he was mounted upon a steed of purest Rabite[1] blood and was habited in a gold-embroidered surcoat; a girdle studded with diamonds girt his loins and on his head was a crown of gold; in fine it was evident from his garb as from his aspect that he was a born ruler of mankind. Thereupon, seeing me all alone on the sea-shore, the knights marvelled with exceeding marvel; then the Prince detached one of his captains to ascertain my history and acquaint him therewith; but albeit the officer plied me with questions I answered him not a word and shed a flood of tears in the deepest silence. So noting the waifage on the sand they thought to themselves, "Perchance some vessel hath been wrecked upon this shore and its planks and timber have been cast upon the land, and doubtless this lady was in that ship and hath been floated ashore on some plank." Whereupon the cavaliers crowded around me and implored me to relate unto them what had befallen me; nevertheless I still answered them not a word. Presently the Prince himself drew near to me and, much amazed, sent away his suite from about me and addressed me in these words, "O my lady, fear naught of ill from me nor distress thyself by needless affright. I would convey thee to my home and under my mother's care; wherefore I am curious to know of thee who thou art. The Queen will assuredly befriend thee and keep thee in comfort and

---

[1] *i.e.*, an Arab of noble strain: see vol. iii. 72.

happiness." And now understanding that his heart was drawn towards me, I told him all that had betided me, and he on hearing the story of my sad destiny became moved with the deepest emotion and his eyes brimmed with tears. Then he comforted me and carried me with him and committed me to the Queen his mother, who also lent kindly ear to my tale of the past, first and last, and hearing it she also was greatly grieved, and wearied not day or night in tending me and (as far as in her lay) striving to make me happy. Seeing, moreover, that her son was deeply enamoured of me and love-distraught she agreed to my becoming his wife, while I also consented when I looked upon his handsome and noble face and figure and to his proved affection for me and his goodness of heart. Accordingly, in due time the marriage was celebrated with royal pomp and circumstance. But what escape is there from Fate? On that very night, the night of the wedding, a King of Zanzibar who dwelt hard by that island, and had erewhile practised against the kingdom, seizing his opportunity, attacked us with a mighty army, and having put many to death, bethought him to take me and my husband alive. But we escaped from his hands and fleeing under the murks of night to the sea-shore found there a fisherman's boat, which we entered thanking our stars and launched it and floated far away on the current, unknowing whither Destiny was directing us. On the third day we espied a vessel making us, whereat we rejoiced with joy excessive, deeming her to be some merchantman coming to our aidance. No sooner had it lain alongside, however, than up there sprang five or six pirates,[1] each brandishing a naked brand in hand, and boarding us tied our arms behind us and carried us to their craft. They then tare the veil from my face and forthwith desired to possess me, each saying to other, "I will enjoy this wench." On this wise wrangling and jangling ensued till right soon it turned to battle and bloodshed, when moment by moment and one by one the ravishers fell dead until all were slain save a single pirate, the bravest of the band. Quoth he to me, "Thou shalt fare with me to Cairo where dwelleth a friend of mine and to him will I give thee, for erewhile I promised him that on this voyage I would secure for him a fair woman for handmaid."

---

[1] In the text "Kazzák" = Cossacks, bandits, mounted highwaymen; the word is well known in India, where it is written in two different ways, and the late Mr. John Shakespear in his excellent Dictionary need hardly have marked the origin "U" (unknown).

Then seeing my husband, whom the pirates had left in bonds he exclaimed, "Who may be this hound? Is he to thee a lover or a friend?" and I made answer, "He is my wedded husband." " 'Tis well," cried he: "in very sooth it behoveth me to release him from the bitter pangs of jealousy and the sight of thee enfolded in another's fond embrace." Whereat the ruffian raised aloft the ill-fated Prince, bound foot and hand, and cast him into the sea, while I shrieked aloud and implored his mercy, but all in vain. Seeing the Prince struggling and drowning in the waves I cried out and screamed and buffetted my face and tare my hair and would fain have cast myself into the waters but I could not, for he held me fast and lashed me to the mainmast. Then, pursuing our course with favouring winds we soon arrived at a small port-village where he bought camels and boy-slaves and journeyed on towards Cairo; but when several stages of the road were left behind us, the Abyssinian who dwelt in this castle suddenly overtook us. From afar we deemed him to be a lofty tower, and when near us could hardly believe him to be a human being. —— And as the morn began to dawn Shahrazad held her peace till

The end of the Five Hundred and Ninety-ninth Night.

THEN said she: —— I have heard, O auspicious King, that the Princesss of Daryabar continued:—At once unsheathing his huge sword the Habashi made for the pirate and ordered him to sur-render himself prisoner, with me and all his slaves, and with pinioned elbows to accompany him. Hereat the robber with hot courage and heading his followers rushed fiercely on the Abys-sinian, and for a long time the fight raged thick and fast, till he and his lay dead upon the field; whereupon the Abyssinian led off the camels and carried me and the pirate's corpse to this castle, and devoured the flesh of his foe at his evening meal. Then turn-ing to me as I wept with bitter weeping he said, "Banish from thy breast this woe and this angry mood; and abide in this castle at perfect ease and in comfort, and solace thyself with my em-braces. However, since thou appearest at this present to be in dire distress, I will excuse thee for to-night, but without fail I shall require thee of thyself on the morrow." He then led me into a separate chamber and locking fast the gates and doors, fell asleep alone in another place. Arising early on the next morning he searched the castle round about, unlocked the wicket which he closed again and sallied forth, according to his custom, in quest of wayfarers. But the caravan escaped him and anon he returned empty-handed when thou didst set upon him and slay him. On this wise the Princess of Daryabar related her history to Prince Khudadad who was moved with ruth for her: then comforting her he said, "Henceforth fear naught nor be on any wise dismayed. These princes are the sons of the King of Harran; and if it please thee, let them lead thee to his court and stablish thee in comfort and luxury: the King also will guard thee from all evil. Or, shouldest thou be loath to fare with them, wilt thou not consent to take for spouse him who hath rescued thee from so great calamity?" The Princess of Daryabar consented to wed with him and forthwith the marriage was celebrated with grand display in the castle and here they found meats and drinks of sundry sorts, and delicious fruits and fine wines wherewith the cannibal would regale himself when a-weary of man's flesh. So Khudadad made ready dishes of every colour and feasted his brothers. Next day taking with them such provaunt as was at hand, all set forth for Harran, and at the close of each stage they chose a suitable stead for nighting; and, when but one day's journey lay before them, the Princes supped that night off what was left to them of their viaticum and drained all the wine that remained. But when the drink had mastered their wits, Khudadad thus addressed his brothers, saying, "Hitherto have I withheld from you the secret of my birth, which now I must disclose. Know ye then that I am your brother, for I also am a son of the King of Harran, whom the Lord of Samaria-land brought up and bade educate; and lastly, my mother is the Princess Firuzah." Then to the Princess of Daryabar, "Thou didst not recognize my rank and pedigree and, had I discovered myself erewhile, haply thou hadst been spared the mortification of being wooed by a man of vulgar blood. But now ease thy mind for that thy husband is a Prince." Quoth she, "Albeit thou discoveredst to me naught until this time, still my heart felt assured that thou wast of noble birth and the son of some potent sovereign." The Princes one and all appeared outwardly well pleased and offered each and every warm congratulations whilst the wedding was celebrating; but inwardly they were filled with envy and sore annoy at such unwelcome issue of events, so much so that when Khudadad retired with the Princess of Daryabar to his tent and slept, those ingrates, forgetful of the service rendered to them by their brother in that he had rescued them when prisoners in the hands of the man-devouring Abyssinian, remained deep in thought and seeking a safe place took counsel one with other to kill him. Quoth the foremost of them, "O my brethren, our father showed him the liveliest affection when he was to us naught save a vagrant and unknown, and indeed made him our ruler and our governor; and now, hearing of his victory won from the ogre and learning that the stranger is his son, will not our sire forthwith appoint this bastard his only heir and give him dominion over us so that we must all be forced to fall at his feet and bear his yoke? My rede is this that we make an end of him in this very spot." Accordingly they stole softly into his tent and dealt him from every side strokes with their swords, so that they slashed him in every limb and fondly thought that they had left him dead on the bed without their awaking the Princess. Next morning they entered the city of Harran and made their salams to the King, who despaired of sighting them again, so he rejoiced with exceeding joy on seeing them restored to him safe and sound and sane, and asked why they had tarried from him so long. In reply they carefully concealed from him their being thrown into the dungeon by the Ghul of Abyssinia and how Khudadad had rescued them: on the contrary all declared that they had been delayed whilst a-hunting and a-visiting the adjacent cities and countries. So the Sultan gave full credence to their account and held his peace. Such was their case; but as regards Khudadad, when the Princess of Daryabar awoke in the morning she found her bridegroom lying drowned in blood gashed and pierced with a score of wounds. —— And as the morn began to dawn Shahrazad held her peace till

The end of the full Six Hundredth Night.

THEN said she: —— I have heard, O auspicious King, that, the Princess, deeming her bridegroom dead, wept at this sight right sore; and, calling to mind his youth and beauty, his valour and his many virtues, she washed his face with her tears and exclaimed, "Well-away and woe is me, O my lover, O Khudadad, do these eyes look upon thee in sudden and violent death? Are these thy brothers (the devils!) whom thy courage hath saved, the destroyers of thee? Nay 'tis I am thy murtheress; I who suffered thee to ally thy Fate with my hapless destiny, a lot that doometh to destruction all who befriend me." Then considering the body attentively she perceived that breath was slowly coming and going through his nostrils, and that his limbs were yet warm. So she made fast the tent-door and ran city-wards to seek a surgeon, and anon having found a skilful leech, she returned with him, but lo and behold! Khudadad was missing. She wist not what had become of him, but thought in her mind that some wild beast had carried him off; then she wept bitterly and bemoaned her mishap, so that the surgeon was moved to ruth and with words of comfort and consolation offered her house and service; and lastly he bore her to the town and assigned to her a separate dwelling. He also appointed two slave-girls to wait upon her, and albeit he knew naught of her condition he was ever in attendance on her with the honour and homage due to the kings. One day, she being somewhat less sad of heart, the surgeon, who had now informed himself of her condition, asked her, saying, "O my lady, be pleased to acquaint me with thine estate and thy misfortunes, and as far as in me lieth I will strive to aid and succour thee." And she, observing the leech to be shrewd and trustworthy withal, made known to him her story. Quoth the surgeon, "An it be thy wish, I would gladly escort thee to thy father-in-law the King of Harran, who is indeed a wise sovereign and a just; and he will rejoice to see thee and will take vengeance on the unnatural Princes, his sons, for the blood of thy husband unjustly shed." These words pleased well the Princess; so the surgeon hired two dromedaries which they mounted and the twain set forth for the city of Harran. Alighting that same evening at a caravanserai the leech asked what news had come from town; and the Keeper answered, "The King of Harran had a son passing valiant and accomplished who abode with him for some years as a stranger; but lately he was lost, nor doth any know of him whether he be dead or alive. The Princess Firuzah his mother hath sent allwheres in search of him, yet hath she found nor trace nor tidings of him. His parents and indeed all the folk, rich and poor, weep and wail for him and albeit the Sultan hath other forty and nine sons, none of them can compare with him for doughty deeds and skilful craft, nor from any one of them deriveth he aught of comfort or consolation. Full quest and search have been made but hitherto all hath been in vain."

The surgeon thereupon made known these words to the Princess of Daryabar, who was minded to go straightway and acquaint the mother of Khudadad with everything that had befallen her husband; but the surgeon, after full reflection, said, "O Princess, shouldst thou fare with this intent, haply ere thou arrive thither the forty-nine Princes may hear of thy coming; and they, by some means or other, will assuredly do thee die, and thy life will be spent to no purpose. Nay, rather let me go first to Prince Khudadad's mother: I will tell her all thy tale and she doubtless will send for thee. Until such time do thou remain secret in this Serai." Accordingly the leech rode on leisurely for the city and on the road he met a lady mounted upon a she-mule[1] whose housings were of the richest and finest, while behind her walked confidential servants, followed by a band of horsemen and foot-soldiers and Habashi slaves; and, as she rode along, the people formed espalier, standing on either side to salute her while she passed. The leech also joined the throng and made his obeisance, after which quoth he to a bystander, which was a Darwaysh, "Methinks this lady must be a queen?" " 'Tis even so," quoth the other, "she is the consort of our Sultan and all the folk honour and esteem her above her sister-wives for that in truth she is the mother of Prince Khudadad and of him thou surely hast heard." Hereupon the surgeon accompanied the cavalcade; and, when the lady dismounted at a cathedral-mosque and gave alms of Ashrafis[2] and gold coins to all around (for the King had enjoined her that until Khudadad's return she should deal charity to the poor with her own hand, and pray for the youth's being restored to his home in peace and safety), the mediciner also mingled with

---

[1] Here and below the Hindostani version mounts the lady upon a camel ("Ushtur" or "Unth") which is not customary in India except when criminals are led about the bazar. An elephant would have been in better form.

[2] The Ashrafí (Port. Xerafim) is a gold coin whose value has greatly varied with its date from four shillings upwards. In The (true) Nights we find (passim) that, according to the minting of the VIth Ommiade, 'Abd al-Malik bin Marwán (A. H. 65-86 = A. D. 685-703), the coinage of Baghdad consisted of three metals. "Ita quoque peregrina suis nummis nomina posuit, aureum Dinar denarium, argentem Dirhen (lege dirham), Drachma, æreum fols (fuls), follem appellans. * * * Nam vera moneta aurea nomine follis lignabatur, ut ærorum sub Aarone Raschido cussorum qui hoc nomen servavit." (O. G. Tychsen p. 8. Introduct. in Rem numariam Muhammedanorum.) For the dinar, daric or miskál see The Nights, vol. i. 32; ix. 294; for the dirham, i. 33, ii. 316, etc.; and for the Fals or Fils = a fish scale, a spangle of metal, vol. i. 321. In the debased currency of the Maroccan Empire the Fals of copper or iron, a substantial coin, is worth 2,160 to the French five-franc piece.

the throng which joined in supplications for their favourite and whispered to a slave saying, "O my brother, it behoveth me that I make known without stay or delay to Queen Firuzah a secret which is with me." Replied he, "An it be aught concerning Prince Khudadad 'tis well: the King's wife will surely give ear to thee; but an it be other, thou wilt hardly win a hearing, for that she is distraught by the absence of her son and careth not for aught beside." The surgeon, still speaking low, made reply, "My secret concerneth that which is on her mind." "If this be so," returned the slave, "do thou follow her train privily till it arrive at the palace gate." Accordingly, when the Lady Firuzah reached her royal apartments, the man made petition to her, saying, "A stranger would fain tell somewhat to thee in private;" and she deigned give permission and command, exclaiming, "'Tis well, let him be brought hither." Hereupon the slave presented to her the surgeon whom the Queen with gracious mien bade approach; and he, kissing ground between her hands, made his petition in these words: "I have a long tale to tell thy Highness whereat thou shalt greatly marvel." Then he described to her Khudadad's condition, the villainy of his brothers and his death at their hands and of his corpse having been carried off by wild beasts. Queen Firuzah hearing of her son's murther fell straightway a-swooning to the ground, and the attendants ran up and, raising her, besprinkled her face with rose-water until she recovered sense and consciousness. Then she gave orders to the surgeon saying, "Hie thee straightway to the Princess of Daryabar and convey to her greetings and expressions of sympathy both from myself and from his sire;" and as the leech departed she called to mind her son and wept with sore weeping. By chance the Sultan, who was passing by that way, seeing Firuzah in tears and sobs and breaking out into sore and bitter lamentation, asked of her the reason thereof. —— And as the morn began to dawn Shahrazad held her peace till

The end of the Six Hundred and First Night.

THEN said she: —— I have heard, O auspicious King, that when her husband enquired of Queen Firuzah why and wherefore she wept and wailed, and moaned and groaned, she told him all she had heard from the leech, and her husband was filled with hot wrath against his sons. So he rose up and went straightway to the audience-chamber, where the townsfolk had gathered together to petition him and to pray for justice and redress; and they, seeing his features working with rage, were all sore afraid. Presently the Sultan seated himself on the throne of his kingship and gave an order to his Grand Wazir, saying, "O Wazir Hasan, take with thee a thousand men of the guard which keepeth watch and ward over the palace and do thou bring hither the forty-and-nine Princes, my unworthy sons, and cast them into the prison appointed unto man-slayers and murtherers; and have a heed that none of them escape." The Wazir did as he was bidden, and seizing the Princes one and all cast them into gaol with the murtherers and other criminals, then reported his action to his liege lord. Hereat the Sultan dismissed sundry claimants and suppliants, saying, "For the space of one full-told month henceforth it besitteth me not to sit in the justice-hall. Depart hence, and, when the thirty days shall have passed away, do ye return hither again." After this rising from the throne he took with him the Wazir Hasan, and entering the apartment of Queen Firuzah, gave command to the Minister that he bring in all haste and with royal state and dignity from the caravanserai, the Princess of Daryabar and the mediciner. The Wazir straightway took horse accompanied by the Emirs and soldiers; and, leading a fine white she-mule richly adorned with jewelled trappings from out of the royal stables, he rode to the caravanserai wherein abode the Princess of Daryabar. Having told her all that the King had done, he seated her upon the animal and, mounting the surgeon upon a steed of Turcoman[1] blood, all three proceeded with pomp and grandeur to the palace. The shop-keepers and townsfolk ran out to greet the lady as the cavalcade wound its way through the streets; and, when they heard say that she was the wife of Prince Khudadad, they rejoiced with exceeding joy for that they should now receive tidings of his whereabouts. As soon as the procession reached the palace gates the Princess of Daryabar saw the Sultan, who had come forth to greet her, and she alighted

---

[1] In the Hindi, as in Galland's version, the horse is naturally enough of Turcoman blood. I cannot but think that in India we have unwisely limited ourselves for cavalry remounts to the Western market that exports chiefly the mongrel "Gulf Arab" and have neglected the far hardier animal, especially the Gútdán blood of the Tartar plains, which supply "excellent horses whose speed and bottom are" say travellers in general, "so justly celebrated throughout Asia." Our predecessors were too wise to "put all the eggs in one basket."

from the mule and kissed his feet. The King then raised her by
the hand and conducted her to the chamber wherein sat Queen
Firuzah awaiting her visit, and all three fell on one another's
necks and wept sore and could on no wise control their grief.
But whenas their sorrow was somewhat assuaged, the Princess of
Daryabar said to the King, "O my lord the Sultan, I would
proffer humble petition that full vengeance may fall upon those,
one and all, by whom my husband hath been so foully and cruelly
murthered."   Replied the King, "O my lady, rest assured that
I will assuredly put to death all those villains in requital for the
blood of Khudadad;" presently adding, " 'Tis true that the
dead body of my brave son hath not been found, still it seemeth
but right to me that a tomb be built, a cenotaph whereby his
greatness and goodness may be held in everlasting remembrance."
Thereupon he summoned the Grand Wazir and bade that a great
Mausoleum of white marble be edified amiddlemost the city
and the Minister straightway appointed workmen and made
choice of a suitable spot in the very centre of the capital. So
there they built a gorgeous cenotaph crowned with a noble dome
under which was sculptured a figure of Khudadad; and, when the
news of its completion reached the King, he appointed a day for
ceremonious mourning and perlections of the Koran. At the appointed time and term the townsfolk gathered together to see the
funeral procession and the obsequies for the departed; and the
Sultan went in state to the Mausoleum together with all the
Wazirs, the Emirs and Lords of the land, and took seat upon carpets of black satin purfled with flowers of gold which were dispread over the marble floor. After a while a bevy of Knights
rode up, with downcast heads and half-closed eyes; and twice
circuiting the dome[1] they halted the third time in front of the
door, and cried out aloud, "O Prince, O son of our Sultan, could
we by the sway of our good swords and the strength of our gallant arms restore thee to life, nor heart nor force would fail us in
the endeavour; but before the fiat of Almighty Allah all must

---

[1] An act of worship, see my Pilgrimage in which "Tawáf" = circuiting, is described in
detail, ii. 38; iii. 201 et seqq. A counterpart of this scene is found in the *Histoire du Sultan
Aqchid* (Ikhshid) who determined to witness his own funeral. Gauttier vol. i. pp. 134-139.
Another and similar incident occurs in the "Nineteenth Vezir's Story" (pp. 213-18 of the
History of the Forty Vezirs, before alluded to): here Hasan of Basrah, an 'Alim who died
in A. H. 110 (=A. D. 728) saw in vision (the "drivel of dreams?") folk of all conditions,
sages, warriors and moon-faced maids seeking, but in vain, to release the sweet soul of the
Prince who had perished.

bow the neck." Then the horsemen rode away to the place
whence they came, followed by one hundred hermits hoar of
head and dwellers of the caves who had passed their lives in
solitude and abstinence nor ever held converse with man or
womankind, neither did they appear in Harran at any time save
for the obsequies of the reigning race. In front came one of these
greybeards steadying with one hand a huge and ponderous tome
which he bore upon his head. Presently all the holy men thrice
compassed the Mausoleum, then standing on the highway the
eldest cried with a loud voice, "O Prince, could we by dint of
orisons and devotions bring thee back to life, these hearts and
souls of ours would be devoted to quickening thee, and on seeing
thee arise once again we would wipe thy feet with our own age-
white beards." And when they also retired came one hundred
maidens of wondrous beauty and loveliness, mounted on white
barbs whose saddles were richly embroidered and set with
jewels: their faces were bare and on their heads they bore golden
canisters filled with precious stones, rubies and diamonds. They
also rode in circuit round the cenotaph and, halting at the door,
the youngest and fairest of them, speaking in the name of her
sisterhood, exclaimed, "O Prince, could our youth and our charms
avail thee aught, we would present ourselves to thee and become
thy handmaids; but alas! thou knowest full well that our beauties are here all in vain nor can our love now warm thy clay."
Then they also departed in the deepest grief. As soon as they
had disappeared the Sultan and all with him rose up and walked
thrice round the figure that had been set up under the dome;
then standing at its feet the father said, "O my beloved son, en-
lighten these eyes which tears for the stress of separation have
thus bedimmed." He then wept bitterly and all his Ministers
and Courtiers and Grandees joined in his mourning and lamentations; and, when they had made an end of the obsequies, the
Sultan and his suite returned palace-wards and the door of the
dome was locked.——And as the morn began to dawn Shahrazad held her peace till

The end of the Six Hundred and Second Night.

THEN said she:——I have heard, O auspicious King, that the
Sultan commanded congregational prayers in all the mosques for

a full told week and he ceased not to mourn and weep and wail
before the cenotaph of his son for eight days. And as soon as
this term was passed he commanded the Grand Wazir that vengeance be meted out for the murther of Prince Khudadad, and
that the Princes be brought out from their dungeons and be done
to death. The tidings were bruited about the city, and preparations were made for executing the assassins and crowds of folk
collected to gaze upon the scaffold, when suddenly came a report
that an enemy whom the King had routed in bygone times was
marching upon the city with a conquering army. Hereat the
Sultan was sore troubled and perplexed and the ministers of
state said one to other, "Alas! had Prince Khudadad been on
life he would forthwith have put to flight the forces of the foe
however fierce and fell." Natheless the Sovran set out from the
city with his suite and host, and eke he made ready for flight to
some other land by way of the river should the enemy's force
prove victorious. Then the two powers met in deadly combat;
and the invader, surrounding the King of Harran's many on
every side, would have cut him to pieces with all his warriors,
when behold, an armed force hitherto unseen rode athwart the
plain at a pace so swift and so sure that the two hostile Kings
gazed upon them in uttermost amazement, nor wist any one
whence that host came. But when it drew near, the horsemen
charged home on the enemies and in the twinkling of an eye
put them to flight; then hotly pursuing felled them with the
biting sword and the piercing spear. Seeing this onslaught the
King of Harran marvelled greatly and rendering thanks to heaven
said to those around him, "Learn ye the name of the Captain of
yonder host, who he may be and whence came he." But when
all the foemen had fallen upon the field save only a few who
escaped hither and thither and the hostile sultan who had been
taken prisoner, the Captain of the friendly forces returned from
pursuit well pleased to greet the King. And, lo and behold! as
the twain drew near one to other the Sultan was certified that the
Captain was none other than his beloved child, Khudadad,
whilome lost and now found. Accordingly, he rejoiced with joy
unspeakable that his enemy had thus been vanquished and that
he had again looked upon his son, Khudadad, who stood before
him alive and safe and sound. "O my sire," presently exclaimed
the Prince, "I am he whom thou deemest to have been slain;
but Allah Almighty hath kept me on life that I might this day

stand thee in good stead and destroy these thine enemies." "O my beloved son," replied the King, "surely I had despaired and never hoped again to see thee with these mine eyes." So father and son dismounted and fell upon each other's necks and quoth the Sultan, clasping the youth's hand, "Long since have I known of thy valiant deeds, and how thou didst save thine ill-omened brothers from the hands of the man-devouring Abyssinian, and of the evil wherewith they requited thee. Go now to thy mother, of whom naught remaineth, through bitter tears for thee, save skin and bone: be thou the first to gladden her heart and give her the good tidings of this thy victory." As they rode along, the Prince enquired of the Sultan, his sire, how he had heard tell of the Habashi and of the rescue of the Princes from the cannibal's clutches. "Hath one of my brothers," added he, "informed thee of this adventure?" "Not so, O my son," replied the King, "not they, but the Princess of Daryabar told me the miserable tale thereof: she hath dwelt for many days with me and 'twas she who first and foremost demanded vengeance for thy blood." When Khudadad heard that the Princess his spouse was his father's guest, he rejoiced with exceeding joy and cried, "Suffer me first to see my mother;[1] then will I go to the Princess of Daryabar." The King of Harran hereat struck off the head of his chief enemy and exposed it publicly throughout the streets of his capital, and all the people exulted mightily not only at the victory but also for the return of Khudadad safe and sound; and dancing and feasting were in every household. Presently Queen Firuzah and the Princess of Daryabar presented themselves before the Sultan and offered their congratulations to him, then they went to see Khudadad both hand in hand and the three falling on one another's necks wept for very joy.——And as the morn began to dawn Shahrazad held her peace till

The end of the Six Hundred and Third Night.

THEN said she:——I have heard, O auspicious King, that after this the King and his Queen and daughter-in-law sat long conversing, and they marvelled much how Khudadad, albeit he was

---

[1] Here, after Moslem fashion, the mother ranks before the wife: "A man can have many wives but only one mother." The idea is old amongst Easterns: see Herodotus and his

sorely gashed and pierced with the sword, had escaped alive from that wildest of wolds, whereupon the Prince at the bidding of his sire told his tale in these words: "A peasant mounted on a camel chanced to pass by my pavilion and seeing me sore wounded and weltering in my blood, set me upon his beast and conveyed me to his house; then, choosing some roots of desert-herbs he placed them on the hurts so that they kindly healed, and I speedily recovered strength. After returning thanks to my benefactor and giving him liberal largesse, I set out for the city of Harran and on the road I saw the forces of the foe in countless numbers marching upon thy city. Wherefore I made the matter known to the folk of the townships and villages round about and besought their aid; then collecting a large force I placed myself at the head thereof, and arriving in the nick of time destroyed the invading hosts." Hereupon the Sultan gave thanks to Allah Almighty and said, "Let all the Princes who conspired against thy life be put to death;" and sent forthright for the Sworder of his vengeance; but Khudadad made request to his sire and said, "In good sooth, O my lord the King, they all deserve the doom thou hast ordained, yet be not these my brethren and eke thine own flesh and blood? I have freely forgiven them their offence against me and I humbly pray thy pardon also, that thou grant them their lives, for that blood ever calleth unto blood." The Sultan at length consented and forgave their offence. Then, summoning all the Ministers, he declared Khudadad his heir and successor, in presence of the Princes whom he bade bring from the prison house. Khudadad caused their chains and fetters to be stricken off and embraced them one by one, showing them the same fondness and affection as he had shown to them in the castle of the cannibal Habashi. All the folk on hearing of this noble conduct of Prince Khudadad raised shouts of applause and loved him yet more than before. The surgeon who had done such good service to the Princess of Daryabar received a robe of honour and much wealth; and on this wise that which began with mishap had issue in all happiness. When Queen Shahrazad ended this story she said to Shahryar, "O my lord, thou art doubtless astonished

---

Christian commentators on the history of Intaphernes' wife (Thalia, cap. cxix). "O King," said that lady of mind logical, "I may get me another mate if God will and other children an I lose these; but as my father and my mother are no longer alive, I may not by any means have another brother," etc., etc.

to find that the Caliph Harún al-Rashid changed his wrath against Ghánim[1] and his mother and sister to feelings of favour and affection, but I am assured that thou wilt be the more surprised on hearing the story of the curious adventures of that same Caliph with the blind man, Bábá Abdullah." Quoth Dunyazad, as was her way, to her sister Shahrazad, "O sister mine, what a rare and delectable tale hast thou told and now prithee favour us with another." She replied, "It is well nigh dawn but, if my life be spared, I will tell thee as the morrow morrows a strange and wonderful history of the Caliph Harun al-Rashid."[2]——And as the morn began to dawn Shahrazad held her peace till

𝕿𝖍𝖊 𝖊𝖓𝖉 𝖔𝖋 𝖙𝖍𝖊 𝕾𝖎𝖝 𝕳𝖚𝖓𝖉𝖗𝖊𝖉 𝖆𝖓𝖉 𝕱𝖔𝖚𝖗𝖙𝖍 𝕹𝖎𝖌𝖍𝖙,

WHEN she began to relate the History of

THE CALIPH'S NIGHT ADVENTURE.

I HAVE heard, O auspicious King, that the Caliph Harun al-Rashid was one night wakeful exceedingly and when he rose in the morning restlessness gat hold of him. Wherefore all about him were troubled for that "Folk aye follow Prince's fashion;" they rejoice exceedingly with his joy and are sorrowful with his sorrows albeit they know not the cause why they are so affected. Presently the Commander of the Faithful sent for Masrúr the Eunuch, and when he came to him cried, "Fetch me my Wazir, Ja'afar the Barmaki, without stay or delay." Accordingly, he went out and returned with the Minister who, finding him alone,

---

[1] In Galland the *Histoire de Ganem, fils d'Abu Aïoub, surnommé l'esclave d'Amour*, precedes Zayn al-Asnám. In the Arab texts Ghanim bin Ayyúb, the Thrall o' Love, occurs much earlier: see The Nights vol. ii. 45.

It is curious to compare the conclusions of these tales with the formula of the latest specimens, the *Contes Arabes Modernes* of Spitta-Bey, *e.g.* "And the twain lived together (p. iii.) and had sons and daughters (p. ii.), cohabiting with perfect harmony (fí al-Kamál pp. 42, 79); and at last they died and were buried and so endeth the story" (wa khalás p. 161).

[2] In Galland and his translators the Adventures of Khudadad and his Brothers is followed by the *Histoire du Dormeur Eveillé* which, as "The Sleeper and the Waker," is to be found in the first of my Supplemental Volumes, pp. 1–29. After this the learned Frenchman introduced, as has been said, the *Histoire de la Lampe merveilleuse* or "Alaeddin" to which I have assigned, for reasons given *in loco*, a place before Khudadad.

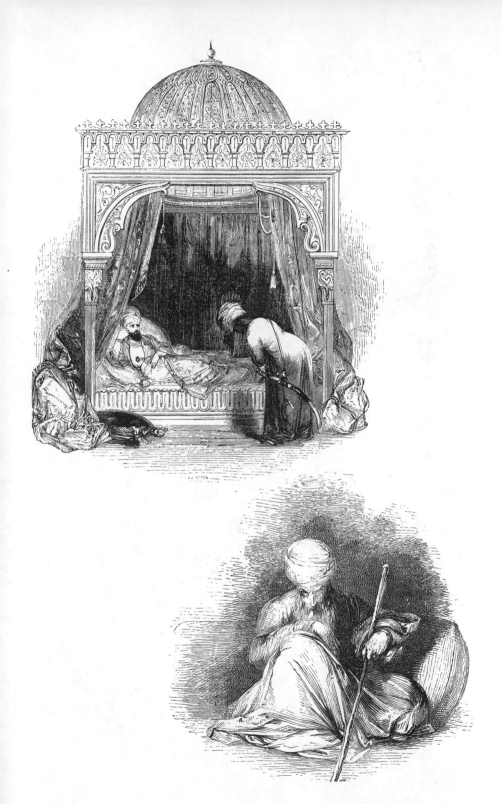

J.W.WHIMPER

which was indeed rare, and seeing as he drew near that he was in a melancholic humour, never even raising his eyes, stopped till his lord would vouchsafe to look upon him. At last the Prince of True Believers cast his glance upon Ja'afar, but forthright turned away his head and sat motionless as before. The Wazir descry-ing naught in the Caliph's aspect that concerned him personally, strengthened his purpose and bespake him on this wise, "O Commander of the Faithful, wilt thine Highness deign suffer me to ask whence cometh this sadness?" and the Caliph answered with a clearer brow, "Verily, O Wazir, these moods have of late become troublesome to me, nor are they to be moved save by hearing strange tales and verses; and, if thou come not hither on a pressing affair, thou wilt gladden me by relating somewhat to dispel my sadness." Replied the Wazir, "O Commander of the Faithful, my office compelleth me to stand on thy service, and I would fain remind thee that this is the day appointed for inform-ing thyself of the good governance of thy capital and its environs, and this matter shall, Inshallah, divert thy mind and dispel its gloom." The Caliph answered, "Thou dost well to remind me, for that I had wholly forgotten it; so fare forth and change thy vestments while I do the same with mine." Presently the twain donned habits of stranger merchants and issued out by a private postern of the palace-garden, which led them into the fields. After they had skirted the city, they reached the Euphrates' bank at some distance from the gate opening on that side, with-out having observed aught of disorder; then they crossed the river in the first ferry-boat they found, and, making a second round on the further side, they passed over the bridge that joined the two halves of Baghdad-town. At the bridge-foot they met with a blind old man who asked alms of them; and the Caliph turned about and crossed his palm with a dinar, whereupon the beggar caught hold of his hand, and held him fast, saying, "O beneficent man, whoso thou ever may be, whom Allah hath in-spired to bestow an alms upon me, refuse not the favour I crave of thee, which is, to strike me a buffet upon the ear, for that I deserve such punishment and a greater still." After these words he quitted his hold of the Caliph's hand that it might smite him, yet for fear lest the stranger pass on without so doing he grasped him fast by his long robe.——And as the morn began to dawn Shahrazad held her peace till

The end of the Six Hundred and Fifth Night.

THEN said she:——I have heard, O auspicious King, that the
Caliph, surprised by the blind man's words and deeds said, "I
may not grant thy request nor will I minish the merit of my
charity, by treating thee as thou wouldst have me entreat thee."
Saying these words, he strove to get away from the blind man,
but he who after his long experience expected this refusal of his
benefactor, did his utmost to keep hold of him, and cried, "O my
lord, forgive my audacity and my persistency; and I implore
thee either give me a cuff on the ear, or take back thine alms,
for I may not receive it save on that condition, without falsing a
solemn oath I have sworn before the face of Allah; and, if thou
knew the reason, thou wouldst accord with me that the penalty
is light indeed." Then the Caliph not caring to be delayed any
longer, yielded to the blind man's importunity, and gave him a
slight cuff: whereupon he loosed him forthright and thanked him
and blessed him. When the Caliph and his Wazir had walked
some way from the blind man, the former exclaimed, "This blind
beggar must assuredly have some right good cause for behaving
himself in such manner to all who give him alms, and I would fain
know it. Do thou return to him and tell him who I am, and bid
him fail not to appear at my palace about mid-afternoon prayer-
time that I may converse with him, and hear whatso he hath to
say." Hereupon Ja'afar went back and bestowed alms on the
blind man giving him another cuff on the ear and apprised him of
the Caliph's command, and returned forthright to his lord. Presently, when the twain reached the town, they found in a square
a vast crowd of folk gazing at a handsome youth and a well-
shaped, who was mounted on a mare which he rode at fullest
speed round the open space, spurring and whipping the beast so
cruelly that she was covered with sweat and blood. Seeing this
the Caliph, amazed at the youth's brutality, stopped to ask the
by-standers an they knew why he tortured and tormented the
mare on such wise; but he could learn naught save that for some
while past, every day at the same time, he had entreated her
after the same fashion. Hereat as they walked along, the Caliph
bid his Wazir especially notice the place and order the young
man to come without failing on the next day, at the hour appointed for the blind man. But ere the Caliph reached his palace,

he saw in a street, which he had not passed through for many months, a newly-built mansion, which seemed to him the palace of some great lord of the land. He asked the Wazir an he knew its owner; and Ja'afar answered he did not but would make inquiry. So he consulted a neighbour who told him that the house-owner was one Khwájah Hasan surnamed Al-Habbál from his handicraft, rope-making; that he himself had seen the man at work in the days of his poverty, that he knew not how Fate and Fortune had befriended him, yet that the same Khwájah had gotten such exceeding wealth that he had been enabled to pay honourably and sumptuously all the expenses he had incurred when building his palace. Then the Wazir returned to the Caliph, and gave him a full account of whatso he had heard, whereat cried the Prince of True Believers, "I must see this Khwajah Hasan al-Habbal: do thou therefore, O Wazir, go and tell him to come to my palace, at the same hour thou hast appointed for the other twain." The Minister did his lord's bidding and the next day, after mid-afternoon prayers, the Caliph retired to his own apartment and Ja'afar introduced the three persons whereof we have been speaking and presented them to the Caliph. All prostrated themselves at his feet and when they rose up, the Commander of the Faithful asked his name of the blind man, who answered he was hight Baba Abdullah. "O Servant of Allah," cried the Caliph, "thy manner of asking alms yesterday seemed so strange to me that, had it not been for certain considerations I should not have granted thy petition; nay, I would have prevented thy giving further offence to the folk. And now I have bidden thee hither that I may know from thyself what impelled thee to swear that rash oath whereof thou toldest me, that I may better judge whether thou have done well or ill, and if I should suffer thee to persist in a practice which meseemeth must set so pernicious an example. Tell me openly how such mad thought entered into thy head, and conceal not aught, for I will know the truth and the full truth."——And as the morn began to dawn Shahrazad held her peace till

The end of the Six Hundred and Sixth Night.

THEN said she:——I have heard, O auspicious King, that Baba Abdullah terrified by these words, cast himself a second time at the Caliph's feet with his face prone to the ground, and when he rose again, said, "O Commander of the Faithful, I crave pardon of thy Highness for my audacity, in that I dared require, and well nigh compelled thee to do a thing which verily seemeth contrary to sound sense. I acknowledge mine offence; but as I knew not thy Highness at that time, I implore thy clemency, and I pray thou wilt consider my ignorance of thine exalted degree. And now as to the extravagance of my action, I readily admit that it must be strange to the sons of Adam; but in the eye of Allah 'tis but a slight penance wherewith I have charged myself for an enormous crime of which I am guilty, and wherefor, an all the people in the world were each and every to give me a cuff on the ear 'twould not be sufficient atonement. Thy Highness shall judge of it thyself, when I, in telling my tale according to thy commandment, will inform thee of what was my offence." And here he began to relate

The Story of the Blind Man, Baba Abdullah.[1]

O my lord the Caliph, I, the humblest of thy slaves, was born in Baghdad, where my father and mother, presently dying within a few days of each other, left me a fortune large enough to last me throughout my lifetime. But I knew not its value and soon I had squandered it in luxury and loose living and I cared naught for thrift or for increasing my store. But when little was left to me of my substance, I repented of my evil courses and toiled and laboured hard by day and night to increase my remaining stock of money. It is truly said, "After waste cometh knowledge of worth." Thus little by little I got together fourscore camels, which I let on hire to merchants, and thus I made goodly gain each time I found occasion: moreover I was wont to engage myself together with my beasts and on this wise I journeyed over all the dominions and domains of thy Highness. Brief, I hoped ere long to reap an abundant crop of gold by the hiring out of my baggage animals.——And as the morn began to dawn Shahrazad held her peace till

---

[1] *i.e.* Daddy Abdullah; the former is used in Pers., Turk. and Hindostani for dad! dear! child! and for the latter, see vol. v. 141.

The end of the Six Hundred and Seventh Night.

THEN said she:——I have heard, O auspicious King, that Baba Abdullah continued his tale in these words:——Once I had carried merchants' stuffs to Bassorah for shipping India-wards and I was returning to Baghdad with my beasts unladen. Now as I fared homewards I chanced pass across a plain of excellent pasturage lying fallow and far from any village, and there unsaddled the camels which I hobbled and tethered together that they might crop the luxuriant herbs and thorns and yet not fare astray. Presently appeared a Darwaysh who was travelling afoot for Bassorah, and he took seat beside me to enjoy ease after unease; whereat I asked him whence he wayfared and whither he was wending. He also asked me the same question and when we had told each to other our own tales, we produced our provisions and brake our fast together, talking of various matters as we ate. Quoth the Darwaysh, "I know a spot hard by which enholdeth a hoard and its wealth is so wonder-great that shouldst thou load upon thy fourscore camels the heaviest burthens of golden coins and costly gems from that treasure there will appear no minishing thereof." Hearing these words I rejoiced with exceeding joy and gathering from his mien and demeanour that he did not deceive me, I arose forthright and falling upon his neck, exclaimed, "O Hallow of Allah, who carest naught for this world's goods and hast renounced all mundane lusts and luxuries, assuredly thou hast full knowledge of this treasure, for naught remaineth hidden from holy men as thou art. I pray thee tell me where it may be found that I may load my fourscore beasts with bales of Ashrafis and jewels: I wot full well that thou hast no greed for the wealth of this world, but take, I pray thee, one of these my fourscore camels as recompense and reward for the favour." Thus spake I with my tongue but in my heart I sorely grieved to think that I must part with a single camel-load of coins and gems; withal I reflected that the other three-score and nineteen camel-loads would contain riches to my heart's content. Accordingly, as I wavered in mind, at one moment consenting and at the next instant repenting, the Darwaysh noting my greed and covetise and avarice, replied, "Not so, O my brother: one camel doth not suffice me that I should shew thee all this hoard. On a single condition only will I tell thee of the place;

to wit, that we twain lead the animals thither and lade them
with the treasure, then shalt thou give me one half thereof and
take the other half to thyself. With forty camels' load of costly
ores and minerals forsure thou canst buy thousands more of
camels." Then, seeing that refusal was impossible, I cried "So
be it! I agree to thy proposal and I will do as thou desirest;"
for in my heart I had conned the matter over and well I wist
that forty camel-loads of gold and gems would suffice me and
many generations of my descendants; and I feared lest an I gainsay him I should repent for ever and ever having let so great a
treasure slip out of hand. Accordingly, giving full consent to
all he said, I got together every one of my beasts and set me a-
wayfaring along with the Fakír.[1] After travelling over some
short distance we came upon a gorge between two craggy
mountain-walls towering high in crescent form and the pass was
exceeding narrow so that the animals were forced to pace in
single file, but further on it flared out and we could thread it
without difficulty into the broad Wady below. No human being
was anywhere to be seen or heard in this wild land, so we were
undisturbed and easy in our minds nor feared aught. Then
quoth the Darwaysh, "Leave here the camels and come with
me."——And as the morn began to dawn Shahrazad held her
peace till

The end of the Six Hundred and Eighth Night.

THEN said she:——I have heard, O auspicious King, that the
blind man Baba Abdullah pursued his tale on this wise:——I did
as the Darwaysh had bidden me; and, nakhing[2] all the camels,
I followed in wake of him. After walking a short way from the
halting-place he produced a flint and steel and struck fire therewith and lit some sticks he had gotten together; then, throwing
a handful of strong-smelling incense upon the flames, he muttered words of incantation which I could by no means understand. At once a cloud of smoke arose, and spireing upwards
veiled the mountains; and presently, the vapour clearing away,
we saw a huge rock with pathway leading to its perpendicular

---

[1] Here the Arab. syn. of the Pers. "Darwaysh," which Egyptians pronounce "Darwísh."
In the Nile-valley the once revered title has been debased to an insult = "poor devil"
(see Pigrimage i., pp. 20-22); "Fakír" also has come to signify a Koran-chaunter.
[2] To "Nakh" is to make the camel kneel. See vo!. ii. 139, and its references.

face. Here the precipice showed an open door, wherethrough appeared in the bowels of the mountain a splendid palace, the workmanship of the Jinns, for no man had power to build aught like it. In due time, after sore toil, we entered therein and found an endless treasure, ranged in mounds with the utmost ordinance and regularity. Seeing a heap of Ashrafis I pounced upon it as a vulture swoopeth upon her quarry, the carrion, and fell to filling the sacks with golden coin to my heart's content. The bags were big, but I was constrained to stuff them only in proportion to the strength of my beasts. The Darwaysh, too, busied himself in like manner, but he charged his sacks with gems and jewels only, counselling me the while to do as he did. So I cast aside the ducats and filled my bags with naught save the most precious of the stonery. When we had wrought our best, we set the well-stuffed sacks upon the camels' backs and we made ready to depart; but, before we left the treasure-house wherein stood ranged thousands of golden vessels, exquisite in shape and workmanship, the Darwaysh went into a hidden chamber and brought from out a silvern casket a little golden box full of some unguent, which he showed to me, and then he placed it in his pocket. Presently, he again threw incense upon the fire and recited his incantations and conjurations, whereat the door closed and the rock became as before. We then divided the camels, he taking one half and I the other; and, passing through the strait and gloomy gorge in single file, we came out upon the open plain. Here our way parted, he wending in the direction of Bassorah and I Baghdad-wards; and when about to leave him I showered thanks upon the Darwaysh who had obtained me all this wealth and riches worth a thousand thousand of gold coins; and farewelled him with deep emotions of gratitude; after which we embraced and wended our several ways. But hardly had I bidden adieu to the Fakir and had gone some little distance from him with my file of camels than the Shaytan tempted me with greed of gain so that I said to myself, "The Darwaysh is alone in the world, without friends or kinsman, and is wholly estranged from matters mundane. What will these camel-loads of filthy lucre advantage him? Moreover, engrossed by the care of the camels, not to speak of the deceitfulness of riches, he may neglect his prayer and worship: therefore it behoveth me to take back from him some few of my beasts." With this resolve I made the camels halt and tying up their forelegs ran back after the holy

man and called out his name. He heard my loud shouts and
awaited me forthright; and, as soon as I approached him I said,
"When I had quitted thee a thought came into my mind; to wit,
that thou art a recluse who keepest thyself aloof from earthly
things, pure in heart and busied only with orison and devotion.
Now care of all these camels will cause thee only toil and moil
and trouble and waste of precious time: 'twere better then to
give them back and not run the risk of these discomforts and
dangers." The Darwaysh replied, "O my son, thou speakest
sooth. The tending of all these animals will bring me naught
save ache of head, so do thou take of them as many as thou listest.
I thought not of the burthen and pother till thou drewest my
attention thereto; but now I am forewarned thereof; so may
Almighty Allah keep thee in His holy keeping!" Accordingly,
I took ten camels of him and was about to gang my gait when
suddenly it struck me, "This Fakir was unconcerned at giving up
ten camels, so 'twere better I ask more of him." Thereupon I
drew nearer to him and said, "Thou canst hardly manage thirty
camels; do give me, I pray thee, other ten." Said he, "O my son,
do whatso thou wishest! Take thee other ten camels; twenty will
suffice me." I did his bidding and driving off the twenty added
them to my forty. Then the spirit of concupiscence possessed
me, and I bethought me more and more to get yet other ten
camels from his share; so I retraced my steps for the third time
and asked him for another ten, and of these, as also the remaining
ten, I wheedled him. The Darwaysh gladly gave up the last of
his camels, and, shaking out his skirts,[1] made ready to depart;
but still my accursed greed stuck to me. Albeit I had got the
fourscore beasts laden with Ashrafis and jewels, and I might have
gone home happy and content, with wealth for fourscore generations, Satan tempted me still more, and urged me also to take
the box of ointment, which I supposed to contain something
more precious than rubies.——And as the morn began to dawn
Shahrazad held her peace till

The end of the Six Hundred and Ninth Night.

THEN said she:——I have heard, O auspicious King, that Baba
Abdullah continued his tale in these words:—So when I had

---

[1] As a sign that he parted willingly with all his possessions.

again farewelled and embraced him I paused awhile and said, "What wilt thou do with the little box of salve thou hast taken to thy portion? I pray thee give me that also." The Fakir would by no means part with it, whereupon I lusted the more to possess it, and resolved in my mind that, should the holy man give it up of his free will, then well and good, but if not I would force it from him. Seeing my intent he drew the box from out his breast-pocket[1] and handed it to me saying, "O my son, an thou wouldst have this box of ointment, then freely do I give it to thee; but first it behoveth thee to learn the virtue of the unguent it con-taineth." Hearing these words I said, "Forasmuch as thou hast shown me all this favour, I beseech thee tell me of this ointment and what of properties it possesseth." Quoth he, "The wonders of this ointment are passing strange and rare. An thou close thy left eye and rub upon the lid the smallest bit of the salve then all the treasures of the world now concealed from thy gaze will come to sight; but an thou rub aught thereof upon thy right eye thou shalt straightway become stone-blind of both." Thereat I bethought me of putting this wondrous unguent to the test and placing in his hand the box I said, "I see thou understandest this matter right well; so now I pray thee apply somewhat of the ointment with thine own hand to my left eyelid." The Darwaysh thereupon closed my left eye and with his finger rubbed a little of the unguent over the lid; and when I opened it and looked around I saw the hidden hoards of the earth in countless quan-tities even as the Fakir had told me I should see them. Then closing my right eyelid, I bade him apply some of the salve to that eye also. Said he, "O my son, I have forewarned thee that if I rub it upon thy right eyelid thou shalt become stone-blind of both. Put far from thee this foolish thought: why shouldst thou bring this evil to no purpose on thyself?" He spake sooth indeed, but by reason of my accursed ill-fate I would not heed his words and considered in my mind, "If applying the salve to the left eyelid hath produced such effect, assuredly far more wondrous still shall be the result when rubbed on the right eye. This fellow doth play me false and keepeth back from me the truth of the matter." When I had thus determined in my mind I laughed and said to the holy man, "Thou art deceiving me to the intent

---

[1] Arab. "'Ubb" prop. = the bulge between the breast and the outer robe which is girdled round the waist to make a pouch. See vol. viii. 205.

that I should not advantage myself by the secret, for that rubbing the unguent upon the right eyelid hath some greater virtue than applying it to the left eye, and thou wouldst withhold the matter from me. It can never be that the same ointment hath qualities so contrary and virtues so diverse." Replied the other, "Allah Almighty is my witness that the marvels of the ointment be none other save these whereof I bespake thee; O dear my friend, have faith in me, for naught hath been told thee save what is sober sooth." Still would I not believe his words, thinking that he dissembled with me and kept secret from me the main virtue of the unguent. Wherefore filled with this foolish thought I pressed him sore and begged that he rub the ointment upon my right eyelid; but he still refused and said, "Thou seest how much of favour I have shown to thee: wherefore should I now do thee so dire an evil? Know for a surety that it would bring thee lifelong grief and misery; and I beseech thee, by Allah the Almighty, abandon this thy purpose and believe my words." But the more he refused so much the more did I persist; and in fine I made oath and sware by Allah, saying, "O Dar-waysh, what things soever I have asked of thee thou gavest freely unto me and now remaineth only this request for me to make. Allah upon thee, gainsay me not and grant me this last of thy boons: and whatever shall betide me I will not hold thee responsible therefor. Let Destiny decide for good or for evil." When the holy man saw that his denial was of no avail and that I irked him with exceeding persistence, he put the smallest bit of ointment on my right lid and, as I opened wide my eyes, lo and behold! both were stone-blind: naught could I see for the black darkness before them and ever since that day have I been sightless and helpless as thou foundest me. When I knew that I was blinded, I exclaimed, "O Darwaysh of ill-omen, what thou didst fore-tell hath come to pass;" and I fell to cursing him and saying, "O would to Heaven thou hadst never brought me to the hoard or hadst given me such wealth. What now avail me all this gold and jewels? Take back thy forty camels and make me whole again." Replied he, "What evil have I done to thee? I showed thee favours more than any man hath ever dealt to another. Thou wouldst not heed my rede, but didst harden thy heart and lustedst to obtain this wealth and to pry into the hidden treas-ures of the earth. Thou wouldst not be content with what thou hadst and thou didst misdoubt my words thinking that I would play thee false. Thy case is beyond all hope, for never more wilt thou regain thy sight; no, never." Then said I with tears and lamentations, "O Fakir, take back thy fourscore camels laden with gold and precious stones and wend thy way: I absolve thee from all blame, natheless I beseech thee by Allah Almighty to restore my sight an thou art able." He answered not a word, but leaving me in miserable plight presently took the load to Bassorah, driving before him the fourscore camels laden with wealth. I cried aloud and besought him to lead me with him away from the life-destroying wilderness, or to put me on the path of some caravan, but he regarded not my cries and abandoned me there.——And as the morn began to dawn Shahrazad held her peace till

The end of the Six Hundred and Tenth Night.

THEN said she:——I have heard, O auspicious King, that Baba Abdullah the blind man resumed his story, saying:—So when the Darwaysh departed from me, I had well nigh died of grief and wrath at the loss of my sight and of my riches, and from the pangs of thirst[1] and hunger. Next day by good fortune a caravan from Bassorah passed that way; and, seeing me in such a grievous condition, the merchants had compassion on me and made me travel with them to Baghdad. Naught could I do save beg my bread in order to keep myself alive; so I became a mendicant and made this vow to Allah Almighty that, as a punishment for this my unlucky greed and cursed covetise, I would require a cuff upon my ear from everyone who might take pity on my case and give an alms. On this wise it was that yesterday I pursued thee with such pertinacity. — When the blind man made an end of his story the Caliph said, "O Baba Abdullah! thine offence was grievous; may Allah have mercy on thee therefor. It now re-maineth to thee to tell thy case to devotees and anchorites that they may offer up their potent prayers in thy behalf. Take no thought for thy daily wants: I have determined that for thy living thou shalt have a dole of four dirhams a day from my royal treasury according to thy need as long as thou mayest live. But

---

[1] Thirst very justly takes precedence of hunger: a man may fast for forty days, but without water in a tropical country he would die within a week. For a description of the horrors of thirst see my "First Footsteps in East Africa," pp. 387-8.

see that thou go no more to ask for alms about my city." So Baba Abdullah returned thanks to the Prince of True Believers, saying, "I will do according to thy bidding." Now when the Caliph Harun al-Rashid had heard the story of Baba Abdullah and the Darwaysh, he turned to and addressed the young man whom he had seen riding at fullest speed upon the mare and savagely lashing and ill-treating her. "What is thy name?" quoth he, and quoth the youth, bowing his brow groundwards, "My name, O Commander of the Faithful, is Sídí Nu'umán."[1] Then said the Caliph, "Hearken now, O Sidi Nu'umán! Ofttimes have I watched the horsemen exercise their horses, and I myself have often done likewise, but never saw I any who rode so mercilessly as thou didst ride thy mare, for thou didst ply both whip and shovel-iron in cruellest fashion. The folk all stood to gaze with wonderment, but chiefly I, who was constrained against my wish to stop and ask the cause of the bystanders. None, however, could make clear the matter, and all men said that thou art wont each day to ride the mare in this most brutal fashion, whereat my mind marvelled all the more. I now would ask of thee the cause of this thy ruthless savagery, and see that thou tell me every whit and leave not aught unsaid." Sidi Nu'uman, hearing the order of the Commander of the Faithful, became aware he was fully bent upon hearing the whole matter and would on no wise suffer him to depart until all was explained. So the colour of his countenance changed and he stood speechless like a statue through fear and trepidation; whereat said the Prince of True Believers, "O Sidi Nu'uman, fear naught but tell me all thy tale. Regard me in the light of one of thy friends and speak without reserve, and explain to me the matter fully as thou wouldst do hadst thou been speaking to thy familiars. Moreover, an thou art afraid of any matter which thou shalt confide to me and if thou dread my indignation, I grant thee immunity and a free pardon." At these comforting words of the Caliph, Sidi Nu'uman took courage, and with clasped hands replied, "I trust

---

[1] In Galland it is Sidi Nouman; in many English translations, as in the "Lucknow" (Newul Kishore Press, 1880), it has become "Sidi Nonman." The word has occurred in King Omar bin al-Nu'uman, vol. ii. 77 and 325, and vol. v. 74. For Sídí = my lord, see vol. v. 283; Byron, in The Corsair, ii. 2, seems to mistake it for "Sayyid."

High in his hall reclines the turban'd Seyd,
Around—the bearded chiefs he came to lead.

I have not in this matter done aught contrary to thy Highness's law and custom, and therefore will I willingly obey thy bidding and relate to thee all my tale. If I have offended in anything then am I worthy of thy punishment. 'Tis true that I have daily exercised the mare and ridden her at speed around the hippodrome as thou sawest me do; and I lashed and gored her with all my might. Thou hadst compassion on the mare and didst deem me cruel-hearted to entreat her thus, but when thou shalt have heard all my adventure thou wilt admit, Inshallah—God willing —that this be only a trifling penalty for her offence, and that not she but I deserve thy pity and pardon! With thy permission I will now begin my story."——And as the morn began to dawn Shahrazad held her peace till

The end of the Six Hundred and Eleventh Night.

THEN said she:——I have heard, O auspicious King, that the Caliph Harun al-Rashid accorded the youth permission to speak and that the rider of the mare began in these words the

History of Sidi Nu'uman.

O LORD of beneficence and benevolence, my parents were possessed of wealth and riches sufficient to provide their son when they died with ample means for a life-long livelihood so that he might pass his days like a Grandee of the land in ease and joyance and delight. I—their only child—had nor care nor trouble about any matter until one day of the days, when in the prime of manhood, I was a minded to take unto me a wife, a woman winsome and comely to look upon, that we might live together in mutual love and double blessedness. But Allah Almighty willed not that a model helpmate become mine; nay, Destiny wedded me to grief and the direst misery. I married a maid who in outward form and features was a model of beauty and loveliness without, however, one single gracious gift of mind or soul; and on the very second day after the wedding her evil nature began to manifest itself. Thou art well aware, O Prince of True Believers, that by Moslem custom none may look upon the face of his betrothed before the marriage contract, nor after wedlock can he complain

should his bride prove a shrew or a fright: he must needs dwell
with her in such content as he may and be thankful for his fate,
be it fair or unfair. When I saw first the face of my bride and
learnt that it was passing comely, I joyed with exceeding joy
and gave thanks to Almighty Allah that He had bestowed on me
so charming a mate. That night I slept with her in joy and love-
delight; but next day when the noon-meal was spread for me and
her I found her not at table and sent to summon her; and after
some delay, she came and sat her down. I dissembled my an-
noyance and forbore for this late-coming to find fault with her;
which I soon had ample reason to do. It so happened that
amongst the many dishes which were served up to us was a fine
pilaff,[1] of which I, according to the custom in our city, began to
eat with a spoon; but she, in lieu of it pulled out an ear-pick from
her pocket and therewith fell to picking up the rice and ate it
grain by grain. Seeing this strange conduct I was sore amazed
and fuming inwardly said in sweet tones, "O my Aminah,[2] what
be this way of eating? hast thou learnt it of thy people or art thou
counting grains of rice purposing to make a hearty meal hereafter? Thou hast eaten but ten or twenty during all this time.
Or haply thou art practising thrift: if so I would have thee know
that Allah Almighty hath given me abundant store and fear not
on that account; but do thou, O my dearling, as all do and eat as
thou seest thy husband eat." I fondly thought that she would
assuredly vouchsafe some words of thanks, but never a syllable
spake she and ceased not picking up grain after grain: nay more,
in order to provoke me to greater displeasure, she paused for a
long time between each. Now when the next course of cakes
came on she idly brake some bread and tossed a crumb or two
into her mouth; in fact she ate less than would satisfy the stomach of a sparrow. I marvelled much to see her so obstinate and
self-willed but I said to myself, in mine innocence, "May be she
hath not been accustomed to eat with men, and especially she
may be too shame-faced to eat heartily in presence of her hus-

---

[1] The Turco-English form of the Persian "Puláo."

[2] *i.e.* the secure (fem.). It was the name of the famous concubine of Solomon to whom he
entrusted his ring (vol. vi. 84); also of the mother of Mohammed who having taken her son
to Al-Medinah (Yathrib) died on the return journey. I cannot understand why the
Apostle of Al-Islam, according to his biographers and commentators, refused to pray for
his parent's soul, she having been born in Al-Fitrah (the interval between the fall of Chris-
tianity and the birth of Al-Islam), when he had not begun to preach his "dispensation."
See Tabari, ii. 450.

band: she will in time do whatso do other folk." I thought also that perchance she hath already broken her fast and lost appetite, or haply it hath been her habit to eat alone. So I said nothing and after dinner went out to smell the air and play the Jaríd[1] and thought no more of the matter. When, however, we two sat again at meat my bride ate after the same fashion as before; nay, she would ever persist in her perversity; whereat I was sore troubled in mind, and marvelled how without food she kept herself alive. One night it chanced that deeming me fast asleep she rose up in stealth from my side, I being wide awake: when I saw her step cautiously from the bed as one fearing lest she might disturb me. I wondered with exceeding wonder why she should arise from sleep to leave me thus and methought I would look into the matter. Wherefore I still feigned sleep and snored but watched her as I lay, and presently saw her dress herself and leave the room; I then sprang off the bed and throwing on my robe and slinging my sword across my shoulder looked out of the window to spy whither she went. Presently she crossed the courtyard and opening the street-door fared forth; and I also ran out through the entrance which she had left unlocked; then followed her by the light of the moon until she entered a cemetery hard by our home. —— And as the morn began to dawn Shahrazad held her peace till

The end of the Six Hundred and Twelfth Night.

THEN said she: —— I have heard, O auspicious King, that Sidi Nu'uman continued his story saying: — But when I beheld Aminah my bride enter the cemetery, I stood without and close to the wall over which I peered so that I could espy her well but she could not discover me. Then what did I behold but Aminah sitting with a Ghúl![2] Thy Highness wotteth well that Ghuls be of the race of devils; to wit, they are unclean spirits which inhabit ruins and which terrify solitary wayfarers and at times seizing them feed upon their flesh; and if by day they find not any traveller to eat they go by night to the graveyards and dig out

---

[1] The cane-play: see vol. vi. 263.
[2] Galland has *une Goule*, *i.e.*, a Ghúlah, a she-Ghúl, an ogress. But the lady was supping with a male of that species, for which see vols. i. 55; vi. 36.

and devour dead bodies. So I was sore amazed and terrified to
see my wife thus seated with a Ghul. Then the twain dug up
from the grave a corpse which had been newly buried, and the
Ghul and my wife Aminah tore off pieces of the flesh which she
ate making merry the while and chatting with her companion;
but inasmuch as I stood at some distance I could not hear what it
was they said. At this sight I trembled with exceeding fear. And
when they had made an end of eating they cast the bones into the
pit and thereover heaped up the earth e'en as it was before. Leaving them thus engaged in their foul and fulsome work, I hastened
home; and, allowing the street-door to remain half-open as my
bride had done, I reached my room, and throwing myself upon
our bed feigned sleep. Presently Aminah came and doffing her
dress calmly lay beside me, and I knew by her manner that she
had not seen me at all, nor guessed that I had followed her to the
cemetery. This gave me great relief of mind, withal I loathed to
bed beside a cannibal and a corpse-eater; howbeit I lay still despite
extreme misliking till the Muezzin's call for dawn-prayers, when
getting up I busied myself with the Wuzú-ablution and set forth
mosque-wards. Then having said my prayers and fulfilled my
ceremonial duties,[1] I strolled about the gardens, and during this
walk having turned over the matter in my mind, determined that
it behoved me to remove my bride from such ill companionship,
and wean her from the habit of devouring dead bodies. With
these thoughts I came back home at dinner-time, when Aminah
on seeing me return bade the servants serve up the noontide-meal
and we twain sat at table; but as before she fell to picking up the
rice grain by grain. Thereat said I to her, "O my wife, it irketh
me much to see thee picking up each grain of rice like a hen. If
this dish suit not thy taste see there are, by Allah's grace and the
Almighty's favour, all kinds of meats before us. Do thou eat of
that which pleaseth thee most; each day the table is bespread
with dishes of different kinds and if these please thee not, thou
hast only to order whatsoever food thy soul desireth. Yet I
would ask of thee one question: Is there no meat upon the table
as rich and toothsome as man's flesh, that thou refuseth every
dish they set before thee?" Ere I had finished speaking my wife

---

[1] In the text "Wazífah" prop. = a task, a stipend, a salary; but here = the "Farz" devotions which he considered to be his duty. In Spitta-Bey (*loc. cit. p. 218*) it is = duty,
office, position.

became assured that I was aware of her night adventure: she suddenly waxed wroth with exceeding wrath, her face flushed red as fire, her eyeballs started out from their sockets and she foamed at the mouth with ungovernable fury. Seeing her in this mood I was terrified and my sense and reason fled by reason of my affright; but presently in the madness of her passion she took up a tasse of water which stood beside her and dipping her fingers in the contents muttered some words which I could not under-stand; then sprinkling some drops over me, cried, "Accursed that thou art! for this thine insolence and betrayal do thou be straightway turned into a dog." At once I became transmewed and she, picking up a staff began to ribroast me right mercilessly and well nigh killed me. I ran about from room to room but she pursued me with the stick, and tunded and belaboured me with might and main, till she was clean exhausted. She then threw the street-door half open and, as I made for it to save my life, attempted violently to close it, so as to squeeze my soul out of my body; but I saw her design and baffled it, leaving behind me, however, the tip of my tail; and piteously yelping hereat I es-caped further basting and thought myself lucky to get away from her without broken bones. When I stood in the street still whin-ing and ailing, the dogs of the quarter seeing a stranger, at once came rushing at me barking and biting;[1] and I with tail between my legs tore along the market-place and ran into the shop of one who sold sheeps' and goats' heads and trotters; and there crouch-ing low hid me in a dark corner. —— And as the morn began to dawn Shahrazad held her peace till

The end of the Six Hundred and Thirteenth Night.

THEN said she: —— I have heard, O auspicious King, that Sidi Nu'uman continued his story as follows: — The shopkeeper, despite his scruples of conscience, which caused him to hold all dogs impure,[2] hath ruth upon my sorry plight and drove away the

---

1 For this scene which is one of every day in the East; see Pilgrimage ii. pp. 52-54.

2 This hate of the friend of man is inherited from Jewish ancestors; and, wherever the Hebrew element prevails, the muzzle, which has lately made its appearance in London, is strictly enforced, as at Trieste. Amongst the many boons which civilisation has conferred upon Cairo I may note hydrophobia; formerly unknown in Egypt the dreadful disease has lately caused more than one death. In India sporadic cases have at rare times occurred in my own knowledge since 1845.

yelling and grinning curs that would have followed me into his shop; and I, escaping this danger of doom, passed all the night hid in my corner. Early next morning the butcher sallied forth to buy his usual wares, sheeps' heads and hooves; and, coming back with a large supply, he began to lay them out for sale within the shop, when I, seeing that a whole pack of dogs had gathered about the place attracted by the smell of flesh, also joined them. The owner noticed me among the ragged tykes and said to himself, "This dog hath tasted naught since yesterday when it ran yelping hungrily and hid within my shop." He then threw me a fair sized piece of meat, but I refused it and went up to him and wagged my tail to the end that he might know my wish to stay with him and be protected by his stall: he, however, thought that I had eaten my sufficiency, and, picking up a staff frightened me away. So when I saw how the butcher heeded not my case, I trotted off and wandering to and fro presently came to a bakery and stood before the door wherethrough I espied the baker at breakfast. Albeit I made no sign as though I wanted aught of food, he threw me a bittock of bread; and I, in lieu of snapping it up and greedily swallowing it, as is the fashion with all dogs, the gentle and simple of them, approached him with it and gazed in his face and wagged my tail by way of thanks. He was pleased by this my well-bred behaviour and smiled at me; whereat I, albeit not one whit anhungered, but merely to humour him, fell to eating the bread, little by little and leisurely, to testify my respect. He was yet more satisfied with my manners and wished to keep me in his shop; and I, noting his intent, sat by the door and looked wistfully at him, whereby he knew that I desired naught of him save his protection. He then caressed me and took charge of me and kept me to guard his store, but I would not enter his house till after he had led the way; he also showed me where to lie o'nights and fed me well at every meal and entreated me right hospitably. I likewise would watch his every movement and always lay down or rose up even as he bade me; and whenas he left his lodging or walked anywhither he took me with him. If ever when I lay asleep he went outside and found me not, he would stand still in the street and call to me crying, "Bakht! Bakht!"[1] an auspicious name he had given to me; and straightway

---

[1] In Galland "Rougeau" = (for Rougeaud?) a red-faced (man), etc., and in the English version "Chance": "Bakht" = luck, good fortune.

on hearing him I would rush about and frisk before the door; and when he set out to taste the air I paced beside him now running on ahead, now following at his heels and ever and anon looking up in his face. Thus some time passed during which I lived with him in all comfort; till one day of the days it so chanced that a woman came to the bakery to buy her bread and gave the owner several dirhams to its price, whereof one was bad coin whilst the others were good. My master tested all the silvers and, finding out the false bit, returned it demanding a true dirham in exchange; but the woman wrangled and would not take it back and swore that it was sound. Quoth the baker, "The dirham is beyond all doubt a worthless: see yonder dog of mine, he is but a beast, yet mark me he will tell thee whether it be true or false silver." So he called me by my name, "Bakht! Bakht!" whereat I sprang up and ran towards him and he, throwing all the moneys upon the ground before me, cried, "Here, look these dirhams over and if there be a false coin among them separate it from all the others." I inspected the silvers each by each and found the counterfeit: then, putting it on one side and all the others on another, I placed my paw upon the false silver and wagging what remained of my tail looked up at my master's face. The baker was delighted with my sagacity, and the woman also, marvelling with excessive marvel at what had happened, took back her bad dirham and paid another in exchange. But when the buyer fared forth, my master called together his neighbours and gossips and related to them this matter; so they threw down on the ground before me coins both good and bad, in order that they might test me and see with their own eyes an I were as clever as my master had said I was. Many times in succession I picked out the false coins from amongst the true and placed my paw upon them without once failing; so all went away astounded and related the case to each and every one they saw and thus the bruit of me spread abroad throughout the city. That live-long day I spent in testing dirhams fair and foul. —— And as the morn began to dawn Shahrazad held her peace till

The end of the Six Hundred and Fourteenth Night.

Then said she: —— I have heard, O auspicious King, that Sidi Nu'uman continued his story saying: — From that day forwards the baker honoured me yet more highly, and all his friends and familiars laughed and said, "Forsooth thou hast in this dog a mighty good Shroff."[1] And some envied my master his luck in having me within the shop, and tried ofttimes to entice me away, but the baker kept me with him nor would he ever allow me to leave his side; for the fame of me brought him a host of customers from every quarter of the town even the farthest. Not many days after there came another woman to buy loaves at our shop and paid the baker six dirhams whereof one was worthless. My master passed them over to me for test and trial, and straightway I picked out the false one, and placing paw thereon looked up in the woman's face. Hereat she waxed confused and confessed that it was miscoined and praised me for that I had found it out; then, going forth the same woman made signs to me that I should follow her unbeknown to the baker. Now I had not ceased praying Allah that somehow He would restore me to my human form and hoped that some good follower of the Almighty would take note of this my sorry condition and vouchsafe me succour. So as the woman turned several times and looked at me, I was persuaded in my mind that she had knowledge of my case; I therefore kept my eyes upon her; which seeing she came back ere she had stepped many paces, and beckoned me to accompany her. I understood her signal and sneaking out of the presence of the baker, who was busy heating his oven, followed in her wake. Pleased beyond all measure to see me obey her, she went straightway home with me, and entering she locked the door and led me into a room where sat a fair maid in embroidered dress whom I judged by her favour to be the good woman's daughter. The damsel was well skilled in arts magical; so the mother said to her, "O my daughter, here is a dog which telleth bad dirhams from good dirhams. When first I heard the marvel I bethought me that the beastie must be a man whom some base wretch and cruel-hearted had turned into a dog. Methought that to-day I would see this animal and test it when buying loaves at the booth of yonder baker and behold, it hath acquitted itself after the fairest of fashions and hath stood the test and trial. Look well, O my daughter, at this dog and see whether it be indeed an animal or a man transformed into a beast by gramarye." The

---

[1] In the text "Sarráf" = a money-changer. See vols. i. 210; iv. 270.

young lady, who had veiled her face,[1] hereupon considered me
attentively and presently cried, "O my mother, 'tis even as thou
sayest, and this I will prove to thee forthright."   Then rising
from her seat she took a basin of water and dipping hand therein
sprinkled some drops upon me saying, "An thou wert born a dog
then do thou abide a dog, but an thou wert born a man then,
by virtue of this water, resume thine human favour and figure."
Immediately I was transformed from the shape of a dog to human
semblance and I fell at the maiden's feet and kissed the ground
before her giving her thanks; then, bussing the hem of her garment, I cried, "O my lady, thou hast been exceeding gracious
unto one unbeknown to thee and a stranger.   How can I find
words wherewith to thank thee and bless thee as thou deservest?
Tell me now, I pray thee, how and whereby I may shew my
gratitude to thee?   From this day forth I am beholden to thy
kindness and am become thy slave."   Then I related all my
case and told her of Aminah's wickedness and what of wrongs
she had wrought me; and I made due acknowledgment to her
mother for that she had brought me to her home.   Herewith
quoth the damsel to me, "O Sidi Nu'uman, I pray thee bestow
not such exceeding thanks upon me, for rather am I glad and
grateful in conferring this service upon one so well-deserving as
thou art.   I have been familiar with thy wife Aminah for a long
time before thou didst marry her; I also knew that she had
skill in witchcraft and she likewise knoweth of my art, for we
twain learnt together of one and the same mistress in the
science. We met ofttimes at the Hammam as friends but, inasmuch as she was ill-mannered and ill-tempered, I declined
further intimacy with her.   Think not that it sufficeth me to have
made thee recover thy form as it was aforetime; nay, verily needs
must I take due vengeance of her for the wrong she hath done
thee.   And this will I do at thy hand, so shalt thou have mastery
over her and find thyself lord of thine own house and home.[2]
Tarry here awhile until I come again."   So saying the damsel
passed into another room and I remained sitting and talking with

---

[1] Galland has forgotten this necessary detail: see vol. i. 30 and elsewhere. In Lane's
story of the man metamorphosed to an ass, the old woman, "quickly covering her face, declared the fact."

[2] In the normal forms of this story, which Galland has told very badly, the maiden
would have married the man she saved.

her mother and praised her excellence and kindness towards me. The ancient dame also related strange and rare deeds of wonder done by her with pure purpose and lawful means, till the girl returned with an ewer in hand and said, "O Sidi Nu'uman, my magical art doth tell me that Aminah is at this present away from home but she will return thither presently. Meanwhile she dissembleth with the domestics and feigneth grief at severance from thee; and she hath pretended that, as thou sattest at meat with her, thou didst suddenly arise and fare forth on some weighty matter, when presently a dog rushed through the open door into the room and she drove it away with a staff." Then giving me a gugglet full of the water the maiden resumed, "O Sidi Nu'uman, go now to thine own house and, keeping this gugglet by thee, await patiently Aminah's coming. Anon she will return and seeing thee will be sore perplexed and will hasten to escape from thee; but before she go forth sprinkle some drops from this gugglet upon her and recite these spells which I shall teach thee. I need not tell thee more; thou wilt espy with thine own eyes what shall happen." Having said these words the young lady taught me magical phrases which I fixed in my memory full firmly, and after this I took my leave and farewelled them both. When I reached home it happened even as the young magician had told me; and I had tarried but a short time in the house when Aminah came in. I held the gugglet in hand and she seeing me trembled with sore trembling and would fain have run away; but I hastily sprinkled some drops upon her and repeated the magical words, whereat she was turned into a mare—the animal thy Highness deigned remark but yesterday. I marvelled greatly to sight this transformation and seizing the mare's mane led her to the stable and secured her with a halter.——And as the morn began to dawn Shahrazad held her peace till

The end of the Six Hundred and Fifteenth Night.

THEN said she:——I have heard, O auspicious King, that Sidi Nu'uman continued his story saying:—When I had secured the mare, I loaded her with reproaches for her wickedness and her base behaviour, and lashed her with a whip till my forearm was

tired.[1] Then I resolved within myself that I would ride her at full
speed round the square each day and thus inflict upon her the
justest penalty.—Herewith Sidi Nu'uman held his peace, having made an end of telling his tale; but presently he resumed,
"O Commander of the Faithful, I trow thou art not displeased at
this my conduct, nay rather thou wouldst punish such a woman
with a punishment still greater than this." He then kissed the
hem of the Caliph's robe and kept silence; and Harun al-Rashid,
perceiving that he had said all his say, exclaimed, "In very sooth
thy story is exceeding strange and rare. The wrong-doing of thy
wife hath no excuse and thy requital is methinks in due measure
and just degree, but I would ask thee one thing—How long wilt
thou chastise her thus, and how long will she remain in bestial
guise? 'Twere better now for thee to seek the young lady by
whose magical skill thy wife was transformed and beg that she
bring her back to human shape. And yet I fear me greatly lest
perchance whenas this sorceress, this Ghulah, shall find herself
restored to woman's form and resumeth her conjurations and
incantations she may—who knoweth?—requite thee with far
greater wrong than she hath done thee heretofore, and from this
thou wilt not be able to escape." After this the Prince of True
Believers forbore to urge the matter, albeit he was mild and
merciful by nature,[2] and addressing the third man whom the
Wazir had brought before him said, "As I was walking in such a
quarter I was astonished to see thy mansion, so great and so
grand is it; and when I made enquiry of the townsfolk they answered each and every, that the palace belongeth to one (thyself)
whom they called Khwájah Hasan. They added that thou wast
erewhile exceeding poor and in straitened case, but that Allah
Almighty had widened thy means and had now sent thee wealth
in such store that thou hast builded the finest of buildings;
moreover, that albeit thou hast so princely a domicile and such
abundance of riches, thou art not unmindful of thy former estate,
and thou dost not waste thy substance in riotous living but thou
addest thereto by lawful trade. The neighbourhood all speaketh
well of thee and not a wight of them hath aught to say against

---

[1] In other similar tales the injured one inflicts such penalty by the express command of
his preserver who takes strong measures to ensure obedience.
[2] In the more finished tales of the true "Nights" the mare would have been restored to
human shape after giving the best security for good conduct in time to come.

thee; so I now would know of thee the certainty of these things, and hear from thine own lips how thou didst gain this abundant wealth. I have summoned thee before me that I might be assured of all such matters by actual hearsay: so fear not to tell me all thy tale; I desire naught of thee save knowledge of this thy case. Enjoy thou to thy heart's content the opulence that Almighty Allah deigned bestow upon thee, and let thy soul have pleasure therein." Thus spake the Caliph and the gracious words reas- sured the man. Then Khwajah Hasan threw himself before the Commander of the Faithful and, kissing the carpet at the foot of the throne, exclaimed, "O Prince of True Believers, I will relate to thee a faithful relation of my adventure, and Almighty Allah be my witness that I have not done aught contrary to thy laws and just commandments, and that all this my wealth is by the favour and goodness of Allah alone." Harun al-Rashid hereupon again bade him speak out boldly and forthwith he began to recount in the following words the

History of Khwajah Hasan al-Habbal.[1]

O Lord of beneficence! obedient to thy royal behest, I will now inform thy Highness of the means and the measures whereby Destiny dowered me with such wealth; but first I would thou hear somewhat of two amongst my friends who abode in the House of Peace, Baghdad. They twain are yet alive and both well know the history which thy slave shall now relate. One of them, men call Sa'd, the other Sa'dí.[2] Now Sa'di opined that without riches no one in this world could be happy and independ- ent; moreover that without hard toil and trouble and wariness and wisdom withal it were impossible to become wealthy. But Sa'd differing therefrom would affirm that affluence cometh not to any save by decree of Destiny and fiat of Fate and Fortune. Sa'd was a poor man while Sa'di had great store of good; yet

---

[1] *i.e.* Master Hasan the Rope-maker. Galland writes, after European fashion, "Hassan," for which see vol. i. 251; and for "Khwájah" vol. vi. 146. "Al-Habbál" was the cognomen of a learned "Háfiz" (= traditionist and Koran reader), Abú Ishák Ibrahim, in Ibn Khall. ii. 262; for another see iv. 410.

[2] "Sa'd" = prosperity and "Sa'dí" = prosperous; the surname of the "Persian moralist," for whom see my friend F. F. Arbuthnot's pleasant booklet, "Persian Portraits" (London, Quaritch, 1887).

there sprang up a firm friendship between them and fond affection each for other; nor were they ever wont to differ upon any matter save only upon this; to wit, that Sa'di relied solely upon deliberation and forethought and Sa'd upon doom and man's lot. It chanced one day that, as they sat talking together on this matter, quoth Sa'di, "A poor man is he who either is born a pauper and passeth all his days in want and penury, or he who having been born to wealth and comfort, doth in the time of manhood squander all he hath and falleth into grievous need; then lacketh he the power to regain his riches and to live at ease by wit and industry." Sa'd made answer, saying, "Nor wit nor industry availeth aught to any one, but Fate alone enableth him to acquire and to preserve riches. Misery and want are but accidents and deliberation is naught. Full many a poor man hath waxed affluent by favour of Fate and richards manifold have, despite their skill and store, been reduced to misery and beggary." Quoth Sa'di, "Thou speakest foolishly. Howbeit put we the matter to fair test and find out for ourselves some handicraftsman scanty of means and living upon his daily wage; him let us provide with money, then will he without a doubt increase his stock and abide in ease and comfort, and so shalt thou be persuaded that my words be true." Now as they twain were walking on, they passed through the lane wherein stood my lodging and saw me a-twisting ropes, which craft my father and grandfather and many generations before me had followed. By the condition of my home and dress they judged that I was a needy man; whereupon Sa'd pointing me out to Sa'di said, "An thou wouldst make trial of this our matter of dispute, see yonder wight. He hath dwelt here for many years and by this trade of rope-making doth gain a bare subsistence for himself and his. I know his case right well of old; he is a worthy subject for the trial; so do thou give him some gold pieces and test the matter." "Right willingly," replied Sa'di, "but first let us take full cognizance of him." So the two friends came up to me, whereat I left my work and saluted them. They returned my salam after which quoth Sa'di, "Prithee what be thy name?" Quoth I, "My name is Hasan, but by reason of my trade of rope-making all men call me Hasan al-Habbál."——And as the morn began to dawn Shahrazad held her peace till

The end of the Six Hundred and Sixteenth Night.

THEN said she:——I have heard, O auspicious King, that Hasan al-Habbal (the Rope-maker) continued his story, saying:——Thereupon Sa'di asked me, "How farest thou by this industry? Methinks thou art blithe and quite content therewith. Thou hast worked long and well and doubtless thou hast laid by large store of hemp and other stock. Thy forbears carried on this craft for many years and must have left thee much of capital and property which thou hast turned to good account and on this wise thou hast largely increased thy wealth." Quoth I, "O my lord, no money have I in pouch whereby I may live happy or even buy me enough to eat. This is my case that every day, from dawn till eve, I spend in making ropes, nor have I one single moment wherein to take rest; and still I am sore straitened to provide even dry bread for myself and family. A wife have I and five small children, who are yet too young to help me ply this business: and 'tis no easy matter to supply their daily wants; how then canst thou suppose that I am enabled to put by large store of hemp and stock? What ropes I twist each day I sell straightway, and of the money earned thereby I spend part upon our needs and with the rest I buy hemp wherewith I twist ropes on the next day. However, praise be to Almighty Allah that, despite this my state of penury, He provideth us with bread sufficing our necessity." When I had made known all my condition Sa'di replied, "O Hasan, now I am certified of thy case and indeed 'tis other than I had supposed; and, given that I gave thee a purse of two hundred Ashrafis, assuredly thou shalt therewith greatly add to thy gains and be enabled to live in ease and affluence: what sayest thou thereto?" Said I, "An thou favour me with such bounty I should hope to grow richer than all and every of my fellow-craftsmen, albeit Baghdad-town is prosperous as it is populous." Then Sa'di, deeming me true and trustworthy, pulled out of his pocket a purse of two hundred gold pieces and handing them to me said, "Take these coins and trade therewith. May Allah advance thee, but see to it that thou use this money with all heed, and waste it not in folly and ungraciousness. I and my friend Sa'd will rejoice with all joy to hear of thy well-being; and, if hereafter we come again and find thee in flourishing condition, 'twill be matter of much satisfaction to us both." Accordingly, O Commander of the Faithful, I took the purse of gold with much gladness and a grateful heart and, placing it in my pocket, thanked Sa'di kissing his garment-hem, whereupon the two friends fared forth. And I, O Prince of True Believers, seeing the twain depart, went on working, but was sore puzzled and perplexed as to where I might bestow the purse; for my house contained neither cupboard nor locker. Howbeit I took it home and kept the matter hidden from my wife and children and when alone and unobserved I drew out ten gold coins by way of spending-money; then, binding the purse-mouth with a bit of string I tied it tightly in the folds of my turband and wound the cloth around my head. Presently, I went off to the market-street and bought me a stock of hemp and coming homewards I laid in some meat for supper, it being now a long while since we had tasted flesh. But as I trudged along the road, meat in hand, a kite[1] came suddenly swooping down, and would have snatched the morsel from out my hand had I not driven off the bird with the other hand. Then it had fain pounced upon the flesh on the left side but again I scared it away and thus, whilst exerting myself with frantic efforts to ward off the bird, by ill luck my turband fell to the ground. At once that accursed kite swooped down and flew off with it in its talons; and I ran pursuing it and shouted aloud. Hearing my cries the Bazar-folk, men and women and a rout of children, did what they could to scare it away and make the beastly bird drop its prey, but they shouted and cast stones in vain: the kite would not let drop the turband and presently flew clean out of sight. I was sore distressed and heavy-hearted to lose the Ashrafis as I hied me home bearing the hemp and what of food I had bought, but chiefly was I vexed and grieved in mind, and ready to die of shame at the thought of what Sa'di would say; especially when I reflected how he would misdoubt my words, nor deem the tale true when I should tell him that a kite had carried off my turband with the gold pieces, but rather would he think that I had practised some deceit and had devised some amusing fable by way of excuse. Howbeit I hugely enjoyed what had remained of the ten Ashrafis and with my wife and children fared sumptuously for some days. Presently, when all the gold was spent and naught remained thereof, I became as poor and needy as before; withal I was content and thankful to Almighty Allah nor blamed my lot.

---

[1] This is true to nature as may be seen any day at Bombay. The crows are equally audacious, and are dangerous to men lying wounded in solitary places.

He had sent in his mercy this purse of gold to me unawares and now He had taken it away, wherefore I was grateful and satisfied, for what He doeth is ever well done.——And as the morn began to dawn Shahrazad held her peace till

The end of the Six Hundred and Seventeenth Night.

Then said she:——I have heard, O auspicious King, that Master Hasan the Ropemaker continued his story in these words:—My wife, who knew not of the matter of the Ashrafis, presently perceived that I was ill at ease and I was compelled for a quiet life to let her know my secret; moreover the neighbours came round to ask me of my case: but I was right loath to tell them all that had betided; they could not bring back what was gone and they would assuredly rejoice at my calamity. However, when they pressed me close I told them every whit; and some thought that I had spoken falsely and derided me and others that I was daft and hare-brained and my words were the wild pratings of an idiot or the drivel of dreams. The youngsters made abundant fun of me and laughed to think that I, who never in my born days had sighted a golden coin, should tell how I had gotten so many Ashrafis, and how a kite had flown away with them. My wife, however, gave full credence to my tale and wept and beat her breast for sorrow. Thus six months passed over us, when it chanced one day that the two friends, to wit, Sa'di and Sa'd, came to my quarter of the town, when quoth Sa'd to Sa'di, "Lo, yonder is the street where dwelleth Hasan al-Habbal. Come let us go and see how he hath added to his stock and how far he hath prospered by means of the two hundred Ashrafis thou gavest him." Sa'di rejoined, " 'Tis well said; indeed, we have not seen him for many days: I would fain visit him and I should rejoice to hear that he hath prospered." So the twain walked along towards my house, Sa'd saying to Sa'di, "Forsooth I perceive that he appeareth the same in semblance, poor and ill-conditioned as before; he weareth old and tattered garments, save that his turband seemeth somewhat newer and cleaner. Look well and judge thyself and 'tis even as I said." Thereupon Sa'di came up closer to me and he also understood that my condition was unaltered; and presently the two friends addressed me. After the usual salutation Sa'd asked, "O Hasan, how fareth it with thee, and how goeth it with thy business and have the two hundred Ashrafis

stood thee in good stead and amended thy trade?" To this answered I, "O my lords, how can I tell you of the sad mishap that
hath befallen me? I dare not speak for very shame, yet cannot I
keep the adventure concealed. Verily a marvellous matter and
a wondrous hath happened to me, the tale whereof will fill you
with wonderment and suspicion, for I wot full well that ye will
not believe it, and that I shall be to you as one that dealeth in
lies; withal needs must I tell you the whole however unwillingly." Hereat I recounted to them every whit that had betided
me first and last, especially that which had befallen me from the
kite; but Sa'di misdoubted me and mistrusted me and cried, "O
Hasan, thou speakest but in jest and dost dissemble with us.
'Tis hard to believe the tale thou tellest. Kites are not wont to
fly off with turbands, but only with such things as they can eat.
Thou wouldst but outwit us and thou art of those who, when
some good fortune cometh to them unforeseen, do straightways
abandon their work or their business and, wasting all in pleasuring, become once more poor and thereafter must nilly-willy eke out
a living as best they may. This methinks be especially the case
with thee; thou hast squandered our gift with all speed and now
art needy as before." "O good my lord, not so," cried I; "this
blame and these hard words ill befit my deserts, for I am wholly
innocent of all thou imputest to me. The strange mishap whereof
I told thee is the truest of truths; and to prove that it is no lie all
the town-folk have knowledge thereof and in good sooth I do not
play thee false. 'Tis certain that kites do not fly away with
turbands; but such mishaps, wondrous and marvellous, may betide mankind especially the miserable of lot." Sa'd also espoused
my cause and said, "O Sa'di, ofttimes have we seen and heard how
kites carry off many things besides comestibles; and his tale may
not be wholly contrary to reason." Then Sa'di pulled out from
his pocket a purseful of gold pieces and counted out and gave me
another two hundred, saying, "O Hasan, take these Ashrafis,
but see that thou keep them with all heed and diligence and beware, and again I say beware, lest thou lose them like the others.
Expend them in such fashion that thou mayst reap full benefit
therefrom and prosper even as thou seest thy neighbours prosper."
I took the money from him and poured out thanks and blessings
upon his head, and when they went their ways I returned to my
rope-walk and thence in due time straight home. My wife and
children were abroad, so again I took ten gold coins of the two

hundred and securely tied up the remainder in a piece of cloth; then I looked around to find a spot wherein to hide my hoard so that my wife and youngsters might not come to know of it and lay hands thereon. Presently, I espied a large earthen jar full of bran standing in a corner of the room, so herein I hid the rag with the gold coins and I misdeemed that it was safely con-cealed from wife and wees.————And as the morn began to dawn Shahrazad held her peace till

The end of the Six Hundred and Eighteenth Night.

Then said she:————I have heard, O auspicious King, that Hasan al-Habbal thus continued his story:—When I had put the Ashrafis a-bottom the jar of bran, my wife came in and I said naught to her of the two friends or of aught had happened, but I set out for the Bazar to buy hemp. Now as soon as I had left the house there came, by evil fate impelled, a man who sold Tafl, or fuller's earth,[1] wherewith the poorer sort of women are wont to wash their hair. My wife would fain have bought some but not a single Kauri[2] or almond had she. Then she took thought and said to herself, "This jar of bran is here to no purpose, I will ex-change it for the clay," and he also, the Tafl-seller, agreed to this proposal and went off taking the jar of bran as the price of the washing-earth. Anon I came back with a load of hemp upon my head and other five on the heads of as many porters who accom-panied me; and I helped them off with their burthens and, after storing the stuff in a room, I paid and dismissed them. Then I stretched me out upon the floor to take rest awhile and looking towards the corner where once stood the jar of bran I found it gone. Words fail me, O Prince of True Believers, to describe the tumult of feelings which filled my heart at the sight. I sprang up with all speed and calling to my wife enquired of her whither the jar had been carried; and she replied that she had exchanged its contents for a trifle of washing-clay. Then cried I aloud, "O wretched, O miserable, what hast thou done? thou hast ruined

---

[1] The Pers. "Gil-i-sar-shúí" (= head-washing clay), the Sindi "Met," and the Arab. "Tafl," a kind of clay much used in Persian, Afghanistan, Sind, etc. Galland turns it into *terre à decrasser* and his English translators into "scouring sand which women use in baths." This argillaceous earth mixed with mustard oil is locally used for clay and when rose-leaves and perfumes are used, it makes a tolerable wash-ball. See "Scinde or The Unhappy Valley," i. 31.

[2] For the "Cowrie" (*Cyprœa moneta*) see vol. iv. 77. The Bádám or Bídám (almond) used by way of small change in India, I have noted elsewhere.

me and thy children; thou hast given away great wealth to that clay-selling fellow!" Then I told her all that had betided me, of the coming of the two friends and how I had hidden the hundred and ninety Ashrafis within the bran-jar; and she, on hearing this wept sore and beat her breast and tore her hair crying, "Where now shall I find that clay-seller? The wight is a stranger, never before did I see him about this quarter or this street." Then turning to me she continued, "Herein thou hast dealt right foolishly, for that thou didst not tell me of the matter, nor didst place any trust in me; otherwise this mishap would never have happened to us; no, never." And she lamented with loud lamentation and bitter whereat I said, "Make not such hubbub nor display such trouble, lest our neighbours overhear thee, and learning of our mishap peradventure laugh at us and call us fools. It behoveth us to rest content with the will of Almighty Allah." However the ten Ashrafis which I had taken from the two hundred sufficed me to carry on my trade and to live with more of ease for some short while; but I ever grieved and I marvelled much anent what could be said to Sa'di when he should come again; for inasmuch as he believed me not the first time I was assured in my mind that now he would denounce me aloud as a cheat and a liar. One day of the days the twain, to wit, Sa'd and Sa'di, came strolling towards my house conversing and, as usual, arguing about me and my case; and I seeing them from afar left off working that I might hide myself, as I could not for very shame come forth and accost them. Seeing this and not guessing the reason they entered my dwelling and, saluting me with the salam, asked me how I had fared. I durst not raise my eyes so abashed and mortified was I, and with bended brow returned the greeting; when they, noting my sorry plight, marvelled saying, "Is all well with thee? Why art thou in this state? Hast thou not made good use of the gold or hast thou wasted thy wealth in lewd living?" Quoth I, "O my lords, the story of the Ashrafis is none other than this. When ye departed from me I went home with the purse of money and, finding no one was in the house for all had gone out somewhere, I took out therefrom ten gold pieces. Then I put the rest together with the purse within a large earthen jar filled full of bran which had long stood in one corner of the room, so might the matter be kept privy from my wife and children. But whilst I was in the market buying me some hemp, my wife returned home; and at that moment there came in to her

a man which sold fuller's earth for washing hair. She had need
thereof withal naught to pay with; so she went out to him and
said, 'I am clean without coin, but I have a quantity of bran; say
me, wilt thou have that in change for thy clay?' The man agreed
and accordingly my wife took the earth of him, and gave him in
exchange the jarful of bran which he carried away with him and
ganged his gait. An ye ask, 'Wherefore didst thou not confide
the matter to thy spouse and tell her that thou hadst put the
money in the jar?' I on my side answer, that ye gave me strict
injunctions to keep the money this time with the utmost heed
and caution. Methought that stead was the safest wherein to
store the gold and I was loath to trust my wife lest haply she
take some coin therefrom and expend it upon her household. O
my lords, I am certified of your goodness and graciousness, but
poverty and penury are writ in my Book of Fate; how then can
I aspire to possessions and prosperity? Withal, never while
I breathe the breath of life, shall I be forgetful of this your generous favour." Quoth Sa'di, "Meseemeth I have disbursed four
hundred Ashrafis to no purpose in giving them to thee; yet the
intent wherewith they were given was that thou shouldst
benefit thereby, not that I claim thy praise and thanksgiving."
So they twain compassionated and condoled with me in my misfortune; and presently Sa'd, an upright man and one who had
acquaintance with me since many a year, produced a leaden coin[1]
which he had picked up from the path and was still carrying in
his pocket; and, after shewing it to Sa'di, said to me, "Seest thou
this bit of lead? Take it and by favour of Fate thou shalt find out
what blessings it will bring to thee." Sa'di on espying it laughed
aloud and made jest of the matter and flouting said, "What advantage will there be to Hasan from this mite of lead and in what
way shall he use it?" Sa'd handing me the leaden coin retorted
in reply, "Give no heed to whatso Sa'di may say, but keep this by
thee. Let him laugh an he please. One day haply shall come to
pass, Inshallah—an it be the will of Almighty Allah—that thou
shalt by means thereof become a wealthy man and a magnifico."
I took the bit of lead and put it in my pocket, and the twain bade
me farewell and went their way.——And as the morn began to
dawn Shahrazad held her peace till

---

1 Galland has *"un morceau de plomb,"* which in the Hindí text becomes "Shíshahká-
paysá" = a (pice) small coin of glass: the translator also terms it a "Faddah," for which

The end of the Six Hundred and Nineteenth Night.

Then said she——I have heard, O auspicious King, that Hasan al-Habbal thus continued his story:—As soon as Sa'd and Sa'di had departed, I went on rope-twisting until night came and when doffing my dress to go to bed the bit of lead which Sa'd had given me fell out of my pocket; so I picked it up and set it carelessly in a small niche in the wall.[1] Now that very night so it happened that a fisherman, one of my neighbours, stood in need of a small coin[2] wherewith to buy some twine for mending his drag-net, as he was wont to do during the dark hours, in order that he might catch the fish ere dawn of day and selling his quarry, buy victuals for himself and his household. So, as he was accustomed to rise while yet somewhat of night remained, he bade his wife go round about to all the neighbours and borrow a copper that he might buy the twine required; and the woman went everywhere, from house to house, but nowhere could she get loan of a farthing, and at last she came home weary and disappointed. Quoth the fisherman to her, "Hast thou been to Hasan al-Habbal?" and quoth she, "Nay, I have not tried at his place. It is the furthest of all the neighbours' houses and fanciest thou, even had I gone there, I could thence have brought back aught?" "Off with thee, O laziest of hussies and good-for-nothing of baggages," cried the fisherman, "away with thee this instant; perchance he hath a copper to lend us." Accordingly the woman, grumbling and muttering, fared forth and coming to my dwelling knocked at the door, saying, "O Hasan al-Habbal, my husband is in sore need of a pice wherewith to buy some twine for mending his nets." Minding me of the coin which Sa'd had given me and where it had been put away, I shouted out to her, "Have patience, my spouse will go forth to thee and give thee what thou needest." My wife, hearing all this hubbub, woke from sleep, and I told her where to find the bit of money, whereupon she fetched it and gave it to the woman, who joyed with exceeding joy, and said, "Thou and thy husband have shown great kindness to my man, wherefore I promise thee that whatsoever fish he may chance to

see Nusf (alias "Nuss"), vols. ii. 37; vi. 214 and ix. 139, 167. Glass tokens, by way of coins, were until late years made at Hebron, in Southern Syria.

[1] For the "Ták" or "Tákah" = the little wall-niche, see vol. vii. 361.

[2] In the French and English versions the coin is a bit of lead for weighting the net. For the "Paysá" (pice) = two farthings, and in weight = half an ounce, see Herklot's Glossary, p. xcviii.

catch at the first throw of the net shall be thine; and I am assured that my goodman, when he shall hear of this my promise, will consent thereto." Accordingly when the woman took the money to her husband and told him of what pledge she had given, he was right willing, and said to her, "Thou hast done well and wisely in that thou madest this covenant." Then having bought some twine and mended all the nets he rose before dawn and hastened riverwards to catch fish according to his custom. But when he cast the net into the stream for the first throw and haled it in, he found that it contained but one fish and that a full span[1] or so in thickness, which he placed apart as my portion. Then he threw the net again and again and at each cast he caught many fishes both small and great, but none reached in size that he first had netted. As soon as he returned home the fisherman came at once to me and brought the fish he had netted in my name, and said, "O our neighbour, my wife promised over night that thou shouldst have whatever fishes should come to ground at the first net-throw; and this fish is the only one I caught. Here it is, prithee take it as a thanks-offering for the kindness of last night, and as fulfilment of the promise. If Allah Almighty had vouch-safed to me of fish a seine-full, all had been thine but 'tis thy fate that only this one was landed at the first cast." Said I, "The mite I gave thee yesternight was not of such value that I should look for somewhat in return;" and refused to accept it. But after much "say and said" he would not take back the fish, and he insisted that it was mine: wherefore I agreed to keep it and gave it to my wife, saying, "O woman, this fish is a return for the mite I gave last night to the fisherman our neighbour. Sa'd hath declared that by means of that coin I shall attain to much riches and abundant opulence." Then I recounted to my wife how my two friends had visited me and what they said and did, and all concerning the leaden coin which Sa'd had given to me. She wondered at seeing but a single fish and said, "How shall I cook it? Meseemeth 'twere best to cut it up and broil it for the children, especially as we have naught of spices and condiments wherewith to dress it otherwise." Then, as she sliced and cleansed the fish she found within its belly a large diamond which she supposed to be a bit of glass or crystal; for she oft had heard

---

[1] In the text "bilisht" = the long span between thumb-tip and minimus-tip. Galland says *long plus d'une coudée et gros à proportion.*

tell of diamonds[1] but never with her own eyes had she beheld one. So she gave it to the youngest of the children for a plaything and when the others saw it, by reason of its brightness and brilliancy all desired to have it and each kept it in turn awhile; moreover when night came and the lamp was lighted they crowded round the stone and gazed upon its beauty, and screamed and shouted with delight.[2] When my wife had spread the table we sat down to supper and the eldest boy set the diamond upon the tray, and as soon as we all had finished eating, the children fought and scrambled as before for it. At first I paid no heed to their noise and hubbub, but when it waxed exceeding loud and irksome I asked my eldest lad the cause why they quarrelled and made such turmoil. Quoth he, "The trouble and dispute are about a piece of glass which giveth forth a light as bright as the lamp." Whereat I told him to produce it and marvelled greatly to see its sparkling water, and enquired of my wife whence she had gotten the piece of crystal. Quoth she, "This I found within the belly of the fish as I was gutting it." Still I did not suppose it to be aught but glass. Presently I bade my wife hide the lamp behind the hearth.——And as the morn began to dawn Shahrazad held her peace till

The end of the Six Hundred and Twentieth Night.

THEN said she: I have heard, O auspicious King, that Hasan al-Habbal thus continued his story:—And when my wife had hidden the lamp from view, such was the brightness of the diamond that we could see right well without other light; where-

---

[1] For the diamond (Arab. "Almás" from ἀδάμας, and in Hind. "Hírá" and "Panná") see vols. vi. 15, i. ix. 325; and in latter correct, "Euritic," a misprint for "dioritic." I still cannot believe diamond-cutting to be an Indian art, and I must hold that it was known to the ancients. It could not have been an unpolished stone, that "Adamas notissimus" which according to Juvenal (vi. 156) Agrippa gave to his sister. Maundeville (A.D. 1322) has a long account of the mineral, "so hard that no man can polish it," and called Hamese ("Almás?"). For Mr. Petrie and his theory, see vol. ix. 325. In most places where the diamond has been discovered of late years it had been used as a magic stone, e.g., by the Pagés or medicine-men of the Brazil, or for children's playthings, which was the case with the South-African "Caffres."

[2] These stones, especially the carbuncle, which give out light in darkness are a commonplace of Eastern folk-lore. For luminous jewels in folk-lore, see Mr. Clouston (i. 412): the belief is not wholly extinct in England, and I have often heard of it in the Brazil and upon the African Gaboon. It appears to me that there may be a basis of fact to this fancy, the abnormal effect of precious stones upon mesmeric "sensitives."

fore I placed it upon the hearth[1] that we might work by it, and said within myself, "The coin that Sa'd left with me hath produced this benefit that we no longer stand in need of a lamp: at least it saveth us oil." When the youngsters saw me put out the lamp and use the glass in its stead they jumped and danced for joy, and screamed and shouted with glee so that all the neighbours round about could hear them when I chid them and sent them to bed; we also went to rest and right soon fell asleep. Next day I woke betimes and went on with my work and thought not of the piece of glass. Now there dwelt hard by us a wealthy Jew, a jeweller who bought and sold all kinds of precious stones; and, as he and his wife essayed to sleep that night, by reason of the noise and clamour of the children they were disturbed for many hours and slumber visited not their eyes. And when morn appeared, the jeweller's wife came to our house to make complaint both for herself and her husband anent the hubbub and shouting. Ere she could say a word of blame my wife, guessing the intent wherewith she came, addressed her saying, "O Rahíl,[2] I fear me that my children pestered thee last night with their laughing and crying. I crave thine indulgence in this matter; well thou must wot how children now cry now laugh at trifles. Come in and see the cause of all their excitement wherefor thou wouldst justly call me to account." She did accordingly and saw the bit of glass about which the youngsters had made such din and uproar; and when she, who had long experience of all manner precious stones, beheld the diamond she was filled with wonderment. My wife then told her how she had found it in the fish's belly, whereupon quoth the Jewess, "This bit of glass is more excellent than all other sorts of glass. I too have such an one as this which I am wont to wear sometimes; and wouldst thou sell it I will buy this thing of thee." Hearing her words the children began to cry and said, "O mother dear, an thou wilt not sell it we promise henceforth to make no noise." Understanding that they would by no means part with it, the women held their peace and presently the Jewess fared forth, but ere she took her leave she whispered my wife, "See that thou tell the matter to none; and, if thou have a mind to sell it at once

---

[1] The chimney and chimney-piece of Galland are not Eastern: the H. V. uses "Bukhárí" = a place for steaming.

[2] *i.e.* "Rachel."

send me word." Now the Jew was sitting in his shop when his
wife went to him and told him of the bit of glass. Quoth he,
"Go straightway back and offer a price for it, saying that 'tis for
me. Begin with some small bidding, then raise the sum until thou
get it." The Jewess thereupon returned to my house and offered
twenty Ashrafis, which my wife deemed a large sum to give for
such a trifle; however, she would not close the bargain. At that
moment I happened to leave my work and, coming home to our
noon-meal, saw the two women talking on the threshold; and
my wife stopped me, saying, "This neighbour biddeth twenty
Ashrafis to price for the piece of glass, but I have as yet given her
no reply. What sayest thou?" Then I bethought me of what
Sa'd had told me; to wit, that much wealth would come to me by
virtue of his leaden coin. The Jewess seeing how I hesitated
bethought her that I would not consent to the price; so quoth
she, "O neighbour, an thou wilt not agree to part with the bit of
glass for twenty pieces of gold, I will e'en give thee fifty." Hereat
I reflected that whereas the Jewess raised her offer so readily from
twenty golden pieces to fifty, this glass must surely be of great
value; so I kept silence and answered her not a word. Then
noting that I still held my peace she cried, "Take then one hundred: this be its full value; nay I know not in very deed if my
husband will consent to so high a price." Said I in reply, "O
my good woman, why talk so foolishly? I will not sell it for aught
less than an hundred thousand[1] gold coins; and thou mayest take
it at that price but only because thou art neighbour to us." The
Jewess raised her offer coin by coin to fifty thousand Ashrafis and
said, "I pray thee wait till morning and sell it not till then, so
that my man may come round and see it." "Right willingly,"
quoth I; "by all manner of means let thy husband drop in and
inspect it."——And as the morn began to dawn Shahrazad held
her peace till

The end of the Six Hundred and Twenty-first Night.

THEN said she:——I have heard, O auspicious King, that Hasan
al-Habbal thus continued his story.——Next day the Jew came
to my house and I drew forth and showed to him the diamond
which shone and glittered in my palm with light as bright as any

---

[1] In the text "lakh," the Anglicised "lac" = 100,000.

lamp's. Presently, assured that all which his wife had told him of its water and lustre was strictly true, he took it in hand and, examining it and turning it about, marvelled with mighty marvel at its beauty saying, "My wife made offer of fifty thousand gold pieces: see now I will give thee yet another twenty thousand." Said I, "Thy wife hath surely named to thee what sum I fixed; to wit, one hundred thousand Ashrafis and naught less: I shall not abate one jot or tittle of this price." The Jew did all he could to buy it for a lesser sum; but I answered only, "It mattereth naught; an thou desire not to come to my terms I must needs sell it to some other jeweller." At length he consented and weighed me out two thousand gold pieces by way of earnest-money, saying, "To-morrow I will bring the amount of my offer and carry off my diamond." To this I gave assent and so, on the day following, he came to me and weighed out the full sum of one hundred thousand Ashrafis, which he had raised amongst his friends and partners in business. Then I gave him the diamond which had brought me such exceeding wealth, and offered thanks to him and praises unto Almighty Allah for this great good Fortune gotten unawares, and much I hoped soon to see my two friends, Sa'd and Sa'di, and to thank them likewise. So first I set my house in order and gave spending-money to my wife for home-necessaries and for clothing herself and children; moreover, I also bought me a fine mansion and furnished it with the best. Then said I to my wife, who thought of nothing save rich clothes and high diet and a life of ease and enjoyment, "It behoveth us not to give up this our craft: we must needs put by some coin and carry on the business." Accordingly, I went to all the rope-makers of the city and buying with much money several manufactories put them to work, and over each establishment I set an overseer, an intelligent man and a trustworthy, so that there is not now throughout Baghdad-city a single ward or quarter that hath not walks and workshops of mine for rope-making. Nay, further, I have in each town and every district of Al-Irak warehouses, all under charge of honest supervisors; and thus it is that I have amassed such a muchel of wealth. Lastly, for my own especial place of business I bought another house, a ruined place with a sufficiency of land adjoining; and, pulling down the old shell, I edified in lieu thereof the new and spacious edifice which thy Highness hath deigned yesterday to look upon. Here all my workmen are lodged and here also are kept my office-books

and accounts; and besides my warehouse it containeth apartments fitted with furniture in simple style all-sufficient for myself
and my family. After some time I quitted my old home, wherein
Sa'd and Sa'di had seen me working, and went and lived in the
new mansion and not long after this removal my two friends and
benefactors bethought them that they would come and visit me.
They marvelled much when, entering my old workshop, they
found me not, and they asked the neighbours, "Where dwelleth
such and such a rope-maker? Is he alive or dead?" Quoth the folk
"He now is a rich merchant; and men no longer call him simply
'Hasan,' but entitle him 'Master Hasan the Rope-maker.' He
hath built him a splendid building and he dwelleth in such and
such a quarter." Whereupon the two familiars set forth in
search of me; and they rejoiced at the good report; albeit Sa'di
would by no means be convinced that all my wealth had sprung
(as Sa'd contended) from its root, that small leaden coin. Presently, conning the matter over in his mind he said to his comrade,
"It delighteth me much to hear of all this good fortune which
hath betided Hasan, despite that he twice deceived me and took
from me four hundred gold pieces, whereby he hath gotten to
himself these riches; for it is absurd to think that it hath come
from the leaden coin thou gavest him. Withal I do forgive him
and owe him no grudge." Replied the other, "Thou art mistaken.
I know Hasan of old to be a good man and true: he would not
delude thee and what he told us is simple sooth I am persuaded
in my mind that he hath won all his wealth and opulence by the
leaden coin: however we shall hear anon what he may have to
say." Conversing thus they came into the street wherein I now
dwell and, seeing a large and magnificent mansion and a new-
made, they guessed it was mine. So they knocked and, on the
porter opening, Sa'di marvelled to see such grandeur and so
many folk sitting within, and feared lest haply they had unwittingly entered the house of some Emir. Then plucking courage
he enquired of the porter, "Is this the dwelling place of Khwajah
Hasan al-Habbal?"——And as the morn began to dawn Shahrazad held her peace till

The end of the Six Hundred and Twenty-second Night.

Then said she: ——I have heard, O auspicious King, that Hasan
al-Habbal continued thus his story:—The porter made reply,

"This is verily the house of Khwajah Hasan al-Habbal; he is within and he sitteth in his office. I pray thee enter and one of the slaves will make known thy coming to him." Hereupon the two friends walked in, and as soon as I saw them I recognised them, and rising up to them I ran and kissed the hems of their garments. They would fain have fallen on my neck and embraced me, but with meekness of mind I would not suffer them so to do; and presently I led them into a large and spacious saloon, and bade them sit upon the highmost seats of honour. They would have constrained me to take the best place, but I exclaimed "O my lords, I am on no wise better than the poor rope-maker Hasan, who not unmindful of your worth and goodness ever prayeth for your welfare, and who deserveth not to sit in higher stead than you." Then they took seat and I opposite them, when quoth Sa'di, "My heart rejoiceth with exceeding joy to see thee in this condition, for that Allah hath given thee all even as thou wishedst. I doubt not thou has gotten all this abundance and opulence by means of the four hundred gold pieces which I gave to thee; but say me truly wherefore didst thou twice deceive me and bespeak me falsely?" Sa'd listened to these words with silent indignation, and ere I could make reply he broke out saying, "O Sa'di, how often have I assured thee that all which Hasan said aforetime anent the losing of the Ashrafis is very sooth and no leasing?" Then they began to dispute each with other; when I, recovering from my surprise, exclaimed, "O my lords, of what avail is this contention? Be not at variance, I beseech you, on my account. All that had befallen me I made known to you; and, whether ye believe my words or ye believe them not, it mattereth but little. Now hearken to the whole truth of my tale." Then I made known to them the story of the piece of lead which I had given to the fisherman and of the diamond found in the fish's belly; brief, I told them every whit even as I have now related to thy Highness. On hearing all my adventure Sa'di said, "O Khwajah Hasan, it seemeth to me passing strange that so great a diamond should be found in the belly of a fish; and I deem it a thing impossible that a kite should fly off with thy turband, or that thy wife should give away the jar of bran in exchange for fuller's earth. Thou sayest the tale is true, still can I not give credit to thy words, for I know full well that the four hundred gold pieces have gotten thee all this wealth." But when they twain rose up to take their leave, I also arose and said, "O my lords, ye have shown favour to me in that ye have thus deigned visit me in my poor home. I beseech you now to taste of my food and to tarry here this night under your servant's roof; as to-morrow I would fain take you by the way of the river to a country-house which I have lately bought." Hereto they consented with some objections; and I, after giving orders for the evening-meal, showed them about the house and displayed the furniture and entertained them with pleasing words and pleasant converse, till a slave came and announced that supper was served. So I led them to the saloon wherein were ranged the trays loaded with many kinds of meats; on all sides stood camphorated wax candles,[1] and before the table were gathered musicians singing and playing on various instruments of mirth and merriment, whilst in the upper part of the saloon men and women were dancing and making much diversion. When we had supped we went to bed, and rising early we prayed the dawn-prayer, and presently embarked on a large and well-appointed boat, and the rowers rowing with a flowing tide soon landed us at my country seat. Then we strolled in a body about the grounds and entered the house, when I showed them our new buildings and displayed to them all that appertained thereto; and hereat they marvelled with great marvel. Thence we repaired to the garden and saw, planted in rows along the walks, fruit-trees of all kinds with ripe fruit bowed down, and watered with water from the river by means of brick-work channels. All round were flowering shrubs whose perfume gladdened the Zephyr; here and there fountains and jets of water shot high in air; and sweet-voiced birds made melody amid the leafy branches hymning the One, the Eternal; in short, the sights and scents on every side filled the soul with joy and gladness. My two friends walked about in joyance and delight, and thanked me again and again for bringing them to so lovely a site and said, "Almighty Allah prosper thee in house and garth." At last I led them to the foot of a tall tree near to one of the garden walls and shewed them a little summer-house wherein I was wont to take rest and refreshment; and the room was furnished with cushions and divans and pillows purfled with virgin gold.——And as the morn began to dawn Shahrazad held her peace till

---

[1] This use of camphor is noted by Gibbon (D. and F. iii. 195).

The end of the Six Hundred and Twenty=third Night.

THEN said she:———I have heard, O auspicious King, that Hasan
al-Habbal thus pursued his tale:———Now so it happened that, as
we sat at rest within that summer-house, two sons of mine,
whom I had sent together with their governor to my country-
place for change of water and air,[1] were roaming about the
garden seeking birds' nests. Presently they came across a big one
upon the top-most boughs and tried to swarm up the trunk and
carry it off, but by reason of their lack of strength and little
practice they durst not venture so high; whereupon they bade a
slave-boy who ever attended on them, climb the tree. He did
their bidding, but when looking into the nest he was amazed
with exceeding amazement to see it mainly made of an old turband. So he brought down the stuff and handed it to the lads.
My eldest son took it from his hands and carried it to the arbour
for me to see, and set it at my feet saying in high glee, "O my
father, look here; this nest is made of cloth." Sa'd and Sa'di
wondered with all wonderment at the sight and the marvel grew
the greater when I, after considering it closely, recognised it for
the very turband whereon the kite had swooped and which had
been borne off by the bird. Then quoth I to my two friends,
"Examine well this turband and certify yourselves that it is the
selfsame one worn upon my head when first ye honoured me
with your presence." Quoth Sa'd, "I know it not," and quoth
Sa'di, "An thou find within it the hundred and ninety gold
pieces, then shalt thou be assured that is thy turband in very
sooth." I said, "O my lord, this is, well I wot, that very turband." And as I held it in my hand, I found it heavy of weight,
and opening out the folds felt somewhat tied up in one of the
corners of the cloth;[2] so I unrolled the swathes when lo and
behold! I came upon the purse of gold pieces. Hereat, shewing
it to Sa'di, I cried, "Canst thou not recognise this purse?" and he
replied, " 'Tis in truth the very purse of Ashrafis which I gave
thee when first we met." Then I opened the mouth and, pouring
out the gold in one heap upon the carpet, bade him count his

---

1 "Áb o hawá" = climate: see vol. ii. 4.
2 Galland makes this article a linen cloth wrapped about the skull-cap or core of the
turban.

money; and he turned it over coin by coin and made the sum thereof one hundred and ninety Ashrafis. Hereat waxing sore ashamed and confounded, he exclaimed, "Now do I believe thy words: nevertheless must thou admit that thou hast earned one-half of this thy prodigious wealth with the two hundred gold pieces I gave thee after our second visit, and the other half by means of the mite thou gottest from Sa'd." To this I made no answer, but my friends ceased not to dispute upon the matter. We then sat down to meat and drink, and when we had eaten our sufficiency, I and my two friends went to sleep in the cool arbour; after which when the sun was well nigh set we mounted and rode off to Baghdad leaving the servants to follow. However, arrived at the city we found all the shops shut and nowhere could we get grain and forage for the horses, and I sent off two slave-boys who had run alongside of us to search for provender. One of them found a jar of bran in the shop of a corn-dealer and paying for the provision brought it, together with the jar, under promise that on the morrow he would carry back the vessel. Then he began to take out the bran by handfuls in the dark and to set it before the horses.——And as the morn began to dawn Shahrazad held her peace till

The end of the Six Hundred and Twenty-fourth Night.

THEN said she:——I have heard, O auspicious king, that Hasan al-Habbal thus continued his story:—So as the slave-boy took out the bran by handfuls and set it before the horses, suddenly his hand came upon a piece of cloth wherein was somewhat heavy. He brought it to me even as he found it and said, "See, is not this cloth the very one of whose loss thou hast ofttimes spoken to us?" I took it and wondering with great wonder knew it was the selfsame piece of stuff wherein I had tied up the hundred and fourscore and ten Ashrafis before hiding them in the jar of bran. Then said I to my friends, "O my lords, it hath pleased Almighty Allah, ere we parted, I and you, to bear me witness of my words and to stablish that I told you naught save whatso was very sooth." And I resumed, addressing Sa'di, "See here the other sum of money, that is, the hundred and ninety Ashrafis which thou gavest me and which I tied up in this very piece of cloth I now recognise." Then I sent for the earthen jar that they might see it, and also bade carry it to my wife that she also might bear witness, an it be or be not the very bran jar which she gave in exchange for fuller's earth. Anon she sent us word and said, "Yea verily I know it well. 'Tis the same jar which I had filled with bran." Accordingly Sa'di owned that he was wrong and said to S'ad, "Now I know that thou speakest truth, and am convinced that wealth cometh not by wealth; but only by the grace of Almighty Allah doth a poor man become a rich man." And he begged pardon for his mistrust and unbelief. We accepted his excuses whereupon we retired to rest and early on the morrow my two friends bade me adieu and journeyed homewards with full persuasion that I had done no wrong and had not squandered the moneys they had given me.——Now when the Caliph Harun al-Rashid had heard the story of Khwajah Hasan to the end, he said, "I have known thee of old by fair report of thee from the folk who, one and all, declare that thou art a good man and true. Moreover the self-same diamond whereby thou hast attained to so great riches is now in my treasury; so I would fain send for Sa'di forthright that he may see it with his own eyes, and weet for certain that not by means of money do men become or rich or poor." The Prince of True Believers said moreover to Khwajah Hasan al-Habbal, "Go now and tell thy tale to my treasurer that he may take it down in writing for an everlasting memorial, and place the writ in the treasury together with the diamond." Then the Caliph with a nod dismissed Khawajah Hasan; and Sidi Nu'uman and Baba Abdullah also kissed the foot of the throne and departed. So when Queen Shahrazad had made an end of relating this history she was about to begin the story of 'Alí Bábá and the Forty Thieves, but King Shahryar prevented her, saying, "O Shahrazad, I am well pleased with this thy tale, but now the dawn appeareth and the chanticleer of morn doth sound his shrill clarion. This day also I spare thy life, to the intent that I may listen at my ease to this new history of thine at the end of the coming night." Hereupon the three took their rest until the fittest time drew near.——And as the morning morrowed Shahrazad held her peace till

𝕿𝖍𝖊 𝖊𝖓𝖉 𝖔𝖋 𝖙𝖍𝖊 𝕾𝖎𝖝 𝕳𝖚𝖓𝖉𝖗𝖊𝖉 𝖆𝖓𝖉 𝕿𝖜𝖊𝖓𝖙𝖞=𝖋𝖎𝖋𝖙𝖍 𝕹𝖎𝖌𝖍𝖙.

With the dawn Dunyazad awoke Queen Shahrazad from slumber sweet and said, "Arise, O my sister, but alas! 'tis a bitter thing to stand in awe of coming doom." Replied Shahrazad, "O dear my sister, be not thou downhearted: if life's span be spent naught can avert the sharp-edged sword. Yet place thy trust in Allah Almighty and put far from thee all such anxious thoughts: my tales are tokens of life prolonged." Whereupon Queen Shah-razad began to tell in these words the story of

ALI BABA AND THE FORTY THIEVES.[1]

IN days of yore and in times and tides long gone before there dwelt in a certain town of Persia two brothers one named Kásim and the other 'Alí Bábá, who at their father's demise had divided the little wealth he had left to them with equitable division, and had lost no time in wasting and spending it all. The elder, however, presently took to himself a wife, the daughter of an opulent merchant; so that when his father-in-law fared to the mercy of Almighty Allah, he became owner of a large shop filled with rare goods and costly wares and of a storehouse stocked with precious stuffs; likewise of much gold that was buried in the ground. Thus was he known throughout the city as a sub-stantial man. But the woman whom Ali Baba had married was poor and needy; they lived, therefore, in a mean hovel and Ali Baba eked out a scanty livelihood by the sale of fuel which he daily collected in the jungle[2] and carried about the town to the Bazar upon his three asses. Now it chanced one day that Ali Baba had cut dead branches and dry fuel sufficient for his need, and had placed the load upon his beasts when suddenly he espied a dust-cloud spireing high in air to his right and moving rapidly towards him; and when he closely considered it he descried a troop of horsemen riding on amain and about to reach him. At this sight he was sore alarmed, and fearing lest perchance they were a band of bandits who would slay him and drive off his donkeys, in his affright he began to run; but forasmuch as they were near hand and he could not escape from out the forest, he

---

[1] Mr. Coote (*loc. cit.*p. 185) is unable to produce a *puramythe* containing all of "Ali Bábá;" but, for the two leading incidents he quotes from Prof. Sakellarios two tales collected in Cyprus. One is Morgiana marking the village doors (p. 187), which has occurred doubtless a hundred times. The other, in the "Story of Drakos," is an ogre, hight "Three Eyes," who attempts the rescue of his wife with a party of blackamoors packed in bales and these are all discovered and slain.

[2] *Dans la forêt*, says Galland.

drove his animals laden with the fuel into a bye-way of the bushes and swarmed up a thick trunk of a huge tree to hide himself therein; and he sat upon a branch whence he could descry everything beneath him whilst none below could catch a glimpse of him above; and that tree grew close beside a rock which towered high above-head. The horsemen, young, active, and doughty riders, came close up to the rock-face and all dismounted; whereat Ali Baba took good note of them and soon he was fully persuaded by their mien and demeanour that they were a troop of highwaymen who, having fallen upon a caravan had despoiled it and carried off the spoil and brought their booty to this place with intent of concealing it safely in some cache. Moreover he observed that they were forty in number.——And as the morn began to dawn Shahrazad held her peace till

The end of the Six Hundred and Twenty-sixth Night.

THEN said she:—I have heard, O auspicious king, that Ali Baba saw the robbers, as soon as they came under the tree, each unbridle his horse and hobble it; then all took off their saddle-bags which proved to be full of gold and silver. The man who seemed to be the captain presently pushed forwards, load on shoulder, through thorns and thickets, till he came up to a certain spot where he uttered these strange words, "Open, O Simsim!"[1] and forthwith appeared a wide doorway in the face of the rock. The robbers went in and last of all their Chief and then the portal shut of itself. Long while they stayed within the cave whilst Ali Baba was constrained to abide perched upon the tree, reflecting that if he came down peradventure the band might issue forth that very moment and seize him and slay him. At last he had determined to mount one of the horses and driving on his asses to return townwards, when suddenly the portal flew open. The robber-chief was first to issue forth; then, standing at the entrance, he saw and counted his men as they came out, and

---

[1] Or "Samsam," The grain = Sesamum Orientale: hence the French, Sesame, ouvre-toi! The term is cabalistical, like Súlem, Súlam or Shúlam in the Directorium Vitæ Humanæ of Johannes di Capuâ: Inquit vir: Ibam in nocte plenilunii et ascendebam super domum ubi furari intendebam, et accedens ad fenestram ubi radii lune ingrediebantur, et dicebam hanc coniurationem, scilicet sulem sulem, septies, deinde amplectebar lumen lune et sine lesione descendebam ad domum, etc. (pp. 24-25) par Joseph Derenbourg, Membre de l'Institut 1re Fascicule, Paris, F. Vieweg, 67, Rue de Richelieu, 1887.

lastly he spake the magical words, "Shut, O Simsim!" whereat
the door closed of itself. When all had passed muster and review,
each slung on his saddle-bags and bridled his own horse and as
soon as ready they rode off, led by the leader, in the direction
whence they came. Ali Baba remained still perched on the tree
and watched their departure; nor would he descend until what
time they were clean gone out of sight, lest perchance one of them
return and look around and descry him. Then he thought within
himself, "I too will try the virtue of those magical words and see
if at my bidding the door will open and close." So he called out
aloud, "Open, O Simsim!" And no sooner had he spoken than
straightway the portal flew open and he entered within. He saw
a large cavern and a vaulted, in height equalling the stature of a
full-grown man and it was hewn in the live stone and lighted up
with light that came through air-holes and bullseyes in the upper
surface of the rock which formed the roof. He had expected to
find naught save outer gloom in this robbers' den, and he was
surprised to see the whole room filled with bales of all manner
stuffs, and heaped up from sole to ceiling with camel-loads of silks
and brocades and embroidered cloths and mounds on mounds of
vari-coloured carpetings; besides which he espied coins golden
and silvern without measure or account, some piled upon the
ground and others bound in leathern bags and sacks. Seeing
these goods and moneys in such abundance, Ali Baba determined in his mind that not during a few years only but for many
generations thieves must have stored their gains and spoils in this
place. When he stood within the cave, its door had closed upon
him, yet he was not dismayed since he had kept in memory the
magical words; and he took no heed of the precious stuffs
around him, but applied himself only and wholly to the sacks of
Ashrafis. Of these he carried out as many as he judged sufficient burthen for the beasts; then he loaded them upon his
animals, and covered this plunder with sticks and fuel, so none
might discern the bags, but might think that he was carrying
home his usual ware. Lastly he called out, "Shut, O Simsim!"
and forthwith the door closed, for the spell so wrought that
whensoever any entered the cave, its portal shut of itself behind
him; and, as he issued therefrom, the same would neither open
nor close again till he had pronounced the words, "Shut, O
Simsim!" Presently, having laden his asses Ali Baba urged them
before him with all speed to the city and reaching home he drove

them into the yard; and, shutting close the outer door, took down first the sticks and fuel and after the bags of gold which he carried in to his wife. She felt them and finding them full of coin suspected that Ali Baba had been robbing and fell to berating and blaming him for that he should do so ill a thing.——And as the morn began to dawn Shahrazad held her peace till

The end of the Six Hundred and Twenty-seventh Night.

THEN said she:——I have heard, O auspicious King, that quoth Ali Baba to his wife:—"Indeed I am no robber and rather do thou rejoice with me at our good fortune." Hereupon he told her of his adventure and began to pour the gold from the bags in heaps before her, and her sight was dazzled by the sheen and her heart delighted at his recital and adventures. Then she began counting the gold, whereat quoth Ali Baba, "O silly woman, how long wilt thou continue turning over the coin? now let me dig a hole wherein to hide this treasure that none may know its secret." Quoth she, "Right is thy rede! still would I weigh the moneys and have some inkling of their amount;" and he replied, "As thou pleasest, but see thou tell no man." So she went off in haste to Kasim's home to borrow weights and scales wherewith she might balance the Ashrafis and make some reckoning of their value; and when she could not find Kasim she said to his wife, "Lend me, I pray thee, thy scales for a moment." Replied her sister-in-law,[1] "Hast thou need of the bigger balance or the smaller?" and the other rejoined, "I need not the large scales, give me the little;" and her sister-in-law cried, "Stay here a moment whilst I look about and find thy want." With this pretext Kasim's wife went aside and secretly smeared wax and suet over the pan of the balance, that she might know what thing it was Ali Baba's wife would weigh, for she made sure that whatso it be some bit thereof would stick to the wax and fat. So the woman took this opportunity to satisfy her curiosity, and Ali Baba's wife suspecting naught thereof carried home the scales and began to weigh the gold, whilst Ali Baba ceased not digging;

---

[1] In the text "Jatháni" = the wife of an elder brother. Hindostani, like other Eastern languages, is rich in terms for kinship whereof English is so exceptionally poor. Mr. Francis Galtson, in his well-known work, "Hereditary Genius," a misnomer by the by for "Hereditary Talent," felt this want severely and was at pains to supply it.

and, when the money was weighed, they twain stowed it into the hole which they carefully filled up with earth. Then the good wife took back the scales to her kinswoman, all unknowing that an Ashrafi had adhered to the cup of the scales; but when Kasim's wife espied the gold coin she fumed with envy and wrath saying to herself, "So ho! they borrowed my balance to weigh out Ashrafis?" and she marvelled greatly whence so poor a man as Ali Baba had gotten such store of wealth that he should be obliged to weigh it with a pair of scales. Now after long pondering the matter, when her husband returned home at eventide, she said to him, "O man, thou deemest thyself a wight of wealth and substance, but lo, thy brother Ali Baba is an Emir by the side of thee and richer far than thou art. He hath such heaps of gold that he must needs weigh his moneys with scales, whilst thou, forsooth, art satisfied to count thy coin." "Whence knowest thou this?" asked Kasim, and in answer his wife related all anent the pair of scales and how she found an Ashrafi stuck to them, and shewed him the gold coin which bore the mark and superscription of some ancient king. No sleep had Kasim all that night by reason of his envy and jealousy and covetise; and next morning he rose betimes and going to Ali Baba said, "O my brother, to all appearance thou art poor and needy; but in effect thou hast a store of wealth so abundant that perforce thou must weigh thy gold with scales." Quoth Ali Baba, "What is this thou sayest? I understand thee not; make clear thy purport;" and quoth Kasim with ready rage, "Feign not that thou art ignorant of what I say and think not to deceive me." Then showing him the Ashrafi he cried, "Thousands of gold coins such as these thou hast put by; and meanwhile my wife found this one stuck to the cup of the scales." Then Ali Baba understood how both Kasim and his wife knew that he had store of Ashrafis, and said in his mind that it would not avail him to keep the matter hidden, but would rather cause ill-will and mischief; and thus he was induced to tell his brother every whit concerning the bandits[1] and also

---

[1] In the text "Thag," our English "Thug," often pronounced moreover by the Briton with the sibilant "th." It means simply a cheat: you say to your servant "Tú bará Thag hai" = thou art a precious rascal; but it has also the secondary meaning of robber, assassin, and the tertiary of Bhawáni-worshippers who offer indiscriminate human sacrifices to the Deëss of Destruction. The word and the thing have been made popular in England through the "Confessions of a Thug" by my late friend Meadows Taylor; and I may record my conviction that were the English driven out of India, "Thuggee," like piracy in Cutch and in the Persian Gulf, would revive at the shortest possible time.

of the treasure trove in the cave. When he had heard the story, Kasim exclaimed, "I would fain learn of thee the certainty of the place where thou foundest the moneys; also the magical words whereby the door opened and closed; and I forewarn thee an thou tell me not the whole truth, I will give notice of those Ashrafis to the Wálí;[1] then shalt thou forfeit all thy wealth and be disgraced and thrown into gaol." Thereupon Ali Baba told him his tale not forgetting the magical words; and Kasim who kept careful heed of all these matters next day set out, driving ten mules he had hired, and readily found the place which Ali Baba had described to him. And when he came to the afore-said rock and to the tree whereon Ali Baba had hidden himself, and he had made sure of the door he cried in great joy, "Open, O Simsim!" The portal yawned wide at once and Kasim went within and saw the piles of jewels and treasures lying ranged all around; and, as soon as he stood amongst them the door shut after him as wont to do. He walked about in ecstasy marvelling at the treasures, and when weary of admiration he gathered to-gether bags of Ashrafis, a sufficient load for his ten mules, and placed them by the entrance in readiness to be carried outside and set upon the beasts. But by the will of Allah Almighty he had clean forgotten the cabalistic words and cried out, "Open, O Barley!" whereat the door refused to move. Astonished and con-fused beyond measure he named the names of all manner of grains save sesame, which had slipped from his memory as though he had never heard the word; whereat in his dire distress he heeded not the Ashrafis that lay heaped at the entrance and paced to and fro, backwards and forwards, within the cave sorely puzzled and per-plexed. The wealth whose sight had erewhile filled his heart with joy and gladness was now the cause of bitter grief and sad-ness.——And as the morn began to dawn Shahrazad held her peace till

The end of the Six Hundred and Twenty-eighth Night.

THEN said she:——I have heard, O auspicious King, that Kasim gave up all hope of the life which he by his greed and envy had so sore imperilled. It came to pass that at noontide the robbers,

---

[1] *i.e.* the Civil Governor, who would want nothing better.

returning by that way, saw from afar some mules standing beside the entrance and much they marvelled at what had brought the beasts to that place; for, inasmuch as Kasim by mischance had failed to tether or hobble them, they had strayed about the jungle and were browsing hither and thither. However, the thieves paid scant regard to the estrays nor cared they to secure them, but only wondered by what means they had wandered so far from the town. Then, reaching the cave the Captain and his troop dismounted and going up to the door repeated the formula and at once it flew open. Now Kasim had heard from within the cave the horse-hooves drawing nigh and yet nigher; and he fell down to the ground in a fit of fear never doubting that it was the clatter of the banditti who would slaughter him without fail. Howbeit he presently took heart of grace and at the moment when the door flew open he rushed out hoping to make good his escape. But the unhappy ran full tilt against the Captain who stood in front of the band, and felled him to the ground; where-upon a robber standing near his chief at once bared his brand and with one cut clave Kasim clean in twain. Thereupon the robbers rushed into the cavern, and put back as they were before the bags of Ashrafis which Kasim had heaped up at the doorway ready for taking away; nor recked they aught of those which Ali Baba had removed, so dazed and amazed were they to dis-cover by what means the strange man had effected an entrance. All knew that it was not possible for any to drop through the skylights so tall and steep was the rock's face, withal slippery of ascent; and also that none could enter by the portal unless he knew the magical words whereby to open it. However they presently quartered the dead body of Kasim and hung it to the door within the cavern, two parts to the right jamb and as many to the left[1] that the sight might be a warning of approaching doom for all who dared enter the cave. Then coming out they closed the hoard door and rode away upon their wonted work. Now when night fell and Kasim came not home, his wife waxed uneasy in mind and running round to Ali Baba said, "O my brother, Kasim hath not returned: thou knowest whither he went, and sore I fear me some misfortune hath betided him." Ali Baba also divined that a mishap had happened to prevent his

---

[1] This is in Galland and it is followed by the H. V. ; but it would be more natural to suppose that of the quarters two were hung up outside the door and the others within.

return; not the less, however, he strove to comfort his sister-in-law with words of cheer and said, "O wife of my brother, Kasim haply exerciseth discretion and, avoiding the city, cometh by a roundabout road and will be here anon. This, I do believe, is the reason why he tarrieth." Thereupon comforted in spirit Kasim's wife fared homewards and sat awaiting her husband's return; but when half the night was spent and still he came not, she was as one distraught. She feared to cry aloud for her grief, lest haply the neighbours hearing her should come and learn the secret; so she wept in silence and upbraiding herself fell to thinking, "Wherefore did I disclose this secret to him and beget envy and jealousy of Ali Baba? this be the fruit thereof and hence the disaster that hath come down upon me." She spent the rest of the night in bitter tears and early on the morrow hied in hottest hurry to Ali Baba and prayed that he would go forth in quest of his brother; so he strove to console her and straightway set out with his asses for the forest. Presently, reaching the rock he wondered to see stains of blood freshly shed and not finding his brother or the ten mules he forefelt a calamity from so evil a sign. He then went to the door and saying, "Open, O Simsim!" he pushed in and saw the dead body of Kasim, two parts hanging to the right, and the rest to the left of the entrance. Albeit he was affrighted beyond measure of affright he wrapped the quarters in two cloths and laid them upon one of his asses, hiding them carefully with sticks and fuel that none might see them. Then he placed the bags of gold upon the two other animals and likewise covered them most carefully; and, when all was made ready he closed the cave-door with the magical words, and set him forth wending homewards with all ward and watchfulness. The asses with the load of Ashrafis he made over to his wife and bade her bury the bags with diligence; but he told her not the condition in which he had come upon his brother Kasim. Then he went with the other ass, to wit, the beast whereon was laid the corpse to the widow's house and knocked gently at the door. Now Kasim had a slave-girl shrewd and sharp-witted, Morgiana[1] hight. She as softly undid the bolt and admitted Ali Baba and the ass into the courtyard of the house, when he let down the body from the beast's back and said, "O Morgiana, haste thee and make thee

---

[1] I am unwilling to alter the time honoured corruption: properly it is written Marjánah = the "Coralline," from Marján = red coral, for which see vols. ii. 100; vii. 373.

ready to perform the rites for the burial of thy lord: I now go to tell the tidings to thy mistress and I will quickly return to help thee in this matter." At that instant Kasim's widow seeing her brother-in-law, exclaimed, "O Ali Baba, what news bringest thou of my spouse? Alas, I see grief tokens written upon thy countenance. Say quickly what hath happened." Then he recounted to her how it had fared with her husband and how he had been slain by the robbers and in what wise he had brought home the dead body.——And as the morn began to dawn Shahrazad held her peace till

The end of the Six Hundred and Twenty-ninth Night.

THEN said she:——I have heard, O auspicious King, that Ali Baba pursued:—"O my lady, what was to happen hath happened but it behoveth us to keep this matter secret, for that our lives depend upon privacy." She wept with sore weeping and made answer, "It hath fared with my husband according to the fiat of Fate; and now for thy safety's sake I give thee my word to keep the affair concealed." He replied, "Naught can avail when Allah hath decreed. Rest thee in patience; until the days of thy widow-hood[1] be accomplisht; after which time I will take thee to wife, and thou shalt live in comfort and happiness; and fear not lest my first spouse vex thee or show aught of jealousy, for that she is kindly and tender of heart." The widow lamenting her loss noisily, cried, "Be it as e'en thou please." Then Ali Baba farewelled her, weeping and wailing for her husband; and joining Morgiana took counsel with her how to manage the burial of his brother. So, after much consultation and many warnings, he left the slave-girl and departed home driving his ass before him. As soon as Ali Baba had fared forth Morgiana went quickly to a druggist's shop; and, that she might the better dissemble with him and not make known the matter, she asked of him a drug often administered to men when diseased with dangerous distemper. He gave it saying, "Who is there in thy house that lieth so ill as to require this medicine?" and said she, "My Master Kasim is sick well nigh unto death: for many days he hath nor spoken nor tasted aught of food, so that almost we despair of his life." Next day Morgiana went again and asked

---

[1] i.e. the " 'Iddah," during which she could not marry. See vol. iii. 292.

the druggist for more of medicine and essences such as are ad-
hibited to the sick when at door of death, that the moribund may
haply rally before the last breath. The man gave the potion and
she taking it sighed aloud and wept, saying, "I fear me he may
not have strength to drink this draught: methinks all will be over
with him ere I return to the house." Meanwhile Ali Baba was
anxiously awaiting to hear sounds of wailing and lamentation in
Kasim's home that he might at such signal hasten thither and
take part in the ceremonies of the funeral. Early on the second
day Morgiana went with veiled face to one Bábá Mustafá,[1] a
tailor well shotten in years whose craft was to make shrouds and
cerecloths; and as soon as she saw him open his shop she gave him
a gold piece and said, "Do thou bind a bandage over thine eyes
and come along with me." Mustafa made as though he would
not go, whereat Morgiana placed a second gold coin in his palm
and entreated him to accompany her. The tailor presently consented for greed of gain, so tying a kerchief tightly over his eyes
she led him by the hand to the house wherein lay the dead body
of her master. Then, taking off the bandage in the darkened
room she bade him sew together the quarters of the corpse, limb
to its limb; and, casting a cloth upon the body, said to the tailor,
"Make haste and sew a shroud according to the size of this dead
man and I will give thee therefor yet another ducat." Baba
Mustafa quickly made the cerecloth of fitting length and breadth,
and Morgiana paid him the promised Ashrafi; then once more
bandaging his eyes led him back to the place whence she had
brought him. After this she returned hurriedly home and with
the help of Ali Baba washed the body in warm water and donning the shroud lay the corpse upon a clean place ready for burial.
This done Morgiana went to the mosque and gave notice to an
Imám[2] that a funeral was awaiting the mourners in a certain
household, and prayed that he would come to read the prayers
for the dead; and the Imám went back with her. Then four
neighbours took up the bier[3] and bore it on their shoulders and

---

[1] In Galland he is a *savetier* * * * *naturellement gai, et qui avait toujours le mot
pour rire*: the H. V. naturally changed him to a tailor as the Chámár or leather-worker
would be inadmissible to polite conversation.

[2] *i.e.* a leader of prayer; the Pers. "Písh-namáz" = fore-prayer, see vols. ii. 203; iv. 111
and 227. Galland has "ímán," which can mean only faith, belief, and in this blunder he is
conscientiously followed by his translators—servum pecus.

[3] Galland nails down the corpse in the bier—a Christian practice—and he certainly knew

fared forth with the Imam and others who were wont to give assistance at such obsequies. After the funeral prayers were ended four other men carried off the coffin; and Morgiana walked before it bare of head, striking her breast and weeping and wailing with exceeding loud lament, whilst Ali Baba and the neighbours came behind. In such order they entered the cemetery and buried him; then, leaving him to Munkar and Nakir [1]—the Questioners of the Dead—all wended their ways. Presently the women of the quarter, according to the custom of the city, gathered together in the house of mourning and sat an hour with Kasim's widow comforting and condoling, presently leaving her somewhat resigned and cheered. Ali Baba stayed forty days at home in ceremonial lamentation for the loss of his brother; so none within the town save himself and his wife (Kasim's widow) and Morgiana knew aught about the secret. And when the forty days of mourning were ended Ali Baba removed to his own quarters all the property belonging to the deceased and openly married the widow; then he appointed his nephew, his brother's eldest son, who had lived a long time with a wealthy merchant and was perfect of knowledge in all matters of trade, such as selling and buying, to take charge of the defunct's shop and to carry on the business.——And as the morn began to dawn Shahrazad held her peace till

The end of the Six Hundred and Thirtieth Night.

THEN said she:——I have heard, O auspicious King, it so chanced one day when the robbers, as was their wont, came to the treasure-cave that they marvelled exceedingly to find nor sign nor trace of Kasim's body whilst they observed that much of gold had been carried off. Quoth the Captain, "Now it behoveth us to make enquiry in this matter; else shall we suffer much of loss and this our treasure, which we and our forefathers have amassed during the course of many years, will little by little be wasted and spoiled." Hereto all assented and with single mind agreed that he whom they had slain had knowledge of the magical words

---

better. Moreover, prayers for the dead are mostly recited over the bier when placed upon the brink of the grave; nor is it usual for a woman to play so prominent a part in the ceremony.

[1] See vols. v. 111; ix. 163 and x. 47.

whereby the door was made to open; moreover that some one beside him had cognizance of the spell and had carried off the body, and also much of gold; wherefore they needs must make diligent research and find out who the man ever might be. They then took counsel and determined that one amongst them, who should be sagacious and deft of wit, must don the dress of some merchant from foreign parts; then, repairing to the city he must go about from quarter to quarter and from street to street, and learn if any townsman had lately died and if so where he wont to dwell, that with this clue they might be enabled to find the wight they sought. Hereat said one of the robbers, "Grant me leave that I fare and find out such tidings in the town and bring thee word anon; and if I fail of my purpose I hold my life in forfeit." Accordingly that bandit, after disguising himself by dress, pushed at night into the town and next morning early he repaired to the market-square and saw that none of the shops had yet been opened, save only that of Baba Mustafa the tailor, who thread and needle in hand sat upon his working-stool. The thief bade him good day and said, " 'Tis yet dark: how canst thou see to sew?" Said the tailor, "I perceive thou art a stranger. Despite my years my eyesight is so keen that only yesterday I sewed together a dead body whilst sitting in a room quite darkened." Quoth the bandit thereupon to himself, "I shall get somewhat of my want from this snip;" and to secure a further clue he asked, "Meseemeth thou wouldst jest with me and thou meanest that a cerecloth for a corpse was stitched by thee and that thy business is to sew shrouds." Answered the tailor, "It mattereth not to thee: question me no more questions." Thereupon the robber placed an Ashrafi in his hand and continued, "I desire not to discover aught thou hidest, albeit my breast like every honest man's is the grave of secrets; and this only would I learn of thee, in what house didst thou do that job? Canst thou direct me thither, or thyself conduct me thereto?" The tailor took the gold with greed and cried, "I have not seen with my own eyes the way to that house. A certain bondswoman led me to a place which I know right well and there she bandaged my eyes and guided me to some tenement and lastly carried me into a darkened room where lay the dead body dismembered. Then she unbound the kerchief and bade me sew together first the corpse and then the shroud, which having done she again blindfolded me and led me back to the stead whence she had brought me and left me there.

Thou seest then I am not able to tell thee where thou shalt find the house." Quoth the robber, "Albeit thou knowest not the dwelling whereof thou speakest, still canst thou take me to the place where thou wast blindfolded; then I will bind a kerchief over thine eyes and lead thee as thou wast led: on this wise per-chance thou mayest hit upon the site. An thou wilt do this favour by me, see here another golden ducat is thine." There-upon the bandit slipped a second Ashrafi into the tailor's palm, and Baba Mustafa thrust it with the first into his pocket; then, leaving his shop as it was, he walked to the place where Morgiana had tied the kerchief around his eyes, and with him went the robber who, after binding on the bandage, led him by the hand. Baba Mustafa, who was clever and keen-witted, presently striking the street whereby he had fared with the handmaid, walked on counting step by step; then, halting suddenly, he said, "Thus far I came with her;" and the twain stopped in front of Kasim's house wherein now dwelt his brother Ali Baba.——— And as the morn began to dawn Shahrazad held her peace till

The end of the Six Hundred and Thirty-first Night.

THEN said she:———I have heard, O auspicious King, that the robber then made marks with white chalk upon the door to the end that he might readily find it at some future time, and removing the bandage from the tailor's eyes said, "O Baba Mustafa, I thank thee for this favour: and Almighty Allah guerdon thee for thy goodness. Tell me now, I pray thee, who dwelleth in yonder house?" Quoth he, "In very sooth I wot not, for I have little knowledge concerning this quarter of the city;" and the bandit, understanding that he could find no further clue from the tailor, dismissed him to his shop with abundant thanks, and hastened back to the tryst-place in the jungle where the band awaited his coming. Not long after it so fortuned that Mor-giana, going out upon some errand, marvelled exceedingly at seeing the chalk-marks showing white in the door; she stood awhile deep in thought and presently divined that some enemy had made the signs that he might recognize the house and play some sleight upon her lord. She therefore chalked the doors of all her neighbours in like manner and kept the matter secret, never entrusting it or to master or to mistress. Meanwhile the robber told his comrades his tale of adventure and how he had found the clue; so the Captain and with him all the band went one after other by different ways till they entered the city; and he who had placed the mark on Ali Baba's door accompanied the Chief to point out the place. He conducted him straightway to the house and shewing the sign exclaimed, "Here dwelleth he of whom we are in search!" But when the Captain looked around him he saw that all the dwellings bore chalk-marks after like fashion and he wondered saying, "By what manner of means knowest thou which house of all these houses that bear similar signs is that whereof thou spakest?" Hereat the robber-guide was confounded beyond measure of confusion, and could make no answer; then with an oath he cried, "I did assuredly set a sign upon a door, but I know not whence came all the marks upon the other entrances; nor can I say for a surety which it was I chalked." Thereupon the Captain returned to the market-place and said to his men, "We have toiled and laboured in vain, nor have we found the house we went forth to seek. Return we now to the forest our rendezvous: I also will fare thither." Then all trooped off and assembled together within the treasure-cave; and, when the robbers had all met, the Captain judged him worthy of punishment who had spoken falsely and had led them through the city to no purpose. So he imprisoned him in presence of them all;[1] and then said he, "To him amongst you will I show special favour who shall go to town and bring me intel-ligence whereby we may lay hands upon the plunderer of our property." Hereat another of the company came forward and said, "I am ready to go and enquire into the case, and 'tis I who will bring thee to thy wish." The Captain after giving him presents and promises despatched him upon his errand; and by the decree of Destiny which none may gainsay, this second robber went first to the house of Baba Mustafa the tailor, as had done the thief who had foregone him. In like manner he also per-suaded the snip with gifts of golden coin that he be led hood-winked and thus too he was guided to Ali Baba's door. Here noting the work of his predecessor, he affixed to the jamb a mark with red chalk the better to distinguish it from the others

---

[1] Galland is less merciful, "*Aussitôt le conducteur fut déclaré digne de mort tout d'une voix, et il s'y condamna lui-même,*" etc. The criminal, indeed, condemns himself and firmly offers his neck to be stricken.

whereon still showed the white. Then hied he back in stealth to his company; but Morgiana on her part also descried the red sign on the entrance and with subtle forethought marked all the others after the same fashion; nor told she any what she had done. Meanwhile the bandit rejoined his band and vauntingly said, "O our Captain, I have found the house and thereon put a mark whereby I shall distinguish it clearly from all its neighbours." ——And as the morn began to dawn Shahrazad held her peace till

The end of the Six Hundred and Thirty-second Night.

THEN said she:——I have heard, O auspicious King, that the Captain despatched another of his men to the city and he found the place, but, as aforetime, when the troop repaired thither they saw each and every house marked with signs of red chalk. So they returned disappointed and the Captain, waxing displeased exceedingly and distraught, clapped also this spy into gaol. Then said the chief to himself, "Two men have failed in their endeavour and have met their rightful meed of punishment; and I trow that none other of my band will essay to follow up their research; so I myself will go and find the house of this wight." Accordingly he fared along and aided by the tailor Baba Mustafa, who had gained much gain of golden pieces in this matter, he hit upon the house of Ali Baba; and here he made no outward show or sign, but marked it on the tablet[1] of his heart and impressed the picture upon the page of his memory. Then returning to the jungle he said to his men, "I have full cognizance of the place and have limned it clearly in my mind; so now there will be no difficulty in finding it. Go forth straightways and buy me and bring hither nineteen mules together with one large leathern jar of mustard oil and seven and thirty vessels of the same kind clean empty. Without me and the two locked up in gaol ye number thirty-seven souls; so I will stow you away armed and accoutred each within his jar and will load two upon each mule, and upon the nineteenth mule there shall be a man in an empty jar on one side, and on the other the jar full of oil. I for my part, in guise of an oil-merchant, will drive the mules into the town, arriving at

---

[1] In the text "Lauh," for which see vol. v. 73.

the house by night, and will ask permission of its master to tarry there until morning. After this we shall seek occasion during the dark hours to rise up and fall upon him and slay him." Furthermore the Captain spake saying, "When we have made an end of him we shall recover the gold and treasure whereof he robbed us and bring it back upon the mules." This counsel pleased the robbers who went forthwith and purchased mules and huge leathern jars, and did as the Captain had bidden them. And after a delay of three days shortly before nightfall they arose; and over-smearing all the jars with oil of mustard, each hid him inside an empty vessel. The Chief then disguised himself in trader's gear and placed the jars upon the nineteen mules; to wit, the thirty-seven vessels in each of which lay a robber armed and accoutred, and the one that was full of oil. This done, he drove the beasts before him and presently he reached Ali Baba's place at nightfall; when it chanced that the house-master was strolling after supper to and fro in front of his home. The Captain saluted him with the salam and said, "I come from such and such a village with oil; and ofttimes have I been here a-selling oil, but now to my grief I have arrived too late and I am sore troubled and perplexed as to where I shall spend the night. An thou have pity on me I pray thee grant that I tarry here in thy courtyard and ease the mules by taking down the jars and giving the beasts somewhat of fodder." Albeit Ali Baba had heard the Captain's voice when perched upon the tree and had seen him enter the cave, yet by reason of the disguise he knew him not for the leader of the thieves, and granted his request with hearty welcome and gave him full license to halt there for the night. He then pointed out an empty shed wherein to tether the mules, and bade one of the slave-boys go fetch grain and water. He also gave orders to the slave-girl Morgiana saying, "A guest hath come hither and tarrieth here to-night. Do thou busy thyself with all speed about his supper and make ready the guest-bed for him." Presently, when the Captain had let down all the jars and had fed and watered his mules, Ali Baba received him with all courtesy and kindness, and summoning Morgiana said in his presence, "See thou fail not in service of this our stranger nor suffer him to lack for aught. To-morrow early I would fare to the Hammam and bathe; so do thou give my slave-boy Abdullah a suit of clean white clothes which I may put on after washing; moreover make thee ready a somewhat of broth overnight that

I may drink it after my return home." Replied she, "I will have
all in readiness as thou hast bidden." So Ali Baba retired to his
rest, and the Captain, having supped, repaired to the shed and
saw that all the mules had their food and drink for the night.——
And as the morn began to dawn Shahrazad held her peace till

The end of the Six Hundred and Thirty-third Night.

THEN said she: I have heard, O auspicious King, that the
Captain, after seeing to the mules and the jars which Ali Baba
and his household held to be full of oil, finding utter privacy,
whispered to his men who were in ambush, "This night at midnight when ye hear my voice, do you quickly open with your
sharp knives the leathern jars from top to bottom and issue forth
without delay." Then passing through the kitchen he reached
the chamber wherein a bed had been dispread for him, Morgiana showing the way with a lamp. Quoth she, "An thou need
aught beside I pray thee command this thy slave who is ever
ready to obey thy say!" He made answer, "Naught else need
I;" then, putting out the light, he lay him down on the bed to
sleep awhile ere the time came to rouse his men and finish off the
work. Meanwhile Morgiana did as her master had bidden her:
she first took out a suit of clean white clothes and made it over to
Abdullah who had not yet gone to rest; then she placed the
pipkin upon the hearth to boil the broth and blew the fire till it
burnt briskly. After a short delay she needs must see an the
broth be boiling, but by that time all the lamps had gone out and
she found that the oil was spent and that nowhere could she
get a light. The slave-boy Abdullah observed that she was
troubled and perplexed hereat, and quoth he to her, "Why make
so much ado? In yonder shed are many jars of oil: go now and
take as much soever as thou listest." Morgiana gave thanks to
him for his suggestion; and Abdullah, who was lying at his ease
in the hall, went off to sleep so that he might wake betimes and
serve Ali Baba in the bath. So the hand-maiden rose [1] and with
oil-can in hand walked to the shed where stood the leathern jars

---

[1] In Arab. "Káma" = he rose, which, in vulgar speech especially in Egypt, = he began.
So in Spitta-Bey's "Contes Arabes Modernes" (p. 124) "Kámat al-Sibhah dhákat fí yad
akhí-h" = the chaplet began (lit. arose) to wax tight in his brother's hand. This sense is
shadowed forth in classical Arabic.

all ranged in rows. Now, as she drew nigh unto one of the vessels, the thief who was hidden therein hearing the tread of footsteps bethought him that it was of his Captain whose summons he awaited; so he whispered, "Is it now time for us to sally forth?" Morgiana started back affrighted at the sound of human accents; but, inasmuch as she was bold and ready of wit, she replied, "The time is not yet come," and said to herself, "These jars are not full of oil and herein I perceive a manner of mystery. Haply the oil merchant hatcheth some treacherous plot against my lord; so Allah, the Compassionating, the Compassionate, protect us from his snares!" Wherefore she answered in a voice made like to the Captain's, "Not yet, the time is not come." Then she went to the next jar and returned the same reply to him who was within, and so on to all the vessels one by one. Then said she in herself, "Laud to the Lord! my master took this fellow in believing him to be an oil-merchant, but lo, he hath admitted a band of robbers, who only await the signal to fall upon him and plunder the place and do him die." Then passed she on to the furthest jar and finding it brimming with oil, filled her can, and returning to the kitchen, trimmed the lamp and lit the wicks; then, bringing forth a large cauldron, she set it upon the fire, and filling it with oil from out the jar heaped wood upon the hearth and fanned it to a fierce flame the readier to boil its contents. When this was done she baled it out in potfuls and poured it seething hot into the leathern vessels one by one while the thieves unable to escape were scalded to death and every jar contained a corpse.[1] Thus did this slave-girl by her subtle wit make a clean end of all noiselessly and unknown even to the dwellers in the house. Now when she had satisfied herself that each and every of the men had been slain, she went back to the kitchen and shutting to the door sat brewing Ali Baba's broth. Scarce had an hour passed before the Captain woke from sleep; and, opening wide his window, saw that all was dark and silent; so he clapped his hands as a signal for his men to come forth but not a sound was heard in return. After awhile he clapped again and called aloud but got no answer; and when he cried out a third

---

[1] So in old Arabian history "Kasír" (the Little One), the Arab Zopyrus, stows away in huge camel-bags the 2,000 warriors intended to surprise masterful Queen Zebba. Chronique de Tabarí, vol. ii., 26. Also the armed men in boxes by which Shamar, King of Al-Yaman, took Shamar-kand = Shamar's-town, now Samarkand. (Ibid. ii. 158.)

time without reply he was perplexed and went out to the shed wherein stood the jars. He thought to himself, "Perchance all are fallen asleep whenas the time for action is now at hand, so I must e'en awaken them without stay or delay." Then approaching the nearest jar he was startled by a smell of oil and seething flesh; and touching it outside he felt it reeking hot; then going to the others one by one, he found all in like condition. Hereat he knew for a surety the fate which had betided his band and, fearing for his own safety, he clomb on to the wall, and thence dropping into a garden made his escape in high dudgeon and sore disappointment. Morgiana awaited awhile to see the Captain return from the shed but he came not; whereat she knew that he had scaled the wall and had taken to flight, for that the street-door was double-locked; and the thieves being all disposed of on this wise Morgiana laid her down to sleep in perfect solace and ease of mind. When two hours of darkness yet remained, Ali Baba awoke and went to the Hammam knowing naught of the night-adventure, for the gallant slave-girl had not aroused him, nor indeed had she deemed such action expedient, because had she sought an opportunity of reporting to him her plan, she might haply have lost her chance and spoiled the project. The sun was high over the horizon when Ali Baba walked back from the Baths; and he marvelled exceedingly to see the jars still standing under the shed and said, "How cometh it that he, the oil-merchant my guest, hath not carried to the market his mules and jars of oil?"———And as the morn began to dawn Shahrazad held her peace till

The end of the Six Hundred and Thirty-fourth Night.

THEN said she:———I have heard, O auspicious King, that Ali Baba presently asked Morgiana what had befallen the oil-merchant his guest whom he had placed under her charge; and she answered, "Allah Almighty vouchsafe to thee six score years and ten of safety! I will tell thee in privacy of this merchant." So Ali Baba went apart with his slave-girl, who taking him without the house first locked the court-door; then showing him a jar she said, "Prithee look into this and see if within there be oil or aught else." Thereupon peering inside it he perceived a man at which sight he cried aloud and fain would have fled in his fright. Quoth Morgiana, "Fear him not, this man hath no longer the force to work thee harm, he lieth dead and stone-dead." Hearing such words of comfort and reassurance Ali Baba asked, "O Morgiana, what evils have we escaped and by what means hath this wretch become the quarry of Fate?" She answered, "Alhamdolillah—Praise be to Almighty Allah!—I will inform thee fully of the case; but hush thee, speak not aloud, lest haply the neighbours learn the secret and it end in our confusion. Look now into all the jars, one by one from first to last." So Ali Baba examined them severally and found in each a man fully armed and accoutred and all lay scalded to death. Hereat speech-less for sheer amazement he stared at the jars, but presently re-covering himself he asked, "And where is he, the oil-merchant?" Answered she, "Of him also I will inform thee. The villain was no trader but a traitorous assassin whose honied words would have ensnared thee to thy doom; and now I will tell thee what he was and what hath happened; but, meanwhile thou art fresh from the Hammam and thou shouldst first drink somewhat of this broth for thy stomach's and thy health's sake." So Ali Baba went within and Morgiana served up the mess; after which quoth her master, "I fain would hear this wondrous story: prithee tell it to me and set my heart at ease." Hereat the handmaid fell to re-lating whatso had betided in these words, "O my master, when thou badest me boil the broth and retiredst to rest, thy slave in obedience to thy command took out a suit of clean white clothes and gave it to the boy Abdullah; then kindled the fire and set on the broth. As soon as it was ready I had need to light a lamp so that I might see to skim it, but all the oil was spent, and, learning this I told my want to the slave-boy Abdullah, who advised me to draw somewhat from the jars which stood under the shed. Accordingly, I took a can and went to the first vessel when sud-denly I heard a voice within whisper with all caution, 'Is it now time for us to sally forth?' I was amazed thereat and judged that the pretended merchant had laid some plot to slay thee; so I re-plied, 'The time is not yet come.' Then I went to the second jar and heard another voice to which I made the like answer, and so on with all of them. I now was certified that these men awaited only some signal from their Chief whom thou didst take to guest within thy walls supposing him to be a merchant in oil; and that after thou receivedst him hospitably the miscreant had brought these men to murther thee and to plunder thy good and spoil thy house. But I gave him no opportunity to win his wish. The last jar I found full of oil and taking somewhat therefrom I lit the lamp; then, putting a large cauldron upon the fire, I filled it up with oil which I brought from the jar and made a fierce blaze under it; and, when the contents were seething hot, I took out sundry cansful with intent to scald them all to death, and going to each jar in due order, I poured within them one by one boiling oil. On this wise having destroyed them utterly, I returned to the kitchen and having extinguished the lamps stood by the window watching what might happen, and how that false merchant would act next. Not long after I had taken my station, the robber-captain awoke and oft-times signalled to his thieves. Then getting no reply he came downstairs and went out to the jars, and finding that all his men were slain he fled through the darkness I know not whither. So when he had clean disappeared I was assured that, the door being double-locked, he had scaled the wall and dropped into the garden and made his escape. Then with my heart at rest I slept." And Morgiana, after telling her story to her master, presently added, "This is the whole truth I have related to thee. For some days indeed have I had inkling of such matter, but withheld it from thee deeming it inexpedient to risk the chance of its meeting the neighbours' ears; now, however, there is no help but to tell thee thereof. One day as I came to the house-door I espied thereon a white chalk-mark, and on the next day a red sign beside the white. I knew not the intent wherewith the marks were made, nevertheless I set others upon the entrances of sundry neighbours, judging that some enemy had done this deed whereby to encompass my master's destruction. Therefore I made the marks on all the other doors in such perfect conformity with those I found, that it would be hard to distinguish amongst them."——And as the morn began to dawn Shahrazad held her peace till

The end of the Six Hundred and Thirty-fifth Night.

THEN said she:——I have heard, O auspicious King, that Morgiana continued to Ali Baba:——"Judge now and see if these signs and all this villainy be not the work of the bandits of the forest, who marked our house that on such wise they might know it again. Of these forty thieves there yet remain two others concerning

whose case I know naught; so beware of them, but chiefly of the
third remaining robber, their Captain, who fled hence alive.
Take good heed and be thou cautious of him, for, shouldst thou
fall into his hands, he will in no wise spare thee but will surely
murther thee. I will do all that lieth in me to save from hurt and
harm thy life and property, nor shall thy slave be found wanting
in any service to my lord." Hearing these words Ali Baba rejoiced with exceeding joyance and said to her, "I am well pleased
with thee for this thy conduct; and say me what wouldst thou
have me do in thy behalf; I shall not fail to remember thy brave
deed so long as breath in me remaineth." Quoth she, "It behoveth us before all things forthright to bury these bodies in the
ground, that so the secret be not known to any one." Hereupon
Ali Baba took with him his slave-boy Abdullah into the garden
and there under a tree they dug for the corpses of the thieves a
deep pit in size proportionate to its contents, and they dragged
the bodies (having carried off their weapons) to the fosse and
threw them in; then, covering up the remains of the seven and
thirty robbers they made the ground appear level and clean as it
wont to be. They also hid the leathern jars and the gear and
arms and presently Ali Baba sent the mules by ones and twos to
the bazar and sold them all with the able aid of his slave-boy
Abdullah. Thus the matter was hushed up nor did it reach the
ears of any; Ali Baba ceased not to be ill at ease lest haply the
Captain or the surviving two robbers should wreak their vengeance on his head. He kept himself private with all caution and
took heed that none learn a word of what had happened and of
the wealth which he had carried off from the bandits' cave.
Meanwhile the Captain of the thieves having escaped with his
life, fled to the forest in hot wrath and sore irk of mind; and his
senses were scattered and the colour of his visage vanished like
ascending smoke. Then he thought the matter over again and
again, and at last he firmly resolved that he needs must take the
life of Ali Baba, else he would lose all the treasure which his
enemy, by knowledge of the magical words, would take away
and turn to his own use. Furthermore, he determined that he
would undertake the business single-handed; and, that after
getting rid of Ali Baba, he would gather together another band
of banditti and would pursue his career of brigandage, as indeed
his forbears had done for many generations. So he lay down to
rest that night, and rising early in the morning donned a dress of

suitable appearance; then going to the city alighted at a caravanserai, thinking to himself, "Doubtless the murther of so many men
hath reached the Wali's ears, and Ali Baba hath been seized and
brought to justice, and his house is levelled and his good is con-
fiscated. The townfolk must surely have heard tidings of these
matters." So he straightway asked of the keeper of the Khán,
"What strange things have happened in the city during the last
few days?" and the other told him all that he had seen and heard,
but the Captain could not learn a whit of that which most concerned him. Hereby he understood that Ali Baba was ware and
wise, and that he had not only carried away such store of treasure
but he had also destroyed so many lives and withal had come off
scatheless; furthermore, that he himself must needs have all his
wits alert not to fall into the hands of his foe and perish. With
this resolve the Captain hired a shop in the Bazar, whither he bore
whole bales of the finest stuffs and goodly merchandise from his
forest treasure-house; and presently he took his seat within the
store and fell to doing merchant's business. By chance his
place fronted the booth of the defunct Kasim where his son, Ali
Baba's nephew, now traded; and the Captain, who called himself Khwajah Hasan, soon formed acquaintance and friendship
with the shop-keepers around about him and treated all with profuse civilities, but he was especially gracious and cordial to the
son of Kasim, a handsome youth and a well-dressed, and ofttimes he would sit and chat with him for a long while. A few
days after it chanced that Ali Baba, as he was sometimes wont to
do, came to see his nephew, whom he found sitting in his shop.
The Captain saw and recognised him at sight and one morning he
asked the young man, saying, "Prithee tell me, who is he that
ever and anon cometh to thee at thy place of sale?" whereto the
youth made answer, "He is my uncle, the brother of my father."
Whereupon the Captain showed him yet greater favour and affection the better to deceive him for his own devices, and gave him
presents and made him sit at meat with him and fed him with the
daintiest of dishes. Presently Ali Baba's nephew bethought him
it was only right and proper that he also should invite the merchant to supper, but whereas his own house was small, and he
was straitened for room and could not make a show of splendour,
as did Khwajah Hasan, he took counsel with his uncle on the
matter.——And as the morn began to dawn Shahrazad held her
peace till

The end of the Six Hundred and Thirty-sixth Night.

THEN said she:——I have heard, O auspicious King, that Ali
Baba replied to his nephew:——"Thou sayest well: it behoveth
thee to entreat thy friend in fairest fashion even as he hath entreated thee. On the morrow, which is Friday, shut thy shop as
do all merchants of repute; then, after the early meal, take
Khwajah Hasan to smell the air,[1] and as thou walkest lead him
hither unawares; meanwhile I will give orders that Morgiana
shall make ready for his coming the best of viands and all necessaries for a feast. Trouble not thyself on any wise, but leave the
matter in my hands." Accordingly on the next day, to wit,
Friday, the nephew of Ali Baba took Khwajah Hasan to walk
about the garden; and, as they were returning he led him by the
street wherein his uncle dwelt. When they came to the house,
the youth stopped at the door and knocking said, "O my lord,
this is my second home: my uncle hath heard much of thee and of
thy goodness me-wards and desireth with exceeding desire to see
thee; so, shouldst thou consent to enter and visit him, I shall
be truly glad and thankful to thee." Albeit Khwajah Hasan
rejoiced in heart that he had thus found means whereby he
might have access to his enemy's house and household, and although he hoped soon to attain his end by treachery, yet he
hesitated to enter in and stood to make his excuses and walk away.
But when the door was opened by the slave-porter, Ali Baba's
nephew seized his companion's hand and after abundant persuasion led him in, whereat he entered with great show of
cheerfulness as though much pleased and honoured. The house-
master received him with all favour and worship and asked him
of his welfare, and said to him "O my lord, I am obliged and
thankful to thee for that thou hast shewn favour to the son of my
brother and I perceive that thou regardest him with an affection
even fonder than my own." Khwajah Hasan replied with pleasant words and said, "Thy nephew vastly taketh my fancy and
in him I am well pleased, for that although young in years yet he
hath been endued by Allah with much of wisdom." Thus they
twain conversed with friendly conversation and presently the

---

[1] *i.e.* for a walk, a "constitutional": the phrase is very common in Egypt, and has
occurred before.

guest rose to depart and said, "O my lord, thy slave must now farewell thee; but on some future day—Inshallah—he will again wait upon thee." Ali Baba, however, would not let him leave and asked, "Whither wendest thou, O my friend? I would invite thee to my table and I pray thee sit at meat with us and after hie thee home in peace. Perchance the dishes are not as delicate as those whereof thou art wont to eat, still deign grant me this request I pray thee and refresh thyself with my victual." Quoth Khwajah Hasan, "O my lord I am beholden to thee for thy gracious invitation, and with pleasure would I sit at meat with thee, but for a special reason must I needs excuse myself; suffer me therefore to depart for I may not tarry longer nor accept thy gracious offer." Hereto the host made reply, "I pray thee, O my lord, tell me what may be the reason so urgent and weighty?" And Khwajah Hasan answered, "The cause is this: I must not, by order of the physician, who cured me lately of my complaint, eat aught of food prepared with salt." Quoth Ali Baba, "An this be all, deprive me not, I pray thee, of the honour thy company will confer upon me: as the meats are not yet cooked, I will forbid the kitchener to make use of any salt. Tarry here awhile and I will return anon to thee." So saying Ali Baba went in to Morgiana and bade her not put salt into any one of the dishes; and she, while busied with her cooking, fell to marvelling greatly at such order and asked her master, "Who is he that eateth meat wherein is no salt?" He answered, "What to thee mattereth it who he may be? only do thou my bidding." She rejoined, " 'Tis well: all shall be as thou wishest;" but in mind she wondered at the man who made such strange request and desired much to look upon him. Wherefore, when all the meats were ready for serv-ing up, she helped the slave-boy Abdullah to spread the table and set on the meal; and no sooner did she see Khwajah Hasan than she knew who he was, albeit he had disguised himself in the dress of a stranger merchant; furthermore, when she eyed him attentively she espied a dagger hidden under his robe. "So ho!" quoth she to herself, "this is the cause why the villain eateth not of salt, for that he seeketh an opportunity to slay my master whose mortal enemy he is; howbeit I will be beforehand with him and despatch him ere he find a chance to harm my lord."——And as the morn began to dawn Shahrazad held her peace till

The end of the Six Hundred and Thirty-seventh Night.

THEN said she:——I have heard, O auspicious King, that Morgiana, having spread a white cloth upon the table and served up the meal, went back to the kitchen and thought out her plot against the robber-Captain. Now when Ali Baba and Khwajah Hasan had eaten their sufficiency, the slave-boy Abdullah brought Morgiana word to serve the dessert, and she cleared the table and set on fruit fresh and dried in salvers, then she placed by the side of Ali Baba a small tripod for three cups with a flagon of wine, and lastly she went off with the slave-boy Abdullah into another room, as though she would herself eat supper. Then Khwajah Hasan, that is, the Captain of the robbers, perceiving that the coast was clear, exulted mightily saying to himself, "The time hath come for me to take full vengeance; with one thrust of my dagger I will despatch this fellow, then escape across the garden and wend my ways. His nephew will not adventure to stay my hand, for an he do but move a finger or toe with that intent another stab will settle his earthly account. Still must I wait awhile until the slave-boy and the cook-maid shall have eaten and lain down to rest them in the kitchen." Morgiana, however, watched him wistfully and divining his purpose said in her mind, "I must not allow this villain advantage over my lord, but by some means I must make void his project and at once put an end to the life of him." Accordingly, the trusty slave-girl changed her dress with all haste and donned such clothes as dancers wear; she veiled her face with a costly kerchief; around her head she bound a fine turband, and about her middle she tied a waist-cloth worked with gold and silver wherein she stuck a dagger, whose hilt was rich in filigree and jewelry. Thus disguised she said to the slave-boy Abdullah, "Take now thy tambourine that we may play and sing and dance in honour of our master's guest." So he did her bidding and the twain went into the room, the lad playing and the lass following. Then, making a low congée, they asked leave to perform and disport and play; and Ali Baba gave permission, saying, "Dance now and do your best that this our guest may be mirthful and merry." Quoth Khwajah Hasan, "O my lord, thou dost indeed provide much pleasant entertainment." Then the slave-boy Abdullah standing by began to strike the tambourine whilst Morgiana rose up and showed her perfect art and pleased them vastly with graceful steps and sportive motion; and suddenly drawing the poniard from her belt she brandished it and paced from side to side, a spectacle which pleased them most of all. At times also she stood before them, now clapping the sharp-edged dagger under her armpit and then setting it against her breast. Lastly she took the tambourine from the slave-boy Abdullah, and still holding the poniard in her right she went round for largesse as is the custom amongst merry-makers. First she stood before Ali Baba who threw a gold coin into the tambourine, and his nephew likewise put in an Ashrafi; then Khwajah Hasan, seeing her about to approach him, fell to pulling out his purse, when she heartened her heart and quick as the blinding leven she plunged the dagger into his vitals, and forthwith the miscreant fell back stone-dead. Ali Baba was dismayed and cried in his wrath, "O unhappy, what is this deed thou hast done to bring about my ruin!" But she replied, "Nay, O my lord, rather to save thee and not to cause thee harm have I slain this man: loosen his garments and see what thou wilt discover thereunder." So Ali Baba searched the dead man's dress and found concealed therein a dagger. Then said Morgiana, "This wretch was thy deadly enemy. Consider him well: he is none other than the oil merchant, the Captain of the band of robbers. Whenas he came hither with intent to take thy life, he would not eat thy salt; and when thou toldest me that he wished not any in the meat I suspected him and at first sight I was assured that he would surely do thee die, Almighty Allah be praised 'tis even as I thought." Then Ali Baba lavished upon her thanks and expressions of gratitude, saying, "Lo, these two times hast thou saved me from his hand," and falling upon her neck he cried, "See thou art free, and as reward for this thy fealty I have wedded thee to my nephew." Then turning to the youth he said, "Do as I bid thee and thou shalt prosper. I would that thou marry Morgiana, who is a model of duty and loyalty: thou seest now yon Khwajah Hasan sought thy friendship only that he might find opportunity to take my life, but this maiden with her good sense and her wisdom hath slain him and saved us."——And as the morn began to dawn Shahrazad held her peace till

The end of the Six Hundred and Thirty-eighth Night.

THEN said she:——I have heard, O auspicious King, that Ali Baba's nephew straightway consented to marry Morgiana.

After which the three, raising the dead body bore it forth with all heed and vigilance and privily buried it in the garden, and for many years no one knew aught thereof. In due time Ali Baba married his brother's son to Morgiana with great pomp, and spread a bride-feast in most sumptuous fashion for his friends and neighbours, and made merry with them and enjoyed singing and all manner of dancing and amusements. He prospered in every undertaking and Time smiled upon him and a new source of wealth was opened to him. For fear of the thieves he had not once visited the jungle-cave wherein lay the treasure, since the day he had carried forth the corpse of his brother Kasim. But some time after, he mounted his hackney one morning and journeyed thither, with all care and caution, till finding no signs of man or horse, and reassured in his mind he ventured to draw near the door. Then alighting from his beast he tied it up to a tree, and going to the entrance pronounced the words which he had not forgotten, "Open, O Simsim!" Hereat, as was its wont, the door flew open, and entering thereby he saw the goods and hoard of gold and silver untouched and lying as he had left them. So he felt assured that not one of all the thieves remained alive, and, that save himself there was not a soul who knew the secret of the place. At once he bound in his saddle-cloth a load of Ashrafis such as his horse could bear and brought it home; and in after days he showed the hoard to his sons and sons' sons and taught them how the door could be caused to open and shut. Thus Ali Baba and his household lived all their lives in wealth and joyance in that city where erst he had been a pauper, and by the blessing of that secret treasure he rose to high degree and dignities.

PRINCE AHMAD AND THE FAIRY PERI-BANU.[1]

In days of yore and times long gone before there was a Sultan of India who begat three sons; the eldest hight Prince Husayn, the second Prince Ali, and the youngest Prince Ahmad; moreover

[1] "Bánú" = a lady, a dame of high degree generally, *e.g.* the (Shah's) Banu-i-Harem in James Morier ("The Mirza," iii. 50), who rightly renders *Pari Banu* = Pari of the first quality. "Peri" (Parí) in its modern form has a superficial resemblance to "Fairy;" but this disappears in the "Pairika" of the Avesta and the "Pairik" of the modern Parsee. In one language only, the Multání, there is a masculine form for the word "Pará" = a he-fairy (Scinde, ii. 203). In Al-Islam these Peris are beautiful feminine spirits who, created after the "Dívs" (Tabari, i. 7), mostly believe in Allah and the Koran and desire the good of mankind: they are often attacked by the said Dívs, giants or demons, who imprison them in cages hung to the highest trees, and here the captives are visited by their friends who feed them with the sweetest of scents. I have already contrasted them with the green-coated pygmies to which the grotesque fancy of Northern Europe has reduced them. Bánú in Pers. = a princess, a lady, and is still much used, *e.g.* Bánú-í-Harim, the Dame of the

he had a niece, named Princess Nur al-Nihár,[1] the daughter of his
cadet brother who, dying early, left his only child under her
uncle's charge.   The King busied himself with abundant diligence
about her instruction and took all care that she should be taught
to read and write, sew and embroider, sing and deftly touch all
instruments of mirth and merriment.   This Princess also in
beauty and loveliness and in wit and wisdom far excelled all the
maidens of her own age in every land.   She was brought up with
the Princes her cousins in all joyance; and they ate together and
played together and slept together; and the king had determined
in his mind that when she reached marriageable age he would
give her in wedlock to some one of the neighbouring royalties;
but, when she came to years of discretion, her uncle perceived
that the three Princes his sons were all three deep in love of her,
and each desired in his heart to woo and to win and to wed her.
Wherefore was the King sore troubled in mind and said to himself, "An I give the Lady Nur al-Nihár in wedlock to any one
of her cousins, the other twain will be dissatisfied and murmur
against my decision; withal my soul cannot endure to see them
grieved and disappointed.   And should I marry her to some
stranger the three Princes my sons will be sore distressed and
saddened in soul; nay, who knoweth that they may not slay
themselves or go forth and betake them to some far and foreign
land?   The matter is a troublous and a perilous; so it behoveth
me their sire to take action on such wise that if one of them
espouse her, the other two be not displeased thereat."   Long
time the Sultan revolved the matter in his mind; and at length
he devised a device; and, sending for the three princes, addressed them saying, "O my sons, ye are in my opinion of equal
merit one with other; nor can I give preference to any of you and
marry him to the Princess Nur al-Nihar; nor yet am I empowered
to wed her with all three.   But I have thought of one plan
whereby she shall be wife to one of you, and yet shall not cause

Serraglio, whom foreigners call "Queen of Persia;" and Árám-Banu = "the calm Princess," a
nickname.   A Greek story equivalent of Prince Ahmad is told by Pio in *Contes Populaires Grecs*
(No. ii. p. 98) and called Τὸ χρυσὸ κουτάκι, the Golden box. Three youths (παλλικάρια)
love the same girl and agree that whoever shall learn the best craft (ὅγεος μάθη πλεία καλὴν
τέχνην) shall marry her; one becomes an astrologer, the second can raise the dead, and the
third can run faster than air.   They find her at death's door, and her soul, which was at her
teeth ready to start, goes down (καὶ πά 'ἡ ψυχή της κάτω, ποῦτανε πλειά στὰ δόντια
της).
[1] Light of the Day.

aught of irk or envy to his brethren; so may your mutual love and affection remain unabated, and one shall never be jealous of the other's happiness. Brief, my device is this: — Go ye and travel to distant countries, each one separating himself from the others; and do ye bring me back the thing most wondrous and marvellous of all sights ye may see upon your wayfarings; and he who shall return with the rarest of curiosities shall be husband to the Princess Nur al-Nihar. Consent ye now to this pro-posal; and whatso of money ye require for travel and for the purchase of objects seld-seen and singular, take ye from the royal treasury as much as ye desire." The three Princes, who were ever submissive to their sire, consented with one voice to this proposal, and each was satisfied and confident that he would bring the King the most extraordinary of gifts and thereby win the Princess to wife. So the Sultan bade give to each what moneys he wanted without stint or account, and counselled them to make ready for the journey without stay or delay and depart their home in the Peace of Allah. —— And as the morn began to dawn Shahrazad held her peace till

The end of the Six Hundred and Forty-fourth Night.

THEN said she: —— I have heard, O auspicious King, that the three princely brothers forthright made them ready for journey and voyage. So they donned disguise, preferring the dress of wandering merchants; and, buying such things as they needed and taking with them each his suite they mounted steeds of purest blood and rode forth in a body from the palace. For several stages they travelled the same road until, reaching a place where it branched off in three different ways, they alighted at a Khan and ate the evening meal. Then they made compact and covenant, that whereas they had thus far travelled together they should at break of day take separate roads and each wend his own way and all seek different and distant regions, agreeing to travel for the space of one year only, after which, should they be in the land of the living, all three would rendezvous at that same caravanserai and return in company to the King their sire. Furthermore, they determined that the first who came back to the Khan should await the arrival of the next, and that two of them should tarry there in expectancy of the third. Then, all this matter duly settled, they retired to rest, and when the morning morrowed they fell on one another's necks and bade farewell; and, lastly, mounting their horses, they rode forth each in his own direction. Now Prince Husayn, the eldest, had oft heard recount the wonders of the land Bishangarh[1], and for a long while had wished to visit it; so he took the road which led thither, and, joining himself to a caravan journeying that way, accompanied it by land and by water and traversed many regions, desert wilds and stony wolds, dense jungles and fertile tracts, with fields and hamlets and gardens and townships. After three months spent in wayfare at length he made Bishangarh, a region over-reigned by manifold rulers, so great was its extent and so far reaching was its power. He put up at a Khan built specially for merchants who came from the farthest lands, and from the folk who dwelt therein he heard tell that the city contained a large central market[2] wherein men bought and sold all manner of rarities and wondrous things. Accordingly, next day Prince Husayn repaired to the Bazar and on sighting it he stood amazed at the

---

[1] Galland has "Bisnagar," which the H. V. corrupts to Bishan-Garh = Vishnu's Fort, an utter misnomer. Bisnagar, like Bijnagar, Beejanuggur, Vizianuggur, etc., is a Prakrit corruption of the Sanskrit Vijáyanagara = City of Victory, the far-famed Hindu city and capital of the Narasingha or Lord of Southern India, mentioned in The Nights, vols. vi. 18; ix. 84. Nicolo de' Conti in the xvth century found it a magnificent seat of Empire some fifteen marches south of the pestilential mountains which contained the diamond mines. Accounts of its renown and condition in the last generation have been given by James Grant ("Remarks on the Dekkan") and by Captain Moore ("Operations of Little's Detachment against Tippoo Sultan"). The latest description of it is in "The Indian Empire," by Sir William W. Hunter. Vijáyanagar, village in Bellary district, Madras, lat. 15° 18′ N., long. 76° 30′ E.; pop. (1871), 437, inhabiting 172 houses. The proper name of this village is *Hampi*, but Vijáyanagar was the name of the dynasty (?) and of the kingdom which had its capital here and was the last great Hindu power of the South. Founded by two adventurers in the middle of the xivth century, it lasted for two centuries till its star went down at Tálikot in A. D. 1565. For a description of the ruins of the old city of Vijáyanagar, which covers a total area of nine square miles, see "Murray's Handbook for Madras," by E. B. Eastwick (1879), vol. ix. p. 235. Authentic history in Southern India begins with the Hindu kingdom of Vijáyanagar, or Narsinha, from A. D. 1118 to 1565. The capital can still be traced within the Madras district of Bellary, on the right bank of the Tungabhadra river—vast ruins of temples, fortifications, tanks and bridges, haunted by hyænas and snakes. For at least three centuries Vijáyanagar ruled over the southern part of the Indian triangle. Its Rajas waged war and made peace on equal terms with the Mohamadan sultans of the Deccan. See vol. iv. p. 335, Sir W. W. Hunter's "Imperial Gazetteer of India," Edit. 1881.

[2] The writer means the great Bazar, the Indian "Chauk," which = our English Carfax or Carfex (Carrefour) and forms the core of ancient cities in the East. It is in some places, as Damascus, large as one of the quarters, and the narrow streets or lanes, vaulted over or thatched, are all closed at night by heavy doors well guarded by men and dogs. Trades are still localised, each owning its own street, after the fashion of older England, where we read of Drapers' Lane and Butchers' Row; Lombard Street, Cheapside and Old Jewry.

prospect of its length and width. It was divided into many streets, all vaulted over but lit up by skylights; and the shops on either side were substantially builded, all after one pattern and nearly of the same size, while each was fronted by an awning which kept off the glare and made a grateful shade. Within these shops were ranged and ordered various kinds of wares; there were bales of "woven air"[1] and linens of finest tissue, plain-white or dyed or adorned with life-like patterns wherefrom beasts and trees and blooms stood out so distinctly that one might believe them to be very ferals, bosquets and gardens. There were more-over silken goods, brocaded stuffs, and finest satins from Persia and Egypt of endless profusion; in the China warehouses stood glass vessels of all kinds, and here and there were stores wherein tapestries and thousands of foot-carpets lay for sale. So Prince Husayn walked on from shop to shop and marvelled much to see such wondrous things whereof he had never even dreamt: and he came at length to the Goldsmiths' Lane and espied gems and jewels and golden and silvern vessels studded with diamonds and rubies, emeralds, pearls and other precious stones, all so lustrous and dazzling bright that the stores were lit up with their singular brilliancy. Hereat he said to himself, "If in one street only there be such wealth and jewels so rare, Allah Almighty and none save He knoweth what may be the riches in all this city." He was not less astonished to behold the Brahmins, how their women-kind for excess of opulence bedecked themselves with the finest gems and were ornamented with the richest gear from front to foot: their very slave-boys and handmaids wore golden necklaces and bracelets and bangles studded with precious stones. Along the length of one market-street were ranged hosts of flower-sellers; for all the folk, both high and low, wore wreaths and garlands: some carried nosegays in hand, other some bound fillets round their heads, while not a few had ropes and festoons surrounding and hanging from their necks. The whole place seemed one huge parterre of bloomery; even traders set bouquets in every shop and stall, and the scented air was heavy with perfume. Strolling to and fro Prince Husayn was

---

[1] The local name of the Patna gauzes. The term was originally applied to the produce of the Coan looms, which, however, was anticipated in ancient Egypt. See p. 287 of "L'Arch-éologie Égyptienne" (Paris, A. Quantin) of the learned Professor G. Maspero, a most able popular work by a savant who has left many regrets on the banks of Nilus.

presently tired and would fain have sat him down somewhere to
rest awhile, when one of the merchants, noting his look of weariness, with kindly courtesy prayed him be seated in his store.
After saluting him with the salam the stranger sat down; and
anon he saw a broker come that way, offering for sale a carpet
some four yards square, and crying, "This be for sale; who
giveth me its worth; to wit, thirty thousand gold pieces?" ——
And as the morn began to dawn Shahrazad held her peace till

The end of the Six Hundred and Forty-fifth Night.

THEN said she: —— I have heard, O auspicious King, that the
Prince marvelled with excessive marvel at the price, and, beckon-
ing the dealer, examined his wares right well; then said he, "A
carpet such as this is selleth for a few silverlings. What special
virtue hath it that thou demand therefor the sum of thirty thousand gold coins?" The broker, believing Husayn to be a merchant
man lately arrived at Bishangarh, answered him saying, "O my
lord, thinkest thou I price this carpet at too high a value? My
master hath bidden me not to sell it for less than forty thousand
Ashrafis." Quoth the Prince, "It surely doth possess some
wondrous virtue, otherwise wouldst thou not demand so prodigious a sum;" and quoth the broker, " 'Tis true, O my lord, its
properties are singular and marvellous. Whoever sitteth on
this carpet and willeth in thought to be taken up and set down
upon other site will, in the twinkling of an eye, be borne thither,
be that place nearhand or distant many a day's journey and
difficult to reach."[1] The Prince hearing these words said to him-

---

[1] The great prototype of the Flying Carpet is that of Sulayman bin Dáúd, a fable which
the Koran (chap. xxi. 81) borrowed from the Talmud, not from "Indian fictions." It was of
green sendal embroidered with gold and silver and studded with precious stones, and its
length and breadth were such that all the Wise King's host could stand upon it, the men to
the left and the Jinns to the right of the throne; and when all were ordered, the Wind, at
royal command, raised it and wafted it whither the Prophet would, while an army of birds
flying overhead canopied the host from the sun. In the Middle Ages the legend assumed
another form. "Duke Richard, surnamed 'Richard sans peur,' walking with his courtiers
one evening in the forest of Moulineaux, near one of his castles on the banks of the Seine,
hearing a prodigious noise coming towards him, sent one of his esquires to know what was
the matter, who brought him word that it was a company of people under a leader or King.
Richard, with five hundred of his bravest Normans, went out to see a sight which the peas-
ants were so accustomed to that they viewed it two or three times a week without fear.
The sight of the troop, preceded by two men, *who spread a cloth on the ground*, made all the

self, "Naught so wonder-rare as this rug can I carry back to the Sultan my sire to my gift, or any that afford him higher satisfaction and delight. Almighty Allah be praised, the aim of my wayfare is attained and hereby, Inshallah! I shall win to my wish. This, if anything, will be to him a joy for ever." Wherefore the Prince, with intent to buy the Flying Carpet, turned to the broker and said, "If indeed it have properties such as thou describest, verily the price thou askest therefor is not over much, and I am ready to pay thee the sum required." The other rejoined, "An thou doubt my words I pray thee put them to the test and by such proof remove thy suspicions. Sit now upon this square of tapestry, and at thy mere wish and will it shall transport us to the caravanserai wherein thou abidest: on this wise shalt thou be certified of my words being sooth, and when assured of their truth thou mayest count out to me, there and then, but not before, the value of my wares." Accordingly, the man spread out the carpet upon the ground behind his shop and seated the Prince thereupon, he sitting by his side. Then, at the mere will[1] and wish of Prince Husayn, the twain were at once transported as though borne by the throne of Solomon to the Khan. So the eldest of the brothers joyed with exceeding joy to think that he had won so rare a thing, whose like could nowhere be found in

---

Normans run away, and leave the Duke alone. He saw the strangers form themselves into a circle on the cloth, and on asking who they were, was told that they were the spirits of Charles V., King of France, and his servants, condemned to expiate their sins by fighting all night against the wicked and the damned. Richard desired to be of their party, and receiving a strict charge not to quit the cloth, was conveyed with them to Mount Sinai, where, leaving them without quitting the cloth, he said his prayers in the Church of St. Catherine's Abbey there, while they were fighting, and returned with them. In proof of the truth of this story, he brought back half the wedding-ring of a knight in that convent, whose wife, after six years, concluded him dead, and was going to take a second husband." (Note in the Lucknow Edition of The Nights.)

1 Amongst Eastern peoples, and especially adepts, the will of man is not a mere term for a mental or cerebral operation, it takes the rank of a substance; it becomes a mighty motive power, like table-turning and other such phenomena which, now looked upon as child's play, will perform a prime part in the Kinetics of the century to come. If a few pair of hands imposed upon a heavy dinner-table can raise it in the air, as I have often seen, what must we expect to result when the new motive force shall find its Franklin and be shown to the world as real "Vril"? The experiment of silently willing a subject to act in a manner not suggested by speech or sign has been repeatedly tried and succeeded in London drawing-rooms; and it has lately been suggested that atrocious crimes have resulted from overpowering volition. In cases of paralysis the Faculty is agreed upon the fact that local symptoms disappear when the will-power returns to the brain. And here I will boldly and baldly state my theory that, in sundry cases, spectral appearances (ghosts) and abnormal smells and sounds are simply the effect of a Will which has, so to speak, created them.

the lands nor amongst the Kings; and his heart and soul were gladdened for that he had come to Bishangarh and hit upon such a prodigy. Accordingly he counted out the forty thousand Ashrafis as payment for the carpet, and gave, moreover, another twenty thousand by way of sweetmeat to the broker. Further-more, he ceased not saying to himself that the King on seeing it would forthright wed him to the Princess Nur al-Nihar; for it were clear impossible that either of his brothers, e'en though they searched the whole world over and over, could find a rarity to compare with this. He longed to take seat upon the carpet that very instant and fly to his own country, or, at least, to await his brothers at the caravanserai where they had parted under promise and covenant, pledged and concluded, to meet again at the year's end. But presently he bethought him that the delay would be long and longsome, and much he feared lest he be tempted to take some rash step; wherefore he resolved upon sojourning in the country whose King and subjects he had ardently desired to behold for many a day, and determined that he would pass the time in sight-seeing and in pleasuring over the lands adjoining. So Prince Husayn tarried in Bishangarh some months. Now the King of that country was wont to hold a high court once every week for hearing disputes and adjudging causes which concerned foreign merchants; and thus the Prince ofttimes saw the King, but to none would he tell a word of his adventure. However, inasmuch as he was comely of countenance, graceful of gait, and courteous of accost, stout hearted and strong, wise and ware and witty, he was held by the folk in higher honour than the Sultan; not to speak of the traders his fellows; and in due time he be-came a favourite at court and learned of the ruler himself all matters concerning his kingdom and his grandeur and greatness. The Prince also visited the most famous Pagodas[1] of that country. The first he saw was wrought in brass and orichalch of most exquisite workmanship: its inner cell measured three yards square and contained amiddlemost a golden image in size and stature like unto a man of wondrous beauty; and so cunning was the workmanship that the face seemed to fix its eyes, two

---

[1] The text has "But-Khánah" = idol-house (or room) syn. with "But-Kadah" = image-cuddy, which has been proposed as the derivation of the disputed "Pagoda." The word "Khánah" also appears in our balcony, origin. "balcony," through the South-Euro-pean tongues, the Persian being "Bálá-khánah" = high room. From "Kadah" also we derive "cuddy," now confined to nautical language.

immense rubies of enormous value, upon all beholders no matter where they stood.[1] He also saw another idol-temple, not less strange and rare than this, builded in a village on a plain surface of some half acre long and broad, wherein bloomed lovely rose-trees and jasmine and herb-basil and many other sweet-scented plants, whose perfume made the air rich with fragrance. Around its court ran a wall three feet high, so that no animal might stray therein; and in the centre was a terrace well-nigh the height of a man, all made of white marble and wavy alabaster, each and every slab being dressed so deftly and joined with such nice joinery that the whole pavement albeit covering so great a space, seemed to the sight but a single stone. In the centre of the terrace stood the domed fane towering some fifty cubits high and conspicuous for many miles around: its length was thirty cubits and its breadth twenty, and the red marbles of the revetment were clean polished as a mirror, so that every image was reflected in it to the life. The dome was exquisitely carved and sumptuously ornamented without; and within were ranged in due rank and sequence rows and rows of idols. To this, the Holy of Holies, from morn till eve thousands of Brahmins, men and women, came flocking for daily worship. They had sports and diversions as well as rites and ceremonies: some feasted and others danced, some sang, others played on instruments of mirth and merriment, while here and there were plays and revels and innocent merry-makings. And hither at every season flocked from distant lands hosts of pilgrims seeking to fulfil their vows and to perform their orisons; all bringing gifts of gold and silver coin and presents rare and costly which they offered to the gods in presence of the royal officers. —— And as the morn began to dawn Shahrazad held her peace till

Œhe end of the Six Hundred and Forty-sixth Night.

THEN said she: —— I have heard, O auspicious King, that Prince Husayn also saw a fête once a year within the city of Bishangarh and the Ryots all, both great and small, gathered together and circumambulated the Pagodas; chiefly circuiting one which

---

[1] Europe contains sundry pictures which have, or are supposed to have, this property; witness the famous Sundarium bearing the head of Jesus. The trick, for it is not Art, is highly admired by the credulous.

in size and grandeur surpassed all others. Great and learned
Pandits versed in the Shástras[1] made journeys of four or five
months and greeted one another at that festival; thither too the
folk from all parts of India pilgrimaged in such crowds that
Prince Husayn was astounded at the sight; and, by reason of the
multitudes that thronged around the temples, he could not see
the mode in which the gods were worshipped. On one side of the
adjacent plain which stretched far and wide, stood a new-made
scaffolding of ample size and great magnificence, nine storeys
high, and the lower part supported by forty pillars; and here one
day in every week the King assembled his Wazirs for the purpose
of meting out justice to all strangers in the land. The palace
within was richly adorned and furnished with costly furniture:
without, upon the wall-faces were limned homely landscapes and
scenes of foreign parts and notably all manner beasts and birds
and insects even gnats and flies, portrayed with such skill of brain
and cunning of hand that they seemed real and alive and the
country-folk and villagers seeing from afar paintings of lions and
tigers and similar ravenous beasts, were filled with awe and dismay. On the other three sides of the scaffolding were pavilions,
also of wood, built for use of the commons, illuminated and decorated inside and outside like the first, and wroughten so cunningly
that men could turn them round, with all the people in them,
and moving them about transfer them to whatsoever quarter
they willed. On such wise they shifted these huge buildings by
aid of machinery;[2] and the folk inside could look upon a succession of sports and games. Moreover, on each side of the
square elephants were ranged in ranks, the number amounting
to well-nigh one thousand, their trunks and ears and hinder parts
being painted with cinnabar and adorned with various lively
figures; their housings were of gold brocade and their howdahs
purfled with silver, carrying minstrels who performed on various
instruments, whilst buffoons delighted the crowd with their
jokes and mimes played their most diverting parts. Of all the
sports, however, which the Prince beheld, the elephant-show
amused him most and filled him with the greatest admiration.

---

[1] *i.e.* the Hindu Scripture or Holy Writ, *e.g.* "Káma-Shastra" = the Cupid-gospel.
[2] This shifting theatre is evidently borrowed by Galland from Pliny (N. H. xxxvi., 24)
who tells that in B. C. 50, C. Curio built two large wooden theatres which could be wheeled
round and formed into an amphitheatre. The simple device seems to stir the bile of the
unmechanical old Roman, so unlike the Greek in powers of invention.

One huge beast, which could be wheeled about where the keepers ever listed, for that his feet rested upon a post which travelled on casters, held in his trunk a flageolet whereon he played so sweetly well that all the people were fain to cry Bravo! There was another but a smaller animal which stood upon one end of a beam laid crosswise upon, and attached with hinges to, a wooden block eight cubits high, and on the further end was placed an iron weight as heavy as the elephant, who would press down for some time upon the beam until the end touched the ground, and then the weight would raise him up again.[1] Thus the beam swung like a see-saw aloft and adown; and, as it moved, the elephant swayed to and fro and kept time with the bands of music, loudly trumpeting the while. The people moreover could wheel about this elephant from place to place as he stood balanced on the beam; and such exhibitions of learned elephants were mostly made in presence of the King. Prince Husayn spent well nigh a year in sight-seeing amongst the fairs and festivals of Bishangarh; and, when the period of the fraternal compact drew near, he spread his carpet upon the court-ground behind the Khan wherein he lodged, and sitting thereon, together with his suite and the steeds and all he had brought with him, mentally wished that he might be transported to the cara-vanserai where the three brothers had agreed to meet. No sooner had he formed the thought than straightway, in the twinkling of an eye, the carpet rose high in air and sped through space and carried them to the appointed stead where, still garbed as a mer-chant he remained in expectation of his brothers' coming. Hearken now, O auspicious King, to what befel Prince Ali, the second brother of Prince Husayn. On the third day after he had parted from the two others, he also joined a caravan and journeyed towards Persia; then, after a march of four months arriving at Shiraz, the capital of Iran-land, he alighted at a Khan, he and his fellow-travellers with whom he had made a manner of friendship; and, passing as a jeweller, there took up his abode with them. Next day the traders fared forth to buy wares and to sell their goods; but Prince Ali, who had brought with him naught of vendible, and only the things he needed, presently doffed his

---

[1] This trick is now common in the circuses and hippodromes of Europe, horses and bulls being easily taught to perform it; but India has as yet not produced anything equal to the "Cyclist elephant" of Paris.

travelling dress, and in company with a comrade of the caravan entered the chief Bazar, known as the Bazistán,[1] or cloth-market. Ali strolled about the place, which was built of brick and where all the shops had arched roofs resting on handsome columns; and he admired greatly to behold the splendid store-houses exposing for sale all manner goods of countless value. He wondered much what wealth was in the town if a single market-street contained riches such as these. And as the brokers went about crying their goods for sale, he saw one of them hending in hand an ivory tube in length about a cubit, which he was offering for sale at the price of thirty thousand Ashrafis. Hearing such demand Prince Ali thought to himself, "Assuredly this fellow is a fool who asketh such a price for so paltry a thing." —— And as the morn began to dawn Shahrazad held her peace till

The end of the Six Hundred and Forty-seventh Night.

Then said she: —— I have heard, O auspicious King, that Prince Ali presently asked one of the shopkeepers with whom he had made acquaintance, saying, "O my friend, is this man a maniac that he asketh a sum of thirty thousand Ashrafis for this little pipe of ivory? Surely none save an idiot would give him such a price and waste upon it such a mint of money." Said the shop-man, "O my lord, this broker is wiser and warier than all the others of his calling, and by means of him I have sold goods worth thousands of sequins. Until yesterday he was in his sound senses; but I cannot say what state is his to-day and whether or no he have lost his wits; but this wot I well, that if he ask thirty thousand for yon ivory tube, 'twill be worth that same or even more. Howbeit we shall see with our own eyes. Sit thee here and rest within the shop until he pass this way." So Prince Ali abode where he was bidden and presently the broker was seen coming up the street. Then the shopman calling to him said, "O man, rare merit hath yon little pipe; for all the folk are astounded to hear thee ask so high a price therefor; nay more, this friend of mine thinketh that thou art crazy." The broker, a

---

[1] This Arab.-Pers. compound, which we have corrupted to "Bezestein" or "Bezettein" and "Bezesten," properly means a market-place for Baz or Bazz = cloth, fine linen; but is used by many writers as = Bazar, see "Kaysariah," vol. i. 266.

man of sense, was on no wise chafed at these words but answered with gentle speech, "O my lord, I doubt not but that thou must deem me a madman to ask so high a price, and set so great a value upon an article so mean; but when I shall have made known to thee its properties and virtues, thou wilt most readily consent to take it at that valuation. Not thou alone but all men who have heard me cry my cry laugh and name me ninny." So saying, the broker showed the Spying Tube to Prince Ali and handing it to him said, "Examine well this ivory, the properties of which I will explain to thee. Thou seest that it is furnished with a piece of glass at either end;[1] and, shouldst thou apply one extremity thereof to thine eye, thou shalt see what thing soe'er thou listest and it shall appear close by thy side though parted from thee by many an hundred of miles." Replied the Prince, "This passeth all conception, nor can I believe it to be veridical until I shall have tested it and I become satisfied that 'tis even as thou sayest." Hereupon the broker placed the little tube in Prince Ali's hand, and showing him the way to handle it said, "Whatso thou mayest wish to descry will be shown to thee by looking through this ivory." Prince Ali silently wished to sight his sire, and when he placed the pipe close to his eye forthwith he saw him hale and hearty, seated on his throne and dispensing justice to the people of his dominion. Then the youth longed with great longing to look upon his lady-love the Princess Nur al-Nihar; and straightway he saw her also sitting upon her bed, sound and sane, talking and laughing, whilst a host of handmaids stood around awaiting her commands. The Prince was astonished

---

[1] The origin of the lens and its applied use to the telescope and the microscope are "lost" (as the Castle-guides of Edinburgh say) "in the glooms of antiquity." Well ground glasses have been discovered amongst the finds of Egypt and Assyria: indeed much of the finer work of the primeval artists could not have been done without such aid. In Europe the "spy-glass" appears first in the Opus Majus of the learned Roger Bacon (circa A. D. 1270); and his "optic tube" (whence his saying "all things are known by perspective"), chiefly contributed to make his wide-spread fame as a wizard. The telescope was popularised by Galileo who (as mostly happens) carried off and still keeps, amongst the vulgar, all the honours of invention. Some "Illustrators" of The Nights confound this "Nazzárah," the Pers. "Dúr-bín," or far-seer, with the "Magic Mirror," a speculum which according to Gower was set up in Rome by Virgilius the Magician; hence the Mirror of Glass in the Squire's tale; Merlin's glassie Mirror of Spenser (F. Q. ii. 24); the mirror in the head of the monstrous fowl which forecast the Spanish invasion to the Mexicans; the glass which in the hands of Cornelius Agrippa (A. D. 1520) showed to the Earl of Surrey fair Geraldine "sick in her bed;" to the globe of glass in The Lusiads; Dr. Dee's show-stone, a bit of cannel-coal; and lastly the zinc and copper disk of the absurdly called "electro-biologist." I have noticed this matter at some length in various places.

exceedingly to behold this strange and wondrous spectacle, and said to himself, "An I should wander the whole world over for ten years or more and search in its every corner and cranny, I shall never find aught so rare and precious as this tube of ivory." Then quoth he to the broker, "The virtues of thy pipe I find are indeed those thou hast described, and right willingly I give to thee its price the thirty thousand Ashrafis." Replied the sales-man, "O my lord, my master hath sworn an oath that he will not part with it for less than forty thousand gold pieces." Here-upon the Prince, understanding that the broker was a just man and a true, weighed out to him the forty thousand sequins and became master of the Spying Tube, enraptured with the thought that assuredly it would satisfy his sire and obtain for him the hand of Princess Nur al-Nihar. So with mind at ease Ali jour-neyed through Shiraz and over sundry parts of Persia; and in fine, when the year was well nigh spent he joined a caravan and, travelling back to India, arrived safe and sound at the ap-pointed caravanserai whither Prince Husayn had foregone him. There the twain tarried awaiting the third brother's safe return. Such, O King Shahryar, is the story of the two brothers; and now I beseech thee incline thine ear and hearken to what befel the youngest, to wit Prince Ahmad; for indeed his adventure is yet more peregrine and seld-seen of all. When he had parted from his brothers, he took the road leading to Samarkand; and, arriving there after long travel, he also like his brothers alighted at a Khan. Next day he fared forth to see the market-square, which folk call the Bazistan, and he found it fairly laid out, the shops wroughten with cunning workmanship and filled with rare stuffs and pre-cious goods and costly merchandise. Now as he wandered to and fro he came across a broker who was hawking a Magical Apple and crying aloud, "Who will buy this fruit, the price whereof be thirty-five thousand gold pieces?" Quoth Prince Ahmad to the man, "Prithee let me see the fruit thou holdest in hand, and explain to me what hidden virtue it possesseth that thou art asking for it so high a value." Quoth the other, smiling and handing to him the apple, "Marvel not at this, O good my lord: in sooth I am certified that when I shall have explained its prop-erties and thou shalt see how it advantageth all mankind, thou wilt not deem my demand exorbitant; nay, rather thou wilt gladly give a treasure-house of gold so thou may possess it." —— And as the morn began to dawn Shahrazad held her peace till

The end of the Six Hundred and Forty=eighth Night.

THEN said she: —— I have heard, O auspicious King, that the broker said moreover to Prince Ahmad, "Now hearken to me, O my lord, and I will tell thee what of virtue lieth in this artificial apple. If anyone be sick of a sickness however sore, nay more if he be ill nigh unto death, and perchance he smell this pome, he will forthwith recover and become well and whole of whatsoever disease he had, plague or pleurisy, fever or other malignant dis-temper, as though he never had been attacked; and his strength will return to him forthright, and after smelling this fruit he will be free from all ailment and malady so long as life shall remain to him." Quoth Prince Ahmad, "How shall I be assured that what thou speakest is truth? If the matter be even as thou sayest, then verily I will give thee right gladly the sum thou demandest." Quoth the broker, "O my lord, all men who dwell in the parts about Samarkand know full well how there once lived in this city a sage of wondrous skill who, after many years of toil and travail, wrought this apple by mixing medicines from herbs and minerals countless in number. All his good, which was great, he expended upon it, and when he had perfected it he made whole thousands of sick folk whom he directed only to smell the fruit. But, alas! his life presently came to an end and death overtook him suddenly ere he could save himself by the marvellous scent; and, as he had won no wealth and left only a bereaved wife and a large family of young children and dependents manifold, his widow had no help but provide for them a maintenance by parting with this prodigy." While the salesman was telling his tale to the Prince a crowd of citizens gathered around them and one amongst the folk, who was well known to the broker, came forward and said, "A friend of mine lieth at home sick to the death: the doctors and surgeons all despair of his life; so I beseech thee let him smell this fruit that he may live." Hearing these words, Prince Ahmad turned to the salesman and said, "O my friend, if this sick man of whom thou hearest can recover strength by smelling the apple, then will I straightway buy it of thee at a valuation of forty thousand Ashrafis." The man had permission to sell it for a sum of thirty-five thousand; so he was satisfied to receive five thousand by way of brokerage, and he rejoined, " 'Tis well, O my lord; now mayest thou test the virtues of this apple and be persuaded in thy mind: hundreds of ailing folk have I made whole by means of it." Accordingly the Prince accompanied the people to the sick man's house and found him lying on his bed with the breath in his nostrils; but, as soon as the dying man smelt the fruit, at once recovering strength he rose in perfect health, sane and sound. Hereupon Ahmad bought the Magical Apple of the dealer and counted out to him the forty thousand Ashrafis. Presently, having gained the object of his travels, he resolved to join some caravan marching Indiawards and return to his father's home; but meanwhile he resolved to solace himself with the sights and marvels of Samarkand. His especial joy was to gaze upon the glorious plain hight Soghd,[1] one of the wonders of this world: the land on all sides was a delight to the sight, emerald-green and bright, with crystal rills like the plains of Paradise; the gardens bore all manner flowers and fruits and the cities and palaces gladdened the stranger's gaze. After some days Prince Ahmad joined a caravan of merchants wending Indiawards; and, when his long and longsome travel was ended, he at last reached the caravanserai where his two brothers, Husayn and Ali, impatiently awaited his arrival. The three rejoiced with exceeding joy to meet once more and fell on one another's necks; thanking Allah who had brought them back safe and sound, hale and hearty, after such prolonged and longsome absence. Then Prince Husayn, being the eldest, turned to them and said, "Now it behoveth us each to recount what hath betided him and announce what rare thing he hath brought back and what be the virtues thereof; and I, being the first-born, will be the foremost to tell my adventures. I bring with me from Bishangarh, a carpet, mean to look at, but such are its properties that should any sit thereon and wish in mind to visit country or city, he will at once be carried thither in ease and safety although it

---

[1] D'Herbelot renders Soghd Samarkand = plain of Samarkand. Hence the old "Sogdiana," the famed and classical capital of Máwaránnahr, our modern Transoxiana, now known as Samarkand. The Hindi translator has turned "Soghd" into "Sadá" and gravely notes that "the village appertained to Arabia." He possibly had a dim remembrance of the popular legend which derives "Samarkand" from Shamir or Samar bin Afrikús, the Tobba King of Al-Yaman, who lay waste Soghd-city ("Shamir kand" = Shamir destroyed); and when rebuilt the place was called by the Arab. corruption Samarkand. See Ibn Khallikan ii. 480. Ibn Haukal (Kitáb al Mamálik wa al-Masálik = Book of Realms and Routes), whose Oriental Geography (xth century) was translated by Sir W. Ouseley (London, Oriental Press, 1800), followed by Abú 'l-Fidá, mentions the Himyaritic inscription upon an iron plate over the Kash portal of Samarkand (Appendix No. iii.).

be distant months, nay years of journey. I have paid forty thousand gold pieces to its price; and, after seeing all the wonders of Bishangarh-land, I took seat upon my purchase and willed myself at this spot. Straightway I found myself here as I wished and have tarried in this caravanserai three months awaiting your arrival. The flying carpet is with me; so let him who listeth make trial of it." When the senior Prince had made an end of telling his tale, Prince Ali spake next and said, "O my brother, this carpet which thou hast brought is marvel-rare and hath most wondrous gifts; nor according to thy statement hath any in all the world seen aught to compare with it." Then bringing forth the Spying Tube, he pursued, "Look ye here, I too have bought for forty thousand Ashrafis somewhat whose merits I will now show forth to you." —— And as the morn began to dawn Shahrazad held her peace till

Ꞧhe end of the Six Hundred and Forty-ninth Night.

THEN said she: —— I have heard, O auspicious King, that Prince Ali enlarged upon the virtues of his purchase and said, "Ye see this ivory pipe? By means of it man may descry objects hidden from his sight and distant from him many a mile. 'Tis truly a most wondrous matter and right worthy your inspection, and you two may try it an ye will. Place but an eye close to the smaller glass and form a wish in mind to see what thing soe'er your soul desireth; and, whether it be near hand or distant many hundreds of miles, this ivory will make the object look clear and close to you." At these words Prince Husayn took the pipe from Prince Ali and, applying his eye to one end as he had been directed, then wished in his heart to behold the Princess Nur al-Nihar;[1] and the two brothers watched him to learn what he would say. Suddenly they saw his face change colour and wither as a wilted flower, while in his agitation and distress a flood of tears gushed from his eyes; and, ere his brothers recovered from their amaze-

---

[1] The wish might have been highly indiscreet and have exposed the wisher to the resentment of the two other brothers. In parts of Europe it is still the belief of the vulgar that men who use telescopes can see even with the naked eye objects which are better kept hidden; and I have heard of troubles in the South of France because the villagers would not suffer the secret charms of their women to become as it were the public property of the lighthouse employés.

ment and could enquire the cause of such strangeness, he cried aloud, "Alas! and well-away. We have endured toil and travail, and we have travelled so far and wide hoping to wed the Princess Nur al-Nihar. But 'tis all in vain: I saw her lying on her bed death-sick and like to breathe her last and around her stood her women all weeping and wailing in the sorest of sorrow. O my brothers, an ye would see her once again for the last time, take ye one final look through the glass ere she be no more." Hereat Prince Ali seized the Spying Tube and peered through it and found the condition of the Princess even as his brother Husayn had described; so he presently passed it over to Prince Ahmad, who also looked and was certified that the Lady Nur al-Nihar was about to give up the ghost. So he said to his elder brothers, "We three are alike love-distraught for the Princess and the dearest wish of each one is to win her. Her life is on the ebb, still I can save her and make her whole if we hasten to her without stay or delay." So saying he pulled from his pocket the Magical Apple and showed it to them crying, "This thing is not less in value than either the Flying Carpet or the Spying Tube. In Samarkand I bought it for forty thousand gold pieces and here is the best opportunity to try its virtues. The folk told me that if a sick man hold it to his nose, although on the point of death, he will wax at once well and hale again: I have myself tested it, and now ye shall see for yourselves its marvel-cure when I shall apply it to the case of Nur al-Nihar. Only, let us seek her presence ere she die." Quoth Prince Husayn, "This were an easy matter: my carpet shall carry us in the twinkling of an eye straight to the bedside of our beloved. Do ye without hesitation sit down with me thereupon, for there is room sufficient to accommodate us three; we shall instantly be carried thither and our servants can follow us." Accordingly, the three Princes disposed themselves upon the Flying Carpet and each willed in his mind to reach the bedside of Nur al-Nihar, when instantly they found themselves within her apartment. The handmaids and eunuchs in waiting were terrified at the sight and marvelled how these stranger men could have entered the chamber; and, as the Castratos were fain fall upon them, brand in hand, they recognised the Princes and drew back still in wonderment at their intrusion. Then the brothers rose forthright from the Flying Carpet and Prince Ahmad came forwards and put the Magical Apple to the nostrils of the lady, who lay stretched on the couch in unconscious state; and as the scent reached her brain the sickness left her and the cure was complete. She opened wide her eyes and sitting erect upon her bed looked all around and chiefly at the Princes as they stood before her; for she felt that she had waxed hale and hearty and as though she awoke after the sweetest of slumber. Presently she arose from her couch and bade her tire-women dress her the while they related to her the sudden coming of the three Princes, her uncle's sons, and how Prince Ahmad had made her smell something whereby she had recovered of her illness. And after she had made the Ablution of Health she joyed with exceeding joy to see the Princes and returned thanks to them, but chiefly to Prince Ahmad in that he had restored her to health and life. —— And as the morn began to dawn Shahrazad held her peace till

The end of the Six Hundred and Fiftieth Night.

THEN she said: —— I have heard, O auspicious King, that the brothers also were gladdened with exceeding gladness to see the Princess Nur al-Nihar recover so suddenly from mortal malady and, presently taking leave of her, they fared to greet their father. Meanwhile the Eunuchs had reported the whole matter to the Sultan, and when the Princes came before him he rose and embraced them tenderly and kissed them on their foreheads, filled with satisfaction to see them again and to hear from them the welfare of the Princess, who was dear to him as she had been his daughter. Then the three brothers produced each one the wondrous thing he had brought from his wayfare; and Prince Husayn first showed the Flying Carpet which in the twinkling of an eye had transported them home from far distant exile and said, "For outward show this carpet hath no merit, but inasmuch as it possesseth such wondrous virtue, methinks 'tis impossible to find in all the world aught that can compare to it for rarity." Next, Prince Ali presented to the King his Spying Tube and said, "The mirror of Jamshíd[1] is as vain and naught beside this pipe, by

---

[1] "Jám-i-Jamshíd" is a well worn commonplace in Moslem folk-lore; but commentators cannnot agree whether "Jám" be = a mirror or a cup. In the latter sense it would represent the Cyathomantic cup of the Patriarch Joseph and the symbolic bowl of Nestor. Jamshíd may be translated either Jam the Bright or the Cup of the Sun: this ancient King is the Solomon of the grand old Guebres.

means whereof all things from East to West and from North to South are made clearly visible to the ken of man." Last of all, Prince Ahmad produced the Magical Apple which wondrously saved the dear life of Nur al-Nihar and said, "By means of this fruit all maladies and grievous distempers are at once made whole." Thus each presented his rarity to the Sultan, saying, "O our lord, deign examine well these gifts we have brought and do thou pronounce which of them all is most excellent and admir-able; so, according to thy promise, he amongst us on whom thy choice may fall shall marry the Princess Nur al-Nihar." When the King had patiently listened to their several claims and had understood how each gift took part in restoring health to his niece, for a while he dove deep in the sea of thought and then answered, "Should I award the palm of merit to Prince Ahmad, whose Magical Apple cured the Princess, then should I deal unfairly by the other two. Albeit his rarity restored her to life and health from mortal illness, yet say me how had he known of her condition save by the virtue of Prince Ali's Spying Tube? In like manner, but for the Flying Carpet of Prince Husayn, which brought you three hither in a moment's space, the Magical Apple would have been of no avail. Wherefore 'tis my rede all three had like part and can claim equal merit in healing her; for it were impossible to have made her whole if any one thing of the three were wanting; furthermore all three objects are won-drous and marvellous without one surpassing other, nor can I, with aught of reason, assign preference or precedence to any. My promise was to marry the Lady Nur al-Nihar to him who should produce the rarest of rarities, but although strange 'tis not less true that all are alike in the one essential condition. The difficulty still remaineth and the question is yet unsolved, whilst I fain would have the matter settled ere the close of day, and without prejudice to any. So needs must I fix upon some plan whereby I may be able to adjudge one of you to be the winner, and bestow upon him the hand of Princess Nur al-Nihar, accord-ing to my plighted word; and thus absolve myself from all responsibility. Now I have resolved upon this course of action; to wit, that ye should mount each one his own steed and all of you be provided with bow and arrows; then do ye ride forth to the Maydán — the hippodrome — whither I and my Ministers of State and Grandees of the kingdom and Lords of the land will follow you. There in my presence ye shall each, turn by turn, shoot a shaft with all your might and main; and he amongst you whose arrow shall fly the farthest will be adjudged by me worthiest to win the Princess Nur al-Nihar to wife." Accordingly the three Princes, who could not gainsay the decision of their sire nor question its wisdom and justice, backed their coursers, and each taking his bow and arrows made straight for the place appointed. The King also, when he had stored the presents in the royal treasury, arrived there with his Wazirs and the dignitaries of his realm; and as soon as all was ready, the eldest son and heir, Prince Husayn, essayed his strength and skill and shot a shaft far along the level plain. After him Prince Ali hent his bow in hand and, discharging an arrow in like direction, overshot the first; and lastly came Prince Ahmad's turn. He too aimed at the same end, but such was the decree of Destiny, that although the knights and courtiers urged on their horses to note where his shaft might strike ground, withal they saw no trace thereof and none of them knew if it had sunk into the bowels of earth or had flown up to the confines of the sky. Some, indeed, there were who with evil mind held that Prince Ahmad had not shot any bolt, and that his arrow had never left his bow. So at last the King bade no more search be made for it and declared himself in favour of Prince Ali and adjudged that he should wed the Princess Nur al-Nihar, forasmuch as his arrow had outsped that of Prince Husayn. Accordingly, in due course the marriage rites and ceremonies were performed after the law and ritual of the land with exceeding pomp and grandeur. But Prince Husayn would not be present at the bride-feast by reason of his disappointment and jealousy, for he had loved the Lady Nur al-Nihar with a love far exceeding that of either of his brothers; and he doffed his princely dress and donning the garb of a Fakir fared forth to live a hermit's life. Prince Ahmad also burned with envy and refused to join the wedding-feast; he did not, however, like Prince Husayn, retire to a hermitage, but he spent all his days in searching for his shaft to find where it had fallen. Now it so fortuned that one morning he went again, alone as was his wont, in quest thereof, and starting from the stead whence they had shot their shafts reached the place where the arrows of Princes Husayn and Ali had been found. Then going straight forwards he cast his glances on every side over hill and dale to his right and to his left. —— And as the morn began to dawn Shahrazad held her peace till

The end of the Six Hundred and Fifty-first Night.

Then said she:——I have heard, O auspicious King, that Prince
Ahmad went searching for his shaft over hill and dale when,
after covering some three parasangs, suddenly he espied it
lying flat upon a rock.[1] Hereat he marvelled greatly, wondering how the arrow had flown so far, but even more so when
he went up to it and saw that it had not stuck in the ground
but appeared to have rebounded and to have fallen flat upon
a slab of stone. Quoth he to himself, "There must assuredly
be some mystery in this matter: else how could anyone shoot a
shaft to such a distance and find it fallen after so strange a
fashion." Then, threading his way amongst the pointed crags
and huge boulders, he presently came to a hollow in the ground
which ended in a subterraneous passage, and after pacing a few
paces he espied an iron door. He pushed this open with all ease,
for that it had no bolt, and entering, arrow in hand, he came upon
an easy slope by which he descended. But whereas he feared to
find all pitch-dark, he discovered at some distance a spacious
square, a widening of the cave, which was lighted on every side
with lamps and candelabra. Then advancing some fifty cubits or
more his glance fell upon a vast and handsome palace, and
presently there issued from within to the portico a lovely
maiden lovesome and lovable, a fairy-form robed in princely
robes and adorned from front to foot with the costliest of jewels.
She walked with slow and stately gait, withal graceful and
blandishing, whilst around her ranged her attendants like the
stars about a moon of the fourteenth night. Seeing this vision
of beauty, Prince Ahmad hastened to salute her with the salam
and she returned it; then coming forwards greeted him graciously
and said in sweetest accents, "Well come and welcome, O Prince
Ahmad: I am pleased to have sight of thee. How fareth it with
thy Highness and why hast thou tarried so long away from me?"
The King's son marvelled greatly to hear her name him by his
name; for that he knew not who she was, as they had never seen
each other aforetime—how then came she to have learnt his
title and condition? Then kissing ground before her he said,

---

[1] This passage may have suggested to Walter Scott one of his descriptions in "The
Monastery."

"O my lady, I owe thee much of thanks and gratitude for that thou art pleased to welcome me with words of cheer in this strange place where I, alone and a stranger, durst enter with exceeding hesitation and trepidation. But it perplexeth me sorely to think how thou camest to learn the name of thy slave." Quoth she with a smile, "O my lord, come hither and let us sit at ease within yon belvedere; and there I will give an answer to thine asking." So they went thither, Prince Ahmad following her footsteps; and on reaching it he was filled with wonder to see its vaulted roof of exquisite workmanship and adorned with gold and lapis lazuli[1] and paintings and ornaments, whose like was nowhere to be found in the world. The lady seeing his astonishment said to the Prince, "This mansion is nothing beside all my others which now, of my free will, I have made thine own; and when thou seest them thou shalt have just cause for wonderment." Then that sylph-like being took seat upon a raised daïs and with abundant show of affection seated Prince Ahmad by her side. Presently quoth she, "Albeit thou know me not, I know thee well, as thou shalt see with surprise when I shall tell thee all my tale. But first it behoveth me disclose to thee who I am. In Holy Writ belike thou hast read that this world is the dwelling-place not only of men, but also of a race hight the Jánn in form likest to mortals. I am the only daughter of a Jinn chief of noblest strain and my name is Perí-Bánú. So marvel not to hear me tell thee who thou art and who is the King thy sire and who is Nur al-Nihar, the daughter of thine uncle. I have full knowledge of all concerning thyself and thy kith and kin; how thou art one of three brothers who all and each were daft for love of Princess Nur al-Nihar and strave to win her from one another to wife. Furthermore thy sire deemed it best to send you all far and wide over foreign lands, and thou faredest to far Samarkand and broughtest back a Magical Apple made with rare art and mystery which thou boughtest for forty thousand Ashrafis; then by means whereof thou madest the Princess thy lady-love whole of a grievous malady, whilst Prince Husayn, thine elder brother, bought for the same sum of money a Flying Carpet at Bishangarh, and Prince Ali also brought home a Spying Tube from Shiraz-city. Let this suffice to show thee that naught is hidden from me of all thy case; and now do thou tell me in

---

[1] In the text "Lájawardí," for which see vols. iii. 33, and ix. 190.

very truth whom dost thou admire the more, for beauty and loveliness, me or the lady Nur al-Nihar thy brother's wife? My heart longeth for thee with excessive longing and desireth that we may be married and enjoy the pleasures of life and the joyance of love. So say me, art thou also willing to wed me, or pinest thou in preference for the daughter of thine uncle? In the fulness of my affection for thee I stood by thy side unseen during the archery-meeting upon the plain of trial, and when thou shottest thy shaft I knew that it would fall far short of Prince Ali's,[1] so I hent it in hand ere it touched ground and carried it away from sight, and striking it upon the iron door caused it rebound and lie flat upon the rock where thou didst find it. And ever since that day I have been sitting in expectancy, wotting well that thou wouldst search for it until thou find it, and by such means I was certified of bringing thee hither to me." Thus spake the beautiful maiden Peri-Banu who with eyes full of love-longing looked up at Prince Ahmad; and then with modest shame bent low her brow and averted her glance.——And as the morn began to dawn Shahrazad held her peace till

The end of the Six Hundred and Fifty-second Night.

THEN said she:——I have heard, O auspicious King, that when Prince Ahmad heard these words of Peri-Banu he rejoiced with joy exceeding, and said to himself, "The Princess Nur al-Nihar is not within my power to win, and Peri-Banu doth outvie her in comeliness of favour and in loveliness of form and in gracefulness of gait." In short so charmed was he and captivated that he clean forgot his love for his cousin; and, noting that the heart of his new enchantress inclined towards him, he replied, "O my lady, O fairest of the fair, naught else do I desire save that I may serve thee and do thy bidding all my life long. But I am of human and thou of non-human birth. Thy friends and family, kith and kin, will haply be displeased with thee an thou unite with me in such union." But she made answer, "I have full sanction of my parents to marry as I list and whomsoever I may prefer. Thou sayest that thou wilt be my servant, nay, rather be thou my lord and master; for I myself and my life and

---

[1] In Galland and the H. V. "Prince Husayn's."

all my good are very thine, and I shall ever be thy bondswoman. Consent now, I beseech thee, to accept me for thy wife: my heart doth tell me thou wilt not refuse my request." Then Peri-Banu added, "I have told thee already that in this matter I act with fullest authority. Besides all this there is a custom and immemorial usage with us fairy-folk that, when we maidens come to marriageable age and years of understanding, each one may wed, according the dictates of her heart, the person that pleaseth her most and whom she judgeth likely to make her days happy. Thus wife and husband live with each other all their lives in harmony and happiness. But if a girl be given away in marriage by the parents, according to their choice and not hers, and she be mated to a helpmate unmeet for her, because ill-shapen or ill-conditioned or unfit to win her affection, then are they twain likely to be at variance each with other for the rest of their days; and endless troubles result to them from such ill-sorted union. Nor are we bound by another law which bindeth modest virgins of the race of Adam; for we freely announce our preference to those we love, nor must we wait and pine to be wooed and won." When Prince Ahmad heard these words of answer, he rejoiced with exceeding joy and stooping down essayed to kiss the skirt of her garment, but she prevented him, and in lieu of her hem gave him her hand. The Prince clasped it with rapture and according to the custom of that place, he kissed it and placed it to his breast and upon his eyes. Hereat quoth the Fairy, smiling a charming smile, "With my hand locked in thine plight me thy troth even as I pledge my faith to thee, that I will alway true and loyal be, nor ever prove faithless or fail of constancy." And quoth the Prince, "O loveliest of beings, O dearling of my soul, thinkest thou that I can ever become a traitor to my own heart, I who love thee to distraction and dedicate to thee my body and my sprite; to thee who art my queen, the very empress of me? Freely I give myself to thee, do thou with me whatso thou wilt." Hereupon Peri-Banu said to Prince Ahmad, "Thou art my husband and I am thy wife.[1] This solemn promise made between thee and me standeth in stead of marriage-contract: no need have we of Kazi, for with us all other forms and ceremonies are

---

[1] This is the "Gandharba-lagana" (fairy wedding) of the Hindus; a marriage which lacked only the normal ceremonies. For the Gandharbas = heavenly choristers see Moor's "Hindú Pantheon," p. 237, etc.

superfluous and of no avail.   Anon I will show thee the chamber
where we shall pass the bride-night; and methinks thou wilt
admire it and confess that there is none like thereto in the whole
world of men." Presently her handmaidens spread the table and
served up dishes of various kinds, and the finest wines in flagons
and goblets of gold dubbed with jewels. So they twain sat at
meat and ate and drank their sufficiency. Then Peri-Banu took
Prince Ahmad by the hand and led him to her private chamber
wherein she slept; and he stood upon the threshold amazed to see
its magnificence and the heaps of gems and precious stones which
dazed his sight, till recovering himself he cried, "Methinks there
is not in the universe a room so splendid and decked with costly
furniture and gemmed articles such as this." Quoth Peri-Banu,
"An thou so admire and praise this palace what wilt thou say
when sighting the mansions and castles of my sire the Jann-
King? Haply too when thou shalt behold my garden thou wilt be
filled with wonder and delight; but now 'tis over late to lead thee
thither and night approacheth." Then she ushered Prince
Ahmad into another room where the supper had been spread,
and the splendour of this saloon yielded in naught to any of the
others; nay, rather it was the more gorgeous and dazzling.
Hundreds of wax candles set in candelabra of the finest amber[1]
and the purest crystal, ranged on all sides, rained floods of light,
whilst golden flowerpots and vessels of finest workmanship and
priceless worth, of lovely shapes and wondrous art, adorned the
niches and the walls.——And as the morn began to dawn Shahrazad held her peace till

The end of the Six Hundred and Fifty-third Night.

THEN said she:——I have heard, O auspicious King, that tongue
of man can never describe the magnificence of that room in which
bands of virgin Peris, loveliest of forms and fairest of features,
garbed in choicest garments played on sweet-toned instruments
of mirth and merriment or sang lays of amorous significance to
strains of heart-bewitching music. Then they twain, to wit the
bride and bridegroom, sat down at meat, ever and anon delaying
to indulge in toyings and bashful love-play and chaste caresses.

---

[1] "Perfumed with amber" (-gris?) says Galland.

Peri-Banu with her own hands passed the choicest mouthfuls to Prince Ahmad and made him taste of each dish and dainty, telling him their names and whereof they were composed. But how shall I, O auspicious King Shahryar, avail to give thee any notion of those Jinn-made dishes or to describe with due meed of praise the delicious flavour of meats such as no mortal ever tasted or ever beheld? Then, when both had supped, they drank the choicest wines, and ate with relish sweet conserves and dry fruit and a dessert of various delicacies. At length, when they had their requirement of eating and drinking, they retired into another room which contained a raised daïs of the grandest, be-decked with gold-purfled cushions and pillows wrought with seed-pearl and Achæmenian tapestries, whereupon they took seat side by side for converse and solace. Then came in a troop of Jinns and fairies who danced and sang before them with wondrous grace and art; and this pretty show pleased Peri-Banu and Prince Ahmad, who watched the sports and displays with ever-renewed delight. At last the newly wedded couple rose and retired, weary of revelry, to another chamber, wherein they found that the slaves had dispread the genial bed, whose frame was gold studded with jewels and whose furniture was of satin and sendal flowered with the rarest embroidery. Here the guests who attended at the marriage festival and the handmaids of the palace, ranged in two lines, hailed the bride and bridegroom as they went within; and then, craving dismissal, they all departed leaving them to take their joyance in bed. On such wise the marriage-festival and nuptial merry-makings were kept up day after day, with new dishes and novel sports, novel dances and new music; and, had Prince Ahmad lived a thousand years with mortal kind, never could he have seen such revels or heard such strains or enjoyed such love-liesse. Thus six months soon passed in the Fairy-land beside Peri-Banu, whom he loved with a love so fond that he would not lose her from his sight for a moment's space; but would feel restless and ill-at-ease whenas he ceased to look upon her. In like manner Peri-Banu was fulfilled with affec-tion for him and strove to please her bridegroom more and more every moment by new arts of dalliance and fresh appliances of pleasure, until so absorbing waxed his passion for her that the thought of home and kindred, kith and kin, faded from his thoughts and fled his mind. But after a time his memory awoke from slumber and at times he found himself longing to look upon

his father, albeit well did he wot that it were impossible to find
out how the far one fared unless he went himself to visit him.
So one day quoth he to Peri-Banu, "An it be thy pleasure, I pray
thee give me thy command that I may leave thee for a few days
to see my sire, who doubtless grieveth at my long absence and
suffereth all the sorrows of separation from his son." Peri-Banu,
hearing these words was dismayed with sore dismay, for that she
thought within herself that this was only an excuse whereby he
might escape and leave her after enjoyment and possession had
made her love pall upon the palate of his mind. So quoth she in
reply, "Hast thou forgotten thy vows and thy plighted troth,
that thou wishest to leave me now? Have love and longing ceased
to stir thee, whilst my heart always throbbeth in raptures as it
hath ever done at the very thought of thee?" Replied the
Prince, "O dearling of my soul, my queen, my empress, what be
these doubts that haunt thy mind, and why such sad misgivings
and sorrowful words? I know full well that the love of thee and
thine affection me-wards are even as thou sayest; and did I not
acknowledge this truth or did I prove unthankful or fail to regard
thee with a passion as warm and deep, as tender and as true as
thine own, I were indeed an ingrate and a traitor of the darkest
dye. Far be it from me to desire severance from thee nor hath
any thought of leaving thee never to return at any time crossed
my mind. But my father is now an old man well shotten in years
and he is sore grieved in mind at this long separation from his
youngest son. If thou wilt deign command, I would fain go visit
him and with all haste return to thine arms; yet I would not do
aught in this matter against thy will; and such is my fond affection
for thee that I would fain be at all hours of the day and watches
of the night by thy side nor leave thee for a moment of time."
Peri-Banu was somewhat comforted by this speech; and from his
looks, words and acts she was certified that Prince Ahmad really
loved her with fondest love and that his heart was true as steel
to her as was his tongue. Whereupon she granted him leave and
liberty to set forth and see his sire, whilst at the same time she
gave him strict commandment not to tarry long with his kith
and kin. Hearken now, O auspicious King Shahryar, to what
befel the Sultan of Hindostan and how it fared with him after the
marriage of Prince Ali to Princess Nur al-Nihar.——And as the
morn began to dawn Shahrazad held her peace till

The end of the Six Hundred and Fifty-fourth Night.

THEN said she:——I have heard, O auspicious King, that not
seeing Prince Husayn and Prince Ahmad for the space of many
days the Sultan waxed exceeding sad and heavy-hearted, and one
morning after Darbár,[1] asked his Wazirs and Ministers what had
betided them and where they were. Hereto the councillors made
answer saying, "O our lord, and shadow of Allah upon earth,
thine eldest son and fruit of thy vitals and heir apparent to thine
Empire the Prince Husayn, in his disappointment and jealousy
and bitter grief hath doffed his royal robes to become a hermit, a
devotee, renouncing all worldly lusts and gusts. Prince Ahmad
thy third son also in high dudgeon hath left the city; and of him
none knoweth aught, whither he hath fled or what hath befallen
him." The King was sore distressed and bade them write without stay or delay and forthright despatch firmans and commands
to all the Nabobs and Governors of the provinces, with strict
injunctions to make straight search for Prince Ahmad and to
send him to his sire the moment he was found. But, albeit the
commandments were carried out to the letter and all the seekers
used the greatest diligence none came upon any trace of him.
Then, with increased sadness of heart, the Sultan ordered his
Grand Wazir to go in quest of the fugitive and the Minister
replied, "Upon my head be it and mine eyes! Thy servant hath
already caused most careful research to be made in every quarter,
but not the smallest clue hath yet come to hand: and this matter
troubleth me the more for that he was dear to me as a son." The
Ministers and Grandees now understood that the King was overwhelmed with woe, tearful-eyed and heavy-hearted by reason
of the loss of Prince Ahmad; whereupon bethought the Grand
Wazir of a certain witch famed for the Black Art who could
conjure down the stars from heaven; and who was a noted
dweller in the capital. So going to the Sultan he spake highly of
her skill in knowledge of the abstruse,[2] saying "Let the King, I

---

[1] The Hind term for the royal levée, as "Selám" is the Persian.
[2] Arab. " 'Ilm al-Ghayb" = the Science of Hidden Things which, says the Hadis, belongeth only to the Lord. Yet amongst Moslems, as with other faiths, the instinctive
longing to pry into the Future has produced a host of pseudo-sciences, Geomancy, Astrology, Prophecy and others which serve only to prove that such knowledge, in the present
condition of human nature, is absolutely unattainable.

pray thee, send for this sorceress and enquire of her concerning his lost son." And the King replied, " 'Tis well said: let her be brought hither and haply she shall give me tidings of the Prince and how he fareth." So they fetched the Sorceress and set her before the Sultan, who said, "O my good woman, I would have thee know that ever since the marriage of Prince Ali with the Lady Nur al-Nihar, my youngest son Prince Ahmad,[1] who was disappointed in her love, hath disappeared from our sight and no man knoweth aught of him. Do thou forthright apply thy magical craft and tell me only this:—Is he yet alive or is he dead? An he live I would learn where is he and how fareth he; more-over, I would ask, Is it written in my book of Destiny that I shall see him yet again?" To this the Witch made reply, "O Lord of the Age and ruler of the times and tide, 'tis not possible for me at once to answer all these questions which belong to the knowledge of Hidden Things; but, if thy Highness deign grant me one day of grace, I will consult my books of gramarye and on the morrow will give thee a sufficient reply and a satisfactory." The Sultan to this assented, saying, "An thou can give me de-tailed and adequate answer, and set my mind at ease after this sorrow, thou shalt have an exceeding great reward and I will honour thee with highmost honour." Next day the Sorceress, accompanied by the Grand Wazir, craved permission to appear before the presence, and when it was granted came forward and said, "I have made ample investigation by my art and mystery and I have assured myself that Prince Ahmad is yet in the land of the living. Be not therefore uneasy in thy mind on his account; but at present, save this only, naught else can I discover regard-ing him, nor can I say for sure where he be or how he is to be found." At these words the Sultan took comfort, and hope sprang up within his breast that he should see his son again ere he died. Now return we to the story of Prince Ahmad. Whenas Peri-Banu understood that he was bent upon visiting his sire and she was convinced that his love her-wards remained firm and steadfast as before, she took thought and determined that it would ill become her to refuse him leave and liberty for such purpose; so she again pondered the matter in her mind and de-

---

[1] In folk-lore and fairy tales the youngest son of mostly three brothers is generally Fortune's favourite: at times also he is the fool or the unlucky one of the family, Cin-derella being his counterpart (Mr. Clouston, i. 321).

bated with herself for many an hour till at length, one day of the days, she turned to her husband and said, "Albeit my heart consenteth not to part from thee for a moment or to lose sight of thee for a single instant, still inasmuch as thou hast ofttimes made entreaty of me and hast shown thyself so solicitous to see thy sire, I will no longer baffle thy wish. But this my favour will depend upon one condition; otherwise I will never grant thy petition and give thee such permission. Swear to me the most binding of oaths that thou wilt haste thee back hither with all possible speed, and thou wilt not by long absence cause me yearning grief and anxious waiting for thy safe return to me." Prince Ahmad, well pleased to win his wish, thanked her saying, "O my beloved, fear not for me after any fashion and rest assured I will come back to thee with all haste as soon as I shall have seen my sire; and life hath no charms for me away from thy presence. Although I must needs be severed from thee for a few days, yet will my heart ever turn to thee and to thee only." These words of Prince Ahmad gladdened the heart of Peri-Banu and drove away the darksome doubts and mysterious misgivings which ever haunted her nightly dreams and her daily musings.——And as the morn began to dawn Shahrazad held her peace till

The end of the Six Hundred and Fifty-fifth Night.

THEN said she:——I have heard, O auspicious King, that Peri-Banu gladdened by these premises addressed her husband, Prince Ahmad, "So now, as soon as thy heart desireth, go thou and pay thy respects to thy sire; but ere thou set out I would charge thee with one charge and look that on no wise thou forget my rede and my counsel. Speak not to any a single word of this thy marriage nor of the strange sights thou hast seen and the wonders thou hast witnessed; but keep them carefully concealed from thy father and thy brethren and from thy kith and kin, one and all. This only shalt thou tell thy sire, so his mind may be set at ease, that thou art buxom and happy; also that thou hast returned home for a while only with the object of seeing him and becoming assured of his welfare." Then she gave orders to her people, bidding them make ready for the journey without delay; and when all things were prepared she appointed twenty horsemen, armed cap-à-pie and fully accoutred, to accompany her husband,

LANDELLS

G. NICHOLLS

and gave him a horse of perfect form and proportions, swift as the blinding leven or the rushing wind; and its housings and furniture were bedeckt with precious ores and studded with jewels. Then she fell on his neck and they embraced with warmest love; and as the twain bade adieu, Prince Ahmad, to set her mind at rest, renewed his protestations and sware to her again his solemn oath. Then mounting his horse and followed by his suite (all Jinn-born cavaliers) he set forth with mighty pomp and circumstance, and riding diligently he soon reached his father's capital. Here he was received with loud acclamations, the like of which had never been known in the land. The Ministers and Officers of State, the citizens and the Ryots all rejoiced with exceeding joy to see him once more, and the folk left their work and with blessings and low obeisances joined the cavalcade; and, crowding around him on every side, escorted him to the palace-gates. When the Prince reached the threshold he dismounted and, entering the audience-hall, fell at his father's feet and kissed them in a transport of filial affection. The Sultan, well nigh distraught for delight at the unexpected sight of Prince Ahmad, rose from his throne and threw himself upon his son's neck weeping for very joy and kissed his forehead saying, "O dear my child, in despair at the loss of the Lady Nur al-Nihar thou didst suddenly fly from thy home, and, despite all research, nor trace nor sign of thee was to be found however sedulously we sought thee; and I, distracted at thy disappearance, am reduced to this condition in which thou seest me. Where hast thou been this long while, and how hast thou lived all this time?" Replied Prince Ahmad, " 'Tis true, O my lord the King, that I was down-hearted and distressed to see Prince Ali gain the hand of my cousin, but that is not the whole cause of my absence. Thou mayest remember how, when we three brothers rode at thy command to yonder plain for a trial of archery, my shaft, albeit the place was large and flat, disappeared from sight and none could find where it had fallen. Now so it fortuned that one day in sore heaviness of mind I fared forth alone and unaccompanied to examine the ground thereabout and try if haply I could find my arrow. But when I reached the spot where the shafts of my brothers, Princes Husayn and Ali, had been picked up, I made search in all directions, right and left, before and behind, thinking that thereabouts mine also might come to hand; but all my trouble was in vain: I found neither shaft nor aught else. So walking onwards in obstinate research, I went a long way, and at last despairing, I would have given up the quest, for full well I knew that my bow could not have carried so far, and indeed that 'twere impossible for any marksman to have driven bolt or pile to such distance, when suddenly I espied it lying flat upon a rock some four parasangs[1] distant from this place." The Sultan marvelled with much marvel at his words and the Prince presently resumed, "So when I picked up the arrow, O my lord, and considered it closely I knew it for the very one I had shot, but admired in my mind how it had come to fly so far, and I doubted not but that there was a somewhat mysterious about the matter. While I thus reflected I came upon the place where I have sojourned ever since that day in perfect solace and happiness. I may not tell thee more of my tale than this; for I came only to ease thy mind on my account, and now I pray thee deign grant me thy supreme permission that I return forthright to my home of delights. From time to time I will not cease to wait upon thee and to enquire of thy welfare with all the affection of a son." Replied the King, "O my child, the sight of thee hath gladdened mine eyes; and I am now satisfied; and not unwillingly I give thee leave to go, since thou art happy in some place so near hand; but shouldst thou at any time delay thy coming hither, say me, how shall I be able to get tidings of thy good health and welfare?" And quoth Prince Ahmad, "O my lord the King, that which thou requirest of me is part of my secret and this must remain deep hidden in my breast: as I said before, I may not discover it to thee nor say aught that might lead to its discovery. However, be not uneasy in thy soul, for I will appear before thee full many a time and haply I may irk thee with continual coming." "O my son," rejoined the Sultan, "I would not learn thy secret an thou would keep it from me, but there is one only thing I desire of thee, which is, that ever and anon I may be assured of thine enduring health and happiness. Thou hast my full permission to hie thee home, but forget not at least once a month to come and see me even as now thou dost, lest such forgetfulness cause me anxiety and trouble, cark and care." So Prince Ahmad tarried with his father three days full-told, but never for a moment did

---

[1] The parasang (Gr. παρασάγγης), which Ibn Khall. (iii. 315) reduces to three miles, has been derived wildly enough from Fars or Pars (Persia proper) sang = (mile) stone. Chardin supports the etymology, "because leagues are marked out with great tall stones in the East as well as the West, *e.g.*, ad primam (vel secundam) lapidem."

the memory of the Lady Peri-Banu fade from his mind; and on the fourth day he mounted horse and returned with the same pomp and pageantry wherewith he came.——And as the morn began to dawn Shahrazad held her peace till

The end of the Six Hundred and Fifty-sixth Night.

THEN said she:——I have heard, O auspicious King, that Peri-Banu joyed with exceeding joy at the sight of Prince Ahmad as he returned to his home; and it seemed to her as though they had been parted for three hundred years: such is love that moments of separation are longsome and weary as twelvemonths. The Prince offered much of excuses for his short absence and his words delighted Peri-Banu yet the more. So these twain, lover and beloved, passed the time in perfect happiness, taking their pleasure one with other. Thus a month went by and Prince Ahmad never once mentioned the name of his sire nor expressed a wish to go visit him according to his promise. Noting this change, the Lady Peri-Banu said to him one day, "Thou toldest me aforetime that once in the beginning of each month thou wouldst fare forth and travel to thy father's court and learn news of his welfare: why then neglectest thou so to do, seeing that he will be distressed and anxiously expecting thee?" Replied Prince Ahmad, " 'Tis even as thou sayest, but, awaiting thy command and thy permission, I have forborne to propose the journey to thee." And she made answer, "Let thy faring and thy returning rest not on my giving thee liberty of leave. At the beginning of each month as it cometh round, do thou ride forth, and from this time forwards thou hast no need to ask permission of me. Stay with thy sire three days full-told and on the fourth come back to me without fail." Accordingly, on the next day betimes in the morning Prince Ahmad took his departure and as aforetime rode forth with abundant pomp and parade and repaired to the palace of the Sultan his sire, to whom he made his obeisance. On like manner continued he to do each month with a suite of horsemen larger and more brilliant than before, whilst he himself was more splendidly mounted and equipped. And whenever the Crescent appeared in the Western sky he fondly farewelled his wife and paid his visit to the King, with whom he tarried three whole days, and on the fourth returned to dwell with Peri-Banu. But, as each and every time he went, his equipage was greater and grander than the last, at length one of the Wazirs, a favourite and cup-companion of the King, was filled with wonderment and jealousy to see Prince Ahmad appear at the palace with such opulence and magnificence. So he said in himself, "None can tell whence cometh this Prince, and by what means he hath obtained so splendid a suite." Then of his envy and malice that Wazir fell to plying the King with deceitful words and said, "O my liege lord and mighty sovran, it ill becometh thee to be thus heedless of Prince Ahmad's proceedings. Seest thou not how day after day his retinue increaseth in numbers and puissance? What an he should plot against thee and cast thee into prison, and take from thee the reins of the realm? Right well thou wottest that inasmuch as thou didst wed Prince Ali to the Lady Nur al-Nihar thou provokedest the wrath of Prince Husayn and Prince Ahmad; so that one of them in the bitterness of his soul renounced the pomps and vanities of this world and hath become a Fakir, whilst the other, to wit; Prince Ahmad, appeareth before thy presence in such inordinate power and majesty. Doubtless they both seek their revenge; and, having gotten thee into their power, the twain will deal treacherously with thee. So I would have thee beware, and again I say beware; and seize the forelock of opportunity ere it be too late; for the wise have said,

'Thou canst bar a spring with a sod of clay * But when grown 'twill bear a big host away.'"

Thus spake that malicious Wazir; and presently he resumed, "Thou knowest also that when Prince Ahmad would end his three days' visits he never asketh thy leave nor farewelleth thee nor biddeth adieu to any one of his family. Such conduct is the beginning of rebellion and proveth him to be rancorous of heart. But 'tis for thee in thy wisdom to decide." These words sank deep in the heart of the simple-minded Sultan and grew a crop of the direst suspicions. He presently thought within himself, "Who knoweth the mind and designs of Prince Ahmad, whether they be dutiful or undutiful towards me? Haply he may be plotting vengeance; so it besitteth me to make enquiries concerning him, to discover where he dwelleth and by what means he hath attained to such puissance and opulence." Filled with these jealous thoughts, he sent in private one day, unbeknown to the

Grand Wazir who would at all times befriend Prince Ahmad, to summon the Witch; and, admitting her by a secret postern to his private chamber, asked of her saying, "Thou didst aforetime learn by thy magical art that Prince Ahmad was alive and didst bring me tidings of him. I am beholden to thee for this good office, and now I would desire of thee to make further quest into his case and ease my mind, which is sore disturbed. Albeit my son still liveth and cometh to visit me every month, yet am I clean ignorant of the place wherein he dwelleth and whence he setteth out to see me; for that he keepeth the matter close hidden from his sire. Go thou forthright and privily, without the knowledge of any, my Wazirs and Nabobs, my courtiers and my household; and make thou diligent research and with all haste bring me word whereabouts he liveth. He now sojourneth here upon his wonted visit; and, on the fourth day, without leave-taking or mention of departure to me or to any of the Ministers and Officers, he will summon his suite and mount his steed; then will he ride to some little distance hence and suddenly disappear. Do thou without stay or delay forego him on the path and lie perdue in some convenient hollow hard by the road whence thou mayest learn where he hometh; then quickly bring me tidings thereof." Accordingly, the Sorceress departed the presence of the King; and, after walking over the four parasangs, she hid herself within a hollow of the rocks hard by the place where Prince Ahmad had found his arrow, and there awaited his arrival. Early on the morrow the Prince, as was his wont, set out upon his journey without taking leave of his sire or fare-welling any of the Ministers. So when they drew nigh, the Sorceress caught sight of the Prince and of the retinue that rode before and beside him; and she saw them enter a hollow way which forked into a many of by-ways; and so steep and dangerous were the cliffs and boulders about the track that hardly could a footman safely pace that path. Seeing this the Sorceress be-thought her that it must surely lead to some cavern or haply to a subterraneous passage, or to a souterrain the abode of Jinns and fairies; when suddenly the Prince and all his suite vanished from her view. So she crept out of the hiding-place wherein she had ensconced herself and wandered far and wide seeking, as dili-gently as she was able, but never finding the subterraneous passage nor yet could she discern the iron door which Prince Ahmad had espied, for none of human flesh and blood had power to see this save he alone to whom it was made visible by the Fairy Peri-Banu; furthermore it was ever concealed from the prying eyes of womankind. Then said the Sorceress to herself, "This toil and moil have I undertaken to no purpose; yea, verily, I have failed to find out that wherefor I came." So she went forthright back to the Sultan and reported to him all that had betided her, how she had lain in wait amid the cliffs and boulders and had seen the Prince and suite ride up the most perilous of paths and, having entered a hollow way, disappear in an eye-twinkling from her sight. And she ended by saying, "Albeit I strove my utmost to find out the spot wherein the Prince abideth, yet could I on no wise succeed; and I pray thy Highness may grant me time to search further into the matter and to find out this mystery which by skill and caution on my part shall not long abide concealed." Answered the Sultan, "Be it as thou wilt: I grant thee leisure to make enquiry and after a time I shall await thy return hither."——And as the morn began to dawn Shahrazad held her peace till

The end of the Six Hundred and Fifty-seventh Night.

THEN said she:——I have heard, O auspicious King, that moreover the King largessed the Witch with a diamond of large size and of great price, saying, "Take this stone to guerdon for thy trouble and travail and in earnest of future favours; so, when thou shalt return and bring me word that thou hast searched and found out the secret, thou shalt have a Bakhshish of far greater worth and I will make thy heart rejoice with choicest joy and honour thee with highmost honour." So the Sorceress looked forwards to the coming of the Prince, for well she knew that at the sight of each crescent he rode home to visit his sire and was bound to abide with him three days, even as the Lady Peri-Banu had permitted and had enjoined him. Now when the moon had waxed and waned, on the day before the Prince would leave home upon his monthly visit, the Witch betook her to the rocks and sat beside the place whence she imagined he would issue forth; and next morning early he and his suite, composed of many a mounted knight with his esquire a-foot, who now always accompanied him in increasing numbers, rode forth gallantly through the iron doorway and passed hard by the place where she lay in wait for him. The Sorceress crouched low upon the ground in her tattered rags; and, seeing a heap by his way, the Prince at first supposed that a slice of stone had fallen from the rocks across his path. But as he drew nigh she fell to weeping and wailing with might and main as though in sore dolour and distress, and she ceased not to crave his countenance and assistance with increase of tears and lamentations. The Prince seeing her sore sorrow had pity on her, and reining in his horse, asked her what she had to require of him and what was the cause of her cries and lamentations. At this the cunning crone but cried the more, and the Prince was affected with compassion still livelier at seeing her tears and hearing her broken, feeble words. So when the Sorceress perceived that Prince Ahmad had ruth on her and would fain show favour to her, she heaved a heavy sigh and in woeful tones, mingled with moans and groans, addressed him in these false words, withal holding the hem of his garment and at times stopping as if convulsed with pain, "O my lord and lord of all loveliness, as I was journeying from my home in yonder city upon an errand to such a place, behold, when I came thus far upon my way, suddenly a hot fit of fever seized me and a shivering and a trembling, so that I lost all strength and fell down helpless as thou seest me; and still no power have I in hand or foot to rise from the ground and to return to my place." Replied the Prince, "Alas, O good woman, there is no house at hand where thou mayest go and be fitly tended and tendered. Howbeit I know a stead whither, an thou wilt, I can convey thee and where by care and kindness thou shalt (Inshallah!) soon recover of thy complaint. Come then with me as best thou canst." With loud moans and groans the Witch made answer, "So weak am I in every limb and helpless that I can by no means rise off the ground or move save with the help of some friendly hand." The Prince then bade one of his horsemen lift up the feeble and ailing old woman and set her upon his steed; and the cavalier did his lord's bidding forthright and mounted her astraddle upon the crupper of his courser: then, Prince Ahmad rode back with her and entering by the iron door carried her to his apartment and sent for Peri-Banu. His wife hurriedly coming forth to the Prince asked him in her flurry, "Is all well and wherefore hast thou come back and what wouldst thou that thou hast sent for me?" Prince Ahmad then told her of the old woman who was healthless and helpless, adding, "Scarce had I set out on my journey

when I espied this ancient dame lying hard by the roadside,
suffering and in sore distress. My heart felt pity for her to see
her in such case and constrained me to bring her hither as I
could not leave her to die among the rocks; and I pray thee of
thy bounty take her in and give her medicines that she may soon
be made whole of this her malady. An thou wilt show this
favour I shall not cease to thank thee and be beholden to thee."
——And as the morn began to dawn Shahrazad held her
peace till

The end of the Six Hundred and Fifty-eighth Night.

THEN said she:——I have heard, O auspicious King, that Peri-
Banu looked at the old woman and charged a twain of her handmaidens that they carry her into a room apart and tend her with
the tenderest care and the uttermost of diligence. The attendants did as she bade them and transported the Sorceress to
the place she had designed. Then Peri-Banu addressed Prince
Ahmad saying, "O my lord, I am pleased to see thy pitiful kindness towards this ancient dame, and I surely will look to her case
even as thou hast enjoined me; but my heart misgiveth me and
much I fear some evil will result from thy goodness. This
woman is not so ill as she doth make believe, but practiseth
deceit upon thee and I ween that some enemy or envier hath
plotted a plot against me and thee. Howbeit go now in peace
upon thy journey." The Prince, who on no wise took to heart
the words of his wife, presently replied to her, "O my lady,
Almighty Allah forfend thee from all offence! With thee to help
and guard me I fear naught of ill: I know of no foeman who
would compass my destruction, for I bear no grudge against any
living being, and I foresee no evil at the hands of man or Jann."
Thereupon the Prince again took leave of Peri-Banu and repaired
with his attendants to the palace of his sire who, by reason of
the malice of his crafty Minister, was inwardly afraid to see his
son; but not the less he welcomed him with great outward show
of love and affection. Meanwhile the two fairy handmaidens,
to whom Peri-Banu had given charge of the Witch, bore her
away to a spacious room splendidly furnished; and laid her on a
bed having a mattress of satin and a brocaded coverlet. Then
one of them sat by her side whilst the other with all speed
fetched, in a cup of porcelain, an essence which was a sovereign

draught for ague and fever. Presently they raised her up and
seated her on the couch saying, "Drain thou this drink. It is the
water of the Lions' Fount and whoso tasteth of the same is forthwith made whole of what disease soever he hath." The Sorceress
took the cup with great difficulty and after swallowing the contents lay back on the bed; and the handmaidens spread the quilt
over her saying, "Now rest awhile and thou shalt soon feel the
virtues of this medicine." Then they left her to sleep for an hour
or so; but presently the Witch, who had feigned sickness to the
intent only that she might learn where Prince Ahmad abode and
might inform the Sultan thereof, being assured that she had discovered all that she desired, rose up and summoning the damsels
said to them, "The drinking of that draught hath restored to me
all my health and strength: I now feel hale and hearty once more
and my limbs are filled with new life and vigour. So at once
acquaint your lady herewith, that I may kiss the hem of her robe
and return my thanks for her goodness me-wards, then depart
and hie me home again." Accordingly, the two handmaidens
took the Sorceress with them and showed her as they went along
the several apartments, each more magnificent and kingly than
the other; and at length they reached the belvedere which was
the noblest saloon of all, and fitted and filled with furniture
exceeding costly and curious. There sat Peri-Banu upon a throne
which was adorned with diamonds and rubies, emeralds, pearls
and other gems of unwonted size and water, whilst round about
her stood fairies of lovely form and features, robed in the richest
raiments and awaiting with folded hands her commandments.
The Sorceress marvelled with extreme marvel to see the splendour of the chambers and their furniture, but chiefly when she
beheld the Lady Peri-Banu seated upon the jewelled throne; nor
could she speak a word for confusion and awe, but she bent
down low and placed her head upon Peri-Banu's feet. Quoth
the Princess in soft speech and reassuring tones, "O good woman,
it pleaseth me greatly to see thee a guest in this my palace, and
I joy even more to learn that thou be wholly quit of thy sickness.
So now solace thy spirits with walking all round about the place
and my servants will accompany thee and show thee what there
is worthy of thine inspection." Hereat the Witch again louted
low and kissed the carpet under Peri-Banu's feet, and took leave
of her hostess in goodly phrase and with great show of gratitude
for her favours. The handmaids then led her round the palace

and displayed to her all the rooms, which dazed and dazzled her sight so that she could not find words to praise them sufficiently. Then she went her ways and the fairies escorted her past the iron doorway whereby Prince Ahmad had brought her in, and left her, bidding her God-speed and blessing her; and the foul crone with many thanks took the road to her own home. But when she had walked to some distance she was minded to see the iron door, so might she with ease know it again; so she went back, but lo and behold! the entrance had vanished and was invisible to her as to all other women. Accordingly, after searching on all sides and pacing to and fro and finding nor sign nor trace of palace or portal, she repaired in despair to the city and, creeping along a deserted path-way, entered the palace, according to her custom, by the private postern. When safely within she straightway sent word by an eunuch to the Sultan, who ordered that she be brought before him. She approached him with troubled countenance, whereat, perceiving that she had failed to carry out her purpose, he asked, "What news? Hast thou accomplished thy design or hast thou been baffled therein?" ——And as the morn began to dawn Shahrazad held her peace till

The end of the Six Hundred and Fifty-ninth Night.

THEN said she:——I have heard, O auspicious King, that the Sorceress, who was a mere creature of the malicious Wazir, replied, "O King of kings, this matter have I fully searched out even as thou gavest command, and I am about to tell thee all that hath betided me. The signs of sorrow and marks of melancholy thou notest upon my countenance are for other cause which narrowly concerneth thy welfare." Then she began to recount her adventure in these terms, "Now when I had reached the rocks I sat me down feigning sickness; and, as Prince Ahmad passed that way and heard my complaining and saw my grievous condition, he had compassion on me. After some 'said and say' he took me with him by a subterranean passage and through an iron door to a magnificent palace and gave me in charge of a fairy, Peri-Banu hight, of passing beauty and loveliness, such as human eye hath never yet seen. Prince Ahmad bade her make me her guest for some few days and bring me a medicine which would complete my cure, and she to please him at once appointed handmaidens to attend upon me. So I was certified that the twain were one flesh, husband and wife. I feigned to be exceeding frail and feeble and made as though I had not strength to walk or even to stand; whereat the two damsels supported me, one on either side, and I was carried into a room where they gave me somewhat to drink and put me upon a bed to rest and sleep. Then thought I to myself:—'Verily I have gained the object wherefor I had feigned sickness'; and I was assured that it availed no more to practise deceit. Accordingly, after a short while I arose and said to the attendants that the draught which they had given me to drink had cut short the fever and had restored strength to my limbs and life to my frame. Then they led me to the presence of the Lady Peri-Banu, who was exceeding pleased to see me once more hale and hearty, and bade her hand-maidens conduct me around the palace and show each room in its beauty and splendour; after which I craved leave to wend my ways and here am I again to work thy will." When thus she had made known to the King all that had betided her, she resumed, "Perchance, on hearing of the might and majesty, opulence and magnificence of the Lady Peri-Banu, thou wilt be gladdened and say within thyself, "Tis well that Prince Ahmad is wedded to this Fairy and hath gotten for himself such wealth and power;' but to the thinking of this thy slave the matter is quite other. It is not well, I dare avouch, that thy son should possess such puissance and treasures, for who knoweth but that he may by good aid of Peri-Banu bring about division and disturbance in the realm? Beware of the wiles and malice of women. The Prince is bewitched with love of her, and peradventure at her incitement he may act towards thee otherwise than right, and lay hands on thy hoards and seduce thy subjects and become master of thy kingdom; and albeit he would not of his own free will do aught to his father and his forbears save what was pious and dutiful, yet the charms of his Princess may work upon him little by little and end by making him a rebel and what more I may not say. Now mayest thou see that the matter is a weighty, so be not heedless but give it full consideration." Then the Sorceress made ready to gang her gait when spake the King, saying, "I am beholden to thee in two things; the first, that thou tookest upon thyself much toil and travail, and on my behalf riskedst thy life to learn the truth anent my son Prince Ahmad. Secondly, I am thankful for that thou hast given me a rede so sound and

such wholesome counsel." So saying, he dismissed her with the
highmost honour; but no sooner had she left the palace than he,
sore distraught, summoned his second Wazir, the malicious
Minister who had incited him against Prince Ahmad, and when
he and his friends appeared in the presence he laid before them
the whole matter and asked of them, saying, "What is your
counsel, and what must I do to protect myself and my kingdom
against the wiles of this Fairy?" Replied one of his councillors,
" 'Tis but a trifling matter and the remedy is simple and nearhand. Command that Prince Ahmad, who is now within the
city if not in the palace, be detained as one taken prisoner. Let
him not be put to death, lest haply the deed may engender rebellion; but at any rate place him under arrest and if he prove
violent clap him in irons."——And as the morn began to dawn
Shahrazad held her peace till

The end of the Six Hundred and Sixtieth Night.

THEN said she:——I have heard, O auspicious King, that this
felon counsel pleased the malicious Minister and all his fautors
and flatterers highly approved his rede. The Sultan kept silence
and made no reply, but on the morrow he sent and summoned the
Sorceress and debated with her whether he should or should not
cast Prince Ahmad into prison. Quoth she, "O King of kings,
this counsel is clean contrary to sound sense and right reason.
An thou throw Prince Ahmad into gaol, so must thou also do
with all his knights and their esquires; and inasmuch as they are
Jinns and Márids, who can tell their power of reprisals? Nor
prison-cells nor gates of adamant can keep them in; they will
forthwith escape and report such violence to the Fairy who,
wroth with extreme wrath to find her husband doomed to
durance vile like a common malefactor, and that too for no default
or crime but by a treacherous arrest, will assuredly deal the
direst of vengeance on thy head and do us a damage we shall not
be able to forfend. An thou wilt confide in me, I will advise
thee how to act, whereby thou mayest win thy wish and no
evil will come nigh thee or thy kingship. Thou knowest well
that to Jinns and Fairies is power given of doing in one short
moment deeds marvellous and wondrous, which mortals fail to
effect after long years of toil and trouble. Now whenas thou

goest a-hunting or on other expedition, thou requirest pavilions
for thyself and many tents for thy retinue and attendants and
soldiery; and in making ready and transporting such store
much time and wealth are wastefully expended. I would advise,
O King of kings, that thou try Prince Ahmad by the following
test: do thou bid him bring to thee a Sháhmiyánah[1] so long and
so broad that it will cover and lodge the whole of thy court and
men-at-arms and camp-followers, likewise the beasts of burthen;
and yet it must be so light that a man may hold it in the hollow
of his hand and carry it whithersoever he listeth." Then, after
holding her peace for a while, she added, still addressing the
Sultan, "And as soon as Prince Ahmad shall acquit himself of
this commission, do thou demand of him a somewhat still greater
and more wondrous wherewith I will make thee ware, and which
he will find grievous of execution. On this wise shalt thou fill
thy treasury with rare inventions and strange, the handicraft of
Jánn, nor will this cease till such time in fine when thy son shall
be at his wits' end to carry out thy requirements. Then, humbled
and abashed, he will never dare to enter thy capital or even thy
presence; and thus shalt thou be saved from fear of harm at his
hands, and thou shalt not have need to put him in gaol or, worse
still, to do him dead." Hearing these words of wisdom, the
Sultan made known the Witch's device to his advisers and asked
them what they deemed thereof. They held their peace and
answered not a word or good or ill; while he himself highly
approved it and said no more. Next day Prince Ahmad came
to visit the King, who welcomed him with overflowing affection
and clasping him to his bosom kissed him on eyes and forehead.
Long time they sat conversing on various subjects, till at length
the Sultan finding an occasion spake thus, "O dear my son, O
Ahmad, for many a day have I been sad at heart and sorrowful
of soul because of separation from thee, and when thou camest
back I was gladdened with great gladness at sight of thee, and
albeit thou didst and dost still withhold from me the knowledge
of thy whereabouts, I refrained from asking thee or seeking to
find out thy secret, since it was not according to thy mind to
tell me of thine abode. Now, however, I have heard say that
thou art wedded to a mighty Jinníyah[2], of passing beauty; and

---

[1] A huge marquee or pavilion-tent in India.
[2] The Jinn feminine; see vol. i. 10. The word hardly corresponds with the Pers. "Peri"

the tidings please me with the highmost possible pleasure. I desire not to learn aught from thee concerning thy Fairy-wife save whatso thou wouldst entrust to me of thine own free will; but, say me, should I at any time require somewhat of thee, canst thou obtain it from her? Doth she regard thee with such favour that she will not deny thee anything thou askest of her?" Quoth the Prince, "O my lord, what dost thou demand of me? My wife is devoted to her husband in heart and soul, so prithee let me learn what it is thou wouldst have of me and her." Replied the Sultan, "Thou knowest that ofttimes I fare a-hunting or on some foray and fray, when I have great need of tents and pavilions and Shahmiyanahs, with herds and troops of camels and mules and other beasts of burden to carry the camp from place to place. I would, therefore, that thou bring me a tent so light that a man may carry it in the hollow of his hand, and yet so large that it may contain my court and all my host and camp and suttlers and bât-animals. An thou wouldst ask the Lady for this gift I know full well that she can give it; and hereby shalt thou save me much of trouble in providing carriage for the tentage and spare me much waste and loss of beasts and men." The Prince replied, "O my sire the Sultan, trouble not thy thought. I will at once make known thy wish to my wife, the Lady Peri-Banu; and, albeit little I wot an fairies have the faculty of making a pavilion such as thou describest, or indeed (supposing that they have such power), an she will grant me or not grant me her aidance; and, moreover, although I cannot promise thee such present, yet whatsoever lieth in my ability to do, that will I gladly do for thy service."——And as the morn began to dawn Shahrazad held her peace till

The end of the Six Hundred and Sixty-first Night.

THEN said she:——I have heard, O auspicious King, that quoth the King to Prince Ahmad, "Shouldst thou perchance fail in this matter and bring me not the gift required, O my son, I will never see thy face again. A sorry husband thou, in good sooth, if thy wife refuse so mean a thing and hasten not to do all thou

---

and Engl. "Fairy," a creation, like the "Dív," of the so-called "Aryan," not "Semitic," race.

biddest her do; giving thee to see that thou art of small value and consequence in her eyes, and that her love for thee is a quantity well nigh to naught. But do thou, O my child, go forth and straightway ask her for the tent. An she give it thee know thou she desireth thee and thou art the dearest of all things to her; and I have been informed that she loveth thee with all her heart and soul and will by no means refuse thee aught thou requirest, were it even the balls of her eyes." Now Prince Ahmad was ever wont to tarry three days each month with the Sultan his sire, and return to his spouse on the fourth; but this time he stayed two days only and farewelled his father on the third. As he passed into the palace Peri-Banu could not but note that he was sad at heart and downcast of face; so she asked of him, "Is all well with thee? Why hast thou come to-day and not to-morrow from the presence of the King thy father, and why carriest thou so triste a countenance?" Whereupon, after kissing her brow and fondly embracing her, he told her the whole matter, first to last, and she made answer, "I will speedily set thy mind at rest, for I would not see thee so saddened for a moment longer. Howbeit, O my love, from this petition of the Sultan thy sire I am certified that his end draweth nigh, and he will soon depart this world to the mercy of Allah the Almighty.[1] Some enemy hath done this deed and much of mischief hath made for thee; and the result is that thy father, all unmindful of his coming doom, doth seek diligently his own destruction." The Prince, anxious and alarmed, thus answered his wife, "Almighty Allah be praised, the King my liege lord is in the best of health and showeth no sign of disorder or decrepitude: 'tis but this morning I left him hale and hearty, and in very sooth I never saw him in better case. Strange, indeed, that thou shouldst ken what shall betide him before I have told thee aught concerning him, and especially how he hath come to learn of our marriage and of our home." Quoth Peri-Banu, "O my Prince, thou knowest what I said to thee whenas I saw the old dame whom thou broughtest hither as one afflicted with the ague and fever. That woman, who is a Witch of Satan's breed, hath disclosed to thy father all he sought to learn concerning this our dwelling-place. And notwithstanding that I saw full clearly she was nor sick nor

---

[1] Galland makes the Fairy most unjustifiably fear that her husband is meditating the murder of his father; and the Hindí in this point has much the advantage of the Frenchman.

sorry, but only feigning a fever, I gave her medicine to drink which cureth complaints of all kinds, and she falsely made believe that by its virtues she had recovered health and strength. So when she came to take leave of me, I sent her with two of my damsels and bid them display to her every apartment in the palace together with its furniture and decorations, that she might better know the condition of me and thee. Now all this did I on thy account only, for thou badest me show compassion to the ancient woman and I was rejoiced to see her departing safe and sound and in the best of spirits. Save her alone, no human being had ever power to know aught of this place, much less to come hither." Prince Ahmad hearing these words thanked and praised her and said, "O sun-faced beauty, I would beg of thee to grant me a boon whereof my father hath made request of me; to wit, a Shahmiyanah of such dimensions that it may shelter him and his many, his camp and bât-cattle and withal may be carried in the hollow of the hand. An such marvel exist I wot not, yet would I do my utmost to procure it, and carry it to him right loyally." Quoth she, "Why trouble thyself for so small a matter? I will forthright send for it and give it thee." Then she summoned one of her handmaids who was treasurer to her and said, "O Nur Jehán,[1] go thou at once and bring me a pavilion of such and such a fashion." So she fared forth without delay and as quickly came back with the pavilion which, at her lady's bidding, she placed in the palm of Prince Ahmad's hand. ——And as the morn began to dawn Shahrazad held her peace till

The end of the Six Hundred and Sixty-second Night.

THEN said she:——I have heard, O auspicious King, that Prince Ahmad hent the pavilion in hand and thought to himself, "What is this Peri-Banu giveth me? Surely she doth make a mock of me." His wife, however, reading his mind in his face fell to laughing aloud, and asked, "What is it, O my dearling Prince? Dost thou think that I am jesting and jibing at thee?" Then she continued, addressing the treasurer Nur Jehan, "Take now yon tent from Prince Ahmad and set it upon the plain that he may see its vast

---

[1] Pers. = "Light of the World"; familiar to Europe as the name of the Grand Moghul Jehángír's principal wife.

size and know if it be such an one as required by the Sultan his
sire." The handmaid took the pavilion and pitched it afar from
the Palace; and yet one end thereof reached thereto from the
outer limit of the plain; and so immense was its size that (as
Prince Ahmad perceived) there was room therein for all the
King's court; and, were two armies ranged under it with their
camp-followers and bât-animals, one would on no wise crowd or
inconvenience the other. He then begged pardon of Peri-Banu
saying, "I wot not that the Shahmiyanah was so prodigious of
extent and of so marvellous a nature; wherefore I misdoubted
when first I saw it." The Treasurer presently struck the tent
and returned it to the palm of his hand; then, without stay or
delay, he took horse and followed by his retinue rode back to the
royal presence, where after obeisance and suit and service he
presented the tent. The Sultan also, at first sight of the gift,
thought it a small matter, but marvelled with extreme marvel to
see its size when pitched, for it would have shaded his capital
and its suburbs. He was not, however, wholly satisfied, for the
size of the pavilion now appeared to him superfluous; but his son
assured him that it would always fit itself to its contents. He
thanked the Prince for bringing him so rare a present, saying,
"O my son, acquaint thy consort with my obligation to her and
offer my grateful thanks for this her bounteous gift. Now indeed
know I of a truth that she doth love thee with the whole of her
heart and soul and all my doubts and fears are well nigh set at
rest." Then the King commanded they should pack up the tent
and store it with all care in the royal treasury. Now strange
it is but true, that when the Sultan received this rare present
from the Prince, the fear and doubt, the envy and jealousy of his
son, which the Witch and the malicious Wazir and his other ill-
advisers had bred in his breast, waxed greater and livelier than
before; because he was now certified that in very truth the
Jinniyah was gracious beyond measure to her mate and that, notwithstanding the great wealth and power of the sovereign, she
could outvie him in mighty deeds for the aidance of her husband.
Accordingly, he feared with excessive fear lest haply she seek
opportunity to slay him in favour of the Prince whom she might
enthrone in his stead. So he bade bring the Witch who had
counselled him aforetime, and upon whose sleight and malice he
now mainly relied. When he related to her the result of her
rede, she took thought for a while; then, raising her brow said,

"O King of kings, thou troublest thyself for naught: thou needest only command Prince Ahmad to bring thee of the water of the Lions' Spring. He must perforce for his honour's sake fulfil thy wish, and if he fail he will for very shame not dare to show his face again at court. No better plan than this canst thou adopt; so look to it nor loiter on thy way." Next day at eventide, as the Sultan was seated in full Darbar surrounded by his Wazirs and Ministers, Prince Ahmad came forwards and making due obeisance took seat by his side and below him. Hereat, the King addressed him, as was his wont, with great show of favour say-ing, "It delighteth me mightily that thou hast brought me the tent I required of thee; for surely in my Treasury there be naught so rare and strange. Yet one other thing lack I, and couldst thou bring it me I shall rejoice with joy exceeding. I have heard tell that the Jinniyah, thy consort, maketh constant use of a water which floweth from the Lions' Spring, the drinking whereof doeth away with fevers and all other deadly diseases. I know thou art anxious that I live in health; and thou wilt gladden me by bringing somewhat of that water, so I may drink thereof when occasion shall require, and well I wot that, as thou valuest my love and affection thee-wards, thou wilt not refuse to grant me my request." Prince Ahmad on hearing this demand was struck with surprise that his sire should so soon make a second demand. So he kept silence awhile, thinking within him-self, "I have managed by some means to obtain the tent from the Lady Peri-Banu, but Allah only knoweth how she will now act, and whether this fresh request will or will not rouse her wrath. Howbeit I know that she will on no wise deny me any boon I may ask of her." So after much hesitation Prince Ahmad made reply, "O my lord the King, I have no power to do aught in this matter, which resteth only with my spouse the Princess; yet will I petition her to give the water; and, if she vouchsafe consent I will bring it straight to thee. Indeed I cannot promise thee such boon with all certainty: I would gladly do my en-deavour in all and everything that can benefit thee, but to ask her for this water is a work more weighty than asking for the tent." Next day the Prince took his departure and returned to Peri-Banu; and after loving embraces and greetings quoth he, "O my lady and light of my eyes, the Sultan my sire sendeth thee his grateful thanks for the granting of his wish; to wit, the pavilion: and now he adventureth himself once more and, certified of thy bounty and beneficence, he would pray from thy hand the boon of a little water from the Lions' Spring. Withal I would assure thee that an the giving of this water please thee not, let the matter be clean forgotten; for to do all thou willest is my one and only wish." Peri-Banu made reply, "Methinks the Sultan, thy sire, would put both me and thee to the test by requiring such boons as those suggested to him by the Sorceress."——And as the morn began to dawn Shahrazad held her peace till

The end of the Six Hundred and Sixty-third Night.

THEN said she:——I have heard, O auspicious King, that Peri-Banu said further to Prince Ahmad, "Natheless I will grant this largesse also as the Sultan hath set his mind upon it, and no harm shall come therefrom to me or to thee, albe 'tis a matter of great risk and danger, and it is prompted by not a little of malice and ungraciousness. But give careful heed to my words, nor neglect thou aught of them, or thy destruction is certain-sure. I now will tell thee what to do. In the hall of yonder castle which riseth on that mountain is a fountain sentinelled by four lions fierce and ravening; and they watch and ward the path that leadeth thereto, a pair standing on guard whilst the other two take their turn to rest, and thus no living thing hath power to pass by them. Yet will I make known to thee the means whereby thou mayest win thy wish without any hurt or harm befalling thee from the furious beasts." Thus saying she drew from an ivory box a clew of thread and, by means of a needle one of those wherewith she had been plying her work, made thereof a ball. This she placed in the hands of her husband, and said, "First, be thou careful that thou keep about thee with all diligence this ball, whose use I shall presently explain to thee. Secondly, choose for thyself two horses of great speed, one for thine own riding, whilst on the other thou shalt load the carcass of a freshly slaughtered sheep cut into four quarters. In the third place, take with thee a phial wherewith I will provide thee, and this is for carrying the water which thou, Inshallah—God willing—shalt bring back. As soon as the morn shall morrow do thou arise with the light and go forth riding thy chosen steed and leading the other alongside of thee by the reins. When thou shalt reach the iron portals which open upon the castle-court, at no great distance from the gate, do

thou cast the ball of thread upon the ground before thee. Forthwith it will begin rolling onwards of its own will towards the
castle door; and do thou follow it through the open entrance
until such time as it stop its course. At this moment thou shalt
see the four lions; and the two that wake and watch will rouse
the twain that sleep and rest. All four will turn their jaws to
the ground and growl and roar with hideous howlings, and make
as though about to fall upon thee and tear thee limb from limb.
However, fear not nor be dismayed, but ride boldly on and
throw to the ground from off the led-horse the sheep's quarters,
one to each lion. See that thou alight not from thy steed, but
gore his ribs with thy shovel-stirrup[1] and ride with all thy might
and main up to the basin which gathereth the water. Here dismount and fill the phial whilst the lions will be busied eating.
Lastly, return with all speed and the beasts will not prevent thy
passing by them." Next day, at peep of morn, Prince Ahmad
did according to all that Peri-Banu had bidden him and rode
forth to the castle. Then, having passed through the iron
portals and crossed the court and opened the door, he entered the
hall, where he threw the quarters of the sheep before the lions,
one to each, and speedily reached the Spring. He filled his phial
with water from the basin and hurried back with all haste. But
when he had ridden some little distance he turned about and saw
two of the guardian lions following upon his track; however, he
was on no wise daunted but drew his sabre from the sheath to
prepare him for self-protection. Hereat one of the twain seeing
him bare his brand for defence, retired a little way from the road
and, standing at gaze, nodded his head and wagged his tail, as
though to pray the Prince to put up his scymitar and to assure
him that he might ride in peace and fear no peril. The other lion
then sprang forwards ahead of him and kept close him, and the
two never ceased to escort him until they reached the city, nay
even the gate of the Palace. The second twain also brought up
the rear till Prince Ahmad had entered the Palace-door; and,
when they were certified of this, all four went back by the way
they came. Seeing such wondrous spectacle, the towns-folk all
fled in dire dismay, albeit the enchanted beasts molested no man;

---

[1] The Arab stirrup, like that of the Argentine Gaucho, was originally made of wood,
liable to break, and forming a frail support for lancer and sworder. A famous chief and
warrior, Abú Sa'íd al-Muhallab (ob. A. H. 83 = 702) first gave orders to forge foot-rests
of iron.

and presently some mounted horsemen espying their lord riding
alone and unattended came up to him and helped him alight.
The Sultan was sitting in his audience-hall conversing with his
Wazirs and Ministers when his son appeared before him; and
Prince Ahmad, having greeted him and blessed him and, in dutiful fashion, prayed for his permanence of existence and prosperity
and opulence, placed before his feet the phial full of the water
from the Lions' Spring, saying, "Lo, I have brought thee the
boon thou desiredst of me. This water is most rare and hard to
obtain; nor is there in all thy Treasure-house aught so notable
and of such value as this. If ever thou fall ill of any malady
(Almighty Allah forfend this should be in thy Destiny!) then
drink a draught thereof and forthwith thou shalt be made whole
of whatso distemper thou hast." When Prince Ahmad had made
an end of speaking, the Sultan, with all love and affection, grace
and honour, embraced him and kissed his head; then, seating him
on his right said, "O my son, I am beholden to thee, beyond
count and measure, for that thou hast adventured thy life and
brought this water with great irk and risk from so perilous a
place." Now the Witch had erewhile informed the King concerning the Lions' Spring and of the mortal dangers which beset
the site; so that he knew right well how gallant was his son's
derring-do; and presently he said, "Say me, O my child, how
couldst thou venture thither and escape from the lions and
broughtest back the water, thyself remaining safe and sound?"
——And as the morn began to dawn Shahrazad held her
peace till

The end of the Six Hundred and Sixty-fourth Night.

THEN said she:——I have heard, O auspicious King, that the
Prince replied, "By thy favour, O my lord the Sultan, have I
returned in safety from that stead mainly because I did according
to the bidding of my spouse, the Lady Peri-Banu; and I have
brought the water from the Lions' Spring only by carrying out
her commands." Then he made known to his father all that had
befallen him in going and returning; and when the Sultan noted
the pre-eminent valiance and prowess of his son he only feared
the more, and the malice and the rancour, envy and jealousy
which filled his heart waxed tenfold greater than before. How-

ever, dissembling his true sentiments he dismissed Prince Ahmad and betaking him to his private chamber at once sent word to bid the Witch appear in the presence; and when she came, he told her of the Prince's visit and all about the bringing of the water from the Lions' Spring. She had already heard somewhat thereof by reason of the hubbub in the city at the coming of the lions; but, as soon as she had given ear to the whole account, she marvelled with mighty marvel and, after whispering in the Sultan's ear her new device, said to him in triumph, "O King of kings, this time thou shalt lay a charge on the Prince and such commandment methinks will trouble him and it shall go hard with him to execute aught thereof." "Thou sayest well," replied the Sovran, "now indeed will I try this plan thou hast projected for me." Wherefore, next day whenas Prince Ahmad came to the presence of his sire, the King said to him, "O dear my child, it delighteth me exceedingly to see thy virtue and valour and the filial love wherewith thou art fulfilled, good gifts chiefly shown by obtaining for me the two rarities I asked of thee. And now one other and final requirement I have of thee; and, shouldst thou avail to satisfy my desire, I shall be well-pleased in my beloved son and render thanks to him for the rest of my days." Prince Ahmad answered, "What is the boon thou requirest? I will for my part do thy bidding as far as in me lieth." Then quoth the King in reply to the Prince, "I would fain have thee bring me a man of size and stature no more than three feet high, with beard full twenty ells in length, who beareth on his shoulder a quarter staff of steel, thirteen score pounds in weight, which he wieldeth with ease and swingeth around his head without wrinkle on brow, even as men wield cudgels of wood." On this wise the Sultan, led astray by the Doom of Destiny and heedless alike of good and evil, asked that which should bring surest destruction upon himself. Prince Ahmad also, with blind obedience out of pure affection to his parent, was ready to supply him with all he required unknowing what was prepared for him in the Secret Purpose. Accordingly he said, "O my sire the Sultan, I trow me 'twill be hard to find, all the world over, a man such as thou desirest, still I will work my best to do thy bidding." Thereupon the Prince retired from the presence and returned, as usual, to his palace where he greeted Peri-Banu with love and gladness; but his face was troubled and his heart was heavy at the thought of the King's last behest. Perceiving his pre-occupation the Princess asked him, saying, "O dear my lord, what tidings bringest thou for me to-day?" Hereto replied he, "The Sultan at each visit requireth of me some new thing and burtheneth me with his requests; and to-day he purposeth to try me and, in the hopes of putting me to shame, he asketh somewhat which 'twere vain to hope I can find in all the world." Thereupon Prince Ahmad told her all the King had said to him.——And as the morn began to dawn Shahrazad held her peace till

The end of the Six Hundred and Sixty-fifth Night.

THEN said she:——I have heard, O auspicious King, that Peri-Banu hearing these words said to the Prince, "Trouble not thyself at all in this matter. Thou didst venture at great risk to carry off for thy father water from the Lions' Spring and thou succeededst in winning thy wish. Now this task is on no wise more difficult or dangerous than was that: nay 'tis the easier for that he thou describest is none other than Shabbar, my brother-german. Although we both have the same parents, yet it pleased Almighty Allah to enform us in different figures and to make him unlike his sister as being in mortal mould can be. Moreover he is valiant and adventurous, always seeking some geste and exploit whereby to further my interest, and right willingly doth he carry out whatso he undertaketh. He is shaped and formed as the Sultan thy sire hath described, nor useth he any weapons save the Nabbút[1] or quarter staff of steel. And see now I will send for him, but be not thou dismayed at sighting him." Replied Prince Ahmad, "If he be in truth thine own brother what matter how he looketh? I shall be pleased to see him as when one welcometh a valued friend or a beloved kinsman. Wherefore should I fear to look upon him?" Hearing these words Peri-Banu despatched one of her attendants who brought to her from her private treasury a chafing-dish of gold; then she bade a fire be lit therein, and sending for a casket of noble metals studded with gems, the gift of her kinsmen, she took therefrom some incense and cast it upon the flames. Herewith issued a dense smoke

---

[1] For this Egyptian and Syrian weapon see vol. i. 234.

spireing high in air and spreading all about the palace; and a few moments after, Peri-Banu who had ceased her conjurations cried, "Lookye my brother Shabbar cometh! canst thou distinguish his form?" The Prince looked up and saw a mannikin in stature dwarfish and no more than three feet high, and with a boss on breast and a hump on back; withal he carried himself with stately mien and majestic air. On his right shoulder was borne his quarter staff of steel thirteen score pounds in weight. His beard was thick and twenty cubits in length but arranged so skilfully that it stood clear off from the ground; he wore also a twisted pair of long mustachios curling up to his ears, and all his face was covered with long pile. His eyes were not unlike unto pig's eyes; and his head, on which was placed a crown-like coiffure, was enormous of bulk, contrasting with the meanness of his stature. Prince Ahmad sat calmly beside his wife, the Fairy, and felt no fear as the figure approached; and presently Shabbar walked up and glancing at him asked Peri-Banu saying, "Who be this mortal who sitteth hard by thee?" Hereto she replied, "O my brother, this is my beloved husband, Prince Ahmad, son of the Sultan of Hindostan. I sent thee not an invitation to the wedding as thou wast then engaged on some great expedition; now, however, by the grace of Almighty Allah thou hast returned triumphant and victorious over thy foes, wherefore I have summoned thee upon a matter which nearly concerneth me." Hearing these words Shabbar looked graciously at Prince Ahmad, saying, "O my beloved sister, is there any service I can render to him?" and she replied, "The Sultan his sire desireth ardently to see thee, and I pray thee go forthright to him and take the Prince with thee by way of guide." Said he, "This instant I am ready to set forth;" but said she, "Not yet, O my brother. Thou art fatigued with journeying; so defer until the morrow thy visit to the King, and this evening I will make known to thee all that concerneth Prince Ahmad." Presently the time came; so Peri-Banu informed her brother Shabbar concerning the King and his ill-counsellors; but she dwelt mainly upon the misdeeds of the old woman, the Witch; and how she had schemed to injure Prince Ahmad and despitefully prevent his going to city or court, and she had gained such influence over the Sultan that he had given up his will to hers and ceased not doing whatso she bade him. Next day at dawn Shabbar the Jinn and Prince Ahmad set out together upon a visit to the Sultan; and when they had reached the city gates,

all the folk, nobles and commons, were struck with consternation
at the dwarf's hideous form; and, flying on every side in affright
and running into shops and houses, barred the doors and closed
the casements and hid themselves therein. So panic-stricken
indeed was their flight that many feet lost shoes and sandals in
running, while from the heads of others their loosened turbands
fell to earth. And when they twain approached the palace
through streets and squares and market-places desolate as the
Desert of Samáwah,[1] all the keepers of the gates took to their
heels at sight of Shabbar and fled, so there was none to hinder
their entering. They walked straight on to the audience-chamber
where the Sultan was holding Darbar, and they found in attendance on him a host of Ministers and Councillors, great and
small, each standing in his proper rank and station. They too on
seeing Shabbar speedily took flight in dire dismay and hid themselves; also the guards had deserted their posts nor cared in any
way to let or stay the twain. The Sovran still sat motionless on
his throne, where Shabbar went up to him with lordly mien and
royal dignity and cried, "O King, thou hast expressed a wish to
see me; and lo, I am here. Say now what wouldst thou have me
do?"——And as the morn began to dawn Shahrazad held her
peace till

The end of the Six Hundred and Sixty-sixth Night.

Then said she;——I have heard, O auspicious King, that the
King made no reply to Shabbar, but held up his hands before his
eyes that he might not behold that frightful figure, and turning
his head would fain have fled in terror. Shabbar was filled with
fury at this rudeness on the part of the Sultan, and was wroth
with exceeding wrath to think that he had troubled himself to
come at the bidding of such a craven, who now on seeing him
would fain run away. So the Jinn, without an instant's delay,
raised his quarter staff of steel, and, swinging it twice in air,
before Prince Ahmad could reach the throne or on any wise
interfere, struck the Sultan so fiercely upon the poll that his
skull was smashed and his brains were scattered over the floor.

---

[1] See vol. vii. 93, where an error of punctuation confounds it with Kerbela,—a desert
with a place of pilgrimage. "Samáwah" in Ibn Khall. (vol. i. 108) is also the name of a
town on the Euphrates.

And when Shabbar had made an end of this offender, he savagely turned upon the Grand Wazir who stood on the Sultan's right, and incontinently would have slain him also, but the Prince craved pardon for his life and said, "Kill him not: he is my friend and hath at no time said one evil word against me. But such is not the case with the others, his fellows." Hearing these words the infuriated Shabbar fell upon the Ministers and ill-counsellors on either side, to wit, all who had devised evil devices against Prince Ahmad, and slew them each and every and suffered none to escape save only those who had taken flight and hidden themselves. Then, going from the hall of justice to the courtyard, the Dwarf said to the Wazir whose life the Prince had saved, "Harkye, there is a Witch who beareth enmity against my brother, the husband of my sister. See that thou produce her forthright; likewise the villain who filled his father's mind with hate and malice, envy and jealousy against him, so may I quite them in full measure for their misdeeds." The Grand Wazir produced them all, first the Sorceress, and then the malicious minister with his rout of fautors and flatterers, and Shabbar felled them one after the other with his quarter staff of steel and killed them pitilessly, crying to the Sorceress, "This is the end of all thy machinations with the King, and this is the fruit of thy deceit and treachery; so learn not to feign thyself sick." And in the blindness of his passion he would have slain all the inhabitants of the city, but Prince Ahmad prevented him and pacified him with soft and flattering words. Hereupon Shabbar habited his brother in the royal habit and seated him on the throne and proclaimed him Sultan of Hindostan. The people all, both high and low, rejoiced with exceeding joy to hear these tidings, for Prince Ahmad was beloved by every one; so they crowded to swear fealty and bring presents and Nazaránahs[1]

---

1 Nazaránah prop. = the gift (or gifts) offered at visits by a Moslem noble or feoffee in India to his feudal superior; and the Kalíchah of Hindú, Malabar, Goa and the Blue Mountains (p. 197). Hence the periodical tributes and especially the presents which represent our "legacy-duty" and the "succession-duty" for Rajahs and Nabobs, the latter so highly lauded by "The Times," as the logical converse of the Corn-laws which ruined our corn. The Nazaránah can always be made a permanent and a considerable source of revenue, far more important than such unpopular and un-Oriental device as an income-tax. But our financiers have yet to learn the A. B. C. of political economy in matters of assessment, which is to work upon familiar lines; and they especially who, like Mr. Wilson "mad as a hatter," hold and hold forth that "what is good for England is good for the world." These myopics decide on theoretical and sentimental grounds that a poll-tax is bad in

and raised shouts of acclamation crying out, "Long live King Ahmad!" When all this was done, Shabbar sent for his sister, Peri-Banu, and made her Queen under the title of Shahr-Banu;[1] and in due time taking leave of her and of King Ahmad, the Jinni returned to his own home.——And as the morn began to dawn Shahrazad held her peace till

The end of the Six Hundred and Sixty-seventh Night.

THEN said she:——I have heard, O auspicious King, that after these things King Ahmad summoned Prince Ali his brother and Nur al-Nihar and made him governor of a large city hard by the capital, and dismissed him thither in high state and splendour. Also he commissioned an official to wait upon Prince Husayn and tell him all the tidings, and sent word saying, "I will appoint thee ruler over any capital or country thy soul desireth; and, if thou consent, I will forward thee letters of appointment." But inasmuch as the Prince was wholly content and entirely happy in Darwaysh-hood, he cared naught for rule or government or aught of worldly vanities; so he sent back the official with his duty and grateful thanks, requesting that he might be left to live his life in solitude and renunciation of matters mundane. Now when Queen Shahrazad had made an end of telling her story and yet the night was not wholly spent, King Shahryar spake saying, "This thy story, admirable and most wonderful, hath given me extreme delight; and I pray thee do thou tell us another tale till such time as the last hours of this our night be passed." She replied, "Be it as thou wilt, O auspicious King: I am thy slave to do as thou shalt bid." Then she began to relate the tale of

THE TWO SISTERS WHO ENVIED THEIR CADETTE.[2]

IN days of yore and in times long gone before there lived a King of Persia, Khusrau Sháh hight, renowned for justice and

---

principle, which it may be, still public opinion sanctions it and it can be increased without exciting discontent. The same with the "Nazaránah;" it has been the custom of ages immemorial, and a little more or a little less does not affect its popularity.

[1] Pers. = City-queen.

[2] Compare with this tale its modern and popular version *Histoire du Rossignol Chanteur* (Spitta-Bey, No. x, p. 123): it contains the rosary (and the ring) that shrinks, the ball that rolls and the water that heals; etc. etc. Mr. Clouston somewhere asserts that the History

righteousness. His father, dying at a good old age, had left him
sole heir to all the realm and, under his rule, the tiger and the kid
drank side by side at the same Ghát;[1] and his treasury was ever
full and his troops and guards were numberless. Now it was his
wont to don disguise and, attended by a trusty Wazir, to wander
about the street at night-time. Whereby things seld-seen and
haps peregrine became known to him, the which, should I tell
thee all thereof, O auspicious King, would weary thee beyond
measure. So he took seat upon the throne of his forbears and
when the appointed days of mourning were ended, according to
the custom of that country, he caused his exalted name, that is
Khusrau Shah, be struck upon all the coins of the kingdom and
entered into the formula of public prayer.[2] And when stablished
in his sovranty he went forth as aforetime on one evening accompanied by his Grand Wazir, both in merchant's habit, walking
the streets and squares, the markets and lanes, the better to note
what might take place both of good and of bad. By chance they

---

of the Envious Sisters, like that of Prince Ahmad and the Perí-Banu, are taken from a MS.
still preserved in the "King's Library," Paris; but he cannot quote his authority, De Sacy
or Langlès. Mr. H. C. Coote (loc. cit. p. 189) declares it to be, and to have been, "an
enormous favourite in Italy and Sicily: no folk-tale exists in those countries at all com-
parable to it in the number of its versions and in the extent of its distribution." He begins
two centuries before Galland, with Straparola (*Notti Piacevoli*), proceeds to Imbriani
(*Novellaja Fiorentina*), Nerucci (*Novelle Montalesi*), Comparetti (*Novelline Italiane*) and
Pitrè (*Fiabe Novelle e Racconti popolari Italiani*, vol. i.); and informs us that "the adventures of the young girl, independently of the joint history of herself and her brother, are
also told in a separate *Fiaba* in Italy. A tale called 'La Favenilla Coraggiosa' is given
by Visentini in his *Fiabe Mantovane* and it is as far as it is a counterpart of the second
portion of Galland's tale." Mr. Coote also finds this story in Hahn's "Griechische Märchen"
entitled "Sun, Moon and Morning Star"—the names of the royal children. The King over-
hears the talk of three girls and marries the youngest despite his stepmother, who sub-
stitutes for her issue a puppy, a kitten and a mouse. The castaways are adopted by a
herdsman whilst the mother is confined in a henhouse; and the King sees his offspring and
exclaims, "These children are like those my wife promised me." His stepmother, hearing
this, threatens the nurse, who goes next morning disguised as a beggar-woman to the girl
and induces her to long for the Bough that makes music, the Magic Mirror, and the bird
Dickierette. The brothers set out to fetch them leaving their shirts which become black
when the mishap befalls them. The sister, directed by a monk, catches the bird and revives
the stones by the Water of Life and the dénouement is brought about by a sausage stuffed
with diamonds. In Miss Stokes' Collection of Hindu Stories (No. xx.) "The Boy who had a
moon on his brow and a star on his chin" also suggests the "Envious Sisters."

[1] Pop. "Ghaut" = The steps (or path) which lead down to a watering-place. Hence the
Hindí saying concerning the "rolling stone"—Dhobi-ka kuttá; na Gharká na Ghát-ká, = a
washerwoman's tyke, nor of the house nor of the Ghát-dyke.

[2] Text "Khatíbah" more usually "Khutbah" = the Friday sermon preached by the
Khatíb: in this the reigning sovereign is prayed for by name and his mention together with
the change of coinage is the proof of his lawful rule. See Lane, M. E. chap. iii.

passed, as the night darkened, through a quarter where dwelt
people of the poorer class; and, as they walked on, the Shah
heard inside a house women talking with loud voices; then going
near, he peeped in by the door-chink, and saw three fair sisters
who having supped together were seated on a divan talking one
to other. The King thereupon applied his ear to the crack and
listened eagerly to what they said, and heard each and every
declaring what was the thing she most desired.[1] Quoth the
eldest, "I would I were married to the Shah's head Baker for then
should I ever have bread to eat, the whitest and choicest in the
city, and your hearts would be fulfilled with envy and jealousy
and malice at my good luck."   Quoth the second, "I would
rather wive with the Shah's chief Kitchener and eat of dainty
dishes that are placed before his Highness, wherewith the royal
bread which is common throughout the Palace cannot compare
for gust and flavour." And quoth the third and youngest of the
three, and by far the most beautiful and lovely of them all, a
maiden of charming nature, full of wit and humour; sharp-
witted, wary and wise, when her turn came to tell her wish,
"O sisters, my ambition is not as ordinary as yours. I care not
for fine bread nor glutton-like do I long for dainty dishes. I look
to somewhat nobler and higher: indeed I would desire nothing
less than to be married by the King and become the mother of a
beautiful Prince, a model of form and in mind as masterful as
valorous. His hair should be golden on one side and silvern on
the other; when weeping he should drop pearls in place of tears,
and when laughing his rosy lips should be fresh as the blossom
new-blown." The Shah was amazed with exceeding amazement
to hear the wishes of the three sisters, but chiefly of the youngest

---

[1] This form of eaves-dropping, in which also the listener rarely hears any good of himself is, I need hardly now say, a favourite incident of Eastern storiology and even of history,
e.g. Three men met together; one of them expressed the wish to obtain a thousand pieces of
gold, so that he might trade with them; the other wished for an appointment under the
Emir of the Moslems; the third wished to possess Yusuf's wife, who was the handsomest of
women and had great political influence. Yusuf, being informed of what they said, sent for
the men, bestowed one thousand dinars on him who wished for that sum, gave an appointment to the other and said to him who wished to possess the lady: "Foolish man! what induced you to wish for that which you can never obtain?" He then sent him to her and she
placed him in a tent where he remained three days, receiving, each day, one and the same
kind of food. She had him then brought to her and said, "What did you eat these days
past?" He replied: "Always the same thing!"—"Well," said she, "all women are the same
thing." She then ordered some money and a dress to be given him, after which, she dismissed him. (Ibn Khallikan iii. 463-64.)

and determined in himself that he would gratify them all. Wherefore quoth he to the Grand Wazir, "Mark well this house and on the morrow bring before me these maidens whom we heard discoursing;" and quoth the Wazir, "O Asylum of the Universe, I hear but to obey." Thereupon the twain walked back to the palace and laid them down to rest. When morning morrowed, the Minister went for the sisters and brought them to the King, who, after greeting them and heartening their hearts, said to them in kindly tone, "O ye maidens of weal, last night what was it that in merry word and jest ye spake one to other? Take heed ye tell the Shah every whit in full detail, for all must become known to us; something have we heard, but now the King would have ye recount your discourse to his royal ears."——And as the morn began to dawn Shahrazad held her peace till

The end of the Six Hundred and Sixty=eighth Night.

THEN said she:——I have heard, O auspicious King, that at these words of the Shah the sisters, confused and filled with shame, durst not reply but stood before him silent with heads bent low; and despite all questioning and encouragement they could not pluck up courage. However, the youngest was of passing comeliness in form and feature and forthwith the Shah became desperately enamoured of her; and of his love began reassuring them and saying, "O ye Princesses of fair ones, be not afraid nor troubled in thought; nor let bashfulness or shyness prevent you telling the Shah what three wishes you wished, for fain would he fulfil them all." Thereat they threw themselves at his feet and, craving his pardon for their boldness and freedom of speech, told him the whole talk, each one repeating the wish she had wished; and on that very day Khusrau Shah married the eldest sister to his chief Baker, and the second sister to his head Cook, and bade make all things ready for his own wedding with the youngest sister. So when the preparations for the royal nuptials had been made after costliest fashion, the King's marriage was celebrated with royal pomp and pageantry, and the bride received the titles of Light of the Harem and Bánú of Irán-land. The other two maidens were likewise married, one to the King's Baker the other to his Cook, after a manner according to their several degrees in life and with little show of grandeur and circumstance. Now it had been only right and reasonable that these twain having won each her own wish, should have passed their time in solace and happiness, but the decree of Destiny doomed other-wise; and, as soon as they saw the grand estate whereto their youngest sister had risen, and the magnificence of her marriage-festival, their hearts were fired with envy and jealousy and sore despite and they resolved upon giving the rein to their hatred and malignancy and to work her some foul mischief. On this wise they remained for many months consumed with rancour, day and night; and they burned with grief and anger whenever they sighted aught of her superior style and state. One morning as the two met at the Hammám and found privacy and opportunity, quoth the eldest sister to the second, "A grievous thing it is in-deed that she, our youngest sister, no lovelier than ourselves, should thus be raised to the dignity and majesty of Queendom and indeed the thought is overhard to bear." Quoth the other, "O sister mine, I also am perplexed and displeased at this thing, and I know not what of merit the Shah could have seen in her that he was tempted to choose her for his consort. She ill be-fitteth that high estate with that face like a monkey's favour; and, save her youth, I know nothing that could commend her to his Highness that he should so exalt her above her fellows. To my mind thou and not she art fit to share the royal bed; and I nurse a grudge against the King for that he hath made this jade his Queen." And the eldest sister rejoined, "I likewise marvel beyond all measure; and I swear that thy youth and beauty, thy well-shaped figure and lovely favour and goodliness of gifts past challenge or compare, might well have sufficed to win the King and have tempted him to wed and bed with thee and make thee his crowned Queen and Sovran Lady in lieu of taking to his arms this paltry strumpet. Indeed he hath shown no sense of what is right and just in leaving thee disappointed; and on this account only the matter troubleth me with exceeding trouble."——And as the morn began to dawn Shahrazad held her peace till

The end of the Six Hundred and Sixty-ninth Night.

Then said she:——I have heard, O auspicious King, that the two sisters took counsel each with other how they might abase their youngest sister in the Shah's sight and cause her downfall and utter ruin. Day and night they conned over the matter in their minds and spoke at great length about it when they ever met together, and pondered endless plans to injure the Queen their sister, and if possible bring about her death; but they could fix upon none. And, whilst they bore this despite and hatred towards her and diligently and deliberately sought the means of gratifying their bitter envy, hatred and malice, she on the other hand regarded them with the same favour and affection as she had done before marriage and thought only how to advantage their low estate. Now when some months of her wedded life had passed, the fair Queen was found to be with child whereof the glad tidings filled the Shah with joy; and straightway he commanded all the people of the capital and throughout the whole Empire keep holiday with feasts and danc-ing and every manner jollity as became so rare and important an occasion. But as soon as the news came to the ears of the two Envious Sisters they were constrained perforce to offer their con-gratulations to the Queen; and, after a long visit, as the twain were about to crave dismissal they said, "Thanks be to Almighty Allah, O our sister, who hath shown us this happy day. One boon have we to ask of thee: to wit, that when the time shall come for thee to be delivered of a child, we may assist as mid-wives at thy confinement, and be with thee and nurse thee for the space of forty days." The Queen in her gladness made reply, "O sisters mine, I fain would have it so; for at a time of such need I know of none on whom to rely with such dependence as upon you. During my coming trial your presence with me will be most welcome and opportune; but I can do only what thing the Shah biddeth nor can I do aught save by his leave. My advice is thus:—Make known this matter to your mates who have always access to the royal presence, and let them personally apply for your attendance as midwives; I doubt not but that the Shah will give you leave to assist me and remain by my side, considering the fond relationship between us three." Then the two sisters returned home full of evil thoughts and malice, and told their wishes to their husbands who, in turn, bespake Khusrau Shah, and proffered their petition with all humility, little knowing what was hidden from them in the Secret Purpose. The King replied, "When I shall have thought the matter over in my mind, I will give you suitable orders." So saying he privately visited the Queen and to her said, "O my lady, an it please thee, methinks 'twould be well to summon thy sisters and secure their aidance, when thou shalt be labouring of child, in lieu of any stranger: and if thou be of the same mind as myself let me at once learn and take steps to obtain their consent and con-cert ere thy time arriveth. They will wait on thee with more loving care than any hired nurse and thou wilt find thyself the safer in their hands." Replied the Queen, "O my lord the Shah, I also venture to think that 'twould be well to have my sisters by my side and not mere aliens at such an hour." Accordingly he sent word to them and from that day they dwelt within the palace to make all ready for the expected confinement; and on this wise they found means to carry out their despiteful plot which during so many days they had devised to scanty purpose. When her full tale of months had been told, the Banu was brought to bed of a man-child marvellous in beauty, whereat the fire of envy and hatred was kindled with redoubled fury in the sisters' breasts. So they again took counsel nor suffered ruth or natural affection to move their cruel hearts; and presently, with great care and secrecy, they wrapped the new-born in a bit of blanket and putting him into a basket cast him into a canal which flowed hard by the Queen's apartment.[1] They then placed a dead puppy in the place of the prince and showed it to the other midwives and nurses, averring that the Queen had given birth to such abortion. When these untoward tidings reached the

---

[1] This ruthless attempt at infanticide was in accordance with the manners of the age nor has it yet disappeared from Rajput-land, China and sundry over-populous countries. Indeed it is a question if civilization may not be compelled to revive the law of Lycurgus which forbade a child, male or female, to be brought up without the approbation of public officers appointed *ad hoc*. One of the curses of the XIXth century is the increased skill of the midwife and physician, who are now able to preserve worthless lives and to bring up semi-abortions whose only effect upon the breed is increased degeneracy. Amongst the Greeks and ancient Arabs the Malthusian practice was carried to excess. Poseidippus declares that in his day —

A man, although poor, will not expose his son;
But however rich, will not preserve his daughter.

See the commentators' descriptions of the Wa'd al-Banát or burial of Mauúdát (living daughters), the barbarous custom of the pagan Arabs (Koran, chaps. xvi. and lxxxi.) one of the many abominations, like the murderous vow of Jephtha, to which Al-Islam put a summary stop. (Ibn Khallikan, iii. 609–616.) For such outcast children reported to be monsters, see pp. 402–412 of Mr. Clouston's "Asiatic and European versions of four of Chaucer's Canterbury Tales," printed by the Chaucer Society.

King's ears he was sore discomforted and waxed wroth with exceeding wrath.——And as the morn began to dawn Shahrazad held her peace till

The end of the Six Hundred and Seventieth Night.

THEN said she:——I have heard, O auspicious King, that the King, inflamed with sudden fierceness, drew his sword and would have slain his Queen had not the Grand Wazir, who happened to be in his presence at the time, restrained his rage and diverted him from his unjust design and barbarous purpose. Quoth he, "O Shadow of Allah upon earth, this mishap is ordained of the Almighty Lord whose will no man hath power to gainsay. The Queen is guiltless of offence against thee, for what is born of her is born without her choice, and she indeed hath no hand therein." With this and other sage counsels he dissuaded his lord from carrying out his fell purpose and saved the guiltless Queen from a sudden and cruel death. Meanwhile the basket wherein lay the newly-born Prince was carried by the current into a rivulet which flowed through the royal gardens; and, as the Intendant of the pleasure grounds and pleasaunces chanced to walk along the bank, by the decree of Destiny he caught sight of the basket floating by, and he called a gardener, bidding him lay hold of it and bring it to him that he might see what was therein. The man ran along the rivulet side; and, with a long stick drawing the basket to land, showed it to the Intendant who opened it and beheld within a new-born babe, a boy of wondrous beauty wrapped in a bit of blanket; at which sight he was astounded beyond measure of surprise. Now it so chanced that the Intendant, who was one of the Emirs and who stood high in favour with the Sovran, had no children: withal he never ceased offering prayers and vows to Almighty Allah that he might have a son to keep alive his memory and continue his name. Delighted at the sight he took home the basket with the babe and giving it to his wife said, "See how Allah hath sent to us this man-child which I just now found floating upon the waters; and do thou apply thee forthright and fetch a wet-nurse to give him milk and nourish him; and bring him up with care and tenderness as though he were thine own." So the Intendant's wife took charge of the child with great gladness and reared him with her whole heart,

diligently as though born of her own womb; nor did the Intendant say aught to any, or seek to find out whose might be the
child lest haply some one claim and take it from him. He was
certified in his mind that the boy came from the Queen's quarter
of the palace, but deemed it inexpedient to make too strict enquiry concerning the matter; and he and his spouse kept the
secret with all secrecy. A year after this the Queen gave birth
to a second son, when her sisters, the Satanesses full of spite, did
with this babe, even as they had done by the first: they wrapped
it in a cloth and set it in a basket which they threw into the
stream, then gave out that the Queen had brought forth a kitten.
But once more, by the mercy of Allah Almighty, this boy came
to the hands of that same Intendant of the gardens who carried
him to his wife and placed him under her charge with strict
injunctions to take care of the second foundling sedulously as she
had done with the first. The Shah, enraged to hear the evil tidings, again rose up to slay the Queen; but as before the Grand
Wazir prevented him and calmed his wrath with words of wholesome rede and a second time saved the unhappy mother's life.
And after another year had gone by the Banu was brought to
bed and this time bore a daughter by whom the sisters did as
they had done by her brothers: they set the innocent inside a
basket and threw her into the stream; and the Intendant found
her also and took her to his wife and bade her rear the infant
together with the other two castaways. Hereupon the Envious
Sisters, wild with malice, reported that the Queen had given
birth to a musk-ratling;[1] whereat King Khusrau could no longer
stay his wrath and indignation. So he cried in furious rage to the
Grand Wazir, "What, shall the Shah suffer this woman, who
beareth naught but vermin and abortions, to share the joys of
his bed? Nay more, the King can no longer allow her to live,
else she will fill the palace with monstrous births: in very sooth,
she is herself a monster, and it behoveth us to rid this place of

---

[1] Hind. Chhuchhundar (*Sorex cærulescens*) which occurs repeatedly in verse; *e.g.*, when
speaking of low men advanced to high degree, the people say:—

Chhuchhúndar-ke sir-par Chambelí-ka tel.
The Jasmine-oil on the musk-rat's head.

In Galland the Sultánah is brought to bed of *un morceau de bois;* and his Indian translator is more consequent. Hahn, as has been seen, also has the mouse but Hahn could
hardly have reached Hindostan.

such unclean creature and accursed." So saying the Shah commanded them do her to death; but the ministers and high officers
of estate who stood before the presence fell at the royal feet and
besought pardon and mercy for the Queen. The Grand Wazir
also said with folded hands, "O Sháhinsháh[1]—O King of the
kings—thy slave would fain represent that 'tis not in accordance
with the course of justice or the laws of the land to take the life
of a woman for no fault of her own. She cannot interfere with
Destiny, nor can she prevent unnatural births such as have thrice
betided her; and such mishaps have oftentimes befallen other
women, whose cases call for compassion and not punishment.
An the King be displeased with her then let him cease to live
with her, and the loss of his gracious favour will be a penalty dire
enough; and, if the Shah cannot suffer the sight of her, then let
her be confined in some room apart, and let her expiate her offence
by alms deeds and charity until 'Izráíl, the Angel of Death,
separate her soul from her flesh." Hearing these words of counsel
from his aged Councillor, Khusrau Shah recognised that it had
been wrong to slay the Queen, for that she could on no wise do
away with aught that was determined by Fate and Destiny;
and presently he said to the Grand Wazir, "Her life is spared at
thine intercession, O wise man and ware; yet will the King doom
her to a weird which, haply, is hardly less hard to bear than death.
And now do thou forthright make ready, by the side of the
Cathedral-mosque, a wooden cage with iron bars and lock the
Queen therein as one would confine a ferocious wild beast.[2]
Then every Mussulman who wendeth his way to public prayers
shall spit in her face ere he set foot within the fane, and if any
fail to carry out this command he shall be punished in like
manner. So place guards and inspectors to enforce obedience and
let me hear if there be aught of gainsaying." The Wazir durst not
make reply but carried out the Shah's commandments; and this
punishment inflicted upon the blameless Queen had far better
befitted her Envious Sisters.——And as the morn began to
dawn Shahrazad held her peace till

---

[1] This title of Sháhinshah was first assumed by Ardashír, the great Persian conqueror,
after slaying the King of Ispahán, Ardawán. (Tabari ii. 73.)

[2] This imprisonment of the good Queen reminds home readers of the "Cage of Clapham"
wherein a woman with child was imprisoned in A.D. 1700, and which was noted by Sir
George Grove as still in existence about 1830.

The end of the Six Hundred and Seventy-first Night.

THEN said she——I have heard, O auspicious King, that the cage was made ready with all speed; and, when the forty days after purification of child-bed[1] had come to an end, the Banu was locked therein; and, according to the King's commandment, all who came to prayer in the Great Mosque would first spit in her face. The hapless woman, well knowing that she was not worthy of this ignominy, bore her sufferings with all patience and fortitude; nor were they few who deemed her blameless and undeserving to endure these torments and tortures inflicted upon her by the Shah; and they pitied her and offered prayers and made vows for her release. Meanwhile the Intendant of the gardens and his wife brought up the two Princes and the Princess with all love and tenderness; and, as the children grew in years, their love for these adopted ones increased in like proportion. They gave the eldest Prince the name Bahman,[2] and to his brother Parwez;[3] and, as the maiden was rare of beauty and passing of loveliness and graciousness, they called her Perízádah.[4] When the Princes became of years to receive instruction, the Intendant of the gardens appointed tutors and masters to teach them reading and writing and all the arts and sciences: the Princess also, showing like eagerness to acquire knowledge, was taught letters by the same instructors, and soon could read and write with as perfect fluency and facility as could her brothers. Then they were placed under the most learned of the Philosophers and the Olema, who taught them the interpretation of the Koran and the sayings of the Apostle; the science of geometry as well as poetry and history, and even the abstruse sciences and the mystic doctrines of the Enlightened; and their teachers were astonished to find how soon

---

[1] Arab. Ayyám al-Nifás = the period of forty days after labour during which, according to Moslem law, a woman may not cohabit with her husband.

[2] A *clarum et venerabile nomen* in Persia; meaning one of the Spirits that preside over beasts of burden; also a king in general, the P.N. of an ancient sovereign, etc.

[3] This is the older pronunciation of the mod. (Khusrau) "Parvíz"; and I owe an apology to Mr. C. J. Lyall (Ancient Arabian Poetry) for terming his "Khusrau Parvêz" an "ugly Indianism" (The Academy, No. 100). As he says (Ibid. vol. x. 85), "the Indians did not invent for Persian words the sounds ê and ô, called *majhúl* (*i.e.* 'not known in Arabic') by the Arabs, but received them at a time when these sounds were universally used in Persia. The substitution by Persians of í and ú for ê and ô is quite modern."

[4] *i.e.* Fairy-born, the Παρυσάτις (Parysatis) of the Greeks which some miswrite Παρύσατις.

and how far all three made progress in their studies and bid fair to outstrip even the sages however learned. Moreover, they all three were reared to horsemanship and skill in the chase, to shooting with shafts and lunging with lance and sway of sabre and jerking the Jeríd, with other manly and warlike sports. Besides all this the Princess Perizadah was taught to sing and play on various instruments of mirth and merriment, wherein she became the peerless pearl of her age and time. The Intendant was exceeding glad of heart to find his adopted children prove themselves such proficients in every branch of knowledge; and presently, forasmuch as his lodging was small and unfit for the growing family, he bought at a little distance from the city a piece of land sufficiently large to contain fields and meadows and copses. Here he fell to building a mansion of great magnificence; and busied himself day and night with supervising the architects and masons and other artificers. He adorned the walls inside and out with sculptural work of the finest and paintings of the choicest, and he fitted every apartment with richest furniture. In the front of his mansion he bade lay out a garden and stocked it with scented flowers and fragrant shrubs and fruit trees whose produce was as that of Paradise. There was moreover a large park girt on all sides by a high wall wherein he reared game, both fur and feather, as sport for the two Princes and their sister. And when the mansion was finished and fit for habitation, the Intendant, who had faithfully served the Shah for many generations of men, craved leave of his lord that he might bid adieu to the city and take up his abode in his new country seat; and the King, who had always looked upon him with the eye of favour, granted to him the required boon right heartily; furthermore, to prove his high opinion of his old servant and his services, he inquired of him if he had aught to request that it might be granted to him. Replied the other, "O my liege lord, thy slave desireth naught save that he may spend the remnant of his days under the shadow of the Shah's protection, with body and soul devoted to his service, even as I served the sire before the son." The Shah dismissed him with words of thanks and comfort, when he left the city and taking with him the two Princes and their sister, he carried them to his newly-built mansion. Some years before this time his wife had departed to the mercy of Allah, and he had passed only five or six months in his second home when he too suddenly fell sick and was admitted into the number of those who have found ruth. Withal he had neglected every occasion of telling his three foundlings the strange tale of their birth and how he had carried them to his home as castaways and had reared them as rearlings and had cherished them as his own children. But he had time to charge them, ere he died, that they three should never cease to live together in love and honour and affection and respect one towards other. The loss of their protector caused them to grieve with bitter grief, for they all thought he was their real father; so they bewailed them and buried him as befitted; after which the two brothers and their sister dwelt together in peace and plenty. But one day of the days the Princes, who were full of daring and of highest mettle, rode forth a-hunting and Princess Perizadah was left alone at home when an ancient woman——And as the morn began to dawn Shahrazad held her peace till

The end of the Six Hundred and Seventy-second Night.

THEN said she:——I have heard, O auspicious King, that perchance an ancient woman of the Moslems, a recluse and a devotee, came to the door and begged leave to enter within and repeat her prayers, as it was then the canonical hour and she had but time to make the Wuzú-ablution. Perizadah bade bring her and saluted her with the salam and kindly welcomed her; then, when the holy woman had made an end of her orisons, the handmaids of the Princess, at her command, conducted her all through the house and grounds, and displayed to her the rooms with their furniture and fittings, and lastly the garden and orchard and game-park. She was well pleased with all she saw and said within herself, "The man who built this mansion and laid out these parterres and vergiers was verily an accomplished artist and a wight of marvellous skill." At last the slaves led her back to the Princess who, awaiting her return, was sitting in the belvedere; and quoth she to the devotee, "Come, O good my mother, do thou sit beside me and make me happy by the company of a pious recluse whom I am fortunate enough to have entertained unawares, and suffer I listen to thy words of grace and thereby gain no small advantage in this world and the next. Thou hast chosen the right path and straight whereon to walk, and that which all men strive for and pine for." The holy woman would fain have seated herself at the feet of the Princess, but she

courteously arose and took her by the hand and constrained her
to sit beside her. Quoth she, "O my lady, mine eyes never yet
beheld one so well-mannered as thou art: indeed, I am unworthy
to sit with thee, natheless, as thou biddest, I will e'en do thy
bidding." As they sat conversing each with other the slave-girls
set before them a table whereon were placed some platters of
bread and cakes with saucers full of fruits both fresh and dried,
and various kinds of cates and sweetmeats. The Princess took
one of the cakes and giving it to the good woman said, "O my
mother, refresh thyself herewith and eat of the fruits such as
thou likest. 'Tis now long since thou didst leave thy home and I
trow thou hast not tasted aught of food upon the road." Replied
the holy woman, "O lady of gentle birth, I am not wont to taste
of dainty dishes such as these, but I can ill refuse thy provision,
since Allah the Almighty deigneth send me food and support by
so liberal and generous a hand as thine." And when they twain
had eaten somewhat and cheered their hearts, the Princess asked
the devotee concerning the manner of her worship and of her
austere life; whereto she made due answer and explained according to her knowledge. The Princess then exclaimed, "Tell me,
I pray thee, what thou thinkest of this mansion and the fashion
of its building and the furniture and the appurtenances; and say
me is all perfect and appropriate, or is aught still lacking in mansion or garden?" And she replied, "Since thou deignest ask my
opinion, I confess to thee that both the building and the parterres
are finished and furnished to perfection; and the belongings are in
the best of taste and in the highest of ordinance. Still to my
thinking there be three things here wanting, which if thou hadst
the place would be most complete." The Princess Perizadah
adjured her saying, "O my aunt, I beseech thee tell me what
three articles yet are lacking, that I may lose nor pains nor toil
to obtain them;" and, as the maiden pressed her with much
entreaty, the devotee was constrained to tell her. Quoth she,
"O gentle lady, the first thing is the Speaking-Bird, called Bul-
bul-i-hazár-dástán;[1] he is very rare and hard to find but, whenever
he poureth out his melodious notes, thousands of birds fly to him

---

[1] In Arab. usually shortened to "Hazár" (bird of a thousand tales = the Thousand),
generally called "'Andalíb:" Galland has *Bulbulhezer* and some of his translators debase
it to *Bulbulkezr*. See vol. v. 148, and the Hazár-dastán of Kazwíní (De Sacy, Chrest. iii.
413). These rarities represent the Rukh's egg in "Alaeddin."

from every side and join him in his harmony. The next thing is the Singing-Tree, whose smooth and glossy leaves when shaken by the wind and rubbed one against other send forth tuneful tones which strike the ear like the notes of sweet-voiced minstrels ravishing the hearts of all who listen. The third thing is the Golden-Water of transparent purity, whereof should but one drop be dripped into a basin and this be placed inside the garden it presently will fill the vessel brimful and will spout upwards in gerbes playing like a fountain that jets: moreover it never ceaseth playing, and all the water as it shooteth up falleth back again inside the basin, not one gout thereof being lost." Replied the Princess, "I doubt not but thou knowest for a certainty the very spot where these wondrous things are to be found; and I pray thee tell me now the place and means whereby I may take action to obtain them."——And as the morn began to dawn Shahrazad held her peace till

The end of the Six Hundred and Seventy-third Night.

THEN said she——I have heard, O auspicious King, that the holy woman thus answered the Princess, "These three rarities are not to be found, save on the boundary-line that lieth between the land of Hind and the confining countries, a score of marches along the road that leadeth Eastwards from this mansion. Let him who goeth forth in quest of them ask the first man he meeteth on the twentieth stage concerning the spot where he may find the Speaking-Bird, the Singing-Tree and the Golden-Water; and he will direct the seeker where to come upon all three." When she had made an end of speaking the Devotee, with many blessings and prayers and vows for her well-being, farewelled the lady Perizadah and fared forth homewards. The Princess, however, ceased not to ponder her words and ever to dwell in memory upon the relation of the holy woman who, never thinking that her hostess had asked for information save by way of curiosity, nor really purposed in mind to set forth with intent of finding the rarities, had heedlessly told all she knew and had given a clue to the discovery. But Perizadah kept these matters deeply graven on the tablets of her heart with firm resolution to follow the directions and, by all means in her power, to gain possession of these three wonders. Withal, the more she

reflected the harder appeared the enterprise, and her fear of failing only added to her unease. Now whilst she sat perplexed
with anxious thought and anon terrified with sore affright, her
brothers rode back from the hunting-ground; and they marvelled
much to see her sad of semblance and low-spirited, wondering
the while what it was that troubled her. Presently quoth Prince
Bahman, "O sister mine, why art thou so heavy of heart this day?
Almighty Allah forbid thou be ill in health or that aught have
betided thee to cause thy displeasure or to make thee melancholy.
Tell us I beseech thee what it is, that we may be sharers in thy
sorrow and be alert to aid thee." The Princess answered not a
word, but after long silence raised her head and looked up at
her brothers; then casting down her eyes she said in curt phrase
that naught was amiss with her. Quoth Prince Bahman, "Full
well I wot that there is a somewhat on thy mind which thou
hesitatest to tell us; and now hear me swear a strong oath that I
will never leave thy side till thou shalt have told us what cause
it is that troubleth thee. Haply thou art aweary of our affection and thou wouldst undo the fraternal tie which hath united
us from our infancy." When she saw her brothers so distressed
and distraught, she was compelled to speak and said, "Albeit,
O my dearlings, to tell you wherefore I am sad and sorrowful
may cause you grief, still there is no help but I explain the
matter to you twain. This mansion, which our dear father
(who hath found ruth) builded for us, is perfect in every attribute
nor lacketh it any condition of comfort or completion. Howbeit
I have found out by chance this day that there are yet three
things which, were they set within these walls, of the house and
grounds, would make our place beyond compare, and in the wide
world there would be naught with it to pair. These three things
are the Speaking-Bird and the Singing-Tree and the Golden-
Water; and ever since I heard of them my heart is filled with
extreme desire to place them within our domain and excessive
longing to obtain them by any means within my power. It now
behoveth you help me with your best endeavour and to consider
what person will aid me in getting possession of these rarities."
Replied Prince Bahman, "My life and that of my brother are at
thy service to carry out thy purpose with heart and soul; and,
couldst thou give me but a clue to the place where these strange
things are found, I would sally forth in quest of them at day-
break as soon as the morning shall morrow." When Prince

Parwez understood that his brother was about to make this journey, he spake saying, "O my brother, thou art eldest of us, so do thou stay at home while I go forth to seek for these three things and bring them to our sister. And indeed it were more fitting for me to undertake a task which may occupy me for years." Replied Prince Bahman, "I have full confidence in thy strength and prowess, and whatso I am able to perform thou canst do as well as I can. Still it is my firm resolve to fare forth upon this adventure alone and unaided, and thou must stay and take care of our sister and our home." So next day Prince Bahman learned from the Princess the road whereon he was to travel and the marks and signs whereby to find the place. Presently, he donned armour and arms and bidding the twain adieu, he took horse and was about to ride forth with the stoutest of hearts, whereat Princess Perizadah's eyes brimmed with tears and in faltering accents she addressed him saying, "O dear my brother, this bitter separation is heart-breaking; and sore sorrowful am I to see thee part from us. This disunion and thine absence in a distant land cause me grief and woe far exceeding that wherewith I mourned and pined for the rarities wherefor thou quittest us. If only we might have some news of thee from day to day then would I feel somewhat comforted and consoled; but now 'tis clear otherwise and regret is of none avail."——— And as the morn began to dawn Shahrazad held her peace till

The end of the Six Hundred and Seventy-fourth Night.

THEN said she:———I have heard, O auspicious King, that Prince Bahman made answer in these words: "O sister mine, I am fully determined in mind to attempt this derring-do: be thou not however anxious or alarmed, for Inshallah—God willing—I shall return successful and triumphant. After my departure shouldst thou at any time feel in fear for my safety, then by this token which I leave thee thou shalt know of my fate and lot, good or evil." Then, drawing from his waist-shawl a little hunting-knife like a whittle, he gave it to Princess Perizadah, saying, "Take now this blade and keep it ever by thee; and shouldst thou at any day or hour be solicitous concerning my condition, draw it from its sheath; and, if the steel be clean and bright as 'tis now then know that I am alive and safe and sound; but an

thou find stains of blood thereon then shalt thou know that I am
slain, and naught remaineth for thee to do save to pray for me
as for one dead." With these words of solace the Prince departed on his journey, and travelled straight along the road to
India, turning nor to right hand nor to left but ever keeping the
same object in view. Thus a score of days was spent in journeying from the land of Iran, and upon the twentieth he reached
the end of his travel. Here he suddenly sighted an ancient man
of frightful aspect sitting beneath a tree hard by his thatched
hut wherein he was wont to shelter himself from the rains of
spring and the heats of summer and the autumnal miasmas and
the wintry frosts. So shotten in years was this Shaykh that hair
and beard, mustachios and whiskers were white as snow, and
the growth of his upper lip was so long and so thick that it
covered and concealed his mouth, while his beard swept the
ground and the nails of his hands and feet had grown to resemble
the claws of a wild beast. Upon his head he wore a broad-
brimmed hat of woven palm-leaves like that of a Malábár fisherman, and all his remaining habit was a strip of matting girded
around his waist. Now this Shaykh was a Darwaysh who for
many years had fled the world and all worldly pleasures; who
lived a holy life of poverty and chastity and other-worldliness
whereby his semblance had become such as I, O auspicious King,
have described to thee. From early dawn that day Prince Bahman
had been watchful and vigilant, ever looking on all sides to descry
some one who could supply him with information touching the
whereabouts of the rarities he sought; and this was the first
human being he had sighted on that stage, the twentieth and last
of his journey. So he rode up to him, being assured that the
Shaykh must be the wight of whom the holy woman had spoken.
Then Prince Bahman dismounting and making low obeisance to
the Darwaysh, said, "O my father, Allah Almighty prolong thy
years and grant thee all thy wishes!" Whereto the Fakir made
answer but in accents so indistinct that the Prince could not distinguish a single word he said; and presently Bahman understood
that his moustache had on such wise closed and concealed his
mouth that his utterance became indistinct and he only muttered
when he would have spoken. He therefore haltered his horse to a
tree and pulling out a pair of scissors said, "O holy man, thy lips
are wholly hidden by this overlong hair; suffer me, I pray thee,
clip the bristling growth which overspreadeth thy face and which

is so long and thick that thou art fearsome to behold; nay, more like to a bear than to a human being." The Darwaysh with a nod consented, and when the Prince had clipped it and trimmed the growth, his face once more looked young and fresh as that of a man in the prime of youth. Presently quoth Bahman to him, "Would Heaven I had a mirror wherein to show thee thy face, so wouldst thou see how youthful thou seemest, and how thy favour hath become far more like that of folk than whilom it was." These flattering words pleased the Darwaysh who smiling said, "I thank thee much for this thy goodly service and kindly offices; and, if in return, I can do aught of favour for thee, I pray thee let me know, and I will attempt to satisfy thee in all things with my very heart and soul." Then said the Prince, "O holy man, I have come hither from far distant lands along a toilsome road in quest of three things; to wit, a certain Speaking-Bird, a Singing-Tree and a Golden-Water; and this know I for certain that they are all to be found hard by this site."——And as the morn began to dawn Shahrazad held her peace till

The end of the Six Hundred and Seventy-fifth Night.

THEN said she:——I have heard, O auspicious King, that the Prince, turning to the Darwaysh, continued, "O Devotee, albeit well I wot that the three things I seek are in this land and near-hand, yet I know not the exact spot wherein to find them. An thou have true information concerning the place and will inform me thereof, I on my part will never forget thy kindness, and I shall have the satisfaction of feeling that this long and toilsome wayfare hath not been wholly vain." Hearing these words of the Prince, the Darwaysh changed countenance and his face waxed troubled and his colour wan; then he bent his glance downwards and sat in deepest silence. Whereat the other said, "O holy father, dost thou not understand the words wherewith I have bespoken thee? An thou art ignorant of the matter prithee let me know straightway that I may again fare onwards until such time as I find a man who can inform me thereof." After a long pause the Darwaysh made reply, "O stranger, 'tis true I ken full well the site whereof thou art in search; but I hold thee dear in that thou hast been of service to me; and I am loath for thine own sake to tell thee where to find that stead." And the Prince rejoined, "Say me, O Fakir, why dost thou withhold this knowledge from me, and wherefore art thou not lief to let me learn it?" Replied the other, " 'Tis a hard road to travel and full of perils and dangers. Besides thyself many have come hither and have asked the path of me, and I refused to tell them, but they heeded not my warning and pressed me sore and compelled me to disclose the secret which I would have buried in my breast. Know, O my son, that all those braves have perished in their pride and not one of them hath returned to me safe and sound. Now, an thy life be dear to thee, follow my counsel and fare no further, but rather turn thee back without stay or delay and make for house and home and family." Hereto Prince Bahman, stern in resolution, made reply, "Thou hast after kindly guise and friendly fashion advised me with the best of advice; and I, having heard all thou hast to say, do thank thee gratefully. But I reck not one jot or tittle of what dangers affront me, nor shall thy threats however fatal deter me from my purpose: moreover, if thieves or foemen haply fall upon me, I am armed at point and can and will protect myself, for I am certified that none can outvie me in strength and stowre." To this the Fakir made reply, "The beings who will cut thy path and bar thy progress to that place are unseen of man, nor will they appear to thee on any wise: how then canst thou defend thyself against them?" And he replied, "So be it, still I fear not and I pray thee only show me the road thither." When the Darwaysh was assured that the Prince had fully determined in mind to attempt the exploit and would by no means turn or be turned back from carrying out his purpose, he thrust his hand into a bag which lay hard by and took therefrom a ball, and said, "Alas, O my son, thou wilt not accept my counsel and I needs must let thee follow thy wilful way. Take this ball and, mounting thy horse, throw it in front of thee, and as long as it shall roll onwards do thou ride after it, but when it shall stop at the hill-foot dismount from thy horse and throw the reins upon his neck and leave him alone, for he will stay there without moving until such time as thou return. Then manfully breast the ascent, and on either side of the path, right and left, thou shalt see a scatter of huge black boulders. Here the sound of many voices in confused clamour and frightful will suddenly strike thine ears, to raise thy wrath and to fill thee with fear and hinder thy higher course uphill. Have a heed that thou be not dismayed, also beware, and again I say beware, lest thou turn thy head at any time, and cast a look backwards. An thy courage fail thee, or thou allow thyself one glance behind thee, thou shalt be transformed that very moment into a black rock; for know thou, O Prince, that all those stones which thou shalt see strewn upon thy way were men whilome and braves like thyself, who went forth with intent to gain the three things thou seekest, but frightened at those sounds lost human shape and became black boulders. However, shouldst thou reach the hill-top safe and sound, thou shalt find on the very summit a cage and perched therein the Speaking-Bird ready to answer all thy queries. So ask of him where thou mayest find the Singing-Tree and the Golden-Water, and he will tell thee all thou requirest. When thou shalt safely have seized all three thou wilt be free from further danger; yet, inasmuch as thou hast not yet set out upon this journey give ear to my counsel. I beg of thee desist from this thy purpose and return home in peace whilst thou hast yet the power."——And as the morn began to dawn Shahrazad held her peace till

𝔗𝔥𝔢 𝔢𝔫𝔡 𝔬𝔣 𝔱𝔥𝔢 𝔖𝔦𝔵 𝔥𝔲𝔫𝔡𝔯𝔢𝔡 𝔞𝔫𝔡 𝔖𝔢𝔳𝔢𝔫𝔱𝔶-𝔰𝔦𝔵𝔱𝔥 𝔑𝔦𝔤𝔥𝔱.

THEN said she:——I have heard, O auspicious King, that the Prince made answer to the Darwaysh, "Until, O thou holy man, such time as I win to my purpose I will not go back; no, never; therefore adieu." So he mounted his horse and threw the ball in front of him; and it rolled forward at racing-speed and he, with gaze intent thereupon, rode after it and did not suffer it to gain upon him. When it had reached the hill whereof the Darwaysh spake, it ceased to make further way, whereupon the Prince dismounted and throwing the reins on his horse's neck left him and fared on afoot to the slope. As far as he could see, the line of his path from the hill-foot to the head was strown with a scatter of huge black boulders; withal his heart felt naught of fear. He had not taken more than some four or five paces before a hideous din and a terrible hubbub of many voices arose, even as the Darwaysh had forewarned him. Prince Bahman, however, walked on valiantly with front erect and fearless tread, but he saw no living thing and heard only the Voices[1] sounding all around him. Some

---

[1] These disembodied "voices" speaking either naturally or through instruments are a recognized phenomenon of the so-called "Spiritualism." See p. 115 of "Supra-mundane

said, "Who is yon fool man and whence hath he come? Stop him, let him not pass!" Others shouted out, "Fall on him, seize this zany and slay him!" Then the report waxed louder and louder still, likest to the roar of thunder, and many Voices yelled out, "Thief! Assassin! Murtherer!" Another muttered in taunting undertones, "Let him be, fine fellow that he is! Suffer him to pass on, for he and he only shall get the cage and the Speaking-Bird." The Prince feared naught but advanced hot foot with his wonted nerve and spirit; presently, however, when the Voices kept approaching nearer and nearer to him and increased in number on every side, he was sore perplexed. His legs began to tremble, he staggered and in fine overcome by fear he clean forgot the warning of the Darwaysh and looked back, whereat he was incontinently turned to stone like the scores of knights and adventurers who had foregone him. Meantime the Princess Perizadah ever carried the hunting-knife, which Bahman her brother had given her, sheathed as it was in her maiden zone. She had kept it there ever since he set out upon his perilous expedition, and whenever she felt disposed she would bare the blade and judge by its sheen how fared her brother. Now until that day when he was transmewed to stone she found it, as often as she looked at it, clean and bright; but on the very evening when that evil fate betided him perchance Prince Parwez said to Perizadah, "O sister mine, give me I pray thee the hunting-knife that I may see how goeth it with our brother." She took it from her waist-belt and handed it to him; and as soon as he unsheathed the knife lo and behold! he saw gouts of gore begin to drop from it. Noting this he dashed the hunting-knife down and burst out into loud lamentations, whilst the Princess who divined what had happened shed a flood of bitter tears and cried with sighs and sobs, "Alas, O my brother, thou hast given thy life for me. Ah, woe is me and well-away! why did I tell thee of the Speaking-Bird and the Singing-Tree and the Golden-Water? Wherefore did I ask that holy woman how she liked our home, and hear of those three things in answer to my question? Would to Heaven she had never crossed our threshold and

Facts," &c., edited by T. J. Nichols, M.D., &c., London, Pitman, 1865. I venture to remark that the medical treatment by Mesmerism, Braidism and hypnotics, which was violently denounced and derided in 1850, is in 1887 becoming a part of the regular professional practice and forms another item in the long list of the Fallacies of the Faculty and the Myopism of the "Scientist."

darkened our doors! Ungrateful hypocrite, dost thou requite me
on such wise for the favour and the honour I was fain to show thee;
and what made me ask of thee the means whereby to win these
things? If now I obtain possession of them what will they
advantage me, seeing that my brother Bahman is no more?
What should I ever do with them?" Thus did Perizadah indulge
her grief bewailing her sad fate; while Parwez in like manner
moaned for his brother Bahman with exceeding bitter mourning.
At last the Prince, who despite his sorrow was assured that his
sister still ardently desired to possess the three marvels, turned
to Perizadah and said, "It behoveth me, O my sister, to set out
forthright and to discover whether Bahman our brother met his
death by doom of Destiny, or whether some enemy have slain
him; and if he hath been killed then must I take full vengeance
on his murtherer." Perizadah besought him with much weeping
and wailing not to leave her, and said, "O joy of my heart, Allah
upon thee, follow not in the footsteps of our dear departed
brother nor quit me in order to attempt a journey so rife in risks.
I care naught for those things in my fear lest I lose thee also
while attempting such enterprise." But Prince Parwez would on
no wise listen to her lament and next day took leave of her, but
ere he fared she said to him, "The hunting-knife which Bahman
left with me was the means of informing us concerning the mishap which happened to him; but, say me how shall I know what
happeneth to thee?" Then he produced a string of pearls which
numbered one hundred and said, "As long as thou shalt see these
pearls all parted one from other and each running loose upon the
string, then do thou know that I am alive; but an thou shouldst
find them fixed and adhering together then be thou ware that I
am dead." The Princess taking the string of pearls hung it
around her neck, determined to observe it hour after hour and
find out how it fared with her second brother. After this Prince
Parwez set out upon his travels and at the twentieth stage came
to the same spot where Bahman had found the Darwaysh and
saw him there in like condition. Then, after saluting him with
the salam, the Prince asked, "Canst thou tell me where to find
the Speaking-Bird and the Singing-Tree and the Golden-Water;
and by what manner of means I may get possession of them? An
thou can I pray thee inform me of this matter."———And as the
morn began to dawn Shahrazad held her peace till

The end of the Six Hundred and Seventy-seventh Night.

Then said she:——I have heard, O auspicious King, that the
Darwaysh strave to stay Prince Parwez from his design and
shewed him all the dangers on the way. Quoth he, "Not many
days ago one like unto thee in years and in features came hither
and enquired of me concerning the matter thou now seekest. I
warned him of the perils of the place and would have weaned
him from his wilful ways, but he paid no wise heed to my warnings and refused to accept my counsel. He went off with full
instructions from me how to find those things he sought; but as
yet he hath not returned, and doubtless he also hath perished
like the many who preceded him upon that perilous enterprise."
Then said Prince Parwez, "O holy father, I know the man of
whom thou speakest, for that he was my brother; and I learned
that he was dead, but have no inkling of the cause whereby he
died." Replied the Darwaysh, "O my lord, I can inform thee on
this matter; he hath been transmewed into a black stone, like the
others of whom I just now spake to thee. If thou wilt not accept
my advice and act according to my counsel thou also shalt perish
by the same means as did thy brother; and I solemnly forewarn
thee to desist from this endeavour." Prince Parwez having
pondered these words, presently made reply, "O Darwaysh, I
thank thee again and again and am much beholden to thee
that thou art fain of my welfare and thou hast given me the
kindest of counsel and the friendliest of advice; nor am I worthy
of such favours bestowed upon a stranger. But now remaineth
naught for me to beseech save that thou wilt point out the path,
for I am fully purposed to fare forwards and on no wise to desist
from my endeavour. I pray thee favour me with full instructions for the road even as thou favouredst my brother." Then
said the Darwaysh, "An thou wilt not lend ear to my warnings
and do as I desire thee, it mattereth to me neither mickle nor
little. Choose for thyself and I by doom of Destiny must perforce forward thy attempt and albeit, by reason of my great age
and infirmities, I may not conduct thee to the place I will not
grudge thee a guide." Then Prince Parwez mounted his horse
and the Darwaysh taking one of many balls from out his scrip
placed it in the youth's hands, directing him the while what to
do, as he had counselled his brother Bahman; and, after giving
him much advice and many warnings he ended with saying, "O

my lord, have a heed not to be perplexed and terrified by the threatening Voices,[1] and sounds from unseen beings, which shall strike thine ear; but advance dauntless to the hill-top where thou shalt find the cage with the Speaking-Bird and the Singing-Tree and the Golden-Water." The Fakir then bid him adieu with words of good omen and the Prince set forth. He threw the ball on the ground before him and, as it rolled up the path, he urged his horse to keep pace with it. But when he reached the hill-foot and saw that the ball had stopped and lay still, he dismounted forthright and paused awhile ere he should begin to climb and conned well in his mind the directions, one and all, given to him by the Darwaysh. Then, with firm courage and fast resolve, he set out afoot to reach the hill-top. But hardly had he begun to climb before he heard a voice beside him threatening him in churlish tongue and crying, "O youth of ill-omen, stand still that I may trounce thee for this thine insolence." Hearing these insulting words of the Invisible Speaker, Prince Parwez felt his blood boil over; he could not refrain his rage and in his passion he clean forgot the words of wisdom wherewith the Fakir had warned him. He seized his sword and drawing it from the scabbard, turned about to slay the man who durst insult him on such wise; but he saw no one and, in the act of looking back both he and his horse became black stones. Meanwhile the Princess ceased not at all hours of the day and watches of the night to consult the string of pearls which Parwez had left her: she counted them overnight when she retired to rest, she slept with them around her neck during the hours of darkness, and when she awoke at the dawn of day she first of all consulted them and noted their condition. Now at the very hour when her second brother was turned to stone she found the pearls sticking one to other so close together that she might not move a single bead apart from its fellows and she knew thereby that Prince Parwez also was lost to her for ever. ———And as the morn began to dawn Shahrazad held her peace till

The end of the Six Hundred and Seventy-eighth Night.

THEN said she:———I have heard, O auspicious King, that the Princess Perizadah was sore grieved at so sudden a blow and said

---

[1] I may also note that the "Hátif," or invisible Speaker, which must be subjective more often than objective, is a common-place of Moslem thaumaturgy.

to herself, "Ah! woe is me and well-away! How bitter will be living without the love of such brothers whose youthtide was sacrificed for me! 'Tis but right that I share their fate whate'er be my lot; else what shall I have to say on the Day of Doom and the Resurrection of the Dead and the Judgment of Mankind?" Wherefore next morning, without further let or stay, she donned disguise of man's attire; and, warning her women and slaves that she would be absent on an errand for a term of days during which they would be in charge of the house and goods, she mounted her hackney and set out alone and unattended. Now, inasmuch as she was skilled in horsemanship and had been wont to accompany her brothers when hunting and hawking, she was better fitted than other women to bear the toils and travails of travel. So on the twentieth day she arrived safe and sound at the hermitage-hut where, seeing the same Shaykh, she took seat beside him and after salaming to him and greeting him she asked him, "O holy father, suffer me to rest and refresh myself awhile in this site of good omen; then deign point out to me, I pray thee, the direction of the place, at no far distance herefrom, wherein are found a certain Speaking-Bird and a Singing-Tree and a Golden-Water. An thou wilt tell me I shall deem this the greatest of favour." Replied the Darwaysh, "Thy voice revealeth to me that thou art a woman and no man, albeit attired in male's apparel. Well I wot the stead whereof thou speakest and which containeth the marvellous things thou hast named. But say me, what is thy purpose in asking me?" The Princess made reply, "I have been told many a tale anent these rare and wondrous things, and I would fain get possession of them and bear them to my home and make them its choicest adornments." And said the Fakir, "O my daughter, in very truth these matters are exceeding rare and admirable: right fit are they for fair ones like thyself to win and take back with thee, but thou hast little inkling of the dangers manifold and dire that encompass them. Better far were it for thee to cast away this vain thought and go back by the road thou camest." Replied the Princess, "O holy father and far-famed anchorite, I come from a distant land whereto I will nevermore return except after winning my wish; no, never! I pray thee tell me the nature of those dangers and what they be, that hearing thereof my heart may judge if I have or have not the strength and the spirit to meet them." Then the Shaykh described to the Princess all the risks of the road as erst he had informed Princes Bahman and Parwez; and he ended with saying, "The dangers will display themselves as soon as thou shalt begin to climb the hill-foot and shall not end till such time as thou wilt have reached the hill-head where is the home of the Speaking-Bird. Then, if thou be fortunate enough to seize him, he will direct thee where to find the Singing-Tree and the Golden-Water. All the time thou climbest the hill, Voices from throats unseen and accents fierce and fell shall resound in thine ears. Furthermore, thou shalt see black rocks and boulders strewn upon thy path; and these, thou must know, are the transformed bodies of men who with exceeding courage attempted the same enterprise, but filled with sudden fear and tempted to turn and to look backwards were changed into stones. Now do thou steadily bear in mind what was their case. At the first they listened to those fearful sounds and cursings with firm souls, but anon their hearts and minds misgave them, or, haply, they fumed with fury to hear the villain words addressed to them and they turned about and gazed behind them, whereat both men and horses became black boulders." But when the Darwaysh had told her every whit, the Princess made reply, "From what thou sayest it seemeth clear to me that these Voices can do nothing but threaten and frighten by their terrible din; furthermore that there is naught to prevent a man climbing up the hill, nor is there any fear of any one attacking him; all he hath to do is on no account to look behind him." And after a short pause she presently added, "O Fakir, albeit a woman yet I have both nerve and thews to carry me through this adventure. I shall not heed the Voices nor be enraged thereat, neither will they have any power to dismay me: moreover, I have devised a device whereby my success on this point is assured." "And what wilt thou do?" asked he, and she answered, "I will stop mine ears with cotton so may not my mind be disturbed and reason perturbed by hearing those awesome sounds." The Fakir marvelled with great marvel and presently exclaimed, "O my lady, methinks thou art destined to get possession of the things thou seekest. This plan hath not occurred to any hitherto[1] and hence it is haply that one and all have failed miserably and have perished in the attempt. Take good heed to thyself however, nor run any risk other than the enterprise requireth." She replied,

---

[1] It may have been borrowed from Ulysses and the Sirens.

"I have no cause for fear since this one and only danger is before me to prevent happy issue. My heart doth bear me witness that I shall surely gain the guerdon wherefor I have undertaken such toil and trouble. But now do thou tell me what I must do, and whither to win my wish I must wend." The Darwaysh once more besought her to return home, but Perizadah refused to listen and remained as firm and resolute as before; so when he saw that she was fully bent upon carrying out her purpose he exclaimed, "Depart, O my daughter, in the peace of Almighty Allah and His blessing; and may He defend thy youth and beauty from all danger." Then taking from his bag a ball he gave it her and said, "When thou art seated in saddle throw this before thee and follow it whitherso it lead thee; and when it shall stop at the hill-foot then dismount and climb the slope. What will happen after I have already told thee."——And as the morn began to dawn Shahrazad held her peace till

The end of the Six Hundred and Seventy-ninth Night.

THEN said she:——I have heard, O auspicious King, that the Princess after farewelling the Fakir straightway bestrode her steed and threw the ball in front of his hooves as she had been bidden do. It rolled along before her in the direction of the hill and she urged her hackney to keep up with it, until reaching the hill it suddenly stopped. Hereat the Princess dismounted forth-with and having carefully plugged both her ears with cotton, began to breast the slope with fearless heart and dauntless soul; and as soon as she had advanced a few steps a hubbub of voices broke out all around her, but she heard not a sound, by reason of her hearing being blunted by the cotton-wool. Then hideous cries arose with horrid din, still she heard them not; and at last they grew to a storm of shouts and shrieks and groans and moans flavoured with foul language such as shameless women use when railing one at other. She caught now and then an echo of the sounds but recked naught thereof and only laughed and said to herself, "What care I for their scoffs and jeers and fulsome taunts? Let them hoot on and bark and bay as they may: this at least shall not turn me from my purpose." As she approached the goal the path became perilous in the extreme and the air was so filled with an infernal din and such awful sounds that even

Rustam would have quailed thereat and the bold spirit of Asfandiyar[1] have quaked with terror. The Princess, however, pressed on with uttermost speed and dauntless heart till she neared the hill-top and espied above her the cage in which the Speaking-Bird was singing with melodious tones; but, seeing the Princess draw nigh, he broke out despite his puny form in thundering tones and cried, "Return, O fool: hie thee back nor dare come nearer." Princess Perizadah heeded not his clamour a whit but bravely reached the hill-top, and running over the level piece of ground made for the cage and seized it saying, "At last I have thee and thou shalt not escape me." She then pulled out the cotton-wool wherewith she had stopped her ears, and heard the Speaking-Bird reply in gentle accents, "O lady valiant and noble, be of good cheer for no harm or evil shall betide thee, as hath happened to those who essayed to make me their prize. Albeit I am encaged I have much secret knowledge of what happeneth in the world of men and I am content to become thy slave, and for thee to be my liege lady. Moreover I am more familiar with all that concerneth thee even than thou art thyself; and one day of the days I will do thee a service which shall deserve thy gratitude. What now is thy command? Speak that I may fulfil thy wish." Princess Perizadah was gladdened by these words, but in the midst of her joy she grieved at the thought of how she had lost her brothers whom she loved with a love so dear, and anon she said to the Speaking-Bird, "Full many a thing I want, but first tell me if the Golden-Water, of which I have heard so much, be nigh unto this place and if so do thou show me where to find it." The Bird directed her accordingly and the Princess took a silver flagon she had brought with her and filled it brimful from the magical fount. Then quoth she to the Bird, "The third and last prize I have come to seek is the Singing-Tree: discover to me where that also can be found." The Bird replied, "O Princess of fair ones, behind thy back in yonder clump that lieth close at hand groweth the Tree;" so she went forthright to the copse and found the Tree she sought singing with sweetest toned voice. But inasmuch as it was huge in girth she returned to her slave the Bird and said, "The Tree indeed I found but 'tis lofty and bulky; how then shall I pull it up?" and

---

1 Two heroes of the Shahnámeh and both the types of reckless daring. The monomachy or duel between these braves lasted through two days.

he made answer, "Pluck but a branchlet of the Tree and plant it in thy garden: 'twill at once take root and in shortest time be as gross and fair a growth as that in yonder copse." So the Princess broke off a twig, and now that she had secured the three things, whereof the holy woman spake to her, she was exceeding joyful and turning to the Bird said, "I have in very deed won my wish, but one thing is yet wanting to my full satisfaction. My brothers who ventured forth with this same purpose are lying hereabouts turned into black stones; and I fain would have them brought to life again and the twain return with me in all satisfaction and assurance of success. Tell me now some plan whereby mine every desire may be fulfilled."——And as the morn began to dawn Shahrazad held her peace till

The end of the Six Hundred and Eightieth Night.

THEN said she:——I have heard, O auspicious King, that the Speaking-Bird replied, "O Princess, trouble not thyself, the thing is easy. Sprinkle some of the Golden-Water from the flagon upon the black stones lying round about, and by virtue thereof each and every shall come to life again, thy two brothers as well as the others." So Princess Perizadah's heart was set at rest and taking the three prizes with her she fared forth and scattered a few drops from the silver flagon upon each black stone as she passed it when, lo and behold! they came to life as men and horses. Amongst them were her brothers whom she at once knew and falling on their necks she embraced them, and asked in tones of surprise, "O my brothers, what do ye here?" To this they answered, "We lay fast asleep." Quoth she, "Strange indeed that ye take delight in slumber away from me and ye forget the purpose wherefor ye left me; to wit, the winning of the Speaking-Bird and the Singing-Tree and the Golden-Water. Did ye not see this place all bestrown with dark hued rocks? Look now and say if there be aught left of them. These men and horses now standing around us were all black stones as ye yourselves also were; but, by the boon of Almighty Allah, all have come to life again and await the signal to depart. And if now ye wish to learn by what strange miracle both ye and they have recovered human shape, know ye that it hath been wrought by virtue of a water contained in this flagon which I sprinkled on the rocks with leave of the Lord of all Living. When I had gained possession of this

cage and its Speaking-Bird, and also of the Singing-Tree, a wand
whereof ye see in my hand, and lastly of the Golden-Water, I
would not take them home with me unless ye twain could also
bear me company; so I asked of this Bird the means whereby ye
could be brought to life again. He made me drop some drops of
the Golden-Water on the boulders and when I had done this ye
two like all the others returned to life and to your proper forms."
Hearing these her words the Princes Bahman and Parwez thanked
and praised their sister Perizadah; and all the others she had
saved showered thanks and blessings on her head saying with
one accord, "O our lady, we are now thy slaves; nor can a life-
long service repay the debt of gratitude we owe thee for this
favour thou hast shown us. Command and we are ready to obey
thee with our hearts and our souls." Quoth Perizadah, "The
bringing back to life of these my brothers were my aim and purpose, and in so doing ye too have profited thereby; and I accept
your acknowledgments as another pleasure. But now do ye
mount each and every man his horse and ride back by the way ye
came to your homes in Allah's peace." On this wise the Princess
dismissed them and made herself also ready to depart; but, as
she was about to bestride her steed, Prince Bahman asked permission of her that he might hold in hand the cage and ride in
front of her. She answered, "Not so, O brother mine; this Bird
is now my slave and I will carry him myself. An thou wilt, take
thou this twig with thee, but hold the cage only till I am seated
in saddle." She then mounted her hackney and, placing the cage
before her on the pommel, bade her brother Parwez take charge
of the Golden-Water in the silver flagon and carry it with all care
and the Prince did her bidding without gainsaying. And when
they all were ready to ride forth, including the knights and the
squires whom Perizadah had brought to life by sprinkling the
Water the Princess turned to them and said, "Why delay we our
departure and how is it that none offereth to lead us?" But as all
hesitated she gave command, "Now let him amongst your number whose noblesse and high degree entitle him to such distinction fare before us and show us the way." Then all with one
accord replied, "O Princess of fair ones, there be none amongst
us worthy of such honour, nor may any wight dare to ride before
thee." So when she saw that none amongst them claimed pre-
eminence or right of guidance, and none desired to take precedence of the rest, she made excuse and said, "O my lords, 'tis

not for me by right to lead the way, but since ye order I must
needs obey." Accordingly she pushed on to the front, and after
came her brothers and behind them the rest. And as they
journeyed on all desired to see the holy man, and thank him for
his favours and friendly rede, but when they reached the spot
where he dwelt they found him dead, and they knew not if old
age had taken him away, or if he perished in his pride because
the Princess Perizadah had found and had carried off the three
things whereof he had been appointed by Destiny guard and
guide.———And as the morn began to dawn Shahrazad held her
peace till

The end of the Six Hundred and Eighty-first Night.

THEN said she:———I have heard, O auspicious King, that all the
company rode on, and as each one arrived at the road which led
him to his natal land he took leave of the Lady Perizadah and
went his way, until all were gone and the Princess and her
brothers were the only left. At last they reached their journey's
end safe and sound, and on entering their mansion Perizadah
hung the cage inside the garden hard by the belvedere and no
sooner did the Speaking-Bird begin to sing than flights of ring-
doves and bulbuls and nightingales and skylarks and parrots and
other songsters came flocking around him from afar and anear.
Likewise she set the twig, which she had taken from the Singing-
Tree, in a choice parterre also hard by the belvedere, and forthright it took root and put forth boughs and buds and grew
goodly in growth, till it became a trunk as large as that from
which she had plucked the twig, whilst from its leafage went
forth bewitching sounds rivalling the music of the parent tree.
She lastly bid them carve her a basin of pure white marble and
set it in the centre of the pleasure grounds; then she poured
therein the Golden-Water and forthright it filled the bowl and
shot upwards like a spouting fountain some twenty feet in height;
moreover the gerbes and jets fell back whence they came and not
one drop was lost: whereby the working of the waters was un-
broken and ever similar. Now but few days passed ere the report
of these three wonders was bruited abroad and flocked the folk
daily from the city to solace themselves with the sight, and the
gates stood always open wide and all who came had entrance to

the house and gardens and free leave to walk about at will and
see these rarities which affected them with admiration and delight. Then also, as soon as both the Princes had recovered from
the toils of travel, they began to go a-hunting as heretofore; and
it chanced one day they rode forth several miles from home
and were both busied in the chase, when the Shah of Irán-land
came by decree of Destiny to the same place for the same purpose. The Princes, seeing a band of knights and huntsmen drawing near, were fain to ride home and to avoid such meeting; so
they left the hunting-grounds and turned them homewards. But
as Fate and lot would have it they hit upon the very road whereby King Khusrau Shah was coming, and so narrow was the path
that they could not avoid the horsemen by wheeling round and
wending another way. So they drew rein perforce and dismounting they salamed and did obeisance to the Shah and stood between
his hands with heads bent low. The Sovran, seeing the horses'
fine trappings and the Princes' costly garments, thought that the
two youths were in the suite of his Wazirs and his Ministers of
state and much wished to look upon their faces; he therefore
bade them raise their heads and stand upright in the presence
and they obeyed his bidding with modest mien and downcast
eyes. He was charmed to behold their comeliness of favour and
their graceful forms and their noble air and their courtly mien;
and, after gazing at them for some time in not a little wonder and
admiration, he asked them who they were and what might be
their names and where they abode. Hereto Prince Bahman made
reply, "O Asylum of the Universe, we are the sons of one whose
life was spent in serving the Shah, the Intendant of the royal
gardens and pleasaunces. As his days drew to a close he builded
him a home without the town for us to dwell in till we should
grow to man's estate and become fit to do thy Highness suit and
service and carry out thy royal commands." The Shah furthermore asked them, "How is it that ye go a-hunting? This is a
special sport of Kings and is not meant for the general of his subjects and dependants." Prince Bahman rejoined, "O Refuge of
the World, we yet are young in years and being brought up at
home we know little of courtly customs; but, as we look to bear
arms in the armies of the Shah we fain would train our bodies
to toil and moil." This answer was honoured by the royal
approof and the King rejoined, "The Shah would see how ye
deal with noble game; so choose ye whatever quarry ye will and

bring it down in the presence." The Princes hereat remounted their horses and joined the Sovran; and when they reached the thickmost of the forest, Prince Bahman started a tiger and Prince Parwez rode after a bear; and the twain used their spears with such skill and good will that each killed his quarry and laid it at the Shah's feet. Then entering the wood again Prince Bahman slew a bear, and Prince Parwez a tiger[1] and did as before; but when they would have ridden off the third time the King forbade them saying, "What! would ye strip the royal preserve of all the game? This be enough and more than enough, the Shah wished only to put your valour to the proof and having seen it with his own eyes he is fully satisfied. Come now with us and stand before us as we sit at meat." Prince Bahman made reply, "We are not worthy of the high honour and dignity wherewith thou favourest us thy humble servants. We dutifully and humbly petition thy Highness to hold us excused for this day; but if the Asylum of the Universe deign appoint some other time thy slaves will right gladly execute thy auspicious orders."——— And as the morn began to dawn Shahrazad held her peace till

The end of the Six Hundred and Eighty-second Night.

THEN said she:——I have heard, O auspicious King, that Khusrau Shah, astonished at their refusal, asked the cause thereof when Prince Bahman answered, "May I be thy sacrifice,[2] O King of kings, we have at home an only sister; and all three are bound together with bonds of the fondest affection; so we brothers go not anywhere without consulting her nor doth she aught save according to our counsel." The King was pleased to see such fraternal love and union and presently quoth he, "By the head of the Shah,[3] he freely giveth you leave to go to-day: consult your sister and meet the Shadow of Allah[4] to-morrow at

---

[1] The "Bágh" or royal tiger, is still found in the jungles of Mázenderán and other regions of Northern Persia.

[2] In addressing the Shah every Persian begins with the formula "Kurbán-at básham" = may I become thy Corban or sacrifice. For this word (Kurbán) see vol. viii. 16.

[3] The King in Persia always speaks of himself in the third person and swears by his own blood and head, soul, life and death. The form of oath is ancient: Joseph, the first (but not the last) Jew-financier of Egypt, emphasises his speech "by the life of Pharaoh." (Gen. xiii. 15, 16.)

[4] Another title of the Shah, making him quasi-divine, at any rate the nearest to the Almighty, like the Czar and the Emperor of China. Hence the subjects bow to him with

this hunting-ground, and tell him what she saith and if she be
content to let you twain come and wait upon the Shah at meat."
So the Princes farewelled and prayed for him; then rode back
home; but they both forgot to tell their sister how they had
fallen in with the King; and of all that passed between them they
remembered not one word.[1] Next day again they went ahunting
and on returning from the chase the Shah enquired of them,
"Have ye consulted with your sister if ye may serve the King,
and what saith she thereto? Have ye obtained permission from
her?" On hearing these words the Princes waxed aghast with
fear; the colour of their faces changed, and each began to look
into the other's eyes. Then Bahman said, "Pardon, O Refuge
of the World, this our transgression. We both forgot the command and remembered not to tell our sister." Replied the King,
"It mattereth naught! ask her to-day and bring me word to-
morrow." But it so happened that on that day also they forgot
the message yet the King was not annoyed at their shortness of
memory, but taking from his pocket three little balls of gold, and
tying them in a kerchief of silk, he handed them to Prince Bahman
saying, "Put these balls in thy waist shawl, so shalt thou not
forget to ask thy sister; and if perchance the matter escape thy
memory, when thou shalt go to bed and take off thy girdle, haply
the sound of them falling to the ground will remind thee of thy
promise." Despite this strict injunction of the Shadow of Allah
the Princes on that day also clean forgot the order and the promise
they had made to the King. When, however, night came on, and
Prince Bahman went to his bed-chamber for sleep, he loosed his
girdle and down fell the golden balls and at the sound the message of the Shah flashed across his thought. So he and his brother
Parwez at once hastened to Perizadah's bower, where she was
about retiring to rest; and, with many excuses for troubling her
at so unseasonable an hour, reported to her all that had happened. She lamented their thoughtlessness which for three successive days had caused them forget the royal behest and ended
with saying, "Fortune hath favoured you, O my brothers, and

---

the body at right angles as David did to Saul (1 Sam. xxiv. 8) or fall upon the face like
Joshua (v. 14).

[1] A most improbable and absurd detail: its sole excuse is the popular superstition of
"blood speaking to blood." The youths being of the royal race felt that they could take
unwarrantable liberties.

brought you suddenly to the notice of the Asylum of the Universe, a chance which often hath led to the height of good. It grieveth me sore that in your over regard for our fraternal love and union ye did not take service with the King when he deigned command you. Moreover ye have far greater cause for regret and repentance than I in that ye failed to plead a sufficient excuse and that which ye offered must have sounded rude and churlish. A right dangerous thing it is to thwart Kingly wishes. In his extreme condescension the Shah commandeth you to take service with him and ye, in rebelling against his exalted orders have done foolishly and ye have caused me much trouble of mind. Howbeit I will sue counsel from my slave the Speaking-Bird and see what he may say; for when I have ever any hard and weighty question to decide I fail not to ask his advice." Hereupon the Princess set the cage by her side and after telling her slave all that her brothers had made known to her, asked admonition of him regarding what they should do. The Speaking-Bird made answer, "It behoveth the Princes to gratify the Shah in all things he requireth of them: moreover, let them make ready a feast for the King and humbly pray him to visit this house, and thereby testify to him loyalty and devotion to his royal person." Then said the Princess, "O Bird, my brothers are most dear to me nor would I suffer them leave my sight for one moment if it were possible; and Allah forfend that this daring on their part do injury to our love and affection." Said the Speaking-Bird, "I have counselled thee for the best and have offered thee the right rede; nor do thou fear aught in following it, for naught save good shall come therefrom." "But," quoth the Princess, "an the Shadow of Allah honour us by crossing the threshold of this house needs must I present myself before him with face unveiled?"[1] "By all means," quoth the Speaking-Bird, "this will not harm thee, nay rather 'twill be to thine advantage."——And as the morn began to dawn Shahrazad held her peace till

The end of the Six Hundred and Eighty-third Night.

THEN said she:——I have heard, O auspicious King, that early next day the two Princes Bahman and Parwez rode as aforetime

---

[1] This is still a Persian custom because all the subjects, women as well as men, are virtually the King's slaves.

to the hunting-ground and met Khusrau Shah, who asked them, saying, "What answer bring ye from your sister?" Hereupon the elder brother advancing said, "O Shadow of Allah, verily we are thy slaves and whatever thou deign bid that we are ready to obey. These less than the least have referred the matter to their sister and have obtained her consent; nay more, she blamed and chided them for that they did not hurry to carry out the commands of the Refuge of the World the moment they were delivered. Therefore being sore displeased at us, she desireth us on her behalf to plead forgiveness with the Sháhinshah[1] for this offence by us offered." Replied the King, "No crime have ye committed to call forth the royal displeasure: nay more, it delighteth the Shadow of Allah exceedingly to see the love ye twain bear towards your sister." Hearing such words of condescension and kindliness from the Shah, the Princes held their peace and hung their heads for shame groundwards; and the King who that day was not keen, according to his custom, after the chase, whenever he saw the brothers hold aloof, called them to his presence and heartened their hearts with words of favour; and presently, when a-weary of sport, he turned the head of his steed palace-wards and deigned order the Princes to ride by his side. The Wazirs and Councillors and Courtiers one and all fumed with envy and jealousy to see two unknowns entreated with such especial favour; and as they rode at the head of the suite adown the market-street all eyes were turned upon the youths and men asked one of other, "Who be the two who ride beside the Shah? Belong they to this city, or come they from some foreign land?" And the folk praised and blessed them saying, "Allah send our King of kings two Princes as goodly and gallant as are these twain who ride beside him. If our hapless Queen who languisheth in durance had brought forth sons, by Allah's favour they would now be of the same age as these young lords." But as soon as the cavalcade reached the palace the King alighted from his horse and led the Princes to his private chamber, a splendid retreat magnificently furnished, wherein a table had been spread with sumptuous meats and rarest cates; and having seated himself thereat he motioned them to do likewise. Hereupon the brothers making low obeisance also took their seats and ate in well-bred silence with respectful mien. Then the

---

[1] i.e. King of kings, the Βασιλεὺς βασιλεύων.

Shah, desiring to warm them into talk[1] and thereby to test their wit and wisdom, addressed them on themes galore and asked of them many questions; and, inasmuch as they had been taught well and trained in every art and science, they answered with propriety and perfect ease. The Shah struck with admiration bitterly regretted that Almighty Allah had not vouchsafed to him sons so handsome in semblance and so apt and so learned as these twain; and, for the pleasure of listening to them, he lingered at meat longer than he was wont to do. And when he rose from table and retired with them to his private apartment he still sat longwhile talking with them and at last in his admira-tion he exclaimed, "Never until this day have I set eyes on youths so well brought up and so comely and so capable as are these, and methinks 'twere hard to find their equals anywhere." In fine quoth he, "The time waxeth late, so now let us cheer our hearts with music." And forthright the royal band of minstrels and musicians began to sing and perform upon instruments of mirth and merriment, whilst dancing-girls and boys displayed their skill, and mimes and mummers played their parts. The Princes enjoyed the spectacle with extreme joy and the last hours of the afternoon passed in royal revelry and regale. But when the sun had set and evening came on, the youths craved dismissal from the Shah with many expressions of gratitude for the exalted favours he had deigned bestow on them; and ere they fared forth the King of kings bespake them, saying, "Come ye again on the morrow to our hunting-ground as heretofore, and thence return to the palace. By the beard of the Shah, he fain would have you always with him, and solace him with your com-panionship and converse." Prince Bahman, prostrating himself before the presence, answered, " 'Tis the very end and aim of all our wishes, O Shadow of Allah upon Earth, that on the morrow when thou shalt come from the chase and pass by our poor house, thou graciously deign enter and rest in it awhile, thereby con-ferring the highmost of honours upon ourselves and upon our sister. Albeit the place is not worthy of the Shahinshah's exalted presence, yet at times do mighty Kings condescend to visit the huts of their slaves." The King, ever more and more enchanted with their comeliness and pleasant speech, vouchsafed a most gracious answer, saying, "The dwelling place of youths in your

---

[1] *Majlis garm karná, i.e.* to give some life to the company.

estate and degree will certainly be goodly and right worthy of you; and the Shah willingly consenteth for the morrow to become the guest of you twain and of your sister whom, albeit he have not yet seen, he is assured to find perfect in all gifts of body and mind. Do ye twain therefore about early dawn-tide expect the Shah at the usual trysting place." The Princes then craved leave to wend their ways; and going home said to their sister, "O Perizadah, the Shah hath decreed that to-morrow he will come to our house and rest here awhile after the hunt." Said she, "An so it be, needs must we see to it that all be made ready for a royal banquet and we may not be put to shame when the Shadow of Allah shall deign shade us. There is no help but that in this matter I ask of my slave, the Speaking-Bird, what counsel he would give; and that I prepare according thereto such meats as are meet for him and are pleasing to the royal palate."——And as the morn began to dawn Shahrazad held her peace till

The end of the Six Hundred and Eighty-fourth Night.

Then said she:——I have heard, O auspicious King, that the Princes both approved of her plan and went to seek repose; whereupon Perizadah sent for the cage and setting it before her said, "O Bird, the Shah hath made a promise and hath decreed that he will deign honour this our house on the morrow, wherefore we must needs make ready for our liege lord the best of banquets and I bid thee say me what dishes should the kitcheners cook for him?" The Speaking-Bird replied, "O my lady, thou hast the most skilful of cooks and confectioners. Do thou bid them dress for thee the choicest dainties, but above all others see thou with thine own eyes that they set before the Shah a dish of new green cucumbers stuffed with pearls." Quoth the Princess in utter wonderment, "Never until this time heard I of such a dainty! How? Cucumbers with a filling of pearls! And what will the King, who cometh to eat bread and not to gaze on stones, say to such meat? Furthermore, I have not in my possession pearls enough to serve for even a single cucumber." Replied the Speaking-Bird, "This were an easy matter: do thou dread naught but only act as I shall advise thee. I seek not aught save thy welfare and would on no wise counsel thee to thy disadvantage. As for the pearls thou shalt collect them on this wise; go thou to-morrow betimes to the pleasure-gardens and bid a hole be dug at the foot of the first tree in the avenue to thy right hand, and there shalt thou find of pearls as large a store as thou shalt require." So after dawn on the next day Princess Perizadah bade a gardener-lad accompany her and fared to the site within the pleasure-gardens whereof the Speaking-Bird had told her. Here the boy dug a hole both deep and wide when suddenly his spade struck upon somewhat hard, and he removed with his hands the earth and discovered to view a golden casket well nigh one foot square. Hereupon the young gardener showed it to the Princess who exclaimed, "I brought thee with me for this very reason. Take heed and see that no harm come to it, but dig it out and bring it to me with all care." When the lad did her bidding she opened it forthright and found it filled with pearls and unions fresh from the sea, round as rings and all of one and the same size perfectly fitted for the purpose which the Speaking-Bird had proposed. Perizadah rejoiced with extreme joy at the sight and taking up the box walked back with it to the house; and the Princes who had seen their sister faring forth betimes with the gardener-lad and had wondered why she went to the park thus early unaccording to her wonted custom, catching sight of her from the casement quickly donned their walking dresses and came to meet her. And as the two brothers walked forwards they saw the Princess approaching them with some-what unusual under her arm, which when they met, proved to be a golden casket whereof they knew naught. Quoth they, "O our sister at early light we espied thee going to the pleasure-grounds with a gardener-lad empty handed, but now thou bring-est back this golden casket; so disclose to us where and how thou hast found it; and haply there may be some hoard close hidden in the parterre?" Perizadah replied, "Sooth ye say, O my brothers: I took this lad with me and made him dig under a cer-tain tree where we came upon this box of pearls, at the sight whereof methinks your hearts will be delighted." The Princess straightway opened the box and her brothers sighting the pearls and unions were amazed with extreme amazement and rejoiced greatly to see them. Quoth the Princess, "Come now ye twain with me, for that I have in hand a weighty matter;" and quoth Prince Bahman, "What is there to do? I pray thee tell us without delay for never yet hast thou kept aught of thy life from us." She made reply, "O my brothers, I have nothing to hide from you, nor think ye any ill of me, for I am now about to tell you all the tale." Then she made known to them what advice the Speaking-Bird had given to her; and they, conning the matter over in their minds, marvelled much why her slave had bidden them set a dish of green cucumbers stuffed with pearls before the Shah, nor could they devise any reason for it. Presently the Princess resumed, "The Speaking-Bird indeed is wise and ware; so methinks this counsel must be for our advantage; and at any rate it cannot be without some object and purpose. It therefore behoveth us to do even as he hath commanded." Hereupon the Princess went to her own chamber and summoning the head cook said to him, "This day the Shah, the Shadow of Allah upon Earth, will condescend here to eat the noon-meal. So do thou take heed that the meats be of choicest flavour and fittest to set before the Asylum of the World, but of all the dishes there is one thou alone must make and let not another have a hand therein. This shall be of the freshest green cucumbers with a stuffing of unions and pearls."——And as the morn began to dawn Shahrazad held her peace till

The end of the Six Hundred and Eighty-fifth Night.

THEN said she:——I have heard, O auspicious King, that the head Cook listened to this order of the Princess with wonderment and said in himself, "Who ever heard of such a dish or dreamed of ordering such an one." The Lady seeing his astonishment betrayed in his semblance without the science of thought-reading,[1] said to him, "It seemeth from thy countenance that thou deemest me daft of wits to give thee such order. I know that no one ever tasted a dish of the kind, but what is that to thee? Do thou e'en as thou art bidden. Thou seest this box brimful of pearls; so take of them as many as thou needest for the dish, and what remaineth over leave in the box." The Kitchener who could answer nothing in his confusion and amazement, chose as many precious stones as he required, and presently fared away to superintend the meats being cooked and made ready for the feast. Meanwhile the Princess went over the house and

---

[1] In Arabic "'Ilm al-Mukáshafah"= the Science by which Eastern adepts discover man's secret thoughts. Of late years it has appeared in England but with the same quackery and imposture which have ruined "Spiritualism" as the Faith of the Future.

grounds and gave directions to the slaves about the ordinance thereof, lending especial attention to the carpets and divans, the lamps and all other furniture. Next day at break of dawn Princes Bahman and Parwez rode forth in rich attire to the appointed place where they first met the Shah, who was also punctual to his promise and vouchsafed to join them in the hunt. Now when the sun had risen high and its rays waxed hot, the King gave up the chase, and set forth with the Princes to their house; and as they drew nigh thereto the cadet pushed forwards and sent word to the Princess that the Asylum of the World was coming in all good omen. Accordingly, she hastened to receive him and stood waiting his arrival at the inner entrance; and after, when the King rode up to the gate and dismounting within the court stepped over the threshold of the house-door, she fell down at his feet and did him worship. Hereat her brothers said, "O Asylum of the World, this is our sister of whom we spake;" and the Shah with gracious kindness and condescension raised her by the hand, and when he saw her face he marvelled much at its wondrous comeliness and loveliness. He thought in himself, "How like she is to her brothers in favour and form, and I trow there be none of all my lieges in city or country who can compare with them for beauty and noble bearing. This country-house also exceedeth all that I have ever seen in splendour and grandeur." The Princess then led the Shah through the house and showed him all the magnificence thereof, while he rejoiced with extreme joy at everything that met his sight. So when King Khusrau had considered whatso was in the mansion he said to the Princess, "This home of thine is far grander than any palace owned by the Shah, who would now stroll about the pleasure-garden, never doubting but that it will be delightsome as the house." Hereat the Princess threw wide open the door whence the grounds could be seen; and at once the King beheld before and above all other things, the fountain which cast up incessantly, in gerbes and jets, water clear as crystal withal golden of hue. Seeing such prodigy he cried, "This is indeed a glorious gusher: never before saw I one so admirable. But say me where is its source, and by what means doth it shoot up in spurts so high? Whence cometh this constant supply and in what fashion was it formed? The Shah would fain see it near hand." "O King of kings, and Lord of the lands," quoth the Princess, "be pleased to do whatso thou desirest." Thereupon they went up to the fountain and the

Shah stood gazing upon it with delight when behold, he heard a concert of sugar-sweet voices choiring with the harmony and melody of wit-ravishing music. So he turned him round and gazed about him to discover the singers, but no one was in sight; and albeit he looketh both far and near all was in vain, he heard the voices but he could descry no songster. At length completely baffled he exclaimed, "Whence come these most musical of sounds; and rise they from the bowels of earth or are they floating in the depths of air? They fill the heart with rapture, but strangely surprise the senses to see that no one singer is in sight." Replied the Princess with a smile, "O Lord of lords, there are no minstrels here and the strains which strike the Shah's ear come from yonder tree. Deign walk on, I pray thee, and examine it well." So he advanced thereto, ever more and more enchanted with the music, and he gazed now at the Golden-Water and now at the Singing-Tree till lost in wonderment and amazement; then, "O Allah," said he to himself, "is all this Nature-made or magical, for in very deed the place is full of mystery?" Presently, turning to the Princess quoth he, "O my lady, prithee whence came ye by this wondrous tree which hath been planted in the middlemost of this garden: did anyone bring it from some far distant land as a rare gift, and by what name is it known?" Quoth Perizadah in reply, "O King of kings, this marvel hight Singing-Tree groweth not in our country. 'Twere long to recount whence and by what means I obtained it; and suffice it for the present to say that the Tree, together with the Golden-Water and the Speaking-Bird, were all found by me at one and the same time. Deign now accompany thy slave and look upon this third rarity; and when the Shah shall have rested and recovered from the toils and travails of hunting, the tale of these three strange things shall be told to the Asylum of the World in fullest detail." Hereto the King replied, "All the Shah's fatigue hath gone for gazing upon these wonders; and now to visit the Speaking-Bird."——And as the morning began to dawn Shahrazad held her peace till

The end of the Six Hundred and Eighty-sixth Night.

THEN said she:——I have heard, O auspicious King, that the Princess took the King and when she had shown to him the Speaking-Bird, they returned to the garden where he never

ceased considering the fountain with extreme surprise and presently exclaimed, "How is this? No spring whence cometh all
this water meeteth the Shah's eye, and no channel; nor is there
any reservoir large enough to contain it." She replied, "Thou
speakest sooth, O King of kings! This jetting fount hath no
source; and it springeth from a small marble basin which I filled
from a single flagon of the Golden-Water; and by the might of
Allah Almighty it increased and waxed copious until it shot up
in this huge gerbe which the Shah seeth. Furthermore it ever
playeth day and night; and, marvellous to relate, the water falling back from that height into the basin minisheth not in quantity
nor is aught of it spilt or wasted." Hereat the King, filled with
wonder and astonishment, bade go back to the Speaking-Bird;
whereupon the Princess led him to the belvedere whence he
looked out upon thousands of all manner fowls carolling in the
trees and filling air with their hymns and praises of the Creator;
so he asked his guide, "O my lady, whence come these countless
songsters which haunt yonder tree and make the welkin resound
with their melodious notes; yet they affect none other of the
trees?" Quoth Perizadah, "O King of kings, they are all attracted
by the Speaking-Bird and flock hither to accompany his song;
and for that his cage hangeth to the window of this belvedere
they prefer only the nearest of the trees; and here he may be
heard singing sweeter notes than any of the others, nay in a
plaint more musical far than that of any nightingale." And as
the Shah drew nigh the cage and gave ear to the Bird's singing,
the Princess called to her captive saying, "Ho, my slave the
Bird, dost thou not perceive the Asylum of the Universe is here
that thou payest him not due homage and worship?" Hearing
these words the Speaking-Bird forthright ceased his shrilling
and at the same moment all the other songsters sat in deepest
silence; for they were loyal to their liege lord nor durst any one
utter a note when he held his peace. The Speaking-Bird then
spake in human voice saying, "O great King, may Almighty
Allah by His Might and Majesty accord thee health and happiness;" so the Shah returned the salutation and the Slave of
Princess Perizadah ceased not to shower blessings upon his head.
Meanwhile the tables were spread after sumptuous fashion and
the choicest meats were set before the company which was seated
in due order and degree, the Shah placing himself hard by the
Speaking-Bird and close to the casement where the cage was

hung. Then the dish of green cucumbers having been set before him, he put forth his hand to help himself, but drew it back in wonderment when he saw that the cucumbers, ranged in order upon the plate, were stuffed with pearls which appeared at either end. He asked the Princess and her brothers, "What is this dish? It cannot be meant for food; then wherefore is it placed before the Shah? Explain to me, I command you, what this thing meaneth." They could not give an answer unknowing what reply to make, and as all held their peace the Speaking-Bird answered for them saying, "O King of the Age and the Time, dost thou deem it strange to see a dish of cucumbers stuffed with pearls? How much stranger then it is that thou wast not astonished to hear that the Queen thy Consort had, contrary to the laws of Allah's ordinance, given birth to such animals as dog and cat and musk-rat. This should have caused thee far more of wonder, for who hath ever heard of woman bearing such as these?" Hereat the Shah made answer to the Speaking-Bird, "All that thou sayest is right indeed and I know that such things are not after the law of Almighty Allah; but I believed the reports of the midwives, the wise women who were with the Queen such time she was brought to bed, for they were not strangers but her own sisters, born of the same parents as herself. How then could I do otherwise than trust their words?" Quoth the Speaking-Bird, "O King of kings, indeed the truth of the matter is not hidden from me. Albeit they be the sisters of thy Queen, yet seeing the royal favours and affection towards their cadette they were consumed with anger and hatred and despite by reason of their envy and jealousy. So they devised evil devices against her and their deceits at last succeeded in diverting thy thoughts from her, and in hiding her virtues from thy sight. Now are their malice and treason made manifest to thee; and, if thou require further proof, do thou summon them and question them of the case. They cannot hide it from thee and will be reduced to confess and crave thy pardon."——And as the morn began to dawn Shahrazad held her peace till

The end of the Six Hundred and Eighty-seventh Night.

THEN said she:——I have heard, O auspicious King, that the Speaking-Bird said also to Khusrau Shah, "These two royal brothers so comely and stalwart and this lovely Princess, their sister, are thine own lawful children to whom the Queen thy Consort gave birth. The midwives, thy sisters-in-law, by reason of the blackness of their hearts and faces bore them away as soon as they were born: indeed every time a child was given to thee they wrapped it in a bit of blanket and putting it in a basket committed it to the stream which floweth by the palace to the intent that it might die an obscure death. But it so fortuned that the Intendant of thy royal gardens espied these baskets one and all as they floated past his grounds, and took charge of the infants he found therein. He then caused them to be nursed and reared with all care and, whilst they were growing up to man's estate, he looked to their being taught every art and science; and whilst his life endured he dealt with them and brought them up in love and tenderness as though they had been his very own. And now, O Khusrau Shah, wake from thy sleep of ignorance and heedlessness, and know that these two Princes Bahman and Parwez and the Princess Perizadah their sister are thine own issue and thy rightful heirs." When the King heard these words and was assured of their purport being true and understood the evil doing of those Satans, his sisters-in-law, he said, "O Bird, I am indeed persuaded of thy soothfastness, for when I first saw these youths at the hunting-ground my bowels yearned with affection towards them and my heart felt constrained to love them as though they had been my own seed. Both they and their sister have drawn my affections to them as a magnet draweth iron: and the voice of blood crieth to me and compelleth me to confess the tie and to acknowledge that they are my true children, borne in the womb of my Queen, whose direful Destiny I have been the means of carrying out." Then turning to the Princes and their sister he said with tearful eyes and broken voice, "Ye are my children and henceforth do ye regard me as your father." At this they ran to him with rare delight and falling on his neck embraced him. Then they all sat down to meat and when they had finished eating, Khusrau Shah said to them, "O my children, I must now leave you, but Inshallah—Allah willing—I will come again to-morrow and bring with me the Queen your mother." So saying he farewelled them fondly and mounting his horse departed to his palace; and no sooner had he seated himself upon his throne than he summoned the Grand Wazir and commanded him saying, "Do thou send this instant and bind in heaviest bonds those vile women, the sisters of my Queen; for their ill deeds have at last come to light and they deserve to die the death of murtherers. Let the Sworder forthright make sharp his sword; for the ground thirsteth for their blood. Go see thyself that they are beheaded without stay or delay: await not other order, but instantly obey my commandment." The Grand Wazir went forth at once and in his presence the Envious Sisters were decapitated and thus underwent fit punishment for their malice and their evil doing. After this, Khusrau Shah with his retinue walked afoot to the Cathedral-mosque whereby the Queen had been imprisoned for so many years in bitter grief and woe, and with his own hands he led her forth from her cage and tenderly embraced her. Then seeing her sad plight and her careworn countenance and wretched attire he wept and cried, "Allah Almighty forgive me this mine unjust and wrongful dealing towards thee. I have put to death thy sisters who deceitfully and despitefully raised my wrath and anger against thee, the innocent, the guiltless; and they have received due retribution for their misdeeds."——And as the morn began to dawn Shahrazad held her peace till

The end of the Six Hundred and Eighty=eighth Night.

THEN said she:——I have heard, O auspicious King, that the King spake kindly and fondly to his Consort, and told her all that had betided him, and what the Speaking-Bird had made known to him, ending with these words, "Come now with me to the palace where thou shalt see thy two sons and daughter grown up to become the loveliest of beings. Hie with me and embrace them and take them to thy bosom, for they are our children, the light of our eyes. But first do thou repair to the Hammam and don thy royal robes and jewels." Meanwhile tidings of these events were noised about the city how the King had at length shown due favour to the Queen, and had released her from bondage with his own hands and prayed forgiveness for the wrongs he had done to her; and how the Princes and the Princess had been proved to be her true-born children, and also how that Khusrau Shah had punished her sisters who conspired against her: so joy and gladness prevailed both in city and kingdom, and all the folk blessed the Shah's Bánú and cursed the Satanesses her sisters. And next day when the Queen had bathed in the Hammam and had donned royal dress and regal jewels, she went to meet her children together with the King who led up to her the Princes Bahman and Parwez and the Princess Perizadah and said, "See, here are thy children, fruit of thy womb and core of thy heart, thine own very sons and thy daughter: embrace them with all a mother's love and extend thy favour and affection to them even as I have done. When thou didst give them birth, thine ill-omened sisters bore them away from thee and cast them into yonder stream and said that thou hadst been delivered first of a puppy, then of a kitten and lastly of a musk-ratling. I cannot console myself for having credited their calumnies and the only recompense I can make is to place in thine embrace these three thou broughtest forth, and whom Allah Almighty hath restored to us and hath made right worthy to be called our children." Then the Princes and Princess fell upon their mother's neck and fondly embraced her weeping tear-floods of joy. After this the Shah and the Banu sat down to meat together with their children; and, when they had made an end of eating, King Khusrau Shah repaired to the garden with his Consort that he might show her the Singing-Tree and the fountain of Golden-Water, whereat the Queen was filled with wonder and delight. Next they turned to the belvedere and visited the Speaking-Bird of whom, as they sat at meat, the King had spoken to her in highest praise, and the Queen rejoiced in his sweet voice and melodious singing. And when they had seen all these things, the King mounted horse, Prince Bahman riding on his right hand and on his left Prince Parwez, while the Queen took Princess Perizadah with her inside her litter, and thus they set forth for the palace. As the royal cavalcade passed the city walls and entered the capital with royal pomp and circumstance, the subjects who had heard the glad tidings thronged in multitudes to see their progress and volleyed shouts of acclamation; and as the lieges had grieved aforetime to see the Queen-consort imprisoned, so now they rejoiced with exceeding joy to find her free once more. But chiefly they marvelled to look upon the Speaking-Bird, for the Princess carried the cage with her, and as they rode along thousands of sweet-toned songsters came swarming round them from every quarter, and flew as an escort to the cage, filling the air with marvellous music; while flocks of others, perching upon the trees and the housetops, carolled and warbled as it were to greet their lord's cage accompanying the royal cavalcade. And when the

palace was reached, the Shah and his Queen and his children sat
down to a sumptuous banquet; and the city was illuminated, and
everywhere dancings and merry-makings testified to the joy of
the lieges; and for many days these revels and rejoicings prevailed throughout the capital and the kingdom where every man
was blithe and happy and had feastings and festivities in his
house. After these festivals King Khusrau Shah made his elder
son Bahman heir to his throne and kingdom and committed to his
hands the affairs of state in their entirety, and the Prince administered affairs with such wisdom and success that the greatness and
glory of the realm were increased twofold. The Shah also entrusted to his youngest son Parwez the charge of his army, both
of horsemen and foot-soldiers; and Princess Perizadah was given
by her sire in marriage to a puissant King who reigned over a
mighty country; and lastly the Queen-mother forgot in perfect
joy and happiness the pangs of her captivity. Destiny ever afterwards endowed them, one and all, with days the most delectable
and they led the liefest of lives until at last there came to them
the Destroyer of delights and the Sunderer of societies and the
Depopulator of palaces and the Garnerer of graveyards and
the Reaper for Resurrection-day, and they became as though
they never had been. So laud be to the Lord who dieth not and
who knoweth no shadow of change.